Medicare Prescription Drug, Improvement, and Modernization Act of 2003

LAW AND EXPLANATION

SECOND EDITION

CCH INCORPORATED
Chicago

A WoltersKluwer Company

This publication is designed to provide accurate and authoritative information in regard to the subject matter covered. It is sold with the understanding that the publisher is not engaged in rendering legal, accounting, or other professional service. If legal advice or other expert assistance is required, the services of a competent professional person should be sought.

ISBN 0-8080-1129-4

©2004, **CCH** INCORPORATED

4025 W. Peterson Ave.
Chicago, IL 60646-6085
1 800 248 3248
health.cch.com

A WoltersKluwer Company

No claim is made to original government works; however, within this Product or Publication, the following are subject to CCH's copyright: (1) the gathering, compilation, and arrangement of such government materials; (2) the magnetic translation and digital conversion of data, if applicable; (3) the historical, statutory and other notes and references; and (4) the commentary and other materials.

All Rights Reserved

Printed in the United States of America

CCH Health Law Group Editorial Staff

LB Brumage
Portfolio Managing Editor

Yvonne Kanak
Managing Editor

Explanation and Law Provisions

Paul Clark

Angela M. Fanelli, J.D.

Rita Matthews-Niles, M.J.

Jay Nawrocki, M.A.

Richard Sarhaddi, J.D.

Susan L. Smith, M.A., J.D.

Sharon M. Sofinski

Geraldine Szuberla, J.D., LL.M.

Suzanne Szymonik, J.D.

Wendy J. Wuchek, J.D.

Production and Support

Annekke L. Bos

Karen Heslop, J.D.

Theresa J. Jensen

Jennifer Lindt

Kathleen M. McEnroe

Dionne Muhammad, J.D.

Denise Schencker

Lora Sendag

Mark Lee Snell, J.D., M.A.

Jennifer Streepy

Amy D. Sutton

Washington News Division

Paula Cruickshank

Jeff Carlson, M.A.

David Hansen, J.D.

Catherine Hubbard, M.A.

Cover Design

Laila Gaidulis

FOREWORD TO SECOND EDITION

The Medicare Prescription Drug, Improvement, and Modernization Act of 2003 (PubLNo 108-173) was enacted on December 8, 2003. It includes a new prescription drug benefit for Medicare beneficiaries, a temporary program to provide prescription drug discount cards to seniors, a new Medicare managed care program, and reimbursement changes under Medicare Parts A and B.

Legislative Background

The idea of adding a prescription drug benefit and privatizing Medicare has been discussed in Congress and by the Administration for years and has generated many bills. A prescription drug benefit for Medicare beneficiaries was included in President Clinton's Health Care Reform Proposal presented to Congress in 1993. In July of 2001, President Bush announced a set of Medicare reform principles, including the option of a subsidized prescription drug benefit for seniors, which the Administration hoped would serve as a foundation for legislation. Both parties agreed on the need for prescription drug coverage for seniors. The President also unveiled a plan to make discount prescription drugs available to all seniors no later than January 2002 through the purchase of discount prescription drug cards. The cards were to be used to purchase medicine from participating pharmacies at a negotiated price. The prescription drug discount card program was pursued through regulatory means but it did not go into effect because the courts determined that Congressional action was required before the program could be offered. The President's plan also included a modernized Medicare system whereby health care coverage could be offered by nongovernmental, private, insurance plans.

On June 27, 2003, the Senate approved the "Prescription Drug and Modernization Act of 2003" (S. 1) and the House approved the "Medicare Prescription Drug and Medicare Improvement Act of 2003 (H.R.1)." Congressional staffers predicted that the conference report would not be available until late in the year because of Senate opposition to provisions in the House bill including drug importation, the generic-drug approval process, and health savings accounts. One of the most contentious issues identified by conferees was the House plan to move seniors from fee-for-service Medicare into private plans. Other issues related to the prescription drug benefit, including access to drug coverage, premium support measures, subsidies to low-income seniors and employers, coverage for dual eligibles, and drug pricing rules. The Congressional Budget Office (CBO) predicted that both the Senate and the House versions would exceed the $400 billion limit on spending authorized by the Congress. But at the end of November 2003, both the House and the Senate passed a version of H.R. 1 that met the agreed upon $400 billion cost over 10 years, according to CBO estimates at the time.

Major Provisions

Two provisions of the legislation, the prescription drug benefit and private fee-for-service coverage, which will allow insurance companies to provide health care to Medicare beneficiaries, are the most significant changes to the Medicare program since its inception in 1965. The prescription drug discount card benefit will become available no later than six months after enactment of the legislation and will end when the prescription drug benefit becomes available in 2006. Both plans provide for subsidies for eligible low-income individuals. The provision establishing the availability of health coverage through traditional fee-for-service or from a private insurance plan will become effective in 2010. Other key provisions include a new managed care program called "Medicare Advantage," which will replace Medicare+Choice;

changes in covered benefits; changes in payment method for drugs and physician services; increases in the Part B premium; establishment of a competitive acquisition program; access to imported drugs; and establishment of health savings accounts.

Highlights of This Book

With this book, CCH INCORPORATED has created a single legal reference tool for its customers. The two main sections of the book include (1) editorial explanations of all of the provisions of the "Medicare Prescription Drug, Improvement, and Modernization Act of 2003," and (2) incorporation of each of the legislative changes into the text of the Social Security Act. These legislative provisions comprise a body of new Medicare and Medicaid law as well as related public law that will affect health care delivery, coverage of benefits, and payment for a long time to come. CCH is committed to assisting health law and health industry professionals by offering this thorough presentation and explanation of the Act.

Second edition. After the first printing of this book was distributed, CCH editors noted a few instances where the incorporation of new law into existing law was incomplete; this edition includes all the legislation, in place. Editors also have corrected some effective dates of different provisions, and made some stylistic changes to the text.

Yvonne Kanak
Managing Editor

March 2004

Table of Contents

How to Use . . . . ¶1
Highlights . . . . ¶5

Explanation

Medicare Prescription Drug Benefit . . . . ¶100
Medicare Advantage . . . . ¶350
Reimbursement and Coverage Issues . . . . ¶501
Regulatory Reduction and Contracting Reform . . . . ¶801
Medicaid, Health Savings Account, and Miscellaneous Provisions . . . . ¶1201

Law

Social Security Act Sections Added, Amended or Repealed . . . . ¶2001
Act Sections Not Amending Social Security Act Sections . . . . ¶10,000

Special Tables

Table of Social Security Act Sections Added, Amended or Repealed . . . . ¶20,001
Table of Act Sections Amending Social Security Act Sections . . . . ¶20,010
Table of Amendments to Other Acts . . . . ¶20,020
Table of Act Sections Not Amending Social Security Act Sections . . . . ¶20,030
Social Security Act Sections to Explanation Table . . . . ¶20,040

                                                                                        Page
Index 637

Detailed Table of Contents

MEDICARE PRESCRIPTION DRUG BENEFIT

Rules for Eligible Individuals

Eligible Individuals .... ¶100
Enrollment Process .... ¶101
Dissemination of Information to Eligible Individuals .... ¶102

Prescription Drug Benefit Defined

Requirements for Prescription Drug Benefits .... ¶103
Standard Prescription Drug Coverage .... ¶104
Protection Against High Out-of-Pocket Expenditures .... ¶105
Alternative Prescription Drug Coverage Requirements .... ¶106
Access to Negotiated Prices .... ¶107
Covered Part D Drug Defined .... ¶108

Beneficiary Protections

Access to Choice of Qualified Prescription Drug Coverage .... ¶109
Beneficiary Protections for Qualified Prescription Drug Coverage .... ¶110

PDP Sponsor Requirements

Access to Covered Part D Drugs .... ¶111
Cost and Utilization Management; Quality Assurance; Medication
Therapy Management Program .... ¶112
Electronic Prescription Program .... ¶113
Grievance Mechanism, Coverage Determinations, Reconsiderations,
Appeals, and Confidentiality of Records .... ¶114

PDP, Limited Risk and Fallback Requirements

Prescription Drug Plan Regions, Submission of Bids, and Plan Approval .... ¶115
Limited Risk Plans and Fallback Prescription Drug Plans .... ¶116
Requirements for and Contracts with Prescription Drug Plans .... ¶117

Premium and Subsidies

Premiums; Late Enrollment Penalty .... ¶118
Premium and Cost-Sharing Subsidies for Low-Income Individuals .... ¶119
Subsidies for Part D Eligible Individuals for Qualified Prescription Drug
Coverage .... ¶120
Medicare Prescription Drug Account in the Federal Supplemental Medical
Insurance Trust Fund .... ¶123
Application to Medicare Advantage and Related Managed Care Programs ...... ¶125
Special Rules for Employer-Sponsored Programs .... ¶127
State Pharmaceutical Assistance Programs .... ¶129
Coordination of Requirements for Plans Providing Prescription Drug
Coverage .... ¶131

Prescription Drug Discount Card Program

Medicare Prescription Drug Discount Card and Transitional Assistance Program	¶150
Eligibility	¶152
Enrollment and Enrollment Fees	¶154
Enrollment Information and Program Features	¶156
Discount Card Features	¶158
Eligibility Procedures for Endorsed Programs and Transitional Assistance	¶160
Transitional Assistance	¶162
Qualifications, Endorsements, and Beneficiary Protections	¶164
Disclosure and Oversight	¶166
Treatment of Territories	¶168
Funding	¶170
Definitions	¶175
Prescription Drug Coverage in Territories and Application of Demonstration Authority	¶178
Legislative Proposal, Study and Report	¶180
Medicare Advantage Conforming Amendments	¶200
Medicaid Provisions Related to the Medicare Prescription Drug Benefit	¶205
Medigap Amendments	¶210
Medicare Prescription Drug Discount Card and Transitional Assistance Program	¶215
State Pharmaceutical Assistance Transition Commission	¶220
Studies and Reports	¶225
Grants to Physicians to Implement Electronic Prescription Drug Programs	¶230
Expanding the Work of Medicare Quality Improvement Organizations to Include Parts C and D	¶235
Conflict of Interest Study	¶240
Study on Employment-Based Retiree Health Coverage	¶245

MEDICARE ADVANTAGE

Implementation of Medicare Advantage Program

Implementation and Transition	¶350

Immediate Improvements

Equalizing MA Payments with Fee-for-Service Costs	¶351
Change in Budget Neutrality for Blended Capitation Rate	¶352
Increasing Minimum Percentage Increase to National Growth Rate	¶353
DoD and VA Costs	¶354
Special Rule for Certain Inpatient Hospital Stays	¶355
MedPAC Study of AAPCC	¶356
Report on Impact of Increased Financial Assistance to MA Plans	¶357
Study on Unreasonable Beneficiary Cost-Sharing	¶358
Announcements Regarding Payment Rates	¶359
Higher Copayments for Non-MA Providers	¶360

©2004, CCH INCORPORATED

Medicare Advantage Regional Plans
Establishment of MA Regional Plans .... ¶361
Definition of MA Regional, Local Plan .... ¶362
Rules for MA Regional Plans .... ¶363
Competition Program Starting in 2006 .... ¶365
Beneficiary Savings .... ¶366
Collection of Premiums .... ¶367
Computation of MA Area-Specific Non-Drug Benchmark .... ¶368
Payment of Plans Based on Bid Amounts .... ¶369
Annual Announcement Process .... ¶370
Uniform Premium and Bid Amounts .... ¶371
Plan Incentives .... ¶372
Enrollees with End-Stage Renal Disease .... ¶373
Facilitating Employer Sponsorship of MA Plans .... ¶374
Medicare Beneficiary Education and Information .... ¶375
Protection Against Beneficiary Selection .... ¶376
Effective Date .... ¶377

Additional Reforms
Special Needs Beneficiaries .... ¶378
Avoiding Duplicative State Regulation .... ¶379
Medicare MSAs .... ¶380
Extension of Reasonable Cost Contracts .... ¶386
Municipal Health Service Demonstration Projects .... ¶387
Payment by PACE Providers .... ¶388
Reimbursement for Federally Qualified Health Centers .... ¶390
Report on Health Care Performance Measures .... ¶394

Comparative Cost Adjustment Program
Comparative Cost Adjustment Program .... ¶396

REIMBURSEMENT AND COVERAGE ISSUES
Provisions Relating to Hospitals and Ambulance Services
Standardized Amount .... ¶501
Labor-Related Share of the Standardized Amount .... ¶503
Market Basket Update .... ¶507
Enhanced Disproportionate Share Hospital (DSH) Treatment .... ¶510
Medicare Inpatient Hospital Payment Adjustment for Low-Volume
Hospitals .... ¶515
Brachytherapy Devices .... ¶545
Hospital Outpatient Department Payments .... ¶547
Payments Connected to Reporting on Quality .... ¶560
Appropriateness of Payments Under IPPS .... ¶562
Revision of the IME Adjustment Percentage .... ¶564
New Medical Technologies .... ¶566
Hospitals in Puerto Rico .... ¶568

8 Medicare Prescription Drug, Improvement, and Modernization Act of 2003

Wage Index Reclassification Reform	¶570
Inpatient Hospital Services Provided by IHS	¶572
Limits on Physician Referrals	¶574
Physician Pathology Services	¶575
One-Time Appeals Process for Hospital Wage Index Classification	¶576
Critical Access Hospitals	¶578
Rural Community Hospital Demonstration Program	¶581
Hold Harmless Provision for Small Rural and Sole Community Hospitals	¶582
Reimbursement for Clinical Laboratory Services Furnished in Certain Rural Areas	¶583
EMTALA Improvements	¶584
MedPAC Study on Rural Payment Adjustments	¶586
Professional Education Costs	¶588
Residency Period for Geriatric Residency or Fellowship Programs	¶590
Resident Training in Non-Hospital Settings	¶592
Frontier Clinics	¶593
Ambulatory Surgical Centers	¶594
Ambulance Services	¶596
Providing Appropriate Coverage of Rural Air Ambulance Services	¶598

Skilled Nursing Facilities

Background Checks	¶601
Additional Information About SNF Benefits	¶604
Payment Adjustment for AIDS Residents in SNFs	¶605
Information on Medicare-Certified SNFs in Hospital Discharge Plans	¶606
Establishing SNFs as Originating Sites for Telehealth Services	¶607
Portable Diagnostic Ultrasound Services in SNFs	¶608
Exclusion from SNF-PPS	¶610

Home Health and Hospice

Demonstration Project to Clarify the Definition of Homebound	¶650
Increase for Home Health Services Furnished in a Rural Area	¶656
Update in Home Health Payment Rates	¶658
Adult Day Care Provided Under the Home Health Benefit	¶660
Provision of Home Health Service by a Religious Nonmedical Health Institution	¶662
MedPAC Study on Medicare Margins of Home Health Agencies	¶664
OASIS Data Collection	¶670
Determination and Delivery of Medical Care	¶671
Rural Hospice Demonstration Project	¶675
Coverage of Hospice Consultation Services	¶677
Voluntary Chronic Care Improvement Programs	¶678
Demonstration Project for Consumer Directed Chronic Outpatient Services	¶679

Physician Services

Payments to Physicians in Rural Areas	¶700

©2004, CCH INCORPORATED

Update to Payments for Physicians' Services .... ¶701
Studies on Access to Physicians' Services................................ ¶703
MedPAC Report on Payment for Physicians' Services .... ¶704
MedPAC Study of Payment for Cardio-Thoracic Surgeons .... ¶705
Private Contracting for Podiatrists, Dentists and Optometrists .... ¶706
Establishment of Floor on Work Geographic Adjustment .... ¶708
Demonstration Project for Coverage of Certain Prescription Drugs and
Biologicals .... ¶710
Treatment of Certain Physician Pathology Services .... ¶720
Modifications to Medicare Payment Advisory Commission (MedPAC) .... ¶721
Physicians' Services Furnished in Alaska................................ ¶722
Review of Physician Practice Expense Geographic Adjustment Data .... ¶725

Other Part B Issues
Indexing Part B Deductible to Inflation .... ¶729
Services Furnished by IHS Hospitals and Clinics .... ¶730

Preventive Services
Preventive Physical Exams .... ¶750
Cardiovascular Screening Tests .... ¶753
Screening Mammography .... ¶754
Diabetes Laboratory Diagnostic Tests .... ¶755
Clinical Laboratory Diagnostic Tests .... ¶756
End-Stage Renal Disease Services .... ¶759
Intravenous Immune Globulin (IVIG) for the Treatment of Primary
Immune Deficiency Diseases in the Home .... ¶760
Orthotics and Prosthetics .... ¶761
Moratorium on Therapy Caps .... ¶762

Cost Containment Provisions
Cost Containment .... ¶765
Presidential Submission of Legislation .... ¶768
House of Representatives Procedures .... ¶771
Senate Procedures .... ¶774
Income-Related Reduction in Part B Premium Subsidy .... ¶776
Military Retirees .... ¶777

Demonstration Projects
Surgical First Assisting Services .... ¶784
Health Care Quality Demonstration Programs............................ ¶785
Medicare Care Management Performance Demonstration Project............. ¶786
Concierge Care .... ¶787
Chiropractic Services .... ¶788
Telemedicine Demonstration Project .... ¶789
Chronically Ill Medicare Beneficiary Research, Data, Demonstration
Strategy .... ¶790

Miscellaneous Provisions

Physical Therapy Services	¶791
Studies Relating To Vision Impairments	¶792
Restoration of Medicare Trust Funds	¶793
Medicare Secondary Payer	¶794
Improvement in Oversight of Technology and Coverage	¶795
Improvements in the National and Local Coverage Determination Process to Respond to Changes in Technology	¶796
Dental Claims	¶797
Medically Underserved Populations	¶798
Office of Rural Health Policy Improvement	¶799
Medicare Advantage Quality Improvement Programs	¶800

REGULATORY REDUCTION AND CONTRACTING REFORM

Regulatory Reform

Administrative Improvement, Regulatory Reduction, and Contracting Reform	¶801
Definition of Supplier	¶825
Issuance of Regulations	¶826
Compliance with Changes in Regulation and Policies	¶827
Reports and Studies Relating to Regulatory Reform	¶828
Flexibility in Medicare Administration	¶829
Requirements for Information Security for Medicare Administrative Contractors	¶830
Provider Education and Technical Assistance	¶831
Medicare Ombudsmen for Providers Beneficiaries	¶832
Small Provider Technical Assistance Demonstration Program	¶833
Beneficiary Outreach Demonstration Programs	¶835

Appeals and Recovery

Transfer of Responsibility for Medicare Appeals	¶901
Process for Expedited Access to Review	¶903
Expedited Review of SNF Appeals	¶905
Revision of Medicare Appeals Process	¶906
Qualified Independent Contractors	¶907
Prepayment Review	¶908
Recovery of Overpayments	¶909
Provider Enrollment Process	¶911
Correction of Minor Errors and Omissions	¶912
Prior Determination Process and ABNs	¶913
Appeals by Providers When There is No Other Party Available	¶915
Revision to Appeals Timeframes and Amounts	¶916
Mediation Process for Local Medical Review Policies	¶917

Miscellaneous Provisions

E & M Documentation Guidelines	¶941

Improvement in Oversight of Technology and Coverage .... ¶942
Treatment of Hospitals for Certain MSP Services .... ¶943
EMTALA Improvements .... ¶944
Emergency Medical Treatment and Labor Act (EMTALA) Technical
Advisory Group .... ¶945
Arrangements to Provide Core Hospice Services in Certain Circumstances .... ¶946
Application of OSHA Bloodborne Pathogens Standard to Certain
Hospitals .... ¶947
BIPA-Related Technical Amendments and Corrections .... ¶948
Authority to Waive a Program Exclusion .... ¶949
Treatment of Certain Dental Claims .... ¶950
Revisions to Reassignment Provisions .... ¶952
Other Provisions .... ¶953

Combatting Waste, Fraud and Abuse
Competitive Acquisition of Certain Items and Services .... ¶1002
Physician Fee Schedule Adjustments .... ¶1004
Competitive Acquisition Program for Drugs and Biologicals .... ¶1006
Extension of Payment Reform .... ¶1008
Adjustments to Payment Amounts for Administration of Drugs and
Biologicals .... ¶1009
Average Sales Price Payment (ASP) Methodology Option .... ¶1010
Payment for Inhalation Drugs .... ¶1011
Demonstration Project for Use of Recovery Audit Contractors .... ¶1012

MEDICAID, HEALTH SAVINGS ACCOUNT, AND MISCELLANEOUS PROVISIONS
Medicaid Provisions
Medicaid DSH Payments .... ¶1201
Increase in Floor for Treatment as a Low DSH State .... ¶1203
Termination of Statewide Waiver .... ¶1204
Reporting Requirements for State Adjustments to DSH Hospitals .... ¶1205
Best Price Exemption for Medicaid Drug Rebate Program .... ¶1206
Extension of Moratorium .... ¶1207

Miscellaneous Provisions
Emergency Health Services for Undocumented Aliens .... ¶1208
Commission on Systemic Interoperability .... ¶1209
Research on Outcomes .... ¶1210
Citizens Health Care Working Group .... ¶1211
Funding Start-Up Costs for Administrative Reform .... ¶1212
Health Care Infrastructure Improvement Program .... ¶1215

Access to Affordable Pharmaceuticals
Hatch-Waxman, Re-Importation Changes .... ¶1301
Federal Trade Commission Review .... ¶1320
Importation of Drugs from Canada .... ¶1330

Health Savings Accounts and Other Tax Provisions
Establishing Health Savings Accounts . . . . ¶1400
Employer Contributions to Health Savings Accounts . . . . ¶1405
Exclusion of Prescription Drug Subsidy . . . . ¶1410
Information Reporting Requirements . . . . ¶1415

¶ 1
How to Use

CCH's *Medicare Prescription Drug, Improvement, and Modernization Act of 2003: Law and Explanation* provides you with CCH explanations of the "Medicare Prescription Drug, Improvement, and Modernization Act of 2003" (PubLNo 108-173), as well as the text of the Social Security Act and related public laws as amended. The Medicare reform legislation was adopted by the U.S. House of Representatives on November 22, 2003, by the U.S. Senate on November 25, 2003, and enacted by President Bush on December 8, 2003.

HIGHLIGHTS

A summary of the Highlights of the Act, located at ¶5, provides a quick overview of the major statutory changes of this Act and a listing of the explanatory paragraphs where the provisions are discussed in more detail. The Highlights are topically arranged.

CCH EXPLANATIONS

CCH-prepared explanations are arranged according to subject matter for easy use. The explanatory paragraphs are followed by boldface citation lines that (1) indicate the section of the Act explained and the corresponding sections of the Social Security Act (or other Acts) that are added, amended, or repealed; and (2) provide a cross-reference to the paragraph numbers at which the statutes as amended by the Act are reproduced. Before each citation line is a sentence indicating the effective date of the provision.

AMENDED SOCIAL SECURITY ACT PROVISIONS

CCH has reflected the Medicare and Medicaid changes mandated by the Act in the Social Security Act provisions affected. The underlying provision making the change is identified for clarity and ease of use. Deleted material, or the text of the Social Security Act provision prior to the amendment, appears in the Amendment Notes that follow each reconstructed Social Security Act provision. **The applicable date for each Amendment Note appears in boldface type.** At the end of each amended Social Security Act provision—and before the Amendment Note—CCH provides references to the CCH explanation of that amended, added, or repealed Social Security Act provision. *The text of the Social Security Act sections affected begins at ¶2001.*

NON-SOCIAL SECURITY ACT PROVISIONS

The sections of the "Medicare Prescription Drug, Improvement, and Modernization Act of 2003" that do not amend the Social Security Act appear in full text in Act section order. Included is the text of the Act sections that amend prior Acts affecting or related to the Social Security Act, such as the Balanced Budget Act of 1997; the Medicare, Medicaid, and SCHIP Benefit and Improvements Act of 2000; Act sections that amend sections of the United States Code other than Social Security sections; and non-code provisions. *The text of these provisions appears in Act section order beginning at ¶10,000.*

SPECIAL FINDING DEVICES

Several tables are provided for assistance in finding Social Security Act sections, Act sections, and explanatory sections. Tables are included that indicate Social Security Act sections added, amended, or repealed cross-referenced to the Act section (see ¶20,001), Act sections are cross-referenced to Social Security Act sections that have been amended (see ¶20,010), provisions of other Acts that were amended by the Act are cross-referenced (see ¶20,020), non-code Act sections are cross-referenced to the CCH paragraph where they are printed (see ¶20,030), and a table cross-referencing Social Security Act sections to the CCH explanation paragraph is also included (see ¶20,040).

¶ 5
Highlights

Below is a brief description of the major provisions of the "Medicare Prescription Drug, Improvement, and Modernization Act of 2003" (PubLNo 108-173) in several subject areas. The paragraph number at the beginning of each section refers to the first Explanation paragraph that discusses the subject matter in greater detail.

PRESCRIPTION DRUG COVERAGE
Starting at ¶ 100

The "Medicare Prescription Drug, Improvement, and Modernization Act of 2003" (PubLNo 108-173) creates a new voluntary prescription drug benefit under a new Part D of the Social Security Act. Beneficiaries entitled to Part A and enrolled in Part B, enrollees in Medicare Advantage private fee-for-service plans, and enrollees in Medicare Savings Account plans will be eligible individuals for the prescription drug benefit. Eligible individuals will have access to at least two prescription drug plans ("PDPs") in their region. In addition, the Act provides for a voluntary Medicare prescription drug discount program, which will provide transitional coverage until coverage under the prescription drug program becomes effective for an individual.

By enrolling in a PDP, eligible individuals will have the choice of either a standard coverage plan or an alternative coverage plan with actuarially equivalent benefits. PDPs also may offer supplemental benefits to the standard coverage plan. For 2006, standard coverage will include a $250 deductible and a 25 percent coinsurance for costs between $251 and $2,250. Beneficiaries will have to pay 100 percent for the cost of prescription drugs for amounts spent between $2,251 and $5,100 each year. At this point, beneficiaries will have spent $3,600 out of their own pocket on the cost of prescription drugs. From this point forward, the beneficiary will pay $2 for generic drugs and $5 for nonpreferred drugs or 5 percent of the cost of the prescription medication, whichever is greater. Subsidies will be established for deductibles, premiums, and cost-sharing for low-income individuals with incomes below 150 percent of the federal poverty line. Eligibility determinations will be made by state Medicaid plans.

The program also provides for transitional assistance to low-income individuals whose income is less than 135 percent of the federal poverty level and who are enrolled in the discount card program. The Secretary will establish a state pharmaceutical assistance transition commission to deal with transitional issues facing state programs and participants due to the implementation of Part D.

MEDICARE ADVANTAGE
Starting at ¶ 350

The Act establishes a new Medicare managed care program, called "Medicare Advantage", which, between 2004 and 2010, will replace the current Medicare+Choice program. Starting in 2004, all plans will be reimbursed at a rate at least as high as the rate for traditional fee-for-service (FFS) Medicare. Health plans also areencouraged to offer coverage not just in one state or one part of a state, but in regional areas that may cover several states. Starting in 2010, CMS will establish up to six demonstration sites for a "comparative cost adjustment program." Health plans will bid to offer coverage to beneficiaries in these sites. All plans, including the traditional Medicare FFS plan offered in that area, will be paid based on the demographic and health risks of enrollees. If the traditional FFS plan disproportionately enrolls high-risk beneficiaries, beneficiary premium changes will be adjusted to compensate.

PROVIDER REIMBURSEMENT
Starting at ¶ 501

Hospitals that do not submit quality data on 10 indicators to be chosen by the Secretary will receive 0.4 percent less of a market basket reimbursement update beginning in fiscal year 2005. For fiscal years 2004 through 2007, hospitals will receive the full market basket increase in their annual reimbursement rate adjustment.

For physicians' services, the conversion factor for 2005 and 2005 fee schedule payments will be at least 1.5 percent. The conversion factor will be exempt from the budget neutrality adjustment that would have resulted in a negative 4.5 percent adjustment in 2005. For payments and services furnished after January 1, 2004, the Secretary will increase the practice expense relative value units (RVUs) for 2004 using supplemental survey data that includes expenses for administering drugs and biologicals. The Secretary also will evaluate Current Procedural Terminology (CPT) codes for physicians' services associated with administering covered outpatient drugs.

Starting for services furnished on or after January 1, 2004, specified covered hospital outpatient drugs (HOPD) will be paid based on a percentage of the reference average wholesale price for the drug. The reference average wholesale price is the average wholesale price for the drug as of May 1, 2003.

COVERAGE
Starting at ¶ 750

Medicare will cover an initial preventive physical examination, subject to deductible and beneficiary cost-sharing. This initial preventive physical examination must be performed no later than six months after the individual's initial coverage date under Part B. Also, cardiovascular screening blood tests are covered starting January 1, 2005.

Decisions regarding national coverage determinations must be made within six months after a request when a technology assessment is not required and nine months when such an assessment is required.

Diabetes screening tests furnished to an individual at risk for diabetes for the purpose of early detection of diabetes are included as a covered medical service.

COST CONTAINMENT
Starting at ¶ 765

The Part B deductible will continue to be $100 for 2004, but will increase in 2005 to $110. In subsequent years it will increase by the same rate as total Part B spending per beneficiary, which is the rate of increase in the Part B premium.

The amount a beneficiary pays for the Part B premium will increase based on income starting in 2007. Over a five-year period, this increase will be phased in so that individuals earning over $200,000 or couples earning over $400,000 eventually will pay 80 percent of the Part B premium. Currently all Medicare beneficiaries pay 25 percent of the Part B premium.

ACCESS TO AFFORDABLE PHARMACEUTICALS
Starting at ¶ 1301

Individuals will be allowed to purchase prescription drugs from Canadian providers subject to U.S. government certification that the drugs offered by these providers are safe.

HEALTH SAVINGS ACCOUNTS
Starting at ¶ 1401

Employees as well as individuals will be able to purchase new Health Savings Accounts (HSAs). HSAs will allow workers up to age 65 to make pre-tax contributions up to $2,250 ($4,500 for families), indexed for inflation, to cover healthcare needs. Individuals aged 55 to 65 can make an additional "catch-up" contribution of as much as $500 annually in 2004, increasing annually until it reaches $1,000 in 2009. HSAs, unlike existing flexible spending accounts, will be portable and assets can accumulate. Recipients will therefore have the opportunity to draw on them for tax-free distributions to cover both current and retirement healthcare costs.

Medicare Prescription Drug Benefit

RULES FOR ELIGIBLE INDIVIDUALS

Eligible Individuals . . . . ¶ 100
Enrollment Process . . . . ¶ 101
Dissemination of Information to
    Eligible Individuals . . . . ¶ 102

PRESCRIPTION DRUG BENEFIT DEFINED

Requirements for Prescription Drug
    Benefits . . . . ¶ 103
Standard Prescription Drug Coverage . . ¶ 104
Protection Against High Out-of-Pocket
    Expenditures . . . . ¶ 105
Alternative Prescription Drug
    Coverage Requirements . . . . ¶ 106
Access to Negotiated Prices . . . . ¶ 107
Covered Part D Drug Defined . . . . ¶ 108

BENEFICIARY PROTECTIONS

Access to Choice of Qualified
    Prescription Drug Coverage . . . . ¶ 109
Beneficiary Protections for Qualified
    Prescription Drug Coverage . . . . ¶ 110

PDP SPONSOR REQUIREMENTS

Access to Covered Part D Drugs . . . . . . ¶ 111
Cost and Utilization Management;
    Quality Assurance; Medication
    Therapy Management Program . . . . ¶ 112
Electronic Prescription Program . . . . . . ¶ 113
Grievance Mechanism, Coverage
    Determinations, Reconsiderations,
    Appeals, and Confidentiality of
    Records . . . . ¶ 114

PDP, LIMITED RISK AND FALLBACK REQUIREMENTS

Prescription Drug Plan Regions,
    Submission of Bids, and Plan
    Approval . . . . ¶ 115
Limited Risk Plans and Fallback
    Prescription Drug Plans . . . . ¶ 116
Requirements for and Contacts with
    Prescription Drug Plans . . . . ¶ 117

PREMIUM AND SUBSIDIES

Premiums; Late Enrollment Penalty . . . . ¶ 118
Premium and Cost-Sharing Subsidies
    for Low-Income Individuals . . . . ¶ 119
Subsidies for Part D Eligible
    Individuals for Qualified
    Prescription Drug Coverage . . . . ¶ 120

Medicare Prescription Drug Account
    in the Federal Supplemental
    Medical Insurance Trust Fund . . . . . . ¶ 123
Application to Medicare Advantage
    and Related Managed Care
    Programs . . . . ¶ 125
Special Rules for Employer-Sponsored
    Programs . . . . ¶ 127
State Pharmaceutical Assistance
    Programs . . . . ¶ 129
Coordination of Requirements for
    Plans Providing Prescription Drug
    Coverage . . . . ¶ 131

PRESCRIPTION DRUG DISCOUNT CARD PROGRAM

Medicare Prescription Drug Discount
    Card and Transitional Assistance
    Program . . . . ¶ 150
Eligibility . . . . ¶ 152
Enrollment and Enrollment Fees . . . . . . ¶ 154
Enrollment Information and Program
    Features . . . . ¶ 156
Discount Card Features . . . . ¶ 158
Eligibility Procedures for Endorsed
    Programs and Transitional
    Assistance . . . . ¶ 160
Transitional Assistance . . . . ¶ 162
Qualifications, Endorsements, and
    Beneficiary Protections . . . . ¶ 164
Disclosure and Oversight . . . . ¶ 166
Treatment of Territories . . . . ¶ 168
Funding . . . . ¶ 170
Definitions . . . . ¶ 175
Prescription Drug Coverage in
    Territories and Application of
    Demonstration Authority . . . . ¶ 178
Legislative Proposal, Study and
    Report . . . . ¶ 180
Medicare Advantage Conforming
    Amendments . . . . ¶ 200
Medicaid Provisions Related to the
    Medicare Prescription Drug Benefit . . ¶ 205
Medigap Amendments . . . . ¶ 210
Medicare Prescription Drug Discount
    Card and Transitional Assistance
    Program . . . . ¶ 215
State Pharmaceutical Assistance
    Transition Commission . . . . ¶ 220
Studies and Reports . . . . ¶ 225

Grants to Physicians to Implement Electronic Prescription Drug Programs .... ¶ 230	Conflict of Interest Study .... ¶ 240
Expanding the Work of Medicare Quality Improvement Organizations to Include Parts C and D .... ¶ 235	Study on Employment-Based Retiree Health Coverage .... ¶ 245

RULES FOR ELIGIBLE INDIVIDUALS

¶ 100
Eligible Individuals

Individuals eligible for prescription drug coverage. Eligibility for prescription drug coverage under Part D for individuals entitled to benefits under Medicare Part A or enrolled in Medicare Part B is as follows:

(1) A fee-for-service enrollee, an individual who is not enrolled in a Medicare Advantage (MA) plan, may obtain prescription drug coverage through enrollment in a prescription drug plan (PDP).

(2) Medicare Advantage (MA) enrollees enrolled in a plan that provides prescription drug coverage (MA-PD) obtain drug coverage through the plan. The MA enrollee may not enroll in a PDP under Part D.

(3) Enrollees in MA private fee-for-service plans that do not provide qualified prescription drug coverage are eligible to enroll in a PDP under Part D.

(4) Enrollees in a Medicare Savings Account (MSA) plan may obtain qualified prescription drug coverage through enrollment in a PDP.

Effective date. Coverage under prescription drug plans and MA-PD plans becomes effective January 1, 2006.

Act Sec. 101(a) adding Sec. 1860D-1(a) of the Social Security Act. Law at ¶ 2261A.

¶ 101
Enrollment Process

Establishment of the enrollment process. The Secretary must establish a process for the enrollment, disenrollment, termination, and change of enrollment of Part D eligible individuals in prescription drug plans (PDPs). The Secretary will use rules similar to the rules established for such a process for MA-PD plans under Sec. 1851 of the Social Security Act, including residence requirements, exercise of choice, election periods, coverage periods, and guaranteed issue and renewal. Except for the initial enrollment period and additional special enrollment periods described below, the election period rules for the prescription drug benefit will follow MA-PD rules related to coverage election periods including initial periods, annual coordinated election periods, special election periods, and election periods for exceptions circumstances. The continuous open enrollment and disenrollment available to MA enrollees for 2005 and the first three months of subsequent years, however, does not apply. The rules applicable to enrollment, disenrollment, termination, and change of enrollment of Part D eligible individuals in MA-PD plans are at Sec. 1851.

Marketing and application forms for PDPs are subject to the rules provided for MA plans under Sec. 1851(h) of the Social Security Act.

Dual eligible individuals. For individuals who are eligible for Part D and are full-benefit dual eligibles who have failed to enroll in a prescription drug plan or MA-PD plan, the enrollment process established by the Secretary will provide for the enrollment in a prescription drug plan that has a monthly benefit that does not exceed the premium assistance available under Part D. If there is more than one plan available that has a premium that does not exceed the premium assistance available, the Secretary will enroll the individual in a plan on a random basis. The individual may decline or change the enrollment in the plan.

Initial enrollment period. An initial enrollment period for individuals who are eligible for Part D as of November 15, 2005, will be established in the same manner as rules for the annual, coordinated open election period for MA plans as described in Sec. 1851(e)(3)(B)(iii) of the Social Security Act. For individuals who become eligible for Part D after November 15, 2005, the initial enrollment period will be similar to the rule for MA plans under Sec. 1851(e)(1) and will be at least six months.

Special enrollment periods. The Secretary will establish special enrollment periods as follows:

Involuntary loss of creditable prescription drug coverage. For an individual who has involuntary lost creditable prescription drug coverage, when establishing the special enrollment period, the Secretary must take into account when the individual received notice of the loss of coverage. A reduction in coverage that results in coverage that no longer meets the requirements under Part D will be considered involuntary loss of coverage. Failure to pay the premium, however, will be considered voluntary loss of coverage.

Errors in enrollment. For errors in enrollment in a prescription drug plan that are the result of an error of an officer, employee, or agent of the federal government, the Secretary must establish a special enrollment period for the prescription drug benefit following the rule for Part B described at Sec. 1837(h) of the Social Security Act. The special enrollment should include a coverage period determined on the basis of the effects of the error and appropriate adjustments of premiums to correct or eliminate the effects of the error.

Other special enrollment periods. The Secretary also will establish special enrollment periods for exceptional circumstances, dual eligibles, and for Part D eligible individuals who discontinue enrollment in an MA-PD plan during the first year of eligibility.

Information to facilitate enrollment. The Secretary may provide prescription drug plan (PDP) sponsors and MA organizations with identifying information about Part D eligible individuals only to the extent the information is necessary to facilitate efficient marketing of plans to the individuals and enrollment of individuals in the plans. The information provided by the Secretary to a PDP sponsor or MA organization may be used only to facilitate marketing of and enrollment in PDPs and MA-PD plans.

Penalties for late enrollment. A late enrollment will be imposed on Part D eligible individuals who enroll in a PDP or an MA-PD after the initial enrollment period and fail to maintain continuous creditable prescription drug coverage during the period of non-enrollment.

Effective date. Coverage becomes effective January 1, 2006.

¶101

Act Sec. 101(a) adding Sec. 1860D-1(b) of the Social Security Act. Law at ¶2261A.

¶ 102

Dissemination of Information to Eligible Individuals

Distribution of information. The Secretary will conduct activities designed to distribute information to eligible and prospective eligible individuals notifying them of the coverage provided under Part D at least 30 days prior to the initial enrollment period described in ¶101. The activities performed by the Secretary for PDPs are similar to those for MA plans under Social Security Act Sec. 1851(d), including publication of comparative information for PDPs and MA-PD plans. The activities must be coordinated with the general rules for distribution of Medicare information under Sec. 1804 as well as Sec. 1851(d). Information also must be available through the toll-free telephone number 1-800-MEDICARE.

Comparative information. The comparative information on prescription drug coverage must include: (1) the benefits provided under the plan, (2) the monthly beneficiary premium under the plan, (3) the quality and performance under the plan, (4) the beneficiary required cost-sharing, and (5) the results of consumer satisfaction surveys conducted as a requirement under the provisions of Part D. The Secretary is not required to provide comparative information for the first plan year in which the PDP is offered and for the next plan year if it is impractical or the information is not available.

Late enrollment. The information distributed to eligible and prospective eligible individuals also must include information concerning the methodology for determining the late enrollment penalty (see ¶118).

Consumer satisfaction survey. To provide comparative information during the enrollment period, the Secretary must conduct consumer satisfaction surveys with respect to PDP sponsors and PDP plans. The surveys must be conducted in a manner similar to the manner in which surveys are conducted for MA organizations and MA plans are conducted under Part C.

Effective date. Effective upon enactment, except that coverage under prescription drug plans and MA-PD plans become effective January 1, 2006.

Act Sec. 101(a) adding Secs. 1860D-1(c) and 1860D-4(d) of the Social Security Act. Law at ¶2261A and 2261D.

PRESCRIPTION DRUG BENEFIT DEFINED

¶ 103

Requirements for Prescription Drug Benefits

Qualified prescription drug coverage. For purposes of Parts C and D, "qualified prescription drug coverage" means either (1) standard prescription drug coverage with access to negotiated prices (see ¶104), or (2) alternative prescription drug coverage with at least actuarially equivalent prices and access to negotiated prices (see ¶106). Alternative prescription drug coverage with at least actuarially equivalent benefits and access to negotiated prices is coverage of covered outpatient drugs that meets the alternative prescription drug coverage requirements and access to negotiated prices, if approved by the Secretary. "Basic prescription drug coverage" also means either standard prescription drug coverage with access to negotiated prices or alternative prescription drug coverage with at least actuarially equivalent benefits and access to negotiated prices without supplemental prescription drug coverage.

Supplemental prescription drug coverage. Qualified prescription drug coverage may include supplemental prescription drug coverage with certain reductions in cost-sharing and/or coverage of optional drugs. Reduction in cost-sharing includes a reduction in the annual deductible, reduction in coinsurance percentage, or an increase in the initial coverage limit with respect to covered Part D drugs or a combination of any of the above. The reduction or increase must increase the actuarial value of benefits above the actuarial value of basic prescription drug coverage. Optional drug coverage is coverage of any product that is excluded from coverage or restricted as defined under Medicaid. A PDP sponsor may not offer a PDP that provides supplemental prescription drug coverage in an area unless the sponsor also offers a PDP in the area that only provides basic prescription drug coverage.

Effective date. Effective upon enactment, except coverage for prescription drugs becomes effective January 1, 2006.

Act Sec. 101(a) adding Sec. 1860D-2(a) of the Social Security Act. Law at ¶2261B.

¶ 104

Standard Prescription Drug Coverage

Requirements. Standard coverage is coverage of covered outpatient drugs that meets the following requirements:

Deductible. The coverage has an annual deductible, which is subject to an annual increase for each subsequent year equal to the annual percentage increase. The annual percentage increase is based on the average per capita aggregate expenditures for covered drugs for Medicare beneficiaries during the 12-month period ending in July of the previous year. The increase in the deductible amount will be rounded to the nearest multiple of $5. The annual deductible for 2006 is $250.

Coinsurance. For costs above the annual deductible and up to the initial coverage limit, the coinsurance is equal to 25 percent of the costs (or is actuarially equivalent to an average expected payment of 25 percent of the costs). PDP sponsors and MA organizations may apply tiered copayments under the plan so long as the tiered copolymers are consistent with the actuarial equivalent of the coinsurance of 25 percent of the cost-sharing requirements.

Initial coverage limit. The coverage has an initial coverage limit on the maximum costs that may be recognized for payment purposes, including the annual deductible. For 2006, the initial limit is $2250. For a subsequent year, the initial coverage limit is equal to the amount specified for the previous year, increased by the annual percentage increase for year involved. The amount determined to be the increase in the initial coverage limit amount will be rounded to the nearest multiple of $10.

Effective date. Effective upon enactment, except coverage of prescription drugs becomes effective January 1, 2006.

Act Sec. 101(a) adding Sec. 1860D-2(b)(1)-(3) and (6) of the Social Security Act. Law at ¶2261B.

¶ 105

Protection Against High Out-of-Pocket Expenditures

Annual out-of-pocket threshold. The prescription drug coverage provides benefits with cost-sharing after an eligible individual has incurred costs for covered Part D drugs in a year equal to the annual out-of-pocket threshold, which is subject to a yearly inflation increase. For 2006, the annual out-of-pocket threshold is $3600. For a year subsequent to 2006, the annual out-of-pocket threshold will be increased by the annual percentage increase. The amount of increase that is not a multiple of $50 will be rounded to the nearest multiple of $50.

The individual will be responsible for cost-sharing in an amount that is equal to the greater of a copayment of $2.00 for a generic drug or a preferred drug that is a multiple source drug, and $5.00 for any other drug; or coinsurance that is equal to five percent. For a year after 2006, the dollar amounts for cost-sharing for the previous year will be increased by the annual percentage increase for the year involved. Any amount that is not a multiple of five cents will be rounded to the nearest multiple of five cents. A PDP or MA-PD may reduce the applicable cost-sharing for generic or preferred drugs to zero.

Incurred costs. Incurred costs only include costs incurred for covered Part D drugs for the annual deductible, cost sharing, and amounts for which benefits are not provided because of the application of the initial coverage limit. Incurred costs do not include any costs incurred for covered Part D drugs that are not included in the plan's formulary. Costs will be treated as incurred only if they are paid by the eligible individual (or by another individual on behalf of the eligible individual); on behalf of a low-income individual under the subsidy provisions; or under a state pharmaceutical assistance program. If an eligible individual is reimbursed for such costs through insurance, a group health plan, or other third-party payment arrangement the costs may not count toward incurred costs.

Determining third-party reimbursement. The Secretary is authorized to establish procedures, in coordination with the Secretary of Treasury and the Secretary of Labor, for determining whether costs for eligible individuals are being reimbursed through insurance, a group health plan, or third-party payment arrangements and inform the PDP sponsors and MA organizations that offer the plans in which the individuals are enrolled about such reimbursement arrangements. In addition, a PDP sponsor or MA organization periodically may ask an eligible individual enrolled in a PDP or MA-PD whether the individual has or expects to receive third-party reimbursement. Material misrepresentation of information related to third-party reimbursement by an eligible individual will constitute grounds for termination of enrollment in the PDP or MA-PD.

Effective date. Effective upon enactment.

Act Sec. 101(a) adding Sec. 1860D-2(b)(4)-(5) of the Social Security Act. Law at ¶ 2261B.

¶ 106

Alternative Prescription Drug Coverage Requirements

Alternate benefit. A PDP or MA-PD plan may provide a different prescription drug benefit design from the standard prescription drug coverage described in ¶ 104 so long as the Secretary determines that certain requirements are met and the plan applies for, and receives, the Secretary's approval of the benefit design. In addition, alternate prescription drug coverage must provide the same protection against high out-of-pocket expenditures as standard prescription drug coverage provides.

Actuarially equivalent coverage. The actuarial value of the total coverage must be at least equal to the actuarial value of standard coverage. The unsubsidized value of the coverage must be at least equal to the unsubsidized value of standard coverage. The unsubsidized value of coverage is the amount by which the actuarial value of the coverage exceeds the actuarial value of the subsidy payments (see ¶ 120).

Assuring standard payment for costs at initial coverage limit. The coverage must be designed (based on actuarially representative patterns of utilization) to provide for the payment of incurred costs that are equal to the initial coverage limit for the year under the standard coverage. The payment is an amount that is at least equal to the product of: (1) the amount by which the initial coverage limit exceeds the deductible, and (2) 100 percent minus the coinsurance.

Deductible. The deductible under the alternative prescription drug coverage benefit cannot exceed the amount of the deductible for the standard prescription drug coverage benefit.

Effective date. Effective upon enactment, except that the prescription drug coverage is not effective until January 1, 2006.

Act Sec. 101(a) adding Sec. 1860D-2(c) of the Social Security Act. Law at ¶ 2261B.

¶ 107

Access to Negotiated Prices

Beneficiary access to negotiated prices. A PDP sponsor offering a PDP plan and a MA organization offering an MA-PD plan must provide beneficiaries with access to negotiated prices for covered Part D drugs, regardless of whether benefits are payable under the plan because of the application of the deductible or other cost-sharing or an initial coverage limit. Negotiated prices include negotiated price concessions such as discounts, direct or indirect subsidies, rebates, and direct or indirect remunerations and any dispensing fees for the drugs.

The prices negotiated by a PDP, by an MA-PD plan, or by a qualified retiree PDP for covered Part D drugs on behalf of an eligible individual will not be taken into account for the purposes of establishing the best price under Medicaid.

Disclosure. The PDP sponsor and MA organization offering an MA-PD plan must disclose to the Secretary the aggregate negotiated price concessions made available to the sponsor or organization by a manufacturer that are passed through in the form of lower subsidies, lower monthly beneficiary prescription drug premiums, and lower prices through pharmacies and other dispensers. Manufacturers are required to disclose pricing information related to negotiated prices under Part D to the Secretary under the same conditions for disclosure of information applicable to the Medicaid program.

Audits and reports. The Secretary periodically may audit the financial statements and records of PDP sponsors and MA organizations offering an MA-PD plan to protect against fraud and abuse and to ensure proper disclosures and accounting in addition to any protections against fraud and abuse provided under new Sec. 1860D-12(b)(3)(C) of the Social Security Act (see ¶ 117).

Effective date. Effective January 1, 2006.

Act Sec. 101(a) adding Sec. 1860D-2(d) of the Social Security Act. Law at ¶ 2261B.

¶ 108
Covered Part D Drug Defined

Covered outpatient drug. A "covered Part D drug" is a drug that may be dispensed only upon prescription, a biological product, or insulin described in Secs. 1927(k)(2)(A)(i)-(iii), (B)(i)- (iii), and (C) of the Social Security Act, respectively, and medical supplies associated with the injection of insulin and vaccines licensed under Sec. 351 of the Public Health Service Act as well as any use of a covered Part D drug for a medically accepted indication. Drugs excluded or restricted from Medicaid coverage are not included in Part D drug coverage except for smoking cessation drugs, or drugs that are added to the list of excluded drugs under Sec. 1927(d)(3).

Avoidance of duplicate coverage. A drug prescribed for an eligible individual that would otherwise be a covered Part D drug will not be covered if payment for the drug is available under Part A or Part B for the individual.

Application of exclusion provisions. Any covered Part D drug for which payment would not be made because it does not meet the Medicare definition of medically necessary may be excluded from qualified prescription drug coverage by a PDP or MA-PD plan. A PDP or MA-PD plan also may exclude any covered Part D drug that is not prescribed in accordance with the plan or Part D. Some exclusions are determinations subject to reconsideration and appeal as described in ¶ 114.

Effective date. Effective upon enactment, except that coverage for prescription drugs becomes effective January 1, 2006.

Act Sec. 101(a) adding Sec. 1860D-2(e) of the Social Security Act. Law at ¶ 2261B.

BENEFICIARY PROTECTIONS

¶ 109
Access to Choice of Qualified Prescription Drug Coverage

Assuring access to a choice of coverage. The Secretary must ensure that each beneficiary has available the choice of at least two qualifying plans in the area in which the individual resides. At least one of the plans must be a PDP. The requirement is not satisfied if only one PDP sponsor or MA organization offers all the qualifying plans in the area; at least two different plan sponsors must offer the plans. If at least two plans are not available, the eligible individual must be given the opportunity to enroll in a fallback PDP.

To ensure access to a plan in an area, the Secretary may approve limited risk plans for the area (see ¶ 116). If access is not provided in the area by limited risk plans, the Secretary must offer a fallback PDP for the area (see ¶ 116).

Qualifying plan defined. A qualifying plan is a PDP or an MA-PD plan that provides the basic prescription drug coverage, or qualified prescription drug coverage, that provides supplemental prescription drug coverage so long as there is no MA monthly supplemental beneficiary premium applied under the plan due to the application of a rebate credited against the premium as described in new Sec. 1854(b)(1)(C) of the Social Security Act (see ¶ 363).

Effective date. Effective upon enactment.

Act Sec. 101(a) adding Sec. 1860D-3 of the Social Security Act. Law at ¶2261C.

¶110

Beneficiary Protections for Qualified Prescription Drug Coverage

Dissemination of information. At the time of enrollment and at least annually thereafter, a PDP sponsor must disclose to each enrollee the information described in Sec. 1852(c)(1) of the Social Security Act related to the benefits provided under Part D. The information that must be disclosed to enrollees of the plan includes:

(1) access to specific covered outpatient drugs, including access through pharmacy networks;

(2) how any formulary used by the sponsor functions, including any tiered formulary structure;

(3) copayments and deductible requirements, including the identification of the tiered or other copayments level applicable to each drug or class of drugs and how the individual may obtain information on the requirements; and

(4) medication therapy management program.

Disclosure of information upon request of an individual. The PDP sponsor must provide individuals with information including general coverage, utilization, and grievance information and appeals as described in Sec. 1852(c)(2)(A), (B) and (C) of the Social Security Act.

Provision of specific information. PDP sponsors must have a mechanism for providing specific information on a timely basis to enrollees who have requested such information. The mechanism should include access to information through a toll-free telephone number and in writing upon request. In addition, PDP sponsors are required to make specific changes in the formulary under the plan available through an Internet website.

Claim information. Each PDP sponsor offering a prescription drug plan must furnish to each enrollee an explanation of benefits and a notice of the benefits in relation to the initial coverage limit and the annual out-of-pocket threshold applicable to the enrollee for the current year, whenever prescription drug benefits are provided. The explanation of benefits must be in a form that is easily understood by enrollees. Notices should take into account incurred costs.

Effective date. Effective upon enactment, except that coverage for prescription drugs becomes effective January 1, 2006.

Act Sec. 101(a) adding Sec. 1860D-4(a) of the Social Security Act. Law at ¶2261D.

PDP SPONSOR REQUIREMENTS

¶111

Access to Covered Part D Drugs

Assuring pharmacy access. A PDP sponsor must permit the participation of any pharmacy that meets the terms and conditions that the plan has established. The PDP sponsor also must ensure a sufficient number of pharmacies participating within its network that dispense (other than by mail order) drugs directly to patients to ensure convenient access. The Secretary must establish rules for convenient access to pharmacies that are no less favorable to enrollees than the rules for convenient access to pharmacies included in the statement of work solicitation of the Department of Defense for the TRICARE Retail Pharmacy program as of March 13, 2003.

Comment: The conference committee report clarified that the minimum in-network pharmacy for each plan offered by a PDP or MA plan in a geographic area must provide access to pharmacies that is not less restrictive than the TRICARE access standards. These standards require that 90 percent of plan enrollees in urban areas will have access to a retail pharmacy within two miles; that 90 percent of suburban plan enrollees will have access to a retail pharmacy within five miles; and that 70 percent of rural plan enrollees will have access to a pharmacy within 15 miles. PDP sponsors or MA sponsors can offer broader networks than those meeting the TRICARE access standards.

Discounts for network pharmacies. For covered Part D drugs dispensed through in-network pharmacies, a PDP may reduce coinsurance or copayments for individuals enrolled in the plan below the level otherwise required. This reduction may not result in an increase in subsidy payments made by the Secretary to the plan.

Other access rules. The rules must include adequate emergency access for enrollees and may include standards for access for enrollees who are residing in long-term care facilities and for pharmacies operated by the Indian Health Service, Indian tribes, and urban Indian organizations. In addition, a PDP sponsor must permit enrollees to receive benefits through a pharmacy (other than a mail order pharmacy), with any differential in charge paid by the enrollees. This may include a 90-day supply of drugs or biologicals.

Participating pharmacies are not required to accept insurance risk as a condition of participation.

Standardized technology. A PDP sponsor of a PDP must issue and reissue a card or other technology that may be used by an enrollee to assure access to negotiated prices. The Secretary must provide for the development, adoption, or recognition of standards relating to a standardized format for the card or other technology that are compatible with the simplification standard requirements established under Part C of Title XI of the Social Security Act. In developing the standards the Secretary must consult with the National Council for Prescription Drug Programs and other standard setting organizations. The standards must be implemented by a date the Secretary determines will ensure that PDP sponsors utilize the standards beginning January 1, 2006.

Requirements for formularies. If a PDP sponsor of a PDP uses a formulary, including the use of tiered cost-sharing, it must meet certain requirements. The requirements for formularies may be met by a PDP sponsor directly or through arrangements with another entity. The PDP sponsor must establish policies and procedures to educate and inform healthcare providers and enrollees about the formulary.

Pharmacy and therapeutic committee. A pharmacy and therapeutic committee must develop and review the formulary. The majority of its members must be practicing physicians or practicing pharmacists or both. The committee must include at least one practicing physician and at least one practicing pharmacist with expertise in the care of elderly or disabled persons and is independent and free of conflict with respect to the sponsor and plan.

Formulary development. The committee must base clinical decisions on the strength of scientific evidence and standards of practice, including assessing peer-reviewed medical literature, such as randomized clinical trials, pharmacoeconomic studies, outcomes research data, and any other appropriate information. It must take into account whether including in the formulary or in a tier of the formulary particular covered Part D drugs has therapeutic advantages in terms of safety and efficacy. The formulary must include drugs within each therapeutic category and class of covered Part D drugs, but not necessarily all drugs within such categories and classifications.

Model guidelines. The Secretary is required to request the United States Pharmacopeia to develop, in consultation with pharmaceutical benefit managers and other interested parties, a list of categories and classes that may be used by PDPs to revise such classification from time to time to reflect changes in therapeutic uses of covered Part D drugs and the additions of new covered Part D drugs.

Drug Information list. The committee must make the reasons for the exclusion of coverage of any drug from the formulary available to the enrollees under the plan through the Internet or other means and must establish policies and procedures to educate and inform healthcare providers and enrollees concerning the formulary.

Limitations on changes in therapeutic class. The PDP sponsor may not change the therapeutic categories and classes in a formulary other than at the beginning of each plan year unless the Secretary permits the PDP to take into account new therapeutic uses and newly approved covered Part D drugs.

Removing a drug from the formulary. Any removal of a covered outpatient drug from a formulary and any change in the preferred or tiered cost-sharing status of the drug may take effect only after notifying beneficiaries, physicians, pharmacies, and pharmacists.

Periodic evaluation of protocols. A PDP must provide for the periodic evaluation and analysis of treatment protocols and procedures relating to the formulary.

Effective date. Effective upon enactment.

Act Sec. 101(a) adding Sec. 1860D-4(b) of the Social Security Act. Law at ¶2261D.

¶112

Cost and Utilization Management; Quality Assurance; Medication Therapy Management Program

Cost and utilization management. The PDP sponsor must have in place, directly or though appropriate arrangements, (1) a cost-effective drug utilization management program, including incentives to reduce costs when medically appropriate; (2) quality assurance measures and systems to reduce medication errors and adverse drug interactions and improve medication use; (3) a medication therapy management program; and (4) a program to control fraud, abuse, and waste. A PDP sponsor or entity may use cost management tools, including differential payments, under all methods of operation.

Medication therapy management program. A medication therapy management program is a program of drug therapy management that may be furnished by a pharmacist and is designed to assure that, for targeted beneficiaries, covered Part D drugs covered under the prescription drug plan are used appropriately to optimize therapeutic outcomes through improved medication use and reduce the risk of adverse events, including adverse drug interactions. The program must be developed in cooperation with licensed and practicing pharmacists and physicians. The Secretary must establish guidelines for the coordination of any medication therapy management program with any care management plan established for a targeted beneficiary under the new chronic care improvement program created by this Act (see ¶678).

Targeted beneficiaries. Targeted beneficiaries are Part D eligible individuals who have multiple chronic diseases such as diabetes, asthma, hypertension, and congestive heart failure; are taking multiple covered Part D drugs; and are identified as likely to incur annual costs for covered Part D drugs that exceed a level specified by the Secretary.

Elements. The program should (1) enhance enrollee understanding to promote the appropriate use of medications by beneficiaries and to reduce the risk of potential adverse events associated with medications through beneficiary education, counseling, and other means; (2) increase enrollee adherence to prescription medication regimens through medication refill reminders, special packaging, and other compliance programs; and (3) detect adverse drug events and patterns of overuse and underuse of prescription drugs.

Establishing fees for pharmacists. In establishing fees for pharmacists and others providing services under the plan, the PDP sponsor must take into account the resources and time required to implement a medication therapy management program. If requested by the Secretary, each sponsor must disclose the amount of management or dispensing fees. The disclosure of the fees will be confidential and handled in the manner provided under the Medicaid program.

Effective date. Effective upon enactment.

Act Sec. 101(a) adding Sec. 1860D-4(c) of the Social Security Act. Law at ¶2261D.

¶113
Electronic Prescription Program

The Secretary must establish uniform standards that meet program requirements for an electronic prescription drug program. The standards apply to prescriptions for covered Part D drugs and required information transmitted electronically under an electronic prescription drug program conducted by a PDP or MA plan. Not later than one year after the date of the promulgation of final standards, prescriptions and other information transmitted electronically for covered Part D drugs prescribed to eligible individuals may be transmitted only in accordance with the final standards.

Program requirements. The electronic prescription drug program must provide for the electronic transmittal to the prescribing healthcare professional and to the dispensing pharmacy and pharmacist of the prescription and information on eligibility and benefits, including the drugs included in the applicable formulary, any tiered formulary structure, and any requirements for prior authorization as well as information on the drug prescribed and other drugs listed on the medication history, including information on drug interactions, warnings, or cautions, and when indicated, dosage adjustments; and information on the availability of a lower cost, therapeutically appropriate alternative for the drug prescribed.

Application of medical history information. Effective on a date specified by the Secretary after appropriate standards have been established, the program must provide for the electronic transmittal of information related to the medical history concerning the individual and related to a covered Part D drug being prescribed or dispensed when requested by the professional or pharmacist involved.

Limitations and timing. Information may only be disclosed if the disclosure of the information is permitted under Sec. 264(c) of the Health Insurance Portability and

Accountability Act of 1996 (HIPAA) privacy rules protecting individually identifiable health information. The information exchanged must be on an interactive real-time basis.

Standards. The standards must be consistent with the objectives of improving patient safety; the quality of care provided to patients; and efficiencies, including cost savings, in the delivery of care. The standards must be designed so that they do not impose an undue administrative burden on prescribing healthcare professionals and dispensing pharmacies and pharmacists. The standards also must be compatible with the HIPAA administrative simplification standards and with general health information technology standards. They must be designed to permit electronic exchange of drug labeling and drug listing information maintained by the Food and Drug Administration and the National Library of Medicine.

The standards must permit the messaging of information if it relates to the appropriate prescribing of drugs, including quality assurance measures and systems. A Part D eligible individual may designate a particular pharmacy to dispense a prescribed drug. Permitting an individual to designate a particular pharmacy does not affect the access required to be provided to pharmacies by the PDP or the application of any differences in benefits or payments under the PDP based on the pharmacy dispensing the covered drug.

Development of initial standards. Not later than September 1, 2005, the Secretary must develop initial uniform standards relating to the requirements for electronic prescription drug programs taking into consideration recommendations from the National Committee on Vital Health and Statistics (NCVHS). The NCVHS must develop recommendations for uniform standards in consultation with standard setting organizations, practicing physicians, hospitals, pharmacies, practicing pharmacists, state boards of pharmacy and medicine, experts on electronic prescribing, and other appropriate federal agencies.

Pilot project. During the one-year period beginning January 1, 2006, the Secretary must conduct a pilot project to test the initial standards prior to the promulgation of final uniform standards to provide for the efficient implementation of the requirements of the electronic prescription program. The Secretary must enter into agreements with physicians, physician groups, pharmacies, hospitals, PDP sponsors, MA organizations, and other entities under which healthcare professionals electronically transmit prescriptions to dispensing pharmacies and pharmacists in accordance with the standards. The Secretary must evaluate the pilot project and report to Congress no later than April 1, 2007.

No pilot testing is required if the Secretary determines in consultation with affected standard setting organizations and industry users that there is adequate industry experience with the standards.

Final standards. Based upon the evaluation of the pilot project, but not later than April 1, 2008, the Secretary must promulgate uniform standards for the electronic prescription program.

The standards will supersede any state law or regulation that is contrary to the standards or restricts the ability to carry out this program and pertains to the electronic transmission of medication history and information on eligibility, benefits, and prescriptions with respect to covered Part D drugs.

Safe harbor. The Secretary must promulgate regulations that provide for a safe harbor from criminal sanctions and the self-referral prohibition with respect to nonmonetary remuneration in the form of hardware, software, or information technology and training services necessary and used solely to receive and transmit

¶113

electronic prescription information in accordance with the standards for the electronic prescription program. The safe harbor applies to: (1) in the case of a hospital, by the hospital to members of its medical staff; (2) in the case of a medical group practice, to the prescribing healthcare professionals who are members of the practice; and (3) in the case of a PDP sponsor or MA organization, by the sponsor or organization to pharmacists and pharmacies participating in its network and to prescribing health professionals.

Effective date. Effective upon enactment.

Act Sec. 101(a) adding Sec. 1860D-4(e) of the Social Security Act. Law at ¶2261D.

¶114
Grievance Mechanism, Coverage Determinations, Reconsiderations, Appeals, and Confidentiality of Records

Grievance procedures. Each PDP sponsor must have meaningful procedures for hearing and resolving grievances between the sponsor (including any entity or individual through which the sponsor provides covered benefits) and enrollees in the PDP sponsor's plan in accordance with MA provisions under Sec. 1852(f) of the Social Security Act.

Coverage determinations and reconsiderations. A PDP sponsor must meet the requirements of Sec. 1852(g)(1)-(3), which provides for determinations, reconsiderations, and expedited determinations and reconsiderations, with respect to covered Part D drug benefits under the PDP it offers in the same manner that the requirements apply to an MA organization with respect to the benefits it offers under an MA plan under Part C.

Request for determination for the treatment of tiered formulary drug. If a PDP sponsor provides for tiered cost-sharing for drugs included within a formulary and provides lower cost-sharing for preferred drugs included within the formulary, an eligible individual may request an exception to the tiered cost-sharing structure. Under an exception, a nonpreferred drug could be covered under the terms applicable for preferred drugs if the prescribing physician determines that the preferred drug for treatment of the same condition either would not be as effective for the individual or would have adverse effects for the individual or both. A PDP sponsor must have an exception process consistent with guidelines established by the Secretary for making a determination when an eligible individual requests that a nonpreferred drug be covered under the terms applicable to preferred drugs. Denial of an exception must be treated as a coverage denial for purposes of an appeal (discussed below).

Appeals. A PDP sponsor must provide for independent review of certain coverage denials and appeals, including a determination related to the application of tiered cost-sharing as required by Sec. 1852(g)(2), (4) and (5) of the Social Security Act, in the same manner as the requirements apply to an MA organization that offers the original Medicare program fee-for-service option under an MA plan under Part C.

Nonformulary determinations. An individual who is enrolled in a prescription drug plan offered by a PDP sponsor may appeal a determination not to provide for coverage of a covered Part D drug that is not on the formulary under the plan only if the prescribing physician determines that all covered Part D drugs on any tier of the formulary for treatment of the same condition would not be as effective for the individual as the nonformulary drug, would have adverse effects for the individual, or both. If the PDP sponsor determines that a plan provides coverage for a covered

Part D drug that is not on the formulary of the plan, the drug must be treated as if it were included on the formulary.

Confidentiality and accuracy of enrollee records. The requirements for confidentiality and accuracy of enrollee records described in Sec. 1852(h) of the Social Security Act apply to a PDP sponsor and prescription drug plan in the same manner as the requirements apply to an MA organization and an MA plan.

Accreditation. The rules related to treatment of accreditation found at Sec. 1852(e)(4) apply to a PDP sponsor in the same manner as they apply to an MA organization with respect to the following requirements: access to covered Part D drugs, quality assurance and medication therapy management, and confidentiality and accuracy of enrollee records.

Public disclosure of pharmaceutical prices for equivalent drugs. A PDP sponsor offering a PDP must ensure that each pharmacy that dispenses a covered Part D drug informs an enrollee of any differential between the price of the drug to the enrollee and the price of the lowest priced generic covered Part D drug under the plan that is therapeutically equivalent and bioequivalent and available at the pharmacy. Notice must be provided at the time of purchase of the drug involved or in the case of dispensing by mail order, at the time of delivery of the drug. This requirement may be waived by the Secretary.

Effective date. Effective upon enactment.

Act Sec. 101(a) adding Secs. 1860D-4(f), (g), (h), (i), (j), and (k) of the Social Security Act. Law at ¶2261D.

PDP, LIMITED RISK AND FALLBACK REQUIREMENTS

¶115

Prescription Drug Plan Regions, Submission of Bids, and Plan Approval

Establishment of prescription drug plan regions. The Secretary must establish and may revise PDP regions in a manner consistent with the requirements for the establishment and revision of MA regions. To the extent possible, PDP regions will be the same as MA regions (see ¶363). The Secretary may establish PDP regions that are not the same as MA regions if the Secretary determines that the establishment of different regions would improve access to benefits. The Secretary also will establish and may revise PDP regions for the territories that are not within the 50 states or District of Columbia. The service area for a prescription drug plan (PDP) will consist of an entire PDP region. A PDP may be offered in more than one PDP region.

Submitting bids and premiums. Each PDP sponsor must submit information to the Secretary with respect to each PDP it offers. The information must be submitted at the same time and in a similar manner as information is submitted by an MA organization under Sec. 1854(a)(6) of the Social Security Act. The Secretary must establish requirements for information submission that promote the offering of such plans in more than one PDP region, including all regions, through the filing of consolidated information. The following information must be submitted:

(1) the prescription drug coverage that will be provided under the plan, including the deductible and cost-sharing;

¶115

(2) the actuarial value of the qualified prescription drug coverage in the region for a Part D eligible individual with a national average risk profile for the factors;

(3) the bid, including an actuarial certification of the:

(a) basis for the actuarial value assumed in the bid;

(b) portion of the bid attributable to the basic prescription drug coverage, and the portion of the bid attributable to supplemental benefits;

(c) assumptions regarding the reinsurance subsidy payments subtracted from the actuarial value to produce the bid; and

(d) administrative expenses assumed in the bid.

(4) the service area for the plan;

(5) whether the PDP sponsor requires a modification of risk level and the extent of the modification. Any modification will apply to all PDPs offered by a PDP sponsor in a PDP region. This does not apply to an MA-PD plan. A modification of risk level may consist of one or more of the following:

(a) an equal percentage point increase in the percents applied in initial risk corridors (see ¶120);

(b) an equal percentage point increase in the percents applied in the second risk corridor;

(c) a decrease in the threshold risk percentages.

(6) Any other information the Secretary may require to carry out this provision.

Actuarial valuation. The Secretary is required to establish processes and methods for determining the actuarial valuation of prescription drug coverage, including: (1) an actuarial valuation of standard prescription drug coverage; (2) actuarial valuations related to alternative prescription drug coverage; (3) an actuarial valuation of the reinsurance subsidy payments; (4) the use of generally accepted actuarial principles and methods; and (5) applying the same methodology for determinations of actuarial valuations for standard prescription drug coverage and alternative prescription drug coverage. The processes and methods for determining actuarial valuation must take into account the effect that providing alternative prescription drug coverage rather than standard prescription drug coverage has on drug utilization.

The PDP sponsors and MA organizations are responsible for the preparation and submission of actuarial valuations required for PDPs and MA-PD plans they offer. Under the processes and methods established by the Secretary to determine the actuarial valuation, PDP sponsors offering PDPs and MA organizations offering MA-PD plans may use actuarial opinions certified by independent, qualified actuaries to establish actuarial values.

Review of information and negotiation. The Secretary must review the information submitted and conduct negotiations with the plan. The Secretary has the authority to negotiate the terms and conditions of the proposed bid submitted and other terms and conditions of a proposed plan. The Secretary has authority similar to the authority of the Director of the Office of Personnel Management with respect to health benefit plans.

Approval of proposed plans. After review and negotiation, the Secretary may approve or disapprove of the PDP. The Secretary may approve a PDP only if the plan and the PDP sponsor offering the plan (1) comply with the requirements including the provision of qualified prescription drug coverage, and (2) meet the requirements relating to actuarial determinations, including alternative prescription drug coverage, and the Secretary determines that the portion of the bid that is attributable to basic prescription drug coverage is supported by the actuarial bases and reasonably and equitably reflects the revenue requirements for benefits provided under the plan less the sum of the insurance repayments. The Secretary also determines the portion of the bid that is attributable to supplemental prescription drug coverage is supported by the actuarial bases and reasonably and equitably reflects the revenue requirements for such coverage under the plan.

The Secretary can only approve the plan if the design of the plan and its benefits, including any formulary and tiered formulary structure, are not likely to substantially discourage enrollment by certain Part D eligible individuals. The plan design of categories and classes within a formulary will not be considered as discouraging to certain individuals if the categories and classes are consistent with the categories and classes established by the United States Pharmacopeia.

Noninterference. To promote competition, the Secretary may not interfere with negotiations between drug manufacturers and pharmacies and PDP sponsors and may not require a particular formulary or institute a price structure for the reimbursement of Part D drugs.

Coordination of benefits. A PDP sponsor offering a prescription drug plan must permit state pharmaceutical assistance programs and prescription drug plans to coordinate benefits with the plan. Fees may not be imposed that are unrelated to coordination.

Effective date. Effective upon enactment.

Act Sec. 101(a) adding Sec. 1860D-11(a), (b), (c), (d), (e), (i), and (j) of the Social Security Act. Law at ¶2262A.

¶116

Limited Risk Plans and Fallback Prescription Drug Plans

Risk plans and fallback entities defined. A "limited risk plan" is a prescription drug plan that provides basic prescription drug coverage and for which the PDP sponsor includes a modification of risk level in its bid submitted for the plan. A limited risk plan does not include a fallback prescription drug plan.

A "full risk plan" is a prescription drug plan that is not a limited risk plan or a fallback prescription drug plan.

An "eligible fallback entity" is an entity that meets the requirements to be PDP sponsor or would meet such requirements, except that it is not a risk-bearing entity, and does not submit a bid for any prescription drug plan for any PDP region for the first year of a contract period. An entity is treated as submitting a bid if the entity is acting as a subcontractor of a PDP sponsor that is offering a plan, except for entities that are subcontractors of an MA organization unless the MA organization is acting as a PDP sponsor.

Application of limited risk plans. The Secretary may only approve a limited risk plan for a PDP region if the access requirements would not be met for the region unless a risk plan was approved. Only the minimum number of risk plans may be approved to meet the access requirement. The Secretary must provide priority in approval for those plans bearing the highest level of risk, but the Secretary may take into account the level of the bids submitted by risk plans. The Secretary may not approve a limited risk plan under which the modification of risk level provides for no or a minimal level of financial risk. There is no limit on the number of full risk plans that may be approved.

Establishing a fallback process. The Secretary must establish a separate process for the solicitation of bids from eligible fallback entities for the offering of a fallback prescription drug plan in all fallback service areas in one or more PDP regions during a contract period. A fallback prescription drug plan is a prescription drug plan that only offers the standard prescription drug coverage and access to negotiated prices and does not include any supplemental prescription drug coverage and meets other requirements that may be specified by the Secretary.

Approval of fallback prescription drug plans. Generally, the rules for approval of PDPs apply to the approval or disapproval of fallback prescription drug plans. The Secretary may approve the offering of only one fallback prescription drug plan with respect to all fallback services in any PDP region for a contract period. The fallback prescription drug plan for a PDP region for a year must be offered at the same time as prescription drug plans would be offered. Competitive contract provisions apply. The Secretary may not enter into a contract with a single fallback entity for the offering of fallback plans throughout the United States.

Fallback service area. A fallback service area is any area within a PDP region that will not meet access requirements for the year based on a determination made by the Secretary before the beginning of the year..

Payments to fallback entities. Payments under the contract provide for payment for the actual costs, taking into account negotiated price concessions for Part D drugs provided to eligible individuals enrolled in a fallback prescription drug plan offered by the entity and payment of management fees that are tied to performance measures established by the Secretary for management, administration, and delivery of the benefits under the contract.

Performance measures. The performance measures established by the Secretary must include measures for cost containment for the Medicare Prescription Drug Account and beneficiaries, such as generic substitution and price discounts; provision of quality programs for enrollees that avoid adverse drug reactions and overutilization and reduce medical errors; provision of timely and accurate delivery of services and pharmacy and beneficiary support services; and efficient and effective benefit administration and claims adjudication.

Monthly beneficiary premium. The monthly beneficiary premium charged under a fallback prescription drug plan must be uniform and equal to 25.5 percent of an amount equal to the Secretary's estimate of the average monthly per capita actuarial cost, including administrative expenses under the fallback prescription drug plan, as calculated by the Chief Actuary of CMS. In calculating the administrative expenses, the Chief Actuary must use a factor that is based on similar expenses of prescription drug plans that are not fallback prescription drug plans.

Contract terms. The terms and conditions of contracts with eligible fallback entities offering fallback prescription drug plans are the same as the terms and conditions of contracts for PDPs. The contract will be for a period of three years and may be renewed after a subsequent bidding process. A contract for a fallback prescription drug plan may be offered in an area for a year only if that area is a fallback service area for that year.

Marketing rules. An eligible fallback entity with a contract may not engage in any marketing or branding of a fallback prescription drug plan.

Annual report on the use of limited risk plans and fallback plans. The Secretary must submit to Congress an annual report that describes instances in which limited risk plans and fallback prescription drug plans were offered. The report must include appropriate recommendations to limit the need for the provision of such plans and to maximize the assumption of financial risk.

Effective date. Effective upon enactment.

Act Sec. 101(a) adding Sec. 1860D-11(f), (g), and (h) of the Social Security Act. Law at ¶2262A.

¶117

Requirements for and Contracts with Prescription Drug Plans

Organizational requirements for prescription drug plan (PDP) sponsors. Each PDP sponsor must meet the following requirements:

(1) The sponsor must be organized and licensed under state law as a risk-bearing entity eligible to offer health insurance or health benefits coverage in each state in which it offers a prescription drug plan.

(2) The entity must assume full financial risk on a prospective basis for benefits it offers under a prescription drug plan and that are not covered by direct subsidy payments (see ¶119 and ¶120). The plan sponsor may obtain insurance or make other arrangements for the cost of coverage provided to any enrollee to the extent that the sponsor is at risk for providing such coverage.

(3) In the case of an unlicensed sponsor and for which a waiver of certain requirements has been approved, the sponsor must meet solvency standards established by the Secretary.

A PDP sponsor that meets the state licensure requirement or has an approved waiver application must meet all other requirements imposed under Part D.

Contract requirements. To offer a prescription drug plan and participate in the prescription drug program under Part D and be eligible for payment, a PDP sponsor must enter into a contract with the Secretary. Under the provisions of the contract, the sponsor agrees to comply with the applicable requirements and standards of Part D and the terms and conditions of payment as provided under Part D. The contract may cover more than one prescription drug plan.

Limitation on entities offering fallback prescription drug plans. The Secretary may not enter into a contract with a PDP sponsor to offer a prescription drug plan (other than a fallback prescription drug plan) in a PDP region for a year if the sponsor:

(1) submitted a bid for a year (as the first year of the contract period) to offer a fallback prescription drug plan in any PDP region;

(2) offers a fallback prescription drug plan in any PDP region during the year; or

(3) offered a fallback prescription drug plan in that PDP region during the previous year.

An entity will be treated as submitting a bid or offering a fallback prescription drug plan if the entity is acting as a subcontractor of a PDP sponsor that is offering a prescription drug plan. This does not apply to entities that are subcontractors of an MA organization unless the organization is acting as a PDP sponsor offering a prescription drug plan.

Incorporation of certain Medicare Advantage contract requirements. Provisions of Sec. 1857 of the Social Security Act apply to contracts under the prescription drug plan program in the same manner as they apply to Medicare Advantage plans. Those provisions include:

(1) minimum enrollment, except that the Secretary may increase the minimum number of enrollees as the Secretary determines is appropriate and the requirement will be waived during the first contract year for an organization in the region;

(2) contract period and effectiveness, except references to payment amounts under Sec. 1853 will be considered payment amounts under Sec. 1860D-15;

(3) protections against fraud and beneficiary protections;

(4) additional contract terms, except that Sec. 1857(e)(2) will apply as specified to PDP sponsors and payments to an MA-PD plan will be treated as expenditures made under Part D.

(5) intermediate sanctions; and

(6) procedures for termination.

Waiver of certain requirements to expand choice. The Secretary may waive the state licensure requirement, however, if the Secretary determines, based on the application and other evidence presented, that any of the grounds for approval of the application have been met. In addition, the provisions of new Sec. 1858(d) of the Social Security Act apply to PDP sponsors in a manner similar to the manner in which the provisions apply to MA organizations (see ¶363). The Secretary may waive the state licensure requirement under circumstances similar to those permitted that apply to provider sponsored organizations under Sec. 1855(a)(2)(B), (C) and (D) and the application by a state of any grounds other than those required under federal law. In addition, no application will be required if a state does not have a licensing process in effect for a PDP sponsor. For plan years beginning before January 1, 2008, if the state does not have a licensing process in effect, the ground for approval of waiver of this requirement is deemed to have been met upon submission of an application.

Application of waiver procedures. Sec. 1855(a)(2)(E), (F) and (G) of the Social Security Act, which deals with the rules for application of waiver to a state, preemption of state law, compliance with consumer protection, and quality standards, and the action the Secretary must take on waiver application apply to PDP sponsors in the same manner as they apply to provider sponsored organizations. If a state does not have a licensing process for PDP sponsors, the limitation of application to only one state, the 36-month effective period, and prohibition against renewal do not apply (Sec. 1855(a)(2)(E)(i) and (ii)).

Solvency standards for non-licensed sponsors. No later than January 1, 2005, the Secretary, in consultation with the National Association of Insurance Commissioners, must establish and publish financial solvency and capital adequacy standards. A PDP sponsor that is not licensed by a state for which a waiver application has been approved must meet the solvency and capital adequacy standards established by the Secretary. The Secretary must establish certification procedures for solvency standards in the manner described in Sec. 1855(c)(2) of the Social Security Act.

Periodic review and revision of standards. The Secretary may periodically review the standards established related to PDP sponsor requirements and revise the standards when appropriate; however, other than at the beginning of a calendar year, the Secretary may not implement regulations that impose new, significant regulatory requirements on a PDP sponsor or prescription drug plan.

Relation to state laws. The standards established under this part supersede any state law or regulation other than state licensing laws or state laws relating to plan solvency. States are prohibited from imposing a premium tax or similar tax with respect to premiums paid to PDP sponsors or payments made to the PDP sponsor by the Secretary.

Effective date. Effective upon enactment.

Act Sec. 101(a) adding Sec. 1860D-12 of the Social Security Act. Law at ¶2262B.

PREMIUM AND SUBSIDIES

¶118

Premiums; Late Enrollment Penalty

Monthly base beneficiary premium. The "monthly beneficiary premium" for a prescription drug plan is defined as the base beneficiary premium, as adjusted. The base beneficiary premium for a month is equal to the product of the beneficiary premium percentage and the national average monthly bid amount for the month.

Calculating the base beneficiary percent. The beneficiary premium percentage is equal to 25.5 percent divided by 100 percent, minus a percentage equal to the total reinsurance payments for the coverage year, divided by the sum of the reinsurance payments and the total payments the Secretary estimates will be paid to PDPs and MA-PD plans that are attributable to the standardized bid amount for the year (taking into account amounts paid by the Secretary and enrollees).

Uniform premium. The monthly beneficiary premium for a prescription drug plan may not vary among eligible individuals enrolled in the plan in the same PDP region; however, the monthly beneficiary premium will increase for individuals subject to a late enrollment penalty or decrease for individuals eligible for a low-income subsidy.

Standardized bid amount. For a PDP that provides basic prescription drug coverage, the "standardized bid amount" is the PDP approved bid. For a PDP that provides supplemental prescription drug coverage, the standardized bid amount is the portion of the PDP approved bid that is attributable to basic prescription drug coverage. "PDP approved bid" is the bid amount approved for the plan.

For MA-PD plans, the standardized bid amount is the portion of the accepted bid amount that is attributable to the basic prescription drug coverage.

Computation of the national average monthly bid amount. For each year beginning with 2006, the Secretary must compute a national average monthly bid amount equal to the average of the standardized bid amount.

If for a month, the standardized bid amount exceeds the adjusted national average monthly bid amount, the base beneficiary premium for the month is adjusted by the excess. If for a month, the adjusted national average monthly bid amount exceeds the standardized bid amount, the base beneficiary premium for the month will be decreased by the amount of the excess. The base beneficiary premium will be increased by the portion of the PDP approved bid that is attributable to supplemental prescription drug benefits.

Late enrollment penalty. Eligible individuals who fail to maintain creditable prescription drug coverage for a 63 days or longer within a continuous period of eligibility beginning on the day after the last date of the individual's initial enrollment period and ending on the date of enrollment under a PDP or MA-PD plan are subject to a late enrollment penalty. The penalty amount is equal to the the greater of (1) the amount the Secretary determines is actuarially sound for each uncovered moth in the same continuous period of eligibility; or (2) one percent of the base beneficiary

¶118

premium for each uncovered month in the period. An uncovered month is any month beginning after the end of the initial enrollment period unless the individual can demonstrate that the individual had creditable prescription drug coverage.

Creditable coverage. An individual is considered to have had creditable prescription drug coverage if the individual establishes that he or she had coverage under one of the following:

(1) a prescription drug plan or MA-PD;

(2) Medicaid;

(3) a group health plan, including a Federal Employee Health Benefits (FEHB) plan and a qualified retiree prescription drug plan;

(4) a state pharmaceutical assistance program;

(5) veterans coverage of prescription drugs;

(6) prescription drug coverage under a Medigap plan;

(7) military coverage including TRICARE; and

(8) other coverage the Secretary determines is appropriate.

Coverage meets the definition of creditable coverage only if the actuarial value of prescription drug coverage equals or exceeds the actuarial value of such coverage under standard prescription drug coverage.

Procedures to document creditable coverage. The Secretary must establish procedures for the documentation of creditable prescription drug coverage, including procedures to assist in determining whether the coverage meets the definition of creditable coverage. Entities that offer creditable prescription drug coverage are required to disclose to the Secretary whether the coverage meets the actuarial equivalence requirement or whether such coverage is changed so that it no longer meets the requirement. If the coverage does not meet the requirement, the disclosure to eligible individuals must include information that because the coverage does not meet the requirements, there are limitations on the periods in a year in which the individuals may enroll in a PDP or MA-PD plan and that the enrollment is subject to a late enrollment penalty.

Waiver of requirement. An eligible individual, who was enrolled in a prescription drug coverage plan described above that is not considered creditable coverage because it does not meet the actuarial equivalence requirement, may apply to the Secretary to treat the coverage as creditable prescription drug coverage, if the individual establishes that the individual was not adequately informed that the coverage did not meet the requirement.

Continuous period of eligibility. "Continuous period of eligibility" is the period that begins with the first day on which the individual is eligible to enroll in a prescription drug plan and ends with the individual's death. Any period during all of which an eligible Part D individual is entitled to hospital insurance benefits under Part A (based on disability, end stage renal disease, widow's insurance benefits, etc.) and which terminated in or before the preceding month in which the individual attained age 65 or for which the basis for eligibility for entitlement changed to eligibility based on the attainment of age 65, will be a separate continuous period of eligibility with respect to the individual.

Collection of monthly beneficiary premiums. Beneficiary premium payments may be paid on a monthly basis directly to the PDP sponsor or MA organization. The beneficiary also has the option of having the amount withheld from his or her Social Security payment or having payment made through an electronic funds transfer mechanism. Payments withheld are to be paid to the PDP sponsor; however, in the case of late enrollment penalties only that portion attributable to increased actuarial costs is to be paid to the plan. The provisions of Sec. 1854(d) of the Social Security Act apply to the collection of monthly beneficiary premiums for the prescription drug benefit in the same manner as they apply to MA organizations.

Late enrollment penalties. The Secretary will specify the portion of the penalty the Secretary estimates is attributable to increased actuarial costs assumed by the PDP sponsor or MA organization as a result of late enrollment. If the individual opts to pay the PDP sponsor or MA organization through withholding from Social Security payments, the Secretary will pay the PDP sponsor or MA organization in which the individual is enrolled only the portion of the penalty that has been estimated as attributable to increased actuarial costs. If the late enrollment penalty is collected by the plan, the Secretary must establish procedures for reducing payments otherwise made to the PDP sponsor or MA organization by an amount equal to the amount of the penalty less the portion of the estimated actuarial costs.

Fallback plans. For individuals enrolled in fallback plans, the monthly beneficiary premium will be collected by withholding payment from Social Security benefits and the fallback plan will not be entitled to a portion of the late enrollment penalty related to actuarial costs to the fallback plan.

Effective date. Effective upon enactment, except that coverage for prescription drugs is effective January 1, 2006.

Act Sec. 101(a) adding Sec. 1860D-13 of the Social Security Act. Law at ¶2262C.

¶119
Premium and Cost-Sharing Subsidies for Low-Income Individuals

Income-related subsidies for individuals with incomes up to 150 percent of the poverty line. The prescription drug benefit program provides premium and cost-sharing subsidies for low-income subsidy-eligible individuals. A subsidy eligible individual is a Part D eligible individual who is enrolled in a prescription drug plan or MA-PD plan, has income below 150 percent of the applicable poverty line, and meets specific resource requirements. There are two groups of subsidy eligible low-income individuals. The first group is composed of persons who:

• are enrolled in a prescription drug plan or MA-PD plan;

• have incomes below 135 percent of poverty;

• have resources in 2006 below $6,000 for an individual and $9,000 for a couple (increased in future years by the percentage increase in the consumer price index (CPI)); or

• are full benefit dual eligibles, regardless of whether they meet other eligibility standards.

The second group of subsidy eligible individuals are persons meeting the same requirements, except that the income level is 150 percent of poverty and an alternative resources standard may be used. The alternative standard in 2006 is $10,000 for an individual and $20,000 for a couple (increased in future years by the percentage increase in the CPI).

Subsidies for individuals with incomes below 135 percent of the poverty line. A subsidy eligible individual, who is determined to have income that is below 135 percent of the poverty line and meets the resource requirements, is eligible for an income-related premium subsidy equal to 100 percent of the low-income benchmark premium amount. The subsidy may not be higher than the actual premium amount for basic coverage under the plan. In addition, the individual is eligible for a premium subsidy of 80 percent of any late enrollment penalties for the first 60 months in which the penalties are imposed and 100 percent for subsequent months. The deductible for these individuals is reduced to $0. The subsidy eligible individual is not subject to the initial coverage limit discussed at ¶104, but is entitled to continuous coverage above the initial coverage limit, subject to reduced cost-sharing for below the out-of-pocket threshold for 2006, as follows:

- institutionalized dual eligible individuals have no cost sharing;

- lowest income dual eligibles with incomes under 100 percent of the poverty line have a copayment of $1 for a generic drug or a preferred drug that is a multiple source drug and $3 for any other drug, or if less, the copayment amount applicable to other individuals described below; and

- other individuals have a copayment of $2 for a generic drug or a preferred drug that is a multiple source drug and $5 for any other drug.

There is no cost-sharing above the annual out-of-pocket threshold.

Individuals with income below 150 percent of poverty line. For other low-income individuals, the premium amount is based on a linear income-related sliding scale ranging from 100 percent of the amount for individuals with incomes at or below 135 percent of the poverty level to 0 percent of the premium amount for individuals with incomes at 150 percent of the poverty level. The deductible is reduced to $50. These individuals are not subject to the initial coverage limit. The individuals are entitled to continuation of coverage subject to a reduced coinsurance of 15 percent for all costs up to the out-of-pocket threshold. Copayment or coinsurance above the annual out-of-pocket threshold amount must not exceed the amount paid for a drug in the year involved by individuals not eligible for low-income subsidies.

Determination of eligibility. Determinations of whether a Part D eligible individual residing in a state is a subsidy eligible individual who meets the requirements are made under the state Medicaid plan or by the Commissioner of Social Security. Determinations will become effective beginning with the month in which the individual applies for a determination that the individual is a subsidy eligible individual and will remain in effect for a period specified by the Secretary, but not more than one year.

Redeterminations and appeals must be made in the same manner as such redeterminations and appeals are made by state Medicaid plans or the Commissioner for the supplemental security income (SSI) program; however, the Commissioner must establish procedures for appeals similar to procedures established for SSI appeals. The Act provides for the authorization of appropriation to the Social Security Administration for sums necessary to make determinations of eligibility.

Treatment of Medicaid beneficiaries. Full dual eligible persons must be treated as subsidy eligible persons. The Secretary may provide that other Medicaid beneficiaries be treated as subsidy eligible.

Income determinations. For a Part D eligible individual who is not treated as subsidy eligible individuals, income will be determined in the same manner as determinations are made for the qualified Medicare beneficiary (QMB) program under Sec. 1905(p)(1)(B) of the Social Security Act; however, Sec. 1902(r)(2), which permits the use of less restrictive methodologies does not apply for determining whether an individual is a low-income subsidy eligible individual. Sec. 1902(r)(2) continues to apply to all state Medicaid eligibility determinations.

Resource standard. The Secretary, jointly with the Commissioner of Social Security, is required to develop a model simplified application form and process for determining and verifying an individual's assets or resources and must provide the forms to states. The application form must consist of an attestation regarding the level of assets or resources and valuations of general classes of assets or resources. The form must be accompanied by recent statements from financial institutions in support of the application.

The resource requirement for 2006 is that an individual's resources (as determined under Sec. 1613 of the Social Security Act for purposes of the SSI program) do not exceed three times the maximum amount of resources that an individual may have and obtain under the program. For a subsequent year, the resource limitation for the previous year is increased by the annual percentage increase in the consumer price index (CPI) as of September of the previous year. Any resource limitation that is not a multiple of $10 will be rounded to the nearest multiple of $10.

Alternative resource standard. The alternative resource standard is that an individual's resources, as determined under Sec. 1613 for purposes of the SSI program, for 2006, do not exceed $10,000 (or $20,000 for a married couple). In the subsequent year, the dollar amounts for the previous year will be increased by the annual increase in the CPI as of September of the previous year. Any resource limitation that is not a multiple of $10 will be rounded to the nearest multiple of $10.

The Secretary may permit a state in making eligibility determinations for premium and cost-sharing subsidies to use the same asset or resource methodologies used to determine eligibility for medical assistance for Medicare cost-sharing so long as the Secretary determines that the use of the methodology will not result in significant differences in the number of individuals determined to be subsidy individuals.

Indexing dollar amounts. For copayments for the lowest income dual eligible individuals, the dollar amount for 2007 will be the dollar amount for 2006 ($1 for generic and multiple source drugs and $3 for other drugs) increased by the annual percentage increase in the CPI as of September of the previous year. For a subsequent year, the dollar amount will be the dollar amount for the previous year increased by the annual percentage increase in the CPI as of September of the previous year.

The deductible for 2007 will be the dollar amount for 2006, $50, increased by the annual percentage increase for 2007 described at ¶104. For a subsequent year, it will be the dollar amount of the previous year increased by the annual percentage increase. Any amount that is not a multiple of $1 will be rounded to the nearest $1.

Premium subsidy amount. The "premium subsidy amount" for an individual residing in a PDP region and enrolled in a PDP or MA-PD plan is the low-income benchmark premium amount for the PDP region in which the individual resides or, if greater, the lowest monthly beneficiary premium for a PDP that offers basic prescription drug coverage in the region. The premium subsidy amount for a PDP region will not be less than the lowest monthly beneficiary premium for a PDP that offers basic prescription drug coverage in the region.

The "low-income benchmark premium amount" for a region equals either: (1) the weighted average of the basic premiums, if all prescription drug plans are offered by the same PDP sponsor; or (2) the weighted average of premiums for prescription drug plans and MA-PD plans, if plans in the region are offered by more than one PDP sponsor.

For purposes of determining the premium subsidy amount, for a PDP that is a basic prescription drug plan, the premium amount is the monthly beneficiary pre-

¶119

mium for the plan. For a PDP that offers alternative prescription drug coverage, the actuarial value of which is greater than that of standard prescription drug coverage, the subsidy amount is the portion of the monthly beneficiary premium is attributable to basic prescription drug coverage. For an MA-PD plan, the subsidy amount is the portion of the MA monthly prescription drug beneficiary premium attributable to basic prescription drug benefits. The premium amounts do not include any amounts attributable to late enrollment penalties.

Administration of subsidy program. The Secretary must develop a process for the administration of the subsidy program that includes the following provisions:

(1) the Secretary provides for notification of the PDP sponsor or MA organization offering the plan that the individual is eligible for a subsidy and the amount of the subsidy;

(2) the sponsor or organization reduces the premiums or cost-sharing otherwise imposed by the amount of the applicable subsidy and submits the amount of the reduction to the Secretary;

(3) the Secretary periodically and on a timely basis reimburses the sponsor or organization for the amount of the reductions; and

(4) The Secretary ensures the confidentiality of individually identifiable information.

The Secretary may compute the reimbursement for cost-sharing subsidies on a capitated basis, taking into account the actuarial value of the subsidies and appropriate adjustments to reflect differences in the risks actually involved.

Relation to Medicaid program. The Part D prescription drug coverage benefit is primary to benefits for prescribed drugs provided under the Medicaid program.

Treatment of territorial residents. A Part D eligible individual who is not a resident of the 50 states or the District of Columbia is not eligible to be a subsidy eligible individual for these provisions, but may be eligible for financial assistance with prescription drug expenses under the Medicaid program.

Effective date. Effective upon enactment.

Act. Sec. 101(a) adding Sec. 1860D-14 of the Social Security Act. Law at ¶2263A.

¶120

Subsidies for Part D Eligible Individuals for Qualified Prescription Drug Coverage

Reduction of premium levels for all beneficiaries. The Secretary is obligated to provide payments to qualifying entities as subsidies for Part D eligible individuals enrolled in a prescription drug program under the prescription drug benefit program. The payments will reduce premium levels applicable to qualified prescription drug coverage for Part D eligible individuals with an overall subsidy level of 74.5 percent for basic prescription drug coverage, reduce adverse selection among PDPs and MA-PD plans, and promote the participation of PDP sponsors and MA organizations. The Secretary must provide for payment to a PDP sponsor that offers a prescription drug plan and an MA organization that offers an MA-PD plan as follows:

(1) *Direct subsidy.* A direct subsidy for each eligible individual enrolled in a prescription drug plan or a MA-PD plan for the month that is equal to the amount of the plan's standardized bid amount, adjusted by health risk factors

and geographic location, and reduced by the base beneficiary premium adjusted for the difference between the bid and the national average bid.

(2) *Subsidy through reinsurance.* The reinsurance payment amount for an enrollee enrolled in a prescription drug plan or an MA-PD plan.

Reinsurance payment amount. The reinsurance payment amount for a coverage year is an amount equal to 80 percent of the allowable reinsurance costs attributable to that portion of gross covered prescription drug costs incurred in the coverage year after the individual has incurred costs that exceed the annual out-of-pocket threshold. The following terms apply to reinsurance payments.

Allowable reinsurance costs. "Allowable reinsurance costs" are the part of the gross covered prescription drug costs under a PDP that are actually paid (net of discounts, chargebacks, and average percentage rebates) by the PDP sponsor or MA organization or by an enrollee under the plan, but not more than the part of the costs that would have been paid by the plan if the drug coverage under the plan were basic coverage, or in the case of supplemental coverage, standard coverage.

Gross covered prescription drug costs. "Gross covered prescription drug costs" are costs incurred under the plan, not including administrative costs, but including costs directly related to the dispensing of covered Part D drugs during the year and costs relating to the deductible. Such costs will be determined regardless of whether they are paid by the individual or under the plan, and regardless of whether coverage under the plan exceeded basic coverage.

Coverage year. "Coverage year" means a calendar year in which covered Part D drugs are dispensed if the claim for the drugs and payment on the claim is made not later than the period after the end of a year specified by the Secretary.

Adjustments of related bids. The Secretary must establish an appropriate methodology for adjusting the standardized bid amount to take into account variations in costs for basic prescription drug coverage among PDPs and MA-PD plans based on the differences in actuarial risk of different enrollees being served and the national average monthly bid amount to take into account differences in prices for covered Part D drugs among PDP regions.

Health status risk adjustments. In establishing the methodology for adjusting the standardized bid amount for health status, the risk adjustment must be designed in a budget neutral manner. The Secretary may take into account similar methodologies used to adjust payments to MA organizations for benefits under the original Medicare fee-for-service option. PDP sponsors are required to submit data regarding drug claims that can be linked at the individual level to Part A and Part B data and other information the Secretary determines is necessary. MA organizations offering MA-PD plans are required to submit data regarding drug claims that can be linked at the individual level to other data the organizations are required to submit to the Secretary and other information the Secretary determines is necessary. The Secretary must publish the risk adjuster established under this section in the year succeeding the year risk adjusters are published for MA organizations.

Geographic adjustment. In establishing the geographic adjustment, if the Secretary determines that price variations are de minimis, no adjustment is to be made. Any adjustments must be applied in a budget neutral manner.

Payment methods. The Secretary must establish a payment method to make interim payments during a year based on the Secretary's best estimate of amounts that will be payable after obtaining all of the information. Payments to the PDP sponsor and MA organization are conditional, subject to the PDP sponsor and MA organization furnishing necessary information to the Secretary. Information may be

¶120

used by officers and employees of HHS only for the purposes of and to the extent necessary to carry out the section. Payments will be made from the Medicare Prescription Drug Trust Account.

The amount of payment may be adjusted to reflect the difference between actual number of individuals enrolled in a PDP plan and the estimated number under the provisions of Sec. 1853(a)(2) of the Social Security Act.

Risk corridors. The Secretary must establish a risk corridor for each PDP and MA-PD plan for each plan year. Risk corridors are defined as specified percentages above and below a target amount. The target amount is defined as total payments paid to the plan, taking into account the amount paid by the Secretary and enrollees, based on the standardized bid amount, risk adjusted, and reduced by total administrative expenses assumed in the bid. The risk corridor for a plan for a year is equal to a range.

First threshold upper and lower limit. The first threshold lower limit is equal to the target amount for the plan *minus* an amount equal to the first threshold risk percentage of the target amount.

The first threshold upper limit is equal to the *sum* of the target amount and an amount equal to the first threshold risk percentage for the plan.

The first threshold risk percentage is 2.5 percent for 2006 and 2007, 5 percent for 2008 through 2011, and for 2012 and subsequent years a percentage established by the Secretary but not less than 5 percent.

Second threshold upper and lower limit. The second threshold lower limit is equal to the target amount for the plan *minus* an amount equal to the second threshold risk percentage of the target amount.

The second threshold upper limit is equal to the *sum* of the target amount for the plan and an amount equal to the second threshold risk percentage of the target amount.

The second threshold risk percentage for 2006 and 2007 is 5 percent, for 2008 through 2011 is 10 percent, and for 2012 and subsequent years a percentage established by the Secretary but not less than 10 percent.

Adjusted allowable risk corridors costs. "Allowable risk corridor costs" are the part of costs (not including administrative costs, but including costs directly related to the dispensing of covered Part D drugs during the year) incurred by the sponsor or organization under the plan that are actually paid (net of discounts, chargebacks, and average percentage rebates) by the sponsor or organization, but not more than the part of the costs that would have been paid under the plan if the prescription drug coverage under the plan were basic coverage, or for supplemental prescription drug coverage, basic coverage taking into account the effect that providing supplemental drug coverage has on drug utilization. Adjusted allowable risk corridor costs for a plan for a coverage year are reduced by total reinsurance payments and subsidy payments. In computing allowable costs, the Secretary will take into account the reduction in cost-sharing above and below the out-of-pocket threshold for subsidy eligible low-income individuals.

Adjustment of payment. No payment adjustments will be made if adjusted allowable costs for the plan are at least equal to the first threshold lower limit of the first risk corridor but not greater than the first threshold upper limit of the risk corridor for the plan the year, i.e., if the plans are within the first risk corridor. A portion of any plan spending above or below these levels is subject to risk adjustment. If adjusted allowable costs exceed the first threshold upper limit, then payments are increased. If adjusted allowable costs are below the first threshold lower limit, then payments are reduced. Payment adjustments will not affect beneficiary premiums.

Increase in payment if adjusted risk corridor costs are above upper limit of risk corridor. If adjusted allowable costs risk corridor costs for the plan for the year exceed the first threshold upper limit, but are not greater than the second threshold upper limit, the Secretary will increase the total of the payments made to the PDP sponsor or MA organization by an amount equal to 50 percent (or, for 2006 and 2007, 75 percent or 90 percent if certain conditions are met for the year) of the difference between the adjusted allowable risk corridor costs and the first threshold upper limit of the risk corridor.

If the adjusted allowable risk corridor costs for the plan for the year are greater than the second threshold upper limit of the risk corridor for the plan for the year, the Secretary will increase the total of the payments made to the sponsor or organization offering the plan for the year an amount equal to the sum of 50 percent (or, for 2006 and 2007, 75 percent or 90 percent)percent if certain conditions are met for the year) of the difference between the second threshold upper limit and the first threshold upper limit and 80 percent of the difference between the adjusted allowable risk corridor costs and the second threshold upper limit of the risk corridor.

The conditions for application of the higher risk sharing percentage for 2006 and 2007 are met if the Secretary determines that at least 60 percent of PDPs and MA-PD plans that are subject to these provisions have adjusted allowable risk corridor costs for the plan for the year that are more than the first threshold upper limit of the risk corridor for the plan for the year and the plans represent at least 60 percent of the Part D eligible individuals enrolled in any PDP or MA-PD. In this case, payment to plans would equal 90 percent of adjusted allowable costs between the first and second upper threshold limits.

Reduction in payment if adjusted allowable risk corridor costs are below lower limit of risk corridor. If the adjusted allowable risk corridor costs for the plan for the year are less than the first threshold lower limit, but not less than the second threshold lower limit, the Secretary will reduce the total of the payments made to the sponsor or organization offering the plan for the year by an amount equal to 50 percent (or for 2006 and 2007, 75 percent) of the difference between the first threshold lower limit of the risk corridor and the adjusted allowable risk corridor costs.

If the adjusted risk corridor costs for the plan for the year are less than the second threshold lower limit of the risk corridor for the plan year, the Secretary will reduce the total payments made to the sponsor or organization offering the plan an amount equal to the sum of 50 percent (or for 2006 and 2007, 75 percent) of the difference between the first threshold lower limit and the second threshold lower limit and 80 percent of the difference between the second threshold upper limit of the risk corridor and the adjusted allowable risk corridor costs.

If payments are reduced, the Secretary may recover amounts from the PDP plan or MA organization.

Comment: The conference committee explanation provides that during 2006 and 2007, plans would be at full risk for adjusted allowable risk corridor costs within 2.5 percent above or below the target. Plans with adjusted allowable costs above this level would receive increased payments. If their costs were between 2.5 percent of the target (first threshold upper limit) and 5 percent of the target (second threshold upper limit), they would be at risk for 25 percent of the increased amount; that is, their payments would equal 75 percent of adjusted allowable costs for spending in this range. If their costs were above 5 percent of the target they would be at risk for 25

¶120

percent of the costs between the first and second threshold upper limits and 20 percent of the costs above that amount. That is, their payments would equal 80 percent of the adjusted allowable costs over the second threshold upper limit. Conversely, if plans fell below the target, they would share the savings with the government. They would have to refund 75 percent of the savings if costs fell between 2.5 percent and 5 percent below the target level, and 80 percent of any amounts below 5 percent of the target.

Plans are at full financial risk for all spending for supplemental prescription drug coverage. The subsidy and risk corridor provisions do not apply to fallback plans.

Disclosure of information. The PDP sponsor and MA organization offering an MA-PD plan must provide the Secretary with information the Secretary determines is necessary to carry out the provisions of this section of the Act. The Secretary will have the right to inspect and audit any books and records of a PDP sponsor or MA organization that pertain to the information regarding costs. The information disclosed or obtained may be used by officers, employees, and contractors of the Department of Health and Human Services only for the purposes of and to the extent necessary to carry out this section.

Effective date. Effective upon enactment, except that prescription drug coverage is effective January 1, 2006.

Act. Sec. 101(a) adding Sec. 1860-D15 of the Social Security Act. Law at ¶2263B.

¶123

Medicare Prescription Drug Account in the Federal Supplemental Medical Insurance Trust Fund

Establishment. An account to be known as the "Medicare Prescription Drug Account" is created within the Federal Supplementary Medical Insurance Trust Fund. The Account will consist of such gifts and bequests as provided in Sec. 201(i)(1) of the Social Security Act, accrued interest on balances in the Account, and amounts deposited in or appropriated to the fund as provided under Part D. Funds provided to the Account must be kept separate from all other funds within the Federal Supplementary Medical Insurance Trust Fund, but can be invested and the investments may be redeemed in the same manner as other funds and investments within the Trust Fund.

Payments from account. The Managing Trustee from time to time will pay amounts from the Account as the Secretary certifies are necessary to make payments to operate the program, including low-income subsidy payments; subsidy payments and fallback payments; payments to sponsors of qualified retiree prescription drug plans; and administrative expenses. Amounts payable from the Account will not be taken into account in computing actuarial rates or premium amounts.

Transfers to Medicaid account. From time to time, the Managing Trustee will transfer, from the Account to the Grants to States for Medicaid account, amounts the Secretary certifies are attributable to increases in payment resulting from increased administrative costs. States would make payments to the Account for dual eligibles as provided for under Sec. 1935(c) of the Social Security Act.

Payments of premiums withheld. The Managing Trustee will pay the premiums and the portion of the late enrollment penalties that are collected from withholding from Social Security benefits to the PDP sponsor or MA organization offering a prescription drug plan.

Deposits into the Account. Amounts paid under rules for dual eligibles and amounts withheld from Social Security benefits are deposited into the Account. Appropriations would be made to the Account equal to the amount of payments and transfers from the Account. To ensure prompt payments of benefits and administrative expenses in the early months of the program, there are appropriated from the Treasury an amount the Secretary certifies as required, but not to exceed 10 percent of the total estimated expenditures from the Account for 2006.

Transfer of remaining balance from Transitional Assistance Account. Any balance in the Transitional Assistance Account will be deposited into the Account.

Effective date. Effective upon enactment.

Act Sec. 101(a) adding Sec. 1860D-16 of the Social Security Act. Law at ¶2264.

¶125

Application to Medicare Advantage and Related Managed Care Programs

Rules relating to offering qualified prescription drug coverage. Beginning January 1, 2006, an MA organization cannot offer an MA plan in an area unless either that plan or another MA plan offered by the organization in the same service area includes required prescription drug coverage and may not offer prescription drug coverage (other than required under Part A and Part B) to an enrollee under an MSA plan or under another MA plan unless such drug coverage under the other plan provides qualified prescription drug coverage and unless the requirements of this section with respect to such coverage are met. Required coverage means basic drug coverage or qualified prescription drug coverage that provides supplemental beneficiary premiums so long as there is no MA monthly supplemental beneficiary premium under the plan.

Default enrollment rules. An individual enrolled in a health benefits plan would not be considered to have been deemed to make an election into an MA-PD plan, unless the plan provides prescription drug coverage. An individual enrolled in an MA plan would not be considered to have been deemed to make an election into an MA-PD plan, unless: (1) for purposes of the January 1, 2006, election, the MA plan provided as of December 31, 2005, any prescription drug coverage; or (2) for periods after January 1, 2006, the MA plan was an MA-PD plan.

Disenrollment. An individual who elects to discontinue enrollment in an MA-PD plan during the first year of eligibility may enroll in a prescription drug plan under Part D at the time of his or her election of coverage under the original Medicare fee-for-service program. If an individual is enrolled in an MA plan (other than an MSA plan) that does not provide qualified prescription drug coverage, and the organization discontinues offering all MA plans without prescription drug coverage, then the individual is deemed to have elected the original Medicare fee-for-service program, unless the individual affirmatively enrolls in an MA-PD plan. This disenrollment will be treated as an involuntary termination of the MA plan.

Application of Part D rules for prescription drug coverage. On and after January 1, 2006, the provisions of Part D apply under Part C of Medicare with respect to prescription drug coverage provided under MA-PD plans in lieu of other Part C provisions that would apply to such coverage. The Secretary could waive these provisions to the extent that they duplicate or are in conflict with provisions applicable to the organization or plan under Part C or as may be necessary to improve coordination. The Secretary may also waive the pharmacy network requirements of Sec. 1860D-4(b)(1)(C) of the Social Security Act in the case of an MA-PD plan that provides access (other than mail order) to qualified prescription drug coverage through pharmacies owned and operated by the MA organizations. The Secretary must determine the organization's pharmacy network is sufficient to provide comparable access for enrollees under the plan.

Rules for private fee-for-service plans. Private fee-for-service (PFFS) plans that offer prescription drug benefits are not required to provide negotiated prices or discounts; however, to the extent a plan did so, it would be required to meet related Part D requirements. The requirements for pharmacy access and public disclosure of pharmaceutical prices for equivalent drugs do not apply if the PFFS plan provides coverage for drugs purchased from all pharmacies, without additional cost-sharing, and without regard to whether they are participating pharmacies in a network or have entered into contracts or agreements with pharmacies to provide drugs to enrollees covered by the plan. The drug utilization management program and the medication therapy management program also is required.

For PFFS plans, the Secretary determines the amount of reinsurance payment using a methodology that bases the amount on the Secretary's estimate of the amount of such payments that would be payable if the plan were an MA-PD plan and that takes into account the average reinsurance payment made for a population of similar risk under MA-PD plans. The risk corridor provisions do not apply, and plans are exempt from negotiations on bid terms. In addition, the exclusion of costs incurred for covered Part D drugs that are not included or treated as not included in a plan's formulary do not apply if the plan does not use a formulary.

Application to reasonable cost reimbursement contractors. If an organization provides benefits under a reasonable cost reimbursement contract and elects to provide qualified prescription drug coverage to a Part D eligible individual who is enrolled under a contract, the provisions of this section and related provisions in Part C apply in the same manner as applied to local MA-PD plans. Coverage under a contract that provides qualified prescription drug coverage will be deemed to be an MA-PD local plan. Individuals, who were not enrolled in the reasonable cost plan, could not enroll in the prescription drug plan. The bid of the reasonable cost plan would not be taken into account in computing the national average monthly bid amount and low-income benchmark premium.

Application to PACE. In general, the provisions of Part D and related provisions of Part C apply to Program of All Inclusive Care to the Elderly (PACE) programs that elect to provide qualified prescription drug coverage to a part D eligible individual who is enrolled in a PACE program in the same manner as they apply to MA-PD plans. A PACE program that provides such coverage will be deemed to be an MA-PD local plan. The organization may not enroll persons not enrolled in the PACE program involved. Bids of a PACE program offering prescription drug coverage are not taken into account in computing any low-income benchmark premium amount and any average benchmark amount.

Effective date. Effective upon enactment.

Act Sec. 101 adding Sec. 1860D-21 of the Social Security Act. Law at ¶2265A.

¶ 127
Special Rules for Employer-Sponsored Programs

Subsidy payment. The Secretary must provide for a special subsidy payment to the sponsor of a qualified retiree prescription drug plan for each qualified covered retiree under the plan. A qualifying covered retiree is a Part D eligible individual who is not enrolled in a PDP or an MA-PD plan but is covered under a qualified prescription drug plan. A qualified retiree prescription drug plan is an employment based retiree health coverage plan if, with respect to a Part D eligible individual covered under the retiree plan, the following requirements are met:

(1) The sponsor of the plan must provide the Secretary, annually or at a time the Secretary may require, with an attestation that the actuarial value of prescription drug coverage under the plan is at least equal to the actuarial value of standard prescription drug coverage.

(2) The sponsor of the plan or administrator of the plan must maintain records and provide access to such records as the Secretary requires for the purposes of audits and other oversight activities necessary to ensure the adequacy of prescription drug coverage and accuracy of payments.

(3) The sponsor of the plan must provide for disclosure of information regarding prescription drug coverage and creditable coverage.

Employer and union special subsidy amount. The special subsidy payment amount for a qualifying covered retiree for a coverage year enrolled with the sponsor of a qualified retiree prescription drug plan equals 28 percent of the retiree's gross covered retiree plan-related prescription drug costs for a year greater than a cost threshold equal to $250, but not greater than the cost limit of $5,000 for plan years that end in 2006. The cost threshold and cost limit amounts will be adjusted annually by the percentage increase in Medicare per capita prescription drug costs.

Definitions. The following terms are defined with respect to qualified retiree prescription drug plans:

Allowable retiree costs. "Allowable retiree costs" are the part of gross covered prescription drug costs that are actually paid (net discounts, chargebacks, and average percentage rebates) by the sponsor or by or on behalf of a qualifying covered retiree under the plan.

Gross covered retiree plan-related prescription drug costs. "Gross covered retiree plan-related prescription drug costs" are the costs incurred under the plan, not including administrative costs, but including costs directly related to the dispensing of a covered Part D drug during a coverage the year. The costs will be determined whether they are paid by the retiree or under the plan.

Employment-based retiree health coverage. "Employment-based retiree health coverage" is health insurance or other coverage of health care costs (whether provided by voluntary insurance coverage or pursuant to statutory or contractual obligation) for part D eligible individuals (or for such individuals and their spouses and dependents) under a group health plan based on their status as retired participants in such plan.

Sponsor. A "sponsor" is a plan sponsor in relation to a group health plan, except that, in the case of a plan maintained jointly by one employer and an employee organization and the employer is the primary source of financing the plan, the term means the employer.

Group health plan. "Group health plan" includes a plan as defined in Sec. 607(1) of the Employee Retirement Income Security Act of 1974 and also includes federal and state governmental plans, collectively bargained plans, and church plans,

Rights of individuals. An individual covered under an employment-based retiree plan is not precluded from enrolling in a PDP plan or MA-PD plan or from having the employment-based plan pay the premium required for coverage under a PDP or MA-PD plan. The PDP or MA-PD plan would constitute primary coverage, not the employer.

Coverage under an employment-based retiree health plan. Employment-based retiree coverage may provide coverage that is better than standard coverage to retirees under a qualified retiree prescription drug plan. Employment-based retiree health coverage may provide coverage that is supplemental to benefits provided under a PDP or MA-PD plan to enrollees in such plans. Employers are not prevented from providing flexibility in benefit design and pharmacy access provisions for basic drug coverage so long as actuarial equivalence requirements are met.

Application of MA waiver authority. The waiver authority under Sec. 1857(i) of the Social Security Act will be applied to prescription drug plans in relation to employment-based retiree health coverage in a similar manner in which they apply to an MA plan, including authorizing the establishment of separate premium amounts for enrollees in a PDP by reason of such coverage and limitations on enrollment to Part D eligible individuals enrolled under such coverage.

Effective date. Effective upon enactment.

Act Sec. 101(a) adding Sec. 1860D-22 of the Social Security Act. Law at ¶2265B.

¶129
State Pharmaceutical Assistance Programs

State pharmaceutical assistance program defined. A state pharmaceutical assistance program (SPAP), for purposes of this provision, is a state program that, on behalf of eligible individuals, (1) provides financial assistance for the purchase or provision of supplemental prescription drug coverage; (2) in determining program eligibility and amount of payment, provides assistance to beneficiaries in all Part D plans and does not discriminate based on the Part D plan in which the individual is enrolled; and (3) satisfies the other requirements of this section.

Coordination elements. Before July 1, 2005, the Secretary must establish requirements for PDPs to ensure effective coordination between a Part D plan (both PDPs and MA-PD plans) and a state pharmaceutical assistance program. The coordination requirements relate to payment of premiums and coverage and payment for supplemental drug benefits for Part D eligible individuals enrolled in PDPs or MA-PD plans, and assistance with cost-sharing. Coordination elements must include requirements for enrollment file-sharing; claims processing, including electronic processing; claims payment; claims reconciliation reports; application of high out-of-pocket expenditure protection; and other administrative procedures specified by the Secretary. The requirements must be consistent with applicable law to safeguard the privacy of any identifiable beneficiary information.

The requirements must include a method for the application by a Part D plan of specified funding amounts from a SPAP for enrolled individuals for supplemental prescription drug benefits. The Secretary is required, when developing the requirements, to consult with state pharmaceutical assistance programs, MA organizations, states, pharmaceutical benefit managers, employers, representatives of Part D eligible individuals, data processing experts, pharmacists, pharmaceutical manufacturers, and other experts.

Related provisions. A prescription drug card used under Part D may also be used for benefits under the state program. The card may have a symbol indicating the connection.

Expenses incurred under a state pharmaceutical program may be counted toward the annual out-of-pocket threshold.

A SPAP is not required to coordinate or provide financial assistance with respect to any Part D plan.

Payments to SPAPs. The Secretary may allocate payments among state pharmaceutical assistance programs that have approved applications for a fiscal year (FY) in proportion to the number of enrollees enrolled in the program as of October 1, 2003. Payments are made to programs for the purpose of educating eligible individuals enrolled in a program about Part D prescription drug coverage; providing technical assistance, phone support, and counseling to facilitate selection and enrollment in plans; and other activities to promote effective coordination of enrollment, coverage, and payment between the programs and the plans. For each of FYs 2005 and 2006, $62.5 million has been appropriated to promote coordination between Medicare prescription drug plans and SPAPs.

Effective date. Effective upon enactment.

Act Sec. 101 adding Sec. 1860D-23 of the Social Security Act. Law at ¶2265C.

¶131

Coordination of Requirements for Plans Providing Prescription Drug Coverage

Application of coordination requirements. The Secretary must apply the coordination requirements established for state pharmaceutical assistance programs under Sec. 1860D-23(a) of the Social Security Act (see ¶129) to other prescription plans including Medicaid (including a plan operating under a waiver under Sec. 1115), group health plans, federal employee health benefits plans, military coverage (including TRICARE), and other prescription drug coverage on behalf of Part D eligible individuals the Secretary specifies. The coordination requirements apply to exchanging information on third-party reimbursement of out-of-pocket costs (see ¶105).

The requirements do not prevent a PDP sponsor or MA organization from applying cost management tools, including differential payments under all methods of operation, or affect the applications of procedures established for exchanging information on third-party payers.

User fees. The Secretary may impose user fees for the transmittal of information necessary for benefit coordination and retain a portion of the fees to defray the Secretary's costs in carrying out the procedures. A user fee, however, may not be imposed on a state pharmaceutical assistance program.

Effective date. Effective upon enactment.

Act Sec. 101 adding Sec. 1860D-24 of the Social Security Act. Law at ¶2266.

PRESCRIPTION DRUG DISCOUNT CARD PROGRAM

¶ 150

Medicare Prescription Drug Discount Card and Transitional Assistance Program

Establishment of prescription drug discount card program. The Secretary is required to establish a program to endorse prescription drug discount card programs that meet certain requirements. Under the program, discount card eligible individuals have access to prescription drug discounts through card sponsors throughout the U.S. The program also provides transitional assistance for low-income persons enrolled in endorsed programs. The program is voluntary for "eligible individuals".

Program implementation. The Secretary must implement the program so that prescription drug discount cards and transitional assistance are available no later than six months after enactment. The Secretary must promulgate regulations to carry out the program and may publish an interim final regulation that becomes effective and final immediately on an interim basis upon the date of publication. If the Secretary promulgates an interim final regulation, a public comment period must be provided. The Secretary may change or revise the regulations after conclusion of the comment period. The program does not, except as provided for during an individual's transition period, apply to covered discount card drugs dispensed after December 31, 2005. Any transitional assistance for low-income persons will be available after that date to the extent the assistance was for drugs dispensed on or before that date.

Special rules for the transition period. Special rules may apply for an individual in a transition period who also is enrolled under a card program as of December 31, 2005. The transition period to the prescription drug benefit under Part D is the period beginning January 1, 2006, and ending on the effective date of the individual's coverage under Part D or, if the individual is not enrolled, at the close of the individual's initial enrollment period for Part D. During this transition period, (1) discounts may continue to apply for drugs dispensed to the individual, (2) no annual enrollment fee will be applicable, (3) the individual *can not* change the endorsed plan in which the individual was enrolled, and (4) the balance of any transitional assistance remaining on January 1, 2006, remain available for drugs dispensed during the individual's period.

Effective date. Effective upon enactment.

Act Sec. 101(a) adding Sec. 1860D-31(a) of the Social Security Act. Law at ¶ 2267.

¶ 152

Eligibility

Discount card eligible individual. A "discount card eligible individual" is an individual who is entitled to benefits, or enrolled in Part A or enrolled under Part B. An individual enrolled in Medicaid (or under any waiver under Sec. 1115 of the Social Security Act) who is entitled to any medical assistance for outpatient prescribed drugs is not considered a discount card eligible individual.

Transitional assistance eligible individual. A "transitional assistance eligible individual" is a discount card eligible individual who resides in one of the 50 states or the District of Columbia, whose income is not more than 135 percent of the official poverty line applicable to the family size involved. Individuals who are not eligible for transitional assistance are persons who have coverage for, or assistance for, covered discount card drugs under: (1) a group health insurance plan or health insurance plan, except for coverage under a plan under Medicare Part C and coverage consisting only of excepted benefits (as defined under Sec. 2791 of the Public Health Service Act); (2) a healthcare plan for members of the uniformed services care; or (3) a plan under the federal employees health benefits program.

Special transitional assistance eligible individual. A "special transitional assistance eligible individual" is a transitional eligible assistance eligible individual whose income is below 100 percent of the poverty line.

Medicaid medically needy. The Secretary is required to provide for appropriate rules for the treatment of medically needy persons as discount eligible individuals and as transitional assistance eligible individuals.

Effective date. Effective upon enactment.

Act Sec. 101(a) adding Sec. 1860D-31(b) of the Social Security Act. Law at ¶2267.

¶ 154
Enrollment and Enrollment Fees

Enrollment process. The Secretary must establish a process through which a discount card eligible individual is enrolled and disenrolled in a discount card program. An eligible individual who is not enrolled in a card program may enroll in an endorsed discount card program and is residing in a state may enroll in an endorsed program that serves residents of the state at any time beginning on the initial enrollment date and before January 1, 2006. The individual must complete a standard enrollment form specified by the Secretary. Each program sponsor is required to transmit to the Secretary (in a form and manner specified by the Secretary) information on individuals who complete the enrollment forms, including information regarding certification as a transitional assistance eligible individual. A discount eligible individual may only be enrolled in one endorsed card program at a time.

Change in election. The Secretary must establish a process that will permit an individual enrolled in an endorsed discount card program during 2004, to enroll in a different endorsed program in 2005. The process must be similar to, and coordinated with, the process established for annual, coordinated elections under Sec. 1851(e)(3) of Part C of the Social Security Act. In addition, the Secretary must permit individuals to change programs in which they were enrolled if they changed residence to outside the service area of the plan or under other exceptional circumstances. Exceptional circumstances may include a change in residential setting, such as placement in a nursing facility, or enrollment or disenrollment from a plan under Part C through which an individual was enrolled in an endorsed program.

Disenrollment. An individual could voluntarily disenroll from an endorsed program at any time. The individual may not enroll in another endorsed program, except during the annual coordinated enrollment period or under the exceptional circumstances specified by the Secretary. An individual, who is not a transitional assistance eligible individual, may be disenrolled by the program sponsor if the individual fails to pay the annual enrollment fee.

Limiting enrollment. For a discount card eligible individual enrolled in a plan under Part C or a reasonable reimbursement cost contract, if the organization is a prescription drug discount card sponsor that offers an endorsed prescription drug discount card program under which the individual may be enrolled, the individual may only enroll in the endorsed discount card program offered by that sponsor. The sponsor must meet the following requirements: (1) the sponsor is not permitted to enroll other individuals in the program, and (2) must provide access through a pharmacy network, not only through mail order. The Secretary may waive these requirements (see ¶ 164).

Enrollment fees. A prescription drug card sponsor may charge each enrollee an annual enrollment fee that does not exceed $30. The sponsor must ensure that the annual enrollment fee (if any) is the same for all enrollees residing in the state and is responsible for collecting the fee. The annual enrollment fee for 2004 and 2005 may not be prorated. There is no annual enrollment fee after 2005.

The Secretary must pay the annual enrollment fee for a transitional assistance eligible individual. The Secretary must establish an arrangement under which a state may pay for some or all of the enrollment fee for enrollees who are not transitional assistance eligible individuals. In the case of such an arrangement, the state must pay the enrollment fee directly to the sponsor. No federal matching payments will be available for expenditures made by a state for enrollment fees. The Secretary must establish special rules for individuals who change the endorsed program in which they are enrolled during the year.

Card issuance. A prescription drug card sponsor is required to issue, to each individual enrolled in its program, a discount card, which is in a standard format specified by the Secretary. The card establishes proof of enrollment and may be used in a coordinated manner to identify the sponsor, program, and individual. The Secretary must specify a date that enrollee access to negotiated prices and transitional assistance, if any, under an endorsed program will become effective.

Effective date. Effective upon enactment.

Act Sec. 101(a) adding Sec. 1860D-31(c) of the Social Security Act. Law at ¶ 2267.

¶ 156

Enrollment Information and Program Features

Secretarial responsibilities. The Secretary must provide for activities that broadly disseminate information to discount card eligible individuals and prospective eligible individuals regarding enrollment in endorsed discount card programs and features of the program, including the availability of transitional assistance. To promote informed choice among endorsed prescription drug discount programs, the Secretary must provide for the dissemination of information that compares the annual enrollment fee and other features of the programs, which may include comparative prices for covered drugs. In addition, the information must include educational materials on the variability of discounts on prices of covered discount drugs under an endorsed program. The Secretary should coordinated these activities with the dissemination of educational material on other Medicare options.

To the extent practicable, the Secretary should ensure that discount card eligible individuals are provided with the required information at least 30 days prior to the initial enrollment date. The Secretary is required to provide for the receipt and response to inquiries and complaints concerning the discount card program and endorsed programs through the use of the Medicare toll-free number (1-800-MEDICARE).

Card sponsor requirements. Each prescription drug card sponsor is required to make available to discount card eligible individuals (through the Internet and otherwise) information the Secretary identifies as being necessary to promote informed choice among discount card programs, including information on enrollment fees and negotiated prices charged to individuals and the amount of available transitional assistance. Each sponsor must have a mechanism, including a toll free number, for providing on request, specific information to individuals enrolled in the program. Each sponsor also is required to inform transitional assistance eligible individuals of the availability of the toll-free number to provide information on the amount of available assistance. Information on the amount of transitional assistance remaining must be made available at the point-of-sale, either electronically or by telephone.

Notification of price difference. Drug card sponsors must provide that each pharmacy that dispensed a covered discount card drug will inform program enrollees of any differential between the price of the drug provided to the enrollee and the price of the lowest priced generic drug covered under the program that is therapeutically equivalent and bioequivalent and available at the pharmacy. This notice must be provided at the time of purchase of the drug, or for a mail order drug, at the time of delivery. The Secretary may waive this requirement under circumstances specified by the Secretary.

Effective date. Effective upon enactment.

Act Sec. 101(a) adding Sec. 1860D-31(d) of the Social Security Act. Law at ¶2267.

¶158

Discount Card Features

Access to negotiated prices. Each prescription drug card sponsor must provide each enrollee with access to negotiated prices. Negotiated prices must take into account negotiated price concessions, such as discounts, direct or indirect subsidies, rebates, and direct or indirect remunerations for covered discount card drugs and must include any dispensing fees. In addition, each sponsor must secure in its network the participation of a sufficient number of pharmacies that dispense drugs directly to enrollees to ensure convenient access to covered drugs at negotiated prices. This requirement may only be met by entities dispensing drugs other than solely by mail order. The Secretary must establish convenient access rules that are no less favorable than standards for convenient access to pharmacies applicable under TRICARE, which are specified in the statement of work solicitation as of March 13, 2003.

Prohibitions on charges. A prescription drug card sponsor (and any pharmacy contracting with the sponsor to provide covered discount card drugs) may not charge enrollees for any items and services required to be provided by the sponsor under the prescription drug card program. This prohibition does not apply to the annual enrollment fee for persons who are not transitional assistance eligible individuals and does not prevent the pharmacy dispensing the drug from imposing a charge for the drug (consistent with the negotiated price) reduced by any transitional assistance. Negotiated prices will not be taken into account for purposes of making best price calculations under the Medicaid rebate program.

Reduction of medication errors. Each endorsed card program is required to implement a system to reduce the likelihood of medication errors and adverse drug interactions and to improve medication use.

Effective date. Effective upon enactment.

Act Sec. 101(a) adding Sec. 1860D-31(e) of the Social Security Act. Law at ¶2267.

¶160

Eligibility Procedures for Endorsed Programs and Transitional Assistance

Determinations. The Secretary must establish procedures for endorsed prescription drug card programs to determine whether an individual is a discount eligible individual, a transitional assistance eligible individual, or a special transitional eligible individual. The Secretary is required to define the terms "income" and "family size" and specify the methods and period for which they are determined. If these methods provide for use of information for prior time periods, the Secretary is required to permit an individual whose circumstances have changed to elect to have eligibility for transitional assistance determined based on income or family size for a more recent period. The Secretary may use a reconsideration process or other method.

Self-certification for transitional assistance. An individual who wishes to be treated as a transitional assistance eligible individual or special transitional eligible individual may self-certify as to his or her income, family size, and prescription drug coverage (if any) through a simplified means specified by the Secretary. A certification may be provided before, on, or after the time of enrollment. The self-certification will be deemed as consent to have the information verified by the Secretary. A verified self-certification as a transitional assistance or special transitional assistance eligible individual will be applicable for the entire period of enrollment in any endorsed program.

Verification The Secretary must establish verification methods, which may include sampling and use of information on Medicaid eligibility provided by the states, financial information from the Commissioner of Social Security, and financial information from the Secretary of the Treasury. The Secretary may find that an eligible individual meets the income requirements for transitional assistance if the individual is within a category of discount card eligible individuals who are enrolled under Medicaid, such as qualified Medicare beneficiaries, specified low-income Medicare beneficiaries, and certain qualified individuals.

States will be required, as a condition of federal financial participation under Medicaid, to provide, on a timely basis, information that allows the Secretary to identify persons eligible for drug coverage under Medicaid, or who are transitional assistance eligible individuals, or special transitional eligible individuals.

Reconsideration. The Secretary is required to establish a reconsideration process for an individual who is determined not to be a transitional assistance eligible or special transitional assistance eligible individual. The results must be communicated to the individual and prescription drug card sponsor involved. The Secretary may enter into contracts to perform the reconsideration function.

Effective date. Effective upon enactment.

Act Sec. 101(a) adding Sec. 1860D-31(f) of the Social Security Act. Law at ¶2267.

¶ 162

Transitional Assistance

Provision of transitional assistance. For 2004, a transitional eligible individual who is enrolled in an endorsed program prior to the initial implementation date is entitled to have the annual enrollment fee paid under the program and payment up to 90 percent of the costs incurred up to $600 for covered discount card drugs obtained through the program taking into account negotiated price for the drug. A special transitional eligible individual who is enrolled in an endorsed program prior to the initial implementation date is entitled have the annual enrollment fee paid under the program and 95 percent of the incurred drug costs up to $600. For 2005, the annual enrollment fee is paid by the program and the percent of coverage remains the same. Payment will be made for the individual's incurred drug costs up to $600 plus any balance left over from 2004, except no rollover will be permitted if the individual voluntarily disenrolled from an endorsed plan. With respect to 2005, the individual must have enrolled an endorsed program and provided certification prior to February 1, 2005. The Secretary must provide a method for the reimbursement of prescription drug card sponsors for assistance provided.

Proration. The Secretary must prorate the $600 annual amount in 2004, for the balance of the year, for persons who have not enrolled in an endorsed program and providing self-certification prior to the program's initial implementation date. For 2005, the amount will be prorated for persons not enrolling in an endorsed program and providing self-certification prior to February 1, 2005. In the case of a transitional assistance individual who enrolls in a different endorsed program, the Secretary must establish a process to provide information to concerning the balance of amount available on behalf of the individual to the new endorsed program. No funds will be available under this program for covered discount card drugs dispensed after December 31, 2005. The Secretary must provide a method for the reimbursement of card sponsors for transitional assistance individuals.

Coverage of coinsurance. Pharmacies are permitted to reduce the coinsurance otherwise applicable. In addition, states are permitted to pay some or all of the coinsurance for some or all transitional assistance eligible enrollees. The state must pay the pharmacy directly. No federal matching payments are available for expenditures made by a state for coinsurance and they will not be considered as Medicare cost-sharing for purposes of the qualified Medicare beneficiary program.

Long-term care facilities and American Indian transitional assistance. The Secretary must establish procedures to ensure access for qualified residents of long-term care facilities. The Secretary could waive requirements of this section as necessary, to negotiate arrangements with sponsors to provide arrangements with pharmacies that support long-term care facilities. The Secretary also must establish procedures and may waive the requirements of the section to ensure that pharmacies operated by the Indian Health Service, Indian tribes and tribal organizations, and urban Indian organizations have the opportunity to participate in the pharmacy networks of at least two endorsed programs in each of the 50 states and the District of Columbia where such a pharmacy operates.

The availability of negotiated prices or transitional assistance could not be taken into account in determining an individual's eligibility for or benefits under any other federal program. Any nonuniformity of benefits resulting from the implementation of the new Sec. 1854(f) (such as the waiver of an enrollment fee) may not be taken into account in calculations of any required additional benefits under Part C.

Effective date. Effective upon enactment.

Act Sec. 101(a) adding Sec. 1860D-31(g) of the Social Security Act. Law at ¶2267.

¶ 164

Qualifications, Endorsements, and Beneficiary Protections

Qualifications for prescription drug card sponsors. Entities eligible to be prescription drug card sponsors are defined and criteria that such entities would have to meet are established. A card sponsor may be any nongovernmental entity that the Secretary determines is appropriate to offer an endorsed discount card program. Entities that could qualify include: (1) a pharmaceutical benefit management company; (2) a wholesale or retail pharmacy delivery system; (3) an insurer (including one that offered Medigap policies); (4) an organization under Part C; or (5) any combination of these. Each program must be operated directly, or through arrangements with an affiliated organization (or organizations), by one or more organizations with demonstrated experience and expertise in operating such a program. Further, the program must meet business stability and integrity requirements specified by the Secretary. The sponsor will be required to have arrangements, satisfactory to the Secretary, to account for transitional assistance provided to eligible individuals.

Applications for endorsement. Each sponsor seeking endorsement must submit an application to the Secretary. The Secretary will review the application and determine whether to endorse the program. The Secretary may not endorse the program unless the program and sponsor comply with the applicable requirements, and the sponsor enters into a contract with the Secretary to carry out the requirements. An endorsement will be for the duration of the discount card and transitional assistance program. The Secretary may, with notice, terminate an endorsement or contract for cause.

Beneficiary protections. The following beneficiary protections are established as follows:

Ensuring choice of programs. The Secretary is required to ensure that at least two endorsed programs (each offered by a different sponsor) are available to each eligible individual. The Secretary also may limit (but not below two) the number of sponsors in a state that are awarded contracts. Card sponsors enrolling individuals in any part of a state are required to permit eligible individuals in all parts of the state to enroll.

Savings to beneficiaries. Each prescription drug card sponsor is required to pass on to discount eligible enrollees the negotiated prices for covered drugs, including discounts negotiated with pharmacies and manufacturers, to the extent such discounts are disclosed under required disclosure rules.

Grievance mechanism. Each card sponsor is required to provide meaningful procedures for hearing and resolving grievances between the sponsor and enrollees in a manner similar to that required under Part C.

Confidentiality. The operations of an endorsed card program are covered functions and a card sponsor is a covered entity for purposes of applying the administrative simplification and privacy provisions of Part C of Title XI of the Social Security Act as established by the Health Insurance Portability and Accountability Act of 1996. The Secretary may waive the relevant portions of privacy regulations for an appropriate limited period of time to promote participation of sponsors.

Additional requirements. The sponsor of an endorsed card program may not provide or market services under the program unless the product or service is directly related to a covered discount card drug or a discount price for a nonprescription drug. Sponsors must meet additional requirements as the Secretary identifies are needed to protect and promote the interest of eligible individuals, including requirements that ensure that enrollees are not charged more than the lower of the negotiated price or the usual and customary price.

Special rules for Part C plans. Special rules apply to Part C organizations or organizations offering a plan or enrollment under a reasonable cost contract. An organization may elect to limit enrollment in its endorsed discount card program to eligible enrollees enrolled in its plan. In this case, special rules apply.

(1) The sponsor may not enroll individuals in an endorsed prescription drug program that are not enrolled in the Part C plan or under the reasonable cost contract.

(2) The pharmacy access requirements applicable to card sponsors are deemed to be met if access is made available through a pharmacy network (and not only through mail order) and the network is approved by the Secretary.

(3) The Secretary may waive requirements applicable to card sponsors to the extent he determined they were duplicative or conflicted with a requirement under Part C or cost contract requirement or were necessary to improve coordination of the card program with Part C or cost contract benefits.

Effective date. Effective upon enactment.

Act Sec. 101(a) adding Sec. 1860D-31(h) of the Social Security Act. Law at ¶2267.

¶166
Disclosure and Oversight

Disclosure. Each card sponsor is required to disclose to the Secretary information relating to: (1) program performance; (2) use of drugs by card program enrollees; (3) the extent to which negotiated price concessions made available by the manufacturer are passed through to enrollees through pharmacies or otherwise; and (4) other information specified by the Secretary. The Medicaid provision providing for the confidentiality of drug information will apply to any drug pricing information (other than aggregate data) disclosed under these requirements.

Oversight. The Secretary must provide appropriate oversight to ensure compliance of endorsed prescription card programs and their sponsors with the requirements of the prescription drug discount card program. The Secretary has the right to audit and inspect any books and records of sponsors (and any affiliated organization) that pertain to the card program, including amounts payable to the sponsor.

Sanctions. The Secretary has the discretion to impose sanctions for abusive practices. The Secretary may implement intermediate sanctions or may revoke the endorsement of a program offered by a sponsor if the Secretary determines that the sponsor or program no longer meet applicable requirements or that the sponsor has engaged in false or misleading marketing practices. Additionally, the Secretary may impose a civil money penalty in an amount not to exceed $10,000 for conduct that a party knows or should know is a violation. The provisions of Sec. 1128A of the Social Security Act (other than subsections (a) and (b) and the second sentence of subsection (f)) 1 apply to a civil money penalty in the same manner as such provisions apply to a penalty or proceeding under Sec. 1128A(a).

Effective date. Effective upon enactment.

Act Sec. 101(a) adding Sec. 1860D-31(i) of the Social Security Act. Law at ¶2267.

¶ 168
Treatment of Territories

Federal assistance is provided to territories that establish a plan to provide transitional assistance for covered discount card drugs to some or all eligible persons residing in the state. Eligible persons are those entitled to benefits under Part A or enrolled in Part B with incomes below 135 percent of the poverty line. The total amount of available federal assistance is $35 million. The amount available for each territory would be determined using the ratio of the total number of Medicare residents in the territory to Medicare residents in all the territories. The amounts received by the state must be used for covered discount card drugs for eligible transitional assistance individuals.

Effective date. Effective upon enactment.

Act Sec. 101(a) adding Sec. 1860D-31(j) of the Social Security Act. Law at ¶ 2267.

¶ 170
Funding

Separate Transitional Assistance Account. A separate account, known as the "Transitional Assistance Account" ("Account") is created within the Federal Supplementary Medical Insurance Trust Fund. Funds in this account will be kept separate from other funds within the Trust fund. Payments will be made from the Account in such amounts as the Secretary certifies are necessary to make payments for transitional assistance. Appropriations to the Account will be made equal to the amount of payments from the Account. Funds necessary to carry out administrative responsibilities are authorized to be appropriated to the Secretary. Payments cannot be made to sponsors for administrative expenses, except for payment of the enrollment fee for transitional eligible individuals. Costs associated with the Medicare prescription drug card and the transitional assistance program are excluded from the calculation of the Part B premium. Any remaining balance in the Account after the Secretary determines that the funds in the Account no longer are necessary to carry out the program will be transferred and deposited into the Medicare Prescription Drug Account.

Effective date. Effective upon enactment.

Act Sec. 101(a) adding Sec. 1860D-31(k) of the Social Security Act. Law at ¶ 2267.

¶ 175
Definitions

Cross references to other sections of the Act are included for definitions of basic prescription drug coverage, covered Part D drugs, creditable prescription drug coverage, Part D eligible individual, fallback prescription drug plan, initial coverage limit, MA plan, MA-PD plan, Medicare Prescription Drug Account, PDP approved bid, PDP region, qualified prescription drug coverage, standard prescription drug coverage, state pharmaceutical assistance program, and subsidy-Part D eligible individual.

"Insurance risk" for a participating pharmacy, is defined as risk of the type commonly assumed only by insurers licensed by a state; it does not include payment variations designed to reflect performance-based measures of activities within control of the pharmacy, such as formulary compliance and generic drug substitution.

A "PDP sponsor" is defined as a nongovernmental agency that is certified under Part D as meeting Part D requirements and standards.

A "prescription drug plan" is defined as prescription drug coverage that: is offered: (1) under a policy, contract, or plan that has been approved under Part D; and (2) by a PDP sponsor pursuant to and in accordance with a contract between the Secretary and the sponsor under Part D.

Application of Part C provisions. Part C requirements will be applied (unless otherwise specified) as if: (1) any reference to a Medicare Advantage plan included a reference to a prescription drug plan; (2) any reference to an MA organization or a provider-sponsored organization included a reference to a PDP sponsor; (3) any reference to a contract included a reference to a drug plan contract, (4) any reference to Part C included a reference to Part D; and (5) any reference to a Part C election period is a reference to a Part D enrollment period.

Effective date. Effective upon enactment.

Act Sec. 101(a) adding new Sec. 1860D-41 of the Social Security Act. Law at ¶2268.

¶ 178
Prescription Drug Coverage in Territories and Application of Demonstration Authority

Access to coverage in territories. The Secretary may waive the Part D requirements, including the requirement for two plans in an area, if the Secretary determines that a waiver necessary to secure access to qualified drug coverage for Part D eligible individuals residing in the territories.

Demonstration authority. The provisions of Sec. 402 of the Social Security Amendments of 1967, which provide for experiments and demonstrations for the purpose of determining appropriate payment and improving quality of care, apply to Part C and Part D in the same manner as they apply to Part A and Part B, except any reference to a Trust Fund in relation to an experiment or demonstration for prescription drug coverage is deemed a reference to the Medicare Prescription Drug Account within the Federal Supplementary Medical Insurance Trust Fund.

Effective date. Effective upon enactment.

Act Sec. 101(a) adding new Sec. 1860D-42 of the Social Security Act. Law at ¶2269.

¶ 180
Legislative Proposal, Study and Report

Submission of legislative proposal and reports to Congress. The Secretary is required to submit a legislative proposal containing necessary technical and conforming amendments to Titles I and II of the Act within six months of enactment. No later than January 1, 2005, the Secretary is required to submit a report to Congress including recommendations for providing benefits under Part D for drugs currently paid for under Part B. By March 1, 2005, the Secretary is required to submit a report to Congress on the progress made in implementing the drug benefit. The report must include specific steps taken, and that need to be taken, to ensure a timely start on January 1, 2006. The report is to include recommendations regarding an appropriate transition form the discount card and transitional assistance program.

Effective date. Effective upon enactment.

Act Sec. 101(b), (c), and (d). Law at ¶ 10,005.

¶ 200
Medicare Advantage Conforming Amendments

Conforming amendments to enrollment periods. Medicare beneficiaries retain the ability to make and change elections to a Medicare+Choice plan through 2006. The current law limitation on changing elections that begins in 2005, is delayed until 2006.

Establishment of special annual, coordinated election period. The annual, coordinated election period will be the six-month period beginning November 2005. The annual coordinated election period for 2004 and 2005 begins on November 15 and ends on December 31. For 2006, the annual coordinated election period begins on November 15 and ends on May 15, 2006. Beginning in 2007, the annual coordinated election period will begin on November 15 and end on December 31.

Special information campaign. The Secretary is required to provide for an education and publicity campaign to inform Medicare Advantage (MA) eligible individuals about the availability of MA plans, including MA-PD plans, offered in different areas and the election process for MA plans.

Coordinating initial enrollment periods. If any portion of an individual's initial enrollment period for Part B occurs after the end of the annual coordinated election period, the individual's initial enrollment period must be extended through the end of the individual's Part B initial enrollment period.

Limitations on one-change rule to same type of plan. The individual's right to change MA plans is limited for plan years beginning on or after January 1, 2006. This limit will not affect an individual's opportunity to make changes during the annual coordinated election period, but it will limit changes during the continuous open enrollment and disenrollment periods in a year. Individuals enrolled in an MA plan that provides qualified prescription drug coverage, may only disenroll from their plan to get coverage through fee-for-service (FFS) Medicare or through another MA plan that does not provide qualified prescription drug coverage. They may not leave their plan to obtain coverage under an MA-PD plan or under a prescription drug plan under Part D. Conversely, individuals enrolled in an MA-PD plan, may only change to another MA-PD plan or they may get coverage under FFS Medicare with coverage under a drug plan under part D. They may not enroll in an MA plan if it does not provide qualified prescription drug coverage.

Promotion of E-prescribing by Medicare Advantage plans. An MA-PD plan is required to provide for a separate or differential payment for a participating physician who prescribes covered Part D drugs in accordance with an electronic prescription program meeting Part D requirements. Such payment is required to take into consideration the implementation costs for the physician and also can be increased for those participating physicians who significantly increased: (1) formulary compliance; (2) lower cost and therapeutically equivalent alternatives; (3) reductions in adverse drug interactions; and (4) efficiencies in filing prescriptions through reduced administrative costs. Additional or increased payment could be structured in the same manner as medication therapy management fees under Sec.1860(D)-4(c)(2)(E) of the Social Security Act.

Effective date. Effective January 1, 2006.

Act Sec. 102(a) amending Sec. 1851(e)(1-4) and (f)(1) of the Social Security Act; Act Sec. 102(b) amending Sec. 1852(j) by adding paragraph (7) of the Social

Security Act; Act Sec. 102(c) amending 1851(a)(1) and 1852(j) of the Social Security Act. Laws at ¶¶ 2255 and 2256.

¶ 205
Medicaid Provisions Related to the Medicare Prescription Drug Benefit

Requirements related to Medicare prescription drug low-income subsidies and transitional assistance. Requirements related to Medicare low-income subsidies and transitional assistance under the prescription drug benefit and the prescription drug discount card program have been established for states as a condition of their state plans under the Medicaid Act and to receive federal Medicaid assistance. The administrative costs expended by a state in providing eligibility information are reimbursable to the state.

Eligibility information. The states are required to provide the Secretary with Medicaid eligibility information necessary to carry out transitional prescription drug assistance verification. The states must: (1) make eligibility determinations for low-income premium and cost-sharing subsidies; (2) inform the Secretary when eligibility has been established; and (3) provide the Secretary with information that may be needed to carry out Part D. Further, as part of the eligibility determination process, states are required to make determinations for Medicare cost-sharing assistance.

Federal assumption of Medicaid responsibility for subsidies for dual eligibles. The states are provided a federal phase-in of the costs of premiums and cost-sharing subsidies for full-benefit dual eligibles and a phased-down state contribution. A full-benefit dual eligible is an individual who has coverage for the month for covered Part D drugs under the prescription drug plan or Medicare Advantage prescription drug plan and is determined eligible by the state for medical assistance under Medicaid.

For each month beginning with January 2006, each state is required to provide for payment to the Secretary an amount equal to the product of:

(1) 1/12 of the product of the base year state Medicaid per capita expenditures for covered Part D drugs for dual eligibles and a proportion equal to 100 percent minus the federal medial assistance percentage applicable to the state for the fiscal year (the state matching rate), increased each year by the applicable growth factor for that year;

(2) the total number of dual eligibles for the state for the month; and

(3) the factor for the month.

Payments will be made in a manner specified by the Secretary similar to the method that payments are made for dual eligibles under Sec. 1843 of the Social Security Act, except that payments must be deposited into the Medicare Prescription Drug Account. A state's failure to make required payments will result in interest charges and in an offset to amounts otherwise payable under Medicaid.

Base year state per capita expenditures. The base year state Medicaid per capita expenditures for covered Part D drugs for dual eligibles is equal to the weighted average of gross per capita Medicaid expenditures (including dispensing fees) for prescription drugs in 2003 and the estimated actuarial value of prescription drug benefits provided under a capitated managed care plan for each dual eligible for 2003.

Gross per capita Medicaid expenditures for prescription drugs. The gross per capita Medicaid expenditures for prescription drugs for 2003 is equal to the state expenditures for covered outpatient drugs, including dispensing fees, during 2003, determined per dual eligible individual for individuals not receiving medial assistance for covered drugs through a Medicare managed care plan. When determining gross expenditures, the Secretary must: (1) use data from the Medicaid Statistical Information System (MSIS) and other available data; (2) exclude expenditures for drugs that are not covered Part D drugs, and (3) reduce the portion of expenditures not attributable to dispensing fees by an adjustment ratio applied to such portion. The adjustment factor is equal to the ratio for the state in 2003 of aggregate payments under rebate agreements under Sec. 1927 of the Social Security Act to gross expenditures under Medicaid for covered outpatient drugs.

Applicable growth factor. The applicable growth factor in 2004, 2005, and 2006 is the average annual percent change of the per capita amount of prescription drug expenditures as determined based on the most recent National Health Expenditure projections for the year involved. In subsequent years, the growth factor is the annual percentage increase average per capita expenditures under Part D. The applicable factor is 90 percent in 2006, phasing down to 75 percent over 10 years. The Secretary is required to notify each state by October 15 of the amount computed under the formula for the following year, beginning in 2006.

Coordination with Medicare prescription drug benefit. Medicare is the primary payer for covered Part D drugs for full-benefit dual eligible individuals. Medicaid coverage is not available for covered Part D drugs or any cost-sharing for covered drugs. States may provide coverage for drugs, other than Part D covered drugs in the manner otherwise provided for non-full benefit dual eligibles or through an arrangement with the prescription drug plan of MA-PD plan.

Treatment of territories. Residents of territories are not eligible for regular low-income subsidies. Territories, however, may apply for additional Medicaid funds if it establishes a plan for providing medical assistance for prescription drugs for low-income Part D eligible individuals. To obtain these funds, territories must provide assurances that additional funds will be used for covered drugs and administrative costs with no more than 10 percent of the total used for administrative expenses for any fiscal period.

Increased amount. The increased amount for a state for a year is equal to the product of the aggregate amount specified below and the ratio of the number of individuals who are entitled to benefits under Part A or enrolled in Part B and reside in the state, to the sum of the numbers for all states that submit a plan. The total amount available for territories is $28,125,000 beginning in the last 3 quarters of 2006, $37,500,000 in 2007, and increasing in subsequent years by the annual percentage increase in prescription drug costs for Medicare beneficiaries.

Report. The Secretary is required to report to Congress on the application of the provision in the territories.

Best price exemption. The prices negotiated from drug manufacturers for covered discount card drugs under an endorsed discount card program and any prices negotiated by a prescription drug plan under Part D or an MA-PD plan under Part C are exempt from the calculation of Medicaid best price.

Medicare cost-sharing. Medicare cost-sharing for Part B premium for qualifying individuals has been extended through September 2004. The total amount available for allocation has been increased to $3,000,000.

Outreach by the Commissioner of Social Security. The outreach requirements for the Commissioner of Social Security have been expanded to include outreach activities for transitional assistance and low-income subsidy individuals and have been extended until September 2004.

Effective date. Effective upon enactment, except that the extension of Medicare-cost sharing for qualifying individuals applies to calendar quarters beginning on or after April 1, 2004.

Act Sec. 103(a)(1) amending Sec. 1902(a) of the Social Security Act by adding paragraph (66); Act Sec. 103(a)(2) redesignating Sec. 1935 as 1936 and adding new Sec. 1935; Act Sec. 103(c) amending new Sec. 1935 by adding subsection (d); Act Sec. 103(d)(1) amending new Sec. 1935(a) and (c)(1) and by adding subsection (e); Act Sec. 103(d)(2) by amending Sec. 1108(f); Act Sec. 103(e) amending 1927(c)(1)(C)(i) by adding subclauses (V) and (VI); Act Sec. 103(f)(1) amending Sec. 1902(a)(10)(E)(iv); Act Sec. 103(f)(2) amending Sec. 1933(g); Act Sec. 103(g) amending Secs. 1144, 1144(a)(1) and (2), 1144(b)(1) and (2). Law at ¶2005, 2025, 2395, 2396A, 2396B, 2396C, 2396D, 2415, 2401E, and 2405.

¶ 210
Medigap Amendments

Medigap policy prohibitions. Effective January 1, 2006, the selling, issuance, or renewal of existing Medigap policies with prescription drug coverage for Part D enrollees is prohibited. The prohibition does not apply to renewal of Medigap prescription policies for individuals who are not Part D enrollees. Individuals enrolling under Part D during the initial enrollment period could enroll in a plan without drug coverage, or continue their previous policy as modified to exclude drugs. Plans H, I, and J, modified to exclude drugs, may continue to be offered to new enrollees. Medigap issuers must notify individuals of these changes 60 days prior to the initial Part D enrollment period.

Enrollment issues. A substitute Medigap policy for individuals enrolling in Part D, who at the time of such enrollment were enrolled in and terminated enrollment in a Medigap policy H, I, or J or a pre-standard policy that included drug coverage, is guaranteed. Evidence of enrollment and termination is required. The guaranteed enrollment applies for any of the Plans A, B, C, and F within the same carrier of issue. The guarantee applies for enrollments occurring in the new Medigap plan within 63 days of termination of enrollment in a Medigap drug Plan H, I, or J.

Insurer limitations. The insurer may not impose an exclusion based on a pre-existing condition for such individuals. Further, the insurer is prohibited from discriminating in the pricing of such policy on the basis of the individual's health status, claims experience, receipt of health care or medical condition.

National Association of Insurance Commissioners. The Secretary is required to request the National Association of Insurance Commissioners to review and revise standards for benefit packages taking into account the changes in benefits resulting form the enactment of this Act and to otherwise update standards to reflect other changes in law included in the Act. To the extent practicable, the revision will provide for implementation of revised standards as of January 1, 2006.

New benefit packages. Two new benefit packages have been created.

First benefit package. The first benefit package will have the following benefits (notwithstanding other provisions of law relating to core benefits): (1) coverage of 50 percent of the cost-sharing otherwise applicable (except coverage of 100 percent cost-sharing applicable for preventive benefits); (2) no coverage of the Part B deductible; (3) coverage of all hospital coinsurance for long stays and 365 extra lifetime days of coverage (as in current core package); and (4) a limitation on annual out-of-pocket costs of $4,000 in 2006 (increased in future years by an appropriate inflation adjustment as specified by the Secretary).

Second benefit package. The second benefit package will have the same benefit structure as the first new package except that: (1) coverage would be provided for 75 percent rather than 50 percent, of cost-sharing otherwise applicable; and (2) the limitation on out-of-pocket costs is $2,000, rather than $4,000. Medigap issuers are not required to participate as a prescription drug plan (PDP) sponsor under the new Part D and a state may not make such a requirement.

Effective date. Effective upon enactment.

Act Sec. 104 (a)(1) amending Sec. 1882 of the Social Security Act by adding subsection (w); Act Sec. 104 (a)(2) amending Sec. 1882(s)(3)(C); Act Sec. 104(b)(1) amending 1882 by adding subsection (w); and Act Sec. 104 (b)(2) amending 1882(g)(1) and (o)(1). Law at ¶2346B, 2346E, 2346F, and 2346G.

¶ 215
Medicare Prescription Drug Discount Card and Transitional Assistance Program

General and administrative provisions. Program costs are excluded from the calculation of the Part B premium. Medicaid confidentiality provisions are applied to drug pricing data reported by manufacturers under the program.

Inapplicable sections of law. The following sections of law do not apply to the card program: (1) new Sec. 1871(a)(3) of the Social Security Act relating to time line for publication of final rules; (2) Chapter 35 of Title 44 of the U.S. Code relating to coordination of federal information policy; (3) Sec. 553(d) of Title 5 of the U.S. Code requiring at least 30 days between issuance and effective date of a substantive rule; and (4) Sec. 801(a)(3)(A) of Title 5 of the U.S. Code providing 60 days for congressional review of a major rule.

Secretary's contracting authority and judicial review. The contracting authority extended to the Secretary under Medicare+Choice also applies to the Secretary with respect to the discount card program. There is no judicial review of a determination not to endorse or enter into a contract with a card sponsor. Further, an order to enjoin any provision of the Sec. 1860D-31 of the Social Security Act does not affect any other provision of the section and all provisions are to be treated as severable.

Taxpayer information disclosure and security. The Secretary of the Treasury, upon written request from the Secretary of HHS, is required to disclose to officers and employees of HHS certain information with respect to a taxpayer for the most recent taxable year for which information is available in the Internal Revenue Service's taxpayer data information system, or if no return was filed for that year, the year before that. Required information will consist of whether the adjusted gross income (as modified by HHS regulations) of the taxpayer, and if applicable the taxpayer's spouse, exceeds amounts that are 100 percent and 135 percent of the official poverty line. This information may only be used to determine eligibility for the transitional low income assistance program.

Effective date. Effective upon enactment.

Act. Sec. 105(a) amending Secs. 1839(g) of the Social Security Act by adding 1839(g) paragraph (2); Act. Sec. 105(b) amending 1927(b)(3)(D) of the Social Security Act; Act Sec. 105(d) amending 1841(a) and (g) of the Social Security Act; Act Sec. 105(e)(1) amending Sec. 6103(l) of the Internal Revenue Code of 1986 by adding paragraph (19); Act Sec. 105(e)(2) amending I.R.C. Sec. 6103(a)(3); Act Sec. 105 (e)(4) amending I.R.C. 6103(p)(4) and Act Sec. 105(e)(4) amending I.R.C. Sec. 7213(a)(2). Law at ¶2165, 2175, 2346B, 2346E, 2346F, 2401D, and 10,020.

¶ 220

State Pharmaceutical Assistance Transition Commission

Establishment of the Commission. The State Pharmaceutical Assistance Transition Commission ("Commission") is established to develop a proposal for dealing with the transitional issues facing state programs and participants due to implementation of the Part D prescription drug program.

Commission members. The Commission, which is to be established as of the first day of the third month following enactment, will include: (1) a representative of each governor from each state with a program that the Secretary identifies as having a benefit package comparable to or more generous than the low-income assistance under the new Sec. 1860D-14 of the Social Security Act; (2) representatives from other states that have pharmaceutical assistance programs, as appointed by the Secretary; (3) representatives (not exceeding the total under 1 and 2) of organizations that have an inherent interest in the participants or the program itself, appointed by the Secretary; (4) representatives of MA organizations, pharmacy benefit managers and other private insurance plans; and 5) the Secretary or the Secretary's designee and other members specified by the Secretary.

Proposal principles. The Commission is required to develop the proposal in accordance with specified principles, including: (1) protection of the interests of program participants in the least disruptive manner; (2) protection of the financial and flexibility interests of states so they are not financially worse off; and (3) principles of Medicare modernization outlined in Title II of the Act.

Commission report. The Commission must report to the President and Congress by January 1, 2005, including specific legislative or administrative recommendations, if any. The Secretary will provide the Commission with administrative support services necessary for the Commission to carry out it responsibilities under this part. The Commission will terminate 30 days later.

Effective date. Effective upon enactment.

Act Sec. 106. Law at ¶ 10,030.

¶ 225

Studies and Reports

Variations in per capita spending. The Secretary is required to study variations in per capita spending for covered Part D drugs among PDP regions to determine the amount of variation that is attributable to price variations and the differences in per capita utilization that is not taken into account in the health status risk adjustment made to PDP bids. Not later than January 1, 2009, the Secretary must submit a report on the study to Congress, which includes: (1) information on the extent of geographic variation in per capita utilization; (2) an analysis of the impact of direct subsidies; (3) whether the subsidies should be adjusted to take into account such variation, and (4) recommendations regarding the appropriateness of applying an additional geographic adjustment factor to bids.

Pharmacy services practice standards study. Not later than 12 months after enactment, the Secretary is required to review the current standards of practice for pharmacy services provided to patients in nursing facilities. Specifically, the Secretary is to assess: (1) the current standards of practice, clinical services, and other service requirements generally utilized for such pharmacy services; and (2) evaluate the impact of those standards with respect to patient safety, reduction of medication errors, and quality of care. The report, which must be submitted to Congress no later than 18 months after enactment, must contain a description of the Secretary's plans to implement this Act in a manner consistent with applicable state and federal laws designed to protect the safety and quality of care of nursing facility patients. The report must also include recommendations regarding necessary actions.

Drug safety and quality issues. The Secretary is required to enter into a contract with the Institute of Medicine ("IOM") to carry out a comprehensive study of drug safety and quality issues to provide a blueprint for system-wide change. The IOM will be constituted of leading experts and key stakeholders in pharmaceutical management and drug safety, including clinicians, health service researchers, pharmacists, system administrators, and payer representatives.

Study objectives. The objectives of the study are to: (1) develop a full understanding of drug safety and quality issues through an evidence-based review of the literature, case studies, and analysis; (2) attempt to develop credible estimates of the incidence, severity and costs of medication errors; (3) evaluate alterative approaches to reducing medication errors; (4) provide guidance on high-priority strategies to achieve drug safety goals; (5) assess opportunities and key impediments to broad nationwide implementation of medication error reductions; and (6) develop an applied research agenda to evaluate the health and cost impacts of alternative interventions. The study must completed within an 18-month period. The study will be funded with sums as may be necessary.

Multi-year contracts study. The agreement requires the Secretary to provide a study on the feasibility and advisability of providing multi-year contracts with PDP sponsors and MA organizations. The Secretary is required to submit a report on this study by January 1, 2007.

Study on utilization and access to Part D drugs for low-income subsidy eligible individuals. The General Accounting Office (GAO) is required to conduct a study to determine the extent to which utilization and access to covered Part D drugs for low-income subsidy eligible individuals differs from that for persons who would qualify as subsidy eligible individuals except for application of the assets test. The report is due to Congress by September 30, 2007.

Study on pharmaceutical information accessibility for the blind and visually impaired. The Secretary is required to undertake a study of how to make prescription pharmaceutical information, including drug labels and usage instructions, accessible to blind and visually-impaired individuals. Included in the study will be a review of existing and emerging technologies, including assistive technology, that makes essential information on the content and prescribed use of pharmaceutical medicines available in a usable format for blind and visually-impaired individuals.

Report. The report will include recommendations for the implementation of usable formats for making prescription pharmaceutical information available to blind and visually-impaired individuals and an estimate of the costs associated with the implementation of each format. This report must be submitted to Congress no later than 18 months after the enactment of the Act.

Effective date. Effective upon enactment.

Act Sec. 107. Law at ¶10,040.

¶ 230
Grants to Physicians to Implement Electronic Prescription Drug Programs

Grants to physicians. The Secretary is authorized to make grants to physicians to assist them to implement electronic prescription programs in compliance with the standards under the new Sec. 1860D-(4)(e) of the Social Security Act. Fifty ($50) million is authorized for fiscal year (FY) 2007, as well as any sums necessary for FY 2008 and FY 2009. The Secretary, in awarding the grant, must give special consideration to physicians who serve a disproportionate number of Medicare patients and give preference to physicians who serve a rural or underserved area. Grant applicants are required to provide the Secretary with information necessary to evaluate the project and to ensure that funding is expended only for the purposes for which it is made. The applicant must agree to make available non-federal contributions totaling at least 50 percent of the costs.

Use of grant funds. Grant funds may be used for purchasing, leasing, and installing hardware and software; making upgrades and other improvements; and providing education and training to eligible physician staff on the use of technology. Only one grant may be awarded per physician or physician group.

Appropriations.

Effective date. Effective upon enactment.

Act Sec. 108. Law at ¶ 10,050.

¶ 235
Expanding the Work of Medicare Quality Improvement Organizations to Include Parts C and D

Quality improvement under Parts C and D. The work of quality improvement organizations (QIOs) is expanded to include Part C and Part D that will offer providers, practitioners, Medicare Advantage (MA) organizations, and prescription drug program (PDP) sponsors quality improvement assistance for prescription drug therapy. The Secretary is required to request that the Institute of Medicine of the National Academy of Sciences conduct a study of the QIO program, including an evaluation of the program and the extent to which other entities could perform similar quality improvement functions as well as or better than QIOs. The Secretary must report to Congress on the study by June 1, 2006. If the Secretary finds, based on the study, that other entities could improve quality as well as or better than QIOs, the Secretary must provide increased competition through such entities.

Effective date. Effective on or after January 1, 2004.

Act Sec. 109(a) amending Sec. 1154(a)(1) of the Social Security Act and Act Sec. 109(b) amending Sec. 1154(a) by adding new paragraph (17). Law at ¶ 2026.

¶ 240
Conflict of Interest Study

Pharmacy benefit manager study and report. The Federal Trade Commission is required to conduct a study of differences in payment amounts for pharmacy services provided to enrollees in group health plans that utilize pharmacy benefit managers (PBMs). The study must include an assessment of the differences in costs incurred by such enrollees and plans for drugs dispensed by mail order pharmacies owned by

PBMs compared to those not owned by PBMs, and community pharmacies. The study also must examine whether such plans are acting in a manner that maximizes competition and results in lower prescription drug prices for enrollees.

Report. The Federal Trade Commission is required to provide a report to Congress within 18 months of enactment. The report must include recommendations regarding any legislation to insure the fiscal integrity of the Part D program.

Effective date. Effective upon enactment.

Act Sec. 110. Law at ¶10,070.

¶ 245
Study on Employment-Based Retiree Health Coverage

Study and report. The Comptroller General of the United States is required to conduct an initial and final study to examine trends in employment-based retiree health coverage as defined under the Social Security Act; the Federal Employees Health Benefits Program (FEHBP); and the options and incentives available under this Act that may have an effect on the voluntary provision of such coverage.

Content of initial study. The initial study must consider:

(1) trends in employment-based retiree health coverage prior to the date of the enactment of this Act;

(2) the opinions of sponsors of employment-based retiree health coverage (sponsors) concerning the options available under this Act that they are most likely to utilize for health coverage to their Medicare-eligible retirees, including an assessment of the administrative burdens associated with the available options;

(3) the likelihood of sponsors to maintain or adjust their levels of retiree health benefits beyond coordination with Medicare, including for prescription drug coverage, provided to Medicare-eligible retirees after the date of the enactment of this Act;

(4) the factors that sponsors expect to consider in making decisions about any changes they may make in the health coverage provided to Medicare-eligible retirees; and

(5) whether PDP options, or the health plan options available under the Medicare Advantage (MA) program, are likely to cause employers and other entities that did not provide health coverage to retirees prior to the date of the enactment of this Act to provide supplemental coverage or contributions toward premium expenses for Medicare-eligible retirees who may enroll in the future.

Content of final study. The final study must consider: (1) changes in the trends in employment-based retiree health coverage since the completion of the initial study by the Comptroller General; (2) factors contributing to any changes in coverage levels; (3) the number and characteristics of sponsors that receive the special subsidy payments for prescription drug coverage to their Medicare-eligible retirees that is of the same or greater actuarial value as the prescription drug coverage available to other Medicare beneficiaries without employment-based retiree health coverage; (4) the extent to which sponsors provide supplemental health coverage or contribute to the premiums for Medicare-eligible retirees who enroll in a PDP or an MA-PD plan; (5) other coverage options the sponsors believe would assist retirees with their future health care needs and their willingness to sponsor such alternative plan designs; (6) the extent to which employers or other entities that did not provide employment-based retiree health coverage prior to the date of the enactment of this Act provided some form of coverage or financial assistance for retiree health care needs after the date of the enactment of this Act; (7) recommendations by employers, benefits experts, academics, and others on ways that the voluntary provision of employment-based retiree health coverage may be improved and expanded.

Reports. The Comptroller General is required to submit a report to Congress on: (1) the initial study no later than one year after the date of the enactment of this Act; and (2) the final study no later than January 1, 2007.

Consultation. The Comptroller General must consult with sponsors of employment-based retiree health coverage, benefits experts, human resources professionals, employee benefits consultants, and academics with experience in health benefits and survey research in the development and design of the initial and final studies under this section.

Effective date. Effective upon enactment.

Act Sec. 111. Law ¶10,080.

Medicare Advantage

IMPLEMENTATION OF MEDICARE ADVANTAGE PROGRAM

Implementation and Transition . . . . ¶ 350

IMMEDIATE IMPROVEMENTS

Equalizing MA Payments with Fee-for-Service Costs . . . . ¶ 351
Change in Budget Neutrality for Blended Capitation Rate . . . . ¶ 352
Increasing Minimum Percentage Increase to National Growth Rate . . ¶ 353
DoD and VA Costs . . . . ¶ 354
Special Rule for Certain Inpatient Hospital Stays. . . . . ¶ 355
MedPAC Study of AAPCC . . . . ¶ 356
Report on Impact of Increased Financial Assistance to MA Plans . . . . ¶ 357
Study on Unreasonable Beneficiary Cost-Sharing . . . . ¶ 358
Announcements Regarding Payment Rates . . . . ¶ 359
Higher Copayments for Non-MA Providers . . . . ¶ 360

MEDICARE ADVANTAGE REGIONAL PLANS

Establishment of MA Regional Plans . . ¶ 361
Definition of MA Regional, Local Plan . . ¶ 362
Rules for MA Regional Plans . . . . ¶ 363
Competition Program Starting in 2006 . . . . ¶ 365
Beneficiary Savings . . . . ¶ 366
Collection of Premiums . . . . ¶ 367
Computation of MA Area-Specific Non-Drug Benchmark . . . . ¶ 368

Payment of Plans Based on Bid Amounts . . . . ¶ 369
Annual Announcement Process . . . . ¶ 370
Uniform Premium and Bid Amounts . . . . ¶ 371
Plan Incentives . . . . ¶ 372
Enrollees with End-Stage Renal Disease . . . . ¶ 373
Facilitating Employer Sponsorship of MA Plans . . . . ¶ 374
Medicare Beneficiary Education and Information . . . . ¶ 375
Protection Against Beneficiary Selection . . . . ¶ 376
Effective Date . . . . ¶ 377

ADDITIONAL REFORMS

Special Needs Beneficiaries . . . . ¶ 378
Avoiding Duplicative State Regulation . . ¶ 379
Medicare MSAs . . . . ¶ 380
Extension of Reasonable Cost Contracts . . . . ¶ 386
Municipal Health Service Demonstration Projects . . . . ¶ 387
Payment by PACE Providers . . . . ¶ 388
Reimbursement for Federally Qualified Health Centers . . . . ¶ 390
Report on Health Care Performance Measures . . . . ¶ 394

COMPARATIVE COST ADJUSTMENT PROGRAM

Comparative Cost Adjustment Program . . . . ¶ 396

IMPLEMENTATION OF MEDICARE ADVANTAGE PROGRAM

¶ 350

Implementation and Transition

CMS is establishing the Medicare Advantage (MA) program under Part C of Title XVIII of the Social Security Act. The MA program will replace the Medicare+Choice (M+C) program. The Secretary of HHS is responsible for providing an appropriate transition in the use of the terms "Medicare+Choice" and "Medicare Advantage" in reference to Medicare Part C. This transition must be fully completed for all materials for plan years beginning not later than January 1, 2006. Before this deadline, references to "Medicare Advantage" or "MA" also include references to "Medicare+Choice."

¶350

Effective date. Effective for plan years beginning January 1, 2006.

Act Sec. 201. Law at ¶10,090.

IMMEDIATE IMPROVEMENTS

¶ 351

Equalizing MA Payments with Fee-for-Service Costs

New payment mechanism. Starting in 2004, the annual Medicare Advantage (MA) capitation rate for an MA payment area will be equal to the largest of the blended capitation rate, the minimum amount, the minimum percentage increase, or a new formula: 100 percent of fee-for-service (FFS) costs. The FFS payment for a given year is the adjusted average per capita cost for the year (with an appropriate risk adjustment) for the MA payment area for Medicare-eligible individuals who are not enrolled in an MA plan for the year, excluding costs attributed to direct graduate medical education payments, but including the amount of additional payments that would have been made in the area if individuals entitled to MA benefits had not received services from the Department of Defense or the Department of Veterans Affairs.

Effective date. Effective for plan years beginning January 1, 2006.

Act Sec. 211(a) amending Sec. 1853(c)(1) of the Social Security Act. Law at ¶2256A.

¶ 352

Change in Budget Neutrality for Blended Capitation Rate

The calculation for the blended capitation rate and the payment adjustment budget neutrality factor is qualified to exclude 2004 from the calculation.

Effective date. Effective for plan years beginning January 1, 2006.

Act Sec. 211(b) amending Secs. 1853(c)(1)(A) and 1853(c)(5) of the Social Security Act. Law at ¶2256A.

¶ 353

Increasing Minimum Percentage Increase to National Growth Rate

For 2004 and each succeeding year, the minimum percentage increase will equal the greater of 102 percent of the previous year's MA capitation rate for the area; or the annual MA capitation rate for the area for the previous year increased by the national per capita MA growth percentage, for that succeeding year, but not taking into account any adjustments for errors in years before 2004. Beginning in 2005 and each subsequent year, the payments to a plan will be based on its prior year rate increased by the revised minimum percentage increase.

Effective date. Effective for plan years beginning January 1, 2006.

Act Sec. 211(c) amending Sec. 1853(c) of the Social Security Act. Law at ¶2256A.

¶ 354
DoD and VA Costs

In determining the area-specific MA capitation rate for a year (beginning with 2004), the annual per capita rate of payment for 1997 (determined at Soc. Sec. Act. Sec. 1876(a)(1)(C)) shall be adjusted to include the Secretary's estimate of the amount of additional payments that would have been made in the area if individuals entitled to MA benefits had not received services from facilities of the Department of Defense or the Department of Veterans Affairs.

Effective date. Effective for plan years beginning January 1, 2006.

Act Sec. 211(d) amending Sec. 1853(c)(3) of the Social Security Act. Law at ¶ 2256A.

¶ 355
Special Rule for Certain Inpatient Hospital Stays

The special rule regarding payment to inpatient hospitals and the financial responsibility of hospitals for Medicare Advantage beneficiaries when they elect or terminate the election of an MA plan is extended to include rehabilitation hospitals, distinct part rehabilitation units, and long-term care hospitals.

Effective date. Effective for plan years beginning January 1, 2004.

Act Sec. 211(e) amending Sec. 1853(g) of the Social Security Act. Law at ¶ 2256A.

¶ 356
MedPAC Study of AAPCC

The Medicare Payment Advisory Commission (MedPAC) must conduct a study that assesses the method used for determining the adjusted average per capita cost (AAPCC). The study must include an examination of (1) the basis for variation in such costs between different areas, including differences in input prices, utilization, and practice patterns; (2) the appropriate geographic area for payment of Medicare Advantage local plans under the MA program; and (3) the accuracy of risk adjustment methods in reflecting differences in costs of providing care to different groups of beneficiaries served under the MA program. MedPAC is required to submit the report to Congress no later than 18 months after enactment of this legislation.

Effective date. Effective upon enactment.

Act Sec. 211(f). Law at ¶ 10,100.

¶ 357
Report on Impact of Increased Financial Assistance to MA Plans

No later than July 1, 2006, the HHS Secretary must send to Congress a report that describes the impact of additional financing provided under this Act and other recent budget Acts on the availability of Medicare Advantage plans in different areas and its impact on lowering premiums and increasing benefits.

Effective date. Effective upon enactment.

Act Sec. 211(g). Law at ¶ 10,100.

¶ 358

Study on Unreasonable Beneficiary Cost-Sharing

The Medicare Payment Advisory Commission (MedPAC), in consultation with beneficiaries, consumer groups, employers, and Medicare Advantage organizations, must conduct a study to determine the extent to which the cost sharing structures under MA plans affect access to covered services or select enrollees based on the health status of eligible individuals. MedPAC must report on the study to Congress no later than December 31, 2004, along with recommendations for appropriate legislative and administrative actions.

Effective date. Effective upon enactment.

Act Sec. 211(h). Law at ¶ 10,100.

¶ 359

Announcements Regarding Payment Rates

Revised MA payment rates. Within six weeks after the date of enactment of this Act, the HHS Secretary must determine and announce revised MA capitation rates for 2004. An MA plan that previously announced its intention to terminate its contract or reduce its service area can rescind its notice.

Special rule for payment rates in 2004. The annual capitation rate for a payment area for January and February 2004 will be calculated and the excess amount under Soc. Sec. Act Sec. 1854(f)(1)(B) will be determined as if the amendments summarized in ¶¶ 351 to 354 above had not been enacted. For March through December 2004, the annual capitation rate for a payment area will be calculated and the excess amount determined in a manner that will ensure that the total payments in 2004 will be the same as they would have been if the capitation rate for January and February had not been enacted.

Notice of plan changes. If a MA organization (MAO) submits a revised notice of premiums to CMS because of the revised payment rates, and the revision results in changes in beneficiary premiums, cost-sharing, or benefits, then the MAO must send written notice of the changes to beneficiaries within three weeks of the date the Secretary approves the changes.

The revised capitation rates for 2004 are not subject to administrative or judicial review.

Effective date. Effective upon enactment.

Act Sec. 211(i). Law at ¶ 10,100.

¶ 360

Higher Copayments for Non-MA Providers

An MA plan may charge a higher copayment if a beneficiary chooses to receive covered healthcare services from providers who do not have contracts or agreements with the MA plan.

Effective date. Effective upon enactment.

Act Sec. 211(j), amending Sec. 1852(d)(4)(B) of the Social Security Act. Law at ¶ 2256, 10,100.

MEDICARE ADVANTAGE REGIONAL PLANS

¶ 361
Establishment of MA Regional Plans

The definition of "coordinated care plans" is expanded to include regional and local preferred provider organization (PPO) plans. The HHS Secretary may not permit the offering of a local PPO plan under the MA program during 2006 or 2007 in a service area unless the plan was offered in the area as of December 7, 2005. The intent is to encourage PPOs to operate at the regional level. PPOs will be able to enter new or expanded service areas again beginning January 1, 2008.

Effective date. Effective for plan years beginning after January 1, 2006.

Act Sec. 221(a), amending Sec. 1851(a)(2)(A) of the Social Security Act. Law at ¶2255.

¶ 362
Definition of MA Regional, Local Plan

The term "MA regional plan" means an MA plan (1) that has a network of providers that have agreed to a contractually specified reimbursement for covered benefits with the organization offering the plan; (2) that provides for reimbursement for all covered benefits regardless of whether such benefits are provided within such network of providers; and (3) that has a service area that spans one or more entire MA regions.

An "MA local plan" is an MA plan that is not an MA regional plan. Under current law, MA local plans are county or equivalent areas as specified by the HHS Secretary.

An MSA plan or MA private fee-for-service plan may have a service area that covers one or more MA regions or even the entire country.

Effective date. Effective for plan years beginning after January 1, 2006.

Act Sec. 221(b) amending Sec. 1859(b) of the Social Security Act. Law at ¶2256F.

¶ 363
Rules for MA Regional Plans

Establishment of MA regions. The service area for a Medicare Advantage regional plan shall consist of an entire MA region. An "MA region" is a region within the 50 states and the District of Columbia.

No later than January 1, 2005, the HHS Secretary must establish and publish MA regions. The Secretary may periodically review and revise MA regions if the Secretary determines such revision to be appropriate. There can be no fewer than 10 regions, and no more than 50 regions. The regions shall maximize the availability of MA regional plans to all MA-eligible individuals without regard to health status, especially those residing in rural areas. Each region should include at least one state, should not divide states across regions, and should include multi-state Metropolitan Statistical Areas in a single region.

Marketing. Before establishing MA regions, the Secretary must conduct a market survey and analysis, including an examination of current insurance markets, to determine how the regions should be established.

An MA regional plan may be offered in more than one MA region, and may even be offered in all MA regions.

Single deductible and out-of-pocket limit. An MA regional plan must have a "single deductible" for both Part A and Part B benefits. The single deductible may be applied differentially for in-network services and waived for preventive or other items and services.

An MA regional plan also must have two catastrophic limits—one for out-of-pocket expenditures for in-network Part A and B benefits and one for out-of-pocket expenditures for all Part A and B benefits.

Risk corridors. CMS will share risk with MA regional plans if costs are above or below a specific risk corridor. MA organizations that offer an MA regional plan in 2006 or 2007 must notify the HHS Secretary of (1) the total costs of providing Part A and B benefits for all enrollees in the region in the year and the portion of such costs attributable to administrative expenses; and (2) the total costs of providing "rebatable integrated benefits" (see below) and the portion of these costs attributable to administrative expenses.

Allowable costs. The term "allowable costs" means, regarding an MA regional plan for a given year, the total costs for the plan and year, reduced by the portion of such costs attributable to administrative expenses incurred in providing the benefits.

Rebatable integrated benefits. The term "rebatable integrated benefits" means non-drug supplemental benefits pursuant to a rebate under Soc. Sec. Act Sec. 1854(b)(1)(C)(ii) (see ¶366 below) that the Secretary determines are integrated with the benefits described in that subparagraph.

Payment adjustments. There will be no payment adjustment if the allowable costs for the plan for the year are at least 97 percent, but do not exceed 103 percent, of the target amount (defined below) for the plan and year. If the allowable costs for the plan for the year are greater than 103 percent, but not greater than 108 percent, of the target amount for the plan and year, the Secretary must increase the total of the monthly payments made to the organization offering the plan by 50 percent of the difference between the allowable costs and 103 percent of the target amount. If allowable costs for the plan for the year are greater than 108 percent of the target amount, the Secretary must increase the total of the monthly payments made to the organization offering the plan by an amount equal to the sum of (1) 2.5 percent of the target amount; and (2) 80 percent of the difference between allowable costs and 108 percent of the target amount.

Reduction in payments. If the allowable costs for the plan are less than 97 percent, but greater than or equal to 92 percent, of the target amount, the Secretary must reduce the total of the monthly payments made to the organization by an amount equal to 50 percent of the difference between 97 percent of the target amount and the allowable costs. If the allowable costs for the plan for the year are less than 92 percent of the target amount, the Secretary must reduce the total of the monthly payments made to the MA organization by an amount equal to the sum of (1) 2.5 percent of the target amount; and (2) 80 percent of the difference between 92 percent of the target amount and the allowable costs.

Target amount. The target amount is defined as an amount equal to the sum of: (1) the total monthly payments made to the organization for enrollees in the plan for the year that are attributable to benefits under the original Medicare FFS program; (2) the total of the MA monthly basic beneficiary premium, collectable for the enrollees for the year; and (3) the total amount of rebatable integrated benefits that the Secretary determines are appropriate for inclusion in the risk corridor calculation.

Disclosure of information. Each MA organization offering an MA regional plan must provide the HHS Secretary with any information the Secretary determines is necessary to carry out this subsection. The Secretary has the right to inspect and audit any books and records of the MA organization pertaining to the information regarding costs.

Organizational and financial requirements. If an MA organization offering an MA regional plan is organized and licensed under state law in a state in the MA region but does not meet the requirements in other states in the region, the HHS Secretary may waive such requirement for an appropriate period of time. The waiver can only be granted if the MA organization has filed the necessary application to meet the other state's requirements. If an MA organization is organized and licensed under more than one state in the region, and the organization does not meet the requirements of each state, the organization may select the rules of one state and apply those rules to the entire service area until such time as the organization meets a state's requirements.

Stabilization fund. To promote greater stability among Medicare Advantage regional plans, the HHS Secretary is required to establish an MA Regional Plan Stabilization Fund. The Fund will be used to provide incentives for plan entry in each region and plan retention in regions with below-average MA penetration. Initially, $10 billion will be available from the Fund beginning on January 1, 2007; these start-up funds will only be available until December 31, 2013.

Funds will be drawn from the Federal Hospital Insurance Trust Fund and the Federal Supplementary Medical Insurance Trust Fund in a proportion that reflects the relative weight that the benefits under Parts A and B represent of the actuarial value of the total benefit. Additional funds will be available in an amount equal to 12.5 percent of average per capita monthly savings from regional plans that bid below the benchmark.

Amounts in the Fund shall be available in advance of appropriations to MA regional plans in qualifying MA regions. The total amount projected to be expended from the Fund in any year may not exceed the amount available in the Fund at the beginning of that year. If the use of the stabilization fund results in increased expenditures, the increased expenditures shall be counted as expenditures from the Fund.

Plan entry funding. Plan entry incentives are available for either a one-year national bonus payment or multi-year adjustments in regional payments; however, in no case can there be a regional payment adjustment if there is a national bonus for that year. The national bonus payment is available to MA organizations entering a particular region, but only if there was no MA plan offered in that region during the previous year. If a national bonus payment is not made, a regional payment adjustment can be made. The regional payment adjustment is an increased payment for an MA regional plan offered in a region that did not have any MA regional plans offered in the previous year.

Multi-year funding. If plan entry funding is provided for two consecutive years in a given region, the HHS Secretary shall submit to Congress a report that describes the underlying market dynamics in the region and includes recommendations concerning changes in the payment methodology for MA regional plans.

Plan retention funding. If market conditions are causing plan withdrawals, the Secretary may use the Fund to encourage MA plans to stay in a particular region. Incentives for plan retention could take the form of an increased payment to plans in regions that meet specific requirements. The requirements are: (1) one or more plans

¶363

inform the Secretary that they will discontinue service in the region in the succeeding year; (2) the Secretary determines that if those plans were not offered, fewer than two MA regional plans, each offered by a different organization, would be offered in the region in the year; (3) for the previous year, the Secretary determines that the proportion of beneficiaries enrolled in MA regional plans in the region is less than the national average of MA regional plan enrollment; and (4) funds have not already been awarded for two consecutive years.

The incentive for plan retention payment may not exceed the greater of: (1) three percent of the benchmark amount applicable in the region; or (2) an amount that, when added to the benchmark, results in a ratio such that the additional amount plus the benchmark for the region divided by the adjusted average per capita cost (AAPCC) equals the weighted average of benchmarks for all regions divided by the AAPCC for the U.S. Any additional payment amount will be treated as if it were an addition to the benchmark amount otherwise applicable, but will not be taken into account in the computation of the benchmark for any subsequent year.

Required reports. Not later than April 1 of each year (beginning in 2008), the HHS Secretary must submit a report to Congress that includes a detailed description of (1) the total amount expended as a result of the Stabilization Fund in the previous year compared to the total amount that would have been expended if the Stabilization Fund had not been established; (2) amounts remaining within the funding limitations; and (3) the steps the Secretary will take to ensure that the expenditures from the Stabilization Fund will not exceed the amount available.

Not later than January 1 of 2009, 2011, 2013 and 2015, the Comptroller General of the United States will submit a report to the HHS Secretary and Congress on the application of payments from the Stabilization Fund. The reports will include an evaluation of: (1) the quality of care provided to individuals for which additional payments were made from the Stabilization Fund; (2) beneficiary satisfaction; (3) the cost of Stabilization Fund payments to the Medicare program; and (4) any improvements in service delivery.

Regional benchmark amounts. Beginning in 2006, the Secretary will compute a "blended benchmark" amount for each MA region. The blended benchmark is designed to allow an MA organization to influence the final benchmark amount, through its plan bid amount. The MA "region-specific non-drug monthly benchmark amount" is the sum of a statutory component and a plan-bid component for the year. The "statutory component" is the product of the statutory region-specific non-drug amount for the region and the year, and the statutory national market share percentage. The "statutory region-specific non-drug amount", the first part of the statutory component, is an amount equal to the sum (for each local MA area within the region) of the product of the MA area-specific non-drug monthly benchmark amount for the area and the year, and the number of MA-eligible individuals residing in the local area, divided by the total number of MA-eligible individuals residing in the region. The "statutory national market share percentage", the second part of the statutory component, is equal to the proportion of MA-eligible individuals nationally who were not enrolled in an MA plan during the most recent month during the previous year for which data are available.

The "plan-bid component" is the product of the weighted average of MA plan bids for the region and the year and the non-statutory market share percentage. The weighted average of plan bids for an MA region is calculated as the sum across MA regional plans, of (for each plan) the products of the unadjusted MA statutory non-drug monthly bid for the plan, and the plan's share of MA enrollment in the region.

¶363

In the first year in which any regional plan is offered in a region, if more than one MA regional plan is offered in that year, the plan's share of MA enrollment in the region is replaced in the formula either by (1) one divided by the number of plans in the region, or (2) a share estimated by the Secretary. The non-statutory market share percentage is one minus the statutory national market share percentage.

Uniform coverage determination. The organization offering an MA regional plan may elect to have a local coverage determination for the entire MA plan based on the local coverage determination applied for any part of the region, as selected by the organization.

Assuring network adequacy. Under current law, a Medicare+Choice organization may select the providers in its network, so long as: (1) the organization makes the benefits available and accessible to each individual within the service area; (2) when medically necessary, the organization makes benefits available and accessible 24 hours a day and 7 days a week; and (3) the plan provides reimbursement for services provided outside of the network when services are medically necessary and immediately required.

The Act maintains all current law network adequacy requirements. However, because regions may encompass areas served by a single hospital, plans may have difficulty meeting their network adequacy requirements if they are unable to reach an agreement with such a hospital. The Secretary, therefore, may provide payment to an "essential hospital" that provides services to enrollees in an area, in cases in which the MA organization offering the plan is unable to reach an agreement with the hospital regarding provision of services to plan enrollees. (An essential hospital is a general acute care hospital that demonstrates to the Secretary that its costs exceed the Medicare Part A payment and is determined by the Secretary to be necessary for an MA plan to meet its network adequacy requirements.) In 2006, $25 million will be available for these payments in 2006, increased each year by the growth in the market basket percentage.

Effective date. Effective for plan years beginning after January 1, 2006.

Act Sec. 221(c) adding new Sec. 1858 of the Social Security Act. Conforming amendments affect Secs. 1851(i)(2), 1852(a), 1853(c), 1853(d), and 1859(c). Law at ¶2255, 2256, 2256A, 2256E, and 2256F.

¶ 365

Competition Program Starting in 2006

Under the current Medicare+Choice program, plans are paid a fixed administrative amount regardless of their efficiency or their actual costs of providing services. Beginning in 2006, an MA organization (other than an MSA) will be required to submit a bid to provide services to Medicare beneficiaries on either a local or a regional level.

Information to be submitted. In submitting its bid, which will be due by the first Monday in June each year (starting in 2006), the MA plan must provide the following information: (1) the monthly aggregate bid amount for the provision of all required items and services, based on average revenue requirements in the payment area for an enrollee with a national average risk profile (including demographic risk factors and health status); (2) the proportion of the bid attributable to the provision of "benefits under the original Medicare fee-for-service program" (defined below), basic prescription drug coverage, and supplemental health care benefits; (3) the actuarial basis for determining the amounts and proportions; (4) a description of deductibles, coinsurance, and copayments applicable under the plan and their actuarial value;

and (5) for qualified prescription drug coverage, the information required under Title I of this Act.

Acceptance and negotiation of bid amounts. The Secretary has the authority to negotiate the monthly bid amount and the proportions, including supplemental benefits, an authority similar to that of the Director of the Office of Personnel Management with respect to the Federal Employees Health Benefits Program. The Secretary may only accept a bid amount and proportion if they are supported by the actuarial bases, and reasonably and equitably reflect the cost of benefits provided under the plan. As under current law, the Secretary does not have the authority to review the bid amounts for private fee-for-service plans. The Secretary may not require: (1) an MA organization to contract with a particular hospital, physician, or other provider to furnish items and services; or (2) a particular price structure for payment under a contract.

Benefits under the FFS option. The term "benefits under the original Medicare fee-for-service program option" means those items and services (other than hospice care) for which benefits are available to eligible individuals under Parts A and B, with cost-sharing as required. In determining the actuarially equivalent level of cost-sharing for required benefits under an MA regional plan, only expenses for in-network providers will be taken into account for the application of the catastrophic limit. Supplemental benefits can include reductions in cost-sharing for Part A and B benefits below the actuarial value of the deductible, coinsurance, and copayments that would be applicable, on average, to individuals in the original fee-for-service program.

Effective date. Effective for plan years beginning after January 1, 2006.

Act Sec. 222(a) amending Sec. 1854 of the Social Security Act. Law at ¶2256 and 2256B.

¶ 366
Beneficiary Savings

Under current law, if a Medicare+Choice plan's adjusted community rate is below the administered monthly payment amount, it must provide reduced cost sharing, additional benefits, or reduced Part B benefits to its enrollees. Under the Act, a Medicare Advantage plan must provide an enrollee with a monthly rebate equal to 75 percent of any "average per capita savings" (the amount by which the risk-adjusted benchmark exceeds the risk-adjusted bid). The remaining 25 percent of the average per capita savings will be retained by the federal government.

Calculating savings. In calculating such savings, and in order to ensure that savings are uniform for all enrollees in a plan, the benchmark and the bid will be risk adjusted according to a statewide (for local plans) or region-wide (for regional plans) risk adjuster.

Alternatively, the Secretary may risk adjust the benchmark and bid on a plan-specific basis for the purpose of calculating savings. The beneficiary rebate can be credited toward providing supplemental healthcare benefits (including a reduction in cost-sharing, additional benefits, or a credit toward any MA monthly supplemental beneficiary premium), the prescription drug premium, or the Part B premium. The plan will inform the Secretary about the form and amount of the rebate, or the actuarial value, in the case of supplemental health care benefits.

Revision of premium terminology. The definitions of several terms relating to the monthly premium have been revised.

The "MA monthly basic beneficiary premium" for plans providing rebates (plans that bid below the benchmark) is zero. For plans with bids above the applicable benchmark, the MA monthly basic beneficiary premium will equal the amount by which the bid exceeds the benchmark.

The "MA monthly prescription drug beneficiary premium" is the portion of the aggregate monthly bid amount that is attributable to the provision of the new prescription drug benefits, less the amount of any rebate.

The "MA monthly supplemental beneficiary premium" is the portion of the aggregate monthly bid amount that is attributable to the provision of supplemental health care benefits, less the amount of any rebate.

The "unadjusted MA statutory non-drug monthly bid" is the portion of the bid submitted by a plan attributable to the provision of required benefits under Medicare fee-for-service.

Effective date. Effective for plan years beginning after January 1, 2006.

Act Sec. 222(b) amending Sec. 1854(b) of the Social Security Act. Law at ¶2256B.

¶ 367

Collection of Premiums

Under current law beneficiaries may have their Part B premiums deducted directly from their Social Security benefits. The Act allows enrollees to have their Medicare Advantage premiums deducted directly from their Social Security benefits, through an electronic funds transfer, or other means, including payment by an employer or under employment-based retiree coverage on behalf of an employee, a former employee, or a dependent. All premium payments deducted from Social Security benefits will be credited to the appropriate Trust Fund as specified by the Secretary and shall be paid to the MA organization.

Effective date. Effective for plan years beginning after January 1, 2006.

Act Sec. 222(c) amending Sec. 1854(d) of the Social Security Act. Law at ¶2256B.

¶ 368

Computation of MA Area-Specific Non-Drug Benchmark

The "Medicare Advantage area-specific non-drug monthly benchmark amount" for a given month, and for a service area that is entirely within an MA local area, is equal to 1/12 of the annual MA capitation rate for the area. For a service area that encompasses more than one MA local area, the amount is equal to the average of the local amounts, weighted by the projected number of enrollees in the plan residing in the respective local area. For an MA region, the MA region-specific benchmark amount for the region for the year is defined as the sum of the statutory component and the plan-bid component. The statutory component is a weighted average of the local MA benchmarks in the region.

Effective date. Effective for plan years beginning after January 1, 2006.

Act Sec. 222(d) adding new Sec. 1853(j) of the Social Security Act. Law at ¶2256A.

¶ 369

Payment of Plans Based on Bid Amounts

Under current law, the Secretary makes monthly payments for each M+C enrollee, reduced by any Part B premium reduction, and adjusted for risk.

Payments before 2006. Under the Act, for payments before 2006, the monthly payment amount will equal 1/12 of the annual MA capitation rate, for an enrollee for that area, reduced by any Part B premium reduction and adjusted for demographic factors such as age, disability status, gender, institutional status, and other factors the Secretary determines to be appropriate, including an adjustment for health status.

Payments for 2006 and after. Beginning in 2006, for plans with "bids below the benchmark," the payment will equal the unadjusted MA statutory non-drug monthly bid amount, with adjustments for demographic factors (including age, disability, and gender) and health status, adjustments for intra-regional variation (if applicable), adjustments relating to risk adjustment, and the monthly rebate.

For plans with "bids at or above the benchmark," the payment amount will equal the MA area-specific non-drug monthly benchmark amount, with the demographic and health status adjustments, adjustments for intra-regional variation (if applicable), and adjustments relating to risk adjustment. The Secretary will continue to be responsible for adjusting payments to MA plans as necessary to ensure that the sum of the monthly payment and the MA monthly basic beneficiary premium equals the unadjusted MA statutory non-drug monthly bid amount, as adjusted.

For an enrollee in an MA plan that offers prescription drug coverage, the plan's payment will include a subsidy payment and reimbursement for premiums and cost-sharing reductions for certain low-income beneficiaries.

Effective date. Effective for plan years beginning after January 1, 2006.

Act Sec. 222(e) amending Sec. 1853(a)(1) of the Social Security Act. Law at ¶ 2256A.

¶ 370

Annual Announcement Process

Under current law, the HHS Secretary is required to announce no later than May 1 (in 2004), and March 1 (in subsequent years), the annual Medicare+Choice capitation rate for each M+C payment area and the risk and other factors to be used in adjusting these rates.

Under the Act, the Secretary must determine and announce the MA capitation rates for each MA payment area for 2005, and the risk and other adjustment factors, by the second Monday in May of 2004. For 2006 and subsequent years, the Secretary will determine and announce, not later than the first Monday in April before the calendar year concerned, the MA capitation rate for each payment area, and the risk and other factors to be used in adjusting such rates. The Secretary will determine and announce, on a timely basis before the calendar year concerned, for each MA region and MA regional plan for which a bid is submitted, the MA region-specific non-drug monthly benchmark amount.

Effective date. Effective for plan years beginning after January 1, 2006.

Act Sec. 222(f) amending Sec. 1853(b) of the Social Security Act. Law at ¶ 2256A.

¶ 371
Uniform Premium and Bid Amounts

Except as permitted to facilitate the offering of MA plans under contracts between MA organizations and employers, labor organizations or the trustees to a fund established by one or more employers or labor organizations, the MA monthly bid amount, the MA monthly basic benefit, prescription drug, and supplemental beneficiary premium may not vary among enrollees in the plan.

Modification of ACR process. Under current law, each Medicare+Choice plan must submit an adjusted community rate (ACR) proposal, estimating the proposed cost of serving Medicare beneficiaries for the following contract year as compared to the estimated cost of providing the same services to a commercial population. The Act replaces the ACR process with the plan bid process noted above at ¶ 365.

Effective date. Effective for plan years beginning after January 1, 2006.

Act Sec. 222(g) amending Secs. 1854, 1854(c), 1854(d)(1), and 1854(f) of the Social Security Act. Law at ¶ 2256B.

¶ 372
Plan Incentives

An MA organization may not operate a physician incentive plan unless it provides information the Secretary requires on any physician incentive plan. Requirements that the organization: (1) conduct periodic surveys, and (2) provide the Secretary with sufficient information regarding the plan, to determine whether or not the plan is in compliance, are replaced.

Effective date. Effective for plan years beginning after January 1, 2006.

Act Sec. 222(h) amending Sec. 1852(j)(4) of the Social Security Act. Law at ¶ 2256.

¶ 373
Enrollees with End-Stage Renal Disease

Under current law, CMS established a separate rate of payment to Medicare+Choice organizations for enrollees who have end-stage renal disease. The Act requires payment rates for ESRD enrollees to be actuarially equivalent to rates that would have been paid with respect to other enrollees in the Medicare Advantage payment area before the enactment of the Act. The Secretary may apply the competitive bidding methodology of this section, with appropriate adjustments to account for the risk adjustment methodology applied to ESRD payments.

Effective date. Effective for plan years beginning after January 1, 2006.

Act Sec. 222(i) amending Sec. 1853(a)(1)(h) of the Social Security Act. Law at ¶ 2256A.

¶ 374
Facilitating Employer Sponsorship of MA Plans

Under current law, employers may sponsor a Medicare+Choice plan or pay premiums for retirees who enroll in an M+C plan. The Act allows the Secretary to waive or modify requirements that hinder the design of, offering of, or enrollment in a Medicare Advantage plan offered by employers, labor organizations, or the trustees of a fund established by one or more employers or labor organizations. The MA plan may restrict enrollment to individuals who are beneficiaries and participants in such a plan.

Effective date. Effective for plan years beginning after January 1, 2006.

Act Sec. 222(j) amending Sec. 1857(i) of the Social Security Act. Law at ¶2256D.

¶ 375
Medicare Beneficiary Education and Information

Under existing law, the Secretary is authorized to collect a user fee from each Medicare+Choice organization for use in carrying out enrollment information dissemination activities as well as the health insurance and counseling assistance. The Act allows the Secretary to also charge a prescription drug plan sponsor under the new Part D for its share of fees related to enrollment information dissemination activities. The authorization for appropriated amounts will be increased from $1 million to $2 million each year, beginning in 2006.

Effective date. Effective for plan years beginning after January 1, 2006.

Act Sec. 222(k) amending Sec. 1857(e)(2) of the Social Security Act. Law at ¶2256D.

¶ 376
Protection Against Beneficiary Selection

The Secretary may not approve a Medicare Advantage plan if the design of the plan and its benefits are likely to substantially discourage enrollment by certain MA-eligible individuals.

Effective date. Effective for plan years beginning after January 1, 2006.

Act Sec. 222(l) amending Sec. 1852(b)(1)(a) of the Social Security Act. Other conforming amendments amend Secs. 1839(a)(2), 1840(i), 1844(c), 1851(a)(3)(B)(ii), 1851(b)(1), 1851(d), 1851(f)(1), and 1857(d)(1) of the Act. Law at ¶¶2256, 2165, 2170, 2245, 2256B, and 2256D.

¶ 377
Effective Date

Title II is effective for plan years beginning on or after January 1, 2006, unless otherwise provided. The Secretary shall revise previously promulgated regulations for the changes due to the provisions of this Act, to carry out Part C of Medicare.

Effective date. Effective for plan years beginning after January 1, 2006.

Act Sec. 223. Law at ¶10,110.

ADDITIONAL REFORMS

¶ 378
Special Needs Beneficiaries

The Act establishes a new Medicare Advantage option—"Specialized Medicare Advantage Plans for Special Needs Beneficiaries." Specialized Medicare Advantage plans are plans that exclusively or disproportionately serve special needs beneficiaries such as those enrolled in the existing Evercare demonstration (which is designed to study the effectiveness of managing the acute-care needs of nursing home residents by pairing physicians and geriatric nurse practitioners).

"Special needs beneficiaries" are defined as Medicare Advantage enrollees who are institutionalized, or entitled to Medicaid, or individuals with severe and disabling conditions that the Secretary deems would benefit from a specialized plan. Specialized Medicare Advantage plans can limit enrollment to special needs beneficiaries until January 1, 2009. No later than one year after enactment of the Act, the Secretary is required to issue final regulations to establish requirements for special needs beneficiaries. No later than December 31, 2007, the Secretary is required to submit a report to Congress that assesses the impact of Specialized Medicare Advantage plans on the cost and quality of care.

The provision does not change current Medicare+Choice quality, oversight, or payment rules.

Effective date. Effective upon enactment.

Act Sec. 231 amending Secs. 1851(a)(2)(A), 1859, and 1859(b) of the Social Security Act. Law at ¶ 2255, 2256F and 10,120.

¶ 379

Avoiding Duplicative State Regulation

Since the Medicare Advantage program is a federal program, state laws do not apply, with the exception of state licensing laws or state laws related to plan solvency. This provision applies prospectively; thus, it would not affect previous and ongoing litigation. Additionally, no state may impose a tax on premiums paid to MA organizations.

Effective date. Effective upon enactment.

Act Sec. 232 amending Secs. 1854(g) and 1856(b)(3) of the Social Security Act. Law at ¶ 2256B and 2256C.

¶ 380

Medicare MSAs

Medicare medical savings accounts (MSAs) were established as a demonstration project in the Medicare+Choice program under the Balanced Budget Act of 1997 (PubLNo 105-33). New enrollments were not allowed after January 1, 2003, or after the number of enrollees reached 390,000. However, no private plan ever established an MSA option for beneficiaries.

Under the Act, the Medicare MSA demonstration becomes a permanent option, the capacity limit is removed, and the deadline for enrollment is eliminated. The requirement that MSAs report on enrollee encounters for an ongoing quality assurance program is eliminated because MSAs are not plans but bank accounts. Non-contract providers furnishing services to enrollees of MSAs are subject to the same balanced billing limitations as non-contract providers furnishing services to enrollees of coordinated care plans.

Effective date. Effective upon enactment, but not applicable until contract years beginning January 1, 2006.

Act Sec. 233 amending Secs. 1851(b)(4), 1851(e)(5)(A), 1852, 1852(e)(1), and 1852(k)(1) of the Social Security Act. Law at ¶ 2255, 2256 and 2256B.

¶ 386
Extension of Reasonable Cost Contracts

Under current law, cost-based plans are reimbursed by Medicare for the actual cost of furnishing covered services to Medicare beneficiaries, less the estimated value of beneficiary cost-sharing. The Secretary cannot extend or renew a reasonable cost reimbursement contract for any period beyond December 31, 2004.

The Act allows these plans to operate indefinitely, unless two other Medicare Advantage plans of the same type (i.e., either 2 local or 2 regional plans) enter the cost contract's service area. These other plans must enroll at least 5,000 beneficiaries for the portion of the area that is within a metropolitan statistical area having more than 250,000 people and counties contiguous to such an area, and at least 1,500 beneficiaries for any other portion of such area.

Effective date. Effective upon enactment.

Act Sec. 234 amending Sec. 1876(h)(5) of the Social Security Act. Law at ¶ 2330 and 2330.

¶ 387
Municipal Health Service Demonstration Projects

The Municipal Health Services Demonstration Project operates in four cities. These cities use their existing public health programs as the nucleus of a coordinated system to provide community-based health care for the underserved urban poor. The project provides comprehensive health services, including a prescription drug benefit and dental services. The demonstration program was scheduled to end December 31, 2004.

The Act extends this demonstration through December 31, 2006.

Effective date. Effective upon enactment.

Act Sec. 235. Law at ¶ 10,150.

¶ 388
Payment by PACE Providers

The Program of All-Inclusive Care for the Elderly (PACE) was created as a demonstration project under the Omnibus Budget Reconciliation Act (PubLNo 101-508) to help community-based organizations provide health and long-term care services on a capitated basis to frail elderly persons at risk of being institutionalized. PACE became a permanent program under the Balanced Budget Act of 1997 (PubLNo 105-33) and a state option for the Medicaid program.

The Act provides that for the Medicare program, protections against balance billing to PACE providers and beneficiaries enrolled under PACE apply in the same manner as applies to Medicare Advantage plans. For the Medicaid program, for services that are furnished to a beneficiary enrolled in a PACE program, the PACE program is not required to pay a provider an amount greater than required under the state plan.

Effective date. Effective for services provided on or after January 1, 2004.

Act Sec. 236 amending Secs. 1866(a)(1)(O), 1894(b), 1902(a), and 1934(b) of the Social Security Act. Law at ¶ 2290, 2375, 2395, 2396A, 2396B, 2396C, 2396D, and 2410.

¶ 390
Reimbursement for Federally Qualified Health Centers

Under current law, services provided by federally qualified health centers (FQHCs) to beneficiaries are reimbursed at no more than 80 percent of the reasonable costs of providing such services less any beneficiary cost sharing. Aside from certain exceptions and safe harbors, persons who offer or pay a kickback, a bribe, or rebate to induce referrals or the provision of services are subject to financial penalties and imprisonment.

Under the Act, FQHCs will receive a wrap-around payment for the reasonable costs of care provided to Medicare managed care patients served at such centers. Reimbursements to FQHCs, combined with Medicare Advantage (MA) payments and cost-sharing payments from beneficiaries, will equal 100 percent of the reasonable costs of providing such services. The safe harbor is extended to include any remuneration between a FQHC and an MA organization.

Effective date. Effective for services provided on or after January 1, 2006, and contract years beginning on or after that date.

Act Sec. 237 amending Secs. 1128B(b)(3), 1833(a)(3), 1853(a), and 1857(e) of the Social Security Act. Law at ¶ 2017, 2121A, 2256A, and 2256D.

¶ 394
Report on Health Care Performance Measures

The Act directs the Institute of Medicine (IOM) to evaluate leading healthcare performance measures in the public and private sectors and options to implement policies that align performance with payment under the Medicare program. The information examined by IOM includes the validity of leading health care performance measures, the success and utility of alternative performance incentive programs, and options to implement policy that aligns performance with payments. A report is due to the Secretary and the congressional committees of jurisdiction within 18 months of enactment.

Effective date. Effective upon enactment.

Act Sec. 238. Law at ¶ 10,180.

COMPARATIVE COST ADJUSTMENT PROGRAM

¶ 396
Comparative Cost Adjustment Program

Establishment. Beginning on January 1, 2010, the Secretary will establish a comparative cost adjustment (CCA) demonstration program, to test whether direct competition between private plans and the original Medicare fee-for-service (FFS) program will enhance competition in Medicare, improve health care delivery for all beneficiaries, and provide for greater beneficiary savings and reductions in government costs.

The demonstration will extend for six years, ending on December 31, 2015. At that point, the Secretary will submit a report to Congress that includes an evaluation of: (1) the financial impact of the demonstration on Medicare, (2) changes in access to physicians and other health care providers, and (3) beneficiary satisfaction under the demonstration and original Medicare fee-for-service. Based upon the results of the evaluation, the Secretary will provide recommendations for any extension or expansion of the demonstration. The demonstration cannot be extended unless there is a reauthorization from Congress.

Requirements for selection of CCA areas. The Secretary will select CCA demonstration areas from among qualifying Metropolitan Statistical Areas (MSAs). To qualify, an MSA in 2010 must have: (1) at least 25 percent of eligible Medicare beneficiaries enrolled in a local coordinated care Medicare Advantage (MA) plan; and (2) at least two coordinated MA local plans offered by different organizations, both of which meet minimum enrollment criteria. The total number of CCA areas is limited to six, or 25 percent of the total number of qualifying MSAs, whichever is lower.

Geographic diversity. The Secretary will select CCA demonstration areas to provide for geographic diversity. At least one of the selected MSAs must be chosen from the four largest that qualify (based on the eligible MA population). At least one MSA must be chosen from among the four with the lowest population density. At least one must include a multi-state area. No more than two CCA areas may be located within the same geographic region. In addition, the Secretary willl also grant priority to qualifying MSAs that have not had a Medicare preferred provider organization (PPO) plan demonstration.

Phase-in of demonstration. The demonstration will be phased in over a four-year period between 2010 and 2013. Both the benchmark and changes to the Part B premiums under the original Medicare fee-for-service program will be phased-in over this four-year period.

Computation of CCA benchmark amount. The CCA competitive benchmark is set at the weighted average of the private plan bids and the FFS amount in the CCA area. In order to provide traditional FFS disproportionate influence in CCA areas, the weight of the benchmark for FFS would equal the nationwide proportion of Medicare beneficiaries enrolled in FFS, or the CCA area's proportion, if higher. The weights for all other private plans would equal the national proportion of beneficiaries enrolled in private plans, or the CCA proportion if lower.

Premium adjustment. Beneficiaries enrolling in plans with bids or FFS amounts below the CCA competitive benchmark will receive 75 percent of the difference between the benchmark and bid/FFS amount, and the government will receive 25 percent of the difference. Beneficiaries enrolling in plans with bids/FFS amounts above the benchmark will pay the excess. Premium adjustments will be moderated over a four-year period for beneficiaries remaining in traditional FFS in CCA areas. An individual residing in a CCA demonstration area who is enrolled in Medicare Part B, but not enrolled in an MA plan, can have an adjustment to his or herPart B premium, either as an increase or a decrease.

Exception. No Part B premium adjustment will be made for individuals with incomes below 150 percent of poverty and who meet the assets requirements to be eligible for a prescription drug subsidy (see ¶119).

Amount of adjustment and limitation. The Part B premium adjustment for FFS beneficiaries in CCA demonstration areas is calculated in the following way: (1) if the FFS area-specific non-drug amount for the month does not exceed the CCA non-drug benchmark, the Part B premium is reduced by 75 percent of the difference; and (2) if the FFS area-specific non-drug amount for the month exceeds the CCA non-drug benchmark, the Part B premium is increased by the full amount of the difference. This adjustment will be phased-in over four years. There is also a five percent limit to the adjustment.

No change in benefits. Nothing in the demonstration project in any way changes the entitlement to defined benefits under Medicare Parts A and B. Throughout the demonstration, beneficiaries will have complete freedom to choose either a private plan or the traditional Medicare fee-for-service program.

Effective date. Effective upon enactment.

Act Sec. 241 adding new Sec. 1860C-1 of the Social Security Act. Law at ¶2256A, 2260 and 10,190.

Reimbursement and Coverage Issues

PROVISIONS RELATING TO HOSPITALS AND AMBULANCE SERVICES

Standardized Amount . . . . ¶ 501
Labor-Related Share of the
 Standardized Amount . . . . ¶ 503
Market Basket Update . . . . ¶ 507
Enhanced Disproportionate Share
 Hospital (DSH) Treatment . . . . ¶ 510
Medicare Inpatient Hospital Payment
 Adjustment for Low-Volume
 Hospitals . . . . ¶ 515
Brachytherapy Devices . . . . ¶ 545
Hospital Outpatient Department
 Payments . . . . ¶ 547
Payments Connected to Reporting on
 Quality . . . . ¶ 560
Appropriateness of Payments Under
 IPPS . . . . ¶ 562
Revision of the IME Adjustment
 Percentage . . . . ¶ 564
New Medical Technologies . . . . ¶ 566
Hospitals in Puerto Rico . . . . ¶ 568
Wage Index Reclassification Reform . . ¶ 570
Inpatient Hospital Services Provided
 by IHS . . . . ¶ 572
Limits on Physician Referrals . . . . ¶ 574
Physician Pathology Services . . . . ¶ 575
One-Time Appeals Process for
 Hospital Wage Index Classification . . ¶ 576
Critical Access Hospitals . . . . ¶ 578
Rural Community Hospital
 Demonstration Program . . . . ¶ 581
Hold Harmless Provision for Small
 Rural and Sole Community
 Hospitals . . . . ¶ 582
Reimbursement for Clinical
 Laboratory Services Furnished in
 Certain Rural Areas . . . . ¶ 583
EMTALA Improvements . . . . ¶ 584
MedPAC Study on Rural Payment
 Adjustments . . . . ¶ 586
Professional Education Costs . . . . ¶ 588
Residency Period for Geriatric
 Residency or Fellowship Programs . . ¶ 590
Resident Training in Non-Hospital
 Settings . . . . ¶ 592
Frontier Clinics . . . . ¶ 593
Ambulatory Surgical Centers . . . . ¶ 594
Ambulance Services . . . . ¶ 596
Providing Appropriate Coverage of
 Rural Air Ambulance Services . . . . . . ¶ 598

SKILLED NURSING FACILITIES

Background Checks . . . . ¶ 601
Additional Information About SNF
 Benefits . . . . ¶ 604
Payment Adjustment for AIDS
 Residents in SNFs . . . . ¶ 605
Information on Medicare-Certified
 SNFs in Hospital Discharge Plans . . ¶ 606
Establishing SNFs as Originating
 Sites for Telehealth Services . . . . ¶ 607
Portable Diagnostic Ultrasound
 Services in SNFs . . . . ¶ 608
Exclusion from SNF-PPS . . . . ¶ 610

HOME HEALTH AND HOSPICE

Demonstration Project to Clarify the
 Definition of Homebound . . . . ¶ 650
Increase for Home Health Services
 Furnished in a Rural Area . . . . ¶ 656
Update in Home Health Payment
 Rates . . . . ¶ 658
Adult Day Care Provided Under the
 Home Health Benefit . . . . ¶ 660
Provision of Home Health Service by
 a Religious Nonmedical Health
 Institution . . . . ¶ 662
MedPAC Study on Medicare Margins
 of Home Health Agencies . . . . ¶ 664
OASIS Data Collection . . . . ¶ 670
Determination and Delivery of
 Medical Care . . . . ¶ 671
Rural Hospice Demonstration Project . . ¶ 675
Coverage of Hospice Consultation
 Services . . . . ¶ 677
Voluntary Chronic Care Improvement
 Programs . . . . ¶ 678
Demonstration Project for Consumer
 Directed Chronic Outpatient
 Services . . . . ¶ 679

PHYSICIAN SERVICES

Payments to Physicians in Rural Areas . . ¶ 700
Update to Payments for Physicians'
 Services . . . . ¶ 701
Studies on Access to Physicians'
 Services . . . . ¶ 703
MedPAC Report on Payment for
 Physicians' Services . . . . ¶ 704
MedPAC Study of Payment for
 Cardio-Thoracic Surgeons . . . . ¶ 705

Private Contracting for Podiatrists, Dentists and Optometrists	¶ 706
Establishment of Floor on Work Geographic Adjustment	¶ 708
Demonstration Project for Coverage of Certain Prescription Drugs and Biologicals	¶ 710
Treatment of Certain Physician Pathology Services	¶ 720
Modifications to Medicare Payment Advisory Commission (MedPAC)	¶ 721
Physicians' Services Furnished in Alaska	¶ 722
Review of Physician Practice Expense Geographic Adjustment Data	¶ 725

OTHER PART B ISSUES

Indexing Part B Deductible to Inflation	¶ 729
Services Furnished by IHS Hospitals and Clinics	¶ 730

PREVENTIVE SERVICES

Preventive Physical Exams	¶ 750
Cardiovascular Screening Tests	¶ 753
Screening Mammography	¶ 754
Diabetes Laboratory Diagnostic Tests	¶ 755
Clinical Laboratory Diagnostic Tests	¶ 756
End-Stage Renal Disease Services	¶ 759
Intravenous Immune Globulin (IVIG) for the Treatment of Primary Immune Deficiency Diseases in the Home	¶ 760
Orthotics and Prosthetics	¶ 761
Moratorium on Therapy Caps	¶ 762

COST CONTAINMENT PROVISIONS

Cost Containment	¶ 765
Presidential Submission of Legislation	¶ 768

House of Representatives Procedures	¶ 771
Senate Procedures	¶ 774
Income-Related Reduction in Part B Premium Subsidy	¶ 776
Military Retirees	¶ 777

DEMONSTRATION PROJECTS

Surgical First Assisting Services	¶ 784
Health Care Quality Demonstration Programs	¶ 785
Medicare Care Management Performance Demonstration Project	¶ 786
Concierge Care	¶ 787
Chiropractic Services	¶ 788
Telemedicine Demonstration Project	¶ 789
Chronically Ill Medicare Beneficiary Research, Data, Demonstration Strategy	¶ 790

MISCELLANEOUS PROVISIONS

Physical Therapy Services	¶ 791
Studies Relating To Vision Impairments	¶ 792
Restoration of Medicare Trust Funds	¶ 793
Medicare Secondary Payer	¶ 794
Improvement in Oversight of Technology and Coverage	¶ 795
Improvements in the National and Local Coverage Determination Process to Respond to Changes in Technology	¶ 796
Dental Claims	¶ 797
Medically Underserved Populations	¶ 798
Office of Rural Health Policy Improvement	¶ 799
Medicare Advantage Quality Improvement Programs	¶ 800

PROVISIONS RELATING TO HOSPITALS AND AMBULANCE SERVICES

¶ 501

Standardized Amount

Equalization of urban and rural standardized amount. Medicare will pay hospitals in rural and small urban areas in the fifty states using the standardized amount that would be used to pay hospitals in large urban areas starting for discharges in FY 2004.

Puerto Rico. The Secretary will compute one local standardized amount for all hospitals in Puerto Rico equal to that for hospitals in large urban areas in Puerto Rico starting for discharges in FY 2004. The existing single standardized amount will continue for hospitals that are not in Puerto Rico are not affected. Hospitals in Puerto Rico will receive the legislated payment increase starting for discharges on April 1, 2004.

Effective date. Effective upon enactment.

Act Sec. 401, amending Secs. 1886(d)(3)(A)(iv) and (d)(3)(d), 1886(d)(9)(A) and (C), 1886(d)(3)(D) of the Social Security Act. Law at ¶2351B and 10,270.

¶ 503
Labor-Related Share of the Standardized Amount

Labor-related share of the standardized amount. For discharges on or after October 1, 2004, the Secretary is required to decrease the labor-related share to 62 percent of the standardized amount when such change will result in higher total payments to the hospital. This provision is applied without regard to certain budget-neutrality requirements. For discharges on or after October 1, 2004, the Secretary is also required to decrease the labor-related share to 62 percent of the standardized amount for hospitals in Puerto Rico when such change results in higher total payments to the hospital.

Effective date. Effective upon enactment.

Act Sec. 403(a), amending Sec. 1886(d)(3)(E) of the Social Security Act; Act Sec. 403(b), amending Sec. 1886(d)(9)(C). Law at ¶2351B.

¶ 507
Market Basket Update

Frequency of updates. The Secretary is required to revise the market basket weights to reflect the most currently available data and to establish a schedule for revising the cost category weights more often than once every five years. The Secretary is required to publish the reasons for and the options considered in establishing such a schedule in the Final rule establishing FY 2006 inpatient hospital payments.

Effective date. Effective upon enactment.

Act Sec. 404. Law at ¶10,280.

Update percentage. For fiscal years 2004 through 2006, the hospital market basket will be updated by the market basket percentage increase minus 0.4 percent for hospitals in all areas. For fiscal year 2007 and subsequent fiscal years, the market basket will be updated by the full market basket percentage increase for hospitals in all areas.

Effective date. This provision is effective upon enactment.

Act Sec. 501, amending Sec. 1886(b)(3)(B)(i) and adding 1886(b)(3)(B)(vii) to the Social Security Act. Law at ¶2351A and 10,280.

¶ 510
Enhanced Disproportionate Share Hospital (DSH) Treatment

Payment calculation. Starting with discharges after April 1, 2004, a hospital that is not a large urban hospital that qualifies for a DSH adjustment will receive its DSH payments using the current DSH adjustment formula for large urban hospitals, subject to a limit. The DSH adjustment for any of these hospitals, except for rural referral centers, will be capped at 12 percent. A Pickle hospital, an urban hospital that receives disproportionate share payments, receiving a DSH adjustment under the alternative formula will not be affected by this provision.

Effective date. This provision is effective for discharges occurring on or after April 1, 2004.

Act Sec. 402, amending Sec. 1886(d)(5)(F) of the Social Security Act. Law at ¶2351B.

Furnishing hospitals with information to compute DSH formula. No later than one year after enactment of this legislation, the Secretary must furnish hospitals with the data necessary to compute the number of patient days used in computing the disproportionate patient percentage for that hospital for the current cost reporting year. This data must also be furnished to other hospitals that would qualify for a disproportionate share payment adjustment based on this data.

Effective date. This provision is effective upon enactment.

Act Sec. 951. Law at ¶11,160.

¶ 515
Medicare Inpatient Hospital Payment Adjustment for Low-Volume Hospitals

Payment adjustment. A payment adjustment will be given to a low-volume hospital which is a hospital that is located more than 25 road miles from another hospital and has less than 800 discharges during the year, including Medicare and non-Medicare patients. The adjustment will be based on the standardized cost per case, the number of discharges and additional incremental costs. In no case shall the adjustment be greater than 25 percent.

Effective date. This provision is effective for discharges starting in FY 2005.

Act Sec. 406. Law at ¶2351B.

¶ 545
Brachytherapy Devices

Special payment for brachytherapy. For a device of brachytherapy furnished on or after January 1, 2004, and before January 1, 2007, payment is equal to the hospital's charges for each device furnished, adjusted to cost. The Secretary is required to conduct a study on sales of drugs and biologicals to large volume purchasers, such as pharmacy benefit managers and health maintenance organizations, to determine whether the price at which such drugs and biologicals are sold to such purchasers does not represent the price at which such drugs and biologicals are made available for purchase to prudent physicians. furnished, adjusted to cost. Charges for such devices will not be included in determining any outlier payment.

The Secretary is required to create additional groups of covered outpatient department services that classify brachytherapy devices separately from other services or groups of services, to reflect the number, isotope, and radioactive intensity of the devices furnished. Separate groups must be created for palladium-103 and iodine-125 devices.

Study. The General Accounting Office (GAO) will conduct a study to determine appropriate payments for devices of brachytherapy. The report on this study must be submitted to Congress and the Secretary no later than January 1, 2005, and should include specific recommendations for appropriate payment for these devices.

Effective date. This provision is effective upon enactment.

Act Sec. 621(b), amending Sec. 1833(t)(16) of the Social Security Act, as redesignated by Act Sec. 411 (b), by adding subparagraph (C); amending Sec. 1833(t)(2) and adding subparagraph (H). Law at ¶2121T.

¶ 547
Hospital Outpatient Department Payments

Payment reform. Starting for services furnished on or after January 1, 2004, specified covered hospital outpatient department (OPD) drugs would be paid based on a percentage of the reference average wholesale price for the drug. The percentage of the reference price for sole-source drugs manufactured by one entity can be no less than 88 percent and no greater than 95 percent in calendar year 2004 and no less than 83 percent and no greater than 95 percent in CY 2005. The percentage of the reference price for innovator multiple source drugs can be no greater than 68 percent in CY 2004 and CY 2005. The percentage of the reference price for non-innovator multiple source drugs can be no greater than 46 percent in CY 2004 and CY 2006.

Definitions. A "specified covered outpatient drug" is a covered outpatient drug for which a separate ambulatory payment classification group (APC) has been established and that is a radiopharmaceutical or a drug or biological for which a pass-through payment was made on or before December 31, 2002. A "specified covered outpatient drug" does not include a drug for which payment is first made on or after January 1, 2003, or a drug for which a temporary Healthcare Common Procedure Coding System (HCPCS) code has not been assigned.

The "reference average wholesale price" is the average wholesale price for the drug as of May 1, 2003.

A "sole source drug" is a biological product approved under a biologics license application under section 351 of the Public Health Services Act or a single source drug produced or distributed under an original new drug application approved by the Food and Drug Administration (FDA); an "innovator multiple source drug" is a multiple source drug that was originally marketed under an original new drug application approved by the FDA.

After transition. In subsequent years, payment will be equal to the average acquisition cost for the drug for that year (which may vary by hospital group, taking into account hospital volume or other hospital characteristics) or if hospital acquisition cost data are not available, the average price for the drug in the year other than radiopharmacuticals established under Social Security Act Secs. 1842(o), 1847A or 1847B as calculated and adjusted by the Secretary.

The covered OPD drugs affected by this provision are outpatient drugs that were paid on a pass-through basis on or before December 31, 2002. These would not include drugs for which pass-through payments are first made on or after January 1, 2003; those drugs for which a temporary HCPCS code has not been assigned; or, during 2004 and 2005, orphan drugs. Drugs for which a temporary HCPCS code has not been assigned will be reimbursed at 95 percent of the AWP. Orphan drugs during this two-year time period will be paid at an amount specified by the Secretary.

Effective date. This provision is effective for services furnished on or after January 1, 2004.

Act Sec. 621, amending Sec. 1833(t) of the Social Security Act. Law at ¶2121T and 10,630.

Functional equivalence test. The Secretary is prohibited from publishing regulations, program memorandum local medical review policies or any other guidance (including the HOPD-PPS payment rate rules) that apply a functional equivalence or similar standard to a drug or biological for transitional pass-through payments under OPPS. This provision does not affect the Secretary's authority to deem a particular drug to be identical to another drug if the two products are pharmaceutically equivalent and bioequivalent, as determined by the Commissioner of the Food and Drug Administration.

Effective date. This provision applies to the application of a functional equivalence standard to a drug or biological on or after the enactment of this legislation, unless the application was made prior to enactment for the purpose of pass-through payments..

Act Sec. 622, amending Sec. 1833(t)(6) by adding new subparagraph (F) to the Social Security Act. Law at ¶2121T.

Small rural hospitals. The hold harmless provision governing outpatient department reimbursement for small rural hospitals has been extended until January 1, 2006.

Effective date. This provision applies to cost reporting periods beginning on or after January 1, 2004.

Act Sec. 407 amending Sec. 1886(b)(3)(I) of the Social Security Act. Law at ¶2351A.

¶ 560
Payments Connected to Reporting on Quality

Quality indicators. An acute care hospital will receive an operating update of the market basket (MB) in fiscal years (FY) 2004 through 2007. However, for FYs 2005 through 2007, receiving this update is contingent on the hospital submitting data before the start of the fiscal year on 10 quality indicators established by the Secretary as of November 1, 2003. (For FY 2005, the Secretary will provide for a 30-day grace period for the submission of the required data.) A hospital that does not submit data to the Secretary will receive an update of the MB minus 0.4 percentage points for the fiscal year in question. The Secretary will not take into account this reduction when computing the applicable percentage increase in subsequent years.

Effective date. Effective upon enactment.

Act Sec. 501(a), amending Sec. 1886(b)(3)(B)(i) and adding clause (vii)(I) to the Social Security Act. Law at ¶2351A.

¶ 562
Appropriateness of Payments Under IPPS

Short-term hospitals. The General Accounting Office is directed to conduct a study to determine (1) the appropriate level and distribution of Medicare payments in relation to costs for short-term general hospitals under the inpatient prospective payment system (IPPS) and (2) the need for geographic adjustments to reflect legitimate differences in hospital costs across geographic areas, kinds of hospitals, and types of cases.

Effective date. Effective upon enactment.

Act Sec. 501(c). Law at ¶ 10,450.

¶ 564
Revision of the IME Adjustment Percentage

Payments related to residents and interns. The indirect medical education (IME) multiplier is set as follows:

- from April 1, 2004, until September 30, 2004—1.47
- fiscal year (FY) 2005—1.42
- fiscal year (FY) 2006—1.37
- fiscal year (FY) 2007—1.32
- starting October 1, 2007—1.35

Effective date. Effective for discharges occurring on or after April 1, 2004.

Act Sec. 502(a), amending Secs. 1886(d)(5)(B)(ii) and 1886(d)(2)(C)(i) of the Social Security Act. Law at ¶ 2351B.

¶ 566
New Medical Technologies

DRG payments. The Secretary is required to add new diagnosis and procedure codes on April 1 of each year but is not required to adjust Medicare's payment or DRG classification until the fiscal year that begins after that date. When determining whether DRG payments are inadequate, the Secretary must apply a threshold that is the lesser of 75 percent of the standardized amount (increased to reflect the difference between costs and charges) or 75 percent of one standard deviation for the DRG involved.

Public input. The Secretary is required to: (1) maintain and update a public list of pending applications for specific services and technologies to be evaluated for eligibility for additional payment; (2) accept comments, recommendations, and data from the public regarding whether a service or technology represents a substantial improvement; and (3) provide for a meeting at which organizations representing physicians, beneficiaries, manufacturers, or other interested parties may present comments, recommendations, and data regarding whether a service or technology represents a substantial improvement. These actions will occur prior to the publication of the proposed regulation.

DRG adjustments. Before establishing an add-on payment as the appropriate reimbursement mechanism, the Secretary is directed to identify one or more DRGs and assign the technology to that DRG, taking into account similar clinical or anatomical characteristics and the relative cost of the technology. The Secretary will assign an eligible technology into a DRG where the average cost of care most closely approximates the cost of the new technology; in such a case, no add-on payment will be made.

Funding for new technology will no longer be budget neutral.

The Secretary is required to automatically reconsider an application as a new technology that was denied for FY 2005 as an application under these new provisions. If such an application is granted, the maximum time period otherwise permitted for such classification as a new technology is extended by 12 months.

Effective date. Effective beginning with fiscal year 2005.

Act Sec. 503 amending Secs. 1886(d)(5)(K), 1886(d)(5)(K)(ii)(I), and 1886(d)(5)(K)(ii)(III) of the Social Security Act. Law at ¶2351B and 10,470.

¶ 568
Hospitals in Puerto Rico

Payment rates. Hospitals in Puerto Rico will receive Medicare payments based on a 50/50 split between federal and local payment rates before April 1, 2004. Starting April 1, 2004, through September 30, 2004, payment will be based on 62.5 percent national amount and 37.5 percent local amount; this will change to 75 percent national and 25 percent local after October 1, 2004, and in subsequent years.

Effective date. Effective upon enactment.

Act Sec. 504, amending Sec. 1886(d)(9)(A) of the Social Security Act and adding new subparagraph (E). Law at ¶2351B.

¶ 570
Wage Index Reclassification Reform

Geographic area. The Secretary is required to establish a process and payment adjustment to recognize the out-migration of hospital employees who reside in a county and work in different area with a higher wage index. A hospital that receives this payment adjustment will be located in a qualifying county that meets criteria established by the Secretary. This criteria will include: (1) a threshold percentage of the weighted average of the area wage index or indices for the higher wage index areas; (2) a threshold of not less than 10 percent for minimum out-migration to a higher wage index area or areas; and (3) a requirement that the average hourly wage of the hospitals in the qualifying county equals or exceeds the average hourly wage of all the hospitals in the area where the county is located.

A qualifying hospital will have its wage index value increased by the percentage of the hospital employees residing in the qualifying county who are employed in any area with a higher wage value. The adjustment will equal the sum of the products of the difference between the wage index value of any higher wage area and the qualifying county multiplied by the number of hospital employee who reside in the qualifying county but are employed in any higher wage index area. The application process for this adjustment is based on the Medicare Geographic Classification Review Board reclassification process and schedule with respect to data submitted. Such an adjustment is effective for three years unless a hospital withdraws or elects to terminate its payment.

The Secretary may require acute hospitals and other hospitals as well as critical access hospitals to submit data regarding the location of their employee's residence or the Secretary may use data from other sources. A hospital that receives a commuting wage adjustment is not eligible for reclassification into another area by the MGCRB. The commuting wage adjustment does not affect the computation of the wage index of the area in which the hospital is located or any other area. It is also exempt from certain budget neutrality requirements. The thresholds and other qualifying criteria for the commuting wage adjustment are not subject to judicial review.

Effective date. Effective for the wage index for discharges occurring on or after October 1, 2004.

Act Sec. 505, amending Sec. 1866(a)(1) of the Social Security Act and adding new Sec. 1886(d)(13)(A) to the Social Security Act. Law at ¶2351B and 10,480.

¶ 572
Inpatient Hospital Services Provided by IHS

Medicare payments. Hospitals that participate in Medicare and that provide Medicare-covered inpatient hospital services under the contract health services program funded by the Indian Health Service (IHS) and operated by the IHS, an Indian tribe, an Indian tribal organization, or an urban Indian organization, will be paid in accordance with regulations promulgated by the Secretary regarding admission practices, payment methodologies, and rates of payments. This will include the requirement to accept these rates as payment in full.

Effective date. Effective no later than one year after enactment.

Act Sec. 506 amending Sec. 1866(a)(1) of the Social Security Act. Law at ¶2290.

¶ 574
Limits on Physician Referrals

Investments in hospitals. Under current law, physicians are generally prohibited from referring Medicare patients to facilities in which they have financial interests. Physicians, however, are not prohibited from referring patients to whole hospitals in which they have ownership or investment interests.

The Act provides that for a period of 18 months from the date of enactment, the "whole hospital" exception is amended to exclude circumstances in which a physician's ownership interest is in a hospital devoted primarily or exclusively to cardiac, orthopedic surgical, or other specialties designated by the Secretary. Specialty hospitals in operation or under development as of November 18, 2003, would be exempt from the provision.

Within 15 months from the date of enactment, the Medicare Payment Advisory Commission (MedPAC), the General Accounting Office (GAO), and HHS would study the effects of the whole-hospital exception for physician-ownership in specialty hospitals.

Effective date. Effective upon enactment.

Act Sec. 507 amending Secs. 1877(d)(2) and (3) and Sec. 1877(h)(7) of the Social Security Act. Law at ¶2335 and 10,500.

¶ 575
Physician Pathology Services

Extension of reimbursement. The Medicare, Medicaid and SCHIP Benefits Improvement and Protection Act of 2000 (BIPA) permitted independent laboratories with existing arrangements with acute care hospitals to bill Medicare separately for the technical components of pathology services provided to hospitals' inpatients and outpatients. Direct payment for these services will be extended during 2005 and 2006.

Effective date. Effective upon enactment.

Act Sec. 732 amending Sec. 542(c) of BIPA. Law at ¶10,890.

¶ 576

One-Time Appeals Process for Hospital Wage Index Classification

Appeal process. The Secretary shall establish no later than January 1, 2004, a one-time process under which a hospital may appeal the wage index classification otherwise applicable to the hospital and select another area within the state (or a contiguous state). The appeal may be filed as soon as possible after the date of the enactment of this Act but must be filed by no later than February 15, 2004. The appeal will be heard by the Medicare Geographic Reclassification Review Board. There is no further administrative or judicial review of this decision. The reclassification will be effective for three years beginning with April 1, 2004. Hospitals can waive reclassification under this provision during the three-year period. The Secretary shall limit the additional expenditures to $900 million.

Effective date. Effective upon enactment.

Act Sec. 508. Law at ¶ 10,510.

¶ 578

Critical Access Hospitals

Increase in payment amounts. Inpatient, outpatient, and covered skilled nursing facility services provided by a critical access hospital (CAH) will be reimbursed at 101 percent of reasonable costs of services furnished to Medicare beneficiaries.

Effective date. This provision applies to cost reporting periods beginning on or after January 1, 2004.

Act Sec. 405(a), amending Secs. 1814(l), 1834(g)(1), and 1883(a)(3) of the Social Security Act. Law at ¶ 2075, 2135, and 2350.

Costs for on-call ER providers. The provision expands reimbursement of on-call emergency room providers to include physician assistants, nurse practitioners, and clinical nurse specialists as well as emergency room physicians for the costs associated with covered Medicare services provided on or after January 1, 2005.

Effective date. This provision applies to costs incurred for services provided on or after January 1, 2005.

Act Sec. 405(b), amending Sec. 1834(g)(5) of the Social Security Act. Law at ¶ 2135.

Periodic interim payments. An eligible CAH will be able to receive payments made on a periodic interim payment (PIP) basis for its inpatient services. The Secretary is required to develop alternative methods for the timing of PIP payments to these CAHs.

Effective date. This provision applies to payments made on or after July 1, 2004.

Act Sec. 405(c), amending Sec. 1815(e)(2) of the Social Security Act. Law at ¶ 2080.

Special professional service payment adjustment. The Secretary cannot require that all physicians or practitioners providing services in a CAH assign their billing rights to the entity in order for the CAH to be able to be paid on the basis of 115 percent of the fee schedule for the professional services provided by the physicians. However, a CAH will not receive payment based on 115 percent of the fee schedule for any individual physician or practitioner who did not assign billing rights to the CAH.

Effective date. This provision applies to cost report periods starting on or after July 1, 2004, except for those CAHs that have already elected payment for physician services on this basis in the past.

Act Sec. 405(d), amending Section 1834(g)(2) of the Social Security Act. Law at ¶2135.

Bed limitation. A CAH will be able to operate up to 25 beds. The requirement that only 15 of the 25 beds be used for acute care at any time will be dropped. The provision will apply to CAH designations made before, on, or after January 1, 2004, but any election made pursuant to the regulations promulgated to implement this provision will only apply prospectively.

Effective date. For designations made before, on, or after January 1, 2004.

Act Sec. 405(e), amending Secs. 1820(c)(2)(B)(iii) and 1820(f) of the Social Security Act. Law at ¶2115.

Grants. The authorization to award rural hospital flexibility grants is established at $35 million each year from fiscal year (FY) 2005 through FY2008. Starting with funds appropriated for FY2005 and in subsequent years, a state is required consult with the hospital association and rural hospitals in the state on the most appropriate way to use such funds. A state may not spend more than 15 percent of the grant amount or the States federally negotiated indirect rate for administrative purposes. Beginning with FY 2005 up to five percent of the total amount appropriated for grants will be available to the Health Resources and Services Administration for administering these grants.

Effective date. Effective upon enactment.

Act Sec. 405(f), amending Sec. 1820(j) and (g) of the Social Security Act. Law at ¶2115.

Distinct part units. A CAH can establish a distinct part psychiatric or rehabilitation unit that meets the applicable requirements for such beds established for a short-term, general hospital, specifically, a subsection (d) hospital as defined in 1886(d)(1)(B). If the distinct part units do not meet these requirements during a cost reporting period, then no Medicare payment will be made to the CAH for services furnished in the unit during the period. Medicare payments will resume only after the CAH demonstrates that the requirements have been met. Medicare payments for services provided in the distinct part units will equal payments that are made on a prospective payment basis to distinct part units of short term general hospitals. The Secretary will not count any beds in the distinct part psychiatric or rehabilitation units toward the CAH bed limit. The total number of beds in these distinct part units cannot exceed 10.

Effective date. This provision applies to cost reporting periods beginning on or after October 1, 2004.

Act Sec. 405(g), amending Secs. 1814(l) and 1820(c)(2) of the Social Security Act. Law at ¶2075, 2115.

Waiver authority. Currently to qualify as a CAH, the rural, for-profit, non profit or public hospital must be located more than 35 miles from another hospital or 15 miles in areas with mountainous terrain or those where only secondary roads are available. These mileage standards may be waived if the hospital has been designated by the State as a necessary provider of health care. This authority is eliminated two years after enactment.

Effective date. Effective upon enactment.

¶578

Act Sec. 405(h), amending Secs. 1820(c)(2)(B)(i)(II) and 1820(h) of the Social Security Act. Law at ¶2115 and 10,290.

¶ 581

Rural Community Hospital Demonstration Program

Testing payment levels. The Secretary is required to establish a demonstration program in rural areas to test different payment methods for under 50 bed rural hospitals. The hospitals are paid their costs for inpatient and extended care (swing-bed) services for 5 years, subject to a cap. The payment methodology is similar to the Tax Equality and Fiscal Responsibility Act (TEFRA) payment system used for Children's hospitals. The hospitals cannot be eligible for the CAH program.

Effective date. The Secretary must implement the demonstration program not later than January 1, 2005, but may not implement the program before October 1, 2004.

Act Sec. 410A. Law at ¶10,330.

¶ 582

Hold Harmless Provision for Small Rural and Sole Community Hospitals

Two-year extension and SCH inclusion. The hold harmless provision governing outpatient department (OPD) reimbursement for small rural hospitals has been extended until January 1, 2006, and extended to sole community hospitals (SCH) located in a rural area for services furnished on or after January 1, 2004, until January 1, 2006.

The Secretary is required to conduct a study to determine if the costs by ambulatory payment classification (APC) groups incurred by rural providers exceed those cost incurred by urban providers and, if appropriate, to make payment adjustments to reflect the higher costs of rural providers by January 1, 2006.

Effective date. Effective upon enactment.

Act Sec. 411 amending Sec. 1833(t)(7)(D)(i) of the Social Security Act. Law at ¶2121T.

¶ 583

Reimbursement for Clinical Laboratory Services Furnished in Certain Rural Areas

100 percent reasonable cost. Hospitals with under 50 beds in low density population rural areas, defined as an area that has a population density that is in the lowest 25 percent of the area, will receive 100 percent reasonable cost reimbursement for clinical diagnostic laboratory tests covered under Part B that are provided as outpatient hospital services. The provision will apply to services furnished during a cost reporting period beginning during the two-year period starting July 1, 2004.

Effective date. Effective upon enactment for a two-year period starting July 1, 2004.

Act Sec. 416. Law at ¶10,370.

¶ 584
EMTALA Improvements

Screening and stabilization services. Emergency room services provided to screen and stabilize a Medicare beneficiary furnished after January 1, 2004, will be evaluated as reasonable and necessary on the basis of the information available to the treating physician or practitioner at the time the services were ordered. The evaluation as to whether the item or service was reasonable and necessary will include the patient's presenting symptoms or complaint and not the patient's principal diagnosis. The Secretary will not be able to consider the frequency with which the item or service was provided to the patient before or after the time of admission or visit.

Investigations. The Secretary will be required to establish a procedure to notify hospitals and physicians when an Emergency Medical Treatment and Active Labor Act (EMTALA) investigation is closed.

QIO Review. Except in the case where a delay would jeopardize the health and safety of individuals, the Secretary will be required to request a quality improvement organization (QIO) review before making a compliance determination that would terminate a hospital's Medicare participation because of EMTALA violations. A period of five days will be allowed for the review, and the QIO must provide a copy of the report on its findings to the hospital or physician involved. This provision will apply to terminations initiated on or after enactment of the Act.

Exceptions. The requirement for an appropriate medical screening examination will not apply in situations where an individual does not request examination or treatment for an emergency condition.

Comment. Providers have reported that some Medicare contractors are looking at final diagnoses (not presenting symptoms) in applying local medical review policies (LMRPs) that match particular tests to particular diagnoses. For example, if a test does not match a listed diagnosis, payment is denied. Other claims are reportedly being denied based on LMRPs that set frequency limits for certain tests. That is, if the test's use in the emergency room exceeds a frequency limit, payment is denied. In its January 2001 report entitled "The Emergency Medical Treatment and Labor Act: The Enforcement Process," the OIG recommended that CMS ensure that peer review occurs before a provider is terminated from the Medicare program for an EMTALA violation. This section implements that recommendation, making the current discretionary QIO review process mandatory in cases that involve a question of medical judgment.

Effective date. Effective upon enactment.

Sec. 944, amending Secs. 1862 by adding subsection (d), 1867(d) by adding new paragraph (4), 1867(d)(3) and 1867(a) of the Social Security Act. Law at ¶ 2295.

¶ 586
MedPAC Study on Rural Payment Adjustments

Payment effects. MedPAC will study the effect on specified rural provisions in this legislation (specifically, Sections 401 through 405, 411, 416, and 504) including total payments, growth in costs, capital spending and other payment factors. An interim report on changes to the critical access hospital program (in Section 405) is due to Congress no later than 18 months from the date of enactment. MedPAC's final report on all topics is due to Congress no later than 3 years from the date of enactment.

Effective date. Effective upon enactment.

Act Sec. 433. Law at ¶ 10,430.

¶ 588
Professional Education Costs

Redistribution of unused resident positions. A teaching hospital's total number of Medicare-reimbursed resident positions will be reduced for cost reporting periods starting July 1, 2005, if its reference resident level is less than its applicable resident limit. Rural hospitals with less than 250 acute care inpatient beds would be exempt from such reductions. For other such hospitals, the reduction will equal 75 percent of the difference between the hospital's limit and its reference resident level. The resident reference level is the highest number of allopathic and osteopathic resident positions (before the application of any weighting factors) for the hospital during the reference period. This reference level is the either: (1) the resident level of the most recent cost reporting period of the hospital for which a cost report has been settled (or submitted, subject to audit) on or before September 30, 2002, or (2) the resident level for the cost reporting period that includes July 1, 2003, if requested on a timely basis by the hospital subject to audit.

Expansions. Upon timely request at the discretion of the Secretary, a hospital's reference level will be adjusted to include the number of medical residents for the cost reporting period that includes July 1, 2003. Upon timely request of the hospital, the Secretary will adjust the reference resident level to include the number of medical residents that were approved in an application to the appropriate accrediting organization before January 1, 2002, if the program was not in operation by the cost reporting period in question (either September 30, 2002 or July 1, 2003 depending upon the hospital's circumstances and the Secretary's approval). The reduction will apply to hospitals that are members of the same affiliated group as of July 1, 2003.

Increase of resident limits. The Secretary is authorized to increase the applicable resident limits for hospitals for portions of cost reporting periods occurring on or after July 1, 2005, by an aggregate number that does not exceed the overall reduction in such limits. The Secretary will take into account the demonstrated likelihood of the hospital filling the positions within the first 3 cost reporting periods beginning on or after July 1, 2005, when determining which hospitals would receive an increase in their resident levels. The Secretary will establish a priority order to distribute the increased resident count first to programs in hospitals located in rural areas, then to hospitals that are not in large urban areas and finally to other hospitals in a state where there is no other training program for a particular specialty. The Secretary shall consider giving special consideration to hospitals that train a large share of graduates from historically large medical colleges. Increases to limits with the same priority category will be determined by the Secretary.

Limitation. Not more than 25 additional full-time equivalent (FTE) residency positions will be given to any hospital. These hospitals will be reimbursed for direct graduate medical education (DGME) for the increase in resident positions at the locality adjusted national average per resident amount. Changes in a hospital's resident count established under this section will affect a hospital's indirect medical education (IME) adjustment; the IME adjustment will be calculated as if "c" is equal to 0.66 for these additional positions starting for discharges after July 1, 2005. These provisions will not apply to reductions in residency programs that occurred as part of the voluntary reduction program or will not affect the ability of certain hospitals to establish new medical residency training programs.

Report. The Secretary is required to submit a report to Congress no later than July 1, 2005, on whether to extend the application deadline for increases in resident limits. Requirement with respect to Federal information policy established by Chapter 35 of Title 44, United States Code will not apply to applications under this section.

Effective date. Effective upon enactment.

Act Sec. 422, amending Secs. 1886(h)(4) and (7) and 1886(d)(5)(B) of the Social Security Act. Law at ¶ 2351B, 2351D, and 10,410.

Freeze on rate of increase for hospitals with FTE approved amounts above 140 percent of locality adjusted national average per resident amount. Payments to hospitals with per resident amounts above 140 percent of the geographically adjusted national average per resident amount are frozen at current levels for fiscal years 2004 through 2013.

Effective date. This provision is effective upon enactment.

Act 711, amending Sec. 1886(h)(2)(D)(iv) of the Social Security Act. Law at ¶ 2351D.

¶ 590

Residency Period for Geriatric Residency or Fellowship Programs

Congress intended to provide an exception to the initial residency period for geriatric residency or fellowship programs so that when a particular approved geriatric training program requires a resident to complete two years of training to initially become board eligible in the geriatric specialty, the 2 years spent in the geriatric training program are treated as part of the resident's initial residency period, but are not counted against any limitation on the initial residency period. The Secretary shall promulgate interim final regulations consistent with this congressional intent to be effective for cost reporting periods beginning on or after October 1, 2003.

Effective date. Effective upon enactment.

Act 712. Law at ¶ 10,830.

¶ 592

Resident Training in Non-Hospital Settings

Payment. During the one-year period beginning on January 1, 2004, the Secretary shall allow all hospitals to count residents in osteopathic and allopathic family practice programs in existence as of January 1, 2002, who are training at non-hospital sites, without regard to the financial arrangement between the hospital and the teaching physician practicing in the non-hospital site to which the resident has been assigned.

The HHS Inspector General shall conduct a study of the appropriateness of alternative payment methodologies for the costs of training residents in non-hospital settings. Not later than one year after the date of the enactment of this Act, the Inspector General shall submit to Congress a report on this study, together with such recommendations as the Inspector General determines appropriate.

Effective date. Effective upon enactment.

Act 713. Law at ¶ 10,840.

¶ 593

Frontier Clinics

Demonstration project. Frontier extended stay clinics will be treated as Medicare providers under a three-year demonstration project. A frontier extended stay clinic is located at least 75 miles from the closest acute care hospital or critical access hospital or inaccessible by public road. Frontier clinics are designed to treat the seriously ill or injured patient who, due to weather conditions or other reasons, cannot be transferred quickly to an acute care center.

Effective date. Effective upon enactment.

Act Sec. 434. Law at ¶ 10,440.

¶ 594

Ambulatory Surgical Centers

Adjustment to payments for ambulatory surgical centers (ASCs) services. In fiscal year 2004, starting April 1, 2004, the ASC update will be be the CPI-U (estimated as of March 31, 2003 minus 3.0 percentage points. In fiscal year 2005, the last quarter of calendar year 2005, and each of the calendar years 2006 through 2009 the update will be 0 percent.

Repeal of survey requirement of new system. Upon implementation of the new ASC payment system, the Secretary is no longer required to update ASC rates based on a survey of the actual audited costs incurred by a representative sample of ASCs every 5 years. Subject to GAO's recommendations, the Secretary will implement a revised payment system for surgical services furnished in an ASC. The new system will be implemented so that it is first effective on or after Jan. 1, 2006, and not later than Jan.1, 2008. There will be no administrative or judicial review of the ASC classification system, relative weights, payment amounts and any geographic adjustment factor.

GAO study and report. GAO is required to conduct a comparative study of the relative costs of procedures furnished in ASCs to those furnished in hospital outpatient departments under OPPS. The study is tol examine the accuracy of the ambulatory payment categories with respect to the procedures furnished in the ASCs.

GAO recommendations. GAO is required to submit recommendations and consider ASC data with respect to (1) the appropriateness of using groups and relative weights established for the outpatient hospital PPS as the basis of the new ASC payment system; (2) if such weights are appropriate, whether the ASC payments should be based on a uniform percentage of such weights, whether the percentages should vary, or whether the weights should be revised for certain procedures or types of services; and (3) the appropriateness of a geographic adjustment in the ASC payment system and if appropriate, the labor and non-labor shares of such payment.

Effective date. Effective upon enactment.

Act Sec. 626, amending Secs. 1833(i)(2)(C) and (A) and adding subparagraph (D) to the Social Security Act; amending 1833(a)(1) by adding subparagraph (G) to the Social Security Act. Law at ¶ 2121I, 2121A and 10,670.

¶ 596
Ambulance Services

Payment for rural and urban ambulance services. The Secretary is required to establish a regional fee schedule for each of the nine census divisions using the methodology used to establish the fee schedule to calculate a regional conversion factor and a regional mileage payment rate, using the same payment adjustments and the same relative value units used in the fee schedule.

Phased implementation. In carrying out the phase-in methodology and fee schedule for each level of service furnished in a year, the portion of the payment amount that is based on the fee schedule must be the greater of the amount determined under the fee schedule or the blended rate for the fee schedule and a regional fee schedule.

- For 2004, the blended rate is based 20 percent on the fee schedule and 80 percent on the regional fee schedule.

- For 2005, the blended rate is based 40 percent on the fee schedule and 60 percent on the regional fee schedule.

- For 2006, the blended rate is based 60 percent on the fee schedule and 40 percent on the regional fee schedule.

- For 2007, 2008, and 2009, the blended rate is based 80 percent on the fee schedule and 20 percent on the regional fee schedule.

- For 2010 and each succeeding year, the blended rate is based 100 percent on the fee schedule.

Regional fee schedule The Secretary is required to establish a regional fee schedule for each of the nine census divisions to calculate a regional conversion factor and a regional mileage payment rate and using the same payment adjustments and the same relative value units as used in the fee schedule under this Sec. 1886(d)(2) of the Social Security Act.

Adjustment to payment for certain long trips. Medicare's payment for ground ambulance services will be increased by one quarter of the amount otherwise established for trips longer than 50 miles occurring on Jan. 1, 2004, and before Jan. 1, 2009. The payment increase applies regardless of where the transportation originated.

Improvement in payments to retain emergency capacity for ambulance services in rural areas. The Secretary is required to provide for a percent increase to the base rate of the fee schedule for ground ambulance services originating in a qualified rural area on or after Jan. 1, 2004. The Secretary must establish the percent increase based on an estimate of the average cost per trip for the base rate in the lowest quartile as compared to the average cost for the base rate for such services in the highest quartile of all rural county populations.

Qualified rural area. Based on the data from the United States decennial census for the year 2000, the Secretary is required to determine for each rural area, the population density for that area. The term "qualified rural area" means a rural area with a the lowest population density weighted by the population, and an aggregate total of 25 percent of the total of the population of all such areas.

Temporary increase for ground air ambulance services. The payments for ground ambulance services originating in a rural area or a rural census tract is to be increased by 2 percent (after application of the long trip and low density payment increases) for services furnished on or after July 1, 2004 through Dec. 31, 2007. The fee schedule for ambulances in other areas (after application of the long trip adjustment) will increase by 1 percent. These increased payments will not affect Medicare payments for covered ambulance services after 2007.

GAO report on cost and access. The Comptroller General is required to submit an initial report to Congress on how costs differ among types of ambulance providers and on access, supply and quality of ambulance services in regions and states that have a reduction in payment under the Medicare ambulance fee schedule by Dec. 31, 2005. The Comptroller General must submit the final report to Congress by Jan. 1, 2007.

Effective date. This provision applies to ambulance services furnished on or after Jan. 1, 2004.

Act Sec. 414 amending Sec. 1834(l) of the Social Security Act. Law at ¶2145 and 10,350.

¶ 598

Providing Appropriate Coverage of Rural Air Ambulance Services

Coverage for air ambulance services. Air ambulance services are reimbursed at the air ambulance rate: (1) if the air ambulance service is reasonable and necessary based on the health condition of the individual being transported or immediately prior to the time of the transport; and (2) if the service complies with equipment and crew requirements established by the Secretary.

Medically necessary air ambulance service. An air ambulance service is considered "medically necessary" if: (1) the service is requested by a physician or a hospital in accordance with the physician's or hospital's responsibilities under the Emergency Medical Treatment and Active Labor Act; (2) the service is provided as a result of a protocol established by a state or regional emergency medical service (EMS) agency; (3) the service is requested by a physician, nurse practitioner, physician assistant, registered nurse, or emergency medical responder who reasonably determines or certifies that the patient's condition is such that the time needed to transport the individual by land or the lack of an appropriate ground ambulance, significantly increases the medical risks for the individual; or (4) the service is requested by a federal or state agency to relocate patients following a natural disaster, an act of war, or a terrorist attack.

Air ambulance defined. The term "air ambulance service" means a fixed wing or rotary wing air ambulance service.

Effective date. This provision applies to services furnished on or after Jan. 1, 2005.

Act Sec. 415 amending Sec. 1834(l) of the Social Security Act. Law at ¶2145 and 2275.

SKILLED NURSING FACILITIES

¶ 601

Background Checks

Pilot program. The Secretary in consultation with the Attorney General is to establish a pilot program to identify efficient, effective, and economical procedures for skilled nursing facilities, nursing facilities, home health agencies, hospice providers, long-term care hospitals, intermediate care facilities, providers of personal care services, and residential care providers to conduct background checks on prospective employees who have direct patient access. $25 million is available over a period from 2004 to 2007 for the pilot program in ten states. States that have existing background check program are eligible for participation in the pilot program.

Providers in the pilot program must notify prospective employees of the background check. As a condition of employment, prospective providers will need to authorize the facility to request a national and state criminal background check and to submit fingerprints. Providers are eligible for reimbursement of the cost of administering the program.

Facilities in states involved in the pilot program may not hire an individual who has a finding of patient or resident abuse. Facilities may allow employees to work on a provisional basis while the background check is being completed. Providers that hire individuals with disqualifying events on their records may be subject to state fines.

The states participating in the pilot are responsible for monitoring compliance with the program and instituting appeal and dispute resolution procedures.

Effective date. Effective upon enactment.

Act Sec. 307. Law at ¶10,260.

¶ 604
Additional Information About SNF Benefits

Effect of provision. Medicare beneficiaries will be provided with additional information on the provision of post-hospital extended care services and inpatient hospital services regarding the number of days remaining of coverage of those services and the spell of illness involved.

Effective date. This subsection will apply to notices provided during calendar quarters beginning more than six months after the date of enactment of this Act.

Act Sec. 925. Law at ¶11,060.

¶ 605
Payment Adjustment for AIDS Residents in SNFs

New payment. Until there is an appropriate adjustment in the case-mix to compensate for increased costs associated with residents with acquired immune deficiency syndrome (AIDS), a 128 percent increase in payment will be made for skilled nursing facility (SNF) services for such residents.

Effective date. Services furnished on or after October 1, 2004 are affected by the Act.

Act Sec. 511 amending Sec. 1888(e) of the Social Security Act. Law at ¶2355.

¶ 606
Information on Medicare-Certified SNFs in Hospital Discharge Plans

Effect of provision. Information on skilled nursing facilities (SNFs) participating in the Medicare program will be made public by the Secretary. This information will enable hospital discharge planners, Medicare beneficiaries and the public to identify the SNFs that are participating in the Medicare program. Hospital discharge plans must then include this information to inform individuals likely to need hospice and post-hospital extended care services of the participating facilities that serve the area in which the beneficiary resides.

Effective date. Applicable to discharge plans made on or after such date as the Secretary specifies, but no longer than six months after the date the Secretary provides for the availability of the information.

Act Sec. 926, amending Section 1861(ee)(2)(D). Law at ¶ 2280B and 11,070.

¶ 607
Establishing SNFs as Originating Sites for Telehealth Services

Study and authorization. The Secretary is to report on demonstration projects under which skilled nursing facilities are treated as originating sites for telehealth services by January 1, 2005 that includes recommendations on mechanism to ensure that telehealth services do not substitute for in-person visits required by physicians, and other medical professionals. If these mechanisms are in place, the Secretary may deem a skilled nursing facility to be an originating site for telehealth services beginning on January 1, 2006.

Effective date. Effective upon enactment.

Act Sec. 418. Law at ¶ 10,390.

¶ 608
Portable Diagnostic Ultrasound Services in SNFs

Study. The Comptroller General is to conduct a study of the use of portable diagnostic ultrasound services furnished to beneficiaries in skilled nursing facilities. The study is to report on the types of equipment used, clinical appropriateness of transporting the equipment, the financial impact of making separate payments for this equipment. The report is to be completed no later than 2 years after enactment.

Effective date. Effective upon enactment.

Act Sec. 513. Law at ¶ 10,540.

¶ 610
Exclusion from SNF-PPS

Services provided by a RHC or FQHC. Services provided by a rural health clinic (RHC) and a federally qualified health center (FQHC) after January 1, 2005, will be excluded from SNF-PPS if such services would have been excluded if furnished by a physician or practitioner who was not affiliated with a RHC or FQHC. The provisions would apply to services furnished on or after January 1, 2005.

Effective date. This provision is effective for services furnished on or after January 1, 2005.

Act Sec. 410 amending Sec. 1888(e)(2)(A) of the Social Security Act by adding clause (iv). Law at ¶ 2355.

HOME HEALTH AND HOSPICE

¶ 650
Demonstration Project to Clarify the Definition of Homebound

Demonstration project. A two-year demonstration program will be conducted under which Medicare beneficiaries with chronic conditions described below are deemed to be homebound for purposes of receiving home health services under the Medicare program. Medicare compliance with current regulations will be waived for those involved in the study for the time period during the study.

A Medicare beneficiary is eligible to be deemed to be homebound, without regard to the purpose, frequency or duration of absences from the home if the beneficiary:

(1) has been certified by one physician as an individual who has a permanent and severe condition that will not improve;

(2) requires assistance from another individual with at least three out of the five activities of daily living for the rest of the beneficiary's life (eating, toileting, transferring, bathing and dressing);

(3) requires skilled nursing services for more than medication management for the rest of the beneficiary's life;

(4) requires an attendant to visit on a daily basis to monitor and treat the beneficiary's medical condition or to assist the beneficiary with activities of daily living;

(5) requires technological assistance or the assistance of another person to leave the home; and

(6) is not employed.

The study must be conducted in three states selected by the Secretary to represent the northeast, Midwest and western regions of the United States. The number of participants may not exceed 15,000. Data collection will include that involved with quality of care, patient outcomes, and additional costs, if any, to the Medicare program. A report on the effectiveness of the program must be submitted to Congress.

Effective date. The project will begin not later than 180 days after the date of the enactment of the Act. A report to Congress will be made not later than one year after the completion of the date of the project using the data collected.

Act Sec. 702. Law at ¶ 10,790.

¶ 656

Increase for Home Health Services Furnished in a Rural Area

Payment increase. A five percent increase in payments will apply to home health services furnished in a rural area on or after April 1, 2004 , and ending on or after April 1, 2005. The Secretary will not have the ability to reduce the standard prospective payment amount to offset the five percent increase in payments.

Effective date. Effective upon enactment of the Act, but effective for services provided on or after April 1, 2004, and before April 1, 2005.

Act Sec. 421. Law at ¶ 10,400.

¶ 658

Update in Home Health Payment Rates

Change in time of update. Home health payment rates will be updated on a calendar year basis as opposed to a fiscal year basis beginning in 2004. During the fourth quarter of 2003 and for the first quarter of 2004, home health agencies will receive the full market basket increase. The update for the last three quarters of 2004,

2005, and 2006 will be equal to the market basket increase minus 0.8 percentage points.

Effective date. Effective upon enactment.

Act Sec. 701 amending Sec. 1895(b) of the Social Security Act, amending Sec. 1895(b)(3)(B)(ii) of the Social Security Act. Law at ¶ 2380.

¶ 660
Adult Day Care Provided Under the Home Health Benefit

Demonstration project. A three-year demonstration project in five states is to be established that will provide adult day care services as part of a home health plan of care. Home health agencies may provide this service directly or under arrangement. In selecting home health agencies to participate, the Secretary is to give preference to home health agencies that are currently licensed to provide adult day care services.

A medical adult day care facility is defined as a facility that is licensed or certified by a state to provide adult day care service for a continuous two-year period and is engaged in providing skilled nursing services and other therapeutic services. The facility must provide the home health services, a program of supervised activities furnished in a group setting, and is designed to promote the physical and mental health of the individual.

Home health agencies will be reimbursed at a rate equal to 95 percent that would otherwise apply. Participation in the demonstration project is limited to 15,000 beneficiaries who voluntarily enroll. Six months after the completion of the project the Secretary is to submit to Congress a report evaluating the project.

Effective date. Effective upon enactment.

Act Sec. 703. Law at ¶ 10,800.

¶ 662
Provision of Home Health Service by a Religious Nonmedical Health Institution

Authorization. Religious nonmedical health institutions are authorized to provide home health services to individuals through December 31, 2006. Annual expenditures for home health services provided by religious nonmedical institutions shall not exceed $700,000.

Effective date. Effective upon enactment.

Act Sec. 706 amending Sec. 1821(a) of the Social Security Act and adding Sec. 1861(aaa). Law at ¶ 2120 and 2280I.

¶ 664
MedPAC Study on Medicare Margins of Home Health Agencies

Study on payment margins. The Medicare Payment Advisory Committee is required to conduct a study of payment margins of home health agencies (HHAs) under the prospective payment system (PPS). The study will examine whether systematic differences in payment margins are related to differences in case mix (as measured by home health resource groups (HHRGs)) among HHAs. Partial or full cost reports filed by HHAs may be used in the study.

Effective date. The report will be submitted to Congress no later than two years after the date of the enactment of this Act.

Act Sec. 705. Law at ¶10,820.

¶670
OASIS Data Collection

Suspension for non-beneficiaries. Prior to this law, all home health agencies participating in the Medicare and Medicaid programs were to conduct patient-specific comprehensive assessments using a standard core assessment data set, the Outcomes and Assessment Information Set (OASIS). Under this law, HHAs will no longer be required to conduct OASIS assessment for non-Medicare/non-Medicaid patients receiving skilled services.

Effective date. The Secretary will prepare a report to Congress not later than 18 months after the date of enactment of this Act.

Act Sec. 704. Law at ¶10,810.

¶671
Determination and Delivery of Medical Care

Nurse practitioner services. In addition to coverage for the physician who certified that a beneficiary is terminally ill, Medicare payments will be made for the services of a nurse practitioner chosen by the beneficiary instead of a physician as having the most significant role in the determination and delivery of the beneficiary's medical care. The nurse practitioner is not authorized to certify the beneficiary as terminally ill, but is able to review hospice plans of care.

Effective date. This provision applies to hospice care furnished on or after October 1, 2004.

Comment. Hospice care is covered by Medicare only for those beneficiaries who are terminally ill. A beneficiary is considered to be terminally ill if there is a medical prognosis that his life expectancy is six months or less. There must be a certification by the beneficiary's attending physician and the medical director (or staff physician) of the hospice program providing the care that the beneficiary is terminally ill.

Act Sec. 408 amending Sec. 1861(dd)(3)(B) and Sec. 1814(a)(7)(i)(I) of the Social Security Act. Law at ¶2280A and 2055.

¶675
Rural Hospice Demonstration Project

Demonstration project. Medicare beneficiaries who live in rural areas and are unable to receive hospice care in the home for lack of an appropriate caregiver will be the subject of this demonstration project. Those beneficiaries will be provided hospice care in a facility of 20 or fewer beds which offers the full range of services provided by hospice programs. No more than three hospice programs will be involved in the study, which will last no longer than five years each.

The hospice programs involved in the study must meet the following requirements:

(1) the programs must comply with otherwise applicable requirements for hospice programs, except that they will not be required to offer services outside of the home; and

(2) payments for the hospice care will be made at the same rates as other hospice programs.

The Secretary may also require the program to comply with additional quality assurance standards that it deems appropriate.

A report will be submitted to Congress by the Secretary including recommendations regarding an extension of the project to hospice programs serving rural areas.

Effective date. Effective upon enactment.

Act Sec. 409. Law at ¶ 10,310.

¶ 677
Coverage of Hospice Consultation Services

Effect of provision. Terminally ill individuals who have not yet elected hospice care will have hospice consultation services covered under Medicare. This provision increases the scope of benefits provided by hospices by adding coverage for the following:

(1) an evaluation of the individual's need for pain and symptom management;

(2) counseling the individual with respect to end-of-life issues and care options; and

(3) advising the individual regarding advanced care planning.

These services are covered when furnished by a physician who is either the medical director or an employee of a hospice program. The payment amount provided to hospices for these consultation services will be equal to the amount established for an office or other outpatient visit for evaluation and management associated with presenting problems of moderate severity under the established Medicare physician fee schedule other than the portion of the amount attributable to the practice expense component.

Effective date. Applicable to services provided by a hospice program on or after January 1, 2004.

Act Sec. 512 amending Secs. 1812(a), 1814(i) and 1861(dd)(2)(A)(i) of the Social Security Act. Law at ¶ 2050, 2065, 2071, and 2280A.

¶ 678
Voluntary Chronic Care Improvement Programs

Programs under traditional fee-for-service. The Secretary will be required to establish and implement chronic care improvement programs. If the programs are established, they are required to improve clinical quality and beneficiary satisfaction and achieve spending targets for Medicare for beneficiaries with certain chronic health conditions. The chronic care improvement (CCI) program is required to (1) have a process to screen each targeted beneficiary for conditions other than the specified chronic conditions, such as impaired cognitive ability and co-morbidities, in order to develop an individualized, goal-oriented care management plan; (2) provide each targeted beneficiary participating in the program with the care management plan; and (3) carry out the plan and other chronic care improvement activities.

Care management plan. The care management plan is required to be developed with the beneficiary and, to the extent appropriate, include: (1) a designated point of contact responsible for communications with the beneficiary and for facilitating communications with other health care providers; (2) self-care education for the beneficiary (through approaches such as disease management or medical nutrition therapy) and education for primary caregivers and family members; (3) education for physicians and other providers and collaboration to enhance communication of relevant clinical information; (4) the use of monitoring technologies that enable patient guidance through the exchange of pertinent clinical information, such as vital signs, symptomatic information, and health self-assessment; and (5) the provision of information about hospice care, pain and palliative care, and end-of-life care. To the extent that a care management plan includes medical nutrition therapy, such services should be delivered by a registered dietician or nutrition professional as defined in Section 1861 of the Social Security Act (42 U.S.C. 1395x.)

The Secretary is required to develop a method for identifying targeted beneficiaries who may benefit from participation in a chronic care improvement program and to communicate with the targeted beneficiary regarding the opportunity to participate. Targeted beneficiaries who are eligible to participate cannot be enrolled in a plan under Medicare Part C and must have one or more of the threshold conditions including; congestive heart failure, diabetes, chronic obstructive pulmonary disease (COPD), or other diseases or conditions specified by the Secretary. Beneficiary participation is voluntary.

Conduct of programs. In carrying out the care management plan, the chronic care improvement organization is required to: (1) guide the participant in managing the participant's health (including all co-morbidities, relevant health care services, and pharmaceutical needs) and in performing activities as specified under the elements of the care management plan of the participant; (2) use decision-support tools such as evidence-based practice guidelines or other criteria as determined by the Secretary; and (3) develop a clinical information database to track and monitor each participant across settings and to evaluate outcomes.

Developmental Phase (Phase I). The establishment of the chronic care improvement program is conducted in two parts. In Phase I, the developmental phase, the Secretary is required to enter into contracts with chronic care improvement organizations for the development, testing, and evaluation of chronic care improvement programs using randomized controlled trials. The first contract is required 12 months after enactment for a three year period. The Secretary is required to enter into contracts to ensure that chronic care improvement programs cover geographic areas in which at least 10 percent of Medicare beneficiaries reside. The Secretary is further required to ensure that each chronic care improvement program includes at least 10,000 targeted beneficiaries along with a sufficient number of Medicare beneficiaries to serve as a control group.

Independent evaluation of Phase I Programs. The Secretary is required to contract for an independent evaluation of each chronic care improvement program. The evaluation is required to include quality improvement measures, such as adherence to evidence-based guidelines and rehospitalization rates; beneficiary and provider satisfaction; health outcomes; and financial outcomes, including any cost savings to Medicare. If the Secretary finds that the chronic care improvement programs have improved the clinical quality of care, improved beneficiary satisfaction, and achieved specified spending targets, then the Secretary is required to expand the program to additional geographic areas not covered during Phase I.

Phase II. Phase II may include national expansion of the program and is required to begin no later than 6 months after the completion of Phase I (nor earlier than 2 years after Phase I began). The Secretary is also required to evaluate Phase II programs using the same criteria used in the Phase I evaluation.

Outcomes report. Chronic care improvement organizations are required to monitor and report to the Secretary on health care quality, cost, and outcomes, in a time

¶678

and manner specified by the Secretary. The organizations are also required to comply with any additional requirements the Secretary may specify.

Accreditation. The Secretary may deem chronic care improvement organizations which are accredited by qualified organizations to have met requirements that the Secretary may specify.

Terms of agreements. The Secretary is not permitted to contract with an organization to operate a chronic care improvement program unless the organization meets the requirements for a chronic care improvement program and such clinical, quality improvement, financial, and other requirements as the Secretary deems to be appropriate for the target beneficiaries to be served; and the organization demonstrates (to the satisfaction of the Secretary) that it is able to assume financial risk for performance under the contract.

Performance standards. Each contract is required to specify performance standards for each of the specified evaluation factors including clinical quality and Medicare spending targets, against which the performance of the chronic care improvement organization under the contract is measured. Contractual adjustments are required if the contractor fails to meet specified performance standards. Further, the contract is required to provide for full recovery by the government of any amount by which the fees paid to the contractor exceed the estimated savings to Medicare that are attributable to the implementation of the contract.

Budget neutral payment condition. The Secretary is required to ensure that aggregate Medicare benefit expenditures for targeted beneficiaries participating in the chronic care improvement program do not exceed estimated Medicare expenditures for a comparable population in the absence of such a program.

Funding. Appropriations of such sums as necessary to provide for contracts with chronic care improvement programs will be authorized from the Medicare Trust Funds, but in no case would the funding be permitted to exceed $100 million over 3 years, beginning October 1, 2003.

Report. The Secretary is required to submit an interim report to Congress on the scope of implementation of the program, the design of the programs, and the preliminary cost and quality findings based on the evaluation criteria no later than two years after implementation. No later than three years and six months after implementation, the Secretary is required to submit an update to the interim report to Congress. The Secretary is further required to submit to Congress two additional biennial reports on the chronic care improvement programs. The first is due no later than two years after the update report.

Effective date. The Secretary will be required to begin implementing the chronic care improvement programs no later than one-year after enactment of the Act.

Sec. 721, adding Sec. 1807 to the Social Security Act. Law at ¶ 2040 and 10,850.

¶ 679

Demonstration Project for Consumer Directed Chronic Outpatient Services

Consumer directed chronic outpatient services. The Secretary will be required to establish demonstration projects, within two years of enactment of this provision, that evaluate methods to improve the quality of care provided to Medicare beneficiaries with chronic conditions and that reduce expenditures that would otherwise be made on their behalf by Medicare. The methods are required to include permitting beneficiaries to direct their own health care needs and services. In designing the demonstrations, the Secretary is required to evaluate practices used by group health plans and practices under State Medicaid programs that permit patients to self-direct the provision of personal care services and to determine the appropriate scope of personal care services that would apply under the demonstration projects. The Secretary must evaluate the practices for a 1-year period and, based on the evaluation, design the demonstration projects. The Secretary also is required to evaluate the clinical and cost effectiveness of the demonstrations.

Demonstration project sites. The Secretary must conduct at least one area that the Secretary determines has a population of individuals entitled to benefits under part A of title XVIII of the Social Security Act, and enrolled under Part B, with a rate of incidence of diabetes that significantly exceeds the national average rate of all areas.

Reports. The Secretary must conduct evaluations of the clinical and cost effectiveness of the demonstration projects. Reports to Congress are required biannually beginning two years after the demonstrations begin. The report on the evaluation must include the following:

(1) an analysis of the patient outcomes and costs of furnishing care to the beneficiaries participating;

(2) an evaluation of patient satisfaction; and

(3) recommendations regarding the extension, expansion or termination of the projects as the Secretary determines appropriate.

Effective date. Effective upon enactment.

Act Sec. 648. Law at ¶10,750.

PHYSICIAN SERVICES

¶700

Payments to Physicians in Rural Areas

Additional incentive payment for certain physician scarcity areas. A new five percent incentive payment program designed to reward both primary care and specialist care physicians for furnishing services in the areas that have fewest physicians available to serve beneficiaries. The incentive payment will be made in counties accounting for 20 percent of Medicare beneficiaries, which is likely to represent more than 20 percent of counties. As with the current HPSA bonus program, the five percent bonus would be added to the amount that Medicare pays after deducting beneficiary cost sharing so that beneficiaries do not pay cost-sharing on the incentive payment.

Determination of ratios. The Secretary will calculate two measures of scarcity. A primary care scarcity area will be determined based on the number of primary care physicians per Medicare beneficiary—the primary care ratio. A specialty care scarcity area will be based on the number of specialty care physicians per Medicare beneficiary—the specialty care ratio. The number of physicians will be based on physicians who actively practice medicine or osteopathy, and will exclude physicians whose practice is exclusively for the Federal Government, physicians who are retired, or physicians who only provide administrative services.

Identification of counties. The provision requires identification of the county in which the service is furnished in order to apply to the bonus. Currently, it is the understanding of the Conferees that the address where the service is furnished,

¶700

including the 5-digit zip code, is contained on the Medicare claim form. Since some zip codes cross county boundaries, the provision allows the Secretary to assign zip codes to counties based on the dominant county of the zip code as determined by the US Postal Service or otherwise. However, nothing would preclude, nor require, the Secretary ultimately to use 9-digit zip codes to determine the county in which the service is furnished. The provision requires periodic review and revision of the counties eligible for the bonus, but not less often than once every three years.

To the extent feasible, the Secretary will treat a rural census tract of a metropolitan statistical area, as determined under the most recent modification of the Goldsmith Modification, as an equivalent area for purposes of qualifying as a primary care scarcity area or specialty care scarcity area. There will be no administrative or judicial review of the designation of the county or area as a scarcity area, the designation of an individual physician's specialty, the assignment of a physician to a county or the assignment of a postal zip code to the county or other area. The Secretary will be required to publish a list of all areas which will qualify as primary care scarcity counties or specialty care scarcity counties as part of the proposed and final rules to implement the physician fee schedule. The list of eligible counties will be published each year in the proposed and final rule implementing the physician fee schedule. The list of counties will be posted on the Internet website of the Centers for Medicare and Medicaid Services (CMS).

Comment: The new five percent bonus for physicians in either primary care scarcity counties or specialty care scarcity counties will increase financial incentives for physicians to provide care to Medicare beneficiaries in these areas with a shortage of physicians. This bonus payment will make it easier to recruit and retain physicians in these scarcity areas.

Effective date. The provision applies to physicians' services furnished on or after January 1, 2005, and before January 1, 2008.

Act Sec. 413(a), amending Sec. 1833 of the Social Security Act by adding subsection (u). Law at ¶2121U.

Improvement to Medicare incentive payment program. For each health professional shortage area that consists of an entire county, the Secretary must provide for the additional payment without any requirement on the physician to identify the health professional shortage area involved. The Secretary must post on the CMS website a list of the health professional shortage areas described above that consist of a partial county to facilitate the additional payment in such areas.

Effective date. This provision applies to physicians' services furnished on or after January 1, 2005.

Act Sec. 413(b), amending 1833(m) of the Social Security Act. Law at ¶2121M and 10,340.

¶701

Update to Payments for Physicians' Services

Conversion factor. The update to the Medicare physician fee schedule conversion factor for 2004 and 2005 will be not less than 1.5 percent. It will be exempt from the budget neutrality adjustment, instead of -4.5% in 2004 and a smaller reduction in 2005.

Sustainable growth rate calculation. Starting in 2003, the gross domestic product (GDP) factor, which is one of four factors used in calculating the SGR, would be modified. The GDP would be based on the annual average change over the preceding

10 years (a 10-year rolling average). The current GDP factor measures the one-year change from the preceding year.

Effective date. Upon enactment.

Act Sec. 601, amending Secs. 1848(d) and 1848(f)(2)(C) of the Social Security Act. Law at ¶2251B, 2251D and 10,550.

¶703

Studies on Access to Physicians' Services

GAO study. The Comptroller General of the United States (GAO) is required to conduct a study on Medicare beneficiaries' access to physicians' services under the Medicare program. The study must include the following: (1) an assessment of beneficiaries' use of physician services through an analysis of claims submitted by physicians under Medicare Part B; (2) an examination of changes in beneficiaries' use of physicians' services over time; and (3) an examination of the extent to which physicians are not accepting new Medicare beneficiaries as patients.

Not later than 18 months after the date of the enactment of this legislation, the Comptroller General must submit to Congress a report on the study that includes a determination whether (1) data from claims submitted by physicians under Medicare Part B indicate potential access problems for Medicare beneficiaries in certain geographic areas; and (2) access by Medicare beneficiaries to physicians' services may have improved, remained constant, or deteriorated over time.

Effective date. Upon enactment.

Act Sec. 604. Law at ¶10,560.

¶704

MedPAC Report on Payment for Physicians' Services

Practice expense component. Not later than one year after the date of the enactment of this legislation, the Medicare Payment Advisory Commission (MedPAC) is required to submit to Congress a report on the effect of refinements to the practice expense component of payments for physicians' services. The report must examine the following issues by physician specialty:

(1) the effect of the practice expense refinements on payment for physicians' services;

(2) the interaction of the practice expense component with other components of and adjustments to payment for physicians' services;

(3) the appropriateness of the amount of physician compensation by reason of such refinements;

(4) the effect of the refinements on Medicare beneficiaries' access to physicians' services; and

(5) the effect of the refinements on physician participation under the Medicare program.

Volume of physician services. MedPAC also must report on the extent to which increases in the volume of physicians' services under Medicare Part B are a result of care that improves the health and well-being of Medicare beneficiaries.

Effective date. Upon enactment.

Act Sec. 606. Law at ¶10,580.

¶ 705
MedPAC Study of Payment for Cardio-Thoracic Surgeons

Practice expense relative values. MedPAC will be required to study the practice expense relative values in the Medicare physician fee schedule for the specialty of thoracic surgery to determine whether such values adequately take into account the attendant costs of nurse assistants at surgery. The study is required to be submitted to Congress by January 1, 2005 and to include recommendations for legislative or administrative action.

Effective date. Effective upon enactment.

Act Sec. 644. Law at ¶ 10,720.

¶ 706
Private Contracting for Podiatrists, Dentists and Optometrists

Private contracts. Podiatrists, dentists and optometrists will be able to enter into private contracts with Medicare beneficiaries.

Effective date. Effective upon enactment.

Act Sec. 603, amending Sec. 1802(b)(5)(B) of the Social Security Act. Law at ¶ 2030.

¶ 708
Establishment of Floor on Work Geographic Adjustment

Work geographic index. The Secretary is required to increase the value of any work geographic index that is below 1.0 to 1.0 for services furnished on or after January 1, 2004, and before January 1, 2007.

Effective date. Upon enactment.

Act Sec. 412, amending Sec. 1848(e)(1) of the Social Security Act. Law at ¶ 2251C.

¶ 710
Demonstration Project for Coverage of Certain Prescription Drugs and Biologicals

Drug and biological replacement demonstration. The Secretary must conduct a demonstration project under which payment is made for drugs or biologics that are prescribed as replacements for drugs and biologicals described in section 1861(s)(2)(A) of the Social Security Act (relating to drugs furnished incident to physicians' services) or Sec.1861(s)(2)(Q) (relating oral anticancer drugs), or both, for which payment is made under Part B. The demonstration project must be conducted in six states covering more than 50,000 patients and is required to begin 90 days following enactment and end no later than December 31, 2005.

Cost sharing. The project is required to provide for cost-sharing applicable with respect to the drugs or biologics in the same manner as the cost-sharing applicable under part D for standard prescription drug coverage. The project is not permitted to cost more than $500 million. No less than 40 percent of the funding shall be for oral cancer.

Report. By January 1, 2006, the Secretary must submit a report on the project to Congress, which includes: (1) an evaluation of patient access to care and patient outcomes under the project, (2) an analysis of the cost effectiveness of the project, including an evaluation of the costs savings to the Medicare program attributable to reduced physicians' services and hospital outpatient departments services for administration of the biological.

Immunomodulating drugs and biologicals. This provision of the demonstration will provide immediate Part B coverage for all immunomodulating drugs and biologicals used when treating multiple sclerosis. Coverage will be extended without regard to whether there is medical or other supervision with respect to the administration of such drug or biological, and include the biological administered via intramuscular injection currently covered under Section 1861(s)(2)(A) or (B) of the Social Security Act.

Effective date. Effective upon enactment.

Act Sec. 641. Law at ¶10,690.

¶720
Treatment of Certain Physician Pathology Services

Technical component. Direct payments for the technical component for these pathology services will be made for services furnished during 2005 and 2006.

Effective date. Effective upon enactment.

Act Sec. 732, amending Sec. 542 of the Benefits Improvement and Protection Act of 2000 (BIPA). Law at ¶10,890.

¶721
Modifications to Medicare Payment Advisory Commission (MedPAC)

Budgetary consequences. MedPAC will be required to examine the budgetary consequences of a recommendation before making the recommendation and to review the factors affecting the efficient provision of expenditures for services in different health care sectors under Medicare fee-for-service. MedPAC will be required to submit two additional reports no later than June 1, 2004. The first report is to study the need for current data and the sources of current data available, to determine the solvency and financial circumstances of hospitals and other Medicare providers. The second report is to address investments and capital financing of hospitals participating under Medicare and access to capital financing for private and not-for-profit hospitals.

Effective date. Effective upon enactment.

Act Sec. 735, amending Secs. 1805(b), 1805(b)(2)(B)(i), and 1805(c)(2)(D) of the Social Security Act. Law at ¶2035 and 10,920.

¶722
Physicians' Services Furnished in Alaska

Adjustments to physician payments. For physicians' services furnished in Alaska in calendar years 2004 and 2005, the Secretary is required to increase the geographic practice cost indices to a level of 1.67 for each of the work, practice expense, and malpractice cost indices.

Effective date. Services furnished between January 1, 2004, and January 1, 2006.

Act Sec. 602, amending Sec. 1848(e)(1) of the Social Security Act. Law at ¶2251C.

¶725
Review of Physician Practice Expense Geographic Adjustment Data

Study. The Secretary shall, in collaboration with State and other appropriate organizations representing physicians, and other appropriate persons, review and consider alternative data sources than those currently used in establishing the geographic index for the practice expense component under the Medicare physician fee schedule. One rural and one statewide localities are to be evaluated. The Secretary is to make a report to Congress on the findings by January 1, 2006.

Effective date. Effective upon enactment.

Act Secs. 605. Law at ¶10,570.

OTHER PART B ISSUES

¶729
Indexing Part B Deductible to Inflation

Increase. The Part B deductible will continue to be $100 through 2004 and then will increase to $110 for 2005. In subsequent years the deductible will be increased by the same percentage as the Part B premium increase. Specifically, the annual percentage increase in the monthly actuarial value of benefits payable from the Federal Supplementary Medical Insurance Trust Fund will be used as the update. The deductible amount will be rounded to the nearest dollar.

In 1966, Medicare's $50 Part B deductible equaled about 45 percent of Part B charges. Today's $100 deductible equals about three percent of such charges. Indexing the Part B deductible to grow at the same rate as total Part B spending per beneficiary would maintain the deductible at 3 percent of such charges over time.

Effective date. Effective upon enactment.

Act Sec. 629, amending Sec. 1833(b) of the Social Security Act. Law at ¶2121B.

¶730
Services Furnished by IHS Hospitals and Clinics

Payment. Medicare Part B payment will be made for all items or services covered under Medicare Part B and provided by a hospital or ambulatory care clinic operated by the Indian Health Service (IHS) or by an Indian tribe or tribal organization. The services must be furnished in or at the direction of the hospital or clinic under the same situations, terms and conditions that apply when such a facility is not operated by IHS or by an Indian tribal organization.

Effective date. Effective during the five-year period beginning on January 1, 2005.

Act Sec. 630, amending Sec. 1880(e) of the Social Security Act. Law at ¶2340.

PREVENTIVE SERVICES

¶ 750

Preventive Physical Exams

Coverage of an initial preventive examination. Medicare coverage for preventive services will be expanded to include coverage of an initial physical preventive physical examination. A covered initial preventive physical examination is one performed no later than six months after the individual's initial coverage date under Part B. The physical examination is defined as physicians' services consisting of a physical examination with the goal of health promotion and disease detection and includes education, counseling, and referral. The examination will include items and services excluding clinical laboratory tests. Initial preventive physical exams will be included in the definition of physician services for purposes of the physicians' fee schedule.

Effective date. These provisions apply to services furnished on or after January 1, 2005, for individuals whose coverage begins on or after such date.

Act Sec. 611, adding Sec. 1861 (ww) and amending Secs. 1861(s)(2), 1833(a)(1), and 1848(j)(3) of the Social Security Act. Law at ¶ 2275, 2280E and 2280J.

¶ 753

Cardiovascular Screening Tests

Coverage. Medicare coverage for cardiovascular screening tests will be authorized. The screening is defined as a blood test for the early detection of cardiovascular disease (or abnormalities associated with an elevated risk of cardiovascular disease) including tests for cholesterol levels and other lipid or triglyceride levels as well as such other indications associated with the presence of (or an elevated risk for) cardiovascular disease as the Secretary may approve for all individuals or for some individuals determined to be at risk for such disease. These indications may include indications measured by non-invasive testing. The Secretary will be required to establish standards regarding the frequency and type of cardiovascular screening tests. However, the screening tests may not be performed more than once every two years.

Effective date. This provision applies to tests furnished on or after January 1, 2005.

Act Sec. 612, amending Secs. 1861(s)(2) and 1862(a)(1) and adding 1861(xx)(1) to the Social Security Act. Law at ¶ 2275, 2280F, and 2280J.

¶ 754

Screening Mammography

Improved payment for mammography services. Screening mammography services as well as unilateral and bilateral diagnostic mammography will not be paid under the outpatient prospective payment system (OPPS). The Secretary is required to provide an appropriate adjustment to the physician fee schedule for the technical component of the diagnostic mammography based on the most recent cost report data available.

Effective date. This provision applies to screening mammography services furnished on or after the date of enactment. The provision applies to diagnostic mammography services furnished on or after January 1, 2005.

¶754

Act Sec. 614, amending Secs. 1833(t)(1)(B)(iv) and 1833(a)(2)(E)(i) of the Social Security Act. Law at ¶2121A and 2121T.

¶755
Diabetes Laboratory Diagnostic Tests

Diabetes screening tests and services. Medicare coverage of diabetes screening tests will be authorized for individuals at risk for diabetes for the purpose of early detection. In this instance, diabetes screening tests include fasting plasma glucose tests as well as other tests and modifications to those tests deemed appropriate by the Secretary after consultation with appropriate organizations. Individuals at risk for diabetes have any or a combination of the following conditions:

(1) hypertension;

(2) dyslipidemia;

(3) obesity, with a body mass index greater than or equal to 30 kg/m2;

(4) previous identification of an elevated impaired fasting glucose;

(5) previous identification of impaired glucose tolerance;

(6) a risk factor of at least 2 of the following characteristics: overweight with a body mass index of greater than 25, but less than 30, kg/m2; a family history of diabetes; a history of gestational diabetes mellitus or delivery of a baby weighing more than 9 pounds; or age of 65 years or more

The Secretary will be required to establish standards, in consultation with appropriate organizations, regarding the frequency of diabetes screening tests. Tests may not be administered more often than twice within the 12-month period following the date of the most recent diabetes screening test of that individual.

Effective date. This provision applies to tests furnished on or after January 1, 2005.

Act Sec. 613, amending Secs. 1862(a)(1) and 1861(s)(2) and adding 1861(yy) to the Social Security Act. Law at ¶2275, 2280G and 2280J.

¶756
Clinical Laboratory Diagnostic Tests

Fee schedules. The annual adjustment in the fee schedules for clinical diagnostic laboratory tests for the years 1998 through 2002 and 2004 through 2008 will be zero percent.

Effective date. Effective upon enactment.

Act Sec. 628, amending Sec. 1833(h)(2)(A)(ii)(IV) of the Social Security Act. Law at ¶2121H.

¶759
End-Stage Renal Disease Services

Composite rate. The end-stage renal disease (ESRD) composite rate will be increased by 1.6 percent for 2005. The prohibition on exceptions will not apply to pediatric ESRD facilities as of October 1, 2002. A pediatric facility is a renal facility with 50 percent of its patients under 18 years old.

Inspector general studies on ESRD drugs. The Inspector General of HHS will be required to conduct two studies regarding drugs and biologicals (including erythropoietin) furnished to ESRD patients and billed separately to Medicare by ESRD facilities. The first study will address existing drugs and biologicals those for which a billing code exists prior to January 1, 2004, and is required to submit a report to the Secretary by April 1, 2004. The second study is of new drugs and biologicals those for which a billing code does not exist prior to January 1, 2004, and is due to the Secretary by April 1, 2006. Each study is required to determine the difference, or spread, between the Medicare payment amount to ESRD facilities for drugs and biologicals, and the facilities' acquisition costs for the drugs and biologicals which are separately billed by the facilities. The studies are also to estimate the rates of growth of expenditures for these drugs and biologicals.

Basic case-mix adjusted prospective payment system. The Secretary will be required to establish a basic case-mix adjusted prospective payment system for dialysis services. The basic case-mix adjusted system is required to begin for services furnished on January 1, 2005. The system is required to adjust for a limited number of patient characteristics (the case-mix).

The basic case-mix adjusted system is composed of two components: (1) those services which currently comprise the composite rate (including the 1.6 percent increase in 2005), and (2) the difference between payment amounts for separately billed drugs and biologicals (including erythropoietin) and acquisition costs as determined by the Inspector General.

Geographic index. The Secretary is also required to adjust the basic case-mix adjusted system payment rates by a geographic index. If the geographic index is different from the one used with the composite rate, then the Secretary is required to phase-in the application over a multi-year period.

Spending and system update. Overall, spending for ESRD services included under the basic case-mix adjusted system is required to result in the same aggregate amount of expenditures as would occur if the current system continued in 2005. The system would be updated in 2006 for growth in drug spending for the portion of the basic case-mix adjusted payment amount that is represented by what is the current spread on separately billed drugs and biologicals. However, the provision does not provide for an update to the composite rate portion of the base rate in 2006 and forward. The increase for drug growth for the spread component would be adjusted downward by its proportionate share (of the spread and composite rate components) and the resulting increase applied to the sum. An adjustment would be made in 2007 for the spread calculated for new drugs and biologicals (those for which a billing code does not exist prior to January 1, 2004) using the 2006 Inspector General study.

Separately billed drugs. Drugs and biologicals (including erythropoietin) currently billed separately, will continue to be billed separately under the basic case-mix adjusted system at acquisition costs. They cannot be bundles into the new system.

Payments. Payments for separately billed drugs and biologicals will be 95 percent of the average wholesale price (AWP) for 2004 and acquisition costs in 2005, and, beginning in 2006 the Secretary has the authority to apply a payment methodology he determines appropriate which may include the average sales price payment methodology or acquisition costs.

Demonstration project. The Secretary is required to establish a three year demonstration project of the fully case-mix adjusted payment system for ESRD services, beginning January 1, 2006. The fully case-mix adjusted system is to include a case-mix system for patient characteristics identified in the report and to bundle separately billed drugs and biologicals and related clinical laboratory tests into the payment rates. The Secretary is required to ensure that sufficient numbers of providers of dialysis services and ESRD facilities participate in the demonstration, but not to

¶759

exceed 500. The Secretary is required to ensure that urban, rural, not-for-profit, for-profit, independent, and specialty providers and facilities are included in the demonstration. During the demonstration, the Secretary is required to increase payment rates that would otherwise apply by 1.6 percent for dialysis services furnished by demonstration participants.

Advisory board. In carrying out the demonstration, the Secretary is required to establish an advisory board comprised of representatives of: patient organizations; individuals with expertise in ESRD services, such as clinicians, economists, and researchers; the Medicare Payment Advisory Commission, the National Institutes of Health, network organizations; Medicare contractors to monitor quality of care; and providers of services and renal dialysis facilities. The advisory panel is required to terminate December 31, 2008. Appropriations are authorized from the Medicare trust funds in the amount of $5 million in fiscal year (FY) 2006 to conduct this demonstration.

Effective date. Effective upon enactment.

Act Sec. 623, amending Sec. 1881(b)(7) Social Security Act and Sec. 422(a)(2) of the Benefits Improvement and Protection Act. Law at ¶2345 and 10,640.

¶760
Intravenous Immune Globulin (IVIG) for the Treatment of Primary Immune Deficiency Diseases in the Home

Extension of coverage. Intravenous immune globulin for the treatment in the home of primary immune deficiency diseases will be a covered medical service under Medicare. Intravenous immune globulin is defined as an approved pooled plasma derivative for the treatment, in the patient's home, of a patient with a diagnosed primary immune deficiency disease, if a physician determines administration of the derivative in the patient's home is medically appropriate. Items or services related to the administration of the derivative are not included in the definition. Intravenous immune globulin is to be paid at 80 percent of the lesser of actual charge or the payment amount.

Effective date. This provision applies to items furnished on or after January 1, 2004.

Act Sec. 642, amending Secs. 1861(s)(2) and 1833(a)(1)(S) and adding 1861(zz) to the Social Security Act. Law at ¶2121A, 2275, and 2280H.

¶761
Orthotics and Prosthetics

Payment for certain shoes and inserts. The Secretary will determine payment amounts for custom molded shoes, extra-depth shoes, and inserts. The Secretary or a carrier will be able to establish lower payment amounts if shoes and inserts of an appropriate quality are readily available at lower amounts. The Secretary will be required to establish a payment amount for an individual substituting modifications to the covered shoe that would assure that there is no net increase in Medicare expenditures.

Effective date. This provision applies to items furnished on or after January 1, 2005.

Act Sec. 627, amending Secs. 1833(o), 1834(h)(4)(c) and 1842(s)(2) of the Social Security Act. Law at ¶2121O, 2140, and 2240.

¶ 762

Moratorium on Therapy Caps

Two-year continuation of moratorium on therapy caps. Application of therapy caps will be suspended through calendar year 2005. The Secretary will be required to submit the reports required by the Balanced Budget Act of 1997 (BBA) and the Benefits Improvement and Protection Act (BIPA) by December 31, 2004. The Secretary will be required to request the Institute of Medicine to identify conditions or diseases that should justify conducting an assessment of the need to waive the therapy caps. The Secretary will be required to submit to Congress a l report, including recommendations, will be due by March 31, , 2004. GAO will be required to submit a report to Congress before October 1, 2004.

Effective date. This provision is effective on enactment.

Act Sec. 624, amending Sec. 1833(g)(4) of the Social Security Act. Law at ¶ 2121G and 10,650.

COST CONTAINMENT PROVISIONS

¶ 765

Cost Containment

Status of Medicare Trust Funds in Annual Report of Medicare Trustees. The Medicare Board of Trustees was established under the Social Security Act to oversee the financial operations of the Medicare Hospital Insurance (HI) trust fund and the Medicare Supplementary Medical Insurance (SMI) trust fund. The Trustees are required to submit annual reports to the Congress. Beginning with their report in 2005, the Trustees' annual report is required to include information on: (1) projections of growth of general revenue Medicare spending as a percentage of the total Medicare outlays for each fiscal year (FY) within the subsequent seven fiscal year reporting period and, 10, 50, and 75 years after the fiscal year, and previous fiscal years; (2) comparisons with the growth trends for the gross domestic product, private health costs, national health expenditures, and other appropriate measures; (3) expenditures and trends in expenditures under Part D; and (4) a financial analysis of the combined Medicare trust funds if general revenue funding for Medicare is limited to 45 percent of total Medicare outlays. The trust fund reports are also required to include a determination as to whether there is projected to be "excess general revenue Medicare funding" (as defined in the paragraph below) for any of the succeeding 6 fiscal years in its annual reports of Medicare's trust funds.

"Excess general revenue Medicare funding" is defined as general revenue Medicare funding expressed as a percentage of total Medicare outlays in excess of 45 percent. This measure is calculated by dividing total Medicare outlays minus dedicated Medicare financing sources by total Medicare outlays. An affirmative determination of excess general revenue funding of Medicare for 2 consecutive annual reports will be treated as funding warning for Medicare in the second year for the purposes of requiring Presidential submission of legislation to Congress. Whenever any Trustees report includes a determination that within the subsequent seven fiscal year period there will be excess general revenue Medicare funding, Congress and the President are advised to address the matter under existing rules and procedures.

Dedicated Medicare financing sources. Dedicated Medicare financing sources include amounts appropriated to the HI trust fund for payroll taxes, transfers from the Railroad Retirement accounts, reimbursements for uninsured persons, and reimbursement for transitional insured coverage; taxation of certain OASDI benefits and tier II railroad retirement taxes, state transfers for Medicare coverage of eligible individuals who receive public assistance; premiums for Parts A, B, and D paid by non-Federal sources including amounts from voluntary enrollees (Part A), adjustments (Part B) and the MA monthly prescription drug beneficiary premiums paid under Part C that are attributable to basic prescription drug coverage (Part D); and gifts received by the Medicare trust funds. The premium amounts will be determined without regard to any reduction in the Part B premiums attributable to the beneficiary rebate under the MA program and Part D premium amounts are deemed to include any penalties for late enrollment.

Other definitions. "Medicare outlays" means total outlays from the Medicare trust funds and include payments made to plans under part C that are attributable to any rebates under the Medicare Advantage program and Medicare administrative expenditures. These outlays are required to be offset by the amount of fraud and abuse collection when applied to or deposited into a Medicare trust fund.

"Medicare trust funds" are defined as the Federal Hospital Insurance Trust Fund and the Federal Supplementary Medical Insurance Trust Fund which includes the Medicare Prescription Drug Account.

Effective date. Effective upon enactment.

Act Sec. 801. Law at ¶10,935.

¶768
Presidential Submission of Legislation

Budget warning. If a Medicare funding warning is made, the President is required to submit proposed legislation to respond to the warning. This must be completed within the fifteen-day period beginning on the date of the budget submission to Congress for the succeeding year it is made. If during the year in which the warning is made, legislation is enacted which eliminates excess general revenue Medicare funding for the seven FY period, then the President is not required to make a legislative proposal. It is the sense of Congress that legislation submitted in this regard should be designed to eliminate excess general revenue Medicare funding for the subsequent seven fiscal year period that begins in such year, as certified by the Board of Trustees not later than 30 days after the date of enactment.

Effective date. Effective upon enactment.

Act Sec. 802. Law at ¶10,940.

¶771
House of Representatives Procedures

Response. The act sets forth procedures for House consideration of the President's legislative request. Within three days of receiving the President's legislative request, the Majority Leader and Minority Leader of the House, or their designees, are required to introduce the proposal. Such legislation must be entitled "A bill to respond to a Medicare funding warning." Any legislation introduced is required to be referred to the appropriate committees which are required to report Medicare funding legislation no later than June 30. The chairman of the Committee on the Budget is required to certify whether or not Medicare funding legislation eliminates excess general revenue Medicare funding for any year within the subsequent seven fiscal year period and whether the legislation would eliminate excess general revenue Medicare funding within the subsequent seven fiscal year period.

Fallback procedures. If the House fails to vote on final passage of the legislation by July 30, the Act provides for fallback procedures. After 30 calendar days (and concurrently five legislative days) after the introduction of the legislation, a move to discharge any committee to which the legislation has been referred is in order, under specified circumstances, and debate on the motion to discharge is limited to one hour. Also, the Act provides for floor consideration in the House of the discharged legislation by the Committee of the Whole no later than three legislative days after discharge.

Effective date. Effective upon enactment.

Act Sec. 803. Law at ¶10,950.

¶774
Senate Procedures

Limited special procedures. Limited special procedures in the Senate for consideration of legislation arising from the Medicare Trustees determination that there will be "excess general revenue Medicare funding" under Section 801 are provided. If the Medicare Trustees report, includes a "Medicare funding warning" and if the President submits the legislative proposal in response to such a warning, that legislation (along with any other qualifying legislation otherwise introduced in the Senate or received from the House) will be entitled to special procedures.

The Majority Leader and the Minority Leader of the Senate (or their designees) are required to introduce the President's legislation. Such legislation must be entitled "A bill to respond to a Medicare funding warning." This bill must be introduced within three days of the session after Congress receives the proposal. Regardless of the subject matter and notwithstanding any jurisdictional precedents of the Senate, the bill will be referred to the Committee on Finance. Any other legislation introduced by any member of the Senate, bearing this same title, shall also be referred to the Committee on Finance.

This Medicare funding legislation will be entitled to the special rules concerning discharge and consideration of the legislation only if: (1) it was passed by the House, or (2) it is limited to matters within the jurisdiction of the Committee on Finance.

Discharge provisions. If the Committee on Finance has not reported any Medicare funding legislation by June 30 then it is in order for any Senator to move to discharge the committee from any one of the pieces of Medicare funding legislation that has been referred to that committee. Only one motion may be made in any session of Congress. This motion is not amendable and debate of the motion and any related appeals is limited to two hours. The two hours is to be equally divided and controlled between the maker of the motion and the Majority Leader (or their designees). If the Senate's Majority Leader supports the motion, then the time in opposition will be controlled by the Senate's Minority Leader (or the Minority Leader's designee) and a point of order may be made at any time during the two hours.

Any appeal made within the two hours may be debated for whatever time remains if any Senator desires to debate the appeal. Also, any motion or appeal made after the two hours shall be decided without debate. It is not in order to move to proceed to the consideration of any other measure or matter while the motion to discharge (or the motion to reconsider the vote with respect to the motion to discharge) is pending. This special motion to discharge is no longer available if the Chairman of the Committee on the Budget certifies that Medicare funding legislation which eliminates the excess general revenue medicare funding for each FY in the subsequent seven fiscal year reporting period has been enacted.

Consideration. Under existing Senate procedures, once Medicare funding legislation has been placed on the calendar (having been either reported or discharged from the committee) it is in order for any member of the Senate to make a motion to proceed to the consideration of that measure. This motion and all subsequent actions in the Senate shall be considered under the Standing Rules of the Senate and the corresponding precedents or pursuant to any unanimous consent agreements reached, as the case may be.

Effective date. Effective upon enactment.

Act Sec. 804. Law at ¶10,960.

¶776

Income-Related Reduction in Part B Premium Subsidy

Increase. To begin to address the fiscal challenges facing the Medicare program, beginning in 2007, Medicare beneficiaries with incomes over $80,000 for an individual or $160,000 for a married couple will be asked to contribute more to the cost of their Medicare benefits through payment of a higher premium. Approximately four percent of Medicare beneficiaries have incomes above these levels. All beneficiaries will continue to receive some level of premium assistance, and all beneficiaries will continue to be eligible for the full range of Medicare benefits.

Subsidy percentages according to income. Beneficiaries with incomes under $80,000 for an individual and $160,000 for a married couple will continue to receive a government subsidy at 75 percent and pay premiums at the 25 percent rate. Those with incomes between $80,000 and $100,000 ($160,000 and $200,000 for a married couple) will receive a 65 percent subsidy and pay 35 percent as a premium. Those with incomes between $100,000 and $150,000 ($200,000 and $300,000 for a couple) will receive a 50 percent subsidy and pay a premium at 50 percent. Those with incomes between $150,000 and $200,000 ($300,000 and $400,000 for a married couple) will receive a 35 percent subsidy and pay a premium at a 65 percent rate. Those with incomes above $200,000 ($400,000 for a married couple) will receive a 20 percent subsidy and pay a premium at an 80 percent rate.

Inflation adjustment. In the case of any calendar year beginning after 2007, the threshold amount and monthly adjustment amount will be adjusted for inflation by multiplying those figures by the percentage (if any) by which the average of the Consumer Price Index for all urban consumers (United States city average) for the twelve-month period ending with August of the preceding calendar year exceeds such average for the twelve-month period ending with August 2006. These amounts will be rounded to the nearest $1,000.

Tax-related issues. To facilitate the income-related reduction in Part B premium subsidy, the conference agreement authorizes the disclosure of certain return information to employees and contractors of the Social Security Administration. Upon written request from the Commissioner of Social Security, the IRS may disclose certain items of return information with respect to a taxpayer whose premium may be subject to adjustment. With respect to such taxpayers, the IRS may disclose (1) taxpayer identity information; (2) filing status; (3) adjusted gross income; (4) the amounts excluded from such taxpayer's gross income under Sections 135 and 911 of the Internal Revenue Code (relating to income from United States Savings bonds used to pay higher education tuition and fees, and foreign earned income); (5) tax-exempt interest received or accrued during the taxable year to the extent such information is available; (6) amounts excluded from such taxpayer's gross income by Sections 931 and 933 of the Internal Revenue Code (relating to income from sources within Guam, American Samoa, the Northern Mariana Islands, or Puerto Rico); (7) for nonfilers only, such other information relating to the liability of the taxpayer as the Secretary may prescribe by regulation, as might indicate that the amount of the premium of the taxpayer may be subject to adjustment (including estimated tax payments and income information derived from Form W-2, Form 1099, or similar information returns); and (8) the taxable year with respect to which the preceding information relates. Return information disclosed under this authority may be used by employees and contractors of the Social Security Administration only for purposes of, and to the extent necessary in, establishing the appropriate amount of any Part B premium adjustment.

Regarding those for whom the Secretary of the Treasury does not have adequate data, including non-filers, the Commissioner of Social Security, in consultation with the Secretary, will prescribe regulations that provide for treatment of the non-filers' premium adjustment. These regulations will provide for (1) the application of the highest applicable percentage of the monthly adjustment amount to the individual if the Commissioner has information that indicates that the individual's modified adjusted gross income might exceed the threshold amount for the taxable year, and (2) proper adjustments in the case of the application of an applicable percentage that is inconsistent with the individual's modified adjusted gross income.

Request for use of more recent taxable year. The Commissioner of Social Security, in consultation with the Secretary of the Treasury, will establish a procedures under which an individual's modified adjusted gross income will, at the request of such individual, be determined by using a more recent taxable year than the taxable year otherwise used, or by a method that the Secretary, in consultation with such Secretary, determines to be appropriate. This may include a methodology for aggregating or disaggregating information from tax returns in the case of marriage or divorce.

A request to use a more recent taxable year may be granted only if (1) the individual furnishes to the Commissioner relevant documentation concerning the year , such as a copy of a filed Federal income tax return or an equivalent document, as the Commissioner specifies for purposes of determining the premium adjustment (if any), and (2) the individual's modified adjusted gross income for such year is significantly less than his or her income for the taxable year originally used by reason of the death of the individual's spouse, the marriage or divorce of the individual, or other major life changing events specified in regulations prescribed by the Commissioner in consultation with the Secretary.

Effective date. Effective upon enactment.

Act Sec. 811, amending Secs. 1839 and 1844 of the Social Security Act and adding to Sec. 1839. Amending Secs. 6103 and 7213 of the Internal Revenue Code of 1986. Law at ¶2165, 2245, and 10,970.

¶ 777

Military Retirees

Waiver of Part B late enrollment penalty. This provision waives the late enrollment penalty for military retirees who did not enroll in Medicare Part B upon becoming eligible for Medicare. The waiver applies to the late enrollment penalty for military retirees, 65 and over, who enroll(ed) in the TRICARE for Life program from

2001 to 2004. The Secretary is required to provide a special Part B enrollment period for these military retirees beginning as soon as possible after enactment and ending December 31, 2004.

Coverage period. For an individual who enrolls during the special enrollment period, the coverage period under part B must begin on the first day of the month following the month in which the individual enrolls.

Effective date. The provision applies to premiums for months beginning January 2004. The Secretary is required to rebate premium penalties paid for months on or after January 2004 for which a penalty does not apply as a result of this provision, but for which a penalty was collected.

Act. Sec. 625, amending Sec. 1839(b) of the Social Security Act. Law at ¶2165 and 10,660.

DEMONSTRATION PROJECTS

¶784

Surgical First Assisting Services

Certified registered nurse first assistants. The Medicare Payment Advisory Commission will be required to study the feasibility and advisability of Medicare Part B payment for surgical first assisting services furnished to Medicare beneficiaries by a certified registered nurse first assistant. MedPAC is required to submit the report by January 1, 2005 and to include recommendations for legislation or administrative action.

Surgical first assisting services. Surgical first assisting services are services consisting of first assisting a physician with surgery and related preoperative, intraoperative, and postoperative care furnished by a certified registered nurse first assistant. The certified registered nurse first assistant must be legally authorized to perform the services by the state in which the services are performed.

Report. The Commission will be required to submit to Congress a report on the study together with recommendations for legislation or administrative action by January 1, 2005.

Effective date. Effective upon enactment.

Act. Sec. 643. Law at ¶10,710.

¶785

Health Care Quality Demonstration Programs

Delivery of care. The conference agreement requires the Secretary to establish a five-year demonstration program that examines the health delivery factors which encourage the delivery of improved patient care quality including: (1) incentives to improve the safety of care provided to beneficiaries; (2) appropriate use of best practice guidelines; (3) reduction of scientific uncertainty through examination of service variation and outcomes measurement; (4) encouragement of shared decision making between providers and patients; (5) the provision of incentives to improve safety, quality, and efficiency; (6) appropriate use of culturally and ethnically sensitive care; and (7) related financial effects associated with these changes.

Health care groups that may participate are physician groups, integrated health care delivery systems, and regional coalitions. These health care groups may implement alternative payment systems that encourage the delivery of high quality care and streamline documentation and reporting requirements. They may also offer benefit packages distinct from those that are currently available under Medicare Parts A and B and under the Part C Medicare Advantage plan.

To qualify for this demonstration, health care groups must meet quality standards; implement quality improvement mechanisms that integrate community-based support, primary care, and referral care; encourage patient participation in decisions; among other requirements. The Secretary may waive Medicare and Peer Review and Administrative Simplification (Title XI) requirements as necessary and may direct agencies within HHS to evaluate, analyze, support, and assist in the demonstration project. The demonstration program is subject to budget-neutrality requirements.

Effective date. Effective upon enactment.

Act. Sec. 646. Law at ¶2291B.

¶786

Medicare Care Management Performance Demonstration Project

Health outcomes. The Secretary would be required to establish a three-year demonstration program to promote continuity of care, help stabilize medical conditions, prevent or minimize acute exacerbations of chronic conditions, and reduce adverse health outcomes. Four sites would be designated for the demonstration: with at least two in urban areas and one in a rural area. One of the demonstration sites would be in a state with a medical school with a geriatrics department that manages rural outreach sites and is capable of managing patients with multiple chronic conditions, one of which is dementia.

Participation. A physician who provides care for a minimum of eligible beneficiaries (as specified by the Secretary) may participate in the demonstration program if the physician agrees to phase in over the course of the three-year period (1) the use of health information technology to manage the clinical care of eligible beneficiaries consistent with the practice standards under the program and (2) the electronic reporting of clinical quality and outcomes measures established by the Secretary.

Practice standards. Each physician participating in the demonstration program must have the ability to:

(1) assesss each eligible beneficiary for conditions other than chronic conditions, such as impaired cognitive ability and co-morbidities, for the purposes of developing care management requirements;

(2) to serve as the primary contact of eligible beneficiaries in accessing items and services for which payment may be made under the Medicare program;

(3) to establish and maintain a health care information system for such beneficiaries;

(4) to promote continuity of care across providers and settings;

(5) to sue evidence-based guidelines and meet such clinical quality and outcome measures as the Secretary requires;

(6) to promote self-care through the provision of patient education and support for patients or, where appropriate, family caregivers;

(7) when appropriate, to refer beneficiaries to community service organizations; and

(8) to meet such other complex care management requirements as the Secretary may specify.

Payment methodology. Under the demonstration program the Secretary must pay a per-beneficiary amount to each participating physician who meets or exceeds specific performance standards established by the Secretary with respect to clinical quality and outcome measures. The amount may vary based on different levels of performance and improvement.

Use of quality improvement organizations. The Secretary must contract with quality improvement organizations or other entities to enroll physicians and evaluate their performance under the demonstration program. The Secretary must require in the contracts that the contractor be responsible for technical assistance and education as needed to physicians enrolled in the demonstration program for the purpose of aiding their adoption of health information technology, meeting practice standards, and implementing required clinical and outcomes measures.

Funding. The Secretary must provide for the transfer from the Federal Supplementary Medical Insurance Trust Fund the funds necessary for the costs of carrying out the demonstration program. The Secretary must ensure that the aggregate payments made by the Secretary do not exceed the amount which the Secretary estimates would have been paid if the demonstration program was not implemented.

Report. The Secretary must submit to Congress a report on the program, together with recommendations for legislation and administrative action, not later than 12 months after the date of completion of the demonstration program.

Effective date. Effective upon enactment.

Act Sec. 649. Law at ¶ 10,760.

¶ 787

Concierge Care

GAO study and report on the propagation of concierge care. The Comptroller General will be required to conduct a study on concierge care to determine the extent to which care is used by Medicare beneficiaries and has impacted upon the access of Medicare beneficiaries (as so defined) to items and services for which reimbursement is provided. Concierge care means an arrangement under which a physician, practitioner (as described in 19 section 1842(b)(18)(C) of the Social Security Act, or other individual (1) charges a membership fee or another incidental fee to an individual desiring to receive the health care item or service from the physician, practitioner, or other individual or (2) requires the individual desiring to receive the health care item or service from such physician, practitioner, or other individual to purchase an item or service.

Report. Not later than 12 months after the date of enactment of this Act, the Comptroller General must submit to Congress a report on the study together with recommendations for legislative or administrative action.

Effective date. Effective upon enactment.

Act Sec. 650. Law at ¶ 10,770.

¶ 788

Chiropractic Services

Demonstration project of coverage of chiropractic services. The Secretary will be required to establish a 2-year demonstration program at four sites to evaluate the feasibility and desirability of covering additional chiropractic services under Medicare. These projects may not be implemented before October 1, 2004. The chiropractic services included in the demonstration shall include, at a minimum, care for neuromusculoskeletal conditions typical among eligible beneficiaries as well as diagnostic and other services that a chiropractor is legally authorized to perform by the State or jurisdiction where treatment occurs. An eligible beneficiary participating in the demonstration project, including those enrolled in Medicare +Choice or Medicare Advantage plans, would not be required to receive approval by physician or other practitioner in order to receive chiropractic services under the demonstration project.

The Secretary will be required to consult with chiropractors, organizations representing chiropractors, beneficiaries and organizations representing beneficiaries in establishing the demonstration projects. Participation by eligible beneficiaries would be on a voluntary basis. The four sites would be equally split between rural and urban areas; at least one of the sites would be in a health professional shortage area.

Evaluation and report. The Secretary would be required to evaluate the demonstration projects to determine (1) whether the participating beneficiaries used fewer Medicare covered services than those who did not participate; (2) the cost of providing such chiropractic services under Medicare; (3) the quality of care and satisfaction of participating beneficiaries; and (4) other appropriate matters. The Secretary will be required to submit a report, including recommendations, to Congress on the evaluation no later than 1 year after the demonstration projects conclude.

Waiver. The Secretary will waive Medicare requirements as necessary.

Funding. The demonstration program will be subject to a budget-neutrality requirement. Appropriations from the Federal Supplementary Insurance Trust Fund are authorized as necessary to conduct this demonstration.

Effective date. Effective upon enactment.

Act Sec. 651. Law at ¶10,780.

¶789

Telemedicine Demonstration Project

Extension of telemedicine demonstration project. The telemedicine demonstration project authorized by the Balanced Budget Refinement Act of 1997 (PubLNo 105-33) is extended for another four years. Funding for this project is increased by $30 million, for a total of $60 million over the eight-year course of the demonstration.

Effective date. Effective upon enactment.

Act Sec. 417, amending Sec. 4207 of the Balanced Budget Act of 1997. Law at ¶10,380.

¶790

Chronically Ill Medicare Beneficiary Research, Data, Demonstration Strategy

Quality of care. The Secretary is required to develop a plan to improve quality of care and to reduce the cost of care for chronically ill Medicare beneficiaries within six months after enactment. The plan is required to use existing data and identify data gaps, develop research initiatives, and propose intervention demonstration programs to provide better health care for chronically ill Medicare beneficiaries.

Plan requirements. The plan is required to: (1) integrate existing datasets including the Medicare Current Beneficiary Survey, the Minimum Data Set, the Outcome and

Assessment Information Set, data from the Quality Improvement Organizations, and claims data; (2) identify any new data needs and a methodology to address new data needs; (3) plan for the collection of such data in a data warehouse; and (4) develop a research agenda using the data. In developing the plan, the Secretary is required to consult with experts in the fields of care for the chronically ill (including clinicians) and is required to enter into contracts with appropriate entities for the development of the plan.

Implementation. The Secretary is required to implement the plan no later than two years after enactment. Appropriations are authorized from amounts in the Treasury not otherwise appropriated, such sums as may be necessary in fiscal years 2004 and 2005 to carry out this provision.

Effective date. Effective upon enactment.

Act Sec. 723. Law at ¶10,870.

MISCELLANEOUS PROVISIONS

¶791

Physical Therapy Services

MedPAC study on direct access to physical therapy services. MedPAC will be required to study the feasibility and advisability of allowing Medicare beneficiaries in fee-for-service direct access to outpatient physical therapy services and those physical therapy services that are furnished as comprehensive rehabilitation facility services. For the purposes of the study, direct access is defined as access to physical therapy services without the requirement that beneficiaries be under the care of, or referred by, a physician. Further, the services provided are not required to be under the supervision of a physician. Finally, either a physician or a qualified physical therapist could satisfy any requirement for certification, recertification and establishment and review of a plan of care. This study, together with recommendations for legislation or administrative actions, must be submitted to Congress no later than January 1, 2005.

Effective date. This provision is effective for services furnished on or after January 1, 2004.

Act Sec. 647. Law at ¶10,740.

¶792

Studies Relating To Vision Impairments

Vision rehabilitation services. The Secretary will be required study the feasibility and advisability of: (1) providing for payment for vision rehabilitation services furnished by vision rehabilitation professionals, and (2) implementing a demonstration project for vision care PPO networks to furnish and pay for conventional eyeglasses subsequent to each cataract surgery with the insertion of intra ocular lens. The Secretary is urged to examine any licensure or certification difficulties faced by vision rehabilitation professionals.

Report. The Secretary is required to submit a report Congress by January 1, 2005, and is to include recommendations for legislation or administrative action. In reviewing reimbursement for vision rehabilitation professionals, the report must examine payments through qualified physicians to vision rehabilitation professionals for either directly supervised services or services delivered under generalized supervision. The report must include an estimate of potential cost savings to the Medicare program taking into consideration quality of service and beneficiary access to services offered by vision care preferred provider organization networks.

Effective date. Upon enactment.

Act Sec. 645. Law at ¶10,730.

¶793

Restoration of Medicare Trust Funds

Correction of trust fund holdings. The Secretary of the Treasury is required to transfer into the Federal Hospital Insurance (HI) Trust Fund an amount that would have been held by that fund if the clerical error had not occurred. Such money is appropriated to the HI Trust Fund. The appropriation is made and transfer is required within 120 days of enactment of this Act. In the case of a clerical error that occurs after April 15, 2001, the Secretary of the Treasury is required to notify the appropriate committees of Congress about the error and the actions to be taken, before such action is taken.

Effective date. Effective upon enactment.

Act Sec. 734. Law at ¶10,910.

¶794

Medicare Secondary Payer

Conditional payments. The Secretary's authority to make conditional payments under the Medicare Secondary Payer provisions if a primary plan has not made or cannot reasonably be expected to promptly make payment. In such circumstances, payment is conditioned on reimbursement to the appropriate Medicare trust fund. The United States may bring an action against any or all entities that were required to make, or responsible for, payment under a primary plan when conditional payment is made. The government may recover double damages under such circumstances.

Effective date. This provision is effective as if included in the enactment of title III of the Medicare and Medicaid Budget Reconciliation Amendments of 1984 (P.L. 98-369).

Conditional payments. Clarifies the Secretary's authority to make conditional payments under the Medicare Secondary Payer provisions if a primary plan has not made or cannot reasonably be expected to promptly make payment. In such circumstances, payment is conditioned on reimbursement to the appropriate Medicare trust fund. An entity that engages in a business, trade, or profession is deemed to have a self-insured plan if it carries its own risk (whether by failure to obtain insurance or otherwise). A primary plan, and an entity that receives payment from a primary plan, must reimburse the appropriate Medicare trust fund for any conditional payment made by the Secretary if the primary plan had responsibility to make payment for the medical item or service. The primary plan's responsibility for payment may be demonstrated by a judgment, a payment conditioned on the recipient's compromise, waiver, or release of payment for items or services included in a claim against the primary plan or the primary plan's insured, or by other means. The United States may bring an action against any or all entities that were required to make, or responsible for, payment under a primary plan when conditional payment is made. The government may recover double damages under such circumstances. In addition, the United States may recover from any entity that received payment from a primary plan or from the proceeds of a primary plan's payment to any entity.

Effective Date. Effective as if included in the enactment of section 953 of the Omnibus Reconciliation Act of 1980.

Act Sec. 301 amending Sec. 1862 of the Social Security Act. Law at ¶2280J, 2280K, 2280L, and 2280M.

Treatment of hospitals for reference laboratory services. The Secretary is prohibited from requiring a hospital or a critical access hospital to ask questions or obtain information relating to the Medicare secondary payer provisions in the case of reference laboratory services if the same requirements are not imposed upon those provided by an independent laboratory. Reference laboratory services are those clinical laboratory diagnostic tests and interpretations of same that are furnished without a face-to-face encounter between the beneficiary and the hospital where the hospital submits a claim for the services.

Effective date. This provision is effective upon enactment.

Act Sec. 943. Law at ¶11,140.

¶795
Improvement in Oversight of Technology and Coverage

Council for technology and innovation. The Secretary will be required to establish a Council for Technology and Innovation within the Centers for Medicare and Medicaid Services (CMS). The council will be composed of senior CMS staff and clinicians and will be chaired by the Executive Coordinator for Technology and Innovation appointed by the Secretary. The Council will coordinate Medicare's coverage, coding, and payment processes with respect to new technologies and procedures, including drug therapies. The Executive Coordinator will serve as the single point of contact for outside groups and entities overseeing the execution of the Council's duties.

Payment basis for new lab tests. The Secretary will be required to establish procedures (by regulation) for determining the basis for and amount of payments for new clinical diagnostic laboratory tests. "New laboratory tests" are those assigned a new, or substantially revised, Health Care Procedure Coding System (HCPCS) code on or after January 1, 2005. The Secretary will be required to:

(1) provide a list of tests for which payments are being establish in that year;

(2) publish a notice of a meeting in the *Federal Register* on the day the list becomes available;

(3) hold the public meeting no earlier than 30 days after the notice to receive public comments and recommendations; and

(4) take into account the comments, recommendations and accompanying data in both proposed and final payment determinations.

The Secretary is also required to make available to the public the criteria and available data considered in making the payment determinations.

GAO study. The General Accounting Office (GAO) will be required to study which external data can be collected in a shorter time frame by CMS to use in calculating payments for inpatient hospital services. The study may include an evaluation of the feasibility and appropriateness of using quarterly samples or special surveys. The study must include an analysis of whether other executive agencies are best suited to collect this information. The report will be due to Congress no later than October 1, 2004.

ICS codes. If the National Committee on Vital and Health Statistics has not made a recommendation to the Secretary by enactment regarding implementation of the ICD-10 coding system for diagnosis and procedures, the Secretary may adopt such standards one year after the date of enactment of the Act.

Effective date. All provisions are effective upon enactment, except as is noted above for HCPCS codes assigned on or after January 1, 2005.

Sec. 942, amending Secs. 1868 and 1833(h) of the Social Security Act. Law at ¶2121H, 2300, and 11,130.

¶796

Improvements in the National and Local Coverage Determination Process to Respond to Changes in Technology

Coverage. The Secretary is required to make available to the public the factors considered in making national coverage determinations of whether an item or service is reasonable and necessary. The Secretary is required to develop guidance documents similar to those required by the Federal Food, Drug and Cosmetic Act (21 U.S.C. 371(h)). The provision establishes a timeframe for decisions regarding national coverage determinations of six months after a request when a technology assessment is not required and nine months when a technology assessment is required and in which a clinical trial is not requested.

Process for public comment. Following the six or nine month period, the Secretary is required to make a draft of the proposed decision available on the HHS website or by other means and provide a 30-day public comment period. Not later than 60 days following the conclusion of the 30-day public comment period the Secretary is required to make a final decision on the request; include clinical evidence and data used in making the decision available to the public when the decision differs from the recommendations of the Medicare Coverage Advisory Committee; and in the case of a decision to grant the coverage determination, assign a temporary or permanent code and implement the coding change. In instances where a request for a national coverage determination is not reviewed by the Medicare Coverage Advisory Committee, the Secretary is required to consult with appropriate outside clinical experts.

Local coverage determination process. The Secretary is also required to develop a plan to evaluate new local coverage determinations to decide which local decisions should be adopted nationally and to decide to what extent greater consistency can be achieved among local coverage decisions, to require the Medicare contractors within an area to consult on new local coverage policies, and to disseminate information on local coverage determination among Medicare contractors to reduce duplication of effort. The provision is effective for national determinations as of January 1, 2004 and for local coverage determinations made on or after July 1, 2004.

Clinical trials. The Secretary is prohibited from excluding from Medicare coverage the routine costs of care incurred by a Medicare beneficiary participating in a category A clinical trial, beginning with routine costs incurred on and after January 1, 2005. This provision does not apply to, or affect, Medicare coverage or payment for a non-experimental/investigational (category B) device.

Effective date. Effective upon enactment.

Sec. 731, amending Sec. 1862 of the Social Security Act. Law at ¶2280J and 10,880.

¶ 797
Dental Claims

Treatment of dental claims. A group health plan providing supplemental or secondary coverage to Medicare beneficiaries will not be able to require dentists to obtain a claim denial from Medicare for noncovered dental services before paying the claim. However, a group health plan may required a claims determination in cases involving inpatient dental hospital services.

Effective date. This provision is effective 60 days after enactment of the Act.

Act. Sec. 950 adding new Sec. 1862(k)(1). Law at ¶ 2280.

¶ 798
Medically Underserved Populations

Safe harbor provisions. Remuneration in the form of a contract, lease, grant, loan or other agreement between a public or non-profit private health center and an individual or entity providing goods or services to the health center will not be a violation of the anti-kickback statute if such an agreement contributes to the ability of the health center to maintain or increase the availability or quality of services provided to a medically underserved population. The Secretary would be required to establish standards, on an expedited basis, related to this safe harbor that would consider whether the arrangement (1) results in savings of federal grant funds or increased revenues to the health center; (2) expands or limits a patient's freedom of choice; and (3) protects a health care professional's independence regarding the provision of medically appropriate treatment. The Secretary may also include other standards that are consistent with Congressional intent in enacting this exception. The Secretary is required to publish a final regulation establishing these standards no later than one year from the date of enactment.

Effective date. Effective upon enactment.

Act Sec. 431, amending 1128B(b)(3). Law at ¶ 2017 and 10,420.

¶ 799
Office of Rural Health Policy Improvement

Functions. The functions of the Office of Rural Health Policy will be expanded. It will be authorized to administer grants, cooperative agreements, and contracts to provide technical assistance and other necessary activities to support activities related to improving rural health care.

Effective date. Effective upon enactment.

Act Sec. 432, amending Sec. 711(b) of the Social Security Act.

¶ 800
Medicare Advantage Quality Improvement Programs

Requirements. Each Medicare Advantage (MA) organization will be required to have an on-going quality improvement program for improving the quality of care provided to enrollees (except for private fee-for-service plans or MSA plans) effective for contract years beginning January 1, 2006. As part of the quality improvement program, each MA organization is required to have a chronic care improvement program. Each chronic care improvement program is required to have a method for monitoring and identifying enrollees with multiple or sufficiently severe chronic conditions that meet criteria established by the organization for participation under the program.

Collection, analysis, and reporting. Each MA organization is required to provide for the collection, analysis and reporting of data that permit measurement of health outcomes and other indicators of quality. The Secretary will establish through regulation appropriate reporting requirements for regional PPOs. The Secretary is permitted to change the types of data that are required of plans only after submitting to Congress a report on the reasons for the changes that was prepared in consultation with MA plans and private accrediting bodies. The Secretary is not permitted to collect data on quality, outcomes, and beneficiary satisfaction for the purposes of consumer choice and program administration if the data were not already being collected as of November 1, 2003. However, these provision regarding data are not to be construed as restricting the ability of the Secretary to carry out the comparative information dissemination provisions regarding plan quality and performance that are contained in section 1851(d)(4)(D).

Each MA organization is deemed to meet the quality improvement program requirements as the Secretary determines to be appropriate if the MA organization is accredited (and periodically reaccredited) by a private accrediting organization under a process that the Secretary has determined ensures that the accrediting organization applies and enforces standards that meet or exceed the standards established by the Secretary.

Effective date. This provision is will apply to contract years beginning on and after January 1, 2006.

Sec. Act 722, amending Sec. 1852(e). Law at ¶ 2256.

Regulatory Reduction and Contracting Reform

REGULATORY REFORM

Administrative Improvement, Regulatory Reduction, and Contracting Reform .... ¶ 801
Definition of Supplier .... ¶ 825
Issuance of Regulations .... ¶ 826
Compliance with Changes in Regulation and Policies .... ¶ 827
Reports and Studies Relating to Regulatory Reform .... ¶ 828
Flexibility in Medicare Administration .. ¶ 829
Requirements for Information Security for Medicare Administrative Contractors .... ¶ 830
Provider Education and Technical Assistance .... ¶ 831
Medicare Ombudsmen for Providers Beneficiaries.................. ¶ 832
Small Provider Technical Assistance Demonstration Program .... ¶ 833
Beneficiary Outreach Demonstration Programs.................... ¶ 835

APPEALS AND RECOVERY

Transfer of Responsibility for Medicare Appeals .... ¶ 901
Process for Expedited Access to Review .... ¶ 903
Expedited Review of SNF Appeals .... ¶ 905
Revision of Medicare Appeals Process .... ¶ 906
Qualified Independent Contractors.... ¶ 907
Prepayment Review .... ¶ 908
Recovery of Overpayments .... ¶ 909
Provider Enrollment Process .... ¶ 911
Correction of Minor Errors and Omissions .... ¶ 912
Prior Determination Process and ABNs .... ¶ 913
Appeals by Providers When There is No Other Party Available .... ¶ 915
Revision to Appeals Timeframes and Amounts .... ¶ 916

Mediation Process for Local Medical Review Policies .... ¶ 917

MISCELLANEOUS PROVISIONS

E & M Documentation Guidelines ..... ¶ 941
Improvement in Oversight of Technology and Coverage .... ¶ 942
Treatment of Hospitals for Certain MSP Services .... ¶ 943
EMTALA Improvements .... ¶ 944
Emergency Medical Treatment and Labor Act (EMTALA) Technical Advisory Group .... ¶ 945
Arrangements to Provide Core Hospice Services in Certain Circumstances .... ¶ 946
Application of OSHA Bloodborne Pathogens Standard to Certain Hospitals .... ¶ 947
BIPA-Related Technical Amendments and Corrections .... ¶ 948
Authority to Waive a Program Exclusion .... ¶ 949
Treatment of Certain Dental Claims .. ¶ 950
Revisions to Reassignment Provisions .. ¶ 952
Other Provisions................. ¶ 953

COMBATTING WASTE, FRAUD AND ABUSE

Competitive Acquisition of Certain Items and Services .... ¶ 1002
Physician Fee Schedule Adjustments .. ¶ 1004
Competitive Acquisition Program for Drugs and Biologicals .... ¶ 1006
Extension of Payment Reform .... ¶ 1008
Adjustments to Payment Amounts for Administration of Drugs and Biologicals .... ¶ 1009
Average Sales Price Payment (ASP) Methodology Option .... ¶ 1010
Payment for Inhalation Drugs .... ¶ 1011
Demonstration Project for Use of Recovery Audit Contractors .... ¶ 1012

REGULATORY REFORM

¶ 801

Administrative Improvement, Regulatory Reduction, and Contracting Reform

Administrative improvements within the Centers for Medicare & Medicaid Services (CMS). A Center is to be established within CMS to: (1) administer Parts C and D of Medicare; (2) provide notice and information to beneficiaries; and (3) provide other such duties specified by the Secretary. The head of the Center is required to report to the Administrator of CMS. The Secretary is required to ensure that the Center carries out these duties by no later than January 1, 2008. The Secretary is permitted to employ management staff as he deems appropriate. If such staff is employed, the staff is required to have demonstrated superior expertise in at least one of the following areas: (1) the review, negotiation, and administration of health care contracts; (2) the design of health care benefit plans; (3) actuarial sciences; (4) consumer education and decision making; (5) any other area specified by the Secretary that requires specialized management or other expertise. The Secretary is required to establish the rate of pay taking into account expertise, experience, and performance. The pay rate cannot exceed the highest rate of basic pay for the Senior Executive Service under Section 5382(b) of title 5, United States Code (currently ES-6).

Requirement for dedicated actuary for Private Health Plans. An actuary within the office of the Chief Actuary of CMS must be permitted to have duties exclusively related to Parts C and D of Medicare and related provisions. The pay grade for the Administrator of CMS is increased to Executive Level III beginning January 1, 2004.

Conforming amendment. This provision changes statutory references from the Health Care Financing Administration to the Centers for Medicare & Medicaid Services.

Effective date. Effective upon enactment.

Act Sec. 900, adding Sec. 1117(b) and 1808 of the Social Security Act. Law at ¶ 2015, 2045, 2256, 2256B, 2256D, 2401F, 2420, and 10,980.

¶ 825

Definition of Supplier

Construction. Nothing in this legislation may be construed to: (1) compromise or affect existing legal remedies for addressing fraud or abuse, whether it be criminal prosecution, civil enforcement or administrative remedies (including the False Claims Act); or (2) prevent or impede the Department of Health and Human Services (HHS) from its efforts to eliminate waste, fraud, or abuse in the Medicare program. The consolidation of Medicare administrative contractors does not constitute the consolidation of the Federal Hospital Insurance Trust Fund and the Federal Supplementary Medical Insurance Trust Fund, or reflect any position on that issue.

Title IX expands the definition of "supplier," and covers contracting reform, education and outreach, appeals and recovery procedures, and miscellaneous changes for providers and suppliers.

Definition of supplier. The term "supplier" means, unless the context otherwise requires, a physician or other practitioner, a facility or other entity (other than a provider of services) furnishing items or services under Medicare.

Effective date. Effective upon enactment.

Act Sec. 901, adding Sec. 1861 of the Social Security Act. Law at ¶ 2270 and 10,990.

¶ 826
Issuance of Regulations

Final regulations. The Secretary, in consultation with the Director of the Office of Management and Budget, is required to establish and publish a regular timeline for the publication of final regulations based on previous publications of a proposed rule or an interim final regulation.

Time frame. The time frame established may not be longer than three years, except under exceptional circumstances. If the Secretary intends to vary the timeline established, the Secretary is required to publish a notice in the Federal Register of the new timeline with an explanation of the variation.

Interim final regulations. If the Secretary does not meet the established time frame, the interim final regulation can not continue in effect unless the Secretary publishes, at the end of each succeeding one-year period, a notice of continuation of the regulation in the *Federal Register* that includes an explanation of why the regular timeline, and any subsequent one-year extensions, had not been complied with.

Limitations on new matter in final regulations. If the Secretary publishes a provision of a final regulation that is not a logical outgrowth of a proposed regulation or interim final regulation, the regulation must be treated as a proposed regulation. The provision will not take effect until public comment has occurred and the provision is published as a final regulation.

The Secretary is required to provide for an appropriate transition to take into account the backlog of previously published interim final regulations.

Effective date. Effective upon enactment.

Act Sec. 902, amending Sec. 1871(a) of the Social Security Act. Law at ¶ 2315.

¶ 827
Compliance with Changes in Regulation and Policies

Substantive change. A substantive change in regulation, manual instructions, interpretative rules, statements of policy, or guidelines of general applicability is not to be applied retroactively to items and services furnished before the effective date of the change, unless the Secretary determines retroactive application is needed to comply with statutory requirements or is in the public interest.

Effective date. Applicable to changes issued on or after the date of enactment.

Timeline for compliance. No substantive change is to go into effect until 30 days after the change is issued or published unless the change is needed to comply with statutory changes or is in the public interest. Compliance actions will be permitted for items and services furnished only on or after the effective date of the change.

Effective date. Applicable to compliance actions undertaken on or after the date of enactment.

Reliance on guidance. If a provider or supplier follows written guidance provided by the Secretary or a Medicare contractor when furnishing items or services or submitting a claim and the guidance is inaccurate, the provider or supplier will not be subject to sanctions of repayment of overpayment, including any penalty or requirement for repayment of any amount, if the provider of services or supplier reasonably relied on such guidance. This is not to be construed as preventing the recoupment or repayment (without any additional penalty) relating to an overpayment insofar as the overpayment was solely the result of a clerical or technical operational error.

Effective date. The reliance on guidance is effective upon enactment, but does not apply to any sanction for which notice is provided on or before the date of enactment.

Act Sec. 903, adding Sec. 1871(e)(1)(A) of the Social Security Act. Law at ¶2315.

¶ 828
Reports and Studies Relating to Regulatory Reform

GAO study on advisory opinion authority. The Comptroller General is required to study the feasibility and appropriateness of the Secretary providing legally binding advisory opinions on appropriate interpretation and application of Medicare regulations. The GAO study must examine the appropriate time frame for issuing such advisory opinions, as well as the need for additional staff and funding to provide such opinions.

GAO report. The Comptroller General is required to submit a report to Congress on the study conducted not later than one year after the date of enactment.

Report from CMS administrator. The Secretary is required to submit to Congress a report on the administration of Medicare and areas of inconsistency or conflict among various provisions under law and regulation. The report must include recommendations for legislation or administrative action that the Secretary determines appropriate to further reduce such inconsistency or conflicts. The Secretary's report must be submitted to Congress no later than two years after enactment, and every three years thereafter.

In preparing the report, the Secretary will collect information from individuals entitled to benefits under Part A, or enrolled under Part B, or both, providers of services, and suppliers, and from the Medicare Beneficiary Ombudsman and the Medicare Provider Ombudsman regarding areas of inconsistency and conflict. The report must include information from Medicare contractors that tracks the nature of written and telephone inquires and provide a description of efforts by the Secretary to reduce inconsistencies or conflicts, and recommendations for administrative action that the Secretary deems appropriate.

Effective date. Effective upon enactment.

Act Sec. 904, amending Sec. 1871 of the Social Security Act. Law at ¶2315 and ¶1,000.

¶ 829
Flexibility in Medicare Administration

Authority to enter into contracts. The Secretary is permitted to contract with any eligible entity to serve as a Medicare administrative contractor. The entity is eligible to contract for the performance of a particular function only if: (a) the entity has demonstrated capability to carry out such function; (b) the entity complies with conflict of interest standards as are generally applicable to federal acquisition and procurement; (c) the entity has sufficient assets to financially support the performance of such functions; and (d) the entity meets other requirements as the Secretary may impose.

Medicare administrative contractors. The term "Medicare administrative contractor" means an agency, organization, or other person with a contract under this section.

Appropriate contractor. With respect to the performance of a particular function, in relation to an individual entitled to benefits under Part A or enrolled under Part B, or both, a specific provider of services or supplier, the appropriate Medicare administrative contractor is contractor that has a contract for the performance of that function in relation to that individual provider of services or supplier or class of provider of services or supplier.

MAC functions. Medicare Administrative Contractors (MAC) will assume all functions including determining the amount of Medicare payments to providers and suppliers, developing local coverage determinations, making the payments, providing education and outreach to beneficiaries, providers and suppliers, technical assistance, providing consultative services to institutions and agencies, communicating with providers and suppliers, and additional functions including functions under the Medicare Integrity Program, as deemed necessary by the Secretary.

Renewal of contracts. The Secretary is required to renew MAC contracts annually, for up to five years. All contracts are subject to a new competition process at least every five years.

Federal Acquisition Regulations (FAR). Federal Acquisition Regulations (FAR) will be applied to these contracts except to the extent any provisions are inconsistent with a specific Medicare requirement, including incentive contracts.

Performance requirements. The contracts are required to contain performance requirements that are to be developed by the Secretary who may consult with beneficiary, provider, and supplier organizations, consistent with written statements of work and used for evaluating contractor performance. The MAC is required to provide the Secretary with timely information and to maintain access to records.

Surety bond. The Secretary may require a surety bond from the MAC, certain MAC officers, and MAC employees certifying payments or disbursing funds pursuant to the contract. The Secretary is prohibited from requiring that the MACs match data from other activities for Medicare secondary payer purposes.

Limitation on liability. The certifying and disbursing officers and the Medicare Administrative Contractors are not liable with respect to Medicare payments except in cases of reckless disregard or the intent to defraud the United States, but this limitation of liability does not limit liability under the False Claims Act. The provision also establishes circumstances where contractors and their employees are indemnified, both in the contract and as the Secretary determines appropriate.

Conforming amendments remove references in the law to "fiscal intermediaries" and "carriers."

The Secretary is required to submit a report to Congress and the GAO by no later than Oct. 1, 2004, that describes the plan for implementing these provisions. The GAO is required to evaluate the Secretary's plan and, within six months of receiving the plan, present an evaluation report to Congress, and make any recommendations the Comptroller General deems appropriate.

The Secretary is also required to report to Congress by Oct. 1, 2008, on: (1) the status of implementing the contracting reform provisions, including the number of contracts that have been competitively bid; (2) the distribution of functions among contracts and contractors; (3) a timeline for complete transition to full competition;

¶829

and (4) a detailed description of how the Secretary has modified oversight and management of Medicare contractors to adapt to full competition.

Effective date. This provision is effective on Oct. 1, 2005. Competitive bidding for the MACs is required for annual contract periods beginning on or after Oct. 1, 2011.

Act Sec. 911, amending Sec. 1816, 1842 and 1874A of the Social Security Act and adding Sec. 1874(A). Law at ¶ 2085, 2180A, 2180B, 2180C, 2180D, 2180E, 2180F, 2180G, 2185, 2190, 2195, 2200, 2205, 2210, 2215, 2220, 2225, 2230, 2235, 2320, and 11,010.

¶ 830
Requirements for Information Security for Medicare Administrative Contractors

Requirements for information security. Medicare Administrative Contractors (as well as fiscal intermediaries and carriers until the MACs are established) must implement a contractor-wide information security program to provide information security for the operation and assets of the contractor for Medicare functions. The information security program must meet requirements for information security programs required of Federal agencies under Title 44 of the United States Code.

Independent audits. MACs must undergo an annual independent evaluation of their information security programs. Existing contractors must undergo the first independent evaluation within one year after the date the contractor begins implementing the information security program. New contractors must have a program in place before beginning claim determination and payment activities.

Evaluation report. The results of the independent evaluations must be submitted to the Secretary and the HHS Inspector General.

The Inspector General of HHS is required to report to Congress annually on the results of the evaluations including assessments of the scope and sufficiency of evaluations.

The Secretary is required to address the results of the evaluations in required management reports.

Effective date. Effective upon enactment.

Act Sec. 912, amending Sec. 1874A of the Social Security Act. Law at ¶ 2320 and 11,020.

¶ 831
Provider Education and Technical Assistance

Contractor education and outreach programs. The Secretary is required to coordinate the educational activities that contractors furnish to providers and suppliers, and report to Congress a description and evaluation of the steps taken to coordinate provider education funding.

Incentives to improve contractor performance. The Secretary is required to use specific claims payment error rates (or similar methodology) to provide incentives for contractors to implement effective education and outreach programs for providers and suppliers.

Reports. By Oct. 1, 2004, the Comptroller General will be required to submit a report to Congress and the Secretary on the adequacy of the methodology and make recommendations to the Secretary. The Secretary is required to report to Congress on how the methodology will be used to assess Medicare contractor performance in implementing effective education and outreach programs, including whether to use such methodology as a basis for performance bonuses.

Provision of access to and prompt responses from Medicare administrative contractors. The Secretary is required to develop a strategy for communicating with beneficiaries, providers, and suppliers. Medicare contractors are required to provide clear, concise, and accurate responses to written inquiries within 45 business days of receipt of the inquiry.

Toll-free telephone number. The Secretary is required to ensure that Medicare contractors have toll-free telephone numbers where beneficiaries, providers, and suppliers can obtain information regarding billing, coding, claims, coverage, and other appropriate Medicare information. Medicare contractors are required to maintain a system for identifying the person supplying information to beneficiaries, providers, and suppliers and to monitor the accuracy, consistency, and timeliness of the information provided.

Monitoring of contractor response. The Secretary is required to establish and make public standards to monitor the accuracy, consistency, and timeliness of written and telephone responses of Medicare contractors as well as to evaluate the contractors against these standards.

Improved provider education and training. This provision authorizes the appropriation of sums as may be necessary in appropriate parts, from the Federal Hospital Insurance Trust Fund and the Federal Supplemental Medical Insurance Trust Funds for fiscal years beginning 2005, for Medicare contractors to increase education and training activities for providers and suppliers. Medicare contractors are required to tailor education and training activities to meet the special needs of small providers or suppliers.

The provision defines a small provider as an institution with fewer than 25 full-time equivalent (FTE) employees and a small supplier as one with fewer than 10 FTEs.

Requirement to maintain Internet sites. The Secretary and the Medicare contractors must maintain Internet sites to answer frequently asked questions and provide published materials of the contractors beginning Oct. 1, 2004.

Additional provider education provisions. This provision bars Medicare contractors from using a record of attendance (or non-attendance) at educational activities to select or track providers or suppliers in conducting any type of audit or prepayment review.

Construction. Nothing in this section is to be construed as providing for disclosure by a Medicare contractor of: (1) the screens used for identifying claims that will be subject to medical review; or (2) information that would compromise pending law enforcement activities or reveal findings of law enforcement-related audits.

Effective date. Effective upon enactment.

Act Sec. 921, adding Sec. 1889 of the Social Security Act. Law at ¶2320, 2360, and 11,025.

¶ 832

Medicare Ombudsmen for Providers Beneficiaries

Medicare ombudsman. A Medicare Provider Ombudsman is to be appointed by the Secretary and located within the Department of Health and Human Services. The

Provider Ombudsman is required to: (1) provide confidential assistance to providers and suppliers regarding complaints, grievances, requests for information, and resolution of unclear or conflicting guidance about Medicare; and (2) submit an annual report of recommendations to Congress and the Secretary regarding improving the administration of Medicare, addressing recurring patterns of confusion under Medicare, and ways to provide for an appropriate and consistent response in cases of self-identified overpayments by providers and suppliers. Such sums, as necessary, are authorized to be appropriated for FY 2004 and subsequent years.

Medicare Beneficiary Ombudsman. A Medicare beneficiary ombudsman is to be appointed by the Secretary and located within HHS. The beneficiary ombudsman is required to have expertise and experience in health care, and education of and assistance to Medicare beneficiaries. The beneficiary ombudsman is required to assist beneficiaries in collecting relevant information to seek an appeal of a decision or determination made by the Secretary, a Medicare contractor, or a Medicare+Choice organization and assisting a beneficiary with any problems arising from disembroiling in a Medicare+Choice plan. The beneficiary ombudsman is required to work with state Health Insurance Counseling Programs, to the extent possible.

Appropriations. Funds are to be appropriated in amounts necessary for FY 2004 and each succeeding fiscal year to carry out the ombudsmen provisions.

Individuals seeking information and assistance will be required to use the 1-800-MEDICARE telephone number for Medicare ombudsman rather than using telephone numbers for Medicare contractors listed in the Medicare handbook; only the 1-800-MEDICARE telephone number will be shown.

Comptroller General study. The Comptroller General is required to study the accuracy and consistency of information provided by the 1-800-MEDICARE line and to assess whether the information sufficiently answers the question of beneficiaries. The report on the study is required to be submitted to Congress not later than one year after enactment.

Effective date. The Secretary is required to appoint both ombudsmen not later than one year from the date of enactment.

Act Sec. 923, amending Sec. 1808 as added and amended by Sec. 900 of the Social Security Act. Law at ¶ 2045 and 11,040.

¶ 833

Small Provider Technical Assistance Demonstration Program

Small provider demonstration program. The Secretary is required to establish a demonstration program under which technical assistance is made available, upon request and on a voluntary basis, to small providers of services or suppliers in order to improve compliance with the applicable requirements of the programs under the Medicare program. The technical assistance is described as: (1) evaluation and recommendations regarding billing and related systems; and (2) information and assistance regarding policies and procedures under the Medicare program, including coding and reimbursement. The term "small provider of services and suppliers" means (1) a provider of services with fewer than 25 full-time-equivalent employees; or (2) a supplier with fewer than 10 full-time-equivalent employees.

Qualification of contractors. In conducting the demonstration program, the Secretary must enter into contracts with qualified organizations (such as peer review organizations or entities described in Sec.1889(g)(2) of the Social Security Act, as inserted by Sec. 921(f)(1)) with appropriate expertise with billing systems of the full range of providers of services and suppliers to provide the technical assistance. In awarding the contracts, the Secretary must consider any prior investigations of the entity's work by the Inspector General of the Department of Health and Human Services or the Comptroller General of the United States.

Description of technical assistance. The technical assistance provided under the demonstration program must include a direct and in-person examination of billing systems and internal controls of small providers of services or suppliers to determine program compliance and to suggest more efficient or effective means of achieving such compliance.

GAO Evaluation. Not later than two years after the date the demonstration program is first implemented, the Comptroller General, in consultation with the Inspector General of the Department of Health and Human Services, shall conduct an evaluation of the demonstration program. The evaluation shall include a determination of whether claims error rates are reduced for small providers of services or suppliers who participated in the program and the extent of improper payments made as a result of the demonstration program. The Comptroller General must submit a report to the Secretary and the Congress on such evaluation and must include in such report recommendations regarding the continuation or extension of the demonstration program.

Financial participation by providers. The provision of technical assistance to a small provider of services or supplier under the demonstration program is conditioned upon the small provider of services or supplier paying an amount estimated (and disclosed in advance of a provider's or supplier's participation in the program) to be equal to 25 percent of the cost of the technical assistance.

Authorization of appropriations. These are authorized to be appropriated, from amounts not otherwise appropriated in the Treasury, such sums as may be necessary to carry out this section. The Secretary is required to establish a demonstration program to provide technical assistance to small providers and suppliers to improve compliance with the applicable requirements of the Medicare program. Technical assistance includes: (1) an evaluation and recommendations on billing and related systems; and (2) information and assistance on policies and procedures including coding and reimbursement policies. The small provider of services or supplies is defined as a provider with fewer than 25 full-time equivalents employees; or a supplier with fewer than 10 full-time equivalent employees.

Qualification of Contractors. In conducting the demonstration program, the Secretary is required to enter into contract with qualified organizations such as peer review organizations or entities with appropriate expertise with billing systems of the full range of providers of services and supplies to provide technical assistance. In awarding the contracts, the Secretary is required to consider any prior investigations of the entity's work by the Inspector General of Department of Health and Human Services or the Comptroller General of the United States.

Description of technical assistance. The technical assistance provided under the demonstration program must include a direct and in-person examination of billing systems and internal controls of small providers of services or supplies to determine program compliance.

GAO evaluation and report. The Inspector General of the Department of Health and Human Services is required to conduct an evaluation of the demonstration program. The evaluation must include an determination of the feasibility of claims error rates for small provider of services or suppliers, and the extent of improper payments made as a result of the demonstration program. The Inspector General is

¶833

required to submit a report to the Secretary and the Congress on the evaluation and recommendations on the continuation or extension of the demonstration program.

Effective date. Effective upon enactment.

Act Sec. 922. Law at ¶ 11,030.

¶ 835

Beneficiary Outreach Demonstration Programs

Demonstration on advice and assistance. The Secretary is required to establish a demonstration program under which Medicare specialists employed by the Department of Health and Human Services can provide advice and assistance to Medicare beneficiaries at existing local offices of the Social Security Administration.

Location. The demonstration program must be conducted in at least six offices or areas. In selecting the offices and areas, the Secretary must provide preference for offices with a high volume of visits by Medicare beneficiaries.

Assistance for rural beneficiaries. The Secretary must provide for the selection of at least two rural areas to participate in the demonstration program. In conducting the demonstration program in such rural areas, the Secretary must provide for Medicare specialists to travel among local offices in a rural area on a scheduled basis.

Duration. The demonstration program must be conducted over a three-year period.

Evaluation.. The Secretary is required to provide for an evaluation of the demonstration program. The evaluation must include an analysis of: (1) the utilization and beneficiary satisfaction with the assistance provided under the program; and (2) the cost-effectiveness of providing beneficiary assistance through out-stationing Medicare specialists at local social security offices.

Report. The Secretary is required to submit to Congress a report on the evaluation and recommendation regarding the feasibility of permanently out-stationing Medicare specialists at local Social Security offices.

Effective date. Effective upon enactment.

Act Sec. 924. Law at ¶ 11,050.

APPEALS AND RECOVERY

¶ 901

Transfer of Responsibility for Medicare Appeals

ALJ functions. No later than April 1, 2004, the Commissioner of Social Security and the Secretary of the Department of Health and Human Services (HHS) are required to develop and send to Congress a plan to transfer responsibility for Medicare appeals. Between July 1, 2005, and October 1, 2005, the transition plan must be implemented and responsibility for administrative law judge (ALJ) hearings under Medicare law will be transferred from the Social Security Administration (SSA) to HHS.

The transfer plan must include information on the following:

  (1) projected workload and staffing requirements;

(2) funding levels required for FY 2005 and subsequent fiscal years to carry out the functions transferred under the plan;

(3) a transition timetable;

(4) specific regulations to govern the appeals process;

(5) development of a unified case tracking system;

(6) the feasibility of developing a process to give binding, precedential authority to decisions of the HHS Departmental Appeals Board (DAB) that address broad legal issues;

(7) the feasibility of filing appeals with ALJs electronically, and conducting hearings using tele-conference or video-conference technologies; and

(8) the steps that should be taken to ensure the independence of ALJs from the Centers for Medicare & Medicaid Services (CMS) and its contractors by placing ALJs in an office that is functionally and operationally separate from CMS;

(9) the steps that should be taken to provide for an appropriate geographic distribution of ALJs;

(10) the steps that should be taken by HHS to hire ALJs and support staff;

(11) the establishment of performance standards for ALJs with respect to timeliness for issuing decisions in Medicare cases, taking into account requirements for the independence of ALJs in decision making;

(12) the feasibility of shared office space, support staff, and other resources between HHS and SSA, with appropriate reimbursement; and

(13) the training that should be provided to ALJs with respect to Medicare laws and regulations.

The Government Accounting Office of the U.S. Comptroller General (GAO) must report to Congress on the plan within six months after the transition plan is submitted to Congress.

Appropriations. Funds may be appropriated from the Federal Hospital Insurance Trust Fund and the Federal Supplemental Medical Insurance Trust Fund to (1) increase the number of ALJs, (2) improve education and training opportunities for ALJs, and (3) increase the staff of the DAB.

Effective date. Effective upon enactment.

Act Sec. 931, adding non-codified provision and amending Sec. 1869(f)(2)(A)(i) of the Social Security Act. Law at ¶2305 and 11,080.

¶ 903

Process for Expedited Access to Review

Access to judicial review. As an exception to the requirement that all administrative review must be completed before judicial review, the Secretary is required to establish a process for expedited review in certain cases. A provider of services, a supplier or an individual Medicare beneficiary who has filed an appeal before the Departmental Appeals Board (DAB) will have access to judicial review when a review entity determines that the DAB does not have the authority to decide the question of law or regulation relevant to the matters in controversy and that there is no material issue of fact in dispute. The appellant may make such a request only once with respect to a question of law or regulation in a case on appeal.

Review entity. A "review entity" is a panel consisting of three members who ALJs or members of the DAB and are appointed by the Secretary to make determinations on expedited review.

Prompt determinations. If an appellant requests a determination by a review entity as described above, and if the appropriate documents and materials accompany the request, the determination of the review entity must be made within 60 days after the date the review entity receives the appellant's request and accompanying materials. The review entity's determination is considered a final decision and not subject to review by the Secretary.

Time limit for court claim. If the appropriate review entity determines that there are no material issues of fact in dispute and that the only issue is one of law or regulation that the DAB does not have the authority to decide, the appellant may bring a civil action by filing a court claim within 60 days of the panel's determination. If the review entity fails to make a determination within 60 days of receiving the request for a determination, the appellant may bring a civil action within 60 days of the review entity's determination or within 60 days after the end of the period provided for the review determination.

Interest. Interest begins to accrue on the amount in controversy on the first day of the first month after the deadline for filing the civil action.

Venue. Court action must be brought in the United States district court for the judicial district in which the appellant is located (or, in the case of an action brought jointly by more than one applicant, the judicial district in which the greatest number of applicants are located) or in the District Court for the District of Columbia.

Provider agreements. Expedited access to judicial review will also be available to providers whose Medicare agreements have been rejected or have not been renewed. Nothing in this provision may be construed to affect the application of any remedy imposed on a skilled nursing facility during the pendency of an appeal under this provision.

Effective date. This provision applies to appeals filed on or after October 1, 2004.

Act Sec. 932(a), amending Sec. 1869(b) and Sec. 932(b), amending Sec. 1866(h)(1). Law at ¶2290 and 2305.

¶ 905
Expedited Review of SNF Appeals

Expedited review of provider agreement determinations. The Secretary must implement a process to expedite review of the following remedies imposed against a skilled nursing facility (SNF): (1) termination of participation, (2) denial of payment for new admissions, (3) appointment of temporary management, or (4) loss of approval for a nurse aide training program due to a finding by CMS of substandard care. Priority is given to cases where termination is imposed.

When a SNF has incurred a civil money penalty that is not related to the quality of care provided to the residents of the facility, the Secretary may waive the statutory requirement that a SNF nurse aide training program may not be approved for a two-year period after the SNF incurs a penalty of $5,000 or more.

Appropriation of funds. Additional funds will be appropriated to reduce by 50 percent the average time for administrative determinations on appeals with respect to SNF conditions of participation. Additional sums will be appropriated for FY 2004 and each subsequent fiscal year as may be necessary to increase the number of administrative law judges (and their staffs) at the DAB and to educate such judges and staff on long-term care issues.

Effective date. This provision applies to appeals filed on or after October 1, 2004.

Act Sec. 932(c) and (d), amending Secs. 1866(h)(1), 1819(f)(2), and 1919(f)(2) of the Social Security Act. Law at ¶2110, 2290, and 2400.

¶ 906
Revision of Medicare Appeals Process

Evidence. A provider of services or a supplier may not introduce evidence in any appeal that was not presented at the reconsideration conducted by the qualified independent contractor, unless there is good cause that precluded the introduction of such evidence at or before that reconsideration.

Use of patients' records. Qualified independent contractors may use patients' records in addition to other evidence when conducting reconsideration of Medicare initial determinations.

Notice required for Medicare appeals. When an initial determination or redetermination results in a denial of a claim for benefits, the notice must be provided in printed form and written in a manner calculated to be understood by the beneficiary. The notice must include: the reasons for the determination or redetermination; the procedures for obtaining additional information concerning the determination or redetermination; and notification of the right to appeal with instructions on how to initiate an appeal.

The person provided the notice may obtain, on request, information on the specific provision of the policy, manual, or regulation used in making the determination or redetermination. Prior to this change, beneficiaries only received a brief statement about the initial determination on the Medicare Summary Notice.

Reconsideration. Any decision with respect to a reconsideration of a qualified independent contractor must be in writing in a manner calculated to be understood by the beneficiary and must include, to the extent appropriate: (1) a detailed explanation of the decision as well as a discussion of the pertinent facts and applicable regulations applied in making the decision; (2) notification of the right to appeal and instructions on how to initiate an appeal; and (3) in the case of a determination of whether an item or service is reasonable and necessary for the diagnosis or treatment of illness or injury, an explanation of the medical or scientific rationale for the decision.

Notice of right to appeal. Notice of the ALJ's decision must be in writing in a manner calculated to be understood by the beneficiary and must include: (1) the specific reasons for the determination (including, to the extent appropriate, a summary of the clinical or scientific evidence used in making the determination); (2) the procedures for obtaining additional information concerning the decision; and (3) notification of the right to appeal the decision and instructions on how to initiate an appeal.

Effective date. Effective upon enactment, except the provision on evidence, which is effective October 1, 2004.

Act Sec. 933, amending Sec. 1869(a) and (b), (c)(3)(B)(i), (c)(3)(E), and (d). Law at ¶2305 and 11,086.

¶ 907

Qualified Independent Contractors

Changes. The Benefits Improvement and Protection Act of 2000 (PubLNo. 106-554) (BIPA) established a new and independent second level of review that would be conducted by at least 12 qualified independent contractors (QICs). That change was not implemented prior to this legislation. The qualifications of the contractors and their reviewer employees have been clarified, and the required number of contractors has been reduced to at least four.

Contractor requirements. The entity or organization serving as a QIC must have sufficient staffing and sufficient medical, legal, and other expertise (including knowledge of the Medicare program) to carry out its duties on a timely basis. A QIC must not conduct any activities in a case unless the QIC: (1) is not a related party; (2) does not have a material familial, financial, or professional relationship with a related party involved in a case; and (3) does not otherwise have a conflict of interest with a related party. A "related party" is:

(1) the Secretary, the Medicare administrative contractor involved, or any fiduciary, officer, director, or employee of HHS or of the contractor;

(2) the individual (or authorized representative);

(3) the health care professional that provides the items or services involved in the case;

(4) the institution at which the items or services (or treatment) involved in the case are provided;

(5) the manufacturer of any drug or other item that is included in the items or services involved in the case; and

(6) any other party determined under any regulations to have a substantial interest in the case involved.

Reviewer requirements. Compensation provided by a QIC to a reviewer in connection with a review must not be contingent on the decision rendered by the reviewer. Each reviewing professional must be a physician or health care professional who is appropriately credentialed or licensed in one or more states to deliver health care services and has medical expertise in the field of practice that is appropriate for the items or services at issue.

Transition. In applying Sec. 1869(g) of the Social Security Act, any reference to a Medicare administrative contractor shall be deemed to include a reference to a fiscal intermediary and a carrier.

Effective date. The eligibility requirements of QICs and QIC reviews are effective as if included in the respective provisions of subtitle C of title V of BIPA , which were amendments to Sec. 1869 effective with respect to determinations made on or after Oct. 1, 2002.

Act Sec. 933(d), amending Sec. 1869(c)(3) and (4). Law at ¶ 2305.

¶ 908

Prepayment Review

Limitation on random reviews. A Medicare administrative contractor may conduct random prepayment review only to develop a contractor-wide or program-wide claims payment error rates or under such additional circumstances as may be provided under regulations, developed in consultation with providers of services and suppliers. The contractor may conduct such review only in accordance with a standard protocol for random prepayment audits developed by the Secretary.

The term "random prepayment review" means a demand for the production of records or documentation absent cause with respect to a claim.

Non-random reviews. Non-random prepayment review of a provider of services or supplier are not permitted when the provider of services or supplier identifies an improper billing practice unless there is a likelihood of sustained or high level of payment error.

Effective date. Effective one year after the date of enactment.

Act Sec. 934, amending Sec. 1874A. Law at ¶ 2320 and 11,090.

¶ 909
Recovery of Overpayments

Use of repayment plans. Applicable to requests for repayment plans made after the date of enactment, when repayment, within 30 days by a provider of services or supplier, of an overpayment would constitute a hardship, the Secretary of HHS is required to enter into a plan with the provider of services or supplier for the repayment (through offset or otherwise) of the overpayment over a period of at least six months but not longer than three years (or not longer than five years in the case of extreme hardship, as determined by the Secretary). Interest will accrue on the balance through the period of repayment.

Limitation on recoupment. Applicable to actions taken after enactment, when a provider has requested reconsideration by a qualified independent contractor (QIC), the Secretary may not recoup the overpayment until the date the decision on the reconsideration has been rendered.

Use of extrapolation. Applicable to samples initiated one year after the date of enactment, a contractor may not use extrapolation to determine overpayment amounts to be recouped unless there is a sustained or high level of payment error; or documented educational intervention has failed to correct the payment error.

Supporting documentation. For a provider of services or supplier previously overpaid, a Medicare contractor may request the periodic production of records or supporting documentation for a limited sample of submitted claims to ensure that the previous practice is not continuing.

Consent settlement. The Secretary may use a consent settlement to settle a projected overpayment.

Payment audits. If a Medicare contractor decides to conduct a post-payment audit of a provider of services or supplier, the contractor must provide the provider of services or supplier with written notice (which may be in electronic form) of the intent to conduct such an audit.

Effective date. Effective upon enactment, with exceptions described above. Not later than one year after enactment, the Secretary is required to establish a process for overutilization of billing codes and establish a standard methodology for selection of sample claims for abnormal billing patterns.

Act Sec. 935, adding Sec. 1893(f). Law at ¶ 2370 and 11,095.

¶ 911

Provider Enrollment Process

Appeals. The Secretary must adopt regulations that would establish procedures under which (1) there are deadlines for actions on applications for enrollment or renewal of enrollment, and (2) there is a mechanism for providers of services, physicians, practitioners, and suppliers to appeal denials of applications to enroll or renew enrollment and a deadline for consideration of such appeals. The Secretary is required to consult with providers and suppliers before changing the provider enrollment forms.

Effective date. The required procedures must be established within six months after the date of enactment. The requirement for consultation before changing the enrollment forms is effective for changes beginning January 1, 2004.

Act Sec. 936, amending Sec. 1866 of the Social Security Act. Law at ¶ 2290 and 11,097.

¶ 912

Correction of Minor Errors and Omissions

Exemption to appeal process. A provider of services or supplier will be given an opportunity to correct an error or omission in a Medicare claim without the need to initiate an appeal. This process will include the ability to resubmit corrected claims.

Effective date. Not later than one year after the date of enactment.

Act Sec. 937. Law at ¶ 11,100.

¶ 913

Prior Determination Process and ABNs

New process. The Secretary shall establish a prior determination process for eligible requesters:

(1) A participating physician who requests a determination with respect to physicians' services to be furnished to a beneficiary who has consented to the physician's request; and

(2) A beneficiary who makes a request for a determination with respect to a physicians' service for which the individual receives from a physician an advance beneficiary notice (ABN).

GAO report. Not later than 18 months after the date of the enactment, the GAO must report on the use of ABNs and the response by beneficiaries. Not later than 36 months, the GAO must report on the use of the prior determination process under this section.

Effective date. Not later than 18 months after the date of the enactment.

Act Sec. 938, amending Sec. 1869 of the Social Security Act. Law at ¶ 2305 and 11,110.

¶ 915

Appeals by Providers When There is No Other Party Available

Deceased beneficiary. If a beneficiary dies before assigning appeal rights, the Secretary must permit a provider or supplier to appeal a payment denial by a Medicare contractor.

Effective date. The provision is effective for items and services furnished on or after enactment.

Act Sec. 939, amending Sec. 1870 of the Social Security Act. Law at ¶2310.

¶916
Revision to Appeals Timeframes and Amounts

Time limits for redeterminations. The time limits for concluding a redetermination of a claim and for reconsideration by a qualified independent contractor are extended to 60 days (from the current limit of 30 days). The minimum amount in controversy for hearings or judicial review will be increased by the percentage increase in the medical care component of the consumer price index for urban consumers, for July 2003 to the July preceding the year involved. The amount will be rounded to the nearest multiple of $10.

Effective date. The adjustment of the minimum amount in controversy is effective beginning in 2005.

Act Sec. 940, amending Secs. 1869(a)(3)(C)(ii); (b)(1)(E); (c)(3)(C)(i); 1852(g)(5), and 1876(b)(5)(B) of the Social Security Act. Law at ¶2305, 2330, and 2256.

¶917
Mediation Process for Local Medical Review Policies

Process. A mediation process will be established, using a physician trained in mediation and employed by the CMS.

The mediator will mediate in disputes between groups representing providers of services, suppliers, and the medical director for a Medicare administrative contractor whenever the regional administrator involved determines that there was a systematic pattern and a large volume of complaints from such groups regarding decisions of the director or there is a complaint from the co-chair of the advisory committee for that contractor to the regional administrator regarding such a dispute.

Effective date. Effective upon enactment.

Act Sec. 940A, adding Sec. 1869(i) and amending Sec. 1874A(b)(3)(A)(i). Law at ¶2305 and 2320.

MISCELLANEOUS PROVISIONS

¶941
E & M Documentation Guidelines

Prohibition. The Secretary will not implement any new or modified documentation guidelines or clinical examples for evaluation and management (E&M) physician services under Medicare unless the Secretary

(1) has developed the guidelines in collaboration with practicing physicians (including both generalists and specialists) and provided for an assessment of the proposed guidelines by the physician community;

(2) has established a plan that contains specific goals, including a schedule, for improving the use of such guidelines;

(3) has conducted appropriate and representative pilot projects to test modifications to the guidelines;

(4) finds that the guidelines have met established objectives; and

(5) has established, and is implementing, a program to educate physicians on the use of the guidelines.

The Secretary must make changes to the manner in which existing evaluation and management documentation guidelines are implemented to reduce paperwork burdens on physicians.

Established objectives for the guidelines are the following:

(1) identify clinically relevant documentation needed to code accurately and assess coding levels accurately;

(2) decrease the level of non-clinically pertinent and burdensome documentation time and content in the physician's medical record;

(3) increase accuracy by reviewers; and

(4) educate both physicians and reviewers.

Pilot project. The Secretary is required to conduct, in development and throughout the planning and operational stages of the project, in consultation with practicing physicians (including both generalists and specialists), representative pilot projects to test the proposed guidelines. The projects will be voluntary less than one-year in duration.

Study of simpler system. The Secretary is required to study the development of a simpler, alternative system of requirements for documentation accompanying claims for evaluation and management physician services for which Medicare payment is made. A study is also required to consider systems other than current coding and documentation requirements for payment for such physician services.

Appropriate coding of office visits. The Secretary is also required to conduct a study of the appropriateness of coding in cases of extended office visits in which there is no diagnosis made. Not later than October 8, 2005, the Secretary must submit a report to Congress on such study and shall include recommendations on how to code appropriately for such visits in a manner that takes into account the amount of time the physician spent with the patient.

Effective date. Effective upon enactment.

Sec. 941. Law at ¶ 11,120.

¶ 942
Improvement in Oversight of Technology and Coverage

Council for technology and innovation. The Secretary will be required to establish a Council for Technology and Innovation within the Centers for Medicare and Medicaid Services (CMS). The council will be composed of senior CMS staff and clinicians and will be chaired by the Executive Coordinator for Technology and Innovation appointed by the Secretary. The Council will coordinate Medicare's coverage, coding, and payment processes with respect to new technologies and procedures, including drug therapies. The Executive Coordinator will serve as the single point of contact for outside groups and entities overseeing the execution of the Council's duties.

Payment basis for new lab tests. The Secretary will be required to establish procedures (by regulation) for determining the basis for and amount of payments for new clinical diagnostic laboratory tests. "New laboratory tests" are those assigned a new, or substantially revised, Health Care Procedure Coding System (HCPCS) code on or after January 1, 2005. The Secretary will be required to:

(1) provide a list of tests for which payments are being establish in that year;

(2) publish a notice of a meeting in the Federal Register on the day the list becomes available;

(3) hold the public meeting no earlier than 30 days after the notice to receive public comments and recommendations; and

(4) take into account the comments, recommendations and accompanying data in both proposed and final payment determinations.

The Secretary is also required to make available to the public the criteria and available data considered in making the payment determinations.

GAO study. The General Accounting Office (GAO) will be required to study which external data can be collected in a shorter time frame by CMS to use in calculating payments for inpatient hospital services. The study may include an evaluation of the feasibility and appropriateness of using quarterly samples or special surveys. The study must include an analysis of whether other executive agencies are best suited to collect this information. The report will be due to Congress no later than October 1, 2004.

ICS codes. If the National Committee on Vital and Health Statistics has not made a recommendation to the Secretary by enactment regarding implementation of the ICD-10 coding system for diagnosis and procedures, the Secretary may adopt such standards one year after the date of enactment of the Act.

Effective date. Effective upon enactment.

Act Sec. 942, amending Sec. 1868 and 1833(h) of the Social Security Act. Law at ¶ 2121H and 2300.

¶ 943

Treatment of Hospitals for Certain MSP Services

Reference laboratory services. The Secretary may not require hospitals, including critical access hospitals, to ask questions or obtain information relating to Medicare secondary payer provisions in the case of reference laboratory services if the Secretary does not require independent laboratories to obtain the same information. Reference laboratory services are clinical laboratory diagnostic tests, or the interpretation of such tests, or both, furnished without a face-to-face encounter between the beneficiary and the hospital involved and in which the hospital submits a claim only for the test or interpretation.

Effective date. Effective upon enactment.

Act Sec. 943. Law at ¶ 11,140.

¶ 944

EMTALA Improvements

Screening and stabilization services. Emergency room services provided to screen and stabilize a Medicare beneficiary furnished after January 1, 2004, will be evaluated as reasonable and necessary on the basis of the information available to the treating physician or practitioner at the time the services were ordered. The evaluation as to whether the item or service was reasonable and necessary will include the patient's presenting symptoms or complaint and not the patient's principal diagnosis. The Secretary will not be able to consider the frequency with which the item or service was provided to the patient before or after the time of admission or visit.

Investigations. The Secretary will be required to establish a procedure to notify hospitals and physicians when an EMTALA investigation is closed.

QIO Review. Except in the case where a delay would jeopardize the health and safety of individuals, the Secretary will be required to request a quality improvement organization (QIO) review before making a compliance determination that would terminate a hospital's Medicare participation because of EMTALA violations. A period of five days will be allowed for the review, and the QIO must provide a copy of the report on its findings to the hospital or physician involved. This provision will apply to terminations initiated on or after enactment of the Act.

Effective date. Effective upon enactment.

Sec. 944, amending Secs. 1862, 1867(d), 1867(d)(3) of the Social Security Act. Law at ¶ 2295.

¶ 945

Emergency Medical Treatment and Labor Act (EMTALA) Technical Advisory Group

EMTALA technical advisory group. The Secretary will establish a 19-member technical advisory group to review issues related to the Emergency Medical Treatment and Active Labor Act (EMTALA) at Sec. 1867 of the law. Members of the technical advisory group will be nominated and will include: the CMS administrator, the Inspector General, four hospital representatives (including two that have not been cited for EMTALA violations), seven practicing physicians with no more than one physician in any particular field, two patient representatives, two staff members involved in EMTALA investigations for different CMS regional offices, one from a state survey office involved in EMTALA investigations and one from a peer review organization.

The advisory group is responsible for reviewing EMTALA regulations and making recommendations regarding the regulations. They will solicit comments and recommendations from hospitals, physicians and the public regarding the regulations. The advisory group will meet twice a year and will end 30 months after its first meeting.

Effective date. Effective upon enactment.

Sec. 945. Law at ¶ 11,150.

¶ 946

Arrangements to Provide Core Hospice Services in Certain Circumstances

Current law. Hospice must currently provide certain core services directly under Medicare. The core services include nursing care, medical social services, and counseling services. Other services may be provided directly by the hospice or under arrangements with other hospices. The hospice, however, maintains responsibility for the management of all services provided, regardless of the facility in which they are furnished.

Explanation of provision. A hospice may, under extraordinary circumstances, enter into arrangements with another hospice to provide core hospice services. These extraordinary circumstances include: unanticipated high patient loads, staffing shortages due to illness or other events, or temporary travel of a patient outside a hospice program's service area. The hospice program making these arrangements will bill and be paid for the hospice care.

Effective date. Applicable to hospice care provided on or after enactment.

Act Sec. 946, amending Sec. 1861(dd)(5) of the Social Security Act. Law at ¶2280A.

¶ 947
Application of OSHA Bloodborne Pathogens Standard to Certain Hospitals

OSHA bloodborne pathogens standard. Hospitals not otherwise subject to the Occupational Safety and Health Act of 1970 (OSHA), must comply with the Bloodborne Pathogens standard. Hospitals failing to comply with this standard will not be terminated from Medicare participation but are subject to a civil money penalty. The penalty will be similar to the penalties imposed under Sec. 17 of OSHA by hospitals that are subject to the provisions of OSHA, and the civil money penalties will be imposed and collected in the same manner as penalties under Sec. 1128A of the Social Security Act.

Effective date. July 1, 2004.

Act Sec. 947, amending Sec. 1866 of the Social Security Act. Law at ¶2290.

¶ 948
BIPA-Related Technical Amendments and Corrections

Terminology. Statutory references in the Medicare, Medicaid and SCHIP Benefits Improvement and Protection Act of 2000 (BIPA) to the Social Security Act are changed to Public Health Service Act, and references to "policy" are changed to "determination."

Effective date. As if included in BIPA.

Act. Sec. 948, amending Secs. 1114, 1154, 1862, 1852, and 1869. Law at ¶2010, 2026, 2256, 2280J, 2280K, 2280L, 2280M, and 2305.

¶ 949
Authority to Waive a Program Exclusion

Waiver of program exclusion. The minimum period of exclusion for mandatory exclusions for convictions of program-related crimes, convictions related to program abuse, or a felony conviction related to health care fraud or related to controlled substances, must be not less than five years. At the request of an administrator of a federal health care program, the Secretary may waive program exclusion, except for an exclusion due to patient abuse or neglect, if (1) the exclusion would impose a hardship on Medicare beneficiaries and (2) the provider is a sole community physician or the sole source of essential specialized services in a community.

Effective date. Upon enactment.

Act Sec. 949, amending section 1128(c)(3)(B). Law at ¶2016.

¶ 950

Treatment of Certain Dental Claims

Supplemental coverage. A group health plan providing supplemental or secondary coverage to Medicare beneficiaries will not be able to require dentists to obtain a claim denial from Medicare for noncovered dental services before paying the claim. However, a group health plan may required a claims determination in cases involving inpatient dental hospital services.

Effective date. This provision is effective 60 days after enactment.

Sec. 950, amending Sec. 1862 adding new Sec. 1862(k)(1) of the Social Security Act. Law at ¶ 2280L.

¶ 952

Revisions to Reassignment Provisions

Billing entities. Entities, as defined by the Secretary, may receive Medicare payment for services provided by a physician or other person if the service is provided under a contractual arrangement. Under this provision, the entity must submit the bill and the contractual arrangement must meet appropriate program integrity and other safeguard requirements.

Effective date. Applicable to payments made on or after the date of enactment.

Sec. 952, amending Sec. 1842(b)(6) of the Social Security Act. Law at ¶ 2180F.

¶ 953

Other Provisions

GAO report on physician compensation. GAO is required to report to Congress, no later than six months from enactment, the appropriateness of updates in the conversion factor including the appropriateness of the sustainable growth rate formula for fiscal year (FY) 2002 and after. The report would include an examination of the stability and predictability of the updates and rate and also alternatives for use of the sustainable growth rate in updates. GAO is also required to report to Congress, no later than 12 months from enactment, all aspects of physician compensation for Medicare services. This report will review alternatives to the physician fee schedule.

Annual publication of the list of National Coverage Determinations. An annual list of national coverage decisions made under Medicare during the previous year must be published by the Secretary. The list of decisions must include information on how to get more information about the determinations and will be published in a publicly available annual publication.

GAO report on flexibility in applying home health conditions of participation to patients who are not Medicare beneficiaries. The GAO is required to report to Congress, no later than six months after enactment, on the implications if there were flexibility in the application of Medicare conditions of participation for home health agencies with respect to groups or types of patients who are not Medicare beneficiaries. The report must include an analysis of the impact such flexible application might have on clinical operations and recipients of such services. The report must also include an analysis of methods for monitoring the quality of care provided to such recipients.

Effective date. Effective upon enactment.

Act. Sec. 953. Law at ¶ 11,170.

OIG report on notices relating to use of hospital lifetime reserve days. No later than one year after the date of enactment, the Office of the Inspector General (OIG) is required to report to Congress on the extent to which hospitals provide notice to Medicare beneficiaries according to applicable requirements, before they use the 60 lifetime reserve days under the hospital benefit. The report must include the appropriateness and feasibility of hospitals providing a notice to beneficiaries before they exhaust the lifetime reserve days.

Effective date. Effective upon enactment.

Act Sec. 953. Law at ¶ 11,170.

COMBATTING WASTE, FRAUD AND ABUSE

¶ 1002

Competitive Acquisition of Certain Items and Services

Quality enhancement and fraud reduction. The Secretary is required to establish and implement quality standards for suppliers of: items and services of durable medical equipment, prosthetics and orthotics, and certain other items and services. Suppliers of the following items and services are included: items of durable medical equipment; prosthetic devices; orthotics and prosthetics; medical supplies; home dialysis supplies and equipment; therapeutic shoes; parenteral and enteral nutrients, equipment, and supplies; electromyogram devices; salivation devices; blood products; and transfusion machines. The Secretary is explicitly authorized to establish the quality standards by program memorandum on a prospective basis after consultation with representatives of relevant parties. The standards are required to be posted on the Internet website of CMS. In addition, the Secretary is required to designate one or more independent accreditation organizations not later than one year after the date the quality standards are implemented. The quality standards may not be less stringent than the quality standards otherwise in place.

Clinical conditions for payment standards. The Secretary is required to establish standards for clinical conditions for payment for covered durable medical equipment that include the specification of types or classes of covered items that require, as a condition of payment, a face-to-face examination and a prescription for the item. The standards are required to be established for those covered items for which there has been a proliferation of use, consistent findings of charges for covered items that are not delivered, or consistent findings of falsification of documentation to provide for payment of such covered items. Beginning with the date of enactment, payment may not be made for motorized or power wheelchairs unless a physician, physician assistant, nurse practitioner, or a clinical nurse specialist has conducted a face-to-face examination of the individual and written a prescription for the item. Medicare payment is not permitted unless the item meets the standards established for clinical condition of coverage.

Competitive acquisition programs. The Secretary is required to establish and implement programs under which competitive acquisition areas are established throughout the United States to award contracts for competitively priced durable medical equipment (DME); items used in infusion; drugs and supplies used in conjunction with DME medical supplies; home dialysis supplies; therapeutic shoes; enteral nutrients, equipment, and supplies; electromyogram devices; salivation devices; blood products; transfusion medicine; and off-the-shelf orthotics (requiring minimal self-adjustment for appropriate use) that would replace the Medicare fee schedule payments. In starting the programs, the Secretary is required to establish competitive acquisition areas, but would be able to exempt rural areas and areas with low population density within urban areas that are not competitive, unless a significant national market exists through mail order for a particular item or service. The Secretary is also permitted to contract with entities to implement the competitive bidding program. Also, the Secretary is permitted to consider the clinical efficiency and the value of specific items within HCPCS codes, including whether some items have a greater therapeutic advantage to individuals in establishing the categories and products that would be subject to bidding.

Physician authorization. The Secretary may also establish a process where a physician would be able to prescribe a particular brand or mode of delivery of an item or service within a particular healthcare procedure code (HCPCS) if the physician determines that use of the item or service would avoid an adverse medical outcome for the beneficiary, as determined by the Secretary, although this could not affect the amount of payment otherwise applicable.

Program phase-in. The programs will be phased-in so that competition under the programs occurs in 10 of the largest metropolitan statistical areas in 2007; 80 of the largest metropolitan statistical areas in 2009; and remaining areas after 2009. The Secretary is permitted to phase-in first items and services with the highest cost and highest volume, or those items and services that the Secretary determines have the largest savings potential. The Secretary may exempt items and services for which competitive acquisition would not be likely to result in significant savings.

Excluded items and services. Exclusions from the competitive acquisition are: inhalation drugs; parenteral nutrients, equipment, and supplies; and class III devices; that is, those that sustain or support life, are implanted, or present potential unreasonable risk (e.g., implantable infusion pumps and heart valve replacements) and are subject to premarket approval by the Food and Drug Administration.

Rented items of DME. The Secretary is required to establish a process where existing rental agreements for covered DME items entered into contract before implementation of this program would not be affected. The supplier would be required to provide for appropriate servicing and replacement of these rental items.

Program requirements. Certain requirements for the competitive acquisition program are established. Specifically, the Secretary cannot award contracts in an area unless the following conditions are met: (1) entities meet quality standards established by the Secretary; (2) entities meet financial standards specified by the Secretary, taking into account the needs of small providers; (3) total amounts paid under the contracts are expected to be less than would otherwise be paid; and (4) beneficiary access to multiple suppliers would be maintained. Contracts are subject to terms and conditions that the Secretary may specify and are required to be re-competed at least every three years. The Secretary is required to award contracts to multiple entities submitting bids in each area for an item or service and has the authority to limit the number of contractors in a competitive acquisition area to the number needed to meet projected demand for covered items and services.

Payments to contractors. Payment for competitively priced items and services will be based on bids submitted and accepted. The Secretary is required to determine a single payment amount for each item or service in each competitive acquisition area. Medicare payment will be equal to 80 percent of the payment amount determined. Beneficiaries will pay the remaining 20 percent (after meeting the Part B deductible). Payment for any item or services can be made only on an assignment-related basis meaning that the supplier bills Medicare and accepts Medicare payment as payment in full. The use of advanced beneficiary notices is not precluded by this program.

The Secretary is required to take appropriate steps to ensure that small suppliers of items and services have an opportunity to be considered for participation in this program. The Secretary cannot pay for items furnished by a contractor unless the contractor has submitted a bid to supply the item and the contract has been awarded. The Secretary is permitted to waive certain provisions of the Federal Acquisition Regulation that are necessary for the efficient implementation of this program, other than those relating to confidentiality of information.

Quality assurance. The Secretary is permitted to contract with an appropriate entity to address beneficiary complaints, provide beneficiary outreach and education services, and monitor the quality of items and services provided.

Judicial review. The conference agreement prohibits administrative or judicial review of the establishment of payments amounts, the awarding of contracts, the designation of competitive acquisition areas, the phased-in implementation, the selection of items and services for competitive acquisition or the bidding structure and number of contractors.

Program Advisory and Oversight Committee established. A Program Advisory and Oversight Committee ("Committee") with members appointed by the Secretary is will be established. The Committee is required to provide advice to the Secretary regarding the implementation of the program; data collection requirements; proposals for efficient interaction among manufacturers and distributors of the items and services, providers, and beneficiaries; the establishment of quality standards, and other functions specified by the Secretary. The provisions of the Federal Advisory Committee Act do not apply to this Committee. The Committee is required to end on December 31, 2009.

Report. The Secretary is required to report to Congress by July 1, 2009, on savings, reductions in cost-sharing, access to items and services, and beneficiary satisfaction under the competitive acquisition program.

Clinical laboratory services demonstration project. The Secretary is required to conduct a demonstration program on using competitive acquisition for clinical laboratory tests that are furnished without a face-to-face encounter between the individual and the hospital personnel or physician performing the test. The terms and conditions of the demonstration are to include the application of CLIA quality standards. An initial report to Congress is required of the Secretary no later than December 31, 2005, with progress and final reports as the Secretary determines appropriate.

Payment updates. For durable medical equipment, prosthetic devices, prosthetics and orthotics, the update will be 0 percentage points in 2004 through 2008. After 2008, for those items not included in competitive bidding the update will be the consumer price index (CPI). For 2005, the payment amount for certain items, oxygen and oxygen equipment, standard wheelchairs, nebulizers, diabetic lancets and testing strips, and hospital beds and air mattresses, will be reduced. The Secretary will take the payment amount otherwise determined and reduce it by the percentage difference between the amount of payment otherwise determined for the specific item for 2002 and the amount of payment for the specific item and HCPC code under chapter 89 of title 5, United States Code. An OIG report on oxygen will be available in the spring of 2004.

Class III medical devices. For class III medical devices the update in 2004, 2005, and 2006 is equal to the percentage increase in the consumer price index for all urban consumers (CPI-U) for the 12- month period ending with June of the previous year. In 2007 the percentage change for class III medical devices is to be determined by the

¶1002

Secretary after taking into account recommendations made by the Comptroller General in a report on class III medical devices. In 2008 the update is determined by the amount paid in 2007 updated by the CPI. In subsequent years the CPI is the update.

Other payment issues and the inherent reasonableness authority. For covered items and services furnished beginning January 1, 2009, items and services included in the competitive acquisition program would be paid as determined under that program and the Secretary would be able to use this payment information to adjust the payment amounts for DME, off-the-shelf orthotics, and other items and services that are supplied in an area that is not a competitive acquisition area. The inherent reasonableness authority for DME; off-the-shelf orthotics; medical supplies; home dialysis supplies; therapeutic shoes; enteral nutrients, equipment, and supplies; electromyogram devices; salivation devices; blood products; and transfusion medicine is not eliminated, but if the Secretary uses the competitive acquisition program information to adjust payments, then inherent reasonableness authority cannot be used.

Prescription solicitation study. The Inspector General of the Department of Health and Human Services (the Inspector General) is required to study the extent to which (if any) suppliers of covered items of DME that are subject to the competitive acquisition program are soliciting physicians to prescribe certain brands or modes of delivery of covered items based on profitability. The report is due to Congress no later than July 1, 2009.

Effective date. Effective upon enactment.

Act Sec. 302 amending Secs. 1833, 1834(a) and (h), 1842(s), and 1847 of the Social Security Act; amends Sec. 4451 of the Balanced Budget Act of 1997. Law at ¶2121A, 2121B, 2121G, 2121H, 2121I, 2121M, 2121O, 2121T, 2121U, 2125, 2140, 2240, 2250, and 10,210.

¶ 1004
Physician Fee Schedule Adjustments

2004 physician fee schedule increases. With respect to payments for services furnished after January 1, 2004, the Secretary will increase the practice expense relative value units (RVUs) for 2004 using supplemental survey data that includes expenses for administering drugs and biologicals (hereafter referred to as drugs). The supplemental survey data will use data that was submitted to the Secretary as of January 1, 2003, by a physician specialty organization as long as it (1) covers practice expenses for oncology drug administration services, and (2) meets criteria established by the Secretary for acceptance of such surveys. In addition, the Secretary will establish work relative value units equal to the work relative value units for a level one office medical visit for an established patient.

CPT code evaluation. The Secretary is required to promptly evaluate existing Current Procedural Terminology (CPT) codes for physicians' services associated with administering covered outpatient drugs to ensure accurate reporting and billing. The Secretary is required to use existing processes for considering coding changes and, to the extent coding changes are made, the Secretary must apply those processes to establish relative values for the services. The Secretary is required to consult with representatives of physician specialties affected by implementation of the average sales price methodology and the competitive bidding program.

Budget neutrality. The Secretary's discretion to adjust practice expense relative value units for years 2004, 2005, or 2006 to ensure budget neutrality will not be limited by the increases in practice expense RVUs for 2004 and 2005.

Non-physician work pool adjustments. The Secretary is required to adjust the non-physician work pool methodology so that the practice expense RVUs for services determined under that methodology are not affected relative to the practice expense RVUs of services not determined under such methodology, as a result of the above changes.

Payment for multiple chemotherapy agents. The Secretary will review the policy in effect as of October 1, 2003, for the administration of more than one chemotherapy agent furnished on a single day through the push technique. After this review, the Secretary has the discretion to modify the policy as appropriate. Any increases made by the Secretary will be exempt from budget neutrality and will be treated as additional expenditures.

Transitional adjustment. To provide a transition during 2004 and 2005 to the amendments to payments made concerning physician's services consisting of drug administration services furnished on or before January 1, 2004, and before January 1, 2006, the physician will receive a payment from the Federal Supplementary Medical Insurance Trust Fund in an amount equal to a percentage of the fee schedule amount, *and in addition to the fee schedule payment.* The percentage is 32 percent for 2004 and three percent in 2005.

Medicare Payment Advisory Commission review and reports. The Medicare Payment Advisory Commission (the Commission) will review the payment changes insofar as they affect payment under Part B of Title XVIII of the Social Security Act (1) for items and services furnished by oncologists; and (2) for drug administration services furnished by other specialists. The Commission will also study effects of the changes relating to: (1) the quality of care furnished to individuals enrolled under part B and the satisfaction of such seven individuals with that care; (2) the adequacy of reimbursement as applied in, and the availability in, different geographic areas and to different physician practice sizes; and (3) the impact on physician practices.

The Commission will submit two reports concerning its review to the Secretary and Congress—one no later than January 1, 2006, and the other no later than January 1, 2007. Each such report may include recommendations regarding further adjustments in such payments as the Commission deems appropriate, and the Secretary has the discretion to make appropriate adjustments utilizing the Commission's reports.

Effective date. Effective upon enactment.

Act Sec. 303, amending Sec. 1848(c)(2) and (i) of the Social Security Act. Law at ¶ 2251A, 2251E, 2275, 2280J, 2401C, and 2401D.

¶ 1006

Competitive Acquisition Program for Drugs and Biologicals

New payment and delivery programs established. Sections 1847A and 1847B are added to the Social Security Act to provide physicians in the Medicare program with an annual choice between two payment and delivery systems: (1) under Sec. 1847A, the physician is reimbursed for covered drugs at the Average Sales Price (ASP) payment methodology, and (2) under Sec. 1847B, a contractor delivers drugs to the physician and is reimbursed using prices established through a competitive bidding process. The ASP method is explained in ¶ 1010.

Competitive acquisition program. The Secretary is required to establish and implement a competitive acquisition program under which:

(1) competitive acquisition areas are established throughout the United States to acquire and pay for covered outpatient drugs;

(2) each physician is given the opportunity annually to elect to obtain drugs under the program or under the ASP option; and

(3) each physician who elects to obtain drugs under the program makes an annual selection of the contractors who will provide drugs.

Competitively biddable drugs and biologicals. The Secretary will establish categories of competitively biddable drugs and biologicals. Competitively biddable drugs and biologicals are those covered under Sec. 1842(o)(1)(C) of the Social Security Act and are furnished on or after January 1, 2006. The Secretary also may exclude other drugs, including entire classes of drugs if the competitive bidding process, when applied to the drugs or biologicals, is (1) not likely to result in significant savings, or (2) likely to have an adverse impact on access to the drugs or biologicals. The Secretary may waive provisions of the Federal Acquisition Regulation as necessary for the efficient implementation of this program, other than provisions relating to confidentiality of information.

Payment methodology. For physician-prescribed outpatient drugs that are supplied under the program, the claim for the drug will be submitted by the contractor that supplied the drug. Collection of any deductible and coinsurance amounts will be the responsibility of the contractor and cannot be collected unless the drug is administered to the specified beneficiary. Payment will be (1) only made to the contractor and (2) conditioned on the administration of the drugs. The Secretary must provide a process for adjustments if payment is made for drugs that were billed at the time of dispensing but were not actually administered.

Contract awards. The Secretary is required to establish a process by which physicians annually select contractors in each competitive acquisition area for each category of covered drugs. The Secretary must make available to physicians on an ongoing basis a list of contractors in the different competitive acquisition areas. Physicians must select a contractor at the time they elect to engage in the competitive acquisition program rather than the average sales price methodology for payment of drugs and biologicals. Contracts awarded by the Secretary will have a term of three years.

For each competitive acquisition area, the Secretary must conduct a competition among entities for acquisition of a competitively biddable drugs and biologicals. For multiple source drugs, the Secretary will conduct a competition among entities for the acquisition of at least one competitively biddable drug and biological within each billing and payment code and each category for each competitive acquisition area. The Secretary cannot award a contract to any entity unless the Secretary finds that the entity has the capacity to supply the competitively biddable drugs and biologicals and meets the quality, service, financial performance, and solvency standards established by the Secretary. Specifically, the Secretary must find that the entity: (1) has arrangements in effect for shipment of competitively biddable drugs at least five days each week; (2) procedures for prompt response and resolution of physician and beneficiary complaints and inquiries regarding shipment of the drugs; and (3) a grievance process for resolving disputes, including review by the Medicare Provider Ombudsman. The Secretary may refuse to contract with an entity that had its license for distributing drugs suspended or revoked by the federal or a state government or that has been excluded from Medicare program participation.

Competitive factors. The Secretary may limit the number of entities that are awarded contracts for any competitive acquisition area and category of drugs, but not below two of such entities. The Secretary must select qualified entities based on the following factors: (1) the bid prices for competitively biddable drugs; (2) the bid price for distribution of those drugs; (3) ability to ensure product integrity; (4) level of customer service; (5) past experience with drug distribution; and (6) any other factors the Secretary specifies. Contracts may be terminated by the Secretary or the entity with appropriate advance notice.

Product acquisition. All drug and biological products distributed by a contractor must be acquired directly from the manufacturer or from a distributor that has acquired the products directly from the manufacturer. Contractors must comply with additional product integrity safeguards as determined by the Secretary for products that are particularly susceptible to counterfeit or diversion.

Contractor requirements. Contractors must comply with requirements regarding storage and handling of covered outpatient drugs and maintaining distribution records. Contractors must still comply with all provisions of the Federal Food, Drug, and Cosmetic Act that relate to the distribution of prescription drugs or biologicals.

The contractor must comply with (1) a code of conduct, specified or recognized by the Secretary, that includes standards regarding conflicts of interest, and (2) all applicable provisions regarding prevention of fraud and abuse, including applicable guidelines of the Department of Justice and the Inspector General of HHS. The contractor must only supply covered drugs directly to physicians and not directly to beneficiaries, except under circumstances and settings where a beneficiary currently receives a drug in the beneficiary's home, or other non-physician office setting as the Secretary may specify. The contractor may only deliver drugs to a physician upon receipt of a prescription for the drugs and other necessary data specified by the Secretary. This provision does not require that a physician submit a prescription for each individual treatment or change a physician's flexibility regarding writing prescriptions for drugs.

Access to drugs and biologicals. The Secretary is required to establish rules under which drugs and biologicals that are acquired through a contractor may be used to resupply inventories of such drugs and biologicals that are administered consistent with safe drug practices and with adequate safeguards against fraud and abuse. Therefore, to carry inventories of the drugs or biologicals, physicians must demonstrate all of the following:

(1) drugs are required immediately;

(2) physician could not have reasonably anticipated the immediate requirement for the drugs;

(3) contractor could not deliver the drugs to the physician in a timely manner; and

(4) drugs were administered in an emergency situation.

This provision does not waive state pharmacy licensing requirements.

Bidding process. In awarding a contract for a category of drugs in a competitive acquisition area, the Secretary is required to consider the bid prices and other factors to acquire and supply the covered outpatient drugs for that category and area.

A bidder may bid either on a national or regional basis. The amount of the bid submitted for any drug in an area must be the same for all portions of that area. The bid price must include (1) all costs related to delivering the drug to the selecting physician (or other point of delivery); (2) the costs of dispensing (including shipping) the drug; and (3) management fees. The bid must not include any costs associated with administering the drug, wastage, spillage, or spoilage. The provisions on confidentiality of bids in Sec. 1927(b)(3)(D) of the Social Security Act apply to the competitive acquisition program.

¶1006

Cost disclosure. Each contract awarded must provide (1) that the contractor disclose to the Secretary the contractor's reasonable, net acquisition costs, not more often than quarterly, and (2) appropriate price adjustments over the two-year period of the contract to reflect significant increases or decreases in a contractor's reasonable, net acquisition costs.

Computation of payment amounts. The Secretary will determine a single payment amount for each competitively biddable drug or biological in an area based on bids submitted and accepted for drugs and biologicals in an area.

Coinsurance. The Secretary will provide a process for adjustments to payments when payment is made for drugs and biologicals that were billed when dispensed, but were not actually administered. Payment for competitively biddable drugs and biologicals will be made in an amount equal to 80 percent of the computed payment amount (see above paragraph). Before coinsurance is applied, the beneficiary must meet the deductible described in Sec. 1833(b) of the Social Security Act. The coinsurance and deductible will be collected by the contractor that supplies the drug or biological.

New drugs or biologicals. For new drugs and biologicals for which a payment and billing code has not been established, and other exceptional cases within the Secretary's discretion, the Secretary may provide for payment to be made under the competitive bidding process or using the average sales price under Sec. 1847A of the Social Security Act.

Assignment and appeal rights. Current rules related to physician assignment of claims for outpatient drugs and beneficiary appeal rights in cases of medical necessity denial remain unchanged.

Judicial review. There shall be no administrative or judicial review under Secs. 1869 and 1878 of the Social Security Act, or otherwise, of (1) the establishment of payment amounts; (2) the awarding of contracts under this section; (3) the establishment of competitive acquisition areas; (4) the phased-in implementation; (5) the selection of categories of competitively biddable drugs and biologicals for competitive acquisition or the selection of a drug in the case of multiple source drugs; (6) the bidding structure and number of contractors selected.

Report. The Secretary is required to submit an annual report on the competitive acquisition program to Congress by 2008. The report must include information on savings, reductions in cost-sharing, access to competitively biddable drugs and biologicals, the range of choices of contractors available to physicians, the satisfaction of physicians and of individuals enrolled under this part, and information comparing prices for drugs and biologicals under the competitive acquisition program and the average sales price methodology, respectively.

Effective date. Effective upon enactment.

Act Sec. 303, adding new Sec. 1847B to the Social Security Act. Law at ¶2250A, 2250B, 2251A, 2275, 2280J, 2401C, 2401D, and 10,220.

¶ 1008
Extension of Payment Reform

Application to other providers. The amendments made by the competitive acquisition program also apply to payments for drugs or biologicals and drug administration services furnished by physicians in specialties other than the specialties of hematology, hematology/oncology, and medical oncology.

Effective date. Effective upon enactment.

Act Sec. 304. Law at ¶10,230.

¶1009

Adjustments to Payment Amounts for Administration of Drugs and Biologicals

Blood clotting factors. For clotting factors furnished on or after January 1, 2005, the Secretary will, after reviewing the January 2003 report to Congress by the Comptroller General of the United States entitled "Payment for Blood Clotting Factor Exceeds Providers Acquisition Cost," provide for a separate payment to an entity that furnishes to the patient blood clotting factors, for items and services related to the furnishing of the factors in an amount that the Secretary determines to be appropriate. The payment amount may take into account any or all of the following:

(1) the mixing (if appropriate) and delivery of factors to an individual, including special inventory management and storage requirements;

(2) ancillary supplies and patient training necessary for the self-administration of the clotting factors.

The separate payment amount for blood clotting factors furnished in 2006 or a subsequent year will be equal to the separate payment amount determined for the previous year increased by the percentage increase in the consumer price index for medical care for the 12-month period ending with June of the previous year.

Pharmacy supplying fee. The Secretary will pay a supplying fee to pharmacies for certain immunosuppressive and oral drugs determined appropriate by the Secretary (less applicable deductible and coinsurance amounts).

Revised drug and administration payments. The Secretary may not implement the revisions in payment amounts for drugs and 22 biologicals administered by physicians for year 2004 unless the Secretary concurrently makes adjustments to the practice expense payment adjustment in the amendments to the 2004 Physician Fee Schedule.

Application to physicians. This payment revisions to blood clotting factors, immunosuppressive and oral drugs, and biologicals furnished by physicians only apply to physicians in the specialties of (1) hematology, (2) hematology/oncology, (3) medical oncology under Title XVIII of the Social Security Act.

Payment for radiopharmaceuticals not affected. The payment methodology under Medicare Part B for radiopharmaceuticals, including carriers' use of invoice pricing methodology, is not affected by the competitive acquisition program established for outpatient drugs.

Prohibition of administrative and judicial review. No administrative or judicial review is allowed under Secs. 1869 and 1878 of the Social Security Act, or otherwise, of determinations of payment amounts, methods, or adjustments relating to blood clotting factors, immunosuppressive, or oral drug payment adjustments

Effective date. Effective upon enactment.

Act Sec. 303, amending Sec. 1842(o). Law at ¶2225, 2250A, 2250B, 2251A, 2275, 2280J, 2401C, and 2401D.

¶ 1010

Average Sales Price Payment (ASP) Methodology Option

Average sales price methodology. Under the competitive acquisition program for outpatient drugs and biologicals (hereafter referred to as drugs) established under Sec. 1847A of the Social Security Act, the physician may elect payment by the Average Sales Price (ASP) method, instead of payment according to the prices established by the competitive bidding process under Sec. 1847B (see ¶ 1006 for an explanation of the competitive bidding process). The average sales price methodology applies to drugs described in Sec. 1842 (o)(1)(C) of the Social Security Act and furnished on or after January 1, 2005.

Payment for multiple source drugs. For a multiple source drug, the payment amount (based on a minimum dosage unit), subject to applicable deductible and coinsurance, is based on the volume-weighted average of manufacturers' reported average sales prices. In calculating the manufacturer's average sales price, volume discounts, prompt pay discounts, cash discounts, free goods to physicians, chargebacks, and rebates other than Medicaid rebates are excluded. For 2005 and subsequent years, the payment amount is 106 percent of the amount calculated using the methods described above.

"Multiple source drug" means, for a calendar quarter, a covered outpatient drug for which there are two or more drug products that: (1) are rated as therapeutically equivalent (under the Food and Drug Administration's (FDA) most recent publication of "Approved Drug Products with Therapeutic Equivalence Evaluations"); (2) are pharmaceutically equivalent and bioequivalent, as determined by the FDA; and (3) are sold or marketed in the United States during the quarter.

The requirement for pharmaceutical equivalence and bioequivalence will not apply if the FDA changes by regulation the requirement that drugs be pharmaceutically equivalent and bioequivalent in order to be considered therapeutically equivalent.

Payment for single source drugs. For single source products, the ASP is calculated using the lower of (1) the multiple source drugs method or (2) the wholesale acquisition cost (WAC). The WAC is the manufacturer's list price for the drug to wholesalers or direct purchasers in the United States, not including prompt pay or other discounts, rebates, or reductions in price, for the most recent month for which the information is available, as reported in wholesale price guides or other publications of drug pricing data. For 2005 and subsequent years, the payment amount is 106 percent of the amount calculated using the methods described above. This amount is also subject to applicable coinsurance and deductible amounts.

"Single source drug" means a covered outpatient drug which is not a multiple source drug and which is produced or distributed under an original new drug application approved by the FDA. This includes a drug product marketed by any cross-licensed producers or distributors operating under the new drug application, or a drug which is a biological. Single source drugs that are within the same billing and payment code as of October 1, 2003, will be treated by the Secretary as if they were multiple source drugs.

Determination of manufacturer's average sales price. The manufacturer's average sales price for a drug or biological for a National Drug Code will be determined by the manufacturer on a quarterly basis. If there is a lag in the reporting of information on rebates and chargebacks so that adequate data are not available on a timely basis, the manufacturer is required to apply a methodology based on a 12-month rolling average for the manufacturer to estimate costs attributable to rebates and chargebacks. For years after 2004, the Secretary may establish a uniform methodology to estimate and apply applicable costs.

Initial period payment determination. For an initial period (not to exceed a calendar quarter) for which sales data is not available, the Secretary may determine the payment amount for a drug, without considering the manufacturer's average sales price, based on (1) the wholesale acquisition cost or (2) methodologies in effect on November 1, 2003, to determine payment amounts for drugs and biologicals. The Secretary is required to update the payment rates on a quarterly basis based on the most recent calendar quarter manufacturer's average sales price. The Secretary may also contract with appropriate entities to determine the payment amount and may implement this program via program memorandum or other method.

Emergency alternative payment. In the case of a public health emergency in which there is an inability to access covered outpatient drugs and a simultaneous price increase that is not reflected in the manufacturer's average sales price for one or more quarters, the Secretary may use the wholesale acquisition cost (or another reasonable measure of drug price) instead of the manufacturer's average sales price, until the price and availability of the drug has stabilized and is reflected in the applicable manufacturer's average sales price.

Monitoring of market prices. The Inspector General of the Department of Health and Human Services (IG), in consultation with the Secretary, is required to conduct studies and surveys to determine the widely available market prices of drugs and biologicals. Based on these studies and other data concerning drugs and biologicals, the IG will compare the average sales price with (1) the "widely available market price" for such drugs and biologicals (if any) and (2) the average manufacturer price for such drugs and biologicals. The "widely available market price" is the price that a prudent physician or supplier would pay for the drug or biological.

The Secretary may disregard the average sales price for a drug or biological that exceeds the widely available market price or the average manufacturer price for such drug or biological by the "applicable threshold percentage". The "applicable threshold percentage" means (1) in 2005, in the case of an average sales price for a drug or biological that exceeds "widely available market price" or the average manufacturer price, five percent; and (2) in 2006 and subsequent years, the percentage applied under this subparagraph subject to such adjustment as the Secretary may specify for the "widely available market price" or the average manufacturer price, or both.

Authority to adjust average sales price. If the IG finds that the average sales price for a drug or biological exceeds the widely available market price or average manufacturer price for a drug or biological by the applicable threshold percentage, the IG will inform the Secretary (at such times as the Secretary may specify) and the Secretary will, effective as of the next quarter, substitute for the amount of payment otherwise determined under this section for the drug or biological the lesser of (1) the widely available market price for the drug or biological (if any) or (2) 103 percent of the average manufacturer price for the drug or biological.

Civil money penalty. If the Secretary determines that a manufacturer has made a misrepresentation in the reporting of the manufacturer's average sales price for a drug or biological, the Secretary may apply a civil money penalty in an amount of up to $10,000 for each such price misrepresentation and for each day when the price misrepresentation was applied.

Report to Congress. The Secretary is required to submit to Congress an annual report on trends in average sales prices, administrative costs associated with compli-

¶1010

ance with the ASP program, the total value of payments made under the ASP program, and a comparison of the average manufacturer price reported under Medicaid with the average sales price.

Administrative and judicial review. Administrative and judicial review is prohibited regarding determinations of manufacturer's average sales price.

Required reports and studies. The Secretary is required to conduct a study on sales of drugs and biologicals to large volume purchasers, such as pharmacy benefit managers and health maintenance organizations, to determine whether the price at which such drugs and biologicals are sold to such purchasers does not represent the price at which such drugs and biologicals are made available for purchase to prudent physicians.

Not later than January 1, 2006, the Secretary will submit a report to Congress on the above study, and will include recommendations on whether such sales to large volume purchasers should be excluded from the computation of a manufacturer's average sales price.

IG report on adequacy of reimbursement rate under average sales price methodology. The Inspector General of the Department of Health and Human Services (IG) shall conduct a study on the ability of physician practices of different sizes in the specialties of hematology, hematology/oncology, and medical oncology, especially particularly large practices, to obtain drugs and biologicals for the treatment of cancer patients at 106 percent of the average sales price for the drugs and biologicals. In conducting the study, the IG shall conduct an audit of a representative sample of such practices to determine the adequacy of reimbursement under the competitive acquisition program.

Not later than October 1, 2005, the IG will submit to Congress a report on the above study. The report is required to include recommendations on the adequacy of reimbursement for competitively biddable drugs and biologicals.

Effective date. Effective upon enactment.

Act Sec. 303, adding Sec. 1847A and amending Secs. 1842(o) and 1927(a) of the Social Security Act. Law at ¶2225, 2250, 2250A, 2250B, 2251A, 2275, 2280J, 2401C and 2401D.

¶ 1011

Payment for Inhalation Drugs

Payment rate. Inhalation drugs or biologicals furnished through covered durable medical equipment that is not described in subparagraph (A)(iv) will be paid at 85 percent of AWP in 2004. In 2005, it will be the amount provided under the average sales price methodology.

The General Accounting Office (GAO) is required to conduct a study to examine the adequacy of current reimbursements for inhalation therapy under the Medicare program and submit the results of the study in a report to Congress no later than one year from the enactment date of this legislation.

Effective date. Effective upon enactment.

Act Sec. 305, amending Sec. 1842(o) of the Social Security Act. Law at ¶2225 and 10,240.

¶ 1012

Demonstration Project for Use of Recovery Audit Contractors

Recovery audit contractors. The Secretary must conduct a demonstration project for up to three years to analyze the use of recovery audit contractors under the Medicare Integrity Program in identifying underpayments and overpayments and recouping overpayments. Payment may be made to such contractors on a contingent basis. A percentage of the amount recovered may be retained by the Secretary and will be available to the CMS program management account. In addition, the Secretary must examine the efficacy of using such contractors regarding duplicative payments, accuracy of coding, and other payment policies in which inaccurate payments arise. The project is required to cover at least two states that are among the states with (1) the highest per capita utilization rates of Medicare services and (2) at least three contractors. No later than six months after the project is completed, the Secretary must submit a report to Congress regarding the project, including information regarding the project's impact on savings to the Medicare program and recommendations on the cost effectiveness of extending or expanding the project.

Qualifications of contractors. The Secretary is authorized to enter into a recovery audit contract only if the contractor's staff possess appropriate clinical knowledge of and experience with Medicare payment rules and regulations or the contractor enters into a contract with another entity whose staff is knowledgeable and experienced. Fiscal intermediaries, carriers, and Medicare administrative contractors are not eligible to serve as recovery audit contractors. In awarding recovery audit contracts, the Secretary is required to give preference to entities that have demonstrated more than three years of direct management experience and a proficiency for cost control or recovery audits with private insurers, health care providers, health plans, or under the Medicaid program.

Investigation of fraud. Recovery of an overpayment by a recovery audit contractor does not preclude the Secretary or the Attorney General from investigating and prosecuting allegations of fraud or abuse arising from overpayments.

Report. The Secretary shall submit to Congress a report on the project not later than six months after the date of its completion. Such reports shall include information (which means information about a conviction for a relevant crime or a finding of patient or resident abuse) on the impact of the project on savings to the Medicare program and recommendations on the cost effectiveness of extending or expanding the project.

Effective date. Effective upon enactment.

Act Sec. 306. Law at ¶ 10,250.

Medicaid, Health Savings Account, and Miscellaneous Provisions

MEDICAID PROVISIONS

Medicaid DSH Payments . . . . ¶ 1201
Increase in Floor for Treatment as a
 Low DSH State . . . . ¶ 1203
Termination of Statewide Waiver . . . . ¶ 1204
Reporting Requirements for State
 Adjustments to DSH Hospitals . . . . . . ¶ 1205
Best Price Exemption for Medicaid
 Drug Rebate Program . . . . ¶ 1206
Extension of Moratorium . . . . ¶ 1207

MISCELLANEOUS PROVISIONS

Emergency Health Services for
 Undocumented Aliens . . . . ¶ 1208
Commission on Systemic
 Interoperability . . . . ¶ 1209
Research on Outcomes . . . . ¶ 1210
Citizens Health Care Working Group . . ¶ 1211
Funding Start-Up Costs for
 Administrative Reform . . . . ¶ 1212

Health Care Infrastructure
 Improvement Program . . . . ¶ 1215

ACCESS TO AFFORDABLE PHARMACEUTICALS

Hatch-Waxman, Re-Importation
 Changes . . . . ¶ 1301
Federal Trade Commission Review . . . . ¶ 1320
Importation of Drugs from Canada . . . . ¶ 1330

HEALTH SAVINGS ACCOUNTS AND OTHER TAX PROVISIONS

Establishing Health Savings Accounts . . ¶ 1400
Employer Contributions to Health
 Savings Accounts . . . . ¶ 1405
Exclusion of Prescription Drug
 Subsidy . . . . ¶ 1410
Information Reporting Requirements . . ¶ 1415

MEDICAID PROVISIONS

¶ 1201

Medicaid DSH Payments

Special, one-time increase. Medicaid disproportionate share hospital (DSH) allotments for any state not paid under special rules for "extremely low DSH states" for fiscal year (FY) 2004 will be equal to 116 percent of the DSH allotment for the state for fiscal year 2003. (See ¶ 1203 for the definition of an extremely low DSH state.)

For each succeeding fiscal year the allotment is equal to the DSH allotment for the state for FY 2004. In the case of fiscal years beginning with the fiscal year when the DSH allotment will no longer exceed the DSH allotment under prior law, the DSH allotment will be the allotment for the state for the previous fiscal year increased by the percentage change in the consumer price index for all urban consumers (all items, U.S. city average) for the previous fiscal year.

Effective date. Effective upon enactment.

Act Sec. 1001(a) amending Sec. 1923(f)(3) of the Social Security Act. Law at ¶ 2401A and 11,180.

¶ 1203

Increase in Floor for Treatment as a Low DSH State

Increase for fiscal years 2004 and 2005. "Extremely low DSH states" for purposes of FY 2001 through 2003 are states whose FY 1999 federal and state DSH expenditures, as reported to CMS as of August 31, 2000, are greater than zero but less than one percent of the state's total Medicaid expenditures for the fiscal year. For FY 2004 and subsequent fiscal years, the relevant expenditures are FY 2000 expenditures as reported to CMS as of August 31, 2003.

Through FY 2008 the DSH allotment for these states will be increased by 16 percent each year. For FY 2009 and subsequent years, the allotment will be increased by the percentage change in the consumer price index for all urban consumers, which is a measure of inflation.

Effective date. Effective upon enactment.

Act Sec. 1001(b) amending subsection 1923(f)(5) of the Social Security Act and adding new subsection 1923(f)(6). Law at ¶ 2401A.

¶ 1204

Termination of Statewide Waiver

Termination of statewide waiver. For fiscal year 2004 or 2005, if a statewide waiver under section 1115 is revoked or terminated before the end of the year and there is no DSH allotment for the state, the Secretary shall permit the state to submit an amendment to its state plan that would describe the methodology to be used by the state to identify and make payments to DSH, including children's hospitals and institutions for mental diseases or other mental health facilities (other than state-owned institutions or facilities), on the basis of the proportion of patients served by such hospitals that are low-income patients with special needs. For FY 2004 and 2005, states with terminated waivers will receive DSH allotments that are the maximum amount, except that the allotment may not result in greater expenditures than would have been made if the waiver had not been revoked or terminated.

Effective date. Effective upon enactment.

Act Sec. 1001(c) amending subsection 1923(f)(3)(A) of the Social Security Act; redesignating subsection (f)(6) as (f)(7); and adding new subsection 1923(f)(6). Law at ¶ 2401A.

¶ 1205

Reporting Requirements for State Adjustments to DSH Hospitals

Increased reporting requirements. To ensure the appropriateness of payment adjustments to DSH hospitals under Medicaid, beginning with fiscal year 2004 and after, states will be required to submit an annual report as a condition of receiving DSH payment adjustments. The annual report must include: identification of each DSH hospital that received a payment adjustment, the amount of the adjustment in the preceding fiscal year, and other information the Secretary determines appropriate.

Effective date. Effective upon enactment.

Act Sec. 1001(d) adding new subsection 1923(j) to the Social Security Act. Law at ¶ 2401B.

¶ 1206
Best Price Exemption for Medicaid Drug Rebate Program

Inpatient drug prices charged to certain public hospitals. Any drug purchased for inpatient use is subject to the auditing and record keeping requirements described in Sec. 340B(a)(5)(C) of the Public Health Service Act. This applies to inpatient drug prices charged to hospitals as described in Sec. 340B(a)(4)(L) of the Public Health Service Act.

Effective date. Effective upon enactment.

Act Sec. 1002 amending Sec. 1927(c)(1)(C) of the Social Security Act. Law at ¶2401E.

¶ 1207
Extension of Moratorium

Extension of moratorium for treatment of certain facilities. The provision that Saginaw Community Hospital in Michigan may not be considered an institution for mental diseases for the purpose of Medicaid is extended permanently.

Effective date. Effective upon enactment.

Act Sec. 1003 amending Sec. 6408(a)(3) of the Omnibus Budget Reconciliation Act of 1989. Law at ¶11,190.

MISCELLANEOUS PROVISIONS

¶ 1208
Emergency Health Services for Undocumented Aliens

Appropriations. The amount of $167,000,000 is appropriated for each of fiscal years 2005 through 2008 for payments to eligible providers based on the percentage of undocumented aliens residing in a particular state as compared to the total number of such aliens residing in all states. The amount of $83,000,000 is appropriated in each of these fiscal year for providers in the six states with the highest number of undocumented alien apprehensions for the year.

Use of funds. The appropriations will be used to make payments to providers to the extent that the provider is not otherwise reimbursed for services to:

(1) undocumented aliens;

(2) aliens who have been paroled into the United States at a U.S. port of entry for the purpose of receiving eligible services; or

(3) Mexican citizens permitted to enter the U.S. for not more than 72 hours under the authority of a biometric machine readable border crossing identification card (also referred to as a "laser visa ") issued in accordance with the requirements of the Immigration and Nationality Act.

Effective date. Effective upon enactment. Not later than Sept. 1, 2004, the Secretary shall establish a process for requesting payments.

Act Sec. 1011. Law at ¶11,200.

¶ 1209

Commission on Systemic Interoperability

Commission on healthcare information technology. A Commission will be established to develop a comprehensive strategy (that includes a timeline and prioritization) for the adoption and implementation of health care information technology standards.

The membership of the Commission will include: individuals with national recognition for their expertise in health finance and economics, health plans and integrated delivery systems, and reimbursement of health facilities; and practicing physicians, practicing pharmacists, and other providers of health services, health care technology and information systems, and other related fields. The commission will provide a mix of different professionals, broad geographic representation, and a balance between urban and rural representatives.

The necessary funds to carry out this section are authorized to be appropriated

Effective date. Effective upon enactment.

Act Sec. 1012. Law at ¶ 11,210.

¶ 1210

Research on Outcomes

Outcomes and quality of care research. The Secretary, acting through the Director of the Agency for Healthcare Research and Quality, must conduct and support research to meet the priorities and requests for scientific evidence and information identified by the Medicare, Medicaid, and Supplemental Security Income (SSI) programs with respect to:

(1) the outcomes, comparative clinical effectiveness, and appropriateness of health care items and services (including prescription drugs); and

(2) strategies for improving the efficiency and effectiveness of the programs, including the ways in which such items and services are organized, managed, and delivered under the programs.

Not later than 18 months after the date of enactment of this Act, the Secretary must identify options that could be undertaken in voluntary collaboration with private and public entities (as appropriate) for the:

(1) provision of more timely information through the Medicare, Medicaid, and Supplemental Security Income (SSI) programs regarding the outcomes and quality of patient care, including clinical and patient-reported outcomes, especially with respect to interventions and conditions for which clinical trials would not be feasible or raise ethical concerns that are difficult to address;

(2) acceleration of the adoption of innovation and quality improvement under such programs; and

(3) development of management tools for the Medicare, Medicaid, and SSI programs.

Effective date. Effective upon enactment.

Act Sec. 1013. Law at ¶ 11,220.

¶ 1211
Citizens Health Care Working Group

Informed public debate. Congress intends to begin a formal nationwide public debate about improving the health care system to provide every American with the ability to obtain quality, affordable health care coverage. Congress will vote on the recommendations that result from the debate.

The Secretary, acting through the Agency for Healthcare Research and Quality, will establish an entity, to be known as the Citizens' Health Care Working Group that will be composed of 15 members. One member will be the Secretary. The Comptroller General of the United States will appoint 14 members.

The working group will hold hearings and report to the general public on the following issues:

(1) the capacity of the public and private health care systems to expand coverage options;

(2) the cost of health care and the effectiveness of care provided at all stages of disease;

(3) innovative State strategies used to expand health care coverage and lower health care costs;

(4) local community solutions to accessing health care coverage;

(5) efforts to enroll individuals currently eligible for public or private health care coverage;

(6) the role of evidence-based medical practices that can be documented as restoring, maintaining, or improving a patient's health, and the use of technology in supporting providers in improving quality of care and lowering costs; and

(7) strategies to assist purchasers of health care, including consumers, to become more aware of the impact of costs, and to lower the costs of health care.

Community meetings. Not later than one year after the date of enactment of this Act, the Working Group must initiate health care community meetings throughout the United States. Such community meetings may be geographically or regionally based and shall be completed within 180 days after the first two meeting.

Appropriations. $3,000,000 is authorized for each of fiscal years 2005 and 2006 to be appropriated for this purpose, and additional funds are authorized for the preparation and dissemination of the Health Report to the public.

Effective date. Effective upon enactment.

Act Sec. 1014. Law at ¶ 11,230.

¶ 1212
Funding Start-Up Costs for Administrative Reform

Start-up amounts. The funds appropriated to carry out this Act from the Federal Hospital Insurance Trust Fund and the Federal Supplementary Medical Insurance Trust Fund are: (1) no more than $1,000,000,000 for the Centers for Medicare and Medicaid Services; and (2) no more than $500,000,000 for the Social Security Administration. These amounts will remain available until September 30, 2005.

Effective date. Effective upon enactment.

Act Sec. 1015. Law at ¶ 11,240.

¶ 1215

Health Care Infrastructure Improvement Program

Loan program. The Secretary will establish a loan program that provides loans to qualifying hospitals for payment of the capital costs of projects described as follows: a project of a qualifying hospital that is designed to improve the health care infrastructure of the hospital, including construction, renovation, or other capital improvements.

No loan may be provided under this section to a qualifying hospital except pursuant to an application that is submitted and approved in a time, manner, and form specified by the Secretary. A loan under this section will be on such terms and conditions and meet such requirements as the Secretary determines appropriate.

Effective date. Effective upon enactment.

Act Sec. 1016. Law at ¶ 2390.

ACCESS TO AFFORDABLE PHARMACEUTICALS

¶ 1301

Hatch-Waxman, Re-Importation Changes

Rules for generic drugs. Under the Hatch-Waxman Act, a generic company may take the initiative to speed the introduction of a generic drug into the marketplace by filing a notice with a name-brand company, detailing its intent to compete and alleging that the name-brand's patent is invalid or will not be infringed. The patent-holder has 45 days in which to file a patent infringement suit against the generic competitor. If the patent-holder does not file a patent infringement suit, the generic company may file a declaratory judgment suit seeking a judicial determination on the validity of a drug patent. If a court decides in favor of the generic company, the Food and Drug Administration (FDA) must approve the company's application to market the generic drug.

Generic companies are given access to highly confidential patent information included in name-brand companies' drug application filings with the FDA, for the purpose of evaluating possible patent infringement. Generic companies are also permitted to counterclaim about allegedly invalid patents when name-brand companies bring patent infringement suits against them.

Under the Hatch-Waxman Act, a generic company that successfully challenges a name-brand patent holder and receives FDA approval to market its generic equivalent of a branded drug receives 180 days of market exclusivity before the FDA will approve other companies' generic copies of the drug. All generic applicants who file with the FDA on the first permissible day will be considered "first applicants." Generic companies forfeit their 180 days of marketing exclusivity if they: fail to market a generic drug within 75 days of receiving FDA approval for it; withdraw an application; amend their certification to a patent; fail to obtain tentative application approval; or enter into non-marketing-type agreements with other generic applicants or patent-holders.

Effective date. Effective upon enactment.

Act Secs. 1101, 1102, and 1103 amending Sec. 505 of the Federal Food, Drug and Cosmetic Act. Law at ¶¶ 11,250, 11,260, and 11,270.

¶ 1320
Federal Trade Commission Review

Anti-trust review of contracts between drug companies. The Federal Trade Commission (FTC) is empowered to conduct an antitrust review of all contracts between generic drug companies and brand-name drug companies, and all contracts between or among two or more generic companies. The contracts include all agreements regarding the manufacture, marketing, or sale of brand-name and/or generic drugs. Failure to submit these contracts to the FTC will result in civil penalties of $11,000 per day, and the FTC may seek equitable relief in federal district courts, enjoining companies that fail to submit contracts for FTC review.

Effective date. Effective 30 days after enactment.

Act Secs. 1111, 1112, 1113, 1114, 1115, 1116, 1117, and 1118. Law at ¶¶ 11,290, 11,300, 11,310, 11,320, 11,330, 11,340, 11,350, and 11,360.

¶ 1330
Importation of Drugs from Canada

Regulations permitting importation of drugs. The FDA is required to promulgate regulations that would permit pharmacists and wholesalers to import cheaper prescription drugs from Canada into the United States. All such drugs must comply with all provisions of the Federal Food, Drug, and Cosmetic Act. Detailed shipping information and chain-of-custody requirements will assure the drugs' authenticity. The FDA is required to grant individuals waivers for personal importation of prescription drugs, as well as issue guidance on enforcement discretion regarding personal-use importation.

The FDA must certify to Congress that this program will not pose any additional risk to the public's health and safety, and that it will result in a significant cost reduction to Americans.

The Secretary of HHS shall conduct a study on the importation of drugs into the United States pursuant to section 804 of the Federal Food, Drug, and Cosmetic Act. Not later than 12 months after the date of the enactment of this Act, the Secretary shall submit to the appropriate committees of Congress a report providing the findings of such study. The President's designees also shall conduct a study and report on issues related to trade and pharmaceuticals.

Effective date. Effective upon enactment, but only if the FDA gives its certification.

Act. Sec. 1121 amending Chapter VIII of the Federal Food, Drug, and Cosmetic Act and adding new Sec. 804; Act Secs. 1122 and 1123. Law at ¶¶ 11,370, 11380, and 11390.

HEALTH SAVINGS ACCOUNTS AND OTHER TAX PROVISIONS

¶ 1400
Establishing Health Savings Accounts

Background. Medical Savings Accounts (MSAs) are tax-favored accounts that can be used to pay medical expenses. Medicare+Choice MSAs are a variation that eligible taxpayers can choose as an alternative to traditional Medicare (Internal

Revenue Code Sec. 138). MSAs operate under rules similar to those governing retirement savings accounts, such as individual retirement accounts (IRAs) and Code Sec. 401(k) plans. Like retirement accounts, MSAs are intended to be long-term accounts that are invested to produce additional income for the account. This distinguishes them from medical flexible spending arrangements (FSAs). FSAs also allow a taxpayer to set aside tax-free funds to pay medical expenses. Unlike MSAs, however, FSA assets are not invested and do not grow beyond the amount of the contributions to the account. Moreover, an FSA lasts only one year, and any amounts that are not spent for medical care are forfeited.

Although MSAs resemble retirement accounts in many respects, they do have one unique feature: both contributions and distributions for medical expenses are tax-free. As a result, money put into an MSA and withdrawn to pay medical expenses is never subject to federal income tax. In contrast, retirement accounts are subject to federal income tax when the contributions and the income attributable to them are eventually distributed to the account beneficiary (or when contributions are made to a Roth IRA).

Because MSAs offer such extraordinary tax shelter opportunities, they have been very restricted. Archer MSAs are available only for self-employed individuals and employees of small businesses whose only health insurance coverage carries high deductibles. The total number of Archer MSAs allowed is capped at 750,000, and no new accounts may be established after 2003. An individual and an employer cannot make deductible contributions to the individual's account during the same tax year. Medicare+Choice MSAs are available only to taxpayers who are eligible for Medicare and are willing to relinquish their traditional Medicare benefits.

Health savings accounts established. The Act establishes health savings accounts (HSAs) that provide tax-favored treatment for amounts that are contributed and used to pay the account beneficiary's medical expenses. The HSAs are much like Archer Medical Savings Accounts MSAs with the existing eligibility restrictions removed.

Overview. An HSA beneficiary is the person on whose behalf the account was established, and may be the taxpayer, the taxpayer's spouse, or the taxpayer's dependents. Generally, the accounts are governed by rules similar to those that govern MSAs. Within limits, contributions are deductible from the account beneficiary income, and an employer's contributions on behalf of an employee are not wages includible in gross income. Distributions are excludable from gross income if they are made for qualified medical expenses. Distributions that are not for qualified medical expenses are included in gross income and are subject to an additional penalty.

Comment. Young workers in particular may benefit by establishing HSAs. The limit on annual HSA contributions means that an account will contain fairly small amounts in its first few years. However, the ability to grow and accrue tax-free income in the account over the worker's lifetime means that very substantial amounts can accrue in an HSA by the time the worker retires.

Nothing in the new Code Section 223 requires an individual to set up an HSA through his or her employer.

Eligible taxpayers. Eligibility for an HSA is determined on a monthly basis. An eligible taxpayer is any individual who, on the first day of the month, is covered under a high deductible health plan, and is not covered under any other kind of health plan, with certain exceptions. The exceptions include plans covering only accidents, disability, dental care, vision care, or long-term care. In addition, a taxpayer can have certain "permitted insurance" plans, which include: (1) a policy under which substantially all of the coverage relates to liabilities incurred under worker's compensation law, tort liabilities, liabilities relating to ownership or use of property (such as auto insurance), or other similar liabilities that the Secretary of the Treasury may specify by regulations; (2) insurance for a specified disease or illness; or (3) insurance that provides a fixed payment for hospitalization (Code Sec. 223(c)(1) and (3), as added by the Medicare Prescription Drug, Improvement and Modernization Act).

Comment. These eligibility rules are similar to those applicable to Archer MSAs but, unlike MSAs, HSAs are not restricted to self-employed taxpayers and taxpayers who work for small employers.

What constitutes a high deductible plan? Generally, a high deductible plan for individual (self-only) coverage has an annual deductible of at least $1,000 (indexed for inflation) and an out-of-pocket expense limit of no more than $5,000; for family coverage, which is anything other than self-only coverage, these amounts are doubled. Out-of-pocket expenses include deductibles, co-payments, and other amounts that the insured person must pay for covered benefits under the plan, but do not include premiums paid for the plan. A plan does not fail to qualify as a high deductible plan if it fails to have a deductible for preventive care. A plan using a network of providers (such as a preferred provider plan or PPO) does not fail to be a high deductible plan if its out-of-pocket expense limit for services provided outside of the network exceeds the out-of-pocket expense limits. Permitted insurance and plans covering only accidents, disability, and dental, vision or long-term care are not high deductible plans (Code Sec. 223(c)(2), as added by the Medicare Prescription Drug, Improvement and Modernization Act).

HSA contribution limits. The maximum annual contribution that can be made to an individual's HSA is the lesser of the annual deductible under the individual's high deductible health plan, or $2,250 for an individual with self-only coverage and $4,500 for an individual with family coverage (Code Sec. 223(b)(1) and (2), as added by the Medicare Prescription Drug, Improvement and Modernization Act). These amounts are adjusted annually for inflation in $50 increments (Code Sec. 223(g), as added by the Medicare Prescription Drug, Improvement and Modernization Act). If an insurance plan uses a network of providers, the plan's deductible for out-of-network services is not taken into account in determining the annual contribution limit; instead, the deductible for in-network services is used (Code Sec. 223(c)(2)(D)(ii), as added by the Medicare Prescription Drug, Improvement and Modernization Act). Contributions from all sources are aggregated for purposes of the annual limit. The maximum annual contribution limit for an HSA is reduced by the aggregate amount that is contributed by the individual's employer and excluded from the individual's income, and the aggregate amount of any contributions to the individual's MSA. Contributions, other than rollovers from other tax-favored accounts, must be in cash.

For individuals who are age 55 or older, the maximum contribution is increased by

- $500 in 2004,
- $600 in 2005,
- $700 in 2006,
- $800 in 2007,
- $900 in 2008, and
- $1,000 in 2009 and thereafter (Code Sec. 223(b)(3), as added by the Medicare Prescription Drug, Improvement and Modernization Act).

¶1400

No contributions, including catch-up contributions, may be made by or for an individual who is eligible for Medicare (Code Sec. 223(b)(7), as added by the Medicare Prescription Drug, Improvement and Modernization Act).

Deduction for individual contributions and exclusion for employer contributions. Within limits, cash contributions made to an HSA by or on behalf of an eligible individual are deductible from that individual's income. The contributions are an above-the-line deduction from gross income and, thus, the deduction is available to taxpayers who do not itemize deductions (Code Sec. 62(a)(19), as added by the Medicare Prescription Drug, Improvement and Modernization Act). To the extent that contributions from an individual's employer do not exceed the annual limit on HSA contributions, they are excluded from the individual's income and exempt from railroad retirement, unemployment and withholding taxes (Code Secs. 106(d), 3231(e)(11), 3306(b)(18) and 3401(a)(22), as added by the Medicare Prescription Drug, Improvement and Modernization Act). Contributions from persons other than the individual's employer are deductible by the individual, but they constitute gifts that may be subject to gift tax. No deduction is allowed to an individual who can be claimed as a taxpayer's dependent (Code Sec. 223(b)(6), as added by the Medicare Prescription Drug, Improvement and Modernization Act). Distributions from an Archer MSA are not treated as taxable distributions if they are rolled over into an HSA within 60 days (Code Sec. 220(f)(5)(A), as amended by the Medicare Prescription Drug, Improvement and Modernization Act).

Married taxpayers. If taxpayers who are married to each other both have family coverage under separate plans, they are both treated as having the family coverage with the lowest annual deductible. If only one spouse has family coverage, both spouses are treated as having the family coverage. The limit on annual deductible contributions to an HSA is reduced by the aggregate amount paid to the spouses' MSAs during the tax year and then is divided equally between them unless they agree on a different division (Code Sec. 223(b)(5), as added by the Medicare Prescription Drug, Improvement and Modernization Act).

HSA contributions are handled similarly to retirement plan contributions. Many rules applicable to IRA contributions also apply to HSA contributions. Distributions from other tax-favored accounts that are rolled over into an HSA are not deductible. Contributions made by the original due date for the taxpayer's return are deemed made in the preceding tax year; in other words, taxpayers may deduct HSA contributions made by April 15 of the following year. Contributions from an employer that exceed the annual limit on contributions are included in the employee's income as compensation subject to income and employment taxes (Code Sec. 223(d)(4)(A), as added by the Medicare Prescription Drug, Improvement and Modernization Act).

Comment. HSA contributions, unlike 401(k) contributions, are free from employment taxes.

An employee cannot deduct employer contributions that are also excluded from the employee's income (Code Sec. 223(b)(4), as added by the Medicare Prescription Drug, Improvement and Modernization Act).

HSA distributions. Distributions from a health account for the account beneficiary's qualified medical expenses are excludable from gross income. Excludable distributions are not treated as deductible medical expenses under Code Sec. 213. Distributions from a health account that are not used for the beneficiary's qualified medical expenses are includible in the beneficiary's gross income. Distributions includible in gross income are also subject to an additional penalty of 10 percent of the includible amount, unless made after the beneficiary's death, disability (as defined at Code Sec. 72(m)), or attainment of the age of Medicare eligibility (Code

Sec. 223(f), as added by the Medicare Prescription Drug, Improvement and Modernization Act).

Returned excess contributions are not taxable. Taxable distributions do not include an excess contribution that is returned to the account beneficiary, as long as the contribution and the net income attributable to it are returned before the due date (with extensions) of the beneficiary's tax return for the year of the contribution. However, the income attributable to the excess contribution is included in the beneficiary's gross income. An excess contribution is a contribution that is not deductible or excludable from income. Taxable distributions also do not include distributions from other tax-favored accounts that are rolled over into the account beneficiary's HSA within 60 days, unless the account beneficiary excluded a rollover distribution within the preceding year (Code Sec. 223(f), as added by the Medicare Prescription Drug, Improvement and Modernization Act).

What expenses may be paid with an HSA distribution? Qualified medical expenses generally are those deductible as medical expenses under Code Sec. 213(d). Thus, they include expenses, not compensated for by insurance or otherwise, for diagnosis, cure, mitigation, treatment, or prevention of disease; transportation primarily for and essential to such care; prescription drugs; and qualified long-term care expenses. Qualification as a medical expense is determined as of the time the expense is incurred. An HSA may not be used to purchase health insurance unless the insurance is (1) for long-term care; (2) for health coverage during any period of continuation coverage required by federal law; (3) for health care coverage while an individual is receiving unemployment compensation under federal or state law; and (4) for health insurance other than a Medicare supplemental policy for an account beneficiary who is eligible for Medicare, (Code Sec. 223(d)(2), as added by the Medicare Prescription Drug, Improvement and Modernization Act)

Transfer of HSA upon divorce. The transfer of an interest in an HSA to the beneficiary's spouse or former spouse under a divorce or separation agreement is not a taxable transfer. The transferred interest is treated as an HSA with the recipient spouse as the account beneficiary (Code Sec. 223(f)(7), as added by the Medicare Prescription Drug, Improvement and Modernization Act).

Transfer of HSA upon death. When an account beneficiary dies and the HSA passes to the surviving spouse as the designated beneficiary, the HSA is treated as if the surviving spouse were the account beneficiary. If an HSA passes to someone other than the surviving spouse at the account beneficiary's death, the HSA ceases to be an HSA. If the transferee is the beneficiary's estate, an amount equal to the account assets is included in the beneficiary's gross income in the year of death. If the transferee is someone other than the beneficiary's estate, an amount equal to the fair market value of the HSA assets is included in the transferee's gross income, but is reduced by the amount of qualified medical expenses incurred by the beneficiary before death and paid by the transferee within one year of the beneficiary's death. In computing taxable income, the transferee may claim a deduction for the portion of the federal estate tax on the decedent's estate that was attributable to the amount of the HSA balance, computed in accordance with the rules in Code Sec. 691(c) (Code Sec. 223(f)(8), as added by the Medicare Prescription Drug, Improvement and Modernization Act).

HSA mechanics. An HSA is a trust created or organized in the United States exclusively for the purpose of paying the qualified medical expenses of the account beneficiary. The trustee must be a bank, insurance company, or other person who demonstrates that the trust will be administered properly. Account assets cannot be invested in life insurance contracts, or commingled with other property except in a

¶1400

common trust fund or investment fund. The individual's interest in the account must be nonforfeitable (Code Sec. 223(d)(1), as added by the Medicare Prescription Drug, Improvement and Modernization Act). An HSA is exempt from tax as long as it remains an HSA, although the accounts are subject to the Code Sec. 511 rules imposing tax on unrelated business income of charitable organizations. The accounts are also subject to rules similar to the IRA rules under Code Sec. 408(e) that terminate the exempt status of an account if the beneficiary engages in prohibited transactions, and that treat as taxable distributions any amounts pledged as security (Code Sec. 223(e), as added by the Medicare Prescription Drug, Improvement and Modernization Act). HSAs are not affected by community property laws. A custodial account can qualify as an HSA (Code Sec. 223(d)(4)(A), as added by the Medicare Prescription Drug, Improvement and Modernization Act).

The Secretary of the Treasury may require reports describing contributions, distributions, the return of excess contributions, and other matters, to be made to the Secretary or the account beneficiary, by the trustee of an HSA or any person who provides an HSA to an individual with a high deductible health plan (Code Sec. 223(h), as added by the Medicare Prescription Drug, Improvement and Modernization Act).

Effective date. The HSA provisions are effective for tax years beginning after December 31, 2003.

Act Sec. 1201(a), redesignating Sec. 223 as 224 of the Internal Revenue Code and adding new Code Sec. 223; Act Sec. 1201(b), adding Code Sec. 62(a)(19); Act Sec. 1201(c), amending Code Sec. 220(f)(5)(A); Act Sec. 1201(d), adding Code Secs. 106(d), 3231(e)(11), 3306(b)(18), 3401(a)(22), and 4980G; Act Sec. 1201(k). Law at ¶ 11,400.

¶ 1405
Employer Contributions to Health Savings Accounts

Background. Employer contributions to an accident or health plan are generally excludable from an employee's gross income (Internal Revenue Code Sec. 106). Such contributions are also generally excludable from wages for employment tax purposes (Code Secs. 3121(a)(2) and 3306(b)(2)). This exclusion generally applies to employees and former employees, their spouses, dependents and survivors. Benefits paid under employer-provided accident or health plans are also generally excludable from income to the extent that they are reimbursements for medical care (Code Sec. 105). In the case of a self-insured medical reimbursement arrangement, the exclusion applies to highly compensated employees only if certain nondiscrimination rules are satisfied (Code Sec. 105(h)). Medical care generally includes amounts paid for qualified long-term care insurance and services (Code Sec. 213). If certain requirements are satisfied, employer-provided accident or health coverage offered under a cafeteria plan is also excludable from an employee's gross income and wages (Code Secs. 125, 3121(a)(5)(G) and 3306(b)(5)(G)). However, long-term care insurance and services cannot be provided through a cafeteria plan.

There are two general employer-provided arrangements that can be used to pay for or reimburse medical expenses of employees outside of a health insurance plan on a tax-favored basis: flexible spending arrangements (FSAs) and health reimbursement arrangements (HRAs). While these arrangements provide similar tax benefits (i.e., the amounts paid under the arrangements for medical care are excludable from gross income and wages for employment tax purposes), they are subject to different rules. A main distinguishing feature between the two arrangements is that while FSAs are generally part of a cafeteria plan and contributions to FSAs are made on a salary reduction basis, HRAs cannot be part of a cafeteria plan and contributions cannot be made on a salary-reduction basis (Notice 2002-45, 2002-28 I.R.B. 93; Rev. Rul. 2002-41, 2002-28 I.R.B. 75).

Amounts paid or accrued by an employer within a tax year for a sickness, accident, hospitalization, medical expense, or similar health plan for its employees are generally deductible as ordinary and necessary business expenses (Code Sec. 162).

Self-employed individuals such as sole proprietors or partners in a partnership are entitled to deduct 100 percent of the amount paid for health insurance for themselves, their spouses and dependents (Code Sec. 162(l)). The exclusion for employer-provided health coverage does not apply to self-employed individuals. Self-employed individuals include "more than two-percent shareholders" of S corporations who are treated as partners for purposes of fringe benefit (Code Sec. 1372) rules.

Employer contributions to health savings accounts. Health savings accounts (HSAs) provide tax-favored treatment for current medical expenses as well as the ability to save on a tax-favored basis for future medical expenses (Code Sec. 223, as added by the Medicare Prescription Drug, Improvement, and Modernization Act of 2003). These accounts are designed to supplement high-deductible health insurance plans and are created exclusively to pay for the qualified medical expenses of the account holder and his or her spouse and dependants. The accounts are subject to rules similar to those applicable to individual retirement arrangements (IRAs).

An employer may set up health savings accounts for its employees and may make contributions to the accounts in addition to any employee contributions. Combined employer and employee contributions may not exceed the limits for account contributions discussed at (generally $2,250 for an individual with self-only coverage and $4,500 for an individual with family coverage) (Code Sec. 223(b)(1) and (2), as added by the Medicare Act).

The Act provides the following rules governing employer contributions to health savings accounts (Act Secs. 1201(d)-(i) of the Medicare Act):

- income exclusions applicable to employer contributions to health savings accounts,
- employment tax exclusions applicable to employer contributions to health savings accounts,
- nondiscrimination rules applicable to employer contributions to health savings accounts,
- a penalty tax on excess contributions to health savings accounts,
- a penalty tax on prohibited transactions involving health savings accounts,
- a penalty for failure to provide reports on health savings accounts,
- an exception from capitalization of policy acquisition costs, and
- the ability to offer health savings accounts under cafeteria plans.

Employer contributions to health savings accounts excluded from employee's taxable income. Health savings account contributions are generally excluded from wages for purposes of determining income and employment taxes (Code Secs. 106(d)(1) and 3401(a)(22), as added by the Medicare Act). Also, the amount contributed to the health savings account of an employee or the employee's spouse must be shown on the employee's W-2 form (Code Sec. 6051(a)(12), as added by the Medicare Act).

¶1405

Comment. Employer contributions are often made through salary reduction contributions deducted from the employee's paycheck.

Employer contributions to any health savings account of an eligible employee are treated as excludable employer-provided coverage for medical expenses under an accident or health plan (Code Sec. 223(c)(1) and (d), as added by the Medicare Act). However, the exclusion applies only to the extent such amounts do not exceed the employee's health savings account dollar "limitations" for the tax year (Code Sec. 223(b), as added by the Medicare Act). The contribution limits are determined without regard to these income exclusion and penalty rules (Code Sec. 106(d)(1), as added by the Medicare Act).

Rules similar to the Archer Medical Savings Account contribution rules apply. Thus, no amount is included in the gross income of any employee solely because the employee can choose between the contributions made to a health savings account and employer contributions to another health plan of the employer. Also, any employer contributions to a health savings account, if otherwise allowable as a deduction, are allowed only for the tax year in which paid. Moreover, every individual required to file an income tax return for the tax year must include on such return the aggregate amount contributed by employers to the health savings accounts of such individual or such individual's spouse for such tax year. Finally, HSA contributions are not part of COBRA (Code Sec. 4980B) coverage (Code Sec. 106(d)(2), as added by the Medicare Act).

Employer contributions excluded from employment taxes. In addition to being excludable from income, HSA contributions are also excludable from wages for purposes of computing employment taxes. When determining railroad retirement taxes, the term compensation does not include any payment made to or for the benefit of an employee if at the time of such payment it is reasonable to believe that the employee will be able to exclude that payment from income under the exclusion (Code Sec. 106(d)) for health savings account contributions (Code Sec. 3231(e)(11), as added by the Medicare Act). Similarly, for purposes of determining unemployment taxes, any payment made to or for the benefit of an employee is excluded from wages if at the time of such payment it is reasonable to believe that the employee will be able to exclude such payment from income under the exclusion (Code Sec. 106(d)) for health savings account contributions (Code Sec. 3306(b)(18), as added by the Medicare Act). Finally, for purposes of determining wages for withholding taxes, any payment made to or for the benefit of an employee is excludable if at the time of such payment it is reasonable to believe that the employee will be able to exclude such payment from income under the exclusion (Code Sec. 106(d)) for health savings account contributions (Code Sec. 3401(a)(22), as added by the Medicare Act).

Nondiscrimination rules governing employer contributions to HSAs. An employer is penalized if it fails to make comparable HSA contributions on behalf of all employees with comparable coverage during the same period. The penalties are identical to those applicable to Archer MSAs (see Code Sec. 4980E). The IRS is authorized to issue regulations to carry out the purposes of this rule, including regulations providing special rules for employers who make contributions to Archer MSAs and health savings accounts during the calendar year (Code Sec. 4980G, as added by the Medicare Act).

Generally, contributions are considered comparable if they are either of the same amount or the same percentage of the deductible under the plan. The comparability rule is applied separately to part-time employees (i.e., employees who are customarily employed for fewer than 30 hours per week). The comparability rule does not apply to amounts transferred from an employee's health savings account, health FSA, or Archer MSA or to contributions made through a cafeteria plan (Code Sec. 4980E(d)). If employer contributions do not satisfy the comparability rule during a period then the employer is subject to an excise tax equal to 35 percent of the aggregate amount contributed by the employer to health savings accounts of the employer for that period (Code Sec. 4980E(b)). The excise tax is designed as a proxy for the denial of the deduction for employer contributions. In the case of a failure to comply with the comparability rule due to reasonable cause and not willful neglect, the IRS may waive part or all of the tax imposed to the extent that the payment of the tax would be excessive relative to the failure involved. For purposes of the comparability rule, employers under common control are aggregated (Code Sec. 4980E(e)).

Excess HSA contributions penalty tax. A tax is imposed in an amount equal to six percent of the amount of the excess contributions to an individual's HSA (determined as of the close of the tax year). According to the Conference Committee Report, the tax is equal to six percent of the cumulative amount of excess contributions that are not distributed from the HSA to the contributor (House Committee Report, H.R. Rep. No. 108-391). The amount of such tax for any tax year shall not exceed six percent of the value of the account or annuity (determined as of the close of the tax year). The tax imposed must be paid by the individual account owner (Code Sec. 4973(a)(5), as added by the Medicare Act).

In the case of HSAs, the term "excess contributions" means the sum of:

(1) the aggregate amount contributed for the tax year to the accounts (other than a rollover contribution) which is neither excludable from gross income nor allowable as a HSA deduction for such year, and

(2) the amount determined under this excess contributions rule for the preceding tax year, reduced by the sum of —

(3) the distributions out of the accounts which were included in gross income as HSA account distributions not used to pay for medical expenses (see Code Sec. 223(f)(2)), and

(4) the excess (if any) of the maximum amount allowable as a HSA deduction for the tax year, as determined without regard to the rule allowing an exclusion for HSA contributions (Code Sec. 106(d)(1)), over the amount contributed to the accounts for the tax year.

Any contribution that is distributed from the HSA as an excess contribution returned before the due date of the individual's tax return (Code Sec. 223(f)(3)) is treated as an amount that was not contributed, for purposes of applying this HSA excess contributions penalty (Code Sec. 4973(a)(5) and (g), as added by the Medicare Act).

Comment. Amounts can be rolled over into a HSA from an Archer MSA or a health FSA on a tax-free basis, according to the House Committee Report. Also, amounts can be rolled over into an HSA from another HSA on a tax-free basis. Amounts transferred from another health savings account or Archer MSA are not taken into account under the annual contribution limits (Conference Committee Report, H.R. Rep. No. 108-391).

HSA prohibited transactions penalty tax. An individual for whose benefit a HSA is established is not subject to the prohibited transactions tax penalty (Code Sec. 4975) with respect to any transaction concerning such account (which would otherwise be taxable under the prohibited transactions rules) if, due to that transaction, the account ceases to be a HSA by reason of the application of the HSA account termination (Code Sec. 223(e)) rules (Code Sec. 4975(c)(6) and (e)(1)(E), as added by the Medicare Act).

¶1405

HSA reporting failure penalty. If a trustee or other person required to file a HSA report fails to file such report at the time and in the manner required, such person must pay a penalty of $50 for each failure. The penalty will not apply if it is shown that the failure is due to reasonable cause (Code Sec. 6693(a)(2)(C), as added by the Medicare Act).

The Conference Committee Report notes that generally trustees of health savings accounts may be required to report to the Secretary of the Treasury amounts with respect to contributions, distributions, and other matters as determined appropriate by the Secretary. In addition, providers of health insurance are required to report information as may be required by the Secretary (Conference Committee Report, H.R. Rep. No. 108-391).

HSA policy acquisition cost capitalization exception. The general requirement applicable to insurance companies that certain policy acquisition cost expenses must be capitalized and amortized does not apply in the case of a contract that is a HSA (Code Sec. 848(e)(1)(v), as added by the Medicare Act).

HSA inclusion in cafeteria plans. Generally, the term "cafeteria plan" does not include any plan which provides for deferred compensation. However, HSAs may be offered under cafeteria plans. The rule excluding plans that provide deferred compensation from the definition of a cafeteria plan does not apply to a plan to the extent of amounts which a covered employee may elect to have the employer pay as contributions to a HSA established on behalf of the employee (Code Sec. 125(d)(2)(D), as added by the Medicare Act).

Effective date. These provisions apply to tax years beginning after December 31, 2003 (Act Sec. 1201(k) of the Medicare Prescription Drug, Improvement, and Modernization Act of 2003).

Act Sec. 1201(d) adding Code Secs. 106(d), 3231(e)(11), 3306(b)(18), 3401(a)(22), 6051(a)(12), and 4980G of the Internal Revenue Code; Act Sec. 1201(e), amending Code Sec. 4973; Act Sec. 1201(f), adding Code Sec. 4975(c)(6) and (e)(1)(E); Act Sec. 1201(g), amending Code Sec. 6693(a)(2); Act Sec. 1201(h), adding Code Sec. 848(e)(1)(v); Act Sec. 1201(i), adding Code Sec. 125(d)(2)(D); Act Sec. 1201(j); Act Sec. 1201(k). Law at ¶11,400.

¶1410
Exclusion of Prescription Drug Subsidy

Background. A government subsidy is available for prescription drugs provided under qualified employer-sponsored retiree prescription drug plans (Section 1860D of the Social Security Act, as added by the Medicare Prescription Drug, Improvement and Modernization Act of 2003). The amount of the subsidy is 28 percent of allowable retiree drug costs between $250 and $5,000. These dollar amounts are indexed annually for inflation.

A qualified retiree prescription drug plan is any employment-based retiree health coverage for which, with respect to an eligible individual/participant, the plan sponsor:

(1) provides to the Secretary of Health and Human Services (HHS) an attestation that the actuarial value of the prescription drug coverage under the plan is at least equal to the actuarial value of standard prescription drug coverage;

(2) maintains adequate records as required by the Secretary of HHS and provides those records to the Secretary of HHS for inspection; and

(3) provides disclosure of information regarding prescription drug coverage as required by law.

Allowable retiree drug costs are those costs actually paid by a plan sponsor or on behalf of a qualifying covered retiree. Accordingly, discounts, chargebacks and rebates are considered in the calculation of allowable costs (Section 1860D-22 of the Social Security Act, as added by the 2003 Medicare Act).

Alternative minimum tax. Alternative minimum tax (AMT) is a system of tax that ensures that high-income corporate and noncorporate taxpayers pay a minimum amount of income tax, rather than escaping liability through the generous use of certain deductions and credits. AMT is the difference between a taxpayer's tentative minimum tax and regular tax. For corporate taxpayers, tentative minimum tax is 20 percent of the excess, if any, of alternative minimum taxable income (AMTI) over the AMTI exemption amount, reduced by the foreign tax credit. AMTI is calculated by adding certain tax preference items to a taxpayer's regular taxable income. A portion of the difference between a corporation's AMTI and adjusted accumulated earnings is treated as a tax preference item. A corporation must increase its AMTI by 75 percent of the amount that its adjusted accumulated earnings exceeds its AMTI (Code Sec. 56).

The adjusted accumulated earnings is the earnings and profits of a corporation calculated with certain adjustments. One such adjustment requires corporations to include tax-exempt income that was excluded from gross income but included in earnings and profits. Income from the discharge of indebtedness and extraterritorial income excluded under Code Sec. 114 are not included in this adjustment (Code Sec. 56(g)(4)(b)).

Subsidy for employer-provided retiree prescription drug coverage excluded from income. Government subsidies provided to employers for prescription drugs under a qualified retiree prescription drug plan are excluded from income (Code Sec. 139A(a), as added by the 2003 Medicare Act).

Comment. According to the House Committee on Ways and Means, the exclusion of retiree prescription drug subsidies increases the value of the subsidy by $18 billion (House Committee on Ways and Means Press Release, November 19, 2003).

Subsidies ignored in calculating employer's deduction. The value of any section 1860D-22 subsidy received by an employer is disregarded in calculating the employer's business deduction for prescription drug costs (Code Sec. 139A, as added by the 2003 Medicare Act). The deduction for contributions to a qualified plan can be calculated as if no subsidy had been received.

Example. Manufacturer contributes $100,000 to its qualified plan to cover actual prescription drug costs for 100 qualified retirees. Manufacturer receives a section 1860D-22 subsidy of $21,000 with respect to its retiree drug costs [($1,000 – 250) × 100 participants × .28]. Manufacturer may deduct the full $100,000 as a business expense, notwithstanding the $21,000 subsidy.

Alternative minimum tax. The subsidies allowed for prescription drugs provided under a qualified retiree prescription drug plan are not included in the adjustment of a corporation's adjusted accumulated earnings for purposes of determining alternative minimum tax (Code Sec. 56(g)(4)(B), as amended by the 2003 Medicare Act).

Effective date. The exclusion of subsidies provided for prescription drugs under a qualified retirement plan applies to tax years ending after the date of enactment of the 2003 Medicare Act (Act Sec. 1202(d) of the Medicare Prescription Drug, Improvement and Modernization Act of 2003).

¶1410

Act Sec. 1202(a) adding Internal Revenue Code Sec. 139A; Act Sec. 1202(b), amending Code Sec. 56(g)(4)(B); Act Sec. 1202(d). Law at ¶11,410.

¶1415
Information Reporting Requirements

Background. Persons in a trade or business who make payments of rent, salaries, wages, premiums, annuities, compensations, remunerations, emoluments, or other fixed or determinable gains, profits, and income totaling $600 or more in the course of that trade or business are required to file an information return. This is sometimes referred to as the "$600-or-more rule." The requirement is designed to remind taxpayers of items of income that should be reflected on their tax returns and assist the IRS in its compliance effort (Code Sec. 6041).

The payments are reported on the appropriate Form 1099. A separate form must be filled out for each person to whom a payment of $600 or more is made.

Certain payments are excluded from this reporting requirement. They include, among others:

(1) the payments of wages and other employment compensation reported on Form W-2;

(2) income taxes withheld from wages, tips, annuities, supplemental unemployment compensation benefit, certain gambling winnings, and third-party payments of sick-pay reported on Form W-2;

(3) payment of rent to real estate agents;

(4) the payment of dividends by corporations reportable under Code Sec. 6042; and

(5) certain foreign-related items (Reg. § 1.6041-4).

Payments made to corporations are not subject to the $600-or-more rule. However, payments made to a corporation providing medical and health care services are reportable (Reg. § 1.6041-3(p)(1)). Payments made to medical service providers through debit, credit and stored-value cards pursuant to a flexible spending account or health reimbursement arrangement must be reported by the employer sponsoring the plan (Rev. Rul. 2003-43).

Exception to information reporting requirements for health arrangements. Payments for medical care made from a flexible spending arrangement or health reimbursement arrangement are excepted from the $600-or-more rule (Code Sec. 6041(f), as amended by the Medicare Prescription Drug, Improvement and Modernization Act of 2003).

Comment. This exclusion specifically addresses the IRS's position in Rev. Rul. 2003-43, which allows tax-free payment/reimbursements to be made via debit or credit cards and other electronic media, provided adequate controls are in place to assure that only medical costs are reimbursed. Under the ruling, employers were required to report the payments on Form 1099-Misc. The exception from the reporting requirements increases the incentives for employers to maintaining such arrangements (House Ways and Mean Committee Press Release, November 21, 2003).

A flexible spending arrangement for purposes of the exception means a benefit program that reimburses employees for specified incurred expenses, the maximum amount of which is less than 500 percent of the value of the coverage (Code Sec. 106(c)(2)). A health reimbursement arrangement is an arrangement treated as employer-provided coverage under Code Sec. 106.

Effective date. The exception to the information reporting requirements of Code Sec. 1041 applies to payments made after December 31, 2002 (Act Sec. 1203(b) of the Medicare Prescription Drug, Improvement and Modernization Act of 2003).

Act Sec. 1203(a) adding Sec. 6041(f) of the Internal Revenue Code; Act Sec. 1203(b). Law at ¶ 11,420.

SOCIAL SECURITY ACT SECTIONS ADDED, AMENDED OR REPEALED

[¶2001]
INTRODUCTION.

The Social Security Act provisions amended by the "Medicare Prescription Drug, Improvement, and Modernization Act of 2003," are shown in the following paragraphs. Deleted Social Security Act material or the text of the Social Security Act Section prior to amendment appears in the amendment notes following each amended Social Security Act provision.

[¶2005] Sec. 1108. LIMITATION ON PAYMENTS TO PUERTO RICO, THE VIRGIN ISLANDS, AND GUAM

[42 U.S.C. §1308]

* * *

(f) Subject to subsection (g) and section 1935(e)(1)(B), the total amount certified by the Secretary under title XIX with respect to a fiscal year for payment to—

* * *

[CCH Explanation at ¶205.]
2003 Amendments:

Section 103(d)(2) of the "Medicare Prescription Drug, Improvement, and Modernization Act of 2003," effective upon enactment, amended section 1108(f) by inserting "and section 1935(e)(1)(B)" after "Subject to subsection (g)".

[¶2010] Sec. 1114. APPOINTMENT OF ADVISORY COUNCIL AND OTHER ADVISORY GROUPS

[42 U.S.C. §1314]

* * *

(i) [Transferred to the end of section 1862 and redesignated as subsection (j).]

[CCH Explanation at ¶948.]
2003 Amendments:

Section 948(a)(1) of the "Medicare Prescription Drug, Improvement, and Modernization Act of 2003," effective upon enactment, transferred section 1114(i) to the end of section 1862 and redesignated it as subsection (j).

Prior to being transferred and redesignated, section 1114(i) read as follows:

(i)(1) Any advisory committee appointed under subsection (f) to advise the Secretary on matters relating to the interpretation, application, or implementation of section 1862(a)(1) shall assure the full participation of a nonvoting member in the deliberations of the advisory committee, and shall provide such nonvoting member access to all information and data made available to voting members of the advisory committee, other than information that—

(A) is exempt from disclosure pursuant to subsection (a) of section 552 of title 5, United States Code, by reason of subsection (b)(4) of such section (relating to trade secrets); or

(B) the Secretary determines would present a conflict of interest relating to such nonvoting member.

(2) If an advisory committee described in paragraph (1) organizes into panels of experts according to types of items or services considered by the advisory committee, any such panel of experts may report any recommendation with respect to such items or services directly to the Secretary without the prior approval of the advisory committee or an executive committee thereof.

[¶2015] Sec. 1117. APPOINTMENT OF THE ADMINISTRATOR AND CHIEF ACTUARY OF THE CENTERS FOR MEDICARE & MEDICAID SERVICES

[42 U.S.C. §1317]

(a) The Administrator of the Centers for Medicare & Medicaid Services shall be appointed by the President by and with the advice and consent of the Senate.

(b)(1) There is established in the Centers for Medicare & Medicaid Services the position of Chief Actuary. The Chief Actuary shall be appointed by, and in direct line of authority to, the Administrator of such Centers. The Chief Actuary shall be appointed from among individuals who have demonstrated, by their education and experience, superior expertise in the actuarial sciences. The Chief Actuary shall exercise such duties as are appropriate for the office of the Chief Actuary and in accordance with professional standards of actuarial independence. The Chief Actuary may be removed only for cause.

* * *

(3) In the office of the Chief Actuary there shall be an actuary whose duties relate exclusively to the programs under parts C and D of title XVIII and related provisions of such title.

[CCH Explanation at ¶ 801.]

2003 Amendments:

Section 900(c) of the "Medicare Prescription Drug, Improvement, and Modernization Act of 2003," effective upon enactment, amended section 1117(b) by adding at the end new paragraph (3).

Section 900(e) of the "Medicare Prescription Drug, Improvement, and Modernization Act of 2003," effective upon enactment, amended section 1117 in the heading to read: "APPOINTMENT OF THE ADMINISTRATOR AND CHIEF ACTUARY OF THE CENTERS FOR MEDICARE & MEDICAID SERVICES".

Section 900(e) of the "Medicare Prescription Drug, Improvement, and Modernization Act of 2003," effective upon enactment, amended section 1117(a) by striking "Health Care Financing Administration" and inserting "Centers for Medicare & Medicaid Services".

Section 900(e) of the "Medicare Prescription Drug, Improvement, and Modernization Act of 2003," effective upon enactment, amended section 1117(b)(1) by striking "Health Care Financing Administration" and inserting "Centers for Medicare & Medicaid Services";

Section 900(e) of the "Medicare Prescription Drug, Improvement, and Modernization Act of 2003," effective upon enactment, amended section 1117(b)(1) by striking "Administration" and inserting "Centers".

[¶ 2016] Sec. 1128. EXCLUSION OF CERTAIN INDIVIDUALS AND ENTITIES FROM PARTICIPATION IN MEDICARE AND STATE HEALTH CARE PROGRAMS

[42 U.S.C. § 1320a-7]

* * *

(c) NOTICE, EFFECTIVE DATE, AND PERIOD OF EXCLUSION.—

* * *

* * *

(3)(B) Subject to subparagraph (G), in the case of an exclusion under subsection (a), the minimum period of exclusion shall be not less than five years, except that, upon the request of the administrator of a Federal health care program (as defined in section 1128B(f)) who determines that the exclusion would impose a hardship on individuals entitled to benefits under part A of title XVIII or enrolled under part B of such title, or both, the Secretary may, after consulting with the Inspector General of the Department of Health and Human Services, waive the exclusion under subsection (a)(1), (a)(3), or (a)(4) with respect to that program in the case of an individual or entity that is the sole community physician or sole source of essential specialized services in a community. The Secretary's decision whether to waive the exclusion shall not be reviewable.

* * *

[CCH Explanation at ¶ 949.]

2003 Amendments:

Section 949 of the "Medicare Prescription Drug, Improvement, and Modernization Act of 2003," effective upon enactment, amended the first sentence of section 1128(c)(3)(B).

Prior to being amended, the first sentence of section 1128(c)(3)(B) read as follows:

Subject to subparagraph (G), in the case of an exclusion under subsection (a), the minimum period of exclusion shall be not less than five years, except that, upon the request of a State, the Secretary may waive the exclusion under subsection (a)(1) in the case of an individual or entity that is the sole community physician or sole source of essential specialized services in a community.

[¶ 2017] Sec. 1128B. CRIMINAL PENALTIES FOR ACTS INVOLVING FEDERAL HEALTH CARE PROGRAMS

[42 U.S.C. § 1320a-7b]

* * *

* * *

(b)(3) Paragraphs (1) and (2) shall not apply to—

* * *

(E) any payment practice specified by the Secretary in regulations promulgated pursuant to section 14(a) of the Medicare and Medicaid Patient and Program Protection Act of 1987;

(F) any remuneration between an organization and an individual or entity providing items or services, or a combination thereof, pursuant to a written agreement between the organization and the individual or entity if the organization is an eligible organization under section 1876 or if the written agreement, through a risk-sharing arrangement, places the individual or entity at substantial financial risk for the cost or utilization of the items or services, or a combination thereof, which the individual or entity is obliged to provide;

(G) the waiver or reduction by pharmacies (including pharmacies of the Indian Health Service, Indian tribes, tribal organizations, and urban Indian organizations) of any cost-sharing imposed under part D of title XVIII, if the conditions described in clauses (i) through (iii) of section 1128A(i)(6)(A) are met with respect to the waiver or reduction (except that, in the case of such a waiver or reduction on behalf of a subsidy eligible individual (as defined in section 1860D-14(a)(3)), section 1128A(i)(6)(A) shall be applied without regard to clauses (ii) and (iii) of that section); and

(H) any remuneration between a Federally qualified health center (or an entity controlled by such a health center) and an MA organization pursuant to a written agreement described in section 1853(a)(4).

(H) [sic] any remuneration between a health center entity described under clause (i) or (ii) of section 1905(l)(2)(B) and any individual or entity providing goods, items, services, donations, loans, or a combination thereof, to such health center entity pursuant to a contract, lease, grant, loan, or other agreement, if such agreement contributes to the ability of the health center entity to maintain or increase the availability, or enhance the quality, of services provided to a medically underserved population served by the health center entity.

* * *

[CCH Explanation at ¶ 390 and 798.]

2003 Amendments:

Section 101(e)(2) of the "Medicare Prescription Drug, Improvement, and Modernization Act of 2003," effective upon enactment, amended section 1128B(b)(3) by striking "and" at the end of subparagraph (E); by striking the period at the end of subparagraph (F) and inserting "; and" and by adding at the end new subparagraph (G).

Section 101(e)(8) of the "Medicare Prescription Drug, Improvement, and Modernization Act of 2003," effective upon enactment, amended section 1128B(b)(3)(C) by inserting "or in regulations under section 1860D-3(e)(6)" after "1987".

CCH Note: section 1128B(b)(3)(C) does not contain the phrase "1987". Therefore, the amendment made by Section 101(e)(8) of the "Medicare Prescription Drug, Improvement, and Modernization Act of 2003," has not been reflected above.

Section 237(d) of the "Medicare Prescription Drug, Improvement, and Modernization Act of 2003," effective upon enactment, amended section 1128B(b)(3) in subparagraph (F) by striking "and" after the semicolon at the end; in subparagraph (G) by striking the period at the end and inserting "; and"; and by adding at the end new subparagraph (H).

The above amendment applies to services provided on or after Jan. 1, 2006, and contract years beginning on or after such date.

Section 431(a) of the "Medicare Prescription Drug, Improvement, and Modernization Act of 2003," effective upon enactment, amended section 1128B(b)(3) in subparagraph (F) by striking "and" after the semicolon at the end; in subparagraph (G) by striking the period at the end and inserting "; and"; and by adding at the end new subparagraph (H).

CCH Note: Both sections 237(d) and 431(a) of the "Medicare Prescription Drug, Improvement, and Modernization Act of 2003," added different subparagraphs "(H)" to the end of section 1128(b)(3). The first subparagraph (H) above was added by section 237(d) and the second subparagraph (H) above was added by section 431(a).

[¶ 2018] Sec. 1140. PROHIBITION OF MISUSE OF SYMBOLS, EMBLEMS, OR NAMES IN REFERENCE TO SOCIAL SECURITY OR MEDICARE

[42 U.S.C. § 1320b-10]

(a)(1) No person may use, in connection with any item constituting an advertisement, solicitation, circular, book, pamphlet, or other communication, or a play, motion picture, broadcast, telecast, or other production, alone or with other words, letters, symbols, or emblems—

(A) the words "Social Security", "Social Security Account", "Social Security System", "Social Security Administration", "Medicare", "Centers for Medicare & Medicaid Services", "Department of Health and Human Services", "Health and Human Services", "Supplemental Security Income Program", or "Medicaid", the letters "SSA", "CMS", "DHHS", "HHS", or "SSI", or any other combination or variation of such words or letters, or

(B) a symbol or emblem of the Social Security Administration, Centers for Medicare & Medicaid Services, or Department of Health and Human Services (including the design of, or a reasonable facsimile of the design of, the social security card issued pursuant to section 205(c)(2)(F) or the Medicare card, the check used for payment of benefits under title II, or envelopes or other stationery used by the Social Security Administration, Centers for Medicare & Medicaid Services, or Department of Health and Human Services), or any other combination or variation of such symbols or emblems,

in a manner which such person knows or should know would convey, or in a manner which reasonably could be interpreted or construed as conveying, the false impression that such item is approved, endorsed, or authorized by the Social Security Administration, the Centers for Medicare & Medicaid Services, or the Department of Health and Human Services or that such person has some connection with, or authorization from, the Social Security Administration, the Centers for Medicare & Medicaid Services, or the Department of Health and Human Services. The preceding provisions of this subsection shall not apply with respect to the use by any agency or instrumentality of a State or political subdivision of a State of any words or letters which identify an agency or instrumentality of such State or of a political subdivision of such State or the use by any such agency or instrumentality of any symbol or emblem of an agency or instrumentality of such State or a political subdivision of such State.

* * *

[CCH Explanation at ¶ 801.]

2003 Amendments:

Section 900(e)(B) of the "Medicare Prescription Drug, Improvement, and Modernization Act of 2003," effective upon enactment, amended section 1140(a)(1) by striking "Health Care Financing Administration" both places it appears in the matter following subparagraph (B) and inserting "Centers for Medicare & Medicaid Services".

Section 900(e)(B) of the "Medicare Prescription Drug, Improvement, and Modernization Act of 2003," effective upon enactment, amended section 1140(a)(1)(A) by striking "Health Care Financing Administration" and inserting "Centers for Medicare & Medicaid Services"; and by striking "HCFA" and inserting "CMS".

Section 900(e)(B) of the "Medicare Prescription Drug, Improvement, and Modernization Act of 2003," effective upon enactment, amended section 1140(a)(1)(B) by striking "Health Care Financing Administration" both places it appears and inserting "Centers for Medicare & Medicaid Services".

[¶ 2020] Sec. 1142. RESEARCH ON OUTCOMES OF HEALTH CARE SERVICES AND PROCEDURES

[42 U.S.C. § 1320b-12]

* * *

(b) PRIORITIES.—

* * *

(3) RELATIONSHIP WITH MEDICARE PROGRAM.—In establishing priorities under paragraph (1) for research and evaluation, and under section 914(a) of the Public Health Service Act for the agenda under such section, the Secretary shall assure that such priorities appropriately reflect the needs and priorities of the program under title XVIII, as set forth by the Administrator of the Centers for Medicare & Medicaid Services.

* * *

[CCH Explanation at ¶ 801.]

2003 Amendments:

Section 900(e)(1)(C) of the "Medicare Prescription Drug, Improvement, and Modernization Act of 2003," effective upon enactment, amended section 1142(b)(3) by striking "Health Care Financing Administration" and inserting "Centers for Medicare & Medicaid Services".

[¶ 2025] Sec. 1144. OUTREACH EFFORTS TO INCREASE AWARENESS OF THE AVAILABILITY OF MEDICARE COST-SHARING AND SUBSIDIES FOR LOW-INCOME INDIVIDUALS UNDER TITLE XVIII

[42 U.S.C. § 1320b-14]

(a) OUTREACH.—

(1) IN GENERAL.—The Commissioner of Social Security (in this section referred to as the "Commissioner") shall conduct outreach efforts to—

(A) identify individuals entitled to benefits under the medicare program under title XVIII who may be eligible for medical assistance for payment of the cost of medicare cost-sharing under the medicaid program pursuant to sections 1902(a)(10)(E) and 1933 for the

Social Security Law Added, Amended or Repealed

transitional assistance under section 1860D-31(f), or for premium and cost-sharing subsidies under section 1860D-14; and

(B) notify such individuals of the availability of such medical assistance, program, and subsidiesunder such sections.

(2) CONTENT OF NOTICE.—Any notice furnished under paragraph (1) shall state that eligibility for medicare cost-sharing assistance, the transitional assistance under section 1860D-31(f), or premium and cost-sharing subsidies under section 1860D-14under such sections is conditioned upon—

(A) the individual providing to the State information about income and resources (in the case of an individual residing in a State that imposes an assets test for eligibility for medicare cost-sharing under the medicaid program); and

* * *

(b) COORDINATION WITH STATES.—

(1) IN GENERAL.—In conducting the outreach efforts under this section, the Commissioner shall—

(A) furnish the agency of each State responsible for the administration of the medicaid program and any other appropriate State agency with information consisting of the name and address of individuals residing in the State that the Commissioner determines may be eligible for medical assistance for payment of the cost of medicare cost-sharing under the medicaid program pursuant to sections 1902(a)(10)(E) and 1933, for transitional assistance under section 1860D-31(f), or for premium and cost-sharing subsidies for low-income individuals under section 1860D-14; and

* * *

(2) INFORMATION IN PERIODIC UPDATES.—The periodic updates described in paragraph (1)(B) shall include information on individuals who are or may be eligible for the medical assistance, program, and subsidiesdescribed in paragraph (1)(A) because such individuals have experienced reductions in benefits under title II.

[CCH Explanation at ¶205.]

2003 Amendments:

Section 103(g) of the "Medicare Prescription Drug, Improvement, and Modernization Act of 2003," effective upon enactment, amended section 1144 in the heading by inserting "AND SUBSIDIES FOR LOW-INCOME INDIVIDUALS UNDER TITLE XVIII" after "COST-SHARING".

Section 103(g) of the "Medicare Prescription Drug, Improvement, and Modernization Act of 2003," effective upon enactment, amended section 1144(a)(1)(A) by inserting "for the transitional assistance under section 1860D-31(f), or for premium and cost-sharing subsidies under section 1860D-14" before the semicolon.

Section 103(g) of the "Medicare Prescription Drug, Improvement, and Modernization Act of 2003," effective upon enactment, amended section 1144(a)(1)(B) by inserting ", program, and subsidies" after "medical assistance".

Section 103(g) of the "Medicare Prescription Drug, Improvement, and Modernization Act of 2003," effective upon enactment, amended section 1144(a)(2) by inserting ", the transitional assistance under section 1860D-31(f), or premium and cost-sharing subsidies under section 1860D-14" after "assistance".

Section 103(g) of the "Medicare Prescription Drug, Improvement, and Modernization Act of 2003," effective upon enactment, amended section 1144(a)(2)(A) by striking "such eligibility" and inserting "eligibility for medicare cost-sharing under the medicaid program".

Section 103(g) of the "Medicare Prescription Drug, Improvement, and Modernization Act of 2003," effective upon enactment, amended section 1144(b)(1)(A) by inserting ", for transitional assistance under section 1860D-31(f), or for premium and cost-sharing subsidies for low-income individuals under section 1860D-14" after "1933".

Section 103(g) of the "Medicare Prescription Drug, Improvement, and Modernization Act of 2003," effective upon enactment, amended section 1144(b)(2) by inserting ", program, and subsidies" after "medical assistance".

[¶2026] Sec. 1154. FUNCTIONS OF PEER REVIEW ORGANIZATIONS

[42 U.S.C. §1320c-3]

(a) Any utilization and quality control peer review organization entering into a contract with the Secretary under this part must perform the following functions:

(1) The organization shall review some or all of the professional activities in the area, subject to the terms of the contract and subject to the requirements of subsection (d), of physicians and other health care practitioners and institutional and noninstitutional providers of health care services in the provision of health care services and items for which payment may be made (in whole or in part) under title XVIII (including where payment is made for such services to eligible

§1154(a)(1) ¶2026

organizations pursuant to contracts under section 1876) to Medicare Advantage organizations pursuant to contracts under part C, and to prescription drug sponsors pursuant to contracts under part D for the purpose of determining whether—

* * *

(17) The organization shall execute its responsibilities under subparagraphs (A) and (B) of paragraph (1) by offering to providers, practitioners, Medicare Advantage organizations offering Medicare Advantage plans under part C, and prescription drug sponsors offering prescription drug plans under part D quality improvement assistance pertaining to prescription drug therapy. For purposes of this part and title XVIII, the functions described in this paragraph shall be treated as a review function.

* * *

(e)(5) [Stricken.]

* * *

[CCH Explanation at ¶ 235 and 948.]

2003 Amendments:

Section 109(a) of the "Medicare Prescription Drug, Improvement, and Modernization Act of 2003," effective upon enactment, amended section 1154(a)(1) by inserting ", to Medicare Advantage organizations pursuant to contracts under part C, and to prescription drug sponsors pursuant to contracts under part D" after "under section 1876".

Section 109(b) of the "Medicare Prescription Drug, Improvement, and Modernization Act of 2003," effective upon enactment, amended section 1154(a) by adding section (17).

Section 948(d) of the "Medicare Prescription Drug, Improvement, and Modernization Act of 2003," effective upon enactment, amended section 1154(e) by striking subsection (5).

Prior to being stricken, section 1154(e)(5) read as follows:

(5) In any review conducted under paragraph (2) or (3), the organization shall solicit the views of the patient involved (or the patient's representative).

[¶ 2030] Sec. 1802. FREE CHOICE BY PATIENT GUARANTEED

[42 U.S.C. § 1395a]

* * *

(b) USE OF PRIVATE CONTRACTS BY MEDICARE BENEFICIARIES.—

* * *

(5) DEFINITIONS.—In this subsection:

* * *

(B) PHYSICIAN.—The term 'physician' has the meaning given such term by paragraphs (1), (2), (3), and (4) of section 1861(r).

* * *

[CCH Explanation at ¶ 706.]

2003 Amendments:

Section 603 of the "Medicare Prescription Drug, Improvement, and Modernization Act of 2003," effective upon enactment, amended section 1802(b)(5)(B) by striking "section 1861(r)(1)" and inserting "paragraphs (1), (2), (3), and (4) of section 1861(r)".

[¶ 2034] Sec. 1804. NOTICE OF MEDICARE BENEFITS; MEDICARE AND MEDIGAP INFORMATION

[42 U.S.C. § 1395b-2]

* * *

(b) The Secretary shall provide information via a toll-free telephone number on the programs under this title. The Secretary shall provide, through the toll-free telephone number 1–800–MEDICARE, for a means by which individuals seeking information about, or assistance with, such programs who phone such toll-free number are transferred (without charge) to appropriate entities for the provision of such information or assistance. Such toll-free number shall be the toll-free number listed for general information and assistance in the annual notice under subsection (a) instead of the listing of numbers of individual contractors.

The Secretary shall provide, through the toll-free telephone number 1–800–MEDICARE, for a means by which individuals seeking information about, or assistance with, such programs who phone such toll-free number are transferred (without charge)to appropriate entities for the provision of such information or assistance. Such toll-free number shall be the toll-free number listed for general information and assistance in the annual notice under subsection (a) instead of the listing of numbers of individual contractors.

* * *

2003 Amendments

Sec. 923(d) of the "Medicare Prescription Drug, Improvement, and Modernization Act of 2003" (PubLNo 108-173), effective date December 8, 2003, amended section 1804(b) by adding at the end the following: "The Secretary shall provide, through the toll-free telephone number 1–800–MEDICARE, for a means by which individuals seeking information about, or assistance with, such programs who phone such toll-free number are transferred (without charge) to appropriate entities for the provision of such information or assistance. Such toll-free number shall be the toll-free number listed for general information and assistance in the annual notice under subsection (a) instead of the listing of numbers of individual contractors."

[¶ 2035] Sec. 1805. MEDICARE PAYMENT ADVISORY COMMISSION

[42 U.S.C. § 1395b-6]

* * *

(b) DUTIES.—

* * *

(2) SPECIFIC TOPICS TO BE REVIEWED.—

* * *

(B) ORIGINAL MEDICARE FEE-FOR-SERVICE SYSTEM.—Specifically, the Commission shall review payment policies under parts A and B, including—

(i) the factors affecting expenditures for the efficient provision of services in different sectors, including the process for updating hospital, skilled nursing facility, physician, and other fees,

* * *

(8) EXAMINATION OF BUDGET CONSEQUENCES.—Before making any recommendations, the Commission shall examine the budget consequences of such recommendations, directly or through consultation with appropriate expert entities.

(c) MEMBERSHIP.—

* * *

(2) QUALIFICATIONS.—

* * *

(B) INCLUSION.—The membership of the Commission shall include (but not be limited to) physicians and other health professionals, experts in the area of pharmaco-economics or prescription drug benefit programs, employers, third-party payers, individuals skilled in the conduct and interpretation of biomedical, health services, and health economics research and expertise in outcomes and effectiveness research and technology assessment. Such membership shall also include representatives of consumers and the elderly.

* * *

(D) ETHICAL DISCLOSURE.—The Comptroller General shall establish a system for public disclosure by members of the Commission of financial and other potential conflicts of interest relating to such members.Members of the Commission shall be treated as employees of Congress for purposes of applying title I of the Ethics in Government Act of 1978 (Public Law 95-521).

* * *

[CCH Explanation at ¶ 721.]

2003 Amendments:

Section 735(a) of the "Medicare Prescription Drug, Improvement, and Modernization Act of 2003," effective upon enactment, amended section 1805(b) by adding new paragraph (8).

Section 735(b) of the "Medicare Prescription Drug, Improvement, and Modernization Act of 2003," effective upon enactment, amended section 1805(b)(2)(B)(i) by inserting "the efficient provision of" after "expenditures for".

Section 735(c)(1) of the "Medicare Prescription Drug, Improvement, and Modernization Act of 2003," effective upon enactment, amended section 1805(c)(2)(D) by adding at the end the following: "Members of the Commission shall be treated as employees of Congress for purposes of applying title I of the Ethics in Government Act of 1978 (Public Law 95-521).".

The amendment made by section 735(c)(1) of the "Medicare Prescription Drug, Improvement, and Modernization Act of 2003," takes effect on January 1, 2004.

Section 735(e) of the "Medicare Prescription Drug, Improvement, and Modernization Act of 2003," effective upon enactment, amended section 1805(c)(2)(B) by inserting "experts in the area of pharmaco-economics or prescription drug benefit programs," after "other health professionals,".

[¶ 2040] Sec. 1807 CHRONIC CARE IMPROVEMENT

(a) IMPLEMENTATION OF CHRONIC CARE IMPROVEMENT PROGRAMS.—

(1) IN GENERAL.—The Secretary shall provide for the phased-in development, testing, evaluation, and implementation of chronic care improvement programs in accordance with this section. Each such program shall be designed to improve clinical quality and beneficiary satisfaction and achieve spending targets with respect to expenditures under this title for targeted beneficiaries with one or more threshold conditions.

(2) DEFINITIONS.—For purposes of this section:

(A) CHRONIC CARE IMPROVEMENT PROGRAM.—The term "chronic care improvement program" means a program described in paragraph (1) that is offered under an agreement under subsection (b) or (c).

(B) CHRONIC CARE IMPROVEMENT ORGANIZATION.—The term "chronic care improvement organization" means an entity that has entered into an agreement under subsection (b) or (c) to provide, directly or through contracts with subcontractors, a chronic care improvement program under this section. Such an entity may be a disease management organization, health insurer, integrated delivery system, physician group practice, a consortium of such entities, or any other legal entity that the Secretary determines appropriate to carry out a chronic care improvement program under this section.

(C) CARE MANAGEMENT PLAN.—The term "care management plan" means a plan established under subsection (d) for a participant in a chronic care improvement program.

(D) THRESHOLD CONDITION.—The term "threshold condition" means a chronic condition, such as congestive heart failure, diabetes, chronic obstructive pulmonary disease (COPD), or other diseases or conditions, as selected by the Secretary as appropriate for the establishment of a chronic care improvement program.

(E) TARGETED BENEFICIARY.—The term "targeted beneficiary" means, with respect to a chronic care improvement program, an individual who—

(i) is entitled to benefits under part A and enrolled under part B, but not enrolled in a plan under part C;

(ii) has one or more threshold conditions covered under such program; and

(iii) has been identified under subsection (d)(1) as a potential participant in such program.

(3) CONSTRUCTION.—Nothing in this section shall be construed as—

(A) expanding the amount, duration, or scope of benefits under this title;

(B) providing an entitlement to participate in a chronic care improvement program under this section;

(C) providing for any hearing or appeal rights under section 1869, 1878, or otherwise, with respect to a chronic care improvement program under this section; or

(D) providing benefits under a chronic care improvement program for which a claim may be submitted to the Secretary by any provider of services or supplier (as defined in section 1861(d)).

(b) DEVELOPMENTAL PHASE (PHASE I).—

(1) IN GENERAL.—In carrying out this section, the Secretary shall enter into agreements consistent with subsection (f) with chronic care improvement organizations for the development, testing, and evaluation of chronic care improvement programs using randomized controlled trials. The first such agreement shall be entered into not later than 12 months after the date of the enactment of this section.

(2) AGREEMENT PERIOD.—The period of an agreement under this subsection shall be for 3 years.

(3) MINIMUM PARTICIPATION.—

(A) IN GENERAL.—The Secretary shall enter into agreements under this subsection in a manner so that chronic care improvement programs offered under this section are offered in geographic areas that, in the aggregate, consist of areas in which at least 10 percent of the aggregate number of medicare beneficiaries reside.

(B) MEDICARE BENEFICIARY DEFINED.—In this paragraph, the term 'medicare beneficiary' means an individual who is entitled to benefits under part A, enrolled under part B, or both, and who resides in the United States.

(4) SITE SELECTION.—In selecting geographic areas in which agreements are entered into under this subsection, the Secretary shall ensure that each chronic care improvement program is conducted in a geographic area in which at least 10,000 targeted beneficiaries reside among other individuals entitled to benefits under part A, enrolled under part B, or both to serve as a control population.

(5) INDEPENDENT EVALUATIONS OF PHASE I PROGRAMS.—The Secretary shall contract for an independent evaluation of the programs conducted under this subsection. Such evaluation shall be done by a contractor with knowledge of chronic care management programs and demonstrated experience in the evaluation of such programs. Each evaluation shall include an assessment of the following factors of the programs:

(A) Quality improvement measures, such as adherence to evidence-based guidelines and rehospitalization rates.

(B) Beneficiary and provider satisfaction.

(C) Health outcomes.

(D) Financial outcomes, including any cost savings to the program under this title.

(c) EXPANDED IMPLEMENTATION PHASE (PHASE II).—

(1) IN GENERAL.—With respect to chronic care improvement programs conducted under subsection (b), if the Secretary finds that the results of the independent evaluation conducted under subsection (b)(6) indicate that the conditions specified in paragraph (2) have been met by a program (or components of such program), the Secretary shall enter into agreements consistent with subsection (f) to expand the implementation of the program (or components) to additional geographic areas not covered under the program as conducted under subsection (b), which may include the implementation of the program on a national basis. Such expansion shall begin not earlier than 2 years after the program is implemented under subsection (b) and not later than 6 months after the date of completion of such program.

(2) CONDITIONS FOR EXPANSION OF PROGRAMS.—The conditions specified in this paragraph are, with respect to a chronic care improvement program conducted under subsection (b) for a threshold condition, that the program is expected to—

(A) improve the clinical quality of care;

(B) improve beneficiary satisfaction; and

(C) achieve targets for savings to the program under this title specified by the Secretary in the agreement within a range determined to be appropriate by the Secretary, subject to the application of budget neutrality with respect to the program and not taking into account any payments by the organization under the agreement under the program for risk under subsection (f)(3)(B).

(3) INDEPENDENT EVALUATIONS OF PHASE II PROGRAMS.—The Secretary shall carry out evaluations of programs expanded under this subsection as the Secretary determines appropriate. Such evaluations shall be carried out in the similar manner as is provided under subsection (b)(5).

(d) IDENTIFICATION AND ENROLLMENT OF PROSPECTIVE PROGRAM PARTICIPANTS.—

(1) IDENTIFICATION OF PROSPECTIVE PROGRAM PARTICIPANTS.—The Secretary shall establish a method for identifying targeted beneficiaries who may benefit from participation in a chronic care improvement program.

(2) INITIAL CONTACT BY SECRETARY.—The Secretary shall communicate with each targeted beneficiary concerning participation in a chronic care improvement program. Such communication may be made by the Secretary and shall include information on the following:

(A) A description of the advantages to the beneficiary in participating in a program.

(B) Notification that the organization offering a program may contact the beneficiary directly concerning such participation.

(C) Notification that participation in a program is voluntary.

(D) A description of the method for the beneficiary to participate or for declining to participate and the method for obtaining additional information concerning such participation.

(3) VOLUNTARY PARTICIPATION.—A targeted beneficiary may participate in a chronic care improvement program on a voluntary basis and may terminate participation at any time.

(e) CHRONIC CARE IMPROVEMENT PROGRAMS.—

(1) IN GENERAL.—Each chronic care improvement program shall—

(A) have a process to screen each targeted beneficiary for conditions other than threshold conditions, such as impaired cognitive ability and co-morbidities, for the purposes of developing an individualized, goaloriented care management plan under paragraph (2);

(B) provide each targeted beneficiary participating in the program with such plan; and

(C) carry out such plan and other chronic care improvement activities in accordance with paragraph (3).

(2) ELEMENTS OF CARE MANAGEMENT PLANS.—A care management plan for a targeted beneficiary shall be developed with the beneficiary and shall, to the extent appropriate, include the following:

(A) A designated point of contact responsible for communications with the beneficiary and for facilitating communications with other health care providers under the plan.

(B) Self-care education for the beneficiary (through approaches such as disease management or medical nutrition therapy) and education for primary caregivers and family members.

(C) Education for physicians and other providers and collaboration to enhance communication of relevant clinical information.

(D) The use of monitoring technologies that enable patient guidance through the exchange of pertinent clinical information, such as vital signs, symptomatic information, and health self-assessment.

(E) The provision of information about hospice care, pain and palliative care, and end-of-life care.

(3) CONDUCT OF PROGRAMS.—In carrying out paragraph (1)(C) with respect to a participant, the chronic care improvement organization shall—

(A) guide the participant in managing the participant's health (including all co-morbidities, relevant health care services, and pharmaceutical needs) and in performing activities as specified under the elements of the care management plan of the participant;

(B) use decision-support tools such as evidencebased practice guidelines or other criteria as determined by the Secretary; and

(C) develop a clinical information database to track and monitor each participant across settings and to evaluate outcomes.

(4) ADDITIONAL RESPONSIBILITIES.—

(A) OUTCOMES REPORT.—Each chronic care improvement organization offering a chronic care improvement program shall monitor and report to the Secretary, in a manner specified by the Secretary, on health care quality, cost, and outcomes.

(B) ADDITIONAL REQUIREMENTS.—Each such organization and program shall comply with such additional requirements as the Secretary may specify.

(5) ACCREDITATION.—The Secretary may provide that chronic care improvement programs and chronic care improvement organizations that are accredited by qualified organizations (as defined by the Secretary) may be deemed to meet such requirements under this section as the Secretary may specify.

(f) TERMS OF AGREEMENTS.—

(1) TERMS AND CONDITIONS.—

(A) IN GENERAL.—An agreement under this section with a chronic care improvement organization shall contain such terms and conditions as the Secretary may specify consistent with this section.

(B) CLINICAL, QUALITY IMPROVEMENT, AND FINANCIAL REQUIREMENTS.—The Secretary may not enter into an agreement with such an organization under this section for the operation of a chronic care improvement program unless—

(i) the program and organization meet the requirements of subsection (e) and such clinical, quality improvement, financial, and other requirements as the Secretary deems to be appropriate for the targeted beneficiaries to be served; and

(ii) the organization demonstrates to the satisfaction of the Secretary that the organization is able to assume financial risk for performance under the agreement (as applied under paragraph (3)(B)) with respect to payments made to the organization under such agreement through available reserves, reinsurance, withholds, or such other means as the Secretary determines appropriate.

(2) MANNER OF PAYMENT.—Subject to paragraph (3)(B), the payment under an agreement under—

(A) subsection (b) shall be computed on a permember per-month basis; or

(B) subsection (c) may be on a per-member permonth basis or such other basis as the Secretary and organization may agree.

(3) APPLICATION OF PERFORMANCE STANDARDS.—

(A) SPECIFICATION OF PERFORMANCE STANDARDS.—Each agreement under this section with a chronic care improvement organization shall specify performance standards for each of the factors specified in subsection (c)(2), including clinical quality and spending targets under this title, against which the performance of the chronic care improvement organization under the agreement is measured.

(B) ADJUSTMENT OF PAYMENT BASED ON PERFORMANCE.—

(i) IN GENERAL.—Each such agreement shall provide for adjustments in payment rates to an organization under the agreement insofar as the Secretary determines that the organization failed to meet the performance standards specified in the agreement under subparagraph (A).

(ii) FINANCIAL RISK FOR PERFORMANCE.—In the case of an agreement under subsection (b) or (c), the agreement shall provide for a full recovery for any amount by which the fees paid to the organization under the agreement exceed the estimated savings to the programs under this title attributable to implementation of such agreement.

(4) BUDGET NEUTRAL PAYMENT CONDITION.—Under this section, the Secretary shall ensure that the aggregate sum of medicare program benefit expenditures for beneficiaries participating in chronic care improvement programs and funds paid to chronic care improvement organizations under this section, shall not exceed the medicare program benefit expenditures that the Secretary estimates would have been made for such targeted beneficiaries in the absence of such programs.

§1807(f)(4) ¶2040

(g) FUNDING.—(1) Subject to paragraph (2), there are appropriated to the Secretary, in appropriate part from the Federal Hospital Insurance Trust Fund and the Federal Supplementary Medical Insurance Trust Fund, such sums as may be necessary to provide for agreements with chronic care improvement programs under this section.

(2) In no case shall the funding under this section exceed $100,000,000 in aggregate increased expenditures under this title (after taking into account any savings attributable to the operation of this section) over the 3-fiscal-year period beginning on October 1, 2003.

[CCH Explanation at ¶ 678.]

2003 Amendments:

Section 721(a) of the "Medicare Prescription Drug, Improvement, and Modernization Act of 2003," effective upon enactment, amended Title XVIII by inserting new section 1807 after section 1806.

[¶ 2045] Sec. 1808. PROVISIONS RELATING TO ADMINISTRATION

(a) COORDINATED ADMINISTRATION OF MEDICARE PRESCRIPTION DRUG AND MEDICARE ADVANTAGE PROGRAMS.—

(1) IN GENERAL.—There is within the Centers for Medicare & Medicaid Services a center to carry out the duties described in paragraph (3).

(2) DIRECTOR.—Such center shall be headed by a director who shall report directly to the Administrator of the Centers for Medicare & Medicaid Services.

(3) DUTIES.—The duties described in this paragraph are the following:

(A) The administration of parts C and D.

(B) The provision of notice and information under section 1804.

(C) Such other duties as the Secretary may specify.

(4) DEADLINE.—The Secretary shall ensure that the center is carrying out the duties described in paragraph (3) by not later than January 1, 2008.

(b) EMPLOYMENT OF MANAGEMENT STAFF.—

(1) IN GENERAL.—The Secretary may employ, within the Centers for Medicare & Medicaid Services, such individuals as management staff as the Secretary determines to be appropriate. With respect to the administration of parts C and D, such individuals shall include individuals with private sector expertise in negotiations with health benefits plans.

(2) ELIGIBILITY.—To be eligible for employment under paragraph (1) an individual shall be required to have demonstrated, by their education and experience (either in the public or private sector), superior expertise in at least one of the following areas:

(A) The review, negotiation, and administration of health care contracts.

(B) The design of health care benefit plans.

(C) Actuarial sciences.

(D) Compliance with health plan contracts.

(E) Consumer education and decision making.

(F) Any other area specified by the Secretary that requires specialized management or other expertise.

(3) RATES OF PAYMENT.—

(A) PERFORMANCE-RELATED PAY.—Subject to subparagraph (B), the Secretary shall establish the rate of pay for an individual employed under paragraph (1). Such rate shall take into account expertise, experience, and performance.

(B) LIMITATION.—In no case may the rate of compensation determined under subparagraph (A) exceed the highest rate of basic pay for the Senior Executive Service under section 5382(b) of title 5, United States Code.

(c) MEDICARE BENEFICIARY OMBUDSMAN.—

(1) IN GENERAL.—The Secretary shall appoint within the Department of Health and Human Services a Medicare Beneficiary Ombudsman who shall have expertise and experience in the fields of health care and education of (and assistance to) individuals entitled to benefits under this title.

(2) DUTIES.—The Medicare Beneficiary Ombudsman shall—

(A) receive complaints, grievances, and requests for information submitted by individuals entitled to benefits under part A or enrolled under part B, or both, with respect to any aspect of the medicare program;

(B) provide assistance with respect to complaints, grievances, and requests referred to in subparagraph (A), including—

(i) assistance in collecting relevant information for such individuals, to seek an appeal of a decision or determination made by a fiscal intermediary, carrier, MA organization, or the Secretary;

(ii) assistance to such individuals with any problems arising from disenrollment from an MA plan under part C; and

(iii) assistance to such individuals in presenting information under section 1839(i)(4)(C) (relating to income-related premium adjustment; and

(C) submit annual reports to Congress and the Secretary that describe the activities of the Office and that include such recommendations for improvement in the administration of this title as the Ombudsman determines appropriate.

The Ombudsman shall not serve as an advocate for any increases in payments or new coverage of services, but may identify issues and problems in payment or coverage policies.

(3) WORKING WITH HEALTH INSURANCE COUNSELING PROGRAMS.—To the extent possible, the Ombudsman shall work with health insurance counseling programs (receiving funding under section 4360 of Omnibus Budget Reconciliation Act of 1990) to facilitate the provision of information to individuals entitled to benefits under part A or enrolled under part B, or both regarding MA plans and changes to those plans. Nothing in this paragraph shall preclude further collaboration between the Ombudsman and such programs.

[CCH Explanation at ¶801 and 832.]

2003 Amendments:

Section 900(a) of the "Medicare Prescription Drug, Improvement, and Modernization Act of 2003," effective upon enactment,, amended Title XVIII by inserting new section 1808 after section 1807.

Section 900(b) of the "Medicare Prescription Drug, Improvement, and Modernization Act of 2003," effective upon enactment,, further amended section 1808 by inserting new subsection (b)

Section 923 of the "Medicare Prescription Drug, Improvement, and Modernization Act of 2003," effective upon enactment,, amended section 1808 by adding new subsection (c) at the end.

[¶2050] Sec. 1812. SCOPE OF BENEFITS

[42 U.S.C. §1395d]

(a) The benefits provided to an individual by the insurance program under this part shall consist of entitlement to have payment made on his behalf or, in the case of payments referred to in section 1814(d)(2) to him (subject to the provisions of this part) for—

* * *

(3) in the case of individuals not enrolled in part B, home health services, and in the case of individuals so enrolled, post-institutional home health services furnished during a home health spell of illness for up to 100 visits during such spell of illness;

(4) in lieu of certain other benefits, hospice care with respect to the individual during up to two periods of 90 days each and an unlimited number of subsequent periods of 60 days each with respect to which the individual makes an election under subsection (d)(1); and.

(5) for individuals who are terminally ill, have not made an election under subsection (d)(1), and have not previously received services under this paragraph, services that are furnished by a physician (as defined in section 1861(r)(1)) who is either the medical director or an employee of a hospice program and that—

(A) consist of—

(i) an evaluation of the individual's need for pain and symptom management, including the individual's need for hospice care; and

(ii) counseling the individual with respect to hospice care and other care options; and

(B) may include advising the individual regarding advanced care planning.

* * *

[CCH Explanation at ¶ 677.]

2003 Amendments:

Section 512(a) of the "Medicare Prescription Drug, Improvement, and Modernization Act of 2003," effective upon enactment, amended section 1812(a) by striking "and" at the end of paragraph (3); by striking the period at the end of paragraph (4) and inserting "; and"; and by inserting after paragraph (4) new paragraph (5).

The amendments made by section 512(a) of the "Medicare Prescription Drug, Improvement, and Modernization Act of 2003," apply to services provided by a hospice program on or after January 1, 2005.

Section 736(c)(1) of the "Medicare Prescription Drug, Improvement, and Modernization Act of 2003," effective upon enactment, amended section 1812(a)(3) by striking "for individuals not" and inserting "in the case of individuals not"; and by striking "for individuals so" and inserting "in the case of individuals so".

[¶ 2055] Sec. 1814. REQUIREMENT OF REQUESTS AND CERTIFICATIONS

[42 U.S.C. § 1395f(a)]

(a) Except as provided in subsections (d) and (g) and in section 1876, payment for services furnished an individual may be made only to providers of services which are eligible therefor under section 1866 and only if—

* * *

(7) in the case of hospice care provided an individual—

(A)(i) in the first 90-day period—

(I) the individual's attending physician (as defined in section 1861(dd)(3)(B))(which for purposes of this subparagraph does not include a nurse practitioner), and

(II) the medical director (or physician member of the interdisciplinary group described in section 1861(dd)(2)(B)) of the hospice program providing (or arranging for) the care,

each certify in writing at the beginning of the period that the individual is terminally ill (as defined in section 1861(dd)(3)(A)), based on the physician's or medical director's clinical judgment regarding the normal course of the individual's illness and

(ii) in a subsequent 90- or 60-day period, the medical director or physician described in clause (i)(II) recertifies at the beginning of the period that the individual is terminally ill based on such clinical judgment;

* * *

(8) in the case of inpatient critical access hospital services, a physician certifies that the individual may reasonably be expected to be discharged or transferred to a hospital within 96 hours after admission to the critical access hospital.

To the extent provided by regulations, the certification and recertification requirements of paragraph (2) shall be deemed satisfied where, at a later date, a physician, nurse practitioner, or clinical nurse specialist (as the case may be) makes certification of the kind provided in subparagraph (A), (B), (C), or (D) of paragraph (2) (whichever would have applied), but only where such certification is accompanied by such medical and other evidence as may be required by such regulations. With respect to the physician certification required by paragraph (2) for home health services furnished to any individual by a home health agency (other than an agency which is a governmental entity) and with respect to the establishment and review of a plan for such services, the Secretary shall prescribe regulations which shall become effective no later than July 1, 1981, and which prohibit a physician who has a significant ownership interest in, or a significant financial or contractual relationship with, such home health agency from performing such certification and from establishing or reviewing such plan, except that such prohibition shall not apply with respect to a home health agency which is a sole community home health agency (as determined by the Secretary). For purposes of the preceding sentence, service by a physician as an uncompensated officer or director of a home health agency shall not constitute having a significant ownership interest in, or a significant financial or contractual relationship with, such agency. For purposes of paragraph (2)(C), an individual shall be considered to be "confined to his home" if the individual has a condition, due to an illness or injury, that restricts the ability of the individual to leave his or her home except with the assistance of another individual or the aid of a supportive device (such as crutches, a cane, a wheelchair, or a walker), or if the individual has a condition such that leaving his or her home is medically contraindicated. While an individual does not have to be bedridden to be considered "confined to his home," the condition of the individual should be such that there exists a normal inability to leave home and that leaving home requires a considerable and taxing effort by the individual. Any absence of an individual from the home attributable to the need to receive health care treatment, including regular absences for the purpose of participating in therapeutic, psychosocial, or medical treatment in an adult day-care program that is licensed or certified by a State, or accredited, to furnish adult day-care services in the State shall not disqualify an individual from being considered to be "confined to his home". Any other absence of an individual from the home shall not so disqualify an individual if the absence is of infrequent or of relatively short duration. For purposes of the preceding sentence, any absence for the purpose of attending a religious service shall be deemed to be an absence of infrequent or short duration.

[CCH Explanation at ¶ 671.]

2003 Amendments:

Section 408(b) of the "Medicare Prescription Drug, Improvement, and Modernization Act of 2003," effective upon enactment, amended section 1814(a)(7)(A)(i)(I) by inserting "(which for purposes of this subparagraph does not include a nurse practitioner)" after "attending physician (as defined in section 1861(dd)(3)(B))".

Section 736(a)(1)(A) of the "Medicare Prescription Drug, Improvement, and Modernization Act of 2003," effective upon enactment, amended section 1814(a) by striking the seventh sentence, as added by section 322(a)(1) of BIPA (PubLNo. 106-554).

Prior to being stricken, the seventh sentence of section 1814(a), as added by section 322(a)(1) of BIPA read as follows:

"The certification regarding terminal illness of an individual under paragraph (7) shall be based on the physician's or medical director's clinical judgment regarding the normal course of the individual's illness."

Section 736(a)(1)(B)(i) of the "Medicare Prescription Drug, Improvement, and Modernization Act of 2003," effective upon enactment, amended section 1814(a)(7)(A) by inserting before the comma at the end the following: "based on the physician's or medical director's clinical judgment regarding the normal course of the individual's illness".

Section 736(a)(1)(B)(ii) of the "Medicare Prescription Drug, Improvement, and Modernization Act of 2003," effective upon enactment, amended section 1814(a)(7)(A) in clause (ii) by inserting before the semicolon at the end the following: "based on such clinical judgment".

Section 736(c)(2)(A) of the "Medicare Prescription Drug, Improvement, and Modernization Act of 2003," effective upon enactment, amended section 1814(a) in the sixth sentence by striking "leave home," and inserting "leave home and".

[¶ 2060] Sec. 1814. AMOUNT PAID TO PROVIDERS
[42 U.S.C. § 1395f(b)]

(b) The amount paid to any provider of services (other than a hospice program providing hospice care, other than a critical access hospital providing inpatient critical access hospital services, and other than a home health agency with respect to durable medical equipment) with respect to services for which payment may be made under this part shall, subject to the provisions of sections 1813, 1886, and 1895 be—

* * *

2003 Amendments:

Section 736(a)(2) of the "Medicare Prescription Drug, Improvement, and Modernization Act of 2003," effective upon enactment, amended section 1814(b) by inserting a comma after "1813".

[¶ 2065] Sec. 1814. PAYMENT FOR HOSPICE CARE
[42 U.S.C. § 1395f(i)]

(i)

* * *

(4) The amount paid to a hospice program with respect to the services under section 1812(a)(5) for which payment may be made under this part shall be equal to an amount established for an office or other outpatient visit for evaluation and management associated with presenting problems of moderate severity and requiring medical decisionmaking of low complexity under the fee schedule established under section 1848(b), other than the portion of such amount attributable to the practice expense component.

(5) In the case of hospice care provided by a hospice program under arrangements under section 1861(dd)(5)(D) made by another hospice program, the hospice program that made the arrangements shall bill and be paid for the hospice care.

[CCH Explanation at ¶ 677 and 946.]

2003 Amendments:

Section 512(b) of the "Medicare Prescription Drug, Improvement, and Modernization Act of 2003," effective upon enactment, amended section 1814(i) by adding at the end a new paragraph (4).

The amendments made by section 512(b) of the "Medicare Prescription Drug, Improvement, and Modernization Act of 2003," apply to services provided by a hospice program on or after January 1, 2005.

Section 946(b) of the "Medicare Prescription Drug, Improvement, and Modernization Act of 2003," effective upon enactment, amended section 1814(i) by adding at the end a new paragraph (5).

[¶ 2075] Sec. 1814. PAYMENT FOR INPATIENT CRITICAL ACCESS HOSPITAL SERVICES

[42 U.S.C. § 1395f(l)]

(l)(1) Except as provided in paragraph (2), the amount of payment under this part for inpatient critical access hospital services is equal to 101 percent of the reasonable costs of the critical access hospital in providing such services.

(2) In the case of a distinct part psychiatric or rehabilitation unit of a critical access hospital described in section 1820(c)(2)(E), the amount of payment for inpatient critical access hospital services of such unit shall be equal to the amount of the payment that would otherwise be made if such services were inpatient hospital services of a distinct part psychiatric or rehabilitation unit, respectively, described in the matter following clause (v) of section 1886(d)(1)(B).

[CCH Explanation at ¶ 578.]

2003 Amendments:

Section 405(a)(1) of the "Medicare Prescription Drug, Improvement, and Modernization Act of 2003," amended section 1814(l) by inserting "equal to 101 percent of" before "the reasonable costs".

The amendments made by section 405(a) of the "Medicare Prescription Drug, Improvement, and Modernization Act of 2003," apply to payments for services furnished during cost reporting periods beginning on or after January 1, 2004.

Section 405(g)(2)(A) of the "Medicare Prescription Drug, Improvement, and Modernization Act of 2003," amended section 1814(l) by striking "(l) The amount" and inserting "(l)(1) Except as provided in paragraph (2), the amount".

Section 405(g)(2)(B) of the "Medicare Prescription Drug, Improvement, and Modernization Act of 2003," amended section 1814(l)(1) by adding at the end a new paragraph (2).

The amendments made by section 405(g) of the "Medicare Prescription Drug, Improvement, and Modernization Act of 2003," apply to cost reporting periods beginning on or after October 1, 2004.

[¶ 2080] Sec. 1815. PAYMENT TO PROVIDERS OF SERVICES

[42 U.S.C. § 1395g]

* * *

(e)(1) The Secretary shall provide payment under this part for inpatient hospital services furnished by a subsection (d) hospital (as defined in section 1886(d)(1)(B), and including a distinct psychiatric or rehabilitation unit of such a hospital) and a subsection (d) Puerto Rico hospital (as defined in section 1386(d)(9)(A)) on a periodic interim payment basis (rather than on the basis of bills actually submitted) in the following cases:

* * *

(B) In the case of a hospital that—

* * *

(C) In the case of a hospital that—

* * *

(2) The Secretary shall provide (or continue to provide) for payment on a periodic interim payment basis (under the standards established under section 405.454(j) of title 42, Code of Federal Regulations, as in effect on October 1, 1986)) in the cases described in subparagraphs (A) through (D)with respect to—

* * *

(C) extended care services;

(D) hospice care;

if the provider of such services elects to receive, and qualifies for, such payments and;

(E) inpatient critical access hospital services;

[CCH Explanation at ¶ 578.]

2003 Amendments:

Section 405(c)(1) of the "Medicare Prescription Drug, Improvement, and Modernization Act of 2003," amended section 1815(e)(2) in the matter before subparagraph (A), by inserting ", in the cases described in subparagraphs (A) through (D)" after "1986"; by striking "and" at the end of subparagraph (C); by adding "and" at the end of subparagraph (D); and by inserting after subparagraph (D) new subparagraph (E).

The above amendments apply to payments made on or after July 1, 2004.

Section 736(a)(3) of the "Medicare Prescription Drug, Improvement, and Modernization Act of 2003," effective upon enactment, amended section 1815(e)(1)(B) in the matter preceding clause (i), by striking "of hospital" and inserting "of a hospital".

[¶ 2085] Sec. 1816. PROVISIONS RELATING TO THE ADMINISTRATION OF PART A

[42 U.S.C. § 1395h]

(a) The administration of this part shall be conducted through contracts with medicare administrative contractors under section 1874A.

(b) [Repealed.]

(c) [Stricken.]

* * *

(2)(A) Each contract under section 1874A that provides for making payments under this part shall provide that payment shall be issued, mailed, or otherwise transmitted with respect to not less than 95 percent of all claims submitted under this title—

* * *

(B) In this paragraph:

* * *

(ii) The term "applicable number of calendar days" means—

* * *

(III) with respect to claims received in the 12-month period beginning October 1, 1988, 25 calendar days,

(IV) with respect to claims received in the 12-month period beginning October 1, 1989, and claims received in any succeeding 12-month period ending on or before September 30, 1993, 24 calendar days, and

* * *

(3)(A) Each contract under section 1874A that provides for making payments under this part shall provide that no payment shall be issued, mailed, or otherwise transmitted with respect to any claim submitted under this title within the applicable number of calendar days after the date on which the claim is received.

* * *

(d) [Repealed.]

(e) [Repealed.]

(f) [Repealed.]

(g) [Repealed.]

(h) [Repealed.]

(i) [Repealed.]

(j) A contract with a medicare administrative contractor under section 1874A with respect to the administration of this part shall require that, with respect to a claim for home health services, extended care services, or post-hospital extended care services submitted by a provider to such medicare administrative contractor that is denied, such medicare administrative contractor—

(k) A contract with a medicare administrative contractor under section 1874A with respect to the administration of this part shall require that such medicare administrative contractor submit an annual report to the Secretary describing the steps taken to recover payments made for items or services for which payment has been or could be made under a primary plan (as defined in section 1862(b)(2)(A)).

(l) [Repealed.]

[CCH Explanation at ¶ 829.]

2003 Amendments:

Section 736(a)(4)(A) of the "Medicare Prescription Drug, Improvement, and Modernization Act of 2003," effective upon enactment, amended section 1816(c)(2)(B)(ii)(III) by striking "and" at the end of subclause (III).

Section 736(a)(4)(B) of the "Medicare Prescription Drug, Improvement, and Modernization Act of 2003," effective upon enactment, amended section 1816(c)(2)(B)(ii)(IV) by striking the period at the end of subclause (IV) and inserting ", and".

Section 911(b)(1) of the "Medicare Prescription Drug, Improvement, and Modernization Act of 2003," effective October 1, 2005, amended the heading of section 1816 to read as follows: "PROVISIONS RELATING TO THE ADMINISTRATION OF PART A".

Prior to amendment the heading of section 1816 read as follows: USE OF PUBLIC AGENCIES OR PRIVATE ORGANIZATIONS TO FACILITATE PAYMENT TO PROVIDERS OF SERVICES.

Section 911(b)(2) of the "Medicare Prescription Drug, Improvement, and Modernization Act of 2003," effective October 1, 2005, amended section 1816(a).

Prior to amendment subsection (a) read as follows:

(a) If any group or association of providers of services wishes to have payments under this part to such providers made through a national, State, or other public or private agency or organization and nominates such agency or organization for this purpose, the Secretary is authorized to enter into an agreement with such agency or organization providing for the determination by such agency or organization (subject to such of the provisions of section 1878 and to review by the Secretary as may be provided for by the agreement) of the amount of the payments required pursuant to this part to be made to such providers (and to providers assigned to such agency or organization under subsection (e)), and for the making of such payments by such agency or organization to such providers (and to providers assigned to such agency or organization under subsection (e)). Such agreement may also include provision for the agency or organization to do all or any part of the following: (1) to provide consultative services to institutions or agencies to enable them to establish and maintain fiscal records necessary for purposes of this part and otherwise to qualify as hospitals, extended care facilities, or home health agencies, and (2) with respect to the providers of services which are to receive payments through it (A) to serve as a center for, and communicate to providers, any information or instructions furnished to it by the Secretary, and serve as a channel of communication from providers to the Secretary; (B) to make such audits of the records of providers as may be necessary to insure that proper payments are made under this part; and (C) to perform such other functions as are necessary to carry out this subsection. As used in this title and part B of title XI, the term "fiscal intermediary" means an agency or organization with a contract under this section.

Section 911(b)(3) of the "Medicare Prescription Drug, Improvement, and Modernization Act of 2003," effective October 1, 2005, repealed section 1816(b).

Prior to being repealed Section 1816(b) read as follows:

(b) The Secretary shall not enter into or renew an agreement with any agency or organization under this section unless—

(1) he finds—

(A) after applying the standards, criteria, and procedures developed under subsection (f), that to do so is consistent with the effective and efficient administration of this part, and

(B) that such agency or organization is willing and able to assist the providers to which payments are made through it under this part in the application of safeguards against unnecessary utilization of services furnished by them to individuals entitled to hospital insurance benefits under section 226, and the agreement provides for such assistance; and

(2) such agency or organization agrees—

(A) to furnish to the Secretary such of the information acquired by it in carrying out its agreement under this section, and

(B) to provide the Secretary with access to all such data, information, and claims processing operations,

as the Secretary may find necessary in performing his functions under this part.

Section 911(b)(4) of the "Medicare Prescription Drug, Improvement, and Modernization Act of 2003," effective October 1, 2005, amended section 1816(c) by striking paragraph (1); and in each of paragraphs (2)(A) and (3)(A), by striking "agreement under this section" and inserting "contract under section 1874A that provides for making payments under this part".

Prior to being stricken, section 1816(c)(1) read as follows:

(1) An agreement with any agency or organization under this section may contain such terms and conditions as the Secretary finds necessary or appropriate, may provide for advances of funds to the agency or organization for the making of payments by it under subsection (a), and shall provide for payment of so much of the cost of administration of the agency or organization as is determined by the Secretary to be necessary and proper for carrying out the functions covered by the agreement. The Secretary shall provide that in determining the necessary and proper cost of administration, the Secretary shall, with respect to each agreement, take into account the amount that is reasonable and adequate to meet the cost which must be incurred by an efficiently and economically operated agency or organization in carrying out the terms of its agreement. The Secretary shall cause to have published in the Federal Register, by not later than September 1 before each fiscal year, data, standards, and methodology to be used to establish budgets for fiscal intermediaries under this section for that fiscal year, and shall cause to be published in the Federal Register for public comment, at least 90 days before such data, standards, and methodology are published, the data, standards, and methodology proposed to be used. The Secretary may not require, as a condition of entering into or renewing an agreement under this section or under section 1871, that a fiscal intermediary match data obtained other than in its activities under this part with data used in the administra-

tion of this part for purposes of identifying situations in which the provisions of section 1862(b) may appear.

Section 911(b)(5) of the "Medicare Prescription Drug, Improvement, and Modernization Act of 2003," effective October 1, 2005, upon enactment, repealed section 1816(d) – (i).

Prior to being repealed Section 1816(d) – (i) read as follows:

(d) If the nomination of an agency or organization as provided in this section is made by a group or association of providers of services, it shall not be binding on members of the group or association which notify the Secretary of their election to that effect. Any provider may, upon such notice as may be specified in the agreement under this section with an agency or organization, withdraw its nomination to receive payments through such agency or organization. Any provider which has withdrawn its nomination, and any provider which has not made a nomination, may elect to receive payments from any agency or organization which has entered into an agreement with the Secretary under this section if the Secretary and such agency or organization agree to it.

(e)(1) Notwithstanding subsections (a) and (d), the Secretary, after taking into consideration any preferences of providers of services, may assign or reassign any provider of services to any agency or organization which has entered into an agreement with him under this section, if he determines, after applying the standards, criteria, and procedures developed under subsection (f), that such assignment or reassignment would result in the more effective and efficient administration of this part.

(2) Notwithstanding subsections (a) and (d), the Secretary may (subject to the provisions of paragraph (4)) designate a national or regional agency or organization which has entered into an agreement with him under this section to perform functions under the agreement with respect to a class of providers of services in the Nation or region (as the case may be), if he determines, after applying the standards, criteria, and procedures developed under subsection (f), that such designation would result in more effective and efficient administration of this part.

(3)(A) Before the Secretary makes an assignment or reassignment under paragraph (1) of a provider of services to other than the agency or organization nominated by the provider, he shall furnish (i) the provider and such agency or organization with a full explanation of the reasons for his determination as to the efficiency and effectiveness of the agency or organization to perform the functions required under this part with respect to the provider, and (ii) such agency or organization with opportunity for a hearing, and such determination shall be subject to judicial review in accordance with chapter 7 of title 5, United States Code.

(B) Before the Secretary makes a designation under paragraph (2) with respect to a class of providers of services, he shall furnish (i) such providers and the agencies and organizations adversely affected by such designation with a full explanation of the reasons for his determination as to the efficiency and effectiveness of such agencies and organizations to perform the functions required under this part with respect to such providers, and (ii) the agencies and organizations adversely affected by such designation with opportunity for a hearing, and such determination shall be subject to judicial review in accordance with chapter 7 of title 5 United States Code.

(4) Notwithstanding subsections (a) and (d) and paragraphs (1), (2), and (3) of this subsection, the Secretary shall designate regional agencies or organizations which have entered into an agreement with him under this section to perform functions under such agreement with respect to home health agencies (as defined in section 1861(o)) in the region, except that in assigning such agencies to such designated regional agencies or organizations the Secretary shall assign a home health agency which is a subdivision of a hospital (and such agency and hospital are affiliated or under common control) only if, after applying such criteria relating to administrative efficiency and effectiveness as he shall promulgate, he determines that such assignment would result in the more effective and efficient administration of this title. By not later than July 1, 1987, the Secretary shall limit the number of such regional agencies or organizations to not more than ten.

(5) Notwithstanding any other provision of this title, the Secretary shall designate the agency or organization which has entered into an agreement under this section to perform functions under such an agreement with respect to each hospice program, except that with respect to a hospice program which is a subdivision of a provider of services (and such hospice program and provider of services are under common control) due regard shall be given to the agency or organization which performs the functions under this section for the provider of services.

(f)(1) In order to determine whether the Secretary should enter into, renew, or terminate an agreement under this section with an agency or organization, whether the Secretary should assign or reassign a provider of services to an agency or organization, and whether the Secretary should designate an agency or organization to perform services with respect to a class of providers of services, the Secretary shall develop standards, criteria, and procedures to evaluate such agency's or organization's (A) overall performance of claims processing (including the agency's or organization's success in recovering payments made under this title for services for which payment has been or could be made under a primary plan (as defined in section $1862(b)(2)(A)$)) and other related functions required to be performed by such an agency or organization under an agreement entered into under this section, and (B) performance of such functions with respect to specific providers of services, and the Secretary shall establish standards and criteria with respect to the efficient and effective administration of this part. No agency or organization shall be found under such standards and criteria not to be efficient or effective or to be less efficient or effective solely on the ground that the agency or organization serves only providers located in a single State.

(2) The standards and criteria established under paragraph (1) shall include—

(A) with respect to claims for services furnished under this part by any provider of services other than a hospital—

(i) whether such agency or organization is able to process 75 percent of reconsiderations within 60 days (except in the case of fiscal year 1989, 66 percent of reconsiderations) and 90 percent of reconsiderations within 90 days, and

(ii) the extent to which such agency's or organization's determinations are reversed on appeal; and

(B) with respect to applications for an exemption from or exception or adjustment to the target amount applicable under section 1886(b) to a hospital that is a not a subsection (d) hospital (as defined in section $1886(d)(1)(B)$)—

(i) if such agency or organization receives a completed application, whether such agency or organization is able to process such application not later than 75 days after the application is filed, and

(ii) if such agency or organization receives an incomplete application, whether such agency or organization is able to return the application with instructions on how to complete the application not later than 60 days after the application is filed.

(g) An agreement with the Secretary under this section may be terminated—

(1) by the agency or organization which entered into such agreement at such time and upon such notice to the Secretary, to the public, and to the providers as may be provided in regulations, or

(2) by the Secretary at such time and upon such notice to the agency or organization, to the providers which have nominated it for purposes of this section, and to the public, as may be provided in regulations, but only if he finds, after

applying the standards, criteria, and procedures developed under subsection (f) and after reasonable notice and opportunity for hearing to the agency or organization, that (A) the agency or organization has failed substantially to carry out the agreement, or (B) the continuation of some or all of the functions provided for in the agreement with the agency or organization is disadvantageous or is inconsistent with the efficient administration of this part.

(h) An agreement with an agency or organization under this section may require any of its officers or employees certifying payments or disbursing funds pursuant to the agreement, or otherwise participating in carrying out the agreement, to give surety bond to the United States in such amount as the Secretary may deem appropriate.

(i)(1) No individual designated pursuant to an agreement under this section as a certifying officer shall, in the absence of gross negligence or intent to defraud the United States, be liable with respect to any payments certified by him under this section.

(2) No disbursing officer shall, in the absence of gross negligence or intent to defraud the United States, be liable with respect to any payment by him under this section if it was based upon a voucher signed by a certifying officer designated as provided in paragraph (1) of this subsection.

(3) No such agency or organization shall be liable to the United States for any payments referred to in paragraph (1) or (2).

Section 911(b)(6)(A) of the "Medicare Prescription Drug, Improvement, and Modernization Act of 2003," effective October 1, 2005, amended section 1816(j) by striking "An agreement with an agency or organization under this section" and inserting "A contract with a medicare administrative contractor under section 1874A with respect to the administration of this part"; and by striking "such agency or organization" and inserting "such medicare administrative contractor" each place it appears.

Section 911(b)(6)(B) of the "Medicare Prescription Drug, Improvement, and Modernization Act of 2003," effective October 1, 2005, amended section 1816(k) by striking "An agreement with an agency or organization under this section" and inserting "A contract with a medicare administrative contractor under section 1874A with respect to the administration of this part"; and by striking "such agency or organization" and inserting "such medicare administrative contractor" each place it appears.

Section 911(b)(7) of the "Medicare Prescription Drug, Improvement, and Modernization Act of 2003," effective October 1, 2005, repealed section 1816(l).

Prior to being repealed Section 1816(l) read as follows:

(l) No agency or organization may carry out (or receive payment for carrying out) any activity pursuant to an agreement under this section to the extent that the activity is carried out pursuant to a contract under the Medicare Integrity Program under section 1893.

[¶ 2090] Sec. 1817. FEDERAL HOSPITAL INSURANCE TRUST FUND

[42 U.S.C. § 1395i]

* * *

(b) With respect to the Trust Fund, there is hereby created a body to be known as the Board of Trustees of the Trust Fund (hereinafter in this section referred to as the "Board of Trustees") composed of the Commissioner of Social Security, the Secretary of the Treasury, the Secretary of Labor, and the Secretary of Health and Human Services, all ex officio, and of two members of the public (both of whom may not be from the same political party), who shall be nominated by the President for a term of four years and subject to confirmation by the Senate. A member of the Board of Trustees serving as a member of the public and nominated and confirmed to fill a vacancy occurring during a term shall be nominated and confirmed only for the remainder of such term. An individual nominated and confirmed as a member of the public may serve in such position after the expiration of such member's term until the earlier of the time at which the member's successor takes office or the time at which a report of the Board is first issued under paragraph (2) after the expiration of the member's term. The Secretary of the Treasury shall be the Managing Trustee of the Board of Trustees (hereinafter in this section referred to as the "Managing Trustee"). The Administrator of the Centers for Medicare & Medicaid Services shall serve as the Secretary of the Board of Trustees. The Board of Trustees shall meet not less frequently than once each calendar year. It shall be the duty of the Board of Trustees to—

* * *

(2) Report to the Congress not later than the first day of April of each year on the operation and status of the Trust Fund during the preceding fiscal year and on its expected operation and status during the current fiscal year and the next 2 fiscal years;Each report provided under paragraph (2) beginning with the report in 2005 shall include the information specified in section 801(a) of Medicare Prescription Drug, Improvement, and Modernization Act of 2003.

* * *

(4) Review the general policies followed in managing the Trust Fund, and recommend changes in such policies, including necessary changes in the provisions of law which govern the way in which the Trust Fund is to be managed.

The report provided for in paragraph (2) shall include a statement of the assets of, and the disbursements made from, the Trust Fund during the preceding fiscal year, an estimate of the expected income to, and disbursements to be made from, the Trust Fund during the current fiscal year and each of the next 2 fiscal years, and a statement of the actuarial status of the Trust Fund. Such report shall also include an actuarial opinion by the Chief Actuary of the Centers for Medicare & Medicaid Services certifying that the techniques and methodologies used are generally accepted within the actuarial profession and that the assumptions and cost estimates used are reasonable. Such report shall be printed as a House document of the session of the Congress to which the report is made. A person serving on the Board of Trustees shall not be considered to be a fiduciary and shall not be personally liable for actions taken in such capacity with respect to the Trust Fund.

* * *

* * *

(k)(3)(A)(i) There are hereby appropriated to the Account from the Trust Fund such sums as the Secretary and the Attorney General certify are necessary to carry out the purposes described in subparagraph (C), to be available without further appropriation, in an amount not to exceed—

(I) for fiscal year 1997, $104,000,000;

* * *

(ii) For each fiscal year, of the amount appropriated in clause (i), the following amounts shall be available only for the purposes of the activities of the Office of the Inspector General of the Department of Health and Human Services with respect to the programs under this title and title XIX—

* * *

* * *

(6) Not later than June 1, 1998, and January 1 of 2000, 2002, and 2004, the Comptroller General of the United States shall submit a report to Congress which—

* * *

(B) identifies any expenditures from the Trust Fund with respect to activities not involving the program under this title;

* * *

[CCH Explanation at ¶ 801.]

2003 Amendments:

Section 736(a)(5)(A) of the "Medicare Prescription Drug, Improvement, and Modernization Act of 2003," effective upon enactment, amended section 1817(k)(3)(A)(i)(I) in clause (i)(I), by striking the comma at the end and inserting a semicolon; and in clause (ii), by striking "the Medicare and medicaid programs" and inserting "the programs under this title and title XIX".

Section 736(a)(6) of the "Medicare Prescription Drug, Improvement, and Modernization Act of 2003," effective upon enactment, amended section 1817(k)(6)(B) by striking "Medicare program under title XVIII" and inserting "program under this title".

Section 801(d)(1) of the "Medicare Prescription Drug, Improvement, and Modernization Act of 2003," effective upon enactment, amended section 1817(b)(2) is amended by adding at the end "Each report provided under paragraph (2) beginning with the report in 2005 shall include the information specified in section 801(a) of Medicare Prescription Drug, Improvement, and Modernization Act of 2003."

Section 900(e)(D) of the "Medicare Prescription Drug, Improvement, and Modernization Act of 2003," effective upon enactment, amended section 1817(b) (i) by striking "Health Care Financing Administration", both in the fifth sentence of the matter preceding paragraph (1) and in the second sentence of the matter following paragraph (4), and inserting "Centers for Medicare & Medicaid Services"; and (ii) by striking "Chief Actuarial Officer" in the second sentence of the matter following paragraph (4) and inserting "Chief Actuary".

[¶ 2095] Sec. 1818. HOSPITAL INSURANCE BENEFITS FOR UNINSURED ELDERLY INDIVIDUALS NOT OTHERWISE ELIGIBLE

[42 U.S.C. § 1395i-2]

(a) Every individual who—

* * *

(4) is not otherwise entitled to benefits under this part,

shall be eligible to enroll in the insurance program established by this part. Except as otherwise provided, any reference to an individual entitled to benefits under this part includes an individual entitled to benefits under this part pursuant to an enrollment under this section or section 1818A.

* * *

* * *

(d)(6)(A) In the case where a State, a political subdivision of a State, or an agency or instrumentality of a State or political subdivision thereof determines to pay, for the life of each individual, the monthly premiums due under paragraph (1) on behalf of each of the individuals in a qualified State or local government retiree group who meets the conditions of subsection (a), the amount of any increase otherwise applicable under section 1839(b) (as applied and modified by subsection (c)(6) of this section) with respect to the monthly premium for benefits under this part for an individual who is a member of such group shall be reduced by the total amount of taxes paid under section 3101(b) of the Internal Revenue Code of 1986 by such individual and under section 3111(b) of such Code by the employers of such individual on behalf of such individual with respect to employment (as defined in section 3121(b) of such Code).

* * *

* * *

* * *

(g)(2)(B) For purposes of this subsection, section 1843(d)(1) shall be applied by substituting "section 1818" for "section 1839" and "subsection (c)(6) (with reference to subsection (b) of section 1839)" for "subsection (b)".

[CCH Explanation at ¶ 101.]

2003 Amendments:

Section 101(e)(5) of the "Medicare Prescription Drug, Improvement, and Modernization Act of 2003," effective upon enactment, amended section 1818(a) is amended by adding at the end the following: "Except as otherwise provided, any reference to an individual entitled to benefits under this part includes an individual entitled to benefits under this part pursuant to an enrollment under this section or section 1818A.".

Section 736(a)(7)(A) of the "Medicare Prescription Drug, Improvement, and Modernization Act of 2003," effective upon enactment, amended section 1818(d)(6)(A) by inserting "of such Code" after "3111(b)".

Section 736(a)(7)(B) of the "Medicare Prescription Drug, Improvement, and Modernization Act of 2003," effective upon enactment, amended section 1818(g)(2)(B) by striking "subsection (b)." and inserting "subsection (b)".

[¶ 2100] Sec. 1819. [Requirements for Provision of Skilled Nursing Facility Services]

[42 U.S.C. § 1395i-3(b)]

(b) REQUIREMENTS RELATING TO PROVISION OF SERVICES.—

* * *

(4) PROVISION OF SERVICES AND ACTIVITIES.—

* * *

(C) REQUIRED NURSING CARE.—

(i) IN GENERAL.—Except as provided in clause (ii), a skilled nursing facility must provide 24-hour licensed nursing service which is sufficient to meet nursing needs of its residents and must use the services of a registered professional nurse at least 8 consecutive hours a day, 7 days a week.

* * *

2003 Amendments:

Section 736(a)(8)(A) of the "Medicare Prescription Drug, Improvement, and Modernization Act of 2003," effective upon enactment, amended section 1819(b)(4)(C)(i) by striking "at least at least" and inserting "at least".

[¶ 2105] Sec. 1819. [Skilled Nursing Facility Administration and Related Requirements]

[42 U.S.C. § 1395i-3(d)]

(d) REQUIREMENTS RELATING TO ADMINISTRATION AND OTHER MATTERS.—

(1) ADMINISTRATION.—

(A) IN GENERAL.—A skilled nursing facility must be administered in a manner that enables it to use its resources effectively and efficiently to attain or maintain the highest practicable physical, mental, and psychosocial well-being of each resident (consistent with requirements established under subsection (f)(5)).

* * *

2003 Amendments:

Section 736(a)(8)(B) of the "Medicare Prescription Drug, Improvement, and Modernization Act of 2003," effective upon enactment, amended section 1819(d)(1)(A) by striking "physical mental" and inserting "physical, mental".

[¶2110] Sec. 1819. [Secretary's Responsibility Regarding SNF Requirements]
[42 U.S.C. § 1395i-3(f)]

(f) RESPONSIBILITIES OF SECRETARY RELATING TO SKILLED NURSING FACILITY REQUIREMENTS.—

* * *

(2) REQUIREMENTS FOR NURSE AIDE TRAINING AND COMPETENCY EVALUATION PROGRAMS AND FOR NURSE AIDE COMPETENCY EVALUATION PROGRAMS.—

* * *

(B) APPROVAL OF CERTAIN PROGRAMS.—Such requirements—

* * *

(iii) Subject to subparagraphs (C) and (D), shall prohibit approval of such a program—

* * *

(D) WAIVER OF DISAPPROVAL OF NURSE-AIDE TRAINING PROGRAMS.—Upon application of a nursing facility, the Secretary may waive the application of subparagraph (B)(iii)(I)(c) if the imposition of the civil monetary penalty was not related to the quality of care provided to residents of the facility. Nothing in this subparagraph shall be construed as eliminating any requirement upon a facility to pay a civil monetary penalty described in the preceding sentence.

* * *

[CCH Explanation at ¶905.]

2003 Amendments:

Section 736(a)(8)(C) of the "Medicare Prescription Drug, Improvement, and Modernization Act of 2003," effective upon enactment, amended section 1819(f)(2)(B)(iii) by moving the last sentence 2 ems to the left.

Section 932(c)(2) of the "Medicare Prescription Drug, Improvement, and Modernization Act of 2003," effective upon enactment, amended section 1819(f)(2)(B)(iii) by striking "subparagraph (C)" and inserting "subparagraphs (C) and (D)".

Section 932(c)(2)(B) of the "Medicare Prescription Drug, Improvement, and Modernization Act of 2003," effective upon enactment, amended section 1819(f)(2) by adding at the end new subparagraph (D).

[¶2115] Sec. 1820. MEDICARE RURAL HOSPITAL FLEXIBILITY PROGRAM
[42 U.S.C. § 1395i-4]

* * *

(c) MEDICARE RURAL HOSPITAL FLEXIBILITY PROGRAM DESCRIBED.—

* * *

(2) STATE DESIGNATION OF FACILITIES.—

* * *

(B) CRITERIA FOR DESIGNATION AS CRITICAL ACCESS HOSPITAL.—A State may designate a facility as a critical access hospital if the facility—

(i) is a hospital that is located in a county (or equivalent unit of local government) in a rural area (as defined in section 1886(d)(2)(D)) or is treated as being located in a rural area pursuant to section 1886(d)(8)(E), and that—

* * *

(II) is certified before January 1, 2006, by the State as being a necessary provider of health care services to residents in the area;

* * *

(iii) provides not more than 25 acute care inpatient beds (meeting such standards as the Secretary may establish) for providing inpatient care for a period that does not exceed, as determined on an annual, average basis, 96 hours per patient; (unless a longer period is required because transfer to a hospital is precluded because of inclement weather or other emergency conditions), except that a peer review organization or equivalent entity may, on request, waive the 96-hour restriction on a case-by-case basis;

* * *

(E) AUTHORITY TO ESTABLISH PSYCHIATRIC AND REHABILITATION DISTINCT PART UNITS.—

(i) IN GENERAL.—Subject to the succeeding provisions of this subparagraph, a critical access hospital may establish—

(I) a psychiatric unit of the hospital that is a distinct part of the hospital; and

(II) a rehabilitation unit of the hospital that is a distinct part of the hospital,

if the distinct part meets the requirements (including conditions of participation) that would otherwise apply to the distinct part if the distinct part were established by a subsection (d) hospital in accordance with the matter following clause (v) of section 1886(d)(1)(B), including any regulations adopted by the Secretary under such section.

(ii) LIMITATION ON NUMBER OF BEDS.—The total number of beds that may be established under clause (i) for a distinct part unit may not exceed 10.

(iii) EXCLUSION OF BEDS FROM BED COUNT.—In determining the number of beds of a critical access hospital for purposes of applying the bed limitations referred to in subparagraph (B)(iii) and subsection (f), the Secretary shall not take into account any bed established under clause (i).

(iv) EFFECT OF FAILURE TO MEET REQUIREMENTS.—If a psychiatric or rehabilitation unit established under clause (i) does not meet the requirements described in such clause with respect to a cost reporting period, no payment may be made under this title to the hospital for services furnished in such unit during such period. Payment to the hospital for services furnished in the unit may resume only after the hospital has demonstrated to the Secretary that the unit meets such requirements.

* * *

(f) PERMITTING MAINTENANCE OF SWING BEDS.—Nothing in this section shall be construed to prohibit a State from designating or the Secretary from certifying a facility as a critical access hospital solely because, at the time the facility applies to the State for designation as a critical access hospital, there is in effect an agreement between the facility and the Secretary under section 1883 under which the facility's inpatient hospital facilities are used for the provision of extended care services, so long as the total number of beds that may be used at any time for the furnishing of either such services or acute care inpatient services does not exceed 25 beds. For purposes of the previous sentence, any bed of a unit of the facility that is licensed as a distinct-part skilled nursing facility at the time the facility applies to the State for designation as a critical access hospital shall not be counted.

* * *

(g)(4) ADDITIONAL REQUIREMENTS WITH RESPECT TO FLEX GRANTS.—With respect to grants awarded under paragraph (1) or (2) from funds appropriated for fiscal year 2005 and subsequent fiscal years—

(A) CONSULTATION WITH THE STATE HOSPITAL ASSOCIATION AND RURAL HOSPITALS ON THE MOST APPROPRIATE WAYS TO USE GRANTS.—A State shall consult with the hospital association of such State and rural hospitals located in such State on the most appropriate ways to use the funds under such grant.

(B) LIMITATION ON USE OF GRANT FUNDS FOR ADMINISTRATIVE EXPENSES.—A State may not expend more than the lesser of—

(i) 15 percent of the amount of the grant for administrative expenses; or

(ii) the State's federally negotiated indirect rate for administering the grant.

(5) USE OF FUNDS FOR FEDERAL ADMINISTRATIVE EXPENSES.—Of the total amount appropriated for grants under paragraphs (1) and (2) for a fiscal year (beginning with fiscal year 2005), up to 5 percent of such amount shall be available to the Health Resources and Services Administration for purposes of administering such grants.

(h) GRANDFATHERING PROVISIONS.—

* * *

(3) STATE AUTHORITY TO WAIVE 35-MILE RULE.—In the case of a facility that was designated as a critical access hospital before January 1, 2006, and was certified by the State as being a necessary provider of health care services to residents in the area under subsection (c)(2)(B)(i)(II), as in effect before such date, the authority under such subsection with respect to any redesignation of such facility shall continue to apply notwithstanding the amendment made by section 405(h)(1) of the Medicare Prescription Drug, Improvement, and Modernization Act of 2003.

AUTHORIZATION OF APPROPRIATIONS.—.—There are authorized to be appropriated from the Federal Hospital Insurance Trust Fund for making grants to all States under subsection (g), $25,000,000 in each of fiscal years 1998 through 2002, *and for making grants to all States under paragraphs (1) and (2) of subsection (g), $35,000,000 in each of fiscal years 2005 through 2008.*.

* * *

[CCH Explanation at ¶ 578.]

2003 Amendments:

Section 405(e)(1) of the "Medicare Prescription Drug, Improvement, and Modernization Act of 2003," amended section 1820(c)(2)(B)(iii) by striking "15 (or, in the case of a facility under an agreement described in subsection (f), 25)" and inserting "25".

Section 405(e)(2) of the "Medicare Prescription Drug, Improvement, and Modernization Act of 2003," amended section 1820(f) by striking "and the number of beds used at any time for acute care inpatient services does not exceed 15 beds".

The amendments made by section 405(e) of the "Medicare Prescription Drug, Improvement, and Modernization Act of 2003," apply to designations made before, on, or after January 1, 2004, but any election made pursuant to regulations promulgated to carry out such amendments shall only apply prospectively.

Section 405(f)(1) of the "Medicare Prescription Drug, Improvement, and Modernization Act of 2003," effective upon enactment, amended section 1820(j) by inserting before the period at the end, the following ", and for making grants to all States under paragraphs (1) and (2) of subsection (g), $35,000,000 in each of fiscal years 2005 through 2008.".

Section 405(f)(2) of the "Medicare Prescription Drug, Improvement, and Modernization Act of 2003," effective upon enactment, amended section 1820(g) by adding at the end new paragraphs (4) and (5).

Section 405(g)(1) of the "Medicare Prescription Drug, Improvement, and Modernization Act of 2003," amended section 1820(c)(2) by adding at the end new clause (E).

The amendments made by section 405(g) of the "Medicare Prescription Drug, Improvement, and Modernization Act of 2003," apply to cost reporting periods beginning on or after October 1, 2004.

Section 405(h)(1) of the "Medicare Prescription Drug, Improvement, and Modernization Act of 2003," effective upon enactment, amended section 1820(c)(2)(B)(i)(II) by inserting "before January 1, 2006," after "is certified".

Section 405(h)(2)(A) of the "Medicare Prescription Drug, Improvement, and Modernization Act of 2003," effective upon enactment, amended section 1820(h) in the heading preceding paragraph (1), by striking "OF CERTAIN FACILITIES" and inserting "PROVISIONS"; and by adding at the end new paragraph (3).

Section 405(h)(2)(B) of the "Medicare Prescription Drug, Improvement, and Modernization Act of 2003," effective upon enactment, amended section 1820(h) by adding at the end new paragraph (3).

[¶ 2120] Sec. 1821. CONDITIONS FOR COVERAGE OF RELIGIOUS NONMEDICAL HEALTH CARE INSTITUTIONAL SERVICES

[42 U.S.C. § 1395i-5]

(a) IN GENERAL.—Subject to subsections (c) and (d), payment under this part may be made for inpatient hospital services or post-hospital extended care services furnished an individual in a religious nonmedical health care institution and for home health services furnished an individual by a religious nonmedical health care institution only if—

* * *

(2) the individual has a condition such that the individual would qualify for benefits under this part for inpatient hospital services, extended care services, or home health services, respectively, if the individual were an inpatient or resident in a hospital or skilled nursing facility, or receiving services from a home health agency that was not such an institution.

* * *

[CCH Explanation at ¶ 662.]

2003 Amendments:

Section 706(a)(1) of the "Medicare Prescription Drug, Improvement, and Modernization Act of 2003," effective upon enactment, amended section 1821(a) in the matter preceding paragraph (1), by inserting "and for home health services furnished an individual by a religious nonmedical health care institution" after "religious nonmedical health care institution".

Section 706(a)(2) of the "Medicare Prescription Drug, Improvement, and Modernization Act of 2003," effective upon enactment, amended section 1821(a)(2) in paragraph (2) by striking "or extended care services" and inserting ", extended care services, or home health services"; and by inserting ", or receiving services from a home health agency," after "skilled nursing facility".

[¶2121A] Sec. 1833. [Amount of Payment]

[42 U.S.C. § 1395l (a)]

(a) Except as provided in section 1876, and subject to the succeeding provisions of this section, there shall be paid from the Federal Supplementary Medical Insurance Trust Fund, in the case of each individual who is covered under the insurance program established by this part and incurs expenses for services with respect to which benefits are payable under this part, amounts equal to—

* * *

(1) in the case of services described in section 1832(a)(1)—80 percent of the reasonable charges for the services; except that—

* * *

(D) with respect to clinical diagnostic laboratory tests for which payment is made under this part—

(i) on the basis of a fee schedule under subsection (h)(1) or section 1834(d)(1), the amount paid shall be equal to 80 percent (or 100 percent, in the case of such tests for which payment is made on an assignment-related basis or which are furnished on an outpatient basis by a critical access hospital of the lesser of the amount determined under such fee schedule,the limitation amount for that test determined under subsection (h)(4)(B), or the amount of the charges billed for the tests,

(ii) on the basis of a negotiated rate established under subsection (h)(6), the amount paid shall be equal to 100 percent of such negotiated rate,

(iii) on the basis of a rate established under a demonstration project under section 1847(e), the amount paid shall be equal to 100 percent of such rate,

* * *

(G) with respect to facility services furnished in connection with a surgical procedure specified pursuant to subsection (i)(1)(A) and furnished to an individual in an ambulatory surgical center described in such subsection, for services furnished beginning with the implementation date of a revised payment system for such services in such facilities specified in subsection (i)(2)(D), the amounts paid shall be 80 percent of the lesser of the actual charge for the services or the amount determined by the Secretary under such revised payment system,

* * *

(S) with respect to drugs and biologicals (including intravenous immune globulin (as defined in section 1861(zz))) not paid on a cost or prospective payment basis as otherwise provided in this part (other than items and services described by subparagraph (B)), the amount paid shall be 80 percent of the lesser of the actual charge or the payment amount established in section 1842(o) (or, if applicable, under section 1847, 1847A, or 1847B),

(T) with respect to medical nutrition therapy services (as defined in section 1861(vv)), the amount paid shall be 80 percent of the lesser of the actual charge for the services or 85 percent of the amount determined under the fee schedule established under section 1848(b) for the same services if furnished by a physician,

(U) with respect to facility fees described in section 1834(m)(2)(B), the amounts paid shall be 80 percent of the lesser of the actual charge or the amounts specified in such section, and

(V) notwithstanding subparagraphs (I) (relating to durable medical equipment), (M) (relating to prosthetic devices and orthotics and prosthetics), and (Q) (relating to 1842(s) items), with respect to competitively priced items and services (described in section 1847(a)(2)) that are furnished in a competitive area, the amounts paid shall be the amounts described in section 1847(b)(5)

(2) in the case of services described in section 1832(a)(2) (except those services described in subparagraphs (C) (D), (E), (F), (G), (H), and (I) of such section and unless otherwise specified in section 1831)—

* * *

(E) with respect to—

(i) outpatient hospital radiology services (including diagnostic and therapeutic radiology, nuclear medicine and CAT scan procedures, magnetic resonance imaging, and ultrasound and other imaging services, but excluding screening mammography) and, for services furnished on or after January 1, 2005, diagnostic mammography, and

* * *

(3) in the case of services described in section 1832(a)(2)(D)—

(A) except as provided in subparagraph (B), the costs which are reasonable and related to the cost of furnishing such services or which are based on such other tests of reasonableness as the Secretary may prescribe in regulations, including those authorized under section 1861(v)(1)(A), less the amount a provider may charge as described in clause (ii) of section 1866(a)(2)(A), but in no case may the payment for such services (other than for items and services described in section 1861(s)(10)(A)) exceed 80 percent of such costs; or

(B) with respect to the services described in clause (ii) of section 1832(a)(2)(D) that are furnished to an individual enrolled with a MA plan under part C pursuant to a written agreement described in section 1853(a)(4), the amount (if any) by which—

(i) the amount of payment that would have otherwise been provided under subparagraph (A) (calculated as if "100 percent" were substituted for "80 percent" in such subparagraph) for such services if the individual had not been so enrolled; exceeds

(ii) the amount of the payments received under such written agreement for such services (not including any financial incentives provided for in such agreement such as risk pool payments, bonuses, or withholds),

less the amount the Federally qualified health center may charge as described in section 1857(e)(3)(B);

* * *

[CCH Explanation at ¶ 390, 594, 754, 760, 1002, 1004, 1006, 1009, and 1010.]

2003 Amendments:

Section 237(a) of the "Medicare Prescription Drug, Improvement, and Modernization Act of 2003," amended section 1833(a)(3).

The above amendment applies to services provided on or after Jan. 1, 2006, and contract years beginning on or after such date.

Prior to amendment, section 1833(a)(3) read as follows:

(3) in the case of services described in section 1832(a)(2)(D), the costs which are reasonable and related to the cost of furnishing such services or which are based on such other tests of reasonableness as the Secretary may prescribe in regulations, including those authorized under section 1861(v)(1)(A), less the amount a provider may charge as described in clause (ii) of section 1866(a)(2)(A), but in no case may the payment for such services (other than for items and services described in section 1861(s)(10)(A) exceed 80 percent of such costs;

Section 302(b)(2)(A) of the "Medicare Prescription Drug, Improvement, and Modernization Act of 2003," effective upon enactment, amended section 1833(a)(1)(T) by striking "and (U)" and inserting "U".

Section 302(b)(2)(B) of the "Medicare Prescription Drug, Improvement, and Modernization Act of 2003," effective upon enactment, amended section 1833(a)(1)(U) by inserting before the semicolon at the end ", and" and adding new subparagraph (V).

Section 302(b)(2)(C) of the "Medicare Prescription Drug, Improvement, and Modernization Act of 2003," effective upon enactment, amended section 1833(a)(1)(D) by striking "or (ii)" and inserting "(ii)" and by adding at the end "or (iii)" and adding new subparagraph (iii).

Section 303(i)(3)(A) of the "Medicare Prescription Drug, Improvement, and Modernization Act of 2003," effective upon enactment, amended section 1833(a)(1)(S) by inserting "(or, if applicable, under section 1847, 1847A, or 1847B)" after "1842(o)".

Section 614(b) of the "Medicare Prescription Drug, Improvement, and Modernization Act of 2003," amended section 1833(a)(2)(E)(i) by inserting "and, for services furnished on or after January 1, 2005, diagnostic mammography" after "screening mammography".

The amendments made by section 614(b) of the "Medicare Prescription Drug, Improvement, and Modernization Act of 2003," apply—

(1) in the case of screening mammography, to services furnished on or after the date of the enactment of the "Medicare Prescription Drug, Improvement, and Modernization Act of 2003,"; and

(2) in the case of diagnostic mammography, to services furnished on or after January 1, 2005.

Section 626(c) of the "Medicare Prescription Drug, Improvement, and Modernization Act of 2003," effective upon enactment, amended section 1833(a)(1) by adding the following new subparagraph (G), prior to amendment, subparagraph (G) was removed.

Section 642(b) of the "Medicare Prescription Drug, Improvement, and Modernization Act of 2003," amended section 1833(a)(1)(S) by inserting "(including intravenous immune globulin (as defined in section 1861(zz)))" after "with respect to drugs and biologicals".

The amendments made by section 642(b) of the "Medicare Prescription Drug, Improvement, and Modernization Act of 2003," apply to items furnished administered on or after January 1, 2004.

Social Security Law Added, Amended or Repealed

[¶2121B] Sec. 1833. [Application of Deductible]
[42 U.S.C. § 1395 *l* (b)]

(b) Before applying subsection (a) with respect to expenses incurred by an individual during any calendar year, the total amount of the expenses incurred by such individual during such year (which would, except for this subsection, constitute incurred expenses from which benefits payable under subsection (a) are determinable) shall be reduced by a deductible of $75 for calendar years before 1991 , $100 for 1991 through 2004, $110 for 2005, and for a subsequent year the amount of such deductible for the previous year increased by the annual percentage increase in the monthly actuarial rate under section 1839(a)(1) ending with such subsequent year (rounded to the nearest $1); except that (1) such total amount shall not include expenses incurred for items and services described in section 1861(s)(10)(A), (2) such deductible shall not apply with respect to home health services (other than a covered osteoporosis drug (as defined in section 1861(kk))). (3) such deductible shall not apply with respect to clinical diagnostic laboratory tests for which payment is made under this part (A) under subsection (a)(1)(D)(i) or (a)(2)(D)(i) on an assignment-related basis, or to a provider having an agreement under section 1866, or (B) on the basis of a negotiated rate determined under subsection (h)(6), (4) such deductible shall not apply to Federally qualified health center services, (5) such deductible shall not apply with respect to screening mammography (as described in section 1861(jj)), and (6) such deductible shall not apply with respect to screening pap smear and screening pelvic exam (as described in 1861(nn)). The total amount of the expenses incurred by an individual as determined under the preceding sentence shall, after the reduction specified in such sentence, be further reduced by an amount equal to the expenses incurred for the first three pints of whole blood (or equivalent quantities of packed red blood cells, as defined under regulations) furnished to the individual during the calendar year, except that such deductible for such blood shall in accordance with regulations be appropriately reduced to the extent that there has been a replacement of such blood (or equivalent quantities of packed red blood cells, as so defined); and for such purposes blood (or equivalent quantities of packed red blood cells, as so defined) furnished such individual shall be deemed replaced when the institution or other person furnishing such blood (or such equivalent quantities of packed red blood cells, as so defined) is given one pint of blood for each pint of blood (or equivalent quantities of packed red blood cells, as so defined) furnished such individual with respect to which a deduction is made under this sentence. The deductible under the previous sentence for blood or blood cells furnished an individual in a year shall be reduced to the extent that a deductible has been imposed under section 1813(a)(2) to blood or blood cells furnished the individual in the year.

[CCH Explanation at ¶729.]
2003 Amendments:

Section 629 of the "Medicare Prescription Drug, Improvement, and Modernization Act of 2003," effective upon enactment, amended section 1833(b) by striking "and $100 for 1991 and subsequent years" and inserting the following: ", $100 for 1991 through 2004, $110 for 2005, and for a subsequent year the amount of such deductible for the previous year increased by the annual percentage increase in the monthly actuarial rate under section 1839(a)(1) ending with such subsequent year (rounded to the nearest $1)".

[¶2121G] Sec. 1833. [Payment Limit on Independent PT and OT Practitioners]
[42 U.S.C. § 1395 *l* (g)]
* * *

(g)(4) This subsection shall not apply to expenses incurred with respect to services furnished during 2000, 2001 2002, 2004, and 2005.

[CCH Explanation at ¶762.]
2003 Amendments:

Section 624(a)(1) of the "Medicare Prescription Drug, Improvement, and Modernization Act of 2003," effective upon enactment, amended section 1833(g)(4) by striking "and 2002" and inserting "2002, 2004, and 2005".

[¶2121H] Sec. 1833. [Clinical Diagnostic Laboratory Tests]
[42 U.S.C. § 1395 *l* (h)]
* * *

* * *

* * *

(h)(2)(A)(ii) Notwithstanding clause (i)—

* * *

(IV) the annual adjustment in the fee schedules determined under clause (i) for each of the years 1994 and 1995, 1998 through 2002, and 2004 through 2008 shall be 0 percent.

* * *

* * *

(5)(D) A person may not bill for a clinical diagnostic laboratory test, including a test performed in a physician's office but excluding a test performed by a rural health clinic, other than on an assignment-related basis. If a person knowingly and willfully and on a repeated basis bills for a clinical diagnostic laboratory test in violation of the previous sentence, the Secretary may apply sanctions against the person in the same manner as the Secretary may apply sanctions against a physician in accordance with paragraph (2) of section 1842(j) in the same manner such paragraphs apply with respect to a physician. Paragraph (4) of such section shall apply in this subparagraph in the same manner as such paragraph applies to such section.

* * *

(8)(A) The Secretary shall establish by regulation procedures for determining the basis for, and amount of, payment under this subsection for any clinical diagnostic laboratory test with respect to which a new or substantially revised HCPCS code is assigned on or after January 1, 2005 (in this paragraph referred to as 'new tests').

(B) Determinations under subparagraph (A) shall be made only after the Secretary—

(i) makes available to the public (through an Internet website and other appropriate mechanisms) a list that includes any such test for which establishment of a payment amount under this subsection is being considered for a year;

(ii) on the same day such list is made available, causes to have published in the Federal Register notice of a meeting to receive comments and recommendations (and data on which recommendations are based) from the public on the appropriate basis under this subsection for establishing payment amounts for the tests on such list;

(iii) not less than 30 days after publication of such notice convenes a meeting, that includes representatives of officials of the Centers for Medicare & Medicaid Services involved in determining payment amounts, to receive such comments and recommendations (and data on which the recommendations are based);

(iv) taking into account the comments and recommendations (and accompanying data) received at such meeting, develops and makes available to the public (through an Internet website and other appropriate mechanisms) a list of proposed determinations with respect to the appropriate basis for establishing a payment amount under this subsection for each such code, together with an explanation of the reasons for each such determination, the data on which the determinations are based, and a request for public written comments on the proposed determination; and

(v) taking into account the comments received during the public comment period, develops and makes available to the public (through an Internet website and other appropriate mechanisms) a list of final determinations of the payment amounts for such tests under this subsection, together with the rationale for each such determination, the data on which the determinations are based, and responses to comments and suggestions received from the public.

(C) Under the procedures established pursuant to subparagraph (A), the Secretary shall—

(i) set forth the criteria for making determinations under subparagraph (A); and

(ii) make available to the public the data (other than proprietary data) considered in making such determinations.

(D) The Secretary may convene such further public meetings to receive public comments on payment amounts for new tests under this subsection as the Secretary deems appropriate.

(E) For purposes of this paragraph:

(i) The term "HCPCS" refers to the Health Care Procedure Coding System.

(ii) A code shall be considered to be "substantially revised" if there is a substantive change to the definition of the test or procedure to which the code applies (such as a new analyte or a new methodology for measuring an existing analyte-specific test).

* * *

(2)(A)(ii) Notwithstanding clause (i)—

* * *

(IV) the annual adjustment in the fee schedules determined under clause (i) for each of the years 1994 and 1995, 1998 through 2002, and 2004 through 2008 shall be 0 percent.

[CCH Explanation at ¶ 756, 795, and 942.]

2003 Amendments:

Section 628 of the "Medicare Prescription Drug, Improvement, and Modernization Act of 2003," effective upon enactment, amended section 1833(h)(2)(A)(ii)(IV) by striking "and 1998 through 2002" and inserting ", 1998 through 2002, and 2004 through 2008".

Section 736(b)(1) of the "Medicare Prescription Drug, Improvement, and Modernization Act of 2003," effective upon enactment, amended section 1833(h)(5)(D) by striking "clinic,," and inserting "clinic,".

Section 942(b) of the "Medicare Prescription Drug, Improvement, and Modernization Act of 2003," effective upon enactment, amended section 1833(h) by adding at the end new subparagraph (8).

[¶ 21211] Sec. 1833. [Outpatient Surgery]

[42 U.S.C. § 1395 *l* (i)]

* * *

(i)(2)(A) For services furnished prior to the implementation of the system described in subparagraph (D), the amount of payment to be made for facility services furnished in connection with a surgical procedure specified pursuant to paragraph (1)(A) and furnished to an individual in an ambulatory surgical center described in such paragraph shall be equal to 80 percent of a standard overhead amount established by the Secretary (with respect to each such procedure) on the basis of the Secretary's estimate of a fair fee which—

(i) takes into account the costs incurred by such centers, or classes of centers, generally in providing services furnished in connection with the performance of such procedure, as determined in accordance with a survey (based upon a representative sample of procedures and facilities) of the actual costs incurred by such centers in providing such services,

(ii) takes such costs into account in such a manner as will assure that the performance of the procedure in such a center will result in substantially less amounts paid under this title than would have been paid if the procedure had been performed on an inpatient basis in a hospital, and

(iii) in the case of insertion of an intraocular lens during or subsequent to cataract surgery includes payment which is reasonable and related to the cost of acquiring the class of lens involved.

Each amount so established shall be reviewed and updated not later than July 1, 1987, and annually thereafter to take account of varying conditions in different areas.

(B) The amount of payment to be made under this part for facility services furnished, in connection with a surgical procedure specified pursuant to paragraph (1)(B), in a physician's office shall be equal to 80 percent of a standard overhead amount established by the Secretary (with respect to each such procedure) on the basis of the Secretary's estimate of a fair fee which—

(i) takes into account additional costs, not usually included in the professional fee, incurred by physicians in securing, maintaining, and staffing the facilities and ancillary services appropriate for the performance of such procedure in the physician's office, and

* * *

(C)(i) Notwithstanding the second sentence of each of subparagraphs (A) and (B), except as otherwise specified in clauses (ii), (iii), and (iv), if the Secretary has not updated amounts established under such subparagraphs or under subparagraph (D), with respect to facility services furnished during a fiscal year (beginning with fiscal year 1986 or a calendar year (beginning with 2006)), such amounts shall be increased by the percentage increase in the Consumer Price Index for all urban consumers (U.S. city average) as estimated by the Secretary for the 12-month period ending with the midpoint of the year involved.

(ii) In each of the fiscal years 1998 through 2002, the increase under this subparagraph shall be reduced (but not below zero) by 2.0 percentage points.

(iii) In fiscal year 2004, beginning with April 1, 2004, the increase under this subparagraph shall be the Consumer Price Index for all urban consumers (U.S. city average) as estimated by the Secretary for the 12-month period ending with March 31, 2003, minus 3.0 percentage points.

(iv) In fiscal year 2005, the last quarter of calendar year 2005, and each of calendar years 2006 through 2009, the increase under this subparagraph shall be 0 percent.

(D)(i) Taking into account the recommendations in the report under section 626(d) of Medicare Prescription Drug, Improvement, and Modernization Act of 2003, the Secretary shall implement a revised payment system for payment of surgical services furnished in ambulatory surgical centers.

(ii) In the year the system described in clause (i) is implemented, such system shall be designed to result in the same aggregate amount of expenditures for such services as would be made if this subparagraph did not apply, as estimated by the Secretary.

(iii) The Secretary shall implement the system described in clause (i) for periods in a manner so that it is first effective beginning on or after January 1, 2006, and not later than January 1, 2008.

(iv) There shall be no administrative or judicial review under section 1869, 1878, or otherwise, of the classification system, the relative weights, payment amounts, and the geographic adjustment factor, if any, under this subparagraph.

* * *

[CCH Explanation at ¶ 594.]

2003 Amendments:

Section 626(a) of the "Medicare Prescription Drug, Improvement, and Modernization Act of 2003," effective upon enactment, amended section 1833(i)(2)(C).

Prior to amendment, section 1833(i)(2)(C) read as follows:

(C) Notwithstanding the second sentence of subparagraph (A) or the second sentence of subparagraph (B), if the Secretary has not updated amounts established under such subparagraphs with respect to facility services furnished during a fiscal year (beginning with fiscal year 1996), such amounts shall be increased by the percentage increase in the consumer price index for all urban consumers (U.S. city average) as estimated by the Secretary for the year involved. In each of the fiscal years 1998 through 2002, the increase under this subparagraph shall be reduced (but not below zero) by 2.0 percentage points.

Section 626(b)(1)(A) of the "Medicare Prescription Drug, Improvement, and Modernization Act of 2003," effective upon enactment, amended section 1833(i)(2)(A), in the matter preceding clause (i), by striking "The" and inserting "For services furnished prior to the implementation of the system described in subparagraph (D), the".

Section 626(b)(1)(B) of the "Medicare Prescription Drug, Improvement, and Modernization Act of 2003," effective upon enactment, amended section 1833(i)(2)(A)(i) by striking "taken not later than January 1, 1995, and every 5 years thereafter,".

Section 626(b)(2) of the "Medicare Prescription Drug, Improvement, and Modernization Act of 2003," effective upon enactment, amended section 1833(i)(2) by adding new subparagraph (D).

[¶ 2121M] Sec. 1833. [Incentive Payments for Physicians' Services Furnished in Underserved Areas]

[42 U.S.C. § 1395*l* (m)]

(m)(1) In the case of physicians' services furnished in a year to an individual, who is covered under the insurance program established by this part and who incurs expenses for such services, in an area that is designated (under section 332(a)(1)(A) of the Public Health Service Act) as a health professional shortage area as identified by the Secretary prior to the beginning of such year, in addition to the amount otherwise paid under this part, there also shall be paid to the physician (or to an employer or facility in the cases described in clause (A) of section 1842(b)(6)) (on a monthly or quarterly basis) from the Federal Supplementary Medical Insurance Trust Fund an amount equal to 10 percent of the payment amount for the service under this part.

(2) For each health professional shortage area identified in paragraph (1) that consists of an entire county, the Secretary shall provide for the additional payment under paragraph (1) without any requirement on the physician to identify the health professional shortage area involved. The Secretary may implement the previous sentence using the method specified in subsection (u)(4)(C).

(3) The Secretary shall post on the Internet website of the Centers for Medicare & Medicaid Services a list of the health professional shortage areas identified in paragraph (1) that consist of a partial county to facilitate the additional payment under paragraph (1) in such areas.

(4) There shall be no administrative or judicial review under section 1869, section 1878, or otherwise, respecting—

> (A) the identification of a county or area;
>
> (B) the assignment of a specialty of any physician under this paragraph;
>
> (C) the assignment of a physician to a county under this subsection; or
>
> (D) the assignment of a postal zip code to a county or other area under this subsection.

[CCH Explanation at ¶ 700.]

2003 Amendments:

Section 413(b)(1)(A) of the "Medicare Prescription Drug, Improvement, and Modernization Act of 2003," amended section 1833(m), by inserting "(1)" after "(m)".

Section 413(b)(1)(B) of the "Medicare Prescription Drug, Improvement, and Modernization Act of 2003," amended section 1833(m)(1), as designated by Section 413(b)(1)(A), by inserting "in a year" after "In the case of physicians' services furnished"; and by inserting "as identified by the Secretary prior to the beginning of such year" after "as a health professional shortage area".

Section 413(b)(1)(C) of the "Medicare Prescription Drug, Improvement, and Modernization Act of 2003," amended section 1833(m) by adding at the end the new paragraphs (2), (3), and (4).

The amendments made by section 413(b) of the "Medicare Prescription Drug, Improvement, and Modernization Act of 2003," apply to physicians' services furnished on or after January 1, 2005.

[¶ 21210] Sec. 1833. [Payment for Therapeutic Shoes for Individuals With Severe Diabetic Foot Disease]

[42 U.S.C. § 1395*l* (o)]

(o)(1) In the case of shoes described in section 1861(s)(12)—

* * *

> (B) with respect to expenses incurred in any calendar year, no more than the amount of payment applicable under paragraph (2) shall be considered as incurred expenses for purposes of subsections (a) and (b).

Payment for shoes (or inserts) under this part shall be considered to include payment for any expenses for the fitting of such shoes (or inserts).

> (2)(A) Except as provided by the Secretary under subparagraphs (B) and (C), the amount of payment under this paragraph for custom molded shoes, extra-depth shoes, and inserts shall be the amount determined for such items by the Secretary under section 1834(h).
>
> (B) The Secretary may establish payment amounts for shoes and inserts that are lower than the amount established under section 1834(h) if the Secretary finds that shoes and inserts of an appropriate quality are readily available at or below the amount established under such section.
>
> (C) In accordance with procedures established by the Secretary, an individual entitled to benefits with respect to shoes described in section 1861(s)(12) may substitute modification of such shoes instead of obtaining one (or more, as specified by the Secretary) pair of inserts (other than the original pair of inserts with respect to such shoes). In such case, the Secretary shall substitute, for the payment amount established under section 1834(h), a payment amount that the Secretary estimates will assure that there is no net increase in expenditures under this subsection as a result of this subparagraph.

* * *

[CCH Explanation at ¶761.]

2003 Amendments:

Section 627(a)(1) of the "Medicare Prescription Drug, Improvement, and Modernization Act of 2003," effective upon enactment, amended section 1833(o)(1)(B) by striking "no more than the limits established under paragraph (2)" and inserting "no more than the amount of payment applicable under paragraph (2)".

Section 627(a)(2) of the "Medicare Prescription Drug, Improvement, and Modernization Act of 2003," effective upon enactment, amended section 1833(o)(2).

The amendments made by section 627(a) of the "Medicare Prescription Drug, Improvement, and Modernization Act of 2003," apply to items furnished on or after January 1, 2005.

Prior to being amended, Section 1833(o)(2), read as follows:

(2)(A) Except as provided by the Secretary under subparagraphs (B) and (C), the limits established under this paragraph—

(i) for the furnishing of—

(I) one pair of custom molded shoes (including any inserts that are provided initially with the shoes) is $300, and

(II) any additional pair of inserts with respect to such shoes is $50; and

(ii) for the furnishing of extra-depth shoes and inserts is—

(I) $100 for the pair of shoes itself, and

(II) $50 for any pairs of inserts for a pair of shoes.

(B) The Secretary or a carrier may establish limits for shoes that are lower than the limits established under subparagraph (A) if the Secretary finds that shoes and inserts of an appropriate quality are readily available at or below such lower limits.

(C) For each year after 1988, each dollar amount under subparagraph (A) or (B) (as previously adjusted under this subparagraph) shall be increased by the same percentage increase as the Secretary provides with respect to durable medical equipment for that year, except that if such increase is not a multiple of $1, it shall be rounded to the nearest multiple of $1.

(D) In accordance with procedures established by the Secretary, an individual entitled to benefits with respect to shoes described in section 1861(s)(12) may substitute modification of such shoes instead of obtaining one (or more, as specified by the Secretary) pairs of inserts (other than the original pair of inserts with respect to such shoes). In such case, the Secretary shall substitute, for the limits established under subparagraph (A), such limits as the Secretary estimates will assure that there is no net increase in expenditures under this subsection as a result of this subparagraph.

[¶2121T] Sec. 1833. PROSPECTIVE PAYMENT SYSTEM FOR HOSPITAL OUTPATIENT DEPARTMENT SERVICES

[42 U.S.C. §1395*l* (t)]

(t) PROSPECTIVE PAYMENT FOR HOSPITAL OUTPATIENT DEPARTMENT SERVICES.—

(1) AMOUNT OF PAYMENT.—

* * *

(B) DEFINITION OF COVERED OPD SERVICES.—For purposes of this subsection, the term "covered OPD services"—

* * *

(iv) does not include any therapy services described in subsection (a)(8) or ambulance services, for which payment is made under a fee schedule described in section 1834(k) or section 1834(l)and does not include screening mammography (as defined in section 1861(jj)) and diagnostic mammography.

(2) SYSTEM REQUIREMENTS.—Under the payment system—

* * *

(F) the Secretary shall develop a method for controlling unnecessary increases in the volume of covered OPD services;

(G) the Secretary shall create additional groups of covered OPD services that classify separately those procedures that utilize contrast agents from those that do not; and

(H) with respect to devices of brachytherapy consisting of a seed or seeds (or radioactive source), the Secretary shall create additional groups of covered OPD services that classify such devices separately from the other services (or group of services) paid for under this subsection in a manner reflecting the number, isotope, and radioactive intensity of such devices furnished, including separate groups for palladium-103 and iodine-125 devices.

* * *

(3) CALCULATION OF BASE AMOUNTS.—

* * *

(C) CALCULATION OF CONVERSION FACTORS.—

* * *

(ii) SUBSEQUENT YEARS.—Subject to paragraph (8)(B), the Secretary shall establish a conversion factor for covered OPD services furnished in subsequent years in an amount equal to the conversion factor established under this subparagraph and applicable to such services furnished in the previous year increased by the OPD fee schedule increase factor specified under clause (iv) for the year involved.

* * *

(5) OUTLIER ADJUSTMENT.—

* * *

(E) EXCLUSION OF SEPARATE DRUG AND BIOLOGICAL APCS FROM OUTLIER PAYMENTS.—No additional payment shall be made under subparagraph (A) in the case of ambulatory payment classification groups established separately for drugs or biologicals.

(6) TRANSITIONAL PASS-THROUGH FOR ADDITIONAL COSTS OF INNOVATIVE MEDICAL DEVICES, DRUGS, AND BIOLOGICALS.—

* * *

(D) AMOUNT OF ADDITIONAL PAYMENT.—Subject to subparagraph (E)(iii), the amount of the payment under this paragraph with respect to a device, drug, or biological provided as part of a covered OPD service is—

(i) in the case of a drug or biological, the amount by which the amount determined under section 1842(o) (or if the drug or biological is covered under a competitive acquisition contract under section 1847B, an amount determined by the Secretary equal to the average price for the drug or biological for all competitive acquisition areas and year established under such section as calculated and adjusted by the Secretary for purposes of this paragraph) for the drug or biological exceeds the portion of the otherwise applicable Medicare OPD fee schedule that the Secretary determines is associated with the drug or biological; or

* * *

(F) LIMITATION OF APPLICATION OF FUNCTIONAL EQUIVALENCE STANDARD.—

(i) IN GENERAL.—The Secretary may not publish regulations that apply a functional equivalence standard to a drug or biological under this paragraph.

(ii) APPLICATION.—Clause (i) shall apply to the application of a functional equivalence standard to a drug or biological on or after the date of enactment of the Medicare Prescription Drug, Improvement, and Modernization Act of 2003 unless—

(I) such application was being made to such drug or biological prior to such date of enactment; and

(II) the Secretary applies such standard to such drug or biological only for the purpose of determining eligibility of such drug or biological for additional payments under this paragraph and not for the purpose of any other payments under this title.

(iii) RULE OF CONSTRUCTION.—Nothing in this subparagraph shall be construed to effect the Secretary's authority to deem a particular drug to be identical to another drug if the 2 products are pharmaceutically equivalent and bioequivalent, as determined by the Commissioner of Food and Drugs.

(7) TRANSITIONAL ADJUSTMENT TO LIMIT DECLINE IN PAYMENT.—

* * *

(D) HOLD HARMLESS PROVISIONS.—

(i) TEMPORARY TREATMENT FOR CERTAIN RURAL HOSPITALS.—In the case of a hospital located in a rural area and that has not more than 100 beds or a sole community hospital (as defined in section 1886(d)(5)(D)(iii)) located in a rural area, for covered OPD services furnished before January 1, 2006, for which the PPS amount is less than the pre-BBA amount, the amount of payment under this subsection shall be increased by the amount of such difference.

* * *

(9) PERIODIC REVIEW AND ADJUSTMENTS COMPONENTS OF PROSPECTIVE PAYMENT SYSTEM.—

* * *

(B) BUDGET NEUTRALITY ADJUSTMENT.—If the Secretary makes adjustments under subparagraph (A), then the adjustments for a year may not cause the estimated amount of expenditures under this part for the year to increase or decrease from the estimated amount of expenditures under this part that would have been made if the adjustments had not been made. In determining adjustments under the preceding sentence for 2004 and 2005, the Secretary shall not take into account under this subparagraph or paragraph (2)(E) any expenditures that would not have been made but for the application of paragraph (14).

* * *

(13) AUTHORIZATION OF ADJUSTMENT FOR RURAL HOSPITALS.—

(A) STUDY.—The Secretary shall conduct a study to determine if, under the system under this subsection, costs incurred by hospitals located in rural areas by ambulatory payment classification groups (APCs) exceed those costs incurred by hospitals located in urban areas.

(B) AUTHORIZATION OF ADJUSTMENT.—Insofar as the Secretary determines under subparagraph (A) that costs incurred by hospitals located in rural areas exceed those costs incurred by hospitals located in urban areas, the Secretary shall provide for an appropriate adjustment under paragraph (2)(E) to reflect those higher costs by January 1, 2006.

(14) DRUG APC PAYMENT RATES.—

(A) IN GENERAL.—The amount of payment under this subsection for a specified covered outpatient drug (defined in subparagraph (B)) that is furnished as part of a covered OPD service (or group of services)—

(i) in 2004, in the case of—

(I) a sole source drug shall in no case be less than 88 percent, or exceed 95 percent, of the reference average wholesale price for the drug;

(II) an innovator multiple source drug shall in no case exceed 68 percent of the reference average wholesale price for the drug; or

(III) a noninnovator multiple source drug shall in no case exceed 46 percent of the reference average wholesale price for the drug;

(ii) in 2005, in the case of—

(I) a sole source drug shall in no case be less than 83 percent, or exceed 95 percent, of the reference average wholesale price for the drug;

(II) an innovator multiple source drug shall in no case exceed 68 percent of the reference average wholesale price for the drug; or

(III) a noninnovator multiple source drug shall in no case exceed 46 percent of the reference average wholesale price for the drug; or

(iii) in a subsequent year, shall be equal, subject to subparagraph (E)—

(I) to the average acquisition cost for the drug for that year (which, at the option of the Secretary, may vary by hospital group (as defined by the Secretary based on volume of covered OPD services or other relevant characteristics)), as determined by the Secretary taking into account the hospital acquisition cost survey data under subparagraph (D); or

(II) if hospital acquisition cost data are not available, the average price for the drug in the year established under section 1842(o), section 1847A, or section 1847B, as the case may be, as calculated and adjusted by the Secretary as necessary for purposes of this paragraph.

§1833(t)(14)(A)(iii)(II) ¶2121T

(B) SPECIFIED COVERED OUTPATIENT DRUG DEFINED.—

(i) IN GENERAL.—In this paragraph, the term "specified covered outpatient drug" means, subject to clause (ii), a covered outpatient drug (as defined in section 1927(k)(2)) for which a separate ambulatory payment classification group (APC) has been established and that is—

(I) a radiopharmaceutical; or

(II) a drug or biological for which payment was made under paragraph (6) (relating to pass-through payments) on or before December 31, 2002.

(ii) EXCEPTION.—Such term does not include—

(I) a drug or biological for which payment is first made on or after January 1, 2003, under paragraph (6);

(II) a drug or biological for which a temporary HCPCS code has not been assigned; or

(III) during 2004 and 2005, an orphan drug (as designated by the Secretary).

(C) PAYMENT FOR DESIGNATED ORPHAN DRUGS DURING 2004 AND 2005.—The amount of payment under this subsection for an orphan drug designated by the Secretary under subparagraph (B)(ii)(III) that is furnished as part of a covered OPD service (or group of services) during 2004 and 2005 shall equal such amount as the Secretary may specify.

(D) ACQUISITION COST SURVEY FOR HOSPITAL OUTPATIENT DRUGS.—

(i) ANNUAL GAO SURVEYS IN 2004 AND 2005.—

(I) IN GENERAL.—The Comptroller General of the United States shall conduct a survey in each of 2004 and 2005 to determine the hospital acquisition cost for each specified covered outpatient drug. Not later than April 1, 2005, the Comptroller General shall furnish data from such surveys to the Secretary for use in setting the payment rates under subparagraph (A) for 2006.

(II) RECOMMENDATIONS.—Upon the completion of such surveys, the Comptroller General shall recommend to the Secretary the frequency and methodology of subsequent surveys to be conducted by the Secretary under clause (ii).

(ii) SUBSEQUENT SECRETARIAL SURVEYS.—The Secretary, taking into account such recommendations, shall conduct periodic subsequent surveys to determine the hospital acquisition cost for each specified covered outpatient drug for use in setting the payment rates under subparagraph (A).

(iii) SURVEY REQUIREMENTS.—The surveys conducted under clauses (i) and (ii) shall have a large sample of hospitals that is sufficient to generate a statistically significant estimate of the average hospital acquisition cost for each specified covered outpatient drug. With respect to the surveys conducted under clause (i), the Comptroller General shall report to Congress on the justification for the size of the sample used in order to assure the validity of such estimates.

(iv) DIFFERENTIATION IN COST.—In conducting surveys under clause (i), the Comptroller General shall determine and report to Congress if there is (and the extent of any) variation in hospital acquisition costs for drugs among hospitals based on the volume of covered OPD services performed by such hospitals or other relevant characteristics of such hospitals (as defined by the Comptroller General).

(v) COMMENT ON PROPOSED RATES.—Not later than 30 days after the date the Secretary promulgated proposed rules setting forth the payment rates under subparagraph (A) for 2006, the Comptroller General shall evaluate such proposed rates and submit to Congress a report regarding the appropriateness of such rates based on the surveys the Comptroller General has conducted under clause (i).

(E) ADJUSTMENT IN PAYMENT RATES FOR OVERHEAD COSTS.—

(i) MEDPAC REPORT ON DRUG APC DESIGN.—The Medicare Payment Advisory Commission shall submit to the Secretary, not later than July 1, 2005, a report on adjustment of payment for ambulatory payment classifications for specified covered outpatient drugs to take into account overhead and related expenses, such as pharmacy services and handling costs. Such report shall include—

(I) a description and analysis of the data available with regard to such expenses;

(II) a recommendation as to whether such a payment adjustment should be made; and

(III) if such adjustment should be made, a recommendation regarding the methodology for making such an adjustment.

(ii) ADJUSTMENT AUTHORIZED.—The Secretary may adjust the weights for ambulatory payment classifications for specified covered outpatient drugs to take into account the recommendations contained in the report submitted under clause (i).

(F) CLASSES OF DRUGS.—For purposes of this paragraph:

(i) SOLE SOURCE DRUGS.—The term "sole source drug" means—

(I) a biological product (as defined under section 1861(t)(1)); or

(II) a single source drug (as defined in section 1927(k)(7)(A)(iv)).

(ii) INNOVATOR MULTIPLE SOURCE DRUGS.—The term "innovator multiple source drug" has the meaning given such term in section 1927(k)(7)(A)(ii).

(iii) NONINNOVATOR MULTIPLE SOURCE DRUGS.—The term "noninnovator multiple source drug" has the meaning given such term in section 1927(k)(7)(A)(iii).

(G) REFERENCE AVERAGE WHOLESALE PRICE.—The term "reference average wholesale price" means, with respect to a specified covered outpatient drug, the average wholesale price for the drug as determined under section 1842(o) as of May 1, 2003.

(H) INAPPLICABILITY OF EXPENDITURES IN DETERMINING CONVERSION, WEIGHTING, AND OTHER ADJUSTMENT FACTORS.—Additional expenditures resulting from this paragraph shall not be taken into account in establishing the conversion, weighting, and other adjustment factors for 2004 and 2005 under paragraph (9), but shall be taken into account for subsequent years.

(15) PAYMENT FOR NEW DRUGS AND BIOLOGICALS UNTIL HCPCS CODE ASSIGNED.—With respect to payment under this part for an outpatient drug or biological that is covered under this part and is furnished as part of covered OPD services for which a HCPCS code has not been assigned, the amount provided for payment for such drug or biological under this part shall be equal to 95 percent of the average wholesale price for the drug or biological.

(16) MISCELLANEOUS PROVISIONS.—

(A) APPLICATION OF RECLASSIFICATION OF CERTAIN HOSPITALS.—If a hospital is being treated as being located in a rural area under section 1886(d)(8)(E), that hospital shall be treated under this subsection as being located in that rural area.

(B) THRESHOLD FOR ESTABLISHMENT OF SEPARATE APCS FOR DRUGS.—The Secretary shall reduce the threshold for the establishment of separate ambulatory payment classification groups (APCs) with respect to drugs or biologicals to $50 per administration for drugs and biologicals furnished in 2005 and 2006.

(C) PAYMENT FOR DEVICES OF BRACHYTHERAPY AT CHARGES ADJUSTED TO COST.—Notwithstanding the preceding provisions of this subsection, for a device of brachytherapy consisting of a seed or seeds (or radioactive source) furnished on or after January 1, 2004, and before January 1, 2007, the payment basis for the device under this subsection shall be equal to the hospital's charges for each device furnished, adjusted to cost. Charges for such devices shall not be included in determining any outlier payment under this subsection.

[CCH Explanation at ¶ 545, 547, 582, and 754.]

2003 Amendments:

Section 411(a) of the "Medicare Prescription Drug, Improvement, and Modernization Act of 2003," amended section 1833(t)(7)(D)(i), in the heading, by striking "SMALL" and inserting "CERTAIN"; by inserting "or a sole community hospital (as defined in section 1886(d)(5)(D)(iii)) located in a rural area" after "100 beds"; and by striking "2004" and inserting "2006".

The amendment made by section 411(a)(1)(B) of the "Medicare Prescription Drug, Improvement, and Modernization Act of 2003" applies to to cost reporting periods beginning on and after January 1, 2004.

Section 411(b)(1) and (2) of the "Medicare Prescription Drug, Improvement, and Modernization Act of 2003," effective upon enactment, amended section 1833(t)(13) by redesignating paragraph (13) as paragraph (16); and by inserting after paragraph (12) the new paragraph (13).

Section 614(a) of the "Medicare Prescription Drug, Improvement, and Modernization Act of 2003," amended section 1833(t)(1)(B)(iv) by inserting before the period at the end the following: "and does not include screening mammography (as defined in section 1861(jj)) and diagnostic mammography".

The amendments made by section 614(a) of the "Medicare Prescription Drug, Improvement, and Modernization Act of 2003," apply—

(1) in the case of screening mammography, to services furnished on or after the date of the enactment of the "Medicare Prescription Drug, Improvement, and Modernization Act of 2003,"; and

(2) in the case of diagnostic mammography, to services furnished on or after January 1, 2005.

Section 621(a)(1) of the "Medicare Prescription Drug, Improvement, and Modernization Act of 2003," amended section 1833(t)(14), as amended by section 411(b), by inserting after paragraph (13) new paragraphs (14) and (15).

The amendments made by section 621(a)(1) of the "Medicare Prescription Drug, Improvement, and Modernization Act of 2003," apply to items and services furnished on or after January 1, 2004.

Section 621(a)(2) of the "Medicare Prescription Drug, Improvement, and Modernization Act of 2003," amended section 1833(t)(16), as redesignated by section 411(b), by adding at the end new subparagraph (B).

The amendments made by section 621(a)(2) of the "Medicare Prescription Drug, Improvement, and Modernization Act of 2003," apply to items and services furnished on or after January 1, 2004.

Section 621(a)(3) of the "Medicare Prescription Drug, Improvement, and Modernization Act of 2003," amended section 1833(t)(5) by adding at the end the new subparagraph (E).

The amendments made by section 621(a)(3) of the "Medicare Prescription Drug, Improvement, and Modernization Act of 2003," apply to items and services furnished on or after January 1, 2004.

Section 621(a)(4) of the "Medicare Prescription Drug, Improvement, and Modernization Act of 2003," amended section 1833(t)(6)(D)(i) by inserting after "under section 1842(o)" the following: "(or if the drug or biological is covered under a competitive acquisition contract under section 1847B, an amount determined by the Secretary equal to the average price for the drug or biological for all competitive acquisition areas and year established under such section as calculated and adjusted by the Secretary for purposes of this paragraph)".

The amendments made by section 621(a)(4) of the "Medicare Prescription Drug, Improvement, and Modernization Act of 2003," apply to items and services furnished on or after January 1, 2004.

Section 621(a)(5) of the "Medicare Prescription Drug, Improvement, and Modernization Act of 2003," amended section 1833(t)(9)(B) by adding at the end the following: "In determining adjustments under the preceding sentence for 2004 and 2005, the Secretary shall not take into account under this subparagraph or paragraph (2)(E) any expenditures that would not have been made but for the application of paragraph (14).".

The amendments made by section 621(a)(5) of the "Medicare Prescription Drug, Improvement, and Modernization Act of 2003," apply to items and services furnished on or after January 1, 2004.

Section 621(b)(1) of the "Medicare Prescription Drug, Improvement, and Modernization Act of 2003," effective upon enactment, amended section 1833(t)(16), as redesignated by section 411(b) and as amended by section 621(a)(2), by adding at the end the new subparagraph C.

Section 621(b)(2) of the "Medicare Prescription Drug, Improvement, and Modernization Act of 2003," effective upon enactment, amended section 1833(t)(2) in subparagraph (F), by striking "and" at the end; in subparagraph (G), by striking the period at the end and inserting "; and"; and by adding at the end the new subparagraph H.

Section 622 of the "Medicare Prescription Drug, Improvement, and Modernization Act of 2003," effective upon enactment, amended section 1833(t)(6) by adding at the end the new subparagraph (F).

Section 736(b)(2) of the "Medicare Prescription Drug, Improvement, and Modernization Act of 2003," effective upon enactment, amended section 1833(t)(3)(C)(ii) by striking "clause (iii)" and inserting "clause (iv)".

[¶ 2121u] Sec. 1833 INCENTIVE PAYMENTS FOR PHYSICIAN SCARCITY AREAS

(u)(1) IN GENERAL.—In the case of physicians' services furnished on or after January 1, 2005, and before January 1, 2008—

(A) by a primary care physician in a primary care scarcity county (identified under paragraph (4)); or

(B) by a physician who is not a primary care physician in a specialist care scarcity county (as so identified),

in addition to the amount of payment that would otherwise be made for such services under this part, there also shall be paid an amount equal to 5 percent of the payment amount for the service under this part.

(2) DETERMINATION OF RATIOS OF PHYSICIANS TO MEDICARE BENEFICIARIES IN AREA.—Based upon available data, the Secretary shall establish for each county or equivalent area in the United States, the following:

(A) NUMBER OF PHYSICIANS PRACTICING IN THE AREA.—The number of physicians who furnish physicians' services in the active practice of medicine or osteopathy in that county or area, other than physicians whose practice is exclusively for the Federal Government, physicians who are retired, or physicians who only provide administrative services. Of such number, the number of such physicians who are—

(i) primary care physicians; or

(ii) physicians who are not primary care physicians.

(B) NUMBER OF MEDICARE BENEFICIARIES RESIDING IN THE AREA.—The number of individuals who are residing in the county and are entitled to benefits under part A or enrolled under this part, or both (in this subsection referred to as "individuals'").

(C) DETERMINATION OF RATIOS.—

(i) PRIMARY CARE RATIO.—The ratio (in this paragraph referred to as the "primary care ratio") of the number of primary care physicians (determined under subparagraph (A)(i)), to the number of individuals determined under subparagraph (B).

(ii) SPECIALIST CARE RATIO.—The ratio (in this paragraph referred to as the "specialist care ratio") of the number of other physicians (determined under subparagraph (A)(ii)), to the number of individuals determined under subparagraph (B).

(3) RANKING OF COUNTIES.—The Secretary shall rank each such county or area based separately on its primary care ratio and its specialist care ratio.

(4) IDENTIFICATION OF COUNTIES.—

(A) IN GENERAL.—The Secretary shall identify—

(i) those counties and areas (in this paragraph referred to as "primary care scarcity counties") with the lowest primary care ratios that represent, if each such county or area were weighted by the number of individuals determined under paragraph (2)(B), an aggregate total of 20 percent of the total of the individuals determined under such paragraph; and

(ii) those counties and areas (in this subsection referred to as "specialist care scarcity counties") with the lowest specialist care ratios that represent, if each such county or area were weighted by the number of individuals determined under paragraph (2)(B), an aggregate total of 20 percent of the total of the individuals determined under such paragraph.

(B) PERIODIC REVISIONS.—The Secretary shall periodically revise the counties or areas identified in subparagraph (A) (but not less often than once every three years) unless the Secretary determines that there is no new data available on the number of physicians practicing in the county or area or the number of individuals residing in the county or area, as identified in paragraph (2).

(C) IDENTIFICATION OF COUNTIES WHERE SERVICE IS FURNISHED.—For purposes of paying the additional amount specified in paragraph (1), if the Secretary uses the 5-digit postal ZIP Code where the service is furnished, the dominant county of the postal ZIP Code (as determined by the United States Postal Service, or otherwise) shall be used to determine whether the postal ZIP Code is in a scarcity county identified in subparagraph (A) or revised in subparagraph (B).

(D) JUDICIAL REVIEW.—There shall be no administrative or judicial review under section 1869, 1878, or otherwise, respecting—

(i) the identification of a county or area;

(ii) the assignment of a specialty of any physician under this paragraph;

(iii) the assignment of a physician to a county under paragraph (2); or

(iv) the assignment of a postal ZIP Code to a county or other area under this subsection.

(5) RURAL CENSUS TRACTS.—To the extent feasible, the Secretary shall treat a rural census tract of a metropolitan statistical area (as determined under the most recent modification of the Goldsmith Modification, originally published in the Federal Register on February 27, 1992 (57 Fed. Reg. 6725)), as an equivalent area for purposes of qualifying as a primary care scarcity county or specialist care scarcity county under this subsection.

(6) PHYSICIAN DEFINED.—For purposes of this paragraph, the term "physician" means a physician described in section 1861(r)(1) and the term "primary care physician" means a physician who is identified in the available data as a general practitioner, family practice practitioner, general internist, or obstetrician or gynecologist.

(7) PUBLICATION OF LIST OF COUNTIES; POSTING ON WEBSITE.—With respect to a year for which a county or area is identified or revised under paragraph (4), the Secretary shall identify such counties or areas as part of the proposed and final rule to implement the physician fee schedule under section 1848 for the applicable year. The Secretary shall post the list of counties identified or revised under paragraph (4) on the Internet website of the Centers for Medicare & Medicaid Services.

[CCH Explanation at ¶ 700.]
2003 Amendments:

Section 413(a) of the "Medicare Prescription Drug, Improvement, and Modernization Act of 2003," effective upon enactment,, amended section 1833 by adding at the end the new subsection (u).

[¶ 2125] Sec. 1834. PAYMENT FOR DURABLE MEDICAL EQUIPMENT

[42 U.S.C. § 1395m(a)]

(a) PAYMENT FOR DURABLE MEDICAL EQUIPMENT.—

(1) GENERAL RULE FOR PAYMENT.—

* * *

(B) PAYMENT BASIS.—Subject to subparagraph (F)(i), the payment basis described in this subparagraph is the lesser of—

* * *

(C) EXCLUSIVE PAYMENT RULE.—Subject to subparagraph (F)(ii), this subsection shall constitute the exclusive provision of this title for payment for covered items under this part or under part A to a home health agency.

* * *

(E) CLINICAL CONDITIONS FOR COVERAGE.—

(i) IN GENERAL.—The Secretary shall establish standards for clinical conditions for payment for covered items under this subsection.

(ii) REQUIREMENTS.—The standards established under clause (i) shall include the specification of types or classes of covered items that require, as a condition of payment under this subsection, a face-to-face examination of the individual by a physician (as defined in section 1861(r)(1)), a physician assistant, nurse practitioner, or a clinical nurse specialist (as those terms are defined in section 1861(aa)(5)) and a prescription for the item.

(iii) PRIORITY OF ESTABLISHMENT OF STANDARDS.—In establishing the standards under this subparagraph, the Secretary shall first establish standards for those covered items for which the Secretary determines there has been a proliferation of use, consistent findings of charges for covered items that are not delivered, or consistent findings of falsification of documentation to provide for payment of such covered items under this part.

(iv) STANDARDS FOR POWER WHEELCHAIRS.—Effective on the date of the enactment of this subparagraph, in the case of a covered item consisting of a motorized or power wheelchair for an individual, payment may not be made for such covered item unless a physician (as defined in section 1861(r)(1)), a physician assistant, nurse practitioner, or a clinical nurse specialist (as those terms are defined in section 1861(aa)(5)) has conducted a face-to-face examination of the individual and written a prescription for the item.

(v) LIMITATION ON PAYMENT FOR COVERED ITEMS.—Payment may not be made for a covered item under this subsection unless the item meets any standards established under this subparagraph for clinical condition of coverage.

(F) APPLICATION OF COMPETITIVE ACQUISITION; LIMITATION OF INHERENT REASONABLENESS AUTHORITY.—In the case of covered items furnished on or after January 1, 2009, that are included in a competitive acquisition program in a competitive acquisition area under section 1847(a)—

(i) the payment basis under this subsection for such items and services furnished in such area shall be the payment basis determined under such competitive acquisition program; and

(ii) the Secretary may use information on the payment determined under such competitive acquisition programs to adjust the payment amount otherwise recognized under subparagraph (B)(ii) for an area that is not a competitive acquisition area under section 1847 and in the case of such adjustment, paragraph (10)(B) shall not be applied.

* * *

(10) EXCEPTIONS AND ADJUSTMENTS.—

* * *

(B) ADJUSTMENT FOR INHERENT REASONABLENESS.—The Secretary is authorized to apply the provisions of paragraphs (8) and (9) of section 1842(b) to covered items and suppliers of such items and payments under this subsection in an area and with respect to covered items and services for which the Secretary does not make a payment amount adjustment under paragraph (1)(F).

* * *

(14) COVERED ITEM UPDATE.—In this subsection, the term "covered item update" means, with respect to a year—

* * *

(E) for 2002, 0 percentage points;

(F) for 2003, the percentage increase in the consumer price index for all urban consumers (U.S. urban average) for the 12-month period ending with June of 2002.

(G) for 2004 through 2006—

(i) subject to clause (ii), in the case of class III medical devices described in section 513(a)(1)(C) of the Federal Food, Drug, and Cosmetic Act (21 U.S.C. 360(c)(1)(C)), the percentage increase described in subparagraph (B) for the year involved; and

(ii) in the case of covered items not described in clause (i), 0 percentage points;

(H) for 2007—

(i) subject to clause (ii), in the case of class III medical devices described in section 513(a)(1)(C) of the Federal Food, Drug, and Cosmetic Act (21 U.S.C. 360(c)(1)(C)), the percentage change determined by the Secretary to be appropriate taking into account recommendations contained in the report of the Comptroller General of the United States under section 302(c)(1)(B) of the Medicare Prescription Drug, Improvement, and Modernization Act of 2003; and

(ii) in the case of covered items not described in clause (i), 0 percentage points; and

(I) for 2008—

(i) subject to clause (ii), in the case of class III medical devices described in section 513(a)(1)(C) of the Federal Food, Drug, and Cosmetic Act (21 U.S.C. 360(c)(1)(C)), the percentage increase described in subparagraph (B) (as applied to the payment amount for 2007 determined after the application of the percentage change under subparagraph (H)(i)); and

(ii) in the case of covered items not described in clause (i), 0 percentage points; and

(J) for a subsequent year, the percentage increase in the consumer price index for all urban consumers (U.S. urban average) for the 12-month period ending with June of the previous year.

* * *

(19) CERTAIN UPGRADED ITEMS.—

(A) INDIVIDUAL'S RIGHT TO CHOOSE UPGRADED ITEM.—Notwithstanding any other provision of this title, the Secretary may issue regulations under which an individual may purchase or rent from a supplier an item of upgraded durable medical equipment for which payment would be made under this subsection if the item were a standard item.

(B) PAYMENTS TO SUPPLIER.—In the case of the purchase or rental of an upgraded item under subparagraph (A)—

(i) the supplier shall receive payment under this subsection with respect to such item as if such item were a standard item; and

(ii) the individual purchasing or renting the item shall pay the supplier an amount equal to the difference between the supplier's charge and the amount under clause (i).

In no event may the supplier's charge for an upgraded item exceed the applicable fee schedule amount (if any) for such item.

(C) CONSUMER PROTECTION SAFEGUARDS.—Any regulations under subparagraph (A) shall provide for consumer protection standards with respect to the furnishing of upgraded equipment under subparagraph (A). Such regulations shall provide for—

(i) determination of fair market prices with respect to an upgraded item;

(ii) full disclosure of the availability and price of standard items and proof of receipt of such disclosure information by the beneficiary before the furnishing of the upgraded item;

(iii) conditions of participation for suppliers in the billing arrangement;

(iv) sanctions of suppliers who are determined to engage in coercive or abusive practices, including exclusion; and

(v) such other safeguards as the Secretary determines are necessary.

(20)(20) IDENTIFICATION OF QUALITY STANDARDS.—

(A) IN GENERAL.—Subject to subparagraph (C), the Secretary shall establish and implement quality standards for suppliers of items and services described in subparagraph (D) to be applied by recognized independent accreditation organizations (as designated under subparagraph (B)) and with which such suppliers shall be required to comply in order to—

(i) furnish any such item or service for which payment is made under this part; and

(ii) receive or retain a provider or supplier number used to submit claims for reimbursement for any such item or service for which payment may be made under this title.

(B) DESIGNATION OF INDEPENDENT ACCREDITATION ORGANIZATIONS.—Not later than the date that is 1 year after the date on which the Secretary implements the quality standards under subparagraph (A), notwithstanding section 1865(b), the Secretary shall designate and approve one or more independent accreditation organizations for purposes of such subparagraph.

(C) QUALITY STANDARDS.—The quality standards described in subparagraph (A) may not be less stringent than the quality standards that would otherwise apply if this paragraph did not apply and shall include consumer services standards.

(D) ITEMS AND SERVICES DESCRIBED.—The items and services described in this subparagraph are the following items and services, as the Secretary determines appropriate:

(i) Covered items (as defined in paragraph (13)) for which payment may otherwise be made under this subsection.

(ii) Prosthetic devices and orthotics and prosthetics described in section 1834(h)(4).

(iii) Items and services described in section 1842(s)(2).

(E) IMPLEMENTATION.—The Secretary may establish by program instruction or otherwise the quality standards under this paragraph, after consultation with representatives of relevant parties. Such standards shall be applied prospectively and shall be published on the Internet website of the Centers for Medicare & Medicaid Services.

(21) SPECIAL PAYMENT RULE FOR SPECIFIED ITEMS AND SUPPLIES.—

(A) IN GENERAL.—Notwithstanding the preceding provisions of this subsection, for specified items and supplies (described in subparagraph (B)) furnished during 2005, the payment amount otherwise determined under this subsection for such specified items and supplies shall be reduced by the percentage difference between—

(i) the amount of payment otherwise determined for the specified item or supply under this subsection for 2002, and

(ii) the amount of payment for the specified item or supply under chapter 89 of title 5, United States Code, as identified in the column entitled "Median FEHP Price" in the table entitled "SUMMARY OF MEDICARE PRICES COMPARED TO VA, MEDICAID, RETAIL, AND FEHP PRICES FOR 16 ITEMS" included in the Testimony of the Inspector General before the Senate Committee on Appropriations, June 12, 2002, or any subsequent report by the Inspector General.

(B) SPECIFIED ITEM OR SUPPLY DESCRIBED.—For purposes of subparagraph (A), a specified item or supply means oxygen and oxygen equipment, standard wheelchairs (including standard power wheelchairs), nebulizers, diabetic supplies consisting of lancets and testing strips, hospital beds, and air mattresses, but only if the HCPCS code for the item or supply is identified in a table referred to in subparagraph (A)(ii).

(C) APPLICATION OF UPDATE TO SPECIAL PAYMENT AMOUNT.—The covered item update under paragraph (14) for specified items and supplies for 2006 and each subsequent year shall be applied to the payment amount under subparagraph (A) unless payment is made for such items and supplies under section 1847.

[CCH Explanation at ¶1002.]
2003 Amendments:

Section 302(a)(1)(A) of the "Medicare Prescription Drug, Improvement, and Modernization Act of 2003," effective upon enactment, amended section 1834(a)(17) by transferring paragraph (17), as added by section 4551(c)(1) of the Balanced Budget Act of 1997 (111 Stat. 458), to the end of such section and redesignating such paragraph as paragraph (19).

Section 302(a)(1)(B) of the "Medicare Prescription Drug, Improvement, and Modernization Act of 2003," effective upon enactment, amended section 1834(a) by adding at the end new paragraph (20).

Section 302(a)(2) of the "Medicare Prescription Drug, Improvement, and Modernization Act of 2003," effective upon enactment, amended section 1834(a)(1) by adding at the end new subparagraph (E).

Section 302(c)(1)(A)(i) of the "Medicare Prescription Drug, Improvement, and Modernization Act of 2003," effective upon enactment, amended section 1834(a)(14)(E) by striking "and" at the end.

Section 302(c)(1)(A)(ii) of the "Medicare Prescription Drug, Improvement, and Modernization Act of 2003," effective upon enactment, amended section 1834(a)(14)(F) (I) by striking "a subsequent year" and inserting "2003"; and (II) by striking "the previous year." and inserting "2002;".

Section 302(c)(1)(A)(iii) of the "Medicare Prescription Drug, Improvement, and Modernization Act of 2003," effective upon enactment, amended section 1834(a)(14) by adding at the end new subparagraphs (G), (H), (I), and (J).

Section 302(c)(2) of the "Medicare Prescription Drug, Improvement, and Modernization Act of 2003," effective upon enactment, amended section 1834(a) by adding at the end new paragraph (21).

Section 302(d)(1)(A) of the "Medicare Prescription Drug, Improvement, and Modernization Act of 2003," effective upon enactment, amended section 1834(a)(1)(B) by striking "The payment basis" and inserting "Subject to subparagraph (F)(i), the payment basis".

Section 302(d)(1)(B) of the "Medicare Prescription Drug, Improvement, and Modernization Act of 2003," effective upon enactment, amended section 1834(a)(1)(C) by striking "This subsection" and inserting "Subject to subparagraph (F)(ii), this subsection".

Section 302(d)(1)(C) of the "Medicare Prescription Drug, Improvement, and Modernization Act of 2003," effective upon enactment, amended section 1834(a)(1) by adding at the end of paragraph (1) new subparagraph (F).

Section 302(d)(1)(D) of the "Medicare Prescription Drug, Improvement, and Modernization Act of 2003," effective upon enactment, amended section 1834(a)(10)(B) by inserting "in an area and with respect to covered items and services for which the Secretary does not make a payment amount adjustment under paragraph (1)(F)" after "under this subsection".

[¶2130] Sec. 1834. FEE SCHEDULES FOR RADIOLOGIST SERVICES
[42 U.S.C. §1395m(b)]

(b) FEE SCHEDULES FOR RADIOLOGIST SERVICES.—

* * *

(4) SAVINGS.—

* * *

(D) 1991 FEE SCHEDULES.—For radiologist services (other than portable X-ray services) furnished under this part during 1991, the conversion factors used in a locality under this subsection shall, subject to clause (vii), be reduced to the adjusted conversion factor for the locality determined as follows:

* * *

Social Security Law Added, Amended or Repealed

(iv) ADJUSTED CONVERSION FACTOR.—The adjusted conversion factor for the professional or technical component of a service in a locality is the sum of $1/2$ of the locally-adjusted amount determined under clause (v) and $1/2$ of the GPCI-adjusted amount determined under clause (vi).

* * *

2003 Amendments:

Section 736(b)(4) of the "Medicare Prescription Drug, Improvement, and Modernization Act of 2003," effective upon enactment, amended section 1834(b)(4)(D)(iv) by striking "clauses (vi)" and inserting "clause (vi)".

[¶2135] Sec. 1834. PAYMENT FOR OUTPATIENT CRITICAL ACCESS HOSPITAL SERVICES

[42 U.S.C. §1395m(g)]

(g) PAYMENT FOR OUTPATIENT CRITICAL ACCESS HOSPITAL SERVICES.—

(1) IN GENERAL.—The amount of payment for outpatient critical access hospital services of a critical access hospital is equal to 101 percent of the reasonable costs of the hospital in providing such services, unless the hospital makes the election under paragraph (2).

(2) ELECTION OF COST BASED HOSPITAL OUTPATIENT SERVICE PAYMENT PLUS FEE SCHEDULE FOR PROFESSIONAL SERVICES.—A critical access hospital may elect to be paid for outpatient critical access hospital services amounts equal to the sum of the following, less the amount that such hospital may charge as described in section 1866(a)(2)(A):

(A) FACILITY FEE.—With respect to facility services, not including any services for which payment may be made under subparagraph (B), the reasonable costs of the critical access hospital in providing such services.

(B) FEE SCHEDULE FOR PROFESSIONAL SERVICES.—With respect to professional services otherwise included within outpatient critical access hospital services, 115 percent of such amounts as would otherwise be paid under this part if such services were not included in outpatient critical access hospital services.

The Secretary may not require, as a condition for applying subparagraph (B) with respect to a critical access hospital, that each physician or other practitioner providing professional services in the hospital must assign billing rights with respect to such services, except that such subparagraph shall not apply to those physicians and practitioners who have not assigned such billing rights.

* * *

(5) COVERAGE OF COSTS FOR CERTAIN EMERGENCY ROOM ON-CALL PROVIDERS.——In determining the reasonable costs of outpatient critical access hospital services under paragraphs (1) and (2)(A), the Secretary shall recognize as allowable costs, amounts (as defined by the Secretary) for reasonable compensation and related costs for physicians, physician assistants, nurse practitioners, and clinical nurse specialists who are on-call (as defined by the Secretary) to provide emergency servicesbut who are not present on the premises of the hospital involved, and are not otherwise furnishing services covered under this title and are not on-call at any other provider or facility.

[CCH Explanation at ¶578.]

2003 Amendments:

Section 405(a)(1) of the "Medicare Prescription Drug, Improvement, and Modernization Act of 2003," amended section 1834(g)(1) by inserting "equal to 101 percent of" before "the reasonable costs".

The amendment made above applies to payments for services furnished during cost reporting periods beginning on or after January 1, 2004.

Section 405(b)(1) of the "Medicare Prescription Drug, Improvement, and Modernization Act of 2003," amended section 1834(g)(5) in the heading by inserting "CERTAIN" before "EMERGENCY"; and by striking "PHYSICIANS" and inserting "PROVIDERS"; by striking "emergency room physicians who are on-call (as defined by the Secretary)" and inserting "physicians, physician assistants, nurse practitioners, and clinical nurse specialists who are on-call (as defined by the Secretary) to provide emergency services"; and by striking "physicians' services" and inserting "services covered under this title".

The amendments made by section 405(b)(1) of the "Medicare Prescription Drug, Improvement, and Modernization Act of 2003," apply with respect to costs incurred for services furnished on or after January 1, 2005.

Section 405(d)(1) of the "Medicare Prescription Drug, Improvement, and Modernization Act of 2003," amended section 1834(g)(2) by adding after and below subparagraph (B) the following: "The Secretary may not require, as a condition for applying subparagraph (B) with respect to a critical access hospital, that each physician or other practitioner providing professional services in the hospital must assign billing rights with respect to such services, except that such subparagraph shall not apply to those physicians and practitioners who have not assigned such billing rights.".

The amendment made by section 405(d)(1) of the "Medicare Prescription Drug, Improvement, and Modernization Act of 2003" applies to cost reporting periods beginning on or after July 1, 2004. In the case of a critical access hospital that made an election under Sec. 1834(g)(2) of the Social Security Act before November 1, 2003, the amendment applies to cost reporting periods beginning on or after July 1, 2001.

[¶2140] Sec. 1834. PAYMENT FOR PROSTHETIC DEVICES AND ORTHOTICS AND PROSTHETICS

[42 U.S.C. §1395m(h)]

(h) PAYMENT FOR PROSTHETIC DEVICES AND ORTHOTICS AND PROSTHETICS.—

(1) GENERAL RULE FOR PAYMENT.—

* * *

(B) PAYMENT BASIS.—Except as provided in subparagraphs (C), (E), and (H)(i), the payment basis described in this subparagraph is the lesser of—

* * *

(D) EXCLUSIVE PAYMENT RULE.—Subject to subparagraph (H)(ii), this subsection shall constitute the exclusive provision of this title for payment for prosthetic devices, orthotics, and prosthetics under this part or under part A to a home health agency.

* * *

(H) APPLICATION OF COMPETITIVE ACQUISITION TO ORTHOTICS; LIMITATION OF INHERENT REASONABLENESS AUTHORITY.—In the case of orthotics described in paragraph (2)(C) of section 1847(a) furnished on or after January 1, 2009, that are included in a competitive acquisition program in a competitive acquisition area under such section—

(i) the payment basis under this subsection for such orthotics furnished in such area shall be the payment basis determined under such competitive acquisition program; and

(ii) the Secretary may use information on the payment determined under such competitive acquisition programs to adjust the payment amount otherwise recognized under subparagraph (B)(ii) for an area that is not a competitive acquisition area under section 1847, and in the case of such adjustment, paragraphs (8) and (9) of section 1842(b) shall not be applied.

* * *

(4) DEFINITIONS.—In this subsection—

(A) the term "applicable percentage increase" means—

* * *

(vii) for 2002, 1 percent;

(viii) for 2003, the percentage increase in the consumer price index for all urban consumers (United States city average) for the 12-month period ending with June of the previous year;

(ix) for 2004, 2005, and 2006, 0 percent; and

(x) for a subsequent year, the percentage increase in the consumer price index for all urban consumers (United States city average) for the 12-month period ending with June of the previous year;

* * *

(C) the term "orthotics and prosthetics" has the meaning given such term in section 1861(s)(9) (and includes shoes described in section 1861(s)(12)), but does not include intraocular lenses or medical supplies (including catheters, catheter supplies, ostomy bags, and supplies related to ostomy care) furnished by a home health agency under section 1861(m)(5).

[CCH Explanation at ¶ 761 and 1002.]

2003 Amendments:

Section 302(c)(3)(A) of the "Medicare Prescription Drug, Improvement, and Modernization Act of 2003," effective upon enactment, amended section 1834(h)(4)(A)(vii) by striking "and" at the end.

Section 302(c)(3)(B) of the "Medicare Prescription Drug, Improvement, and Modernization Act of 2003," effective upon enactment, amended section 1834(h)(4)(A)(viii) by striking "a subsequent year" and inserting "2003".

Section 302(c)(3)(C) of the "Medicare Prescription Drug, Improvement, and Modernization Act of 2003," effective upon enactment, amended section 1834(h)(4)(A) by adding at the end new clauses (ix) and (x).

Section 302(d)(2)(A) of the "Medicare Prescription Drug, Improvement, and Modernization Act of 2003," effective upon enactment, amended section 1834(h)(1)(B) by striking "and (E)" and inserting ", (E), and (H)(i)".

Section 302(d)(2)(B) of the "Medicare Prescription Drug, Improvement, and Modernization Act of 2003," effective upon enactment, amended section 1834(h)(1)(D) by striking "This subsection" and inserting "Subject to subparagraph (H)(ii), this subsection".

Section 302(d)(2)(C) of the "Medicare Prescription Drug, Improvement, and Modernization Act of 2003," effective upon enactment, amended section 1834(h)(1) by adding at the end of paragraph (1) new subparagraph (H).

Section 627(b)(1) of the "Medicare Prescription Drug, Improvement, and Modernization Act of 2003," amended section 1834(h)(4)(C) by inserting "(and includes shoes described in section 1861(s)(12))" after "in section 1861(s)(9)".

The amendments made by section 627(b) of the "Medicare Prescription Drug, Improvement, and Modernization Act of 2003," apply to items furnished on or after January 1, 2005.

[¶ 2145] Sec. 1834. [Prospective Fee Schedule for Ambulance Services]

[42 U.S.C. § 1395m(l)]

(l) ESTABLISHMENT OF FEE SCHEDULE FOR AMBULANCE SERVICES.—

* * *

(2) CONSIDERATIONS.—In establishing such fee schedule, the Secretary shall—

* * *

(E) phase in the application of the payment rates under the fee schedule in an efficient and fair manner consistent with paragraph (11), except that such phase-in shall provide for full payment of any national mileage rate for ambulance services provided by suppliers that are paid by carriers in any of the 50 States where payment by a carrier for such services for all such suppliers in such State did not, prior to the implementation of the fee schedule, include a separate amount for all mileage within the county from which the beneficiary is transported.

* * *

(9) TRANSITIONAL ASSISTANCE FOR RURAL PROVIDERS.—In the case of ground ambulance services furnished on or after July 1, 2001, and before January 1, 2004, for which the transportation originates in a rural area (as defined in section 1886(d)(2)(D)) or in a rural census tract of a metropolitan statistical area (as determined under the most recent modification of the Goldsmith Modification, originally published in the Federal Register on February 27, 1992 (57 Fed. Reg. 6725)), the fee schedule established under this subsection shall provide that, with respect to the payment rate for mileage for a trip above 17 miles, and up to 50 miles, the rate otherwise established shall be increased by not less than $1/2$ of the additional payment per mile established for the first 17 miles of such a trip originating in a rural area.

(10) PHASE-IN PROVIDING FLOOR USING BLEND OF FEE SCHEDULE AND REGIONAL FEE SCHEDULES.—In carrying out the phase-in under paragraph (2)(E) for each level of ground service furnished in a year, the portion of the payment amount that is based on the fee schedule shall be the greater of the amount determined under such fee schedule (without regard to this paragraph) or the following blended rate of the fee schedule under paragraph (1) and of a regional fee schedule for the region involved:

(A) For 2004 (for services furnished on or after July 1, 2004), the blended rate shall be based 20 percent on the fee schedule under paragraph (1) and 80 percent on the regional fee schedule.

(B) For 2005, the blended rate shall be based 40 percent on the fee schedule under paragraph (1) and 60 percent on the regional fee schedule.

(C) For 2006, the blended rate shall be based 60 percent on the fee schedule under paragraph (1) and 40 percent on the regional fee schedule.

(D) For 2007, 2008, and 2009, the blended rate shall be based 80 percent on the fee schedule under paragraph (1) and 20 percent on the regional fee schedule.

(E) For 2010 and each succeeding year, the blended rate shall be based 100 percent on the fee schedule under paragraph (1).

For purposes of this paragraph, the Secretary shall establish a regional fee schedule for each of the nine census divisions (referred to in section 1886(d)(2)) using the methodology (used in establishing the fee schedule under paragraph (1)) to calculate a regional conversion factor and a regional mileage payment rate and using the same payment adjustments and the same relative value units as used in the fee schedule under such paragraph.

(11) ADJUSTMENT IN PAYMENT FOR CERTAIN LONG TRIPS.—In the case of ground ambulance services furnished on or after July 1, 2004, and before January 1, 2009, regardless of where the transportation originates, the fee schedule established under this subsection shall provide that, with respect to the payment rate for mileage for a trip above 50 miles the per mile rate otherwise established shall be increased by 1/4 of the payment per mile otherwise applicable to miles in excess of 50 miles in such trip.

(12) ASSISTANCE FOR RURAL PROVIDERS FURNISHING SERVICES IN LOW POPULATION DENSITY AREAS.—

(A) IN GENERAL.—In the case of ground ambulance services furnished on or after July 1, 2004, and before January 1, 2010, for which the transportation originates in a qualified rural area (identified under subparagraph (B)(iii)), the Secretary shall provide for a percent increase in the base rate of the fee schedule for a trip established under this subsection. In establishing such percent increase, the Secretary shall estimate the average cost per trip for such services (not taking into account mileage) in the lowest quartile as compared to the average cost per trip for such services (not taking into account mileage) in the highest quartile of all rural county populations.

(B) IDENTIFICATION OF QUALIFIED RURAL AREAS.—

(i) DETERMINATION OF POPULATION DENSITY IN AREA.—Based upon data from the United States decennial census for the year 2000, the Secretary shall determine, for each rural area, the population density for that area.

(ii) RANKING OF AREAS.—The Secretary shall rank each such area based on such population density.

(iii) IDENTIFICATION OF QUALIFIED RURAL AREAS.—The Secretary shall identify those areas (in subparagraph (A) referred to as "qualified rural areas") with the lowest population densities that represent, if each such area were weighted by the population of such area (as used in computing such population densities), an aggregate total of 25 percent of the total of the population of all such areas.

(iv) RURAL AREA.—For purposes of this paragraph, the term "rural area" has the meaning given such term in section 1886(d)(2)(D). If feasible, the Secretary shall treat a rural census tract of a metropolitan statistical area (as determined under the most recent modification of the Goldsmith Modification, originally published in the Federal Register on February 27, 1992 (57 Fed. Reg. 6725) as a rural area for purposes of this paragraph.

(v) JUDICIAL REVIEW.—There shall be no administrative or judicial review under section 1869, 1878, or otherwise, respecting the identification of an area under this subparagraph.

(13) TEMPORARY INCREASE FOR GROUND AMBULANCE SERVICES.—

(A) IN GENERAL.—After computing the rates with respect to ground ambulance services under the other applicable provisions of this subsection, in the case of such services furnished on or after July 1, 2004, and before January 1, 2007, for which the transportation originates in—

(i) a rural area described in paragraph (9) or in a rural census tract described in such paragraph, the fee schedule established under this section shall provide that the rate for the service otherwise established, after the application of any increase under paragraphs (11) and (12), shall be increased by 2 percent; and

(ii) an area not described in clause (i), the fee schedule established under this subsection shall provide that the rate for the service otherwise established, after the application of any increase under paragraph (11), shall be increased by 1 percent.

§1834(l)(13)(A)(ii) ¶2145

(B) APPLICATION OF INCREASED PAYMENTS AFTER 2006.—The increased payments under subparagraph (A) shall not be taken into account in calculating payments for services furnished after the period specified in such subparagraph.

(14) PROVIDING APPROPRIATE COVERAGE OF RURAL AIR AMBULANCE SERVICES.—

(A) IN GENERAL.—The regulations described in section 1861(s)(7) shall provide, to the extent that any ambulance services (whether ground or air) may be covered under such section, that a rural air ambulance service (as defined in subparagraph (C)) is reimbursed under this subsection at the air ambulance rate if the air ambulance service—

(i) is reasonable and necessary based on the health condition of the individual being transported at or immediately prior to the time of the transport; and

(ii) complies with equipment and crew requirements established by the Secretary.

(B) SATISFACTION OF REQUIREMENT OF MEDICALLY NECESSARY.—The requirement of subparagraph (A)(i) is deemed to be met for a rural air ambulance service if—

(i) subject to subparagraph (D), such service is requested by a physician or other qualified medical personnel (as specified by the Secretary) who reasonably determines or certifies that the individual's condition is such that the time needed to transport the individual by land or the instability of transportation by land poses a threat to the individual's survival or seriously endangers the individual's health; or

(ii) such service is furnished pursuant to a protocol that is established by a State or regional emergency medical service (EMS) agency and recognized or approved by the Secretary under which the use of an air ambulance is recommended, if such agency does not have an ownership interest in the entity furnishing such service.

(C) RURAL AIR AMBULANCE SERVICE DEFINED.—For purposes of this paragraph, the term "rural air ambulance service" means fixed wing and rotary wing air ambulance service in which the point of pick up of the individual occurs in a rural area (as defined in section 1886(d)(2)(D)) or in a rural census tract of a metropolitan statistical area (as determined under the most recent modification of the Goldsmith Modification, originally published in the Federal Register on February 27, 1992 (57 Fed. Reg. 6725)).

(D) LIMITATION.—

(i) IN GENERAL.—Subparagraph (B)(i) shall not apply if there is a financial or employment relationship between the person requesting the rural air ambulance service and the entity furnishing the ambulance service, or an entity under common ownership with the entity furnishing the air ambulance service, or a financial relationship between an immediate family member of such requester and such an entity.

(ii) EXCEPTION.—Where a hospital and the entity furnishing rural air ambulance services are under common ownership, clause (i) shall not apply to remuneration (through employment or other relationship) by the hospital of the requester or immediate family member if the remuneration is for provider-based physician services furnished in a hospital (as described in section 1887) which are reimbursed under part A and the amount of the remuneration is unrelated directly or indirectly to the provision of rural air ambulance services.

[CCH Explanation at ¶ 596 and 598.]
2003 Amendments:

Section 414(a)(1) of the "Medicare Prescription Drug, Improvement, and Modernization Act of 2003," effective upon enactment, amended section 1834(l)(2)(E) by inserting "consistent with paragraph (11)" after "in an efficient and fair manner".

Section 414(a)(2) of the "Medicare Prescription Drug, Improvement, and Modernization Act of 2003," effective upon enactment, amended section 1834(l)(8) by redesignating paragraph (8), as added by section 221(a) of BIPA (114 Stat. 2763A-486), as paragraph (9).

Section 414(a)(3) of the "Medicare Prescription Drug, Improvement, and Modernization Act of 2003," effective upon enactment, amended section 1834(l) by adding at the end new paragraph (10).

Section 414(b) of the "Medicare Prescription Drug, Improvement, and Modernization Act of 2003," effective upon enactment, amended section 1834(l) by adding at the end new paragraph (11).

Section 414(c) of the "Medicare Prescription Drug, Improvement, and Modernization Act of 2003," effective upon enactment, amended section 1834(l) by adding at the end new paragraph (12).

Section 414(d) of the "Medicare Prescription Drug, Improvement, and Modernization Act of 2003," effective upon enactment, amended section 1834(l) by adding at the end new paragraph (13).

Section 415(a) of the "Medicare Prescription Drug, Improvement, and Modernization Act of 2003," effective upon enactment, amended section 1834(l) by adding at the end new paragraph (14).

The amendments made by section 415(a) of the "Medicare Prescription Drug, Improvement, and Modernization Act of 2003," apply to services furnished on or after January 1, 2005.

[¶ 2150] Sec. 1834. PAYMENT FOR TELEHEALTH SERVICES

[42 U.S.C. § 1395m(m)]

(m) PAYMENT FOR TELEHEALTH SERVICES.—

* * *

(4) DEFINITIONS.—For purposes of this subsection:

* * *

(C) ORIGINATING SITE.—

* * *

(ii) SITES DESCRIBED.—The sites referred to in clause (i) are the following sites:

* * *

(III) A rural health clinic (as defined in section 1861(aa)(2)).

* * *

2003 Amendments:

Section 736(b)(5) of the "Medicare Prescription Drug, Improvement, and Modernization Act of 2003," effective upon enactment, amended section 1834(m)(4)(C)(ii)(III) by striking "1861(aa)(s)" and inserting "1861(aa)(2)".

[¶ 2155] Sec. 1835. PROCEDURE FOR PAYMENT OF CLAIMS OF PROVIDERS OF SERVICES

[42 U.S.C. § 1395n]

(a) Except as provided in subsections (b), (c), and (e), payment for services described in section 1832(a)(2) furnished an individual may be made only to providers of services which are eligible therefor under section 1866(a), and only if—

* * *

(2) a physician certifies (and recertifies, where such services are furnished over a period of time, in such cases, with such frequency, and accompanied by such supporting material, appropriate to the case involved, as may be provided by regulations) that—

* * *

To the extent provided by regulations, the certification and recertification requirements of paragraph (2) shall be deemed satisfied where, at a later date, a physician makes a certification of the kind provided in subparagraph (A) or (B) of paragraph (2) (whichever would have applied), but only where such certification is accompanied by such medical and other evidence as may be required by such regulations. For purposes of this section, the term "provider of services" shall include a clinic, rehabilitation agency, or public health agency if, in the case of a clinic or rehabilitation agency, such clinic or agency meets the requirements of section 1861(p)(4)(A) (or meets the requirements of such section through the operation of section 1861(g)), or if, in the case of a public health agency, such agency meets the requirements of section 1861(p)(4)(B)(or meets the requirements of such section through the operation of section 1861(g)), but only with respect to the furnishing of outpatient physical therapy services (as therein defined) or (though the operation of section 1861(g)) with respect to the furnishing of outpatient occupational therapy services. With respect to the physician certification required by paragraph (2) for home health services furnished to any individual by a home health agency (other than an agency which is a governmental entity) and with respect to the establishment and review of a plan for such services, the Secretary shall prescribe regulations which shall become effective no later than July 1, 1981, and which prohibit a physician who has a significant ownership interest in, or a significant financial or contractual relationship with, such home health agency from performing such certification and from establishing or reviewing such plan, except that such prohibition shall not apply with respect to a home health agency which is a sole community home health agency (as determined by the Secretary). For purposes of the preceding sentence, service by a physician as an uncompensated officer or director of a home health agency shall not constitute having a significant ownership interest in, or a significant financial or contractual relationship with, such agency. For purposes of paragraph (2)(A), an individual shall be considered to be "confined to his home" if the individual has a condition, due to an illness or injury, that restricts the ability of the individual to leave his or her home except with the assistance of another individual or the aid of a supportive device (such as crutches, a cane, a wheelchair, or a walker), or if the individual has a condition such that leaving his or her home is medically contraindicated. While an individual does not have to be bedridden to be considered "confined to his home", the condition of the individual should be such that there exists a normal inability to leave home and that leaving home requires a considerable and taxing effort by the individual, Any absence of an individual from the home attributable to the need to receive health care treatment, including regular absences for the purpose of participating in therapeutic, psychosocial, or medical treatment in an adult day-care program that is licensed or certified by a State, or accredited, to furnish adult day-care services in the State shall not disqualify an individual from being considered to be "confined to his home". Any other absence of an individual from the home shall not so disqualify an individual if the absence is of infrequent or of relatively short duration. For purposes of the preceding sentence, any absence for the purpose of attending a religious service shall be deemed to be an absence of infrequent or short duration.

* * *

2003 Amendments:

Section 736(c)(2)(B) of the "Medicare Prescription Drug, Improvement, and Modernization Act of 2003," effective upon enactment, amended section 1835(a) in the seventh sentence by striking "leave home," and inserting "leave home and".

[¶ 2160] Sec. 1838. COVERAGE PERIOD

[42 U.S.C. § 1395q]

(a) The period during which an individual is entitled to benefits under the insurance program established by this part (hereinafter referred to as his "coverage period") shall begin on whichever of the following is the latest:

(1) July 1, 1966, or (in the case of a disabled individual who has not attained age 65) July 1, 1973; or

* * *

2003 Amendments:

Section 736(b)(6) of the "Medicare Prescription Drug, Improvement, and Modernization Act of 2003," effective upon enactment, amended section 1838(a)(1) by inserting a comma after "1966".

[¶ 2165] Sec. 1839. AMOUNTS OF PREMIUMS

[42 U.S.C. § 1395r]

(a)

* * *

(2) The monthly premium of each individual enrolled under this part for each month after December 1983 shall be the amount determined under paragraph (3), adjusted as required in accordance with subsections (b), (c), (f), and (i), and to reflect any credit provided under section 1854(b)(1)(C)(ii)(III).

* * *

(4) The Secretary shall also, during September of 1983 and of each year thereafter, determine the monthly actuarial rate for disabled enrollees under age 65 which shall be applicable for the succeeding calendar year. Such actuarial rate shall be the amount the Secretary estimates to be necessary so that the aggregate amount for such calendar year with respect to disabled enrollees under age 65 will equal one-half of the total of the benefits and administrative costs which he estimates will be payable from the Federal Supplementary Medical Insurance Trust Fund for services performed and related administrative costs incurred in such calendar year with respect to such enrollees. In calculating the monthly actuarial rate under this paragraph, the Secretary shall include an appropriate amount for a contingency margin.

(b) In the case of an individual whose coverage period began pursuant to an enrollment after his initial enrollment period (determined pursuant to subsection (c) or (d) of section 1837) and not pursuant to a special enrollment period under section 1837(i)(4), the monthly premium determined under subsection (a) (without regard to any adjustment under subsection (i))shall be increased by 10 percent of the monthly premium so determined for each full 12 months (in the same continuous period of eligibility) in which he could have been but was not enrolled. For purposes of the preceding sentence, there shall be taken into account (1) the months which elapsed between the close of his initial enrollment period and the close of the enrollment period in which he enrolled, plus (in the case of an individual who reenrolls) (2) the months which elapsed between the date of termination of a previous coverage period and the close of the enrollment period in which he reenrolled, but there shall not be taken into account months for which the individual can demonstrate that the individual was enrolled in a group health plan described in section 1862(b)(1)(A)(v) by reason of the individual's (or the individual's spouse's) current employment status or months during which the individual has not attained the age of 65 and for which the individual can demonstrate that the individual was enrolled in a large group health plan (as that term is defined in section 1862(b)(1)(B)(iv)) by reason of the individual's current employment status (or the current employment status of a family member of the individual). Any increase in an individual's monthly premium under the first sentence of this subsection with respect to a particular continuous period of eligibility shall not be applicable with respect to any other continuous period of eligibility which such individual may have. No increase in the premium shall be effected for a month in the case of an individual who enrolls under this part during 2001, 2002, 2003, or 2004 and who demonstrates to the Secretary before December 31, 2004, that the individual is a covered beneficiary (as defined in section 1072(5) of title 10, United States Code). The Secretary of Health and Human Services shall consult with the Secretary of Defense in identifying individuals described in the previous sentence.

* * *

(f) For any calendar year after 1988, if an individual is entitled to monthly benefits under section 202 or 223 or to a monthly annuity under section 3(a), 4(a), or 4(f) of the Railroad Retirement Act of 1974 for November and December of the preceding year, ifthe monthly premium of the individual under this section for December and for January is deducted from those benefits under section 1840(a)(1) or section 1840(b)(1) and if the amount of the individual's premium is not adjusted for such January under subsection (i), the monthly premium otherwise determined under this section for an individual for that year shall not be increased, pursuant to this subsection, to the extent that such increase would reduce the amount of benefits payable to that individual for that December below the amount of benefits payable to that individual for that November (after the deduction of the premium under this section). For purposes of this subsection, retroactive adjustments or payments and deductions on account of work shall not be taken into account in determining the monthly benefits to which an individual is entitled under section 202 or 223 or under the Railroad Retirement Act of 1974.

(g) In estimating the benefits and administrative costs which will be payable from the Federal Supplementary Medical Insurance Trust Fund for a year for purposes of determining the monthly premium rate under subsection (a)(3), the Secretary shall exclude an estimate of any benefits and administrative costs attributable to—

(1) the application of section 1861(v)(1)(L)(viii) or to the establishment under section 1861(v)(1)(L)(i)(V) of a per visit limit at 106 percent of the median (instead of 105 percent of the median), but only to the extent payment for home health services under this title is not being made under section 1895 (relating to prospective payment for home health services); and

(2) the medicare prescription drug discount card and transitional assistance program under section 1860D-31.

(h) POTENTIAL APPLICATION OF COMPARATIVE COST ADJUSTMENT IN CCA AREAS.—

(1) IN GENERAL.—Certain individuals who are residing in a CCA area under section 1860C-1 who are not enrolled in an MA plan under part C may be subject to a premium adjustment under subsection (f) of such section for months in which the CCA program under such section is in effect in such area.

(2) NO EFFECT ON LATE ENROLLMENT PENALTY OR INCOME-RELATED ADJUSTMENT IN SUBSIDIES.— Nothing in this subsection or section 1860C-1(f) shall be construed as affecting the amount of any premium adjustment under subsection (b) or (i). Subsection (f) shall be applied without regard to any premium adjustment referred to in paragraph (1).

(3) IMPLEMENTATION.—In order to carry out a premium adjustment under this subsection and section 1860C-1(f) (insofar as it is effected through the manner of collection of premiums under section 1840(a)), the Secretary shall transmit to the Commissioner of Social Security—

(A) at the beginning of each year, the name, social security account number, and the amount of the premium adjustment (if any) for each individual enrolled under this part for each month during the year; and

(B) periodically throughout the year, information to update the information previously transmitted under this paragraph for the year.

§1839(h)(3)(B) ¶2165

(i) REDUCTION IN PREMIUM SUBSIDY BASED ON INCOME.—

(1) IN GENERAL.—In the case of an individual whose modified adjusted gross income exceeds the threshold amount under paragraph (2), the monthly amount of the premium subsidy applicable to the premium under this section for a month after December 2006 shall be reduced (and the monthly premium shall be increased) by the monthly adjustment amount specified in paragraph (3).

(2) THRESHOLD AMOUNT.—For purposes of this subsection, the threshold amount is—

(A) except as provided in subparagraph (B), $80,000, and

(B) in the case of a joint return, twice the amount applicable under subparagraph (A) for the calendar year.

(3) MONTHLY ADJUSTMENT AMOUNT.—

(A) IN GENERAL.—Subject to subparagraph (B), the monthly adjustment amount specified in this paragraph for an individual for a month in a year is equal to the product of the following:

(i) SLIDING SCALE PERCENTAGE.—The applicable percentage specified in the table in subparagraph (C) for the individual minus 25 percentage points.

(ii) UNSUBSIDIZED PART B PREMIUM AMOUNT.—200 percent of the monthly actuarial rate for enrollees age 65 and over (as determined under subsection (a)(1) for the year).

(B) 5-YEAR PHASE IN.—The monthly adjustment amount specified in this paragraph for an individual for a month in a year before 2011 is equal to the following percentage of the monthly adjustment amount specified in subparagraph (A):

(i) For 2007, 20 percent.

(ii) For 2008, 40 percent.

(iii) For 2009, 60 percent.

(iv) for 2010, 80 percent.

(C) APPLICABLE PERCENTAGE.—

(i) IN GENERAL.—

If the modified adjusted gross income is:	The applicable percentage is:
More than $80,000 but not more than $100,000	35 percent
More than $100,000 but not more than $150,000	50 percent
More than $150,000 but not more than $200,000	65 percent
More than $200,000	80 percent

(ii) JOINT RETURNS.—In the case of a joint return, clause (i) shall be applied by substituting dollar amounts which are twice the dollar amounts otherwise applicable under clause (i) for the calendar year.

(iii) MARRIED INDIVIDUALS FILING SEPARATE RETURNS.—In the case of an individual who—

(I) is married as of the close of the taxable year (within the meaning of section 7703 of the Internal Revenue Code of 1986) but does not file a joint return for such year, and

(II) does not live apart from such individual's spouse at all times during the taxable year,

clause (i) shall be applied by reducing each of the dollar amounts otherwise applicable under such clause for the calendar year by the threshold amount for such year applicable to an unmarried individual.

(4) MODIFIED ADJUSTED GROSS INCOME.—

(A) IN GENERAL.—For purposes of this subsection, the term "modified adjusted gross income" means adjusted gross income (as defined in section 62 of the Internal Revenue Code of 1986)—

(i) determined without regard to sections 135, 911, 931, and 933 of such Code; and

(ii) increased by the amount of interest received or accrued during the taxable year which is exempt from tax under such Code.

In the case of an individual filing a joint return, any reference in this subsection to the modified adjusted gross income of such individual shall be to such return's modified adjusted gross income.

(B) TAXABLE YEAR TO BE USED IN DETERMINING MODIFIED ADJUSTED GROSS INCOME.—

(i) IN GENERAL.—In applying this subsection for an individual's premiums in a month in a year, subject to clause (ii) and subparagraph (C), the individual's modified adjusted gross income shall be such income determined for the individual's last taxable year beginning in the second calendar year preceding the year involved.

(ii) TEMPORARY USE OF OTHER DATA.—If, as of October 15 before a calendar year, the Secretary of the Treasury does not have adequate data for an individual in appropriate electronic form for the taxable year referred to in clause (i), the individual's modified adjusted gross income shall be determined using the data in such form from the previous taxable year. Except as provided in regulations prescribed by the Commissioner of Social Security in consultation with the Secretary, the preceding sentence shall cease to apply when adequate data in appropriate electronic form are available for the individual for the taxable year referred to in clause (i), and proper adjustments shall be made to the extent that the premium adjustments determined under the preceding sentence were inconsistent with those determined using such taxable year.

(iii) NON-FILERS.—In the case of individuals with respect to whom the Secretary of the Treasury does not have adequate data in appropriate electronic form for either taxable year referred to in clause (i) or clause (ii), the Commissioner of Social Security, in consultation with the Secretary, shall prescribe regulations which provide for the treatment of the premium adjustment with respect to such individual under this subsection, including regulations which provide for—

(I) the application of the highest applicable percentage under paragraph (3)(C) to such individual if the Commissioner has information which indicates that such individual's modified adjusted gross income might exceed the threshold amount for the taxable year referred to in clause (i), and

(II) proper adjustments in the case of the application of an applicable percentage under subclause (I) to such individual which is inconsistent with such individual's modified adjusted gross income for such taxable year.

(C) USE OF MORE RECENT TAXABLE YEAR.—

(i) IN GENERAL.—The Commissioner of Social Security in consultation with the Secretary of the Treasury shall establish a procedures under which an individual's modified adjusted gross income shall, at the request of such individual, be determined under this subsection—

(I) for a more recent taxable year than the taxable year otherwise used under subparagraph (B), or

(II) by such methodology as the Commissioner, in consultation with such Secretary, determines to be appropriate, which may include a methodology for aggregating or disaggregating information from tax returns in the case of marriage or divorce.

(ii) STANDARD FOR GRANTING REQUESTS.—A request under clause (i)(I) to use a more recent taxable year may be granted only if—

(I) the individual furnishes to such Commissioner with respect to such year such documentation, such as a copy of a filed Federal income tax return or an equivalent document, as the Commissioner specifies for purposes of determining the premium adjustment (if any) under this subsection; and

(II) the individual's modified adjusted gross income for such year is significantly less than such income for the taxable year determined under subparagraph (B) by reason of the death of such individual's spouse, the marriage or divorce of such individual, or other major life changing events specified in regulations prescribed by the Commissioner in consultation with the Secretary.

(5) INFLATION ADJUSTMENT.—

(A) IN GENERAL.—In the case of any calendar year beginning after 2007, each dollar amount in paragraph (2) or (3) shall be increased by an amount equal to—

(i) such dollar amount, multiplied by

(ii) the percentage (if any) by which the average of the Consumer Price Index for all urban consumers (United States city average) for the 12-month period ending with August of the preceding calendar year exceeds such average for the 12-month period ending with August 2006.

(B) ROUNDING.—If any dollar amount after being increased under subparagraph (A) is not a multiple of $1,000, such dollar amount shall be rounded to the nearest multiple of $1,000.

(6) JOINT RETURN DEFINED.—For purposes of this subsection, the term "joint return" has the meaning given to such term by section 7701(a)(38) of the Internal Revenue Code of 1986.

[CCH Explanation at ¶ 215, 376, 396, 776, and 777.]

2003 Amendments:

Section 105(a) of the "Medicare Prescription Drug, Improvement, and Modernization Act of 2003," effective upon enactment, amended section 1839(g) by striking "attributable to the application of section" and inserting "attributable to—(1) the application of section"; by striking the period and inserting "; and"; and by adding at the end new paragraph (2).

Section 222(l)(2)(A) of the "Medicare Prescription Drug, Improvement, and Modernization Act of 2003," amended section 1839(a)(2) by striking "80 percent of any reduction elected under section 1854(f)(1)(E)" and inserting "any credit provided under section 1854(b)(1)(C)(ii)(III)".

The above amendment applies to plan years beginning on or after January 1, 2006.

Section 241(b)(2)(A) of the "Medicare Prescription Drug, Improvement, and Modernization Act of 2003," effective upon enactment, amended section 1839 by adding at the end new subsection (h).

Section 625(a)(1) of the "Medicare Prescription Drug, Improvement, and Modernization Act of 2003," amended section 1839(b) by adding at the end the following new sentence: "No increase in the premium shall be effected for a month in the case of an individual who enrolls under this part during 2001, 2002, 2003, or 2004 and who demonstrates to the Secretary before December 31, 2004, that the individual is a covered beneficiary (as defined in section 1072(5) of title 10, United States Code). The Secretary of Health and Human Services shall consult with the Secretary of Defense in identifying individuals described in the previous sentence.".

The amendment above applies to premiums for months beginning January 2004.

Section 736(b)(7) of the "Medicare Prescription Drug, Improvement, and Modernization Act of 2003," effective upon enactment, amended section 1839(a)(4) in the second sentence by striking "which will" and inserting "will".

Section 811 of the "Medicare Prescription Drug, Improvement, and Modernization Act of 2003," effective upon enactment, amended section 1839, as amended by section 241(c), by adding at the end new subsection (i).

Section 811(b)(1) of the "Medicare Prescription Drug, Improvement, and Modernization Act of 2003," effective upon enactment, amended section 1839(a)(2) by striking "and (f)" and inserting "(f), and (i)".

Section 811(b)(1) of the "Medicare Prescription Drug, Improvement, and Modernization Act of 2003," effective upon enactment, amended section 1839(b) by inserting "(without regard to any adjustment under subsection (i))" after "subsection (a)".

Section 811(b)(1) of the "Medicare Prescription Drug, Improvement, and Modernization Act of 2003," effective upon enactment, amended section 1839(f) by striking "and if" and inserting "if"; and by inserting "and if the amount of the individual's premium is not adjusted for such January under subsection (i)," after "section 1840(b)(1),".

[¶ 2170] Sec. 1840. PAYMENT OF PREMIUMS

[42 U.S.C. §1395s]

* * *

(i) In the case of an individual enrolled in a Medicare+Choice plan, the Secretary shall provide for necessary adjustments of the monthly beneficiary premium to reflect 80 percent of any reduction elected under section 1854(f)(1)(E) and to reflect any credit provided under section 1854(b)(1)(C)(iv). To the extent to which the Secretary determines that such an adjustment is appropriate, with the concurrence of any agency responsible for the administration of such benefits, such premium adjustment may be provided directly, as an adjustment to any social security, railroad retirement, or civil service retirement benefits, or, in the case of an individual who receives medical assistance under title XIX for medicare costs described in section 1905(p)(3)(A)(ii), as an adjustment to the amount otherwise owed by the State for such medical assistance.

[CCH Explanation at ¶ 376.]

2003 Amendments:

Section 222(l)(2)(b) of the "Medicare Prescription Drug, Improvement, and Modernization Act of 2003," effective upon enactment, amended section 1840(i) by inserting "and to reflect any credit provided under section 1854(b)(1)(C)(iv)" after "section 1854(f)(1)(E)".

The above amendment applies to plan years beginning on or after January 1, 2006.

[¶ 2175] Sec. 1841. FEDERAL SUPPLEMENTARY MEDICAL INSURANCE TRUST FUND

[42 U.S.C. § 1395t]

(a) There is hereby created on the books of the Treasury of the United States a trust fund to be known as the "Federal Supplementary Medical Insurance Trust Fund" (hereinafter in this section referred to as the "Trust Fund"). The Trust Fund shall consist of such gifts and bequests as may be made as provided in section 201(i)(1), such amounts as may be deposited in, or appropriated to, such fund as provided in this part, and such amounts as may be deposited in, or appropriated to, the Medicare Prescription Drug Account established by section 1860D-16 or the Transitional Assistance Account established by section 1860D-31(k)(1).

(b) With respect to the Trust Fund, there is hereby created a body to be known as the Board of Trustees of the Trust Fund (hereinafter in this section referred to as the "Board of Trustees") composed of the Commissioner of Social Security, the Secretary of the Treasury, the Secretary of Labor, and the Secretary of Health and Human Services, all ex officio, and of two members of the public (both of whom may not be from the same political party), who shall be nominated by the President for a term of four years and subject to confirmation by the Senate. A member of the Board of Trustees serving as a member of the public and nominated and confirmed to fill a vacancy occurring during a term shall be nominated and confirmed only for the remainder of such term. An individual nominated and confirmed as a member of the public may serve in such position after the expiration of such member's term until the earlier of the time at which the member's successor takes office or the time at which a report of the Board is first issued under paragraph (2) after the expiration of the member's term. The Secretary of the Treasury shall be the Managing Trustee of the Board of Trustees (hereinafter in this section referred to as the "Managing Trustee"). The Administrator of the Centers for Medicare & Medicaid Services shall serve as the Secretary of the Board of Trustees. The Board of Trustees shall meet not less frequently than once each calendar year. It shall be the duty of the Board of Trustees to—

* * *

(2) Report to the Congress not later than the first day of April of each year on the operation and status of the Trust Fund during the preceding fiscal year and on its expected operation and status during the current fiscal year and the next 2 fiscal years;

Each report provided under paragraph (2) beginning with the report in 2005 shall include the information specified in section 801(a) of Medicare Prescription Drug, Improvement, and Modernization Act of 2003.

* * *

(4) Review the general policies followed in managing the Trust Fund, and recommend changes in such policies, including necessary changes in the provisions of law which govern the way in which the Trust Fund is to be managed.

The report provided for in paragraph (2) shall include a statement of the assets of, and the disbursements made from, the Trust Fund during the preceding fiscal year, an estimate of the expected income to, and disbursements to be made from, the Trust Fund during the current fiscal year and each of the next 2 fiscal years, and a statement of the actuarial status of the Trust Fund. Such report shall also include an actuarial opinion by the Chief Actuary of the Centers for Medicare & Medicaid Services certifying that the techniques and methodologies used are generally accepted within the actuarial profession and that the assumptions and cost estimates used are reasonable. Such report shall be printed as a House document of the session of the Congress to which the report is made. A person serving on the Board of Trustees shall not be considered to be a fiduciary and shall not be personally liable for actions taken in such capacity with respect to the Trust Fund.

* * *

(g) The Managing Trustee shall pay from time to time from the Trust Fund such amounts as the Secretary of Health and Human Services certifies are necessary to make the payments provided for by this part, and the payments with respect to administrative expenses in accordance with section 201(g)(1). The payments provided for under part D, other than under section 1860D-31(k)(2), shall be made from the Medicare Prescription Drug Account in the Trust Fund. The payments provided for under section 1860D-31(k)(2) shall be made from the Transitional Assistance Account in the Trust Fund.

(h) The Managing Trustee shall pay from time to time from the Trust Fund such amounts as the Secretary of Health and Human Services certifies are necessary to pay the costs incurred by the Director of the Office of Personnel Management in making deductions pursuant to section 1840(d)or pursuant to section 1860D-13(c)(1) or 1854(d)(2)(A)(inwhich case payments shall be made in appropriate part from the Medicare Prescription Drug Account in the Trust Fund). During each fiscal year, or after the close of such fiscal year, the Director of the Office of Personnel Management shall certify to the Secretary the amount of the costs the Director incurred in making such deductions, and such certified amount shall be the basis for the amount of such costs certified by the Secretary to the Managing Trustee.

(i) The Managing Trustee shall pay from time to time from the Trust Fund such amounts as the Secretary of Health and Human Services certifies are necessary to pay the costs incurred by the Railroad Retirement Board for services performed pursuant to section 1840(b)(1) and section 1842(g)and pursuant to sections 1860D-13(c)(1) and 1854(d)(2)(A) (in which case payments shall be made in appropriate part from the Medicare Prescription Drug Account in the Trust Fund). During each fiscal year, or after the close of such fiscal year, the Railroad Retirement Board shall certify to the Secretary the amount of the costs it incurred in performing such services and such certified amount shall be the basis for the amount of such costs certified by the Secretary to the Managing Trustee.

[CCH Explanation at ¶215 and 801.]

2003 Amendments:

Section 101(e)(3)(C) of the "Medicare Prescription Drug, Improvement, and Modernization Act of 2003," effective upon enactment, amended section 1841(a) by striking "and" before "such amounts" and by inserting before the period the following:", and such amounts as may be deposited in, or appropriated to, the Medicare Prescription Drug Account established by section 1860D-16".

Section 101(e)(3)(C) of the "Medicare Prescription Drug, Improvement, and Modernization Act of 2003," effective upon enactment, amended section 1841(g) by adding at the end the following: "The payments provided for under part D, other than under section 1860D-31(k)(2), shall be made from the Medicare Prescription Drug Account in the Trust Fund.".

Section 101(e)(3)(C) of the "Medicare Prescription Drug, Improvement, and Modernization Act of 2003," effective upon enactment, amended section 1841(h) by inserting "or pursuant to section 1860D-13(c)(1) or 1854(d)(2)(A) (in which case payments shall be made in appropriate part from the Medicare Prescription Drug Account in the Trust Fund)" after "1840(d)".

Section 101(e)(3)(C) of the "Medicare Prescription Drug, Improvement, and Modernization Act of 2003," effective upon enactment, amended section 1841(i) by inserting after "and section 1842(g)" the following: "and pursuant to sections 1860D-13(c)(1) and 1854(d)(2)(A) (in which case payments shall be made in appropriate part from the Medicare Prescription Drug Account in the Trust Fund)".

Section 105(d) of the "Medicare Prescription Drug, Improvement, and Modernization Act of 2003," effective upon enactment, amended section 1841(a) in the last sentence of subsection (a), by inserting after "section 1860D-16" the following: "or the Transitional Assistance Account established by section 1860D-31(k)(1)".

Section 105(d) of the "Medicare Prescription Drug, Improvement, and Modernization Act of 2003," effective upon enactment, amended section 1841(g) by adding at the end the following: "The payments provided for under section 1860D-31(k)(2) shall be made from the Transitional Assistance Account in the Trust Fund.".

Section 801(d)(2) of the "Medicare Prescription Drug, Improvement, and Modernization Act of 2003," effective upon enactment, amended section 1841(b)(2) by adding at the end the following: "Each report provided under paragraph (2) beginning with the report in 2005 shall include the information specified in section 801(a) of Medicare Prescription Drug, Improvement, and Modernization Act of 2003.".

Section 900(e)(1)(E) of the "Medicare Prescription Drug, Improvement, and Modernization Act of 2003," effective upon enactment, amended section 1841(b) by striking "Health Care Financing Administration", both in the fifth sentence of the matter preceding paragraph (1) and in the second sentence of the matter following paragraph (4), and inserting "Centers for Medicare & Medicaid Services".

Section 900(e)(1)(E) of the "Medicare Prescription Drug, Improvement, and Modernization Act of 2003," effective upon enactment, amended section 1841(b) by striking "Chief Actuarial Officer" in the second sentence of the matter following paragraph (4) and inserting "Chief Actuary".

[¶2180A] Sec. 1842. PROVISIONS RELATING TO THE ADMINISTRATION OF PART B

[42 U.S.C. §1395u]

(a) The administration of this part shall be conducted through contracts with medicare administrative contractors under section 1874A.

Social Security Law Added, Amended or Repealed

[CCH Explanation at ¶ 829.]
2003 Amendments:

Section 911(c)(1) of the "Medicare Prescription Drug, Improvement, and Modernization Act of 2003," effective October 1, 2005, amended the heading of section 1842 to read as follows: "PROVISIONS RELATING TO THE ADMINISTRATION OF PART B".

Section 911(c)(2) of the "Medicare Prescription Drug, Improvement, and Modernization Act of 2003," effective October 1, 2005, amended section 1842(a).

Prior to amendment section 1842(a) read as follows:

(a) In order to provide for the administration of the benefits under this part with maximum efficiency and convenience for individuals entitled to benefits under this part and for providers of services and other persons furnishing services to such individuals, and with a view to furthering coordination of the administration of the benefits under part A and under this part, the Secretary is authorized to enter into contracts with carriers, including carriers with which agreements under section 1816 are in effect, which will perform some or all of the following functions (or, to the extent provided in such contracts, will secure performance thereof by other organizations); and, with respect to any of the following functions which involve payments for physicians' services on a reasonable charge basis, the Secretary shall to the extent possible enter into such contracts:

(1)(A) make determinations of the rates and amounts of payments required pursuant to this part to be made to providers of services and other persons on a reasonable cost or reasonable charge basis (as may be applicable);

(B) receive, disburse, and account for funds in making such payments; and

(C) make such audits of the records of providers of services as may be necessary to assure that proper payments are made under this part;

(2)(A) determine compliance with the requirements of section 1861(k) as to utilization reviews; and

(B) assist providers of services and other persons who furnish services for which payment may be made under this part in the development of procedures relating to utilization practices, make studies of the effectiveness of such procedures and methods for their improvement, assist in the application of safeguards against unnecessary utilization of services furnished by providers of services and other persons to individuals entitled to benefits under this part, and provide procedures for and assist in arranging, where necessary, the establishment of groups outside hospitals (meeting the requirements of section 1861(k)(2)) to make reviews of utilization;

(3) serve as a channel of communication of information relating to the administration of this part; and

(4) otherwise assist, in such manner as the contract may provide, in discharging administrative duties necessary to carry out the purposes of this part.

[¶ 2180B] Sec. 1842. [Carrier Contracts; General]
[42 U.S.C. § 1395u(b)(1)]

(b)(1) [Stricken.]

[CCH Explanation at ¶ 829 and 952.]
2003 Amendments:

Section 911(c)(3)(A) of the "Medicare Prescription Drug, Improvement, and Modernization Act of 2003," effective upon enactment,, amended section 1842(b) by striking paragraph (1).

Prior to being stricken, paragraph (1) read as follows:

(b)(1) Contracts with carriers under subsection (a) may be entered into without regard to section 3709 of the Revised Statutes or any other provision of law requiring competitive bidding.

[¶ 2180C] Sec. 1842. [Carrier Performance Requirements]
[42 U.S.C. § 1395u(b)(2)]

(b)(2)(A) [Stricken.]

(B) [Stricken.]

(C) In the case of residents of nursing facilities who receive services described in clause (i) or (ii) of section 1861(s)(2)(K) performed by a member of a team, the Secretary shall instruct medicare administrative contractors to develop mechanisms which permit routine payment under this part for up to 1.5 visits per month per resident. In the previous sentence, the term "team" refers to a physician and includes a physician assistant acting under the supervision of the physician or a nurse practitioner working in collaboration with that physician, or both.

(D) [Stricken.]

(E) [Stricken.]

[CCH Explanation at ¶ 829 and 952.]
2003 Amendments:

Section 911(c)(3)(B) of the "Medicare Prescription Drug, Improvement, and Modernization Act of 2003," effective upon enactment, amended section 1842(b)(2) by striking subparagraphs (A) and (B); in subparagraph (C), by striking "carriers" and inserting "medicare administrative contractors"; and by striking subparagraphs (D) and (E).

Prior to being amended, Section 1842(b)(2) read as follows:

(2)(A) No such contract shall be entered into with any carrier unless the Secretary finds that such carrier will perform its obligations under the contract efficiently and effectively and will meet such requirements as to financial responsibility, legal authority, and other matters as he finds pertinent. The Secretary shall publish in the Federal Register standards and criteria for the efficient and effective performance of contract obligations under this section, and opportunity shall be provided for public comment prior to implementation. In establishing such standards and criteria, the Secretary shall provide a system to measure a carrier's performance of responsibilities described in paragraph (3)(H), subsection (h), and section 1845(e)(2). The Secretary may not require, as a condition of entering into or renewing a contract under this section or under section 1871, that a carrier match data obtained other than in its activities under this part with data used in the administration of this part for purposes of identifying situations in which section 1862(b) may apply.

(B) The Secretary shall establish standards for evaluating carriers' performance of reviews of initial carrier determinations and of fair hearings under paragraph (3)(C), under which a carrier is expected—

(i) to complete such reviews, within 45 days after the date of a request by an individual enrolled under this part for such a review, in 95 percent of such requests, and

(ii) to make a final determination, within 120 days after the date of receipt of a request by an individual enrolled under this part for a fair hearing under paragraph (3)(C), in 90 percent of such cases.

(C) In the case of residents of nursing facilities who receive services described in clause (i) or (ii) of section 1861(s)(2)(K) performed by a member of a team, the Secretary shall instruct carriers to develop mechanisms which permit routine payment under this part for up to 1.5 visits per month per resident. In the previous sentence, the term "team" refers to a physician and includes a physician assistant acting under the supervision of the physician or a nurse practitioner working in collaboration with that physician, or both.

(D) In addition to any other standards and criteria established by the Secretary for evaluating carrier performance under this paragraph relating to avoiding erroneous payments, the carrier shall be subject to standards and criteria relating to the carrier's success in recovering payments made under this part for items or services for which payment has been or could be made under a primary plan (as defined in section 1862(b)(2)(A)).

(E) With respect to the payment of claims for home health services under this part that, but for the amendments made by section 4611 of the Balanced Budget Act of 1997, would be payable under part A instead of under this part, the Secretary shall continue administration of such claims through fiscal intermediaries under section 1816.

[¶ 2180D] Sec. 1842. [Payment on Reasonable Cost or Reasonable Charge Basis; Claims for Payment; Assignment; Fair Hearings; Customary and Prevailing Charges]

[42 U.S.C. § 1395u(b)(3)]

(b)(3) The Secretary—

(A) shall take such action as may be necessary to assure that, where payment under this part for a service is on a cost basis, the cost is reasonable cost (as determined under section 1861(v));

(B) shall take such action as may be necessary to assure that, where payment under this part for a service is on a charge basis, such charge will be reasonable and not higher than the charge applicable, for a comparable service and under comparable circumstances, to the policyholders and subscribers of the medicare administrative contractor, and such payment will (except as otherwise provided in section 1870(f) be made—

* * *

(C) [Stricken.]

(D) [Stricken.]

(E) [Stricken.]

* * *

(F) shall take such action as may be necessary to assure that where payment under this part for a service rendered is on a charge basis, such payment shall be determined on the basis of the charge that is determined in accordance with this section on the basis of customary and prevailing charge levels in effect at the time the service was rendered or, in the case of services rendered more than 12 months before the year in which the bill is submitted or request for payment is made, on the basis of such levels in effect for the 12-month period preceding such year;

(G) shall, for a service that is furnished with respect to an individual enrolled under this part, that is not paid on an assignment-related basis, and that is subject to a limiting charge under section 1848(g)—

* * *

(H) , shall implement—

(i) programs to recruit and retain physicians as participating physicians in the area served by the medicare administrative contractor, including educational and outreach activities and the use of professional relations personnel to handle billing and other problems relating to payment of claims of participating physicians; and

* * *

(L) shall monitor and profile physicians' billing patterns within each area or locality and provide comparative data to physicians whose utilization patterns vary significantly from other physicians in the same payment area or locality.

In determining the reasonable charge for services for purposes of this paragraph, there shall be taken into consideration the customary charges for similar services generally made by the physician or other person furnishing such services, as well as the prevailing charges in the locality for similar services. No charge may be determined to be reasonable in the case of bills submitted or requests for payment made under this part after December 31, 1970, if it exceeds the higher of (i) the prevailing charge recognized by the carrier and found acceptable by the Secretary for similar services in the same locality in administering this part on December 31, 1970, or (ii) the prevailing charge level that, on the basis of statistical data and methodology acceptable to the Secretary, would cover 75 percent of the customary charges made for similar services in the same locality during the 12-month period ending on the June 30 last preceding the start of the calendar year in which the service is rendered. In the case of physicians' services the prevailing charge level determined for purposes of clause (ii) of the preceding sentence for any twelve-month period (beginning after June 30, 1973) specified in clause (ii) of such sentence may not exceed (in the aggregate) the level determined under such clause for the fiscal year ending June 30, 1973, or (with respect to physicians' services furnished in a year after 1987) the level determined under this sentence (or under any other provision of law affecting the prevailing charge level) for the previous year except to the extent that the Secretary finds, on the basis of appropriate economic index data, that such higher level is justified by year-to-year economic changes. With respect to power-operated wheelchairs for which payment may be made in accordance with section 1861(s)(6), charges determined to be reasonable may not exceed the lowest charge at which power-operated wheelchairs are available in the locality. In the case of medical services, supplies, and equipment (including equipment servicing) that, in the judgment of the Secretary, do not generally vary significantly in quality from one supplier to another, the charges incurred after December 31, 1972, determined to be reasonable may not exceed the lowest charge levels at which such services, supplies, and equipment are widely and consistently available in a locality except to the extent and under the circumstances specified by the Secretary. The requirement in subparagraph (B) that a bill be submitted or request for payment be made by the close of the following calendar year shall not apply if (I) failure to submit the bill or request the payment by the close of such year is due to the error or misrepresentation of an officer, employee, fiscal intermediary, carrier, medicare administrative contractor, or agent of the Department of Health and Human Services performing functions under this title and acting within the scope of his or its authority, and (II) the bill is submitted or the payment is requested promptly after such error or misrepresentation is eliminated or corrected. Notwithstanding the provisions of the third and fourth sentences preceding this sentence, the prevailing charge level in the case of a physician service in a particular locality determined pursuant to such third and fourth sentences for any calendar year after 1974, shall, if lower than the prevailing charge level for the fiscal year ending June 30, 1975, in the case of a similar physician service in the same locality by reason of the application of economic index data, be raised to such prevailing charge level for the fiscal year ending June 30, 1975, and shall remain at such prevailing charge level until the prevailing charge for a year (as adjusted by economic index data) equals or exceeds such prevailing charge level. The amount of any charges for outpatient services which shall be considered reasonable shall be subject to the limitations established by regulations issued by the Secretary pursuant to section 1861(v)(1)(K), and in determining the reasonable charge for such services, the Secretary may limit such reasonable charge to a percentage of the amount of the prevailing charge for similar services furnished in a physician's office, taking into account the extent to which overhead costs associated with such outpatient services have been included in the reasonable cost or charge of the facility.

[CCH Explanation at ¶ 829.]

2003 Amendments:

Section 911(c)(3)(C) of the "Medicare Prescription Drug, Improvement, and Modernization Act of 2003," effective October 1, 2005, amended section 1842(b)(3) in the matter before subparagraph (A), by striking "Each such contract shall provide that the carrier" and inserting "The Secretary"; by striking "will" the first place it appears in each of subparagraphs (A), (B), (F), (G), (H), and (L) and inserting "shall"; in subparagraph (B), in the matter before clause (i), by striking "to the policyholders and subscribers of the carrier" and inserting "to the policyholders and subscribers of the medicare administrative contractor"; by striking subparagraphs (C), (D), and (E); in subparagraph (H)—by striking "if it makes determinations or payments with respect to physicians' services," in the matter preceding clause (i); and by striking "carrier" and inserting "medicare administrative contractor" in clause (i); by striking subparagraph (I); in subparagraph (L), by striking the semicolon and inserting a period; in the first sentence, after subparagraph (L), by striking "and shall contain" and all that follows through the period; and in the seventh sentence, by inserting "medicare administrative contractor," after "carrier,".

Prior to being amended, Section 1842(b)(3) read as follows:

(3) Each such contract shall provide that the carrier—

(A) will take such action as may be necessary to assure that, where payment under this part for a service is on a cost basis, the cost is reasonable cost (as determined under section 1861(v));

(B) will take such action as may be necessary to assure that, where payment under this part for a service is on a charge basis, such charge will be reasonable and not higher than the charge applicable, for a comparable service and under comparable circumstances, to the policyholders and

§1842(b)(3)(L)   ¶2180D

subscribers of the carrier, and such payment will (except as otherwise provided in section 1870(f) be made—

(i) on the basis of an itemized bill; or

(ii) on the basis of an assignment under the terms of which (I) the reasonable charge is the full charge for the service (except in the case of physicians' services and ambulance service furnished as described in section 1862(a)(4), other than for purposes of section 1870(f), (II) the physician or other person furnishing such service agrees not to charge (and to refund amounts already collected) for services for which payment under this title is denied under section 1154(a)(2) by reason of a determination under section 1154(a)(1)(B), and (III) the physician or other person furnishing such service agrees not to charge (and to refund amounts already collected) for such service if payment may not be made therefor by reason of the provisions of paragraph (1) of section 1862(a), and if the individual to whom such service was furnished was without fault in incurring the expenses of such service, and if the Secretary's determination that payment (pursuant to such assignment) was incorrect and was made subsequent to the third year following the year in which notice of such payment was sent to such individual; except that the Secretary may reduce such three-year period to not less than one year if he finds such reduction is consistent with the objectives of this title;

but (in the case of bills submitted, or requests for payment made, after March 1968) only if the bill is submitted, or a written request for payment is made in such other form as may be permitted under regulations, no later than the close of the calendar year following the year in which such service if furnished (deeming any service furnished in the last 3 months of any calendar year to have been furnished in the succeeding calendar year);

(C) will establish and maintain procedures pursuant to which an individual enrolled under this part will be granted an opportunity for a fair hearing by the carrier, in any case where the amount in controversy is at least $100, but less than $500, when requests for payment under this part with respect to services furnished him are denied or are not acted upon with reasonable promptness or when the amount of such payment is in controversy;

(D) will furnish to the Secretary such timely information and reports as he may find necessary in performing his functions under this part;

(E) will maintain such records and afford such access thereto as the Secretary finds necessary to assure the correctness and verification of the information and reports under subparagraph (D) and otherwise to carry out the purposes of this part;

(F) will take such action as may be necessary to assure that where payment under this part for a service rendered is on a charge basis, such payment shall be determined on the basis of the charge that is determined in accordance with this section on the basis of customary and prevailing charge levels in effect at the time the service was rendered or, in the case of services rendered more than 12 months before the year in which the bill is submitted or request for payment is made, on the basis of such levels in effect for the 12-month period preceding such year;

(G) will, for a service that is furnished with respect to an individual enrolled under this part, that is not paid on an assignment-related basis, and that is subject to a limiting charge under section 1848(g)—

(i) determine, prior to making payment, whether the amount billed for such service exceeds the limiting charge applicable under section 1848(g)(2);

(ii) notify the physician, supplier, or other person periodically (but not less often than once every 30 days) of determinations that amounts billed exceeded such applicable limiting charges; and

(iii) provide for prompt response to inquiries of physicians, suppliers, and other persons concerning the accuracy of such limiting charges for their services;

(H) if it makes determinations or payments with respect to physicians' services, will implement—

(i) programs to recruit and retain physicians as participating physicians in the area served by the carrier, including educational and outreach activities and the use of professional relations personnel to handle billing and other problems relating to payment of claims of participating physicians; and

(ii) programs to familiarize beneficiaries with the participating physician program and to assist such beneficiaries in locating participating physicians;

(I) will submit annual reports to the Secretary describing the steps taken to recover payments made under this part for items or services for which payment has been or could be made under a primary plan (as defined in section 1862(b)(2)(A)); and

(J) [Repealed.]

(K) [Repealed.] [; and]

(L) will monitor and profile physicians' billing patterns within each area or locality and provide comparative data to physicians whose utilization patterns vary significantly from other physicians in the same payment area or locality;

and shall contain such other terms and conditions not inconsistent with this section as the Secretary may find necessary or appropriate. In determining the reasonable charge for services for purposes of this paragraph, there shall be taken into consideration the customary charges for similar services generally made by the physician or other person furnishing such services, as well as the prevailing charges in the locality for similar services. No charge may be determined to be reasonable in the case of bills submitted or requests for payment made under this part after December 31, 1970, if it exceeds the higher of (i) the prevailing charge recognized by the carrier and found acceptable by the Secretary for similar services in the same locality in administering this part on December 31, 1970, or (ii) the prevailing charge level that, on the basis of statistical data and methodology acceptable to the Secretary, would cover 75 percent of the customary charges made for similar services in the same locality during the 12-month period ending on the June 30 last preceding the start of the calendar year in which the service is rendered. In the case of physicians' services the prevailing charge level determined for purposes of clause (ii) of the preceding sentence for any twelve-month period (beginning after June 30, 1973) specified in clause (ii) of such sentence may not exceed (in the aggregate) the level determined under such clause for the fiscal year ending June 30, 1973, or (with respect to physicians' services furnished in a year after 1987) the level determined under this sentence (or under any other provision of law affecting the prevailing charge level) for the previous year except to the extent that the Secretary finds, on the basis of appropriate economic index data, that such higher level is justified by year-to-year economic changes. With respect to power-operated wheelchairs for which payment may be made in accordance with section 1861(s)(6), charges determined to be reasonable may not exceed the lowest charge at which power-operated wheelchairs are available in the locality. In the case of medical services, supplies, and equipment (including equipment servicing) that, in the judgment of the Secretary, do not generally vary significantly in quality from one supplier to another, the charges incurred after December 31, 1972, determined to be reasonable may not exceed the lowest charge levels at which such services, supplies, and equipment are widely and consistently available in a locality except to the extent and under the circumstances specified by the Secretary. The requirement in subparagraph (B) that a bill be submitted or request for payment be made by the close of the following calendar year shall not apply if (I) failure to submit the bill or request the payment by the close of such year is due to the error or misrepresentation of an officer, employee, fiscal intermediary, carrier, or agent of the Department of Health and Human Services performing functions under this title and acting within the scope of his or its authority, and (II) the bill is submitted or the payment is requested promptly after such error or misrepresentation is eliminated or corrected. Notwithstanding the provisions of the third and fourth sentences preceding this sentence, the prevailing charge level in the case of a physician service in a particular locality determined pursuant to such third and fourth sentences for any calendar year after 1974, shall, if lower than the prevailing charge level for the fiscal year ending June 30, 1975, in the case of a similar physician service in the same locality by reason of the application of economic index data, be raised to such prevailing charge level for the fiscal year ending June 30, 1975, and shall remain at such prevailing charge level until the prevailing charge for a year (as adjusted by economic index data) equals or exceeds such prevailing charge level. The amount of any charges for outpatient services which shall be considered reasonable shall be subject to the limitations established by regulations issued by the Secretary pursuant to section 1861(v)(1)(K), and in determining the reasonable charge for such services, the Secretary may limit such reasonable charge to a percentage of the amount of the prevailing charge for similar services furnished in a physician's office, taking into account the extent to which overhead costs associated with such outpatient services have been included in the reasonable cost or charge of the facility.

[¶ 2180E] Sec. 1842. [Duration; Renewability; Termination of Carrier Contracts]

[42 U.S.C. § 1395u(b)(5)]

(b)(5) [Stricken.]

[CCH Explanation at ¶ 829.]

2003 Amendments:

Section 911(c)(3)(D) of the "Medicare Prescription Drug, Improvement, and Modernization Act of 2003," effective upon enactment,, amended section 1842(b) by striking paragraph (5).

Prior to being stricken, Section 1842(b)(5), read as follows:

(b)(5) Each contract under the section shall be for a term of at least one year, and may be automatically renewable from term to term in the absence of notice by either party of intention to terminate at the end of the current term; except that the Secretary may terminate any such contract at any time (after such reasonable notice and opportunity for hearing to the carrier involved as he may provide in regulations) if he finds that the carrier has failed substantially to carry out the contract or is carrying out the contract in a manner inconsistent with the efficient and effective administration of the insurance program established by this part.

[¶ 2180F] Sec. 1842. [Prohibition Against Reassignment]

[42 U.S.C. § 1395u(b)(6)]

(b)(6) No payment under this part for a service provided to any individual shall (except as provided in section 1870) be made to anyone other than such individual or (pursuant to an assignment described in subparagraph (B)(ii) of paragraph (3)) the physician or other person who provided the service, except that (A) payment may be made (i) to the employer of such physician or other person if such physician or other person is required as a condition of his employment to turn over his fee for such service to his employer, or (ii) where the service was provided under a contractual arrangement between such physician or other person and an entity, to the entity if, under the contractual arrangement, the entity submits the bill for the service and the contractual arrangement meets such program integrity and other safeguards as the Secretary may determine to be appropriate,(B) payment may be made to an entity (i) which provides coverage of the services under a health benefits plan, but only to the extent that payment is not made under this part, (ii) which has paid the person who provided the service an amount (including the amount payable under this part) which that person has accepted as payment in full for the service, and (iii) to which the individual has agreed in writing that payment may be made under this part, (C) in the case of services described in clause (i) of section 1861(s)(2)(K), payment shall be made to either (i) the employer of the physician assistant involved, or (ii) with respect to a physician assistant who was the owner of a rural health clinic (as described in section 1861(aa)(2)) for a continuous period beginning prior to the date of the enactment of the Balanced Budget Act of 1997 and ending on the date that the Secretary determines such rural health clinic no longer meets the requirements of section 1861(aa)(2), payment may be made directly to the physician assistant, (D) payment may be made to a physician for physicians' services (and services furnished incident to such services) furnished by a second physician to patients of the first physician if (i) the first physician is unavailable to provide the services; (ii) the services are furnished pursuant to an arrangement between the two physicians that (I) is informal and reciprocal, or (II) involves per diem or other fee-for-time compensation for such services; (iii) the services are not provided by the second physician over a continuous period of more than 60 days; and (iv) the claim form submitted to the medicare administrative contractor for such services includes the second physician's unique identifier (provided under the system established under subsection (r)) and indicates that the claim meets the requirements of this subparagraph for payment to the first physician. No payment which under the preceding sentence may be made directly to the physician or other person providing the service involved (pursuant to an assignment described in subparagraph (B)(ii) of paragraph (3)) shall be made to anyone else under a reassignment or power of attorney (except to an employer or entity as described in subparagraph (A) of such sentence); but nothing in this subsection shall be construed (I) to prevent the making of such a payment in accordance with an assignment from the individual to whom the service was provided or a reassignment from the physician or other person providing such service if such assignment or reassignment is made to a governmental agency or entity or is established by or pursuant to the order of a court of competent jurisdiction, or (II) to preclude an agent of the physician or other person providing the service from receiving any such payment if (but only if) such agent does so pursuant to an agency agreement under which the compensation to be paid to the agent for his services for or in connection with the billing or collection of payments due such physician or other person under this title is unrelated (directly or indirectly) to the amount of such payments or the billings therefor, and is not dependent upon the actual collection of any such payment, (E) in the case of an item or service (other than services described in section 1888(e)(2)(A)(ii)) furnished by, or under arrangements made by, a skilled nursing facility to an individual who (at the time the item or service is furnished) is a resident of a skilled nursing facility, payment shall be made to the facility, (F) in the case of home health services "(including medical supplies described in section 1861(m)(5), but excluding durable medical equipment to the extent provided for in such section)" furnished to an individual who (at the time the item or service is furnished) is under a plan of care of a home health agency, payment shall be made to the agency (without regard to whether or not the item or service was furnished by the agency, by others under arrangement with them made by the agency, or when any other contracting or consulting arrangement, or otherwise). For purposes of subparagraph (C) of the first sentence of this paragraph, an employment relationship may include any independent contractor arrangement, and employer status shall be determined in accordance with the law of the State in which the services described in such clause are performed, and (G) in the case of services in a hospital or clinic to which section 1880(e) applies, payment shall be made to such hospital or clinic.

[CCH Explanation at ¶ 952.]

2003 Amendments:

Section 911(c)(3)(E) of the "Medicare Prescription Drug, Improvement, and Modernization Act of 2003," effective upon enactment,, amended section 1842(b)(6)(D)(iv) by striking "carrier" and inserting "medicare administrative contractor".

Section 952(a) of the "Medicare Prescription Drug, Improvement, and Modernization Act of 2003," effective upon enactment,, amended section 1842(b)(6)(A) by striking "or (ii) (where the service was provided in a hospital, critical access hospital, clinic, or other facility) to the facility in which the service was provided if there is a contractual arrangement between such physician or other person and such facility under which such facility submits the bill for such service," and inserting "or (ii) where the service was provided under a contractual arrangement between such physician or other person and an entity, to the entity if, under the contractual arrangement, the entity submits the bill for the service and the contractual arrangement meets such program integrity and other safeguards as the Secretary may determine to be appropriate,".

Section 952(b) of the "Medicare Prescription Drug, Improvement, and Modernization Act of 2003," effective upon enactment,, amended the second sentence of 1842(b)(6) by striking "except to an employer or facility as described in clause (A)" and inserting "except to an employer or entity as described in subparagraph (A)".

[¶ 2180G] Sec. 1842. [Payment for Physicians' Services in Teaching Setting]

[42 U.S.C. § 1395u(b)(7)]

(b)(7)(A) In the case of physicians' services furnished to a patient in a hospital with a teaching program approved as specified in section 1861(b)(6) but which does not meet the conditions described in section 1861(b)(7), the Secretary shall not provide (except on the basis described in subparagraph (C)) for payment for such services under this part—

***

(B) The customary charge for such services in a hospital shall be determined in accordance with regulations issued by the Secretary and taking into account the following factors:

(i) In the case of a physician who is not a teaching physician (as defined by the Secretary), the Secretary shall take into account the amounts the physician charges for similar services in the physician's practice outside the teaching setting.

(ii) In the case of a teaching physician, if the hospital, its physicians, or other appropriate billing entity has established one or more schedules of charges which are collected for medical and surgical services, the Secretary shall base payment under this title on the greatest of—

***

(C) In the case of physicians' services furnished to a patient in a hospital with a teaching program approved as specified in section 1861(b)(6) but which does not meet the conditions described in section 1861(b)(7), if the conditions described in subclauses (I) and (II) of subparagraph (A)(i) are met and if the physician elects payment to be determined under this subparagraph, the Secretary shall provide for payment for such services under this part on the basis of regulations of the Secretary governing reimbursement for the services of hospital-based physicians (and not on any other basis).

(D)

***

(iii) The Secretary shall determine appropriate methods of reimbursement of assistants at surgery where such services are reimbursable under this part.

If all the teaching physicians in a hospital agree to have payment made for all of their physicians' services under this part furnished patients in the hospital on the basis of an assignment described in paragraph (3)(B)(ii) or under the procedure described in section 1870(f)(1), notwithstanding clause (ii) of this subparagraph, the Secretary shall provide for payment in an amount equal to 90 percent of the prevailing charges paid for similar services in the same locality.

[CCH Explanation at ¶ 829.]
2003 Amendments:

Section 911(c)(3)(F) of the "Medicare Prescription Drug, Improvement, and Modernization Act of 2003," effective October 1, 2005, amended section 1842(b)(7) by striking "the carrier" and inserting "the Secretary" each place it appears.

[¶ 2185] Sec. 1842. [Claims Processing Requirements]

[42 U.S.C. § 1395u(c)]

(c)(1) [Stricken.]

(2)(A) Each contract under section 1874A that provides for making payments under this part shall provide that payment shall be issued, mailed, or otherwise transmitted with respect to not less than 95 percent of all claims submitted under this part—

***

(B) In this paragraph:

***

(ii) The term "applicable number of calendar days" means—

***

(III) with respect to claims received in the 12-month period beginning October 1, 1988, 25 calendar days (or 18 calendar days with respect to claims submitted by participating physicians),

(IV) with respect to claims received in the 12-month period beginning October 1, 1989, and claims received in any succeeding 12-month period ending on or before September 30, 1993, 24 calendar days (or 17 calendar days with respect to claims submitted by participating physicians), and

(V) with respect to claims received in the 12-month period beginning October 1, 1993, and claims received in any succeeding 12-month period, 30 calendar days.

***

(3)(A) Each contract under this section which provides for the disbursement of funds, as described in section 1847A(a)(3)(B, shall provide that no payment shall be issued, mailed, or otherwise transmitted with respect to any claim submitted under this title within the applicable number of calendar days after the date on which the claim is received.

***

(4) Neither a medicare administrative contractornor the Secretary may impose a fee under this title—

***

(5) [Stricken.]

(6) [Stricken.]

Social Security Law Added, Amended or Repealed

[CCH Explanation at ¶ 829.]
2003 Amendments:

Section 736(b)(8)(A) of the "Medicare Prescription Drug, Improvement, and Modernization Act of 2003," effective upon enactment, amended section 1842(c)(2)(B)(ii) by striking "and" at the end of subclause (III); and by striking the period at the end of subclause (IV) and inserting ", and".

Section 911(c)(4)(A) of the "Medicare Prescription Drug, Improvement, and Modernization Act of 2003," effective October 1, 2005, amended section 1842(c) by striking paragraph (1).

Prior to being stricken, paragraph (1) read as follows:

(1) Any contract entered into with a carrier under this section shall provide for advances of funds to the carrier for the making of payments by it under this part, and shall provide for payment of the cost of administration of the carrier, as determined by the Secretary to be necessary and proper for carrying out the functions covered by the contract. The Secretary shall provide that in determining a carier's necessary and proper cost of administration, the Secretary shall, with respect to each contract, take into account the amount that is reasonable and adequate to meet the costs which must be incurred by an efficiently and economically operated carrier in carrying out the terms of its contract. The Secretary shall cause to have published in the Federal Register, by not later than September 1 before each fiscal year, data, standards, and methodology to be used to establish budgets for carriers under this section for that fiscal year, and shall cause to be published in the Federal Register for public comment, at least 90 days before such data, standards, and methodlogy are published, the data, standards, and methodology proposed to be used.

Section 911(c)(4)(B) of the "Medicare Prescription Drug, Improvement, and Modernization Act of 2003," effective October 1, 2005, amended section 1842(c)(2)(A) by striking "contract under this section which provides for the disbursement of funds, as described in subsection (a)(1)(B)," and inserting "contract under section 1874A that provides for making payments under this part".

Section 911(c)(4)(C) of the "Medicare Prescription Drug, Improvement, and Modernization Act of 2003," effective October 1, 2005, amended section 1842(c)(3)(A) by striking "subsection (a)(1)(B)" and inserting "section 1874A(a)(3)(B)".

Section 911(c)(4)(D) of the "Medicare Prescription Drug, Improvement, and Modernization Act of 2003," effective October 1, 2005, amended section 1842(c)(4) in the matter preceding subparagraph (A), by striking "carrier" and inserting "medicare administrative contractor".

Section 911(c)(4)(E) of the "Medicare Prescription Drug, Improvement, and Modernization Act of 2003," effective October 1, 2005, amended section 1842(c) by striking paragraphs (5) and (6).

Prior to being stricken paragraphs (5) and (6) read as follows:

(5) Each contract under this section which provides for the disbursement of funds, as described in subsection (a)(1)(B), shall require the carrier to meet criteria developed by the Secretary to measure the timeliness of carrier responses to requests for payment of items described in section 1834(a)(15)(C).

(6) No carrier may carry out (or receive payment for carrying out) any activity pursuant to a contract under this subsection to the extent that the activity is carried out pursuant to a contract under the Medicare Integrity Program under section 1893. The previous sentence shall not apply with respect to the activity described in section 1893(b)(5) (relating to prior authorization of certain items of durable medical equipment under section 1834(a)(15)).

[¶ 2190] Sec. 1842. [Surety Bond Requirement]

[42 U.S.C. § 1395u(d)]

(d) [Repealed.]

[CCH Explanation at ¶ 829.]
2003 Amendments:

Section 911(c)(5) of the "Medicare Prescription Drug, Improvement, and Modernization Act of 2003," effective October 1, 2005, repealed section 1842(d).

Prior to being repealed, section 1842(d) read as follows:

(d) Any contract with a carrier under this section may require such carrier or any of its officers or employees certifying payments or disbursing funds pursuant to the contract, or otherwise participating in carrying out the contract, to give surety bond to the United States in such amount as the Secretary may deem appropriate.

[¶ 2195] Sec. 1842. [Immunity]

[42 U.S.C. § 1395u(e)]

(e) [Repealed.]

[CCH Explanation at ¶ 829.]
2003 Amendments:

Section 911(c)(5) "Medicare Prescription Drug, Improvement, and Modernization Act of 2003," effective October 1, 2005, repealed section 1842(e).

Prior to being repealed, section 1842(e) read as follows:

(e)(1) No individual designated pursuant to a contract under this section as a certifying officer shall, in the absence of gross negligence or intent to defraud the United States, be liable with respect to any payments certified by him under this section.

(2) No disbursing officer shall, in the absence of gross negligence or intent to defraud the United States, be liable with respect to any payment by him under this section if it was based upon a voucher signed by a certifying officer designated as provided in paragraph (1) of this subsection.

(3) No such carrier shall be liable to the United States for any payments referred to in paragraph (1) or (2).

[¶ 2200] Sec. 1842. ["Carrier" Defined]

[42 U.S.C. § 1395u(f)]

(f) [Repealed.]

[CCH Explanation at ¶ 829.]
2003 Amendments:

Section 911(c)(5) of the "Medicare Prescription Drug, Improvement, and Modernization Act of 2003," effective October 1, 2005, repealed section 1842(f).

Prior to being repealed, section 1842(f) read as follows:

(f) For purposes of this part, the term "carrier" means—

(1) with respect to providers of services and other persons, a voluntary association, corporation, partnership or other nongovernmental organization which is lawfully engaged in providing, paying for, or reimbursing the cost of, health services under group insurance policies or contracts, medical or hospital service agreements, membership or subscription contracts, or similar group arrangements, in consideration of premiums or other periodic charges payable to the carrier, including a health benefits plan duly sponsored or underwritten by an employee organization; and

(2) with respect to providers of services only, any agency or organization (not described in paragraph (1)) with which an agreement is in effect under section 1816.

[¶ 2205] Sec. 1842. [Carrier Contracts with Railroad Retirement Board]

[42 U.S.C. § 1395u(g)]

(g) The Railroad Retirement Board shall, in accordance with such regulations as the Secretary may prescribe, contract with a medicare administrative contractor or contractors to perform the functions set out in this section with respect to individuals entitled to benefits as qualified railroad retirement beneficiaries pursuant to section 226(a) of this Act and section 7(d) of the Railroad Retirement Act of 1974.

[CCH Explanation at ¶ 829.]
2003 Amendments:

Section 911(c)(6) of the "Medicare Prescription Drug, Improvement, and Modernization Act of 2003," effective October 1, 2005, amended section 1842(g) by striking "carrier or carriers" and inserting "medicare administrative contractor or contractors".

[¶ 2210] Sec. 1842. [Participating Physician and Supplier Program]

[42 U.S.C. § 1395u(h)]

* * *

(h)(2) The Secretary shall maintain a toll-free telephone number or numbers at which individuals enrolled under this part may obtain the names, addresses, specialty, and telephone numbers of participating physicians and suppliers and may request a copy of an appropriate directory published under paragraph (4). The Secretary shall, without charge, mail a copy of such directory upon such a request.

(3)(A) In any case in which medicare administrative contractor having a contract under section 1874A that provides for making payments under this part is able to develop a system for the electronic transmission to such contractor of bills for services, such contractor shall establish direct lines for the electronic receipt of claims from participating physicians and suppliers.

(B) The Secretary shall establish a procedure whereby an individual enrolled under this part may assign, in an appropriate manner on the form claiming a benefit under this part for an item or service furnished by a participating physician or supplier, the individual's rights of payment under a medicare supplemental policy (described in section 1882(g)(1)) in which the individual is enrolled. In the case such an assignment is properly executed and a payment determination is made by a medicare administrative contractor with a contract under this section, the contractor shall transmit to the private entity issuing the medicare supplemental policy notice of such fact and shall include an explanation of benefits and any additional information that the Secretary may determine to be appropriate in order to enable the entity to decide whether (and the amount of) any payment is due under the policy. The Secretary may enter into agreements for the transmittal of such information to entities electronically. The Secretary shall impose user fees for the transmittal of information under this subparagraph by a medicare administrative contractor, whether electronically or otherwise, and such user fees shall be collected and retained by the contractor.

* * *

(5)(A) The Secretary shall promptly notify individuals enrolled under this part through an annual mailing of the participation program under this subsection and the publication and availability of the directories and shall make the appropriate area directory or directories available in each district and branch office of the Social Security Administration, in the offices of medicare administrative contractors, and to senior citizen organizations.

(B) The annual notice provided under subparagraph (A) shall include—

* * *

(iii) an explanation of the assistance offered by medicare administrative contractors in obtaining the names of participating physicians and suppliers, and

* * *

[CCH Explanation at ¶ 829.]
2003 Amendments:

Section 911(c)(7)(A) of the "Medicare Prescription Drug, Improvement, and Modernization Act of 2003," effective October 1, 2005, amended section 1842(h)(2) by striking "Each carrier having an agreement with the Secretary under subsection (a)" and inserting "The Secretary".

Section 911(c)(7)(B) of the "Medicare Prescription Drug, Improvement, and Modernization Act of 2003," effective October 1, 2005, amended section 1842(h)(3)(A) by striking "a carrier having an agreement with the Secretary under subsection (a)" and inserting "medicare administrative contractor having a contract under section 1874A that provides for making payments under this part"; and by striking "such carrier" and inserting "such contractor".

Section 911(c)(7)(C) of the "Medicare Prescription Drug, Improvement, and Modernization Act of 2003," effective October 1, 2005, amended section 1842(h)(3)(B) by striking "a carrier" and inserting "a medicare administrative contractor" each place it appears; and by striking "the carrier" and inserting "the contractor" each place it appears.

Section 911(c)(7)(D) of the "Medicare Prescription Drug, Improvement, and Modernization Act of 2003," effective October 1, 2005, amended secs. 1842(h)(5)(A) and (B) by striking "carriers" and inserting "medicare administrative contractors" each place it appears.

[¶ 2215] Sec. 1842. [Definitions Relating to Participating Physicians]

[42 U.S.C. § 1395u(i)]

(i) For purposes of this title:

* * *

(2) The term "participating physician" refers, with respect to the furnishing of services, to a physician who at the time of furnishing the services is a participating physician (under subsection (h)(1)); the term "nonparticipating physician" refers, with respect to the furnishing of services, to a physician who at the time of furnishing the services is not a participating physician; and the term "nonparticipating supplier or other person" means a supplier or other person (excluding a provider of services) that is not a participating physician or supplier (as defined in subsection (h)(1)).

* * *

[CCH Explanation at ¶ 829.]
2003 Amendments:

Section 736(b)(9) of the "Medicare Prescription Drug, Improvement, and Modernization Act of 2003," effective upon enactment, amended section 1842(i)(2) by striking "services, a physician" and inserting "services, to a physician".

[¶ 2220] Sec. 1842. [Refund Requirement When Services Not Covered]

[42 U.S.C. § 1395u(l)]

(l)(1)(A) Subject to subparagraph (C), if—

* * *

(iii) (I) a medicare administrative contractor determines under this part or a peer review organization determines under part B of title XI that payment may not be made by reason of section 1862(a)(1) because a service otherwise covered under this title is not reasonable and necessary under the standards described in that section or (II) payment under this title for such services is denied under section 1154(a)(2) by reason of a determination under section 1154(a)(1)(B), and

* * *

(2) Each medicare administrative contractor with a contract in effect under this section with respect to physicians and each peer review organization with a contract under part B of title XI shall send any notice of denial of payment for physicians' services based on section 1862(a)(1)

and for which payment is not requested on an assignment-related basis to the physician and the individual involved.

* * *

[CCH Explanation at ¶ 829.]
2003 Amendments:

Section 911(c)(8) of the "Medicare Prescription Drug, Improvement, and Modernization Act of 2003," effective October 1, 2005, amended section 1842(l)(1)(A)(iii) by striking "carrier" and inserting "medicare administrative contractor".

Section 911(c)(8) of the "Medicare Prescription Drug, Improvement, and Modernization Act of 2003," effective October 1, 2005, amended section 1842 (l)(2) by striking "carrier" and inserting "medicare administrative contractor".

[¶ 2225] Sec. 1842. [Reimbursement for Drugs and Biologicals]

[42 U.S.C. § 1395u(o)]

(o)(1) If a physician's, supplier's, or any other person's bill or request for payment for services includes a charge for a drug or biological for which payment may be made under this part and the drug or biological is not paid on a cost or prospective payment basis as otherwise provided in this part, the amount payable for the drug or biological is equal to the following:

(A) In the case of any of the following drugs or biologicals, 95 percent of the average wholesale price:

(i) A drug or biological furnished before January 1, 2004.

(ii) Blood clotting factors furnished during 2004.

(iii) A drug or biological furnished during 2004 that was not available for payment under this part as of April 1, 2003.

(iv) A vaccine described in subparagraph (A) or (B) of section 1861(s)(10) furnished on or after January 1, 2004.

(v) A drug or biological furnished during 2004 in connection with the furnishing of renal dialysis services if separately billed by renal dialysis facilities.

(B) In the case of a drug or biological furnished during 2004 that is not described in

(i) clause (ii), (iii), (iv), or (v) of subparagraph (A),

(ii) subparagraph (D)(i), or

(iii) subparagraph (F),

the amount determined under paragraph (4).

(C) In the case of a drug or biological that is not described in subparagraph (A)(iv), (D)(i), or (F) furnished on or after January 1, 2005, the amount provided under section 1847, section 1847A, section 1847B, or section 1881(b)(13), as the case may be for the drug or biological.

(D)(i) Except as provided in clause (ii), in the case of infusion drugs furnished through an item of durable medical equipment covered under section 1861(n) on or after January 1, 2004, 95 percent of the average wholesale price for such drug in effect on October 1, 2003.

(ii) In the case of such infusion drugs furnished in a competitive acquisition area under section 1847 on or after January 1, 2007, the amount provided under section 1847.

(E) In the case of a drug or biological, consisting of intravenous immune globulin, furnished

(i) in 2004, the amount of payment provided under paragraph (4); and

(ii) in 2005 and subsequent years, the amount of payment provided under section 1847A.

(F) In the case of blood and blood products (other than blood clotting factors), the amount of payment shall be determined in the same manner as such amount of payment was determined on October 1, 2003.

(G) In the case of inhalation drugs or biologicals furnished through durable medical equipment covered under section 1861(n) that are furnished

(i) in 2004, the amount provided under paragraph (4) for the drug or biological; and

(ii) in 2005 and subsequent years, the amount provided under section 1847A for the drug or biological.

(2) If payment for a drug or biological is made to a licensed pharmacy approved to dispense drugs or biologicals under this part, the Secretary may pay a dispensing fee (less the applicable deductible and coinsurance amounts) to the pharmacy. This paragraph shall not apply in the case of payment under paragraph (1)(C).

* * *

(4)(A) Subject to the succeeding provisions of this paragraph, the amount of payment for a drug or biological under this paragraph furnished in 2004 is equal to 85 percent of the average wholesale price (determined as of April 1, 2003) for the drug or biological.

(B) The Secretary shall substitute for the percentage under subparagraph (A) for a drug or biological the percentage that would apply to the drug or biological under the column entitled "Average of GAO and OIG data (percent)" in the table entitled "Table 3.—Medicare Part B Drugs in the Most Recent GAO and OIG Studies" published on August 20, 2003, in the Federal Register (68 Fed. Reg. 50445).

(C)(i) The Secretary may substitute for the percentage under subparagraph (A) a percentage that is based on data and information submitted by the manufacturer of the drug or biological by October 15, 2003.

(ii) The Secretary may substitute for the percentage under subparagraph (A) with respect to drugs and biologicals furnished during 2004 on or after April 1, 2004, a percentage that is based on data and information submitted by the manufacturer of the drug or biological after October 15, 2003, and before January 1, 2004.

(D) In no case may the percentage substituted under subparagraph (B) or (C) be less than 80 percent.

(5)(A) Subject to subparagraph (B), in the case of clotting factors furnished on or after January 1, 2005, the Secretary shall, after reviewing the January 2003 report to Congress by the Comptroller General of the United States entitled "Payment for Blood Clotting Factor Exceeds Providers Acquisition Cost", provide for a separate payment, to the entity which furnishes to the patient blood clotting factors, for items and services related to the furnishing of such factors in an amount that the Secretary determines to be appropriate. Such payment amount may take into account any or all of the following:

(i) The mixing (if appropriate) and delivery of factors to an individual, including special inventory management and storage requirements.

(ii) Ancillary supplies and patient training necessary for the self-administration of such factors.

(B) In determining the separate payment amount under subparagraph (A) for blood clotting factors furnished in 2005, the Secretary shall ensure that the total amount of payments under this part (as estimated by the Secretary) for such factors under paragraph (1)(C) and such separate payments for such factors does not exceed the total amount of payments that would have been made for such factors under this part (as estimated by the Secretary) if the amendments made by section 303 of the Medicare Prescription Drug, Improvement, and Modernization Act of 2003 had not been enacted.

(C) The separate payment amount under this subparagraph for blood clotting factors furnished in 2006 or a subsequent year shall be equal to the separate payment amount determined under this paragraph for the previous year increased by the percentage increase in the consumer price index for medical care for the 12-month period ending with June of the previous year.

(6) In the case of an immunosuppressive drug described in subparagraph (J) of section 1861(s)(2) and an oral drug described in subparagraph (Q) or (T) of such section, the Secretary shall pay to the pharmacy a supplying fee for such a drug determined appropriate by the Secretary (less the applicable deductible and coinsurance amounts).

(7) There shall be no administrative or judicial review under section 1869, section 1878, or otherwise, of determinations of payment amounts, methods, or adjustments under paragraphs (4) through (6).

Social Security Law Added, Amended or Repealed

[CCH Explanation at ¶¶ 1004, 1006, 1009, 1010, and 1011.]

2003 Amendments:

Section 303(b)(1) of the "Medicare Prescription Drug, Improvement, and Modernization Act of 2003," effective upon enactment, amended section 1842(o)(1).

Prior to being amended section 1842(o)(1) read as follows:

(1) If a physician's, supplier's, or any other person's bill or request for payment for services includes a charge for a drug or biological for which payment may be made under this part and the drug or biological is not paid on a cost or prospective payment basis as otherwise provided in this part, the amount payable for the drug or biological is equal to 95 percent of the average wholesale price.

Section 303(b)(2) of the "Medicare Prescription Drug, Improvement, and Modernization Act of 2003," effective upon enactment, amended section 1842(o) by adding new paragraph (4).

Section 303(e)(1) of the "Medicare Prescription Drug, Improvement, and Modernization Act of 2003," effective upon enactment, amended section 1842(o) by adding new paragraph (5).

Section 303(e)(2) of the "Medicare Prescription Drug, Improvement, and Modernization Act of 2003," effective upon enactment, amended section 1842(o) by adding new paragraph (6).

Section 303(g)(1) of the "Medicare Prescription Drug, Improvement, and Modernization Act of 2003," effective upon enactment, amended section 1842(o) by adding new paragraph 7.

Section 303(i)(1) of the "Medicare Prescription Drug, Improvement, and Modernization Act of 2003," effective upon enactment, amended section 1842(o)(2) by adding at the end the following: "This paragraph shall not apply in the case of payment under paragraph (1)(C).".

Section 305(a) of the "Medicare Prescription Drug, Improvement, and Modernization Act of 2003," effective upon enactment, amended section 1842(o)(1)(G), as added by section 303(b).

Prior to being amended by Section 305(a), paragraph (G) read as follows:

(G) The provisions of subparagraphs (A) through (F) of this paragraph shall not apply to an inhalation drug or biological furnished through durable medical equipment covered under section 1861(n).

[¶ 2230] Sec. 1842. [Required Diagnostic Coding]

[42 U.S.C. § 1395u(p)]

* * *

(p)(3) In the case of a request for payment for an item or service furnished by a physician not submitted on an assignment-related basis and which does not include the code (or codes) required under paragraph (1)—

(A) if the physician knowingly and willfully fails to provide the code (or codes) promptly upon request of the Secretary or a medicare administrative contractor, the physician may be subject to a civil money penalty in an amount not to exceed $2,000, and

* * *

[CCH Explanation at ¶ 829.]

2003 Amendments:

Section 911(c)(9) of the "Medicare Prescription Drug, Improvement, and Modernization Act of 2003," effective October 1, 2005, amended section 1842(p)(3)(A) by striking "carrier" and inserting "medicare administrative contractor".

[¶ 2235] Sec. 1842. [Anesthesia Services]

[42 U.S.C. § 1395u(q)]

(q)(1)(A) The Secretary, in consultation with groups representing physicians who furnish anesthesia services, shall establish by regulation a relative value guide for use in all localities in making payment for physician anesthesia services furnished under this part. Such guide shall be designed so as to result in expenditures under this title for such services in an amount that would not exceed the amount of such expenditures which would otherwise occur.

* * *

[CCH Explanation at ¶ 829.]

2003 Amendments:

Section 911(c)(10) of the "Medicare Prescription Drug, Improvement, and Modernization Act of 2003," effective October 1, 2005, amended section 1842(q)(1)(A) by striking "carrier".

[¶2240] Sec. 1842. REPLACEMENT OF REASONABLE CHARGE METHODOLOGY BY FEE SCHEDULES

[42 U.S.C. §1395u(s)]

(s)(1) Subject to paragraph (3), the Secretary may implement a statewide or other areawide fee schedule to be used for payment of any item or service described in paragraph (2) which is paid on a reasonable charge basis. Any fee schedule established under this paragraph for such item or service shall be updated each year by the percentage increase in the consumer price index for all urban consumers (United States city average) for the 12-month period ending with June of the preceding year, except that in no event shall a fee schedule for an item described in paragraph (2)(D) be updated before 2003.

(2) The items and services described in this paragraph are as follows:

* * *

(C) [Stricken.]

* * *

(3) In the case of items and services described in paragraph (2)(D) that are included in a competitive acquisition program in a competitive acquisition area under section 1847(a)

(A) the payment basis under this subsection for such items and services furnished in such area shall be the payment basis determined under such competitive acquisition program; and

(B) the Secretary may use information on the payment determined under such competitive acquisition programs to adjust the payment amount otherwise applicable under paragraph (1) for an area that is not a competitive acquisition area under section 1847, and in the case of such adjustment, paragraphs (8) and (9) of section 1842(b) shall not be applied.

[CCH Explanation at ¶761 and 1002.]

2003 Amendments:

Section 302(d)(3) of the "Medicare Prescription Drug, Improvement, and Modernization Act of 2003," effective upon enactment,, amended section 1842(s) in the first sentence of paragraph (1), by striking "The Secretary" and inserting "Subject to paragraph (3), the Secretary"; and by adding at the end new paragraph (3).

Section 627(b)(2) of the "Medicare Prescription Drug, Improvement, and Modernization Act of 2003," amended section 1842(s)(2) by striking subparagraph (C).

The amendments made by section 627(b) of the "Medicare Prescription Drug, Improvement, and Modernization Act of 2003," apply to items furnished on or after January 1, 2005.

Prior to being stricken subparagraph (C) read as follows:

(C) Therapeutic shoes.

[¶2245] Sec. 1844. APPROPRIATIONS TO COVER GOVERNMENT CONTRIBUTIONS AND CONTINGENCY RESERVE

[42 U.S.C. §1395w]

(a) There are authorized to be appropriated from time to time, out of any moneys in the Treasury not otherwise appropriated, to the Federal Supplementary Medical Insurance Trust Fund—

(1)

* * *

(B) a Government contribution equal to the aggregate premiums payable for a month for enrollees under age 65 under this part and deposited in the Trust Fund, multiplied by the ratio of—

* * *

(ii) the dollar amount of the premium per enrollee for such month; minus

(C) the aggregate amount of additional premium payments attributable to the application of section 1839(i); plus

* * *

(c) The Secretary shall determine the Government contribution under subparagraphs (A) and (B) of subsection (a)(1) without regard to any premium reduction resulting from an election under section 1854(f)(1)(E) or any credits provided under section 1854(b)(1)(C)(iv) and without regard to any premium adjustment effected under sections 1839(h) and 1860C-1(f).

[CCH Explanation at ¶ 376 and 776.]

2003 Amendments:

Section 222(l)(2)(C) of the "Medicare Prescription Drug, Improvement, and Modernization Act of 2003," effective upon enactment, amended section 1844(c) by inserting "or any credits provided under section 1854(b)(1)(C)(iv)" after "section 1854(f)(1)(E)".

The above amendment applies to plan years beginning on or after January 1, 2006.

Section 241(b)(2)(B) of the "Medicare Prescription Drug, Improvement, and Modernization Act of 2003," effective upon enactment, amended section 1844(c) by inserting "and without regard to any premium adjustment effected under sections 1839(h) and 1860C-1(f)" before the period at the end.

Section 811(b)(2) of the "Medicare Prescription Drug, Improvement, and Modernization Act of 2003," effective upon enactment, amended section 1844(a)(1) in subparagraph (B), by striking "plus" at the end and inserting "minus"; and by adding at the end new subparagraph (C).

[¶ 2250] Sec. 1847. COMPETITIVE ACQUISITION OF CERTAIN ITEMS AND SERVICES

[42 U.S.C. § 1395w-3]

(a) ESTABLISHMENT OF COMPETITIVE ACQUISITION PROGRAMS.—

(1) IMPLEMENTATION OF PROGRAMS.—

(A) IN GENERAL.—The Secretary shall establish and implement programs under which competitive acquisition areas are established throughout the United States for contract award purposes for the furnishing under this part of competitively priced items and services (described in paragraph (2)) for which payment is made under this part. Such areas may differ for different items and services.

(B) PHASED-IN IMPLEMENTATION.—The programs—

(i) shall be phased in among competitive acquisition areas in a manner so that the competition under the programs occurs in—

(I) 10 of the largest metropolitan statistical areas in 2007;

(II) 80 of the largest metropolitan statistical areas in 2009; and

(III) additional areas after 2009; and

(ii) may be phased in first among the highest cost and highest volume items and services or those items and services that the Secretary determines have the largest savings potential.

(C) WAIVER OF CERTAIN PROVISIONS.—In carrying out the programs, the Secretary may waive such provisions of the Federal Acquisition Regulation as are necessary for the efficient implementation of this section, other than provisions relating to confidentiality of information and such other provisions as the Secretary determines appropriate.

(2) ITEMS AND SERVICES DESCRIBED.—The items and services referred to in paragraph (1) are the following:

(A) DURABLE MEDICAL EQUIPMENT AND MEDICAL SUPPLIES.—Covered items (as defined in section 1834(a)(13)) for which payment would otherwise be made under section 1834(a), including items used in infusion and drugs (other than inhalation drugs) and supplies used in conjunction with durable medical equipment, but excluding class III devices under the Federal Food, Drug, and Cosmetic Act.

(B) OTHER EQUIPMENT AND SUPPLIES.—Items and services described in section 1842(s)(2)(D), other than parenteral nutrients, equipment, and supplies.

(C) OFF-THE-SHELF ORTHOTICS.—Orthotics described in section 1861(s)(9) for which payment would otherwise be made under section 1834(h) which require minimal self-adjustment for appropriate use and do not require expertise in trimming, bending, molding, assembling, or customizing to fit to the individual.

(3) EXCEPTION AUTHORITY.—In carrying out the programs under this section, the Secretary may exempt—

(A) rural areas and areas with low population density within urban areas that are not competitive, unless there is a significant national market through mail order for a particular item or service; and

(B) items and services for which the application of competitive acquisition is not likely to result in significant savings.

(4) SPECIAL RULE FOR CERTAIN RENTED ITEMS OF DURABLE MEDICAL EQUIPMENT AND OXYGEN.—In the case of a covered item for which payment is made on a rental basis under section 1834(a) and in the case of payment for oxygen under section 1834(a)(5), the Secretary shall establish a process by which rental agreements for the covered items and supply arrangements with oxygen suppliers entered into before the application of the competitive acquisition program under this section for the item may be continued notwithstanding this section. In the case of any such continuation, the supplier involved shall provide for appropriate servicing and replacement, as required under section 1834(a).

(5) PHYSICIAN AUTHORIZATION.—

(A) IN GENERAL.—With respect to items or services included within a particular HCPCS code, the Secretary may establish a process for certain items and services under which a physician may prescribe a particular brand or mode of delivery of an item or service within such code if the physician determines that use of the particular item or service would avoid an adverse medical outcome on the individual, as determined by the Secretary.

(B) NO EFFECT ON PAYMENT AMOUNT.—A prescription under subparagraph (A) shall not affect the amount of payment otherwise applicable for the item or service under the code involved.

(6) APPLICATION.—For each competitive acquisition area in which the program is implemented under this subsection with respect to items and services, the payment basis determined under the competition conducted under subsection (b) shall be substituted for the payment basis otherwise applied under section 1834(a), section 1834(h), or section 1842(s), as appropriate.

(b) PROGRAM REQUIREMENTS.—

(1) IN GENERAL.—The Secretary shall conduct a competition among entities supplying items and services described in subsection (a)(2) for each competitive acquisition area in which the program is implemented under subsection (a) with respect to such items and services.

(2) CONDITIONS FOR AWARDING CONTRACT.—

(A) IN GENERAL.—The Secretary may not award a contract to any entity under the competition conducted in an competitive acquisition area pursuant to paragraph (1) to furnish such items or services unless the Secretary finds all of the following:

(i) The entity meets applicable quality standards specified by the Secretary under section 1834(a)(20).

(ii) The entity meets applicable financial standards specified by the Secretary, taking into account the needs of small providers.

(iii) The total amounts to be paid to contractors in a competitive acquisition area are expected to be less than the total amounts that would otherwise be paid.

(iv) Access of individuals to a choice of multiple suppliers in the area is maintained.

(B) TIMELY IMPLEMENTATION OF PROGRAM.—Any delay in the implementation of quality standards under section 1834(a)(20) or delay in the receipt of advice from the program oversight committee established under subsection (c) shall not delay the implementation of the competitive acquisition program under this section.

(3) CONTENTS OF CONTRACT.—

(A) IN GENERAL.—A contract entered into with an entity under the competition conducted pursuant to paragraph (1) is subject to terms and conditions that the Secretary may specify.

(B) TERM OF CONTRACTS.—The Secretary shall recompete contracts under this section not less often than once every 3 years.

(4) LIMIT ON NUMBER OF CONTRACTORS.—

(A) IN GENERAL.—The Secretary may limit the number of contractors in a competitive acquisition area to the number needed to meet projected demand for items and services covered under the contracts. In awarding contracts, the Secretary shall take into account the ability of bidding entities to furnish items or services in sufficient quantities to meet the anticipated needs of individuals for such items or services in the geographic area covered under the contract on a timely basis.

(B) MULTIPLE WINNERS.—The Secretary shall award contracts to multiple entities submitting bids in each area for an item or service.

(5) PAYMENT.—

(A) IN GENERAL.—Payment under this part for competitively priced items and services described in subsection (a)(2) shall be based on bids submitted and accepted under this section for such items and services. Based on such bids the Secretary shall determine a single payment amount for each item or service in each competitive acquisition area.

(B) REDUCED BENEFICIARY COST-SHARING.—

(i) APPLICATION OF COINSURANCE.—Payment under this section for items and services shall be in an amount equal to 80 percent of the payment basis described in subparagraph (A).

(ii) APPLICATION OF DEDUCTIBLE.—Before applying clause (i), the individual shall be required to meet the deductible described in section 1833(b).

(C) PAYMENT ON ASSIGNMENT-RELATED BASIS.—Payment for any item or service furnished by the entity may only be made under this section on an assignment-related basis.

(D) CONSTRUCTION.—Nothing in this section shall be construed as precluding the use of an advanced beneficiary notice with respect to a competitively priced item and service.

(6) PARTICIPATING CONTRACTORS.—

(A) IN GENERAL.—Except as provided in subsection (a)(4), payment shall not be made for items and services described in subsection (a)(2) furnished by a contractor and for which competition is conducted under this section unless—

(i) the contractor has submitted a bid for such items and services under this section; and

(ii) the Secretary has awarded a contract to the contractor for such items and services under this section.

(B) BID DEFINED.—In this section, the term 'bid' means an offer to furnish an item or service for a particular price and time period that includes, where appropriate, any services that are attendant to the furnishing of the item or service.

(C) RULES FOR MERGERS AND ACQUISITIONS.—In applying subparagraph (A) to a contractor, the contractor shall include a successor entity in the case of a merger or acquisition, if the successor entity assumes such contract along with any liabilities that may have occurred thereunder.

(D) PROTECTION OF SMALL SUPPLIERS.—In developing procedures relating to bids and the awarding of contracts under this section, the Secretary shall take appropriate steps to ensure that small suppliers of items and services have an opportunity to be considered for participation in the program under this section.

(7) CONSIDERATION IN DETERMINING CATEGORIES FOR BIDS.—The Secretary may consider the clinical efficiency and value of specific items within codes, including whether some items have a greater therapeutic advantage to individuals.

(8) AUTHORITY TO CONTRACT FOR EDUCATION, MONITORING, OUTREACH, AND COMPLAINT SERVICES.—The Secretary may enter into contracts with appropriate entities to address complaints from individuals who receive items and services from an entity with a contract under this section and to conduct appropriate education of and outreach to such individuals and monitoring quality of services with respect to the program.

(9) AUTHORITY TO CONTRACT FOR IMPLEMENTATION.—The Secretary may contract with appropriate entities to implement the competitive bidding program under this section.

(10) NO ADMINISTRATIVE OR JUDICIAL REVIEW.—There shall be no administrative or judicial review under section 1869, section 1878, or otherwise, of—

(A) the establishment of payment amounts under paragraph (5);

(B) the awarding of contracts under this section;

(C) the designation of competitive acquisition areas under subsection (a)(1)(A);

(D) the phased-in implementation under subsection (a)(1)(B);

(E) the selection of items and services for competitive acquisition under subsection (a)(2); or

(F) the bidding structure and number of contractors selected under this section.

(c) PROGRAM ADVISORY AND OVERSIGHT COMMITTEE.—

(1) ESTABLISHMENT.—The Secretary shall establish a Program Advisory and Oversight Committee (hereinafter in this section referred to as the 'Committee').

(2) MEMBERSHIP; TERMS.—The Committee shall consist of such members as the Secretary may appoint who shall serve for such term as the Secretary may specify.

(3) DUTIES.—

(A) ADVICE.—The Committee shall provide advice to the Secretary with respect to the following functions:

(i) The implementation of the program under this section.

(ii) The establishment of financial standards for purposes of subsection (b)(2)(A)(ii).

(iii) The establishment of requirements for collection of data for the efficient management of the program.

(iv) The development of proposals for efficient interaction among manufacturers, providers of services, suppliers (as defined in section 1861(d)), and individuals.

(v) The establishment of quality standards under section 1834(a)(20).

(B) ADDITIONAL DUTIES.—The Committee shall perform such additional functions to assist the Secretary in carrying out this section as the Secretary may specify.

(4) INAPPLICABILITY OF FACA.—The provisions of the Federal Advisory Committee Act (5 U.S.C. App.) shall not apply.

(5) TERMINATION.—The Committee shall terminate on December 31, 2009.

(d) REPORT.—Not later than July 1, 2009, the Secretary shall submit to Congress a report on the programs under this section. The report shall include information on savings, reductions in cost-sharing, access to and quality of items and services, and satisfaction of individuals.

(e) DEMONSTRATION PROJECT FOR CLINICAL LABORATORY SERVICES.—

(1) IN GENERAL.—The Secretary shall conduct a demonstration project on the application of competitive acquisition under this section to clinical diagnostic laboratory tests—

(A) for which payment would otherwise be made under section 1833(h) (other than for pap smear laboratory tests under paragraph (7) of such section) or section 1834(d)(1) (relating to colorectal cancer screening tests); and

(B) which are furnished by entities that did not have a face-to-face encounter with the individual.

(2) TERMS AND CONDITIONS.—

(A) IN GENERAL.—Except as provided in subparagraph (B), such project shall be under the same conditions as are applicable to items and services described in subsection (a)(2), excluding subsection (b)(5)(B) and other conditions as the Secretary determines to be appropriate.

Social Security Law Added, Amended or Repealed

(B) APPLICATION OF CLIA QUALITY STANDARDS.—The quality standards established by the Secretary under section 353 of the Public Health Service Act for clinical diagnostic laboratory tests shall apply to such tests under the demonstration project under this section in lieu of quality standards described in subsection (b)(2)(A)(i).

(3) REPORT.—The Secretary shall submit to Congress—

(A) an initial report on the project not later than December 31, 2005; and

(B) such progress and final reports on the project after such date as the Secretary determines appropriate..

[CCH Explanation at ¶1002.]

2003 Amendments:

Section 302(b)(1) of the "Medicare Prescription Drug, Improvement, and Modernization Act of 2003," effective upon enactment, amended section 1847.

Prior to amendment section 1847 read as follows:

Sec. 1847. DEMONSTRATION PROJECTS FOR COMPETITIVE ACQUISITION OF ITEMS AND SERVICES

(a) ESTABLISHMENT OF DEMONSTRATION PROJECT BIDDING AREAS.—

(1) IN GENERAL.—The Secretary shall implement not more than 5 demonstration projects under which competitive acquisition areas are established for contract award purposes for the furnishing under this part of the items and services described in subsection (d).

(2) PROJECT REQUIREMENTS.—Each demonstration project under paragraph (1)—

(A) shall include such group of items and services as the Secretary may prescribe,

(B) shall be conducted in not more than 3 competitive acquisition areas, and

(C) shall be operated over a 3-year period.

(3) CRITERIA FOR ESTABLISHMENT OF COMPETITIVE ACQUISITION AREAS.—Each competitive acquisition area established under a demonstration project implemented under paragraph (1)—

(A) shall be, or shall be within, a metropolitan statistical area (as defined by the Secretary of Commerce), and

(B) shall be chosen based on the availability and accessibility of entities able to furnish items and services, and the probable savings to be realized by the use of competitive bidding in the furnishing of items and services in such area.

(b) AWARDING OF CONTRACTS IN AREAS.—

(1) IN GENERAL.—The Secretary shall conduct a competition among individuals and entities supplying items and services described in subsection (c) for each competitive acquisition area established under a demonstration project implemented under subsection (a).

(2) CONDITIONS FOR AWARDING CONTRACT.—The Secretary may not award a contract to any entity under the competition conducted pursuant to paragraph (1) to furnish an item or service unless the Secretary finds that the entity meets quality standards specified by the Secretary and that the total amounts to be paid under the contract are expected to be less than the total amounts that would otherwise be paid.

(3) CONTENTS OF CONTRACT.—A contract entered into with an entity under the competition conducted pursuant to paragraph (1) is subject to terms and conditions that the Secretary may specify.

(4) LIMIT ON NUMBER OF CONTRACTORS.—The Secretary may limit the number of contractors in a competitive acquisition area to the number needed to meet projected demand for items and services covered under the contracts.

(c) EXPANSION OF PROJECTS.—

(1) EVALUATIONS.—The Secretary shall evaluate the impact of the implementation of the demonstration projects on Medicare program payments, access, diversity of product selection, and quality. The Secretary shall make annual reports to the Committees on Ways and Means and Commerce of the House of Representatives and the Committee on Finance of the Senate on the results of the evaluation described in the preceding sentence and a final report not later than 6 months after the termination date specified in subsection (e).

(2) EXPANSION.—If the Secretary determines from the evaluations under paragraph (1) that there is clear evidence that any demonstration project—

(A) results in a decrease in Federal expenditures under this title, and

(B) does not reduce program access, diversity of product selection, and quality under this title,

the Secretary may expand the project to additional competitive acquisition areas.

(d) SERVICES DESCRIBED.—The items and services to which this section applies are all items and services covered under this part (except for physicians' services as defined in section 1861(s)(1)) that the Secretary may specify. At least one demonstration project shall include oxygen and oxygen equipment.

(e) TERMINATION.—Notwithstanding any other provision of this section, all projects under this section shall terminate not later than December 31, 2002.

[¶2250A] Sec. 1847A. USE OF AVERAGE SALES PRICE PAYMENT METHODOLOGY

(a) APPLICATION.—

(1) IN GENERAL.—Except as provided in paragraph (2), this section shall apply to payment for drugs and biologicals that are described in section 1842(o)(1)(C) and that are furnished on or after January 1, 2005.

(2) ELECTION.—This section shall not apply in the case of a physician who elects under subsection (a)(1)(A)(ii) of section 1847B for that section to apply instead of this section for the payment for drugs and biologicals.

(b) PAYMENT AMOUNT.—

(1) IN GENERAL.—Subject to subsections (d)(3)(C) and (e), the amount of payment determined under this section for the billing and payment code for a drug or biological (based on a minimum dosage unit) is, subject to applicable deductible and coinsurance—

(A) in the case of a multiple source drug (as defined in subsection (c)(6)(C)), 106 percent of the amount determined under paragraph (3); or

(B) in the case of a single source drug or biological (as defined in subsection (c)(6)(D)), 106 percent of the amount determined under paragraph (4).

(2) SPECIFICATION OF UNIT.—

(A) SPECIFICATION BY MANUFACTURER.—The manufacturer of a drug or biological shall specify the unit associated with each National Drug Code (including package size) as part of the submission of data under section 1927(b)(3)(A)(iii).

(B) UNIT DEFINED.—In this section, the term "unit" means, with respect to each National Drug Code (including package size) associated with a drug or biological, the lowest identifiable quantity (such as a capsule or tablet, milligram of molecules, or grams) of the drug or biological that is dispensed, exclusive of any diluent without reference to volume measures pertaining to liquids. For years after 2004, the Secretary may establish the unit for a manufacturer to report and methods for counting units as the Secretary determines appropriate to implement this section.

(3) MULTIPLE SOURCE DRUG.—For all drug products included within the same multiple source drug billing and payment code, the amount specified in this paragraph is the volume-weighted average of the average sales prices reported under section 1927(b)(3)(A)(iii) determined by—

(A) computing the sum of the products (for each National Drug Code assigned to such drug products) of—

(i) the manufacturer's average sales price (as defined in subsection (c)); and

(ii) the total number of units specified under paragraph (2) sold; and

(B) dividing the sum determined under subparagraph (A) by the sum of the total number of units under subparagraph (A)(ii) for all National Drug Codes assigned to such drug products.

(4) SINGLE SOURCE DRUG OR BIOLOGICAL.—The amount specified in this paragraph for a single source drug or biological is the lesser of the following:

(A) AVERAGE SALES PRICE.—The average sales price as determined using the methodology applied under paragraph (3) for all National Drug Codes assigned to such drug or biological product.

(B) WHOLESALE ACQUISITION COST (WAC).—The wholesale acquisition cost (as defined in subsection (c)(6)(B)) using the methodology applied under paragraph (3) for all National Drug Codes assigned to such drug or biological product.

(5) BASIS FOR PAYMENT AMOUNT.—The payment amount shall be determined under this subsection based on information reported under subsection (f) and without regard to any special packaging, labeling, or identifiers on the dosage form or product or package.

(c) MANUFACTURER'S AVERAGE SALES PRICE.—

(1) IN GENERAL.—For purposes of this section, subject to paragraphs (2) and (3), the manufacturer's "average sales price" means, of a drug or biological for a National Drug Code for a calendar quarter for a manufacturer for a unit—

(A) the manufacturer's sales to all purchasers (excluding sales exempted in paragraph (2)) in the United States for such drug or biological in the calendar quarter; divided by

(B) the total number of such units of such drug or biological sold by the manufacturer in such quarter.

(2) CERTAIN SALES EXEMPTED FROM COMPUTATION.—In calculating the manufacturer's average sales price under this subsection, the following sales shall be excluded:

(A) SALES EXEMPT FROM BEST PRICE.—Sales exempt from the inclusion in the determination of "best price" under section 1927(c)(1)(C)(i).

(B) SALES AT NOMINAL CHARGE.—Such other sales as the Secretary identifies as sales to an entity that are merely nominal in amount (as applied for purposes of section 1927(c)(1)(C)(ii)(III), except as the Secretary may otherwise provide).

(3) SALE PRICE NET OF DISCOUNTS.—In calculating the manufacturer's average sales price under this subsection, such price shall include volume discounts, prompt pay discounts, cash discounts, free goods that are contingent on any purchase requirement, chargebacks, and rebates (other than rebates under section 1927). For years after 2004, the Secretary may include in such price other price concessions, which may be based on recommendations of the Inspector General, that would result in a reduction of the cost to the purchaser.

(4) PAYMENT METHODOLOGY IN CASES WHERE AVERAGE SALES PRICE DURING FIRST QUARTER OF SALES IS UNAVAILABLE.—In the case of a drug or biological during an initial period (not to exceed a full calendar quarter) in which data on the prices for sales for the drug or biological is not sufficiently available from the manufacturer to compute an average sales price for the drug or biological, the Secretary may determine the amount payable under this section for the drug or biological based on—

(A) the wholesale acquisition cost; or

(B) the methodologies in effect under this part on November 1, 2003, to determine payment amounts for drugs or biologicals.

(5) FREQUENCY OF DETERMINATIONS.—

(A) IN GENERAL ON A QUARTERLY BASIS.—The manufacturer's average sales price, for a drug or biological of a manufacturer, shall be calculated by such manufacturer under this subsection on a quarterly basis. In making such calculation insofar as there is a lag in the reporting of the information on rebates and chargebacks under paragraph (3) so that adequate data are not available on a timely basis, the manufacturer shall apply a methodology based on a 12-month rolling average for the manufacturer to estimate costs attributable to rebates and chargebacks. For years after 2004, the Secretary may establish a uniform methodology under this subparagraph to estimate and apply such costs.

(B) UPDATES IN PAYMENT AMOUNTS.—The payment amounts under subsection (b) shall be updated by the Secretary on a quarterly basis and shall be applied based upon the manufacturer's average sales price calculated for the most recent calendar quarter for which data is available.

(C) USE OF CONTRACTORS; IMPLEMENTATION.—The Secretary may contract with appropriate entities to calculate the payment amount under subsection (b). Notwithstanding any other provision of law, the Secretary may implement, by program instruction or otherwise, any of the provisions of this section.

(6) DEFINITIONS AND OTHER RULES.—In this section:

(A) MANUFACTURER.—The term "manufacturer" means, with respect to a drug or biological, the manufacturer (as defined in section 1927(k)(5)).

(B) WHOLESALE ACQUISITION COST.—The term "wholesale acquisition cost" means, with respect to a drug or biological, the manufacturer's list price for the drug or biological to wholesalers or direct purchasers in the United States, not including prompt pay or other discounts, rebates or reductions in price, for the most recent month for which the information is available, as reported in wholesale price guides or other publications of drug or biological pricing data.

(C) MULTIPLE SOURCE DRUG.—

(i) IN GENERAL.—The term "multiple source drug" means, for a calendar quarter, a drug for which there are 2 or more drug products which—

(I) are rated as therapeutically equivalent (under the Food and Drug Administration's most recent publication of "Approved Drug Products with Therapeutic Equivalence Evaluations"),

§1847A(c)(6)(C)(i)(I) ¶2250A

(II) except as provided in subparagraph (E), are pharmaceutically equivalent and bioequivalent, as determined under subparagraph (F) and as determined by the Food and Drug Administration, and

(III) are sold or marketed in the United States during the quarter.

(ii) EXCEPTION.—With respect to single source drugs or biologicals that are within the same billing and payment code as of October 1, 2003, the Secretary shall treat such single source drugs or biologicals as if the single source drugs or biologicals were multiple source drugs.

(D) SINGLE SOURCE DRUG OR BIOLOGICAL.—The term "single source drug or biological" means—

(i) a biological; or

(ii) a drug which is not a multiple source drug and which is produced or distributed under a new drug application approved by the Food and Drug Administration, including a drug product marketed by any cross-licensed producers or distributors operating under the new drug application.

(E) EXCEPTION FROM PHARMACEUTICAL EQUIVALENCE AND BIOEQUIVALENCE REQUIREMENT.—Subparagraph (C)(ii) shall not apply if the Food and Drug Administration changes by regulation the requirement that, for purposes of the publication described in subparagraph (C)(i), in order for drug products to be rated as therapeutically equivalent, they must be pharmaceutically equivalent and bioequivalent, as defined in subparagraph (F).

(F) DETERMINATION OF PHARMACEUTICAL EQUIVALENCE AND BIOEQUIVALENCE.—For purposes of this paragraph—

(i) drug products are pharmaceutically equivalent if the products contain identical amounts of the same active drug ingredient in the same dosage form and meet compendial or other applicable standards of strength, quality, purity, and identity; and

(ii) drugs are bioequivalent if they do not present a known or potential bioequivalence problem, or, if they do present such a problem, they are shown to meet an appropriate standard of bioequivalence.

(G) INCLUSION OF VACCINES.—In applying provisions of section 1927 under this section, "other than a vaccine" is deemed deleted from section 1927(k)(2)(B).

(d) MONITORING OF MARKET PRICES.—

(1) IN GENERAL.—The Inspector General of the Department of Health and Human Services shall conduct studies, which may include surveys, to determine the widely available market prices of drugs and biologicals to which this section applies, as the Inspector General, in consultation with the Secretary, determines to be appropriate.

(2) COMPARISON OF PRICES.—Based upon such studies and other data for drugs and biologicals, the Inspector General shall compare the average sales price under this section for drugs and biologicals with—

(A) the widely available market price for such drugs and biologicals (if any); and

(B) the average manufacturer price (as determined under section 1927(k)(1)) for such drugs and biologicals.

(3) LIMITATION ON AVERAGE SALES PRICE.—

(A) IN GENERAL.—The Secretary may disregard the average sales price for a drug or biological that exceeds the widely available market price or the average manufacturer price for such drug or biological by the applicable threshold percentage (as defined in subparagraph (B)).

(B) APPLICABLE THRESHOLD PERCENTAGE DEFINED.—In this paragraph, the term "applicable threshold percentage" means—

(i) in 2005, in the case of an average sales price for a drug or biological that exceeds widely available market price or the average manufacturer price, 5 percent; and

(ii) in 2006 and subsequent years, the percentage applied under this subparagraph subject to such adjustment as the Secretary may specify for the widely available market price or the average manufacturer price, or both.

(C) AUTHORITY TO ADJUST AVERAGE SALES PRICE.—If the Inspector General finds that the average sales price for a drug or biological exceeds such widely available market price or average manufacturer price for such drug or biological by the applicable threshold percentage, the Inspector General shall inform the Secretary (at such times as the Secretary may specify to carry out this subparagraph) and the Secretary shall, effective as of the next quarter, substitute for the amount of payment otherwise determined under this section for such drug or biological the lesser of—

(i) the widely available market price for the drug or biological (if any); or

(ii) 103 percent of the average manufacturer price (as determined under section 1927(k)(1)) for the drug or biological.

(4) CIVIL MONEY PENALTY.—

(A) IN GENERAL.—If the Secretary determines that a manufacturer has made a misrepresentation in the reporting of the manufacturer's average sales price for a drug or biological, the Secretary may apply a civil money penalty in an amount of up to $10,000 for each such price misrepresentation and for each day in which such price misrepresentation was applied.

(B) PROCEDURES.—The provisions of section 1128A (other than subsections (a) and (b)) shall apply to civil money penalties under subparagraph (B) in the same manner as they apply to a penalty or proceeding under section 1128A(a).

(5) WIDELY AVAILABLE MARKET PRICE.—

(A) IN GENERAL.—In this subsection, the term "widely available market price" means the price that a prudent physician or supplier would pay for the drug or biological. In determining such price, the Inspector General shall take into account the discounts, rebates, and other price concessions routinely made available to such prudent physicians or suppliers for such drugs or biologicals.

(B) CONSIDERATIONS.—In determining the price under subparagraph (A), the Inspector General shall consider information from one or more of the following sources:

(i) Manufacturers.

(ii) Wholesalers.

(iii) Distributors.

(iv) Physician supply houses.

(v) Specialty pharmacies.

(vi) Group purchasing arrangements.

(vii) Surveys of physicians.

(viii) Surveys of suppliers.

(ix) Information on such market prices from insurers.

(x) Information on such market prices from private health plans.

(e) AUTHORITY TO USE ALTERNATIVE PAYMENT IN RESPONSE TO PUBLIC HEALTH EMERGENCY.—In the case of a public health emergency under section 319 of the Public Health Service Act in which there is a documented inability to access drugs and biologicals, and a concomitant increase in the price, of a drug or biological which is not reflected in the manufacturer's average sales price for one or more quarters, the Secretary may use the wholesale acquisition cost (or other reasonable measure of drug or biological price) instead of the manufacturer's average sales price for such quarters and for subsequent quarters until the price and availability of the drug or biological has stabilized and is substantially reflected in the applicable manufacturer's average sales price.

(f) QUARTERLY REPORT ON AVERAGE SALES PRICE.—For requirements for reporting the manufacturer's average sales price (and, if required to make payment, the manufacturer's wholesale acquisition cost) for the drug or biological under this section, see section 1927(b)(3).

(g) JUDICIAL REVIEW.—There shall be no administrative or judicial review under section 1869, section 1878, or otherwise, of—

(1) determinations of payment amounts under this section, including the assignment of National Drug Codes to billing and payment codes;

(2) the identification of units (and package size) under subsection (b)(2);

(3) the method to allocate rebates, chargebacks, and other price concessions to a quarter if specified by the Secretary;

(4) the manufacturer's average sales price when it is used for the determination of a payment amount under this section; and

(5) the disclosure of the average manufacturer price by reason of an adjustment under subsection (d)(3)(C) or (e)..

[CCH Explanation at ¶1006, 1009, and 1010.]

2003 Amendments:

Section 303(c)(1) of the "Medicare Prescription Drug, Improvement, and Modernization Act of 2003," effective upon enactment, amended Title XVIII by adding new section 1847A.

[¶2250B] Sec. 1847B. COMPETITIVE ACQUISITION OF OUTPATIENT DRUGS AND BIOLOGICALS

(a) IMPLEMENTATION OF COMPETITIVE ACQUISITION.—

(1) IMPLEMENTATION OF PROGRAM.—

(A) IN GENERAL.—The Secretary shall establish and implement a competitive acquisition program under which—

(i) competitive acquisition areas are established for contract award purposes for acquisition of and payment for categories of competitively biddable drugs and biologicals (as defined in paragraph (2)) under this part;

(ii) each physician is given the opportunity annually to elect to obtain drugs and biologicals under the program, rather than under section 1847A; and

(iii) each physician who elects to obtain drugs and biologicals under the program makes an annual selection under paragraph (5) of the contractor through which drugs and biologicals within a category of drugs and biologicals will be acquired and delivered to the physician under this part.

This section shall not apply in the case of a physician who elects section 1847A to apply.

(B) IMPLEMENTATION.—For purposes of implementing the program, the Secretary shall establish categories of competitively biddable drugs and biologicals. The Secretary shall phase in the program with respect to those categories beginning in 2006 in such manner as the Secretary determines to be appropriate.

(C) WAIVER OF CERTAIN PROVISIONS.—In order to promote competition, in carrying out the program the Secretary may waive such provisions of the Federal Acquisition Regulation as are necessary for the efficient implementation of this section, other than provisions relating to confidentiality of information and such other provisions as the Secretary determines appropriate.

(D) EXCLUSION AUTHORITY.—The Secretary may exclude competitively biddable drugs and biologicals (including a class of such drugs and biologicals) from the competitive bidding system under this section if the application of competitive bidding to such drugs or biologicals—

(i) is not likely to result in significant savings; or

(ii) is likely to have an adverse impact on access to such drugs or biologicals.

(2) COMPETITIVELY BIDDABLE DRUGS AND BIOLOGICALS AND PROGRAM DEFINED.—For purposes of this section—

(A) COMPETITIVELY BIDDABLE DRUGS AND BIOLOGICALS DEFINED.—The term "competitively biddable drugs and biologicals" means a drug or biological described in section 1842(o)(1)(C) and furnished on or after January 1, 2006.

(B) PROGRAM.—The term "program" means the competitive acquisition program under this section.

(C) COMPETITIVE ACQUISITION AREA; AREA.—The terms "competitive acquisition area" and "area" mean an appropriate geographic region established by the Secretary under the program.

(D) "CONTRACTOR.—The term "contractor" means an entity that has entered into a contract with the Secretary under this section.

(3) APPLICATION OF PROGRAM PAYMENT METHODOLOGY.—

(A) IN GENERAL.—With respect to competitively biddable drugs and biologicals which are supplied under the program in an area and which are prescribed by a physician who has elected this section to apply—

(i) the claim for such drugs and biologicals shall be submitted by the contractor that supplied the drugs and biologicals;

(ii) collection of amounts of any deductible and coinsurance applicable with respect to such drugs and biologicals shall be the responsibility of such contractor and shall not be collected unless the drug or biological is administered to the individual involved; and

(iii) the payment under this section (and related amounts of any applicable deductible and coinsurance) for such drugs and biologicals—

(I) shall be made only to such contractor; and

(II) shall be conditioned upon the administration of such drugs and biologicals.

(B) PROCESS FOR ADJUSTMENTS.—The Secretary shall provide a process for adjustments to payments in the case in which payment is made for drugs and biologicals which were billed at the time of dispensing but which were not actually administered.

(C) INFORMATION FOR PURPOSES OF COST-SHARING.—The Secretary shall provide a process by which physicians submit information to contractors for purposes of the collection of any applicable deductible or coinsurance amounts under subparagraph (A)(ii).

(4) CONTRACT REQUIRED.—Payment may not be made under this part for competitively biddable drugs and biologicals prescribed by a physician who has elected this section to apply within a category and a competitive acquisition area with respect to which the program applies unless—

(A) the drugs or biologicals are supplied by a contractor with a contract under this section for such category of drugs and biologicals and area; and

(B) the physician has elected such contractor under paragraph (5) for such category and area.

(5) CONTRACTOR SELECTION PROCESS.—

(A) ANNUAL SELECTION.—

(i) IN GENERAL.—The Secretary shall provide a process for the selection of a contractor, on an annual basis and in such exigent circumstances as the Secretary may provide and with respect to each category of competitively biddable drugs and biologicals for an area by selecting physicians.

(ii) TIMING OF SELECTION.—The selection of a contractor under clause (i) shall be made at the time of the election described in section 1847A(a) for this section to apply and shall be coordinated with agreements entered into under section 1842(h).

(B) INFORMATION ON CONTRACTORS.—The Secretary shall make available to physicians on an ongoing basis, through a directory posted on the Internet website of the Centers for

Medicare & Medicaid Services or otherwise and upon request, a list of the contractors under this section in the different competitive acquisition areas.

(C) SELECTING PHYSICIAN DEFINED.—For purposes of this section, the term "selecting physician" means, with respect to a contractor and category and competitive acquisition area, a physician who has elected this section to apply and has selected to apply under this section such contractor for such category and area.

(b) PROGRAM REQUIREMENTS.—

(1) CONTRACT FOR COMPETITIVELY BIDDABLE DRUGS AND BIOLOGICALS.—The Secretary shall conduct a competition among entities for the acquisition of competitively biddable drugs and biologicals. Notwithstanding any other provision of this title, in the case of a multiple source drug, the Secretary shall conduct such competition among entities for the acquisition of at least one competitively biddable drug and biological within each billing and payment code within each category for each competitive acquisition area.

(2) CONDITIONS FOR AWARDING CONTRACT.—

(A) IN GENERAL.—The Secretary may not award a contract to any entity under the competition conducted in a competitive acquisition area pursuant to paragraph (1) with respect to the acquisition of competitively biddable drugs and biologicals within a category unless the Secretary finds that the entity meets all of the following with respect to the contract period involved:

(i) CAPACITY TO SUPPLY COMPETITIVELY BIDDABLE DRUG OR BIOLOGICAL WITHIN CATEGORY.—

(I) IN GENERAL.—The entity has sufficient arrangements to acquire and to deliver competitively biddable drugs and biologicals within such category in the area specified in the contract.

(II) SHIPMENT METHODOLOGY.—The entity has arrangements in effect for the shipment at least 5 days each week of competitively biddable drugs and biologicals under the contract and for the timely delivery (including for emergency situations) of such drugs and biologicals in the area under the contract.

(ii) QUALITY, SERVICE, FINANCIAL PERFORMANCE AND SOLVENCY STANDARDS.—The entity meets quality, service, financial performance, and solvency standards specified by the Secretary, including—

(I) the establishment of procedures for the prompt response and resolution of complaints of physicians and individuals and of inquiries regarding the shipment of competitively biddable drugs and biologicals; and

(II) a grievance and appeals process for the resolution of disputes.

(B) ADDITIONAL CONSIDERATIONS.—The Secretary may refuse to award a contract under this section, and may terminate such a contract, with an entity based upon—

(i) the suspension or revocation, by the Federal Government or a State government, of the entity's license for the distribution of drugs or biologicals (including controlled substances); or

(ii) the exclusion of the entity under section 1128 from participation under this title.

(C) APPLICATION OF MEDICARE PROVIDER OMBUDSMAN.—For provision providing for a programwide Medicare Provider Ombudsman to review complaints, see section 1868(b), as added by section 923 of the Medicare Prescription Drug, Improvement, and Modernization Act of 2003.

(3) AWARDING MULTIPLE CONTRACTS FOR A CATEGORY AND AREA.—The Secretary may limit (but not below 2) the number of qualified entities that are awarded such contracts for any category and area. The Secretary shall select among qualified entities based on the following:

(A) The bid prices for competitively biddable drugs and biologicals within the category and area.

(B) Bid price for distribution of such drugs and biologicals.

(C) Ability to ensure product integrity.

(D) Customer service.

(E) Past experience in the distribution of drugs and biologicals, including controlled substances.

(F) Such other factors as the Secretary may specify.

(4) TERMS OF CONTRACTS.—

(A) IN GENERAL.—A contract entered into with an entity under the competition conducted pursuant to paragraph (1) is subject to terms and conditions that the Secretary may specify consistent with this section.

(B) PERIOD OF CONTRACTS.—A contract under this section shall be for a term of 3 years, but may be terminated by the Secretary or the entity with appropriate, advance notice.

(C) INTEGRITY OF DRUG AND BIOLOGICAL DISTRIBUTION SYSTEM.—A contractor (as defined in subsection (a)(2)(D)) shall—

(i) acquire all drug and biological products it distributes directly from the manufacturer or from a distributor that has acquired the products directly from the manufacturer; and

(ii) comply with any product integrity safeguards as may be determined to be appropriate by the Secretary.

Nothing in this subparagraph shall be construed to relieve or exempt any contractor from the provisions of the Federal Food, Drug, and Cosmetic Act that relate to the wholesale distribution of prescription drugs or biologicals.

(D) COMPLIANCE WITH CODE OF CONDUCT AND FRAUD AND ABUSE RULES.—Under the contract—

(i) the contractor shall comply with a code of conduct, specified or recognized by the Secretary, that includes standards relating to conflicts of interest; and

(ii) the contractor shall comply with all applicable provisions relating to prevention of fraud and abuse, including compliance with applicable guidelines of the Department of Justice and the Inspector General of the Department of Health and Human Services.

(E) DIRECT DELIVERY OF DRUGS AND BIOLOGICALS TO PHYSICIANS.—Under the contract the contractor shall only supply competitively biddable drugs and biologicals directly to the selecting physicians and not directly to individuals, except under circumstances and settings where an individual currently receives a drug or biological in the individual's home or other non-physician office setting as the Secretary may provide. The contractor shall not deliver drugs and biologicals to a selecting physician except upon receipt of a prescription for such drugs and biologicals, and such necessary data as may be required by the Secretary to carry out this section. This section does not—

(i) require a physician to submit a prescription for each individual treatment; or

(ii) change a physician's flexibility in terms of writing a prescription for drugs or biologicals for a single treatment or a course of treatment.

(5) PERMITTING ACCESS TO DRUGS AND BIOLOGICALS.—The Secretary shall establish rules under this section under which drugs and biologicals which are acquired through a contractor under this section may be used to resupply inventories of such drugs and biologicals which are administered consistent with safe drug practices and with adequate safeguards against fraud and abuse. The previous sentence shall apply if the physicians can demonstrate to the Secretary all of the following:

(A) The drugs or biologicals are required immediately.

(B) The physician could not have reasonably anticipated the immediate requirement for the drugs or biologicals.

(C) The contractor could not deliver to the physician the drugs or biologicals in a timely manner.

(D) The drugs or biologicals were administered in an emergency situation.

(6) CONSTRUCTION.—Nothing in this section shall be construed as waiving applicable State requirements relating to licensing of pharmacies.

(c) BIDDING PROCESS.—

(1) IN GENERAL.—In awarding a contract for a category of drugs and biologicals in an area under the program, the Secretary shall consider with respect to each entity seeking to be awarded a contract the bid price and the other factors referred to in subsection (b)(3).

(2) BID DEFINED.—In this section, the term "bid" means an offer to furnish a competitively biddable drug or biological for a particular price and time period.

(3) BIDDING ON A NATIONAL OR REGIONAL BASIS.—Nothing in this section shall be construed as precluding a bidder from bidding for contracts in all areas of the United States or as requiring a bidder to submit a bid for all areas of the United States.

(4) UNIFORMITY OF BIDS WITHIN AREA.—The amount of the bid submitted under a contract offer for any competitively biddable drug or biological for an area shall be the same for that drug or biological for all portions of that area.

(5) CONFIDENTIALITY OF BIDS.—The provisions of subparagraph (D) of section 1927(b)(3) shall apply to periods during which a bid is submitted with respect to a competitively biddable drug or biological under this section in the same manner as it applies to information disclosed under such section, except that any reference—

(A) in that subparagraph to a "manufacturer or wholesaler" is deemed a reference to a "bidder" under this section;

(B) in that section to "prices charged for drugs" is deemed a reference to a "bid" submitted under this section; and

(C) in clause (i) of that section to "this section", is deemed a reference to "part B of title XVIII".

(6) INCLUSION OF COSTS.—The bid price submitted in a contract offer for a competitively biddable drug or biological shall—

(A) include all costs related to the delivery of the drug or biological to the selecting physician (or other point of delivery); and

(B) include the costs of dispensing (including shipping) of such drug or biological and management fees, but shall not include any costs related to the administration of the drug or biological, or wastage, spillage, or spoilage.

(7) PRICE ADJUSTMENTS DURING CONTRACT PERIOD; DISCLOSURE OF COSTS.—Each contract awarded shall provide for—

(A) disclosure to the Secretary the contractor's reasonable, net acquisition costs for periods specified by the Secretary, not more often than quarterly, of the contract; and

(B) appropriate price adjustments over the period of the contract to reflect significant increases or decreases in a contractor's reasonable, net acquisition costs, as so disclosed.

(d) COMPUTATION OF PAYMENT AMOUNTS.—

(1) IN GENERAL.—Payment under this section for competitively biddable drugs or biologicals shall be based on bids submitted and accepted under this section for such drugs or biologicals in an area. Based on such bids the Secretary shall determine a single payment amount for each competitively biddable drug or biological in the area.

(2) SPECIAL RULES.—The Secretary shall establish rules regarding the use under this section of the alternative payment amount provided under section 1847A to the use of a price for specific competitively biddable drugs and biologicals in the following cases:

(A) NEW DRUGS AND BIOLOGICALS.—A competitively biddable drug or biological for which a payment and billing code has not been established.

(B) OTHER CASES.—Such other exceptional cases as the Secretary may specify in regulations.

(e) COST-SHARING.—

(1) APPLICATION OF COINSURANCE.—Payment under this section for competitively biddable drugs and biologicals shall be in an amount equal to 80 percent of the payment basis described in subsection (d)(1).

(2) DEDUCTIBLE.—Before applying paragraph (1), the individual shall be required to meet the deductible described in section 1833(b).

(3) COLLECTION.—Such coinsurance and deductible shall be collected by the contractor that supplies the drug or biological involved. Subject to subsection (a)(3)(B), such coinsurance and deductible may be collected in a manner similar to the manner in which the coinsurance and deductible are collected for durable medical equipment under this part.

(f) SPECIAL PAYMENT RULES.—

(1) USE IN EXCLUSION CASES.—If the Secretary excludes a drug or biological (or class of drugs or biologicals) under subsection (a)(1)(D), the Secretary may provide for payment to be made under this part for such drugs and biologicals (or class) using the payment methodology under section 1847A.

(2) APPLICATION OF REQUIREMENT FOR ASSIGNMENT.—For provision requiring assignment of claims for competitively biddable drugs and biologicals, see section 1842(o)(3).

(3) PROTECTION FOR BENEFICIARY IN CASE OF MEDICAL NECESSITY DENIAL.—For protection of individuals against liability in the case of medical necessity determinations, see section 1842(b)(3)(B)(ii)(III).

(g) JUDICIAL REVIEW.—There shall be no administrative or judicial review under section 1869, section 1878, or otherwise, of—

(1) the establishment of payment amounts under subsection (d)(1);

(2) the awarding of contracts under this section;

(3) the establishment of competitive acquisition areas under subsection (a)(2)(C);

(4) the phased-in implementation under subsection (a)(1)(B);

(5) the selection of categories of competitively biddable drugs and biologicals for competitive acquisition under such subsection or the selection of a drug in the case of multiple source drugs; or

(6) the bidding structure and number of contractors selected under this section..

[CCH Explanation at ¶ 1006, 1009, and 1010.]
2003 Amendments:

Section 303(d)(1) of the "Medicare Prescription Drug, Improvement, and Modernization Act of 2003," effective upon enactment, amended Title XVIII by adding section 1847B.

[¶ 2251A] Sec. 1848(c). DETERMINATION OF RELATIVE VALUES FOR PHYSICIANS' SERVICES

[42 U.S.C. § 1395w-4(c)]

(c) DETERMINATION OF RELATIVE VALUES FOR PHYSICIANS' SERVICES.—

* * *

(2) DETERMINATION OF RELATIVE VALUES.—

* * *

(B) PERIODIC REVIEW AND ADJUSTMENTS IN RELATIVE VALUES.—

* * *

(ii) ADJUSTMENTS.—

* * *

(II) LIMITATION ON ANNUAL ADJUSTMENTS.—Subject to clause (iv), the adjustments under subclause (I) for a year may not cause the amount of expenditures under this part for the year to differ by more than $20,000,000 from the amount of expenditures under this part that would have been made if such adjustments had not been made.

* * *

(iv) EXEMPTION FROM BUDGET NEUTRALITY.—The additional expenditures attributable to—

(I) subparagraph (H) shall not be taken into account in applying clause (ii)(II) for 2004;

(II) subparagraph (I) insofar as it relates to a physician fee schedule for 2005 or 2006 shall not be taken into account in applying clause (ii)(II) for drug administration services under the fee schedule for such year for a specialty described in subparagraph (I)(ii)(II); and

(III) subparagraph (J) insofar as it relates to a physician fee schedule for 2005 or 2006 shall not be taken into account in applying clause (ii)(II) for drug administration services under the fee schedule for such year.

* * *

(H) ADJUSTMENTS IN PRACTICE EXPENSE RELATIVE VALUE UNITS FOR CERTAIN DRUG ADMINISTRATION SERVICES BEGINNING IN 2004

(i) USE OF SURVEY DATA.—In establishing the physician fee schedule under subsection (b) with respect to payments for services furnished on or after January 1, 2004, the Secretary shall, in determining practice expense relative value units under this subsection, utilize a survey submitted to the Secretary as of January 1, 2003, by a physician specialty organization pursuant to section 212 of the Medicare, Medicaid, and SCHIP Balanced Budget Refinement Act of 1999 if the survey—

(I) covers practice expenses for oncology drug administration services; and

(II) meets criteria established by the Secretary for acceptance of such surveys.

(ii) PRICING OF CLINICAL ONCOLOGY NURSES IN PRACTICE EXPENSE METHODOLOGY.—If the survey described in clause (i) includes data on wages, salaries, and compensation of clinical oncology nurses, the Secretary shall utilize such data in the methodology for determining practice expense relative value units under subsection (c).

(iii) WORK RELATIVE VALUE UNITS FOR CERTAIN DRUG ADMINISTRATION SERVICES.—In establishing the relative value units under this paragraph for drug administration services described in clause (iv) furnished on or after January 1, 2004, the Secretary shall establish work relative value units equal to the work relative value units for a level 1 office medical visit for an established patient.

(iv) DRUG ADMINISTRATION SERVICES DESCRIBED.—The drug administration services described in this clause are physicians' services—

(I) which are classified as of October 1, 2003, within any of the following groups of procedures: therapeutic or diagnostic infusions (excluding chemotherapy); chemotherapy administration services; and therapeutic, prophylactic, or diagnostic injections;

(II) for which there are no work relative value units assigned under this subsection as of such date; and

(III) for which national relative value units have been assigned under this subsection as of such date.

(I) ADJUSTMENTS IN PRACTICE EXPENSE RELATIVE VALUE UNITS FOR CERTAIN DRUG ADMINISTRATION SERVICES BEGINNING WITH 2005.—

(i) IN GENERAL.—In establishing the physician fee schedule under subsection (b) with respect to payments for services furnished on or after January 1, 2005 or 2006, the Secretary shall adjust the practice expense relative value units for such year consistent with clause (ii).

Social Security Law Added, Amended or Repealed

(ii) USE OF SUPPLEMENTAL SURVEY DATA.—

(I) IN GENERAL.—Subject to subclause (II), if a specialty submits to the Secretary by not later than March 1, 2004, for 2005, or March 1, 2005, for 2006, data that includes expenses for the administration of drugs and biologicals for which the payment amount is determined pursuant to section 1842(o), the Secretary shall use such supplemental survey data in carrying out this subparagraph for the years involved insofar as they are collected and provided by entities and organizations consistent with the criteria established by the Secretary pursuant to section 212(a) of the Medicare, Medicaid, and SCHIP Balanced Budget Refinement Act of 1999.

(II) LIMITATION ON SPECIALTY.—Subclause (I) shall apply to a specialty only insofar as not less than 40 percent of payments for the specialty under this title in 2002 are attributable to the administration of drugs and biologicals, as determined by the Secretary.

(III) APPLICATION.—This clause shall not apply with respect to a survey to which subparagraph (H)(i) applies.

(J) PROVISIONS FOR APPROPRIATE REPORTING AND BILLING FOR PHYSICIANS' SERVICES ASSOCIATED WITH THE ADMINISTRATION OF COVERED OUTPATIENT DRUGS AND BIOLOGICALS.—

(i) EVALUATION OF CODES.—The Secretary shall promptly evaluate existing drug administration codes for physicians' services to ensure accurate reporting and billing for such services, taking into account levels of complexity of the administration and resource consumption.

(ii) USE OF EXISTING PROCESSES.—In carrying out clause (i), the Secretary shall use existing processes for the consideration of coding changes and, to the extent coding changes are made, shall use such processes in establishing relative values for such services.

(iii) IMPLEMENTATION.—In carrying out clause (i), the Secretary shall consult with representatives of physician specialties affected by the implementation of section 1847A or section 1847B, and shall take such steps within the Secretary's authority to expedite such considerations under clause (ii).

(iv) SUBSEQUENT, BUDGET NEUTRAL ADJUSTMENTS PERMITTED.—Nothing in subparagraph (H) or (I) or this subparagraph shall be construed as preventing the Secretary from providing for adjustments in practice expense relative value units under (and consistent with) subparagraph (B) for years after 2004, 2005, or 2006, respectively.

[CCH Explanation at ¶ 1004, 1006, 1009, and 1010.]

2003 Amendments:

Section 303(a)(1)(A)(i) of the "Medicare Prescription Drug, Improvement, and Modernization Act of 2003," effective upon enactment, amended section 1848(c)(2)(B)(ii)(II) by striking "The adjustments" and inserting "Subject to clause (iv), the adjustments".

Section 303(a)(1)(A)(ii) of the "Medicare Prescription Drug, Improvement, and Modernization Act of 2003," effective upon enactment, amended section 1848(c)(2)(B) by adding new subclause (iv).

Section 303(a)(1)(B) of the "Medicare Prescription Drug, Improvement, and Modernization Act of 2003," effective upon enactment, amended section 1848(c)(2) by adding new subparagraphs (H), (I), and (J).

[¶ 2251B] Sec. 1848(d). CONVERSION FACTORS

[42 U.S.C. § 1395w-4(d)]

(d) CONVERSION FACTORS.—

(4) UPDATE FOR YEARS BEGINNING WITH 2001.—

* * *

(B) UPDATE ADJUSTMENT FACTOR.—For purposes of subparagraph (A)(ii), subject to subparagraph (D) and paragraph (5), the "update adjustment factor" for a year is equal (as estimated by the Secretary) to the sum of the following:

* * *

(5) UPDATE FOR 2004 AND 2005.—The update to the single conversion factor established in paragraph (1)(C) for each of 2004 and 2005 shall be not less than 1.5 percent.

[CCH Explanation at ¶ 701.]
2003 Amendments:

Section 601(a)(1) of the "Medicare Prescription Drug, Improvement, and Modernization Act of 2003," effective upon enactment, amended section 1848(d) by adding new paragraph (5).

Section 601(a)(2) of the "Medicare Prescription Drug, Improvement, and Modernization Act of 2003," effective upon enactment, amended section 1848(d)(4)(B) by inserting in the matter before clause (i), "and paragraph (5)" after "subparagraph (D)" before clause (i).

[¶ 2251C] Sec. 1848(e). GEOGRAPHIC ADJUSTMENT FACTORS

[42 U.S.C. § 1395w-4(e)]

(e) GEOGRAPHIC ADJUSTMENT FACTORS.—

(1) ESTABLISHMENT OF GEOGRAPHIC INDICES.—

(A) IN GENERAL.—Subject to subparagraphs (B), (C), (E), (F) and (G), the Secretary shall establish—

* * *

(E) FLOOR AT 1.0 ON WORK GEOGRAPHIC INDEX.—After calculating the work geographic index in subparagraph (A)(iii), for purposes of payment for services furnished on or after January 1, 2004, and before January 1, 2007, the Secretary shall increase the work geographic index to 1.00 for any locality for which such work geographic index is less than 1.00."

(G) [SIC] FLOOR FOR PRACTICE EXPENSE, MALPRACTICE, AND WORK GEOGRAPHIC INDICES FOR SERVICES FURNISHED IN ALASKA.—For purposes of payment for services furnished in Alaska on or after January 1, 2004, and before January 1, 2006, after calculating the practice expense, malpractice, and work geographic indices in clauses (i), (ii), and (iii) of subparagraph (A) and in subparagraph (B), the Secretary shall increase any such index to 1.67 if such index would otherwise be less than 1.67.

* * *

[CCH Explanation at ¶ 708 and 722.]
2003 Amendments:

Section 412(1) of the "Medicare Prescription Drug, Improvement, and Modernization Act of 2003," effective upon enactment, amended section 1848(e)(1)(A) by striking "subparagraphs (B) and (C)" and inserting "subparagraphs (B), (C), and (E)".

Section 412(2) of the "Medicare Prescription Drug, Improvement, and Modernization Act of 2003," effective upon enactment, amended section 1848(e)(1) by adding a new section (E).

Section 602(1) of the "Medicare Prescription Drug, Improvement, and Modernization Act of 2003," effective upon enactment, amended section 1848(e)(1)(A) by striking "subparagraphs (B), (C), (E), and (F)" and inserting "subparagraphs (B), (C), (E), (F) and (G)".

Section 602(2) of the "Medicare Prescription Drug, Improvement, and Modernization Act of 2003," effective upon enactment, amended 1848(e)(1) by adding a new section (G).

[¶ 2251D] Sec. 1848(f). SUSTAINABLE GROWTH RATE

[42 U.S.C. § 1395w-4(f)]

(f) SUSTAINABLE GROWTH RATE.—

* * *

(2) SPECIFICATION OF GROWTH RATE.—The sustainable growth rate for all physicians' services for a fiscal year (beginning with fiscal year 1998 and ending with fiscal year 2000) and a year beginning with 2000 shall be equal to the product of—

* * *

(C) 1 plus the Secretary's estimate of the annual average percentage growth in real gross domestic product per capita (divided by 100) during the 10-year period ending with the applicable period involved, and

* * *

Social Security Law Added, Amended or Repealed

[CCH Explanation at ¶701.]

2003 Amendments:

Section 601(b)(1) of the "Medicare Prescription Drug, Improvement, and Modernization Act of 2003," effective upon enactment, amended section 1848(f)(2)(C) by striking "projected" and inserting "annual average"; and by striking "from the previous applicable period to the applicable period involved" and inserting "during the 10-year period ending with the applicable period involved".

The amendments made by section 601(b) of the "Medicare Prescription Drug, Improvement, and Modernization Act of 2003," apply to computations of the sustainable growth rate for years beginning with 2003.

[¶2251E] Sec. 1848(i). MISCELLANEOUS PROVISIONS

[42 U.S.C. §1395w-4(i)]

(i) MISCELLANEOUS PROVISIONS.—

(1) RESTRICTION ON ADMINISTRATIVE AND JUDICIAL REVIEW.—There shall be no administrative or judicial review under section 1869 or otherwise of—

* * *

(B) the determination of relative values and relative value units under subsection (c) including adjustments under subsections (c)(2)(F), (c)(2)(H), and (c)(2)(I), and section 13515(b) of the Omnibus Budget Reconciliation Act of 1993,

* * *

(3) NO COMPARABILITY ADJUSTMENT.—For physicians' services for which payment under this part is determined under this section—

(A) a carrier may not make any adjustment in the payment amount under section 1842(b)(3)(B) on the basis that the payment amount is higher than the charge applicable, for comparable services and under comparable circumstances, to the policyholders and subscribers of the carrier,

* * *

[CCH Explanation at ¶1004, 1006, 1009, and 1010.]

2003 Amendments:

Section 303(g)(2) of the "Medicare Prescription Drug, Improvement, and Modernization Act of 2003," effective upon enactment, amended section 1848(i)(1)(B) by striking "subsection (c)(2)(F)" and inserting "subsections (c)(2)(F), (c)(2)(H), and (c)(2)(I)".

Section 736(b)(10) of the "Medicare Prescription Drug, Improvement, and Modernization Act of 2003," effective upon enactment, amended section by striking "a comparable services" and inserting "comparable services"

[¶2251F] Sec. 1848(j). DEFINITIONS

[42 U.S.C. §1395w-4(j)]

(j) DEFINITIONS.—In this section:

* * *

(3) PHYSICIANS' SERVICES.—The term "physicians' services" includes items and services described in paragraphs (1), (2)(A), (2)(D), (2)(G), (2)(P) (with respect to services described in subparagraphs (A) and (C) of section 1861(oo)(2)), (2)(R) (with respect to services described in subparagraphs (B), (C), and (D) of section 1861(pp)(1)), (2)(S), (2)(W),(3), (4), (13), (14) (with respect to services described in section 1861(nn)(2)), and (15) of section 1861(s) (other than clinical diagnostic laboratory tests and such other items and services as the Secretary may specify).

* * *

[CCH Explanation at ¶1103.]

2003 Amendments:

Section 611(c) of the "Medicare Prescription Drug, Improvement, and Modernization Act of 2003," amended section 1848(j)(3) by inserting "(2)(W)," after "(2)(S),".

The amendments made by section 611(c) of the "Medicare Prescription Drug, Improvement, and Modernization Act of 2003," apply to services furnished on or after January 1, 2005, but only for individuals whose coverage period under part B of the "Medicare Prescription Drug, Improvement, and Modernization Act of 2003," begins on or after such date.

[¶ 2255] **Sec. 1851. ELIGIBILITY, ELECTION, AND ENROLLMENT**

[42 U.S.C. §1395w-21]

(a) CHOICE OF MEDICARE BENEFITS THROUGH MEDICARE + CHOICE PLANS.—

(1) IN GENERAL.—Subject to the provisions of this section, each Medicare + Choice eligible individual (as defined in paragraph (3)) is entitled to elect to receive benefits (other than qualified prescription drug benefits) under this title—

* * *

(B) through enrollment in a Medicare + Choice plan under this part,

and may elect qualified prescription drug coverage in accordance with section 1860D-1.

(2) TYPES OF MEDICARE + CHOICE PLANS THAT MAY BE AVAILABLE.—A Medicare + Choice plan may be any of the following types of plans of health insurance:

(A) COORDINATED CARE PLANS (INCLUDING REGIONAL PLANS).—

(i) IN GENERAL.—Coordinated care plans which provide health care services, including but not limited to health maintenance organization plans (with or without point of service options), plans offered by provider-sponsored organizations (as defined in section 1855(d)), and regional or local preferred provider organization plans(including MA regional plans).

(ii) SPECIALIZED MA PLANS FOR SPECIAL NEEDS INDIVIDUALS.——Specialized MA plans for special needs individuals (as defined in section 1859(b)(6)) may be any type of coordinated care plan.

* * *

(3) MEDICARE + CHOICE ELIGIBLE INDIVIDUAL.—

* * *

(B) SPECIAL RULE FOR END-STAGE RENAL DISEASE.—Such term shall not include an individual medically determined to have end-stage renal disease, except that—

* * *

(ii) in the case of such an individual who is enrolled in a Medicare+Choice plan under clause (i) (or subsequently under this clause), if the enrollment is discontinued under circumstances described in subsection (e)(4)(A), then the individual will be treated as a "Medicare+Choice eligible individual" for purposes of electing to continue enrollment in another Medicare+Choice plan.

(b) SPECIAL RULES.—

(1) RESIDENCE REQUIREMENT.—

* * *

(B) CONTINUATION OF ENROLLMENT PERMITTED.—Pursuant to rules specified by the Secretary, the Secretary shall provide that an MA local plan may offer to all individuals residing in a geographic area the option to continue enrollment in the plan, notwithstanding that the individual no longer resides in the service area of the plan, so long as the plan provides that individuals exercising this option have, as part of the benefits under the original medicare fee-for-service program option, reasonable access within that geographic area to the full range of basic benefits, subject to reasonable cost sharing liability in obtaining such benefits.

(C) CONTINUATION OF ENROLLMENT PERMITTED WHERE SERVICE CHANGED.—Notwithstanding subparagraph (A) and in addition to subparagraph (B), if a Medicare+Choice organization eliminates from its service area a Medicare+Choice payment area that was previously within its service area, the organization may elect to offer individuals residing in all or portions of the affected area who would otherwise be ineligible to continue enrollment the option to continue enrollment in an MA local plan it offers so long as—

* * *
* * *

(4) COVERAGE UNDER MSA PLANS.—

(A) IN GENERAL.—Under rules established by the Secretary, an individual is not eligible to enroll (or continue enrollment) in an MSA plan for a year unless the individual provides assurances satisfactory to the Secretary that the individual will reside in the United States for at least 183 days during the year.

* * *

(C) REPORTS.—The Secretary shall submit to Congress periodic reports on the numbers of individuals enrolled in such plans and on the evaluation being conducted under subparagraph (B).

* * *

(d) PROVIDING INFORMATION TO PROMOTE INFORMED CHOICE.—

* * *

(3) GENERAL INFORMATION.—General information under this paragraph, with respect to coverage under this part during a year, shall include the following:

* * *

(F) CATASTROPHIC COVERAGE AND SINGLE DEDUCTIBLE.—In the case of an MA regional plan, a description of the catastrophic coverage and single deductible applicable under the plan.

(4) INFORMATION COMPARING PLAN OPTIONS.—Information under this paragraph, with respect to a Medicare + Choice plan for a year, shall include the following:

(A) BENEFITS.—The benefits covered under the plan, including the following:

* * *

(ii) Any beneficiary cost sharing, including information on the single deductible (if applicable) under section 1858(b)(1).

* * *

(B) PREMIUMS.—

(i) IN GENERAL.—The monthly amount of the premium charged to an individual.

* * *

(E) SUPPLEMENTAL BENEFITS.—Supplemental health care benefits, including any reductions in costsharing under section 1852(a)(3) and the terms and conditions (including premiums) for such benefits.

* * *

(e) COVERAGE ELECTION PERIODS.—

(1) INITIAL CHOICE UPON ELIGIBILITY TO MAKE ELECTION IF MEDICARE + CHOICE PLANS AVAILABLE TO INDIVIDUAL.—If, at the time an individual first becomes entitled to benefits under part A and enrolled under part B, there is one or more Medicare + Choice plans offered in the area in which the individual resides, the individual shall make the election under this section during a period specified by the Secretary such that if the individual elects a Medicare + Choice plan during the period, coverage under the plan becomes effective as of the first date on which the individual may receive such coverage. If any portion of an individual's initial enrollment period under part B occurs after the end of the annual, coordinated election period described in paragraph (3)(B)(iii), the initial enrollment period under this part shall further extend through the end of the individual's initial enrollment period under part B.

(2) OPEN ENROLLMENT AND DISENROLLMENT OPPORTUNITIES.—Subject to paragraph (5)—

(A) CONTINUOUS OPEN ENROLLMENT AND DISENROLLMENT THROUGH 2005.—At any time during the time period beginning January 1, 1998, and ending on December 31, 2005, a Medicare + Choice eligible individual may change the election under subsection (a)(1).

(B) Continuous open enrollment and disenrollment for first 6 months during 2006.—

(i) In general.—Subject to clause (ii), subparagraph (C)(iii), and subparagraph (D), at any time during the first 6 months of 2006, or, if the individual first becomes a Medicare + Choice eligible individual during 2006, during the first 6 months during 2006 in which the individual is a Medicare + Choice eligible individual, a Medicare + Choice eligible individual may change the election under subsection (a)(1).

* * *

(C) Continuous open enrollment and disenrollment for first 3 months in subsequent years.—

(i) In general.—Subject to clauses (ii) and (iii) and subparagraph (D), at any time during the first 3 months of a year after 2006, or, if the individual first becomes a Medicare + Choice eligible individual during a year after 2006, during the first 3 months of such year in which the individual is a Medicare + Choice eligible individual, a Medicare + Choice eligible individual may change the election under subsection (a)(1).

* * *

(iii) Limitation on exercise of right with respect to prescription drug coverage.—Effective for plan years beginning on or after January 1, 2006, in applying clause (i) (and clause (i) of subparagraph (B)) in the case of an individual who—

(I) is enrolled in an MA plan that does provide qualified prescription drug coverage, the individual may exercise the right under such clause only with respect to coverage under the original fee-for-service plan or coverage under another MA plan that does not provide such coverage and may not exercise such right to obtain coverage under an MA-PD plan or under a prescription drug plan under part D; or

(II) is enrolled in an MA-PD plan, the individual may exercise the right under such clause only with respect to coverage under another MA-PD plan (and not an MA plan that does not provide qualified prescription drug coverage) or under the original fee-for-service plan and coverage under a prescription drug plan under part D.

(D) Continuous open enrollment for institutionalized individuals.—At any time after 2005 in the case of a Medicare+Choice eligible individual who is institutionalized (as defined by the Secretary), the individual may elect under subsection (a)(1)—

* * *

(3) Annual, coordinated election period.—

* * *

(B) Annual, coordinated election period.—For purposes of this section, the term "annual, coordinated election period" means—

(i) with respect to a year before 2002, the month of November before such year;

(ii) with respect to 2002, 2003, 2004, and 2005, the period beginning on November 15 and ending on December 31 of the year before such year;

(iii) with respect to 2006, the period beginning on November 15, 2005, and ending on May 15, 2006; and

(iv) with respect to 2007 and succeeding years, the period beginning on November 15 and ending on December 31 of the year before such year.

(C) Medicare + Choice health information fairs.—During the fall season of each year (beginning with 1999) and during the period described in subparagraph (B)(iii), in conjunction with the annual coordinated election period defined in subparagraph (B), the Secretary shall provide for a nationally coordinated educational and publicity campaign to inform Medicare + Choice eligible individuals about Medicare + Choice plans and the election process provided under this section.

(D) Special information campaigns.—During November 1998 the Secretary shall provide for an educational and publicity campaign to inform Medicare + Choice eligible individuals about the availability of Medicare + Choice plans, and eligible organizations with risk-sharing contracts under section 1876, offered in different areas and the election process provided under this section. During the period described in subparagraph (B)(iii), the Secretary shall provide for an educational and publicity campaign to inform MA eligible individuals about the availability of MA plans (including MA-PD plans) offered in different areas and the election process provided under this section.

(4) SPECIAL ELECTION PERIODS.—Effective as of January 1, 2006, an individual may discontinue an election of a Medicare + Choice plan offered by a Medicare + Choice organization other than during an annual, coordinated election period and make a new election under this section if—

* * *

(5) SPECIAL RULES FOR MSA PLANS.—Notwithstanding the preceding provisions of this subsection, an individual—

(A) may elect an MSA plan only during—

(i) an initial open enrollment period described in paragraph (1), or

(ii) an annual, coordinated election period described in paragraph (3)(B);

(iii) [Stricken.]

* * *

(f) EFFECTIVENESS OF ELECTIONS AND CHANGES OF ELECTIONS.—

(1) DURING INITIAL COVERAGE ELECTION PERIOD.—An election of coverage made during the initial coverage election period under subsection (e)(1) shall take effect upon the date the individual becomes entitled to benefits under part A and enrolled under part B, except as the Secretary may provide (consistent with section 1838) in order to prevent retroactive coverage.

* * *

(3) ANNUAL, COORDINATED ELECTION PERIOD.—An election or change of coverage made during an annual, coordinated election period (as defined in subsection (e)(3)(B)), other than the period described in clause (iii) of such subsection in a year shall take effect as of the first day of the following year.

* * *

(i) EFFECT OF ELECTION OF MEDICARE + CHOICE PLAN OPTION.—

(1) PAYMENTS TO ORGANIZATIONS.—Subject to sections 1852(a)(5), 1853(a)(4), 1853(g), 1853(h), 1886(d)(11), and 1886(h)(3)(D), payments under a contract with a Medicare + Choice organization under section 1853(a) with respect to an individual electing a Medicare + Choice plan offered by the organization shall be instead of the amounts which (in the absence of the contract) would otherwise be payable under parts A and B for items and services furnished to the individual.

(2) ONLY ORGANIZATION ENTITLED TO PAYMENT.—Subject to sections 1853(a)(4), 1853(e), 1853(g), 1853(h), 1857(f)(2), 1858(h), 1886(d)(11), and 1886(h)(3)(D), only the Medicare + Choice organization shall be entitled to receive payments from the Secretary under this title for services furnished to the individual.

[CCH Explanation at ¶ 200, 361, 376, 378, 380, and 390.]

2003 Amendments:

Section 102(a)(1) of the "Medicare Prescription Drug, Improvement, and Modernization Act of 2003," effective upon enactment, amended section 1851(e) in paragraph (2), by striking "2004" and "2005" and inserting "2005" and "2006" each place it appears; and in paragraph (3), by striking "2005" and inserting "2006" each place it appears.

Section 102(a)(2) of the "Medicare Prescription Drug, Improvement, and Modernization Act of 2003," effective upon enactment, amended section 1851(e)(3)(B).

Prior to amendment section 1851(e)(3)(B) read as follows:

(B) ANNUAL, COORDINATED ELECTION PERIOD.—For purposes of this section, the term "annual, coordinated election period" means, with respect to a year before 2003 and after 2005, the month of November before such year and with respect to 2003, 2004, and 2005, the period beginning on November 15 and ending on December 31 of the year before such year.

Section 102(a)(3) of the "Medicare Prescription Drug, Improvement, and Modernization Act of 2003," effective upon enactment, amended section 1851(e)(3) in subparagraph (C), by inserting "and during the period described in subparagraph (B)(iii)" after "(beginning with 1999)"; and in subparagraph (D) in the heading by striking "CAMPAIGN IN 1998" and inserting "CAMPAIGNS"; and in subparagraph (D) by adding at the end the following: "During the period described in subparagraph (B)(iii), the Secretary shall provide for an educational and publicity campaign to inform MA eligible individuals about the availability of MA plans (including MA-PD plans) offered in different areas and the election process provided under this section.".

Section 102(a)(4) of the "Medicare Prescription Drug, Improvement, and Modernization Act of 2003," effective upon enactment, amended section 1851(e)(1) by adding at the end the following new sentence: "If any portion of an individual's initial enrollment period under part B occurs after the end of the annual, coordinated election period described in paragraph (3)(B)(iii), the initial enrollment period under this part shall further extend through the end of the individual's initial enrollment period under part B.".

Section 102(a)(5) of the "Medicare Prescription Drug, Improvement, and Modernization Act of 2003," effective upon enactment, amended section 1851(f)(3) by inserting ", other than the period described in clause (iii) of such subsection" after "subsection (e)(3)(B)".

Section 102(a)(6) of the "Medicare Prescription Drug, Improvement, and Modernization Act of 2003," effective upon enactment, amended section 1851(e)(2) in subparagraph (B)(i), by inserting ", subparagraph (C)(iii)," after "clause (ii)"; in subparagraph (C)(i), by striking "clause (ii)" and inserting "clauses (ii) and (iii)"; and by adding at the end of subparagraph (C) new clause (iii).

Section 102(c) of the "Medicare Prescription Drug, Improvement, and Modernization Act of 2003," effective upon enactment, amended section 1851(a)(1) by inserting "(other than qualified prescription drug benefits)" after "benefits"; by striking the period at the end of subparagraph (B) and inserting a comma; and by adding after and below subparagraph (B) the following: "and may elect qualified prescription drug coverage in accordance with section 1860D-1.".

Section 221(a) of the "Medicare Prescription Drug, Improvement, and Modernization Act of 2003," effective upon enactment, amended section 1851(a)(2)(A) by striking "COORDINATED CARE PLANS.—Coordinated" and inserting the following: "COORDINATED CARE PLANS (INCLUDING REGIONAL PLANS).—(i) IN GENERAL.—Coordinated"; by inserting "regional or local" before "preferred provider organization plans"; and by inserting "(including MA regional plans)" after "preferred provider organization plans".

The above amendment applies to plan years beginning on or after January 1, 2006.

Section 221(d)(5) of the "Medicare Prescription Drug, Improvement, and Modernization Act of 2003," effective upon enactment, amended section 1851(i)(2) by inserting "1858(h)," after "1857(f)(2),".

The above amendment applies to plan years beginning on or after January 1, 2006.

Section 222(l)(3)(A) of the "Medicare Prescription Drug, Improvement, and Modernization Act of 2003," effective upon enactment, amended section 1851(b)(1) in subparagraph (B), by striking "a plan" and inserting "an MA local plan"; in subparagraph (B), by striking "basic benefits described in section 1852(a)(1)(A)" and inserting "benefits under the original medicare fee-for-service program option"; and in subparagraph (C), by striking "in a Medicare+Choice plan" and inserting "in an MA local plan".

The above amendment applies to plan years beginning on or after January 1, 2006.

Section 222(l)(3)(B)(i) of the "Medicare Prescription Drug, Improvement, and Modernization Act of 2003," effective upon enactment, amended section 1851(d) in paragraph (3), by adding at the end new subparagraph (F); in paragraph (4)(A)(ii), by inserting ", including information on the single deductible (if applicable) under section 1858(b)(1)" after "cost sharing"; in paragraph (4)(B)(i), by striking "Medicare+Choice monthly basic" and all that follows and inserting "monthly amount of the premium charged to an individual."; and amended subparagraph (E) of subsection (d)(4).

Prior to amendment section 1851(d)(4)(E) read as follows:

(E) SUPPLEMENTAL BENEFITS.—Whether the organization offering the plan includes mandatory supplemental benefits in its base benefit package or offers optional supplemental benefits and the terms and conditions (including premiums) for such coverage.

The above amendment applies to plan years beginning on or after January 1, 2006.

Section 222(l)(3)(D) of the "Medicare Prescription Drug, Improvement, and Modernization Act of 2003," effective upon enactment, amended section 1851(a)(3)(B)(ii) by striking "section 1851(e)(4)(A)" and inserting "subsection (e)(4)(A)".

The above amendment applies to plan years beginning on or after January 1, 2006.

Section 222(l)(3)(E) of the "Medicare Prescription Drug, Improvement, and Modernization Act of 2003," effective upon enactment, amended section 1851(f)(1) by striking "subsection (e)(1)(A)" and inserting "subsection (e)(1)".

The above amendment applies to plan years beginning on or after January 1, 2006.

Section 231(a) of the "Medicare Prescription Drug, Improvement, and Modernization Act of 2003," effective upon enactment, amended section 1851(a)(2)(A) by adding at the end new clause (ii).

Section 233(b) of the "Medicare Prescription Drug, Improvement, and Modernization Act of 2003," effective upon enactment, amended section 1851(b)(4) in the heading, by striking "ON A DEMONSTRATION BASIS"; by striking the first sentence of subparagraph (A); and by striking the second sentence of subparagraph (C).

Prior to amendment the first sentence of subparagraph (A) read as follows:

(A) An individual is not eligible to enroll in an MSA plan under this part—

(i) on or after January 1, 2003, unless the enrollment is the continuation of such an enrollment in effect as of such date; or

(ii) as of any date if the number of such individuals so enrolled as of such date has reached 390,000.

Prior to amendment the second sentence of subparagraph (C) read as follows:

The Secretary shall submit such a report, by not later than March 1, 2002, on whether the time limitation under subparagraph (A)(i) should be extended or removed and whether to change the numerical limitation under subparagraph (A)(ii).

Section 233(d)(1) of the "Medicare Prescription Drug, Improvement, and Modernization Act of 2003," effective upon enactment, amended section 1851(e)(5)(A) by adding "or" at the end of clause (i); by striking ", or" at the end of clause (ii) and inserting a semicolon; and by striking clause (iii).

Prior to being stricken clause (iii) read as follows:

(iii) the month of November 1998;

Section 237(b)(2)(A) of the "Medicare Prescription Drug, Improvement, and Modernization Act of 2003," effective upon enactment, amended section 1851(i) in paragraph (1), by inserting "1853(a)(4)," after "Subject to sections 1852(a)(5),"; and in paragraph (2), by inserting "1853(a)(4)," after "Subject to sections".

The above amendment applies to services provided on or after Jan. 1, 2006, and contract years beginning on or after such date.

[¶ 2256] Sec. 1852. BENEFITS AND BENEFICIARY PROTECTIONS
[42 U.S.C. § 1395w-22]

(a) BASIC BENEFITS.—

(1)(A) REQUIREMENT.— IN GENERAL.—Except as provided in section 1859(b)(3) for MSA plans, and except as provided in paragraph (6) for MA regional plans each Medicare + Choice plan shall provide to members enrolled under this part, through providers and other persons that meet the applicable requirements of this title and part A of title XI, benefits under the original medicare fee-for-service program option (and, for plan years before 2006, additional benefits required under section 1854(f)(1)(A)).

(B) BENEFITS UNDER THE ORIGINAL MEDICARE FEE-FOR-SERVICE PROGRAM OPTION DEFINED.—

(i) IN GENERAL.—For purposes of this part, the term 'benefits under the original medicare feefor-service program option' means those items and services (other than hospice care) for which benefits are available under parts A and B to individuals entitled to benefits under part A and enrolled under part B, with cost-sharing for those services as required under parts A and B or an actuarially equivalent level of cost-sharing as determined in this part.

(ii) SPECIAL RULE FOR REGIONAL PLANS.—In the case of an MA regional plan in determining an actuarially equivalent level of cost-sharing with respect to benefits under the original medicare fee-for-service program option, there shall only be taken into account, with respect to the application of section 1858(b)(2), such expenses only with respect to subparagraph (A) of such section.

(2) SATISFACTION OF REQUIREMENT.—

* * *

(C) ELECTION OF UNIFORM COVERAGE DETERMINATION.—In the case of a Medicare+Choice organization that offers a Medicare+Choice plan in an area in which more than one local coverage determinationis applied with respect to different parts of the area, the organization may elect to have the local coverage determinationfor the part of the area that is most beneficial to Medicare+Choice enrollees (as identified by the Secretary) apply with respect to all Medicare+Choice enrollees enrolled in the plan.

(3) SUPPLEMENTAL BENEFITS.—

* * *

(C) APPLICATION TO MEDICARE + CHOICE PRIVATE FEE-FOR-SERVICE PLANS.—Nothing in this paragraph shall be construed as preventing a Medicare + Choice private fee-for-service plan from offering supplemental benefits that include payment for some or all of the balance billing amounts permitted consistent with section 1852(k) and coverage of additional services that the plan finds to be medically necessary. Such benefits may include reductions in cost-sharing below the actuarial value specified in section 1854(e)(4)(B).

* * *

(5) NATIONAL COVERAGE DETERMINATIONS AND LEGISLATIVE CHANGES IN BENEFITS.—If there is a national coverage determination or legislative change in benefits required to be provided under this part made in the period beginning on the date of an announcement under section 1853(b) and ending on the date of the next announcement under such section and the Secretary projects that the determination will result in a significant change in the costs to a Medicare + Choice organization of providing the benefits that are the subject of such national coverage determination and that such change in costs was not incorporated in the determination of the annual Medicare + Choice capitation rate under section 1853 included in the announcement made at the beginning of such period, then, unless otherwise required by law—

* * *

The projection under the previous sentence shall be based on an analysis by the Chief Actuary of the Centers for Medicare & Medicaid Services of the actuarial costs associated with the coverage determination or legislative change in benefits.

(6) SPECIAL BENEFIT RULES FOR REGIONAL PLANS.—In the case of an MA plan that is an MA regional plan, benefits under the plan shall include the benefits described in paragraphs (1) and (2) of section 1858(b).

(b) ANTIDISCRIMINATION.—

(1) BENEFICIARIES.—

(A) IN GENERAL.—A Medicare + Choice organization may not deny, limit, or condition the coverage or provision of benefits under this part, for individuals permitted to be enrolled with the organization under this part, based on any health status-related factor described in section 2702(a)(1) of the Public Health Service Act. The Secretary shall not approve a plan of an organization if the Secretary determines that the design of the plan and its benefits are likely to substantially discourage enrollment by certain MA eligible individuals with the organization.

* * *

(c) DISCLOSURE REQUIREMENTS.—

(1) DETAILED DESCRIPTION OF PLAN PROVISIONS.—A Medicare + Choice organization shall disclose, in clear, accurate, and standardized form to each enrollee with a Medicare + Choice plan offered by the organization under this part at the time of enrollment and at least annually thereafter, the following information regarding such plan:

* * *

(I) QUALITY IMPROVEMENT PROGRAM.—A description of the organization's quality improvement program under subsection (e) if required under such section.

* * *

(d) ACCESS TO SERVICES.—

* * *

(4) ASSURING ACCESS TO SERVICES IN MEDICARE + CHOICE PRIVATE FEE-FOR-SERVICE PLANS.—In addition to any other requirements under this part, in the case of a Medicare + Choice private fee-for-service plan, the organization offering the plan must demonstrate to the Secretary that the organization has sufficient number and range of health care professionals and providers willing to provide services under the terms of the plan. The Secretary shall find that an organization has met such requirement with respect to any category of health care professional or provider if. with respect to that category of provider—

* * *

(B) the plan has contracts or agreements (other than deemed contracts or agreements under subsection (j)(6)) with a sufficient number and range of providers within such category to provide covered services under the terms of the plan,

or a combination of both.
The previous sentence shall not be construed as restricting the persons from whom enrollees under such a plan may obtain covered benefits, except that, if a plan entirely meets such requirement with respect to a category of health care professional or provider on the basis of subparagraph (B), it may provide for a higher beneficiary copayment in the case of health care professionals and providers of that category who do not have contracts or agreements (other than deemed contracts or agreements under subsection (j)(6)) to provide covered services under the terms of the plan.

(e) QUALITY IMPROVEMENT PROGRAM.—

(1) IN GENERAL.—Each MA organization shall have an ongoing quality improvement program for the purpose of improving the quality of care provided to enrollees in each MA plan offered by such organization (other than an MA private fee-for-service plan or an MSA plan).

(2) CHRONIC CARE IMPROVEMENT PROGRAMS.—As part of the quality improvement program under paragraph (1), each MA organization shall have a chronic care improvement program. Each chronic care improvement program shall have a method for monitoring and identifying

enrollees with multiple or sufficiently severe chronic conditions that meet criteria established by the organization for participation under the program.

(3) DATA.—

(A) COLLECTION, ANALYSIS, AND REPORTING.—

(i) IN GENERAL.—Except as provided in clauses (ii) and (iii) with respect to plans described in such clauses and subject to subparagraph (B), as part of the quality improvement program under paragraph (1), each MA organization shall provide for the collection, analysis, and reporting of data that permits the measurement of health outcomes and other indices of quality.

(ii) APPLICATION TO MA REGIONAL PLANS.—The Secretary shall establish as appropriate by regulation requirements for the collection, analysis, and reporting of data that permits the measurement of health outcomes and other indices of quality for MA organizations with respect to MA regional plans. Such requirements may not exceed the requirements under this subparagraph with respect to MA local plans that are preferred provider organization plans.

(iii) APPLICATION TO PREFERRED PROVIDER ORGANIZATIONS.—Clause (i) shall apply to MA organizations with respect to MA local plans that are preferred provider organization plans only insofar as services are furnished by providers or services, physicians, and other health care practitioners and suppliers that have contracts with such organization to furnish services under such plans.

(iv) DEFINITION OF PREFERRED PROVIDER ORGANIZATION PLAN.—In this subparagraph, the term 'preferred provider organization plan' means an MA plan that—

(I) has a network of providers that have agreed to a contractually specified reimbursement for covered benefits with the organization offering the plan;

(II) provides for reimbursement for all covered benefits regardless of whether such benefits are provided within such network of providers; and

(III) is offered by an organization that is not licensed or organized under State law as a health maintenance organization.

(B) LIMITATIONS.—

(i) TYPES OF DATA.—The Secretary shall not collect under subparagraph (A) data on quality, outcomes, and beneficiary satisfaction to facilitate consumer choice and program administration other than the types of data that were collected by the Secretary as of November 1, 2003.

(ii) CHANGES IN TYPES OF DATA.—Subject to subclause (iii), the Secretary may only change the types of data that are required to be submitted under subparagraph (A) after submitting to Congress a report on the reasons for such changes that was prepared in consultation with MA organizations and private accrediting bodies.

(iii) CONSTRUCTION.—Nothing in the subsection shall be construed as restricting the ability of the Secretary to carry out the duties under section 1851(d)(4)(D);

(4) TREATMENT OF ACCREDITATION.—

* * *

(B) REQUIREMENTS DESCRIBED.—The provisions described in this subparagraph are the following:

(i) Paragraphs (1) through (3) of this subsection (relating to quality improvement programs).

* * *

(vii) The requirements described in section 1860D-4(j), to the extent such requirements apply under section 1860D-21(c).

* * *
* * *

§1852(e)(4)(B)(vii)   ¶2256

(g) Coverage Determinations, Reconsiderations, and Appeals.—

* * *

(5) Appeals.—An enrollee with a Medicare + Choice plan of a Medicare + Choice organization under this part who is dissatisfied by reason of the enrollee's failure to receive any health service to which the enrollee believes the enrollee is entitled and at no greater charge than the enrollee believes the enrollee is required to pay is entitled, if the amount in controversy is $100 or more, to a hearing before the Secretary to the same extent as is provided in section 205(b), and in any such hearing the Secretary shall make the organization a party. If the amount in controversy is $1,000 or more, the individual or organization shall, upon notifying the other party, be entitled to judicial review of the Secretary's final decision as provided in section 205(g), and both the individual and the organization shall be entitled to be parties to that judicial review. In applying subsections (b) and (g) of section 205 as provided in this paragraph, and in applying section 205(l) thereto, any reference therein to the Commissioner of Social Security or the Social Security Administration shall be considered a reference to the Secretary or the Department of Health and Human Services, respectively The provisions of section 1869(b)(1)(E)(iii) shall apply with respect to dollar amounts specified in the first 2 sentences of this paragraph in the same manner as they apply to the dollar amounts specified in section 1869(b)(1)(E)(i).

* * *

(j) Rules Regarding Provider Participation.—

* * *

(4) Limitations on Physician Incentive Plans.—

(A) In general.—No Medicare + Choice organization may operate any physician incentive plan (as defined in subparagraph (B)) unless the organization provides assurances satisfactory to the Secretary that the following requirements are met:

* * *

(ii) If the plan places a physician or physician group at substantial financial risk (as determined by the Secretary) for services not provided by the physician or physician group, the organization provides stop-loss protection for the physician or group that is adequate and appropriate, based on standards developed by the Secretary that take into account the number of physicians placed at such substantial financial risk in the group or under the plan and the number of individuals enrolled with the organization who receive services from the physician or group.

* * *

(7) Promotion of E-Prescribing by MA Plans.—

(A) In general.—An MA-PD plan may provide for a separate payment or otherwise provide for a differential payment for a participating physician that prescribes covered part D drugs in accordance with an electronic prescription drug program that meets standards established under section 1860D-4(e).

(B) Considerations.—Such payment may take into consideration the costs of the physician in implementing such a program and may also be increased for those participating physicians who significantly increase—

(i) formulary compliance;

(ii) lower cost, therapeutically equivalent alternatives;

(iii) reductions in adverse drug interactions; and

(iv) efficiencies in filing prescriptions through reduced administrative costs.

(C) Structure.—Additional or increased payments under this subsection may be structured in the same manner as medication therapy management fees are structured under section 1860D-4(c)(2)(E).

(k) Treatment of Services Furnished by Certain Providers.—

(1) In general.—Except as provided in paragraph (2), a physician or other entity (other than a provider of services) that does not have a contract establishing payment amounts for services

furnished to an individual enrolled under this part with a Medicare + Choice organization described in section 1851(a)(2)(A) or with an organization offering an MSA plan shall accept as payment in full for covered services under this title that are furnished to such an individual the amounts that the physician or other entity could collect if the individual were not so enrolled. Any penalty or other provision of law that applies to such a payment with respect to an individual entitled to benefits under this title (but not enrolled with a Medicare + Choice organization under this part) also applies with respect to an individual so enrolled.

* * *

[CCH Explanation at ¶ 200, 360, 365, 372, 376, 380, 800, 801, 916, and 948.]

2003 Amendments:

Section 102(b) of the "Medicare Prescription Drug, Improvement, and Modernization Act of 2003," effective upon enactment, amended section 1852(j) by adding at the end new subparagrah (7).

Section 211(j) of the "Medicare Prescription Drug, Improvement, and Modernization Act of 2003," effective upon enactment, amended section 1852(d)(4)(B) by inserting "(other than deemed contracts or agreements under subsection (j)(6))" after "the plan has contracts or agreements", and in the last sentence, by inserting before the period at the end the following: ", except that, if a plan entirely meets such requirement with respect to a category of health care professional or provider on the basis of subparagraph (B), it may provide for a higher beneficiary copayment in the case of health care professionals and providers of that category who do not have contracts or agreements (other than deemed contracts or agreements under subsection (j)(6)) to provide covered services under the terms of the plan".

Section 221(d)(3) of the "Medicare Prescription Drug, Improvement, and Modernization Act of 2003," amended section 1852(a)(1) by inserting "and except as provided in paragraph (6) for MA regional plans" after "MSA plans", and by adding new paragraph (6).

The above amendment applies to plan years beginning on or after January 1, 2006.

Section 222(a)(2) of the "Medicare Prescription Drug, Improvement, and Modernization Act of 2003," effective upon enactment, amended section 1852(a)(1) by striking "IN GENERAL.—Except" and inserting "REQUIREMENT.— .(A) IN GENERAL.—Except" and by striking "title XI" and all that follows and inserting the following: "title XI, benefits under the original medicare fee-for-service program option (and, for plan years before 2006, additional benefits required under section 1854(f)(1)(A))" and new subsection (B).

Prior to amendment, section 1852(a)(1)(A) and (B) read as follows:

(A) those items and services (other than hospice care) for which benefits are available under parts A and B to individuals residing in the area served by the plan, and

(B) additional benefits required under section 1854(f)(1)(A).

Section 222(a)(3) of the "Medicare Prescription Drug, Improvement, and Modernization Act of 2003," amended section 1852(a)(3) by adding at the end the following: "Such benefits may include reductions in cost-sharing below the actuarial value specified in section 1854(e)(4)(B).".

The above amendment applies to plan years beginning on or after January 1, 2006.

Section 222(h)(1)of the "Medicare Prescription Drug, Improvement, and Modernization Act of 2003," amended section 1852(j)(4) by inserting "the organization provides assurances satisfactory to the Secretary that" after "unless".

The above amendment applies to plan years beginning on or after January 1, 2006.

Section 222(h)(2) of the "Medicare Prescription Drug, Improvement, and Modernization Act of 2003," amended section 1852(j)(4)(ii) by striking "the organization—"and all that follows through "(I) provides" and inserting "the organization provides"; by striking ", and" and inserting a period; and by striking subclause (II).

Prior to amendment, subclause (II) read as follows:

(II) conducts periodic surveys of both individuals enrolled and individuals previously enrolled with the organization to determine the degree of access of such individuals to services provided by the organization and satisfaction with the quality of such services.

The above amendment applies to plan years beginning on or after January 1, 2006.

Section 222(h)(3) of the "Medicare Prescription Drug, Improvement, and Modernization Act of 2003," amended section 1852(j)(4) by striking clause (iii).

Prior to being striken, clause (iii) read as follows:

(iii) The organization provides the Secretary with descriptive information regarding the plan, sufficient to permit the Secretary to determine whether the plan is in compliance with the requirements of this subparagraph.

The above amendment applies to plan years beginning on or after January 1, 2006.

Section 222(l)(1)of the "Medicare Prescription Drug, Improvement, and Modernization Act of 2003," amended section 1852(b)(1)(A) is amended by adding at the end the following: "The Secretary shall not approve a plan of an organization if the Secretary determines that the design of the plan and its benefits are likely to substantially discourage enrollment by certain MA eligible individuals with the organization.".

The above amendment applies to plan years beginning on or after January 1, 2006.

Section 233(a) of the "Medicare Prescription Drug, Improvement, and Modernization Act of 2003," amended section 1852(e)(1) by inserting "(other than MSA plans)" after "plans"; amended section 1852(c)(1)(I) by inserting before the period at the end the following: ", if required under such section"; amended section 1852(e)(2)(A) by striking ", a nonnetwork MSA plan,"; amended section 1852(e)(2)(B) by striking ", NONNETWORK MSA PLANS," and ", a nonnetwork MSA plan,".

The amendments made by section 233(a) of the "Medicare Prescription Drug, Improvement, and Modernization Act of 2003," apply on and after the date of enactment of the Act but do not apply to contract years beginning on or after January 1, 2006.

Section 233(c) of the "Medicare Prescription Drug, Improvement, and Modernization Act of 2003," effective upon enactment, amended section 1852(k)(1) by inserting "or with an organization offering an MSA plan" after "section 1851(a)(2)(A)".

Section 722(a)(1) of the "Medicare Prescription Drug, Improvement, and Modernization Act of 2003," amended section 1852(e) by striking "ASSURANCE" and inserting "IMPROVEMENT" in the heading.

The amendments made by section 722(a)(1) of the "Medicare Prescription Drug, Improvement, and Modernization Act of 2003," apply with respect to contract years beginning on and after January 1, 2006.

Section 722(a)(2) of the "Medicare Prescription Drug, Improvement, and Modernization Act of 2003," amended section 1852(e)(1) through (3). to read as follows:

The amendments made by section 722(a)(2) of the "Medicare Prescription Drug, Improvement, and Modernization Act of 2003," apply with respect to contract years beginning on and after January 1, 2006.

Prior to amendment, 1852(e)(1) — (3) read as follows:

(1) In general.—Each Medicare + Choice organization must have arrangements, consistent with any regulation, for an ongoing quality assurance program for health care services it provides to individuals enrolled with Medicare + Choice plans (other than MSA plans) of the organization.

(2) (A) In general.—The quality assurance program of an organization with respect to a Medicare + Choice plan (other than a Medicare + Choice private fee-for-service plan or a preferred provider organization plan) it offers shall—

(i) stress health outcomes and provide for the collection, analysis, and reporting of data (in accordance with a quality measurement system that the Secretary recognizes) that will permit measurement of outcomes and other indices of the quality of Medicare + Choice plans and organizations;

(ii) monitor and evaluate high volume and high risk services and the care of acute and chronic conditions;

(iii) evaluate the continuity and coordination of care that enrollees receive;

(iv) be evaluated on an ongoing basis as to its effectiveness;

(v) include measures of consumer satisfaction;

(vi) provide the Secretary with such access to information collected as may be appropriate to monitor and ensure the quality of care provided under this part;

(vii) provide review by physicians and other health care professionals of the process followed in the provision of such health care services;

(viii) provide for the establishment of written protocols for utilization review, based on current standards of medical practice;

(ix) have mechanisms to detect both underutilization and overutilization of services;

(x) after identifying areas for improvement, establish or alter practice parameters;

(xi) take action to improve quality and assesses the effectiveness of such action through systematic followup; and

(xii) make available information on quality and outcomes measures to facilitate beneficiary comparison and choice of health coverage options (in such form and on such quality and outcomes measures as the Secretary determines to be appropriate).

Such program shall include a separate focus (with respect to all the elements described in this subparagraph) on racial and ethnic minorities.

ELEMENTS OF PROGRAM FOR ORGANIZATIONS OFFERING MEDICARE + CHOICE PRIVATE FEE-FOR-SERVICE PLANS, AND PREFERRED PROVIDER ORGANIZATION PLANS

The quality assurance program of an organization with respect to a Medicare + Choice private fee-for-service plan, or a preferred provider organization plan it offers shall—

(i) meet the requirements of clauses (i) through (vi) of subparagraph (A);

(ii) insofar as it provides for the establishment of written protocols for utilization review. base such protocols on current standards of medical practice; and

(iii) have mechanisms to evaluate utilization of services and inform providers and enrollees of the results of such evaluation.

Such program shall include a separate focus (with respect to all the elements described in this subparagraph) on racial and ethnic minorities.

(C) DEFINITION OF NON-NETWORK MSA PLAN

In this subsection, the term "non-network MSA plan" means an MSA plan offered by a Medicare + Choice organization that does not provide benefits required to be provided by this part, in whole or in part, through a defined set of providers under contract, or under another arrangement, with the organization.

(D) DEFINITION OF PREFERRED PROVIDER ORGANIZATION PLAN

In this paragraph, the term 'preferred provider organization plan' means a Medicare+Choice plan that—

(i) has a network of providers that have agreed to a contractually specified reimbursement for covered benefits with the organization offering the plan;

(ii) provides for reimbursement for all covered benefits regardless of whether such benefits are provided within such network of providers; and

(iii) is offered by an organization that is not licensed or organized under State law as a health maintenance organization.

(3) EXTERNAL REVIEW

(A) IN GENERAL.—Each Medicare + Choice organization shall, for each Medicare + Choice plan it operates, have an agreement with an independent quality review and improvement organization approved by the Secretary to perform functions of the type described in sections 1154(a)(4)(B) and 1154(a)(14) with respect to services furnished by Medicare + Choice plans for which payment is made under this title. The previous sentence shall not apply to a Medicare + Choice private fee-for-service plan or a non-network MSA plan that does not employ utilization review.

(B) NONDUPLICATION OF ACCREDITATION.—Except in the case of the review of quality complaints, and consistent with subparagraph (C), the Secretary shall ensure that the external review activities conducted under subparagraph (A) are not duplicative of review activities conducted as part of the accreditation process.

(C) WAIVER AUTHORITY.—The Secretary may waive the requirement described in subparagraph (A) in the case of an organization if the Secretary determines that the organization has consistently maintained an excellent record of quality assurance and compliance with other requirements under this part.

Section 722(a)(3)(A) of the "Medicare Prescription Drug, Improvement, and Modernization Act of 2003," amended section 1852(e)(4)(B)(i) by amending clause (i).

The amendments made by section 722(a)(3) of the "Medicare Prescription Drug, Improvement, and Modernization Act of 2003," apply with respect to contract years beginning on and after January 1, 2006.

Prior to amendment, clause (i) read as follows:

Paragraphs (1) and (2) of this subsection (relating to quality assurance programs).

Section 722(a)(3)(B) of the "Medicare Prescription Drug, Improvement, and Modernization Act of 2003," amended section 1852(e)(4)(B)(vii) by adding at the end the following new clause:

"(vii) The requirements described in section 1860D-4(j), to the extent such requirements apply under section 1860D-21(c)."

The amendments made by section 722(a)(3) of the "Medicare Prescription Drug, Improvement, and Modernization Act of 2003," apply with respect to contract years beginning on and after January 1, 2006.

Section 722(a)(4) of the "Medicare Prescription Drug, Improvement, and Modernization Act of 2003," amended section 1852(e)(5) by striking paragraph (5).

The amendments made by section 722(a)(4) of the "Medicare Prescription Drug, Improvement, and Modernization Act of 2003," apply with respect to contract years beginning on and after January 1, 2006.

Section 722(b) of the "Medicare Prescription Drug, Improvement, and Modernization Act of 2003," amended section 1852(c)(1)(I).

The amendments made by section 722(b) of the "Medicare Prescription Drug, Improvement, and Modernization Act of 2003," apply with respect to contract years beginning on and after January 1, 2006.

Prior to amendment 1852(c)(1)(I) read as follows:

"(I) Quality Assurance Program.—A description of the organization's quality assurance program under subsection (e)."

Section 900(e)(1)(F) of the "Medicare Prescription Drug, Improvement, and Modernization Act of 2003," effective upon enactment, amended section 1852(a)(5) by striking "Health Care Financing Administration" in the matter following subparagraph (B) and inserting "Centers for Medicare & Medicaid Services".

Section 940(b)(2)(A)of the "Medicare Prescription Drug, Improvement, and Modernization Act of 2003," effective upon enactment, amended section 1852(g)(5) by adding at the end the following:

"The provisions of section 1869(b)(1)(E)(iii) shall apply with respect to dollar amounts specified in the first 2 sentences of this paragraph in the same manner as they apply to the dollar amounts specified in section 1869(b)(1)(E)(i)."

Section 948(b)(2)(B) of the "Medicare Prescription Drug, Improvement, and Modernization Act of 2003," effective upon enactment, amended section 1852(a)(2)(C) by striking "policy" and "POLICY" and inserting "determination" each place it appears and "DETERMINATION", respectively.

[¶2256A] Sec. 1853. PAYMENTS TO MEDICARE + CHOICE ORGANIZATIONS

[42 U.S.C. § 1395w-23]

(a) PAYMENTS TO ORGANIZATIONS.—

(1) MONTHLY PAYMENTS.—

(A) IN GENERAL.—Under a contract under section 1857 and subject to subsections (e), (g) and (i) and section 1859(e)(4), the Secretary shall make monthly payments under this section in advance to each Medicare + Choice organization, with respect to coverage of an individual under this part in a Medicare + Choice payment area for a month, in an amount determined as follows:

(i) PAYMENT BEFORE 2006.—For years before 2006, the payment amount shall be equal to 112 of the annual MA capitation rate (as calculated under subsection (c)(1)) with respect to that individual for that area, adjusted under subparagraph (C) and reduced by the amount of any reduction elected under section 1854(f)(1)(E).

(ii) PAYMENT FOR ORIGINAL FEE-FOR-SERVICE BENEFITS BEGINNING WITH 2006.—For years beginning with 2006, the amount specified in subparagraph (B).

(B) PAYMENT AMOUNT FOR ORIGINAL FEE-FORSERVICE BENEFITS BEGINNING WITH 2006.—

(i) PAYMENT OF BID FOR PLANS WITH BIDS BELOW BENCHMARK.—In the case of a plan for which there are average per capita monthly savings described in section 1854(b)(3)(C) or 1854(b)(4)(C), as the case may be, the amount specified in this subparagraph is equal to the unadjusted MA statutory non-drug monthly bid amount, adjusted under subparagraph (C) and (if applicable) under subparagraphs (F) and (G), plus the amount (if any) of any rebate under subparagraph (E).

(ii) PAYMENT OF BENCHMARK FOR PLANS WITH BIDS AT OR ABOVE BENCHMARK.—In the case of a plan for which there are no average per capita monthly savings described in section 1854(b)(3)(C) or 1854(b)(4)(C), as the case may be, the amount specified in this subparagraph is equal to the MA area-specific non-drug monthly benchmark amount, adjusted under subparagraph (C) and (if applicable) under subparagraphs (F) and (G).

(iii) PAYMENT OF BENCHMARK FOR MSA PLANS.—Notwithstanding clauses (i) and (ii), in the case of an MSA plan, the amount specified in this subparagraph is equal to the MA area-specific non-drug monthly benchmark amount, adjusted under subparagraph (C).

(C) DEMOGRAPHIC ADJUSTMENT, INCLUDING ADJUSTMENT FOR HEALTH STATUS.—The Secretary shall adjust the payment amount under subparagraph (A)(i) and the amount specified under subparagraph (B)(i), (B)(ii), and (B)(iii) for such risk factors as age, disability status, gender, institutional status, and such other factors as the Secretary determines to be appropriate, including adjustment for health status under paragraph (3), so as to ensure actuarial equivalence. The Secretary may add to, modify, or substitute for such adjustment factors if such changes will improve the determination of actuarial equivalence.

§1853(a)(1)(C) ¶2256A

(D) SEPARATE PAYMENT FOR FEDERAL DRUG SUBSIDIES.—In the case of an enrollee in an MA-PD plan, the MA organization offering such plan also receives—

(i) subsidies under section 1860D-15 (other than under subsection (g)); and

(ii) reimbursement for premium and costsharing reductions for low-income individuals under section 1860D-14(c)(1)(C).

(E) PAYMENT OF REBATE FOR PLANS WITH BIDS BELOW BENCHMARK.—In the case of a plan for which there are average per capita monthly savings described in section 1854(b)(3)(C) or 1854(b)(4)(C), as the case may be, the amount specified in this subparagraph is the amount of the monthly rebate computed under section 1854(b)(1)(C)(i) for that plan and year (as reduced by the amount of any credit provided under section 1854(b)(1)(C)(iv)).

(F) ADJUSTMENT FOR INTRA-AREA VARIATIONS.—

(i) INTRA-REGIONAL VARIATIONS.—In the case of payment with respect to an MA regional plan for an MA region, the Secretary shall also adjust the amounts specified under subparagraphs (B)(i) and (B)(ii) in a manner to take into account variations in MA local payment rates under this part among the different MA local areas included in such region.

(ii) INTRA-SERVICE AREA VARIATIONS.—In the case of payment with respect to an MA local plan for a service area that covers more than one MA local area, the Secretary shall also adjust the amounts specified under subparagraphs (B)(i) and (B)(ii) in a manner to take into account variations in MA local payment rates under this part among the different MA local areas included in such service area.

(G) ADJUSTMENT RELATING TO RISK ADJUSTMENT.—The Secretary shall adjust payments with respect to MA plans as necessary to ensure that—

(i) the sum of—

(I) the monthly payment made under subparagraph (A)(ii); and

(II) the MA monthly basic beneficiary premium under section 1854(b)(2)(A); equals

(ii) the unadjusted MA statutory non-drug monthly bid amount, adjusted in the manner described in subparagraph (C) and, for an MA regional plan, subparagraph (F).

(H) SPECIAL RULE FOR END-STAGE RENAL DISEASE.—The Secretary shall establish separate rates of payment to a Medicare + Choice organization with respect to classes of individuals determined to have endstage renal disease and enrolled in a Medicare + Choice plan of the organization. Such rates of payment shall be actuarially equivalent to rates that would have been paid with respect to other enrollees in the MA payment area (or such other area as specified by the Secretary) under the provisions of this section as in effect before the date of the enactment of the Medicare Prescription Drug, Improvement, and Modernization Act of 2003.In accordance with regulations, the Secretary shall provide for the application of the seventh sentence of section. 1881(b)(7) to payments under this section covering the provision of renal dialysis treatment in the same manner as such sentence applies to composite rate payments described in such sentence. In establishing such rates, the Secretary shall provide for appropriate adjustments to increase each rate to reflect the demonstration rate (including the risk adjustment methodology associated with such rate) of the social health maintenance organization end-stage renal disease capitation demonstrations (established by section 2355 of the Deficit Reduction Act of 1984, as amended by section 13567(b) of the Omnibus Budget Reconciliation Act of 1993), and shall compute such rates by taking into account such factors as renal treatment modality, age, and the underlying cause of the end-stage renal disease. The Secretary may apply the competitive bidding methodology provided for in this section, with appropriate adjustments to account for the risk adjustment methodology applied to end stage renal disease payments.

* * *

(3) ESTABLISHMENT OF RISK ADJUSTMENT FACTORS.—

* * *

(C)

* * *

(ii) PHASE-IN.—Except as provided in clause (iv), such risk adjustment methodology shall be implemented in a phased-in manner so that the methodology insofar as it makes adjustments to capitation rates for health status applies to—

* * *

(4) PAYMENT RULE FOR FEDERALLY QUALIFIED HEALTH CENTER SERVICES.—If an individual who is enrolled with an MA plan under this part receives a service from a Federally qualified health center that has a written agreement with the MA organization that offers such plan for providing such a service (including any agreement required under section 1857(e)(3))—

(A) the Secretary shall pay the amount determined under section 1833(a)(3)(B) directly to the Federally qualified health center not less frequently than quarterly; and

(B) the Secretary shall not reduce the amount of the monthly payments under this subsection as a result of the application of subparagraph (A).

(b) ANNUAL ANNOUNCEMENT OF PAYMENT RATES.—

(1) ANNUAL ANNOUNCEMENTS.—

(A) FOR 2005.—The Secretary shall determine, and shall announce (in a manner intended to provide notice to interested parties), not later than the second Monday in May of 2004, with respect to each MA payment area, the following:

(i) MA CAPITATION RATES.—The annual MA capitation rate for each MA payment area for 2005.

(ii) ADJUSTMENT FACTORS.—The risk and other factors to be used in adjusting such rates under subsection (a)(1)(C) for payments for months in 2005.

(B) FOR 2006 AND SUBSEQUENT YEARS.—For a year after 2005—

(i) INITIAL ANNOUNCEMENT.—The Secretary shall determine, and shall announce (in a manner intended to provide notice to interested parties), not later than the first Monday in April before the calendar year concerned, with respect to each MA payment area, the following:

(I) MA CAPITATION RATES; MA LOCAL AREA BENCHMARK.—The annual MA capitation rate for each MA payment area for the year.

(II) ADJUSTMENT FACTORS.—The risk and other factors to be used in adjusting such rates under subsection (a)(1)(C) for payments for months in such year.

(ii) REGIONAL BENCHMARK ANNOUNCEMENT.—The Secretary shall determine, and shall announce (in a manner intended to provide notice to interested parties), on a timely basis before the calendar year concerned, with respect to each MA region and each MA regional plan for which a bid was submitted under section 1854, the MA region-specific non-drug monthly benchmark amount for that region for the year involved; and

(iii) BENCHMARK ANNOUNCEMENT FOR CCA LOCAL AREAS.—The Secretary shall determine, and shall announce (in a manner intended to provide notice to interested parties), on a timely basis before the calendar year concerned, with respect to each CCA area (as defined in section 1860C-1(b)(1)(A)), the CCA non-drug monthly benchmark amount under section 1860C-1(e)(1) for that area for the year involved.

(2) ADVANCE NOTICE OF METHODOLOGICAL CHANGES.—At least 45 days before making the announcement under paragraph (1) for a year, the Secretary shall provide for notice to Medicare + Choice organizations of proposed changes to be made in the methodology from the methodology and assumptions used in the previous announcement and shall provide such organizations an opportunity to comment on such proposed changes.

(3) EXPLANATION OF ASSUMPTIONS.—In each announcement made under paragraph (1), the Secretary shall include an explanation of the assumptions and changes in methodology used in such announcement.

(4) CONTINUED COMPUTATION AND PUBLICATION OF COUNTY-SPECIFIC PER CAPITA FEE-FOR-SERVICE EXPENDITURE INFORMATION.—The Secretary, through the Chief Actuary of the Centers for Medicare & Medicaid Services, shall provide for the computation and publication, on an annual basis beginning with 2001 at the time of publication of the annual Medicare+Choice capitation rates under paragraph (1), of the following information for the original medicare fee-for-service program under parts A and B (exclusive of individuals eligible for coverage under section 226A) for each Medicare+Choice payment area for the second calendar year ending before the date of publication:

* * *

(c) CALCULATION OF ANNUAL MEDICARE + CHOICE CAPITATION RATES.—

(1) IN GENERAL.—For purposes of this part, subject to paragraphs (6)(C) and (7), each annual Medicare + Choice capitation rate, for a Medicare + Choice payment areathat is an MA local area for a contract year consisting of a calendar year, is equal to the largest of the amounts specified in the following subparagraph (A), (B), (C), or (D):

(A) BLENDED CAPITATION RATE.—For a year before 2005, the sum of—

* * *

(ii) the national percentage (as specified under paragraph (2) for the year) of the input-price-adjusted annual national Medicare + Choice capitation rate, as determined under paragraph (4) for the year.

multiplied (for a year other than 2004) by the budget neutrality adjustment factor determined under paragraph (5).

(B) MINIMUM AMOUNT.—12 multiplied by the following amount:

* * *

(iv) For 2002 2003, and 2004, the minimum amount specified in this clause (or clause (iii)) for the preceding year increased by the national per capita Medicare + Choice growth percentage, described in paragraph (6)(A) for that succeeding year.

(C) MINIMUM PERCENTAGE INCREASE.—

* * *

(iv) For 2002 and 2003, 102 percent of the annual Medicare + Choice capitation rate under this paragraph for the area for the previous year.

(v) For 2004 and each succeeding year, the greater of—

(I) 102 percent of the annual MA capitation rate under this paragraph for the area for the previous year; or

(II) the annual MA capitation rate under this paragraph for the area for the previous year increased by the national per capita MA growth percentage, described in paragraph (6) for that succeeding year, but not taking into account any adjustment under paragraph (6)(C) for a year before 2004.

(D) 100 PERCENT OF FEE-FOR-SERVICE COSTS.—

(i) IN GENERAL.—For each year specified in clause (ii), the adjusted average per capita cost for the year involved, determined under section 1876(a)(4) and adjusted as appropriate for the purpose of risk adjustment, for the MA payment area for individuals who are not enrolled in an MA plan under this part for the year, but adjusted to exclude costs attributable to payments under section 1886(h).

(ii) PERIODIC REBASING.—The provisions of clause (i) shall apply for 2004 and for subsequent years as the Secretary shall specify (but not less than once every 3 years).

(iii) INCLUSION OF COSTS OF VA AND DOD MILITARY FACILITY SERVICES TO MEDICARE-ELIGIBLE BENEFICIARIES.—In determining the adjusted average per capita cost under clause (i) for a year, such cost shall be adjusted to include the Secretary's estimate, on a per capita basis, of the amount of additional payments that would have been made in the area involved under this title if individuals entitled to benefits under this title had not received services from facilities of the Department of Defense or the Department of Veterans Affairs.

* * *

(3) ANNUAL AREA-SPECIFIC MEDICARE + CHOICE CAPITATION RATE.—

(A) IN GENERAL.—For purposes of paragraph (1)(A), subject to subparagraphs (B) and (E), the annual area-specific Medicare + Choice capitation rate for a Medicare + Choice payment area—

* * *

(E) INCLUSION OF COSTS OF DOD AND VA MILITARY FACILITY SERVICES TO MEDICARE-ELIGIBLE BENEFICIARIES.—In determining the area-specific MA capitation rate under subparagraph (A) for a year (beginning with 2004), the annual per capita rate of payment for 1997 determined under section 1876(a)(1)(C) shall be adjusted to include in the rate the Secretary's estimate, on a per capita basis, of the amount of additional payments that would have been made in the area involved under this title if individuals entitled to benefits under this title had not received services from facilities of the Department of Defense or the Department of Veterans Affairs.

* * *

(5) PAYMENT ADJUSTMENT BUDGET NEUTRALITY FACTOR.—For purposes of paragraph (1)(A), for each year (other than 2004), the Secretary shall determine a budget neutrality adjustment factor so that the aggregate of the payments under this part (other than those attributable to subsections (a)(3)(C)(iv) and (i)) shall equal the aggregate payments that would have been made under this part if payment were based entirely on area-specific capitation rates.

(6) NATIONAL PER CAPITA MEDICARE + CHOICE GROWTH PERCENTAGE DEFINED.—

* * *

(C) ADJUSTMENT FOR OVER OR UNDER PROJECTION OF NATIONAL PER CAPITA MEDICARE+CHOICE GROWTH PERCENTAGE.—Beginning with rates calculated for 1999, before computing rates for a year as described in paragraph (1), the Secretary shall adjust all area-specific and national Medicare + Choice capitation rates (and beginning in 2000, the minimum amount) for the previous year for the differences between the projections of the national per capita Medicare + Choice growth percentage for that year and previous years and the current estimate of such percentage for such years, except that for purposes of paragraph (1)(C)(v)(II), no such adjustment shall be made for a year before 2004.

(7) ADJUSTMENT FOR NATIONAL COVERAGE DETERMINATIONS AND LEGISLATIVE CHANGES IN BENEFITS.—If the Secretary makes a determination with respect to coverage under this title or there is a change in benefits required to be provided under this part that the Secretary projects will result in a significant increase in the costs to Medicare+Choice of providing benefits under contracts under this part (for periods after any period described in section 1852(a)(5)), the Secretary shall adjust appropriately the payments to such organizations under this part. Such projection and adjustment shall be based on an analysis by the Chief Actuary of the Centers for Medicare & Medicaid Services of the actuarial costs associated with the new benefits.

(d) MA PAYMENT AREA; MA LOCAL AREA; MA REGION DEFINED—

(1) MA PAYMENT AREA.—In this part, except as provided in this subsection, the term "MA payment area" means—

(A) with respect to an MA local plan, an MA local area (as defined in paragraph (2)); and

(B) with respect to an MA regional plan, an MA region (as established under section 1858(a)(2)).;

(2) MA LOCAL AREA.—The term "MA local area" means a county or equivalent area specified by the Secretary.; and

* * *

§1853(d)(2) ¶2256A

(4) GEOGRAPHIC ADJUSTMENT.—

(A) IN GENERAL.—Upon written request of the chief executive officer of a State for a contract year (beginning after 1998) made by not later than February 1 of the previous year, the Secretary shall make a geographic adjustment to a Medicare + Choice payment area in the State otherwise determined under paragraph (1) for MA local plans—

* * *

(iii) to consolidating into a single Medicare + Choice payment area noncontiguous counties (or equivalent areas described in paragraph (1)(A)) within a State.

Such adjustment shall be effective for payments for months beginning with January of the year following the year in which the request is received.

(B) BUDGET NEUTRALITY ADJUSTMENT.—In the case of a State requesting an adjustment under this paragraph, the Secretary shall initially (and annually thereafter) adjust the payment rates otherwise established under this subsection with respect to MA local plans for Medicare + Choice payment areas in the State in a manner so that the aggregate of the payments under this section for such plans in the State shall not exceed the aggregate payments that would have been made under this section for such plans for Medicare + Choice payment areas in the State in the absence of the adjustment under this paragraph.

* * *

(f) PAYMENTS FROM TRUST FUNDS.—The payment to a Medicare + Choice organization under this section for individuals enrolled under this part with the organization and payments to a Medicare + Choice MSA under subsection (e)(1) shall be made from the Federal Hospital Insurance Trust Fund and the Federal Supplementary Medical Insurance Trust Fund in such proportion as the Secretary determines reflects the relative weight that benefits under part A and under part B represents of the actuarial value of the total benefits under this title. Payments to MA organizations for statutory drug benefits provided under this title are made from the Medicare Prescription Drug Account in the Federal Supplementary Medical Insurance Trust Fund. Monthly payments otherwise payable under this section for October 2000 shall be paid on the first business day of such month. Monthly payments otherwise payable under this section for October 2001 shall be paid on the last business day of September 2001. Monthly payments otherwise payable under this section for October 2006 shall be paid on the first business day of October 2006.

(g) SPECIAL RULE FOR CERTAIN INPATIENT HOSPITAL STAYS.—In the case of an individual who is receiving inpatient hospital services from a subsection (d) hospital (as defined in section 1886(d)(1)(B)), a rehabilitation hospital described in section 1886(d)(1)(B)(ii) or a distinct part rehabilitation unit described in the matter following clause (v) of section 1886(d)(1)(B), or a long-term care hospital (described in section 1886(d)(1)(B)(iv)) as of the effective date of the individual's—

* * *

(2) termination of election with respect to a Medicare + Choice organization under this part—

* * *

(B) payment for such services during the stay shall not be made under section 1886(d) or other payment provision under this title for inpatient services for the type of facility, hospital, or unit involved, described in the matter preceding paragraph (1), as the case may be, or by any succeeding Medicare + Choice organization, and

* * *

(j) COMPUTATION OF BENCHMARK AMOUNTS.—For purposes of this part, the term "MA area-specific non-drug monthly benchmark amount" means for a month in a year—

(1) with respect to—

(A) a service area that is entirely within an MA local area, subject to section 1860C-1(d)(2)(A), an amount equal to 112 of the annual MA capitation rate under section 1853(c)(1) for the area for the year, adjusted as appropriate for the purpose of risk adjustment; or

(B) a service area that includes more than one MA local area, an amount equal to the average of the amounts described in subparagraph (A) for each such local MA area, weighted by the projected number of enrollees in the plan residing in the respective local MA areas (as used by the plan for purposes of the bid and disclosed to the Secretary under section 1854(a)(6)(A)(iii)), adjusted as appropriate for the purpose of risk adjustment; or

(2) with respect to an MA region for a month in a year, the MA region-specific non-drug monthly benchmark amount, as defined in section 1858(f) for the region for the year.

[CCH Explanation at ¶351, 352, 353, 354, 355, 368, 369, 370, 373, 390, 396, and 801.]

2003 Amendments:

Section 101(e)(3)(D)of the "Medicare Prescription Drug, Improvement, and Modernization Act of 2003," effective upon enactment, amended section 1853(f) in the heading by striking "TRUST FUND" and inserting "TRUST FUNDS"; and by inserting after the first sentence the following: "Payments to MA organizations for statutory drug benefits provided under this title are made from the Medicare Prescription Drug Account in the Federal Supplementary Medical Insurance Trust Fund.".

Section 211(a) of the "Medicare Prescription Drug, Improvement, and Modernization Act of 2003," effective upon enactment, amended section 1853(c)(1) by adding at the end new subparagraph (D); and in the matter before subparagraph (A), by striking "or (C)" and inserting "(C), or (D)".

Section 211(b)(1) of the "Medicare Prescription Drug, Improvement, and Modernization Act of 2003," effective upon enactment, amended section 1853(c) in paragraph (1)(A), by inserting "(for a year other than 2004)" after "multiplied"; and in paragraph (5), by inserting "(other than 2004)" after "for each year".

Section 211(c)(1) of the "Medicare Prescription Drug, Improvement, and Modernization Act of 2003," effective upon enactment, amended section 1853(c)(1) in subparagraph (A), by striking "The sum" and inserting "For a year before 2005, the sum"; in subparagraph (B)(iv), by striking "and each succeeding year" and inserting ", 2003, and 2004"; in subparagraph (C)(iv), by striking "and each succeeding year" and inserting "and 2003"; and by adding at the end of subparagraph (C) new clause (v).

Section 211(c)(2) of the "Medicare Prescription Drug, Improvement, and Modernization Act of 2003," effective upon enactment, amended section 1853(c)(6)(C) by inserting before the period at the end the following: ", except that for purposes of paragraph (1)(C)(v)(II), no such adjustment shall be made for a year before 2004".

Section 211(d) of the "Medicare Prescription Drug, Improvement, and Modernization Act of 2003," effective upon enactment, amended section 1853(c)(3) in subparagraph (A), by striking "subparagraph (B)" and inserting "subparagraphs (B) and (E)"; and by adding at the end new subparagraph (E).

Section 211(e)(1) of the "Medicare Prescription Drug, Improvement, and Modernization Act of 2003," effective upon enactment, amended section 1853(g) in the matter preceding paragraph (1), by inserting ", a rehabilitation hospital described in section 1886(d)(1)(B)(ii) or a distinct part rehabilitation unit described in the matter following clause (v) of section 1886(d)(1)(B), or a long-term care hospital (described in section 1886(d)(1)(B)(iv))" after "1886(d)(1)(B))"; and in paragraph (2)(B), by inserting "or other payment provision under this title for inpatient services for the type of facility, hospital, or unit involved, described in the matter preceding paragraph (1), as the case may be," after "1886(d)".

Section 221(d)(1) of the "Medicare Prescription Drug, Improvement, and Modernization Act of 2003," effective upon enactment, amended section 1853(d) by amending the heading to read as follows: "MA PAYMENT AREA; MA LOCAL AREA; MA REGION DEFINED"; by redesignating paragraphs (2) and (3) as paragraphs (3) and (4), respectively; by amending paragraph (1); by inserting after paragraph (1) new paragraph (2); in paragraph (4), as so redesignated—in subparagraph (A), by inserting "for MA local plans" after "paragraph (1)"; in subparagraph (A)(iii), by striking "paragraph (1)" and inserting "paragraph (1)(A)"; and in subparagraph (B)—by inserting "with respect to MA local plans" after "established under this section"; by inserting "for such plans" after "payments under this section"; and by inserting "for such plans" after "made under this section".

Prior to amendment section 1853(d) read as follows.

(d) MEDICARE + CHOICE PAYMENT AREA DEFINED.—

(1) IN GENERAL.—In this part, except as provided in paragraph (3), the term "Medicare + Choice payment area" means a county, or equivalent area specified by the Secretary.

(2) RULE FOR ESRD BENEFICIARIES.—In the case of individuals who are determined to have end stage renal disease, the Medicare + Choice payment area shall be a State or such other payment area as the Secretary specifies.

(3) GEOGRAPHIC ADJUSTMENT.—

(A) IN GENERAL.—Upon written request of the chief executive officer of a State for a contract year (beginning after 1998) made by not later than February 1 of the previous year, the Secretary shall make a geographic adjustment to a Medicare + Choice payment area in the State otherwise determined under paragraph (1)—

(i) to a single statewide Medicare + Choice payment area,

(ii) to the metropolitan based system described in subparagraph (C), or

(iii) to consolidating into a single Medicare + Choice payment area noncontiguous counties (or equivalent areas described in paragraph (1)) within a State.

Such adjustment shall be effective for payments for months beginning with January of the year following the year in which the request is received.

(B) BUDGET NEUTRALITY ADJUSTMENT.—In the case of a State requesting an adjustment under this paragraph, the Secretary shall initially (and annually thereafter) adjust the payment rates otherwise established under this section for Medicare + Choice payment areas in the State in a manner so that the aggregate of the payments under this section in the State shall not exceed the aggregate payments that would have been made under this section for Medicare + Choice payment areas in the State in the absence of the adjustment under this paragraph.

(C) METROPOLITAN BASED SYSTEM.—The metropolitan based system described in this subparagraph is one in which—

(i) all the portions of each metropolitan statistical area in the State or in the case of a consolidated metropolitan statistical area, all of the portions of each primary metropolitan statistical area within the consolidated area within the State, are treated as a single Medicare + Choice payment area, and

(ii) all areas in the State that do not fall within a metropolitan statistical area are treated as a single Medicare + Choice payment area.

(D) AREAS.—In subparagraph (C), the terms "metropolitan statistical area", "consolidated metropolitan statistical area", and "primary metropolitan statistical area" mean any area designated as such by the Secretary of Commerce.

The above amendment applies to plan years beginning on or after January 1, 2006.

Section 221(d)(4) of the "Medicare Prescription Drug, Improvement, and Modernization Act of 2003," effective upon enactment, amended section 1853(c)(1) by inserting "that is an MA local area" after "for a Medicare+Choice payment area".

§1853(j)(2) ¶2256A

Section 222(d) of the "Medicare Prescription Drug, Improvement, and Modernization Act of 2003," effective upon enactment, amended section 1853 by adding at the end new subsection (j).

The above amendment applies to plan years beginning on or after January 1, 2006.

Section 222(e)(1) of the "Medicare Prescription Drug, Improvement, and Modernization Act of 2003," effective upon enactment, amended section 1853(a)(1) by redesignating subparagraph (B) as subparagraph (H); and amended subparagraph (A).

Prior to amendment subparagraph (A) read as follows:

(A) IN GENERAL.—Under a contract under section 1857 and subject to subsections (e), (g) and (i) and section 1859(e)(4), the Secretary shall make monthly payments under this section in advance to each Medicare + Choice organization, with respect to coverage of an individual under this part in a Medicare + Choice payment area for a month, in an amount equal to 1/12 of the annual Medicare + Choice capitation rate (as calculated under subsection (c)) with respect to that individual for that area, reduced by the amount of any reduction elected under section 1854(f)(1)(E) and adjusted for such risk factors as age, disability status, gender, institutional status, and such other factors as the Secretary determines to be appropriate, so as to ensure actuarial equivalence. The Secretary may add to, modify, or substitute for such factors, if such changes will improve the determination of actuarial equivalence.

The above amendment applies to plan years beginning on or after January 1, 2006.

Section 222(f)(1) and (2) of the "Medicare Prescription Drug, Improvement, and Modernization Act of 2003," effective upon enactment, amended section 1853(b) by amending paragraph (1); and in paragraph (3), by striking "in the announcement" and all that follows and inserting "in such announcement.".

Prior to amendment paragraph (1) read as follows:

(1) ANNUAL ANNOUNCEMENT.—The Secretary shall annually determine, and shall announce (in a manner intended to provide notice to interested parties) for years before 2004 and after 2005 not later than March 1 before the calendar year concerned and for 2004 and 2005 not later than the second Monday in May before the respective calendar year—

(A) the annual Medicare + Choice capitation rate for each Medicare + Choice payment area for the year, and

(B) the risk and other factors to be used in adjusting such rates under subsection (a)(1)(A) for payments for months in that year.

The above amendment applies to plan years beginning on or after January 1, 2006.

Section 222(i) of the "Medicare Prescription Drug, Improvement, and Modernization Act of 2003," effective upon enactment, amended section 1853(a)(1)(H), as redesignated under subsection (d)(1)(A), by amending the second sentence to read as follows: "Such rates of payment shall be actuarially equivalent to rates that would have been paid with respect to other enrollees in the MA payment area (or such other area as specified by the Secretary) under the provisions of this section as in effect before the date of the enactment of the Medicare Prescription Drug, Improvement, and Modernization Act of 2003."; and by adding at the end the following new sentence: "The Secretary may apply the competitive bidding methodology provided for in this section, with appropriate adjustments to account for the risk adjustment methodology applied to end stage renal disease payments.".

The above amendment applies to plan years beginning on or after January 1, 2006.

Section 237(b)(1) of the "Medicare Prescription Drug, Improvement, and Modernization Act of 2003," effective upon enactment, amended section 1853(a) by adding at the end new paragraph (4).

Section 237(b)(2)(B) of the "Medicare Prescription Drug, Improvement, and Modernization Act of 2003," effective upon enactment, amended section 1853(c)(5) by striking "subsections (a)(3)(C)(iii) and (i)" and inserting "subsections (a)(3)(C)(iii), (a)(4), and (i)".

The amendments made by Sections 237(b)(1) and 237(b)(2)(B) of the "Medicare Prescription Drug, Improvement, and Modernization Act of 2003," apply to services provided on or after Jan. 1, 2006, and contract years beginning on or after such date.

Section 241(b)(1)(A) of the "Medicare Prescription Drug, Improvement, and Modernization Act of 2003," effective upon enactment, amended section 1853(j)(1)(A) by inserting "subject to section 1860C-1(d)(2)(A)," after "within an MA local area,".

Section 241(b)(1)(B) of the "Medicare Prescription Drug, Improvement, and Modernization Act of 2003," effective upon enactment, amended section 1853(b)(1)(B), as amended by section 222(f)(1), by adding at the end new clause (iii).

Section 736(d)(1) of the "Medicare Prescription Drug, Improvement, and Modernization Act of 2003," effective upon enactment, amended section 1853 in subsection (a)(3)(C)(ii), by striking "clause (iii)" and inserting "clause (iv)"; in subsection (a)(3)(C), by redesignating the clause (iii) added by such section 607 as clause (iv); and in subsection (c)(5), by striking "(a)(3)(C)(iii)" and inserting "(a)(3)(C)(iv)".

Section 900(e)(1)(G) of the "Medicare Prescription Drug, Improvement, and Modernization Act of 2003," effective upon enactment, amended section 1853 in subsection (b)(4), by striking "Health Care Financing Administration" in the first sentence and inserting "Centers for Medicare & Medicaid Services"; and in subsection (c)(7), by striking "Health Care Financing Administration" in the last sentence and inserting "Centers for Medicare & Medicaid Services".

[¶ 2256B] Sec. 1854. PREMIUMS AND BID AMOUNTS

[42 U.S.C. § 1395w-24]

(a) SUBMISSION OF PROPOSED PREMIUMS, BID AMOUNTS AND RELATED INFORMATION.—

(1) IN GENERAL.—

(A) INITIAL SUBMISSION.—Not later than the second Monday in September of 2002, 2003, and 2004 (or the first Monday in June of each subsequent year), each MA organization shall submit to the Secretary, in a form and manner specified by the Secretary and for each MA plan for the service area (or segment of such an area if permitted under subsection (h)) in which it intends to be offered in the following year the following:

(i) The information described in paragraph (2), (3), (4), or (6)(A) for the type of plan and year involved.

(ii) The plan type for each plan.

(iii) The enrollment capacity (if any) in relation to the plan and area.

(B) BENEFICIARY REBATE INFORMATION.—In the case of a plan required to provide a monthly rebate under subsection (b)(1)(C) for a year, the MA organization offering the plan shall submit to the Secretary, in such form and manner and at such time as the Secretary specifies, information on—

(i) the manner in which such rebate will be provided under clause (ii) of such subsection; and

(ii) the MA monthly prescription drug beneficiary premium (if any) and the MA monthly supplemental beneficiary premium (if any).

(C) PAPERWORK REDUCTION FOR OFFERING OF MA REGIONAL PLANS NATIONALLY OR IN MULTI-REGION AREAS.—The Secretary shall establish requirements for information submission under this subsection in a manner that promotes the offering of MA regional plans in more than one region (including all regions) through the filing of consolidated information.

(2) INFORMATION REQUIRED FOR COORDINATED CARE PLANS BEFORE 2006.—For a Medicare + Choice plan described in section 1851(a)(2)(A) for a year before 2006, the information described in this paragraph is as follows:

* * *

(3) REQUIREMENTS FOR MSA PLANS.—For an MSA plan for any year, the information described in this paragraph is as follows:

* * *

(4) REQUIREMENTS FOR PRIVATE FEE-FOR-SERVICE PLANS BEFORE 2006.—For a Medicare + Choice plan described in section 1851(a)(2)(C) for benefits described in section 1852(a)(1)(A) for a year before 2006, the information described in this paragraph is as follows:—

* * *

(5) REVIEW.—

(A) IN GENERAL.—Subject to subparagraph (B), the Secretary shall review the adjusted community rates, the amounts of the basic and supplemental premiums, and values filed under paragraphs (2) and (4) of this subsection and shall approve or disapprove such rates, amounts, and values so submitted. The Chief Actuary of the Centers for Medicare & Medicaid Services shall review the actuarial assumptions and data used by the Medicare+Choice organization with respect to such rates, amounts, and values so submitted to determine the appropriateness of such assumptions and data.

(B) EXCEPTION.—The Secretary shall not review, approve, or disapprove the amounts submitted under paragraph (3) or, in the case of an MA private fee-for-service plan, subparagraphs (A)(ii) and (B) of paragraph (4).

(6) SUBMISSION OF BID AMOUNTS BY MA ORGANIZATIONS BEGINNING IN 2006.—

(A) INFORMATION TO BE SUBMITTED.—For an MA plan (other than an MSA plan) for a plan year beginning on or after January 1, 2006, the information described in this subparagraph is as follows:

(i) The monthly aggregate bid amount for the provision of all items and services under the plan, which amount shall be based on average revenue requirements (as used for purposes of section 1302(8) of the Public Health Service Act) in the payment area for an enrollee with a national average risk profile for the factors described in section 1853(a)(1)(C) (as specified by the Secretary).

(ii) The proportions of such bid amount that are attributable to—

(I) the provision of benefits under the original medicare fee-for-service program option (as defined in section 1852(a)(1)(B));

(II) the provision of basic prescription drug coverage; and

(III) the provision of supplemental health care benefits.

(iii) The actuarial basis for determining the amount under clause (i) and the proportions described in clause (ii) and such additional information as the Secretary may require to verify such actuarial bases and the projected number of enrollees in each MA local area.

(iv) A description of deductibles, coinsurance, and copayments applicable under the plan and the actuarial value of such deductibles, coinsurance, and copayments, described in subsection (e)(4)(A).

(v) With respect to qualified prescription drug coverage, the information required under section 1860D-4, as incorporated under section 1860D-11(b)(2), with respect to such coverage.

In the case of a specialized MA plan for special needs individuals, the information described in this subparagraph is such information as the Secretary shall specify.

(B) ACCEPTANCE AND NEGOTIATION OF BID AMOUNTS.—

(i) AUTHORITY.—Subject to clauses (iii) and (iv), the Secretary has the authority to negotiate regarding monthly bid amounts submitted under subparagraph (A) (and the proportions described in subparagraph (A)(ii)), including supplemental benefits provided under subsection (b)(1)(C)(ii)(I) and in exercising such authority the Secretary shall have authority similar to the authority of the Director of the Office of Personnel Management with respect to health benefits plans under chapter 89 of title 5, United States Code.

(ii) APPLICATION OF FEHBP STANDARD.—Subject to clause (iv), the Secretary may only accept such a bid amount or proportion if the Secretary determines that such amount and proportions are supported by the actuarial bases provided under subparagraph (A) and reasonably and equitably reflects the revenue requirements (as used for purposes of section 1302(8) of the Public Health Service Act) of benefits provided under that plan.

(iii) NONINTERFERENCE.—In order to promote competition under this part and part D and in carrying out such parts, the Secretary may not require any MA organization to contract with a particular hospital, physician, or other entity or individual to furnish items and services under this title or require a particular price structure for payment under such a contract to the extent consistent with the Secretary's authority under this part.

(iv) EXCEPTION.—In the case of a plan described in section 1851(a)(2)(C), the provisions of clauses (i) and (ii) shall not apply and the provisions of paragraph (5)(B), prohibiting the review, approval, or disapproval of amounts described in such paragraph, shall apply to the negotiation and rejection of the monthly bid amounts and the proportions referred to in subparagraph (A).

(b) MONTHLY PREMIUM CHARGED.—

(1) IN GENERAL.—

(A) RULE FOR OTHER THAN MSA PLANS.—Subject to the rebate under subparagraph (C), the monthly amount (if any) of the premium charged to an individual enrolled in a Medicare + Choice plan (other than an MSA plan) offered by a Medicare + Choice organization shall be equal to the sum of the Medicare + Choice monthly basic beneficiary premium, the Medicare + Choice monthly supplementary beneficiary premium (if any), and, if the plan provides qualified prescription drug coverage, the MA monthly prescription drug beneficiary premium.

* * *

(C) BENEFICIARY REBATE RULE.—

(i) REQUIREMENT.—The MA plan shall provide to the enrollee a monthly rebate equal to 75 percent of the average per capita savings (if any) described in paragraph (3)(C) or (4)(C), as applicable to the plan and year involved.

(ii) FORM OF REBATE.—A rebate required under this subparagraph shall be provided through the application of the amount of the rebate toward one or more of the following:

(I) PROVISION OF SUPPLEMENTAL HEALTH CARE BENEFITS AND PAYMENT FOR PREMIUM FOR SUPPLEMENTAL BENEFITS.—The provision of supplemental health care benefits described in section 1852(a)(3) in a manner specified under the plan, which may include the reduction of cost-sharing otherwise applicable as well as additional health care benefits which are not benefits under the original medicare fee-for-service program option, or crediting toward an MA monthly supplemental beneficiary premium (if any).

(II) PAYMENT FOR PREMIUM FOR PRESCRIPTION DRUG COVERAGE.—Crediting toward the MA monthly prescription drug beneficiary premium.

(III) PAYMENT TOWARD PART B PREMIUM.—Crediting toward the premium imposed under part B (determined without regard to the application of subsections (b), (h), and (i) of section 1839).

(iii) DISCLOSURE RELATING TO REBATES.—The plan shall disclose to the Secretary information on the form and amount of the rebate provided under this subparagraph or the actuarial value in the case of supplemental health care benefits.

(iv) APPLICATION OF PART B PREMIUM REDUCTION.—Insofar as an MA organization elects to provide a rebate under this subparagraph under a plan as a credit toward the part B premium under clause (ii)(III), the Secretary shall apply such credit to reduce the premium under section 1839 of each enrollee in such plan as provided in section 1840(i).

(2) PREMIUM AND BID TERMINOLOGY DEFINED.—For purposes of this part:

(A) MA MONTHLY BASIC BENEFICIARY PREMIUM.—The term "MA monthly basic beneficiary premium" means, with respect to an MA plan—

(i) described in section 1853(a)(1)(B)(i) (relating to plans providing rebates), zero; or

(ii) described in section 1853(a)(1)(B)(ii), the amount (if any) by which the unadjusted MA statutory non-drug monthly bid amount (as defined in subparagraph (E)) exceeds the applicable unadjusted MA area-specific non-drug monthly benchmark amount (as defined in section 1853(j)).

(B) MA MONTHLY PRESCRIPTION DRUG BENEFICIARY PREMIUM.—The term "MA monthly prescription drug beneficiary premium" means, with respect to an MA plan, the base beneficiary premium (as determined under section 1860D-13(a)(2) and as adjusted under section 1860D-13(a)(1)(B)), less the amount of rebate credited toward such amount under section 1854(b)(1)(C)(ii)(II).

(C) MA MONTHLY SUPPLEMENTAL BENEFICIARY PREMIUM.—The term "MA monthly supplemental beneficiary premium" means, with respect to an MA plan, the portion of the aggregate monthly bid amount submitted under clause (i) of subsection (a)(6)(A) for the year that is attributable under clause (ii)(III) of such subsection to the provision of supplemental health care benefits, less the amount of rebate credited toward such portion under section 1854(b)(1)(C)(ii)(I).

(D) MEDICARE + CHOICE MONTHLY MSA PREMIUM.—The term "Medicare + Choice monthly MSA premium" means, with respect to a Medicare + Choice plan, the amount of such premium filed under subsection (a)(3)(A) for the plan.

(E) UNADJUSTED MA STATUTORY NON-DRUG MONTHLY BID AMOUNT.—The term "unadjusted MA statutory non-drug monthly bid amount" means the portion of the bid amount submitted under clause (i) of subsection (a)(6)(A) for the year that is attributable under clause (ii)(I) of such subsection to the provision of benefits under the original medicare fee-for-service program option (as defined in section 1852(a)(1)(B)).

(3) COMPUTATION OF AVERAGE PER CAPITA MONTHLY SAVINGS FOR LOCAL PLANS.—For purposes of paragraph (1)(C)(i), the average per capita monthly savings referred to in such paragraph for an MA local plan and year is computed as follows:

(A) DETERMINATION OF STATEWIDE AVERAGE RISK ADJUSTMENT FOR LOCAL PLANS.—

(i) IN GENERAL.—Subject to clause (iii), the Secretary shall determine, at the same time rates are promulgated under section 1853(b)(1) (beginning with 2006) for each

State, the average of the risk adjustment factors to be applied under section 1853(a)(1)(C) to payment for enrollees in that State for MA local plans.

(ii) TREATMENT OF STATES FOR FIRST YEAR IN WHICH LOCAL PLAN OFFERED.—In the case of a State in which no MA local plan was offered in the previous year, the Secretary shall estimate such average. In making such estimate, the Secretary may use average risk adjustment factors applied to comparable States or applied on a national basis.

(iii) AUTHORITY TO DETERMINE RISK ADJUSTMENT FOR AREAS OTHER THAN STATES.—The Secretary may provide for the determination and application of risk adjustment factors under this subparagraph on the basis of areas other than States or on a plan-specific basis.

(B) DETERMINATION OF RISK ADJUSTED BENCHMARK AND RISK-ADJUSTED BID FOR LOCAL PLANS.—For each MA plan offered in a local area in a State, the Secretary shall—

(i) adjust the applicable MA area-specific non-drug monthly benchmark amount (as defined in section 1853(j)(1)) for the area by the average risk adjustment factor computed under subparagraph (A); and

(ii) adjust the unadjusted MA statutory nondrug monthly bid amount by such applicable average risk adjustment factor.

(C) DETERMINATION OF AVERAGE PER CAPITA MONTHLY SAVINGS.—The average per capita monthly savings described in this subparagraph for an MA local plan is equal to the amount (if any) by which—

(i) the risk-adjusted benchmark amount computed under subparagraph (B)(i); exceeds

(ii) the risk-adjusted bid computed under subparagraph (B)(ii).

(4) COMPUTATION OF AVERAGE PER CAPITA MONTHLY SAVINGS FOR REGIONAL PLANS.—For purposes of paragraph (1)(C)(i), the average per capita monthly savings referred to in such paragraph for an MA regional plan and year is computed as follows:

(A) DETERMINATION OF REGIONWIDE AVERAGE RISK ADJUSTMENT FOR REGIONAL PLANS.—

(i) IN GENERAL.—The Secretary shall determine, at the same time rates are promulgated under section 1853(b)(1) (beginning with 2006) for each MA region the average of the risk adjustment factors to be applied under section 1853(a)(1)(C) to payment for enrollees in that region for MA regional plans.

(ii) TREATMENT OF REGIONS FOR FIRST YEAR IN WHICH REGIONAL PLAN OFFERED.—In the case of an MA region in which no MA regional plan was offered in the previous year, the Secretary shall estimate such average. In making such estimate, the Secretary may use average risk adjustment factors applied to comparable regions or applied on a national basis.

(iii) AUTHORITY TO DETERMINE RISK ADJUSTMENT FOR AREAS OTHER THAN REGIONS.—The Secretary may provide for the determination and application of risk adjustment factors under this subparagraph on the basis of areas other than MA regions or on a plan-specific basis.

(B) DETERMINATION OF RISK-ADJUSTED BENCHMARK AND RISK-ADJUSTED BID FOR REGIONAL PLANS.—For each MA regional plan offered in a region, the Secretary shall—

(i) adjust the applicable MA area-specific non-drug monthly benchmark amount (as defined in section 1853(j)(2)) for the region by the average risk adjustment factor computed under subparagraph (A); and

(ii) adjust the unadjusted MA statutory nondrug monthly bid amount by such applicable average risk adjustment factor.

(C) DETERMINATION OF AVERAGE PER CAPITA MONTHLY SAVINGS.—The average per capita monthly savings described in this subparagraph for an MA regional plan is equal to the amount (if any) by which—

(i) the risk-adjusted benchmark amount computed under subparagraph (B)(i); exceeds

(ii) the risk-adjusted bid computed under subparagraph (B)(ii).

(c) UNIFORM PREMIUM AND BID AMOUNTS.—Except as permitted under section 1857(i), the MA monthly bid amount submitted under subsection (a)(6), the amounts of the MA monthly basic, prescription drug, and supplemental beneficiary premiums, and the MA monthly MSA premium charged under subsection (b) of an MA organization under this part may not vary among individuals enrolled in the plan.

(d) TERMS AND CONDITIONS OF IMPOSING PREMIUMS.—(1) IN GENERAL.—Each Medicare + Choice organization shall permit the payment of Medicare + Choice monthly basic, prescription drug, and supplemental beneficiary premiums on a monthly basis, may terminate election of individuals for a Medicare + Choice plan for failure to make premium payments only in accordance with section 1851(g)(3)(B)(i), and may not provide for cash or other monetary rebates as an inducement for enrollment or otherwise.

(2) BENEFICIARY'S OPTION OF PAYMENT THROUGH WITHHOLDING FROM SOCIAL SECURITY PAYMENT OR USE OF ELECTRONIC FUNDS TRANSFER MECHANISM.—In accordance with regulations, an MA organization shall permit each enrollee, at the enrollee's option, to make payment of premiums (if any) under this part to the organization through—

(A) withholding from benefit payments in the manner provided under section 1840 with respect to monthly premiums under section 1839;

(B) an electronic funds transfer mechanism (such as automatic charges of an account at a financial institution or a credit or debit card account); or

(C) such other means as the Secretary may specify, including payment by an employer or under employment-based retiree health coverage (as defined in section 1860D-22(c)(1)) on behalf of an employee or former employee (or dependent).

All premium payments that are withheld under subparagraph (A) shall be credited to the appropriate Trust Fund (or Account thereof), as specified by the Secretary, under this title and shall be paid to the MA organization involved. No charge may be imposed under an MA plan with respect to the election of the payment option described in subparagraph (A). The Secretary shall consult with the Commissioner of Social Security and the Secretary of the Treasury regarding methods for allocating premiums withheld under subparagraph (A) among the appropriate Trust Funds and Account.

(3) INFORMATION NECESSARY FOR COLLECTION.—In order to carry out paragraph (2)(A) with respect to an enrollee who has elected such paragraph to apply, the Secretary shall transmit to the Commissioner of Social Security—

(A) by the beginning of each year, the name, social security account number, consolidated monthly beneficiary premium described in paragraph (4) owed by such enrollee for each month during the year, and other information determined appropriate by the Secretary, in consultation with the Commissioner of Social Security; and

(B) periodically throughout the year, information to update the information previously transmitted under this paragraph for the year.

(4) CONSOLIDATED MONTHLY BENEFICIARY PREMIUM.—In the case of an enrollee in an MA plan, the Secretary shall provide a mechanism for the consolidation of—

(A) the MA monthly basic beneficiary premium (if any);

(B) the MA monthly supplemental beneficiary premium (if any); and

(C) the MA monthly prescription drug beneficiary premium (if any).

(e) LIMITATION ON ENROLLEE LIABILITY.—

(1) FOR BASIC AND ADDITIONAL BENEFITS BEFORE 2006.—For periods before 2006, in no event may—

* * *

(2) FOR SUPPLEMENTAL BENEFITS BEFORE 2006.—For periods before 2006, if the Medicare + Choice organization provides to its members enrolled under this part in a Medicare + Choice plan described in section 1851(a)(2)(A) with respect to supplemental benefits described in section 1852(a)(3), the sum of the Medicare + Choice monthly supplemental beneficiary premium (multiplied by 12) charged and the actuarial value of its deductibles, coinsurance, and copay-

ments charged with respect to such benefits may not exceed the adjusted community rate for such benefits (as defined in subsection (f)(3)).

(3) DETERMINATION ON OTHER BASIS.—If the Secretary determines that adequate data are not available to determine the actuarial value under paragraph (1)(A), (2), or (4), the Secretary may determine such amount with respect to all individuals in same geographic area, the State, or in the United States, eligible to enroll in the Medicare + Choice plan involved under this part or on the basis of other appropriate data.

(4) SPECIAL RULE FOR PRIVATE FEE-FOR-SERVICE PLANS AND FOR BASIC BENEFITS BEGINNING IN 2006.—With respect to a Medicare + Choice private fee-for-service plan (other than a plan that is an MSA plan)and for periods beginning with 2006, with respect to an MA plan described in section 1851(a)(2)(A). in no event may—

(A) the actuarial value of the deductibles, coinsurance, and copayments applicable on average to individuals enrolled under this part with such a plan of an organization with respect to benefits under the original medicare fee-for-service program option, exceed

(B) the actuarial value of the deductibles, coinsurance, and copayments that would be applicable with respect to such benefits on average to individuals entitled to benefits under part A and enrolled under part B if they were not members of a Medicare + Choice organization for the year.

(f) REQUIREMENT FOR ADDITIONAL BENEFITSBEFORE 2006.—

(1) REQUIREMENT.—

(A) IN GENERAL.—For years before 2006, each Medicare + Choice organization (in relation to a Medicare + Choice plan, other than an MSA plan, it offers) shall provide that if there is an excess amount (as defined in subparagraph (B)) for the plan for a contract year, subject to the succeeding provisions of this subsection, the organization shall provide to individuals such additional benefits (as the organization may specify) in a value which the Secretary determines is at least equal to the adjusted excess amount (as defined in subparagraph (C)).

* * *

(g) PROHIBITION OF STATE IMPOSITION OF PREMIUM TAXES.—No State may impose a premium tax or similar tax with respect to payments to Medicare + Choice organizations under section 1853 or premiums paid to such organizations under this part.

* * *

[CCH Explanation at ¶ 365, 366, 371, 376, 379, 380, and 801.]

2003 Amendments:

Section 222(a)(1)(A) of the "Medicare Prescription Drug, Improvement, and Modernization Act of 2003," effective upon enactment, amended section 1854(a)(1).

Prior to amendment, section 1854(a)(1) read as follows:

(1) IN GENERAL.—Not later than the second Monday in September of 2002, 2003, and 2004 (or July 1 of each other year), each Medicare + Choice organization shall submit to the Secretary, in a form and manner specified by the Secretary and for each Medicare + Choice plan for the service area (or segment of such an area if permitted under subsection (h)) in which it intends to be offered in the following year—

(A) the information described in paragraph (2), (3), or (4) for the type of plan involved; and

(B) the enrollment capacity (if any) in relation to the plan and area.

Section 222(a)(1)(B) of the "Medicare Prescription Drug, Improvement, and Modernization Act of 2003," effective upon enactment, amended section 1854(a) by adding at the end of subsection (a) new subsection (6).

Section 222(b)(1) of the "Medicare Prescription Drug, Improvement, and Modernization Act of 2003," effective upon enactment, amended section 1854(b)(1) in subparagraph (A), by striking "The monthly amount" and inserting "Subject to the rebate under subparagraph (C), the monthly amount (if any)"; and by adding at the end new subparagraph (C).

Section 222(b)(2)(A) of the "Medicare Prescription Drug, Improvement, and Modernization Act of 2003," effective upon enactment, amended section 1854(b)(2) in the heading, by inserting "AND BID" after "PREMIUM".

Section 222(b)(2)(B) of the "Medicare Prescription Drug, Improvement, and Modernization Act of 2003," effective upon enactment, amended section 1854(b)(2) by redesignating subparagraph (C) as subparagraph (D).

Section 222(b)(2)(C) of the "Medicare Prescription Drug, Improvement, and Modernization Act of 2003," effective upon enactment, amended section 1854(b)(2) by striking subparagraphs (A) and (B) and inserting new subparagraphs (A), (B) and (C).

Prior to amendment, subparagraphs (A) and (B) read as follows:

(A) THE MEDICARE + CHOICE MONTHLY BASIC BENEFICIARY PREMIUM.—The term "Medicare + Choice monthly basic beneficiary premium" means, with respect to a Medicare + Choice plan, the amount authorized to be charged under subsection (e)(1) for the plan, or, in the case of a Medicare + Choice private fee-for-service plan, the amount filed under subsection (a)(4)(A)(ii).

(B) MEDICARE + CHOICE MONTHLY SUPPLEMENTAL BENEFICIARY PREMIUM.—The term "Medicare + Choice monthly supplemental beneficiary premium" means, with respect to a Medicare + Choice plan, the amount authorized to be charged under subsection (e)(2) for the plan or, in the case of a MSA plan or Medicare + Choice private fee-for-service plan, the amount filed under paragraph (3)(B) or (4)(B) of subsection (a).

Section 222(b)(2)(D) of the "Medicare Prescription Drug, Improvement, and Modernization Act of 2003," effective upon enactment, amended section 1854(b)(2) by adding new subparagraph (E).

Section 222(b)(3) of the "Medicare Prescription Drug, Improvement, and Modernization Act of 2003," effective upon enactment, amended section 1854(b) by adding new paragraphs (3) and (4).

Section 222(c)(1) of the "Medicare Prescription Drug, Improvement, and Modernization Act of 2003," effective upon enactment, amended section 1854(d) by striking "PREMIUMS.—Each" and inserting "PREMIUMS.—(1) In General.—Each; and by adding new paragraphs (2) – (4).

Section 222(g)(1) of the "Medicare Prescription Drug, Improvement, and Modernization Act of 2003," effective upon enactment, amended section 1854 by amending the section heading to read as follows: "premiums and bid amounts"; in the heading of subsection (a), by inserting ", BID AMOUNTS," after "PREMIUMS";. in subsection (a)(2) by inserting "BEFORE 2006" after "FOR COORDINATED CARE PLANS"; and by inserting "for a year before 2006" after "section 1851(a)(2)(A)"; in subsection (a)(3), by striking "described" and inserting "for any year"; in subsection (a)(4) by inserting "BEFORE 2006" after "FOR PRIVATE FEE-FOR-SERVICE PLANS"; and by inserting "for a year before 2006" after "section 1852(a)(1)(A)"; in subsection (a)(5)(A), by inserting "paragraphs (2) and (4) of" after "filed under"; in subsection (a)(5)(B), by inserting after "paragraph (3) or" the following: ", in the case of an MA private fee-for-service plan,"; in subsection (b)(1)(A) by striking "and" and inserting a comma and by inserting before the period at the end the following: ", and, if the plan provides qualified prescription drug coverage, the MA monthly prescription drug beneficiary premium".

Section 222(g)(2) of the "Medicare Prescription Drug, Improvement, and Modernization Act of 2003," effective upon enactment, amended section 1854(c).

Prior to amendment 1854(c) read as follows:

(c) UNIFORM PREMIUM.—The Medicare + Choice monthly basic and supplemental beneficiary premium, the Medicare + Choice monthly MSA premium charged under subsection (b) of a Medicare + Choice organization under this part may not vary among individuals enrolled in the plan.

Section 222(g)(3) of the "Medicare Prescription Drug, Improvement, and Modernization Act of 2003," effective upon enactment, amended section 1854(d)(1) as amended by subsection (c)(1), by inserting ", prescription drug," after "basic".

Section 222(g)(4)(A) of the "Medicare Prescription Drug, Improvement, and Modernization Act of 2003," effective upon enactment, amended section 1854(e) in paragraph (1), by striking ".—In" and inserting "BEFORE 2006.—For periods before 2006, in"; in paragraph (2), by striking ".—If" and insert "BEFORE 2006.—For periods before 2006, if"; in paragraph (3), by striking "or (2)" and inserting ", (2), or (4)"; and in paragraph (4) by inserting "AND FOR BASIC BENEFITS BEGINNING IN 2006" after "PLANS"; in the matter before subparagraph (A), by inserting "and for periods beginning with 2006, with respect to an MA plan described in section 1851(a)(2)(A)" after "MSA plan"; in subparagraph (A), by striking "required benefits described in section 1852(a)(1)" and inserting "benefits under the original medicare fee-for-service program option"; and in subparagraph (B), by inserting "with respect to such benefits" after "would be applicable".

Section 222(g)(5)(A) of the "Medicare Prescription Drug, Improvement, and Modernization Act of 2003," effective upon enactment, amended section 1854(f) in the heading, by inserting "BEFORE 2006" after "ADDITIONAL BENEFITS"; and in paragraph (1)(A), by striking "Each" and inserting "For years before 2006, each".

The amendments made by section 222 of the "Medicare Prescription Drug, Improvement, and Modernization Act of 2003" are effective with respect to plan years beginning on or after January 1, 2006.

Section 232(b) of the "Medicare Prescription Drug, Improvement, and Modernization Act of 2003," amended section 1854(g) by inserting "or premiums paid to such organizations under this part" after "section 1853".

The amendment made by section 232(b) of the "Medicare Prescription Drug, Improvement, and Modernization Act of 2003," is effective upon enactment of the "Medicare Prescription Drug, Improvement, and Modernization Act of 2003."

Section 900(e)(1)(H) of the "Medicare Prescription Drug, Improvement, and Modernization Act of 2003," effective upon enactment, amended section 1854(a)(5)(A) by striking "Health Care Financing Administration" and inserting "Centers for Medicare & Medicaid Services".

[¶2256C] Sec. 1856. ESTABLISHMENT OF STANDARDS

[42 U.S.C. §1395w-26]

* * *

(b) ESTABLISHMENT OF OTHER STANDARDS.—

* * *

(3) RELATION TO STATE LAWS.—The standards established under this part shall supersede any State law or regulation (other than State licensing laws or State laws relating to plan solvency) with respect to MA plans which are offered by MA organizations under this part.

* * *

[CCH Explanation at ¶379.]
2003 Amendments:

Section 232(a) of the "Medicare Prescription Drug, Improvement, and Modernization Act of 2003," effective upon enactment, amended section 1856(b)(3).

Prior to amendment 1856(b)(3) read as follows:

(3) RELATION TO STATE LAWS.—

(A) IN GENERAL.—The standards established under this subsection shall supersede any State law or regulation (including standards described in subparagraph (B)) with respect to Medicare + Choice plans which are offered by

Medicare + Choice organizations under this part to the extent such law or regulation is inconsistent with such standards.

(B) STANDARDS SPECIFICALLY SUPERSEDED.—State standards relating to the following are superseded under this paragraph:

(i) Benefit requirements (including cost-sharing requirements).

(ii) Requirements relating to inclusion or treatment of providers.

(iii) Coverage determinations (including related appeals and grievance processes).

(iv) Requirements relating to marketing materials and summaries and schedules of benefits regarding a Medicare+Choice plan.

[¶ 2256D] Sec. 1857. CONTRACTS WITH MEDICARE + CHOICE ORGANIZATIONS

[42 U.S.C. § 1395w-27]

* * *

(d) PROTECTIONS AGAINST FRAUD AND BENEFICIARY PROTECTIONS.—

(1) PERIODIC AUDITING.—The Secretary shall provide for the annual auditing of the financial records (including data relating to Medicare utilizationand costs, including allowable costs under section 1858(c)) of at least one-third of the Medicare + Choice organizations offering Medicare + Choice plans under this part. The Comptroller General shall monitor auditing activities conducted under this subsection.

* * *

(4) DISCLOSURE.—

(A) IN GENERAL.—Each Medicare + Choice organization shall, in accordance with regulations of the Secretary, report to the Secretary financial information which shall include the following:

* * *

(ii) A copy of the report, if any, filed with the Secretarycontaining the information required to be reported under section 1124 by disclosing entities.

* * *

(e) ADDITIONAL CONTRACT TERMS.—

* * *

(2) COST-SHARING IN ENROLLMENT-RELATED COSTS.—

(A) IN GENERAL.—A Medicare + Choice organization and a PDP sponsor under part D shall pay the fee established by the Secretary under subparagraph (B).

(B) AUTHORIZATION.—The Secretary is authorized to charge a fee to each Medicare + Choice organization with a contract under this part and each PDP sponsor with a contract under Part d that is equal to the organization's or sponsor's pro rata share (as determined by the Secretary) of the aggregate amount of fees which the Secretary is directed to collect in a fiscal year. Any amounts collected shall be available without further appropriation to the Secretary for the purpose of carrying out section 1851 (relating to enrollment and dissemination of information), section 1860D-1(c), and section 4360 of the Omnibus Budget Reconciliation Act of 1990 (relating to the health insurance counseling and assistance program).

(C) AUTHORIZATION OF APPROPRIATIONS.—There are authorized to be appropriated for the purposes described in subparagraph (B) for each fiscal year beginning with fiscal year 2001 and ending with fiscal year 2005 an amount equal to $100,000,000, and for each fiscal year beginning with fiscal year 2006 an amount equal to $200,000,000, reduced by the amount of fees authorized to be collected under this paragraph and section 1860D-12(b)(3)(D) for the fiscal year.

(D) LIMITATION.—In any fiscal year the fees collected by the Secretary under subparagraph (B) shall not exceed the lesser of—

(i) the estimated costs to be incurred by the Secretary in the fiscal year in carrying out the activities described in section 1851 and section 1860D-1(c) and section 4360 of the Omnibus Budget Reconciliation Act of 1990; or

* * *

Social Security Law Added, Amended or Repealed

(ii)(III) $100,000,000 in fiscal year 2000;

(IV) the Medicare+Choice portion (as defined in subparagraph (E)) of $100,000,000 in fiscal year 2001 and each succeeding fiscal year before fiscal year 2006; and

(V) the applicable portion (as defined in subparagraph (F)) of $200,000,000 in fiscal year 2006 and each succeeding fiscal year.

* * *

(F) APPLICABLE PORTION DEFINED.—In this paragraph, the term "applicable portion" means, for a fiscal year—

(i) with respect to MA organizations, the Secretary's estimate of the total proportion of expenditures under this title that are attributable to expenditures made under this part (including payments under part D that are made to such organizations); or

(ii) with respect to PDP sponsors, the Secretary's estimate of the total proportion of expenditures under this title that are attributable to expenditures made to such sponsors under part D.

(3) AGREEMENTS WITH FEDERALLY QUALIFIED HEALTH CENTERS.—

(A) PAYMENT LEVELS AND AMOUNTS.—A contract under this section with an MA organization shall require the organization to provide, in any written agreement described in section 1853(a)(4) between the organization and a Federally qualified health center, for a level and amount of payment to the Federally qualified health center for services provided by such health center that is not less than the level and amount of payment that the plan would make for such services if the services had been furnished by a entity providing similar services that was not a Federally qualified health center.

(B) COST-SHARING.—Under the written agreement referred to in subparagraph (A), a Federally qualified health center must accept the payment amount referred to in such subparagraph plus the Federal payment provided for in section 1833(a)(3)(B) as payment in full for services covered by the agreement, except that such a health center may collect any amount of cost-sharing permitted under the contract under this section, so long as the amounts of any deductible, coinsurance, or copayment comply with the requirements under section 1854(e).

* * *

(i) MEDICARE+CHOICE PROGRAM COMPATIBILITY WITH EMPLOYER OR UNION GROUP HEALTH PLANS.—
(1) CONTRACTS WITH MA ORGANIZATIONS.—To facilitate the offering of Medicare+Choice plans under contracts between Medicare+Choice organizations and employers, labor organizations, or the trustees of a fund established by 1 or more employers or labor organizations (or combination thereof) to furnish benefits to the entity's employees, former employees (or combination thereof) or members or former members (or combination thereof) of the labor organizations, the Secretary may waive or modify requirements that hinder the design of, the offering of, or the enrollment in such Medicare+Choice plans.

(2) EMPLOYER SPONSORED MA PLANS.—To facilitate the offering of MA plans by employers, labor organizations, or the trustees of a fund established by one or more employers or labor organizations (or combination thereof) to furnish benefits to the entity's employees, former employees (or combination thereof) or members or former members (or combination thereof) of the labor organizations, the Secretary may waive or modify requirements that hinder the design of, the offering of, or the enrollment in such MA plans. Notwithstanding section 1851(g), an MA plan described in the previous sentence may restrict the enrollment of individuals under this part to individuals who are beneficiaries and participants in such plan.

[CCH Explanation at ¶ 374, 375, 376, 390, and 801.]

2003 Amendments:

Section 222(j) of the "Medicare Prescription Drug, Improvement, and Modernization Act of 2003," amended section 1857(i)(1) by designating the matter following the heading as a paragraph (1) with the heading "CONTRACTS WITH MA ORGANIZATIONS.—"and appropriate indentation; and by adding at the end new paragraph (2).

The above amendment applies to plan years beginning on or after January 1, 2006.

Section 222(k) of the "Medicare Prescription Drug, Improvement, and Modernization Act of 2003," amended section 1857(e)(2) in subparagraph (A) by inserting "and a PDP sponsor under part D" after "organization"; in subparagraph (B) by inserting "and each PDP sponsor with a con-

§1857(i)(2) ¶2256D

tract under part D" after "contract under this part"; by inserting "or sponsor's" after "organization's"; and by inserting ", section 1860D-1(c)," after "information)"; in subparagraph (C) by inserting "and ending with fiscal year 2005" after "beginning with fiscal year 2001"; by inserting "and for each fiscal year beginning with fiscal year 2006 an amount equal to $200,000,000," after "$100,000,000,"; and by inserting "and section 1860D-12(b)(3)(D)" after "under this paragraph"; in subparagraph (D) in clause (i) by inserting "and section 1860D-1(c)" after "section 1851"; in clause (ii)(III), by striking "and" at the end of subclause (III); in clause (ii)(IV), by striking "each succeeding fiscal year." and inserting "each succeeding fiscal year before fiscal year 2006; and"; and in clause (ii), by adding at the end new subclause (V); and by adding at the end new subparagraph (F).

The above amendment applies to plan years beginning on or after January 1, 2006.

Section 222(l)(3)(C) of the "Medicare Prescription Drug, Improvement, and Modernization Act of 2003," amended section 1857(d)(1) by striking ", costs, and computation of the adjusted community rate" and inserting "and costs, including allowable costs under section 1858(c)".

Section 237(c) of the "Medicare Prescription Drug, Improvement, and Modernization Act of 2003," effective upon enactment, amended section 1857(e) by adding new subsection (3).

The above amendment applies to services provided on or after Jan. 1, 2006, and contract years beginning on or after such date.

Section 900(e)(I) of the "Medicare Prescription Drug, Improvement, and Modernization Act of 2003," effective upon enactment, amended section 1857(d)(4)(A)(ii), by striking "Health Care Financing Administration" and inserting "Secretary".

[¶ 2256E] Sec. 1858. SPECIAL RULES FOR MA REGIONAL PLANS

(a) REGIONAL SERVICE AREA; ESTABLISHMENT OF MA REGIONS.—

(1) COVERAGE OF ENTIRE MA REGION.—The service area for an MA regional plan shall consist of an entire MA region established under paragraph (2) and the provisions of section 1854(h) shall not apply to such a plan.

(2) ESTABLISHMENT OF MA REGIONS.—

(A) MA REGION.—For purposes of this title, the term "MA region" means such a region within the 50 States and the District of Columbia as established by the Secretary under this paragraph.

(B) ESTABLISHMENT.—

(i) INITIAL ESTABLISHMENT.—Not later than January 1, 2005, the Secretary shall first establish and publish MA regions.

(ii) PERIODIC REVIEW AND REVISION OF SERVICE AREAS.—The Secretary may periodically review MA regions under this paragraph and, based on such review, may revise such regions if the Secretary determines such revision to be appropriate.

(C) REQUIREMENTS FOR MA REGIONS.—The Secretary shall establish, and may revise, MA regions under this paragraph in a manner consistent with the following:

(i) NUMBER OF REGIONS.—There shall be no fewer than 10 regions, and no more than 50 regions.

(ii) MAXIMIZING AVAILABILITY OF PLANS.—The regions shall maximize the availability of MA regional plans to all MA eligible individuals without regard to health status, especially those residing in rural areas.

(D) MARKET SURVEY AND ANALYSIS.—Before establishing MA regions, the Secretary shall conduct a market survey and analysis, including an examination of current insurance markets, to determine how the regions should be established.

(3) NATIONAL PLAN.—Nothing in this subsection shall be construed as preventing an MA regional plan from being offered in more than one MA region (including all regions).

(b) APPLICATION OF SINGLE DEDUCTIBLE AND CATASTROPHIC LIMIT ON OUT-OF-POCKET EXPENSES.—An MA regional plan shall include the following:

(1) SINGLE DEDUCTIBLE.—Any deductible for benefits under the original medicare fee-for-service program option shall be a single deductible (instead of a separate inpatient hospital deductible and a part B deductible) and may be applied differentially for in-network services and may be waived for preventive or other items and services.

(2) CATASTROPHIC LIMIT.—

(A) IN-NETWORK.—A catastrophic limit on out-of-pocket expenditures for in-network benefits under the original medicare fee-for-service program option.

(B) TOTAL.—A catastrophic limit on out-of-pocket expenditures for all benefits under the original medicare fee-for-service program option.

(c) PORTION OF TOTAL PAYMENTS TO AN ORGANIZATION SUBJECT TO RISK FOR 2006 AND 2007.—

(1) APPLICATION OF RISK CORRIDORS.—

(A) IN GENERAL.—This subsection shall only apply to MA regional plans offered during 2006 or 2007.

(B) NOTIFICATION OF ALLOWABLE COSTS UNDER THE PLAN.—In the case of an MA organization that offers an MA regional plan in an MA region in 2006 or 2007, the organization shall notify the Secretary, before such date in the succeeding year as the Secretary specifies, of—

(i) its total amount of costs that the organization incurred in providing benefits covered under the original medicare fee-for-service program option for all enrollees under the plan in the region in the year and the portion of such costs that is attributable to administrative expenses described in subparagraph (C); and

(ii) its total amount of costs that the organization incurred in providing rebatable integrated benefits (as defined in subparagraph (D)) and with respect to such benefits the portion of such costs that is attributable to administrative expenses described in subparagraph (C) and not described in clause (i) of this subparagraph.

(C) ALLOWABLE COSTS DEFINED.—For purposes of this subsection, the term 'allowable costs' means, with respect to an MA regional plan for a year, the total amount of costs described in subparagraph (B) for the plan and year, reduced by the portion of such costs attributable to administrative expenses incurred in providing the benefits described in such subparagraph.

(D) REBATABLE INTEGRATED BENEFITS.—For purposes of this subsection, the term 'rebatable integrated benefits' means such non-drug supplemental benefits under subclause (I) of section 1854(b)(1)(C)(ii) pursuant to a rebate under such section that the Secretary determines are integrated with the benefits described in subparagraph (B)(i).

(2) ADJUSTMENT OF PAYMENT.—

(A) NO ADJUSTMENT IF ALLOWABLE COSTS WITHIN 3 PERCENT OF TARGET AMOUNT.—If the allowable costs for the plan for the year are at least 97 percent, but do not exceed 103 percent, of the target amount for the plan and year, there shall be no payment adjustment under this subsection for the plan and year.

(B) INCREASE IN PAYMENT IF ALLOWABLE COSTS ABOVE 103 PERCENT OF TARGET AMOUNT.—

(i) COSTS BETWEEN 103 AND 108 PERCENT OF TARGET AMOUNT.—If the allowable costs for the plan for the year are greater than 103 percent, but not greater than 108 percent, of the target amount for the plan and year, the Secretary shall increase the total of the monthly payments made to the organization offering the plan for the year under section 1853(a) by an amount equal to 50 percent of the difference between such allowable costs and 103 percent of such target amount.

(ii) COSTS ABOVE 108 PERCENT OF TARGET AMOUNT.—If the allowable costs for the plan for the year are greater than 108 percent of the target amount for the plan and year, the Secretary shall increase the total of the monthly payments made to the organization offering the plan for the year under section 1853(a) by an amount equal to the sum of—

(I) 2.5 percent of such target amount; and

(II) 80 percent of the difference between such allowable costs and 108 percent of such target amount.

(C) REDUCTION IN PAYMENT IF ALLOWABLE COSTS BELOW 97 PERCENT OF TARGET AMOUNT.—

(i) COSTS BETWEEN 92 AND 97 PERCENT OF TARGET AMOUNT.—If the allowable costs for the plan for the year are less than 97 percent, but greater than or equal to 92 percent, of the target amount for the plan and year, the Secretary shall reduce the total of the monthly payments made to the organization offering the plan for the year under section 1853(a) by an amount (or otherwise recover from the plan an amount) equal to 50 percent of the difference between 97 percent of the target amount and such allowable costs.

(ii) COSTS BELOW 92 PERCENT OF TARGET AMOUNT.—If the allowable costs for the plan for the year are less than 92 percent of the target amount for the plan and year, the Secretary shall reduce the total of the monthly payments made to the organization offering the plan for the year under section 1853(a) by an amount (or otherwise recover from the plan an amount) equal to the sum of—

(I) 2.5 percent of such target amount; and

(II) 80 percent of the difference between 92 percent of such target amount and such allowable costs.

(D) TARGET AMOUNT DESCRIBED.—For purposes of this paragraph, the term 'target amount' means, with respect to an MA regional plan offered by an organization in a year, an amount equal to—

(i) the sum of—

(I) the total monthly payments made to the organization for enrollees in the plan for the year that are attributable to benefits under the original medicare fee-for-service program option (as defined in section 1852(a)(1)(B));

(II) the total of the MA monthly basic beneficiary premium collectable for such enrollees for the year; and

(III) the total amount of the rebates under section 1854(b)(1)(C)(ii) that are attributable to rebatable integrated benefits; reduced by

(ii) the amount of administrative expenses assumed in the bid insofar as the bid is attributable to benefits described in clause (i)(I) or (i)(III).

(3) DISCLOSURE OF INFORMATION.—

(A) IN GENERAL.—Each contract under this part shall provide—

(i) that an MA organization offering an MA regional plan shall provide the Secretary with such information as the Secretary determines is necessary to carry out this subsection; and

(ii) that, pursuant to section 1857(d)(2)(B), the Secretary has the right to inspect and audit any books and records of the organization that pertain to the information regarding costs provided to the Secretary under paragraph (1)(B).

(B) RESTRICTION ON USE OF INFORMATION.—Information disclosed or obtained pursuant to the provisions of this subsection may be used by officers, employees, and contractors of the Department of Health and Human Services only for the purposes of, and to the extent necessary in, carrying out this subsection.

(d) ORGANIZATIONAL AND FINANCIAL REQUIREMENTS.—

(1) IN GENERAL.—In the case of an MA organization that is offering an MA regional plan in an MA region and—

(A) meets the requirements of section 1855(a)(1) with respect to at least one such State in such region; and

(B) with respect to each other State in such region in which it does not meet requirements, it demonstrates to the satisfaction of the Secretary that it has filed the necessary application to meet such requirements,

the Secretary may waive such requirement with respect to each State described in subparagraph (B) for such period of time as the Secretary determines appropriate for the timely processing of such an application by the State (and, if such application is denied, through the end of such plan year as the Secretary determines appropriate to provide for a transition).

(2) SELECTION OF APPROPRIATE STATE.—In applying paragraph (1) in the case of an MA organization that meets the requirements of section 1855(a)(1) with respect to more than one State in a region, the organization shall select, in a manner specified by the Secretary among such States, one State the rules of which shall apply in the case of the States described in paragraph (1)(B).

(e) STABILIZATION FUND.—

(1) ESTABLISHMENT.—The Secretary shall establish under this subsection an MA Regional Plan Stabilization Fund (in this subsection referred to as the "Fund") which shall be available for 2 purposes:

(A) PLAN ENTRY.—To provide incentives to have MA regional plans offered in each MA region under paragraph (3).

(B) PLAN RETENTION.—To provide incentives to retain MA regional plans in certain MA regions with below-national-average MA market penetration under paragraph (4).

(2) FUNDING.—

(A) INITIAL FUNDING.—

(i) IN GENERAL.—There shall be available to the Fund, for expenditures from the Fund during the period beginning on January 1, 2007, and ending on December 31, 2013, a total of $10,000,000,000.

(ii) PAYMENT FROM TRUST FUNDS.—Such amount shall be available to the Fund, as expenditures are made from the Fund, from the Federal Hospital Insurance Trust Fund and the Federal Supplementary Medical Insurance Trust Fund in the proportion specified in section 1853(f).

(B) ADDITIONAL FUNDING FROM SAVINGS.—

(i) IN GENERAL.—There shall also be made available to the Fund, 50 percent of savings described in clause (ii).

(ii) SAVINGS.—The savings described in this clause are 25 percent of the average per capita savings described in section 1854(b)(4)(C) for which monthly rebates are provided under section 1854(b)(1)(C) in the fiscal year involved that are attributable to MA regional plans.

(iii) AVAILABILITY.—Funds made available under this subparagraph shall be transferred into a special account in the Treasury from the Federal Hospital Insurance Trust Fund and the Federal Supplementary Medical Insurance Trust Fund in the proportion specified in section 1853(f) on a monthly basis.

(C) OBLIGATIONS.—Amounts in the Fund shall be available in advance of appropriations to MA regional plans in qualifying MA regions only in accordance with paragraph (5).

(D) ORDERING.—Expenditures from the Fund shall first be made from amounts made available under subparagraph (A).

(3) PLAN ENTRY FUNDING.—

(A) IN GENERAL.—Funding is available under this paragraph for a year only as follows:

(i) NATIONAL PLAN.—For a national bonus payment described in subparagraph (B) for the offering by a single MA organization of an MA regional plan in each MA region in the year, but only if there was not such a plan offered in each such region in the previous year. Funding under this clause is only available with respect to any individual MA organization for a single year, but may be made available to more than one such organization in the same year.

(ii) REGIONAL PLANS.—Subject to clause (iii), for an increased amount under subparagraph (C) for an MA regional plan offered in an MA region which did not have any MA regional plan offered in the prior year.

(iii) LIMITATION ON REGIONAL PLAN FUNDING IN CASE OF NATIONAL PLAN.—In no case shall there be any payment adjustment under subparagraph (C) for a year for which a national payment adjustment is made under subparagraph (B).

(B) NATIONAL BONUS PAYMENT.—The national bonus payment under this subparagraph shall—

§1858(e)(3)(B) ¶2256E

(i) be available to an MA organization only if the organization offers MA regional plans in every MA region;

(ii) be available with respect to all MA regional plans of the organization regardless of whether any other MA regional plan is offered in any region; and

(iii) subject to amounts available under paragraph (5) for a year, be equal to 3 percent of the benchmark amount otherwise applicable for each MA regional plan offered by the organization.

(C) REGIONAL PAYMENT ADJUSTMENT.—

(i) IN GENERAL.—The increased amount under this subparagraph for an MA regional plan in an MA region for a year shall be an amount, determined by the Secretary, based on the bid submitted for such plan (or plans) and shall be available to all MA regional plans offered in such region and year. Such amount may be based on the mean, mode, or median, or other measure of such bids and may vary from region to region. The Secretary may not limit the number of plans or bids in a region.

(ii) MULTI-YEAR FUNDING.—

(I) IN GENERAL.—Subject to amounts available under paragraph (5), funding under this subparagraph shall be available for a period determined by the Secretary.

(II) REPORT.—If the Secretary determines that funding will be provided for a second consecutive year with respect to an MA region, the Secretary shall submit to the Congress a report that describes the underlying market dynamics in the region and that includes recommendations concerning changes in the payment methodology otherwise provided for MA regional plans under this part.

(iii) APPLICATION TO ALL PLANS IN A REGION.—Funding under this subparagraph with respect to an MA region shall be made available with respect to all MA regional plans offered in the region.

(iv) LIMITATION ON AVAILABILITY OF PLAN RETENTION FUNDING IN NEXT YEAR.—If an increased amount is made available under this subparagraph with respect to an MA region for a period determined by the Secretary under clause (ii)(I), in no case shall funding be available under paragraph (4) with respect to MA regional plans offered in the region in the year following such period.

(D) APPLICATION.—Any additional payment under this paragraph provided for an MA regional plan for a year shall be treated as if it were an addition to the benchmark amount otherwise applicable to such plan and year, but shall not be taken into account in the computation of any benchmark amount for any subsequent year.

(4) PLAN RETENTION FUNDING.—

(A) IN GENERAL.—Funding is available under this paragraph for a year with respect to MA regional plans offered in an MA region for the increased amount specified in subparagraph (B) but only if the region meets the requirements of subparagraphs (C) and (E).

(B) PAYMENT INCREASE.—The increased amount under this subparagraph for an MA regional plan in an MA region for a year shall be an amount, determined by the Secretary, that does not exceed the greater of—

(i) 3 percent of the benchmark amount applicable in the region; or

(ii) such amount as (when added to the benchmark amount applicable to the region) will result in the ratio of—

(I) such additional amount plus the benchmark amount computed under section 1854(b)(4)(B)(i) for the region and year, to the adjusted average per capita cost for the region and year, as estimated by the Secretary under section 1876(a)(4) and adjusted as appropriate for the purpose of risk adjustment; being equal to

(II) the weighted average of such benchmark amounts for all the regions and such year, to the average per capita cost for the United States and such year, as estimated by the Secretary under section 1876(a)(4) and adjusted as appropriate for the purpose of risk adjustment.

(C) REGIONAL REQUIREMENTS.—The requirements of this subparagraph for an MA region for a year are as follows:

(i) NOTIFICATION OF PLAN EXIT.—The Secretary has received notice (in such form and manner as the Secretary specifies) before a year that one or more MA regional plans that were offered in the region in the previous year will not be offered in the succeeding year.

(ii) REGIONAL PLANS AVAILABLE FROM FEWER THAN 2 MA ORGANIZATIONS IN THE REGION.—The Secretary determines that if the plans referred to in clause (i) are not offered in the year, fewer than 2 MA organizations will be offering MA regional plans in the region in the year involved.

(iii) PERCENTAGE ENROLLMENT IN MA REGIONAL PLANS BELOW NATIONAL AVERAGE.—For the previous year, the Secretary determines that the average percentage of MA eligible individuals residing in the region who are enrolled in MA regional plans is less than the average percentage of such individuals in the United States enrolled in such plans.

(D) APPLICATION.—Any additional payment under this paragraph provided for an MA regional plan for a year shall be treated as if it were an addition to the benchmark amount otherwise applicable to such plan and year, but shall not be taken into account in the computation of any benchmark amount for any subsequent year.

(E) 2-CONSECUTIVE-YEAR LIMITATION.—

(i) IN GENERAL.—In no case shall any funding be available under this paragraph in an MA region in a period of consecutive years that exceeds 2 years.

(ii) REPORT.—If the Secretary determines that funding will be provided under this paragraph for a second consecutive year with respect to an MA region, the Secretary shall submit to the Congress a report that describes the underlying market dynamics in the region and that includes recommendations concerning changes in the payment methodology otherwise provided for MA regional plans under this part.

(5) FUNDING LIMITATION.—

(A) IN GENERAL.—The total amount expended from the Fund as a result of the application of this subsection through the end of a calendar year may not exceed the amount available to the Fund as of the first day of such year. For purposes of this subsection, amounts that are expended under this title insofar as such amounts would not have been expended but for the application of this subsection shall be counted as amounts expended as a result of such application.

(B) APPLICATION OF LIMITATION.—The Secretary may obligate funds from the Fund for a year only if the Secretary determines (and the Chief Actuary of the Centers for Medicare & Medicaid Services and the appropriate budget officer certify) that there are available in the Fund at the beginning of the year sufficient amounts to cover all such obligations incurred during the year consistent with subparagraph (A). The Secretary shall take such steps, in connection with computing additional payment amounts under paragraphs (3) and (4) and including limitations on enrollment in MA regional plans receiving such payments, as will ensure that sufficient funds are available to make such payments for the entire year. Funds shall only be made available from the Fund pursuant to an apportionment made in accordance with applicable procedures.

(6) SECRETARY REPORTS.—Not later than April 1 of each year (beginning in 2008), the Secretary shall submit a report to Congress and the Comptroller General of the United States that includes—

(A) a detailed description of—

(i) the total amount expended as a result of the application of this subsection in the previous year compared to the total amount that would have been expended under this title in the year if this subsection had not been enacted;

(ii) the projections of the total amount that will be expended as a result of the application of this subsection in the year in which the report is submitted compared to the total amount that would have been expended under this title in the year if this subsection had not been enacted;

§1858(e)(6)(A)(ii) ¶2256E

(iii) amounts remaining within the funding limitation specified in paragraph (5); and

(iv) the steps that the Secretary will take under paragraph (5)(B) to ensure that the application of this subsection will not cause expenditures to exceed the amount available in the Fund; and

(B) a certification from the Chief Actuary of the Centers for Medicare & Medicaid Services that the description provided under subparagraph (A) is reasonable, accurate, and based on generally accepted actuarial principles and methodologies.

(7) BIENNIAL GAO REPORTS.—Not later than January 1 of 2009, 2011, 2013, and 2015, the Comptroller General of the United States shall submit to the Secretary and Congress a report on the application of additional payments under this subsection. Each report shall include—

(A) an evaluation of—

(i) the quality of care provided to individuals enrolled in MA regional plans for which additional payments were made under this subsection;

(ii) the satisfaction of such individuals with benefits under such a plan;

(iii) the costs to the medicare program for payments made to such plans; and

(iv) any improvements in the delivery of health care services under such a plan;

(B) a comparative analysis of the performance of MA regional plans receiving payments under this subsection with MA regional plans not receiving such payments; and

(C) recommendations for such legislation or administrative action as the Comptroller General determines to be appropriate.

(f) COMPUTATION OF APPLICABLE MA REGION-SPECIFIC NON-DRUG MONTHLY BENCHMARK AMOUNTS.—

(1) COMPUTATION FOR REGIONS.—For purposes of section 1853(j)(2) and this section, subject to subsection (e), the term 'MA region-specific non-drug monthly benchmark amount' means, with respect to an MA region for a month in a year, the sum of the 2 components described in paragraph (2) for the region and year. The Secretary shall compute such benchmark amount for each MA region before the beginning of each annual, coordinated election period under section 1851(e)(3)(B) for each year (beginning with 2006).

(2) 2 COMPONENTS.—For purposes of paragraph (1), the 2 components described in this paragraph for an MA region and a year are the following:

(A) STATUTORY COMPONENT.—The product of the following:

(i) STATUTORY REGION-SPECIFIC NON-DRUG AMOUNT.—The statutory region-specific non-drug amount (as defined in paragraph (3)) for the region and year.

(ii) STATUTORY NATIONAL MARKET SHARE.—The statutory national market share percentage, determined under paragraph (4) for the year.

(B) PLAN-BID COMPONENT.—The product of the following:

(i) WEIGHTED AVERAGE OF MA PLAN BIDS IN REGION.—The weighted average of the plan bids for the region and year (as determined under paragraph (5)(A)).

(ii) NON-STATUTORY MARKET SHARE.—1 minus the statutory national market share percentage, determined under paragraph (4) for the year.

(3) STATUTORY REGION-SPECIFIC NON-DRUG AMOUNT.—For purposes of paragraph (2)(A)(i), the term 'statutory region-specific non-drug amount' means, for an MA region and year, an amount equal the sum (for each MA local area within the region) of the product of—

(A) MA area-specific non-drug monthly benchmark amount under section 1853(j)(1)(A) for that area and year; and

(B) the number of MA eligible individuals residing in the local area, divided by the total number of MA eligible individuals residing in the region.

(4) COMPUTATION OF STATUTORY MARKET SHARE PERCENTAGE.—

(A) IN GENERAL.—The Secretary shall determine for each year a statutory national market share percentage that is equal to the proportion of MA eligible individuals nationally who were not enrolled in an MA plan during the reference month.

(B) REFERENCE MONTH DEFINED.—For purposes of this part, the term 'reference month' means, with respect to a year, the most recent month during the previous year for which the Secretary determines that data are available to compute the percentage specified in subparagraph (A) and other relevant percentages under this part.

(5) DETERMINATION OF WEIGHTED AVERAGE MA BIDS FOR A REGION.—

(A) IN GENERAL.—For purposes of paragraph (2)(B)(i), the weighted average of plan bids for an MA region and a year is the sum, for MA regional plans described in subparagraph (D) in the region and year, of the products (for each such plan) of the following:

(i) MONTHLY MA STATUTORY NON-DRUG BID AMOUNT.—The unadjusted MA statutory non-drug monthly bid amount for the plan.

(ii) PLAN'S SHARE OF MA ENROLLMENT IN REGION.—The factor described in subparagraph (B) for the plan.

(B) PLAN'S SHARE OF MA ENROLLMENT IN REGION.—

(i) IN GENERAL.—Subject to the succeeding provisions of this subparagraph, the factor described in this subparagraph for a plan is equal to the number of individuals described in subparagraph (C) for such plan, divided by the total number of such individuals for all MA regional plans described in subparagraph (D) for that region and year.

(ii) SINGLE PLAN RULE.—In the case of an MA region in which only a single MA regional plan is being offered, the factor described in this subparagraph shall be equal to 1.

(iii) EQUAL DIVISION AMONG MULTIPLE PLANS IN YEAR IN WHICH PLANS ARE FIRST AVAILABLE.—In the case of an MA region in the first year in which any MA regional plan is offered, if more than one MA regional plan is offered in such year, the factor described in this subparagraph for a plan shall (as specified by the Secretary) be equal to—

(I) 1 divided by the number of such plans offered in such year; or

(II) a factor for such plan that is based upon the organization's estimate of projected enrollment, as reviewed and adjusted by the Secretary to ensure reasonableness and as is certified by the Chief Actuary of the Centers for Medicare & Medicaid Services.

(C) COUNTING OF INDIVIDUALS.—For purposes of subparagraph (B)(i), the Secretary shall count for each MA regional plan described in subparagraph (D) for an MA region and year, the number of individuals who reside in the region and who were enrolled under such plan under this part during the reference month.

(D) PLANS COVERED.—For an MA region and year, an MA regional plan described in this subparagraph is an MA regional plan that is offered in the region and year and was offered in the region in the reference month.

(g) ELECTION OF UNIFORM COVERAGE DETERMINATION.—Instead of applying section 1852(a)(2)(C) with respect to an MA regional plan, the organization offering the plan may elect to have a local coverage determination for the entire MA region be the local coverage determination applied for any part of such region (as selected by the organization).

(h) ASSURING NETWORK ADEQUACY.—

(1) IN GENERAL.—For purposes of enabling MA organizations that offer MA regional plans to meet applicable provider access requirements under section 1852 with respect to such plans, the Secretary may provide for payment under this section to an essential hospital that provides inpatient hospital services to enrollees in such a plan where the MA organization offering the plan certifies to the Secretary that the organization was unable to reach an agreement between

the hospital and the organization regarding provision of such services under the plan. Such payment shall be available only if—

(A) the organization provides assurances satisfactory to the Secretary that the organization will make payment to the hospital for inpatient hospital services of an amount that is not less than the amount that would be payable to the hospital under section 1886 with respect to such services; and

(B) with respect to specific inpatient hospital services provided to an enrollee, the hospital demonstrates to the satisfaction of the Secretary that the hospital's costs of such services exceed the payment amount described in subparagraph (A).

(2) PAYMENT AMOUNTS.—The payment amount under this subsection for inpatient hospital services provided by a subsection (d) hospital to an enrollee in an MA regional plan shall be, subject to the limitation of funds under paragraph (3), the amount (if any) by which—

(A) the amount of payment that would have been paid for such services under this title if the enrollees were covered under the original medicare fee-for-service program option and the hospital were a critical access hospital; exceeds

(B) the amount of payment made for such services under paragraph (1)(A).

(3) AVAILABLE AMOUNTS.—There shall be available for payments under this subsection—

(A) in 2006, $25,000,000; and

(B) in each succeeding year the amount specified in this paragraph for the preceding year increased by the market basket percentage increase (as defined in section 1886(b)(3)(B)(iii)) for the fiscal year ending in such succeeding year.

Payments under this subsection shall be made from the Federal Hospital Insurance Trust Fund.

(4) ESSENTIAL HOSPITAL.—In this subsection, the term 'essential hospital' means, with respect to an MA regional plan offered by an MA organization, a subsection (d) hospital (as defined in section 1886(d)) that the Secretary determines, based upon an application filed by the organization with the Secretary, is necessary to meet the requirements referred to in paragraph (1) for such plan.

[CCH Explanation at ¶363.]
2003 Amendments:

Section 221(c) of the "Medicare Prescription Drug, Improvement, and Modernization Act of 2003," effective upon enactment, added new section 1858.

The above amendment applies to plan years beginning on or after January 1, 2006.

[¶2256F] Sec. 1859. DEFINITIONS; MISCELLANEOUS PROVISIONS

[42 U.S.C. §1395w-28]

* * *

(b) DEFINITIONS RELATING TO MEDICARE + CHOICE PLANS.—

* * *

(4) MA REGIONAL PLAN.—The term "MA regional plan" means an MA plan described in section 1851(a)(2)(A)(i)—

(A) that has a network of providers that have agreed to a contractually specified reimbursement for covered benefits with the organization offering the plan;

(B) that provides for reimbursement for all covered benefits regardless of whether such benefits are provided within such network of providers; and

(C) the service area of which is one or more entire MA regions.

(5) MA LOCAL PLAN.—The term "MA local plan" means an MA plan that is not an MA regional plan.

(6) SPECIALIZED MA PLANS FOR SPECIAL NEEDS INDIVIDUALS.—

(A) IN GENERAL.—The term "specialized MA plan for special needs individuals" means an MA plan that exclusively serves special needs individuals (as defined in subparagraph (B)).

(B) SPECIAL NEEDS INDIVIDUAL.—The term "special needs individual" means an MA eligible individual who—

(i) is institutionalized (as defined by the Secretary);

(ii) is entitled to medical assistance under a State plan under title XIX; or

(iii) meets such requirements as the Secretary may determine would benefit from enrollment in such a specialized MA plan described in subparagraph (A) for individuals with severe or disabling chronic conditions.

The Secretary may waive application of section 1851(a)(3)(B) in the case of an individual described in clause (i), (ii), or (iii) of this subparagraph and may apply rules similar to the rules of section 1894(c)(4) for continued eligibility of special needs individuals.

(c) OTHER REFERENCES TO OTHER TERMS.—

* * *

(5) MA LOCAL AREA.—The term 'MA local area' is defined in section 1853(d)(2).

* * *

(f) RESTRICTION ON ENROLLMENT FOR SPECIALIZED MA PLANS FOR SPECIAL NEEDS INDIVIDUALS.—In the case of a specialized MA plan for special needs individuals (as defined in subsection (b)(6)), notwithstanding any other provision of this part and in accordance with regulations of the Secretary and for periods before January 1, 2009, the plan may restrict the enrollment of individuals under the plan to individuals who are within one or more classes of special needs individuals.

[CCH Explanation at ¶362 and 378.]

2003 Amendments:

Section 221(b) of the "Medicare Prescription Drug, Improvement, and Modernization Act of 2003," effective upon enactment, amended section 1859(b) by adding at the end new paragraphs (4) and (5).

The above amendment applies to plan years beginning on or after January 1, 2006.

Section 221(d)(2) of the "Medicare Prescription Drug, Improvement, and Modernization Act of 2003," effective upon enactment, amended section 1859(c) by adding new paragraph (5).

Section 231(b) of the "Medicare Prescription Drug, Improvement, and Modernization Act of 2003," effective upon enactment, amended section 1859(b) by adding new paragraph (6).

Section 231(c) of the "Medicare Prescription Drug, Improvement, and Modernization Act of 2003," effective upon enactment, amended section 1859 by adding new subsection (f).

[¶2260] Sec. 1860C-1. COMPARATIVE COST ADJUSTMENT (CCA) PROGRAM

(a) ESTABLISHMENT OF PROGRAM.—

(1) IN GENERAL.—The Secretary shall establish a program under this section (in this section referred to as the "CCA program") for the application of comparative cost adjustment in CCA areas selected under this section.

(2) DURATION.—The CCA program shall begin January 1, 2010, and shall extend over a period of 6 years, and end on December 31, 2015.

(3) REPORT.—Upon the completion of the CCA program, the Secretary shall submit a report to Congress. Such report shall include the following, with respect to both this part and the original medicare fee-for-service program:

(A) An evaluation of the financial impact of the CCA program.

(B) An evaluation of changes in access to physicians and other health care providers.

(C) Beneficiary satisfaction.

(D) Recommendations regarding any extension or expansion of the CCA program.

(b) REQUIREMENTS FOR SELECTION OF CCA AREAS.—

(1) CCA AREA DEFINED.—

(A) IN GENERAL.—For purposes of this section, the term "CCA area" means an MSA that meets the requirements of paragraph (2) and is selected by the Secretary under subsection (c).

(B) MSA DEFINED.—For purposes of this section, the term "MSA" means a Metropolitan Statistical Area (or such similar area as the Secretary recognizes).

(2) REQUIREMENTS FOR CCA AREAS.—The requirements of this paragraph for an MSA to be a CCA area are as follows:

(A) MA ENROLLMENT REQUIREMENT.—For the reference month (as defined under section 1858(f)(4)(B)) with respect to 2010, at least 25 percent of the total number of MA eligible individuals who reside in the MSA were enrolled in an MA local plan described in section 1851(a)(2)(A)(i).

(B) 2 PLAN REQUIREMENT.—There will be offered in the MSA during the annual, coordinated election period under section 1851(e)(3)(B) before the beginning of 2010 at least 2 MA local plans described in section 1851(a)(2)(A)(i) (in addition to the fee-for-service program under parts A and B), each offered by a different MA organization and each of which met the minimum enrollment requirements of paragraph (1) of section 1857(b) (as applied without regard to paragraph (3) thereof) as of the reference month.

(c) SELECTION OF CCA AREAS.—

(1) GENERAL SELECTION CRITERIA.—The Secretary shall select CCA areas from among those MSAs qualifying under subsection (b) in a manner that—

(A) seeks to maximize the opportunity to test the application of comparative cost adjustment under this title;

(B) does not seek to maximize the number of MA eligible individuals who reside in such areas; and

(C) provides for geographic diversity consistent with the criteria specified in paragraph (2).

(2) SELECTION CRITERIA.—With respect to the selection of MSAs that qualify to be CCA areas under subsection (b), the following rules apply, to the maximum extent feasible:

(A) MAXIMUM NUMBER.—The number of such MSAs selected may not exceed the lesser of (i) 6, or (ii) 25 percent of the number of MSAs that meet the requirement of subsection (b)(2)(A).

(B) ONE OF 4 LARGEST AREAS BY POPULATION.—At least one such qualifying MSA shall be selected from among the 4 such qualifying MSAs with the largest total population of MA eligible individuals.

(C) ONE OF 4 AREAS WITH LOWEST POPULATION DENSITY.—At least one such qualifying MSA shall be selected from among the 4 such qualifying MSAs with the lowest population density (as measured by residents per square mile or similar measure of density).

(D) MULTISTATE AREA.—At least one such qualifying MSA shall be selected that includes a multiState area. Such an MSA may be an MSA described in subparagraph (B) or (C).

(E) LIMITATION WITHIN SAME GEOGRAPHIC REGION.—No more than 2 such MSAs shall be selected that are, in whole or in part, within the same geographic region (as specified by the Secretary) of the United States.

(F) PRIORITY TO AREAS NOT WITHIN CERTAIN DEMONSTRATION PROJECTS.—Priority shall be provided for those qualifying MSAs that do not have a demonstration project in effect as of the date of the enactment of this section for medicare preferred provider organization plans under this part.

(d) APPLICATION OF COMPARATIVE COST ADJUSTMENT.—

(1) IN GENERAL.—In the case of a CCA area for a year—

(A) for purposes of applying this part with respect to payment for MA local plans, any reference to an MA area-specific non-drug monthly benchmark amount shall be treated as a reference to such benchmark computed as if the CCA area-specific non-drug monthly benchmark amount (as defined in subsection (e)(1)) were substituted for the amount described in section 1853(j)(1)(A) for the CCA area and year involved, as phased in under paragraph (3); and

(B) with respect to months in the year for individuals residing in the CCA area who are not enrolled in an MA plan, the amount of the monthly premium under section 1839 is subject to adjustment under subsection (f).

(2) EXCLUSION OF MA LOCAL AREAS WITH FEWER THAN 2 ORGANIZATIONS OFFERING MA PLANS.—

(A) IN GENERAL.—In no case shall an MA local area that is within an MSA be included as part of a CCA area unless for 2010 (and, except as provided in subparagraph (B), for a subsequent year) there is offered in each part of such MA local area at least 2 MA local plans described in section 1851(a)(2)(A)(i) each of which is offered by a different MA organization.

(B) CONTINUATION.—If an MA local area meets the requirement of subparagraph (A) and is included in a CCA area for 2010, such local area shall continue to be included in such CCA area for a subsequent year notwithstanding that it no longer meets such requirement so long as there is at least one MA local plan described in section 1851(a)(2)(A)(i) that is offered in such local area.

(3) PHASE-IN OF CCA BENCHMARK.—

(A) IN GENERAL.—In applying this section for a year before 2013, paragraph (1)(A) shall be applied as if the phase-in fraction under subparagraph (B) of the CCA non-drug monthly benchmark amount for the year were substituted for such fraction of the MA area-specific non-drug monthly benchmark amount.

(B) PHASE-IN FRACTION.—The phase-in fraction under this subparagraph is—

(i) for 2010 14; and

(ii) for a subsequent year is the phase-in fraction under this subparagraph for the previous year increased by 14, but in no case more than 1.

(e) COMPUTATION OF CCA BENCHMARK AMOUNT.—

(1) CCA NON-DRUG MONTHLY BENCHMARK AMOUNT.—For purposes of this section, the term "CCA non-drug monthly benchmark amount" means, with respect to a CCA area for a month in a year, the sum of the 2 components described in paragraph (2) for the area and year. The Secretary shall compute such benchmark amount for each such CCA area before the beginning of each annual, coordinated election period under section 1851(e)(3)(B) for each year (beginning with 2010) in which the CCA area is so selected.

(2) 2 COMPONENTS.—For purposes of paragraph (1), the 2 components described in this paragraph for a CCA area and a year are the following:

(A) MA LOCAL COMPONENT.—The product of the following:

(i) WEIGHTED AVERAGE OF MEDICARE ADVANTAGE PLAN BIDS IN AREA.—The weighted average of the plan bids for the area and year (as determined under paragraph (3)(A)).

(ii) NON-FFS MARKET SHARE.—1 minus the fee-for-service market share percentage, determined under paragraph (4) for the area and year.

(B) FEE-FOR-SERVICE COMPONENT.—The product of the following:

(i) FEE-FOR-SERVICE AREA-SPECIFIC NONDRUG AMOUNT.—The fee-for-service area-specific non-drug amount (as defined in paragraph (5)) for the area and year.

(ii) FEE-FOR-SERVICE MARKET SHARE.—The fee-for-service market share percentage, determined under paragraph (4) for the area and year.

§1860C-1(e)(2)(B)(ii)

(3) DETERMINATION OF WEIGHTED AVERAGE MA BIDS FOR A CCA AREA.—

(A) IN GENERAL.—For purposes of paragraph (2)(A)(i), the weighted average of plan bids for a CCA area and a year is, subject to subparagraph (D), the sum of the following products for MA local plans described in subparagraph (C) in the area and year:

(i) MONTHLY MEDICARE ADVANTAGE STATUTORY NON-DRUG BID AMOUNT.—The accepted unadjusted MA statutory non-drug monthly bid amount.

(ii) PLAN'S SHARE OF MEDICARE ADVANTAGE ENROLLMENT IN AREA.—The number of individuals described in subparagraph (B), divided by the total number of such individuals for all MA plans described in subparagraph (C) for that area and year.

(B) COUNTING OF INDIVIDUALS.—The Secretary shall count, for each MA local plan described in subparagraph (C) for an area and year, the number of individuals who reside in the area and who were enrolled under such plan under this part during the reference month for that year.

(C) EXCLUSION OF PLANS NOT OFFERED IN PREVIOUS YEAR.—For an area and year, the MA local plans described in this subparagraph are MA local plans described in section 1851(a)(2)(A)(i) that are offered in the area and year and were offered in the CCA area in the reference month.

(D) COMPUTATION OF WEIGHTED AVERAGE OF PLAN BIDS.—In calculating the weighted average of plan bids for a CCA area under subparagraph (A)—

(i) in the case of an MA local plan that has a service area only part of which is within such CCA area, the MA organization offering such plan shall submit a separate bid for such plan for the portion within such CCA area; and

(ii) the Secretary shall adjust such separate bid (or, in the case of an MA local plan that has a service area entirely within such CCA area, the plan bid) as may be necessary to take into account differences between the service area of such plan within the CCA area and the entire CCA area and the distribution of plan enrollees of all MA local plans offered within the CCA area.

(4) COMPUTATION OF FEE-FOR-SERVICE MARKET SHARE PERCENTAGE.—The Secretary shall determine, for a year and a CCA area, the proportion (in this subsection referred to as the "fee-for-service market share percentage") equal to—

(A) the total number of MA eligible individuals residing in such area who during the reference month for the year were not enrolled in any MA plan; divided by

(B) the sum of such number and the total number of MA eligible individuals residing in such area who during such reference month were enrolled in an MA local plan described in section 1851(a)(2)(A)(i), or, if greater, such proportion determined for individuals nationally.

(5) FEE-FOR-SERVICE AREA-SPECIFIC NON-DRUG AMOUNT.—(A) IN GENERAL.—For purposes of paragraph (2)(B)(i) and subsection (f)(2)(A), subject to subparagraph (C), the term "fee-for-service area-specific nondrug amount" means, for a CCA area and a year, the adjusted average per capita cost for such area and year involved, determined under section 1876(a)(4) and adjusted as appropriate for the purpose of risk adjustment for benefits under the original medicare fee-forservice program option for individuals entitled to benefits under part A and enrolled under part B who are not enrolled in an MA plan for the year, but adjusted to exclude costs attributable to payments under section 1886(h).

(B) USE OF FULL RISK ADJUSTMENT TO STANDARDIZE FEE-FOR-SERVICE COSTS TO TYPICAL BENEFICIARY.—In determining the adjusted average per capita cost for an area and year under subparagraph (A), such costs shall be adjusted to fully take into account the demographic and health status risk factors established under section 1853(a)(1)(A)(iv) so that such per capita costs reflect the average costs for a typical beneficiary residing in the CCA area.

(C) INCLUSION OF COSTS OF VA AND DOD MILITARY FACILITY SERVICES TO MEDICARE-ELIGIBLE BENEFICIARIES.—In determining the adjusted average per capita cost under subparagraph (A) for a year, such cost shall be adjusted to include the Secretary's estimate, on a per capita basis, of the amount of additional payments that would have been made in the area involved under this title if individuals entitled to benefits under this title had not received services from facilities of the Department of Veterans Affairs or the Department of Defense.

(f) PREMIUM ADJUSTMENT.—

(1) APPLICATION.—

(A) IN GENERAL.—Except as provided in subparagraph (B), in the case of an individual who is enrolled under part B, who resides in a CCA area, and who is not enrolled in an MA plan under this part, the monthly premium otherwise applied under part B (determined without regard to subsections (b), (f), and (i) of section 1839 or any adjustment under this subsection) shall be adjusted in accordance with paragraph (2), but only in the case of premiums for months during the period in which the CCA program under this section for such area is in effect.

(B) NO PREMIUM ADJUSTMENT FOR SUBSIDY ELIGIBLE BENEFICIARIES.—No premium adjustment shall be made under this subsection for a premium for a month if the individual is determined to be a subsidy eligible individual (as defined in section 1860D-14(a)(3)(A)) for the month.

(2) AMOUNT OF ADJUSTMENT.—

(A) IN GENERAL.—Under this paragraph, subject to the exemption under paragraph (1)(B) and the limitation under subparagraph (B), if the fee-for-service area-specific non-drug amount (as defined in section (e)(5)) for a CCA area in which an individual resides for a month—

(i) does not exceed the CCA non-drug monthly benchmark amount (as determined under subsection (e)(1)) for such area and month, the amount of the premium for the individual for the month shall be reduced, by an amount equal to 75 percent of the amount by which such CCA benchmark exceeds such fee-for-service area-specific nondrug amount; or

(ii) exceeds such CCA non-drug benchmark, the amount of the premium for the individual for the month shall be adjusted to ensure, that—

(I) the sum of the amount of the adjusted premium and the CCA non-drug benchmark for the area; is equal to

(II) the sum of the unadjusted premium plus the amount of such fee-for-service areaspecific non-drug amount for the area.

(B) LIMITATION.—In no case shall the actual amount of an adjustment under subparagraph (A) for an area and month in a year result in an adjustment that exceeds the maximum adjustment permitted under subparagraph (C) for the area and year, or, if less, the maximum annual adjustment permitted under subparagraph (D) for the area and year.

(C) PHASE-IN OF ADJUSTMENT.—The amount of an adjustment under subparagraph (A) for a CCA area and year may not exceed the product of the phase-in fraction for the year under subsection (d)(3)(B) multiplied by the amount of the adjustment otherwise computed under subparagraph (A) for the area and year, determined without regard to this subparagraph and subparagraph (D).

(D) 5-PERCENT LIMITATION ON ADJUSTMENT.—The amount of the adjustment under this subsection for months in a year shall not exceed 5 percent of the amount of the monthly premium amount determined for months in the year under section 1839 without regard to subsections (b), (f), and (i) of such section and this subsection.".

[CCH Explanation at ¶ 396.]

2003 Amendments:

Section 241(a) of the "Medicare Prescription Drug, Improvement, and Modernization Act of 2003," effective upon enactment, added new section 1860C-1.

TITLE 1—MEDICARE PRESCRIPTION DRUG BENEFIT
SEC. 101 MEDICARE PRESCRIPTION DRUG BENEFIT.
PART D—VOLUNTARY PRESCRIPTION DRUG BENEFIT PROGRAM

Subpart 1—Part D Eligible Individuals and Prescription Drug Benefits

[¶2261A] Sec. 1860D-1. ELIGIBILITY, ENROLLMENT, AND INFORMATION

(a) PROVISION OF QUALIFIED PRESCRIPTION DRUG COVERAGE THROUGH ENROLLMENT IN PLANS.—

(1) IN GENERAL.—Subject to the succeeding provisions of this part, each part D eligible individual (as defined in paragraph (3)(A)) is entitled to obtain qualified prescription drug coverage (described in section 1860D-2(a)) as follows:

(A) FEE-FOR-SERVICE ENROLLEES MAY RECEIVE COVERAGE THROUGH A PRESCRIPTION DRUG PLAN.—A part D eligible individual who is not enrolled in an MA plan may obtain qualified prescription drug coverage through enrollment in a prescription drug plan (as defined in section 1860D-41(a)(14)).

(B) MEDICARE ADVANTAGE ENROLLEES.—

(i) ENROLLEES IN A PLAN PROVIDING QUALIFIED PRESCRIPTION DRUG COVERAGE RECEIVE COVERAGE THROUGH THE PLAN.—A part D eligible individual who is enrolled in an MA-PD plan obtains such coverage through such plan.

(ii) LIMITATION ON ENROLLMENT OF MA PLAN ENROLLEES IN PRESCRIPTION DRUG PLANS.—Except as provided in clauses (iii) and (iv), a part D eligible individual who is enrolled in an MA plan may not enroll in a prescription drug plan under this part.

(iii) PRIVATE FEE-FOR-SERVICE ENROLLEES IN MA PLANS NOT PROVIDING QUALIFIED PRESCRIPTION DRUG COVERAGE PERMITTED TO ENROLL IN A PRESCRIPTION DRUG PLAN.—A part D eligible individual who is enrolled in an MA private fee-for-service plan (as defined in section 1859(b)(2)) that does not provide qualified prescription drug coverage may obtain qualified prescription drug coverage through enrollment in a prescription drug plan.

(iv) ENROLLEES IN MSA PLANS PERMITTED TO ENROLL IN A PRESCRIPTION DRUG PLAN.—A part D eligible individual who is enrolled in an MSA plan (as defined in section 1859(b)(3)) may obtain qualified prescription drug coverage through enrollment in a prescription drug plan.

(2) COVERAGE FIRST EFFECTIVE JANUARY 1, 2006.—Coverage under prescription drug plans and MA-PD plans shall first be effective on January 1, 2006.

(3) DEFINITIONS.—For purposes of this part:

(A) PART D ELIGIBLE INDIVIDUAL.—The term 'part D eligible individual' means an individual who is entitled to benefits under part A or enrolled under part B.

(B) MA PLAN.—The term 'MA plan' has the meaning given such term in section 1859(b)(1).

(C) MA-PD PLAN.—The term 'MA-PD plan' means an MA plan that provides qualified prescription drug coverage.

(b) ENROLLMENT PROCESS FOR PRESCRIPTION DRUG PLANS.—

(1) ESTABLISHMENT OF PROCESS.—

(A) IN GENERAL.—The Secretary shall establish a process for the enrollment, disenrollment, termination, and change of enrollment of part D eligible individuals in prescription drug plans consistent with this subsection.

(B) APPLICATION OF MA RULES.—In establishing such process, the Secretary shall use rules similar to (and coordinated with) the rules for enrollment, disenrollment, termination, and change of enrollment with an MA-PD plan under the following provisions of section 1851:

(i) RESIDENCE REQUIREMENTS.—Section 1851(b)(1)(A), relating to residence requirements.

(ii) EXERCISE OF CHOICE.—Section 1851(c) (other than paragraph (3)(A) of such section), relating to exercise of choice.

(iii) COVERAGE ELECTION PERIODS.—Subject to paragraphs (2) and (3) of this subsection, section 1851(e) (other than subparagraphs (B) and (C) of paragraph (2) and the second sentence of paragraph (4) of such section), relating to coverage election periods, including initial periods, annual coordinated election periods, special election periods, and election periods for exceptional cir-cumstances.

(iv) COVERAGE PERIODS.—Section 1851(f), relating to effectiveness of elections and changes of elections.

(v) GUARANTEED ISSUE AND RENEWAL.—Section 1851(g) (other than paragraph (2) of such section and clause (i) and the second sentence of clause (ii) of paragraph (3)(C) of such section), relating to guaranteed issue and renewal.

(vi) MARKETING MATERIAL AND APPLICATION FORMS.—Section 1851(h), relating to approval of marketing material and application forms.

In applying clauses (ii), (iv), and (v) of this subparagraph, any reference to section 1851(e) shall be treated as a reference to such section as applied pursuant to clause (iii) of this subparagraph.

(C) SPECIAL RULE.—The process established under subparagraph (A) shall include, in the case of a part D eligible individual who is a full-benefit dual eligible individual (as defined in section 1935(c)(6)) who has failed to enroll in a prescription drug plan or an MA-PD plan, for the enrollment in a prescription drug plan that has a monthly beneficiary premium that does not exceed the premium assistance available under section 1860D-14(a)(1)(A)). If there is more than one such plan available, the Secretary shall enroll such an individual on a random basis among all such plans in the PDP region. Nothing in the previous sentence shall prevent such an individual from declining or changing such enrollment.

(2) INITIAL ENROLLMENT PERIOD.—

(A) PROGRAM INITIATION.—In the case of an individual who is a part D eligible individual as of November 15, 2005, there shall be an initial enrollment period that shall be the same as the annual, coordinated open election period described in section 1851(e)(3)(B)(iii), as applied under paragraph (1)(B)(iii).

(B) CONTINUING PERIODS.—In the case of an individual who becomes a part D eligible individual after November 15, 2005, there shall be an initial enrollment period which is the period under section 1851(e)(1), as applied under paragraph (1)(B)(iii) of this section, as if 'entitled to benefits under part A or enrolled under part B' were substituted for 'entitled to benefits under part A and enrolled under part B', but in no case shall such period end before the period described in subparagraph (A).

(3) ADDITIONAL SPECIAL ENROLLMENT PERIODS.—The Secretary shall establish special enrollment periods, including the following:

(A) INVOLUNTARY LOSS OF CREDITABLE PRESCRIPTION DRUG COVERAGE.—

(i) IN GENERAL.—In the case of a part D eligible individual who involuntarily loses creditable prescription drug coverage (as defined in section 1860D-13(b)(4)).

(ii) NOTICE.—In establishing special enrollment periods under clause (i), the Secretary shall take into account when the part D eligible individuals are provided notice of the loss of creditable prescription drug coverage.

(iii) FAILURE TO PAY PREMIUM.—For purposes of clause (i), a loss of coverage shall be treated as voluntary if the coverage is terminated because of failure to pay a required beneficiary premium.

(iv) REDUCTION IN COVERAGE.—For purposes of clause (i), a reduction in coverage so that the coverage no longer meets the requirements under section 1860D-13(b)(5) (relating to actuarial equivalence) shall be treated as an involuntary loss of coverage.

§1860D-1(b)(3)(A)(iv) ¶2261A

(B) ERRORS IN ENROLLMENT.—In the case described in section 1837(h) (relating to errors in enrollment), in the same manner as such section applies to part B.

(C) EXCEPTIONAL CIRCUMSTANCES.—In the case of part D eligible individuals who meet such exceptional conditions (in addition to those conditions applied under paragraph (1)(B)(iii)) as the Secretary may provide.

(D) MEDICAID COVERAGE.—In the case of an individual (as determined by the Secretary) who is a full-benefit dual eligible individual (as defined in section 1935(c)(6)).

(E) DISCONTINUANCE OF MA-PD ELECTION DURING FIRST YEAR OF ELIGIBILITY.—In the case of a part D eligible individual who discontinues enrollment in an MA-PD plan under the second sentence of section 1851(e)(4) at the time of the election of coverage under such sentence under the original medicare fee-for-service program.

(4) INFORMATION TO FACILITATE ENROLLMENT.—

(A) IN GENERAL.—Notwithstanding any other provision of law but subject to subparagraph (B), the Secretary may provide to each PDP sponsor and MA organization such identifying information about part D eligible individuals as the Secretary determines to be necessary to facilitate efficient marketing of prescription drug plans and MA-PD plans to such individuals and enrollment of such individuals in such plans.

(B) LIMITATION.—

(i) PROVISION OF INFORMATION.—The Secretary may provide the information under subparagraph (A) only to the extent necessary to carry out such subparagraph.

(ii) USE OF INFORMATION.—Such information provided by the Secretary to a PDP sponsor or an MA organization may be used by such sponsor or organization only to facilitate marketing of, and enrollment of part D eligible individuals in, prescription drug plans and MA-PD plans.

(5) REFERENCE TO ENROLLMENT PROCEDURES FOR MA-PD PLANS.—For rules applicable to enrollment, disenrollment, termination, and change of enrollment of part D eligible individuals in MA-PD plans, see section 1851.

(6) REFERENCE TO PENALTIES FOR LATE ENROLLMENT.—Section 1860D-13(b) imposes a late enrollment penalty for part D eligible individuals who—

(A) enroll in a prescription drug plan or an MA-PD plan after the initial enrollment period described in paragraph (2); and

(B) fail to maintain continuous creditable prescription drug coverage during the period of non-enrollment.

(c) PROVIDING INFORMATION TO BENEFICIARIES.—

(1) ACTIVITIES.—The Secretary shall conduct activities that are designed to broadly disseminate information to part D eligible individuals (and prospective part D eligible individuals) regarding the coverage provided under this part. Such activities shall ensure that such information is first made available at least 30 days prior to the initial enrollment period described in subsection (b)(2)(A).

(2) REQUIREMENTS.—The activities described in paragraph (1) shall—

(A) be similar to the activities performed by the Secretary under section 1851(d), including dissemination (including through the toll-free telephone number 1-800-MEDI-CARE) of comparative information for prescription drug plans and MA-PD plans; and

(B) be coordinated with the activities performed by the Secretary under such section and under section 1804.

(3) COMPARATIVE INFORMATION.—

(A) IN GENERAL.—Subject to subparagraph (B), the comparative information referred to in paragraph (2)(A) shall include a comparison of the following with respect to qualified prescription drug coverage:

(i) BENEFITS.—The benefits provided under the plan.

(ii) MONTHLY BENEFICIARY PREMIUM.—The monthly beneficiary premium under the plan.

(iii) QUALITY AND PERFORMANCE.—The quality and performance under the plan.

(iv) BENEFICIARY COST-SHARING.—The cost-sharing required of part D eligible individuals under the plan.

(v) CONSUMER SATISFACTION SURVEYS.—The results of consumer satisfaction surveys regarding the plan conducted pursuant to section 1860D-4(d).

(B) EXCEPTION FOR UNAVAILABILITY OF INFORMATION.—The Secretary is not required to provide comparative information under clauses (iii) and (v) of subparagraph (A) with respect to a plan—

(i) for the first plan year in which it is of-fered; and

(ii) for the next plan year if it is impracticable or the information is otherwise unavailable.

(4) INFORMATION ON LATE ENROLLMENT PENALTY.—The information disseminated under paragraph (1) shall include information concerning the methodology for determining the late enrollment penalty under section 1860D-13(b).

[CCH Explanation at ¶ 100.]
2003 Amendments:

Section 101(a) of the "Medicare Prescription Drug, Improvement, and Modernization Act of 2003," effective upon enactment, added new section 1860D-1.

The above amendment applies to coverage effective January 1, 2006.

[¶ 2261B] Sec. 1860D-2. PRESCRIPTION DRUG BENEFITS

(a) REQUIREMENTS.—

(1) IN GENERAL.—For purposes of this part and part C, the term 'qualified prescription drug coverage' means either of the following:

(A) STANDARD PRESCRIPTION DRUG COVERAGE WITH ACCESS TO NEGOTIATED PRICES.—Standard prescription drug coverage (as defined in subsection (b)) and access to negotiated prices under subsection (d).

(B) ALTERNATIVE PRESCRIPTION DRUG COVERAGE WITH AT LEAST ACTUARIALLY EQUIVALENT BENEFITS AND ACCESS TO NEGOTIATED PRICES.—Coverage of covered part D drugs which meets the alternative prescription drug coverage requirements of subsection (c) and access to negotiated prices under subsection (d), but only if the benefit design of such coverage is approved by the Secretary, as provided under subsection (c).

(2) PERMITTING SUPPLEMENTAL PRESCRIPTION DRUG COVERAGE.—

(A) IN GENERAL.—Subject to subparagraph (B), qualified prescription drug coverage may include supplemental prescription drug coverage consisting of either or both of the following:

(i) CERTAIN REDUCTIONS IN COST-SHARING.—

(I) IN GENERAL.—A reduction in the annual deductible, a reduction in the coinsurance percentage, or an increase in the initial coverage limit with respect to covered part D drugs, or any combination thereof, insofar as such a reduction or increase increases the actuarial value of benefits above the actuarial value of basic prescription drug coverage.

(II) CONSTRUCTION.—Nothing in this paragraph shall be construed as affecting the application of subsection (c)(3).

(ii) OPTIONAL DRUGS.—Coverage of any product that would be a covered part D drug but for the application of subsection (e)(2)(A).

(B) REQUIREMENT.—A PDP sponsor may not offer a prescription drug plan that provides supplemental prescription drug coverage pursuant to subparagraph (A) in an area unless the sponsor also offers a prescription drug plan in the area that only provides basic prescription drug coverage.

(3) BASIC PRESCRIPTION DRUG COVERAGE.—For purposes of this part and part C, the term 'basic prescription drug coverage' means either of the following:

(A) Coverage that meets the requirements of paragraph (1)(A).

(B) Coverage that meets the requirements of paragraph (1)(B) but does not have any supplemental prescription drug coverage described in paragraph (2)(A).

(4) APPLICATION OF SECONDARY PAYOR PROVISIONS.—The provisions of section 1852(a)(4) shall apply under this part in the same manner as they apply under part C.

(5) CONSTRUCTION.—Nothing in this subsection shall be construed as changing the computation of incurred costs under subsection (b)(4).

(b) STANDARD PRESCRIPTION DRUG COVERAGE.—For purposes of this part and part C, the term 'standard prescription drug coverage' means coverage of covered part D drugs that meets the following requirements:

(1) DEDUCTIBLE.—

(A) IN GENERAL.—The coverage has an annual deductible—

(i) for 2006, that is equal to $250; or

(ii) for a subsequent year, that is equal to the amount specified under this paragraph for the previous year increased by the percentage specified in paragraph (6) for the year involved.

(B) ROUNDING.—Any amount determined under subparagraph (A)(ii) that is not a multiple of $5 shall be rounded to the nearest multiple of $5.

(2) BENEFIT STRUCTURE.—

(A) 25 PERCENT COINSURANCE.—The coverage has coinsurance (for costs above the annual deductible specified in paragraph (1) and up to the initial coverage limit under paragraph (3)) that is—

(i) equal to 25 percent; or

(ii) actuarially equivalent (using processes and methods established under section 1860D-11(c)) to an average expected payment of 25 percent of such costs.

(B) USE OF TIERS.—Nothing in this part shall be construed as preventing a PDP sponsor or an MA organization from applying tiered copayments under a plan, so long as such tiered copayments are consistent with subparagraph (A)(ii).

(3) INITIAL COVERAGE LIMIT.—

(A) IN GENERAL.—Except as provided in paragraph (4), the coverage has an initial coverage limit on the maximum costs that may be recognized for payment purposes (including the annual deductible)—

(i) for 2006, that is equal to $2,250; or

(ii) for a subsequent year, that is equal to the amount specified in this paragraph for the previous year, increased by the annual percentage increase described in paragraph (6) for the year involved.

(B) ROUNDING.—Any amount determined under subparagraph (A)(ii) that is not a multiple of $10 shall be rounded to the nearest multiple of $10.

(4) PROTECTION AGAINST HIGH OUT-OF-POCKET EXPENDITURES.—

(A) IN GENERAL.—

(i) IN GENERAL.—The coverage provides benefits, after the part D eligible individual has incurred costs (as described in subparagraph (C)) for covered part D drugs in a year equal to the annual out-of-pocket threshold specified in subparagraph (B), with cost-sharing that is equal to the greater of—

(I) a copayment of $2 for a generic drug or a preferred drug that is a multiple source drug (as defined in section 1927(k)(7)(A)(i)) and $5 for any other drug; or

(II) coinsurance that is equal to 5 percent.

(ii) ADJUSTMENT OF AMOUNT.—For a year after 2006, the dollar amounts specified in clause (i)(I) shall be equal to the dollar amounts specified in this subparagraph for the previous year, increased by the annual percentage increase described in paragraph (6) for the year involved. Any amount established under this clause that is not a multiple of a 5 cents shall be rounded to the nearest multiple of 5 cents.

(B) ANNUAL OUT-OF-POCKET THRESHOLD.—

(i) IN GENERAL.—For purposes of this part, the 'annual out-of-pocket threshold' specified in this subparagraph—

(I) for 2006, is equal to $3,600; or

(II) for a subsequent year, is equal to the amount specified in this subparagraph for the previous year, increased by the annual percentage increase described in paragraph (6) for the year involved.

(ii) ROUNDING.—Any amount determined under clause (i)(II) that is not a multiple of $50 shall be rounded to the nearest multiple of $50.

(C) APPLICATION.—In applying subparagraph (A)—

(i) incurred costs shall only include costs incurred with respect to covered part D drugs for the annual deductible described in paragraph (1), for cost-sharing described in paragraph (2), and for amounts for which benefits are not provided because of the application of the initial coverage limit described in paragraph (3), but does not include any costs incurred for covered part D drugs which are not included (or treated as being included) in the plan's formulary; and

(ii) such costs shall be treated as incurred only if they are paid by the part D eligible individual (or by another person, such as a family member, on behalf of the individual), under section 1860D-14, or under a State Pharmaceutical Assistance Program and the part D eligible individual (or other person) is not reimbursed through insurance or otherwise, a group health plan, or other third-party payment arrangement (other than under such section or such a Program) for such costs.

(D) INFORMATION REGARDING THIRD-PARTY REIMBURSEMENT.—

(i) PROCEDURES FOR EXCHANGING INFORMATION.—In order to accurately apply the requirements of subparagraph (C)(ii), the Secretary is authorized to establish procedures, in coordination with the Secretary of the Treasury and the Secretary of Labor—

(I) for determining whether costs for part D eligible individuals are being reimbursed through insurance or otherwise, a group health plan, or other third-party payment arrangement; and

(II) for alerting the PDP sponsors and MA organizations that offer the prescription drug plans and MA-PD plans in which such individuals are enrolled about such reimbursement arrangements.

(ii) AUTHORITY TO REQUEST INFORMATION FROM ENROLLEES.—A PDP sponsor or an MA organization may periodically ask part D eligible individuals enrolled in a prescription drug plan or an MA-PD plan offered by the sponsor or organization whether such individuals have or expect to receive such third-party reimbursement. A material misrepresentation of the information described in the preceding sentence by an individual (as defined in standards set by the Secretary and determined through a process established by the Secretary) shall constitute grounds for termination of enrollment in any plan under section 1851(g)(3)(B) (and as applied under this part under section 1860D-1(b)(1)(B)(v)) for a period specified by the Secretary.

(5) CONSTRUCTION.—Nothing in this part shall be construed as preventing a PDP sponsor or an MA organization offering an MA-PD plan from reducing to 0 the cost-sharing otherwise applicable to preferred or generic drugs.

(6) ANNUAL PERCENTAGE INCREASE.—The annual percentage increase specified in this paragraph for a year is equal to the annual percentage increase in average per capita aggregate expenditures for covered part D drugs in the United States for part D eligible individuals, as determined by the Secretary for the 12-month period ending in July of the previous year using such methods as the Secretary shall specify.

(c) ALTERNATIVE PRESCRIPTION DRUG COVERAGE REQUIREMENTS.—A prescription drug plan or an MA-PD plan may provide a different prescription drug benefit design from standard prescription drug coverage so long as the Secretary determines (consistent with section 1860D-11(c)) that the following requirements are met and the plan applies for, and receives, the approval of the Secretary for such benefit design:

(1) ASSURING AT LEAST ACTUARIALLY EQUIVALENT COVERAGE.—

(A) ASSURING EQUIVALENT VALUE OF TOTAL COVERAGE.—The actuarial value of the total coverage is at least equal to the actuarial value of standard prescription drug coverage.

(B) ASSURING EQUIVALENT UNSUBSIDIZED VALUE OF COVERAGE.—The unsubsidized value of the coverage is at least equal to the unsubsidized value of standard prescription drug coverage. For purposes of this subparagraph, the unsubsidized value of coverage is the amount by which the actuarial value of the coverage exceeds the actuarial value of the subsidy payments under section 1860D-15 with respect to such coverage.

(C) ASSURING STANDARD PAYMENT FOR COSTS AT INITIAL COVERAGE LIMIT.—The coverage is designed, based upon an actuarially representative pattern of utilization, to provide for the payment, with respect to costs incurred that are equal to the initial coverage limit under subsection (b)(3) for the year, of an amount equal to at least the product of—

(i) the amount by which the initial coverage limit described in subsection (b)(3) for the year exceeds the deductible described in subsection (b)(1) for the year; and

(ii) 100 percent minus the coinsurance percentage specified in subsection (b)(2)(A)(i).

(2) MAXIMUM REQUIRED DEDUCTIBLE.—The deductible under the coverage shall not exceed the deductible amount specified under subsection (b)(1) for the year.

(3) SAME PROTECTION AGAINST HIGH OUT-OF-POCKET EXPENDITURES.—The coverage provides the coverage required under subsection (b)(4).

(d) ACCESS TO NEGOTIATED PRICES.—

(1) ACCESS.—

(A) IN GENERAL.—Under qualified prescription drug coverage offered by a PDP sponsor offering a prescription drug plan or an MA organization offering an MA-PD plan, the sponsor or organization shall provide enrollees with access to negotiated prices used for payment for covered part D drugs, regardless of the fact that no benefits may be payable under the coverage with respect to such drugs because of the application of a deductible or other cost-sharing or an initial coverage limit (described in subsection (b)(3)).

(B) NEGOTIATED PRICES.—For purposes of this part, negotiated prices shall take into account negotiated price concessions, such as discounts, direct or indirect subsidies, rebates, and direct or indirect remunerations, for covered part D drugs, and include any dispensing fees for such drugs.

(C) MEDICAID-RELATED PROVISIONS.—The prices negotiated by a prescription drug plan, by an MA-PD plan with respect to covered part D drugs, or by a qualified retiree prescription drug plan (as defined in section 1860D-22(a)(2)) with respect to such drugs on behalf of part D eligible individuals, shall (notwith-standing any other provision of law) not be taken into account for the purposes of establishing the best price under section 1927(c)(1)(C).

(2) DISCLOSURE.—A PDP sponsor offering a prescription drug plan or an MA organization offering an MA-PD plan shall disclose to the Secretary (in a manner specified by the Secretary) the aggregate negotiated price con-cessions described in paragraph (1)(B) made available to the sponsor or organization by a manufacturer which are passed through in the form of lower subsidies, lower monthly beneficiary prescription drug premiums, and lower prices through

pharmacies and other dispensers. The provisions of section 1927(b)(3)(D) apply to information disclosed to the Secretary under this paragraph.

(3) AUDITS.—To protect against fraud and abuse and to ensure proper disclosures and accounting under this part and in accordance with section 1857(d)(2)(B) (as applied under section 1860D-12(b)(3)(C)), the Secretary may conduct periodic audits, directly or through contracts, of the financial statements and records of PDP sponsors with respect to prescription drug plans and MA organizations with respect to MA-PD plans.

(e) COVERED PART D DRUG DEFINED.—

(1) IN GENERAL.—Except as provided in this subsection, for purposes of this part, the term 'covered part D drug' means—

(A) a drug that may be dispensed only upon a prescription and that is described in subparagraph (A)(i), (A)(ii), or (A)(iii) of section 1927(k)(2); or

(B) a biological product described in clauses (i) through (iii) of subparagraph (B) of such section or insulin described in subparagraph (C) of such section and medical supplies associated with the injection of insulin (as defined in regulations of the Secretary),

and such term includes a vaccine licensed under section 351 of the Public Health Service Act and any use of a covered part D drug for a medically accepted indication (as defined in section 1927(k)(6)).

(2) EXCLUSIONS.—

(A) IN GENERAL.—Such term does not include drugs or classes of drugs, or their medical uses, which may be excluded from coverage or otherwise restricted under section 1927(d)(2), other than subparagraph (E) of such section (relating to smoking cessation agents), or under section 1927(d)(3).

(B) MEDICARE COVERED DRUGS.—A drug prescribed for a part D eligible individual that would otherwise be a covered part D drug under this part shall not be so considered if payment for such drug as so prescribed and dispensed or administered with respect to that individual is available (or would be available but for the application of a deductible) under part A or B for that individual.

(3) APPLICATION OF GENERAL EXCLUSION PROVISIONS.—A prescription drug plan or an MA-PD plan may exclude from qualified prescription drug coverage any covered part D drug—

(A) for which payment would not be made if section 1862(a) applied to this part; or

(B) which is not prescribed in accordance with the plan or this part.

Such exclusions are determinations subject to reconsideration and appeal pursuant to subsections (g) and (h), respectively, of section 1860D-4.

[CCH Explanation at ¶ 103.]
2003 Amendments:

Section 101(a) of the "Medicare Prescription Drug, Improvement, and Modernization Act of 2003," effective upon enactment, added new section 1860D-2.

The above amendment applies to coverage effective January 1, 2006.

[¶ 2261C] Sec. 1860D-3. ACCESS TO A CHOICE OF QUALIFIED PRESCRIPTION DRUG COVERAGE

(a) ASSURING ACCESS TO A CHOICE OF COVERAGE.—

(1) CHOICE OF AT LEAST TWO PLANS IN EACH AREA.—The Secretary shall ensure that each part D eligible individual has available, consistent with paragraph (2), a choice of enrollment in at least 2 qualifying plans (as defined in paragraph (3)) in the area in which the individual resides, at least one of which is a prescription drug plan. In any such case in which such plans are not available, the part D eligible individual shall be given the opportunity to enroll in a fallback prescription drug plan.

(2) REQUIREMENT FOR DIFFERENT PLAN SPONSORS.—The requirement in paragraph (1) is not satisfied with respect to an area if only one entity offers all the qualifying plans in the area.

(3) QUALIFYING PLAN DEFINED.—For purposes of this section, the term 'qualifying plan' means—

(A) a prescription drug plan; or

(B) an MA-PD plan described in section 1851(a)(2)(A)(i) that provides—

(i) basic prescription drug coverage; or

(ii) qualified prescription drug coverage that provides supplemental prescription drug coverage so long as there is no MA monthly supplemental beneficiary premium applied under the plan, due to the application of a credit against such premium of a rebate under section 1854(b)(1)(C).

(b) FLEXIBILITY IN RISK ASSUMED AND APPLICATION OF FALLBACK PLAN.—In order to ensure access pursuant to subsection (a) in an area—

(1) the Secretary may approve limited risk plans under section 1860D-11(f) for the area; and

(2) only if such access is still not provided in the area after applying paragraph (1), the Secretary shall provide for the offering of a fallback prescription drug plan for that area under section 1860D-11(g).

[CCH Explanation at ¶109.]

2003 Amendments:

Section 101(a) of the "Medicare Prescription Drug, Improvement, and Modernization Act of 2003," effective upon enactment, added new section 1860D-3.

The above amendment applies to coverage effective January 1, 2006.

[¶2261D] Sec. 1860D-4. BENEFICIARY PROTECTIONS FOR QUALIFIED PRESCRIPTION DRUG COVERAGE

(a) DISSEMINATION OF INFORMATION.—

(1) GENERAL INFORMATION.—

(A) APPLICATION OF MA INFORMATION.—A PDP sponsor shall disclose, in a clear, accurate, and standardized form to each enrollee with a prescription drug plan offered by the sponsor under this part at the time of enrollment and at least annually thereafter, the information described in section 1852(c)(1) relating to such plan, insofar as the Secretary determines appropriate with respect to benefits provided under this part, and including the information described in subparagraph (B).

(B) DRUG SPECIFIC INFORMATION.—The information described in this subparagraph is information concerning the following:

(i) Access to specific covered part D drugs, including access through pharmacy networks.

(ii) How any formulary (including any tiered formulary structure) used by the sponsor functions, including a description of how a part D eligible individual may obtain information on the formulary consistent with paragraph (3).

(iii) Beneficiary cost-sharing requirements and how a part D eligible individual may obtain information on such requirements, including tiered or other copayment level applicable to each drug (or class of drugs), consistent with paragraph (3).

(iv) The medication therapy management program required under subsection (c).

(2) DISCLOSURE UPON REQUEST OF GENERAL COVERAGE, UTILIZATION, AND GRIEVANCE INFORMATION.—Upon request of a part D eligible individual who is eligible to enroll in a prescription drug plan, the PDP sponsor offering such plan shall provide information similar (as determined by the Secretary) to the information described in subparagraphs (A), (B), and (C) of section 1852(c)(2) to such individual.

(3) PROVISION OF SPECIFIC INFORMATION.—

(A) RESPONSE TO BENEFICIARY QUESTIONS.—Each PDP sponsor offering a prescription drug plan shall have a mechanism for providing specific information on a timely basis to enrollees upon request. Such mechanism shall include access to information through the use of a toll-free telephone number and, upon request, the provision of such information in writing.

(B) AVAILABILITY OF INFORMATION ON CHANGES IN FORMULARY THROUGH THE INTERNET.—A PDP sponsor offering a prescription drug plan shall make available on a timely basis through an Internet website information on specific changes in the formulary under the plan (including changes to tiered or preferred status of covered part D drugs).

(4) CLAIMS INFORMATION.—A PDP sponsor offering a prescription drug plan must furnish to each enrollee in a form easily understandable to such enrollees—

(A) an explanation of benefits (in accordance with section 1806(a) or in a comparable manner); and

(B) when prescription drug benefits are provided under this part, a notice of the benefits in relation to—

(i) the initial coverage limit for the current year; and

(ii) the annual out-of-pocket threshold for the current year.

Notices under subparagraph (B) need not be provided more often than as specified by the Secretary and notices under subparagraph (B)(ii) shall take into account the application of section 1860D-2(b)(4)(C) to the extent practicable, as specified by the Secretary.

(b) ACCESS TO COVERED PART D DRUGS.—

(1) ASSURING PHARMACY ACCESS.—

(A) PARTICIPATION OF ANY WILLING PHARMACY.—A prescription drug plan shall permit the participation of any pharmacy that meets the terms and conditions under the plan.

(B) DISCOUNTS ALLOWED FOR NETWORK PHARMACIES.—For covered part D drugs dispensed through in-network pharmacies, a prescription drug plan may, notwithstanding subparagraph (A), reduce coinsurance or copayments for part D eligible individuals enrolled in the plan below the level otherwise required. In no case shall such a reduction result in an increase in payments made by the Secretary under section 1860D-15 to a plan.

(C) CONVENIENT ACCESS FOR NETWORK PHARMACIES.—

(i) IN GENERAL.—The PDP sponsor of the prescription drug plan shall secure the participation in its network of a sufficient number of pharmacies that dispense (other than by mail order) drugs directly to patients to ensure convenient access (consistent with rules established by the Secretary).

(ii) APPLICATION OF TRICARE STANDARDS.—The Secretary shall establish rules for convenient access to in-network pharmacies under this subparagraph that are no less favorable to enrollees than the rules for convenient access to pharmacies included in the statement of work of solicitation (#MDA906-03-R-0002) of the Department of Defense under the TRICARE Retail Pharmacy (TRRx) as of March 13, 2003.

(iii) ADEQUATE EMERGENCY ACCESS.—Such rules shall include adequate emergency access for enrollees.

(iv) CONVENIENT ACCESS IN LONG-TERM CARE FACILITIES.—Such rules may include standards with respect to access for enrollees who are residing in long-term care facilities and for pharmacies operated by the Indian Health Service, Indian tribes and tribal organizations, and urban Indian organizations (as defined in section 4 of the Indian Health Care Improvement Act).

(D) LEVEL PLAYING FIELD.—Such a sponsor shall permit enrollees to receive benefits (which may include a 90-day supply of drugs or biologicals) through a pharmacy (other than a mail order pharmacy), with any differential in charge paid by such enrollees.

(E) NOT REQUIRED TO ACCEPT INSURANCE RISK.—The terms and conditions under subparagraph (A) may not require participating pharmacies to accept insurance risk as a condition of participation.

(2) USE OF STANDARDIZED TECHNOLOGY.—

(A) IN GENERAL.—The PDP sponsor of a prescription drug plan shall issue (and reissue, as appropriate) such a card (or other technology) that may be used by an enrollee to assure access to negotiated prices under section 1860D-2(d).

§1860D-4(b)(2)(A) ¶2261D

(B) STANDARDS.—

(i) IN GENERAL.—The Secretary shall provide for the development, adoption, or recognition of standards relating to a standardized format for the card or other technology required under subparagraph (A). Such standards shall be compatible with part C of title XI and may be based on standards developed by an appropriate standard setting organization.

(ii) CONSULTATION.—In developing the standards under clause (i), the Secretary shall consult with the National Council for Prescription Drug Programs and other standard setting organizations determined appropriate by the Secretary.

(iii) IMPLEMENTATION.—The Secretary shall develop, adopt, or recognize the standards under clause (i) by such date as the Secretary determines shall be sufficient to ensure that PDP sponsors utilize such standards beginning January 1, 2006.

(3) REQUIREMENTS ON DEVELOPMENT AND APPLICATION OF FORMULARIES.—If a PDP sponsor of a prescription drug plan uses a formulary (including the use of tiered cost-sharing), the following requirements must be met:

(A) DEVELOPMENT AND REVISION BY A PHARMACY AND THERAPEUTIC (P&T) COMMITTEE.—

(i) IN GENERAL.—The formulary must be developed and reviewed by a pharmacy and therapeutic committee. A majority of the members of such committee shall consist of individuals who are practicing physicians or practicing pharmacists (or both).

(ii) INCLUSION OF INDEPENDENT EXPERTS.—Such committee shall include at least one practicing physician and at least one practicing pharmacist, each of whom—

(I) is independent and free of conflict with respect to the sponsor and plan; and

(II) has expertise in the care of elderly or disabled persons.

(B) FORMULARY DEVELOPMENT.—In developing and reviewing the formulary, the committee shall—

(i) base clinical decisions on the strength of scientific evidence and standards of practice, including assessing peer-reviewed medical literature, such as randomized clinical trials, pharmacoeconomic studies, outcomes research data, and on such other information as the committee determines to be appropriate; and

(ii) take into account whether including in the formulary (or in a tier in such formulary) particular covered part D drugs has therapeutic advantages in terms of safety and efficacy.

(C) INCLUSION OF DRUGS IN ALL THERAPEUTIC CATEGORIES AND CLASSES.—

(i) IN GENERAL.—The formulary must include drugs within each therapeutic category and class of covered part D drugs, although not necessarily all drugs within such categories and classes.

(ii) MODEL GUIDELINES.—The Secretary shall request the United States Pharmacopeia to develop, in consultation with pharmaceutical benefit managers and other interested parties, a list of categories and classes that may be used by prescription drug plans under this paragraph and to revise such classification from time to time to reflect changes in therapeutic uses of covered part D drugs and the additions of new covered part D drugs.

(iii) LIMITATION ON CHANGES IN THERAPEUTIC CLASSIFICATION.—The PDP sponsor of a prescription drug plan may not change the therapeutic categories and classes in a formulary other than at the beginning of each plan year except as the Secretary may permit to take into account new therapeutic uses and newly approved covered part D drugs.

(D) PROVIDER AND PATIENT EDUCATION.—The PDP sponsor shall establish policies and procedures to educate and inform health care providers and enrollees concerning the formulary.

(E) NOTICE BEFORE REMOVING DRUG FROM FORMULARY OR CHANGING PREFERRED OR TIER STATUS OF DRUG.—Any removal of a covered part D drug from a formulary and any change in the preferred or tiered cost-sharing status of such a drug shall take effect only after appropriate notice is made available (such as under subsection (a)(3)) to the Secretary, affected enrollees, physicians, pharmacies, and pharmacists.

(F) PERIODIC EVALUATION OF PROTOCOLS.—In connection with the formulary, the sponsor of a prescription drug plan shall provide for the periodic evaluation and analysis of treatment protocols and procedures.

The requirements of this paragraph may be met by a PDP sponsor directly or through arrangements with another entity.

(c) COST AND UTILIZATION MANAGEMENT; QUALITY ASSURANCE; MEDICATION THERAPY MANAGEMENT PROGRAM.—

(1) IN GENERAL.—The PDP sponsor shall have in place, directly or through appropriate arrangements, with respect to covered part D drugs, the following:

(A) A cost-effective drug utilization management program, including incentives to reduce costs when medically appropriate, such as through the use of multiple source drugs (as defined in section 1927(k)(7)(A)(i)).

(B) Quality assurance measures and systems to reduce medication errors and adverse drug interactions and improve medication use.

(C) A medication therapy management program described in paragraph (2).

(D) A program to control fraud, abuse, and waste.

Nothing in this section shall be construed as impairing a PDP sponsor from utilizing cost management tools (including differential payments) under all methods of operation.

(2) MEDICATION THERAPY MANAGEMENT PROGRAM.—

(A) DESCRIPTION.—

(i) IN GENERAL.—A medication therapy management program described in this paragraph is a program of drug therapy management that may be furnished by a pharmacist and that is designed to assure, with respect to targeted beneficiaries described in clause (ii), that covered part D drugs under the prescription drug plan are appropriately used to optimize therapeutic outcomes through improved medication use, and to reduce the risk of adverse events, including adverse drug interactions. Such a program may distinguish between services in ambulatory and institutional settings.

(ii) TARGETED BENEFICIARIES DESCRIBED.—Targeted beneficiaries described in this clause are part D eligible individuals who—

(I) have multiple chronic diseases (such as diabetes, asthma, hypertension, hyperlipidemia, and congestive heart failure);

(II) are taking multiple covered part D drugs; and

(III) are identified as likely to incur annual costs for covered part D drugs that exceed a level specified by the Secretary.

(B) ELEMENTS.—Such program may include elements that promote—

(i) enhanced enrollee understanding to promote the appropriate use of medications by enrollees and to reduce the risk of potential adverse events associated with medications, through beneficiary education, counseling, and other appropriate means;

(ii) increased enrollee adherence with prescription medication regimens through medication refill reminders, special packaging, and other compliance programs and other appropriate means; and

(iii) detection of adverse drug events and patterns of overuse and underuse of prescription drugs.

(C) DEVELOPMENT OF PROGRAM IN COOPERATION WITH LICENSED PHARMACISTS.—Such program shall be developed in cooperation with licensed and practicing pharmacists and physicians.

§1860D-4(c)(2)(C) ¶2261D

(D) COORDINATION WITH CARE MANAGEMENT PLANS.—The Secretary shall establish guidelines for the coordination of any medication therapy management program under this paragraph with respect to a targeted beneficiary with any care management plan established with respect to such beneficiary under a chronic care improvement program under section 1807.

(E) CONSIDERATIONS IN PHARMACY FEES.—The PDP sponsor of a prescription drug plan shall take into account, in establishing fees for pharmacists and others providing services under such plan, the resources used, and time required to, implement the medication therapy management program under this paragraph. Each such sponsor shall disclose to the Secretary upon request the amount of any such management or dispensing fees. The provisions of section 1927(b)(3)(D) apply to information disclosed under this subparagraph.

(d) CONSUMER SATISFACTION SURVEYS.—In order to provide for comparative information under section 1860D-1(c)(3)(A)(v), the Secretary shall conduct consumer satisfaction surveys with respect to PDP sponsors and prescription drug plans in a manner similar to the manner such surveys are conducted for MA organizations and MA plans under part C.

(e) ELECTRONIC PRESCRIPTION PROGRAM.—

(1) APPLICATION OF STANDARDS.—As of such date as the Secretary may specify, but not later than 1 year after the date of promulgation of final standards under paragraph (4)(D), prescriptions and other information described in paragraph (2)(A) for covered part D drugs prescribed for part D eligible individuals that are transmitted electronically shall be transmitted only in accordance with such standards under an electronic prescription drug program that meets the requirements of paragraph (2).

(2) PROGRAM REQUIREMENTS.—Consistent with uniform standards established under paragraph (3)—

(A) PROVISION OF INFORMATION TO PRESCRIBING HEALTH CARE PROFESSIONAL AND DISPENSING PHARMACIES AND PHARMACISTS.—An electronic prescription drug program shall provide for the electronic transmittal to the prescribing health care professional and to the dispensing pharmacy and pharmacist of the prescription and information on eligibility and benefits (including the drugs included in the applicable formulary, any tiered formulary structure, and any requirements for prior authorization) and of the following information with respect to the prescribing and dispensing of a covered part D drug:

(i) Information on the drug being prescribed or dispensed and other drugs listed on the medication history, including information on drug-drug interactions, warnings or cautions, and, when indicated, dosage adjustments.

(ii) Information on the availability of lower cost, therapeutically appropriate alternatives (if any) for the drug prescribed.

(B) APPLICATION TO MEDICAL HISTORY INFORMATION.—Effective on and after such date as the Secretary specifies and after the establishment of appropriate standards to carry out this subparagraph, the program shall provide for the electronic transmittal in a manner similar to the manner under subparagraph (A) of information that relates to the medical history concerning the individual and related to a covered part D drug being prescribed or dispensed, upon request of the professional or pharmacist involved.

(C) LIMITATIONS.—Information shall only be disclosed under subparagraph (A) or (B) if the disclosure of such information is permitted under the Federal regulations (concerning the privacy of individually identifiable health information) promulgated under section 264(c) of the Health Insurance Portability and Accountability Act of 1996.

(D) TIMING.—To the extent feasible, the information exchanged under this paragraph shall be on an interactive, real-time basis.

(3) STANDARDS.—

(A) IN GENERAL.—The Secretary shall provide consistent with this subsection for the promulgation of uniform standards relating to the requirements for electronic prescription drug programs under paragraph (2).

(B) OBJECTIVES.—Such standards shall be consistent with the objectives of improving—

(i) patient safety;

(ii) the quality of care provided to patients; and

(iii) efficiencies, including cost savings, in the delivery of care.

(C) DESIGN CRITERIA.—Such standards shall—

(i) be designed so that, to the extent practicable, the standards do not impose an undue administrative burden on prescribing health care professionals and dispensing pharmacies and pharmacists;

(ii) be compatible with standards established under part C of title XI, standards established under subsection (b)(2)(B)(i), and with general health information technology standards; and

(iii) be designed so that they permit electronic exchange of drug labeling and drug listing information maintained by the Food and Drug Administration and the National Library of Medicine.

(D) PERMITTING USE OF APPROPRIATE MESSAGING.—Such standards shall allow for the messaging of information only if it relates to the appropriate prescribing of drugs, including quality assurance measures and systems referred to in subsection (c)(1)(B).

(E) PERMITTING PATIENT DESIGNATION OF DISPENSING PHARMACY.—

(i) IN GENERAL.—Consistent with clause (ii), such standards shall permit a part D eligible individual to designate a particular pharmacy to dispense a prescribed drug.

(ii) NO CHANGE IN BENEFITS.—Clause (i) shall not be construed as affecting—

(I) the access required to be provided to pharmacies by a prescription drug plan; or

(II) the application of any differences in benefits or payments under such a plan based on the pharmacy dispensing a covered part D drug.

(4) DEVELOPMENT, PROMULGATION, AND MODIFICATION OF STANDARDS.—

(A) INITIAL STANDARDS.—Not later than September 1, 2005, the Secretary shall develop, adopt, recognize, or modify initial uniform standards relating to the requirements for electronic prescription drug programs described in paragraph (2) taking into consideration the recommendations (if any) from the National Committee on Vital and Health Statistics (as established under section 306(k) of the Public Health Service Act (42 U.S.C. 242k(k))) under subparagraph (B).

(B) ROLE OF NCVHS.—The National Committee on Vital and Health Statistics shall develop recommendations for uniform standards relating to such requirements in consultation with the following:

(i) Standard setting organizations (as defined in section 1171(8))

(ii) Practicing physicians.

(iii) Hospitals.

(iv) Pharmacies.

(v) Practicing pharmacists.

(vi) Pharmacy benefit managers.

(vii) State boards of pharmacy.

(viii) State boards of medicine.

(ix) Experts on electronic prescribing.

(x) Other appropriate Federal agencies.

(C) PILOT PROJECT TO TEST INITIAL STANDARDS.—

(i) IN GENERAL.—During the 1-year period that begins on January 1, 2006, the Secretary shall conduct a pilot project to test the initial standards developed under subparagraph (A) prior to the promulgation of the final uniform standards under subparagraph (D) in order to provide for the efficient implementation of the requirements described in paragraph (2).

(ii) EXCEPTION.—Pilot testing of standards is not required under clause (i) where there already is adequate industry experience with such standards, as determined by the Secretary after consultation with effected standard setting organizations and industry users.

(iii) VOLUNTARY PARTICIPATION OF PHYSICIANS AND PHARMACIES.—In order to conduct the pilot project under clause (i), the Secretary shall enter into agreements with physicians, physician groups, pharmacies, hospitals, PDP sponsors, MA organizations, and other appropriate entities under which health care professionals electronically transmit prescriptions to dispensing pharmacies and pharmacists in accordance with such standards.

(iv) EVALUATION AND REPORT.—

(I) EVALUATION.—The Secretary shall conduct an evaluation of the pilot project conducted under clause (i).

(II) REPORT TO CONGRESS.—Not later than April 1, 2007, the Secretary shall submit to Congress a report on the evaluation conducted under subclause (I).

(D) FINAL STANDARDS.—Based upon the evaluation of the pilot project under subparagraph (C)(iv)(I) and not later than April 1, 2008, the Secretary shall promulgate uniform standards relating to the requirements described in paragraph (2).

(5) RELATION TO STATE LAWS.—The standards promulgated under this subsection shall supersede any State law or regulation that—

(A) is contrary to the standards or restricts the ability to carry out this part; and

(B) pertains to the electronic transmission of medication history and of information on eligibility, benefits, and prescriptions with respect to covered part D drugs under this part.

(6) ESTABLISHMENT OF SAFE HARBOR.—The Secretary, in consultation with the Attorney General, shall promulgate regulations that provide for a safe harbor from sanctions under paragraphs (1) and (2) of section 1128B(b) and an exception to the prohibition under subsection (a)(1) of section 1877 with respect to the provision of nonmonetary remuneration (in the form of hardware, software, or information technology and training services) necessary and used solely to receive and transmit electronic prescription information in accordance with the standards promulgated under this subsection—

(A) in the case of a hospital, by the hospital to members of its medical staff;

(B) in the case of a group practice (as defined in section 1877(h)(4)), by the practice to prescribing health care professionals who are members of such practice; and

(C) in the case of a PDP sponsor or MA organization, by the sponsor or organization to pharmacists and pharmacies participating in the network of such sponsor or organization, and to prescribing health care professionals.

(f) GRIEVANCE MECHANISM.—Each PDP sponsor shall provide meaningful procedures for hearing and resolving grievances between the sponsor (including any entity or individual through which the sponsor provides covered benefits) and enrollees with prescription drug plans of the sponsor under this part in accordance with section 1852(f).

(g) COVERAGE DETERMINATIONS AND RECONSIDERATIONS.—

(1) APPLICATION OF COVERAGE DETERMINATION AND RECONSIDERATION PROVISIONS.—A PDP sponsor shall meet the requirements of paragraphs (1) through (3) of section 1852(g) with respect to covered benefits under the prescription drug plan it offers under this part in the same manner as such requirements apply to an MA organization with respect to benefits it offers under an MA plan under part C.

(2) REQUEST FOR A DETERMINATION FOR THE TREATMENT OF TIERED FORMULARY DRUG.—In the case of a prescription drug plan offered by a PDP sponsor that provides for tiered cost-sharing for drugs included within a formulary and provides lower cost-sharing for preferred drugs included within the formulary, a part D eligible individual who is enrolled in the plan may request an exception to the tiered cost-sharing structure. Under such an exception, a nonpreferred drug could be covered under the terms applicable for preferred drugs if the prescribing physician determines that the preferred drug for treatment of the same condition either would not be as

effective for the individual or would have adverse effects for the individual or both. A PDP sponsor shall have an exceptions process under this paragraph consistent with guidelines established by the Secretary for making a determination with respect to such a request. Denial of such an exception shall be treated as a coverage denial for purposes of applying subsection (h).

(h) APPEALS.—

(1) IN GENERAL.—Subject to paragraph (2), a PDP sponsor shall meet the requirements of paragraphs (4) and (5) of section 1852(g) with respect to benefits (including a determination related to the application of tiered cost-sharing described in subsection (g)(2)) in a manner similar (as determined by the Secretary) to the manner such requirements apply to an MA organization with respect to benefits under the original medicare fee-for-service program option it offers under an MA plan under part C. In applying this paragraph only the part D eligible individual shall be entitled to bring such an appeal.

(2) LIMITATION IN CASES ON NONFORMULARY DETERMINATIONS.—A part D eligible individual who is enrolled in a prescription drug plan offered by a PDP sponsor may appeal under paragraph (1) a determination not to provide for coverage of a covered part D drug that is not on the formulary under the plan only if the prescribing physician determines that all covered part D drugs on any tier of the formulary for treatment of the same condition would not be as effective for the individual as the nonformulary drug, would have adverse effects for the individual, or both.

(3) TREATMENT OF NONFORMULARY DETERMINATIONS.—If a PDP sponsor determines that a plan provides coverage for a covered part D drug that is not on the formulary of the plan, the drug shall be treated as being included on the formulary for purposes of section 1860D-2(b)(4)(C)(i).

(i) PRIVACY, CONFIDENTIALITY, AND ACCURACY OF ENROLLEE RECORDS.—The provisions of section 1852(h) shall apply to a PDP sponsor and prescription drug plan in the same manner as it applies to an MA organization and an MA plan.

(j) TREATMENT OF ACCREDITATION.—Subparagraph (A) of section 1852(e)(4) (relating to treatment of accreditation) shall apply to a PDP sponsor under this part with respect to the following requirements, in the same manner as it applies to an MA organization with respect to the requirements in subparagraph (B) (other than clause (vii) thereof) of such section:

(1) Subsection (b) of this section (relating to access to covered part D drugs).

(2) Subsection (c) of this section (including quality assurance and medication therapy management).

(3) Subsection (i) of this section (relating to confidentiality and accuracy of enrollee records).

(k) PUBLIC DISCLOSURE OF PHARMACEUTICAL PRICES FOR EQUIVALENT DRUGS.—

(1) IN GENERAL.—A PDP sponsor offering a prescription drug plan shall provide that each pharmacy that dispenses a covered part D drug shall inform an enrollee of any differential between the price of the drug to the enrollee and the price of the lowest priced generic covered part D drug under the plan that is therapeutically equivalent and bioequivalent and available at such pharmacy.

(2) TIMING OF NOTICE.—

(A) IN GENERAL.—Subject to subparagraph (B), the information under paragraph (1) shall be provided at the time of purchase of the drug involved, or, in the case of dispensing by mail order, at the time of delivery of such drug.

(B) WAIVER.—The Secretary may waive subparagraph (A) in such circumstances as the Secretary may specify.

[CCH Explanation at ¶ 110, 111, 112, 113, and 114.]

2003 Amendments:

Section 101(a) of the "Medicare Prescription Drug, Improvement, and Modernization Act of 2003," effective upon enactment, added new section 1860D-4.

The above amendment applies to coverage effective January 1, 2006.

Subpart 2—Prescription Drug Plans; PDP Sponsors; Financing

[¶2262A] Sec. 1860D-11. PDP REGIONS; SUBMISSION OF BIDS; PLAN APPROVAL

(a) ESTABLISHMENT OF PDP REGIONS; SERVICE AREAS.—

(1) COVERAGE OF ENTIRE PDP REGION.—The service area for a prescription drug plan shall consist of an entire PDP region established under paragraph (2).

(2) ESTABLISHMENT OF PDP REGIONS.—

(A) IN GENERAL.—The Secretary shall establish, and may revise, PDP regions in a manner that is consistent with the requirements for the establishment and revision of MA regions under subparagraphs (B) and (C) of section 1858(a)(2).

(B) RELATION TO MA REGIONS.—To the extent practicable, PDP regions shall be the same as MA regions under section 1858(a)(2). The Secretary may establish PDP regions which are not the same as MA regions if the Secretary determines that the establishment of different regions under this part would improve access to benefits under this part.

(C) AUTHORITY FOR TERRITORIES.—The Secretary shall establish, and may revise, PDP regions for areas in States that are not within the 50 States or the District of Columbia.

(3) NATIONAL PLAN.—Nothing in this subsection shall be construed as preventing a prescription drug plan from being offered in more than one PDP region (including all PDP regions).

(b) SUBMISSION OF BIDS, PREMIUMS, AND RELATED INFORMATION.—

(1) IN GENERAL.—A PDP sponsor shall submit to the Secretary information described in paragraph (2) with respect to each prescription drug plan it offers. Such information shall be submitted at the same time and in a similar manner to the manner in which information described in paragraph (6) of section 1854(a) is submitted by an MA organization under paragraph (1) of such section.

(2) INFORMATION DESCRIBED.—The information described in this paragraph is information on the following:

(A) COVERAGE PROVIDED.—The prescription drug coverage provided under the plan, including the deductible and other cost-sharing.

(B) ACTUARIAL VALUE.—The actuarial value of the qualified prescription drug coverage in the region for a part D eligible individual with a national average risk profile for the factors described in section 1860D-15(c)(1)(A) (as specified by the Secretary).

(C) BID.—Information on the bid, including an actuarial certification of—

(i) the basis for the actuarial value described in subparagraph (B) assumed in such bid;

(ii) the portion of such bid attributable to basic prescription drug coverage and, if applicable, the portion of such bid attributable to supplemental benefits;

(iii) assumptions regarding the reinsurance subsidy payments provided under section 1860D-15(b) subtracted from the actuarial value to produce such bid; and

(iv) administrative expenses assumed in the bid.

(D) SERVICE AREA.—The service area for the plan.

(E) LEVEL OF RISK ASSUMED.—

(i) IN GENERAL.—Whether the PDP sponsor requires a modification of risk level under clause (ii) and, if so, the extent of such modification. Any such modification shall apply with respect to all prescription drug plans offered by a PDP sponsor in a PDP region. This subparagraph shall not apply to an MA-PD plan.

(ii) RISK LEVELS DESCRIBED.—A modification of risk level under this clause may consist of one or more of the following:

(I) INCREASE IN FEDERAL PERCENTAGE ASSUMED IN INITIAL RISK CORRIDOR.—An equal percentage point increase in the percents applied under subparagraphs (B)(i),

(B)(ii)(I), (C)(i), and (C)(ii)(I) of section 1860D-15(e)(2). In no case shall the application of previous sentence prevent the application of a higher percentage under section 1869D-15(e)(2)(B)(iii).

(II) INCREASE IN FEDERAL PERCENTAGE ASSUMED IN SECOND RISK CORRIDOR.—An equal percentage point increase in the percents applied under subparagraphs (B)(ii)(II) and (C)(ii)(II) of section 1860D-15(e)(2).

(III) DECREASE IN SIZE OF RISK CORRIDORS.—A decrease in the threshold risk percentages specified in section 1860D-15(e)(3)(C).

(F) ADDITIONAL INFORMATION.—Such other information as the Secretary may require to carry out this part.

(3) PAPERWORK REDUCTION FOR OFFERING OF PRESCRIPTION DRUG PLANS NATIONALLY OR IN MULTI-REGION AREAS.—The Secretary shall establish requirements for information submission under this subsection in a manner that promotes the offering of such plans in more than one PDP region (including all regions) through the filing of consolidated information.

(c) ACTUARIAL VALUATION.—

(1) PROCESSES.—For purposes of this part, the Secretary shall establish processes and methods for determining the actuarial valuation of prescription drug coverage, including—

(A) an actuarial valuation of standard prescription drug coverage under section 1860D-2(b);

(B) actuarial valuations relating to alternative prescription drug coverage under section 1860D-2(c)(1);

(C) an actuarial valuation of the reinsurance subsidy payments under section 1860D-15(b);

(D) the use of generally accepted actuarial principles and methodologies; and

(E) applying the same methodology for determinations of actuarial valuations under subparagraphs (A) and (B).

(2) ACCOUNTING FOR DRUG UTILIZATION.—Such processes and methods for determining actuarial valuation shall take into account the effect that providing alternative prescription drug coverage (rather than standard prescription drug coverage) has on drug utilization.

(3) RESPONSIBILITIES.—

(A) PLAN RESPONSIBILITIES.—PDP sponsors and MA organizations are responsible for the preparation and submission of actuarial valuations required under this part for prescription drug plans and MA-PD plans they offer.

(B) USE OF OUTSIDE ACTUARIES.—Under the processes and methods established under paragraph (1), PDP sponsors offering prescription drug plans and MA organizations offering MA-PD plans may use actuarial opinions certified by independent, qualified actuaries to establish actuarial values.

(d) REVIEW OF INFORMATION AND NEGOTIATION.—

(1) REVIEW OF INFORMATION.—The Secretary shall review the information filed under subsection (b) for the purpose of conducting negotiations under paragraph (2).

(2) NEGOTIATION REGARDING TERMS AND CONDITIONS.—Subject to subsection (i), in exercising the authority under paragraph (1), the Secretary—

(A) has the authority to negotiate the terms and conditions of the proposed bid submitted and other terms and conditions of a proposed plan; and

(B) has authority similar to the authority of the Director of the Office of Personnel Management with respect to health benefits plans under chapter 89 of title 5, United States Code.

(e) APPROVAL OF PROPOSED PLANS.—

(1) IN GENERAL.—After review and negotiation under subsection (d), the Secretary shall approve or disapprove the prescription drug plan.

(2) REQUIREMENTS FOR APPROVAL.—The Secretary may approve a prescription drug plan only if the following requirements are met:

(A) COMPLIANCE WITH REQUIREMENTS.—The plan and the PDP sponsor offering the plan comply with the requirements under this part, including the provision of qualified prescription drug coverage.

(B) ACTUARIAL DETERMINATIONS.—The Secretary determines that the plan and PDP sponsor meet the requirements under this part relating to actuarial determinations, including such requirements under section 1860D-2(c).

(C) APPLICATION OF FEHBP STANDARD.—

(i) IN GENERAL.—The Secretary determines that the portion of the bid submitted under subsection (b) that is attributable to basic prescription drug coverage is supported by the actuarial bases provided under such subsection and reasonably and equitably reflects the revenue requirements (as used for purposes of section 1302(8)(C) of the Public Health Service Act) for benefits provided under that plan, less the sum (determined on a monthly per capita basis) of the actuarial value of the reinsurance payments under section 1860D-15(b).

(ii) SUPPLEMENTAL COVERAGE.—The Secretary determines that the portion of the bid submitted under subsection (b) that is attributable to supplemental prescription drug coverage pursuant to section 1860D-2(a)(2) is supported by the actuarial bases provided under such subsection and reasonably and equitably reflects the revenue requirements (as used for purposes of section 1302(8)(C) of the Public Health Service Act) for such coverage under the plan.

(D) PLAN DESIGN.—

(i) IN GENERAL.—The Secretary does not find that the design of the plan and its benefits (including any formulary and tiered formulary structure) are likely to substantially discourage enrollment by certain part D eligible individuals under the plan.

(ii) USE OF CATEGORIES AND CLASSES IN FORMULARIES.—The Secretary may not find that the design of categories and classes within a formulary violates clause (i) if such categories and classes are consistent with guidelines (if any) for such categories and classes established by the United States Pharmacopeia.

(f) APPLICATION OF LIMITED RISK PLANS.—

(1) CONDITIONS FOR APPROVAL OF LIMITED RISK PLANS.—The Secretary may only approve a limited risk plan (as defined in paragraph (4)(A)) for a PDP region if the access requirements under section 1860D-3(a) would not be met for the region but for the approval of such a plan (or a fallback prescription drug plan under subsection (g)).

(2) RULES.—The following rules shall apply with respect to the approval of a limited risk plan in a PDP region:

(A) LIMITED EXERCISE OF AUTHORITY.—Only the minimum number of such plans may be approved in order to meet the access requirements under section 1860D-3(a).

(B) MAXIMIZING ASSUMPTION OF RISK.—The Secretary shall provide priority in approval for those plans bearing the highest level of risk (as computed by the Secretary), but the Secretary may take into account the level of the bids submitted by such plans.

(C) NO FULL UNDERWRITING FOR LIMITED RISK PLANS.—In no case may the Secretary approve a limited risk plan under which the modification of risk level provides for no (or a de minimis) level of financial risk.

(3) ACCEPTANCE OF ALL FULL RISK CONTRACTS.—There shall be no limit on the number of full risk plans that are approved under subsection (e).

(4) RISK-PLANS DEFINED.—For purposes of this subsection:

(A) LIMITED RISK PLAN.—The term 'limited risk plan' means a prescription drug plan that provides basic prescription drug coverage and for which the PDP sponsor includes a modification of risk level described in subparagraph (E) of subsection (b)(2) in its bid submitted for the plan under such subsection. Such term does not include a fallback prescription drug plan.

(B) FULL RISK PLAN.—The term 'full risk plan' means a prescription drug plan that is not a limited risk plan or a fallback prescription drug plan.

(g) GUARANTEEING ACCESS TO COVERAGE.—

(1) SOLICITATION OF BIDS.—

(A) IN GENERAL.—Separate from the bidding process under subsection (b), the Secretary shall provide for a process for the solicitation of bids from eligible fallback entities (as defined in paragraph (2)) for the offering in all fallback service areas (as defined in paragraph (3)) in one or more PDP regions of a fallback prescription drug plan (as defined in paragraph (4)) during the contract period specified in paragraph (5)).

(B) ACCEPTANCE OF BIDS.—

(i) IN GENERAL.—Except as provided in this subparagraph, the provisions of subsection (e) shall apply with respect to the approval or disapproval of fallback prescription drug plans. The Secretary shall enter into contracts under this subsection with eligible fallback entities for the offering of fall-back prescription drug plans so approved in fallback service areas.

(ii) LIMITATION OF 1 PLAN FOR ALL FALL-BACK SERVICE AREAS IN A PDP REGION.—With respect to all fallback service areas in any PDP region for a contract period, the Secretary shall approve the offering of only 1 fallback prescription drug plan.

(iii) COMPETITIVE PROCEDURES.—Competitive procedures (as defined in section 4(5) of the Office of Federal Procurement Policy Act (41 U.S.C. 403(5))) shall be used to enter into a contract under this subsection. The provisions of subsection (d) of section 1874A shall apply to a contract under this section in the same manner as they apply to a contract under such section.

(iv) TIMING.—The Secretary shall approve a fallback prescription drug plan for a PDP region in a manner so that, if there are any fallback service areas in the region for a year, the fallback prescription drug plan is offered at the same time as prescription drug plans would otherwise be offered.

(v) NO NATIONAL FALLBACK PLAN.—The Secretary shall not enter into a contract with a single fallback entity for the offering of fallback plans throughout the United States.

(2) ELIGIBLE FALLBACK ENTITY.—For purposes of this section, the term 'eligible fallback entity' means, with respect to all fallback service areas in a PDP region for a contract period, an entity that—

(A) meets the requirements to be a PDP sponsor (or would meet such requirements but for the fact that the entity is not a risk-bearing entity); and

(B) does not submit a bid under section 1860D11(b) for any prescription drug plan for any PDP region for the first year of such contract period.

For purposes of subparagraph (B), an entity shall be treated as submitting a bid with respect to a prescription drug plan if the entity is acting as a subcontractor of a PDP sponsor that is offering such a plan. The previous sentence shall not apply to entities that are subcontractors of an MA organization except insofar as such organization is acting as a PDP sponsor with respect to a prescription drug plan.

(3) FALLBACK SERVICE AREA.—For purposes of this subsection, the term 'fallback service area' means, for a PDP region with respect to a year, any area within such region for which the Secretary determines before the beginning of the year that the access requirements of the first sentence of section 1860D-3(a) will not be met for part D eligible individuals residing in the area for the year.

(4) FALLBACK PRESCRIPTION DRUG PLAN.—For purposes of this part, the term 'fallback prescription drug plan' means a prescription drug plan that—

§1860D-11(g)(4) ¶2262A

(A) only offers the standard prescription drug coverage and access to negotiated prices described in section 1860D-2(a)(1)(A) and does not include any supplemental prescription drug coverage; and

(B) meets such other requirements as the Secretary may specify.

(5) PAYMENTS UNDER THE CONTRACT.—

(A) IN GENERAL.—A contract entered into under this subsection shall provide for—

(i) payment for the actual costs (taking into account negotiated price concessions described in section 1860D-2(d)(1)(B)) of covered part D drugs provided to part D eligible individuals enrolled in a fallback prescription drug plan offered by the entity; and

(ii) payment of management fees that are tied to performance measures established by the Secretary for the management, administration, and delivery of the benefits under the contract.

(B) PERFORMANCE MEASURES.—The performance measures established by the Secretary pursuant to subparagraph (A)(ii) shall include at least measures for each of the following:

(i) COSTS.—The entity contains costs to the Medicare Prescription Drug Account and to part D eligible individuals enrolled in a fallback prescription drug plan offered by the entity through mechanisms such as generic substitution and price discounts.

(ii) QUALITY PROGRAMS.—The entity provides such enrollees with quality programs that avoid adverse drug reactions and overutilization and reduce medical errors.

(iii) CUSTOMER SERVICE.—The entity provides timely and accurate delivery of services and pharmacy and beneficiary support services.

(iv) BENEFIT ADMINISTRATION AND CLAIMS ADJUDICATION.—The entity provides efficient and effective benefit administration and claims adjudication.

(6) MONTHLY BENEFICIARY PREMIUM.—Except as provided in section 1860D-13(b) (relating to late enrollment penalty) and subject to section 1860D-14 (relating to low-income assistance), the monthly beneficiary premium to be charged under a fallback prescription drug plan offered in all fallback service areas in a PDP region shall be uniform and shall be equal to 25.5 percent of an amount equal to the Secretary's estimate of the average monthly per capita actuarial cost, including administrative expenses, under the fallback prescription drug plan of providing coverage in the region, as calculated by the Chief Actuary of the Centers for Medicare & Medicaid Services. In calculating such administrative expenses, the Chief Actuary shall use a factor that is based on similar expenses of prescription drug plans that are not fallback prescription drug plans.

(7) GENERAL CONTRACT TERMS AND CONDITIONS.—

(A) IN GENERAL.—Except as may be appropriate to carry out this section, the terms and conditions of contracts with eligible fallback entities offering fallback prescription drug plans under this subsection shall be the same as the terms and conditions of contracts under this part for prescription drug plans.

(B) PERIOD OF CONTRACT.—

(i) IN GENERAL.—Subject to clause (ii), a contract approved for a fallback prescription drug plan for fallback service areas for a PDP region under this section shall be for a period of 3 years (except as may be renewed after a subsequent bidding process).

(ii) LIMITATION.—A fallback prescription drug plan may be offered under a contract in an area for a year only if that area is a fallback service area for that year.

(C) ENTITY NOT PERMITTED TO MARKET OR BRAND FALLBACK PRESCRIPTION DRUG PLANS.—An eligible fallback entity with a contract under this subsection may not engage in any marketing or branding of a fallback prescription drug plan.

(h) ANNUAL REPORT ON USE OF LIMITED RISK PLANS AND FALLBACK PLANS.—The Secretary shall submit to Congress an annual report that describes instances in which limited risk plans and fallback prescription drug plans were offered under subsections (f) and (g). The Secretary shall include in such

Social Security Law Added, Amended or Repealed

report such recommendations as may be appropriate to limit the need for the provision of such plans and to maximize the assumption of financial risk under section subsection (f).

(i) NONINTERFERENCE.—In order to promote competition under this part and in carrying out this part, the Secretary—

(1) may not interfere with the negotiations between drug manufacturers and pharmacies and PDP sponsors; and

(2) may not require a particular formulary or institute a price structure for the reimbursement of covered part D drugs.

(j) COORDINATION OF BENEFITS.—A PDP sponsor offering a prescription drug plan shall permit State Pharmaceutical Assistance Programs and Rx plans under sections 1860D-23 and 1860D-24 to coordinate benefits with the plan and, in connection with such coordination with such a Program, not to impose fees that are unrelated to the cost of coordination.

[CCH Explanation at ¶115.]

2003 Amendments:

Section 101(a) of the "Medicare Prescription Drug, Improvement, and Modernization Act of 2003," effective upon enactment, added new section 1860D-11.

The above amendment applies to coverage effective January 1, 2006.

[¶2262B] Sec. 1860D-12. REQUIREMENTS FOR AND CONTRACTS WITH PRESCRIPTION DRUG PLAN (PDP) SPONSORS

(a) GENERAL REQUIREMENTS.—Each PDP sponsor of a prescription drug plan shall meet the following requirements:

(1) LICENSURE.—Subject to subsection (c), the sponsor is organized and licensed under State law as a riskbearing entity eligible to offer health insurance or health benefits coverage in each State in which it offers a prescription drug plan.

(2) ASSUMPTION OF FINANCIAL RISK FOR UNSUBSIDIZED COVERAGE.—

(A) IN GENERAL.—Subject to subparagraph (B), to the extent that the entity is at risk the entity assumes financial risk on a prospective basis for benefits that it offers under a prescription drug plan and that is not covered under section 1860D-15(b).

(B) REINSURANCE PERMITTED.—The plan sponsor may obtain insurance or make other arrangements for the cost of coverage provided to any enrollee to the extent that the sponsor is at risk for providing such coverage.

(3) SOLVENCY FOR UNLICENSED SPONSORS.—In the case of a PDP sponsor that is not described in paragraph (1) and for which a waiver has been approved under subsection (c), such sponsor shall meet solvency standards established by the Secretary under subsection (d).

(b) CONTRACT REQUIREMENTS.—

(1) IN GENERAL.—The Secretary shall not permit the enrollment under section 1860D-1 in a prescription drug plan offered by a PDP sponsor under this part, and the sponsor shall not be eligible for payments under section 1860D-14 or 1860D-15, unless the Secretary has entered into a contract under this subsection with the sponsor with respect to the offering of such plan. Such a contract with a sponsor may cover more than one prescription drug plan. Such contract shall provide that the sponsor agrees to comply with the applicable requirements and standards of this part and the terms and conditions of payment as provided for in this part.

(2) LIMITATION ON ENTITIES OFFERING FALLBACK PRESCRIPTION DRUG PLANS.—The Secretary shall not enter into a contract with a PDP sponsor for the offering of a prescription drug plan (other than a fallback prescription drug plan) in a PDP region for a year if the sponsor—

(A) submitted a bid under section 1860D-11(g) for such year (as the first year of a contract period under such section) to offer a fallback prescription drug plan in any PDP region;

(B) offers a fallback prescription drug plan in any PDP region during the year; or

(C) offered a fallback prescription drug plan in that PDP region during the previous year.

For purposes of this paragraph, an entity shall be treated as submitting a bid with respect to a prescription drug plan or offering a fallback prescription drug plan if the entity is acting as a subcontractor of a PDP sponsor that is offering such a plan. The previous sentence shall not apply to entities that are subcontractors of an MA organization except insofar as such organization is acting as a PDP sponsor with respect to a prescription drug plan.

(3) INCORPORATION OF CERTAIN MEDICARE ADVANTAGE CONTRACT REQUIREMENTS.—Except as otherwise provided, the following provisions of section 1857 shall apply to contracts under this section in the same manner as they apply to contracts under section 1857(a):

(A) MINIMUM ENROLLMENT.—Paragraphs (1) and (3) of section 1857(b), except that—

(i) the Secretary may increase the minimum number of enrollees required under such paragraph (1) as the Secretary determines appropriate; and

(ii) the requirement of such paragraph (1) shall be waived during the first contract year with respect to an organization in a region.

(B) CONTRACT PERIOD AND EFFECTIVENESS.—Section 1857(c), except that in applying paragraph (4)(B) of such section any reference to payment amounts under section 1853 shall be deemed payment amounts under section 1860D-15.

(C) PROTECTIONS AGAINST FRAUD AND BENEFICIARY PROTECTIONS.—Section 1857(d).

(D) ADDITIONAL CONTRACT TERMS.—Section 1857(e); except that section 1857(e)(2) shall apply as specified to PDP sponsors and payments under this part to an MA-PD plan shall be treated as expenditures made under part D.

(E) INTERMEDIATE SANCTIONS.—Section 1857(g) (other than paragraph (1)(F) of such section), except that in applying such section the reference in section 1857(g)(1)(B) to section 1854 is deemed a reference to this part.

(F) PROCEDURES FOR TERMINATION.—Section 1857(h).

(c) WAIVER OF CERTAIN REQUIREMENTS TO EXPAND CHOICE.—

(1) AUTHORIZING WAIVER.—

(A) IN GENERAL.—In the case of an entity that seeks to offer a prescription drug plan in a State, the Secretary shall waive the requirement of subsection (a)(1) that the entity be licensed in that State if the Secretary determines, based on the application and other evidence presented to the Secretary, that any of the grounds for approval of the application described in paragraph (2) have been met.

(B) APPLICATION OF REGIONAL PLAN WAIVER RULE.—In addition to the waiver available under subparagraph (A), the provisions of section 1858(d) shall apply to PDP sponsors under this part in a manner similar to the manner in which such provisions apply to MA organizations under part C, except that no application shall be required under paragraph (1)(B) of such section in the case of a State that does not provide a licensing process for such a sponsor.

(2) GROUNDS FOR APPROVAL.—

(A) IN GENERAL.—The grounds for approval under this paragraph are—

(i) subject to subparagraph (B), the grounds for approval described in subparagraphs (B), (C), and (D) of section 1855(a)(2); and

(ii) the application by a State of any grounds other than those required under Federal law.

(B) SPECIAL RULES.—In applying subparagraph (A)(i)—

(i) the ground of approval described in section 1855(a)(2)(B) is deemed to have been met if the State does not have a licensing process in effect with respect to the PDP sponsor; and

(ii) for plan years beginning before January 1, 2008, if the State does have such a licensing process in effect, such ground for approval described in such section is deemed to have been met upon submission of an application described in such section.

(3) APPLICATION OF WAIVER PROCEDURES.—With respect to an application for a waiver (or a waiver granted) under paragraph (1)(A) of this subsection, the provisions of subparagraphs (E), (F), and (G) of section 1855(a)(2) shall apply, except that clauses (i) and (ii) of such subparagraph (E) shall not apply in the case of a State that does not have a licensing process described in paragraph (2)(B)(i) in effect.

(4) REFERENCES TO CERTAIN PROVISIONS.—In applying provisions of section 1855(a)(2) under paragraphs (2) and (3) of this subsection to prescription drug plans and PDP sponsors—

(A) any reference to a waiver application under section 1855 shall be treated as a reference to a waiver application under paragraph (1)(A) of this subsection; and

(B) any reference to solvency standards shall be treated as a reference to solvency standards established under subsection (d) of this section.

(d) SOLVENCY STANDARDS FOR NON-LICENSED ENTITIES.—

(1) ESTABLISHMENT AND PUBLICATION.—The Secretary, in consultation with the National Association of Insurance Commissioners, shall establish and publish, by not later than January 1, 2005, financial solvency and capital adequacy standards for entities described in paragraph (2).

(2) COMPLIANCE WITH STANDARDS.—A PDP sponsor that is not licensed by a State under subsection (a)(1) and for which a waiver application has been approved under subsection (c) shall meet solvency and capital adequacy standards established under paragraph (1). The Secretary shall establish certification procedures for such sponsors with respect to such solvency standards in the manner described in section 1855(c)(2).

(e) LICENSURE DOES NOT SUBSTITUTE FOR OR CONSTITUTE CERTIFICATION.—The fact that a PDP sponsor is licensed in accordance with subsection (a)(1) or has a waiver application approved under subsection (c) does not deem the sponsor to meet other requirements imposed under this part for a sponsor.

(f) PERIODIC REVIEW AND REVISION OF STANDARDS.—

(1) IN GENERAL.—Subject to paragraph (2), the Secretary may periodically review the standards established under this section and, based on such review, may revise such standards if the Secretary determines such revision to be appropriate.

(2) PROHIBITION OF MIDYEAR IMPLEMENTATION OF SIGNIFICANT NEW REGULATORY REQUIREMENTS.—The Secretary may not implement, other than at the beginning of a calendar year, regulations under this section that impose new, significant regulatory requirements on a PDP sponsor or a prescription drug plan.

(g) PROHIBITION OF STATE IMPOSITION OF PREMIUM TAXES; RELATION TO STATE LAWS.—The provisions of sections 1854(g) and 1856(b)(3) shall apply with respect to PDP sponsors and prescription drug plans under this part in the same manner as such sections apply to MA organizations and MA plans under part C.

[CCH Explanation at ¶ 117.]
2003 Amendments:

Section 101(a) of the "Medicare Prescription Drug, Improvement, and Modernization Act of 2003," effective upon enactment, added new section 1860D-12.

The above amendment applies to coverage effective January 1, 2006.

[¶ 2262C] SEC. 1860D-13. PREMIUMS; LATE ENROLLMENT PENALTY

(a) MONTHLY BENEFICIARY PREMIUM.—

(1) COMPUTATION.—

(A) IN GENERAL.—The monthly beneficiary premium for a prescription drug plan is the base beneficiary premium computed under paragraph (2) as adjusted under this paragraph.

(B) ADJUSTMENT TO REFLECT DIFFERENCE BETWEEN BID AND NATIONAL AVERAGE BID.—

(i) ABOVE AVERAGE BID.—If for a month the amount of the standardized bid amount (as defined in paragraph (5)) exceeds the amount of the adjusted national average monthly bid amount (as defined in clause (iii)), the base beneficiary premium for the month shall be increased by the amount of such excess.

(ii) BELOW AVERAGE BID.—If for a month the amount of the adjusted national average monthly bid amount for the month exceeds the standardized bid amount, the base beneficiary premium for the month shall be decreased by the amount of such excess.

(iii) ADJUSTED NATIONAL AVERAGE MONTHLY BID AMOUNT DEFINED.—For purposes of this subparagraph, the term 'adjusted national average monthly bid amount' means the national average monthly bid amount computed under paragraph (4), as adjusted under section 1860D-15(c)(2).

(C) INCREASE FOR SUPPLEMENTAL PRESCRIPTION DRUG BENEFITS.—The base beneficiary premium shall be increased by the portion of the PDP approved bid that is attributable to supplemental prescription drug benefits.

(D) INCREASE FOR LATE ENROLLMENT PENALTY.—The base beneficiary premium shall be increased by the amount of any late enrollment penalty under subsection (b).

(E) DECREASE FOR LOW-INCOME ASSISTANCE.—The monthly beneficiary premium is subject to decrease in the case of a subsidy eligible individual under section 1860D-14.

(F) UNIFORM PREMIUM.—Except as provided in subparagraphs (D) and (E), the monthly beneficiary premium for a prescription drug plan in a PDP region is the same for all part D eligible individuals enrolled in the plan.

(2) BASE BENEFICIARY PREMIUM.—The base beneficiary premium under this paragraph for a prescription drug plan for a month is equal to the product—

(A) the beneficiary premium percentage (as specified in paragraph (3)); and

(B) the national average monthly bid amount (computed under paragraph (4)) for the month.

(3) BENEFICIARY PREMIUM PERCENTAGE.—For purposes of this subsection, the beneficiary premium percentage for any year is the percentage equal to a fraction—

(A) the numerator of which is 25.5 percent; and

(B) the denominator of which is 100 percent minus a percentage equal to—

(i) the total reinsurance payments which the Secretary estimates are payable under section 1860D-15(b) with respect to the coverage year; divided by

(ii) the sum of—

(I) the amount estimated under clause (i) for the year; and

(II) the total payments which the Secretary estimates will be paid to prescription drug plans and MA-PD plans that are attributable to the standardized bid amount during the year, taking into account amounts paid by the Secretary and enrollees.

(4) COMPUTATION OF NATIONAL AVERAGE MONTHLY BID AMOUNT.—

(A) IN GENERAL.—For each year (beginning with 2006) the Secretary shall compute a national average monthly bid amount equal to the average of the standardized bid amounts (as defined in paragraph (5)) for each prescription drug plan and for each MA-PD plan described in section 1851(a)(2)(A)(i). Such average does not take into account the bids submitted for MSA plans, MA private fee-for-service plan, and specialized MA plans for special needs individuals, PACE programs under section 1894 (pursuant to section 1860D-21(f)), and under reasonable cost reimbursement contracts under section 1876(h) (pursuant to section 1860D-21(e)).

(B) WEIGHTED AVERAGE.—

(i) IN GENERAL.—The monthly national average monthly bid amount computed under subparagraph (A) for a year shall be a weighted average, with the weight for each plan being equal to the average number of part D eligible individuals enrolled in such plan in the reference month (as defined in section 1858(f)(4)).

(ii) SPECIAL RULE FOR 2006.—For purposes of applying this paragraph for 2006, the Secretary shall establish procedures for determining the weighted average under clause (i) for 2005.

(5) STANDARDIZED BID AMOUNT DEFINED.—For purposes of this subsection, the term 'standardized bid amount' means the following:

(A) PRESCRIPTION DRUG PLANS.—

(i) BASIC COVERAGE.—In the case of a prescription drug plan that provides basic prescription drug coverage, the PDP approved bid (as defined in paragraph (6)).

(ii) SUPPLEMENTAL COVERAGE.—In the case of a prescription drug plan that provides supplemental prescription drug coverage, the portion of the PDP approved bid that is attributable to basic prescription drug coverage.

(B) MA-PD PLANS.—In the case of an MA-PD plan, the portion of the accepted bid amount that is attributable to basic prescription drug coverage.

(6) PDP APPROVED BID DEFINED.—For purposes of this part, the term 'PDP approved bid' means, with respect to a prescription drug plan, the bid amount approved for the plan under this part.

(b) LATE ENROLLMENT PENALTY.—

(1) IN GENERAL.—Subject to the succeeding provisions of this subsection, in the case of a part D eligible individual described in paragraph (2) with respect to a continuous period of eligibility, there shall be an increase in the monthly beneficiary premium established under subsection (a) in an amount determined under paragraph (3).

(2) INDIVIDUALS SUBJECT TO PENALTY.—A part D eligible individual described in this paragraph is, with respect to a continuous period of eligibility, an individual for whom there is a continuous period of 63 days or longer (all of which in such continuous period of eligibility) beginning on the day after the last date of the individual's initial enrollment period under section 1860D-1(b)(2) and ending on the date of enrollment under a prescription drug plan or MA-PD plan during all of which the individual was not covered under any creditable prescription drug coverage.

(3) AMOUNT OF PENALTY.—

(A) IN GENERAL.—The amount determined under this paragraph for a part D eligible individual for a continuous period of eligibility is the greater of—

(i) an amount that the Secretary determines is actuarially sound for each uncovered month (as defined in subparagraph (B)) in the same continuous period of eligibility; or

(ii) 1 percent of the base beneficiary premium (computed under subsection (a)(2)) for each such uncovered month in such period.

(B) UNCOVERED MONTH DEFINED.—For purposes of this subsection, the term 'uncovered month' means, with respect to a part D eligible individual, any month beginning after the end of the initial enrollment period under section 1860D-1(b)(2) unless the individual can demonstrate that the individual had creditable prescription drug coverage (as defined in paragraph (4)) for any portion of such month.

(4) CREDITABLE PRESCRIPTION DRUG COVERAGE DEFINED.—For purposes of this part, the term 'creditable prescription drug coverage' means any of the following coverage, but only if the coverage meets the requirement of paragraph (5):

(A) COVERAGE UNDER PRESCRIPTION DRUG PLAN OR MA-PD PLAN.—Coverage under a prescription drug plan or under an MA-PD plan.

(B) MEDICAID.—Coverage under a medicaid plan under title XIX or under a waiver under section 1115.

(C) GROUP HEALTH PLAN.—Coverage under a group health plan, including a health benefits plan under chapter 89 of title 5, United States Code (commonly known as the Federal employees health benefits program), and a qualified retiree prescription drug plan (as defined in section 1860D-22(a)(2)).

(D) STATE PHARMACEUTICAL ASSISTANCE PROGRAM.—Coverage under a State pharmaceutical assistance program described in section 1860D-23(b)(1).

§1860D-13(b)(4)(D) ¶2262C

(E) VETERANS' COVERAGE OF PRESCRIPTION DRUGS.—Coverage for veterans, and survivors and dependents of veterans, under chapter 17 of title 38, United States Code.

(F) PRESCRIPTION DRUG COVERAGE UNDER MEDIGAP POLICIES.—Coverage under a medicare supplemental policy under section 1882 that provides benefits for prescription drugs (whether or not such coverage conforms to the standards for packages of benefits under section 1882(p)(1)).

(G) MILITARY COVERAGE (INCLUDING TRICARE).—Coverage under chapter 55 of title 10, United States Code.

(H) OTHER COVERAGE.—Such other coverage as the Secretary determines appropriate.

(5) ACTUARIAL EQUIVALENCE REQUIREMENT.—Coverage meets the requirement of this paragraph only if the coverage is determined (in a manner specified by the Secretary) to provide coverage of the cost of prescription drugs the actuarial value of which (as defined by the Secretary) to the individual equals or exceeds the actuarial value of standard prescription drug coverage (as determined under section 1860D-11(c)).

(6) PROCEDURES TO DOCUMENT CREDITABLE PRESCRIPTION DRUG COVERAGE.—

(A) IN GENERAL.—The Secretary shall establish procedures (including the form, manner, and time) for the documentation of creditable prescription drug coverage, including procedures to assist in determining whether coverage meets the requirement of paragraph (5).

(B) DISCLOSURE BY ENTITIES OFFERING CREDITABLE PRESCRIPTION DRUG COVERAGE.—

(i) IN GENERAL.—Each entity that offers prescription drug coverage of the type described in subparagraphs (B) through (H) of paragraph (4) shall provide for disclosure, in a form, manner, and time consistent with standards established by the Secretary, to the Secretary and part D eligible individuals of whether the coverage meets the requirement of paragraph (5) or whether such coverage is changed so it no longer meets such requirement.

(ii) DISCLOSURE OF NON-CREDITABLE COVERAGE.—In the case of such coverage that does not meet such requirement, the disclosure to part D eligible individuals under this subparagraph shall include information regarding the fact that because such coverage does not meet such requirement there are limitations on the periods in a year in which the individuals may enroll under a prescription drug plan or an MA-PD plan and that any such enrollment is subject to a late enrollment penalty under this subsection.

(C) WAIVER OF REQUIREMENT.—In the case of a part D eligible individual who was enrolled in prescription drug coverage of the type described in subparagraphs (B) through (H) of paragraph (4) which is not creditable prescription drug coverage because it does not meet the requirement of paragraph (5), the individual may apply to the Secretary to have such coverage treated as creditable prescription drug coverage if the individual establishes that the individual was not adequately informed that such coverage did not meet such requirement.

(7) CONTINUOUS PERIOD OF ELIGIBILITY.—

(A) IN GENERAL.—Subject to subparagraph (B), for purposes of this subsection, the term 'continuous period of eligibility' means, with respect to a part D eligible individual, the period that begins with the first day on which the individual is eligible to enroll in a prescription drug plan under this part and ends with the individual's death.

(B) SEPARATE PERIOD.—Any period during all of which a part D eligible individual is entitled to hospital insurance benefits under part A and—

(i) which terminated in or before the month preceding the month in which the individual attained age 65; or

(ii) for which the basis for eligibility for such entitlement changed between section 226(b) and section 226(a), between 226(b) and section 226A, or between section 226A and section 226(a), shall be a separate continuous period of eligibility with respect to the individual (and each such period which terminates shall be deemed not to have existed for purposes of subsequently applying this paragraph).

(c) COLLECTION OF MONTHLY BENEFICIARY PREMIUMS.—

(1) IN GENERAL.—Subject to paragraphs (2) and (3), the provisions of section 1854(d) shall apply to PDP sponsors and premiums (and any late enrollment penalty) under this part in the same manner as they apply to MA organizations and beneficiary premiums under part C, except that any reference to a Trust Fund is deemed for this purpose a reference to the Medicare Prescription Drug Account.

(2) CREDITING OF LATE ENROLLMENT PENALTY.—

(A) PORTION ATTRIBUTABLE TO INCREASED ACTUARIAL COSTS.—With respect to late enrollment penalties imposed under subsection (b), the Secretary shall specify the portion of such a penalty that the Secretary estimates is attributable to increased actuarial costs assumed by the PDP sponsor or MA organization (and not taken into account through risk adjustment provided under section 1860D-15(c)(1) or through reinsurance payments under section 1860D-15(b)) as a result of such late enrollment.

(B) COLLECTION THROUGH WITHHOLDING.—In the case of a late enrollment penalty that is collected from a part D eligible individual in the manner described in section 1854(d)(2)(A), the Secretary shall provide that only the portion of such penalty estimated under subparagraph (A) shall be paid to the PDP sponsor or MA organization offering the part D plan in which the individual is enrolled.

(C) COLLECTION BY PLAN.—In the case of a late enrollment penalty that is collected from a part D eligible individual in a manner other than the manner described in section 1854(d)(2)(A), the Secretary shall establish procedures for reducing payments otherwise made to the PDP sponsor or MA organization by an amount equal to the amount of such penalty less the portion of such penalty estimated under subparagraph (A).

(3) FALLBACK PLANS.—In applying this subsection in the case of a fallback prescription drug plan, paragraph (2) shall not apply and the monthly beneficiary premium shall be collected in the manner specified in section 1854(d)(2)(A) (or such other manner as may be provided under section 1840 in the case of monthly premiums under section 1839).

[CCH Explanation at ¶118.]

2003 Amendments:

Section 101(a) of the "Medicare Prescription Drug, Improvement, and Modernization Act of 2003," effective upon enactment, added new section 1860D-13.

The above amendment applies to coverage effective January 1, 2006.

[¶2263A] SEC. 1860D-14. PREMIUM AND COST-SHARING SUBSIDIES FOR LOW-INCOME INDIVIDUALS

(a) INCOME-RELATED SUBSIDIES FOR INDIVIDUALS WITH INCOME UP TO 150 PERCENT OF POVERTY LINE.—

(1) INDIVIDUALS WITH INCOME BELOW 135 PERCENT OF POVERTY LINE.—In the case of a subsidy eligible individual (as defined in paragraph (3)) who is determined to have income that is below 135 percent of the poverty line applicable to a family of the size involved and who meets the resources requirement described in paragraph (3)(D) or who is covered under this paragraph under paragraph (3)(B)(i), the individual is entitled under this section to the following:

(A) FULL PREMIUM SUBSIDY.—An income-related premium subsidy equal to—

(i) 100 percent of the amount described in subsection (b)(1), but not to exceed the premium amount specified in subsection (b)(2)(B); plus

(ii) 80 percent of any late enrollment penalties imposed under section 1860D-13(b) for the first 60 months in which such penalties are imposed for that individual, and 100 percent of any such penalties for any subsequent month.

(B) ELIMINATION OF DEDUCTIBLE.—A reduction in the annual deductible applicable under section 1860D-2(b)(1) to $0.

§1860D-14(a)(1)(B) ¶2263A

(C) CONTINUATION OF COVERAGE ABOVE THE INITIAL COVERAGE LIMIT.—The continuation of coverage from the initial coverage limit (under paragraph (3) of section 1860D-2(b)) for expenditures incurred through the total amount of expenditures at which benefits are available under paragraph (4) of such section, subject to the reduced cost-sharing described in subparagraph (D).

(D) REDUCTION IN COST-SHARING BELOW OUTOF-POCKET THRESHOLD.—

(i) INSTITUTIONALIZED INDIVIDUALS.—In the case of an individual who is a full-benefit dual eligible individual and who is an institutionalized individual or couple (as defined in section 1902(q)(1)(B)), the elimination of any beneficiary coinsurance described in section 1860D-2(b)(2) (for all amounts through the total amount of expenditures at which benefits are available under section 1860D-2(b)(4)).

(ii) LOWEST INCOME DUAL ELIGIBLE INDIVIDUALS.—In the case of an individual not described in clause (i) who is a full-benefit dual eligible individual and whose income does not exceed 100 percent of the poverty line applicable to a family of the size involved, the substitution for the beneficiary coinsurance described in section 1860D2(b)(2) (for all amounts through the total amount of expenditures at which benefits are available under section 1860D-2(b)(4)) of a copayment amount that does not exceed $1 for a generic drug or a preferred drug that is a multiple source drug (as defined in section 1927(k)(7)(A)(i)) and $3 for any other drug, or, if less, the copayment amount applicable to an individual under clause (iii).

(iii) OTHER INDIVIDUALS.—In the case of an individual not described in clause (i) or (ii), the substitution for the beneficiary coinsurance described in section 1860D-2(b)(2) (for all amounts through the total amount of expenditures at which benefits are available under section 1860D2(b)(4)) of a copayment amount that does not exceed the copayment amount specified under section 1860D-2(b)(4)(A)(i)(I) for the drug and year involved.

(E) ELIMINATION OF COST-SHARING ABOVE ANNUAL OUT-OF-POCKET THRESHOLD.—The elimination of any cost-sharing imposed under section 1860D2(b)(4)(A).

(2) OTHER INDIVIDUALS WITH INCOME BELOW 150 PERCENT OF POVERTY LINE.—In the case of a subsidy eligible individual who is not described in paragraph (1), the individual is entitled under this section to the following:

(A) SLIDING SCALE PREMIUM SUBSIDY.—An income-related premium subsidy determined on a linear sliding scale ranging from 100 percent of the amount described in paragraph (1)(A) for individuals with incomes at or below 135 percent of such level to 0 percent of such amount for individuals with incomes at 150 percent of such level.

(B) REDUCTION OF DEDUCTIBLE.—A reduction in the annual deductible applicable under section 1860D-2(b)(1) to $50.

(C) CONTINUATION OF COVERAGE ABOVE THE INITIAL COVERAGE LIMIT.—The continuation of coverage from the initial coverage limit (under paragraph (3) of section 1860D-2(b)) for expenditures incurred through the total amount of expenditures at which benefits are available under paragraph (4) of such section, subject to the reduced coinsurance described in subparagraph (D).

(D) REDUCTION IN COST-SHARING BELOW OUTOF-POCKET THRESHOLD.—The substitution for the beneficiary coinsurance described in section 1860D2(b)(2) (for all amounts above the deductible under subparagraph (B) through the total amount of expenditures at which benefits are available under section 1860D-2(b)(4)) of coinsurance of '15 percent' instead of coinsurance of '25 percent' in section 1860D2(b)(2).

(E) REDUCTION OF COST-SHARING ABOVE ANNUAL OUT-OF-POCKET THRESHOLD.—Subject to subsection (c), the substitution for the cost-sharing imposed under section 1860D-2(b)(4)(A) of a copayment or coinsurance not to exceed the copayment or coinsurance amount specified under section 1860D-2(b)(4)(A)(i)(I) for the drug and year involved.

(3) DETERMINATION OF ELIGIBILITY.—

(A) SUBSIDY ELIGIBLE INDIVIDUAL DEFINED.—For purposes of this part, subject to subparagraph (F), the term 'subsidy eligible individual' means a part D eligible individual who—

(i) is enrolled in a prescription drug plan or MA-PD plan;

(ii) has income below 150 percent of the poverty line applicable to a family of the size involved; and

(iii) meets the resources requirement described in subparagraph (D) or (E).

(B) DETERMINATIONS.—

(i) IN GENERAL.—The determination of whether a part D eligible individual residing in a State is a subsidy eligible individual and whether the individual is described in paragraph (1) shall be determined under the State plan under title XIX for the State under section 1935(a) or by the Commissioner of Social Security. There are authorized to be appropriated to the Social Security Administration such sums as may be necessary for the determination of eligibility under this subparagraph.

(ii) EFFECTIVE PERIOD.—Determinations under this subparagraph shall be effective beginning with the month in which the individual applies for a determination that the individual is a subsidy eligible individual and shall remain in effect for a period specified by the Secretary, but not to exceed 1 year.

(iii) REDETERMINATIONS AND APPEALS THROUGH MEDICAID.—Redeterminations and appeals, with respect to eligibility determinations under clause (i) made under a State plan under title XIX, shall be made in accordance with the frequency of, and manner in which, redeterminations and appeals of eligibility are made under such plan for purposes of medical assistance under such title.

(iv) REDETERMINATIONS AND APPEALS THROUGH COMMISSIONER.—With respect to eligibility determinations under clause (i) made by the Commissioner of Social Security—

(I) redeterminations shall be made at such time or times as may be provided by the Commissioner; and

(II) the Commissioner shall establish procedures for appeals of such determinations that are similar to the procedures described in the third sentence of section 1631(c)(1)(A).

(v) TREATMENT OF MEDICAID BENEFICIARIES.—Subject to subparagraph (F), the Secretary—

(I) shall provide that part D eligible individuals who are full-benefit dual eligible individuals (as defined in section 1935(c)(6)) or who are recipients of supplemental security income benefits under title XVI shall be treated as subsidy eligible individuals described in paragraph (1); and

(II) may provide that part D eligible individuals not described in subclause (I) who are determined for purposes of the State plan under title XIX to be eligible for medical assistance under clause (i), (iii), or (iv) of section 1902(a)(10)(E) are treated as being determined to be subsidy eligible individuals described in paragraph (1).

Insofar as the Secretary determines that the eligibility requirements under the State plan for medical assistance referred to in subclause (II) are sub-stantially the same as the requirements for being treated as a subsidy eligible individual described in paragraph (1), the Secretary shall provide for the treatment described in such subclause.

(C) INCOME DETERMINATIONS.—For purposes of applying this section—

(i) in the case of a part D eligible individual who is not treated as a subsidy eligible individual under subparagraph (B)(v), income shall be determined in the manner described in section 1905(p)(1)(B), without regard to the application of section 1902(r)(2); and

(ii) the term 'poverty line' has the meaning given such term in section 673(2) of the Community Services Block Grant Act (42 U.S.C. 9902(2)), including any revision required by such section.

Nothing in clause (i) shall be construed to affect the application of section 1902(r)(2) for the determination of eligibility for medical assistance under title XIX.

(D) Resource Standard Applied to Full Low-Income Subsidy to be Based on Three Times SSI Resource Standard.—The resources requirement of this subparagraph is that an individual's resources (as determined under section 1613 for purposes of the supplemental security income program) do not exceed—

(i) for 2006 three times the maximum amount of resources that an individual may have and obtain benefits under that program; and

(ii) for a subsequent year the resource limitation established under this clause for the previous year increased by the annual percentage increase in the consumer price index (all items; U.S. city average) as of September of such previous year.

Any resource limitation established under clause (ii) that is not a multiple of $10 shall be rounded to the nearest multiple of $10.

(E) Alternative Resource Standard.—

(i) In General.—The resources requirement of this subparagraph is that an individual's resources (as determined under section 1613 for purposes of the supplemental security income program) do not exceed—

(I) for 2006, $10,000 (or $20,000 in the case of the combined value of the individual's assets or resources and the assets or resources of the individual's spouse); and

(II) for a subsequent year the dollar amounts specified in this subclause (or subclause (I)) for the previous year increased by the annual percentage increase in the consumer price index (all items; U.S. city average) as of September of such previous year.

Any dollar amount established under subclause (II) that is not a multiple of $10 shall be rounded to the nearest multiple of $10.

(ii) Use of Simplified Application Form and Process.—The Secretary, jointly with the Commissioner of Social Security, shall—

(I) develop a model, simplified application form and process consistent with clause (iii) for the determination and verification of a part D eligible individual's assets or resources under this subparagraph; and

(II) provide such form to States.

(iii) Documentation and Safeguards.—Under such process—

(I) the application form shall consist of an attestation under penalty of perjury regarding the level of assets or resources (or combined assets and resources in the case of a married part D eligible individual) and valuations of general classes of assets or resources;

(II) such form shall be accompanied by copies of recent statements (if any) from financial institutions in support of the application; and

(III) matters attested to in the application shall be subject to appropriate methods of verification.

(iv) Methodology Flexibility.—The Secretary may permit a State in making eligibility determinations for premium and cost-sharing subsidies under this section to use the same asset or resource methodologies that are used with respect to eligibility for medical assistance for medicare cost-sharing described in section 1905(p) so long as the Secretary determines that the use of such methodologies will not result in any significant differences in the number of individuals determined to be subsidy eligible individuals.

(F) Treatment of Territorial Residents.—In the case of a part D eligible individual who is not a resident of the 50 States or the District of Columbia, the individual is not eligible to be a subsidy eligible individual under this section but may be eligible for financial assistance with prescription drug expenses under section 1935(e).

(4) INDEXING DOLLAR AMOUNTS.—

(A) COPAYMENT FOR LOWEST INCOME DUAL ELIGIBLE INDIVIDUALS.—The dollar amounts applied under paragraph (1)(D)(ii)—

(i) for 2007 shall be the dollar amounts specified in such paragraph increased by the annual percentage increase in the consumer price index (all items; U.S. city average) as of September of such previous year; or

(ii) for a subsequent year shall be the dollar amounts specified in this clause (or clause (i)) for the previous year increased by the annual percentage increase in the consumer price index (all items; U.S. city average) as of September of such previous year.

Any amount established under clause (i) or (ii), that is based on an increase of $1 or $3, that is not a multiple of 5 cents or 10 cents, respectively, shall be rounded to the nearest multiple of 5 cents or 10 cents, respectively.

(B) REDUCED DEDUCTIBLE.—The dollar amount applied under paragraph (2)(B)—

(i) for 2007 shall be the dollar amount specified in such paragraph increased by the annual percentage increase described in section 1860D2(b)(6) for 2007; or

(ii) for a subsequent year shall be the dollar amount specified in this clause (or clause (i)) for the previous year increased by the annual percentage increase described in section 1860D-2(b)(6) for the year involved.

Any amount established under clause (i) or (ii) that is not a multiple of $1 shall be rounded to the nearest multiple of $1.

(b) PREMIUM SUBSIDY AMOUNT.—

(1) IN GENERAL.—The premium subsidy amount described in this subsection for a subsidy eligible individual residing in a PDP region and enrolled in a prescription drug plan or MA-PD plan is the low-income benchmark premium amount (as defined in paragraph (2)) for the PDP region in which the individual resides or, if greater, the amount specified in paragraph (3).

(2) LOW-INCOME BENCHMARK PREMIUM AMOUNT DEFINED.—

(A) IN GENERAL.—For purposes of this subsection, the term 'low-income benchmark premium amount' means, with respect to a PDP region in which—

(i) all prescription drug plans are offered by the same PDP sponsor, the weighted average of the amounts described in subparagraph (B)(i) for such plans; or

(ii) there are prescription drug plans offered by more than one PDP sponsor, the weighted average of amounts described in subparagraph (B) for prescription drug plans and MA-PD plans described in section 1851(a)(2)(A)(i) offered in such region.

(B) PREMIUM AMOUNTS DESCRIBED.—The premium amounts described in this subparagraph are, in the case of—

(i) a prescription drug plan that is a basic prescription drug plan, the monthly beneficiary premium for such plan;

(ii) a prescription drug plan that provides alternative prescription drug coverage the actuarial value of which is greater than that of standard prescription drug coverage, the portion of the monthly beneficiary premium that is attributable to basic prescription drug coverage; and

(iii) an MA-PD plan, the portion of the MA monthly prescription drug beneficiary premium that is attributable to basic prescription drug benefits (described in section 1852(a)(6)(B)(ii)).

The premium amounts described in this subparagraph do not include any amounts attributable to late enrollment penalties under section 1860D-13(b).

(3) ACCESS TO 0 PREMIUM PLAN.—In no case shall the premium subsidy amount under this subsection for a PDP region be less than the lowest monthly beneficiary premium for a prescription drug plan that offers basic prescription drug coverage in the region.

§1860D-14(b)(3)   ¶2263A

(c) ADMINISTRATION OF SUBSIDY PROGRAM.—

(1) IN GENERAL.—The Secretary shall provide a process whereby, in the case of a part D eligible individual who is determined to be a subsidy eligible individual and who is enrolled in a prescription drug plan or is enrolled in an MA-PD plan—

(A) the Secretary provides for a notification of the PDP sponsor or the MA organization offering the plan involved that the individual is eligible for a subsidy and the amount of the subsidy under subsection (a);

(B) the sponsor or organization involved reduces the premiums or cost-sharing otherwise imposed by the amount of the applicable subsidy and submits to the Secretary information on the amount of such reduction;

(C) the Secretary periodically and on a timely basis reimburses the sponsor or organization for the amount of such reductions; and

(D) the Secretary ensures the confidentiality of individually identifiable information.

In applying subparagraph (C), the Secretary shall compute reductions based upon imposition under subsections (a)(1)(D) and (a)(2)(E) of unreduced copayment amounts applied under such subsections.

(2) USE OF CAPITATED FORM OF PAYMENT.—The reimbursement under this section with respect to cost-sharing subsidies may be computed on a capitated basis, taking into account the actuarial value of the subsidies and with appropriate adjustments to reflect differences in the risks actually involved.

(d) RELATION TO MEDICAID PROGRAM.—For special provisions under the medicaid program relating to medicare prescription drug benefits, see section 1935.

[CCH Explanation at ¶ 119.]

2003 Amendments:

Section 101(a) of the "Medicare Prescription Drug, Improvement, and Modernization Act of 2003," effective upon enactment, added new section 1860D-14.

The above amendment applies to coverage effective January 1, 2006.

[¶ 2263B] SEC. 1860D-15. SUBSIDIES FOR PART D ELIGIBLE INDIVIDUALS FOR QUALIFIED PRESCRIPTION DRUG COVERAGE

(a) SUBSIDY PAYMENT.—In order to reduce premium levels applicable to qualified prescription drug coverage for part D eligible individuals consistent with an overall subsidy level of 74.5 percent for basic prescription drug coverage, to reduce adverse selection among prescription drug plans and MA-PD plans, and to promote the participation of PDP sponsors under this part and MA organizations under part C, the Secretary shall provide for payment to a PDP sponsor that offers a prescription drug plan and an MA organization that offers an MA-PD plan of the following subsidies in accordance with this section:

(1) DIRECT SUBSIDY.—A direct subsidy for each part D eligible individual enrolled in a prescription drug plan or MA-PD plan for a month equal to—

(A) the amount of the plan's standardized bid amount (as defined in section 1860D-13(a)(5)), adjusted under subsection (c)(1), reduced by

(B) the base beneficiary premium (as computed under paragraph (2) of section 1860D-13(a) and as adjusted under paragraph (1)(B) of such section).

(2) SUBSIDY THROUGH REINSURANCE.—The reinsurance payment amount (as defined in subsection (b)).

This section constitutes budget authority in advance of appropriations Acts and represents the obligation of the Secretary to provide for the payment of amounts provided under this section.

(b) REINSURANCE PAYMENT AMOUNT.—

(1) IN GENERAL.—The reinsurance payment amount under this subsection for a part D eligible individual enrolled in a prescription drug plan or MA-PD plan for a coverage year is an amount equal to 80 percent of the allowable reinsurance costs (as specified in paragraph (2)) attributable to that portion of gross covered prescription drug costs as specified in paragraph (3)

incurred in the coverage year after such individual has incurred costs that exceed the annual out-of-pocket threshold specified in section 1860D-2(b)(4)(B).

(2) ALLOWABLE REINSURANCE COSTS.—For purposes of this section, the term 'allowable reinsurance costs' means, with respect to gross covered prescription drug costs under a prescription drug plan offered by a PDP sponsor or an MA-PD plan offered by an MA organization, the part of such costs that are actually paid (net of discounts, chargebacks, and average percentage rebates) by the sponsor or organization or by (or on behalf of) an enrollee under the plan, but in no case more than the part of such costs that would have been paid under the plan if the prescription drug coverage under the plan were basic prescription drug coverage, or, in the case of a plan providing supplemental prescription drug coverage, if such coverage were standard prescription drug coverage.

(3) GROSS COVERED PRESCRIPTION DRUG COSTS.—For purposes of this section, the term 'gross covered prescription drug costs' means, with respect to a part D eligible individual enrolled in a prescription drug plan or MAPD plan during a coverage year, the costs incurred under the plan, not including administrative costs, but including costs directly related to the dispensing of covered part D drugs during the year and costs relating to the deductible. Such costs shall be determined whether they are paid by the individual or under the plan, regardless of whether the coverage under the plan exceeds basic prescription drug coverage.

(4) COVERAGE YEAR DEFINED.—For purposes of this section, the term 'coverage year' means a calendar year in which covered part D drugs are dispensed if the claim for such drugs (and payment on such claim) is made not later than such period after the end of such year as the Secretary specifies.

(c) ADJUSTMENTS RELATING TO BIDS.—

(1) HEALTH STATUS RISK ADJUSTMENT.—

(A) ESTABLISHMENT OF RISK ADJUSTORS.—The Secretary shall establish an appropriate methodology for adjusting the standardized bid amount under subsection (a)(1)(A) to take into account variation in costs for basic prescription drug coverage among prescription drug plans and MA-PD plans based on the differences in actuarial risk of different enrollees being served. Any such risk adjustment shall be designed in a manner so as not to result in a change in the aggregate amounts payable to such plans under subsection (a)(1) and through that portion of the monthly beneficiary prescription drug premiums described in subsection (a)(1)(B) and MA monthly prescription drug beneficiary premiums.

(B) CONSIDERATIONS.—In establishing the methodology under subparagraph (A), the Secretary may take into account the similar methodologies used under section 1853(a)(3) to adjust payments to MA organizations for benefits under the original medicare fee-forservice program option.

(C) DATA COLLECTION.—In order to carry out this paragraph, the Secretary shall require—

(i) PDP sponsors to submit data regarding drug claims that can be linked at the individual level to part A and part B data and such other information as the Secretary determines necessary; and

(ii) MA organizations that offer MA-PD plans to submit data regarding drug claims that can be linked at the individual level to other data that such organizations are required to submit to the Secretary and such other information as the Secretary determines necessary.

(D) PUBLICATION.—At the time of publication of risk adjustment factors under section 1853(b)(1)(B)(i)(II), the Secretary shall publish the risk adjusters established under this paragraph for the succeeding year.

(2) GEOGRAPHIC ADJUSTMENT.—

(A) IN GENERAL.—Subject to subparagraph (B), for purposes of section 1860D-13(a)(1)(B)(iii), the Secretary shall establish an appropriate methodology for adjusting the national average monthly bid amount (computed under section 1860D-13(a)(4)) to take into account differences in prices for covered part D drugs among PDP regions.

§1860D-15(c)(2)(A) ¶2263B

(B) DE MINIMIS RULE.—If the Secretary determines that the price variations described in subparagraph (A) among PDP regions are de minimis, the Secretary shall not provide for adjustment under this paragraph.

(C) BUDGET NEUTRAL ADJUSTMENT.—Any adjustment under this paragraph shall be applied in a manner so as to not result in a change in the aggregate payments made under this part that would have been made if the Secretary had not applied such adjustment.

(d) PAYMENT METHODS.—

(1) IN GENERAL.—Payments under this section shall be based on such a method as the Secretary determines. The Secretary may establish a payment method by which interim payments of amounts under this section are made during a year based on the Secretary's best estimate of amounts that will be payable after obtaining all of the information.

(2) REQUIREMENT FOR PROVISION OF INFORMATION.—

(A) REQUIREMENT.—Payments under this section to a PDP sponsor or MA organization are conditioned upon the furnishing to the Secretary, in a form and manner specified by the Secretary, of such information as may be required to carry out this section.

(B) RESTRICTION ON USE OF INFORMATION.—Information disclosed or obtained pursuant to subparagraph (A) may be used by officers, employees, and contractors of the Department of Health and Human Services only for the purposes of, and to the extent necessary in, carrying out this section.

(3) SOURCE OF PAYMENTS.—Payments under this section shall be made from the Medicare Prescription Drug Account.

(4) APPLICATION OF ENROLLEE ADJUSTMENT.—The provisions of section 1853(a)(2) shall apply to payments to PDP sponsors under this section in the same manner as they apply to payments to MA organizations under section 1853(a).

(e) PORTION OF TOTAL PAYMENTS TO A SPONSOR OR ORGANIZATION SUBJECT TO RISK (APPLICATION OF RISK CORRIDORS).—

(1) COMPUTATION OF ADJUSTED ALLOWABLE RISK CORRIDOR COSTS.—

(A) IN GENERAL.—For purposes of this subsection, the term 'adjusted allowable risk corridor costs' means, for a plan for a coverage year (as defined in subsection (b)(4))—

(i) the allowable risk corridor costs (as defined in subparagraph (B)) for the plan for the year, reduced by

(ii) the sum of (I) the total reinsurance payments made under subsection (b) to the sponsor of the plan for the year, and (II) the total subsidy payments made under section 1860D-14 to the sponsor of the plan for the year.

(B) ALLOWABLE RISK CORRIDOR COSTS.—For purposes of this subsection, the term 'allowable risk corridor costs' means, with respect to a prescription drug plan offered by a PDP sponsor or an MA-PD plan offered by an MA organization, the part of costs (not including administrative costs, but including costs directly related to the dispensing of covered part D drugs during the year) incurred by the sponsor or organization under the plan that are actually paid (net of discounts, chargebacks, and average percentage rebates) by the sponsor or organization under the plan, but in no case more than the part of such costs that would have been paid under the plan if the prescription drug coverage under the plan were basic prescription drug coverage, or, in the case of a plan providing supplemental prescription drug coverage, if such coverage were basic prescription drug coverage taking into account the adjustment under section 1860D-11(c)(2). In computing allowable costs under this paragraph, the Secretary shall compute such costs based upon imposition under paragraphs (1)(D) and (2)(E) of section 1860D-14(a) of the maximum amount of copayments permitted under such paragraphs.

(2) ADJUSTMENT OF PAYMENT.—

(A) NO ADJUSTMENT IF ADJUSTED ALLOWABLE RISK CORRIDOR COSTS WITHIN RISK CORRIDOR.—If the adjusted allowable risk corridor costs (as defined in paragraph (1)) for the plan for the year are at least equal to the first threshold lower limit of the risk corridor (specified in paragraph (3)(A)(i)), but not greater than the first threshold upper limit of the risk corridor (specified in paragraph (3)(A)(iii)) for the plan for the year, then no payment adjustment shall be made under this subsection.

(B) INCREASE IN PAYMENT IF ADJUSTED ALLOWABLE RISK CORRIDOR COSTS ABOVE UPPER LIMIT OF RISK CORRIDOR.—

(i) COSTS BETWEEN FIRST AND SECOND THRESHOLD UPPER LIMITS.—If the adjusted allowable risk corridor costs for the plan for the year are greater than the first threshold upper limit, but not greater than the second threshold upper limit, of the risk corridor for the plan for the year, the Secretary shall increase the total of the payments made to the sponsor or organization offering the plan for the year under this section by an amount equal to 50 percent (or, for 2006 and 2007, 75 percent or 90 percent if the conditions described in clause (iii) are met for the year) of the difference between such adjusted allowable risk corridor costs and the first threshold upper limit of the risk corridor.

(ii) COSTS ABOVE SECOND THRESHOLD UPPER LIMITS.—If the adjusted allowable risk corridor costs for the plan for the year are greater than the second threshold upper limit of the risk corridor for the plan for the year, the Secretary shall increase the total of the payments made to the sponsor or organization offering the plan for the year under this section by an amount equal to the sum of—

(I) 50 percent (or, for 2006 and 2007, 75 percent or 90 percent if the conditions described in clause (iii) are met for the year) of the difference between the second threshold upper limit and the first threshold upper limit; and

(II) 80 percent of the difference between such adjusted allowable risk corridor costs and the second threshold upper limit of the risk corridor.

(iii) CONDITIONS FOR APPLICATION OF HIGHER PERCENTAGE FOR 2006 AND 2007.—The conditions described in this clause are met for 2006 or 2007 if the Secretary determines with respect to such year that—

(I) at least 60 percent of prescription drug plans and MA-PD plans to which this subsection applies have adjusted allowable risk corridor costs for the plan for the year that are more than the first threshold upper limit of the risk corridor for the plan for the year; and

(II) such plans represent at least 60 percent of part D eligible individuals enrolled in any prescription drug plan or MA-PD plan.

(C) REDUCTION IN PAYMENT IF ADJUSTED ALLOWABLE RISK CORRIDOR COSTS BELOW LOWER LIMIT OF RISK CORRIDOR.—

(i) COSTS BETWEEN FIRST AND SECOND THRESHOLD LOWER LIMITS.—If the adjusted allowable risk corridor costs for the plan for the year are less than the first threshold lower limit, but not less than the second threshold lower limit, of the risk corridor for the plan for the year, the Secretary shall reduce the total of the payments made to the sponsor or organization offering the plan for the year under this section by an amount (or otherwise recover from the sponsor or organization an amount) equal to 50 percent (or, for 2006 and 2007, 75 percent) of the difference between the first threshold lower limit of the risk corridor and such adjusted allowable risk corridor costs.

(ii) COSTS BELOW SECOND THRESHOLD LOWER LIMIT.—If the adjusted allowable risk corridor costs for the plan for the year are less the second threshold lower limit of the risk corridor for the plan for the year, the Secretary shall reduce the total of the payments made to the sponsor or organization offering the plan for the year under this section by an amount (or otherwise recover from the sponsor or organization an amount) equal to the sum of—

(I) 50 percent (or, for 2006 and 2007, 75 percent) of the difference between the first threshold lower limit and the second threshold lower limit; and

(II) 80 percent of the difference between the second threshold upper limit of the risk corridor and such adjusted allowable risk corridor costs.

§1860D-15(e)(2)(C)(ii)(II) ¶2263B

(3) ESTABLISHMENT OF RISK CORRIDORS.—

(A) IN GENERAL.—For each plan year the Secretary shall establish a risk corridor for each prescription drug plan and each MA-PD plan. The risk corridor for a plan for a year shall be equal to a range as follows:

(i) FIRST THRESHOLD LOWER LIMIT.—The first threshold lower limit of such corridor shall be equal to—

(I) the target amount described in subparagraph (B) for the plan; minus

(II) an amount equal to the first threshold risk percentage for the plan (as determined under subparagraph (C)(i)) of such target amount.

(ii) SECOND THRESHOLD LOWER LIMIT.—The second threshold lower limit of such corridor shall be equal to—

(I) the target amount described in subparagraph (B) for the plan; minus

(II) an amount equal to the second threshold risk percentage for the plan (as determined under subparagraph (C)(ii)) of such target amount.

(iii) FIRST THRESHOLD UPPER LIMIT.—The first threshold upper limit of such corridor shall be equal to the sum of—

(I) such target amount; and

(II) the amount described in clause (i)(II).

(iv) SECOND THRESHOLD UPPER LIMIT.—The second threshold upper limit of such corridor shall be equal to the sum of—

(I) such target amount; and

(II) the amount described in clause (ii)(II).

(B) TARGET AMOUNT DESCRIBED.—The target amount described in this paragraph is, with respect to a prescription drug plan or an MA-PD plan in a year, the total amount of payments paid to the PDP sponsor or MA-PD organization for the plan for the year, taking into account amounts paid by the Secretary and enrollees, based upon the standardized bid amount (as defined in section 1860D-13(a)(5) and as risk adjusted under subsection (c)(1)), reduced by the total amount of administrative expenses for the year assumed in such standardized bid.

(C) FIRST AND SECOND THRESHOLD RISK PERCENTAGE DEFINED.—

(i) FIRST THRESHOLD RISK PERCENTAGE.—Subject to clause (iii), for purposes of this section, the first threshold risk percentage is—

(I) for 2006 and 2007, and 2.5 percent;

(II) for 2008 through 2011, 5 percent; and

(III) for 2012 and subsequent years, a percentage established by the Secretary, but in no case less than 5 percent.

(ii) SECOND THRESHOLD RISK PERCENTAGE.—Subject to clause (iii), for purposes of this section, the second threshold risk percentage is—

(I) for 2006 and 2007, 5 percent;

(II) for 2008 through 2011, 10 percent; and

(III) for 2012 and subsequent years, a percentage established by the Secretary that is greater than the percent established for the year under clause (i)(III), but in no case less than 10 percent.

(iii) REDUCTION OF RISK PERCENTAGE TO ENSURE 2 PLANS IN AN AREA.—Pursuant to section 1860D-11(b)(2)(E)(ii), a PDP sponsor may submit a bid that requests a decrease in the applicable first or second threshold risk percentages or an increase in the percents applied under paragraph (2).

(4) PLANS AT RISK FOR ENTIRE AMOUNT OF SUPPLEMENTAL PRESCRIPTION DRUG COVERAGE.—A PDP sponsor and MA organization that offers a plan that provides supplemental prescription drug benefits shall be at full financial risk for the provision of such supplemental benefits.

(5) NO EFFECT ON MONTHLY PREMIUM.—No adjustment in payments made by reason of this subsection shall affect the monthly beneficiary premium or the MA monthly prescription drug beneficiary premium.

(f) DISCLOSURE OF INFORMATION.—

(1) IN GENERAL.—Each contract under this part and under part C shall provide that—

(A) the PDP sponsor offering a prescription drug plan or an MA organization offering an MA-PD plan shall provide the Secretary with such information as the Secretary determines is necessary to carry out this section; and

(B) the Secretary shall have the right in accordance with section 1857(d)(2)(B) (as applied under section 1860D-12(b)(3)(C)) to inspect and audit any books and records of a PDP sponsor or MA organization that pertain to the information regarding costs provided to the Secretary under subparagraph (A).

(2) RESTRICTION ON USE OF INFORMATION.—Information disclosed or obtained pursuant to the provisions of this section may be used by officers, employees, and contractors of the Department of Health and Human Services only for the purposes of, and to the extent necessary in, carrying out this section.

(g) PAYMENT FOR FALLBACK PRESCRIPTION DRUG PLANS.—In lieu of the amounts otherwise payable under this section to a PDP sponsor offering a fallback prescription drug plan (as defined in section 1860D-3(c)(4)), the amount payable shall be the amounts determined under the contract for such plan pursuant to section 1860D-11(g)(5).

[CCH Explanation at ¶ 120.]

2003 Amendments:

Section 101(a) of the "Medicare Prescription Drug, Improvement, and Modernization Act of 2003," effective upon enactment, added new section 1860D-15.

The above amendment applies to coverage effective January 1, 2006.

[¶ 2264] SEC. 1860D-16. MEDICARE PRESCRIPTION DRUG ACCOUNT IN THE FEDERAL SUPPLEMENTARY MEDICAL INSURANCE TRUST FUND

(a) ESTABLISHMENT AND OPERATION OF ACCOUNT.—

(1) ESTABLISHMENT.—There is created within the Federal Supplementary Medical Insurance Trust Fund established by section 1841 an account to be known as the 'Medicare Prescription Drug Account' (in this section referred to as the 'Account').

(2) FUNDING.—The Account shall consist of such gifts and bequests as may be made as provided in section 201(i)(1), accrued interest on balances in the Account, and such amounts as may be deposited in, or appropriated to, such Account as provided in this part.

(3) SEPARATE FROM REST OF TRUST FUND.—Funds provided under this part to the Account shall be kept separate from all other funds within the Federal Supplementary Medical Insurance Trust Fund, but shall be invested, and such investments redeemed, in the same manner as all other funds and investments within such Trust Fund.

(b) PAYMENTS FROM ACCOUNT.—

(1) IN GENERAL.—The Managing Trustee shall pay from time to time from the Account such amounts as the Secretary certifies are necessary to make payments to operate the program under this part, including—

(A) payments under section 1860D-14 (relating to low-income subsidy payments);

(B) payments under section 1860D-15 (relating to subsidy payments and payments for fallback plans);

(C) payments to sponsors of qualified retiree prescription drug plans under section 1860D-22(a); and

(D) payments with respect to administrative expenses under this part in accordance with section 201(g).

(2) TRANSFERS TO MEDICAID ACCOUNT FOR INCREASED ADMINISTRATIVE COSTS.—The Managing Trustee shall transfer from time to time from the Account to the Grants to States for Medicaid

account amounts the Secretary certifies are attributable to increases in payment resulting from the application of section 1935(b).

(3) PAYMENTS OF PREMIUMS WITHHELD.—The Managing Trustee shall make payment to the PDP sponsor or MA organization involved of the premiums (and the portion of late enrollment penalties) that are collected in the manner ner described in section 1854(d)(2)(A) and that are payable under a prescription drug plan or MA-PD plan offered by such sponsor or organization.

(4) TREATMENT IN RELATION TO PART B PREMIUM.—Amounts payable from the Account shall not be taken into account in computing actuarial rates or premium amounts under section 1839.

(c) DEPOSITS INTO ACCOUNT.—

(1) LOW-INCOME TRANSFER.—Amounts paid under section 1935(c) (and any amounts collected or offset under paragraph (1)(C) of such section) are deposited into the Account.

(2) AMOUNTS WITHHELD.—Pursuant to sections 1860D-13(c) and 1854(d) (as applied under this part), amounts that are withheld (and allocated) to the Account are deposited into the Account.

(3) APPROPRIATIONS TO COVER GOVERNMENT CONTRIBUTIONS.—There are authorized to be appropriated from time to time, out of any moneys in the Treasury not otherwise appropriated, to the Account, an amount equivalent to the amount of payments made from the Account under subsection (b) plus such amounts as the Managing Trustee certifies is necessary to maintain an appropriate contingency margin, reduced by the amounts deposited under paragraph (1) or subsection (a)(2).

(4) INITIAL FUNDING AND RESERVE.—In order to assure prompt payment of benefits provided under this part and the administrative expenses thereunder during the early months of the program established by this part and to provide an initial contingency reserve, there are authorized to be appropriated to the Account, out of any moneys in the Treasury not otherwise appropriated, such amount as the Secretary certifies are required, but not to exceed 10 percent of the estimated total expenditures from such Account in 2006.

(5) TRANSFER OF ANY REMAINING BALANCE FROM TRANSITIONAL ASSISTANCE ACCOUNT.—Any balance in the Transitional Assistance Account that is transferred under section 1860D-31(k)(5) shall be deposited into the Account.

[CCH Explanation at ¶ 123.]

2003 Amendments:

Section 101(a) of the "Medicare Prescription Drug, Improvement, and Modernization Act of 2003," effective upon enactment, added new section 1860D-16.

The above amendment applies to coverage effective January 1, 2006.

Subpart 3—Application to Medicare Advantage Program and Treatment of Employer-Sponsored Programs and Other Prescription Drug Plans

[¶ 2265A] Sec. 1860D-21. APPLICATION TO MEDICARE ADVANTAGE PROGRAM AND RELATED MANAGED CARE PROGRAMS

(a) SPECIAL RULES RELATING TO OFFERING OF QUALIFIED PRESCRIPTION DRUG COVERAGE.—

(1) IN GENERAL.—An MA organization on and after January 1, 2006—

(A) may not offer an MA plan described in section 1851(a)(2)(A) in an area unless either that plan (or another MA plan offered by the organization in that same service area) includes required prescription drug coverage (as defined in paragraph (2)); and

(B) may not offer prescription drug coverage (other than that required under parts A and B) to an enrollee under an MSA plan or under another MA plan unless such drug coverage under such other plan provides qualified prescription drug coverage and unless the requirements of this section with respect to such coverage are met.

(2) QUALIFYING COVERAGE.—For purposes of paragraph (1)(A), the term 'required coverage' means with respect to an MA-PD plan—

(A) basic prescription drug coverage; or

(B) qualified prescription drug coverage that provides supplemental prescription drug coverage, so long as there is no MA monthly supplemental beneficiary premium applied under the plan (due to the application of a credit against such premium of a rebate under section 1854(b)(1)(C)).

(b) APPLICATION OF DEFAULT ENROLLMENT RULES.—

(1) SEAMLESS CONTINUATION.—In applying section 1851(c)(3)(A)(ii), an individual who is enrolled in a health benefits plan shall not be considered to have been deemed to make an election into an MA-PD plan unless such health benefits plan provides any prescription drug coverage.

(2) MA CONTINUATION.—In applying section 1851(c)(3)(B), an individual who is enrolled in an MA plan shall not be considered to have been deemed to make an election into an MA-PD plan unless—

(A) for purposes of the election as of January 1, 2006, the MA plan provided as of December 31, 2005, any prescription drug coverage; or

(B) for periods after January 1, 2006, such MA plan is an MA-PD plan.

(3) DISCONTINUANCE OF MA-PD ELECTION DURING FIRST YEAR OF ELIGIBILITY.—In applying the second sentence of section 1851(e)(4) in the case of an individual who is electing to discontinue enrollment in an MA-PD plan, the individual shall be permitted to enroll in a prescription drug plan under part D at the time of the election of coverage under the original medicare fee-for-service program.

(4) RULES REGARDING ENROLLEES IN MA PLANS NOT PROVIDING QUALIFIED PRESCRIPTION DRUG COVERAGE.—In the case of an individual who is enrolled in an MA plan (other than an MSA plan) that does not provide qualified prescription drug coverage, if the organization offering such coverage discontinues the offering with respect to the individual of all MA plans that do not provide such coverage—

(i) the individual is deemed to have elected the original medicare fee-for-service program option, unless the individual affirmatively elects to enroll in an MA-PD plan; and

(ii) in the case of such a deemed election, the disenrollment shall be treated as an involuntary termination of the MA plan described in subparagraph (B)(ii) of section 1882(s)(3) for purposes of applying such section.

The information disclosed under section 1852(c)(1) for individuals who are enrolled in such an MA plan shall include information regarding such rules.

(c) APPLICATION OF PART D RULES FOR PRESCRIPTION DRUG COVERAGE.—With respect to the offering of qualified prescription drug coverage by an MA organization under this part on and after January 1, 2006—

(1) IN GENERAL.—Except as otherwise provided, the provisions of this part shall apply under part C with respect to prescription drug coverage provided under MA-PD plans in lieu of the other provisions of part C that would apply to such coverage under such plans.

(2) WAIVER.—The Secretary shall waive the provisions referred to in paragraph (1) to the extent the Secretary determines that such provisions duplicate, or are in conflict with, provisions otherwise applicable to the organization or plan under part C or as may be necessary in order to improve coordination of this part with the benefits under this part.

(3) TREATMENT OF MA OWNED AND OPERATED PHARMACIES.—The Secretary may waive the requirement of section 1860D-4(b)(1)(C) in the case of an MA-PD plan that provides access (other than mail order) to qualified prescription drug coverage through pharmacies owned and operated by the MA organization, if the Secretary determines that the organization's pharmacy network is sufficient to provide comparable access for enrollees under the plan.

(d) SPECIAL RULES FOR PRIVATE FEE-FOR-SERVICE PLANS THAT OFFER PRESCRIPTION DRUG COVERAGE.—With respect to an MA plan described in section 1851(a)(2)(C) that offers qualified prescription drug coverage, on and after January 1, 2006, the following rules apply:

(1) REQUIREMENTS REGARDING NEGOTIATED PRICES.—Subsections (a)(1) and (d)(1) of section 1860D2 and section 1860D-4(b)(2)(A) shall not be construed to require the plan to provide

§ 1860D-21(d)(1) ¶ 2265A

negotiated prices (described in subsection (d)(1)(B) of such section), but shall apply to the extent the plan does so.

(2) MODIFICATION OF PHARMACY ACCESS STANDARD AND DISCLOSURE REQUIREMENT.—If the plan provides coverage for drugs purchased from all pharmacies, without charging additional cost-sharing, and without regard to whether they are participating pharmacies in a network or have entered into contracts or agreements with pharmacies to provide drugs to enrollees covered by the plan, subsections (b)(1)(C) and (k) of section 1860D-4 shall not apply to the plan.

(3) DRUG UTILIZATION MANAGEMENT PROGRAM AND MEDICATION THERAPY MANAGEMENT PROGRAM NOT REQUIRED.—The requirements of subparagraphs (A) and (C) of section 1860D-4(c)(1) shall not apply to the plan.

(4) APPLICATION OF REINSURANCE.—The Secretary shall determine the amount of reinsurance payments under section 1860D-15(b) using a methodology that—

(A) bases such amount on the Secretary's estimate of the amount of such payments that would be payable if the plan were an MA-PD plan described in section 1851(a)(2)(A)(i) and the previous provisions of this subsection did not apply; and

(B) takes into account the average reinsurance payments made under section 1860D-15(b) for populations of similar risk under MA-PD plans described in such section.

(5) EXEMPTION FROM RISK CORRIDOR PROVISIONS.—The provisions of section 1860D-15(e) shall not apply.

(6) EXEMPTION FROM NEGOTIATIONS.—Subsections (d) and (e)(2)(C) of section 1860D-11 shall not apply and the provisions of section 1854(a)(5)(B) prohibiting the review, approval, or disapproval of amounts described in such section shall apply to the proposed bid and terms and conditions described in section 1860D-11(d).

(7) TREATMENT OF INCURRED COSTS WITHOUT REGARD TO FORMULARY.—The exclusion of costs incurred for covered part D drugs which are not included (or treated as being included) in a plan's formulary under section 1860D2(b)(4)(B)(i) shall not apply insofar as the plan does not utilize a formulary.

(e) APPLICATION TO REASONABLE COST REIMBURSEMENT CONTRACTORS.—

(1) IN GENERAL.—Subject to paragraphs (2) and (3) and rules established by the Secretary, in the case of an organization that is providing benefits under a reasonable cost reimbursement contract under section 1876(h) and that elects to provide qualified prescription drug coverage to a part D eligible individual who is enrolled under such a contract, the provisions of this part (and related provisions of part C) shall apply to the provision of such coverage to such enrollee in the same manner as such provisions apply to the provision of such coverage under an MAPD local plan described in se ction 1851(a)(2)(A)(i) and coverage under such a contract that so provides qualified prescription drug coverage shall be deemed to be an MAPD local plan.

(2) LIMITATION ON ENROLLMENT.—In applying paragraph (1), the organization may not enroll part D eligible individuals who are not enrolled under the reasonable cost reimbursement contract involved.

(3) BIDS NOT INCLUDED IN DETERMINING NATIONAL AVERAGE MONTHLY BID AMOUNT.—The bid of an organization offering prescription drug coverage under this subsection shall not be taken into account in computing the national average monthly bid amount and low-income benchmark premium amount under this part.

(f) APPLICATION TO PACE.—

(1) IN GENERAL.—Subject to paragraphs (2) and (3) and rules established by the Secretary, in the case of a PACE program under section 1894 that elects to provide qualified prescription drug coverage to a part D eligible individual who is enrolled under such program, the provisions of this part (and related provisions of part C) shall apply to the provision of such coverage to such enrollee in the same manner as such provisions apply to the provision of such coverage under an MA-PD local plan described in section 1851(a)(2)(A)(ii) and a PACE program that so provides such coverage shall be deemed to be an MA-PD local plan.

(2) LIMITATION ON ENROLLMENT.—In applying paragraph (1), the organization may not enroll part D eligible individuals who are not enrolled under the PACE program involved.

Social Security Law Added, Amended or Repealed

(3) BIDS NOT INCLUDED IN DETERMINING STANDARDIZED BID AMOUNT.—The bid of an organization offering prescription drug coverage under this subsection is not be taken into account in computing any average benchmark bid amount and low-income benchmark premium amount under this part.

[CCH Explanation at ¶ 125.]

2003 Amendments:

Section 101(a) of the "Medicare Prescription Drug, Improvement, and Modernization Act of 2003," effective upon enactment, added new section 1860D-21.

The above amendment applies to coverage effective January 1, 2006.

[¶ 2265B] Sec 1860D-22. SPECIAL RULES FOR EMPLOYER-SPONSORED PROGRAMS

(a) SUBSIDY PAYMENT.—

(1) IN GENERAL.—The Secretary shall provide in accordance with this subsection for payment to the sponsor of a qualified retiree prescription drug plan (as defined in paragraph (2)) of a special subsidy payment equal to the amount specified in paragraph (3) for each qualified covered retiree under the plan (as defined in paragraph (4)). This subsection constitutes budget authority in advance of appropriations Acts and represents the obligation of the Secretary to provide for the payment of amounts provided under this section.

(2) QUALIFIED RETIREE PRESCRIPTION DRUG PLAN DEFINED.—For purposes of this subsection, the term 'qualified retiree prescription drug plan' means employment-based retiree health coverage (as defined in subsection (c)(1)) if, with respect to a part D eligible individual who is a participant or beneficiary under such coverage, the following requirements are met:

(A) ATTESTATION OF ACTUARIAL EQUIVALENCE TO STANDARD COVERAGE.—The sponsor of the plan provides the Secretary, annually or at such other time as the Secretary may require, with an attestation that the actuarial value of prescription drug coverage under the plan (as determined using the processes and methods described in section 1860D-11(c)) is at least equal to the actuarial value of standard prescription drug coverage.

(B) AUDITS.—The sponsor of the plan, or an administrator of the plan designated by the sponsor, shall maintain (and afford the Secretary access to) such records as the Secretary may require for purposes of audits and other oversight activities necessary to ensure the adequacy of prescription drug coverage and the accuracy of payments made under this section. The provisions of section 1860D-2(d)(3) shall apply to such information under this section (including such actuarial value and attestation) in a manner similar to the manner in which they apply to financial records of PDP sponsors and MA organizations.

(C) PROVISION OF DISCLOSURE REGARDING PRESCRIPTION DRUG COVERAGE.—The sponsor of the plan shall provide for disclosure of information regarding prescription drug coverage in accordance with section 1860D-13(b)(6)(B).

(3) EMPLOYER AND UNION SPECIAL SUBSIDY AMOUNTS.—

(A) IN GENERAL.—For purposes of this subsection, the special subsidy payment amount under this paragraph for a qualifying covered retiree for a coverage year enrolled with the sponsor of a qualified retiree prescription drug plan is, for the portion of the retiree's gross covered retiree plan-related prescription drug costs (as defined in subparagraph (C)(ii)) for such year that exceeds the cost threshold amount specified in subparagraph (B) and does not exceed the cost limit under such subparagraph, an amount equal to 28 percent of the allowable retiree costs (as defined in subparagraph (C)(i)) attributable to such gross covered prescription drug costs.

(B) COST THRESHOLD AND COST LIMIT APPLICABLE.—

(i) IN GENERAL.—Subject to clause (ii)—

(I) the cost threshold under this subparagraph is equal to $250 for plan years that end in 2006; and

(II) the cost limit under this subparagraph is equal to $5,000 for plan years that end in 2006.

(ii) INDEXING.—The cost threshold and cost limit amounts specified in subclauses (I) and (II) of clause (i) for a plan year that ends after 2006 shall be adjusted in the same manner as the annual deductible and the annual out-of-pocket threshold, respectively, are annually adjusted under paragraphs (1) and (4)(B) of section 1860D-2(b).

(C) DEFINITIONS.—For purposes of this paragraph:

(i) ALLOWABLE RETIREE COSTS.—The term 'allowable retiree costs' means, with respect to gross covered prescription drug costs under a qualified retiree prescription drug plan by a plan sponsor, the part of such costs that are actually paid (net of discounts, chargebacks, and average percentage rebates) by the sponsor or by or on behalf of a qualifying covered retiree under the plan.

(ii) GROSS COVERED RETIREE PLAN-RELATED PRESCRIPTION DRUG COSTS.—For purposes of this section, the term 'gross covered retiree planrelated prescription drug costs' means, with respect to a qualifying covered retiree enrolled in a qualified retiree prescription drug plan during a coverage year, the costs incurred under the plan, not including administrative costs, but including costs directly related to the dispensing of covered part D drugs during the year. Such costs shall be determined whether they are paid by the retiree or under the plan.

(iii) COVERAGE YEAR.—The term 'coverage year' has the meaning given such term in section 1860D15(b)(4).

(4) QUALIFYING COVERED RETIREE DEFINED.—For purposes of this subsection, the term 'qualifying covered retiree' means a part D eligible individual who is not enrolled in a prescription drug plan or an MA-PD plan but is covered under a qualified retiree prescription drug plan.

(5) PAYMENT METHODS, INCLUDING PROVISION OF NECESSARY INFORMATION.—The provisions of section 1860D-15(d) (including paragraph (2), relating to requirement for provision of information) shall apply to payments under this subsection in a manner similar to the manner in which they apply to payment under section 1860D15(b).

(6) CONSTRUCTION.—Nothing in this subsection shall be construed as—

(A) precluding a part D eligible individual who is covered under employment-based retiree health coverage from enrolling in a prescription drug plan or in an MA-PD plan;

(B) precluding such employment-based retiree health coverage or an employer or other person from paying all or any portion of any premium required for coverage under a prescription drug plan or MA-PD plan on behalf of such an individual;

(C) preventing such employment-based retiree health coverage from providing coverage—

(i) that is better than standard prescription drug coverage to retirees who are covered under a qualified retiree prescription drug plan; or

(ii) that is supplemental to the benefits provided under a prescription drug plan or an MA-PD plan, including benefits to retirees who are not covered under a qualified retiree prescription drug plan but who are enrolled in such a prescription drug plan or MA-PD plan; or

(D) preventing employers to provide for flexibility in benefit design and pharmacy access provisions, without regard to the requirements for basic prescription drug coverage, so long as the actuarial equivalence requirement of paragraph (2)(A) is met.

(b) APPLICATION OF MA WAIVER AUTHORITY.—The provisions of section 1857(i) shall apply with respect to prescription drug plans in relation to employment-based retiree health coverage in a manner similar to the manner in which they apply to an MA plan in relation to employers, including authorizing the establishment of separate premium amounts for enrollees in a prescription drug plan by reason of such coverage and limitations on enrollment to part D eligible individuals enrolled under such coverage.

(c) DEFINITIONS.—For purposes of this section:

(1) EMPLOYMENT-BASED RETIREE HEALTH COVERAGE.—The term 'employment-based retiree health coverage' means health insurance or other coverage of health care costs (whether provided by voluntary insurance coverage or pursuant to statutory or contractual obligation) for

part D eligible individuals (or for such individuals and their spouses and dependents) under a group health plan based on their status as retired participants in such plan.

(2) SPONSOR.—The term 'sponsor' means a plan sponsor, as defined in section 3(16)(B) of the Employee Retirement Income Security Act of 1974, in relation to a group health plan, except that, in the case of a plan maintained jointly by one employer and an employee organization and with respect to which the employer is the primary source of financing, such term means such employer.

(3) GROUP HEALTH PLAN.—The term 'group health plan' includes such a plan as defined in section 607(1) of the Employee Retirement Income Security Act of 1974 and also includes the following:

(A) FEDERAL AND STATE GOVERNMENTAL PLANS.—Such a plan established or maintained for its employees by the Government of the United States, by the government of any State or political subdivision thereof, or by any agency or instrumentality of any of the foregoing, including a health benefits plan offered under chapter 89 of title 5, United States Code.

(B) COLLECTIVELY BARGAINED PLANS.—Such a plan established or maintained under or pursuant to one or more collective bargaining agreements.

(C) CHURCH PLANS.—Such a plan established and maintained for its employees (or their beneficiaries) by a church or by a convention or association of churches which is exempt from tax under section 501 of the Internal Revenue Code of 1986.

[CCH Explanation at ¶ 127.]
2003 Amendments:

Section 101(a) of the "Medicare Prescription Drug, Improvement, and Modernization Act of 2003," effective upon enactment, added new section 1860D-22.

The above amendment applies to coverage effective January 1, 2006.

[¶ 2265C] Sec. 1860D-23. STATE PHARMACEUTICAL ASSISTANCE PROGRAMS

(a) REQUIREMENTS FOR BENEFIT COORDINATION.—

(1) IN GENERAL.—Before July 1, 2005, the Secretary shall establish consistent with this section requirements for prescription drug plans to ensure the effective coordination between a part D plan (as defined in paragraph (5)) and a State Pharmaceutical Assistance Program (as defined in subsection (b)) with respect to—

(A) payment of premiums and coverage; and

(B) payment for supplemental prescription drug benefits,

for part D eligible individuals enrolled under both types of plans.

(2) COORDINATION ELEMENTS.—The requirements under paragraph (1) shall include requirements relating to coordination of each of the following:

(A) Enrollment file sharing.

(B) The processing of claims, including electronic processing.

(C) Claims payment.

(D) Claims reconciliation reports.

(E) Application of the protection against high out-of-pocket expenditures under section 1860D-2(b)(4).

(F) Other administrative processes specified by the Secretary.

Such requirements shall be consistent with applicable law to safeguard the privacy of any individually identifiable beneficiary information.

(3) USE OF LUMP SUM PER CAPITA METHOD.—Such requirements shall include a method for the application by a part D plan of specified funding amounts from a State Pharmaceutical Assistance Program for enrolled individuals for supplemental prescription drug benefits.

(4) CONSULTATION.—In establishing requirements under this subsection, the Secretary shall consult with State Pharmaceutical Assistance Programs, MA organizations, States, pharmaceuti-

cal benefit managers, employers, representatives of part D eligible individuals, the data processing experts, pharmacists, pharmaceutical manufacturers, and other experts.

(5) PART D PLAN DEFINED.—For purposes of this section and section 1860D-24, the term 'part D plan' means a prescription drug plan and an MA-PD plan.

(b) STATE PHARMACEUTICAL ASSISTANCE PROGRAM.—For purposes of this part, the term 'State Pharmaceutical Assistance Program' means a State program—

(1) which provides financial assistance for the purchase or provision of supplemental prescription drug coverage or benefits on behalf of part D eligible individuals;

(2) which, in determining eligibility and the amount of assistance to part D eligible individuals under the Program, provides assistance to such individuals in all part D plans and does not discriminate based upon the part D plan in which the individual is enrolled; and

(3) which satisfies the requirements of subsections (a) and (c).

(c) RELATION TO OTHER PROVISIONS.—

(1) MEDICARE AS PRIMARY PAYOR.—The requirements of this section shall not change or affect the primary payor status of a part D plan.

(2) USE OF A SINGLE CARD.—A card that is issued under section 1860D-4(b)(2)(A) for use under a part D plan may also be used in connection with coverage of benefits provided under a State Pharmaceutical Assistance Program and, in such case, may contain an emblem or symbol indicating such connection.

(3) OTHER PROVISIONS.—The provisions of section 1860D-24(c) shall apply to the requirements under this section.

(4) SPECIAL TREATMENT UNDER OUT-OF-POCKET RULE.—In applying section 1860D-2(b)(4)(C)(ii), expenses incurred under a State Pharmaceutical Assistance Program may be counted toward the annual out-of-pocket threshold.

(5) CONSTRUCTION.—Nothing in this section shall be construed as requiring a State Pharmaceutical Assistance Program to coordinate or provide financial assistance with respect to any part D plan.

(d) FACILITATION OF TRANSITION AND COORDINATION WITH STATE PHARMACEUTICAL ASSISTANCE PROGRAMS.—

(1) TRANSITIONAL GRANT PROGRAM.—The Secretary shall provide payments to State Pharmaceutical Assistance Programs with an application approved under this subsection.

(2) USE OF FUNDS.—Payments under this section may be used by a Program for any of the following:

(A) Educating part D eligible individuals enrolled in the Program about the prescription drug coverage available through part D plans under this part.

(B) Providing technical assistance, phone support, and counseling for such enrollees to facilitate selection and enrollment in such plans.

(C) Other activities designed to promote the effective coordination of enrollment, coverage, and payment between such Program and such plans.

(3) ALLOCATION OF FUNDS.—Of the amount appropriated to carry out this subsection for a fiscal year, the Secretary shall allocate payments among Programs that have applications approved under paragraph (4) for such fiscal year in proportion to the number of enrollees enrolled in each such Program as of October 1, 2003.

(4) APPLICATION.—No payments may be made under this subsection except pursuant to an application that is submitted and approved in a time, manner, and form specified by the Secretary.

(5) FUNDING.—Out of any funds in the Treasury not otherwise appropriated, there are appropriated for each of fiscal years 2005 and 2006, $62,500,000 to carry out this subsection.

[CCH Explanation at ¶ 129.]

2003 Amendments:

Section 101(a) of the "Medicare Prescription Drug, Improvement, and Modernization Act of 2003," effective upon enactment, added new section 1860D-23.

The above amendment applies to coverage effective January 1, 2006.

[¶ 2266] Sec. 1860D-24. COORDINATION REQUIREMENTS FOR PLANS PROVIDING PRESCRIPTION DRUG COVERAGE

(a) APPLICATION OF BENEFIT COORDINATION REQUIREMENTS TO ADDITIONAL PLANS.—

(1) IN GENERAL.—The Secretary shall apply the coordination requirements established under section 1860D-23(a) to Rx plans described in subsection (b) in the same manner as such requirements apply to a State Pharmaceutical Assistance Program.

(2) APPLICATION TO TREATMENT OF CERTAIN OUTOF-POCKET EXPENDITURES.—To the extent specified by the Secretary, the requirements referred to in paragraph (1) shall apply to procedures established under section 1860D-2(b)(4)(D).

(3) USER FEES.—

(A) IN GENERAL.—The Secretary may impose user fees for the transmittal of information necessary for benefit coordination under section 1860D-2(b)(4)(D) in a manner similar to the manner in which user fees are imposed under section 1842(h)(3)(B), except that the Secretary may retain a portion of such fees to defray the Secretary's costs in carrying out procedures under section 1860D-2(b)(4)(D).

(B) APPLICATION.—A user fee may not be imposed under subparagraph (A) with respect to a State Pharmaceutical Assistance Program.

(b) RX PLAN.—An Rx plan described in this subsection is any of the following:

(1) MEDICAID PROGRAMS.—A State plan under title XIX, including such a plan operating under a waiver under section 1115, if it meets the requirements of section 1860D-23(b)(2).

(2) GROUP HEALTH PLANS.—An employer group health plan.

(3) FEHBP.—The Federal employees health benefits plan under chapter 89 of title 5, United States Code.

(4) MILITARY COVERAGE (INCLUDING TRICARE).—Coverage under chapter 55 of title 10, United States Code.

(5) OTHER PRESCRIPTION DRUG COVERAGE.—Such other health benefit plans or programs that provide coverage or financial assistance for the purchase or provision of prescription drug coverage on behalf of part D eligible individuals as the Secretary may specify.

(c) RELATION TO OTHER PROVISIONS.—

(1) USE OF COST MANAGEMENT TOOLS.—The requirements of this section shall not impair or prevent a PDP sponsor or MA organization from applying cost management tools (including differential payments) under all methods of operation.

(2) NO AFFECT ON TREATMENT OF CERTAIN OUTOF-POCKET EXPENDITURES.—The requirements of this section shall not affect the application of the procedures established under section 1860D-2(b)(4)(D).

[CCH Explanation at ¶ 131.]

2003 Amendments:

Section 101(a) of the "Medicare Prescription Drug, Improvement, and Modernization Act of 2003," effective upon enactment, added new section 1860D-24.

The above amendment applies to coverage effective January 1, 2006.

Subpart 4—Medicare Prescription Drug Discount Card and Transitional Assistance Program

[¶ 2267] Sec. 1860D-31. MEDICARE PRESCRIPTION DRUG DISCOUNT CARD AND TRANSITIONAL ASSISTANCE PROGRAM

(a) ESTABLISHMENT OF PROGRAM.—

(1) IN GENERAL.—The Secretary shall establish a program under this section—

(A) to endorse prescription drug discount card programs that meet the requirements of this section in order to provide access to prescription drug discounts through prescription drug card sponsors for discount card eligible individuals throughout the United States; and

(B) to provide for transitional assistance for transitional assistance eligible individuals enrolled in such endorsed programs.

(2) PERIOD OF OPERATION.—

(A) IMPLEMENTATION DEADLINE.—The Secretary shall implement the program under this section so that discount cards and transitional assistance are first available by not later than 6 months after the date of the enactment of this section.

(B) EXPEDITING IMPLEMENTATION.—The Secretary shall promulgate regulations to carry out the program under this section which may be effective and final immediately on an interim basis as of the date of publication of the interim final regulation. If the Secretary provides for an interim final regulation, the Secretary shall provide for a period of public comments on such regulation after the date of publication. The Secretary may change or revise such regulation after completion of the period of public comment.

(C) TERMINATION AND TRANSITION.—

(i) IN GENERAL.—Subject to clause (ii)—

(I) the program under this section shall not apply to covered discount card drugs dispensed after December 31, 2005; and

(II) transitional assistance shall be available after such date to the extent the assistance relates to drugs dispensed on or before such date.

(ii) TRANSITION.—In the case of an individual who is enrolled in an endorsed discount card program as of December 31, 2005, during the individual's transition period (if any) under clause (iii), in accordance with transition rules specified by the Secretary—

(I) such endorsed program may continue to apply to covered discount card drugs dispensed to the individual under the program during such transition period;

(II) no annual enrollment fee shall be applicable during the transition period;

(III) during such period the individual may not change the endorsed program plan in which the individual is enrolled; and

(IV) the balance of any transitional assistance remaining on January 1, 2006, shall remain available for drugs dispensed during the individual's transition period.

(iii) TRANSITION PERIOD.—The transition period under this clause for an individual is the period beginning on January 1, 2006, and ending in the case of an individual who—

(I) is enrolled in a prescription drug plan or an MA-PD plan before the last date of the initial enrollment period under section 1860D-1(b)(2)(A), on the effective date of the individual's coverage under such part; or

(II) is not so enrolled, on the last day of such initial period.

(3) VOLUNTARY NATURE OF PROGRAM.—Nothing in this section shall be construed as requiring a discount card eligible individual to enroll in an endorsed discount card program under this section.

(4) GLOSSARY AND DEFINITIONS OF TERMS.—For purposes of this section:

(A) COVERED DISCOUNT CARD DRUG.—The term 'covered discount card drug' has the meaning given the term 'covered part D drug' in section 1860D-2(e).

(B) DISCOUNT CARD ELIGIBLE INDIVIDUAL.—The term 'discount card eligible individual' is defined in subsection (b)(1)(A).

(C) ENDORSED DISCOUNT CARD PROGRAM; ENDORSED PROGRAM.—The terms 'endorsed discount card program' and 'endorsed program' mean a prescription drug discount card program that is endorsed (and for which the sponsor has a contract with the Secretary) under this section.

(D) NEGOTIATED PRICE.—Negotiated prices are described in subsection (c)(1)(A)(ii).

(E) PRESCRIPTION DRUG CARD SPONSOR; SPONSOR.—The terms 'prescription drug card sponsor' and 'sponsor' are defined in subsection (h)(1)(A).

(F) STATE.—The term 'State' has the meaning given such term for purposes of title XIX.

(G) TRANSITIONAL ASSISTANCE ELIGIBLE INDIVIDUAL.—The term 'transitional assistance eligible individual' is defined in subsection (b)(2).

(b) ELIGIBILITY FOR DISCOUNT CARD AND FOR TRANSITIONAL ASSISTANCE.—For purposes of this section:

(1) DISCOUNT CARD ELIGIBLE INDIVIDUAL.—

(A) IN GENERAL.—The term 'discount card eligible individual' means an individual who—

(i) is entitled to benefits, or enrolled, under part A or enrolled under part B; and

(ii) subject to paragraph (4), is not an individual described in subparagraph (B).

(B) INDIVIDUAL DESCRIBED.—An individual described in this subparagraph is an individual described in subparagraph (A)(i) who is enrolled under title XIX (or under a waiver under section 1115 of the requirements of such title) and is entitled to any medical assistance for outpatient prescribed drugs described in section 1905(a)(12).

(2) TRANSITIONAL ASSISTANCE ELIGIBLE INDIVIDUAL.—

(A) IN GENERAL.—Subject to subparagraph (B), the term 'transitional assistance eligible individual' means a discount card eligible individual who resides in one of the 50 States or the District of Columbia and whose income (as determined under subsection (f)(1)(B)) is not more than 135 percent of the poverty line (as defined in section 673(2) of the Community Services Block Grant Act, 42 U.S.C. 9902(2), including any revision required by such section) applicable to the family size involved (as determined under subsection (f)(1)(B)).

(B) EXCLUSION OF INDIVIDUALS WITH CERTAIN PRESCRIPTION DRUG COVERAGE.—Such term does not include an individual who has coverage of, or assistance for, covered discount card drugs under any of the following:

(i) A group health plan or health insurance coverage (as such terms are defined in section 2791 of the Public Health Service Act), other than coverage under a plan under part C and other than coverage consisting only of excepted benefits (as defined in such section).

(ii) Chapter 55 of title 10, United States Code (relating to medical and dental care for members of the uniformed services).

(iii) A plan under chapter 89 of title 5, United States Code (relating to the Federal employees' health benefits program).

(3) SPECIAL TRANSITIONAL ASSISTANCE ELIGIBLE INDIVIDUAL.—The term 'special transitional assistance eligible individual' means a transitional assistance eligible individual whose income (as determined under subsection (f)(1)(B)) is not more than 100 percent of the poverty line (as defined in section 673(2) of the Community Services Block Grant Act, 42 U.S.C. 9902(2), including any revision required by such section) applicable to the family size involved (as determined under subsection (f)(1)(B)).

(4) TREATMENT OF MEDICAID MEDICALLY NEEDY.—For purposes of this section, the Secretary shall provide for appropriate rules for the treatment of medically needy individuals described in

section 1902(a)(10)(C) as discount card eligible individuals and as transitional assistance eligible individuals.

(c) ENROLLMENT AND ENROLLMENT FEES.—

(1) ENROLLMENT PROCESS.—The Secretary shall establish a process through which a discount card eligible individual is enrolled and disenrolled in an endorsed discount card program under this section consistent with the following:

(A) CONTINUOUS OPEN ENROLLMENT.—Subject to the succeeding provisions of this paragraph and subsection (h)(9), a discount card eligible individual who is not enrolled in an endorsed discount card program and is residing in a State may enroll in any such endorsed program—

(i) that serves residents of the State; and

(ii) at any time beginning on the initial enrollment date, specified by the Secretary, and before January 1, 2006.

(B) USE OF STANDARD ENROLLMENT FORM.—An enrollment in an endorsed program shall only be effected through completion of a standard enrollment form specified by the Secretary. Each sponsor of an endorsed program shall transmit to the Secretary (in a form and manner specified by the Secretary) information on individuals who complete such enrollment forms and, to the extent provided under subsection (f), information regarding certification as a transitional assistance eligible individual.

(C) ENROLLMENT ONLY IN ONE PROGRAM.—

(i) IN GENERAL.—Subject to clauses (ii) and (iii), a discount card eligible individual may be enrolled in only one endorsed discount card program under this section.

(ii) CHANGE IN ENDORSED PROGRAM PERMITTED FOR 2005.—The Secretary shall establish a process, similar to (and coordinated with) the process for annual, coordinated elections under section 1851(e)(3) during 2004, under which an individual enrolled in an endorsed discount card program may change the endorsed program in which the individual is enrolled for 2005.

(iii) ADDITIONAL EXCEPTIONS.—The Secretary shall permit an individual to change the endorsed discount card program in which the individual is enrolled in the case of an individual who changes residence to be outside the service area of such program and in such other exceptional cases as the Secretary may provide (taking into account the circumstances for special election periods under section 1851(e)(4)). Under the previous sentence, the Secretary may consider a change in residential setting (such as placement in a nursing facility) or enrollment in or disenrollment from a plan under part C through which the individual was enrolled in an endorsed program to be an exceptional circumstance.

(D) DISENROLLMENT.—

(i) VOLUNTARY.—An individual may voluntarily disenroll from an endorsed discount card program at any time. In the case of such a voluntary disenrollment, the individual may not enroll in another endorsed program, except under such exceptional circumstances as the Secretary may recognize under subparagraph (C)(iii) or during the annual coordinated enrollment period provided under subparagraph (C)(ii).

(ii) INVOLUNTARY.—An individual who is enrolled in an endorsed discount card program and not a transitional assistance eligible individual may be disenrolled by the sponsor of the program if the individual fails to pay any annual enrollment fee required under the program.

(E) APPLICATION TO CERTAIN ENROLLEES.—In the case of a discount card eligible individual who is enrolled in a plan described in section 1851(a)(2)(A) or under a reasonable cost reimbursement contract under section 1876(h) that is offered by an organization that also is a prescription discount card sponsor that offers an endorsed discount card program under which the individual may be enrolled and that has made an election to apply the special rules under subsection (h)(9)(B) for such an endorsed program, the individual may only enroll in such an endorsed discount card program offered by that sponsor.

(2) ENROLLMENT FEES.—

(A) IN GENERAL.—Subject to the succeeding provisions of this paragraph, a prescription drug card sponsor may charge an annual enrollment fee for each discount card eligible individual enrolled in an endorsed discount card program offered by such sponsor. The annual enrollment fee for either 2004 or 2005 shall not be prorated for portions of a year. There shall be no annual enrollment fee for a year after 2005.

(B) AMOUNT.—No annual enrollment fee charged under subparagraph (A) may exceed $30.

(C) UNIFORM ENROLLMENT FEE.—A prescription drug card sponsor shall ensure that the annual enrollment fee (if any) for an endorsed discount card program is the same for all discount card eligible individuals enrolled in the program and residing in the State.

(D) COLLECTION.—The annual enrollment fee (if any) charged for enrollment in an endorsed program shall be collected by the sponsor of the program.

(E) PAYMENT OF FEE FOR TRANSITIONAL ASSISTANCE ELIGIBLE INDIVIDUALS.—Under subsection (g)(1)(A), the annual enrollment fee (if any) otherwise charged under this paragraph with respect to a transitional assistance eligible individual shall be paid by the Secretary on behalf of such individual.

(F) OPTIONAL PAYMENT OF FEE BY STATE.—

(i) IN GENERAL.—The Secretary shall establish an arrangement under which a State may provide for payment of some or all of the enrollment fee for some or all enrollees who are not transitional assistance eligible individuals in the State, as specified by the State under the arrangement. Insofar as such a payment arrangement is made with respect to an enrollee, the amount of the enrollment fee shall be paid directly by the State to the sponsor.

(ii) NO FEDERAL MATCHING AVAILABLE UNDER MEDICAID OR SCHIP.—Expenditures made by a State for enrollment fees described in clause (i) shall not be treated as State expenditures for purposes of Federal matching payments under title XIX or XXI.

(G) RULES IN CASE OF CHANGES IN PROGRAM ENROLLMENT DURING A YEAR.—The Secretary shall provide special rules in the case of payment of an annual enrollment fee for a discount card eligible individual who changes the endorsed program in which the individual is enrolled during a year.

(3) ISSUANCE OF DISCOUNT CARD.—Each prescription drug card sponsor of an endorsed discount card program shall issue, in a standard format specified by the Secretary, to each discount card eligible individual enrolled in such program a card that establishes proof of enrollment and that can be used in a coordinated manner to identify the sponsor, program, and individual for purposes of the program under this section.

(4) PERIOD OF ACCESS.—In the case of a discount card eligible individual who enrolls in an endorsed program, access to negotiated prices and transitional assistance, if any, under such endorsed program shall take effect on such date as the Secretary shall specify.

(d) PROVISION OF INFORMATION ON ENROLLMENT AND PROGRAM FEATURES.—

(1) SECRETARIAL RESPONSIBILITIES.—

(A) IN GENERAL.—The Secretary shall provide for activities under this subsection to broadly disseminate information to discount card eligible individuals (and prospective eligible individuals) regarding—

(i) enrollment in endorsed discount card programs; and

(ii) the features of the program under this section, including the availability of transitional assistance.

(B) PROMOTION OF INFORMED CHOICE.—In order to promote informed choice among endorsed prescription drug discount card programs, the Secretary shall provide for the dissemination of information which—

(i) compares the annual enrollment fee and other features of such programs, which may include comparative prices for covered discount card drugs; and

(ii) includes educational materials on the variability of discounts on prices of covered discount card drugs under an endorsed program.

The dissemination of information under clause (i) shall, to the extent practicable, be coordinated with the dissemination of educational information on other medicare options.

(C) SPECIAL RULE FOR INITIAL ENROLLMENT DATE UNDER THE PROGRAM.—To the extent practicable, the Secretary shall ensure, through the activities described in subparagraphs (A) and (B), that discount card eligible individuals are provided with such information at least 30 days prior to the initial enrollment date specified under subsection (c)(1)(A)(ii).

(D) USE OF MEDICARE TOLL-FREE NUMBER.—The Secretary shall provide through the toll-free telephone number 1-800-MEDICARE for the receipt and response to inquiries and complaints concerning the program under this section and endorsed programs.

(2) PRESCRIPTION DRUG CARD SPONSOR RESPONSIBILITIES.—

(A) IN GENERAL.—Each prescription drug card sponsor that offers an endorsed discount card program shall make available to discount card eligible individuals (through the Internet and otherwise) information that the Secretary identifies as being necessary to promote informed choice among endorsed discount card programs by such individuals, including information on enrollment fees and negotiated prices for covered discount card drugs charged to such individuals.

(B) RESPONSE TO ENROLLEE QUESTIONS.—Each sponsor offering an endorsed discount card program shall have a mechanism (including a toll-free telephone number) for providing upon request specific information (such as negotiated prices and the amount of transitional assistance remaining available through the program) to discount card eligible individuals enrolled in the program. The sponsor shall inform transitional assistance eligible individuals enrolled in the program of the availability of such toll-free telephone number to provide information on the amount of available transitional assistance.

(C) INFORMATION ON BALANCE OF TRANSITIONAL ASSISTANCE AVAILABLE AT POINT-OF-SALE.—Each sponsor offering an endorsed discount card program shall have a mechanism so that information on the amount of transitional assistance remaining under subsection (g)(1)(B) is available (electronically or by telephone) at the point-of-sale of covered discount card drugs.

(3) PUBLIC DISCLOSURE OF PHARMACEUTICAL PRICES FOR EQUIVALENT DRUGS.—

(A) IN GENERAL.—A prescription drug card sponsor offering an endorsed discount card program shall provide that each pharmacy that dispenses a covered discount card drug shall inform a discount card eligible individual enrolled in the program of any differential between the price of the drug to the enrollee and the price of the lowest priced generic covered discount card drug under the program that is therapeutically equivalent and bioequivalent and available at such pharmacy.

(B) TIMING OF NOTICE.—

(i) IN GENERAL.—Subject to clause (ii), the information under subparagraph (A) shall be provided at the time of purchase of the drug involved, or, in the case of dispensing by mail order, at the time of delivery of such drug.

(ii) WAIVER.—The Secretary may waive clause (i) in such circumstances as the Secretary may specify.

(e) DISCOUNT CARD FEATURES.—

(1) SAVINGS TO ENROLLEES THROUGH NEGOTIATED PRICES.—

(A) ACCESS TO NEGOTIATED PRICES.—

(i) IN GENERAL.—Each prescription drug card sponsor that offers an endorsed discount card program shall provide each discount card eligible individual enrolled in the program with access to negotiated prices.

(ii) NEGOTIATED PRICES.—For purposes of this section, negotiated prices shall take into account negotiated price concessions, such as discounts, direct or indirect subsidies, rebates, and direct or indirect remunerations, for covered discount card drugs, and include any dispensing fees for such drugs.

(B) ENSURING PHARMACY ACCESS.—Each prescription drug card sponsor offering an endorsed discount card program shall secure the participation in its network of a sufficient number of pharmacies that dispense (other than solely by mail order) drugs directly to enrollees to ensure convenient access to covered discount card drugs at negotiated prices (consistent with rules established by the Secretary). The Secretary shall establish convenient access rules under this clause that are no less favorable to enrollees than the standards for convenient access to pharmacies included in the statement of work of solicitation (#MDA906-03-R-0002) of the Department of Defense under the TRICARE Retail Pharmacy (TRRx) as of March 13, 2003.

(C) PROHIBITION ON CHARGES FOR REQUIRED SERVICES.—

(i) IN GENERAL.—Subject to clause (ii), a prescription drug card sponsor (and any pharmacy contracting with such sponsor for the provision of covered discount card drugs to individuals enrolled in such sponsor's endorsed discount card program) may not charge an enrollee any amount for any items and services required to be provided by the sponsor under this section.

(ii) CONSTRUCTION.—Nothing in clause (i) shall be construed to prevent—

(I) the sponsor from charging the annual enrollment fee (except in the case of a transitional assistance eligible individual); and

(II) the pharmacy dispensing the covered discount card drug, from imposing a charge (consistent with the negotiated price) for the covered discount card drug dispensed, reduced by the amount of any transitional assistance made available.

(D) INAPPLICABILITY OF MEDICAID BEST PRICE RULES.—The prices negotiated from drug manufacturers for covered discount card drugs under an endorsed discount card program under this section shall (notwithstanding any other provision of law) not be taken into account for the purposes of establishing the best price under section 1927(c)(1)(C).

(2) REDUCTION OF MEDICATION ERRORS AND ADVERSE DRUG INTERACTIONS.—Each endorsed discount card program shall implement a system to reduce the likelihood of medication errors and adverse drug interactions and to improve medication use.

(f) ELIGIBILITY PROCEDURES FOR ENDORSED PROGRAMS AND TRANSITIONAL ASSISTANCE.—

(1) DETERMINATIONS.—

(A) PROCEDURES.—The determination of whether an individual is a discount card eligible individual or a transitional assistance eligible individual or a special transitional assistance eligible individual (as defined in subsection (b)) shall be determined under procedures specified by the Secretary consistent with this subsection.

(B) INCOME AND FAMILY SIZE DETERMINATIONS.—For purposes of this section, the Secretary shall define the terms 'income' and 'family size' and shall specify the methods and period for which they are determined. If under such methods income or family size is determined based on the income or family size for prior periods of time, the Secretary shall permit (whether through a process of reconsideration or otherwise) an individual whose income or family size has changed to elect to have eligibility for transitional assistance determined based on income or family size for a more recent period.

(2) USE OF SELF-CERTIFICATION FOR TRANSITIONAL ASSISTANCE.—

(A) IN GENERAL.—Under the procedures specified under paragraph (1)(A) an individual who wishes to be treated as a transitional assistance eligible individual or a special transitional assistance eligible individual under this section (or another qualified person on such individual's behalf) shall certify on the enrollment form under subsection (c)(1)(B) (or similar form specified by the Secretary), through a simplified means specified by the Secretary and under penalty of perjury or similar sanction for false statements, as to the amount of the individual's income, family size, and individual's prescription drug coverage (if any) insofar as they relate to eligibility to be a transitional assistance eligible individual or a special transitional assistance eligible individual. Such certification shall be deemed as consent to verification of respective eligibility under paragraph (3). A certification under this paragraph may be provided before, on, or after the time of enrollment under an endorsed program.

(B) TREATMENT OF SELF-CERTIFICATION.—The Secretary shall treat a certification under subparagraph (A) that is verified under paragraph (3) as a determination that the individual involved is a transitional assistance eligible individual or special transitional assistance eligible individual (as the case may be) for the entire period of the enrollment of the individual in any endorsed program.

(3) VERIFICATION.—

(A) IN GENERAL.—The Secretary shall establish methods (which may include the use of sampling and the use of information described in subparagraph (B)) to verify eligibility for individuals who seek to enroll in an endorsed program and for individuals who provide a certification under paragraph (2).

(B) INFORMATION DESCRIBED.—The information described in this subparagraph is as follows:

(i) MEDICAID-RELATED INFORMATION.—Information on eligibility under title XIX and provided to the Secretary under arrangements between the Secretary and States in order to verify the eligibility of individuals who seek to enroll in an endorsed program and of individuals who provide certification under paragraph (2).

(ii) SOCIAL SECURITY INFORMATION.—Financial information made available to the Secretary under arrangements between the Secretary and the Commissioner of Social Security in order to verify the eligibility of individuals who provide such certification.

(iii) INFORMATION FROM SECRETARY OF THE TREASURY.—Financial information made available to the Secretary under section 6103(l)(19) of the Internal Revenue Code of 1986 in order to verify the eligibility of individuals who provide such certification.

(C) VERIFICATION IN CASES OF MEDICAID ENROLLEES.—

(i) IN GENERAL.—Nothing in this section shall be construed as preventing the Secretary from finding that a discount card eligible individual meets the income requirements under subsection (b)(2)(A) if the individual is within a category of discount card eligible individuals who are enrolled under title XIX (such as qualified medicare beneficiaries (QMBs), specified low-income medicare beneficiaries (SLMBs), and certain qualified individuals (QI-1s)).

(ii) AVAILABILITY OF INFORMATION FOR VERIFICATION PURPOSES.—As a condition of provision of Federal financial participation to a State that is one of the 50 States or the District of Columbia under title XIX, for purposes of carrying out this section, the State shall provide the information it submits to the Secretary relating to such title in a manner specified by the Secretary that permits the Secretary to identify individuals who are described in subsection (b)(1)(B) or are transitional assistance eligible individuals or special transitional assistance eligible individuals.

(4) RECONSIDERATION.—

(A) IN GENERAL.—The Secretary shall establish a process under which a discount card eligible individual, who is determined through the certification and verification methods under paragraphs (2) and (3) not to be a transitional assistance eligible individual or a special transitional assistance eligible individual, may request a reconsideration of the determination.

(B) CONTRACT AUTHORITY.—The Secretary may enter into a contract to perform the reconsiderations requested under subparagraph (A).

(C) COMMUNICATION OF RESULTS.—Under the process under subparagraph (A) the results of such reconsideration shall be communicated to the individual and the prescription drug card sponsor involved.

Social Security Law Added, Amended or Repealed 387

(g) TRANSITIONAL ASSISTANCE.—

(1) PROVISION OF TRANSITIONAL ASSISTANCE.—An individual who is a transitional assistance eligible individual (as determined under this section) and who is enrolled with an endorsed program is entitled—

(A) to have payment made of any annual enrollment fee charged under subsection (c)(2) for enrollment under the program; and

(B) to have payment made, up to the amount specified in paragraph (2), under such endorsed program of 90 percent (or 95 percent in the case of a special transitional assistance eligible individual) of the costs incurred for covered discount card drugs obtained through the program taking into account the negotiated price (if any) for the drug under the program.

(2) LIMITATION ON DOLLAR AMOUNT.—

(A) IN GENERAL.—Subject to subparagraph (B), the amount specified in this paragraph for a transitional assistance eligible individual—

(i) for costs incurred during 2004, is $600; or

(ii) for costs incurred during 2005, is—

(I) $600, plus

(II) except as provided in subparagraph (E), the amount by which the amount available under this paragraph for 2004 for that individual exceeds the amount of payment made under paragraph (1)(B) for that individual for costs incurred during 2004.

(B) PRORATION.—

(i) IN GENERAL.—In the case of an individual not described in clause (ii) with respect to a year, the Secretary may prorate the amount specified in subparagraph (A) for the balance of the year involved in a manner specified by the Secretary.

(ii) INDIVIDUAL DESCRIBED.—An individual described in this clause is a transitional assistance eligible individual who—

(I) with respect to 2004, enrolls in an endorsed program, and provides a certification under subsection (f)(2), before the initial implementation date of the program under this section; and

(II) with respect to 2005, is enrolled in an endorsed program, and has provided such a certification, before February 1, 2005.

(C) ACCOUNTING FOR AVAILABLE BALANCES IN CASES OF CHANGES IN PROGRAM ENROLLMENT.—In the case of a transitional assistance eligible individual who changes the endorsed discount card program in which the individual is enrolled under this section, the Secretary shall provide a process under which the Secretary provides to the sponsor of the endorsed program in which the individual enrolls information concerning the balance of amounts available on behalf of the individual under this paragraph.

(D) LIMITATION ON USE OF FUNDS.—Pursuant to subsection (a)(2)(C), no assistance shall be provided under paragraph (1)(B) with respect to covered discount card drugs dispensed after December 31, 2005.

(E) NO ROLLOVER PERMITTED IN CASE OF VOLUNTARY DISENROLLMENT.—Except in such exceptional cases as the Secretary may provide, in the case of a transitional assistance eligible individual who voluntarily disenrolls from an endorsed plan, the provisions of subclause (II) of subparagraph (A)(ii) shall not apply.

(3) PAYMENT.—The Secretary shall provide a method for the reimbursement of prescription drug card sponsors for assistance provided under this subsection.

(4) COVERAGE OF COINSURANCE.—

(A) WAIVER PERMITTED BY PHARMACY.—Nothing in this section shall be construed as precluding a pharmacy from reducing or waiving the application of coinsurance imposed under paragraph (1)(B) in accordance with section 1128B(b)(3)(G).

§1860D-31(g)(4)(A) ¶2267

(B) OPTIONAL PAYMENT OF COINSURANCE BY STATE.—

(i) IN GENERAL.—The Secretary shall establish an arrangement under which a State may provide for payment of some or all of the coinsurance under paragraph (1)(B) for some or all enrollees in the State, as specified by the State under the arrangement. Insofar as such a payment arrangement is made with respect to an enrollee, the amount of the coinsurance shall be paid directly by the State to the pharmacy involved.

(ii) NO FEDERAL MATCHING AVAILABLE UNDER MEDICAID OR SCHIP.—Expenditures made by a State for coinsurance described in clause (i) shall not be treated as State expenditures for purposes of Federal matching payments under title XIX or XXI.

(iii) NOT TREATED AS MEDICARE COST-SHARING.—Coinsurance described in paragraph (1)(B) shall not be treated as coinsurance under this title for purposes of section 1905(p)(3)(B).

(C) TREATMENT OF COINSURANCE.—The amount of any coinsurance imposed under paragraph (1)(B), whether paid or waived under this paragraph, shall not be taken into account in applying the limitation in dollar amount under paragraph (2).

(5) ENSURING ACCESS TO TRANSITIONAL ASSISTANCE FOR QUALIFIED RESIDENTS OF LONG-TERM CARE FACILITIES AND AMERICAN INDIANS.—

(A) RESIDENTS OF LONG-TERM CARE FACILITIES.—The Secretary shall establish procedures and may waive requirements of this section as necessary to negotiate arrangements with sponsors to provide arrangements with pharmacies that support long-term care facilities in order to ensure access to transitional assistance for transitional assistance eligible individuals who reside in long-term care facilities.

(B) AMERICAN INDIANS.—The Secretary shall establish procedures and may waive requirements of this section to ensure that, for purposes of providing transitional assistance, pharmacies operated by the Indian Health Service, Indian tribes and tribal organizations, and urban Indian organizations (as defined in section 4 of the Indian Health Care Improvement Act) have the opportunity to participate in the pharmacy networks of at least two endorsed programs in each of the 50 States and the District of Columbia where such a pharmacy operates.

(6) NO IMPACT ON BENEFITS UNDER OTHER PROGRAMS.—The availability of negotiated prices or transitional assistance under this section shall not be treated as benefits or otherwise taken into account in determining an individual's eligibility for, or the amount of benefits under, any other Federal program.

(7) DISREGARD FOR PURPOSES OF PART C.—Nonuniformity of benefits resulting from the implementation of this section (including the provision or nonprovision of transitional assistance and the payment or waiver of any enrollment fee under this section) shall not be taken into account in applying section 1854(f).

(h) QUALIFICATION OF PRESCRIPTION DRUG CARD SPONSORS AND ENDORSEMENT OF DISCOUNT CARD PROGRAMS; BENEFICIARY PROTECTIONS.—

(1) PRESCRIPTION DRUG CARD SPONSOR AND QUALIFICATIONS.—

(A) PRESCRIPTION DRUG CARD SPONSOR AND SPONSOR DEFINED.—For purposes of this section, the terms 'prescription drug card sponsor' and 'sponsor' mean any nongovernmental entity that the Secretary determines to be appropriate to offer an endorsed discount card program under this section, which may include—

(i) a pharmaceutical benefit management company;

(ii) a wholesale or retail pharmacy delivery system;

(iii) an insurer (including an insurer that offers medicare supplemental policies under section 1882);

(iv) an organization offering a plan under part C; or

(v) any combination of the entities described in clauses (i) through (iv).

(B) ADMINISTRATIVE QUALIFICATIONS.—Each endorsed discount card program shall be operated directly, or through arrangements with an affiliated organization (or organizations), by one or more entities that have demonstrated experience and expertise in operating such a program or a similar program and that meets such business stability and integrity requirements as the Secretary may specify.

(C) ACCOUNTING FOR TRANSITIONAL ASSISTANCE.—The sponsor of an endorsed discount card program shall have arrangements satisfactory to the Secretary to account for the assistance provided under subsection (g) on behalf of transitional assistance eligible individuals.

(2) APPLICATIONS FOR PROGRAM ENDORSEMENT.—

(A) SUBMISSION.—Each prescription drug card sponsor that seeks endorsement of a prescription drug discount card program under this section shall submit to the Secretary, at such time and in such manner as the Secretary may specify, an application containing such information as the Secretary may require.

(B) APPROVAL; COMPLIANCE WITH APPLICABLE REQUIREMENTS.—The Secretary shall review the application submitted under subparagraph (A) and shall determine whether to endorse the prescription drug discount card program. The Secretary may not endorse such a program unless—

(i) the program and prescription drug card sponsor offering the program comply with the applicable requirements under this section; and

(ii) the sponsor has entered into a contract with the Secretary to carry out such requirements.

(C) TERMINATION OF ENDORSEMENT AND CONTRACTS.—An endorsement of an endorsed program and a contract under subparagraph (B) shall be for the duration of the program under this section (including any transition applicable under subsection (a)(2)(C)(ii)), except that the Secretary may, with notice and for cause (as defined by the Secretary), terminate such endorsement and contract.

(D) ENSURING CHOICE OF PROGRAMS.—

(i) IN GENERAL.—The Secretary shall ensure that there is available to each discount card eligible individual a choice of at least 2 endorsed programs (each offered by a different sponsor).

(ii) LIMITATION ON NUMBER.—The Secretary may limit (but not below 2) the number of sponsors in a State that are awarded contracts under this paragraph.

(3) SERVICE AREA ENCOMPASSING ENTIRE STATES.—Except as provided in paragraph (9), if a prescription drug card sponsor that offers an endorsed program enrolls in the program individuals residing in any part of a State, the sponsor must permit any discount card eligible individual residing in any portion of the State to enroll in the program.

(4) SAVINGS TO MEDICARE BENEFICIARIES.—Each prescription drug card sponsor that offers an endorsed discount card program shall pass on to discount card eligible individuals enrolled in the program negotiated prices on covered discount card drugs, including discounts negotiated with pharmacies and manufacturers, to the extent disclosed under subsection (i)(1).

(5) GRIEVANCE MECHANISM.—Each prescription drug card sponsor shall provide meaningful procedures for hearing and resolving grievances between the sponsor (including any entity or individual through which the sponsor carries out the endorsed discount card program) and enrollees in endorsed discount card programs of the sponsor under this section in a manner similar to that required under section 1852(f).

(6) CONFIDENTIALITY OF ENROLLEE RECORDS.—

(A) IN GENERAL.—For purposes of the program under this section, the operations of an endorsed program are covered functions and a prescription drug card sponsor is a covered entity for purposes of applying part C of title XI and all regulatory provisions promulgated thereunder, including regulations (relating to privacy) adopted pursuant to the authority of the Secretary under section 264(c) of the Health Insurance Portability and Accountability Act of 1996 (42 U.S.C. 1320d-2 note).

(B) WAIVER AUTHORITY.—In order to promote participation of sponsors in the program under this section, the Secretary may waive such relevant portions of regulations relating to privacy referred to in subparagraph (A), for such appropriate, limited period of time, as the Secretary specifies.

(7) LIMITATION ON PROVISION AND MARKETING OF PRODUCTS AND SERVICES.—The sponsor of an endorsed discount card program—

(A) may provide under the program—

(i) a product or service only if the product or service is directly related to a covered discount card drug; or

(ii) a discount price for nonprescription drugs; and

(B) may, to the extent otherwise permitted under paragraph (6) (relating to application of HIPAA requirements), market a product or service under the program only if the product or service is directly related to—

(i) a covered discount card drug; or

(ii) a drug described in subparagraph (A)(ii) and the marketing consists of information on the discounted price made available for the drug involved.

(8) ADDITIONAL PROTECTIONS.—Each endorsed discount card program shall meet such additional requirements as the Secretary identifies to protect and promote the interest of discount card eligible individuals, including requirements that ensure that discount card eligible individuals enrolled in endorsed discount card programs are not charged more than the lower of the price based on negotiated prices or the usual and customary price.

(9) SPECIAL RULES FOR CERTAIN ORGANIZATIONS.—

(A) IN GENERAL.—In the case of an organization that is offering a plan under part C or enrollment under a reasonable cost reimbursement contract under section 1876(h) that is seeking to be a prescription drug card sponsor under this section, the organization may elect to apply the special rules under subparagraph (B) with respect to enrollees in any plan described in section 1851(a)(2)(A) that it offers or under such contract and an endorsed discount card program it offers, but only if it limits enrollment under such program to individuals enrolled in such plan or under such contract.

(B) SPECIAL RULES.—The special rules under this subparagraph are as follows:

(i) LIMITATION ON ENROLLMENT.—The sponsor limits enrollment under this section under the endorsed discount card program to discount card eligible individuals who are enrolled in the part C plan involved or under the reasonable cost reimbursement contract involved and is not required nor permitted to enroll other individuals under such program.

(ii) PHARMACY ACCESS.—Pharmacy access requirements under subsection (e)(1)(B) are deemed to be met if the access is made available through a pharmacy network (and not only through mail order) and the network used by the sponsor is approved by the Secretary.

(iii) SPONSOR REQUIREMENTS.—The Secretary may waive the application of such requirements for a sponsor as the Secretary determines to be duplicative or to conflict with a requirement of the organization under part C or section 1876 (as the case may be) or to be necessary in order to improve coordination of this section with the benefits under such part or section.

(i) DISCLOSURE AND OVERSIGHT.—

(1) DISCLOSURE.—Each prescription drug card sponsor offering an endorsed discount card program shall disclose to the Secretary (in a manner specified by the Secretary) information relating to program performance, use of prescription drugs by discount card eligible individuals enrolled in the program, the extent to which negotiated price concessions described in subsection (e)(1)(A)(ii) made available to the entity by a manufacturer are passed through to enrollees through pharmacies or otherwise, and such other information as the Secretary may specify. The provisions of section 1927(b)(3)(D) shall apply to drug pricing data reported under the previous sentence (other than data in aggregate form).

(2) OVERSIGHT; AUDIT AND INSPECTION AUTHORITY.—The Secretary shall provide appropriate oversight to ensure compliance of endorsed discount card programs and their sponsors with the requirements of this section. The Secretary shall have the right to audit and inspect any books and records of a prescription discount card sponsor (and of any affiliated organization referred to in subsection (h)(1)(B)) that pertain to the endorsed discount card program under this section, including amounts payable to the sponsor under this section.

(3) SANCTIONS FOR ABUSIVE PRACTICES.—The Secretary may implement intermediate sanctions or may revoke the endorsement of a program offered by a sponsor under this section if the Secretary determines that the sponsor or the program no longer meets the applicable requirements of this section or that the sponsor has engaged in false or misleading marketing practices. The Secretary may impose a civil money penalty in an amount not to exceed $10,000 for conduct that a party knows or should know is a violation of this section. The provisions of section 1128A (other than subsections (a) and (b) and the second sentence of subsection (f)) shall apply to a civil money penalty under the previous sentence in the same manner as such provisions apply to a penalty or proceeding under section 1128A(a).

(j) TREATMENT OF TERRITORIES.—

(1) IN GENERAL.—The Secretary may waive any provision of this section (including subsection (h)(2)(D)) in the case of a resident of a State (other than the 50 States and the District of Columbia) insofar as the Secretary determines it is necessary to secure access to negotiated prices for discount card eligible individuals (or, at the option of the Secretary, individuals described in subsection (b)(1)(A)(i)).

(2) TRANSITIONAL ASSISTANCE.—

(A) IN GENERAL.—In the case of a State, other than the 50 States and the District of Columbia, if the State establishes a plan described in subparagraph (B) (for providing transitional assistance with respect to the provision of prescription drugs to some or all individuals residing in the State who are described in subparagraph (B)(i)), the Secretary shall pay to the State for the entire period of the operation of this section an amount equal to the amount allotted to the State under subparagraph (C).

(B) PLAN.—The plan described in this subparagraph is a plan that—

(i) provides transitional assistance with respect to the provision of covered discount card drugs to some or all individuals who are entitled to benefits under part A or enrolled under part B, who reside in the State, and who have income below 135 percent of the poverty line; and

(ii) assures that amounts received by the State under this paragraph are used only for such assistance.

(C) ALLOTMENT LIMIT.—The amount described in this subparagraph for a State is equal to $35,000,000 multiplied by the ratio (as estimated by the Secretary) of—

(i) the number of individuals who are entitled to benefits under part A or enrolled under part B and who reside in the State (as determined by the Secretary as of July 1, 2003), to

(ii) the sum of such numbers for all States to which this paragraph applies.

(D) CONTINUED AVAILABILITY OF FUNDS.—Amounts made available to a State under this paragraph which are not used under this paragraph shall be added to the amount available to that State for purposes of carrying out section 1935(e).

(k) FUNDING.—

(1) ESTABLISHMENT OF TRANSITIONAL ASSISTANCE ACCOUNT.—

(A) IN GENERAL.—There is created within the Federal Supplementary Medical Insurance Trust Fund established by section 1841 an account to be known as the 'Transitional Assistance Account' (in this subsection referred to as the 'Account').

(B) FUNDS.—The Account shall consist of such gifts and bequests as may be made as provided in section 201(i)(1), accrued interest on balances in the Account, and such amounts as may be deposited in, or appropriated to, the Account as provided in this subsection.

(C) SEPARATE FROM REST OF TRUST FUND.—Funds provided under this subsection to the Account shall be kept separate from all other funds within the Federal Supplementary Medical Insurance Trust Fund, but shall be invested, and such investments redeemed, in the same manner as all other funds and investments within such Trust Fund.

(2) PAYMENTS FROM ACCOUNT.—

(A) IN GENERAL.—The Managing Trustee shall pay from time to time from the Account such amounts as the Secretary certifies are necessary to make payments for transitional assistance provided under subsections (g) and (j)(2).

(B) TREATMENT IN RELATION TO PART B PREMIUM.—Amounts payable from the Account shall not be taken into account in computing actuarial rates or premium amounts under section 1839.

(3) APPROPRIATIONS TO COVER BENEFITS.—There are appropriated to the Account in a fiscal year, out of any moneys in the Treasury not otherwise appropriated, an amount equal to the payments made from the Account in the year.

(4) FOR ADMINISTRATIVE EXPENSES.—There are authorized to be appropriated to the Secretary such sums as may be necessary to carry out the Secretary's responsibilities under this section.

(5) TRANSFER OF ANY REMAINING BALANCE TO MEDICARE PRESCRIPTION DRUG ACCOUNT.—Any balance remaining in the Account after the Secretary determines that funds in the Account are no longer necessary to carry out the program under this section shall be transferred and deposited into the Medicare Prescription Drug Account under section 1860D-16.

(6) CONSTRUCTION.—Nothing in this section shall be construed as authorizing the Secretary to provide for payment (other than payment of an enrollment fee on behalf of a transitional assistance eligible individual under subsection (g)(1)(A)) to a sponsor for administrative expenses incurred by the sponsor in carrying out this section (including in administering the transitional assistance provisions of subsections (f) and (g)).

[CCH Explanation at ¶ 150, 152, 154, 156, 158, 160, 162, 164, 166, 168, and 170.]

2003 Amendments:

Section 101(a) of the "Medicare Prescription Drug, Improvement, and Modernization Act of 2003," effective upon enactment, added new section 1860D-31.

The above amendment applies to coverage effective January 1, 2006.

Subpart 5—Definitions and Miscellaneous Provisions

[¶ 2268] SEC. 1860D-41. DEFINITIONS; TREATMENT OF REFERENCES TO PROVISIONS IN PART C

(a) DEFINITIONS.—For purposes of this part:

(1) BASIC PRESCRIPTION DRUG COVERAGE.—The term 'basic prescription drug coverage' is defined in section 1860D-2(a)(3).

(2) COVERED PART D DRUG.—The term 'covered part D drug' is defined in section 1860D-2(e).

(3) CREDITABLE PRESCRIPTION DRUG COVERAGE.—The term 'creditable prescription drug coverage' has the meaning given such term in section 1860D-13(b)(4).

(4) PART D ELIGIBLE INDIVIDUAL.—The term 'part D eligible individual' has the meaning given such term in section 1860D-1(a)(4)(A).

(5) FALLBACK PRESCRIPTION DRUG PLAN.—The term 'fallback prescription drug plan' has the meaning given such term in section 1860D-11(g)(4).

(6) INITIAL COVERAGE LIMIT.—The term 'initial coverage limit' means such limit as established under section 1860D-2(b)(3), or, in the case of coverage that is not standard prescription drug coverage, the comparable limit (if any) established under the coverage.

(7) INSURANCE RISK.—The term 'insurance risk' means, with respect to a participating pharmacy, risk of the type commonly assumed only by insurers licensed by a State and does not

include payment variations designed to reflect performance-based measures of activities within the control of the pharmacy, such as formulary compliance and generic drug substitution.

(8) MA PLAN.—The term 'MA plan' has the meaning given such term in section 1860D-1(a)(4)(B).

(9) MA-PD PLAN.—The term 'MA-PD plan' has the meaning given such term in section 1860D-1(a)(4)(C).

(10) MEDICARE PRESCRIPTION DRUG ACCOUNT.—The term 'Medicare Prescription Drug Account' means the Account created under section 1860D-16(a).

(11) PDP APPROVED BID.—The term 'PDP approved bid' has the meaning given such term in section 1860D-13(a)(6).

(12) PDP REGION.—The term 'PDP region' means such a region as provided under section 1860D-11(a)(2).

(13) PDP SPONSOR.—The term 'PDP sponsor' means a nongovernmental entity that is certified under this part as meeting the requirements and standards of this part for such a sponsor.

(14) PRESCRIPTION DRUG PLAN.—The term 'prescription drug plan' means prescription drug coverage that is offered—

(A) under a policy, contract, or plan that has been approved under section 1860D-11(e); and

(B) by a PDP sponsor pursuant to, and in accordance with, a contract between the Secretary and the sponsor under section 1860D-12(b).

(15) QUALIFIED PRESCRIPTION DRUG COVERAGE.—The term 'qualified prescription drug coverage' is defined in section 1860D-2(a)(1).

(16) STANDARD PRESCRIPTION DRUG COVERAGE.—The term 'standard prescription drug coverage' is defined in section 1860D-2(b).

(17) STATE PHARMACEUTICAL ASSISTANCE PROGRAM.—The term 'State Pharmaceutical Assistance Program' has the meaning given such term in section 1860D-23(b).

(18) SUBSIDY ELIGIBLE INDIVIDUAL.—The term 'subsidy eligible individual' has the meaning given such term in section 1860D-14(a)(3)(A).

(b) APPLICATION OF PART C PROVISIONS UNDER THIS PART.—For purposes of applying provisions of part C under this part with respect to a prescription drug plan and a PDP sponsor, unless otherwise provided in this part such provisions shall be applied as if—

(1) any reference to an MA plan included a reference to a prescription drug plan;

(2) any reference to an MA organization or a provider-sponsored organization included a reference to a PDP sponsor;

(3) any reference to a contract under section 1857 included a reference to a contract under section 1860D-12(b);

(4) any reference to part C included a reference to this part; and

(5) any reference to an election period under section 1851 were a reference to an enrollment period under section 1860D-1.

[CCH Explanation at ¶ 175.]
2003 Amendments:

Section 101(a) of the "Medicare Prescription Drug, Improvement, and Modernization Act of 2003," effective upon enactment, added new section 1860D-41.

The above amendment applies to coverage effective January 1, 2006.

[¶ 2269] SEC. 1860D-42. MISCELLANEOUS PROVISIONS

(a) ACCESS TO COVERAGE IN TERRITORIES.—The Secretary may waive such requirements of this part, including section 1860D-3(a)(1), insofar as the Secretary determines it is necessary to secure access to qualified prescription drug coverage for part D eligible individuals residing in a State (other than the 50 States and the District of Columbia).

(b) APPLICATION OF DEMONSTRATION AUTHORITY.—The provisions of section 402 of the Social Security Amendments of 1967 (Public Law 90-248) shall apply with respect to this part and part C in the same manner it applies with respect to parts A and B, except that any reference with respect to a Trust Fund in relation to an experiment or demonstration project relating to prescription drug coverage under this part shall be deemed a reference to the Medicare Prescription Drug Account within the Federal Supplementary Medical Insurance Trust Fund.".

[CCH Explanation at ¶178.]
2003 Amendments:

Section 101(a) of the "Medicare Prescription Drug, Improvement, and Modernization Act of 2003," effective upon enactment, added new section 1860D-42.

The above amendment applies to coverage effective January 1, 2006.

[¶2270] Sec. 1861. SUPPLIER
[42 U.S.C. §1395x(d)]

(d) The term "supplier" means, unless the context otherwise requires, a physician or other practitioner, a facility, or other entity (other than a provider of services) that furnishes items or services under this title.

[CCH Explanation at ¶825.]
2003 Amendments:

Section 901(b) of the "Medicare Prescription Drug, Improvement, and Modernization Act of 2003," effective upon enactment, amended section 1861 by inserting after subsection (c) new subsection (d), defining the term "supplier".

[¶2275] Sec. 1861. MEDICAL AND OTHER HEALTH SERVICES
[42 U.S.C. §1395x(s)]

(s) The term "medical and other health services" means any of the following items or services:

* * *

(2)(A) services and supplies (including drugs and biologicals which are not usually self-administered by the patient) furnished as an incident to a physician's professional service, of kinds which are commonly furnished in physicians' offices and are commonly either rendered without charge or included in the physicians' bills (or would have been so included but for the application of section 1847B);

* * *

(K)(i) services which would be physicians' services and services described in subsection (ww)(1) if furnished by a physician (as defined in subsection (r)(1) of this section) and which are performed by a physician assistant (as defined in subsection (aa)(5) of this section) under the supervision of a physician (as so defined) and which the physician assistant is legally authorized to perform by the State in which the services are performed, and such services and supplies furnished as incident to such services as would be covered under subparagraph (A) if furnished incident to a physician's professional service, but only if no facility or other provider charges or is paid any amounts with respect to the furnishing of such services,

(ii) services which would be physicians' services and services described in subsection (ww)(1) if furnished by a physician (as defined in subsection (r)(1)) and which are performed by a nurse practitioner or clinical nurse specialist (as defined in subsection (aa)(5)) working in collaboration (as defined in subsection (aa)(6)) with a physician (as defined in subsection (r)(1)) which the nurse practitioner or clinical nurse specialist is legally authorized to perform by the State in which the services are performed, and such services and supplies furnished as an incident to such services as would be covered under subparagraph (A) if furnished incident to a physician's professional service, but only if no facility or other provider charges or is paid any amounts with respect to the furnishing of such services;

* * *

(W) an initial preventive physical examination (as defined in subsection (ww));

(X) cardiovascular screening blood tests (as defined in subsection (xx)(1));

Social Security Law Added, Amended or Repealed

(Y) diabetes screening tests (as defined in subsection (yy)); and

(Z) intravenous immune globulin for the treatment of primary immune deficiency diseases in the home (as defined in subsection (zz));

* * *

(7) ambulance service where the use of other methods of transportation is contraindicated by the individual's condition, but, subject to section 1834(l)(14), only to the extent provided in regulations;

* * *

[CCH Explanation at ¶ 598, 750, 753, 755, 760, 1004, 1006, 1009, and 1010.]

2003 Amendments:

Section 303(i)(2) of the "Medicare Prescription Drug, Improvement, and Modernization Act of 2003," effective upon enactment, amended section 1861(s)(2)(A) by inserting "(or would have been so included but for the application of section 1847B)" after "included in the physicians' bills".

Section 415(b) of the "Medicare Prescription Drug, Improvement, and Modernization Act of 2003," amended section 1861(s)(7) by inserting ", subject to section 1834(l)(14)," after "but".

The amendments made by section 415(b) of the "Medicare Prescription Drug, Improvement, and Modernization Act of 2003," apply to services furnished on or after January 1, 2005.

Section 611(a) of the "Medicare Prescription Drug, Improvement, and Modernization Act of 2003," amended section 1861(s)(2) in subparagraph (U), by striking "and" at the end; in subparagraph (V)(iii), by inserting "and" at the end; and by adding at the end new subparagraph (W).

The amendments made by section 611(a) of the "Medicare Prescription Drug, Improvement, and Modernization Act of 2003," apply to services furnished on or after January 1, 2005, but only for individuals whose coverage period under part B begins on or after such date.

Section 611(d)(2) of the "Medicare Prescription Drug, Improvement, and Modernization Act of 2003," amended clauses (i) and (ii) of section 1861(s)(2)(K) by inserting "and services described in subsection (ww)(1)" after "services which would be physicians' services".

The amendments made by section 611(d) of the "Medicare Prescription Drug, Improvement, and Modernization Act of 2003," apply to services furnished on or after January 1, 2005, but only for individuals whose coverage period under part B begins on or after such date.

Section 612(a) of the "Medicare Prescription Drug, Improvement, and Modernization Act of 2003," amended section 1861(s)(2) in subparagraph (V)(iii), by striking "and" at the end; in subparagraph (W), by inserting "and" at the end; and by adding at the end new subparagraph (X).

The amendments made by section 612(a) of the "Medicare Prescription Drug, Improvement, and Modernization Act of 2003," apply to tests furnished on or after January 1, 2005.

Section 613(a) of the "Medicare Prescription Drug, Improvement, and Modernization Act of 2003," amended section 1861(s)(2) in subparagraph (W), by striking "and" at the end; in subparagraph (X), by adding "and" at the end; and by adding at the end new subparagraph (Y).

The above amendment applies to tests furnished on or after Jan. 1, 2005.

Section 642(a)(1) of the "Medicare Prescription Drug, Improvement, and Modernization Act of 2003," amended section 1861(s)(2) by striking "and" at the end of subparagraph (X); by adding "and" at the end of subparagraph (Y); and by adding at the end new subparagraph (Z).

The amendments made by section 642(a) of the "Medicare Prescription Drug, Improvement, and Modernization Act of 2003," apply to items furnished administered on or after January 1, 2004.

Section 736(b)(11) of the "Medicare Prescription Drug, Improvement, and Modernization Act of 2003," effective upon enactment, amended section 1861(s)(2)(K)(i) by striking "; and but" and inserting ", but"

[¶ 2280] Sec. 1861. REASONABLE COST

[42 U.S.C. § 1395x(v)]

* * *

* * *

* * *

(v)(1)(S)(ii)(III) Subclauses (I) and (II) shall not apply to payments with respect to the costs of hospital outpatient services provided by any hospital that is a sole community hospital (as defined in section 1886(d)(5)(D)(iii))or a critical access hospital (as defined in section 1861(mm)(1)).

* * *

[CCH Explanation at ¶ 578.]

2003 Amendments:

Section 414(g) of the "Medicare Prescription Drug, Improvement, and Modernization Act of 2003," effective upon enactment, amended section 1861(v)(1) by moving subparagraph (U) 4 ems to the left.

[CCH Note: Existing law text reflects this change.]

Section 736(b)(3) of the "Medicare Prescription Drug, Improvement, and Modernization Act of 2003," effective upon enactment, amended section 1861(v)(1)(S)(ii)(III) by striking "(as defined in section 1886(d)(5)(D)(iii)" and inserting "(as defined in section 1886(d)(5)(D)(iii))".

Section 736(c)(4) of the "Medicare Prescription Drug, Improvement, and Modernization Act of 2003," effective upon enactment, amended section 1861(v) by moving paragraph (8) (including clauses (i) through (v) of such paragraph) 2 ems to the left.

[CCH Note: Existing law text reflects this change.]

[¶2280A] Sec. 1861. HOSPICE CARE; HOSPICE PROGRAM
[42 U.S.C. §1395x(dd)]

* * *

(dd)(2) The term "hospice program" means a public agency or private organization (or a subdivision thereof) which—

(A)(i) is primarily engaged in providing the care and services described in paragraph (1) and makes such services available (as needed) on a 24-hour basis and which also provides bereavement counseling for the immediate family of terminally ill individuals and services described in section 1812(a)(5),

* * *

* * *

(3)(B) The term "attending physician" means, with respect to an individual, the physician (as defined in subsection (r)(1)) or nurse practitioner (as defined in subsection (aa)(5)), who may be employed by a hospice program, whom the individual identifies as having the most significant role in the determination and delivery of medical care to the individual at the time the individual makes an election to receive hospice care.

* * *

(5)

* * *

(D) In extraordinary, exigent, or other non-routine circumstances, such as unanticipated periods of high patient loads, staffing shortages due to illness or other events, or temporary travel of a patient outside a hospice program's service area, a hospice program may enter into arrangements with another hospice program for the provision by that other program of services described in paragraph (2)(A)(ii)(I). The provisions of paragraph (2)(A)(ii)(II) shall apply with respect to the services provided under such arrangements.

(E) A hospice program may provide services described in paragraph (1)(A) other than directly by the program if the services are highly specialized services of a registered professional nurse and are provided non-routinely and so infrequently so that the provision of such services directly would be impracticable and prohibitively expensive.

[CCH Explanation at ¶ 671, 677, and 946.]
2003 Amendments:

Section 408(a) of the "Medicare Prescription Drug, Improvement, and Modernization Act of 2003," effective upon enactment, amended section 1861(dd)(3)(B) by inserting "or nurse practitioner (as defined in subsection (aa)(5))" after "the physician (as defined in subsection (r)(1))".

Section 512(c) of the "Medicare Prescription Drug, Improvement, and Modernization Act of 2003," amended section 1861(dd)(2)(A)(i) by inserting before the comma at the end the following: "and services described in section 1812(a)(5)".

The amendments made by section 512(c) of the "Medicare Prescription Drug, Improvement, and Modernization Act of 2003," apply to services provided by a hospice program on or after January 1, 2005.

Section 946 of the "Medicare Prescription Drug, Improvement, and Modernization Act of 2003," effective upon enactment, amended section 1861(dd)(5) by adding new subparagraphs (D) and (E).

[¶2280B] Sec. 1861. DISCHARGE PLANNING PROCESS
[42 U.S.C. §1395x(ee)]

* * *

(ee)(2) The Secretary shall develop guidelines and standards for the discharge planning process in order to ensure a timely and smooth transition to the most appropriate type of and setting for post-hospital or rehabilitative care. The guidelines and standards shall include the following:

* * *

Social Security Law Added, Amended or Repealed

(D) A discharge planning evaluation must include an evaluation of a patient's likely need for appropriate post-hospital services, including hospice care and post-hospital extended care services, and the availability of those services including the availability of home health services through individuals and entities that participate in the program under this title and that serve the area in which the patient resides and that request to be listed by the hospital as availableand, in the case of individuals who are likely to need post-hospital extended care services, the availability of such services through facilities that participate in the program under this title and that serve the area in which the patient resides.

* * *

[CCH Explanation at ¶606.]

2003 Amendments:

Section 926(b) of the "Medicare Prescription Drug, Improvement, and Modernization Act of 2003," effective upon enactment, amended section 1861(ee)(2)(D) by striking "hospice services" and inserting "hospice care and post-hospital extended care services"; and by inserting before the period at the end the following: "and, in the case of individuals who are likely to need post-hospital extended care services, the availability of such services through facilities that participate in the program under this title and that serve the area in which the patient resides".

[¶2280C] Sec. 1861(mm) CRITICAL ACCESS HOSPITAL; CRITICAL ACCESS HOSPITAL SERVICES

[42 U.S.C. §1395x(mm)]

2003 Amendments:

Section 736(a)(10) of the "Medicare Prescription Drug, Improvement, and Modernization Act of 2003," effective upon enactment, amended the heading of subsection (mm) of section 1861 to read as follows: "Critical Access Hospital; Critical Access Hospital Services".

[¶2280D] Sec. 1861. POST-INSTITUTIONAL HOME HEALTH SERVICES; HOME HEALTH SPELL OF ILLNESS

[42 U.S.C. §1395x(tt)]

(tt)(1) The term "post-institutional home health services" means home health services furnished to an individual—

(A) after discharge from a hospital or critical accesshospital in which the individual was an inpatient for not less than 3 consecutive days before such discharge if such home health services were initiated within 14 days after the date of such discharge; or

* * *

(2) The term "home health spell of illness" with respect to any individual means a period of consecutive days—

* * *

(B) ending with the close of the first period of 60 consecutive days thereafter on each of which the individual is neither an inpatient of a hospital or critical access hospital nor an inpatient of a facility described in section 1819(a)(1) or subsection (y)(1) nor provided home health services.

2003 Amendments:

Section 736(a)(11) of the "Medicare Prescription Drug, Improvement, and Modernization Act of 2003," effective upon enactment, amended paragraphs (1) and (2) of section 1861(tt) by striking "rural primary care" and inserting "critical access".

[¶2280E] Sec. 1861. INITIAL PREVENTATIVE PHYSICAL EXAMINATION

(ww)(1) The term "initial preventive physical examination" means physicians' services consisting of a physical examination (including measurement of height, weight, and blood pressure, and an electrocardiogram) with the goal of health promotion and disease detection and includes education, counseling, and referral with respect to screening and other preventive services described in paragraph (2), but does not include clinical laboratory tests.

(2) The screening and other preventive services described in this paragraph include the following:

(A) Pneumococcal, influenza, and hepatitis B vaccine and administration under subsection (s)(10).

(B) Screening mammography as defined in subsection (jj).

(C) Screening pap smear and screening pelvic exam as defined in subsection (nn).

(D) Prostate cancer screening tests as defined in subsection (oo).

Social Security Law Added, Amended or Repealed

(E) Colorectal cancer screening tests as defined in subsection (pp).

(F) Diabetes outpatient self-management training services as defined in subsection (qq)(1).

(G) Bone mass measurement as defined in subsection (rr).

(H) Screening for glaucoma as defined in subsection (uu).

(I) Medical nutrition therapy services as defined in subsection (vv).

(J) Cardiovascular screening blood tests as defined in subsection (xx)(1).

(K) Diabetes screening tests as defined in subsection (yy).

[CCH Explanation at ¶750 and 1103.]

2003 Amendments:

Section 611(b) of the "Medicare Prescription Drug, Improvement, and Modernization Act of 2003," amended section 1861 by adding at the end new subsection (ww).

The amendments made by this section apply to services furnished on or after January 1, 2005, but only for individuals whose coverage period under part B begins on or after such date.

[¶2280F] Sec. 1861. CARDIOVASCULAR SCREENING BLOOD TEST

(xx)(1) The term "cardiovascular screening blood test" means a blood test for the early detection of cardiovascular disease (or abnormalities associated with an elevated risk of cardiovascular disease) that tests for the following:

(A) Cholesterol levels and other lipid or triglyceride levels.

(B) Such other indications associated with the presence of, or an elevated risk for, cardiovascular disease as the Secretary may approve for all individuals (or for some individuals determined by the Secretary to be at risk for cardiovascular disease), including indications measured by noninvasive testing.

The Secretary may not approve an indication under subparagraph (B) for any individual unless a blood test for such is recommended by the United States Preventive Services Task Force.

(2) The Secretary shall establish standards, in consultation with appropriate organizations, regarding the frequency for each type of cardiovascular screening blood tests, except that such frequency may not be more often than once every 2 years.

[CCH Explanation at ¶753.]

2003 Amendments:

Section 612(b) of the "Medicare Prescription Drug, Improvement, and Modernization Act of 2003," amended section 1861 by adding at the end new subsection (xx).

The amendments made by this section shall apply to tests furnished on or after January 1, 2005.

[¶2280G] Sec. 1861. DIABETES SCREENING TESTS

(yy)(1) The term "diabetes screening tests" means testing furnished to an individual at risk for diabetes (as defined in paragraph (2)) for the purpose of early detection of diabetes, including—

(A) a fasting plasma glucose test; and

(B) such other tests, and modifications to tests, as the Secretary determines appropriate, in consultation with appropriate organizations.

(2) For purposes of paragraph (1), the term "individual at risk for diabetes" means an individual who has any of the following risk factors for diabetes:

(A) Hypertension.

(B) Dyslipidemia.

(C) Obesity, defined as a body mass index greater than or equal to 30 kg/m2.

(D) Previous identification of an elevated impaired fasting glucose.

(E) Previous identification of impaired glucose tolerance.

(F) A risk factor consisting of at least 2 of the following characteristics:

(i) Overweight, defined as a body mass index greater than 25, but less than 30, kg/m2.

(ii) A family history of diabetes.

(iii) A history of gestational diabetes mellitus or delivery of a baby weighing greater than 9 pounds.

(iv) 65 years of age or older.

(3) The Secretary shall establish standards, in consultation with appropriate organizations, regarding the frequency of diabetes screening tests, except that such frequency may not be more often than twice within the 12-month period following the date of the most recent diabetes screening test of that individual.

[CCH Explanation at ¶755 and 1016.]

2003 Amendments:

Section 613(b) of the "Medicare Prescription Drug, Improvement, and Modernization Act of 2003," amended section 1861 as amended by section 612(b), is amended by adding at the end new subsection (yy).

The amendment above applies to tests furnished on or after January 1, 2005.

[¶2280H] Sec. 1861. INTRAVENOUS IMMUNE GLOBULIN

(zz) The term "intravenous immune globulin" means an approved pooled plasma derivative for the treatment in the patient's home of a patient with a diagnosed primary immune deficiency disease, but not including items or services related to the administration of the derivative, if a physician determines administration of the derivative in the patient's home is medically appropriate.

[CCH Explanation at ¶760.]

2003 Amendments:

Section 642(a)(2) of the "Medicare Prescription Drug, Improvement, and Modernization Act of 2003," amended section 1861 by adding at the end the following new subsection (zz).

The amendments made by this section apply to items administered on or after January 1, 2004.

[¶2280I] Sec. 1861. EXTENDED CARE IN RELIGIOUS NONMEDICAL HEALTH CARE INSTITUTIONS

(aaa)(1) The term "home health agency" also includes a religious nonmedical health care institution (as defined in subsection (ss)(1)), but only with respect to items and services ordinarily furnished by such an institution to individuals in their homes, and that are comparable to items and services furnished to individuals by a home health agency that is not religious nonmedical health care institution.

(2)(A) Subject to subparagraphs (B), payment may be made with respect to services provided by such an institution only to such extent and under such conditions, limitations, and requirements (in addition to or in lieu of the conditions, limitations, and requirements otherwise applicable) as may be provided in regulations consistent with section 1821.

(B) Notwithstanding any other provision of this title, payment may not be made under subparagraph (A)—

(i) in a year insofar as such payments exceed $700,000; and

(ii) after December 31, 2006.

[CCH Explanation at ¶662.]

2003 Amendments:

Section 706(b) of the "Medicare Prescription Drug, Improvement, and Modernization Act of 2003," effective upon enactment, amended section 1861(aaa) as amended by section 642, by adding at the end the new section "Extended Care in Religious Nonmedical Health Care Institutions.".

[¶2280J] Sec. 1862. [Exclusions From Coverage; Basic Guidelines]

[42 U.S.C. §1395y(a)]

(a) Notwithstanding any other provision of this title, no payment may be made under part A or part B for any expenses incurred for items or services—

* * *

(1)(H) in the case of colorectal cancer screening tests, which are performed more frequently than is covered under section 1834(d),

(I) the frequency and duration of home health services which are in excess of normative guidelines that the Secretary shall establish by regulation,

(J) in the case of a drug or biological specified in section 1847A(c)(6)(C) for which payment is made under part B that is furnished in a competitive area under section 1847B, that is not furnished by an entity under a contract under such section,

(K) in the case of an initial preventive physical examination, which is performed not later than 6 months after the date the individual's first coverage period begins under part B,

(L) in the case of cardiovascular screening blood tests (as defined in section 1861(xx)(1)), which are performed more frequently than is covered under section 1861(xx)(2), and

(M) in the case of a diabetes screening test (as defined in section 1861(yy)(1)), which is performed more frequently than is covered under section 1861(yy)(3);

* * *

(7) where such expenses are for routine physical checkups, eyeglasses (other than eyewear described in section 1861(s)(8)) or eye examinations for the purpose of prescribing, fitting, or changing eyeglasses, procedures performed (during the course of any eye examination) to determine the refractive state of the eyes, hearing aids or examinations therefor, or immunizations (except as otherwise allowed under section 1861(s)(10) and subparagraph (B), (F), (G), (H), or (K) of paragraph (1));

* * *

Paragraph (7) shall not apply to Federally qualified health center services described in section 1861(aa)(3)(B); or

In making a national coverage determination (as defined in paragraph (1)(B) of section 1869(f)) the Secretary shall ensure consistent with subsection (l) that the public is afforded notice and opportunity to comment prior to implementation by the Secretary of the determination; meetings of advisory committees established under section 1114(f) with respect to the determination are made on the record; in making the determination, the Secretary has considered applicable information (including clinical experience and medical, technical, and scientific evidence) with respect to the subject matter of the determination; and in the determination, provide a clear statement of the basis for the determination (including responses to comments received from the public), the assumptions underlying that basis, and make available to the public the data (other than proprietary data) considered in making the determination.

[CCH Explanation at ¶ 584, 750, 753, 755, 796, 948, 1004, 1006, 1009 and 1010.]

2003 Amendments:

Section 303(i)(3)(B) of the "Medicare Prescription Drug, Improvement, and Modernization Act of 2003," effective upon enactment, amended section 1862(a)(1) by striking "and" at the end of subparagraph (H); by striking the semicolon at the end of subparagraph (I) and inserting ", and"; and by adding at the end new subparagraph (J).

Section 611(d)(1)(A) of the "Medicare Prescription Drug, Improvement, and Modernization Act of 2003," amended section 1862(a)(1), as amended by section 303(i)(3)(B), by striking "and" at the end of subparagraph (I); by striking the semicolon at the end of subparagraph (J) and inserting ", and"; and by adding at the end new subparagraph (K).

The amendments made by section 611(d) of the "Medicare Prescription Drug, Improvement, and Modernization Act of 2003," apply to services furnished on or after January 1, 2005, but only for individuals whose coverage period under part B of the "Medicare Prescription Drug, Improvement, and Modernization Act of 2003," begins on or after such date.

Section 611(d)(1)(B) of the "Medicare Prescription Drug, Improvement, and Modernization Act of 2003," amended section 1862(a)(7) by striking "or (H)" and inserting "(H), or (K)".

The amendments made by section 611(d) of the "Medicare Prescription Drug, Improvement, and Modernization Act of 2003," apply to services furnished on or after January 1, 2005, but only for individuals whose coverage period under part B of the "Medicare Prescription Drug, Improvement, and Modernization Act of 2003," begins on or after such date.

Section 612(c) of the "Medicare Prescription Drug, Improvement, and Modernization Act of 2003," amended section 1862(a)(1), as amended by section 611(d), by striking "and" at the end of subparagraph (J); by striking the semicolon at the end of subparagraph (K) and inserting ", and"; and by adding at the end new subparagraph (L).

The amendments made by section 612(c) of the "Medicare Prescription Drug, Improvement, and Modernization Act of 2003," apply to tests furnished on or after January 1, 2005.

Section 613(c) of the "Medicare Prescription Drug, Improvement, and Modernization Act of 2003," amended section 1862(a)(1), as amended by section 612(c), by striking "and" at the end of subparagraph (K); by striking the semicolon at the end of subparagraph (L) and inserting ", and"; and by adding at the end new subparagraph (M).

The amendments made by section 613(c) of the "Medicare Prescription Drug, Improvement, and Modernization Act of 2003," apply to tests furnished on or after Jan. 1, 2005.

Section 731(a)(1)(A) of the "Medicare Prescription Drug, Improvement, and Modernization Act of 2003," effective upon enactment, amended section 1862, as amended by sections 948 and 950, in the third sentence of subsection (a), by inserting "consistent with subsection (l)" after "the Secretary shall ensure"; and by adding at the end new subsection (l).

[¶ 2280K] **Sec. 1862. MEDICARE AS SECONDARY PAYER**

[42 U.S.C. § 1395y(b)]

(b) MEDICARE AS SECONDARY PAYER.—

* * *

(2) MEDICARE SECONDARY PAYER.—

(A) IN GENERAL.—Payment under this title may not be made, except as provided in subparagraph (B), with respect to any item or service to the extent that—

(i) payment has been made, or can reasonably be expected to be made, with respect to the item or service as required under paragraph (1), or

(ii) payment has been made or can reasonably be expected to be made under a workmen's compensation law or plan of the United States or a State or under an automobile or liability insurance policy or plan (including a self-insured plan) or under no fault insurance.

In this subsection, the term "primary plan" means a group health plan or large group health plan, to the extent that clause (i) applies, and a workmen's compensation law or plan, an automobile or liability insurance policy or plan (including a self-insured plan) or no fault insurance, to the extent that clause (ii) applies. An entity that engages in a business, trade, or profession shall be deemed to have a self-insured plan if it carries its own risk (whether by a failure to obtain insurance, or otherwise) in whole or in part.

(B) REPAYMENT REQUIRED.—

(i) AUTHORITY TO MAKE CONDITIONAL PAYMENT.—The Secretary may make payment under this title with respect to an item or service if a primary plan described in subparagraph (A)(ii) has not made or cannot reasonably be expected to make payment with respect to such item or service promptly (as determined in accordance with regulations). Any such payment by the Secretary shall be conditioned on reimbursement to the appropriate Trust Fund in accordance with the succeeding provisions of this subsection.

(ii) PRIMARY PLANS.—A primary plan, and an entity that receives payment from a primary plan, shall reimburse the appropriate Trust Fund for any payment made by the Secretary under this title with respect to an item or service if it is demonstrated that such primary plan has or had a responsibility to make payment with respect to such item or service. A primary plan's responsibility for such payment may be demonstrated by a judgment, a payment conditioned upon the recipient's compromise, waiver, or release (whether or not there is a determination or admission of liability) of payment for items or services included in a claim against the primary plan or the primary plan's insured, or by other means. If reimbursement is not made to the appropriate Trust Fund before the expiration of the 60-day period that begins on the date notice of, or information related to, a primary plan's responsibility for such payment or other information is received, the Secretary may charge interest (beginning with the date on which the notice or other information is received) on the amount of the reimbursement until reimbursement is made (at a rate determined by the Secretary in accordance with regulations of the Secretary of the Treasury applicable to charges for late payments).

(iii) ACTION BY UNITED STATES.—In order to recover payment made under this title for an item or service, the United States may bring an action against any or all entities that are or were required or responsible (directly, as an insurer or self-insurer, as a third-party administrator, as an employer that sponsors or contributes to a group health plan, or large group health plan, or otherwise) to make payment with respect to the same item or service (or any portion thereof) under a primary plan. The United States may, in accordance with paragraph (3)(A) collect double damages against any such entity. In addition, the United States may recover under this clause from any entity that has received payment from a primary plan or from the proceeds of a primary plan's payment to any entity. The United States may not recover from a third-party administrator under this clause in cases where the third-party administrator would not be able to recover the amount at issue from the employer or group health plan and is not employed by or under contract with the employer or group health plan at the time the

Social Security Law Added, Amended or Repealed

action for recovery is initiated by the United States or for whom it provides administrative services due to the insolvency or bankruptcy of the employer or plan.

(iv) SUBROGATION RIGHTS.—The United States shall be subrogated (to the extent of payment made under this title for such an item or service) to any right under this subsection of an individual or any other entity to payment with respect to such item or service under a primary plan.

(v) WAIVER OF RIGHTS.—The Secretary may waive (in whole or in part) the provisions of this subparagraph in the case of an individual claim if the Secretary determines that the waiver is in the best interests of the program established under this title.

(vi) CLAIMS-FILING PERIOD.—Notwithstanding any other time limits that may exist for filing a claim under an employer group health plan, the United States may seek to recover conditional payments in accordance with this subparagraph where the request for payment is submitted to the entity required or responsible under this subsection to pay with respect to the item or service (or any portion thereof) under a primary plan within the 3-year period beginning on the date on which the item or service was furnished.

* * *

(3) ENFORCEMENT.—

(A) PRIVATE CAUSE OF ACTION.—There is established a private cause of action for damages (which shall be in an amount double the amount otherwise provided) in the case of a primary plan which fails to provide for primary payment (or appropriate reimbursement) in accordance with paragraphs (1) and (2)(A).

* * *

(5) IDENTIFICATION OF SECONDARY PAYER SITUATIONS.—

(A) REQUESTING MATCHING INFORMATION.—

* * *

(ii) ADMINISTRATOR.—The Administrator of the Centers for Medicare & Medicaid Services shall request, not less often than annually, the Commissioner of the Social Security Administration to disclose to the Administrator the information described in subparagraph (B) of section 6103(l)(12) of the Internal Revenue Code of 1986.

* * *

(d) *For purposes of subsection (a)(1)(A), in the case of any item or service that is required to be provided pursuant to section 1867 to an individual who is entitled to benefits under this title, determinations as to whether the item or service is reasonable and necessary shall be made on the basis of the information available to the treating physician or practitioner (including the patient's presenting symptoms or complaint) at the time the item or service was ordered or furnished by the physician or practitioner (and not on the patient's principal diagnosis). When making such determinations with respect to such an item or service, the Secretary shall not consider the frequency with which the item or service was provided to the patient before or after the time of the admission or visit.*

[CCH Explanation at ¶ 801.]

2003 Amendments:

Section 301(a)(1) of the "Medicare Prescription Drug, Improvement, and Modernization Act of 2003," amended section 1862(b)(2) in subparagraph (A)(ii), by striking "promptly (as determined in accordance with regulations)".

Section 301(a)(2) of the "Medicare Prescription Drug, Improvement, and Modernization Act of 2003," amended section 1862(b)(2) in subparagraph (B) by redesignating clauses (i) through (v) as clauses (ii) through (vi), respectively; and by inserting before clause (ii), as so redesignated, new clause (i).

The amendments made by section 301(a) of the "Medicare Prescription Drug, Improvement, and Modernization Act of 2003," are effective as if included in the enactment of title II of the Medicare and Medicaid Budget Reconciliation Act of 1980 (PubLNo 96-499).

Section 301(b)(1) of the "Medicare Prescription Drug, Improvement, and Modernization Act of 2003," amended section 1862(b)(2)(A) in the matter following clause (ii), by inserting the following sentence at the end: "An entity that engages in a business, trade, or profession shall be deemed to have a self-insured plan if it carries its own risk (whether by a failure to obtain insurance, or otherwise) in whole or in part."

Section 301(b)(2) of the "Medicare Prescription Drug, Improvement, and Modernization Act of 2003," amended section 1862(b)(2)(B)(ii), as redesignated by subsection (a)(2)(A), by striking the first sentence and inserting the following: "A primary plan, and an entity that receives payment from a primary plan, shall reimburse the appropriate Trust Fund for any payment made by the Secretary under this title with respect to an item or service if it is demonstrated that such primary plan has or had a responsibility to make payment with respect to such item or service. A primary plan's responsibility for such payment may be demonstrated by a judgment, a payment conditioned upon the recipient's compromise, waiver, or release (whether or not there is a determination or admission of liability) of payment for items or services included in a claim against the primary plan or the primary plan's insured, or by other means."; and in the final sentence, by striking "on the date such notice or other information is received" and inserting "on the date notice of, or information related to, a primary plan's responsibility for such payment or other information is received".

Prior to being redesignated and amended, section 1862(b)(2)(B)(i) read as follows:

"(i) PRIMARY PLANS. Any payment under this title with respect to any item or service to which subparagraph (A) applies shall be conditioned on reimbursement to the appropriate Trust Fund established by this title when notice or other information is received that payment for such item or service has been or could be made under such subparagraph. If reimbursement is not made to the appropriate Trust Fund before the expiration of the 60-day period that begins on the date such notice or other information is received, the Secretary may charge interest (beginning with the date on which the notice or other information is received) on the amount of the reimbursement until reimbursement is made (at a rate determined by the Secretary in accordance with regulations of the Secretary of the Treasury applicable to charges for late payments)."

Section 301(b)(2) of the "Medicare Prescription Drug, Improvement, and Modernization Act of 2003," effective upon enactment, amended section 1862(b)(2)(B)(iii), as redesignated by subsection (a)(2)(A), by striking the first sentence and inserting the following: "In order to recover payment made under this title for an item or service, the United States may bring an action against any or all entities that are or were required or responsible (directly, as an insurer or self-insurer, as a third-party administrator, as an employer that sponsors or contributes to a group health plan, or large group health plan, or otherwise) to make payment with respect to the same item or service (or any portion thereof) under a primary plan. The United States may, in accordance with paragraph (3)(A) collect double damages against any such entity. In addition, the United States may recover under this clause from any entity that has received payment from a primary plan or from the proceeds of a primary plan's payment to any entity."

Prior to being redesignated and amended, section 1862(b)(2)(B)(ii) read as follows:

(ii) ACTION BY UNITED STATES."In order to recover payment under this title for such an item or service, the United States may bring an action against any entity which is required or responsible (directly, as a third-party administrator, or otherwise) to make payment with respect to such item or service (or any portion thereof) under a primary plan (and may, in accordance with paragraph (3)(A) collect double damages against that entity), or against any other entity (including any physician or provider) that has received payment from that entity with respect to the item or service, and may join or intervene in any action related to the events that gave rise to the need for the item or service. The United States may not recover from a third-party administrator under this clause in cases where the third-party administrator would not be able to recover the amount at issue from the employer or group health plan and is not employed by or under contract with the employer or group health plan at the time the action for recovery is initiated by the United States or for whom it provides administrative services due to the insolvency or bankruptcy of the employer or plan."

The amendments made by section 301(b) of the "Medicare Prescription Drug, Improvement, and Modernization Act of 2003," are effective as if included in the enactment of section 953 of the Omnibus Reconciliation Act of 1980 (PubLNo. 96-499).

Section 301(c) of the "Medicare Prescription Drug, Improvement, and Modernization Act of 2003," amended section 1862(b) in paragraph (1)(A), by moving the indentation of clauses (ii) through (v) 2 ems to the left; and in paragraph (3)(A), by striking "such" before "paragraphs".

The amendments made by section 301(c) of the "Medicare Prescription Drug, Improvement, and Modernization Act of 2003," are effective as if included in the enactment of section 953 of the Omnibus Reconciliation Act of 1980 (PubLNo. 96-499).

Section 900(e)(1)(J) of the "Medicare Prescription Drug, Improvement, and Modernization Act of 2003," effective upon enactment, amended section 1862(b)(5)(A)(ii) by striking "Health Care Financing Administration" and inserting "Centers for Medicare & Medicaid Services".

Section 944(a)(1) of the "Medicare Prescription Drug, Improvement, and Modernization Act of 2003," amended section 1862 by inserting after subsection (c), a new subsection (d).

This amendment is effective for items and services furnished on or after January 1, 2004.

[¶ 2280L] Sec. 1862. NATIONAL AND LOCAL COVERAGE DETERMINATION PROCESS

(k)(1) *Subject to paragraph (2), a group health plan (as defined in subsection (a)(1)(A)(v)) providing supplemental or secondary coverage to individuals also entitled to services under this title shall not require a medicare claims determination under this title for dental benefits specifically excluded under subsection (a)(12) as a condition of making a claims determination for such benefits under the group health plan.*

(2) *A group health plan may require a claims determination under this title in cases involving or appearing to involve inpatient dental hospital services or dental services expressly covered under this title pursuant to actions taken by the Secretary.*

(l)(1) FACTORS AND EVIDENCE USED IN MAKING NATIONAL COVERAGE DETERMINATIONS.—The Secretary shall make available to the public the factors considered in making national coverage determinations of whether an item or service is reasonable and necessary. The Secretary shall develop guidance documents to carry out this paragraph in a manner similar to the development of guidance documents under section 701(h) of the Federal Food, Drug, and Cosmetic Act (21 U.S.C. 371(h)).

(2) TIMEFRAME FOR DECISIONS ON REQUESTS FOR NATIONAL COVERAGE DETERMINATIONS.—In the case of a request for a national coverage determination that—

(A) does not require a technology assessment from an outside entity or deliberation from the Medicare Coverage Advisory Committee, the decision on the request shall be made not later than 6 months after the date of the request; or

§ 1862(l)(2)(A) ¶ 2280L

(B) requires such an assessment or deliberation and in which a clinical trial is not requested, the decision on the request shall be made not later than 9 months after the date of the request.

(3) PROCESS FOR PUBLIC COMMENT IN NATIONAL COVERAGE DETERMINATIONS.—

(A) PERIOD FOR PROPOSED DECISION.—Not later than the end of the 6-month period (or 9-month period for requests described in paragraph (2)(B)) that begins on the date a request for a national coverage determination is made, the Secretary shall make a draft of proposed decision on the request available to the public through the Internet website of the Centers for Medicare & Medicaid Services or other appropriate means.

(B) 30-DAY PERIOD FOR PUBLIC COMMENT.—Beginning on the date the Secretary makes a draft of the proposed decision available under subparagraph (A), the Secretary shall provide a 30-day period for public comment on such draft.

(C) 60-DAY PERIOD FOR FINAL DECISION.—Not later than 60 days after the conclusion of the 30-day period referred to under subparagraph (B), the Secretary shall—

(i) make a final decision on the request;

(ii) include in such final decision summaries of the public comments received and responses to such comments;

(iii) make available to the public the clinical evidence and other data used in making such a decision when the decision differs from the recommendations of the Medicare Coverage Advisory Committee; and

(iv) in the case of a final decision under clause (i) to grant the request for the national coverage determination, the Secretary shall assign a temporary or permanent code (whether existing or unclassified) and implement the coding change.

(4) CONSULTATION WITH OUTSIDE EXPERTS IN CERTAIN NATIONAL COVERAGE DETERMINATIONS.—With respect to a request for a national coverage determination for which there is not a review by the Medicare Coverage Advisory Committee, the Secretary shall consult with appropriate outside clinical experts.

(5) LOCAL COVERAGE DETERMINATION PROCESS.—

(A) PLAN TO PROMOTE CONSISTENCY OF COVERAGE DETERMINATIONS.—The Secretary shall develop a plan to evaluate new local coverage determinations to determine which determinations should be adopted nationally and to what extent greater consistency can be achieved among local coverage determinations.

(B) CONSULTATION.—The Secretary shall require the fiscal intermediaries or carriers providing services within the same area to consult on all new local coverage determinations within the area.

(C) DISSEMINATION OF INFORMATION.—The Secretary should serve as a center to disseminate information on local coverage determinations among fiscal intermediaries and carriers to reduce duplication of effort.

(6) NATIONAL AND LOCAL COVERAGE DETERMINATION DEFINED.—For purposes of this subsection—

(A) NATIONAL COVERAGE DETERMINATION.—The term "national coverage determination" means a determination by the Secretary with respect to whether or not a particular item or service is covered nationally under this title.

(B) LOCAL COVERAGE DETERMINATION.—The term "local coverage determination" has the meaning given that in section 1869(f)(2)(B).

[CCH Explanation at ¶ 796.]

2003 Amendments:

Section 731(a)(1)(B) of the "Medicare Prescription Drug, Improvement, and Modernization Act of 2003," amended 1862 by adding new section (l).

The amendments made by paragraph (l) shall apply to national coverage determinations as of January 1, 2004,

and section 1862(l)(5) of the Social Security Act, as added by such paragraph, shall apply to local coverage determinations made on or after July 1, 2004.

Section 950(a) of the "Medicare Prescription Drug, Improvement, and Modernization Act of 2003," amended section 1862 by adding at the end, new subsection (k).

The above amendment is effective 60 days after enactment of the Medicare Prescription Drug, Improvement, and Modernization Act of 2003.

[¶ 2280M] Sec. 1862. COVERAGE OF ROUTINE COSTS ASSOCIATED WITH CERTAIN CLINICAL TRIALS OF CATEGORY A DEVICES

(m)(1) IN GENERAL.—In the case of an individual entitled to benefits under part A, or enrolled under part B, or both who participates in a category A clinical trial, the Secretary shall not exclude under subsection (a)(1) payment for coverage of routine costs of care (as defined by the Secretary) furnished to such individual in the trial.

(2) CATEGORY A CLINICAL TRIAL.—For purposes of paragraph (1), a "category A clinical trial" means a trial of a medical device if—

(A) the trial is of an experimental/investigational (category A) medical device (as defined in regulations under section 405.201(b) of title 42, Code of Federal Regulations (as in effect as of September 1, 2003));

(B) the trial meets criteria established by the Secretary to ensure that the trial conforms to appropriate scientific and ethical standards; and

(C) in the case of a trial initiated before January 1, 2010, the device involved in the trial has been determined by the Secretary to be intended for use in the diagnosis, monitoring, or treatment of an immediately life-threatening disease or condition.

[CCH Explanation at ¶ 796.]

2003 Amendments:

Section 731(b)(1) of the "Medicare Prescription Drug, Improvement, and Modernization Act of 2003," amended section 1862, as amended by section 731(a), by adding at the end the following new subsection (m).

The amendment made by paragraph (1) shall apply to routine costs incurred on and after January 1, 2005, and, as of such date, section 411.15(o) of title 42, Code of Federal Regulations, is superseded to the extent inconsistent with section 1862(m) of the Social Security Act, as added by such paragraph.

[¶ 2285] Sec. 1865. EFFECT OF ACCREDITATION

[42 U.S.C. § 1395bb]

* * *

* * *

* * *

(b)(3)(B) The 210-day and 60-day deadlines specified in subparagraph (A) shall not apply in the case of any request for a finding with respect to accreditation of a provider entity to which the conditions and requirements of sections 1819 and 1861(j) apply.

* * *

2003 Amendments:

Section 736(a)(12) of the "Medicare Prescription Drug, Improvement, and Modernization Act of 2003," effective upon enactment, amended section 1865(b)(3)(B) by striking "section 1819 and 1861(j)" and inserting "sections 1819 and 1861(j)".

[¶ 2290] Sec. 1866 AGREEMENTS WITH PROVIDERS OF SERVICES; ENROLLMENT PROCESSES

[42 U.S.C. § 1395cc]

(a)(1) Any provider of services (except a fund designated for purposes of section 1814(g) and section 1835(e)) shall be qualified to participate under this title and shall be eligible for payments under this title if it files with the Secretary an agreement—

* * *

(O) to accept as payment in full for services that are covered under this title and are furnished to any individual enrolled with a Medicare+Choice organization under part C, with a PACE provider under section 1894 or 1934, or with an eligible organization with a risk-sharing contract under section 1876, under section 1876(i)(2)(A) (as in effect before February 1, 1985), under section 402(a) of the Social Security Amendments of 1967, or under section 222(a) of the Social Security Amendments of 1972, which does not have a contract (or, in the case of a PACE provider, contract or other agreement) establishing payment amounts for services furnished to members of the organization or PACE program eligible individuals enrolled with the PACE provider, the amounts that would be made as a payment in full under this title (less any payments under sections 1886(d)(11) and 1886(h)(3)(D)) if the individuals were not so enrolled,

* * *

(R) to contract only with a health care clearinghouse (as defined in section 1171) that meets each standard and implementation specification adopted or established under part C of title XI on or after the date on which the health care clearinghouse is required to comply with the standard or specification,

(S) in the case of a hospital that has a financial interest (as specified by the Secretary in regulations) in an entity to which individuals are referred as described in section 1861(ee)(2)(H)(ii), or in which such an entity has such a financial interest, or in which another entity has such a financial interest (directly or indirectly) with such hospital and such an entity, to maintain and disclose to the Secretary (in a form and manner specified by the Secretary) information on—

* * *

(iii) the percentage of such individuals who received such services from such provider (or another such provider),

(T) in the case of hospitals and critical access hospitals, to furnish to the Secretary such data as the Secretary determines appropriate pursuant to subparagraph (E) of section 1886(d)(12) to carry out such section,

(U) in the case of hospitals which furnish inpatient hospital services for which payment may be made under this title, to be a participating provider of medical care both—

(i) under the contract health services program funded by the Indian Health Service and operated by the Indian Health Service, an Indian tribe, or tribal organization (as those terms are defined in section 4 of the Indian Health Care Improvement Act), with respect to items and services that are covered under such program and furnished to an individual eligible for such items and services under such program; and

(ii) under any program funded by the Indian Health Service and operated by an urban Indian organization with respect to the purchase of items and services for an eligible urban Indian (as those terms are defined in such section 4),

in accordance with regulations promulgated by the Secretary regarding admission practices, payment methodology, and rates of payment (including the acceptance of no more than such payment rate as payment in full for such items and services, and

(V) in the case of hospitals that are not otherwise subject to the Occupational Safety and Health Act of 1970 (or a State occupational safety and health plan that is approved under 18(b) of such Act), to comply with the Bloodborne Pathogens standard under section 1910.1030 of title 29 of the Code of Federal Regulations (or as subsequently redesignated).

* * *
* * *

(b)(4)(A) A hospital that fails to comply with the requirement of subsection (a)(1)(V) (relating to the Bloodborne Pathogens standard) is subject to a civil money penalty in an amount described in subparagraph (B), but is not subject to termination of an agreement under this section.

(B) The amount referred to in subparagraph (A) is an amount that is similar to the amount of civil penalties that may be imposed under section 17 of the Occupational Safety and Health Act of 1970 for a violation of the Bloodborne Pathogens standard referred to in subsection (a)(1)(U) by a hospital that is subject to the provisions of such Act.

(C) A civil money penalty under this paragraph shall be imposed and collected in the same manner as civil money penalties under subsection (a) of section 1128A are imposed and collected under that section.

* * *

(h)(1)(A) Except as provided in paragraph (2), an institution or agency dissatisfied with a determination by the Secretary that it is not a provider of services or with a determination described in subsection (b)(2) shall be entitled to a hearing thereon by the Secretary (after reasonable notice) to the same extent as is provided in section 205(b), and to judicial review of the Secretary's final decision after such hearing as is provided in section 205(g), except that, in so applying such sections and in applying section 205(l) thereto, any reference therein to the Commissioner of Social Security or the Social Security Administration shall be considered a reference to the Secretary or the Department of Health and Human Services, respectively.

(B) An institution or agency described in subparagraph (A) that has filed for a hearing under subparagraph (A) shall have expedited access to judicial review under this subparagraph in the same manner as providers of services, suppliers, and individuals entitled to benefits under part A or enrolled under part B, or both, may obtain expedited access to judicial review under the process established under section 1869(b)(2). Nothing in this subparagraph shall be construed to affect the application of any remedy imposed under section 1819 during the pendency of an appeal under this subparagraph.

(C)(i) The Secretary shall develop and implement a process to expedite proceedings under this subsection in which—

(I) the remedy of termination of participation has been imposed;

(II) "a remedy described in clause (i) or (iii) of section 1819(h)(2)(B) has been imposed, but only if such remedy has been imposed on an immediate basis; or

(III) a determination has been made as to a finding of substandard quality of care that results in the loss of approval of a skilled nursing facility's nurse aide training program.

(ii) Under such process under clause (i), priority shall be provided in cases of termination described in clause (i)(I).

(iii) Nothing in this subparagraph shall be construed to affect the application of any remedy imposed under section 1819 during the pendency of an appeal under this subparagraph.

* * *

(j) ENROLLMENT PROCESS FOR PROVIDERS OF SERVICES AND SUPPLIERS.—

(1) ENROLLMENT PROCESS.—

(A) IN GENERAL.—The Secretary shall establish by regulation a process for the enrollment of providers of services and suppliers under this title.

(B) DEADLINES.—The Secretary shall establish by regulation procedures under which there are deadlines for actions on applications for enrollment (and, if applicable, renewal of enrollment). The Secretary shall monitor the performance of medicare administrative contractors in meeting the deadlines established under this subparagraph.

(C) CONSULTATION BEFORE CHANGING PROVIDER ENROLLMENT FORMS.—The Secretary shall consult with providers of services and suppliers before making changes in the provider enrollment forms required of such providers and suppliers to be eligible to submit claims for which payment may be made under this title.

(2) HEARING RIGHTS IN CASES OF DENIAL OR NONRENEWAL.—A provider of services or supplier whose application to enroll (or, if applicable, to renew enrollment) under this title is denied may have a hearing and judicial review of such denial under the procedures that apply under subsection (h)(1)(A) to a provider of services that is dissatisfied with a determination by the Secretary.

[CCH Explanation at ¶ 905 and 911.]
2003 Amendments:

Section 236(a)(1) of the "Medicare Prescription Drug, Improvement, and Modernization Act of 2003," amended section 1866(a)(1)(O) by striking "part C or" and inserting "part C, with a PACE provider under section 1894 or 1934, or"; by striking "(i)"; by striking "and (ii)"; by inserting "(or, in the case of a PACE provider, contract or other agreement)" after "have a contract"; and by striking "members of the organization" and inserting "members of the organization or PACE program eligible individuals enrolled with the PACE provider,".

The above amendment applies to services furnished on or after Jan. 1, 2004.

Section 505(b) of the "Medicare Prescription Drug, Improvement, and Modernization Act of 2003," amended section 1866(a)(1)(R) by striking "and" at the end; amended section 1866(a)(1)(S) by striking the period at the end and inserting ", and"; and by inserting after subparagraph (S) new subparagraph (T).

This amendment first applies to the wage index for discharges occurring on or after October 1, 2004.

Section 506(a)(1) of the "Medicare Prescription Drug, Improvement, and Modernization Act of 2003," amended section 1866(a)(1)(S) by striking "and" at the end; in subparagraph (T), by striking the period and inserting ", and"; and by inserting after subparagraph (T) new subparagraph (U).

This amendment applies as of a date specified by the Secretary of HHS, but in no case later than one year after the date of enactment, to Medicare participation agreements in effect (or entered into) on or after such date.

Section 736(a)(13) of the "Medicare Prescription Drug, Improvement, and Modernization Act of 2003," effective upon enactment, amended section 1866(b)(2) by moving subparagraph (D) 2 ems to the left.

[CCH Note: Existing law text reflects this change.]

Section 932(b) of the "Medicare Prescription Drug, Improvement, and Modernization Act of 2003," effective upon enactment, amended section 1866(h)(1) by inserting "(A)" after "(h)(1)"; and by adding at the end new subparagraph (B).

Section 932(c)(1) of the "Medicare Prescription Drug, Improvement, and Modernization Act of 2003," effective upon enactment, amended section 1866(h)(1), as amended by subsection (b), by adding at the end new subparagraph (C).

Section 936(a) of the "Medicare Prescription Drug, Improvement, and Modernization Act of 2003," effective upon enactment, amended section 1866 by adding at the end of the heading the following: "; ENROLLMENT PROCESSES" and by adding at the end new subsection (j).

Section 947(a)(1) of the "Medicare Prescription Drug, Improvement, and Modernization Act of 2003," effective upon enactment, amended section 1866(a)(1) in subparagraph (T), by striking "and" at the end; in subparagraph (U), by striking the period at the end and inserting ", and"; and by inserting after subparagraph (U) new subparagraph (V).

Section 947(a)(2) of the "Medicare Prescription Drug, Improvement, and Modernization Act of 2003," effective upon enactment, amended section 1866(b) by adding at the end new paragraph (4).

[¶2291A] Sec. 1866B. PROVISIONS FOR ADMINISTRATION OF DEMONSTRATION PROGRAM

* * *

(b) CONTRACTS FOR PROGRAM ADMINISTRATION.—

* * *

(7) FUNCTIONS OF PROGRAM ADMINISTRATOR.—A program administrator shall perform any or all of the following functions, as specified by the Secretary:

* * *

(D) PAYMENT OF BONUSES.—Using such guidelines as the Secretary shall establish, and subject to the approval of the Secretary, make bonus payments as described in subsection (c)(2)(B) to entities furnishing items or services for which payment may be made under the program.

* * *

2003 Amendments:

Section 736(c)(5) of the "Medicare Prescription Drug, Improvement, and Modernization Act of 2003," effective upon enactment, amended section 1866B(b)(7)(D) by striking "(c)(2)(A)(ii)" and inserting "(c)(2)(B)".

[¶2291B] Sec. 1866C. HEALTH CARE QUALITY DEMONSTRATION PROGRAM

(a) DEFINITIONS.—In this section:

(1) BENEFICIARY.—The term "beneficiary" means n individual who is entitled to benefits under part A and enrolled under part B, including any individual who is enrolled in a Medicare Advantage plan under part C.

(2) HEALTH CARE GROUP.—

(A) IN GENERAL.—The term "health care group" means—

(i) a group of physicians that is organized at least in part for the purpose of providing physician's services under this title;

(ii) an integrated health care delivery system that delivers care through coordinated hospitals, clinics, home health agencies, ambulatory surgery centers, skilled nursing facilities, rehabilitation facilities and clinics, and employed, independent, or contracted physicians; or

(iii) an organization representing regional coalitions of groups or systems described in clause (i) or (ii).

(B) INCLUSION.—As the Secretary determines appropriate, a health care group may include a hospital or any other individual or entity furnishing items or services for which payment may be made under this title that is affiliated with the health care group under an arrangement structured so that such hospital, individual, or entity participates in a demonstration project under this section.

(3) PHYSICIAN.—Except as otherwise provided for by the Secretary, the term "physician" means any individual who furnishes services that may be paid for as physicians' services under this title.

(b) DEMONSTRATION PROJECTS.—The Secretary shall establish a 5-year demonstration program under which the Secretary shall approve demonstration projects that examine health delivery factors that encourage the delivery of improved quality in patient care, including—

(1) the provision of incentives to improve the safety of care provided to beneficiaries;

(2) the appropriate use of best practice guidelines by providers and services by beneficiaries;

(3) reduced scientific uncertainty in the delivery of care through the examination of variations in the utilization and allocation of services, and outcomes measurement and research;

(4) encourage shared decision making between providers and patients;

(5) the provision of incentives for improving the quality and safety of care and achieving the efficient allocation of resources;

(6) the appropriate use of culturally and ethnically sensitive health care delivery; and

(7) the financial effects on the health care marketplace of altering the incentives for care delivery and changing the allocation of resources.

(c) ADMINISTRATION BY CONTRACT.—

(1) IN GENERAL.—Except as otherwise provided in this section, the Secretary may administer the demonstration program established under this section in a manner that is similar to the manner in which the demonstration program established under section 1866A is administered in accordance with section 1866B.

(2) ALTERNATIVE PAYMENT SYSTEMS.—A health care group that receives assistance under this section may, with respect to the demonstration project to be carried out with such assistance, include proposals for the use of alternative payment systems for items and services provided to beneficiaries by the group that are designed to—

(A) encourage the delivery of high quality care while accomplishing the objectives described in subsection (b); and

(B) streamline documentation and reporting requirements otherwise required under this title.

(3) BENEFITS.—A health care group that receives assistance under this section may, with respect to the demonstration project to be carried out with such assistance, include modifications to the package of benefits available under the original medicare fee-for-service program under parts A and B or the package of benefits available through a Medicare Advantage plan under part C. The criteria employed under the demonstration program under this section to evaluate outcomes and determine best practice guidelines and incentives shall not be used as a basis for the denial of medicare benefits under the demonstration program to patients against their wishes (or if the patient is incompetent, against the wishes of the patient's surrogate) on the basis of the patient's age or expected length of life or of the patient's present or predicted disability, degree of medical dependency, or quality of life.

(d) ELIGIBILITY CRITERIA.—To be eligible to receive assistance under this section, an entity shall—

(1) be a health care group;

(2) meet quality standards established by the Secretary, including—

(A) the implementation of continuous quality improvement mechanisms that are aimed at integrating community-based support services, primary care, and referral care;

(B) the implementation of activities to increase the delivery of effective care to beneficiaries;

(C) encouraging patient participation in preference-based decisions;

(D) the implementation of activities to encourage the coordination and integration of medical service delivery; and

(E) the implementation of activities to measure and document the financial impact on the health care marketplace of altering the incentives of health care delivery and changing the allocation of resources; and

(3) meet such other requirements as the Secretary may establish.

(e) WAIVER AUTHORITY.—The Secretary may waive such requirements of titles XI and XVIII as may be necessary to carry out the purposes of the demonstration program established under this section.

(f) BUDGET NEUTRALITY.—With respect to the 5-year period of the demonstration program under subsection (b), the aggregate expenditures under this title for such period shall not exceed the aggregate expenditures that would have been expended under this title if the program established under this section had not been implemented.

(g) NOTICE REQUIREMENTS.—In the case of an individual that receives health care items or services under a demonstration program carried out under this section, the Secretary shall ensure that such individual is notified of any waivers of coverage or payment rules that are applicable to such individual under this title as a result of the participation of the individual in such program.

(h) PARTICIPATION AND SUPPORT BY FEDERAL AGENCIES.—In carrying out the demonstration program under this section, the Secretary may direct—

(1) the Director of the National Institutes of Health to expand the efforts of the Institutes to evaluate current medical technologies and improve the foundation for evidence-based practice;

(2) the Administrator of the Agency for Healthcare Research and Quality to, where possible and appropriate, use the program under this section as a laboratory for the study of quality improvement strategies and to evaluate, monitor, and disseminate information relevant to such program; and

(3) the Administrator of the Centers for Medicare & Medicaid Services and the Administrator of the Center for Medicare Choices to support linkages of relevant medicare data to registry information from participating health care groups for the beneficiary populations served by the participating groups, for analysis supporting the purposes of the demonstration program, consistent with the applicable provisions of the Health Insurance Portability and Accountability Act of 1996.

[CCH Explanation at ¶785.]

2003 Amendments:

Section 646 of the "Medicare Prescription Drug, Improvement, and Modernization Act of 2003," effective upon enactment, added section 1866C.

[¶2295] Sec. 1867. EXAMINATION AND TREATMENT FOR EMERGENCY MEDICAL CONDITIONS AND WOMEN IN LABOR

[42 U.S.C. §1395dd]

* * *

(d) ENFORCEMENT.—

(1) CIVIL MONETARY PENALTIES.—

* * *

(B) Subject to subparagraph (C), any physician who is responsible for the examination, treatment, or transfer of an individual in a participating hospital, including a physician on-call for the care of such an individual, and who negligently violates a requirement of this section, including a physician who—

* * *

(ii) misrepresents an individual's condition or other information, including a hospital's obligations under this section,

is subject to a civil money penalty of not more than $50,000 for each such violation and, if the violation is gross and flagrant or is repeated, to exclusion from participation in this title and State health care programs. The provisions of section 1128A (other than the first and second sentences of subsection (a) and subsection (b)) shall apply to a civil money penalty and exclusion under this subparagraph in the same manner as such provisions apply with respect to a penalty, exclusion, or proceeding under section 1128A(a).

Social Security Law Added, Amended or Repealed

* * *

(3) CONSULTATION WITH PEER REVIEW ORGANIZATIONS.—In considering allegations of violations of the requirements of this section in imposing sanctions under paragraph (1) or in terminating a hospital's participation under this title, the Secretary shall request the appropriate utilization and quality control peer review organization (with a contract under part B of title XI) to assess whether the individual involved had an emergency medical condition which had not been stabilized, and provide a report on its findings. Except in the case in which a delay would jeopardize the health or safety of individuals, the Secretary shall request such a review before effecting a sanction under paragraph (1) and shall provide a period of at least 60 days for such review. Except in the case in which a delay would jeopardize the health or safety of individuals, the Secretary shall also request such a review before making a compliance determination as part of the process of terminating a hospital's participation under this title for violations related to the appropriateness of a medical screening examination, stabilizing treatment, or an appropriate transfer as required by this section, and shall provide a period of 5 days for such review. The Secretary shall provide a copy of the organization's report to the hospital or physician consistent with confidentiality requirements imposed on the organization under such part B.

(4) NOTICE UPON CLOSING AN INVESTIGATION.—The Secretary shall establish a procedure to notify hospitals and physicians when an investigation under this section is closed.

(e) DEFINITIONS.—In this section:

(1) The term "emergency medical condition" means—

* * *

(B) with respect to a pregnant woman who is having contractions—

* * *

(2) The term "participating hospital" means a hospital that has entered into a provider agreement under section 1866.

* * *

[CCH Explanation at ¶584.]
2003 Amendments:

Section 736(a)(14)(A) of the "Medicare Prescription Drug, Improvement, and Modernization Act of 2003," effective upon enactment, amended section 1867(d)(1)(B)(ii) in the matter following clause (ii), by striking "is is" and inserting "is".

Section 736(a)(14)(B) of the "Medicare Prescription Drug, Improvement, and Modernization Act of 2003," effective upon enactment, amended section 1867(e)(1)(B), by striking "a pregnant women" and inserting "a pregnant woman".

Section 736(a)(14)(C) of the "Medicare Prescription Drug, Improvement, and Modernization Act of 2003," effective upon enactment, amended section 1867(e)(2), by striking "means hospital" and inserting "means a hospital".

Section 944(b) of the "Medicare Prescription Drug, Improvement, and Modernization Act of 2003," effective upon enactment, amended section 1867(d) by adding at the end new paragraph (4).

Section 944(c) of the "Medicare Prescription Drug, Improvement, and Modernization Act of 2003," effective upon enactment, amended section 1867(d)(3) in the first sentence, by inserting "or in terminating a hospital's participation under this title" after "in imposing sanctions under paragraph (1)"; and by adding at the end the following new sentences: "Except in the case in which a delay would jeopardize the health or safety of individuals, the Secretary shall also request such a review before making a compliance determination as part of the process of terminating a hospital's participation under this title for violations related to the appropriateness of a medical screening examination, stabilizing treatment, or an appropriate transfer as required by this section, and shall provide a period of 5 days for such review. The Secretary shall provide a copy of the organization's report to the hospital or physician consistent with confidentiality requirements imposed on the organization under such part B.".

The amendments made by section 944(c) of the "Medicare Prescription Drug, Improvement, and Modernization Act of 2003," apply to terminations of participation initiated on or after the date of the enactment of the "Medicare Prescription Drug, Improvement, and Modernization Act of 2003."

[¶2300] Sec. 1868. PRACTICING PHYSICIANS ADVISORY COUNCIL; COUNCIL FOR TECHNOLOGY AND INNOVATION

[42 U.S.C. §1395ee]

(a) PRACTICING PHYSICIANS ADVISORY COUNCIL.—

(1) The Secretary shall appoint, based upon nominations submitted by medical organizations representing physicians, a Practicing Physicians Advisory Council (in this subsection referred to as the "Council") to be composed of 15 physicians, each of whom has submitted at least 250 claims for physicians' services under this title in the previous year. At least 11 of the members of the Council shall be physicians described in section 1861(r)(1) and the members of

the Council shall include both participating and nonparticipating physicians and physicians practicing in rural areas and underserved urban areas.

* * *

(b) COUNCIL FOR TECHNOLOGY AND INNOVATION.—(1) ESTABLISHMENT.—The Secretary shall establish a Council for Technology and Innovation within the Centers for Medicare & Medicaid Services (in this section referred to as "CMS").

(2) COMPOSITION.—The Council shall be composed of senior CMS staff and clinicians and shall be chaired by the Executive Coordinator for Technology and Innovation (appointed or designated under paragraph (4)).

(3) DUTIES.—The Council shall coordinate the activities of coverage, coding, and payment processes under this title with respect to new technologies and procedures, including new drug therapies, and shall coordinate the exchange of information on new technologies between CMS and other entities that make similar decisions.

(4) EXECUTIVE COORDINATOR FOR TECHNOLOGY AND INNOVATION.—The Secretary shall appoint (or designate) a noncareer appointee (as defined in section 3132(a)(7) of title 5, United States Code) who shall serve as the Executive Coordinator for Technology and Innovation. Such executive coordinator shall report to the Administrator of CMS, shall chair the Council, shall oversee the execution of its duties, and shall serve as a single point of contact for outside groups and entities regarding the coverage, coding, and payment processes under this title.

[CCH Explanation at ¶ 795 and 942.]

2003 Amendments:

Section 942(a)(1) of the "Medicare Prescription Drug, Improvement, and Modernization Act of 2003," effective upon enactment, amended section 1868 by adding at the end of the heading the following: "; COUNCIL FOR TECHNOLOGY AND INNOVATION"; by inserting "PRACTICING PHYSICIANS ADVISORY COUNCIL.—(1)" after "(a)"; in paragraph (1), as redesignated under paragraph (2) of this Act, by striking "in this section" and inserting "in this subsection"; by redesignating subsections (b) and (c) as paragraphs (2) and (3), respectively; and by adding at the end new subsection (b).

[¶ 2305] Sec. 1869. DETERMINATIONS; APPEALS

[42 U.S.C. § 1395ff]

(a) INITIAL DETERMINATIONS.—

* * *

(3) REDETERMINATIONS.—

* * *

(C) DEADLINES.—

* * *

(ii) CONCLUDING REDETERMINATIONS.—Redeterminations shall be concluded by not later than the 60-day period beginning on the date the fiscal intermediary or the carrier, as the case may be, receives a request for a redetermination. Notice of such determination shall be mailed to the individual filing the claim before the conclusion of such 60-day period.

* * *

(4) REQUIREMENTS OF NOTICE OF DETERMINATIONS.—With respect to an initial determination insofar as it results in a denial of a claim for benefits—

(A) the written notice on the determination shall include—

(i) the reasons for the determination, including whether a local medical review policy or a local coverage determination was used;

(ii) the procedures for obtaining additional information concerning the determination, including the information described in subparagraph (B); and

(iii) notification of the right to seek a redetermination or otherwise appeal the determination and instructions on how to initiate such a redetermination under this section;

(B) such written notice shall be provided in printed form and written in a manner calculated to be understood by the individual entitled to benefits under part A or enrolled under part B, or both; and

(C) the individual provided such written notice may obtain, upon request, information on the specific provision of the policy, manual, or regulation used in making the redetermination.

(5) REQUIREMENTS OF NOTICE OF REDETERMINATIONS.—With respect to a redetermination insofar as it results in a denial of a claim for benefits—

(A) the written notice on the redetermination shall include—

(i) the specific reasons for the redetermination;

(ii) as appropriate, a summary of the clinical or scientific evidence used in making the redetermination;

(iii) a description of the procedures for obtaining additional information concerning the redetermination; and

(iv) notification of the right to appeal the redetermination and instructions on how to initiate such an appeal under this section;

(B) such written notice shall be provided in printed form and written in a manner calculated to be understood by the individual entitled to benefits under part A or enrolled under part B, or both; and

(C) the individual provided such written notice may obtain, upon request, information on the specific provision of the policy, manual, or regulation used in making the redetermination.

(b) APPEAL RIGHTS.—

(1) IN GENERAL.—

(A) RECONSIDERATION OF INITIAL DETERMINATION.—Subject to subparagraph (D), any individual dissatisfied with any initial determination under subsection (a)(1) shall be entitled to reconsideration of the determination, and, subject to subparagraphs (D) and (E), a hearing thereon by the Secretary to the same extent as is provided in section 205(b) and, subject to paragraph (2), to judicial review of the Secretary's final decision after such hearing as is provided in section 205(g). For purposes of the preceding sentence, any reference to the 'Commissioner of Social Security' or the 'Social Security Administration' in subsection (g) or (l) of section 205 shall be considered a reference to the "Secretary" or the "Department of Health and Human Services", respectively.

* * *

(E) AMOUNTS IN CONTROVERSY.—

* * *

(iii) ADJUSTMENT OF DOLLAR AMOUNTS.—For requests for hearings or judicial review made in a year after 2004, the dollar amounts specified in clause (i) shall be equal to such dollar amounts increased by the percentage increase in the medical care component of the consumer price index for all urban consumers (U.S. city average) for July 2003 to the July preceding the year involved. Any amount determined under the previous sentence that is not a multiple of $10 shall be rounded to the nearest multiple of $10.

(F) EXPEDITED PROCEEDINGS.—

* * *

(ii) REFERENCE TO EXPEDITED ACCESS TO JUDICIAL REVIEW.—For the provision relating to expedited access to judicial review, see paragraph (2).

* * *

(2) EXPEDITED ACCESS TO JUDICIAL REVIEW.—

(A) IN GENERAL.—The Secretary shall establish a process under which a provider of services or supplier that furnishes an item or service or an individual entitled to benefits under part A or enrolled under part B, or both, who has filed an appeal under paragraph (1) (other than an appeal filed under paragraph (1)(F)(i)) may obtain access to judicial review when a review entity (described in subparagraph (D)), on its own motion or at the request of the appellant, determines that the Departmental Appeals Board does not have the authority to decide the question of law or regulation relevant to the matters in controversy and that there is no material issue of fact in dispute. The appellant may make such request only once with respect to a question of law or regulation for a specific matter in dispute in a case of an appeal.

(B) PROMPT DETERMINATIONS.—If, after or coincident with appropriately filing a request for an administrative hearing, the appellant requests a determination by the appropriate review entity that the Departmental Appeals Board does not have the authority to decide the question of law or regulations relevant to the matters in controversy and that there is no material issue of fact in dispute, and if such request is accompanied by the documents and materials as the appropriate review entity shall require for purposes of making such determination, such review entity shall make a determination on the request in writing within 60 days after the date such review entity receives the request and such accompanying documents and materials. Such a determination by such review entity shall be considered a final decision and not subject to review by the Secretary.

(C) ACCESS TO JUDICIAL REVIEW.—

(i) IN GENERAL.—If the appropriate review entity—

(I) determines that there are no material issues of fact in dispute and that the only issues to be adjudicated are ones of law or regulation that the Departmental Appeals Board does not have authority to decide; or

(II) fails to make such determination within the period provided under subparagraph (B), then the appellant may bring a civil action as described in this subparagraph.

(ii) DEADLINE FOR FILING.—Such action shall be filed, in the case described in—

(I) clause (i)(I), within 60 days of the date of the determination described in such clause; or

(II) clause (i)(II), within 60 days of the end of the period provided under subparagraph (B) for the determination.

(iii) VENUE.—Such action shall be brought in the district court of the United States for the judicial district in which the appellant is located (or, in the case of an action brought jointly by more than one applicant, the judicial district in which the greatest number of applicants are located) or in the District Court for the District of Columbia.

(iv) INTEREST ON ANY AMOUNTS IN CONTROVERSY.—Where a provider of services or supplier is granted judicial review pursuant to this paragraph, the amount in controversy (if any) shall be subject to annual interest beginning on the first day of the first month beginning after the 60-day period as determined pursuant to clause (ii) and equal to the rate of interest on obligations issued for purchase by the Federal Supplementary Medical Insurance Trust Fund for the month in which the civil action authorized under this paragraph is commenced, to be awarded by the reviewing court in favor of the prevailing party. No interest awarded pursuant to the preceding sentence shall be deemed income or cost for the purposes of determining reimbursement due providers of services or suppliers under this title.

(D) REVIEW ENTITY DEFINED.—For purposes of this subsection, the term 'review entity' means an entity of up to three reviewers who are administrative law judges or members of the Departmental Appeals Board selected for purposes of making determinations under this paragraph.".

(3) REQUIRING FULL AND EARLY PRESENTATION OF EVIDENCE BY PROVIDERS.—A provider of services or supplier may not introduce evidence in any appeal under this section that was not presented at the reconsideration conducted by the qualified independent contractor under subsection (c),

unless there is good cause which precluded the introduction of such evidence at or before that reconsideration.

(c) CONDUCT OF RECONSIDERATIONS BY INDEPENDENT CONTRACTORS.—

* * *

(3) REQUIREMENTS.—Any qualified independent contractor entering into a contract with the Secretary under this subsection shall meet all of the following requirements:

(A) IN GENERAL.—The qualified independent contractor shall perform such duties and functions and assume such responsibilities as may be required by the Secretary to carry out the provisions of this subsection, and shall have sufficient medical, legal, and other expertise (including knowledge of the program under this title) and sufficient staffing to make reconsiderations under this subsection.

(B) RECONSIDERATIONS.—

(i) IN GENERAL.—The qualified independent contractor shall review initial determinations. Where an initial determination is made with respect to whether an item or service is reasonable and necessary for the diagnosis or treatment of illness or injury (under section 1862(a)(1)(A)), such review shall include consideration of the facts and circumstances of the initial determination by a panel of physicians or other appropriate health care professionals and any decisions with respect to the reconsideration shall be based on applicable information, including clinical experience (including the medical records of the individual involved) and medical, technical, and scientific evidence.

* * *

(C) DEADLINES FOR DECISIONS.—

(i) RECONSIDERATIONS.—Except as provided in clauses (iii) and (iv), the qualified independent contractor shall conduct and conclude a reconsideration under subparagraph (B), and mail the notice of the decision with respect to the reconsideration by not later than the end of the 60-day period beginning on the date a request for reconsideration has been timely filed.

* * *

(D) QUALIFICATIONS FOR REVIEWERS.—The requirements of subsection (g) shall be met (relating to qualifications of reviewing professionals).

(E) EXPLANATION OF DECISION.—Any decision with respect to a reconsideration of a qualified independent contractor shall be in writing, be written in a manner calculated to be understood by the individual entitled to benefits under part A or enrolled under part B, or both, and shall include (to the extent appropriate), and shall include a detailed explanation of the decision as well as a discussion of the pertinent facts and applicable regulations applied in making such decision and a notification of the right to appeal such determination and instructions on how to initiate such appeal under this section, and in the case of a determination of whether an item or service is reasonable and necessary for the diagnosis or treatment of illness or injury (under section 1862(a)(1)(A)) an explanation of the medical and scientific rationale for the decision.

* * *

(I) DATA COLLECTION.—

* * *

(ii) TYPE OF DATA COLLECTED.—Each qualified independent contractor shall keep accurate records of each decision made, consistent with standards established by the Secretary for such purpose. Such records shall be maintained in an electronic database in a manner that provides for identification of the following:

* * *

(III) Situations suggesting the need for changes in national or local coverage determination.

§1869(c)(3)(I)(ii)(III) ¶2305

(IV) Situations suggesting the need for changes in local coverage determinations.

* * *

(J) Hearings by the Secretary.—The qualified independent contractor shall (i) submit such information as is required for an appeal of a decision of the contractor, and (ii) participate in such hearings as required by the Secretary.

(K) Independence Requirements.—

(i) In general.—Subject to clause (ii), a qualified independent contractor shall not conduct any activities in a case unless the entity—

(I) is not a related party (as defined in subsection (g)(5));

(II) does not have a material familial, financial, or professional relationship with such a party in relation to such case; and

(III) does not otherwise have a conflict of interest with such a party.

(ii) Exception for reasonable compensation.—Nothing in clause (i) shall be construed to prohibit receipt by a qualified independent contractor of compensation from the Secretary for the conduct of activities under this section if the compensation is provided consistent with clause (iii).

(iii) Limitations on entity compensation.—Compensation provided by the Secretary to a qualified independent contractor in connection with reviews under this section shall not be contingent on any decision rendered by the contractor or by any reviewing professional.

(4) Number of Qualified Independent Contractors.—The Secretary shall enter into contracts with a sufficient number of qualified independent contractors (but not fewer than 4 such contractors) to conduct reconsiderations consistent with the timeframes applicable under this subsection.

* * *

(d) Deadlines for Hearings by the Secretary; Notice.—

* * *

(4) Notice.—Notice of the decision of an administrative law judge shall be in writing in a manner calculated to be understood by the individual entitled to benefits under part A or enrolled under part B, or both, and shall include—

(A) the specific reasons for the determination (including, to the extent appropriate, a summary of the clinical or scientific evidence used in making the determination);

(B) the procedures for obtaining additional information concerning the decision; and

(C) notification of the right to appeal the decision and instructions on how to initiate such an appeal under this section.

* * *

(f) Review of Coverage Determinations.—

* * *

(2) Local Coverage Determination.—

(A) In General.—Review of any local coverage determination shall be subject to the following limitations:

(i) Upon the filing of a complaint by an aggrieved party, such a determination shall be reviewed by an administrative law judge. The administrative law judge—

* * *

(4) Pending National Coverage Determinations.—

(A) In General.—In the event the Secretary has not issued a national coverage or noncoverage determination with respect to a particular type or class of items or services, an aggrieved person (as described in paragraph (5)) may submit to the Secretary a request to make such a determination with respect to such items or services. By not later than the end of the 90-day period beginning on the date the Secretary receives such a request (notwithstanding the receipt by the Secretary of new evidence (if any) during such 90-day period), the Secretary shall take one of the following actions:

* * *

(iv) Issue a notice that states that the Secretary has not completed a review of the request for a national coverage determination and that includes an identification of the remaining steps in the Secretary's review process and a deadline by which the Secretary will complete the review and take an action described in clause (i), (ii), or(iii).

(B) Deemed Action by the Secretary.—In the case of an action described in subparagraph (A)(iv), if the Secretary fails to take an action referred to in such clause by the deadline specified by the Secretary under such clause, then the Secretary is deemed to have taken an action described in subparagraph (A)(iii) as of the deadline.

(C) Explanation of Determination.—When issuing a determination under subparagraph (A), the Secretary shall include an explanation of the basis for the determination. An action taken under subparagraph (A) (other than clause (iv)) is deemed to be a national coverage determination for purposes of review under (paragraph (1)(A).

* * *

(g) Qualifications of Reviewers.—

(1) In general.—In reviewing determinations under this section, a qualified independent contractor shall assure that—

(A) each individual conducting a review shall meet the qualifications of paragraph (2);

(B) compensation provided by the contractor to each such reviewer is consistent with paragraph (3); and

(C) in the case of a review by a panel described in subsection (c)(3)(B) composed of physicians or other health care professionals (each in this subsection referred to as a 'reviewing professional'), a reviewing professional meets the qualifications described in paragraph (4) and, where a claim is regarding the furnishing of treatment by a physician (allopathic or osteopathic) or the provision of items or services by a physician (allopathic or osteopathic), a reviewing professional shall be a physician (allopathic or osteopathic).

(2) Independence.—

(A) In general.—Subject to subparagraph (B), each individual conducting a review in a case shall—

(i) not be a related party (as defined in paragraph (5));

(ii) not have a material familial, financial, or professional relationship with such a party in the case under review; and

(iii) not otherwise have a conflict of interest with such a party.

(B) Exception.—Nothing in subparagraph (A) shall be construed to—

(i) prohibit an individual, solely on the basis of a participation agreement with a fiscal intermediary, carrier, or other contractor, from serving as a reviewing professional if—

(I) the individual is not involved in the provision of items or services in the case under review;

(II) the fact of such an agreement is disclosed to the Secretary and the individual entitled to benefits under part A or enrolled under part B, or both, or such individual's authorized representative, and neither party objects; and

(III) the individual is not an employee of the intermediary, carrier, or contractor and does not provide services exclusively or primarily to or on behalf of such intermediary, carrier, or contractor;

(ii) prohibit an individual who has staff privileges at the institution where the treatment involved takes place from serving as a reviewer merely on the basis of having such staff privileges if the existence of such privileges is disclosed to the Secretary and such individual (or authorized representative), and neither party objects; or

(iii) prohibit receipt of compensation by a reviewing professional from a contractor if the compensation is provided consistent with paragraph (3).

For purposes of this paragraph, the term 'participation agreement' means an agreement relating to the provision of health care services by the individual and does not include the provision of services as a reviewer under this subsection.

(3) LIMITATIONS ON REVIEWER COMPENSATION.—Compensation provided by a qualified independent contractor to a reviewer in connection with a review under this section shall not be contingent on the decision rendered by the reviewer.

(4) LICENSURE AND EXPERTISE.—Each reviewing professional shall be—

(A) a physician (allopathic or osteopathic) who is appropriately credentialed or licensed in one or more States to deliver health care services and has medical expertise in the field of practice that is appropriate for the items or services at issue; or

(B) a health care professional who is legally authorized in one or more States (in accordance with State law or the State regulatory mechanism provided by State law) to furnish the health care items or services at issue and has medical expertise in the field of practice that is appropriate for such items or services.

(5) RELATED PARTY DEFINED.—For purposes of this section, the term 'related party' means, with respect to a case under this title involving a specific individual entitled to benefits under part A or enrolled under part B, or both, any of the following:

(A) The Secretary, the medicare administrative contractor involved, or any fiduciary, officer, director, or employee of the Department of Health and Human Services, or of such contractor.

(B) The individual (or authorized representative).

(C) The health care professional that provides the items or services involved in the case.

(D) The institution at which the items or services (or treatment) involved in the case are provided.

(E) The manufacturer of any drug or other item that is included in the items or services involved in the case.

(F) Any other party determined under any regulations to have a substantial interest in the case involved.

(h) PRIOR DETERMINATION PROCESS FOR CERTAIN ITEMS AND SERVICES.—(1) ESTABLISHMENT OF PROCESS.—(A) IN GENERAL.—.—With respect to a medicare administrative contractor that has a contract under section 1874A that provides for making payments under this title with respect to physicians' services (as defined in section 1848(j)(3)), the Secretary shall establish a prior determination process that meets the requirements of this subsection and that shall be applied by such contractor in the case of eligible requesters.

(B) ELIGIBLE REQUESTER.—For purposes of this subsection, each of the following shall be an eligible requester:

(i) A participating physician, but only with respect to physicians' services to be furnished to an individual who is entitled to benefits under this title and who has consented to the physician making the request under this subsection for those physicians' services.

(ii) An individual entitled to benefits under this title, but only with respect to a physicians' service for which the individual receives, from a physician, an advance beneficiary notice under section 1879(a).

(2) SECRETARIAL FLEXIBILITY.—The Secretary shall establish by regulation reasonable limits on the physicians' services for which a prior determination of coverage may be requested under this subsection. In establishing such limits, the Secretary may consider the dollar amount involved with respect to the physicians' service, administrative costs and burdens, and other relevant factors.

(3) REQUEST FOR PRIOR DETERMINATION.—(A) IN GENERAL.—Subject to paragraph (2), under the process established under this subsection an eligible requester may submit to the contractor a request for a determination, before the furnishing of a physicians' service, as to whether the physicians' service is covered under this title consistent with the applicable requirements of section 1862(a)(1)(A) (relating to medical necessity).

(B) ACCOMPANYING DOCUMENTATION.—The Secretary may require that the request be accompanied by a description of the physicians' service, supporting documentation relating to the medical necessity for the physicians' service, and any other appropriate documentation. In the case of a request submitted by an eligible requester who is described in paragraph (1)(B)(ii), the Secretary may require that the request also be accompanied by a copy of the advance beneficiary notice involved.

(4) RESPONSE TO REQUEST.—(A) IN GENERAL.—Under such process, the contractor shall provide the eligible requester with written notice of a determination as to whether—

(i) the physicians' service is so covered;

(ii) the physicians' service is not so covered; or

(iii) the contractor lacks sufficient information to make a coverage determination with respect to the physicians' service.

(B) CONTENTS OF NOTICE FOR CERTAIN DETERMINATIONS.—(i) NONCOVERAGE.—If the contractor makes the determination described in subparagraph (A)(ii), the contractor shall include in the notice a brief explanation of the basis for the determination, including on what national or local coverage or noncoverage determination (if any) the determination is based, and a description of any applicable rights under subsection (a).

(ii) INSUFFICIENT INFORMATION.—If the contractor makes the determination described in subparagraph (A)(iii), the contractor shall include in the notice a description of the additional information required to make the coverage determination.

(C) DEADLINE TO RESPOND.—Such notice shall be provided within the same time period as the time period applicable to the contractor providing notice of initial determinations on a claim for benefits under subsection (a)(2)(A).

(D) INFORMING BENEFICIARY IN CASE OF PHYSICIAN REQUEST.—In the case of a request by a participating physician under paragraph (1)(B)(i), the process shall provide that the individual to whom the physicians' service is proposed to be furnished shall be informed of any determination described in subparagraph (A)(ii) (relating to a determination of non-coverage) and the right (referred to in paragraph (6)(B)) to obtain the physicians' service and have a claim submitted for the physicians' service.

(5) BINDING NATURE OF POSITIVE DETERMINATION.—If the contractor makes the determination described in paragraph (4)(A)(i), such determination shall be binding on the contractor in the absence of fraud or evidence of misrepresentation of facts presented to the contractor.

(6) LIMITATION ON FURTHER REVIEW.—(A) IN GENERAL.—Contractor determinations described in paragraph (4)(A)(ii) or (4)(A)(iii) (relating to pre-service claims) are not subject to further administrative appeal or judicial review under this section or otherwise.

(B) DECISION NOT TO SEEK PRIOR DETERMINATION OR NEGATIVE DETERMINATION DOES NOT IMPACT RIGHT TO OBTAIN SERVICES, SEEK REIMBURSEMENT, OR APPEAL RIGHTS.—Nothing in this subsection shall be construed as affecting the right of an individual who—

(i) decides not to seek a prior determination under this subsection with respect to physicians' services; or

(ii) seeks such a determination and has received a determination described in paragraph (4)(A)(ii), from receiving (and submitting a claim for) such physicians' services and from obtaining administrative or judicial review respecting such claim under the other applicable provisions of this section. Failure to seek a prior determination under this subsection with respect to physicians' service shall not be taken into account in such administrative or judicial review.

(C) NO PRIOR DETERMINATION AFTER RECEIPT OF SERVICES.—Once an individual is provided physicians' services, there shall be no prior determination under this subsection with respect to such physicians' services.

(i) MEDIATION PROCESS FOR LOCAL COVERAGE DETERMINATIONS.—(1) ESTABLISHMENT OF PROCESS

The Secretary shall establish a mediation process under this subsection through the use of a physician trained in mediation and employed by the Centers for Medicare & Medicaid Services.

(2) RESPONSIBILITY OF MEDIATOR.—Under the process established in paragraph (1), such a mediator shall mediate in disputes between groups representing providers of services, suppliers (as defined in section 1861(d)), and the medical director for a medicare administrative contractor whenever the regional administrator (as defined by the Secretary) involved determines that there was a systematic pattern and a large volume of complaints from such groups regarding decisions of such director or there is a complaint from the co-chair of the advisory committee for that contractor to such regional administrator regarding such dispute.

[CCH Explanation at ¶ 901, 903, 905, 906, 907, 916, and 948.]

2003 Amendments:

Section 931(d) of the "Medicare Prescription Drug, Improvement, and Modernization Act of 2003," effective upon enactment, amended section 1869(f)(2)(A)(i) by striking "of the Social Security Administration".

Section 932 of the "Medicare Prescription Drug, Improvement, and Modernization Act of 2003," effective upon enactment, amended section 1869(b) in paragraph (1)(A), by inserting ", subject to paragraph (2)," before "to judicial review of the Secretary's final decision"; and by adding at the end new paragraph (2).

Section 932(a)(2) of the "Medicare Prescription Drug, Improvement, and Modernization Act of 2003," effective upon enactment, amended section 1869(b)(1)(F)(ii) to read as follows: "(ii) Reference to expedited access to judicial review.—For the provision relating to expedited access to judicial review, see paragraph (2).".

Prior to amendment section 1869(b)(1)(F)(ii) read as follows:

(ii) Expedited hearing.—In a hearing by the Secretary under this section, in which the moving party alleges that no material issues of fact are in dispute, the Secretary shall make an expedited determination as to whether any such facts are in dispute and, if not, shall render a decision expeditiously.

Section 933(a) of the "Medicare Prescription Drug, Improvement, and Modernization Act of 2003," effective upon enactment, amended section 1869(b) by adding at the end new paragraph (3).

Section 933(b) of the "Medicare Prescription Drug, Improvement, and Modernization Act of 2003," effective upon enactment, amended section 1869(c)(3)(B)(i) by inserting "(including the medical records of the individual involved)" after "clinical experience".

Section 933(c)(1) of the "Medicare Prescription Drug, Improvement, and Modernization Act of 2003," effective upon enactment, amended section 1869(a) by adding at the end new paragraphs (4) and (5).

Section 933(c)(2) of the "Medicare Prescription Drug, Improvement, and Modernization Act of 2003," effective upon enactment, amended section 1869(c)(3)(E) by inserting "be written in a manner calculated to be understood by the individual entitled to benefits under part A or enrolled under part B, or both, and shall include (to the extent appropriate)" after "in writing,"; and by inserting "and a notification of the right to appeal such determination and instructions on how to initiate such appeal under this section" after "such decision,".

Section 933(c)(3) of the "Medicare Prescription Drug, Improvement, and Modernization Act of 2003," effective upon enactment, amended section 1869(d) in the heading, by inserting "; NOTICE" after "SECRETARY"; and by adding at the end new paragraph (4).

Section 933(c)(4) of the "Medicare Prescription Drug, Improvement, and Modernization Act of 2003," effective upon enactment, amended section 1869(c)(3)(J)(i) by striking "prepare" and inserting "submit" and by striking "with respect to" and all that follows through "and relevant policies".

Section 933(d)(1) of the "Medicare Prescription Drug, Improvement, and Modernization Act of 2003," effective upon enactment, amended section 1869(c)(3) in subparagraph (A), by striking "sufficient training and expertise in medical science and legal matters" and inserting "sufficient medical, legal, and other expertise (including knowledge of the program under this title) and sufficient staffing"; and by adding at the end new subparagraph (K).

Section 933(d)(2)(A) of the "Medicare Prescription Drug, Improvement, and Modernization Act of 2003," effective upon enactment, amended section 1869(c)(3)(D) to read as follows "Qualifications for reviewers The requirements of subsection (g) shall be met (relating to qualifications of reviewing professionals)."; and by adding at the end new subsection (g).

Prior to amendment, section 1869(c)(3)(D) read as follows:

(D) LIMITATION ON INDIVIDUAL REVIEWING DETERMINATIONS.—

(i) PHYSICIANS AND HEALTH CARE PROFESSIONAL.—No physician or health care professional under the employ of a qualified independent contractor may review—

(I) determinations regarding health care services furnished to a patient if the physician or health care professional was directly responsible for furnishing such services; or

(II) determinations regarding health care services provided in or by an institution, organization, or agency, if the physician or any member of the family of the physician or health care professional has, directly or indirectly, a significant financial interest in such institution, organization, or agency.

(ii) FAMILY DESCRIBED.—For purposes of this paragraph, the family of a physician or health care professional includes the spouse (other than a spouse who is legally separated from the physician or health care professional under a decree of divorce or separate maintenance), children (including stepchildren and legally adopted children), grandchildren, parents, and grandparents of the physician or health care professional.

Section 933(d)(3) of the "Medicare Prescription Drug, Improvement, and Modernization Act of 2003," effective upon enactment, amended section 1869(c)(4) by striking "not fewer than 12 qualified independent contractors under this subsection" and inserting "a sufficient number of qualified independent contractors (but not fewer than 4 such contractors) to conduct reconsiderations consistent with the timeframes applicable under this subsection".

Section 938 of the "Medicare Prescription Drug, Improvement, and Modernization Act of 2003," effective upon enactment, amended section 1869, as amended by 933(d)(2)(B), by adding at the end new subsection (h).

Section 940(a)(1) of the "Medicare Prescription Drug, Improvement, and Modernization Act of 2003," effective upon enactment, amended section 1869(a)(3)(C)(ii) by striking "30-day period" each place it appears and inserting "60-day period".

Section 940(a)(2) of the "Medicare Prescription Drug, Improvement, and Modernization Act of 2003," effective upon enactment, amended section 1869(c)(3)(C)(i), by striking "30-day period" and inserting "60-day period".

Section 940(b)(1) of the "Medicare Prescription Drug, Improvement, and Modernization Act of 2003," effective upon enactment, amended section 1869(b)(1)(E) by adding at the end new clause (iii).

Section 940A of the "Medicare Prescription Drug, Improvement, and Modernization Act of 2003," effective upon enactment, amended section 1869 as amended by 938(a) adding new subsection (i).

Section 948(b)(1) of the "Medicare Prescription Drug, Improvement, and Modernization Act of 2003," effective upon enactment, amended section 1869(c)(3)(I)(ii) in subclause (III), by striking "policy" and inserting "determination"; and in subclause (IV), by striking "medical review policies" and inserting "coverage determinations".

Section 948(c) of the "Medicare Prescription Drug, Improvement, and Modernization Act of 2003," effective upon enactment, amended section 1869(f)(4) in subparagraph (A)(iv), by striking "subclause (I), (II), or (III)" and inserting "clause (i), (ii), or (iii)"; in subparagraph (B), by striking "clause (i)(IV)" and "clause (i)(III)" and inserting "subparagraph (A)(iv)" and "subparagraph (A)(iii)", respectively; and in subparagraph (C), by striking "clause (i)", "subclause (IV)" and "subparagraph (A)" and inserting "subparagraph (A)", "clause (iv)" and "paragraph (1)(A)", respectively each place it appears.

[¶ 2310] Sec. 1870. OVERPAYMENT ON BEHALF OF INDIVIDUALS AND SETTLEMENT OF CLAIMS FOR BENEFITS ON BEHALF OF DECEASED INDIVIDUALS

[42 U.S.C. § 1395gg]

* * *

(h) Notwithstanding subsection (f) or any other provision of law, the Secretary shall permit a provider of services or supplier to appeal any determination of the Secretary under this title relating to services rendered under this title to an individual who subsequently dies if there is no other party available to appeal such determination.

[CCH Explanation at ¶ 915.]
2003 Amendments:

Section 939 of the "Medicare Prescription Drug, Improvement, and Modernization Act of 2003," effective upon enactment, amended section 1870 adding at the end new subsection (h).

[¶ 2315] Sec. 1871. REGULATIONS

[42 U.S.C. § 1395hh]

* * *

(a)(3)(A) The Secretary, in consultation with the Director of the Office of Management and Budget, shall establish and publish a regular timeline for the publication of final regulations based on the previous publication of a proposed regulation or an interim final regulation.

(B) Such timeline may vary among different regulations based on differences in the complexity of the regulation, the number and scope of comments received, and other relevant factors, but shall not be longer than 3 years except under exceptional circumstances. If the Secretary intends to vary such timeline with respect to the publication of a final regulation, the Secretary shall cause to have published in the Federal Register notice of the different timeline by not later than the timeline previously established with respect to such regulation. Such notice shall include a brief explanation of the justification for such variation.

(C) In the case of interim final regulations, upon the expiration of the regular timeline established under this paragraph for the publication of a final regulation after opportunity for public comment, the interim final regulation shall not continue in effect unless the Secretary publishes (at the end of the regular timeline and, if applicable, at the end of each succeeding 1-year period) a notice of continuation of the regulation that includes an explanation of why the regular timeline (and any subsequent 1-year extension) was not complied with. If such a notice is published, the regular timeline (or such timeline as previously extended under this paragraph) for publication of the final regulation shall be treated as having been extended for 1 additional year.

(D) The Secretary shall annually submit to Congress a report that describes the instances in which the Secretary failed to publish a final regulation within the applicable regular timeline under this paragraph and that provides an explanation for such failures.

(4) If the Secretary publishes a final regulation that includes a provision that is not a logical outgrowth of a previously published notice of proposed rulemaking or interim final rule, such provision shall be treated as a proposed regulation and shall not take effect until there is the further opportunity for public comment and a publication of the provision again as a final regulation.

* * *

(e)(1)(A) [sic] A substantive change in regulations, manual instructions, interpretative rules, statements of policy, or guidelines of general applicability under this title shall not be applied (by extrapolation or otherwise) retroactively to items and services furnished before the effective date of the change, unless the Secretary determines that—

(i) such retroactive application is necessary to comply with statutory requirements; or

(ii) failure to apply the change retroactively would be contrary to the public interest.

(B)(i) Except as provided in clause (ii), a substantive change referred to in subparagraph (A) shall not become effective before the end of the 30-day period that begins on the date that the Secretary has issued or published, as the case may be, the substantive change.

(ii) The Secretary may provide for such a substantive change to take effect on a date that precedes the end of the 30-day period under clause (i) if the Secretary finds that waiver of such 30-day period is necessary to comply with statutory requirements or that the application of such 30-day period is contrary to the public interest. If the Secretary provides for an earlier effective date pursuant to this clause, the Secretary shall include in the issuance or publication of the substantive change a finding described in the first sentence, and a brief statement of the reasons for such finding.

(C) No action shall be taken against a provider of services or supplier with respect to noncompliance with such a substantive change for items and services furnished before the effective date of such a change.

(2)(A) If—

(i) a provider of services or supplier follows the written guidance (which may be transmitted electronically) provided by the Secretary or by a medicare contractor (as defined in section 1889(g)) acting within the scope of the contractor's contract authority, with respect to the furnishing of items or services and submission of a claim for benefits for such items or services with respect to such provider or supplier;

(ii) the Secretary determines that the provider of services or supplier has accurately presented the circumstances relating to such items, services, and claim to the contractor in writing; and

(iii) the guidance was in error;

the provider of services or supplier shall not be subject to any penalty or interest under this title or the provisions of title XI insofar as they relate to this title (including interest under a repayment plan under section 1893 or otherwise) relating to the provision of such items or service or such claim if the provider of services or supplier reasonably relied on such guidance.

(B) Subparagraph (A) shall not be construed as preventing the recoupment or repayment (without any additional penalty) relating to an overpayment insofar as the overpayment was solely the result of a clerical or technical operational error.

(f)(1) Not later than 2 years after the date of the enactment of this subsection, and every 3 years thereafter, the Secretary shall submit to Congress a report with respect to the administration of this title and areas of inconsistency or conflict among the various provisions under law and regulation.

(2) In preparing a report under paragraph (1), the Secretary shall collect—

(A) information from individuals entitled to benefits under part A or enrolled under part B, or both, providers of services, and suppliers and from the Medicare Beneficiary Ombudsman with respect to such areas of inconsistency and conflict; and

(B) information from medicare contractors that tracks the nature of written and telephone inquiries.

(3) A report under paragraph (1) shall include a description of efforts by the Secretary to reduce such inconsistency or conflicts, and recommendations for legislation or administrative action that the Secretary determines appropriate to further reduce such inconsistency or conflicts.

[CCH Explanation at ¶ 826, 827, 828.]

2003 Amendments:

Section 902(a) of the "Medicare Prescription Drug, Improvement, and Modernization Act of 2003," effective upon enactment, amended section 1871(a) by adding at the end new paragraph (3).

Section 902(b) of the "Medicare Prescription Drug, Improvement, and Modernization Act of 2003," effective upon enactment, amended section 1871(a) by adding at the end new paragraph (4).

Section 903(a) of the "Medicare Prescription Drug, Improvement, and Modernization Act of 2003," effective upon enactment, amended section 1871 as amended by 902(a), adding new subsection (e)(1)(A).

This amendment applies to final regulations published on or after the date of enactment.

Section 903(b) of the "Medicare Prescription Drug, Improvement, and Modernization Act of 2003," effective upon enactment, amended section 1871 as amended by 902(a), adding new subsection (e)(1)(B).

This amendment applies to compliance actions undertaken on or after the date of enactment.

Section 903(c) of the "Medicare Prescription Drug, Improvement, and Modernization Act of 2003," effective upon enactment, amended section 1871 as amended by 902(a), adding new subsection (e)(2).

This amendment applies only to a penalty or interest imposed with respect to guidance provided on or after July 24, 2003.

[CCH Note: Section 903 of the "Medicare Prescription Drug, Improvement, and Modernization Act of 2003," added new subsection (e) to section 1871 of the Social Security Act, however, a subsection (d) has not been added to section 1871.]

Section 904(2)(b) of the "Medicare Prescription Drug, Improvement, and Modernization Act of 2003," effective upon enactment, amended section 1871, as amended by section 903 by adding at the end new subsection (f).

[CCH Note: Section 904(2)(b) of the "Medicare Prescription Drug, Improvement, and Modernization Act of 2003," added new subsection (f) to section 1871 of the Social Security Act, following subsection (e) as added by section 903, however, a subsection (d) has not been added to section 1871.]

[¶ 2320] Sec. 1874A. CONTRACTS WITH MEDICARE ADMINISTRATIVE CONTRACTORS

(a) AUTHORITY.—

(1) AUTHORITY TO ENTER INTO CONTRACTS.—The Secretary may enter into contracts with any eligible entity to serve as a medicare administrative contractor with respect to the performance of any or all of the functions described in paragraph (4) or parts of those functions (or, to the extent provided in a contract, to secure performance thereof by other entities).

(2) ELIGIBILITY OF ENTITIES.—An entity is eligible to enter into a contract with respect to the performance of a particular function described in paragraph (4) only if—

(A) the entity has demonstrated capability to carry out such function;

(B) the entity complies with such conflict of interest standards as are generally applicable to Federal acquisition and procurement;

(C) the entity has sufficient assets to financially support the performance of such function; and

(D) the entity meets such other requirements as the Secretary may impose.

(3) MEDICARE ADMINISTRATIVE CONTRACTOR DEFINED.—For purposes of this title and title XI—

(A) IN GENERAL.—The term "medicare administrative contractor" means an agency, organization, or other person with a contract under this section.

(B) APPROPRIATE MEDICARE ADMINISTRATIVE CONTRACTOR.—With respect to the performance of a particular function in relation to an individual entitled to benefits under part A or enrolled under part B, or both, a specific provider of services or supplier (or class of such providers of services or suppliers), the 'appropriate' medicare administrative contractor is the medicare administrative contractor that has a contract under this section with respect to the performance of that function in relation to that individual, provider of services or supplier or class of provider of services or supplier.

§1874A(a)(3)(B) ¶2320

(4) FUNCTIONS DESCRIBED.—The functions referred to in paragraphs (1) and (2) are payment functions (including the function of developing local coverage determinations, as defined in section 1869(f)(2)(B)), provider services functions, and functions relating to services furnished to individuals entitled to benefits under part A or enrolled under part B, or both, as follows:

(A) DETERMINATION OF PAYMENT AMOUNTS.—Determining (subject to the provisions of section 1878 and to such review by the Secretary as may be provided for by the contracts) the amount of the payments required pursuant to this title to be made to providers of services, suppliers and individuals.

(B) MAKING PAYMENTS.—Making payments described in subparagraph (A) (including receipt, disbursement, and accounting for funds in making such payments).

(C) BENEFICIARY EDUCATION AND ASSISTANCE.—Providing education and outreach to individuals entitled to benefits under part A or enrolled under part B, or both, and providing assistance to those individuals with specific issues, concerns, or problems.

(D) PROVIDER CONSULTATIVE SERVICES.—Providing consultative services to institutions, agencies, and other persons to enable them to establish and maintain fiscal records necessary for purposes of this title and otherwise to qualify as providers of services or suppliers.

(E) COMMUNICATION WITH PROVIDERS.—Communicating to providers of services and suppliers any information or instructions furnished to the medicare administrative contractor by the Secretary, and facilitating communication between such providers and suppliers and the Secretary.

(F) PROVIDER EDUCATION AND TECHNICAL ASSISTANCE.—Performing the functions relating to provider education, training, and technical assistance.

(G) ADDITIONAL FUNCTIONS.—Performing such other functions, including (subject to paragraph (5)) functions under the Medicare Integrity Program under section 1893, as are necessary to carry out the purposes of this title.

(5) RELATIONSHIP TO MIP CONTRACTS.—

(A) NONDUPLICATION OF DUTIES.—In entering into contracts under this section, the Secretary shall assure that functions of medicare administrative contractors in carrying out activities under parts A and B do not duplicate activities carried out under a contract entered into under the Medicare Integrity Program under section 1893. The previous sentence shall not apply with respect to the activity described in section 1893(b)(5) (relating to prior authorization of certain items of durable medical equipment under section 1834(a)(15)).

(B) CONSTRUCTION.—An entity shall not be treated as a medicare administrative contractor merely by reason of having entered into a contract with the Secretary under section 1893.

(6) APPLICATION OF FEDERAL ACQUISITION REGULATION.—Except to the extent inconsistent with a specific requirement of this section, the Federal Acquisition Regulation applies to contracts under this section.

(b) CONTRACTING REQUIREMENTS.—

(1) USE OF COMPETITIVE PROCEDURES.—

(A) IN GENERAL.—Except as provided in laws with general applicability to Federal acquisition and procurement or in subparagraph (B), the Secretary shall use competitive procedures when entering into contracts with medicare administrative contractors under this section, taking into account performance quality as well as price and other factors.

(B) RENEWAL OF CONTRACTS.—The Secretary may renew a contract with a medicare administrative contractor under this section from term to term without regard to section 5 of title 41, United States Code, or any other provision of law requiring competition, if the medicare administrative contractor has met or exceeded the performance requirements applicable with respect to the contract and contractor, except that the Secretary shall provide for the application of competitive procedures under such a contract not less frequently than once every 5 years.

(C) TRANSFER OF FUNCTIONS.—The Secretary may transfer functions among medicare administrative contractors consistent with the provisions of this paragraph. The Secretary shall ensure that performance quality is considered in such transfers. The Secretary shall provide public notice (whether in the Federal Register or otherwise) of any such transfer (including a description of the functions so transferred, a description of the providers of services and suppliers affected by such transfer, and contact information for the contractors involved).

(D) INCENTIVES FOR QUALITY.—The Secretary shall provide incentives for medicare administrative contractors to provide quality service and to promote efficiency.

(2) COMPLIANCE WITH REQUIREMENTS.—No contract under this section shall be entered into with any medicare administrative contractor unless the Secretary finds that such medicare administrative contractor will perform its obligations under the contract efficiently and effectively and will meet such requirements as to financial responsibility, legal authority, quality of services provided, and other matters as the Secretary finds pertinent.

(3) PERFORMANCE REQUIREMENTS.—

(A) DEVELOPMENT OF SPECIFIC PERFORMANCE REQUIREMENTS.—

(i) IN GENERAL.—The Secretary shall develop contract performance requirements to carry out the specific requirements applicable under this title to a function described in subsection (a)(4) and shall develop standards for measuring the extent to which a contractor has met such requirements. Such requirements shall include specific performance duties expected of a medical director of a medicare administrative contractor, including requirements relating to professional relations and the availability of such director to conduct medical determination activities within the jurisdiction of such a contractor

(ii) CONSULTATION.—In developing such performance requirements and standards for measurement, the Secretary shall consult with providers of services, organizations representative of beneficiaries under this title, and organizations and agencies performing functions necessary to carry out the purposes of this section with respect to such performance requirements.

(iii) PUBLICATION OF STANDARDS.—The Secretary shall make such performance requirements and measurement standards available to the public.

(B) CONSIDERATIONS.—The Secretary shall include, as one of the standards developed under subparagraph (A), provider and beneficiary satisfaction levels.

(C) INCLUSION IN CONTRACTS.—All contractor performance requirements shall be set forth in the contract between the Secretary and the appropriate medicare administrative contractor. Such performance requirements—

(i) shall reflect the performance requirements published under subparagraph (A), but may include additional performance requirements;

(ii) shall be used for evaluating contractor performance under the contract; and

(iii) shall be consistent with the written statement of work provided under the contract.

(4) INFORMATION REQUIREMENTS.—The Secretary shall not enter into a contract with a medicare administrative contractor under this section unless the contractor agrees—

(A) to furnish to the Secretary such timely information and reports as the Secretary may find necessary in performing his functions under this title; and

(B) to maintain such records and afford such access thereto as the Secretary finds necessary to assure the correctness and verification of the information and reports under subparagraph (A) and otherwise to carry out the purposes of this title.

(5) SURETY BOND.—A contract with a medicare administrative contractor under this section may require the medicare administrative contractor, and any of its officers or employees certifying payments or disbursing funds pursuant to the contract, or otherwise participating in carrying out the contract, to give surety bond to the United States in such amount as the Secretary may deem appropriate.

§1874A(b)(5) ¶2320

(c) TERMS AND CONDITIONS.—

(1) IN GENERAL.—A contract with any medicare administrative contractor under this section may contain such terms and conditions as the Secretary finds necessary or appropriate and may provide for advances of funds to the medicare administrative contractor for the making of payments by it under subsection (a)(4)(B).

(2) PROHIBITION ON MANDATES FOR CERTAIN DATA COLLECTION.—The Secretary may not require, as a condition of entering into, or renewing, a contract under this section, that the medicare administrative contractor match data obtained other than in its activities under this title with data used in the administration of this title for purposes of identifying situations in which the provisions of section 1862(b) may apply.

(d) LIMITATION ON LIABILITY OF MEDICARE ADMINISTRATIVE CONTRACTORS AND CERTAIN OFFICERS.—

(1) CERTIFYING OFFICER.—No individual designated pursuant to a contract under this section as a certifying officer shall, in the absence of the reckless disregard of the individual's obligations or the intent by that individual to defraud the United States, be liable with respect to any payments certified by the individual under this section.

(2) DISBURSING OFFICER.—No disbursing officer shall, in the absence of the reckless disregard of the officer's obligations or the intent by that officer to defraud the United States, be liable with respect to any payment by such officer under this section if it was based upon an authorization (which meets the applicable requirements for such internal controls established by the Comptroller General of the United States) of a certifying officer designated as provided in paragraph (1) of this subsection.

(3) LIABILITY OF MEDICARE ADMINISTRATIVE CONTRACTOR.—

(A) IN GENERAL.—No medicare administrative contractor shall be liable to the United States for a payment by a certifying or disbursing officer unless, in connection with such payment, the medicare administrative contractor acted with reckless disregard of its obligations under its medicare administrative contract or with intent to defraud the United States.

(B) RELATIONSHIP TO FALSE CLAIMS ACT.—Nothing in this subsection shall be construed to limit liability for conduct that would constitute a violation of sections 3729 through 3731 of title 31, United States Code.

(4) INDEMNIFICATION BY SECRETARY.—

(A) IN GENERAL.—Subject to subparagraphs (B) and (D), in the case of a medicare administrative contractor (or a person who is a director, officer, or employee of such a contractor or who is engaged by the contractor to participate directly in the claims administration process) who is made a party to any judicial or administrative proceeding arising from or relating directly to the claims administration process under this title, the Secretary may, to the extent the Secretary determines to be appropriate and as specified in the contract with the contractor, indemnify the contractor and such persons.

(B) CONDITIONS.—The Secretary may not provide indemnification under subparagraph (A) insofar as the liability for such costs arises directly from conduct that is determined by the judicial proceeding or by the Secretary to be criminal in nature, fraudulent, or grossly negligent. If indemnification is provided by the Secretary with respect to a contractor before a determination that such costs arose directly from such conduct, the contractor shall reimburse the Secretary for costs of indemnification.

(C) SCOPE OF INDEMNIFICATION.—Indemnification by the Secretary under subparagraph (A) may include payment of judgments, settlements (subject to subparagraph (D)), awards, and costs (including reasonable legal expenses).

(D) WRITTEN APPROVAL FOR SETTLEMENTS OR COMPROMISES.—A contractor or other person described in subparagraph (A) may not propose to negotiate a settlement or compromise of a proceeding described in such subparagraph without the prior written approval of the Secretary to negotiate such settlement or compromise. Any indemnification under subparagraph (A) with respect to amounts paid under a settlement or compromise of a proceeding described in such subparagraph are conditioned upon prior written approval by the Secretary of the final settlement or compromise.

(E) CONSTRUCTION.—Nothing in this paragraph shall be construed—

(i) to change any common law immunity that may be available to a medicare administrative contractor or person described in subparagraph (A); or

(ii) to permit the payment of costs not otherwise allowable, reasonable, or allocable under the Federal Acquisition Regulation..

(e) REQUIREMENTS FOR INFORMATION SECURITY.—

(1) DEVELOPMENT OF INFORMATION SECURITY PROGRAM.—A medicare administrative contractor that performs the functions referred to in subparagraphs (A) and (B) of subsection (a)(4) (relating to determining and making payments) shall implement a contractor-wide information security program to provide information security for the operation and assets of the contractor with respect to such functions under this title. An information security program under this paragraph shall meet the requirements for information security programs imposed on Federal agencies under paragraphs (1) through (8) of section 3544(b) of title 44, United States Code (other than the requirements under paragraphs (2)(D)(i), (5)(A), and (5)(B) of such section).

(2) INDEPENDENT AUDITS.—

(A) PERFORMANCE OF ANNUAL EVALUATIONS.—Each year a medicare administrative contractor that performs the functions referred to in subparagraphs (A) and (B) of subsection (a)(4) (relating to determining and making payments) shall undergo an evaluation of the information security of the contractor with respect to such functions under this title. The evaluation shall—

(i) be performed by an entity that meets such requirements for independence as the Inspector General of the Department of Health and Human Services may establish; and

(ii) test the effectiveness of information security control techniques of an appropriate subset of the contractor's information systems (as defined in section 3502(8) of title 44, United States Code) relating to such functions under this title and an assessment of compliance with the requirements of this subsection and related information security policies, procedures, standards and guidelines, including policies and procedures as may be prescribed by the Director of the Office of Management and Budget and applicable information security standards promulgated under section 11331 of title 40, United States Code.

(B) DEADLINE FOR INITIAL EVALUATION.—

(i) NEW CONTRACTORS.—In the case of a medicare administrative contractor covered by this subsection that has not previously performed the functions referred to in subparagraphs (A) and (B) of subsection (a)(4) (relating to determining and making payments) as a fiscal intermediary or carrier under section 1816 or 1842, the first independent evaluation conducted pursuant to subparagraph (A) shall be completed prior to commencing such functions.

(ii) OTHER CONTRACTORS.—In the case of a medicare administrative contractor covered by this subsection that is not described in clause (i), the first independent evaluation conducted pursuant to subparagraph (A) shall be completed within 1 year after the date the contractor commences functions referred to in clause (i) under this section.

(C) REPORTS ON EVALUATIONS.—

(i) TO THE DEPARTMENT OF HEALTH AND HUMAN SERVICES.—The results of independent evaluations under subparagraph (A) shall be submitted promptly to the Inspector General of the Department of Health and Human Services and to the Secretary.

(ii) TO CONGRESS.—The Inspector General of the Department of Health and Human Services shall submit to Congress annual reports on the results of such evaluations, including assessments of the scope and sufficiency of such evaluations.

(iii) AGENCY REPORTING.—The Secretary shall address the results of such evaluations in reports required under section 3544(c) of title 44, United States Code.

(f) INCENTIVES TO IMPROVE CONTRACTOR PERFORMANCE IN PROVIDER EDUCATION AND OUTREACH.—The Secretary shall use specific claims payment error rates or similar methodology of medicare administrative contractors in the processing or reviewing of medicare claims in order to give such contractors an incentive to implement effective education and outreach programs for providers of services and suppliers.

(g) COMMUNICATIONS WITH BENEFICIARIES, PROVIDERS OF SERVICES AND SUPPLIERS.—

(1) COMMUNICATION STRATEGY.—The Secretary shall develop a strategy for communications with individuals entitled to benefits under part A or enrolled under part B, or both, and with providers of services and suppliers under this title.

(2) RESPONSE TO WRITTEN INQUIRIES.—Each medicare administrative contractor shall, for those providers of services and suppliers which submit claims to the contractor for claims processing and for those individuals entitled to benefits under part A or enrolled under part B, or both, with respect to whom claims are submitted for claims processing, provide general written responses (which may be through electronic transmission) in a clear, concise, and accurate manner to inquiries of providers of services, suppliers, and individuals entitled to benefits under part A or enrolled under part B, or both, concerning the programs under this title within 45 business days of the date of receipt of such inquiries.

(3) RESPONSE TO TOLL-FREE LINES.—The Secretary shall ensure that each medicare administrative contractor shall provide, for those providers of services and suppliers which submit claims to the contractor for claims processing and for those individuals entitled to benefits under part A or enrolled under part B, or both, with respect to whom claims are submitted for claims processing, a toll-free telephone number at which such individuals, providers of services, and suppliers may obtain information regarding billing, coding, claims, coverage, and other appropriate information under this title.

(4) MONITORING OF CONTRACTOR RESPONSES.—

(A) IN GENERAL.—Each medicare administrative contractor shall, consistent with standards developed by the Secretary under subparagraph (B)—

(i) maintain a system for identifying who provides the information referred to in paragraphs (2) and (3); and

(ii) monitor the accuracy, consistency, and timeliness of the information so provided.

(B) DEVELOPMENT OF STANDARDS.—

(i) IN GENERAL.—The Secretary shall establish and make public standards to monitor the accuracy, consistency, and timeliness of the information provided in response to written and telephone inquiries under this subsection. Such standards shall be consistent with the performance requirements established under subsection (b)(3).

(ii) EVALUATION.—In conducting evaluations of individual medicare administrative contractors, the Secretary shall take into account the results of the monitoring conducted under subparagraph (A) taking into account as performance requirements the standards established under clause (i). The Secretary shall, in consultation with organizations representing providers of services, suppliers, and individuals entitled to benefits under part A or enrolled under part B, or both, establish standards relating to the accuracy, consistency, and timeliness of the information so provided.

(C) DIRECT MONITORING.—Nothing in this paragraph shall be construed as preventing the Secretary from directly monitoring the accuracy, consistency, and timeliness of the information so provided.

(5) AUTHORIZATION OF APPROPRIATIONS.—There are authorized to be appropriated such sums as are necessary to carry out this subsection.

(h) CONDUCT OF PREPAYMENT REVIEW.—

(1) (1) CONDUCT OF RANDOM PREPAYMENT REVIEW.—

(A) IN GENERAL.—A medicare administrative contractor may conduct random prepayment review only to develop a contractor-wide or program-wide claims payment error rates or under such additional circumstances as may be provided under regulations, developed in consultation with providers of services and suppliers.

(B) USE OF STANDARD PROTOCOLS WHEN CONDUCTING PREPAYMENT REVIEWS.—When a medicare administrative contractor conducts a random prepayment review, the contractor may conduct such review only in accordance with a standard protocol for random prepayment audits developed by the Secretary.

(C) CONSTRUCTION.—Nothing in this paragraph shall be construed as preventing the denial of payments for claims actually reviewed under a random prepayment review.

(D) RANDOM PREPAYMENT REVIEW.—For purposes of this subsection, the term 'random prepayment review' means a demand for the production of records or documentation absent cause with respect to a claim.

(2) LIMITATIONS ON NON-RANDOM PREPAYMENT REVIEW.—

(A) LIMITATIONS ON INITIATION OF NON-RANDOM PREPAYMENT REVIEW.—A medicare administrative contractor may not initiate non-random prepayment review of a provider of services or supplier based on the initial identification by that provider of services or supplier of an improper billing practice unless there is a likelihood of sustained or high level of payment error under section 1893(f)(3)(A).

(B) TERMINATION OF NON-RANDOM PREPAYMENT REVIEW.—The Secretary shall issue regulations relating to the termination, including termination dates, of non-random prepayment review. Such regulations may vary such a termination date based upon the differences in the circumstances triggering prepayment review.

[CCH Explanation at ¶ 830, 831, 908, and 917.]

2003 Amendments:

Section 911(a) of the "Medicare Prescription Drug, Improvement, and Modernization Act of 2003," effective October 1, 2005, amended section 1874A by adding such section as new.

Section 912(a) of the "Medicare Prescription Drug, Improvement, and Modernization Act of 2003," effective upon enactment, amended section 1874A by adding new subsection (e).

Section 921(b)(1) of the "Medicare Prescription Drug, Improvement, and Modernization Act of 2003," effective October 1, 2004, amended section 1874A by adding new subsection (f).

This amendment applies to each fiscal intermediary and each carrier in the same manner as they apply to Medicare administrative contractors.

Section 921(c) of the "Medicare Prescription Drug, Improvement, and Modernization Act of 2003," effective October 1, 2004, amended section 1874A by adding new subsection (g).

Section 934(a) of the "Medicare Prescription Drug, Improvement, and Modernization Act of 2003," effective upon enactment, amended section 1874A by adding new subsection (h).

Section 940A(b) of the "Medicare Prescription Drug, Improvement, and Modernization Act of 2003," effective upon enactment, amended section 1874A(b)(3)(A)(i) is amended by adding at the end the following: "Such requirements shall include specific performance duties expected of a medical director of a medicare administrative contractor, including requirements relating to professional relations and the availability of such director to conduct medical determination activities within the jurisdiction of such a contractor.".

[¶ 2325] Sec. 1875. STUDIES AND RECOMMENDATIONS

[42 U.S.C. § 1395*ll*]

* * *

(b) The Secretary shall make a continuing study of the operation and administration of the this title (including a validation of the accreditation process of the Joint Commission on Accreditation of Hospitals, the operation and administration of health maintenance organizations authorized by section 226 of the Social Security Amendments of 1972, the experiments and demonstration projects authorized by section 402 of the Social Security Amendments of 1967 and the experiments and demonstration projects authorized by section 222(a) of the Social Security Amendments of 1972), and shall transmit to the Congress annually a report concerning the operation of such programs.

2003 Amendments:

Section 101(e)(7) of the "Medicare Prescription Drug, Improvement, and Modernization Act of 2003," effective upon enactment, amended section 1875(b) is amended by striking "the insurance programs under parts A and B" and inserting "this title".

[¶ 2330] Sec. 1876. PAYMENTS TO HEALTH MAINTENANCE ORGANIZATIONS AND COMPETITIVE MEDICAL PLANS

[42 U.S.C. § 1395mm]

* * *

(b) For purposes of this section, the term "eligible organization" means a public or private entity (which may be a health maintenance organization or a competitive medical plan), organized under the laws of any State, which—

* * *

(5)(B) [sic] The provisions of section 1869(b)(1)(E)(iii) shall apply with respect to dollar amounts specified in the first 2 sentences of this subparagraph in the same manner as they apply to the dollar amounts specified in section 1869(b)(1)(E)(i).

* * *

* * *

(c)(2)(B) If there is a national coverage determination made in the period beginning on the date of an announcement under subsection (a)(1)(A) and ending on the date of the next announcement under such subsection that the Secretary projects will result in a significant change in the costs to the organization of providing the benefits that are the subject of such national coverage determination and that was not incorporated in the determination of the per capita rate of payment included in the announcement made at the beginning of such period—

* * *

* * *

(h)(5)

* * *

(C)(i) Subject to clause (ii), a reasonable cost reimbursement contract under this subsection may be extended or renewed indefinitely.

(ii) For any period beginning on or after January 1, 2008, a reasonable cost reimbursement contract under this subsection may not be extended or renewed for a service area insofar as such area during the entire previous year was within the service area of—

(I) 2 or more MA regional plans described in clause (iii); or

(II) 2 or more MA local plans described in clause (iii).

(iii) A plan described in this clause for a year for a service area is a plan described in section 1851(a)(2)(A)(i) if the service area for the year meets the following minimum enrollment requirements:

(I) With respect to any portion of the area involved that is within a Metropolitan Statistical Area with a population of more than 250,000 and counties contiguous to such Metropolitan Statistical Area, 5,000 individuals.

(II) With respect to any other portion of such area, 1,500 individuals.

* * *

* * *

(j)(2) The physicians' services or renal dialysis services described in this paragraph are physicians' services or renal dialysis services which are furnished to an enrollee of an eligible organization under this section by a physician, provider of services, or renal dialysis facility who is not under a contract with the organization.

* * *

[CCH Explanation at ¶386 and 916.]
2003 Amendments:

Section 234 of the "Medicare Prescription Drug, Improvement, and Modernization Act of 2003," effective upon enactment, amended section 1876(h)(5)(C) is amended.

Prior to amendment section 1876(h)(5)(C) read as follows:

(C) The Secretary may not extend or renew a reasonable cost reimbursement contract under this subsection for any period beyond December 31, 2004.

Section 736(d)(2)(A) of the "Medicare Prescription Drug, Improvement, and Modernization Act of 2003," effective upon enactment, amended section 1876(c)(2)(B) by striking "signifcant" and inserting "significant".

Section 736(d)(2)(B) of the "Medicare Prescription Drug, Improvement, and Modernization Act of 2003," effective upon enactment, amended section 1876(j)(2) by striking "this setion" and inserting "this section".

Section 940(b)(2)(B) of the "Medicare Prescription Drug, Improvement, and Modernization Act of 2003," effective upon enactment, amended section 1876(b)(5)(B) by adding at the end the following: "The provisions of section 1869(b)(1)(E)(iii) shall apply with respect to dollar amounts specified in the first 2 sentences of this subparagraph in the same manner as they apply to the dollar amounts specified in section 1869(b)(1)(E)(i).".

[Section 940(b)(2)(B) of the "Medicare Prescription Drug, Improvement, and Modernization Act of 2003," amended section 1876(b)(5)(B) of the Social Security Act, however, paragraphs (b)(3), (b)(4) and (b)(5) do not exist in the law.]

[¶ 2335] Sec. 1877. LIMITATION ON CERTAIN PHYSICIAN REFERRALS

[42 U.S.C. § 1395nn]

* * *

(b) GENERAL EXCEPTIONS TO BOTH OWNERSHIP AND COMPENSATION ARRANGEMENT PROHIBITIONS.—Subsection (a)(1) shall not apply in the following cases:

* * *

(5) ELECTRONIC PRESCRIBING.—An exception established by regulation under section 1860D-3(e)(6).

* * *

(d) ADDITIONAL EXCEPTIONS RELATED ONLY TO OWNERSHIP OR INVESTMENT PROHIBITION.—The following, if not otherwise excepted under subsection (b), shall not be considered to be an ownership or investment interest described in subsection (a)(2)(A):

* * *

(2) RURAL PROVIDERS.—In the case of designated health services furnished in a rural area (as defined in section 1886(d)(2)(D)) by an entity, if—

(A) substantially all of the designated health services furnished by the entity are furnished to individuals residing in such a rural area; and

(B) effective for the 18-month period beginning on November 18, 2003, the entity is not a specialty hospital (as defined in subsection (h)(7)).

(3) HOSPITAL OWNERSHIP.—In the case of designated health services provided by a hospital (other than a hospital described in paragraph (1)) if—

(A) the referring physician is authorized to perform services at the hospital;

(B) effective for the 18-month period beginning on November 18, 2003, the hospital is not a specialty hospital (as defined in subsection (h)(7)); and

* * *

(h) DEFINITIONS AND SPECIAL RULES.—For purposes of this section:

* * *

(7) SPECIALTY HOSPITAL.—

(A) IN GENERAL.—For purposes of this section, except as provided in subparagraph (B), the term "specialty hospital" means a subsection (d) hospital that is primarily or exclusively engaged in the care and treatment of one of the following categories:

(i) Patients with a cardiac condition.

(ii) Patients with an orthopedic condition.

(iii) Patients receiving a surgical procedure.

(iv) Any other specialized category of services that the Secretary designates as inconsistent with the purpose of permitting physician ownership and investment interests in a hospital under this section.

(B) EXCEPTION.—For purposes of this section, the term "specialty hospital" does not include any hospital—

(i) determined by the Secretary—

(I) to be in operation before November 18, 2003; or

(II) under development as of such date;

(ii) for which the number of physician investors at any time on or after such date is no greater than the number of such investors as of such date;

(iii) for which the type of categories described in subparagraph (A) at any time on or after such date is no different than the type of such categories as of such date;

(iv) for which any increase in the number of beds occurs only in the facilities on the main campus of the hospital and does not exceed 50 percent of the number of beds in the hospital as of November 18, 2003, or 5 beds, whichever is greater; and

(v) that meets such other requirements as the Secretary may specify.

[CCH Explanation at ¶574.]
2003 Amendments:

Section 101(e)(8) of the "Medicare Prescription Drug, Improvement, and Modernization Act of 2003," effective upon enactment, amended section 1877(b) by adding at the end new paragraph (5).

Section 507(a)(1)(A) of the "Medicare Prescription Drug, Improvement, and Modernization Act of 2003," effective upon enactment, amended section 1877(d)(3)(A) by striking ", and" at the end of subparagraph (A) and inserting a semicolon; and by redesignating subparagraph (B) as subparagraph (C) and inserting after subparagraph (A) new subparagraph (B).

Section 507(a)(1)(B) of the "Medicare Prescription Drug, Improvement, and Modernization Act of 2003," effective upon enactment, amended section 1877(h) by adding new paragraph (7).

Section 507(a)(2) of the "Medicare Prescription Drug, Improvement, and Modernization Act of 2003," effective upon enactment, amended section 1877(d)(2) is amended.

Prior to amendment section 1877(d)(2) read as follows:

(2) RURAL PROVIDER.—In the case of designated health services furnished in a rural area (as defined in section 1886(d)(2)(D)) by an entity, if substantially all of the designated health services furnished by such entity are furnished to individuals residing in such a rural area.

[¶2340] Sec. 1880. INDIAN HEALTH SERVICE FACILITIES
[42 U.S.C. §1395qq]

* * *

(e)(1)(A) Notwithstanding section 1835(d), subject to subparagraph (B), the Secretary shall make payment under part B to a hospital or an ambulatory care clinic (whether provider-based or freestanding) that is operated by the Indian Health Service or by an Indian tribe or tribal organization (as defined for purposes of subsection (a)) for services described in paragraph (2) (and for items and services furnished during the 5-year period beginning on January 1, 2005, all items and services for which payment may be made under part B) furnished in or at the direction of the hospital or clinic under the same situations, terms, and conditions as would apply if the services were furnished in or at the direction of such a hospital or clinic that was not operated by such Service, tribe, or organization.

* * *

[CCH Explanation at ¶730.]
2003 Amendments:

Section 630 of the "Medicare Prescription Drug, Improvement, and Modernization Act of 2003," effective upon enactment, amended section 1880(e)(1)(A) by inserting "(and for items and services furnished during the 5-year period beginning on January 1, 2005, all items and services for which payment may be made under part B)" after "for services described in paragraph (2)".

[¶2345] Sec. 1881. MEDICARE COVERAGE FOR END STAGE RENAL DISEASE PATIENTS
[42 U.S.C. §1395rr]

* * *

* * *

(b)(7) Subject to paragraph (12), the Secretary shall provide by regulation for a method (or methods) for determining prospectively the amounts of payments to be made for dialysis services furnished by providers of services and renal dialysis facilities to individuals in a facility and to such individuals at home. Such method (or methods) shall provide for the prospective determination of a rate (or rates) for each mode of care based on a single composite weighted formula (which takes into account the mix of patients who receive dialysis services at a facility or at home and the relative costs of providing such services in such settings) for hospital-based facilities and such a single composite weighted formula for other renal dialysis facilities, or based on such other method or combination of methods which differentiate between hospital-based facilities and other renal dialysis facilities and which the Secretary determines, after detailed analysis, will more effectively encourage the more efficient delivery of dialysis services and will provide greater incentives for increased use of home dialysis than through the single composite weighted formulas. The amount of a payment made under any method other than a method based on a single composite weighted formula may not exceed the amount (or, in the case of continuous cycling peritoneal dialysis, 130 percent of the amount) of the median payment that would have been made under the formula for hospital-based facilities. Subject to section 422(a)(2) of the Medicare, Medicaid, and SCHIP Benefits Improvement and Protection Act of 2000, the Secretary shall provide for such exceptions to such methods as may be warranted by unusual circumstances (including the special circumstances of sole facilities located in isolated, rural areas and of pediatric facilities). Each application for such an exception shall be deemed to be approved unless the Secretary disapproves it by not later than 60 working days after the date the application is filed. The Secretary may provide that such method will serve in lieu of any target reimbursement rate that would otherwise be established under paragraph (6). The Secretary shall reduce the amount of each composite rate payment under this paragraph for each treatment by 50 cents (subject to such adjustments as may be required to reflect modes of dialysis other than hemodialysis) and provide for payment of such amount to the organizations (designated under subsection (c)(1)(A)) for such organizations' necessary and proper administrative costs incurred in carrying out the responsibilities described in subsection (c)(2). The Secretary shall provide that amounts paid under the previous sentence shall be distributed to the organizations described in subsection (c)(1)(A) to ensure equitable treatment of all such network organizations. The Secretary in distributing any such payments to network organizations shall take into account—

* * *

(D) the proportion of the aggregate administrative funds collected in the network area.

The Secretary shall increase the amount of each composite rate payment for dialysis services furnished during 2000 by 1.2 percent above such composite rate payment amounts for such services furnished on December 31, 1999, for such services furnished on or after January 1, 2001, and before January 1, 2005, by 2.4 percent above such composite rate payment amounts for such services furnished on December 31, 2000, and for such services furnished on or after January 1, 2005, by 1.6 percent above such composite rate payment amounts for such services furnished on December 31, 2004.

* * *

* * *

(11)(B) Erythropoietin, when provided to a patient determined to have end stage renal disease, shall not be included as a dialysis service for purposes of payment under any prospective payment amount or comprehensive fee established under this section, and subject to paragraphs (12) and (13) payment for such item shall be made separately—

* * *

(12)(A) In lieu of payment under paragraph (7) beginning with services furnished on January 1, 2005, the Secretary shall establish a basic case-mix adjusted prospective payment system for dialysis services furnished by providers of services and renal dialysis facilities in a year to individuals in a facility and to such individuals at home. The case-mix under such system shall be for a limited number of patient characteristics.

(B) The system described in subparagraph (A) shall include—

(i) the services comprising the composite rate established under paragraph (7); and

(ii) the difference between payment amounts under this title for separately billed drugs and biologicals (including erythropoietin) and acquisition costs of such drugs and biologicals, as determined by the Inspector General reports to the Secretary as required by section 623(c) of the Medicare Prescription Drug, Improvement, and Modernization Act of 2003—

(I) beginning with 2005, for such drugs and biologicals for which a billing code exists prior to January 1, 2004; and

(II) beginning with 2007, for such drugs and biologicals for which a billing code does not exist prior to January 1, 2004,

adjusted to 2005, or 2007, respectively, as determined to be appropriate by the Secretary.

(C)(i) In applying subparagraph (B)(ii) for 2005, such payment amounts under this title shall be determined using the methodology specified in paragraph (13)(A)(i).

(ii) For 2006, the Secretary shall provide for an adjustment to the payments under clause (i) to reflect the difference between the payment amounts using the methodology under paragraph (13)(A)(i) and the payment amount determined using the methodology applied by the Secretary under paragraph (13)(A)(iii) of such paragraph, as estimated by the Secretary.

(D) The Secretary shall adjust the payment rates under such system by a geographic index as the Secretary determines to be appropriate. If the Secretary applies a geographic index under this paragraph that differs from the index applied under paragraph (7) the Secretary shall phase-in the application of the index under this paragraph over a multiyear period.

(E)(i) Such system shall be designed to result in the same aggregate amount of expenditures for such services, as estimated by the Secretary, as would have been made for 2005 if this paragraph did not apply.

(ii) The adjustment made under subparagraph (B)(ii)(II) shall be done in a manner to result in the same aggregate amount of expenditures after such adjustment as would otherwise have been made for such services for 2006 or 2007, respectively, as estimated by the Secretary, if this paragraph did not apply.

(F) Beginning with 2006, the Secretary shall annually increase the basic case-mix adjusted payment amounts established under this paragraph, by an amount determined by—

(i) applying the estimated growth in expenditures for drugs and biologicals (including erythropoietin) that are separately billable to the component of the basic case-mix adjusted system described in subparagraph (B)(ii); and

(ii) converting the amount determined in clause (i) to an increase applicable to the basic case-mix adjusted payment amounts established under subparagraph (B).

Nothing in this paragraph shall be construed as providing for an update to the composite rate component of the basic case-mix adjusted system under subparagraph (B).

(G) There shall be no administrative or judicial review under section 1869, section 1878, or otherwise, of the case-mix system, relative weights, payment amounts, the geographic adjustment factor, or the update for the system established under this paragraph, or the determination of the difference between medicare payment amounts and acquisition costs for separately billed drugs and biologicals (including erythropoietin) under this paragraph and paragraph (13).

(13)(A) The payment amounts under this title for separately billed drugs and biologicals furnished in a year, beginning with 2004, are as follows:

(i) For such drugs and biologicals (other than erythropoietin) furnished in 2004, the amount determined under section 1842(o)(1)(A)(v) for the drug or biological.

(ii) For such drugs and biologicals (including erythropoietin) furnished in 2005, the acquisition cost of the drug or biological, as determined by the Inspector General reports to the Secretary as required by section 623(c) of the Medicare Prescription Drug, Improvement, and Modernization Act of 2003. Insofar as the Inspector General has not determined the acquisition cost with respect to a drug or biological, the Secretary shall determine the payment amount for such drug or biological.

(iii) For such drugs and biologicals (including erythropoietin) furnished in 2006 and subsequent years, such acquisition cost or the amount determined under section 1847A for the drug or biological, as the Secretary may specify.

(B)(i) Drugs and biologicals (including erythropoietin) which were separately billed under this subsection on the day before the date of the enactment of the Medicare Prescription Drug, Improvement, and Modernization Act of 2003 shall continue to be separately billed on and after such date.

(ii) Nothing in this paragraph, section 1842(o), section 1847A, or section 1847B shall be construed as requiring or authorizing the bundling of payment for drugs and biologicals into the basic case-mix adjusted payment system under this paragraph.

* * *

Social Security Law Added, Amended or Repealed

[CCH Explanation at ¶759.]

2003 Amendments:

Section 623(a) of the "Medicare Prescription Drug, Improvement, and Modernization Act of 2003," effective upon enactment, amended the last sentence of section 1881(b)(7) by striking "and" before "for such services" the second place it appears; by inserting "and before January 1, 2005," after "January 1, 2001,"; and by inserting before the period at the end the following: ", and for such services furnished on or after January 1, 2005, by 1.6 percent above such composite rate payment amounts for such services furnished on December 31, 2004".

Section 623(b)(2) of the "Medicare Prescription Drug, Improvement, and Modernization Act of 2003," effective upon enactment, amended the fourth sentence of section 1881(b)(7) by striking "The Secretary" and inserting "Subject to section 422(a)(2) of the Medicare, Medicaid, and SCHIP Benefits Improvement and Protection Act of 2000, the Secretary".

Section 623(d)(1) of the "Medicare Prescription Drug, Improvement, and Modernization Act of 2003," effective upon enactment, amended section 1881(b) by adding new paragraphs (12) and (13).

Section 623(d)(2) of the "Medicare Prescription Drug, Improvement, and Modernization Act of 2003," effective upon enactment, amended section 1881(b)(7) in the first sentence by striking "The Secretary" and inserting "Subject to paragraph (12), the Secretary".

Section 623(d)(3) of the "Medicare Prescription Drug, Improvement, and Modernization Act of 2003," effective upon enactment, amended section 1881(b)(11)(B) by inserting "subject to paragraphs (12) and (13)" before "payment for such item".

[¶2346A] Sec. 1882. CRIMINAL PENALTIES; CIVIL PENALTIES FOR CERTAIN VIOLATIONS

[42 U.S.C. §1395ss(d)]

* * *

(d)(3)(A)(i) It is unlawful for a person to sell or issue to an individual entitled to benefits under part A or enrolled under part B of this title (including an individual electing a Medicare+Choice plan under section 1851)—

* * *

(II) in the case of an individual not electing a Medicare+Choice plan, a Medicare supplemental policy with knowledge that the individual is entitled to benefits under another Medicare supplemental policy or in the case of an individual electing a Medicare+Choice plan, a Medicare supplemental policy with knowledge that the policy duplicates health benefits to which the individual is otherwise entitled under the Medicare+Choice plan or under another Medicare supplemental policy, or

* * *

* * *

* * *

(B)(iii)(II) Subclause (I) shall not apply in the case of an individual who has another policy, if the individual indicates in writing, as part of the application for purchase, that the policy being purchased replaces such other policy and indicates an intent to terminate the policy being replaced when the new policy becomes effective and the issuer or seller certifies in writing that such policy will not, to the best of the issuer's or seller's knowledge, duplicate coverage (taking into account any such replacement).

* * *

2003 Amendments:

Section 736(e)(1) of the "Medicare Prescription Drug, Improvement, and Modernization Act of 2003," effective upon enactment, amended section 1882(d)(3)(A)(i)(II) by striking "plan a medicare supplemental policy" and inserting "plan, a medicare supplemental policy".

Section 736(e)(2) of the "Medicare Prescription Drug, Improvement, and Modernization Act of 2003," effective upon enactment, amended section 1882(d)(3)(B)(iii)(II) by striking "to the best of the issuer or seller's knowledge" and inserting "to the best of the issuer's or seller's knowledge".

[¶2346B] Sec. 1882. DEFINITIONS

[42 U.S.C. §1395ss(g)]

(g)(1) For purposes of this section, a Medicare supplemental policy is a health insurance policy or other health benefit plan offered by a private entity to individuals who are entitled to have payment made under this title, which provides reimbursement for expenses incurred for services and items for which payment may be made under this title but which are not reimbursable by reason of the applicability of deductibles, coinsurance amounts, or other limitations imposed pursuant to this title; but does not include a prescription drug plan under part D or a Medicare+Choice plan or any such policy or plan of one or more employers or labor organizations, or of the trustees of a fund established by one or more employers or labor organizations (or combination thereof), for employers or former employees (or combination thereof) or for members or former members (or combination thereof) of the labor organizations and does not include a policy or plan of an eligible organization (as defined in section 1876(b)) if the policy or plan provides benefits pursuant to a contract under section 1876 or an approved demonstration project described in section 603(c) of the Social Security Amendments of 1983, section 2355 of the Deficit Reduction Act of 1984, of 1986, or a policy or plan of an organization if the policy or plan provides benefits pursuant to an agreement under section 1833(a)(1)(A). For purposes of this section, the term "policy" includes a certificate issued under such policy.

(2) For purposes of this section:

(A) The term "NAIC Model Standards" means the "NAIC Model Regulation to Implement the Individual Accident and Sickness Insurance Minimum Standards Act", adopted by the National Association of Insurance Commissioners on June 6, 1979, as it applies to medicare supplemental policies.

* * *

[CCH Explanation at ¶ 210 and 215.]

2003 Amendments:

Section 104(b)(2)(A) of the "Medicare Prescription Drug, Improvement, and Modernization Act of 2003," effective upon enactment, amended section 1882(g)(1) by inserting "a prescription drug plan under part D or" after "but does not include".

Section 736(e)(3) of the "Medicare Prescription Drug, Improvement, and Modernization Act of 2003," effective upon enactment, amended section 1882(g)(2)(A) by striking "medicare supplement policies" and inserting "medicare supplemental policies"

[¶ 2346C] Sec. 1882. REQUIREMENTS OF GROUP BENEFITS; CORE GROUP BENEFITS; UNIFORM OUTLINE OF COVERAGE

[42 U.S.C. § 1395ss(o)]

(o) The requirements of this subsection are as follows:

(1) Each medicare supplemental policy shall provide for coverage of a group of benefits consistent with subsections (p), (v), and (w).

* * *

[CCH Explanation at ¶ 210 and 215.]

2003 Amendments:

Section 104(b)(2)(B) of the "Medicare Prescription Drug, Improvement, and Modernization Act of 2003," effective upon enactment, amended section 1882(o)(1) by striking "subsection (p)" and inserting "subsections (p), (v), and (w)".

[¶ 2346D] Sec. 1882. STANDARDS FOR GROUP BENEFITS

[42 U.S.C. § 1395ss(p)]

* * *

(p)(2) The benefits under the 1991 NAIC Model Regulation or 1991 Federal Regulation shall provide—

* * *

(B) for identification of a core group of basic benefits common to all policies; and

* * *

2003 Amendments:

Section 736(e)(4) of the "Medicare Prescription Drug, Improvement, and Modernization Act of 2003," effective upon enactment, amended section 1882(p)(2)(B) by striking ", and" and inserting "; and".

[¶ 2346E] Sec. 1882. COVERAGE OF PREEXISTING CONDITIONS

[42 U.S.C. § 1395ss(s)]

* * *

(s)(3)(A) The issuer of a Medicare supplemental policy—

* * *

(iii) may not impose an exclusion of benefits based on a preexisting condition under such policy,

* * *

* * *

(C)(ii)(I) Subject to subclause (II), only for purposes of an individual described in subparagraph (B)(v), a Medicare supplemental policy described in this subparagraph is the same Medicare supplemental policy referred to in such subparagraph in which the individual was most recently previously enrolled, if available from the same issuer, or, if not so available, a policy described in clause (i).

(II) If the medicare supplemental policy referred to in subparagraph (B)(v) was a medigap Rx policy (as defined in subsection (v)(6)(A)), a medicare supplemental policy described in this subparagraph is such policy in which the individual was most recently enrolled as modified under subsection (v)(2)(C)(i) or, at the election of the individual, a policy referred to in subsection (v)(3)(A)(i).

(iii) Only for purposes of an individual described in subparagraph (B)(vi) and subject to subsection (v)(1), a Medicare supplemental policy described in this subparagraph shall include any Medicare supplemental policy.

* * *

[CCH Explanation at ¶ 210 and 215.]

2003 Amendments:

Section 104(a)(2)(A) of the "Medicare Prescription Drug, Improvement, and Modernization Act of 2003," effective upon enactment, amended section 1882(s)(3)(C)(ii) by striking "(ii) Only" and inserting "(ii)(I) Subject to subclause (II), only"; and by adding at the end new subclause (II).

Section 104(a)(2)(B) of the "Medicare Prescription Drug, Improvement, and Modernization Act of 2003," effective upon enactment, amended section 1882(s)(3)(C)(iii) by inserting "and subject to subsection (v)(1)" after "subparagraph (B)(vi)"

Section 736(e)(5) of the "Medicare Prescription Drug, Improvement, and Modernization Act of 2003," effective upon enactment, amended section 1882(s)(3)(A)(iii) by striking "pre-existing" and inserting "preexisting".

[¶ 2346F] Sec. 1882. RULES RELATING TO MEDIGAP POLICIES THAT PROVIDE PRESCRIPTION DRUG COVERAGE

(v)(1) PROHIBITION ON SALE, ISSUANCE, AND RENEWAL OF NEW POLICIES THAT PROVIDE PRESCRIPTION DRUG COVERAGE.—

(A) IN GENERAL.—Notwithstanding any other provision of law, on or after January 1, 2006, a medigap Rx policy (as defined in paragraph (6)(A)) may not be sold, issued, or renewed under this section—

(i) to an individual who is a part D enrollee (as defined in paragraph (6)(B)); or

(ii) except as provided in subparagraph (B), to an individual who is not a part D enrollee.

(B) CONTINUATION PERMITTED FOR NON-PART D ENROLLEES.—Subparagraph (A)(ii) shall not apply to the renewal of a medigap Rx policy that was issued before January 1, 2006.

(C) CONSTRUCTION.—Nothing in this subsection shall be construed as preventing the offering on and after January 1, 2006, of "H", "I", and "J" policies described in paragraph (2)(D)(i) if the benefit packages are modified in accordance with paragraph (2)(C).

(2) ELIMINATION OF DUPLICATIVE COVERAGE UPON PART D ENROLLMENT.—

(A) IN GENERAL.—In the case of an individual who is covered under a medigap Rx policy and enrolls under a part D plan—

(i) before the end of the initial part D enrollment period, the individual may—

(I) enroll in a medicare supplemental policy without prescription drug coverage under paragraph (3); or

(II) continue the policy in effect subject to the modification described in subparagraph (C)(i); or

(ii) after the end of such period, the individual may continue the policy in effect subject to such modification.

§1882(v)(2)(A)(ii) ¶2346F

(B) NOTICE REQUIRED TO BE PROVIDED TO CURRENT POLICYHOLDERS WITH MEDIGAP RX POLICY.—No medicare supplemental policy of an issuer shall be deemed to meet the standards in subsection (c) unless the issuer provides written notice (in accordance with standards of the Secretary established in consultation with the National Association of Insurance Commissioners) during the 60-day period immediately preceding the initial part D enrollment period, to each individual who is a policyholder or certificate holder of a medigap Rx policy (at the most recent available address of that individual) of the following:

(i) If the individual enrolls in a plan under part D during the initial enrollment period under section 1860D-1(b)(2)(A), the individual has the option of—

(I) continuing enrollment in the individual's current plan, but the plan's coverage of prescription drugs will be modified under subparagraph (C)(i); or

(II) enrolling in another medicare supplemental policy pursuant to paragraph (3).

(ii) If the individual does not enroll in a plan under part D during such period, the individual may continue enrollment in the individual's current plan without change, but—

(I) the individual will not be guaranteed the option of enrollment in another medicare supplemental policy pursuant to paragraph (3); and

(II) if the current plan does not provide creditable prescription drug coverage (as defined in section 1860D-13(b)(4)), notice of such fact and that there are limitations on the periods in a year in which the individual may enroll under a part D plan and any such enrollment is subject to a late enrollment penalty.

(iii) Such other information as the Secretary may specify (in consultation with the National Association of Insurance Commissioners), including the potential impact of such election on premiums for medicare supplemental policies.

(C) MODIFICATION.—

(i) IN GENERAL.—The policy modification described in this subparagraph is the elimination of prescription coverage for expenses of prescription drugs incurred after the effective date of the individual's coverage under a part D plan and the appropriate adjustment of premiums to reflect such elimination of coverage.

(ii) CONTINUATION OF RENEWABILITY AND APPLICATION OF MODIFICATION.—No medicare supplemental policy of an issuer shall be deemed to meet the standards in subsection (c) unless the issuer—

(I) continues renewability of medigap Rx policies that it has issued, subject to subclause (II); and

(II) applies the policy modification described in clause (i) in the cases described in clauses (i)(II) and (ii) of subparagraph (A).

(D) REFERENCES TO RX POLICIES.—

(i) H, I, AND J POLICIES.—Any reference to a benefit package classified as "H" "I", or "J" (including the benefit package classified as "J" with a high deductible feature, as described in subsection (p)(11)) under the standards established under subsection (p)(2) shall be construed as including a reference to such a package as modified under subparagraph (C) and such packages as modified shall not be counted as a separate benefit package under such subsection.

(ii) APPLICATION IN WAIVERED STATES.—Except for the modification provided under subparagraph (C), the waivers previously in effect under subsection (p)(2) shall continue in effect.

(3) AVAILABILITY OF SUBSTITUTE POLICIES WITH GUARANTEED ISSUE.—

(A) IN GENERAL.—The issuer of a medicare supplemental policy—

(i) may not deny or condition the issuance or effectiveness of a medicare supplemental policy that has a benefit package classified as "A", "B", "C", or "F" (including the benefit package classified as "F" with a high deductible feature, as described in subsection (p)(11)), under the standards established under subsection (p)(2), or a benefit package described in subparagraph (A) or (B) of subsection (w)(2) and that is offered and is available for issuance to new enrollees by such issuer;

(ii) may not discriminate in the pricing of such policy, because of health status, claims experience, receipt of health care, or medical condition; and

(iii) may not impose an exclusion of benefits based on a pre-existing condition under such policy,

in the case of an individual described in subparagraph (B) who seeks to enroll under the policy not later than 63 days after the effective date of the individual's coverage under a part D plan.

(B) INDIVIDUAL COVERED.—An individual described in this subparagraph with respect to the issuer of a medicare supplemental policy is an individual who—

(i) enrolls in a part D plan during the initial part D enrollment period;

(ii) at the time of such enrollment was enrolled in a medigap Rx policy issued by such issuer; and

(iii) terminates enrollment in such policy and submits evidence of such termination along with the application for the policy under subparagraph (A).

(C) SPECIAL RULE FOR WAIVERED STATES.—For purposes of applying this paragraph in the case of a State that provides for offering of benefit packages other than under the classification referred to in subparagraph (A)(i), the references to benefit packages in such subparagraph are deemed references to comparable benefit packages offered in such State.

(4) ENFORCEMENT.—

(A) PENALTIES FOR DUPLICATION.—The penalties described in subsection (d)(3)(A)(ii) shall apply with respect to a violation of paragraph (1)(A).

(B) GUARANTEED ISSUE.—The provisions of paragraph (4) of subsection (s) shall apply with respect to the requirements of paragraph (3) in the same manner as they apply to the requirements of such subsection.

(5) CONSTRUCTION.—Any provision in this section or in a medicare supplemental policy relating to guaranteed renewability of coverage shall be deemed to have been met with respect to a part D enrollee through the continuation of the policy subject to modification under paragraph (2)(C) or the offering of a substitute policy under paragraph (3). The previous sentence shall not be construed to affect the guaranteed renewability of such a modified or substitute policy.

(6) DEFINITIONS.—For purposes of this subsection:

(A) MEDIGAP RX POLICY.—The term "medigap Rx policy" means a medicare supplemental policy—

(i) which has a benefit package classified as "H", "I", or ""J" (including the benefit package classified as "J" with a high deductible feature, as described in subsection (p)(11)) under the standards established under subsection (p)(2), without regard to this subsection; and

(ii) to which such standards do not apply (or to which such standards have been waived under subsection (p)(6)) but which provides benefits for prescription drugs.

Such term does not include a policy with a benefit package as classified under clause (i) which has been modified under paragraph (2)(C)(i).

(B) PART D ENROLLEE.—The term "part D enrollee" means an individual who is enrolled in a part D plan.

(C) PART D PLAN.—The term "part D enrollee'" means a prescription drug plan or an MA-PD plan (as defined for purposes of part D).

(D) INITIAL PART D ENROLLMENT PERIOD.—The term "initial part D enrollment period" means the initial enrollment period described in section 1860D-1(b)(2)(A).

§1882(v)(6)(D)   ¶2346F

[CCH Explanation at ¶ 210 and 215.]

2003 Amendments:

Section 104(a)(1) of the "Medicare Prescription Drug, Improvement, and Modernization Act of 2003," effective upon enactment, amended section 1882 by adding at the end new subsection (v).

[¶ 2346G] Sec. 1882. DEVELOPMENT OF NEW STANDARDS FOR MEDICARE SUPPLEMENTAL POLICIES

(w)(1) IN GENERAL.—The Secretary shall request the National Association of Insurance Commissioners to review and revise the standards for benefit packages under subsection (p)(1), taking into account the changes in benefits resulting from enactment of the Medicare Prescription Drug, Improvement, and Modernization Act of 2003 and to otherwise update standards to reflect other changes in law included in such Act. Such revision shall incorporate the inclusion of the 2 benefit packages described in paragraph (2). Such revisions shall be made consistent with the rules applicable under subsection (p)(1)(E) with the reference to the "1991 NAIC Model Regulation" deemed a reference to the NAIC Model Regulation as published in the Federal Register on December 4, 1998, and as subsequently updated by the National Association of Insurance Commissioners to reflect previous changes in law (and subsection (v)) and the reference to "date of enactment of this subsection" deemed a reference to the date of enactment of the Medicare Prescription Drug, Improvement, and Modernization Act of 2003. To the extent practicable, such revision shall provide for the implementation of revised standards for benefit packages as of January 1, 2006.

(2) NEW BENEFIT PACKAGES.—The benefit packages described in this paragraph are the following (notwithstanding any other provision of this section relating to a core benefit package):

(A) FIRST NEW BENEFIT PACKAGE.—A benefit package consisting of the following:

(i) Subject to clause (ii), coverage of 50 percent of the cost-sharing otherwise applicable under parts A and B, except there shall be no coverage of the part B deductible and coverage of 100 percent of any cost-sharing otherwise applicable for preventive benefits.

(ii) Coverage for all hospital inpatient coinsurance and 365 extra lifetime days of coverage of inpatient hospital services (as in the current core benefit package).

(iii) A limitation on annual out-of-pocket expenditures under parts A and B to $4,000 in 2006 (or, in a subsequent year, to such limitation for the previous year increased by an appropriate inflation adjustment specified by the Secretary).

(B) SECOND NEW BENEFIT PACKAGE.—A benefit package consisting of the benefit package described in subparagraph (A), except as follows:

(i) Substitute "75 percent" for "50 percent" in clause (i) of such subparagraph.

(ii) Substitute "$2,000" for "$4,000" in clause (iii) of such subparagraph.

[CCH Explanation at ¶ 210 and 215.]

2003 Amendments:

Section 104(b)(1) of the "Medicare Prescription Drug, Improvement, and Modernization Act of 2003," effective upon enactment, amended section 1882 by adding at the end new (w).

[¶ 2350] Sec. 1883. HOSPITAL PROVIDERS OF EXTENDED CARE SERVICES

[42 U.S.C. § 1395tt]

* * *

(a)(3) Notwithstanding any other provision of this title, a critical access hospital shall be paid for covered skilled nursing facility services furnished under an agreement entered into under this section on the basis of equal to 101 percent of the reasonable costs of such services (as determined under section 1861(v)).

* * *

2003 Amendments:

Section 405(a)(1) of the "Medicare Prescription Drug, Improvement, and Modernization Act of 2003," effective upon enactment, amended section 1883(a)(3) by inserting "equal to 101 percent of" before "the reasonable costs".

The amendment made above applies to payments for services furnished during cost reporting periods beginning on or after January 1, 2004.

[¶ 2351A] Sec. 1886. [Rate of Increase in Target Amounts for Inpatient Hospital Services]

[42 U.S.C. § 1395ww(b)]

* * *

* * *

(b)(3)(B)(i) For purposes of subsection (d) and subsection (j) for discharges occurring during a fiscal year, the "applicable percentage increase" shall be—

* * *

(XVIII) for fiscal year 2003, the market basket percentage increase minus 0.55 percentage points for hospitals in all areas,

(XIX) for each of fiscal years 2004 through 2007, subject to clause (vii), the market basket percentage increase for hospitals in all areas; and

(XX) for fiscal year 2008 and each subsequent fiscal year, the market basket percentage increase for hospitals in all areas.

* * *

(vii)(I) For purposes of clause (i)(XIX) for each of fiscal years 2005 through 2007, in a case of a subsection (d) hospital that does not submit data to the Secretary in accordance with subclause (II) with respect to such a fiscal year, the applicable percentage increase under such clause for such fiscal year shall be reduced by 0.4 percentage points. Such reduction shall apply only with respect to the fiscal year involved, and the Secretary shall not take into account such reduction in computing the applicable percentage increase under clause (i)(XIX) for a subsequent fiscal year.

(II) Each subsection (d) hospital shall submit to the Secretary quality data (for a set of 10 indicators established by the Secretary as of November 1, 2003) that relate to the quality of care furnished by the hospital in inpatient settings in a form and manner, and at a time, specified by the Secretary for purposes of this clause, but with respect to fiscal year 2005, the Secretary shall provide for a 30-day grace period for the submission of data by a hospital.

* * *

(I)(i) For cost reporting periods beginning on or after October 1, 2000, in the case of a sole community hospital there shall be substituted for the amount otherwise determined under subsection (d)(5)(D)(i), if such substitution results in a greater amount of payment under this section for the hospital—

(I) with respect to discharges occurring in fiscal year 2001, 75 percent of the amount otherwise applicable to the hospital under subsection (d)(5)(D)(i) (referred to in this clause as the "subsection (d)(5)(D)(i) amount") and 25 percent of the rebased target amount (as defined in clause (ii));

* * *

(iii) In no case shall a hospital be denied treatment as a sole community hospital or payment (on the basis of a target rate as such as a hospital) because data are unavailable for any cost reporting period due to changes in ownership, changes in fiscal intermediaries, or other extraordinary circumstances, so long as data for at least one applicable base cost reporting period is available.

* * *

[CCH Explanation at ¶ 560.]

2003 Amendments:

Section 407(a) of the "Medicare Prescription Drug, Improvement, and Modernization Act of 2003," amended section 1886(b)(3)(I) by adding at the end new clause (iii).

The amendments made by section 407(a) of the "Medicare Prescription Drug, Improvement, and Modernization Act of 2003," apply to cost reporting periods beginning on or after January 1, 2004.

Section 501(a) of the "Medicare Prescription Drug, Improvement, and Modernization Act of 2003," effective upon enactment, amended section 1886(b)(3)(B)(i) by striking "and" at the end of subclause (XVIII); by striking subclause

(XIX); and by inserting after subclause (XVIII) new subclauses (XIX) and (XX).

Prior to being stricken subclause XIX read as follows:

(XIX) for fiscal year 2004 and each subsequent fiscal year, the market basket percentage increase for hospitals in all areas.

Section 501(b) of the "Medicare Prescription Drug, Improvement, and Modernization Act of 2003," effective upon enactment, amended section 1886(b)(3)(B) by adding at the end new clause (vii).

Section 736(a)(9) of the "Medicare Prescription Drug, Improvement, and Modernization Act of 2003," effective upon enactment, amended section 1886(b)(3)(I)(i)(I) by striking "the the" and inserting "the".

[¶ 2351B] Sec. 1886. [PPS Transition Period; DRG Classification System; Exceptions and Adjustments to PPS]

[42 U.S.C. § 1395ww(d)]

* * *

(d)(2) The Secretary shall determine a national adjusted DRG prospective payment rate, for each inpatient hospital discharge in fiscal year 1984 involving inpatient hospital services of a subsection (d) hospital in the United States, and shall determine a regional adjusted DRG prospective payment rate for such discharges in each region, for which payment may be made under part A of this title. Each such rate shall be determined for hospitals located in urban or rural areas within the United States or within each such region, respectively, as follows:

* * *

(C) STANDARDIZING AMOUNTS.—The Secretary shall standardize the amount updated under subparagraph (B) for each hospital by—

(i) excluding an estimate of indirect medical education costs (taking into account, for discharges occurring after September 30, 1986, the amendments made by section 9104(a) of the Medicare and Medicaid Budget Reconciliation Amendments of 1985), except that the Secretary shall not take into account any reduction in the amount of additional payments under paragraph (5)(B)(ii) resulting from the amendment made by section 4621(a)(1) of the Balanced Budget Act of 1997, or any additional payments under such paragraph resulting from the application of section 111 of the Medicare, Medicaid, and SCHIP Balanced Budget Refinement Act of 1999, of section 302 of the Medicare, Medicaid, and SCHIP Benefits Improvement and Protection Act of 2000, or the Medicare Prescription Drug, Improvement, and Modernization Act of 2003,

* * *

(iv) for discharges occurring on or after October 1, 1986, excluding an estimate of the additional payments to certain hospitals to be made under paragraph (5)(F), except that the Secretary shall not exclude additional payments under such paragraph made as a result of the enactment of section 6003(c) of the Omnibus Budget Reconciliation Act of 1989 the enactment of section 4002(b) of the Omnibus Budget Reconciliation Act of 1990, the enactment of section 303 of the Medicare, Medicaid, and SCHIP Benefits Improvement and Protection Act of 2000, or the enactment of section 402(a)(1) of the Medicare Prescription Drug, Improvement, and Modernization Act of 2003.

* * *

(3) The Secretary shall determine a national adjusted DRG prospective payment rate, for each inpatient hospital discharge in a fiscal year after fiscal year 1984 involving inpatient hospital services of a subsection (d) hospital in the United States, and shall determine, for fiscal years before fiscal year 1997, a regional adjusted DRG prospective payment rate for such discharges in each region for which payment may be made under part A of this title. Each such rate shall be determined for hospitals located in large urban, other urban, or rural areas within the United States and within each such region, respectively, as follows:

* * *

(A) UPDATING PREVIOUS STANDARDIZED AMOUNTS.—

* * *

(iii) For discharges occurring in the fiscal year beginning on October 1, 1994, the average standardized amount for hospitals located in a rural area shall be equal to the average standardized amount for hospitals located in an urban area.

Social Security Law Added, Amended or Repealed

(iv)(I) Subject to subclause (II), for discharges occurring in a fiscal year beginning on or after October 1, 1995, the Secretary shall compute an average standardized amount for hospitals located in a large urban area and for hospitals located in other areas within the United States and within each region equal to the respective average standardized amount computed for the previous fiscal year under this subparagraph increased by the applicable percentage increase under subsection (b)(3)(B)(i) with respect to hospitals located in the respective areas for the fiscal year involved.

(II) For discharges occurring in a fiscal year (beginning with fiscal year 2004), the Secretary shall compute a standardized amount for hospitals located in any area within the United States and within each region equal to the standardized amount computed for the previous fiscal year under this subparagraph for hospitals located in a large urban area (or, beginning with fiscal year 2005, for all hospitals in the previous fiscal year) increased by the applicable percentage increase under subsection (b)(3)(B)(i) for the fiscal year involved.

* * *

(D) COMPUTING DRG-SPECIFIC RATES FOR HOSPITALS.—For each discharge classified within a diagnosis-related group, the Secretary shall establish for the fiscal year a national DRG prospective payment rate and shall establish, for fiscal years before fiscal year 1997, a regional DRG prospective payment rate for each region which is equal—

(i) for fiscal years before fiscal year 2004, for hospitals located in a large urban area in the United States or that region (respectively), to the product of—

* * *

(II) the weighting factor (determined under paragraph (4)(B)) for that diagnosis-related group;

(ii) for fiscal years before fiscal year 2004, for hospitals located in other areas in the United States or that region (respectively), to the product of—

* * *

(II) the weighting factor (determined under paragraph (4)(B)) for that diagnosis-related group; and

(iii) for a fiscal year beginning after fiscal year 2003, for hospitals located in all areas, to the product of—

(I) the applicable standardized amount (computed under subparagraph (A)), reduced under subparagraph (B), and adjusted or reduced under subparagraph (C) for the fiscal year; and

(II) the weighting factor (determined under paragraph (4)(B)) for that diagnosis-related group.

(E) ADJUSTING FOR DIFFERENT AREA WAGE LEVELS.—(i) IN GENERAL.—Except as provided in clause (ii), the Secretary shall adjust the proportion (as estimated by the Secretary from time to time) of hospitals' costs which are attributable to wages and wage-related costs, of the DRG prospective payment rates computed under subparagraph (D) for area differences in hospital wage levels by a factor (established by the Secretary) reflecting the relative hospital wage level in the geographic area of the hospital compared to the national average hospital wage level. Not later than October 1, 1990, and October 1, 1993 (and at least every 12 months thereafter), the Secretary shall update the factor under the preceding sentence on the basis of a survey conducted by the Secretary (and updated as appropriate) of the wages and wage-related costs of subsection (d) hospitals in the United States. Not less often than once every 3 years the Secretary (through such survey or otherwise) shall measure the earnings and paid hours of employment by occupational category and shall exclude data with respect to the wages and wage-related costs incurred in furnishing skilled nursing facility services. Any adjustments or updates made under this subparagraph for a fiscal year (beginning with fiscal year 1991) shall be made in a manner that assures that the aggregate payments under this subsection in the fiscal year are not greater or less than those that would have been made in the year without such adjustment. The Secretary shall apply the previous sentence for any period as if the amendments made by section 403(a)(1) of the Medicare Prescription Drug, Improvement, and Modernization Act of 2003 had not been enacted.

§1886(d)(3)(E)(i)   ¶2351B

(ii) ALTERNATIVE PROPORTION TO BE ADJUSTED BEGINNING IN FISCAL YEAR 2005.—For discharges occurring on or after October 1, 2004, the Secretary shall substitute "62 percent" for the proportion described in the first sentence of clause (i), unless the application of this clause would result in lower payments to a hospital than would otherwise be made.

* * *

(5)

* * *

(B) The Secretary shall provide for an additional payment amount for subsection (d) hospitals with indirect costs of medical education, in an amount computed in the same manner as the adjustment for such costs under regulations (in effect as of January 1, 1983) under subsection (a)(2), except as follows:

* * *

(ii) For purposes of clause (i)(II), the indirect teaching adjustment factor is equal to c $(((1+r)$ to the nth power) - 1), where "r" is the ratio of the hospital's full-time equivalent interns and residents to beds and "n" equals .405. Subject to clause (ix), for discharges occurring—

* * *

(VI) during fiscal year 2002, "c" is equal to 1.6;

(VII) on or after October 1, 2002, and before April 1, 2004, "c" is equal to 1.35.

(VIII) on or after April 1, 2004, and before October 1, 2004, "c" is equal to 1.47;

(IX) during fiscal year 2005, "c" is equal to 1.42;

(X) during fiscal year 2006, "c" is equal to 1.37;

(XI) during fiscal year 2007, "c" is equal to 1.32; and

(XII) on or after October 1, 2007, "c" is equal to 1.35.

* * *

(v) In determining the adjustment with respect to a hospital for discharges occurring on or after October 1, 1997, the total number of full-time equivalent interns and residents in the fields of allopathic and osteopathic medicine in either a hospital or nonhospital setting may not exceed the number (or, 130 percent of such number in the case of a hospital located in a rural area) of such full-time equivalent interns and residents in the hospital with respect to the hospital's most recent cost reporting period ending on or before December 31, 1996. Rules similar to the rules of subsection (h)(4)(F)(ii) shall apply for purposes of this clause. The provisions of subsection (h)(7) shall apply with respect to the first sentence of this clause in the same manner as it applies with respect to subsection (h)(4)(F)(i).

* * *

(ix) For discharges occurring on or after July 1, 2005, insofar as an additional payment amount under this subparagraph is attributable to resident positions redistributed to a hospital under subsection (h)(7)(B), in computing the indirect teaching adjustment factor under clause (ii) the adjustment shall be computed in a manner as if "c" were equal to 0.66 with respect to such resident positions.

* * *

* * *

(F)(iv) The disproportionate share adjustment percentage for a cost reporting period for a hospital that is not described in clause (i)(II) and that—

* * *

(II) is located in an urban area and has less than 100 beds, is equal to 5 percent or, subject to clause (xiv) and for discharges occurring on or after April 1, 2001, is equal to the percent determined in accordance with clause (xiii);

(III) is located in a rural area and is not described in subclause (IV) or (V) or in the second sentence of clause (v), is equal to 4 percent or, subject to clause (xiv) and for discharges occurring on or after April 1, 2001, is equal to the percent determined in accordance with clause (xii);

(IV) is located in a rural area, is classified as a rural referral center under subparagraph (C), and is classified as a sole community hospital under subparagraph (D), is equal to 10 percent or, if greater, the percent determined in accordance with the applicable formula described in clause (viii) or, subject to clause (xiv) and for discharges occuring on or after April 1, 2001, the greater of the percentages determined under clause (x) or (xi);

(V) is located in a rural area, is classified as a rural referral center under subparagraph (C), and is not classified as a sole community hospital under subparagraph (D), is equal to the percent determined in accordance with the applicable formula described in clause (viii) or, subject to clause (xiv) and for discharges occurring on or after April 1, 2001, is equal to the percent determined in accordance with clause (xi); or

* * *

(viii) Subject to clause (xiv), the formula used to determine the disproportionate share adjustment percentage for a cost reporting period for a hospital described in clause (iv)(IV) or (iv)(V) is the percentage determined in accordance with the following formula: $(P-30)(.6)+4.0$, where "P" is the hospital's disproportionate patient percentage (as defined in clause (vi)).

* * *

(x) Subject to clause (xiv), for purposes of clause (iv)(VI) (relating to sole community hospitals), in the case of a hospital for a cost reporting period with a disproportionate patient percentage (as defined in clause (vi)) that—

* * *

(xi) Subject to clause (xiv), for purposes of clause (iv)(V) (relating to rural referral centers), in the case of a hospital for a cost reporting period with a disproportionate patient percentage (as defined in clause (vi)) that—

* * *

(xii) Subject to clause (xiv), for purposes of clause (iv)(III) (relating to small rural hospitals generally), in the case of a hospital for a cost reporting period with a disproportionate patient percentage (as defined in clause (vi)) that—

* * *

(xiii) Subject to clause (xiv), for purposes of clause (iv)(II) (relating to urban hospitals with less than 100 beds), in the case of a hospital for a cost reporting period with a disproportionate patient percentage (as defined in clause (vi)) that—

* * *

(xiv)(I) In the case of discharges occurring on or after April 1, 2004, subject to subclause (II), there shall be substituted for the disproportionate share adjustment percentage otherwise determined under clause (iv) (other than subclause (I)) or under clause (viii), (x), (xi), (xii), or (xiii), the disproportionate share adjustment percentage determined under clause (vii) (relating to large, urban hospitals).

(II) Under subclause (I), the disproportionate share adjustment percentage shall not exceed 12 percent for a hospital that is not classified as a rural referral center under subparagraph (C).

* * *

(K)(i) Effective for discharges beginning on or after October 1, 2001, the Secretary shall establish a mechanism to recognize the costs of new medical services and technologies under the payment system established under this subsection. Such mechanism shall be established after notice and opportunity for public comment (in the publications required by subsection (e)(5) for a fiscal year or otherwise). Such mechanism shall be modified to meet the requirements of clause (viii).

(ii) The mechanism established pursuant to clause (i) shall—

(I) apply to a new medical service or technology if, based on the estimated costs incurred with respect to discharges involving such service or technology, the DRG prospective payment rate otherwise applicable to such discharges under this subsection is inadequate (applying a threshold specified by the Secretary that is the lesser of 75 percent of the standardized amount (increased to reflect the difference between cost and charges) or 75 percent of one standard deviation for the diagnosis-related group involved);

* * *

(III) provide for additional payment to be made under this subsection with respect to discharges involving a new medical service or technology described in subclause (I) that occur during the period described in subclause (II) in an amount that adequately reflects the estimated average cost of such service or technology; and

* * *

(vii) Under the mechanism under this subparagraph, the Secretary shall provide for the addition of new diagnosis and procedure codes in April 1 of each year, but the addition of such codes shall not require the Secretary to adjust the payment (or diagnosis-related group classification) under this subsection until the fiscal year that begins after such date.

(viii) The mechanism established pursuant to clause (i) shall be adjusted to provide, before publication of a proposed rule, for public input regarding whether a new service or technology represents an advance in medical technology that substantially improves the diagnosis or treatment of individuals entitled to benefits under part A as follows:

(I) The Secretary shall make public and periodically update a list of all the services and technologies for which an application for additional payment under this subparagraph is pending.

(II) The Secretary shall accept comments, recommendations, and data from the public regarding whether the service or technology represents a substantial improvement.

(III) The Secretary shall provide for a meeting at which organizations representing hospitals, physicians, such individuals, manufacturers, and any other interested party may present comments, recommendations, and data to the clinical staff of the Centers for Medicare & Medicaid Services before publication of a notice of proposed rulemaking regarding whether service or technology represents a substantial improvement.

(ix) Before establishing any add-on payment under this subparagraph with respect to a new technology, the Secretary shall seek to identify one or more diagnosis-related groups associated with such technology, based on similar clinical or anatomical characteristics and the cost of the technology. Within such groups the Secretary shall assign an eligible new technology into a diagnosis-related group where the average costs of care most closely approximate the costs of care of using the new technology. No add-on payment under this subparagraph shall be made with respect to such new technology and this clause shall not affect the application of paragraph (4)(C)(iii).

* * *

(7) There shall be no administrative or judicial review under section 1878 or otherwise of—

(A) the determination of the requirement, or the proportional amount, of any adjustment effected pursuant to subsection (e)(1)or the determination of the applicable percentage increase under paragraph (12)(A)(ii), and

* * *

(9)(A) Notwithstanding section 1814(b) but subject to the provisions of section 1813, the amount of the payment with respect to the operating costs of inpatient hospital services of a subsection (d) Puerto Rico hospital for inpatient hospital discharges is equal to the sum of—

(i) the applicable Puerto Rico percentage (specified in subparagraph (E))of the Puerto Rico adjusted DRG prospective payment rate (determined under subparagraph (B) or (C)) for such discharges,

(ii) the applicable Federal percentage (specified in subparagraph (E)) of—

(I) for discharges beginning in a fiscal year beginning on or after October 1, 1997, and before October 1, 2003, the discharge-weighted average of—

(aa) the national adjusted DRG prospective payment rate (determined under paragraph (3)(D)) for hospitals located in a large urban area,

(bb) such rate for hospitals located in other urban areas, and

(cc) such rate for hospitals located in a rural area,

for such discharges, adjusted in the manner provided in paragraph (3)(E) for different area wage levels; and

(II) for discharges in a fiscal year beginning on or after October 1, 2003, the national DRG prospective payment rate determined under paragraph (3)(D)(iii) for hospitals located in any area for such discharges, adjusted in the manner provided in paragraph (3)(E) for different area wage levels.

As used in this section, the term "subsection (d) Puerto Rico hospital" means a hospital that is located in Puerto Rico and that would be a subsection (d) hospital (as defined in paragraph (1)(B)) if it were located in one of the 50 States.

* * *

(C) The Secretary shall determine a Puerto Rico adjusted DRG prospective payment rate, for each inpatient hospital discharge after fiscal year 1988 involving inpatient hospital services of a subsection (d) Puerto Rico hospital for which payment may be made under part A of this title. Such rate shall be determined for hospitals located in urban or rural areas within Puerto Rico as follows:

(i)(I) For discharges in a fiscal year after fiscal year 1988 and before fiscal year 2004, the Secretary shall compute an average standardized amount for hospitals located in an urban area and for hospitals located in a rural area equal to the respective average standardized amount computed for the previous fiscal year under subparagraph (B)(iii) or under this clause, increased for fiscal year 1989 by the applicable percentage increase under subsection (b)(3)(B), and adjusted for subsequent fiscal years in accordance with the final determination of the Secretary under subsection (e)(4), and adjusted to reflect the most recent case-mix data available.

(II) For discharges occurring in a fiscal year (beginning with fiscal year 2004), the Secretary shall compute an average standardized amount for hospitals located in any area of Puerto Rico that is equal to the average standardized amount computed under subclause (I) for fiscal year 2003 for hospitals in a large urban area (or, beginning with fiscal year 2005, for all hospitals in the previous fiscal year) increased by the applicable percentage increase under subsection (b)(3)(B) for the fiscal year involved.

(ii) The Secretary shall reduce each of the average standardized amounts (or for fiscal year 2004 and thereafter, the average standardized amount) by a proportion equal to the proportion (estimated by the Secretary) of the amount of payments under this paragraph which are additional payments described in subparagraph (D)(i) (relating to outlier payments).

(iii) For each discharge classified within a diagnosis-related group for hospitals located in an urban or rural area, respectively, the Secretary shall establish a Puerto Rico DRG prospective payment rate equal to the product of—

(I) the average standardized amount (computed under clause (i) and reduced under clause (ii)), and

* * *

(iv)(I) The Secretary shall adjust the proportion (as estimated by the Secretary from time to time) of hospitals' costs which are attributable to wages and wage-related costs, of the Puerto Rico DRG prospective payment rate computed under clause (iii) for area differences in hospital wage levels by a factor (established by the Secretary) reflecting the relative hospital wage level in the geographic area of the hospital compared to the Puerto Rico average hospital wage level. The second and third sentences of paragraph (3)(E)(i) shall apply to subsection (d) Puerto Rico hospitals under this clause in the same manner as they apply to subsection (d) hospitals under such paragraph and, for purposes of this clause, any reference in such paragraph to a subsection (d) hospital is deemed a reference to a subsection (d) Puerto Rico hospital.

(II) For discharges occurring on or after October 1, 2004, the Secretary shall substitute "62 percent" for the proportion described in the first sentence of clause (i), unless the application of this subclause would result in lower payments to a hospital than would otherwise be made.

* * *

(E) For purposes of subparagraph (A), for discharges occurring—

(i) on or after October 1, 1987, and before October 1, 1997, the applicable Puerto Rico percentage is 75 percent and the applicable Federal percentage is 25 percent;

(ii) on or after October 1, 1997, and before April 1, 2004, the applicable Puerto Rico percentage is 50 percent and the applicable Federal percentage is 50 percent;

(iii) on or after April 1, 2004, and before October 1, 2004, the applicable Puerto Rico percentage is 37.5 percent and the applicable Federal percentage is 62.5 percent; and

(iv) on or after October 1, 2004, the applicable Puerto Rico percentage is 25 percent and the applicable Federal percentage is 75 percent.

* * *

(12) PAYMENT ADJUSTMENT FOR LOW-VOLUME HOSPITALS.—

(A) IN GENERAL.—In addition to any payments calculated under this section for a subsection (d) hospital, for discharges occurring during a fiscal year (beginning with fiscal year 2005), the Secretary shall provide for an additional payment amount to each low-volume hospital (as defined in subparagraph (C)(i)) for discharges occurring during that fiscal year that is equal to the applicable percentage increase (determined under subparagraph (B) for the hospital involved) in the amount paid to such hospital under this section for such discharges (determined without regard to this paragraph).

(B) APPLICABLE PERCENTAGE INCREASE.—The Secretary shall determine an applicable percentage increase for purposes of subparagraph (A) as follows:

(i) The Secretary shall determine the empirical relationship for subsection (d) hospitals between the standardized cost-per-case for such hospitals and the total number of discharges of such hospitals and the amount of the additional incremental costs (if any) that are associated with such number of discharges.

(ii) The applicable percentage increase shall be determined based upon such relationship in a manner that reflects, based upon the number of such discharges for a subsection (d) hospital, such additional incremental costs.

(iii) In no case shall the applicable percentage increase exceed 25 percent.

(C) DEFINITIONS.—

(i) LOW-VOLUME HOSPITAL.—For purposes of this paragraph, the term "low-volume hospital" means, for a fiscal year, a subsection (d) hospital (as defined in paragraph (1)(B)) that the Secretary determines is located more than 25 road miles from another subsection (d) hospital and has less than 800 discharges during the fiscal year.

(ii) DISCHARGE.—For purposes of subparagraph (B) and clause (i), the term "discharge" means an inpatient acute care discharge of an individual regardless of whether the individual is entitled to benefits under part A.

(13)(A) In order to recognize commuting patterns among geographic areas, the Secretary shall establish a process through application or otherwise for an increase of the wage index applied under paragraph (3)(E) for subsection (d) hospitals located in a qualifying county described in subparagraph (B) in the amount computed under subparagraph (D) based on out-migration of hospital employees who reside in that county to any higher wage index area.

(B) The Secretary shall establish criteria for a qualifying county under this subparagraph based on the out-migration referred to in subparagraph (A) and differences in the area wage indices. Under such criteria the Secretary shall, utilizing such data as the Secretary determines to be appropriate, establish—

(i) a threshold percentage, established by the Secretary, of the weighted average of the area wage index or indices for the higher wage index areas involved;

(ii) a threshold (of not less than 10 percent) for minimum out-migration to a higher wage index area or areas; and

(iii) a requirement that the average hourly wage of the hospitals in the qualifying county equals or exceeds the average hourly wage of all the hospitals in the area in which the qualifying county is located.

(C) For purposes of this paragraph, the term "higher wage index area" means, with respect to a county, an area with a wage index that exceeds that of the county.

(D) The increase in the wage index under subparagraph (A) for a qualifying county shall be equal to the percentage of the hospital employees residing in the qualifying county who are employed in any higher wage index area multiplied by the sum of the products, for each higher wage index area of—

(i) the difference between—

(I) the wage index for such higher wage index area, and

(II) the wage index of the qualifying county; and

(ii) the number of hospital employees residing in the qualifying county who are employed in such higher wage index area divided by the total number of hospital employees residing in the qualifying county who are employed in any higher wage index area.

(E) The process under this paragraph may be based upon the process used by the Medicare Geographic Classification Review Board under paragraph (10). As the Secretary determines to be appropriate to carry out such process, the Secretary may require hospitals (including subsection (d) hospitals and other hospitals) and critical access hospitals, as required under section 1866(a)(1)(T), to submit data regarding the location of residence, or the Secretary may use data from other sources.

(F) A wage index increase under this paragraph shall be effective for a period of 3 fiscal years, except that the Secretary shall establish procedures under which a subsection (d) hospital may elect to waive the application of such wage index increase.

(G) A hospital in a county that has a wage index increase under this paragraph for a period and that has not waived the application of such an increase under subparagraph (F) is not eligible for reclassification under paragraph (8) or (10) during that period.

(H) Any increase in a wage index under this paragraph for a county shall not be taken into account for purposes of—

(i) computing the wage index for portions of the wage index area (not including the county) in which the county is located; or

(ii) applying any budget neutrality adjustment with respect to such index under paragraph (8)(D).

(I) The thresholds described in subparagraph (B), data on hospital employees used under this paragraph, and any determination of the Secretary under the process described in subparagraph (E) shall be final and shall not be subject to judicial review.

[CCH Explanation at ¶ 501, 503, 510, 515, 564, 566, 568, 570, and 588.]

2003 Amendments:

Section 401(a)(1) of the "Medicare Prescription Drug, Improvement, and Modernization Act of 2003," effective upon enactment, amended section 1886(d)(3)(A)(iv) by striking "(iv) For discharges" and inserting "(iv)(I) Subject to subclause (II), for discharges"; and by adding at the end new subclause (II).

Section 401(b)(1)(A) of the "Medicare Prescription Drug, Improvement, and Modernization Act of 2003," effective upon enactment, amended section 1886(d)(3)(D) in the heading, by striking "IN DIFFERENT AREAS".

Section 401(b)(1)(B) of the "Medicare Prescription Drug, Improvement, and Modernization Act of 2003," effective upon enactment, amended section 1886(d)(3)(D) in the matter preceding clause (i), by striking ", each of".

Section 401(b)(1)(C) of the "Medicare Prescription Drug, Improvement, and Modernization Act of 2003," effective upon enactment, amended section 1886(d)(3)(D)(i) in the matter preceding subclause (I), by inserting "for fiscal years before fiscal year 2004," before "for hospitals"; and in subclause (II), by striking "and" after the semicolon at the end.

Section 401(b)(1)(D) of the "Medicare Prescription Drug, Improvement, and Modernization Act of 2003," effective upon enactment, amended section 1886(d)(3)(D)(ii) in the matter preceding subclause (I), by inserting "for fiscal years before fiscal year 2004," before "for hospitals"; and in subclause (II), by striking the period at the end and inserting "; and".

Section 401(b)(1)(E) of the "Medicare Prescription Drug, Improvement, and Modernization Act of 2003," effective upon enactment, amended section 1886(d)(3)(D) by adding at the end new clause (iii).

Section 401(b)(2)(A) of the "Medicare Prescription Drug, Improvement, and Modernization Act of 2003," effective upon enactment, amended section 1886(d)(3) in the matter preceding subparagraph (A), by inserting ", for fiscal years before fiscal year 1997," before "a regional adjusted DRG prospective payment rate".

Section 401(b)(2)(B) of the "Medicare Prescription Drug, Improvement, and Modernization Act of 2003," effective upon enactment, amended section 1886(d)(3)(D) in the matter preceding clause (i), by inserting ", for fiscal years before fiscal year 1997," before "a regional DRG prospective payment rate for each region,".

Section 401(b)(3) of the "Medicare Prescription Drug, Improvement, and Modernization Act of 2003," effective upon enactment, amended section 1886(d)(3)(A)(iii) by striking "in an other urban area" and inserting "in an urban area".

Section 401(c)(1)(A) of the "Medicare Prescription Drug, Improvement, and Modernization Act of 2003," effective upon enactment, amended section 1886(d)(9)(A)(i) by striking "and" after the comma at the end.

Section 401(c)(1)(B) of the "Medicare Prescription Drug, Improvement, and Modernization Act of 2003," effective upon enactment, amended section 1886(d)(9)(A)(ii) by striking clause (ii) and inserting a new clause (ii).

Prior to being stricken clause (ii) read as follows:

(ii) the applicable Federal percentage (specified in subparagraph (E)) of the discharge-weighted average of—

(I) the national adjusted DRG prospective payment rate (determined under paragraph (3)(D)) for hospitals located in a large urban area,

(II) such rate for hospitals located in other urban areas, and

(III) such rate for hospitals located in a rural area,

for such discharges, adjusted in the manner provided in paragraph (3)(E) for different area wage levels. As used in this section, the term "subsection (d) Puerto Rico hospital" means a hospital that is located in Puerto Rico and that would be a subsection (d) hospital (as defined in paragraph (1)(B)) if it were located in one of the fifty States.

Section 401(c)(2)(A)(i) and (ii) of the "Medicare Prescription Drug, Improvement, and Modernization Act of 2003," effective upon enactment, amended section 1886(d)(9)(C)(i) by striking "(i) The Secretary" and inserting "(i)(I) For discharges in a fiscal year after fiscal year 1988 and before fiscal year 2004, the Secretary"; and by adding at the end new subclause (II).

Section 401(c)(2)(B) of the "Medicare Prescription Drug, Improvement, and Modernization Act of 2003," effective upon enactment, amended section 1886(d)(9)(C)(ii) by inserting "(or for fiscal year 2004 and thereafter, the average standardized amount)" after "each of the average standardized amounts".

Section 401(c)(2)(C) of the "Medicare Prescription Drug, Improvement, and Modernization Act of 2003," effective upon enactment, amended section 1886(d)(9)(C)(iii)(I) by striking "for hospitals located in an urban or rural area, respectively".

Section 402(a) of the "Medicare Prescription Drug, Improvement, and Modernization Act of 2003," effective upon enactment, amended section 1886(d)(5)(F) by adding at the end new clause (xiv).

Section 402(b)(1) of the "Medicare Prescription Drug, Improvement, and Modernization Act of 2003," effective upon enactment, amended section 1886(d)(5)(F) in each of subclauses (II), (III), (IV), (V), and (VI) of clause (iv), by inserting "subject to clause (xiv)" before "for discharges occurring"; in clause (viii), by striking "The formula" and inserting "Subject to clause (xiv), the formula"; and in each of clauses (x), (xi), (xii), and (xiii), by striking "For purposes" and inserting "Subject to clause (xiv), for purposes".

Section 402(b)(2) of the "Medicare Prescription Drug, Improvement, and Modernization Act of 2003," effective upon enactment, amended section 1886(d)(2)(C)(iv) by striking "or" before "the enactment of section 303"; and by inserting before the period at the end the following: ", or the enactment of section 402(a)(1) of the Medicare Prescription Drug, Improvement, and Modernization Act of 2003".

Section 403(a)(1)(A) of the "Medicare Prescription Drug, Improvement, and Modernization Act of 2003," effective upon enactment, amended section 1886(d)(3)(E) by striking "WAGE LEVELS.—The Secretary" and inserting "WAGE LEVELS.—(i) IN GENERAL.—Except as provided in clause (ii), the Secretary".

Section 403(a)(1)(B) of the "Medicare Prescription Drug, Improvement, and Modernization Act of 2003," effective upon enactment, amended section 1886(d)(3)(E) by adding at the end new clause (ii).

Section 403(a)(2) of the "Medicare Prescription Drug, Improvement, and Modernization Act of 2003," effective upon enactment, amended section 1886(d)(3)(E) by adding at the end of clause (i) the following new sentence: "The Secretary shall apply the previous sentence for any period as if the amendments made by section 403(a)(1) of the Medicare Prescription Drug, Improvement, and Modernization Act of 2003 had not been enacted.".

Section 403(b) of the "Medicare Prescription Drug, Improvement, and Modernization Act of 2003," effective upon enactment, amended section 1886(d)(9)(C)(iv) by inserting "(I)" after "(iv)"; by striking "paragraph (3)(E)" and inserting "paragraph (3)(E)(i)"; and by adding at the end subclause (II).

Section 406(a) of the "Medicare Prescription Drug, Improvement, and Modernization Act of 2003," effective upon enactment, amended section 1886(d) by adding at the end new paragraph (12).

Section 406(b) of the "Medicare Prescription Drug, Improvement, and Modernization Act of 2003," effective upon enactment, amended section 1886(d)(7)(A) by inserting after "to subsection (e)(1)" the following: "or the determination of the applicable percentage increase under paragraph (12)(A)(ii)".

Section 422(b)(1) of the "Medicare Prescription Drug, Improvement, and Modernization Act of 2003," effective upon enactment, amended section 1886(d)(5)(B) in the second sentence of clause (ii), by striking "For discharges" and inserting "Subject to clause (ix), for discharges"; in clause (v), by adding at the end the following: "The provisions of subsection (h)(7) shall apply with respect to the first sentence of this clause in the same manner as it applies with respect to subsection (h)(4)(F)(i)."; and by adding at the end new clause (ix).

Section 502(a) of the "Medicare Prescription Drug, Improvement, and Modernization Act of 2003," amended section 1886(d)(5)(B)(ii) in subclause (VI), by striking "and" after the semicolon at the end; in subclause (VII) by inserting "and before April 1, 2004," after "on or after October 1, 2002," and by striking the period at the end and inserting a semicolon; and by adding at the end new subclauses (VIII), (IX), (X), (XI), and (XII).

The amendments made by section 502(a) of the "Medicare Prescription Drug, Improvement, and Modernization Act of 2003," apply to discharges occurring on or after April 1, 2004.

Section 502(b) of the "Medicare Prescription Drug, Improvement, and Modernization Act of 2003," amended section 1886(d)(2)(C)(i) by striking "1999 or" and inserting "1999,"; and by inserting ", or the Medicare Prescription Drug, Improvement, and Modernization Act of 2003" after "2000".

Social Security Law Added, Amended or Repealed

The amendments made by section 502(b) apply to discharges occurring on or after April 1, 2004.

Section 503(a) of the "Medicare Prescription Drug, Improvement, and Modernization Act of 2003," amended section 1886(d)(5)(K) by adding at the end new clause (vii).

Section 503(b)(1) of the "Medicare Prescription Drug, Improvement, and Modernization Act of 2003," amended section 1886(d)(5)(K)(ii)(I) by inserting "(applying a threshold specified by the Secretary that is the lesser of 75 percent of the standardized amount (increased to reflect the difference between cost and charges) or 75 percent of one standard deviation for the diagnosis-related group involved)" after "is inadequate".

Section 503(b)(2) of the "Medicare Prescription Drug, Improvement, and Modernization Act of 2003," amended section 1886(d)(5)(K) in clause (i), by adding at the end the following: "Such mechanism shall be modified to meet the requirements of clause (viii)."; and by adding at the end new clause (viii).

Section 503(c) of the "Medicare Prescription Drug, Improvement, and Modernization Act of 2003," amended section 1886(d)(5)(K) by adding at the end the following new clause (ix).

Section 503(d)(1) of the "Medicare Prescription Drug, Improvement, and Modernization Act of 2003," effective upon enactment, amended section 1886(d)(5)(K)(ii)(III) by striking "subject to paragraph (4)(C)(iii),".

The amendments made by section 503 apply to classification for fiscal years beginning with fiscal year 2005.

Section 504 of the "Medicare Prescription Drug, Improvement, and Modernization Act of 2003," effective upon enactment, amended section 1886(d)(9)(A) in clause (i), by striking "for discharges beginning on or after October 1, 1997, 50 percent (and for discharges between October 1, 1987, and September 30, 1997, 75 percent)" and inserting "the applicable Puerto Rico percentage (specified in subparagraph (E))";

and in clause (ii), by striking "for discharges beginning in a fiscal year beginning on or after October 1, 1997, 50 percent (and for discharges between October 1, 1987, and September 30, 1997, 25 percent)" and inserting "the applicable Federal percentage (specified in subparagraph (E))";

and by adding at the end new subparagraph (E).

Section 1886(d)(9)(A)(ii) does not exist in the law, therefore no amendment was made to this section.

Section 505(a) of the "Medicare Prescription Drug, Improvement, and Modernization Act of 2003," amended section 1886(d) by adding at the end new paragraph (13).

The amendment made by section 505(a) shall first apply to the wage index for discharges occurring on or after October 1, 2004.

[¶ 2351C] Sec. 1886. [Capital-Related Costs for Inpatient Hospital Services; Return on Equity Capital]

[42 U.S.C. § 1395ww(g)]

* * *

* * *

(g)(3)(B) Subparagraph (A) shall not apply to payments with respect to the capital-related costs of any hospital that is a sole community hospital (as defined in subsection (d)(5)(D)(iii)), subsection (d)(5)(D)(iii) or a critical access hospital (as defined in section 1861(mm)(1)).

* * *

2003 Amendments:

Section 736(a)(15) of the "Medicare Prescription Drug, Improvement, and Modernization Act of 2003," effective upon enactment, amended section 1886(g)(3) by striking "(as defined in subsection (d)(5)(D)(iii))" and inserting "(as defined in subsection (d)(5)(D)(iii))".

[¶ 2351D] Sec. 1886. [Direct Medical Education Costs]

[42 U.S.C. § 1395ww(h)]

(h) PAYMENTS FOR DIRECT GRADUATE MEDICAL EDUCATION COSTS.—

* * *

(2) DETERMINATION OF HOSPITAL-SPECIFIC APPROVED FTE RESIDENT AMOUNTS.—The Secretary shall determine, for each hospital with an approved medical residency training program, an approved FTE resident amount for each cost reporting period beginning on or after July 1, 1985, as follows:

* * *

(D) AMOUNT FOR SUBSEQUENT COST REPORTING PERIODS.—

* * *

(iv) ADJUSTMENT IN RATE OF INCREASE FOR HOSPITALS WITH FTE APPROVED AMOUNT ABOVE 140 PERCENT OF LOCALOTY ADJUSTED NATIONAL AVERAGE PER RESIDENT AMOUNT.—

(I) FREEZE FOR FISCAL YEARS 2001 AND 2002 AND 2004 THROUGH 2013.—For a cost reporting period beginning during fiscal year 2001 or fiscal year 2002 or during the period beginning with fiscal year 2004 and ending with fiscal year 2013, if the approved FTE resident amount for a hospital for the preceding cost reporting period exceeds 140 percent of the locality adjusted national average per resident amount computed under subparagraph (E) for that hospital and period, subject to subclause (III), the approved FTE resident amount for the period involved shall be the same as the approved FTE resident amount for the hospital for such preceding cost reporting period.

(II) 2 PERCENT DECREASE IN UPDATE FOR FISCAL YEARS 2003, 2004, AND 2005.—For the cost reporting period beginning during fiscal year 2003, if the approved FTE resident amount for a hospital for the preceding cost reporting period exceeds 140 percent of the locality adjusted national average per resident amount computed under subparagraph (E) for that hospital and preceding period, the approved FTE resident amount for the period involved shall be updated in the manner described in subparagraph (D)(i) except that, subject to subclause (III), the consumer price index applied for a 12-month period shall be reduced (but not below zero) by 2 percentage points.

* * *

(3) HOSPITAL PAYMENT AMOUNT PER RESIDENT.—

* * *

(D) PAYMENT FOR MANAGED CARE ENROLLEES.—

* * *

(ii) APPLICABLE PERCENTAGE.—For purposes of clause (i), the applicable percentage is—

* * *

(III) 60 percent in 2000,

* * *

(4) DETERMINATION OF FULL-TIME-EQUIVALENT RESIDENTS.—

* * *

(F) LIMITATION ON NUMBER OF RESIDENTS IN ALLOPATHIC AND OSTEOPATHIC MEDICINE.—

(i) IN GENERAL.—Such rules shall provide that for purposes of a cost reporting period beginning on or after October 1, 1997, subject to paragraph (7), the total number of full-time equivalent residents before application of weighting factors (as determined under this paragraph) with respect to a hospital's approved medical residency training program in the fields of allopathic medicine and osteopathic medicine may not exceed the number of such full-time equivalent residents for the hospital's most recent cost reporting period ending on or before December 31, 1996.

* * *

(H) SPECIAL RULES FOR APPLICATION OF SUBPARAGRAPHS (F) AND (G).—

(i) NEW FACILITIES.—The Secretary shall, consistent with the principles of subparagraphs (F) and (G) and subject to paragraph (7), prescribe rules for the application of such subparagraphs in the case of medical residency training programs established on or after January 1, 1995. In promulgating such rules for purposes of subparagraph (F), the Secretary shall give special consideration to facilities that meet the needs of underserved rural areas.

* * *

(7) REDISTRIBUTION OF UNUSED RESIDENT POSITIONS.—

(A) REDUCTION IN LIMIT BASED ON UNUSED POSITIONS.—

(i) PROGRAMS SUBJECT TO REDUCTION.—

(I) IN GENERAL.—Except as provided in subclause (II), if a hospital's reference resident level (specified in clause (ii)) is less than the otherwise applicable resident limit (as defined in subparagraph (C)(ii)), effective for portions of cost reporting periods occurring on or after July 1, 2005, the otherwise applicable resident limit shall be reduced by 75 percent of the difference between such otherwise applicable resident limit and such reference resident level.

(II) EXCEPTION FOR SMALL RURAL HOSPITALS.—This subparagraph shall not apply to a hospital located in a rural area (as defined in subsection (d)(2)(D)(ii)) with fewer than 250 acute care inpatient beds.

(ii) REFERENCE RESIDENT LEVEL.—

(I) IN GENERAL.—Except as otherwise provided in subclauses (II) and (III), the reference resident level specified in this clause for a hospital is the resident level for the most recent cost reporting period of the hospital ending on or before September 30, 2002, for which a cost report has been settled (or, if not, submitted (subject to audit)), as determined by the Secretary.

(II) USE OF MOST RECENT ACCOUNTING PERIOD TO RECOGNIZE EXPANSION OF EXISTING PROGRAMS.—If a hospital submits a timely request to increase its resident level due to an expansion of an existing residency training program that is not reflected on the most recent settled cost report, after audit and subject to the discretion of the Secretary, the reference resident level for such hospital is the resident level for the cost reporting period that includes July 1, 2003, as determined by the Secretary.

(III) EXPANSIONS UNDER NEWLY APPROVED PROGRAMS.—Upon the timely request of a hospital, the Secretary shall adjust the reference resident level specified under subclause (I) or (II) to include the number of medical residents that were approved in an application for a medical residency training program that was approved by an appropriate accrediting organization (as determined by the Secretary) before January 1, 2002, but which was not in operation during the cost reporting period used under subclause (I) or (II), as the case may be, as determined by the Secretary.

(iii) AFFILIATION.—The provisions of clause (i) shall be applied to hospitals which are members of the same affiliated group (as defined by the Secretary under paragraph (4)(H)(ii)) as of July 1, 2003.

(B) REDISTRIBUTION.—

(i) IN GENERAL.—The Secretary is authorized to increase the otherwise applicable resident limit for each qualifying hospital that submits a timely application under this subparagraph by such number as the Secretary may approve for portions of cost reporting periods occurring on or after July 1, 2005. The aggregate number of increases in the otherwise applicable resident limits under this subparagraph may not exceed the Secretary's estimate of the aggregate reduction in such limits attributable to subparagraph (A).

(ii) CONSIDERATIONS IN REDISTRIBUTION.—In determining for which hospitals the increase in the otherwise applicable resident limit is provided under clause (i), the Secretary shall take into account the demonstrated likelihood of the hospital filling the positions within the first 3 cost reporting periods beginning on or after July 1, 2005, made available under this subparagraph, as determined by the Secretary.

(iii) PRIORITY FOR RURAL AND SMALL URBAN AREAS.—In determining for which hospitals and residency training programs an increase in the otherwise applicable resident limit is provided under clause (i), the Secretary shall distribute the increase to programs of hospitals located in the following priority order:

(I) First, to hospitals located in rural areas (as defined in subsection (d)(2)(D)(ii)).

(II) Second, to hospitals located in urban areas that are not large urban areas (as defined for purposes of subsection (d)).

(III) Third, to other hospitals in a State if the residency training program involved is in a specialty for which there are not other residency training programs in the State.

Increases of residency limits within the same priority category under this clause shall be determined by the Secretary.

(iv) LIMITATION.—In no case shall more than 25 full-time equivalent additional residency positions be made available under this subparagraph with respect to any hospital.

(v) APPLICATION OF LOCALITY ADJUSTED NATIONAL AVERAGE PER RESIDENT AMOUNT.—With respect to additional residency positions in a hospital attributable to the increase provided under this subparagraph, notwithstanding any other provision of this subsection, the approved FTE resident amount is deemed to be equal to the locality adjusted national average per resident amount computed under paragraph (4)(E) for that hospital.

(vi) CONSTRUCTION.—Nothing in this subparagraph shall be construed as permitting the redistribution of reductions in residency positions attributable to voluntary reduction programs under paragraph (6), under a demonstration project approved as of October 31, 2003, under the authority of section 402 of Public Law 90-248, or as affecting the ability of a hospital to establish new medical residency training programs under paragraph (4)(H).

(C) RESIDENT LEVEL AND LIMIT DEFINED.—In this paragraph:

(i) RESIDENT LEVEL.—The term "resident level" means, with respect to a hospital, the total number of full-time equivalent residents, before the application of weighting factors (as determined under paragraph (4)), in the fields of allopathic and osteopathic medicine for the hospital.

(ii) OTHERWISE APPLICABLE RESIDENT LIMIT.—The term "otherwise applicable resident limit" means, with respect to a hospital, the limit otherwise applicable under subparagraphs (F)(i) and (H) of paragraph (4) on the resident level for the hospital determined without regard to this paragraph.

(D) JUDICIAL REVIEW.—There shall be no administrative or judicial review under section 1869, 1878, or otherwise, with respect to determinations made under this paragraph.

[CCH Explanation at ¶ 588.]

2003 Amendments:

Section 422(a)(1) of the "Medicare Prescription Drug, Improvement, and Modernization Act of 2003," effective upon enactment, amended section 1886(h)(4)(F)(i) by inserting "subject to paragraph (7)," after "October 1, 1997,".

Section 422(a)(2) of the "Medicare Prescription Drug, Improvement, and Modernization Act of 2003," effective upon enactment, amended section 1886(h)(4)(H)(i) by inserting "and subject to paragraph (7)" after "subparagraphs (F) and (G)".

Section 422(a)(3) of the "Medicare Prescription Drug, Improvement, and Modernization Act of 2003," effective upon enactment, amended section 1886(h) by adding new paragraph (7).

Section 711(1)(A) and (B) of the "Medicare Prescription Drug, Improvement, and Modernization Act of 2003," effective upon enactment, amended section 1886(h)(2)(D)(iv)(I) by inserting "AND 2004 THROUGH 2013" after "AND 2002"; and by inserting "or during the period beginning with fiscal year 2004 and ending with fiscal year 2013" after "during fiscal year 2001 or fiscal year 2002".

Section 711(2)(A) and (B) of the "Medicare Prescription Drug, Improvement, and Modernization Act of 2003," effective upon enactment, amended section 1886(h)(2)(D)(iv)(II) by striking "fiscal year 2004, or fiscal year 2005," and by striking "For a" and inserting "For the".

Section 736(c)(6) of the "Medicare Prescription Drug, Improvement, and Modernization Act of 2003," effective upon enactment, amended section 1886(h)(3)(D)(ii)(III) by striking "and" after the comma at the end.

[¶ 2355] Sec. 1888. PAYMENT TO SKILLED NURSING FACILITIES FOR ROUTINE SERVICE COSTS

[42 U.S.C. § 1395yy]

* * *

* * *

(e)(2) DEFINITIONS.—For purposes of this subsection:

(A) COVERED SKILLED NURSING FACILITY SERVICES.—

(i) IN GENERAL.—The term "covered skilled nursing facility services"—

***

(II) includes all items and services (other than items and services described in clauses (ii), (iii), and (iv)) for which payment may be made under part B and which are furnished to an individual who is a resident of a skilled nursing facility during the period in which the individual is provided covered post-hospital extended care services.

***

(iv) EXCLUSION OF CERTAIN RURAL HEALTH CLINIC AND FEDERALLY QUALIFIED HEALTH CENTER SERVICES.—Services described in this clause are—

(I) rural health clinic services (as defined in paragraph (1) of section 1861(aa)); and

(II) Federally qualified health center services (as defined in paragraph (3) of such section);

that would be described in clause (ii) if such services were not furnished by an individual affiliated with a rural health clinic or a Federally qualified health center.

***

(12) ADJUSTMENT FOR RESIDENTS WITH AIDS.—

(A) IN GENERAL.—Subject to subparagraph (B), in the case of a resident of a skilled nursing facility who is afflicted with acquired immune deficiency syndrome (AIDS), the per diem amount of payment otherwise applicable (determined without regard to any increase under section 101 of the Medicare, Medicaid, and SCHIP Balanced Budget Refinement Act of 1999, or under section 314(a) of Medicare, Medicaid, and SCHIP Benefits Improvement and Protection Act of 2000), shall be increased by 128 percent to reflect increased costs associated with such residents.

(B) SUNSET.—Subparagraph (A) shall not apply on and after such date as the Secretary certifies that there is an appropriate adjustment in the case mix under paragraph (4)(G)(i) to compensate for the increased costs associated with residents described in such subparagraph.

[CCH Explanation at ¶ 605 and 610.]

2003 Amendments:

Section 410(a)(1) of the "Medicare Prescription Drug, Improvement, and Modernization Act of 2003," amended section 1888(e)(2)(A)(i)(II) by striking "clauses (ii) and (iii)" and inserting "clauses (ii), (iii), and (iv)"; and.by adding at the end new clause (iv).

The amendments made by section 410(a) of the "Medicare Prescription Drug, Improvement, and Modernization Act of 2003," apply to services furnished on or after January 1, 2005.

Section 511(a) of the "Medicare Prescription Drug, Improvement, and Modernization Act of 2003," amended section 1888(e)(12).

The amendments made by section 511(a) of the "Medicare Prescription Drug, Improvement, and Modernization Act of 2003," apply to services furnished on or after October 1, 2004.

Prior to amendment, section 1888(e)(12) read as follows:

(12) PAYMENT RULE FOR CERTAIN FACILITIES.—

(A) IN GENERAL.—In the case of a qualified acute skilled nursing facility described in subparagraph (B), the per diem amount of payment shall be determined by applying the non-Federal percentage and Federal percentage specified in paragraph (2)(C)(ii).

(B) FACILITY DESCRIBED.—For purposes of subparagraph (A), a qualified acute skilled nursing facility is a facility that—

(i) was certified by the Secretary as a skilled nursing facility eligible to furnish services under this title before July 1, 1992;

(ii) is a hospital-based facility; and

(iii) for the cost reporting period beginning in fiscal year 1998, the facility had more than 60 percent of total patient days comprised of patients who are described in subparagraph (C).

(C) DESCRIPTION OF PATIENTS.—For purposes of subparagraph (B), a patient described in this subparagraph is an individual who—

(i) is entitled to benefits under part A; and

(ii) is immuno-compromised secondary to an infectious disease, with specific diagnoses as specified by the Secretary.

[¶ 2360] Sec. 1889. PROVIDER EDUCATION AND TECHNICAL ASSISTANCE

(a) COORDINATION OF EDUCATION FUNDING.—The Secretary shall coordinate the educational activities provided through medicare contractors (as defined in subsection (g), including under section 1893) in order to maximize the effectiveness of Federal education efforts for providers of services and suppliers.

(b) ENHANCED EDUCATION AND TRAINING.—

(1) ADDITIONAL RESOURCES.—There are authorized to be appropriated to the Secretary (in appropriate part from the Federal Hospital Insurance Trust Fund and the Federal Supplementary Medical Insurance Trust Fund) such sums as may be necessary for fiscal years beginning with fiscal year 2005.

(2) USE.—The funds made available under paragraph (1) shall be used to increase the conduct by medicare contractors of education and training of providers of services and suppliers regarding billing, coding, and other appropriate items and may also be used to improve the accuracy, consistency, and timeliness of contractor responses.

(c) TAILORING EDUCATION AND TRAINING ACTIVITIES FOR SMALL PROVIDERS OR SUPPLIERS.—

(1) IN GENERAL.—Insofar as a medicare contractor conducts education and training activities, it shall tailor such activities to meet the special needs of small providers of services or suppliers (as defined in paragraph (2)). Such education and training activities for small providers of services and suppliers may include the provision of technical assistance (such as review of billing systems and internal controls to determine program compliance and to suggest more efficient and effective means of achieving such compliance).

(2) SMALL PROVIDER OF SERVICES OR SUPPLIER.—In this subsection, the term "small provider of services or supplier" means—

(A) a provider of services with fewer than 25 full-time-equivalent employees; or

(B) a supplier with fewer than 10 full-time-equivalent employees.

(d) INTERNET WEBSITES; FAQS.—The Secretary, and each medicare contractor insofar as it provides services (including claims processing) for providers of services or suppliers, shall maintain an Internet website which—

(1) provides answers in an easily accessible format to frequently asked questions, and

(2) includes other published materials of the contractor,

that relate to providers of services and suppliers under the programs under this title (and title XI insofar as it relates to such programs).

(e) ENCOURAGEMENT OF PARTICIPATION IN EDUCATION PROGRAM ACTIVITIES.—A medicare contractor may not use a record of attendance at (or failure to attend) educational activities or other information gathered during an educational program conducted under this section or otherwise by the Secretary to select or track providers of services or suppliers for the purpose of conducting any type of audit or prepayment review.

(f) CONSTRUCTION.—Nothing in this section or section 1893(g) shall be construed as providing for disclosure by a medicare contractor—

(1) of the screens used for identifying claims that will be subject to medical review; or

(2) of information that would compromise pending law enforcement activities or reveal findings of law enforcement-related audits.

(g) DEFINITIONS.—For purposes of this section, the term "medicare contractor" includes the following:

(1) A medicare administrative contractor with a contract under section 1874A, including a fiscal intermediary with a contract under section 1816 and a carrier with a contract under section 1842.

(2) An eligible entity with a contract under section 1893.

Such term does not include, with respect to activities of a specific provider of services or supplier an entity that has no authority under this title or title IX with respect to such activities and such provider of services or supplier.

[CCH Explanation at ¶831.]

2003 Amendments:

Section 921(a)(1) of the "Medicare Prescription Drug, Improvement, and Modernization Act of 2003," effective October 1, 2004, added new section 1889.

Section 921(d) of the "Medicare Prescription Drug, Improvement, and Modernization Act of 2003," effective October 1, 2004, amended section 1889 adding new subsections (b) and (c).

Section 921(e) of the "Medicare Prescription Drug, Improvement, and Modernization Act of 2003," effective October 1, 2004, amended section 1889 by adding new subsection (d).

Section 921(f) of the "Medicare Prescription Drug, Improvement, and Modernization Act of 2003," effective October 1, 2004, amended section 1889 adding new subsections (e) – (g).

[¶ 2365] Sec. 1891. CONDITIONS OF PARTICIPATION FOR HOME HEALTH AGENCIES; HOME HEALTH QUALITY

[42 U.S.C. § 1395bbb]

* * *

(d)(1) Not later than January 1, 1989, the Secretary shall designate an assessment instrument (or instruments) for use by an agency in complying with subsection (c)(2)(C)(i)(I).

* * *

2003 Amendments:

Section 736(c)(3) of the "Medicare Prescription Drug, Improvement, and Modernization Act of 2003," effective upon enactment, amended section 1891(d)(1) by striking "subsection (c)(2)(C)(I)" and inserting "subsection (c)(2)(C)(i)(I)".

[¶ 2370] Sec. 1893. MEDICARE INTEGRITY PROGRAM

[42 U.S.C. § 1395ddd]

(a) ESTABLISHMENT OF PROGRAM.—There is hereby established the Medicare Integrity Program (in this section referred to as the "Program") under which the Secretary shall promote the integrity of the medicare program by entering into contracts in accordance with this section with eligible entities to carry out the activities described in subsection (b).

* * *

(f) RECOVERY OF OVERPAYMENTS.—

(1) USE OF REPAYMENT PLANS.—

(A) IN GENERAL.—If the repayment, within 30 days by a provider of services or supplier, of an overpayment under this title would constitute a hardship (as described in subparagraph (B)), subject to subparagraph (C), upon request of the provider of services or supplier the Secretary shall enter into a plan with the provider of services or supplier for the repayment (through offset or otherwise) of such overpayment over a period of at least 6 months but not longer than 3 years (or not longer than 5 years in the case of extreme hardship, as determined by the Secretary). Interest shall accrue on the balance through the period of repayment. Such plan shall meet terms and conditions determined to be appropriate by the Secretary.

(B) HARDSHIP.—

(i) IN GENERAL.—For purposes of subparagraph (A), the repayment of an overpayment (or overpayments) within 30 days is deemed to constitute a hardship if—

(I) in the case of a provider of services that files cost reports, the aggregate amount of the overpayments exceeds 10 percent of the amount paid under this title to the provider of services for the cost reporting period covered by the most recently submitted cost report; or

(II) in the case of another provider of services or supplier, the aggregate amount of the overpayments exceeds 10 percent of the amount paid under this title to the provider of services or supplier for the previous calendar year.

(ii) RULE OF APPLICATION.—The Secretary shall establish rules for the application of this subparagraph in the case of a provider of services or supplier that was not paid under this title during the previous year or was paid under this title only during a portion of that year.

(iii) TREATMENT OF PREVIOUS OVERPAYMENTS.—If a provider of services or supplier has entered into a repayment plan under subparagraph (A) with respect to a specific overpayment amount, such payment amount under the repayment plan shall not be taken into account under clause (i) with respect to subsequent overpayment amounts.

(C) EXCEPTIONS.—Subparagraph (A) shall not apply if—

(i) the Secretary has reason to suspect that the provider of services or supplier may file for bankruptcy or otherwise cease to do business or discontinue participation in the program under this title; or

(ii) there is an indication of fraud or abuse committed against the program.

(D) IMMEDIATE COLLECTION IF VIOLATION OF REPAYMENT PLAN.—If a provider of services or supplier fails to make a payment in accordance with a repayment plan under this paragraph, the Secretary may immediately seek to offset or otherwise recover the total balance outstanding (including applicable interest) under the repayment plan.

(E) RELATION TO NO FAULT PROVISION.—Nothing in this paragraph shall be construed as affecting the application of section 1870(c) (relating to no adjustment in the cases of certain overpayments).

(2) LIMITATION ON RECOUPMENT.—

(A) IN GENERAL.—In the case of a provider of services or supplier that is determined to have received an overpayment under this title and that seeks a reconsideration by a qualified independent contractor on such determination under section 1869(b)(1), the Secretary may not take any action (or authorize any other person, including any medicare contractor, as defined in subparagraph (C)) to recoup the overpayment until the date the decision on the reconsideration has been rendered. If the provisions of section 1869(b)(1) (providing for such a reconsideration by a qualified independent contractor) are not in effect, in applying the previous sentence any reference to such a reconsideration shall be treated as a reference to a redetermination by the fiscal intermediary or carrier involved.

(B) COLLECTION WITH INTEREST.—Insofar as the determination on such appeal is against the provider of services or supplier, interest on the overpayment shall accrue on and after the date of the original notice of overpayment. Insofar as such determination against the provider of services or supplier is later reversed, the Secretary shall provide for repayment of the amount recouped plus interest at the same rate as would apply under the previous sentence for the period in which the amount was recouped.

(C) MEDICARE CONTRACTOR DEFINED.—For purposes of this subsection, the term "medicare contractor" has the meaning given such term in section 1889(g).

(3) LIMITATION ON USE OF EXTRAPOLATION.—A medicare contractor may not use extrapolation to determine overpayment amounts to be recovered by recoupment, offset, or otherwise unless the Secretary determines that—

(A) there is a sustained or high level of payment error; or

(B) documented educational intervention has failed to correct the payment error.

There shall be no administrative or judicial review under section 1869, section 1878, or otherwise, of determinations by the Secretary of sustained or high levels of payment errors under this paragraph.

(4) PROVISION OF SUPPORTING DOCUMENTATION.—In the case of a provider of services or supplier with respect to which amounts were previously overpaid, a medicare contractor may request the periodic production of records or supporting documentation for a limited sample of submitted claims to ensure that the previous practice is not continuing.

(5) CONSENT SETTLEMENT REFORMS.—

(A) IN GENERAL.—The Secretary may use a consent settlement (as defined in subparagraph (D)) to settle a projected overpayment.

(B) OPPORTUNITY TO SUBMIT ADDITIONAL INFORMATION BEFORE CONSENT SETTLEMENT OFFER.—Before offering a provider of services or supplier a consent settlement, the Secretary shall—

(i) communicate to the provider of services or supplier—

(I) that, based on a review of the medical records requested by the Secretary, a preliminary evaluation of those records indicates that there would be an overpayment;

(II) the nature of the problems identified in such evaluation; and

(III) the steps that the provider of services or supplier should take to address the problems; and

(ii) provide for a 45-day period during which the provider of services or supplier may furnish additional information concerning the medical records for the claims that had been reviewed.

(C) CONSENT SETTLEMENT OFFER.—The Secretary shall review any additional information furnished by the provider of services or supplier under subparagraph (B)(ii). Taking into consideration such information, the Secretary shall determine if there still appears to be an overpayment. If so, the Secretary—

(i) shall provide notice of such determination to the provider of services or supplier, including an explanation of the reason for such determination; and

(ii) in order to resolve the overpayment, may offer the provider of services or supplier—

(I) the opportunity for a statistically valid random sample; or

(II) a consent settlement.

The opportunity provided under clause (ii)(I) does not waive any appeal rights with respect to the alleged overpayment involved.

(D) CONSENT SETTLEMENT DEFINED.—For purposes of this paragraph, the term "consent settlement" means an agreement between the Secretary and a provider of services or supplier whereby both parties agree to settle a projected overpayment based on less than a statistically valid sample of claims and the provider of services or supplier agrees not to appeal the claims involved.

(6) NOTICE OF OVER-UTILIZATION OF CODES.—The Secretary shall establish, in consultation with organizations representing the classes of providers of services and suppliers, a process under which the Secretary provides for notice to classes of providers of services and suppliers served by the contractor in cases in which the contractor has identified that particular billing codes may be overutilized by that class of providers of services or suppliers under the programs under this title (or provisions of title XI insofar as they relate to such programs).

(7) PAYMENT AUDITS.—

(A) WRITTEN NOTICE FOR POST-PAYMENT AUDITS.—Subject to subparagraph (C), if a medicare contractor decides to conduct a post-payment audit of a provider of services or supplier under this title, the contractor shall provide the provider of services or supplier with written notice (which may be in electronic form) of the intent to conduct such an audit.

(B) EXPLANATION OF FINDINGS FOR ALL AUDITS.—Subject to subparagraph (C), if a medicare contractor audits a provider of services or supplier under this title, the contractor shall—

(i) give the provider of services or supplier a full review and explanation of the findings of the audit in a manner that is understandable to the provider of services or supplier and permits the development of an appropriate corrective action plan;

(ii) inform the provider of services or supplier of the appeal rights under this title as well as consent settlement options (which are at the discretion of the Secretary);

(iii) give the provider of services or supplier an opportunity to provide additional information to the contractor; and

(iv) take into account information provided, on a timely basis, by the provider of services or supplier under clause (iii).

(C) EXCEPTION.—Subparagraphs (A) and (B) shall not apply if the provision of notice or findings would compromise pending law enforcement activities, whether civil or criminal, or reveal findings of law enforcement-related audits.

(8) STANDARD METHODOLOGY FOR PROBE SAMPLING.—The Secretary shall establish a standard methodology for medicare contractors to use in selecting a sample of claims for review in the case of an abnormal billing pattern.

[CCH Explanation at ¶ 909.]

2003 Amendments:

Section 736(c)(7) of the "Medicare Prescription Drug, Improvement, and Modernization Act of 2003," effective upon enactment, amended section 1893(a) by striking "Medicare program" and inserting "medicare program".

Section 935(a) of the "Medicare Prescription Drug, Improvement, and Modernization Act of 2003," effective upon enactment, amended section 1893 by adding at the end new subsection (f).

[¶ 2375] Sec. 1894. [Benefits and Safeguards]

[42 U.S.C. § 1395eee(b)]

(b) SCOPE OF BENEFITS; BENEFICIARY SAFEGUARDS.—

* * *

(3) TREATMENT OF MEDICARE SERVICES FURNISHED BY NONCONTRACT PHYSICIANS AND OTHER ENTITIES.—

(A) APPLICATION OF MEDICARE ADVANTAGE REQUIREMENT WITH RESPECT TO MEDICARE SERVICES FURNISHED BY NONCONTRACT PHYSICIANS AND OTHER ENTITIES.—Section 1852(k)(1) (relating to limitations on balance billing against MA organizations for noncontract physicians and other entities with respect to services covered under this title) shall apply to PACE providers, PACE program eligible individuals enrolled with such PACE providers, and physicians and other entities that do not have a contract or other agreement establishing payment amounts for services furnished to such an individual in the same manner as such section applies to MA organizations, individuals enrolled with such organizations, and physicians and other entities referred to in such section.

(B) REFERENCE TO RELATED PROVISION FOR NONCONTRACT PROVIDERS OF SERVICES.—For the provision relating to limitations on balance billing against PACE providers for services covered under this title furnished by noncontract providers of services, see section 1866(a)(1)(O).

(4) REFERENCE TO RELATED PROVISION FOR SERVICES COVERED UNDER TITLE XIX BUT NOT UNDER THIS TITLE.—For provisions relating to limitations on payments to providers participating under the State plan under title XIX that do not have a contract or other agreement with a PACE provider establishing payment amounts for services covered under such plan (but not under this title) when such services are furnished to enrollees of that PACE provider, see section 1902(a)(66).

2003 Amendments:

Section 236(a)(2) of the "Medicare Prescription Drug, Improvement, and Modernization Act of 2003," amended section 1894(b) by adding at the end new paragraphs (3) and (4).

The above amendment applies to services furnished on or after January 1, 2004.

[¶ 2380] Sec. 1895. PROSPECTIVE PAYMENT FOR HOME HEALTH SERVICES

[42 U.S.C. § 1395fff]

* * *

(b) SYSTEM OF PROSPECTIVE PAYMENT FOR HOME HEALTH SERVICES.—

* * *

(3) PAYMENT BASIS.—

* * *

(B) ANNUAL UPDATE.—

(i) IN GENERAL.—The standard prospective payment amount (or amounts) shall be adjusted for fiscal year 2002 and for fiscal year 2003 and for each subsequent year (beginning with 2004) in a prospective manner specified by the Secretary by the home health applicable increase percentage (as defined in clause (ii)) applicable to the fiscal yearor year involved.

(ii) HOME HEALTH APPLICABLE INCREASE PERCENTAGE.—For purposes of this subparagraph, the term "home health applicable increase percentage" means, with respect to—

(I) each of fiscal years 2002 and 2003, the home health market basket percentage increase (as defined in clause (iii)) minus 1.1 percentage points;

(II) for the last calendar quarter of 2003 and the first calendar quarter of 2004, the home health market basket percentage increase;

(III) the last 3 calendar quarters of 2004, and each of 2005 and 2006 the home health market basket percentage increase minus 0.8 percentage points; or

(IV) 2007 and any subsequent year, the home health market basket percentage increase.

(iii) HOME HEALTH MARKET BASKET PERCENTAGE INCREASE.—For purposes of this subsection, the term "home health market basket percentage increase" means, with respect to a fiscal year or year, a percentage (estimated by the Secretary before the beginning of the fiscal year or year) determined and applied with respect to the mix of goods and services included in home health services in the same manner as the market basket percentage increase under section 1886(b)(3)(B)(iii) is determined and applied to the mix of goods and services comprising inpatient hospital services for the fiscal year or year.

(iv) ADJUSTMENT FOR CASE MIX CHANGES.—Insofar as the Secretary determines that the adjustments under paragraph (4)(A)(i) for a previous fiscal year or year (or estimates that such adjustments for a future fiscal year or year) did (or are likely to) result in a change in aggregate payments under this subsection during the fiscal year or year that are a result of changes in the coding or classification of different units of services that do not reflect real changes in case mix, the Secretary may adjust the standard prospective payment amount (or amounts) under paragraph (3) for subsequent fiscal years or years so as to eliminate the effect of such coding or classification changes.

* * *

(5) OUTLIERS.—The Secretary may provide for an addition or adjustment to the payment amount otherwise made in the case of outliers because of unusual variations in the type or amount of medically necessary care. The total amount of the additional payments or payment adjustments made under this paragraph with respect to a fiscal year or year may not exceed 5 percent of the total payments projected or estimated to be made based on the prospective payment system under this subsection in that year.

* * *

[CCH Explanation at ¶ 658.]

2003 Amendments:

Section 701(a)(1) of the "Medicare Prescription Drug, Improvement, and Modernization Act of 2003," effective upon enactment, amended section 1895(b)(3)(B)(i) by striking "each fiscal year (beginning with fiscal year 2002)" and inserting "fiscal year 2002 and for fiscal year 2003 and for each subsequent year (beginning with 2004)"; and by inserting "or year" after "the fiscal year".

Section 701(a)(2) of the "Medicare Prescription Drug, Improvement, and Modernization Act of 2003," effective upon enactment, amended section 1895(b)(3)(B)(ii) in subclause (I), by striking "or" at the end; by redesignating subclause (II) as subclause (III); in subclause (III), as so redesignated, by striking "any subsequent fiscal year" and inserting "2004 and any subsequent year"; and by inserting after subclause (I) the new subclause (II).

Section 701(a)(3) of the "Medicare Prescription Drug, Improvement, and Modernization Act of 2003," effective upon enactment, amended section 1895(b)(3)(B)(iii) by inserting "or year" after "fiscal year" each place it appears.

Section 701(a)(4) of the "Medicare Prescription Drug, Improvement, and Modernization Act of 2003," effective upon enactment, amended section 1895(b)(3)(B)(iv) by inserting "or year" after "fiscal year" each place it appears; and by inserting "or years" after "fiscal years".

Section 701(a)(5) of the "Medicare Prescription Drug, Improvement, and Modernization Act of 2003," effective upon enactment, amended section 1895(b)(5) by inserting "or year" after "fiscal year".

Section 701(b) of the "Medicare Prescription Drug, Improvement, and Modernization Act of 2003," effective upon enactment, amended section 1895(b)(3)(B)(ii), as amended by subsection 701(a)(2), by striking "or" at the end of subclause (II); by redesignating subclause (III) as subclause (IV); in subclause (IV), as so redesignated, by striking "2004" and inserting "2007"; and by inserting after subclause (II) the new subclause (III).

[¶ 2385] Sec. 1896. MEDICARE SUBVENTION PROGRAM FOR MILITARY RETIREES

[42 U.S.C. § 1395ggg]

* * *

(b) PROGRAM.—

* * *

(4) DURATION.—The administering Secretaries shall conduct the program during the 4-year period beginning on January 1, 1998, except that the administering Secretaries may negotiate and (subject to section 712(f) of the Floyd D. Spence National Defense Authorization Act for Fiscal Year 2001) enter into a new or revised agreement under paragraph (1)(A) to continue the program after the end of such period. If the program is so continued, the administering Secretaries may terminate the agreement under which the program operates after providing notice to Congress in accordance with subsection (k)(2)(B)(v).

* * *

2003 Amendments:

Section 736(c)(8) of the "Medicare Prescription Drug, Improvement, and Modernization Act of 2003," effective upon enactment, amended section 1896(b)(4) by striking "701(f)" and inserting "712(f)".

[¶ 2390] Sec. 1897 HEALTH CARE INFRASTRUCTURE IMPROVEMENT PROGRAM

(a) ESTABLISHMENT.—The Secretary shall establish a loan program that provides loans to qualifying hospitals for payment of the capital costs of projects described in subsection (d).

(b) APPLICATION.—No loan may be provided under this section to a qualifying hospital except pursuant to an application that is submitted and approved in a time, manner, and form specified by the Secretary. A loan under this section shall be on such terms and conditions and meet such requirements as the Secretary determines appropriate.

(c) SELECTION CRITERIA.—

(1) IN GENERAL.—The Secretary shall establish criteria for selecting among qualifying hospitals that apply for a loan under this section. Such criteria shall consider the extent to which the project for which loan is sought is nationally or regionally significant, in terms of expanding or improving the health care infrastructure of the United States or the region or in terms of the medical benefit that the project will have.

(2) QUALIFYING HOSPITAL DEFINED.—For purposes of this section, the term "qualifying hospital" means a hospital that—

(A) is engaged in research in the causes, prevention, and treatment of cancer; and

(B) is designated as a cancer center for the National Cancer Institute or is designated by the State as the official cancer institute of the State.

(d) PROJECTS.—A project described in this subsection is a project of a qualifying hospital that is designed to improve the health care infrastructure of the hospital, including construction, renovation, or other capital improvements.

(e) STATE AND LOCAL PERMITS.—The provision of a loan under this section with respect to a project shall not—

(1) relieve any recipient of the loan of any obligation to obtain any required State or local permit or approval with respect to the project;

(2) limit the right of any unit of State or local government to approve or regulate any rate of return on private equity invested in the project; or

(3) otherwise supersede any State or local law (including any regulation) applicable to the construction or operation of the project.

(f) FORGIVENESS OF INDEBTEDNESS.—The Secretary may forgive a loan provided to a qualifying hospital under this section under terms and conditions that are analogous to the loan forgiveness provision for student loans under part D of title IV of the Higher Education Act of 1965 (20 U.S.C. 1087a et seq.), except that the Secretary shall condition such forgiveness on the establishment by the hospital of—

(A) an outreach program for cancer prevention, early diagnosis, and treatment that provides services to a substantial majority of the residents of a State or region, including residents of rural areas;

(B) an outreach program for cancer prevention, early diagnosis, and treatment that provides services to multiple Indian tribes; and

Social Security Law Added, Amended or Repealed

(C)(i) unique research resources (such as population databases); or

(ii) an affiliation with an entity that has unique research resources.

(g) FUNDING.—

(1) IN GENERAL.—There are appropriated, out of amounts in the Treasury not otherwise appropriated, to carry out this section, $200,000,000, to remain available during the period beginning on July 1, 2004, and ending on September 30, 2008.

(2) ADMINISTRATIVE COSTS.—From funds made available under paragraph (1), the Secretary may use, for the administration of this section, not more than $2,000,000 for each of fiscal years 2004 through 2008.

(3) AVAILABILITY.—Amounts appropriated under this section shall be available for obligation on July 1, 2004.

(h) REPORT TO CONGRESS.—Not later than 4 years after the date of the enactment of this section, the Secretary shall submit to Congress a report on the projects for which loans are provided under this section and a recommendation as to whether the Congress should authorize the Secretary to continue loans under this section beyond fiscal year 2008.

[CCH Explanation at ¶1215.]

2003 Amendments:

Section 1016 of the "Medicare Prescription Drug, Improvement, and Modernization Act of 2003," effective upon enactment, amended Title XVIII by adding new section 1897.

[¶2395] Sec. 1902. [Eligibility, Amount, Duration, and Scope of Benefits]

[42 U.S.C. §1396a(a)(10)]

(a)(10) provide—

* * *

* * *

(E)(iv) subject to sections 1933 and 1905(p)(4), for making medical assistance available (but only for premiums payable with respect to months during the period beginning with January 1998, ending with September 2004 for Medicare cost-sharing described in section 1905(p)(3)(A)(ii) for individuals who would be qualified Medicare beneficiaries described in section 1905(p)(1) but for the fact that their income exceeds the income level established by the State under section 1905(p)(2) and is at least 120 percent, but less than 135 percent, of the official poverty line (referred to in such section) for a family of the size involved and who are not otherwise eligible for medical assistance under the State plan;

* * *

[CCH Explanation at ¶205.]

2003 Amendments:

Section 103(f)(1) of the "Medicare Prescription Drug, Improvement, and Modernization Act of 2003," effective upon enactment, amended section 1902(a)(10)(E)(iv), as amended by section 401(a) of Public Law 108-89, by striking "ending with March 2004" and inserting "ending with September 2004".

[¶2396A] Sec. 1902. [Beneficiary Reports]

[42 U.S.C. §1396a(a)(64)]

(a)(64) provide, not later than 1 year after the date of the enactment of this paragraph, a mechanism to receive reports from beneficiaries and others and compile data concerning alleged instances of waste, fraud, and abuse relating to the operation of this title;

[CCH Explanation at ¶ 205.]
2003 Amendments:

Section 103(a)(1)(A) of the "Medicare Prescription Drug, Improvement, and Modernization Act of 2003," effective upon enactment, amended section 1902(a)(64) by striking "and" at the end.

[¶ 2396B] Sec. 1902. [Provider Numbers]
[42 U.S.C. § 1396a(a)(65)]

* * *

(a)(65) The requirement of clause (A) of paragraph (37) with respect to a State plan may be waived by the Secretary if he finds that the State has exercised good faith in trying to meet such requirement. Notwithstanding paragraph (10)(B) or any other provision of this subsection, a State plan shall provide medical assistance with respect to an alien who is not lawfully admitted for permanent residence or otherwise permanently residing in the United States under color of law only in accordance with section 1903(v);

[CCH Explanation at ¶ 205.]
2003 Amendments:

Section 103(a)(1)(B) of the "Medicare Prescription Drug, Improvement, and Modernization Act of 2003," effective upon enactment, amended section 1902(a)(65) by striking the period at the end of paragraph (65) and inserting "; and".

Section 236(b)(1)(A) of the "Medicare Prescription Drug, Improvement, and Modernization Act of 2003," amended section 1902(a)(65) by striking "and" at the end.

The above amendment applies to services furnished on or after January 1, 2004.

[¶ 2396C] Sec. 1902. [Eligibility]

(a)(66) provide for making eligibility determinations under section 1935(a); and

[CCH Explanation at ¶ 205.]
2003 Amendments:

Section 103(a)(1)(C) of the Medicare Prescription Drug, Improvement, and Modernization Act of 2003, effective upon enactment, added new section 1902(a)(66).

Section 236(b)(1)(B) of the "Medicare Prescription Drug, Improvement, and Modernization Act of 2003," effective upon enactment, amended section 1902(a)(66) by striking the period at the end and inserting "; and".

[¶ 2396D] Sec. 1902. [PACE Provider Requirements]

(a)(67) provide, with respect to services covered under the State plan (but not under title XVIII) that are furnished to a PACE program eligible individual enrolled with a PACE provider by a provider participating under the State plan that does not have a contract or other agreement with the PACE provider that establishes payment amounts for such services, that such participating provider may not require the PACE provider to pay the participating provider an amount greater than the amount that would otherwise be payable for the service to the participating provider under the State plan for the State where the PACE provider is located (in accordance with regulations issued by the Secretary).

2003 Amendments:

Section 236(b)(1)(C) of the Medicare Prescription Drug, Improvement, and Modernization Act of 2003, effective upon enactment, added new section 1902(a)(67).

The above amendment applies to services furnished on or after Jan. 1, 2004.

[¶ 2400] Sec. 1919. RESPONSIBILITIES OF SECRETARY RELATING TO NURSING FACILITY REQUIREMENTS
[42 U.S.C. § 1396r(f)]

(f) RESPONSIBILITIES OF SECRETARY RELATING TO NURSING FACILITY REQUIREMENTS.—

* * *

(2) REQUIREMENTS FOR NURSE AIDE TRAINING AND COMPETENCY EVALUATION PROGRAMS AND FOR NURSE AIDE COMPETENCY EVALUATION PROGRAMS.—

* * *

(B) APPROVAL OF CERTAIN PROGRAMS.—Such requirements—

* * *

(iii) subject to subparagraphs (C) and (D), shall prohibit approval of such a program—

* * *

(D) WAIVER OF DISAPPROVAL OF NURSE-AIDE TRAINING PROGRAMS.—Upon application of a nursing facility, the Secretary may waive the application of subparagraph (B)(iii)(I)(c) if the imposition of the civil monetary penalty was not related to the quality of care provided to residents of the facility. Nothing in this subparagraph shall be construed as eliminating any requirement upon a facility to pay a civil monetary penalty described in the preceding sentence.

* * *

[CCH Explanation at ¶ 905.]

2003 Amendments:

Section 932(c)(2) of the "Medicare Prescription Drug, Improvement, and Modernization Act of 2003," effective upon enactment, amended section 1919(f)(2) in subparagraph (B)(iii) by striking "subparagraph (C)" and inserting "subparagraphs (C) and (D)"; and by adding at the end the new subparagraph D.

[¶ 2401A] Sec. 1923. LIMITATION ON FEDERAL FINANCIAL PARTICIPATION

[42 U.S.C. § 1396r-4(f)]

(f) LIMITATION ON FEDERAL FINANCIAL PARTICIPATION.—

* * *

(3) STATE DSH ALLOTMENTS FOR FISCAL YEAR 2003 AND THEREAFTER.—

(A) IN GENERAL.—Except as provided in paragraph (6), the DSH allotment for any State for fiscal year 2003 and each succeeding fiscal year is equal to the DSH allotment for the State for the preceding fiscal year under paragraph (2) or this paragraph, increased, subject to subparagraphs (B) and (C) and paragraph (5), by the percentage change in the consumer price index for all urban consumers (all items; U.S. city average), for the previous fiscal year.

* * *

(C) SPECIAL, TEMPORARY INCREASE IN ALLOTMENTS ON A ONE-TIME, NON-CUMULATIVE BASIS.— The DSH allotment for any State (other than a State with a DSH allotment determined under paragraph (5))—

(i) for fiscal year 2004 is equal to 116 percent of the DSH allotment for the State for fiscal year 2003 under this paragraph, notwithstanding subparagraph (B); and

(ii) for each succeeding fiscal year is equal to the DSH allotment for the State for fiscal year 2004 or, in the case of fiscal years beginning with the fiscal year specified in subparagraph (D) for that State, the DSH allotment for the State for the previous fiscal year increased by the percentage change in the consumer price index for all urban consumers (all items; U.S. city average), for the previous fiscal year.

(D) FISCAL YEAR SPECIFIED.—For purposes of subparagraph (C)(ii), the fiscal year specified in this subparagraph for a State is the first fiscal year for which the Secretary estimates that the DSH allotment for that State will equal (or no longer exceed) the DSH allotment for that State under the law as in effect before the date of the enactment of this subparagraph.

* * *

(5) SPECIAL RULE FOR LOW DSH STATES.—(A) FOR FISCAL YEARS 2001 THROUGH 2003 FOR EXTREMELY LOW DSH STATES.—In the case of a State in which the total expenditures under the State plan (including Federal and State shares) for disproportionate share hospital adjustments under this section for fiscal year 1999, as reported to the Administrator of the Health Care Financing Administration as of August 31, 2000, is greater than 0 but less than 1 percent of the State's total amount of expenditures under the State plan for medical assistance during the fiscal year, the DSH allotment for fiscal year 2001 shall be increased to 1 percent of the State's total amount of expenditures under such plan for such assistance during such fiscal year. In subsequent fiscal years before fiscal year 2004, such increased allotment is subject to an increase for inflation as provided in paragraph (3)(A).

(B) For fiscal year 2004 and subsequent fiscal years.—In the case of a State in which the total expenditures under the State plan (including Federal and State shares) for disproportionate share hospital adjustments under this section for fiscal year 2000, as reported to the Administrator of the Centers for Medicare & Medicaid Services as of August 31, 2003, is greater than 0 but less than 3 percent of the State's total amount of expenditures under the State plan for medical assistance during the fiscal year, the DSH allotment for the State with respect to—

(i) fiscal year 2004 shall be the DSH allotment for the State for fiscal year 2003 increased by 16 percent;

(ii) each succeeding fiscal year before fiscal year 2009 shall be the DSH allotment for the State for the previous fiscal year increased by 16 percent; and

(iii) fiscal year 2009 and any subsequent fiscal year, shall be the DSH allotment for the State for the previous year subject to an increase for inflation as provided in paragraph (3)(A).

(6) Allotment Adjustment.—Only with respect to fiscal year 2004 or 2005, if a statewide waiver under section 1115 is revoked or terminated before the end of either such fiscal year and there is no DSH allotment for the State, the Secretary shall—

(A) permit the State whose waiver was revoked or terminated to submit an amendment to its State plan that would describe the methodology to be used by the State (after the effective date of such revocation or termination) to identify and make payments to disproportionate share hospitals, including children's hospitals and institutions for mental diseases or other mental health facilities (other than State-owned institutions or facilities), on the basis of the proportion of patients served by such hospitals that are low-income patients with special needs; and

(B) provide for purposes of this subsection for computation of an appropriate DSH allotment for the State for fiscal year 2004 or 2005 (or both) that would not exceed the amount allowed under paragraph (3)(B)(ii) and that does not result in greater expenditures under this title than would have been made if such waiver had not been revoked or terminated.

In determining the amount of an appropriate DSH allotment under subparagraph (B) for a State, the Secretary shall take into account the level of DSH expenditures for the State for the fiscal year preceding the fiscal year in which the waiver commenced.

* * *

[CCH Explanation at ¶ 1201, 1203, and 1204.]

2003 Amendments:

Section 1001(a)(1) of the "Medicare Prescription Drug, Improvement, and Modernization Act of 2003," effective upon enactment, amended section 1923(f)(3)(A) by striking "subparagraph (B)" and inserting "subparagraphs (B) and (C)".

Section 1001(a)(2) of the "Medicare Prescription Drug, Improvement, and Modernization Act of 2003," effective upon enactment, amended section 1923(f)(3) by adding new subparagraphs (C) and (D).

Section 1001(b) of the "Medicare Prescription Drug, Improvement, and Modernization Act of 2003," effective upon enactment, amended section 1923(f)(5) in the paragraph heading, by striking "Extremely"; by striking "In the case of" and inserting the following: "(A) "For fiscal years 2001 through 2003 for extremely low dsh states.—In the case of"; by inserting "before fiscal year 2004" after "In subsequent years"; and by adding clause (B).

Section 1001(c) of the "Medicare Prescription Drug, Improvement, and Modernization Act of 2003," effective upon enactment, amended section 1923(f)(3)(A) by striking "The DSH" and inserting "Except as provided in paragraph (6), the DSH"; by redesignating paragraph (6) as paragraph (7); and by inserting new paragraph (6).

[¶ 2401B] Sec. 1923. ANNUAL REPORTS AND OTHER REQUIREMENTS REGARDING PAYMENT ADJUSTMENTS

(j) With respect to fiscal year 2004 and each fiscal year thereafter, the Secretary shall require a State, as a condition of receiving a payment under section 1903(a)(1) with respect to a payment adjustment made under this section, to do the following:

(1) Report.—The State shall submit an annual report that includes the following:

(A) An identification of each disproportionate share hospital that received a payment adjustment under this section for the preceding fiscal year and the amount of the payment adjustment made to such hospital for the preceding fiscal year.

(B) Such other information as the Secretary determines necessary to ensure the appropriateness of the payment adjustments made under this section for the preceding fiscal year.

(2) INDEPENDENT CERTIFIED AUDIT.—The State shall annually submit to the Secretary an independent certified audit that verifies each of the following:

(A) The extent to which hospitals in the State have reduced their uncompensated care costs to reflect the total amount of payment adjustments under this section.

(B) Payments under this section to hospitals that comply with the requirements of subsection (g).

(C) Only the uncompensated care costs of providing inpatient hospital and outpatient hospital services to individuals described in paragraph (1)(A) of such subsection are included in the calculation of the hospital-specific limits under such subsection.

(D) The State included all payments under this title, including supplemental payments, in the calculation of such hospital-specific limits.

(E) The State has separately documented and retained a record of all of its costs under this title, claimed expenditures under this title, uninsured costs in determining payment adjustments under this section, and any payments made on behalf of the uninsured from payment adjustments under this section.

2003 Amendments:

Section 1001(d) of the "Medicare Prescription Drug, Improvement, and Modernization Act of 2003," effective upon enactment, amended 1923 by adding new subsection (j).

[¶ 2401C] Sec. 1927. REQUIREMENT FOR REBATE AGREEMENT

[42 U.S.C. § 1396r-8(a)]

(a) REQUIREMENT FOR REBATE AGREEMENT.—

(1) IN GENERAL.—In order for payment to be available under section 1903(a) or under part B of title XVIII for covered outpatient drugs of a manufacturer, the manufacturer must have entered into and have in effect a rebate agreement described in subsection (b) with the Secretary, on behalf of States (except that, the Secretary may authorize a State to enter directly into agreements with a manufacturer), and must meet the requirements of paragraph (5) (with respect to drugs purchased by a covered entity on or after the first day of the first month that begins after the date of the enactment of title VI of the Veterans Health Care Act of 1992) and paragraph (6). Any agreement between a State and a manufacturer prior to April 1, 1991, shall be deemed to have been entered into on January 1, 1991, and payment to such manufacturer shall be retroactively calculated as if the agreement between the manufacturer and the State had been entered into on January 1, 1991. If a manufacturer has not entered into such an agreement before March 1, 1991, such an agreement, subsequently entered into, shall become effective as of the date on which the agreement is entered into or, at State option, on any date thereafter on or before the first day of the calendar quarter that begins more than 60 days after the date the agreement is entered into.

* * *

[CCH Explanation at ¶ 1004, 1006, 1009, and 1010.]

2003 Amendments:

Section 303(i)(4)(A) of the "Medicare Prescription Drug, Improvement, and Modernization Act of 2003," effective upon enactment, amended section 1927(a)(1) by inserting "or under part B of title XVIII" after "section 1903(a)".

[¶ 2401D] Sec. 1927. TERMS OF REBATE AGREEMENT

[42 U.S.C. § 1396r-8(b)]

(b) TERMS OF REBATE AGREEMENT.—

* * *

(3) MANUFACTURER PROVISION OF PRICE INFORMATION.—

(A) IN GENERAL.—Each manufacturer with an agreement in effect under this section shall report to the Secretary—

(i) not later than 30 days after the last day of each rebate period under the agreement (beginning on or after January 1, 1991), on the average manufacturer price (as defined in subsection (k)(1)) and, (for single source drugs and innovator multiple source drugs), the manufacturer's best price (as defined in subsection (c)(2)(B)) for covered outpatient drugs for the rebate period under the agreement;

(ii) not later than 30 days after the date of entering into an agreement under this section on the average manufacturer price (as defined in subsection (k)(1)) as of October 1, 1990 for each of the manufacturer's covered outpatient drugs; and

(iii) for calendar quarters beginning on or after January 1, 2004, in conjunction with reporting required under clause (i) and by National Drug Code (including package size)—

(I) the manufacturer's average sales price (as defined in section 1847A(c)) and the total number of units specified under section 1847A(b)(2)(A);

(II) if required to make payment under section 1847A, the manufacturer's wholesale acquisition cost, as defined in subsection (c)(6) of such section; and

(III) information on those sales that were made at a nominal price or otherwise described in section 1847A(c)(2)(B);

for a drug or biological described in subparagraph (C), (D), (E), or (G) of section 1842(o)(1) or section 1881(b)(13)(A)(ii).

Information reported under this subparagraph is subject to audit by the Inspector General of the Department of Health and Human Services.

(B) VERIFICATION SURVEYS OF AVERAGE MANUFACTURER PRICE AND MANUFACTURER'S AVERAGE SALES PRICE.—The Secretary may survey wholesalers and manufacturers that directly distribute their covered outpatient drugs, when necessary, to verify manufacturer prices and manufacturer's average sales prices (including wholesale acquisition cost) if required to make payment reported under subparagraph (A). The Secretary may impose a civil monetary penalty in an amount not to exceed $100,000 on a wholesaler, manufacturer, or direct seller, if the wholesaler, manufacturer, or direct seller of a covered outpatient drug refuses a request for information about charges or prices by the Secretary in connection with a survey under this subparagraph or knowingly provides false information. The provisions of section 1128A (other than subsections (a) (with respect to amounts of penalties or additional assessments) and (b)) shall apply to a civil money penalty under this subparagraph in the same manner as such provisions apply to a penalty or proceeding under section 1128A(a).

* * *

(D) CONFIDENTIALITY OF INFORMATION.—Notwithstanding any other provision of law, information disclosed by manufacturers or wholesalers under this paragraph or under an agreement with the Secretary of Veterans Affairs described in subsection (a)(6)(A)(ii) (other than the wholesale acquisition cost for purposes of carrying out section 1847A) is confidential and shall not be disclosed by the Secretary or the Secretary of Veterans Affairs or a State agency (or contractor therewith) in a form which discloses the identity of a specific manufacturer or wholesaler, prices charged for drugs by such manufacturer or wholesaler, except—

(i) as the Secretary determines to be necessary to carry out this section, to carry out section 1847A (including the determination and implementation of the payment amount), or to carry out section 1847B,

(iii) to permit the Director of the Congressional Budget Office to review the information provided.

The previous sentence shall also apply to information disclosed under section 1860D-2(d)(2) or 1860D-4(c)(2)(E)and drug pricing data reported under the first sentence of section 1860D-31(i)(1).

* * *

[CCH Explanation at ¶ 215, 1004, 1006, 1009, and 1010.]
2003 Amendments:

Section 101(e)(4) of the "Medicare Prescription Drug, Improvement, and Modernization Act of 2003," effective upon enactment, amended section 1927(b)(3)(D) by adding the sentence following clause (iii).

Section 105(b)of the "Medicare Prescription Drug, Improvement, and Modernization Act of 2003," effective upon enactment, amended section 1927(b)(3)(D) by amending the last sentence as added by section 101(e)(4) by inserting "and drug pricing data reported under the first sentence of section 1860D-31(i)(1)" after "section 1860D-4(c)(2)(E)".

Section 303(i)(4)(B)(i) of the "Medicare Prescription Drug, Improvement, and Modernization Act of 2003," effective upon enactment, amended section 1927(b)(3)(A)(i) by striking "and" at the end and inserting a semi-colon.

Section 303(i)(4)(B)(ii) of the "Medicare Prescription Drug, Improvement, and Modernization Act of 2003," effective upon enactment, amended section 1927(b)(3)(A)(ii) by striking the period and inserting "; and".

Section 303(i)(4)(B)(iii) of the "Medicare Prescription Drug, Improvement, and Modernization Act of 2003," effective upon enactment, amended section 1927(b)(3)(A) by adding new paragraph iii.

Section 303(i)(4)(C)(i) of the "Medicare Prescription Drug, Improvement, and Modernization Act of 2003," effective upon enactment, amended section 1927(b)(3)(B) in the heading by inserting "AND MANUFACTURER'S AVERAGE SALES PRICE" after "PRICE".

Section 303(i)(4)(C)(ii) of the "Medicare Prescription Drug, Improvement, and Modernization Act of 2003," effective upon enactment, amended section 1927(b)(3)(B) by inserting "and manufacturer's average sales prices (including wholesale acquisition cost) if required to make payment" after "manufacturer prices".

Section 303(i)(4)(D)(i) of the "Medicare Prescription Drug, Improvement, and Modernization Act of 2003," effective upon enactment, amended section 1927(b)(3)(D) in the matter preceding clause (i), by inserting "(other than the wholesale acquisition cost for purposes of carrying out section 1847A)" after "subsection (a)(6)(A)(ii)".

Section 303(i)(4)(D)(ii) of the "Medicare Prescription Drug, Improvement, and Modernization Act of 2003," effective upon enactment, amended section 1927(b)(3)(D)(i) by inserting ", to carry out section 1847A (including the determination and implementation of the payment amount), or to carry out section 1847B" after "this section".

[¶ 2401E] Sec. 1927. DETERMINATION OF AMOUNT OF REBATE
[42 U.S.C. § 1396r-8(c)]

(c) DETERMINATION OF AMOUNT OF REBATE.—

(1) BASIC REBATE FOR SINGLE SOURCE DRUGS AND INNOVATOR MULTIPLE SOURCE DRUGS.—

* * *

(C) BEST PRICE DEFINED.—For purposes of this section—

(i) IN GENERAL.—The term 'best price' means, with respect to a single source drug or innovator multiple source drug of a manufacturer, the lowest price available from the manufacturer during the rebate period to any wholesaler, retailer, provider, health maintenance organization, nonprofit entity, or governmental entity within the United States, excluding—

(I) any prices charged on or after October 1, 1992, to the Indian Health Service, the Department of Veterans Affairs, a State home receiving funds under section 1741 of title 38, United States Code, the Department of Defense, the Public Health Service, or a covered entity described in subsection (a)(5)(B) (including inpatient prices charged to hospitals described in section 340B(a)(4)(L) of the Public Health Service Act);

* * *

(IV) any depot prices and single award contract prices, as defined by the Secretary, of any agency of the Federal Government;

(V) the prices negotiated from drug manufacturers for covered discount card drugs under an endorsed discount card program under section 1860D-31; and

(VI) any prices charged which are negotiated by a prescription drug plan under part D of title XVIII, by an MA-PD plan under part C of such title with respect to covered part D drugs or by a qualified retiree prescription drug plan (as defined in section 1860D-22(a)(2)) with respect to such drugs on behalf of individuals entitled to benefits under part A or enrolled under part B of such title.

* * *

(iii) APPLICATION OF AUDITING AND RECORDKEEPING REQUIREMENTS.—With respect to a covered entity described in section 340B(a)(4)(L) of the Public Health Service Act, any drug purchased for inpatient use shall be subject to the auditing and recordkeeping requirements described in section 340B(a)(5)(C) of the Public Health Service Act.

* * *

[CCH Explanation at ¶ 205 and 1206.]

2003 Amendments:

Section 103(e)(1) of the "Medicare Prescription Drug, Improvement, and Modernization Act of 2003," effective upon enactment, amended section 1927(c)(1)(C)(i), by striking "and" at the end of subclause (III); by striking the period at the end of subclause (IV) and inserting a semicolon; and by adding new subclauses (V) and (VI).

New subclause (VI) applies to prices charged for drugs dispensed on or after January 1, 2006.

Section 1002(a) of the "Medicare Prescription Drug, Improvement, and Modernization Act of 2003," effective upon enactment, amended section 1927(c)(1)(C)(i)(I) by inserting before the semicolon the following:"(including inpatient prices charged to hospitals described in section 340B(a)(4)(L) of the Public Health Service Act)".

Section 1002(b) of the "Medicare Prescription Drug, Improvement, and Modernization Act of 2003," effective upon enactment, amended section 1927(c)(1)(C) by adding clause (iii).

[¶2401F] Sec. 1927. TREATMENT OF PHARMACY REIMBURSEMENT LIMITS

[42 U.S.C. §1396r-8(e)]

(e) TREATMENT OF PHARMACY REIMBURSEMENT LIMITS.—

* * *

(4) ESTABLISHMENT OF UPPER PAYMENT LIMITS.—The Secretary shall establish a Federal upper reimbursement limit for each multiple source drug for which the FDA has rated three or more products therapeutically and pharmaceutically equivalent, regardless of whether all such additional formulations are rated as such and shall use only such formulations when determining any such upper limit.

[CCH Explanation at ¶ 801.]

2003 Amendments:

Section 900(e)(K) of the "Medicare Prescription Drug, Improvement, and Modernization Act of 2003," effective upon enactment, amended section 1927(e)(4), by striking "HCFA" and inserting "The Secretary".

[¶2401G] Sec. 1927. DRUG USE REVIEW

[42 U.S.C. §1396r-8(g)]

(g) DRUG USE REVIEW.—

(1) IN GENERAL.—

* * *

(B) The program shall assess data on drug use against predetermined standards, consistent with the following:

(i) compendia which shall consist of the following:

(I) American Hospital Formulary Service Drug Information;

(II) United States Pharmacopeia-Drug Information;and

(III) the DRUGDEX Information System; and

* * *

2003 Amendments:

Section 101(e)(9) of the "Medicare Prescription Drug, Improvement, and Modernization Act of 2003," effective upon enactment, amended section 1927(g)(1)(B)(i) by adding "and" at the end of subclause (II); and by striking subclause (IV).

Prior to being stricken, subclause (IV) read as follows:

(IV) American Medical Association Drug Evaluations; and

[¶2405] Sec. 1933. STATE COVERAGE OF MEDICARE COST-SHARING FOR ADDITIONAL LOW-INCOME MEDICARE BENEFICIARIES

[42 U.S.C. §1396u-3]

* * *

(g) SPECIAL RULE.—With respect to the period that begins on January 1, 2004, and ends on September 30, 2004, a State shall select qualifying individuals, and provide such individuals with assistance, in accordance with the provisions of this section as in effect with respect to calendar year 2003, except that for such purpose—

* * *

(2) the total allocation amount under subsection (c) for such period shall be $300,000,000.

[CCH Explanation at ¶ 205.]

2003 Amendments:

Section 103(f)(2) of the "Medicare Prescription Drug, Improvement, and Modernization Act of 2003," effective upon enactment, amended section 1933(g) as added by section 401(c) of Public Law 108-89, in the matter preceding paragraph (1), by striking "March 31, 2004" and inserting "September 30, 2004"; and in paragraph (2), by striking "$100,000,000" and inserting "$300,000,000".

[¶ 2410] Sec. 1934. PROGRAM OF ALL-INCLUSIVE CARE FOR THE ELDERLY (PACE)

[42 U.S.C. § 1396u-4]

* * *

(b) SCOPE OF BENEFITS; BENEFICIARY SAFEGUARDS.—

* * *

(3) TREATMENT OF MEDICARE SERVICES FURNISHED BY NONCONTRACT PHYSICIANS AND OTHER ENTITIES.—

(A) APPLICATION OF MEDICAID ADVANTAGE REQUIREMENT WITH RESPECT TO MEDICARE SERVICES FURNISHED BY NONCONTRACT PHYSICIANS AND OTHER ENTITIES.—Section 1852(k)(1) (relating to limitations on balance billing against MA organizations for noncontract physicians and other entities with respect to services covered under title XVIII) shall apply to PACE providers, PACE program eligible individuals enrolled with such PACE providers, and physicians and other entities that do not have a contract or other agreement establishing payment amounts for services furnished to such an individual in the same manner as such section applies to MA organizations, individuals enrolled with such organizations, and physicians and other entities referred to in such section.

(B) REFERENCE TO RELATED PROVISION FOR NONCONTRACT PROVIDERS OF SERVICES.—For the provision relating to limitations on balance billing against PACE providers for services covered under title XVIII furnished by noncontract providers of services, see section 1866(a)(1)(O).

(4) REFERENCE TO RELATED PROVISION FOR SERVICES COVERED UNDER THIS TITLE BUT NOT UNDER TITLE XVIII.—For provisions relating to limitations on payments to providers participating under the State plan under this title that do not have a contract or other agreement with a PACE provider establishing payment amounts for services covered under such plan (but not under title XVIII) when such services are furnished to enrollees of that PACE provider, see section 1902(a)(67).

* * *

2003 Amendments:

Section 236(b)(2) of the "Medicare Prescription Drug, Improvement, and Modernization Act of 2003," amended section 1934(b) by adding at the end new paragraphs (3) and (4).

The above amendment applies to services furnished on or after January 1, 2004.

[¶ 2415] Sec. 1935. SPECIAL PROVISIONS RELATING TO MEDICARE PRESCRIPTION DRUG BENEFIT

(a) REQUIREMENTS RELATING TO MEDICARE PRESCRIPTION DRUG LOW-INCOME SUBSIDIES AND MEDICARE TRANSITIONAL PRESCRIPTION DRUG ASSISTANCE.—As a condition of its State plan under this title under section 1902(a)(66) and receipt of any Federal financial assistance under section 1903(a) subject to subsection (e), a State shall do the following:

(1) INFORMATION FOR TRANSITIONAL PRESCRIPTION DRUG ASSISTANCE VERIFICATION.—The State shall provide the Secretary with information to carry out section 1860D-31(f)(3)(B)(i).

(2) ELIGIBILITY DETERMINATIONS FOR LOW-INCOME SUBSIDIES.—The State shall—

(A) make determinations of eligibility for premium and cost-sharing subsidies under and in accordance with section 1860D-14;

(B) inform the Secretary of such determinations in cases in which such eligibility is established; and

(C) otherwise provide the Secretary with such information as may be required to carry out part D, other than subpart 4, of title XVIII (including section 1860D-14).

(3) SCREENING FOR ELIGIBILITY, AND ENROLLMENT OF, BENEFICIARIES FOR MEDICARE COST-SHARING.—As part of making an eligibility determination required under paragraph (2) for an individual, the State shall make a determination of the individual's eligibility for medical assistance for any medicare cost-sharing described in section 1905(p)(3) and, if the individual is eligible for any such medicare cost-sharing, offer enrollment to the individual under the State plan (or under a waiver of such plan).

(b) REGULAR FEDERAL SUBSIDY OF ADMINISTRATIVE COSTS.—The amounts expended by a State in carrying out subsection (a) are expenditures reimbursable under the appropriate paragraph of section 1903(a).

(c) FEDERAL ASSUMPTION OF MEDICAID PRESCRIPTION DRUG COSTS FOR DUALLY ELIGIBLE INDIVIDUALS.—

(1) PHASED-DOWN STATE CONTRIBUTION.—

(A) IN GENERAL.—Each of the 50 States and the District of Columbia for each month beginning with January 2006 shall provide for payment under this subsection to the Secretary of the product of—

(i) the amount computed under paragraph (2)(A) for the State and month;

(ii) the total number of full-benefit dual eligible individuals (as defined in paragraph (6)) for such State and month; and

(iii) the factor for the month specified in paragraph (5).

(B) FORM AND MANNER OF PAYMENT.—Payment under subparagraph (A) shall be made in a manner specified by the Secretary that is similar to the manner in which State payments are made under an agreement entered into under section 1843, except that all such payments shall be deposited into the Medicare Prescription Drug Account in the Federal Supplementary Medical Insurance Trust Fund.

(C) COMPLIANCE.—If a State fails to pay to the Secretary an amount required under subparagraph (A), interest shall accrue on such amount at the rate provided under section 1903(d)(5). The amount so owed and applicable interest shall be immediately offset against amounts otherwise payable to the State under section 1903(a), in accordance with the Federal Claims Collection Act of 1996 and applicable regulations.

(D) DATA MATCH.—The Secretary shall perform such periodic data matches as may be necessary to identify and compute the number of full-benefit dual eligible individuals for purposes of computing the amount under subparagraph (A).

(2) AMOUNT.—

(A) IN GENERAL.—The amount computed under this paragraph for a State described in paragraph (1) and for a month in a year is equal to—

(i) $1/12$ of the product of—

(I) the base year state medicaid per capita expenditures for covered part D drugs for full-benefit dual eligible individuals (as computed under paragraph (3)); and

(II) a proportion equal to 100 percent minus the Federal medical assistance percentage (as defined in section 1905(b)) applicable to the State for the fiscal year in which the month occurs; and

(ii) increased for each year (beginning with 2004 up to and including the year involved) by the applicable growth factor specified in paragraph (4) for that year.

(B) NOTICE.—The Secretary shall notify each State described in paragraph (1) not later than October 15 before the beginning of each year (beginning with 2006) of the amount computed under subparagraph (A) for the State for that year.

Social Security Law Added, Amended or Repealed 473

(3) BASE YEAR STATE MEDICAID PER CAPITA EXPENDITURES FOR COVERED PART D DRUGS FOR FULLBENEFIT DUAL ELIGIBLE INDIVIDUALS.—

(A) IN GENERAL.—For purposes of paragraph (2)(A), the 'base year State medicaid per capita expenditures for covered part D drugs for full-benefit dual eligible individuals' for a State is equal to the weighted average (as weighted under subparagraph (C)) of—

(i) the gross per capita medicaid expenditures for prescription drugs for 2003, determined under subparagraph (B); and

(ii) the estimated actuarial value of prescription drug benefits provided under a capitated managed care plan per full-benefit dual eligible individual for 2003, as determined using such data as the Secretary determines appropriate.

(B) GROSS PER CAPITA MEDICAID EXPENDITURES FOR PRESCRIPTION DRUGS.—

(i) IN GENERAL.—The gross per capita medicaid expenditures for prescription drugs for 2003 under this subparagraph is equal to the expenditures, including dispensing fees, for the State under this title during 2003 for covered outpatient drugs, determined per full-benefit-dual-eligible-individual for such individuals not receiving medical assistance for such drugs through a medicaid managed care plan.

(ii) DETERMINATION.—In determining the amount under clause (i), the Secretary shall—

(I) use data from the Medicaid Statistical Information System (MSIS) and other available data;

(II) exclude expenditures attributable to covered outpatient prescription drugs that are not covered part D drugs (as defined in section 1860D-2(e)); and

(III) reduce such expenditures by the product of such portion and the adjustment factor (described in clause (iii)).

(iii) ADJUSTMENT FACTOR.—The adjustment factor described in this clause for a State is equal to the ratio for the State for 2003 of—

(I) aggregate payments under agreements under section 1927; to

(II) the gross expenditures under this title for covered outpatient drugs referred to in clause (i).

Such factor shall be determined based on information reported by the State in the medicaid financial management reports (form CMS-64) for the 4 quarters of calendar year 2003 and such other data as the Secretary may require.

(C) WEIGHTED AVERAGE.—The weighted average under subparagraph (A) shall be determined taking into account—

(i) with respect to subparagraph (A)(i), the average number of full-benefit dual eligible individuals in 2003 who are not described in clause (ii); and

(ii) with respect to subparagraph (A)(ii), the average number of full-benefit dual eligible individuals in such year who received in 2003 medical assistance for covered outpatient drugs through a medicaid managed care plan.

(4) APPLICABLE GROWTH FACTOR.—The applicable growth factor under this paragraph for—

(A) each of 2004, 2005, and 2006, is the average annual percent change (to that year from the previous year) of the per capita amount of prescription drug expenditures (as determined based on the most recent National Health Expenditure projections for the years involved); and

(B) a succeeding year, is the annual percentage increase specified in section 1860D-2(b)(6) for the year.

(5) FACTOR.—The factor under this paragraph for a month—

(A) in 2006 is 90 percent;

(B) in 2007 is 88-13 percent;

(C) in 2008 is 86-23 percent;

(D) in 2009 is 85 percent;

§1935(c)(5)(D) ¶2415

(E) in 2010 is 83-13 percent;

(F) in 2011 is 81-23 percent;

(G) in 2012 is 80 percent;

(H) in 2013 is 78-13 percent;

(I) in 2014 is 76-23 percent; or

(J) after December 2014, is 75 percent.

(6) FULL-BENEFIT DUAL ELIGIBLE INDIVIDUAL DEFINED.—

(A) IN GENERAL.—For purposes of this section, the term 'full-benefit dual eligible individual' means for a State for a month an individual who—

(i) has coverage for the month for covered part D drugs under a prescription drug plan under part D of title XVIII, or under an MA-PD plan under part C of such title; and

(ii) is determined eligible by the State for medical assistance for full benefits under this title for such month under section 1902(a)(10)(A) or 1902(a)(10)(C), by reason of section 1902(f), or under any other category of eligibility for medical assistance for full benefits under this title, as determined by the Secretary.

(B) TREATMENT OF MEDICALLY NEEDY AND OTHER INDIVIDUALS REQUIRED TO SPEND DOWN.—In applying subparagraph (A) in the case of an individual determined to be eligible by the State for medical assistance under section 1902(a)(10)(C) or by reason of section 1902(f), the individual shall be treated as meeting the requirement of subparagraph (A)(ii) for any month if such medical assistance is provided for in any part of the month.

(d) COORDINATION OF PRESCRIPTION DRUG BENEFITS.—

(1) MEDICARE AS PRIMARY PAYOR.—In the case of a part D eligible individual (as defined in section 1860D-1(a)(3)(A)) who is described in subsection (c)(6)(A)(ii), notwithstanding any other provision of this title, medical assistance is not available under this title for such drugs (or for any cost-sharing respecting such drugs), and the rules under this title relating to the provision of medical assistance for such drugs shall not apply. The provision of benefits with respect to such drugs shall not be considered as the provision of care or services under the plan under this title. No payment may be made under section 1903(a) for prescribed drugs for which medical assistance is not available pursuant to this paragraph.

(2) COVERAGE OF CERTAIN EXCLUDABLE DRUGS.—In the case of medical assistance under this title with respect to a covered outpatient drug (other than a covered part D drug) furnished to an individual who is enrolled in a prescription drug plan under part D of title XVIII or an MA-PD plan under part C of such title, the State may elect to provide such medical assistance in the manner otherwise provided in the case of individuals who are not full-benefit dual eligible individuals or through an arrangement with such plan.

(e) TREATMENT OF TERRITORIES.—

(1) IN GENERAL.—In the case of a State, other than the 50 States and the District of Columbia—

(A) the previous provisions of this section shall not apply to residents of such State; and

(B) if the State establishes and submits to the Secretary a plan described in paragraph (2) (for providing medical assistance with respect to the provision of prescription drugs to part D eligible individuals), the amount otherwise determined under section 1108(f) (as increased under section 1108(g)) for the State shall be increased by the amount for the fiscal period specified in paragraph (3).

(2) PLAN.—The Secretary shall determine that a plan is described in this paragraph if the plan—

(A) provides medical assistance with respect to the provision of covered part D drugs (as defined in section 1860D-2(e)) to low-income part D eligible individuals;

(B) provides assurances that additional amounts received by the State that are attributable to the operation of this subsection shall be used only for such assistance and related administrative expenses and that no more than 10 percent of the amount specified in paragraph (3)(A) for the State for any fiscal period shall be used for such administrative expenses; and

(C) meets such other criteria as the Secretary may establish.

(3) INCREASED AMOUNT.—

(A) IN GENERAL.—The amount specified in this paragraph for a State for a year is equal to the product of—

(i) the aggregate amount specified in subparagraph (B); and

(ii) the ratio (as estimated by the Secretary) of—

(I) the number of individuals who are entitled to benefits under part A or enrolled under part B and who reside in the State (as determined by the Secretary based on the most recent available data before the beginning of the year); to

(II) the sum of such numbers for all States that submit a plan described in paragraph (2).

(B) AGGREGATE AMOUNT.—The aggregate amount specified in this subparagraph for—

(i) the last 3 quarters of fiscal year 2006, is equal to $28,125,000;

(ii) fiscal year 2007, is equal to $37,500,000; or

(iii) a subsequent year, is equal to the aggregate amount specified in this subparagraph for the previous year increased by annual percentage increase specified in section 1860D-2(b)(6) for the year involved.

(4) REPORT.—The Secretary shall submit to Congress a report on the application of this subsection and may include in the report such recommendations as the Secretary deems appropriate.

[CCH Explanation at ¶ 205.]

2003 Amendments:

Section 103(a)(2) of the "Medicare Prescription Drug, Improvement, and Modernization Act of 2003," effective upon enactment, amended Title XVIII by adding new section 1935.

Section 103(b) of the "Medicare Prescription Drug, Improvement, and Modernization Act of 2003," effective upon enactment, amended section 1935, as added by section 103(a)(2), by adding at the end new subsection (c).

Section 103(c) of the "Medicare Prescription Drug, Improvement, and Modernization Act of 2003," effective upon enactment, further amended section 1935, as inserted and amended by Sections 103(a)(2) and 103(b) by adding at the end new subsection (d).

Section 103(d)(1)(A) of the "Medicare Prescription Drug, Improvement, and Modernization Act of 2003," effective upon enactment, amended section 1935(a), in the matter preceding paragraph (1), by inserting "subject to subsection (e)" after "section 1903(a)".

Section 103(d)(1)(B) of the "Medicare Prescription Drug, Improvement, and Modernization Act of 2003," effective upon enactment, amended section 1935(c)(1) by inserting "subject to subsection (e)" after "1903(a)(1)".

CCH Note: Section 1935(c)(1) does not contain the phrase "1903(a)(1)". Therefore, the amendment made by Section 103(d)(1)(B) of the "Medicare Prescription Drug, Improvement, and Modernization Act of 2003," has not been reflected above.

Section 103(d)(1)(C) of the "Medicare Prescription Drug, Improvement, and Modernization Act of 2003,", effective upon enactment, further amended section 1935 by adding at the end new subsection (e).

[¶ 2416] Sec. 1936. REFERENCES TO LAWS DIRECTLY AFFECTING MEDICAID PROGRAM

[42 U.S.C. § 1396v]

(a) AUTHORITY OR REQUIREMENTS TO COVER ADDITIONAL INDIVIDUALS.—For provisions of law which make additional individuals eligible for medical assistance under this title, see the following:

(1) AFDC.—(A) Section 402(a)(32) of this Act (relating to individuals who are deemed recipients of aid but for whom a payment is not made).

(B) Section 402(a)(37) of this Act (relating to individuals who lose AFDC eligibility due to increased earnings).

(C) Section 406(h) of this Act (relating to individuals who lose AFDC eligibility due to increased collection of child or spousal support).

(D) Section 482(e)(6) of this Act (relating to certain individuals participating in work supplementation programs).

(2) SSI.—(A) Section 1611(e) of this Act (relating to treatment of couples sharing an accommodation in a facility).

(B) Section 1619 of this Act (relating to benefits for individuals who perform substantial gainful activity despite severe medical impairment).

(C) Section 1634(b) and (c) of this Act (relating to preservation of benefit status for disabled widows and widowers who lost SSI benefits because of 1983 changes in actuarial reduction formula).

(D) Section 1634(c) of this Act (relating to individuals who lose eligibility for SSI benefits due to entitlement to child's insurance benefits under section 202(d) of this Act).

(E) Section 1634(d) of this Act (relating to individuals who lose eligibility for SSI benefits due to entitlement to early widow's or widower's insurance benefits under section 202 (e) or (f) of this Act).

(3) FOSTER CARE AND ADOPTION ASSISTANCE.—Sections 472(h) and 473(b) of this Act (relating to medical assistance for children in foster care and for adopted children).

(4) REFUGEE ASSISTANCE.—Section 412(e)(5) of the Immigration and Nationality Act (relating to medical assistance for certain refugees).

(5) MISCELLANEOUS.—(A) Section 230 of Public Law 93-66 (relating to deeming eligible for medical assistance certain essential persons).

(B) Section 231 of Public Law 93-66 (relating to deeming eligible for medical assistance certain persons in medical institutions).

(C) Section 232 of Public Law 93-66 (relating to deeming eligible for medical assistance certain blind and disabled medically indigent persons).

(D) Section 13(c) of Public Law 93-233 (relating to deeming eligible for medical assistance certain individuals receiving mandatory State supplementary payments).

(E) Section 503 of Public Law 94-566 (relating to deeming eligible for medical assistance certain individuals who would be eligible for supplemental security income benefits but for cost-of-living increases in social security benefits).

(F) Section 310(b)(1) of Public Law 96-272 (relating to continuing Medicaid eligibility for certain recipients of Veteran's Administration pensions).

(b) ADDITIONAL STATE PLAN REQUIREMENTS.—For other provisions of law that establish additional requirements for State plans to be approved under this title, see the following:

(1) Section 1618 of this Act (relating to requirement for operation of certain State supplementation programs).

(2) Section 212(a) of Public Law 93-66 (relating to requiring mandatory minimum State supplementation of SSI benefits program).

2003 Amendments:

Section 103(a)(2)(A) of the "Medicare Prescription Drug, Improvement, and Modernization Act of 2003," effective upon enactment, redesignated section 1935 as section 1936.

[¶ 2420] Sec. 2104. ALLOTMENTS
[42 U.S.C. § 1397dd]

* * *

(g) RULE FOR REDISTRIBUTION AND EXTENDED AVAILABILITY OF FISCAL YEARS 1998 AND 1999 ALLOTMENTS—

* * *

(3) DETERMINATION OF AMOUNTS.—For purposes of calculating the amounts described in paragraphs (1) and (2) relating to the allotment for fiscal year 1998 or fiscal year 1999, the Secretary shall use the amounts reported by the States not later than December 15, 2000, or November 30, 2001, respectively, on HCFA Form 64 or HCFA Form 21 or CMS Form 64 or CMS Form 21, as the case may be, as approved by the Secretary.

[CCH Explanation at ¶ 801.]

2003 Amendments:

Section 900(e)(1)(M) of the "Medicare Prescription Drug, Improvement, and Modernization Act of 2003," effective upon enactment, amended section 2104(g)(3) by inserting "or CMS Form 64 or CMS Form 21, as the case may be," after "HCFA Form 64 or HCFA Form 21".

ACT SECTIONS NOT AMENDING SOCIAL SECURITY ACT SECTIONS

MEDICARE ACT OF 2003

[¶ 10,000] ACT SEC. 1. SHORT TITLE; AMENDMENTS TO SOCIAL SECURITY ACT; REFERENCES TO BIPA AND SECRETARY; TABLE OF CONTENTS.

(a) SHORT TITLE.—This Act may be cited as the "Medicare Prescription Drug, Improvement, and Modernization Act of 2003".

(b) AMENDMENTS TO SOCIAL SECURITY ACT.—Except as otherwise specifically provided, whenever in division A of this Act an amendment is expressed in terms of an amendment to or repeal of a section or other provision, the reference shall be considered to be made to that section or other provision of the Social Security Act.

(c) BIPA; SECRETARY.—In this Act:

(1) BIPA.—The term "BIPA" means the Medicare, Medicaid, and SCHIP Benefits Improvement and Protection Act of 2000, as enacted into law by section 1(a)(6) of Public Law 106-554.

(2) SECRETARY.—The term "Secretary" means the Secretary of Health and Human Services.

. . .

TITLE I—MEDICARE PRESCRIPTION DRUG BENEFIT

[¶ 10,005] ACT SEC. 101. MEDICARE PRESCRIPTION DRUG BENEFIT.

. . .

(b) SUBMISSION OF LEGISLATIVE PROPOSAL.—Not later than 6 months after the date of the enactment of this Act, the Secretary shall submit to the appropriate committees of Congress a legislative proposal providing for such technical and conforming amendments in the law as are required by the provisions of this title and title II.

(c) STUDY ON TRANSITIONING PART B PRESCRIPTION DRUG COVERAGE.—Not later than January 1, 2005, the Secretary shall submit a report to Congress that makes recommendations regarding methods for providing benefits under subpart 1 of part D of title XVIII of the Social Security Act for outpatient prescription drugs for which benefits are provided under part B of such title.

(d) REPORT ON PROGRESS IN IMPLEMENTATION OF PRESCRIPTION DRUG BENEFIT.—Not later than March 1, 2005, the Secretary shall submit a report to Congress on the progress that has been made in implementing the prescription drug benefit under this title. The Secretary shall include in the report specific steps that have been taken, and that need to be taken, to ensure a timely start of the program on January 1, 2006. The report shall include recommendations regarding an appropriate transition from the program under section 1860D-31 of the Social Security Act to prescription drug benefits under subpart 1 of part D of title XVIII of such Act.

(e) ADDITIONAL CONFORMING CHANGES.—

(1) CONFORMING REFERENCES TO PREVIOUS PART D.—Any reference in law (in effect before the date of the enactment of this Act) to part D of title XVIII of the Social Security Act is deemed a reference to part E of such title (as in effect after such date).

. . .

(6) DISCLOSURE.—Section 6103(l)(7)(D)(ii) of the Internal Revenue Code of 1986 is amended by inserting "or subsidies provided under section 1860D-14 of such Act" after "Social Security Act".

. . .

[CCH Explanation at ¶ 125, 129, and 131.]

[¶ 10,010] ACT SEC. 104. MEDIGAP AMENDMENTS.

. . .

(c) RULE OF CONSTRUCTION.—

(1) IN GENERAL.—Nothing in this Act shall be construed to require an issuer of a medicare supplemental policy under section 1882 of the Social Security Act (42 U.S.C. 1395rr) to participate as a PDP sponsor under part D of title XVIII of such Act, as added by section 101, as a condition for issuing such policy.

(2) PROHIBITION ON STATE REQUIREMENT.—A State may not require an issuer of a medicare supplemental policy under section 1882 of the Social Security Act (42 U.S.C. 1395rr) to participate as a PDP sponsor under such part D as a condition for issuing such policy.

[CCH Explanation at ¶210.]

[¶10,020] ACT SEC. 105. ADDITIONAL PROVISIONS RELATING TO MEDICARE PRESCRIPTION DRUG DISCOUNT CARD AND TRANSITIONAL ASSISTANCE PROGRAM.

. . .

(c) RULES FOR IMPLEMENTATION.—The following rules shall apply to the medicare prescription drug discount card and transitional assistance program under section 1860D-31 of the Social Security Act, as added by section 101(a):

(1) In promulgating regulations pursuant to subsection (a)(2)(B) of such section 1860D-31—

(A) section 1871(a)(3) of the Social Security Act (42 U.S.C. 1395hh(a)(3)), as added by section 902(a)(1), shall not apply;

(B) chapter 35 of title 44, United States Code, shall not apply; and

(C) sections 553(d) and 801(a)(3)(A) of title 5, United States Code, shall not apply.

(2) Section 1857(c)(5) of the Social Security Act (42 U.S.C. 1395w-27(c)(5)) shall apply with respect to section 1860D-31 of such Act, as added by section 101(a), in the same manner as it applies to part C of title XVIII of such Act.

(3) The administration of such program shall be made without regard to chapter 35 of title 44, United States Code.

(4)(A) There shall be no judicial review of a determination not to endorse, or enter into a contract, with a prescription drug card sponsor under section 1860D-31 of the Social Security Act.

(B) In the case of any order issued to enjoin any provision of section 1860D-31 of the Social Security Act (or of any provision of this section), such order shall not affect any other provision of such section (or of this section) and all such provisions shall be treated as severable.

. . .

(e) DISCLOSURE OF RETURN INFORMATION FOR PURPOSES OF PROVIDING TRANSITIONAL ASSISTANCE UNDER MEDICARE DISCOUNT CARD PROGRAM.—

(1) IN GENERAL.—Subsection (l) of section 6103 of the Internal Revenue Code of 1986 (relating to disclosure of returns and return information for purposes other than tax administration) is amended by adding at the end the following new paragraph:

(19) DISCLOSURE OF RETURN INFORMATION FOR PURPOSES OF PROVIDING TRANSITIONAL ASSISTANCE UNDER MEDICARE DISCOUNT CARD PROGRAM.—

(A) IN GENERAL.—The Secretary, upon written request from the Secretary of Health and Human Services pursuant to carrying out section 1860D-31 of the Social Security Act, shall disclose to officers, employees, and contractors of the Department of Health and Human Services with respect to a taxpayer for the applicable year—

(i)(I) whether the adjusted gross income, as modified in accordance with specifications of the Secretary of Health and Human Services for purposes of carrying out such section, of such taxpayer and, if applicable, such taxpayer's spouse, for the applicable year, exceeds the amounts specified by the Secretary of Health and Human Services in order to apply the 100 and 135 percent of the poverty lines under such section, (II) whether the return was a joint return, and (III) the applicable year, or

(ii) if applicable, the fact that there is no return filed for such taxpayer for the applicable year.

Non-Code Provisions

(B) DEFINITION OF APPLICABLE YEAR.—For the purposes of this subsection, the term 'applicable year' means the most recent taxable year for which information is available in the Internal Revenue Service's taxpayer data information systems, or, if there is no return filed for such taxpayer for such year, the prior taxable year.

(C) RESTRICTION ON USE OF DISCLOSED INFORMATION.—Return information disclosed under this paragraph may be used only for the purposes of determining eligibility for and administering transitional assistance under section 1860D-31 of the Social Security Act."

(2) CONFIDENTIALITY.—Paragraph (3) of section 6103(a) of such Code is amended by striking "or (16)" and inserting "(16), or (19)".

(3) PROCEDURES AND RECORDKEEPING RELATED TO DISCLOSURES.—Subsection (p)(4) of section 6103 of such Code is amended by striking "(l)(16) or (17)" each place it appears and inserting "(l)(16), (17), or (19)".

(4) UNAUTHORIZED DISCLOSURE OR INSPECTION.—Paragraph (2) of section 7213(a) of such Code is amended by striking "or (16)" and inserting " (16), or (19)".

[CCH Explanation at ¶215.]

[¶10,030] ACT SEC. 106. STATE PHARMACEUTICAL ASSISTANCE TRANSITION COMMISSION.

(a) ESTABLISHMENT.—

(1) IN GENERAL.—There is established, as of the first day of the third month beginning after the date of the enactment of this Act, a State Pharmaceutical Assistance Transition Commission (in this section referred to as the "Commission") to develop a proposal for addressing the unique transitional issues facing State pharmaceutical assistance programs, and program participants, due to the implementation of the voluntary prescription drug benefit program under part D of title XVIII of the Social Security Act, as added by section 101.

(2) DEFINITIONS.—For purposes of this section:

(A) STATE PHARMACEUTICAL ASSISTANCE PROGRAM DEFINED.—The term "State pharmaceutical assistance program" means a program (other than the medicaid program) operated by a State (or under contract with a State) that provides as of the date of the enactment of this Act financial assistance to medicare beneficiaries for the purchase of prescription drugs.

(B) PROGRAM PARTICIPANT.—The term "program participant" means a low-income medicare beneficiary who is a participant in a State pharmaceutical assistance program.

(b) COMPOSITION.—The Commission shall include the following:

(1) A representative of each Governor of each State that the Secretary identifies as operating on a statewide basis a State pharmaceutical assistance program that provides for eligibility and benefits that are comparable or more generous than the low-income assistance eligibility and benefits offered under section 1860D-14 of the Social Security Act.

(2) Representatives from other States that the Secretary identifies have in operation other State pharmaceutical assistance programs, as appointed by the Secretary.

(3) Representatives of organizations that have an inherent interest in program participants or the program itself, as appointed by the Secretary but not to exceed the number of representatives under paragraphs (1) and (2).

(4) Representatives of Medicare Advantage organizations, pharmaceutical benefit managers, and other private health insurance plans, as appointed by the Secretary.

(5) The Secretary (or the Secretary's designee) and such other members as the Secretary may specify.

The Secretary shall designate a member to serve as Chair of the Commission and the Commission shall meet at the call of the Chair.

(c) DEVELOPMENT OF PROPOSAL.—The Commission shall develop the proposal described in subsection (a) in a manner consistent with the following principles:

(1) Protection of the interests of program participants in a manner that is the least disruptive to such participants and that includes a single point of contact for enrollment and processing of benefits.

(2) Protection of the financial and flexibility interests of States so that States are not financially worse off as a result of the enactment of this title.

(3) Principles of medicare modernization under this Act.

(d) REPORT.—By not later than January 1, 2005, the Commission shall submit to the President and Congress a report that contains a detailed proposal (including specific legislative or administrative recommendations, if any) and such other recommendations as the Commission deems appropriate.

(e) SUPPORT.—The Secretary shall provide the Commission with the administrative support services necessary for the Commission to carry out its responsibilities under this section.

(f) TERMINATION.—The Commission shall terminate 30 days after the date of submission of the report under subsection (d).

[CCH Explanation at ¶ 220.]

[¶ 10,040] ACT SEC. 107. STUDIES AND REPORTS.

(a) STUDY REGARDING REGIONAL VARIATIONS IN PRESCRIPTION DRUG SPENDING.—

(1) IN GENERAL.—The Secretary shall conduct a study that examines variations in per capita spending for covered part D drugs under part D of title XVIII of the Social Security Act among PDP regions and, with respect to such spending, the amount of such variation that is attributable to—

(A) price variations (described in section 1860D-15(c)(2) of such Act); and

(B) differences in per capita utilization that is not taken into account in the health status risk adjustment provided under section 1860D-15(c)(1) of such Act.

(2) REPORT AND RECOMMENDATIONS.—Not later than January 1, 2009, the Secretary shall submit to Congress a report on the study conducted under paragraph (1). Such report shall include—

(A) information regarding the extent of geographic variation described in paragraph (1)(B);

(B) an analysis of the impact on direct subsidies under section 1860D-15(a)(1) of the Social Security Act in different PDP regions if such subsidies were adjusted to take into account the variation described in subparagraph (A); and

(C) recommendations regarding the appropriateness of applying an additional geographic adjustment factor under section 1860D-15(c)(2) that reflects some or all of the variation described in subparagraph (A).

(b) REVIEW AND REPORT ON CURRENT STANDARDS OF PRACTICE FOR PHARMACY SERVICES PROVIDED TO PATIENTS IN NURSING FACILITIES.—

(1) REVIEW.—

(A) IN GENERAL.—Not later than 12 months after the date of the enactment of this Act, the Secretary shall conduct a thorough review of the current standards of practice for pharmacy services provided to patients in nursing facilities.

(B) SPECIFIC MATTERS REVIEWED.—In conducting the review under subparagraph (A), the Secretary shall—

(i) assess the current standards of practice, clinical services, and other service requirements generally used for pharmacy services in long-term care settings; and

(ii) evaluate the impact of those standards with respect to patient safety, reduction of medication errors and quality of care.

(2) REPORT.—

(A) IN GENERAL.—Not later than the date that is 18 months after the date of the enactment of this Act, the Secretary shall submit a report to Congress on the study conducted under paragraph (1)(A).

(B) CONTENTS.—The report submitted under subparagraph (A) shall contain—

(i) a description of the plans of the Secretary to implement the provisions of this Act in a manner consistent with applicable State and Federal laws designed to protect the safety and quality of care of nursing facility patients; and

(ii) recommendations regarding necessary actions and appropriate reimbursement to ensure the provision of prescription drugs to medicare beneficiaries residing in nursing facilities in a manner consistent with existing patient safety and quality of care standards under applicable State and Federal laws.

(c) IOM STUDY ON DRUG SAFETY AND QUALITY.—

(1) IN GENERAL.—The Secretary shall enter into a contract with the Institutes of Medicine of the National Academies of Science (such Institutes referred to in this subsection as the "IOM") to carry out a comprehensive study (in this subsection referred to as the "study") of drug safety and quality issues in order to provide a blueprint for system-wide change.

(2) OBJECTIVES.—

(A) The study shall develop a full understanding of drug safety and quality issues through an evidence-based review of literature, case studies, and analysis. This review will consider the nature and causes of medication errors, their impact on patients, the differences in causation, impact, and prevention across multiple dimensions of health care delivery- including patient populations, care settings, clinicians, and institutional cultures.

(B) The study shall attempt to develop credible estimates of the incidence, severity, costs of medication errors that can be useful in prioritizing resources for national quality improvement efforts and influencing national health care policy.

(C) The study shall evaluate alternative approaches to reducing medication errors in terms of their efficacy, cost-effectiveness, appropriateness in different settings and circumstances, feasibility, institutional barriers to implementation, associated risks, and the quality of evidence supporting the approach.

(D) The study shall provide guidance to consumers, providers, payers, and other key stakeholders on high-priority strategies to achieve both short-term and long-term drug safety goals, to elucidate the goals and expected results of such initiatives and support the business case for them, and to identify critical success factors and key levers for achieving success.

(E) The study shall assess the opportunities and key impediments to broad nationwide implementation of medication error reductions, and to provide guidance to policy-makers and government agencies (including the Food and Drug Administration, the Centers for Medicare & Medicaid Services, and the National Institutes of Health) in promoting a national agenda for medication error reduction.

(F) The study shall develop an applied research agenda to evaluate the health and cost impacts of alternative interventions, and to assess collaborative public and private strategies for implementing the research agenda through AHRQ and other government agencies.

(3) CONDUCT OF STUDY.—

(A) EXPERT COMMITTEE.—In conducting the study, the IOM shall convene a committee of leading experts and key stakeholders in pharmaceutical management and drug safety, including clinicians, health services researchers, pharmacists, system administrators, payer representatives, and others.

(B) COMPLETION.—The study shall be completed within an 18-month period.

(4) REPORT.—A report on the study shall be submitted to Congress upon the completion of the study.

(5) AUTHORIZATION OF APPROPRIATIONS.—There are authorized to be appropriated to carry out this section such sums as may be necessary.

(d) STUDY OF MULTI-YEAR CONTRACTS.—

(1) IN GENERAL.—The Secretary shall provide for a study on the feasibility and advisability of providing for contracting with PDP sponsors and MA organizations under parts C and D of title XVIII on a multi-year basis.

(2) REPORT.—Not later than January 1, 2007, the Secretary shall submit to Congress a report on the study under paragraph (1). The report shall include such recommendations as the Secretary deems appropriate.

(e) GAO STUDY REGARDING IMPACT OF ASSETS TEST FOR SUBSIDY ELIGIBLE INDIVIDUALS.—

(1) STUDY.—The Comptroller General of the United States shall conduct a study to determine the extent to which drug utilization and access to covered part D drugs under part D of title XVIII of the Social Security Act by subsidy eligible individuals differs from such utilization and access for individuals who would qualify as such subsidy eligible individuals but for the application of section 1860D-14(a)(3)(A)(iii) of such Act.

(2) REPORT.—Not later than September 30, 2007, the Comptroller General shall submit a report to Congress on the study conducted under paragraph (1) that includes such recommendations for legislation as the Comptroller General determines are appropriate.

(f) STUDY ON MAKING PRESCRIPTION PHARMACEUTICAL INFORMATION ACCESSIBLE FOR BLIND AND VISUALLY-IMPAIRED INDIVIDUALS.—

(1) STUDY.—

(A) IN GENERAL.—The Secretary shall undertake a study of how to make prescription pharmaceutical information, including drug labels and usage instructions, accessible to blind and visually-impaired individuals.

(B) STUDY TO INCLUDE EXISTING AND EMERGING TECHNOLOGIES.—The study under subparagraph (A) shall include a review of existing and emerging technologies, including assistive technology, that makes essential information on the content and prescribed use of pharmaceutical medicines available in a usable format for blind and visually-impaired individuals.

(2) REPORT.—

(A) IN GENERAL.—Not later than 18 months after the date of the enactment of this Act, the Secretary shall submit a report to Congress on the study required under paragraph (1).

(B) CONTENTS OF REPORT.—The report required under paragraph (1) shall include recommendations for the implementation of usable formats for making prescription pharmaceutical information available to blind and visually-impaired individuals and an estimate of the costs associated with the implementation of each format.

[CCH Explanation at ¶225.]

[¶10,050] ACT SEC. 108. GRANTS TO PHYSICIANS TO IMPLEMENT ELECTRONIC PRESCRIPTION DRUG PROGRAMS.

(a) IN GENERAL.—The Secretary is authorized to make grants to physicians for the purpose of assisting such physicians to implement electronic prescription drug programs that comply with the standards promulgated or modified under section 1860D-4(e) of the Social Security Act, as inserted by section 101(a).

(b) AWARDING OF GRANTS.—

(1) APPLICATION.—No grant may be made under this section except pursuant to a grant application that is submitted and approved in a time, manner, and form specified by the Secretary.

(2) CONSIDERATIONS AND PREFERENCES.—In awarding grants under this section, the Secretary shall—

(A) give special consideration to physicians who serve a disproportionate number of medicare patients; and

(B) give preference to physicians who serve a rural or underserved area.

(3) LIMITATION ON GRANTS.—Only 1 grant may be awarded under this section with respect to any physician or group practice of physicians.

(c) TERMS AND CONDITIONS.—

(1) IN GENERAL.—Grants under this section shall be made under such terms and conditions as the Secretary specifies consistent with this section.

(2) USE OF GRANT FUNDS.—Funds provided under grants under this section may be used for any of the following:

(A) For purchasing, leasing, and installing computer software and hardware, including handheld computer technologies.

(B) Making upgrades and other improvements to existing computer software and hardware to enable eprescribing.

(C) Providing education and training to eligible physician staff on the use of technology to implement the electronic transmission of prescription and patient information.

(3) PROVISION OF INFORMATION.—As a condition for the awarding of a grant under this section, an applicant shall provide to the Secretary such information as the Secretary may require in order to—

(A) evaluate the project for which the grant is made; and

(B) ensure that funding provided under the grant is expended only for the purposes for which it is made.

(4) AUDIT.—The Secretary shall conduct appropriate audits of grants under this section.

(5) MATCHING REQUIREMENT.—The applicant for a grant under this section shall agree, with respect to the costs to be incurred by the applicant in implementing an electronic prescription drug program, to make available (directly or through donations from public or private entities) non-Federal contributions toward such costs in an amount that is not less than 50 percent of such costs. Non-Federal contributions under the previous sentence may be in cash or in kind, fairly evaluated, including plant, equipment, or services. Amounts provided by the Federal Government, or services assisted or subsidized to any significant extent by the Federal Government, may not be included in determining the amount of such contributions.

(d) AUTHORIZATION OF APPROPRIATIONS.—There are authorized to be appropriated to carry out this section $50,000,000 for fiscal year 2007 and such sums as may be necessary for each of fiscal years 2008 and 2009.

[CCH Explanation at ¶230.]

[¶10,060] ACT SEC. 109. EXPANDING THE WORK OF MEDICARE QUALITY IMPROVEMENT ORGANIZATIONS TO INCLUDE PARTS C AND D.

. . .

(d) IOM STUDY OF QIOS.—

(1) IN GENERAL.—The Secretary shall request the Institute of Medicine of the National Academy of Sciences to conduct an evaluation of the program under part B of title XI of the Social Security Act. The study shall include a review of the following:

(A) An overview of the program under such part.

(B) The duties of organizations with contracts with the Secretary under such part.

(C) The extent to which quality improvement organizations improve the quality of care for medicare beneficiaries.

(D) The extent to which other entities could perform such quality improvement functions as well as, or better than, quality improvement organizations.

(E) The effectiveness of reviews and other actions conducted by such organizations in carrying out those duties.

(F) The source and amount of funding for such organizations.

(G) The conduct of oversight of such organizations.

(2) REPORT TO CONGRESS.—Not later than June 1, 2006, the Secretary shall submit to Congress a report on the results of the study described in paragraph (1), including any recommendations for legislation.

(3) INCREASED COMPETITION.—If the Secretary finds based on the study conducted under paragraph (1) that other entities could improve quality in the medicare program as well as, or better than, the current quality improvement organizations, then the Secretary shall provide for such increased competition through the addition of new types of entities which may perform quality improvement functions.

[CCH Explanation at ¶ 235.]

[¶ 10,070] ACT SEC. 110. CONFLICT OF INTEREST STUDY.

(a) STUDY.—The Federal Trade Commission shall conduct a study of differences in payment amounts for pharmacy services provided to enrollees in group health plans that utilize pharmacy benefit managers. Such study shall include the following:

(1) An assessment of the differences in costs incurred by such enrollees and plans for prescription drugs dispensed by mail-order pharmacies owned by pharmaceutical benefit managers compared to mail-order pharmacies not owned by pharmaceutical benefit managers, and community pharmacies.

(2) Whether such plans are acting in a manner that maximizes competition and results in lower prescription drug prices for enrollees.

(b) REPORT.—Not later than 18 months after the date of the enactment of this Act, the Commission shall submit to Congress a report on the study conducted under subsection (a). Such report shall include recommendations regarding any need for legislation to ensure the fiscal integrity of the voluntary prescription drug benefit program under part D of title XVIII, as added by section 101, that may be appropriated as the result of such study.

(c) EXEMPTION FROM PAPERWORK REDUCTION ACT.—Chapter 35 of title 44, United States Code, shall not apply to the collection of information under subsection (a).

[CCH Explanation at ¶ 240.]

[¶ 10,080] ACT SEC. 111. STUDY ON EMPLOYMENT-BASED RETIREE HEALTH COVERAGE.

(a) STUDY.—The Comptroller General of the United States shall conduct an initial and final study under this subsection to examine trends in employment-based retiree health coverage (as defined in 1860D-22(c)(1) of the Social Security Act, as added by section 101), including coverage under the Federal Employees Health Benefits Program (FEHBP), and the options and incentives available under this Act which may have an effect on the voluntary provision of such coverage.

(b) CONTENT OF INITIAL STUDY.—The initial study under this section shall consider the following:

(1) Trends in employment-based retiree health coverage prior to the date of the enactment of this Act.

(2) The opinions of sponsors of employment-based retiree health coverage concerning which of the options available under this Act they are most likely to utilize for the provision of health coverage to their medicare-eligible retirees, including an assessment of the administrative burdens associated with the available options.

(3) The likelihood of sponsors of employment-based retiree health coverage to maintain or adjust their levels of retiree health benefits beyond coordination with medicare, including for prescription drug coverage, provided to medicare-eligible retirees after the date of the enactment of this Act.

(4) The factors that sponsors of employment-based retiree health coverage expect to consider in making decisions about any changes they may make in the health coverage provided to medicare-eligible retirees.

(5) Whether the prescription drug plan options available, or the health plan options available under the Medicare Advantage program, are likely to cause employers and other entities that did not provide health coverage to retirees prior to the date of the enactment of this Act to provide supplemental coverage or contributions toward premium expenses for medicare-eligible retirees who may enroll in such options in the future.

(c) CONTENTS OF FINAL STUDY.—The final study under this section shall consider the following:

(1) Changes in the trends in employment-based retiree health coverage since the completion of the initial study by the Comptroller General.

(2) Factors contributing to any changes in coverage levels.

(3) The number and characteristics of sponsors of employment-based retiree health coverage who receive the special subsidy payments under section 1860D-22 of the Social Security Act, as added by section 101, for the provision of prescription drug coverage to their medicare-eligible retirees that is the same or greater actuarial value as the prescription drug coverage available to other medicare beneficiaries without employment-based retiree health coverage.

(4) The extent to which sponsors of employment-based retiree health coverage provide supplemental health coverage or contribute to the premiums for medicare-eligible retirees who enroll in a prescription drug plan or an MAPD plan.

(5) Other coverage options, including tax-preferred retirement or health savings accounts, consumer-directed health plans, or other vehicles that sponsors of employment-based retiree health coverage believe would assist retirees with their future health care needs and their willingness to sponsor such alternative plan designs.

(6) The extent to which employers or other entities that did not provide employment-based retiree health coverage prior to the date of the enactment of this Act provided some form of coverage or financial assistance for retiree health care needs after the date of the enactment of this Act.

(7) Recommendations by employers, benefits experts, academics, and others on ways that the voluntary provision of employment-based retiree health coverage may be improved and expanded.

(d) REPORTS.—The Comptroller General shall submit a report to Congress on—

(1) the initial study under subsection (b) not later than 1 year after the date of the enactment of this Act; and

(2) the final study under subsection (c) not later than January 1, 2007.

(e) CONSULTATION.—The Comptroller General shall consult with sponsors of employment-based retiree health coverage, benefits experts, human resources professionals, employee benefits consultants, and academics with experience in health benefits and survey research in the development and design of the initial and final studies under this section.

[CCH Explanation at ¶245.]

TITLE II—MEDICARE ADVANTAGE

Subtitle A—Implementation of Medicare Advantage Program

[¶10,090] ACT SEC. 201. IMPLEMENTATION OF MEDICARE ADVANTAGE PROGRAM.

(a) IN GENERAL.—There is hereby established the Medicare Advantage program. The Medicare Advantage program shall consist of the program under part C of title XVIII of the Social Security Act (as amended by this Act).

(b) REFERENCES.—Subject to subsection (c), any reference to the program under part C of title XVIII of the Social Security Act shall be deemed a reference to the Medicare Advantage program and, with respect to such part, any reference to "Medicare+Choice" is deemed a reference to "Medicare Advantage" and "MA".

(c) TRANSITION.—In order to provide for an orderly transition and avoid beneficiary and provider confusion, the Secretary shall provide for an appropriate transition in the use of the terms "Medicare+Choice" and "Medicare Advantage" (or "MA") in reference to the program under part C of title XVIII of the Social Security Act. Such transition shall be fully completed for all materials for plan years beginning not later than January 1, 2006. Before the completion of such transition, any reference to "Medicare Advantage" or "MA" shall be deemed to include a reference to "Medicare+Choice".

[CCH Explanation at ¶350.]

Subtitle B—Immediate Improvements

[¶ 10,100] ACT SEC. 211. IMMEDIATE IMPROVEMENTS.

. . .

(f) MEDPAC STUDY OF AAPCC.—

(1) STUDY.—The Medicare Payment Advisory Commission shall conduct a study that assesses the method used for determining the adjusted average per capita cost (AAPCC) under section 1876(a)(4) of the Social Security Act (42 U.S.C. 1395mm(a)(4)) as applied under section 1853(c)(1)(A) of such Act (as amended by subsection (a)). Such study shall include an examination of—

(A) the bases for variation in such costs between different areas, including differences in input prices, utilization, and practice patterns;

(B) the appropriate geographic area for payment of MA local plans under the Medicare Advantage program under part C of title XVIII of such Act; and

(C) the accuracy of risk adjustment methods in reflecting differences in costs of providing care to different groups of beneficiaries served under such program.

(2) REPORT.—Not later than 18 months after the date of the enactment of this Act, the Commission shall submit to Congress a report on the study conducted under paragraph (1).

(g) REPORT ON IMPACT OF INCREASED FINANCIAL ASSISTANCE TO MEDICARE ADVANTAGE PLANS.—Not later than July 1, 2006, the Secretary shall submit to Congress a report that describes the impact of additional financing provided under this Act and other Acts (including the Medicare, Medicaid, and SCHIP Balanced Budget Refinement Act of 1999 and BIPA) on the availability of Medicare Advantage plans in different areas and its impact on lowering premiums and increasing benefits under such plans.

(h) MEDPAC STUDY AND REPORT ON CLARIFICATION OF AUTHORITY REGARDING DISAPPROVAL OF UNREASONABLE BENEFICIARY COST-SHARING.—

(1) STUDY.—The Medicare Payment Advisory Commission, in consultation with beneficiaries, consumer groups, employers, and organizations offering plans under part C of title XVIII of the Social Security Act, shall conduct a study to determine the extent to which the cost-sharing structures under such plans affect access to covered services or select enrollees based on the health status of eligible individuals described in section 1851(a)(3) of the Social Security Act (42 U.S.C. 1395w-21(a)(3)).

(2) REPORT.—Not later than December 31, 2004, the Commission shall submit a report to Congress on the study conducted under paragraph (1) together with recommendations for such legislation and administrative actions as the Commission considers appropriate.

(i) IMPLEMENTATION OF PROVISIONS.—

(1) ANNOUNCEMENT OF REVISED MEDICARE ADVANTAGE PAYMENT RATES.—Within 6 weeks after the date of the enactment of this Act, the Secretary shall determine, and shall announce (in a manner intended to provide notice to interested parties) MA capitation rates under section 1853 of the Social Security Act (42 U.S.C. 1395w-23) for 2004, revised in accordance with the provisions of this section.

(2) TRANSITION TO REVISED PAYMENT RATES.—The provisions of section 604 of BIPA (114 Stat. 2763A-555) (other than subsection (a)) shall apply to the provisions of subsections (a) through (d) of this section for 2004 in the same manner as the provisions of such section 604 applied to the provisions of BIPA for 2001.

(3) SPECIAL RULE FOR PAYMENT RATES IN 2004.—

(A) JANUARY AND FEBRUARY.—Notwithstanding the amendments made by subsections (a) through (d), for purposes of making payments under section 1853 of the Social Security Act (42 U.S.C. 1395w-23) for January and February 2004, the annual capitation rate for a payment area shall be calculated and the excess amount under section 1854(f)(1)(B) of such Act (42 U.S.C. 1395w-24(f)(1)(B)) shall be determined as if such amendments had not been enacted.

(B) MARCH THROUGH DECEMBER.—Notwith-standing the amendments made by subsections (a) through (d), for purposes of making payments under section 1853 of the Social Security Act (42 U.S.C. 1395w-23) for March through December 2004, the annual capitation rate for a payment area shall be calculated and the excess amount under section 1854(f)(1)(B) of such Act (42 U.S.C. 1395w-24(f)(1)(B)) shall be determined, in such manner as the Secretary estimates will ensure that the total of such payments with respect to 2004 is the same as the amounts that would have been if subparagraph (A) had not been enacted.

(C) CONSTRUCTION.—Subparagraphs (A) and (B) shall not be taken into account in computing such capitation rate for 2005 and subsequent years.

(4) PLANS REQUIRED TO PROVIDE NOTICE OF CHANGES IN PLAN BENEFITS.—In the case of an organization offering a plan under part C of title XVIII of the Social Security Act that revises its submission of the information described in section 1854(a)(1) of such Act (42 U.S.C. 1395w-23(a)(1)) for a plan pursuant to the application of paragraph (2), if such revision results in changes in beneficiary premiums, beneficiary cost-sharing, or benefits under the plan, then by not later than 3 weeks after the date the Secretary approves such submission, the organization offering the plan shall provide each beneficiary enrolled in the plan with written notice of such changes.

(5) LIMITATION ON REVIEW.—There shall be no administrative or judicial review under section 1869 or section 1878 of the Social Security Act (42 U.S.C. 1395ff and 1395oo), or otherwise of any determination made by the Secretary under this subsection or the application of the payment rates determined pursuant to this subsection.

(j) ADDITIONAL AMENDMENTS.—Section 1852(d)(4) (42 U.S.C. 1395w-22(d)(4)) is amended—

(1) in subparagraph (B), by inserting "(other than deemed contracts or agreements under subsection (j)(6))" after "the plan has contracts or agreements"; and

(2) in the last sentence, by inserting before the period at the end the following: ", except that, if a plan entirely meets such requirement with respect to a category of health care professional or provider on the basis of subparagraph (B), it may provide for a higher beneficiary copayment in the case of health care professionals and providers of that category who do not have contracts or agreements (other than deemed contracts or agreements under subsection (j)(6)) to provide covered services under the terms of the plan".

[CCH Explanation at ¶356]

Subtitle C—Offering of Medicare Advantage (MA) Regional Plans; Medicare Advantage Competition

. . .

[¶10,110] ACT SEC. 223. EFFECTIVE DATE.

(a) EFFECTIVE DATE.—The amendments made by this subtitle shall apply with respect to plan years beginning on or after January 1, 2006.

(b) ISSUANCE OF REGULATIONS.—The Secretary shall revise the regulations previously promulgated to carry out part C of title XVIII of the Social Security Act to carry out the provisions of this Act.

[CCH Explanation at ¶377.]

Subtitle D—Additional Reforms

[¶10,120] ACT SEC. 231. SPECIALIZED MA PLANS FOR SPECIAL NEEDS INDIVIDUALS.

. . .

(d) AUTHORITY TO DESIGNATE OTHER PLANS AS SPECIALIZED MA PLANS.—In promulgating regulations to carry out section 1851(a)(2)(A)(ii) of the Social Security Act (as added by subsection (a)) and section 1859(b)(6) of such Act (as added by subsection (b)), the Secretary may provide (notwithstanding section 1859(b)(6)(A) of such Act) for the offering of specialized MA plans for special needs individuals by MA plans that disproportionately serve special needs individuals.

(e) REPORT TO CONGRESS.—Not later than December 31, 2007, the Secretary shall submit to Congress a report that assesses the impact of specialized MA plans for special needs individuals on the cost and quality of services provided to enrollees. Such report shall include an assessment of the costs and savings to the medicare program as a result of amendments made by subsections (a), (b), and (c).

(f) EFFECTIVE DATES.—

(1) IN GENERAL.—The amendments made by subsections (a), (b), and (c) shall take effect upon the date of the enactment of this Act.

(2) DEADLINE FOR ISSUANCE OF REQUIREMENTS FOR SPECIAL NEEDS INDIVIDUALS; TRANSITION.—No later than 1 year after the date of the enactment of this Act, the Secretary shall issue final regulations to establish requirements for special needs individuals under section 1859(b)(6)(B)(iii) of the Social Security Act, as added by subsection (b).

[CCH Explanation at ¶378.]

[¶10,150] ACT SEC. 235. 2-YEAR EXTENSION OF MUNICIPAL HEALTH SERVICE DEMONSTRATION PROJECTS.

The last sentence of section 9215(a) of the Consolidated Omnibus Budget Reconciliation Act of 1985 (42 U.S.C. 1395b-1 note), as amended by section 6135 of the Omnibus Budget Reconciliation Act of 1989, section 13557 of the Omnibus Budget Reconciliation Act of 1993, section 4017 of BBA, section 534 of BBRA (113 Stat. 1501A-390), and section 633 of BIPA, is amended by striking " December 31, 2004" and inserting "December 31, 2006".

[CCH Explanation at ¶387.]

[¶10,180] ACT SEC. 238. INSTITUTE OF MEDICINE EVALUATION AND REPORT ON HEALTH CARE PERFORMANCE MEASURES.

(a) EVALUATION.—

(1) IN GENERAL.—Not later than the date that is 2 months after the date of the enactment of this Act, the Secretary shall enter into an arrangement under which the Institute of Medicine of the National Academy of Sciences (in this section referred to as the "Institute") shall conduct an evaluation of leading health care performance measures in the public and private sectors and options to implement policies that align performance with payment under the medicare program under title XVIII of the Social Security Act (42 U.S.C. 1395 et seq.).

(2) SPECIFIC MATTERS EVALUATED.—In conducting the evaluation under paragraph (1), the Institute shall—

(A) catalogue, review, and evaluate the validity of leading health care performance measures;

(B) catalogue and evaluate the success and utility of alternative performance incentive programs in public or private sector settings; and

(C) identify and prioritize options to implement policies that align performance with payment under the medicare program that indicate—

(i) the performance measurement set to be used and how that measurement set will be updated;

(ii) the payment policy that will reward performance; and

(iii) the key implementation issues (such as data and information technology requirements) that must be addressed.

(3) SCOPE OF HEALTH CARE PERFORMANCE MEASURES.—The health care performance measures described in paragraph (2)(A) shall encompass a variety of perspectives, including physicians, hospitals, other health care providers, health plans, purchasers, and patients.

(4) CONSULTATION WITH MEDPAC.—In evaluating the matters described in paragraph (2)(C), the Institute shall consult with the Medicare Payment Advisory Commission established under section 1805 of the Social Security Act (42 U.S.C. 1395b-6).

(b) REPORT.—Not later than the date that is 18 months after the date of enactment of this Act, the Institute shall submit to the Secretary and appropriate committees of jurisdiction of the Senate and House of Representatives a report on the evaluation conducted under subsection (a)(1) describing the findings of such evaluation and recommendations for an overall strategy and approach for aligning

Non-Code Provisions

payment with performance, including options for updating performance measures, in the original medicare fee-for-service program under parts A and B of title XVIII of the Social Security Act, the Medicare Advantage program under part C of such title, and any other programs under such title XVIII.

(c) AUTHORIZATION OF APPROPRIATIONS.—There are authorized to be appropriated such sums as may be necessary for purposes of conducting the evaluation and preparing the report required by this section.

[CCH Explanation at ¶394.]

Subtitle E—Comparative Cost Adjustment (CCA) Program

[¶10,190] ACT SEC. 241. COMPARATIVE COST ADJUSTMENT (CCA) PROGRAM.

. . .

(c) NO CHANGE IN MEDICARE'S DEFINED BENEFIT PACKAGE.—Nothing in this part (or the amendments made by this part) shall be construed as changing the entitlement to defined benefits under parts A and B of title XVIII of the Social Security Act.

[CCH Explanation at ¶396.]

TITLE III—COMBATTING WASTE, FRAUD, AND ABUSE

. . .

[¶10,210] ACT SEC. 302. PAYMENT FOR DURABLE MEDICAL EQUIPMENT; COMPETITIVE ACQUISITION OF CERTAIN ITEMS AND SERVICES.

. . .

(b) COMPETITIVE ACQUISITION.—

. . .

(3) GAO REPORT ON IMPACT OF COMPETITIVE ACQUISITION ON SUPPLIERS.—

(A) STUDY.—The Comptroller General of the United States shall conduct a study on the impact of competitive acquisition of durable medical equipment under section 1847 of the Social Security Act, as amended by paragraph (1), on suppliers and manufacturers of such equipment and on patients. Such study shall specifically examine the impact of such competitive acquisition on access to, and quality of, such equipment and service related to such equipment.

(B) REPORT.—Not later than January 1, 2009, the Comptroller General shall submit to Congress a report on the study conducted under subparagraph (A) and shall include in the report such recommendations as the Comptroller General determines appropriate.

(c) TRANSITIONAL FREEZE.—

(1) DME.—

. . .

(B) GAO REPORT ON CLASS III MEDICAL DEVICES.—Not later than March 1, 2006, the Comptroller General of the United States shall submit to Congress, and transmit to the Secretary, a report containing recommendations on the appropriate update percentage under section 1834(a)(14) of the Social Security Act (42 U.S.C. 1395m(a)(14)) for class III medical devices described in section 513(a)(1)(C) of the Federal Food, Drug, and Cosmetic Act (21 U.S.C. 360(a)(1)(C)) furnished to medicare beneficiaries during 2007 and 2008.

. . .

(e) REPORT ON ACTIVITIES OF SUPPLIERS.—The Inspector General of the Department of Health and Human Services shall conduct a study to determine the extent to which (if any) suppliers of covered items of durable medical equipment that are subject to the competitive acquisition program under section 1847 of the Social Security Act, as amended by subsection (a), are soliciting physicians to prescribe certain brands or modes of delivery of covered items based on profitability. Not later than July 1, 2009, the Inspector General shall submit to Congress a report on such study.

[CCH Explanation at ¶1002.]

[¶10,220] ACT SEC. 303. PAYMENT REFORM FOR COVERED OUTPATIENT DRUGS AND BIOLOGICALS.

(a) ADJUSTMENT TO PHYSICIAN FEE SCHEDULE.—

. . .

(2) TREATMENT OF OTHER SERVICES CURRENTLY IN THE NONPHYSICIAN WORK POOL.—The Secretary shall make adjustments to the nonphysician work pool methodology (as such term is used in the final rule promulgated by the Secretary in the Federal Register on December 31, 2002 (67 Fed. Reg. 251)), for the determination of practice expense relative value units under the physician fee schedule under section 1848(c)(2)(C)(ii) of the Social Security Act (42 U.S.C. 1395w-4(c)(2)(C)(ii)), so that the practice expense relative value units for services determined under such methodology are not affected relative to the practice expense relative value units of services not determined under such methodology, as a result of the amendments made by paragraph (1).

(3) PAYMENT FOR MULTIPLE CHEMOTHERAPY AGENTS FURNISHED ON A SINGLE DAY THROUGH THE PUSH TECHNIQUE.—

(A) REVIEW OF POLICY.—The Secretary shall review the policy, as in effect on October 1, 2003, with respect to payment under section 1848 of the Social Security Act (42 U.S.C. 1395w-4) for the administration of more than 1 drug or biological to an individual on a single day through the push technique.

(B) MODIFICATION OF POLICY.—After conducting the review under subparagraph (A), the Secretary shall modify such payment policy as the Secretary determines to be appropriate.

(C) EXEMPTION FROM BUDGET NEUTRALITY UNDER PHYSICIAN FEE SCHEDULE.—If the Secretary modifies such payment policy pursuant to subparagraph (B), any increased expenditures under title XVIII of the Social Security Act resulting from such modification shall be treated as additional expenditures attributable to subparagraph (H) of section 1848(c)(2) of the Social Security Act (42 U.S.C. 1395w-4(c)(2)), as added by paragraph (1)(B), for purposes of applying the exemption to budget neutrality under subparagraph (B)(iv) of such section, as added by paragraph (1)(A).

(4) TRANSITIONAL ADJUSTMENT.—

(A) IN GENERAL.—In order to provide for a transition during 2004 and 2005 to the payment system established under the amendments made by this section, in the case of physicians' services consisting of drug administration services described in subparagraph (H)(iv) of section 1848(c)(2) of the Social Security Act (42 U.S.C. 1395w-4(c)(2)), as added by paragraph (1)(B), furnished on or after January 1, 2004, and before January 1, 2006, in addition to the amount determined under the fee schedule under section 1848(b) of such Act (42 U.S.C. 1395w-4(b)) there also shall be paid to the physician from the Federal Supplementary Medical Insurance Trust Fund an amount equal to the applicable percentage specified in subparagraph (B) of such fee schedule amount for the services so determined.

(B) APPLICABLE PERCENTAGE.—The applicable percentage specified in this subparagraph for services furnished—

(i) during 2004, is 32 percent; and

(ii) during 2005, is 3 percent.

(5) MEDPAC REVIEW AND REPORTS; SECRETARIAL RESPONSE.—

(A) REVIEW.—The Medicare Payment Advisory Commission shall review the payment changes made under this section insofar as they affect payment under part B of title XVIII of the Social Security Act—

(i) for items and services furnished by oncologists; and

(ii) for drug administration services furnished by other specialists.

(B) OTHER MATTERS STUDIED.—In conducting the review under subparagraph (A), the Commission shall also review such changes as they affect—

(i) the quality of care furnished to individuals enrolled under part B and the satisfaction of such individuals with that care;

(ii) the adequacy of reimbursement as applied in, and the availability in, different geographic areas and to different physician practice sizes; and

(iii) the impact on physician practices.

(C) REPORTS.—The Commission shall submit to the Secretary and Congress—

(i) not later than January 1, 2006, a report on the review conducted under subparagraph (A)(i); and

(ii) not later than January 1, 2007, a report on the review conducted under subparagraph (A)(ii).

Each such report may include such recommendations regarding further adjustments in such payments as the Commission deems appropriate.

(D) SECRETARIAL RESPONSE.—As part of the rulemaking with respect to payment for physicians services under section 1848 of the Social Security Act (42 U.S.C. 1395w-4) for 2007, the Secretary may make appropriate adjustments to payment for items and services described in subparagraph (A)(i), taking into account the report submitted under such subparagraph (C)(i).

. . .

(c) APPLICATION OF AVERAGE SALES PRICE METHODS BEGINNING IN 2005.—

. . .

(2) REPORT ON SALES TO PHARMACY BENEFIT MANAGERS.—

(A) STUDY.—The Secretary shall conduct a study on sales of drugs and biologicals to large volume purchasers, such as pharmacy benefit managers and health maintenance organizations, for purposes of determining whether the price at which such drugs and biologicals are sold to such purchasers does not represent the price such drugs and biologicals are made available for purchase to prudent physicians.

(B) REPORT.—Not later than January 1, 2006, the Secretary shall submit to Congress a report on the study conducted under paragraph (1), and shall include recommendations on whether such sales to large volume purchasers should be excluded from the computation of a manufacturer's average sales price under section 1847A of the Social Security Act, as added by paragraph (1).

(3) INSPECTOR GENERAL REPORT ON ADEQUACY OF REIMBURSEMENT RATE UNDER AVERAGE SALES PRICE METHODOLOGY.—

(A) STUDY.—The Inspector General of the Department of Health and Human Services shall conduct a study on the ability of physician practices in the specialties of hematology, hematology/oncology, and medical oncology of different sizes, especially particularly large practices, to obtain drugs and biologicals for the treatment of cancer patients at 106 percent of the average sales price for the drugs and biologicals. In conducting the study, the Inspector General shall conduct an audit of a representative sample of such practices to determine the adequacy of reimbursement under section 1847A of the Social Security Act, as added by paragraph (1).

(B) REPORT.—Not later October 1, 2005, the Inspector General shall submit to Congress a report on the study conducted under subparagraph (A), and shall include recommendations on the adequacy of reimbursement for such drugs and biologicals under such section 1847A.

(d) PAYMENT BASED ON COMPETITION.—

. . .

(2) REPORT.—Not later than July 1, 2008, the Secretary shall submit to Congress a report on the program conducted under section 1847B of the Social Security Act, as added by paragraph (1). Such report shall include information on savings, reductions in cost-sharing, access to

competitively biddable drugs and biologicals, the range of choices of contractors available to physicians, the satisfaction of physicians and of individuals enrolled under this part, and information comparing prices for drugs and biologicals under such section and section 1847A of such Act, as added by subsection (c).

. . .

(f) LINKAGE OF REVISED DRUG PAYMENTS AND INCREASES FOR DRUG ADMINISTRATION.—The Secretary shall not implement the revisions in payment amounts for drugs and biologicals administered by physicians as a result of the amendments made by subsection (b) with respect to 2004 unless the Secretary concurrently makes adjustments to the practice expense payment adjustment under the amendments made by subsection (a).

(g) PROHIBITION OF ADMINISTRATIVE AND JUDICIAL REVIEW.—

. . .

(3) MULTIPLE CHEMOTHERAPY AGENTS, OTHER SERVICES CURRENTLY ON THE NON-PHYSICIAN WORK POOL, AND TRANSITIONAL ADJUSTMENT.—There shall be no administrative or judicial review under section 1869, section 1878, or otherwise, of determinations of payment amounts, methods, or adjustments under paragraphs (2) through (4) of subsection (a).

(h) CONTINUATION OF PAYMENT METHODOLOGY FOR RADIOPHARMACEUTICALS.—Nothing in the amendments made by this section shall be construed as changing the payment methodology under part B of title XVIII of the Social Security Act for radiopharmaceuticals, including the use by carriers of invoice pricing methodology.

(i) CONFORMING AMENDMENTS.—

. . .

(5) IMPLEMENTATION.—The provisions of chapter 8 of title 5, United States Code, shall not apply with respect to regulations implementing the amendments made by subsections (a), (b), and (e)(3), to regulations implementing section 304, and to regulations implementing the amendment made by section 305(a), insofar as such regulations apply in 2004.

(6) REPEAL OF STUDY.—Section 4556 of the Balanced Budget Act of 1997 (42 U.S.C. 1395u note) is amended by striking subsection (c).

(j) APPLICATION TO CERTAIN PHYSICIAN SPECIALTIES.—Insofar as the amendments made by this section apply to payments for drugs or biologicals and drug administration services furnished by physicians, such amendments shall only apply to physicians in the specialties of hematology, hematology/oncology, and medical oncology under title XVIII of the Social Security Act.

[CCH Explanations at ¶101, 1004, 1006, and 1009.]

[¶10,230] ACT SEC. 304. EXTENSION OF APPLICATION OF PAYMENT REFORM FOR COVERED OUTPATIENT DRUGS AND BIOLOGICALS TO OTHER PHYSICIAN SPECIALTIES.

Notwithstanding section 303(j), the amendments made by section 303 shall also apply to payments for drugs or biologicals and drug administration services furnished by physicians in specialties other than the specialties of hematology, hematology/oncology, and medical oncology.

[CCH Explanation at ¶1008.]

[¶10,240] ACT SEC. 305. PAYMENT FOR INHALATION DRUGS.

. . .

(b) GAO STUDY OF MEDICARE PAYMENT FOR INHALATION THERAPY.—

(1) STUDY.—The Comptroller General of the United States shall conduct a study to examine the adequacy of current reimbursements for inhalation therapy under the medicare program.

(2) REPORT.—Not later than 1 year after the date of the enactment of this Act, the Comptroller General shall submit to Congress a report on the study conducted under paragraph (1).

[CCH Explanation at ¶1011.]

[¶10,250] ACT SEC. 306. DEMONSTRATION PROJECT FOR USE OF RECOVERY AUDIT CONTRACTORS.

(a) IN GENERAL.—The Secretary shall conduct a demonstration project under this section (in this section referred to as the "project") to demonstrate the use of recovery audit contractors under the Medicare Integrity Program in identifying underpayments and overpayments and recouping overpayments under the medicare program for services for which payment is made under part A or B of title XVIII of the Social Security Act. Under the project—

(1) payment may be made to such a contractor on a contingent basis;

(2) such percentage as the Secretary may specify of the amount recovered shall be retained by the Secretary and shall be available to the program management account of the Centers for Medicare & Medicaid Services; and

(3) the Secretary shall examine the efficacy of such use with respect to duplicative payments, accuracy of coding, and other payment policies in which inaccurate payments arise.

(b) SCOPE AND DURATION.—

(1) SCOPE.—The project shall cover at least 2 States that are among the States with—

(A) the highest per capita utilization rates of medicare services, and

(B) at least 3 contractors.

(2) DURATION.—The project shall last for not longer than 3 years.

(c) WAIVER.—The Secretary shall waive such provisions of title XVIII of the Social Security Act as may be necessary to provide for payment for services under the project in accordance with subsection (a).

(d) QUALIFICATIONS OF CONTRACTORS.—

(1) IN GENERAL.—The Secretary shall enter into a recovery audit contract under this section with an entity only if the entity has staff that has the appropriate clinical knowledge of and experience with the payment rules and regulations under the medicare program or the entity has or will contract with another entity that has such knowledgeable and experienced staff.

(2) INELIGIBILITY OF CERTAIN CONTRACTORS.—The Secretary may not enter into a recovery audit contract under this section with an entity to the extent that the entity is a fiscal intermediary under section 1816 of the Social Security Act (42 U.S.C. 1395h), a carrier under section 1842 of such Act (42 U.S.C. 1395u), or a Medicare Administrative Contractor under section 1874A of such Act.

(3) PREFERENCE FOR ENTITIES WITH DEMONSTRATED PROFICIENCY.—In awarding contracts to recovery audit contractors under this section, the Secretary shall give preference to those risk entities that the Secretary determines have demonstrated more than 3 years direct management experience and a proficiency for cost control or recovery audits with private insurers, health care providers, health plans, or under the medicaid program under title XIX of the Social Security Act.

(e) CONSTRUCTION RELATING TO CONDUCT OF INVESTIGATION OF FRAUD.—A recovery of an overpayment to a provider by a recovery audit contractor shall not be construed to prohibit the Secretary or the Attorney General from investigating and prosecuting, if appropriate, allegations of fraud or abuse arising from such overpayment.

(f) REPORT.—The Secretary shall submit to Congress a report on the project not later than 6 months after the date of its completion. Such reports shall include information on the impact of the project on savings to the medicare program and recommendations on the cost-effectiveness of extending or expanding the project.information' means information about a conviction for a relevant crime or a finding of patient or resident abuse.

[CCH Explanation at ¶1012.]

[¶10,260] ACT SEC. 307. PILOT PROGRAM FOR NATIONAL AND STATE BACKGROUND CHECKS ON DIRECT PATIENT ACCESS EMPLOYEES OF LONG-TERM CARE FACILITIES OR PROVIDERS.

(a) AUTHORITY TO CONDUCT PROGRAM.—The Secretary, in consultation with the Attorney General, shall establish a pilot program to identify efficient, effective, and economical procedures for long term care facilities or providers to conduct background checks on prospective direct patient access employees.

(b) REQUIREMENTS.—

(1) IN GENERAL.—Under the pilot program, a longterm care facility or provider in a participating State, prior to employing a direct patient access employee that is first hired on or after the commencement date of the pilot program in the State, shall conduct a background check on the employee in accordance with such procedures as the participating State shall establish.

(2) PROCEDURES.—

(A) IN GENERAL.—The procedures established by a participating State under paragraph (1) should be designed to—

(i) give a prospective direct access patient employee notice that the long-term care facility or provider is required to perform background checks with respect to new employees;

(ii) require, as a condition of employment, that the employee—

(I) provide a written statement disclosing any disqualifying information;

(II) provide a statement signed by the employee authorizing the facility to request national and State criminal history background checks;

(III) provide the facility with a rolled set of the employee's fingerprints; and

(IV) provide any other identification information the participating State may require;

(iii) require the facility or provider to check any available registries that would be likely to contain disqualifying information about a prospective employee of a long-term care facility or provider; and

(iv) permit the facility or provider to obtain State and national criminal history background checks on the prospective employee through a 10-fingerprint check that utilizes State criminal records and the Integrated Automated Fingerprint Identification System of the Federal Bureau of Investigation.

(B) ELIMINATION OF UNNECESSARY CHECKS.—The procedures established by a participating State under paragraph (1) shall permit a long-term care facility or provider to terminate the background check at any stage at which the facility or provider obtains disqualifying information regarding a prospective direct patient access employee.

(3) PROHIBITION ON HIRING OF ABUSIVE WORKERS.—

(A) IN GENERAL.—A long-term care facility or provider may not knowingly employ any direct patient access employee who has any disqualifying information.

(B) PROVISIONAL EMPLOYMENT.—

(i) IN GENERAL.—Under the pilot program, a participating State may permit a long-term care facility or provider to provide for a provisional period of employment for a direct patient access employee pending completion of a background check, subject to such supervision during the employee's provisional period of employment as the participating State determines appropriate.

(ii) SPECIAL CONSIDERATION FOR CERTAIN FACILITIES AND PROVIDERS.—In determining what constitutes appropriate supervision of a provisional employee, a participating State shall take into account cost or other burdens that would be imposed on small rural long-term care facilities or providers, as well as the nature of care delivered by such facilities or providers that are home health agencies or providers of hospice care.

(4) USE OF INFORMATION; IMMUNITY FROM LIABILITY.—

(A) USE OF INFORMATION.—A participating State shall ensure that a long-term care facility or provider that obtains information about a direct patient access employee pursuant to a background check uses such information only for the purpose of determining the suitability of the employee for employment.

Non-Code Provisions

(B) IMMUNITY FROM LIABILITY.—A participating State shall ensure that a long-term care facility or provider that, in denying employment for an individual selected for hire as a direct patient access employee (including during any period of provisional employment), reasonably relies upon information obtained through a background check of the individual, shall not be liable in any action brought by the individual based on the employment determination resulting from the information.

(5) AGREEMENTS WITH EMPLOYMENT AGENCIES.—A participating State may establish procedures for facilitating the conduct of background checks on prospective direct patient access employees that are hired by a long-term care facility or provider through an employment agency (including a temporary employment agency).

(6) PENALTIES.—A participating State may impose such penalties as the State determines appropriate to enforce the requirements of the pilot program conducted in that State.

(c) PARTICIPATING STATES.—

(1) IN GENERAL.—The Secretary shall enter into agreements with not more than 10 States to conduct the pilot program under this section in such States.

(2) REQUIREMENTS FOR STATES.—An agreement entered into under paragraph (1) shall require that a participating State—

(A) be responsible for monitoring compliance with the requirements of the pilot program;

(B) have procedures by which a provisional employee or an employee may appeal or dispute the accuracy of the information obtained in a background check performed under the pilot program; and

(C) agree to—

(i) review the results of any State or national criminal history background checks conducted regarding a prospective direct patient access employee to determine whether the employee has any conviction for a relevant crime;

(ii) immediately report to the entity that requested the criminal history background checks the results of such review; and

(iii) in the case of an employee with a conviction for a relevant crime that is subject to reporting under section 1128E of the Social Security Act (42 U.S.C. 1320a-7e), report the existence of such conviction to the database established under that section.

(3) APPLICATION AND SELECTION CRITERIA.—

(A) APPLICATION.—A State seeking to participate in the pilot program established under this section, shall submit an application to the Secretary containing such information and at such time as the Secretary may specify.

(B) SELECTION CRITERIA.—

(i) IN GENERAL.—In selecting States to participate in the pilot program, the Secretary shall establish criteria to ensure—

(I) geographic diversity;

(II) the inclusion of a variety of long-term care facilities or providers;

(III) the evaluation of a variety of payment mechanisms for covering the costs of conducting the background checks required under the pilot program; and

(IV) the evaluation of a variety of penalties (monetary and otherwise) used by participating States to enforce the requirements of the pilot program in such States.

(ii) ADDITIONAL CRITERIA.—The Secretary shall, to the greatest extent practicable, select States to participate in the pilot program in accordance with the following:

(I) At least one participating State should permit long-term care facilities or providers to provide for a provisional period of employment pending completion of a background check and at least one such State should not permit such a period of employment.

Act Sec. 307(c)(3)(B)(ii)(I) ¶10,260

(II) At least one participating State should establish procedures under which employment agencies (including temporary employment agencies) may contact the State directly to conduct background checks on prospective direct patient access employees.

(III) At least one participating State should include patient abuse prevention training (including behavior training and interventions) for managers and employees of long-term care facilities and providers as part of the pilot program conducted in that State.

(iii) INCLUSION OF STATES WITH EXISTING PROGRAMS.—Nothing in this section shall be construed as prohibiting any State which, as of the date of the enactment of this Act, has procedures for conducting background checks on behalf of any entity described in subsection (g)(5) from being selected to participate in the pilot program conducted under this section.

(d) PAYMENTS.—Of the amounts made available under subsection (f) to conduct the pilot program under this section, the Secretary shall—

(1) make payments to participating States for the costs of conducting the pilot program in such States; and

(2) reserve up to 4 percent of such amounts to conduct the evaluation required under subsection (e).

(e) EVALUATION.—The Secretary, in consultation with the Attorney General, shall conduct by grant, contract, or interagency agreement an evaluation of the pilot program conducted under this section. Such evaluation shall—

(1) review the various procedures implemented by participating States for long-term care facilities or providers to conduct background checks of direct patient access employees and identify the most efficient, effective, and economical procedures for conducting such background checks;

(2) assess the costs of conducting such background checks (including start-up and administrative costs);

(3) consider the benefits and problems associated with requiring employees or facilities or providers to pay the costs of conducting such background checks;

(4) consider whether the costs of conducting such background checks should be allocated between the medicare and medicaid programs and if so, identify an equitable methodology for doing so;

(5) determine the extent to which conducting such background checks leads to any unintended consequences, including a reduction in the available workforce for such facilities or providers;

(6) review forms used by participating States in order to develop, in consultation with the Attorney General, a model form for such background checks;

(7) determine the effectiveness of background checks conducted by employment agencies; and

(8) recommend appropriate procedures and payment mechanisms for implementing a national criminal background check program for such facilities and providers.

(f) FUNDING.—Out of any funds in the Treasury not otherwise appropriated, there are appropriated to the Secretary to carry out the pilot program under this section for the period of fiscal years 2004 through 2007, $25,000,000.

(g) DEFINITIONS.—In this section:

(1) CONVICTION FOR A RELEVANT CRIME.—The term "conviction for a relevant crime" means any Federal or State criminal conviction for—

(A) any offense described in section 1128(a) of the Social Security Act (42 U.S.C. 1320a-7); and

(B) such other types of offenses as a participating State may specify for purposes of conducting the pilot program in such State.

(2) DISQUALIFYING INFORMATION.—The term "disqualifying information" means a conviction for a relevant crime or a finding of patient or resident abuse.

(3) FINDING OF PATIENT OR RESIDENT ABUSE.—The term "finding of patient or resident abuse" means any substantiated finding by a State agency under section 1819(g)(1)(C) or 1919(g)(1)(C) of the Social Security Act (42 U.S.C. 1395i-3(g)(1)(C), 1396r(g)(1)(C)) or a Federal agency that a direct patient access employee has committed—

(A) an act of patient or resident abuse or neglect or a misappropriation of patient or resident property; or

(B) such other types of acts as a participating State may specify for purposes of conducting the pilot program in such State.

(4) DIRECT PATIENT ACCESS EMPLOYEE.—The term "direct patient access employee" means any individual (other than a volunteer) that has access to a patient or resident of a long-term care facility or provider through employment or through a contract with such facility or provider, as determined by a participating State for purposes of conducting the pilot program in such State.

(5) LONG-TERM CARE FACILITY OR PROVIDER.—

(A) IN GENERAL.—The term "long-term care facility or provider" means the following facilities or providers which receive payment for services under title XVIII or XIX of the Social Security Act:

(i) A skilled nursing facility (as defined in section 1819(a) of the Social Security Act) (42 U.S.C. 1395i-3(a)).

(ii) A nursing facility (as defined in section 1919(a) in such Act) (42 U.S.C. 1396r(a)).

(iii) A home health agency.

(iv) A provider of hospice care (as defined in section 1861(dd)(1) of such Act) (42 U.S.C. 1395x(dd)(1)).

(v) A long-term care hospital (as described in section 1886(d)(1)(B)(iv) of such Act) (42 U.S.C. 1395ww(d)(1)(B)(iv)).

(vi) A provider of personal care services.

(vii) A residential care provider that arranges for, or directly provides, long-term care services.

(viii) An intermediate care facility for the mentally retarded (as defined in section 1905(d) of such Act) 42 U.S.C. 1396d(d)).

(B) ADDITIONAL FACILITIES OR PROVIDERS.—During the first year in which a pilot program under this section is conducted in a participating State, the State may expand the list of facilities or providers under subparagraph (A) (on a phased-in basis or otherwise) to include such other facilities or providers of long-term care services under such titles as the participating State determines appropriate.

(C) EXCEPTIONS.—Such term does not include—

(i) any facility or entity that provides, or is a provider of, services described in subparagraph (A) that are exclusively provided to an individual pursuant to a self-directed arrangement that meets such requirements as the participating State may establish in accordance with guidance from the Secretary; or

(ii) any such arrangement that is obtained by a patient or resident functioning as an employer.

(6) PARTICIPATING STATE.—The term "participating State" means a State with an agreement under subsection (c)(1).

[CCH Explanation at ¶601.]

TITLE IV—RURAL PROVISIONS

Subtitle A—Provisions Relating to Part A Only

[¶10,270] ACT SEC. 401. EQUALIZING URBAN AND RURAL STANDARDIZED PAYMENT AMOUNTS UNDER THE MEDICARE INPATIENT HOSPITAL PROSPECTIVE PAYMENT SYSTEM.

. . .

(d) IMPLEMENTATION.—

(1) IN GENERAL.—The amendments made by subsections (a), (b), and (c)(1) of this section shall have no effect on the authority of the Secretary, under subsection (b)(2) of section 402 of Public Law 108-89, to delay implementation of the extension of provisions equalizing urban and rural standardized inpatient hospital payments under subsection (a) of such section 402.

(2) APPLICATION OF PUERTO RICO STANDARDIZED AMOUNT BASED ON LARGE URBAN AREAS.—The authority of the Secretary referred to in paragraph (1) shall apply with respect to the amendments made by subsection (c)(2) of this section in the same manner as that authority applies with respect to the extension of provisions equalizing urban and rural standardized inpatient hospital payments under subsection (a) of such section 402, except that any reference in subsection (b)(2)(A) of such section 402 is deemed to be a reference to April 1, 2004.

. . .

[CCH Explanation at ¶501.]

[¶10,280] ACT SEC. 404. MORE FREQUENT UPDATE IN WEIGHTS USED IN HOSPITAL MARKET BASKET.

(a) MORE FREQUENT UPDATES IN WEIGHTS.—After revising the weights used in the hospital market basket under section 1886(b)(3)(B)(iii) of the Social Security Act (42 U.S.C. 1395ww(b)(3)(B)(iii)) to reflect the most current data available, the Secretary shall establish a frequency for revising such weights, including the labor share, in such market basket to reflect the most current data available more frequently than once every 5 years.

(b) INCORPORATION OF EXPLANATION IN RULEMAKING.—The Secretary shall include in the publication of the final rule for payment for inpatient hospital services under section 1886(d) of the Social Security Act (42 U.S.C. 1395ww(d)) for fiscal year 2006, an explanation of the reasons for, and options considered, in determining frequency established under subsection (a).

[CCH Explanation at ¶507.]

[¶10,290] ACT SEC. 405. IMPROVEMENTS TO CRITICAL ACCESS HOSPITAL PROGRAM.

. . .

(c) AUTHORIZATION OF PERIODIC INTERIM PAYMENT (PIP).—

. . .

(2) DEVELOPMENT OF ALTERNATIVE TIMING METHODS OF PERIODIC INTERIM PAYMENTS.—With respect to periodic interim payments to critical access hospitals for inpatient critical access hospital services under section 1815(e)(2)(E) of the Social Security Act, as added by paragraph (1), the Secretary shall develop alternative methods for the timing of such payments.

. . .

(d) CONDITION FOR APPLICATION OF SPECIAL PROFESSIONAL SERVICE PAYMENT ADJUSTMENT.—

. . .

(2) EFFECTIVE DATE.—

(A) IN GENERAL.—Except as provided in subparagraph (B), the amendment made by paragraph (1) shall apply to cost reporting periods beginning on or after July 1, 2004.

(B) RULE OF APPLICATION.—In the case of a critical access hospital that made an election under section 1834(g)(2) of the Social Security Act (42 U.S.C. 1395m(g)(2)) before November 1, 2003, the amendment made by paragraph (1) shall apply to cost reporting periods beginning on or after July 1, 2001.

...

[CCH Explanation at ¶ 578.]

[¶ 10,310] ACT SEC. 409. RURAL HOSPICE DEMONSTRATION PROJECT.

(a) IN GENERAL.—The Secretary shall conduct a demonstration project for the delivery of hospice care to medicare beneficiaries in rural areas. Under the project medicare beneficiaries who are unable to receive hospice care in the facility for lack of an appropriate caregiver are provided such care in a facility of 20 or fewer beds which offers, within its walls, the full range of services provided by hospice programs under section 1861(dd) of the Social Security Act (42 U.S.C. 1395x(dd)).

(b) SCOPE OF PROJECT.—The Secretary shall conduct the project under this section with respect to no more than 3 hospice programs over a period of not longer than 5 years each.

(c) COMPLIANCE WITH CONDITIONS.—Under the demonstration project—

(1) the hospice program shall comply with otherwise applicable requirements, except that it shall not be required to offer services outside of the home or to meet the requirements of section 1861(dd)(2)(A)(iii) of the Social Security Act; and

(2) payments for hospice care shall be made at the rates otherwise applicable to such care under title XVIII of such Act.

The Secretary may require the program to comply with such additional quality assurance standards for its provision of services in its facility as the Secretary deems appropriate.

(d) REPORT.—Upon completion of the project, the Secretary shall submit a report to Congress on the project and shall include in the report recommendations regarding extension of such project to hospice programs serving rural areas.

...

[CCH Explanation at ¶ 675.]

[¶ 10,330] ACT SEC. 410A. RURAL COMMUNITY HOSPITAL DEMONSTRATION PROGRAM.

(a) ESTABLISHMENT OF RURAL COMMUNITY HOSPITAL (RCH) DEMONSTRATION PROGRAM.—

(1) IN GENERAL.—The Secretary shall establish a demonstration program to test the feasibility and advisability of the establishment of rural community hospitals (as defined in subsection (f)(1)) to furnish covered inpatient hospital services (as defined in subsection (f)(2)) to medicare beneficiaries.

(2) DEMONSTRATION AREAS.—The program shall be conducted in rural areas selected by the Secretary in States with low population densities, as determined by the Secretary.

(3) APPLICATION.—Each rural community hospital that is located in a demonstration area selected under paragraph (2) that desires to participate in the demonstration program under this section shall submit an application to the Secretary at such time, in such manner, and containing such information as the Secretary may require.

(4) SELECTION OF HOSPITALS.—The Secretary shall select from among rural community hospitals submitting applications under paragraph (3) not more than 15 of such hospitals to participate in the demonstration program under this section.

(5) DURATION.—The Secretary shall conduct the demonstration program under this section for a 5-year period.

(6) IMPLEMENTATION.—The Secretary shall implement the demonstration program not later than January 1, 2005, but may not implement the program before October 1, 2004.

(b) PAYMENT.—

(1) IN GENERAL.—The amount of payment under the demonstration program for covered inpatient hospital services furnished in a rural community hospital, other than such services furnished in a psychiatric or rehabilitation unit of the hospital which is a distinct part, is—

(A) for discharges occurring in the first cost reporting period beginning on or after the implementation of the demonstration program, the reasonable costs of providing such services; and

(B) for discharges occurring in a subsequent cost reporting period under the demonstration program, the lesser of—

(i) the reasonable costs of providing such services in the cost reporting period involved; or

(ii) the target amount (as defined in paragraph (2), applicable to the cost reporting period involved.

(2) TARGET AMOUNT.—For purposes of paragraph (1)(B)(ii), the term "target amount" means, with respect to a rural community hospital for a particular 12-month cost reporting period—

(A) in the case of the second such reporting period for which this subsection is in effect, the reasonable costs of providing such covered inpatient hospital services as determined under paragraph (1)(A), and

(B) in the case of a later reporting period, the target amount for the preceding 12-month cost reporting period,

increased by the applicable percentage increase (under clause (i) of section 1886(b)(3)(B) of the Social Security Act (42 U.S.C. 1395ww(b)(3)(B))) in the market basket percentage increase (as defined in clause (iii) of such section) for that particular cost reporting period.

(c) FUNDING.—

(1) IN GENERAL.—The Secretary shall provide for the transfer from the Federal Hospital Insurance Trust Fund under section 1817 of the Social Security Act (42 U.S.C. 1395i) of such funds as are necessary for the costs of carrying out the demonstration program under this section.

(2) BUDGET NEUTRALITY.—In conducting the demonstration program under this section, the Secretary shall ensure that the aggregate payments made by the Secretary do not exceed the amount which the Secretary would have paid if the demonstration program under this section was not implemented.

(d) WAIVER AUTHORITY.—The Secretary may waive such requirements of title XVIII of the Social Security Act (42 U.S.C. 1395 et seq.) as may be necessary for the purpose of carrying out the demonstration program under this section.

(e) REPORT.—Not later than 6 months after the completion of the demonstration program under this section, the Secretary shall submit to Congress a report on such program, together with recommendations for such legislation and administrative action as the Secretary determines to be appropriate.

(f) DEFINITIONS.—In this section:

(1) RURAL COMMUNITY HOSPITAL DEFINED.—

(A) IN GENERAL.—The term "rural community hospital" means a hospital (as defined in section 1861(e) of the Social Security Act (42 U.S.C. 1395x(e))) that—

(i) is located in a rural area (as defined in section 1886(d)(2)(D) of such Act (42 U.S.C. 1395ww(d)(2)(D))) or treated as being so located pursuant to section 1886(d)(8)(E) of such Act (42 U.S.C. 1395ww(d)(8)(E));

(ii) subject to paragraph (2), has fewer than 51 acute care inpatient beds, as reported in its most recent cost report;

(iii) makes available 24-hour emergency care services; and

(iv) is not eligible for designation, or has not been designated, as a critical access hospital under section 1820.

(B) TREATMENT OF PSYCHIATRIC AND REHABILITATION UNITS.—For purposes of paragraph (1)(B), beds in a psychiatric or rehabilitation unit of the hospital which is a distinct part of the hospital shall not be counted.

(2) COVERED INPATIENT HOSPITAL SERVICES.—The term "covered inpatient hospital services" means inpatient hospital services, and includes extended care services furnished under an agreement under section 1883 of the Social Security Act (42 U.S.C. 1395tt).

[CCH Explanation at ¶ 581.]

Subtitle B—Provisions Relating to Part B Only

. . .

[¶ 10,340] ACT SEC. 413. MEDICARE INCENTIVE PAYMENT PROGRAM IMPROVEMENTS FOR PHYSICIAN SCARCITY.

. . .

(c) GAO STUDY OF GEOGRAPHIC DIFFERENCES IN PAYMENTS FOR PHYSICIANS' SERVICES.—

(1) STUDY.—The Comptroller General of the United States shall conduct a study of differences in payment amounts under the physician fee schedule under section 1848 of the Social Security Act (42 U.S.C. 1395w-4) for physicians' services in different geographic areas. Such study shall include—

(A) an assessment of the validity of the geographic adjustment factors used for each component of the fee schedule;

(B) an evaluation of the measures used for such adjustment, including the frequency of revisions;

(C) an evaluation of the methods used to determine professional liability insurance costs used in computing the malpractice component, including a review of increases in professional liability insurance premiums and variation in such increases by State and physician specialty and methods used to update the geographic cost of practice index and relative weights for the malpractice component; and

(D) an evaluation of the effect of the adjustment to the physician work geographic index under section 1848(e)(1)(E) of the Social Security Act, as added by section 412, on physician location and retention in areas affected by such adjustment, taking into account—

(i) differences in recruitment costs and retention rates for physicians, including specialists, between large urban areas and other areas; and

(ii) the mobility of physicians, including specialists, over the last decade.

(2) REPORT.—Not later than 1 year after the date of the enactment of this Act, the Comptroller General shall submit to Congress a report on the study conducted under paragraph (1). The report shall include recommendations regarding the use of more current data in computing geographic cost of practice indices as well as the use of data directly representative of physicians' costs (rather than proxy measures of such costs).

[CCH Explanation at ¶ 700.]

[¶ 10,350] ACT SEC. 414. PAYMENT FOR RURAL AND URBAN AMBULANCE SERVICES.

. . .

(e) IMPLEMENTATION.—The Secretary may implement the amendments made by this section, and revise the conversion factor applicable under section 1834(l) of the Social Security Act (42 U.S.C. 1395m(l)) for purposes of implementing such amendments, on an interim final basis, or by program instruction.

(f) GAO REPORT ON COSTS AND ACCESS.—Not later than December 31, 2005, the Comptroller General of the United States shall submit to Congress an initial report on how costs differ among the types of ambulance providers and on access, supply, and quality of ambulance services in those regions and States that have a reduction in payment under the medicare ambulance fee schedule (under section 1834(l) of the Social Security Act, as amended by this Act). Not later than December 31, 2007, the Comptroller General shall submit to Congress a final report on such access and supply.

(g) TECHNICAL AMENDMENTS.—(1) Section 221(c) of BIPA (114 Stat. 2763A-487) is amended by striking "subsection (b)(2)" and inserting "subsection (b)(3)".

(2) Section 1861(v)(1) (42 U.S.C. 1395x(v)(1)) is amended by moving subparagraph (U) 4 ems to the left.

. . .

[CCH Explanation at ¶ 596.]

[¶ 10,370] ACT SEC. 416. TREATMENT OF CERTAIN CLINICAL DIAGNOSTIC LABORATORY TESTS FURNISHED TO HOSPITAL OUTPATIENTS IN CERTAIN RURAL AREAS.

(a) IN GENERAL.—Notwithstanding subsections (a), (b), and (h) of section 1833 of the Social Security Act (42 U.S.C. 1395l) and section 1834(d)(1) of such Act (42 U.S.C. 1395m(d)(1)), in the case of a clinical diagnostic laboratory test covered under part B of title XVIII of such Act that is furnished during a cost reporting period described in subsection (b) by a hospital with fewer than 50 beds that is located in a qualified rural area (identified under paragraph (12)(B)(iii) of section 1834(l) of the Social Security Act (42 U.S.C. 1395m(l)), as added by section 414(c)) as part of outpatient services of the hospital, the amount of payment for such test shall be 100 percent of the reasonable costs of the hospital in furnishing such test.

(b) APPLICATION.—A cost reporting period described in this subsection is a cost reporting period beginning during the 2-year period beginning on July 1, 2004.

(c) PROVISION AS PART OF OUTPATIENT HOSPITAL SERVICES.—For purposes of subsection (a), in determining whether clinical diagnostic laboratory services are furnished as part of outpatient services of a hospital, the Secretary shall apply the same rules that are used to determine whether clinical diagnostic laboratory services are furnished as an outpatient critical access hospital service under section 1834(g)(4) of the Social Security Act (42 U.S.C. 1395m(g)(4)).

[CCH Explanation at ¶ 583.]

[¶ 10,380] ACT SEC. 417. EXTENSION OF TELEMEDICINE DEMONSTRATION PROJECT.

Section 4207 of the Balanced Budget Act of 1997 (Public Law 105-33) is amended—

(1) in subsection (a)(4), by striking "4-year" and inserting " 8-year"; and

(2) in subsection (d)(3), by striking "$30,000,000" and inserting "$60,000,000".

[CCH Explanation at ¶ 789.]

[¶ 10,390] ACT SEC. 418. REPORT ON DEMONSTRATION PROJECT PERMITTING SKILLED NURSING FACILITIES TO BE ORIGINATING TELEHEALTH SITES; AUTHORITY TO IMPLEMENT.

(a) EVALUATION.—The Secretary, acting through the Administrator of the Health Resources and Services Administration in consultation with the Administrator of the Centers for Medicare & Medicaid Services, shall evaluate demonstration projects conducted by the Secretary under which skilled nursing facilities (as defined in section 1819(a) of the Social Security Act (42 U.S.C. 1395i-3(a)) are treated as originating sites for telehealth services.

(b) REPORT.—Not later than January 1, 2005, the Secretary shall submit to Congress a report on the evaluation conducted under subsection (a). Such report shall include recommendations on mechanisms to ensure that permitting a skilled nursing facility to serve as an originating site for the use of telehealth services or any other service delivered via a telecommunications system does not serve as a substitute for in-person visits furnished by a physician, or for in-person visits furnished by a physician assistant, nurse practitioner or clinical nurse specialist, as is otherwise required by the Secretary.

(c) AUTHORITY TO EXPAND ORIGINATING TELEHEALTH SITES TO INCLUDE SKILLED NURSING FACILITIES.—Insofar as the Secretary concludes in the report required under subsection (b) that it is advisable to permit a skilled nursing facility to be an originating sites for telehealth services under section 1834(m)

Non-Code Provisions

of the Social Security Act (42 U.S.C. 1395m(m)), and that the Secretary can establish the mechanisms to ensure such permission does not serve as a substitute for in-person visits furnished by a physician, or for in-person visits furnished by a physician assistant, nurse practitioner or clinical nurse specialist, the Secretary may deem a skilled nursing facility to be an originating site under paragraph (4)(C)(ii) of such section beginning on January 1, 2006.

[CCH Explanation at ¶ 607.]

Subtitle C—Provisions Relating to Parts A and B

[¶ 10,400] ACT SEC. 421. 1-YEAR INCREASE FOR HOME HEALTH SERVICES FURNISHED IN A RURAL AREA.

(a) IN GENERAL.—With respect to episodes and visits ending on or after April 1, 2004, and before April 1, 2005, in the case of home health services furnished in a rural area (as defined in section 1886(d)(2)(D) of the Social Security Act (42 U.S.C. 1395ww(d)(2)(D))), the Secretary shall increase the payment amount otherwise made under section 1895 of such Act (42 U.S.C. 1395fff) for such services by 5 percent.

(b) WAIVING BUDGET NEUTRALITY.—The Secretary shall not reduce the standard prospective payment amount (or amounts) under section 1895 of the Social Security Act (42 U.S.C. 1395fff) applicable to home health services furnished during a period to offset the increase in payments resulting from the application of subsection (a).

(c) NO EFFECT ON SUBSEQUENT PERIODS.—The payment increase provided under subsection (a) for a period under such subsection—

(1) shall not apply to episodes and visits ending after such period; and

(2) shall not be taken into account in calculating the payment amounts applicable for episodes and visits occurring after such period.

[CCH Explanation at ¶ 656.]

[¶ 10,410] ACT SEC. 422. REDISTRIBUTION OF UNUSED RESIDENT POSITIONS.

. . .

(b) CONFORMING PROVISIONS.—

. . .

(2) Chapter 35 of title 44, United States Code, shall not apply with respect to applications under section 1886(h)(7) of the Social Security Act, as added by subsection (a)(3).

(c) REPORT ON EXTENSION OF APPLICATIONS UNDER REDISTRIBUTION PROGRAM.—Not later than July 1, 2005, the Secretary shall submit to Congress a report containing recommendations regarding whether to extend the deadline for applications for an increase in resident limits under section 1886(h)(4)(I)(ii)(II) of the Social Security Act (as added by subsection (a)).

[CCH Explanation at ¶ 588.]

Subtitle D—Other Provisions

[¶ 10,420] ACT SEC. 431. PROVIDING SAFE HARBOR FOR CERTAIN COLLABORATIVE EFFORTS THAT BENEFIT MEDICALLY UNDERSERVED POPULATIONS.

. . .

(b) RULEMAKING FOR EXCEPTION FOR HEALTH CENTER ENTITY ARRANGEMENTS.—

(1) ESTABLISHMENT.—

(A) IN GENERAL.—The Secretary shall establish, on an expedited basis, standards relating to the exception described in section 1128B(b)(3)(H) of the Social Security Act, as added by subsection (a), for health center entity arrangements to the antikickback penalties.

(B) FACTORS TO CONSIDER.—The Secretary shall consider the following factors, among others, in establishing standards relating to the exception for health center entity arrangements under subparagraph (A):

(i) Whether the arrangement between the health center entity and the other party results in savings of Federal grant funds or increased revenues to the health center entity.

(ii) Whether the arrangement between the health center entity and the other party restricts or limits an individual's freedom of choice.

(iii) Whether the arrangement between the health center entity and the other party protects a health care professional's independent medical judgment regarding medically appropriate treatment.

The Secretary may also include other standards and criteria that are consistent with the intent of Congress in enacting the exception established under this section.

(2) DEADLINE.—Not later than 1 year after the date of the enactment of this Act the Secretary shall publish final regulations establishing the standards described in paragraph (1).

. . .

[CCH Explanation at ¶798.]

[¶10,430] ACT SEC. 433. MEDPAC STUDY ON RURAL HOSPITAL PAYMENT ADJUSTMENTS.

(a) IN GENERAL.—The Medicare Payment Advisory Commission shall conduct a study of the impact of sections 401 through 406, 411, 416, and 505. The Commission shall analyze the effect on total payments, growth in costs, capital spending, and such other payment effects under those sections.

(b) REPORTS.—

(1) INTERIM REPORT.—Not later than 18 months after the date of the enactment of this Act, the Commission shall submit to Congress an interim report on the matters studied under subsection (a) with respect only to changes to the critical access hospital provisions under section 405.

(2) FINAL REPORT.—Not later than 3 years after the date of the enactment of this Act, the Commission shall submit to Congress a final report on all matters studied under subsection (a).

[CCH Explanation at ¶586.]

[¶10,440] ACT SEC. 434. FRONTIER EXTENDED STAY CLINIC DEMONSTRATION PROJECT.

(a) AUTHORITY TO CONDUCT DEMONSTRATION PROJECT.—The Secretary shall waive such provisions of the medicare program established under title XVIII of the Social Security Act (42 U.S.C. 1395 et seq.) as are necessary to conduct a demonstration project under which frontier extended stay clinics described in subsection (b) in isolated rural areas are treated as providers of items and services under the medicare program.

(b) CLINICS DESCRIBED.—A frontier extended stay clinic is described in this subsection if the clinic—

(1) is located in a community where the closest shortterm acute care hospital or critical access hospital is at least 75 miles away from the community or is inaccessible by public road; and

(2) is designed to address the needs of—

(A) seriously or critically ill or injured patients who, due to adverse weather conditions or other reasons, cannot be transferred quickly to acute care referral centers; or

(B) patients who need monitoring and observation for a limited period of time.

(c) SPECIFICATION OF CODES.—The Secretary shall determine the appropriate life-safety codes for such clinics that treat patients for needs referred to in subsection (b)(2).

Non-Code Provisions

(d) FUNDING.—

(1) IN GENERAL.—Subject to paragraph (2), there are authorized to be appropriated, in appropriate part from the Federal Hospital Insurance Trust Fund and the Federal Supplementary Medical Insurance Trust Fund, such sums as are necessary to conduct the demonstration project under this section.

(2) BUDGET NEUTRAL IMPLEMENTATION.—In conducting the demonstration project under this section, the Secretary shall ensure that the aggregate payments made by the Secretary under the medicare program do not exceed the amount which the Secretary would have paid under the medicare program if the demonstration project under this section was not implemented.

(e) 3-YEAR PERIOD.—The Secretary shall conduct the demonstration under this section for a 3-year period.

(f) REPORT.—Not later than the date that is 1 year after the date on which the demonstration project concludes, the Secretary shall submit to Congress a report on the demonstration project, together with such recommendations for legislation or administrative action as the Secretary determines appropriate.

(g) DEFINITIONS.—In this section, the terms "hospital" and " critical access hospital" have the meanings given such terms in subsections (e) and (mm), respectively, of section 1861 of the Social Security Act (42 U.S.C. 1395x).

[CCH Explanation at ¶ 593.]

TITLE V—PROVISIONS RELATING TO PART A

Subtitle A—Inpatient Hospital Services

[¶ 10,450] ACT SEC. 501. REVISION OF ACUTE CARE HOSPITAL PAYMENT UPDATES.

. . .

(c) GAO STUDY AND REPORT ON APPROPRIATENESS OF PAYMENTS UNDER THE PROSPECTIVE PAYMENT SYSTEM FOR INPATIENT HOSPITAL SERVICES.—

(1) STUDY.—The Comptroller General of the United States, using the most current data available, shall conduct a study to determine—

(A) the appropriate level and distribution of payments in relation to costs under the prospective payment system under section 1886 of the Social Security Act (42 U.S.C. 1395ww) for inpatient hospital services furnished by subsection (d) hospitals (as defined in subsection (d)(1)(B) of such section); and

(B) whether there is a need to adjust such payments under such system to reflect legitimate differences in costs across different geographic areas, kinds of hospitals, and types of cases.

(2) REPORT.—Not later than 24 months after the date of the enactment of this Act, the Comptroller General of the United States shall submit to Congress a report on the study conducted under paragraph (1) together with such recommendations for legislative and administrative action as the Comptroller General determines appropriate.

. . .

[¶ 10,470] ACT SEC. 503. RECOGNITION OF NEW MEDICAL TECHNOLOGIES UNDER INPATIENT HOSPITAL PROSPECTIVE PAYMENT SYSTEM.

. . .

(d) ESTABLISHMENT OF NEW FUNDING FOR HOSPITAL INPATIENT TECHNOLOGY.—

. . .

(2) NOT BUDGET NEUTRAL.—There shall be no reduction or other adjustment in payments under section 1886 of the Social Security Act because an additional payment is provided under subsection (d)(5)(K)(ii)(III) of such section.

(e) EFFECTIVE DATE.—

(1) IN GENERAL.—The Secretary shall implement the amendments made by this section so that they apply to classification for fiscal years beginning with fiscal year 2005.

(2) RECONSIDERATIONS OF APPLICATIONS FOR FISCAL YEAR 2004 THAT ARE DENIED.—In the case of an application for a classification of a medical service or technology as a new medical service or technology under section 1886(d)(5)(K) of the Social Security Act (42 U.S.C. 1395ww(d)(5)(K)) that was filed for fiscal year 2004 and that is denied—

(A) the Secretary shall automatically reconsider the application as an application for fiscal year 2005 under the amendments made by this section; and

(B) the maximum time period otherwise permitted for such classification of the service or technology shall be extended by 12 months.

. . .

[CCH Explanation at ¶566.]

[¶10,480] ACT SEC. 505. WAGE INDEX ADJUSTMENT RECLASSIFICATION REFORM.

. . .

(c) EFFECTIVE DATE.—The amendments made by this section shall first apply to the wage index for discharges occurring on or after October 1, 2004. In initially implementing such amendments, the Secretary may modify the deadlines otherwise applicable under clauses (ii) and (iii)(I) of section 1886(d)(10)(C) of the Social Security Act (42 U.S.C. 1395ww(d)(10)(C)), for submission of, and actions on, applications relating to changes in hospital geographic reclassification.

[CCH Explanation at ¶570.]

[¶10,490] ACT SEC. 506. LIMITATION ON CHARGES FOR INPATIENT HOSPITAL CONTRACT HEALTH SERVICES PROVIDED TO INDIANS BY MEDICARE PARTICIPATING HOSPITALS.

. . .

(b) EFFECTIVE DATE.—The amendments made by this section shall apply as of a date specified by the Secretary of Health and Human Services (but in no case later than 1 year after the date of enactment of this Act) to medicare participation agreements in effect (or entered into) on or after such date.

(c) PROMULGATION OF REGULATIONS.—The Secretary shall promulgate regulations to carry out the amendments made by subsection (a).

[CCH Explanation at ¶572.]

[¶10,500] ACT SEC. 507. CLARIFICATIONS TO CERTAIN EXCEPTIONS TO MEDICARE LIMITS ON PHYSICIAN REFERRALS.

. . .

(b) APPLICATION OF EXCEPTION FOR HOSPITALS UNDER DEVELOPMENT.—For purposes of section 1877(h)(7)(B)(i)(II) of the Social Security Act, as added by subsection (a)(1)(B), in determining whether a hospital is under development as of November 18, 2003, the Secretary shall consider—

(1) whether architectural plans have been completed, funding has been received, zoning requirements have been met, and necessary approvals from appropriate State agencies have been received; and

(2) any other evidence the Secretary determines would indicate whether a hospital is under development as of such date.

(c) STUDIES.—

(1) MEDPAC STUDY.—The Medicare Payment Advisory Commission, in consultation with the Comptroller General of the United States, shall conduct a study to determine—

(A) any differences in the costs of health care services furnished to patients by physician-owned specialty hospitals and the costs of such services furnished by local full-service community hospitals within specific diagnosis-related groups;

(B) the extent to which specialty hospitals, relative to local full-service community hospitals, treat patients in certain diganosis-related groups within a category, such as cardiology, and an analysis of the selection;

(C) the financial impact of physician-owned specialty hospitals on local full-service community hospitals;

(D) how the current diagnosis-related group system should be updated to better reflect the cost of delivering care in a hospital setting; and

(E) the proportions of payments received, by type of payer, between the specialty hospitals and local fullservice community hospitals.

(2) HHS STUDY.—The Secretary shall conduct a study of a representative sample of specialty hospitals—

(A) to determine the percentage of patients admitted to physician-owned specialty hospitals who are referred by physicians with an ownership interest;

(B) to determine the referral patterns of physician owners, including the percentage of patients they referred to physician-owned specialty hospitals and the percentage of patients they referred to local full-service community hospitals for the same condition;

(C) to compare the quality of care furnished in physician-owned specialty hospitals and in local fullservice community hospitals for similar conditions and patient satisfaction with such care; and

(D) to assess the differences in uncompensated care, as defined by the Secretary, between the specialty hospital and local full-service community hospitals, and the relative value of any tax exemption available to such hospitals.

(3) REPORTS.—Not later than 15 months after the date of the enactment of this Act, the Commission and the Secretary, respectively, shall each submit to Congress a report on the studies conducted under paragraphs (1) and (2), respectively, and shall include any recommendations for legislation or administrative changes.

[CCH Explanation at ¶574.]

[¶10,510] ACT SEC. 508. 1-TIME APPEALS PROCESS FOR HOSPITAL WAGE INDEX CLASSIFICATION.

(a) ESTABLISHMENT OF PROCESS.—

(1) IN GENERAL.—The Secretary shall establish by instruction or otherwise a process under which a hospital may appeal the wage index classification otherwise applicable to the hospital and select another area within the State (or, at the discretion of the Secretary, within a contiguous State) to which to be reclassified.

(2) PROCESS REQUIREMENTS.—The process established under paragraph (1) shall be consistent with the following:

(A) Such an appeal shall be filed by not later than April 1, 2004.

(B) Such an appeal shall be heard by the Medicare Geographic Reclassification Review Board.

(C) There shall be no further administrative or judicial review of a decision of such Board.

(3) RECLASSIFICATION UPON SUCCESSFUL APPEAL.—If the Medicare Geographic Reclassification Review Board determines that the hospital is a qualifying hospital (as defined in subsection (c)), the hospital shall be reclassified to the area selected under paragraph (1). Such reclassification shall apply with respect to discharges occurring during the 3-fiscal-year period beginning with fiscal year 2005.

(4) INAPPLICABILITY OF CERTAIN PROVISIONS.—Except as the Secretary may provide, the provisions of paragraphs (8) and (10) of section 1886(d) of the Social Security Act (42 U.S.C. 1395ww(d)) shall not apply to an appeal under this section.

(b) APPLICATION OF RECLASSIFICATION.—In the case of an appeal decided in favor of a qualifying hospital under subsection (a), the wage index reclassification shall not affect the wage index computation for any area or for any other hospital and shall not be effected in a budget neutral manner. The provisions of this section shall not affect payment for discharges occurring after the end of the 3-fiscal-year-period referred to in subsection (a).

(c) QUALIFYING HOSPITAL DEFINED.—For purposes of this section, the term "qualifying hospital" means a subsection (d) hospital (as defined in section 1886(d)(1)(B) of the Social Security Act, 42 U.S.C. 1395ww(d)(1)(B)) that—

(1) does not qualify for a change in wage index classification under paragraph (8) or (10) of section 1886(d) of the Social Security Act (42 U.S.C. 1395ww(d)) on the basis of requirements relating to distance or commuting; and

(2) meets such other criteria, such as quality, as the Secretary may specify by instruction or otherwise.

The Secretary may modify the wage comparison guidelines promulgated under section 1886(d)(10)(D) of such Act (42 U.S.C. 1395ww(d)(10)(D)) in carrying out this section.

(d) WAGE INDEX CLASSIFICATION.—For purposes of this section, the term "wage index classification" means the geographic area in which it is classified for purposes of determining for a fiscal year the factor used to adjust the DRG prospective payment rate under section 1886(d) of the Social Security Act (42 U.S.C. 1395ww(d)) for area differences in hospital wage levels that applies to such hospital under paragraph (3)(E) of such section.

(e) LIMITATION ON EXPENDITURES.—The aggregate amount of additional expenditures resulting from the application of this section shall not exceed $500,000,000.

(f) TRANSITIONAL EXTENSION.—Any reclassification of a county or other area made by Act of Congress for purposes of making payments under section 1886(d) of the Social Security Act (42 U.S.C. 1395ww(d)) that expired on September 30, 2003, shall be deemed to be in effect during the period beginning on January 1, 2004, and ending on September 30, 2004.

[CCH Explanation at ¶576.]

Subtitle B—Other Provisions

. . .

[¶10,540] ACT SEC. 513. STUDY ON PORTABLE DIAGNOSTIC ULTRASOUND SERVICES FOR BENEFICIARIES IN SKILLED NURSING FACILITIES.

(a) STUDY.—The Comptroller General of the United States shall conduct a study of portable diagnostic ultrasound services furnished to medicare beneficiaries in skilled nursing facilities. Such study shall consider the following:

(1) TYPES OF EQUIPMENT; TRAINING.—The types of portable diagnostic ultrasound services furnished to such beneficiaries, the types of portable ultrasound equipment used to furnish such services, and the technical skills, or training, or both, required for technicians to furnish such services.

(2) CLINICAL APPROPRIATENESS.—The clinical appropriateness of transporting portable diagnostic ultrasound diagnostic and technicians to patients in skilled nursing facilities as opposed to transporting such patients to a hospital or other facility that furnishes diagnostic ultrasound services.

(3) FINANCIAL IMPACT.—The financial impact if Medicare were make a separate payment for portable ultrasound diagnostic services, including the impact of separate payments—

(A) for transportation and technician services for residents during a resident in a part A stay, that would otherwise be paid for under the prospective payment system for covered skilled nursing facility services (under section 1888(e) of the Social Security Act (42 U.S.C. 1395yy(e)); and

Non-Code Provisions

(B) for such services for residents in a skilled nursing facility after a part A stay.

(4) CREDENTIALING REQUIREMENTS.—Whether the Secretary should establish credentialing or other requirements for technicians that furnish diagnostic ultrasound services to medicare beneficiaries.

(b) REPORT.—Not later than 2 years after the date of the enactment of this Act, the Comptroller General shall submit to Congress a report on the study conducted under subsection (a), and shall include any recommendations for legislation or administrative change as the Comptroller General determines appropriate.

[CCH Explanation at ¶ 608.]

TITLE VI—PROVISIONS RELATING TO PART B

Subtitle A—Provisions Relating to Physicians' Services

[¶ 10,550] ACT SEC. 601. REVISION OF UPDATES FOR PHYSICIANS' SERVICES.

(a) UPDATE FOR 2004 AND 2005.—

. . .

(3) NOT TREATED AS CHANGE IN LAW AND REGULATION IN SUSTAINABLE GROWTH RATE DETERMINATION.—The amendments made by this subsection shall not be treated as a change in law for purposes of applying section 1848(f)(2)(D) of the Social Security Act (42 U.S.C. 1395w-4(f)(2)(D)).

. . .

[CCH Explanation at ¶ 701.]

[¶ 10,560] ACT SEC. 604. GAO STUDY ON ACCESS TO PHYSICIANS' SERVICES.

(a) STUDY.—The Comptroller General of the United States shall conduct a study on access of medicare beneficiaries to physicians' services under the medicare program. The study shall include—

(1) an assessment of the use by beneficiaries of such services through an analysis of claims submitted by physicians for such services under part B of the medicare program;

(2) an examination of changes in the use by beneficiaries of physicians' services over time; and

(3) an examination of the extent to which physicians are not accepting new medicare beneficiaries as patients.

(b) REPORT.—Not later than 18 months after the date of the enactment of this Act, the Comptroller General shall submit to Congress a report on the study conducted under subsection (a). The report shall include a determination whether—

(1) data from claims submitted by physicians under part B of the medicare program indicate potential access problems for medicare beneficiaries in certain geographic areas; and

(2) access by medicare beneficiaries to physicians' services may have improved, remained constant, or deteriorated over time.

[CCH Explanation at ¶ 703.]

[¶ 10,570] ACT SEC. 605. COLLABORATIVE DEMONSTRATION-BASED REVIEW OF PHYSICIAN PRACTICE EXPENSE GEOGRAPHIC ADJUSTMENT DATA.

(a) IN GENERAL.—Not later than January 1, 2005, the Secretary shall, in collaboration with State and other appropriate organizations representing physicians, and other appropriate persons, review and consider alternative data sources than those currently used in establishing the geographic index for the practice expense component under the medicare physician fee schedule under section 1848(e)(1)(A)(i) of the Social Security Act (42 U.S.C. 1395w-4(e)(1)(A)(i)).

(b) SITES.—The Secretary shall select two physician payment localities in which to carry out subsection (a). One locality shall include rural areas and at least one locality shall be a statewide locality that includes both urban and rural areas.

(c) REPORT AND RECOMMENDATIONS.—

(1) REPORT.—Not later than January 1, 2006, the Secretary shall submit to Congress a report on the review and consideration conducted under subsection (a). Such report shall include information on the alternative developed data sources considered by the Secretary under subsection (a), including the accuracy and validity of the data as measures of the elements of the geographic index for practice expenses under the medicare physician fee schedule as well as the feasibility of using such alternative data nationwide in lieu of current proxy data used in such index, and the estimated impacts of using such alternative data.

(2) RECOMMENDATIONS.—The report submitted under paragraph (1) shall contain recommendations on which data sources reviewed and considered under subsection (a) are appropriate for use in calculating the geographic index for practice expenses under the medicare physician fee schedule.

[CCH Explanation at ¶725.]

[¶10,580] ACT SEC. 606. MEDPAC REPORT ON PAYMENT FOR PHYSICIANS' SERVICES.

(a) PRACTICE EXPENSE COMPONENT.—Not later than 1 year after the date of the enactment of this Act, the Medicare Payment Advisory Commission shall submit to Congress a report on the effect of refinements to the practice expense component of payments for physicians' services, after the transition to a full resource-based payment system in 2002, under section 1848 of the Social Security Act (42 U.S.C. 1395w-4). Such report shall examine the following matters by physician specialty:

(1) The effect of such refinements on payment for physicians' services.

(2) The interaction of the practice expense component with other components of and adjustments to payment for physicians' services under such section.

(3) The appropriateness of the amount of compensation by reason of such refinements.

(4) The effect of such refinements on access to care by medicare beneficiaries to physicians' services.

(5) The effect of such refinements on physician participation under the medicare program.

(b) VOLUME OF PHYSICIANS' SERVICES.—Not later than 1 year after the date of the enactment of this Act, the Medicare Payment Advisory Commission shall submit to Congress a report on the extent to which increases in the volume of physicians' services under part B of the medicare program are a result of care that improves the health and well-being of medicare beneficiaries. The study shall include the following:

(1) An analysis of recent and historic growth in the components that the Secretary includes under the sustainable growth rate (under section 1848(f) of the Social Security Act (42 U.S.C. 1395w-4(f))).

(2) An examination of the relative growth of volume in physicians' services between medicare beneficiaries and other populations.

(3) An analysis of the degree to which new technology, including coverage determinations of the Centers for Medicare & Medicaid Services, has affected the volume of physicians' services.

(4) An examination of the impact on volume of demographic changes.

(5) An examination of shifts in the site of service or services that influence the number and intensity of services furnished in physicians' offices and the extent to which changes in reimbursement rates to other providers have effected these changes.

(6) An evaluation of the extent to which the Centers for Medicare & Medicaid Services takes into account the impact of law and regulations on the sustainable growth rate.

. . .

[CCH Explanation at ¶704.]

Subtitle C—Other Provisions

[¶10,630] ACT SEC. 621. HOSPITAL OUTPATIENT DEPARTMENT (HOPD) PAYMENT REFORM.

. . .

Non-Code Provisions

(b) SPECIAL PAYMENT FOR BRACHYTHERAPY.—

. . .

(3) GAO REPORT.—The Comptroller General of the United States shall conduct a study to determine appropriate payment amounts under section 1833(t)(16)(C) of the Social Security Act, as added by paragraph (1), for devices of brachytherapy. Not later than January 1, 2005, the Comptroller General shall submit to Congress and the Secretary a report on the study conducted under this paragraph, and shall include specific recommendations for appropriate payments for such devices.

. . .

[CCH Explanation at ¶ 547.]

[¶ 10,640] ACT SEC. 623. PAYMENT FOR RENAL DIALYSIS SERVICES.

. . .

(c) INSPECTOR GENERAL STUDIES ON ESRD DRUGS.—

(1) IN GENERAL.—The Inspector General of the Department of Health and Human Services shall conduct two studies with respect to drugs and biologicals (including erythropoietin) furnished to end-stage renal disease patients under the medicare program which are separately billed by end stage renal disease facilities.

(2) STUDIES ON ESRD DRUGS.—

(A) EXISTING DRUGS.—The first study under paragraph (1) shall be conducted with respect to such drugs and biologicals for which a billing code exists prior to January 1, 2004.

(B) NEW DRUGS.—The second study under paragraph (1) shall be conducted with respect to such drugs and biologicals for which a billing code does not exist prior to January 1, 2004.

(3) MATTERS STUDIED.—Under each study conducted under paragraph (1), the Inspector General shall—

(A) determine the difference between the amount of payment made to end stage renal disease facilities under title XVIII of the Social Security Act for such drugs and biologicals and the acquisition costs of such facilities for such drugs and biologicals and which are separately billed by end stage renal disease facilities, and

(B) estimate the rates of growth of expenditures for such drugs and biologicals billed by such facilities.

(4) REPORTS.—

(A) EXISTING ESRD DRUGS.—Not later than April 1, 2004, the Inspector General shall report to the Secretary on the study described in paragraph (2)(A).

(B) NEW ESRD DRUGS.—Not later than April 1, 2006, the Inspector General shall report to the Secretary on the study described in paragraph (2)(B).

. . .

(e) DEMONSTRATION OF BUNDLED CASE-MIX ADJUSTED PAYMENT SYSTEM FOR ESRD SERVICES.—

(1) IN GENERAL.—The Secretary shall establish a demonstration project of the use of a fully case-mix adjusted payment system for end stage renal disease services under section 1881 of the Social Security Act (42 U.S.C. 1395rr) for patient characteristics identified in the report under subsection (f) that bundles into such payment rates amounts for—

(A) drugs and biologicals (including erythropoietin) furnished to end stage renal disease patients under the medicare program which are separately billed by end stage renal disease facilities (as of the date of the enactment of this Act); and

(B) clinical laboratory tests related to such drugs and biologicals.

(2) FACILITIES INCLUDED IN THE DEMONSTRATION.—In conducting the demonstration under this subsection, the Secretary shall ensure the participation of a sufficient number of providers of dialysis services and renal dialysis facilities, but in no case to exceed 500. In selecting such

providers and facilities, the Secretary shall ensure that the following types of providers are included in the demonstration:

(A) Urban providers and facilities.

(B) Rural providers and facilities.

(C) Not-for-profit providers and facilities.

(D) For-profit providers and facilities.

(E) Independent providers and facilities.

(F) Specialty providers and facilities, including pediatric providers and facilities and small providers and facilities.

(3) TEMPORARY ADD-ON PAYMENT FOR DIALYSIS SERVICES FURNISHED UNDER THE DEMONSTRATION.—

(A) IN GENERAL.—During the period of the demonstration project, the Secretary shall increase payment rates that would otherwise apply under section 1881(b) of such Act (42 U.S.C. 1395rr(b)) by 1.6 percent for dialysis services furnished in facilities in the demonstration site.

(B) RULES OF CONSTRUCTION.—Nothing in this subsection shall be construed as—

(i) as an annual update under section 1881(b) of the Social Security Act (42 U.S.C. 1395rr(b));

(ii) as increasing the baseline for payments under such section; or

(iii) requiring the budget neutral implementation of the demonstration project under this subsection.

(4) 3-YEAR PERIOD.—The Secretary shall conduct the demonstration under this subsection for the 3-year period beginning on January 1, 2006.

(5) USE OF ADVISORY BOARD.—

(A) IN GENERAL.—In carrying out the demonstration under this subsection, the Secretary shall establish an advisory board comprised of representatives described in subparagraph (B) to provide advice and recommendations with respect to the establishment and operation of such demonstration.

(B) REPRESENTATIVES.—Representatives referred to in subparagraph (A) include representatives of the following:

(i) Patient organizations.

(ii) Individuals with expertise in end stage renal dialysis services, such as clinicians, economists, and researchers.

(iii) The Medicare Payment Advisory Commission, established under section 1805 of the Social Security Act (42 U.S.C. 1395b-6).

(iv) The National Institutes of Health.

(v) Network organizations under section 1881(c) of the Social Security Act (42 U.S.C. 1395rr(c)).

(vi) Medicare contractors to monitor quality of care.

(vii) Providers of services and renal dialysis facilities furnishing end stage renal disease services.

(C) TERMINATION OF ADVISORY PANEL.—The advisory panel shall terminate on December 31, 2008.

(6) AUTHORIZATION OF APPROPRIATIONS.—There are authorized to be appropriated, in appropriate part from the Federal Hospital Insurance Trust Fund and the Federal Supplementary Medical Insurance Trust Fund, $5,000,000 in fiscal year 2006 to conduct the demonstration under this subsection.

Non-Code Provisions

(f) REPORT ON A BUNDLED PROSPECTIVE PAYMENT SYSTEM FOR END STAGE RENAL DISEASE SERVICES.—

(1) REPORT.—

(A) IN GENERAL.—Not later than October 1, 2005, the Secretary shall submit to Congress a report detailing the elements and features for the design and implementation of a bundled prospective payment system for services furnished by end stage renal disease facilities including, to the maximum extent feasible, bundling of drugs, clinical laboratory tests, and other items that are separately billed by such facilities. The report shall include a description of the methodology to be used for the establishment of payment rates, including components of the new system described in paragraph (2).

(B) RECOMMENDATIONS.—The Secretary shall include in such report recommendations on elements, features, and methodology for a bundled prospective payment system or other issues related to such system as the Secretary determines to be appropriate.

(2) ELEMENTS AND FEATURES OF A BUNDLED PROSPECTIVE PAYMENT SYSTEM.—The report required under paragraph (1) shall include the following elements and features of a bundled prospective payment system:

(A) BUNDLE OF ITEMS AND SERVICES.—A description of the bundle of items and services to be included under the prospective payment system.

(B) CASE MIX.—A description of the case-mix adjustment to account for the relative resource use of different types of patients.

(C) WAGE INDEX.—A description of an adjustment to account for geographic differences in wages.

(D) RURAL AREAS.—The appropriateness of establishing a specific payment adjustment to account for additional costs incurred by rural facilities.

(E) OTHER ADJUSTMENTS.—Such other adjustments as may be necessary to reflect the variation in costs incurred by facilities in caring for patients with end stage renal disease.

(F) UPDATE FRAMEWORK.—A methodology for appropriate updates under the prospective payment system.

(G) ADDITIONAL RECOMMENDATIONS.—Such other matters as the Secretary determines to be appropriate.

[CCH Explanation at ¶759.]

[¶10,650] ACT SEC. 624. 2-YEAR MORATORIUM ON THERAPY CAPS; PROVISIONS RELATING TO REPORTS.

(a) ADDITIONAL MORATORIUM ON THERAPY CAPS.—

. . .

(2) REMAINDER OF 2003.—For the period beginning on the date of the enactment of this Act and ending of December 31, 2003, the Secretary shall not apply the provisions of paragraphs (1), (2), and (3) of section 1833(g) to expenses incurred with respect to services described in such paragraphs during such period. Nothing in the preceding sentence shall be construed as affecting the application of such paragraphs by the Secretary before the date of the enactment of this Act.

(b) PROMPT SUBMISSION OF OVERDUE REPORTS ON PAYMENT AND UTILIZATION OF OUTPATIENT THERAPY SERVICES.—Not later than March 31, 2004, the Secretary shall submit to Congress the reports required under section 4541(d)(2) of the Balanced Budget Act of 1997 (Public Law 105-33; 111 Stat. 457) (relating to alternatives to a single annual dollar cap on outpatient therapy) and under section 221(d) of the Medicare, Medicaid, and SCHIP Balanced Budget Refinement Act of 1999 (Appendix F, 113 Stat. 1501A-352), as enacted into law by section 1000(a)(6) of Public Law 106-113 (relating to utilization patterns for outpatient therapy).

Medicare Act of 2003

(c) GAO REPORT IDENTIFYING CONDITIONS AND DISEASES JUSTIFYING WAIVER OF THERAPY CAP.—

(1) STUDY.—The Comptroller General of the United States shall identify conditions or diseases that may justify waiving the application of the therapy caps under section 1833(g) of the Social Security Act (42 U.S.C. 1395l(g)) with respect to such conditions or diseases.

(2) REPORT TO CONGRESS.—Not later than October 1, 2004, the Comptroller General shall submit to Congress a report on the conditions and diseases identified under paragraph (1), and shall include a recommendation of criteria, with respect to such conditions and disease, under which a waiver of the therapy caps would apply.

[CCH Explanation at ¶762.]

[¶10,660] ACT SEC. 625. WAIVER OF PART B LATE ENROLLMENT PENALTY FOR CERTAIN MILITARY RETIREES; SPECIAL ENROLLMENT PERIOD.

(a) WAIVER OF PENALTY.—

. . .

(2) EFFECTIVE DATE.—The amendment made by paragraph (1) shall apply to premiums for months beginning with January 2004. The Secretary shall establish a method for providing rebates of premium penalties paid for months on or after January 2004 for which a penalty does not apply under such amendment but for which a penalty was previously collected.

(b) MEDICARE PART B SPECIAL ENROLLMENT PERIOD.—

(1) IN GENERAL.—In the case of any individual who, as of the date of the enactment of this Act, is eligible to enroll but is not enrolled under part B of title XVIII of the Social Security Act and is a covered beneficiary (as defined in section 1072(5) of title 10, United States Code), the Secretary of Health and Human Services shall provide for a special enrollment period during which the individual may enroll under such part. Such period shall begin as soon as possible after the date of the enactment of this Act and shall end on December 31, 2004.

(2) COVERAGE PERIOD.—In the case of an individual who enrolls during the special enrollment period provided under paragraph (1), the coverage period under part B of title XVIII of the Social Security Act shall begin on the first day of the month following the month in which the individual enrolls.

[CCH Explanation at ¶777.]

[¶10,670] ACT SEC. 626. PAYMENT FOR SERVICES FURNISHED IN AMBULATORY SURGICAL CENTERS.

. . .

(d) GAO STUDY OF AMBULATORY SURGICAL CENTER PAYMENTS.—

(1) STUDY.—

(A) IN GENERAL.—The Comptroller General of the United States shall conduct a study that compares the relative costs of procedures furnished in ambulatory surgical centers to the relative costs of procedures furnished in hospital outpatient departments under section 1833(t) of the Social Security Act (42 U.S.C. 1395l(t)). The study shall also examine how accurately ambulatory payment categories reflect procedures furnished in ambulatory surgical centers.

(B) CONSIDERATION OF ASC DATA.—In conducting the study under paragraph (1), the Comptroller General shall consider data submitted by ambulatory surgical centers regarding the matters described in clauses (i) through (iii) of paragraph (2)(B).

(2) REPORT AND RECOMMENDATIONS.—

(A) REPORT.—Not later than January 1, 2005, the Comptroller General shall submit to Congress a report on the study conducted under paragraph (1).

(B) RECOMMENDATIONS.—The report submitted under subparagraph (A) shall include recommendations on the following matters:

Non-Code Provisions

(i) The appropriateness of using the groups of covered services and relative weights established under the outpatient prospective payment system as the basis of payment for ambulatory surgical centers.

(ii) If the relative weights under such hospital outpatient prospective payment system are appropriate for such purpose—

(I) whether the payment rates for ambulatory surgical centers should be based on a uniform percentage of the payment rates or weights under such outpatient system; or

(II) whether the payment rates for ambulatory surgical centers should vary, or the weights should be revised, based on specific procedures or types of services (such as ophthalmology and pain management services).

(iii) Whether a geographic adjustment should be used for payment of services furnished in ambulatory surgical centers, and if so, the labor and nonlabor shares of such payment.

. . .

[CCH Explanation at ¶594.]

Subtitle D—Additional Demonstrations, Studies, and Other Provisions

[¶10,690] ACT SEC. 641. DEMONSTRATION PROJECT FOR COVERAGE OF CERTAIN PRESCRIPTION DRUGS AND BIOLOGICALS.

(a) DEMONSTRATION PROJECT.—The Secretary shall conduct a demonstration project under part B of title XVIII of the Social Security Act under which payment is made for drugs or biologicals that are prescribed as replacements for drugs and biologicals described in section 1861(s)(2)(A) or 1861(s)(2)(Q) of such Act (42 U.S.C. 1395x(s)(2)(A), 1395x(s)(2)(Q)), or both, for which payment is made under such part. Such project shall provide for cost-sharing applicable with respect to such drugs or biologicals in the same manner as cost-sharing applies with respect to part D drugs under standard prescription drug coverage (as defined in section 1860D-2(b) of the Social Security Act, as added by section 101(a)).

(b) DEMONSTRATION PROJECT SITES.—The project established under this section shall be conducted in sites selected by the Secretary.

(c) DURATION.—The Secretary shall conduct the demonstration project for the 2-year period beginning on the date that is 90 days after the date of the enactment of this Act, but in no case may the project extend beyond December 31, 2005.

(d) LIMITATION.—Under the demonstration project over the duration of the project, the Secretary may not provide—

(1) coverage for more than 50,000 patients; and

(2) more than $500,000,000 in funding.

(e) REPORT.—Not later than July 1, 2006, the Secretary shall submit to Congress a report on the project. The report shall include an evaluation of patient access to care and patient outcomes under the project, as well as an analysis of the cost effectiveness of the project, including an evaluation of the costs savings (if any) to the medicare program attributable to reduced physicians' services and hospital outpatient departments services for administration of the biological.

. . .

[CCH Explanation at ¶710.]

[¶10,710] ACT SEC. 643. MEDPAC STUDY OF COVERAGE OF SURGICAL FIRST ASSISTING SERVICES OF CERTIFIED REGISTERED NURSE FIRST ASSISTANTS.

(a) STUDY.—The Medicare Payment Advisory Commission (in this section referred to as the "Commission") shall conduct a study on the feasibility and advisability of providing for payment under part B of title XVIII of the Social Security Act for surgical first assisting services furnished by a certified registered nurse first assistant to medicare beneficiaries.

(b) REPORT.—Not later than January 1, 2005, the Commission shall submit to Congress a report on the study conducted under subsection (a) together with recommendations for such legislation or administrative action as the Commission determines to be appropriate.

(c) DEFINITIONS.—In this section:

(1) SURGICAL FIRST ASSISTING SERVICES.—The term "surgical first assisting services" means services consisting of first assisting a physician with surgery and related preoperative, intraoperative, and postoperative care (as determined by the Secretary) furnished by a certified registered nurse first assistant (as defined in paragraph (2)) which the certified registered nurse first assistant is legally authorized to perform by the State in which the services are performed.

(2) CERTIFIED REGISTERED NURSE FIRST ASSISTANT.—The term " certified registered nurse first assistant" means an individual who—

(A) is a registered nurse and is licensed to practice nursing in the State in which the surgical first assisting services are performed;

(B) has completed a minimum of 2,000 hours of first assisting a physician with surgery and related preoperative, intraoperative, and postoperative care; and

(C) is certified as a registered nurse first assistant by an organization recognized by the Secretary.

[CCH Explanation at ¶784.]

[¶10,720] ACT SEC. 644. MEDPAC STUDY OF PAYMENT FOR CARDIOTHORACIC SURGEONS.

(a) STUDY.—The Medicare Payment Advisory Commission (in this section referred to as the "Commission") shall conduct a study on the practice expense relative values established by the Secretary of Health and Human Services under the medicare physician fee schedule under section 1848 of the Social Security Act (42 U.S.C. 1395w-4) for the specialty of thoracic surgery to determine whether such values adequately take into account the attendant costs of nurse assistants at surgery.

(b) REPORT.—Not later than January 1, 2005, the Commission shall submit to Congress a report on the study conducted under subsection (a) together with recommendations for such legislation or administrative action as the Commission determines to be appropriate.

[CCH Explanation at ¶705.]

[¶10,730] ACT SEC. 645. STUDIES RELATING TO VISION IMPAIRMENTS.

(a) COVERAGE OF OUTPATIENT VISION SERVICES FURNISHED BY VISION REHABILITATION PROFESSIONALS UNDER PART BK.—

(1) STUDY.—The Secretary shall conduct a study to determine the feasibility and advisability of providing for payment for vision rehabilitation services furnished by vision rehabilitation professionals.

(2) REPORT.—Not later than January 1, 2005, the Secretary shall submit to Congress a report on the study conducted under paragraph (1) together with recommendations for such legislation or administrative action as the Secretary determines to be appropriate.

(3) VISION REHABILITATION PROFESSIONAL DEFINED.—In this subsection, the term "vision rehabilitation professional" means an orientation and mobility specialist, a rehabilitation teacher, or a low vision therapist.

(b) REPORT ON APPROPRIATENESS OF A DEMONSTRATION PROJECT TO TEST FEASIBILITY OF USING PPO NETWORKS TO REDUCE COSTS OF ACQUIRING EYEGLASSES FOR MEDICARE BENEFICIARIES AFTER CATARACT SURGERY.—Not later than 1 year after the date of the enactment of this Act, the Secretary shall submit to Congress a report on the feasibility of establishing a two-year demonstration project under which the Secretary enters into arrangements with vision care preferred provider organization networks to furnish and pay for conventional eyeglasses subsequent to each cataract surgery with insertion of an intraocular lens on behalf of Medicare beneficiaries. In such report, the Secretary shall include an estimate of potential cost savings to the Medicare program through the use of such networks, taking into consideration quality of service and beneficiary access to services offered by vision care preferred provider organization networks.

[CCH Explanation at ¶792.]

[¶10,740] ACT SEC. 647. MEDPAC STUDY ON DIRECT ACCESS TO PHYSICAL THERAPY SERVICES.

(a) STUDY.—The Medicare Payment Advisory Commission (in this section referred to as the "Commission") shall conduct a study on the feasibility and advisability of allowing medicare fee-for-service beneficiaries direct access to outpatient physical therapy services and physical therapy services furnished as comprehensive rehabilitation facility services.

(b) REPORT.—Not later than January 1, 2005, the Commission shall submit to Congress a report on the study conducted under subsection (a) together with recommendations for such legislation or administrative action as the Commission determines to be appropriate.

(c) DIRECT ACCESS DEFINED.—The term "direct access" means, with respect to outpatient physical therapy services and physical therapy services furnished as comprehensive outpatient rehabilitation facility services, coverage of and payment for such services in accordance with the provisions of title XVIII of the Social Security Act, except that sections 1835(a)(2), 1861(p), and 1861(cc) of such Act (42 U.S.C. 1395n(a)(2), 1395x(p), and 1395x(cc), respectively) shall be applied—

(1) without regard to any requirement that—

(A) an individual be under the care of (or referred by) a physician; or

(B) services be provided under the supervision of a physician; and

(2) by allowing a physician or a qualified physical therapist to satisfy any requirement for—

(A) certification and recertification; and

(B) establishment and periodic review of a plan of care.

[CCH Explanation at ¶791.]

[¶10,750] ACT SEC. 648. DEMONSTRATION PROJECT FOR CONSUMER DIRECTED CHRONIC OUTPATIENT SERVICES.

(a) ESTABLISHMENT.—

(1) IN GENERAL.—Subject to the succeeding provisions of this section, the Secretary shall establish demonstration projects (in this section referred to as "demonstration projects") under which the Secretary shall evaluate methods that improve the quality of care provided to individuals with chronic conditions and that reduce expenditures that would otherwise be made under the medicare program on behalf of such individuals for such chronic conditions, such methods to include permitting those beneficiaries to direct their own health care needs and services.

(2) INDIVIDUALS WITH CHRONIC CONDITIONS DEFINED.—In this section, the term "individuals with chronic conditions" means an individual entitled to benefits under part A of title XVIII of the Social Security Act, and enrolled under part B of such title, but who is not enrolled under part C of such title who is diagnosed as having one or more chronic conditions (as defined by the Secretary), such as diabetes.

(b) DESIGN OF PROJECTS.—

(1) EVALUATION BEFORE IMPLEMENTATION OF PROJECT.—

(A) IN GENERAL.—In establishing the demonstration projects under this section, the Secretary shall evaluate best practices employed by group health plans and practices under State plans for medical assistance under the medicaid program under title XIX of the Social Security Act, as well as best practices in the private sector or other areas, of methods that permit patients to self-direct the provision of personal care services. The Secretary shall evaluate such practices for a 1-year period and, based on such evaluation, shall design the demonstration project.

(B) REQUIREMENT FOR ESTIMATE OF BUDGET NEUTRAL COSTS.—As part of the evaluation under subparagraph (A), the Secretary shall evaluate the costs of furnishing care under the projects. The Secretary may not implement the demonstration projects under this section unless the Secretary determines that the costs of providing care to individuals with chronic conditions under the project will not exceed the costs, in the aggregate, of furnishing care to such individuals under title XVIII of the Social Security Act, that would otherwise be paid without regard to the demonstration projects for the period of the project.

(2) SCOPE OF SERVICES.—The Secretary shall determine the appropriate scope of personal care services that would apply under the demonstration projects.

(c) VOLUNTARY PARTICIPATION.—Participation of providers of services and suppliers, and of individuals with chronic conditions, in the demonstration projects shall be voluntary.

(d) DEMONSTRATION PROJECTS SITES.—Not later than 2 years after the date of the enactment of this Act, the Secretary shall conduct at least one area that the Secretary determines has a population of individuals entitled to benefits under part A of title XVIII of the Social Security Act, and enrolled under part B of such title, with a rate of incidence of diabetes that significantly exceeds the national average rate of all areas.

(e) EVALUATION AND REPORT.—

(1) EVALUATIONS.—The Secretary shall conduct evaluations of the clinical and cost effectiveness of the demonstration projects.

(2) REPORTS.—Not later than 2 years after the commencement of the demonstration projects, and biannually thereafter, the Secretary shall submit to Congress a report on the evaluation, and shall include in the report the following:

(A) An analysis of the patient outcomes and costs of furnishing care to the individuals with chronic conditions participating in the projects as compared to such outcomes and costs to other individuals for the same health conditions.

(B) Evaluation of patient satisfaction under the demonstration projects.

(C) Such recommendations regarding the extension, expansion, or termination of the projects as the Secretary determines appropriate.

(f) WAIVER AUTHORITY.—The Secretary shall waive compliance with the requirements of title XVIII of the Social Security Act (42 U.S.C. 1395 et seq.) to such extent and for such period as the Secretary determines is necessary to conduct demonstration projects.

(g) AUTHORIZATION OF APPROPRIATIONS.—(1) Payments for the costs of carrying out the demonstration project under this section shall be made from the Federal Supplementary Medical Insurance Trust Fund under section 1841 of such Act (42 U.S.C. 1395t).

(2) There are authorized to be appropriated from such Trust Fund such sums as may be necessary for the Secretary to enter into contracts with appropriate organizations for the deign, implementation, and evaluation of the demonstration project.

(3) In no case may expenditures under this section exceed the aggregate expenditures that would otherwise have been made for the provision of personal care services.

[CCH Explanation at ¶679.]

[¶10,760] ACT SEC. 649. MEDICARE CARE MANAGEMENT PERFORMANCE DEMONSTRATION.

(a) ESTABLISHMENT.—

(1) IN GENERAL.—The Secretary shall establish a pay-for-performance demonstration program with physicians to meet the needs of eligible beneficiaries through the adoption and use of health information technology and evidence-based outcomes measures for—

(A) promoting continuity of care;

(B) helping stabilize medical conditions;

(C) preventing or minimizing acute exacerbations of chronic conditions; and

(D) reducing adverse health outcomes, such as adverse drug interactions related to polypharmacy.

(2) SITES.—The Secretary shall designate no more than 4 sites at which to conduct the demonstration program under this section, of which—

(A) 2 shall be in an urban area;

(B) 1 shall be in a rural area; and

(C) 1 shall be in a State with a medical school with a Department of Geriatrics that manages rural outreach sites and is capable of managing patients with multiple chronic conditions, one of which is dementia.

(3) DURATION.—The Secretary shall conduct the demonstration program under this section for a 3-year period.

(4) CONSULTATION.—In carrying out the demonstration program under this section, the Secretary shall consult with private sector and non-profit groups that are undertaking similar efforts to improve quality and reduce avoidable hospitalizations for chronically ill patients.

(b) PARTICIPATION.—

(1) IN GENERAL.—A physician who provides care for a minimum number of eligible beneficiaries (as specified by the Secretary) may participate in the demonstration program under this section if such physician agrees, to phasein over the course of the 3-year demonstration period and with the assistance provided under subsection (d)(2)—

(A) the use of health information technology to manage the clinical care of eligible beneficiaries consistent with paragraph (3); and

(B) the electronic reporting of clinical quality and outcomes measures in accordance with requirements established by the Secretary under the demonstration program.

(2) SPECIAL RULE.—In the case of the sites referred to in subparagraphs (B) and (C) of subsection (a)(2), a physician who provides care for a minimum number of beneficiaries with two or more chronic conditions, including dementia (as specified by the Secretary), may participate in the program under this section if such physician agrees to the requirements in subparagraphs (A) and (B) of paragraph (1).

(3) PRACTICE STANDARDS.—Each physician participating in the demonstration program under this section must demonstrate the ability—

(A) to assess each eligible beneficiary for conditions other than chronic conditions, such as impaired cognitive ability and co-morbidities, for the purposes of developing care management requirements;

(B) to serve as the primary contact of eligible beneficiaries in accessing items and services for which payment may be made under the medicare program;

(C) to establish and maintain health care information system for such beneficiaries;

(D) to promote continuity of care across providers and settings;

(E) to use evidence-based guidelines and meet such clinical quality and outcome measures as the Secretary shall require;

(F) to promote self-care through the provision of patient education and support for patients or, where appropriate, family caregivers;

(G) when appropriate, to refer such beneficiaries to community service organizations; and

(H) to meet such other complex care management requirements as the Secretary may specify.

The guidelines and measures required under subparagraph (E) shall be designed to take into account beneficiaries with multiple chronic conditions.

(c) PAYMENT METHODOLOGY.—Under the demonstration program under this section the Secretary shall pay a per beneficiary amount to each participating physician who meets or exceeds specific performance standards established by the Secretary with respect to the clinical quality and outcome measures reported under subsection (b)(1)(B). Such amount may vary based on different levels of performance or improvement.

(d) ADMINISTRATION.—

(1) USE OF QUALITY IMPROVEMENT ORGANIZATIONS.—The Secretary shall contract with quality improvement organizations or such other entities as the Secretary deems appropriate to enroll physicians and evaluate their performance under the demonstration program under this section.

(2) TECHNICAL ASSISTANCE.—The Secretary shall require in such contracts that the contractor be responsible for technical assistance and education as needed to physicians enrolled in the demonstration program under this section for the purpose of aiding their adoption of health information technology, meeting practice standards, and implementing required clinical and outcomes measures.

(e) FUNDING.—

(1) IN GENERAL.—The Secretary shall provide for the transfer from the Federal Supplementary Medical Insurance Trust Fund established under section 1841 of the Social Security Act (42 U.S.C. 1395t) of such funds as are necessary for the costs of carrying out the demonstration program under this section.

(2) BUDGET NEUTRALITY.—In conducting the demonstration program under this section, the Secretary shall ensure that the aggregate payments made by the Secretary do not exceed the amount which the Secretary estimates would have been paid if the demonstration program under this section was not implemented.

(f) WAIVER AUTHORITY.—The Secretary may waive such requirements of titles XI and XVIII of the Social Security Act (42 U.S.C. 1301 et seq.; 1395 et seq.) as may be necessary for the purpose of carrying out the demonstration program under this section.

(g) REPORT.—Not later than 12 months after the date of completion of the demonstration program under this section, the Secretary shall submit to Congress a report on such program, together with recommendations for such legislation and administrative action as the Secretary determines to be appropriate.

(h) DEFINITIONS.—In this section:

(1) ELIGIBLE BENEFICIARY.—The term "eligible beneficiary" means any individual who—

(A) is entitled to benefits under part A and enrolled for benefits under part B of title XVIII of the Social Security Act and is not enrolled in a plan under part C of such title; and

(B) has one or more chronic medical conditions specified by the Secretary (one of which may be cognitive impairment).

(2) HEALTH INFORMATION TECHNOLOGY.—The term "health information technology" means email communication, clinical alerts and reminders, and other information technology that meets such functionality, interoperability, and other standards as prescribed by the Secretary.

[CCH Explanation at ¶786.]

[¶10,770] ACT SEC. 650. GAO STUDY AND REPORT ON THE PROPAGATION OF CONCIERGE CARE.

(a) STUDY.—

(1) IN GENERAL.—The Comptroller General of the United States shall conduct a study on concierge care (as defined in paragraph (2)) to determine the extent to which such care—

(A) is used by medicare beneficiaries (as defined in section 1802(b)(5)(A) of the Social Security Act (42 U.S.C. 1395a(b)(5)(A))); and

(B) has impacted upon the access of medicare beneficiaries (as so defined) to items and services for which reimbursement is provided under the medicare program under title XVIII of the Social Security Act (42 U.S.C. 1395 et seq.).

(2) CONCIERGE CARE.—In this section, the term "concierge care" means an arrangement under which, as a prerequisite for the provision of a health care item or service to an individual, a physician, practitioner (as described in section 1842(b)(18)(C) of the Social Security Act (42 U.S.C. 1395u(b)(18)(C))), or other individual—

(A) charges a membership fee or another incidental fee to an individual desiring to receive the health care item or service from such physician, practitioner, or other individual; or

(B) requires the individual desiring to receive the health care item or service from such physician, practitioner, or other individual to purchase an item or service.

(b) REPORT.—Not later than the date that is 12 months after the date of enactment of this Act, the Comptroller General of the United States shall submit to Congress a report on the study conducted under subsection (a)(1) together with such recommendations for legislative or administrative action as the Comptroller General determines to be appropriate.

[CCH Explanation at ¶787.]

[¶10,780] ACT SEC. 651. DEMONSTRATION OF COVERAGE OF CHIROPRACTIC SERVICES UNDER MEDICARE.

(a) DEFINITIONS.—In this section:

(1) CHIROPRACTIC SERVICES.—The term "chiropractic services" has the meaning given that term by the Secretary for purposes of the demonstration projects, but shall include, at a minimum—

(A) care for neuromusculoskeletal conditions typical among eligible beneficiaries; and

(B) diagnostic and other services that a chiropractor is legally authorized to perform by the State or jurisdiction in which such treatment is provided.

(2) DEMONSTRATION PROJECT.—The term "demonstration project" means a demonstration project established by the Secretary under subsection (b)(1).

(3) ELIGIBLE BENEFICIARY.—The term "eligible beneficiary" means an individual who is enrolled under part B of the medicare program.

(4) MEDICARE PROGRAM.—The term "medicare program" means the health benefits program under title XVIII of the Social Security Act (42 U.S.C. 1395 et seq.).

(b) DEMONSTRATION OF COVERAGE OF CHIROPRACTIC SERVICES UNDER MEDICARE.—

(1) ESTABLISHMENT.—The Secretary shall establish demonstration projects in accordance with the provisions of this section for the purpose of evaluating the feasibility and advisability of covering chiropractic services under the medicare program (in addition to the coverage provided for services consisting of treatment by means of manual manipulation of the spine to correct a subluxation described in section 1861(r)(5) of the Social Security Act (42 U.S.C. 1395x(r)(5))).

(2) NO PHYSICIAN APPROVAL REQUIRED.—In establishing the demonstration projects, the Secretary shall ensure that an eligible beneficiary who participates in a demonstration project, including an eligible beneficiary who is enrolled for coverage under a Medicare+Choice plan (or, on and after January 1, 2006, under a Medicare Advantage plan), is not required to receive approval from a physician or other health care provider in order to receive a chiropractic service under a demonstration project.

(3) CONSULTATION.—In establishing the demonstration projects, the Secretary shall consult with chiropractors, organizations representing chiropractors, eligible beneficiaries, and organizations representing eligible beneficiaries.

(4) PARTICIPATION.—Any eligible beneficiary may participate in the demonstration projects on a voluntary basis.

(c) CONDUCT OF DEMONSTRATION PROJECTS.—

(1) DEMONSTRATION SITES.—

(A) SELECTION OF DEMONSTRATION SITES.—The Secretary shall conduct demonstration projects at 4 demonstration sites.

(B) GEOGRAPHIC DIVERSITY.—Of the sites described in subparagraph (A)—

(i) 2 shall be in rural areas; and

(ii) 2 shall be in urban areas.

(C) SITES LOCATED IN HPSAS.—At least 1 site described in clause (i) of subparagraph (B) and at least 1 site described in clause (ii) of such subparagraph shall be located in an area that is designated under section 332(a)(1)(A) of the Public Health Service Act (42 U.S.C. 254e(a)(1)(A)) as a health professional shortage area.

(2) IMPLEMENTATION; DURATION.—

(A) IMPLEMENTATION.—The Secretary shall not implement the demonstration projects before October 1, 2004.

(B) DURATION.—The Secretary shall complete the demonstration projects by the date that is 2 years after the date on which the first demonstration project is implemented.

(d) EVALUATION AND REPORT.—

(1) EVALUATION.—The Secretary shall conduct an evaluation of the demonstration projects—

(A) to determine whether eligible beneficiaries who use chiropractic services use a lesser overall amount of items and services for which payment is made under the medicare program than eligible beneficiaries who do not use such services;

(B) to determine the cost of providing payment for chiropractic services under the medicare program;

(C) to determine the satisfaction of eligible beneficiaries participating in the demonstration projects and the quality of care received by such beneficiaries; and

(D) to evaluate such other matters as the Secretary determines is appropriate.

(2) REPORT.—Not later than the date that is 1 year after the date on which the demonstration projects conclude, the Secretary shall submit to Congress a report on the evaluation conducted under paragraph (1) together with such recommendations for legislation or administrative action as the Secretary determines is appropriate.

(e) WAIVER OF MEDICARE REQUIREMENTS.—The Secretary shall waive compliance with such requirements of the medicare program to the extent and for the period the Secretary finds necessary to conduct the demonstration projects.

(f) FUNDING.—

(1) DEMONSTRATION PROJECTS.—

(A) IN GENERAL.—Subject to subparagraph (B) and paragraph (2), the Secretary shall provide for the transfer from the Federal Supplementary Insurance Trust Fund under section 1841 of the Social Security Act (42 U.S.C. 1395t) of such funds as are necessary for the costs of carrying out the demonstration projects under this section.

(B) LIMITATION.—In conducting the demonstration projects under this section, the Secretary shall ensure that the aggregate payments made by the Secretary under the medicare program do not exceed the amount which the Secretary would have paid under the medicare program if the demonstration projects under this section were not implemented.

(2) EVALUATION AND REPORT.—There are authorized to be appropriated such sums as are necessary for the purpose of developing and submitting the report to Congress under subsection (d).

[CCH Explanation at ¶788.]

TITLE VII—PROVISIONS RELATING TO PARTS A AND B

Subtitle A—Home Health Services

. . .

[¶10,790] ACT SEC. 702. DEMONSTRATION PROJECT TO CLARIFY THE DEFINITION OF HOMEBOUND.

(a) DEMONSTRATION PROJECT.—Not later than 180 days after the date of the enactment of this Act, the Secretary shall conduct a 2-year demonstration project under part B of title XVIII of the Social Security Act under which medicare beneficiaries with chronic conditions described in subsection (b) are deemed to be homebound for purposes of receiving home health services under the medicare program.

(b) MEDICARE BENEFICIARY DESCRIBED.—For purposes of subsection (a), a medicare beneficiary is eligible to be deemed to be homebound, without regard to the purpose, frequency, or duration of absences from the home, if—

(1) the beneficiary has been certified by one physician as an individual who has a permanent and severe, disabling condition that is not expected to improve;

(2) the beneficiary is dependent upon assistance from another individual with at least 3 out of the 5 activities of daily living for the rest of the beneficiary's life;

(3) the beneficiary requires skilled nursing services for the rest of the beneficiary's life and the skilled nursing is more than medication management;

(4) an attendant is required to visit the beneficiary on a daily basis to monitor and treat the beneficiary's medical condition or to assist the beneficiary with activities of daily living;

(5) the beneficiary requires technological assistance or the assistance of another person to leave the home; and

(6) the beneficiary does not regularly work in a paid position full-time or part-time outside the home.

(c) DEMONSTRATION PROJECT SITES.—The demonstration project established under this section shall be conducted in 3 States selected by the Secretary to represent the Northeast, Midwest, and Western regions of the United States.

(d) LIMITATION ON NUMBER OF PARTICIPANTS.—The aggregate number of such beneficiaries that may participate in the project may not exceed 15,000.

(e) DATA.—The Secretary shall collect such data on the demonstration project with respect to the provision of home health services to medicare beneficiaries that relates to quality of care, patient outcomes, and additional costs, if any, to the medicare program.

(f) REPORT TO CONGRESS.—Not later than 1 year after the date of the completion of the demonstration project under this section, the Secretary shall submit to Congress a report on the project using the data collected under subsection (e). The report shall include the following:

(1) An examination of whether the provision of home health services to medicare beneficiaries under the project has had any of the following effects:

(A) Has adversely affected the provision of home health services under the medicare program.

(B) Has directly caused an increase of expenditures under the medicare program for the provision of such services that is directly attributable to such clarification.

(2) The specific data evidencing the amount of any increase in expenditures that is directly attributable to the demonstration project (expressed both in absolute dollar terms and as a percentage) above expenditures that would otherwise have been incurred for home health services under the medicare program.

(3) Specific recommendations to exempt permanently and severely disabled homebound beneficiaries from restrictions on the length, frequency, and purpose of their absences from the home to qualify for home health services without incurring additional costs to the medicare program.

(g) WAIVER AUTHORITY.—The Secretary shall waive compliance with the requirements of title XVIII of the Social Security Act (42 U.S.C. 1395 et seq.) to such extent and for such period as the Secretary determines is necessary to conduct demonstration projects.

(h) CONSTRUCTION.—Nothing in this section shall be construed as waiving any applicable civil monetary penalty, criminal penalty, or other remedy available to the Secretary under title XI or title XVIII of the Social Security Act for acts prohibited under such titles, including penalties for false certifications for purposes of receipt of items or services under the medicare program.

(i) AUTHORIZATION OF APPROPRIATIONS.—Payments for the costs of carrying out the demonstration project under this section shall be made from the Federal Supplementary Medical Insurance Trust Fund under section 1841 of such Act (42 U.S.C. 1395t).

(j) DEFINITIONS.—In this section:

(1) MEDICARE BENEFICIARY.—The term "medicare beneficiary" means an individual who is enrolled under part B of title XVIII of the Social Security Act.

(2) HOME HEALTH SERVICES.—The term "home health services" has the meaning given such term in section 1861(m) of the Social Security Act (42 U.S.C. 1395x(m)).

(3) ACTIVITIES OF DAILY LIVING DEFINED.—The term "activities of daily living" means eating, toileting, transferring, bathing, and dressing.

[CCH Explanation at ¶ 650.]

[¶ 10,800] ACT SEC. 703. DEMONSTRATION PROJECT FOR MEDICAL ADULT DAY-CARE SERVICES.

(a) ESTABLISHMENT.—Subject to the succeeding provisions of this section, the Secretary shall establish a demonstration project (in this section referred to as the "demonstration project") under which the Secretary shall, as part of a plan of an episode of care for home health services established for a medicare beneficiary, permit a home health agency, directly or under arrangements with a medical adult day-care facility, to provide medical adult day-care services as a substitute for a portion of home health services that would otherwise be provided in the beneficiary's home.

(b) PAYMENT.—

(1) IN GENERAL.—Subject to paragraph (2), the amount of payment for an episode of care for home health services, a portion of which consists of substitute medical adult day-care services, under the demonstration project shall be made at a rate equal to 95 percent of the amount that would otherwise apply for such home health services under section 1895 of the Social Security Act (42 U.S.C. 1395fff). In no case may a home health agency, or a medical adult day-care facility under arrangements with a home health agency, separately charge a beneficiary for medical adult day-care services furnished under the plan of care.

(2) ADJUSTMENT IN CASE OF OVERUTILIZATION OF SUBSTITUTE ADULT DAY-CARE SERVICES TO ENSURE BUDGET NEUTRALITY.—The Secretary shall monitor the expenditures under the demonstration project and under title XVIII of the Social Security Act for home health services. If the Secretary estimates that the total expenditures under the demonstration project and under such title XVIII for home health services for a period determined by the Secretary exceed expenditures that would have been made under such title XVIII for home health services for such period if the demonstration project had not been conducted, the Secretary shall adjust the rate of payment to medical adult day-care facilities under paragraph (1) in order to eliminate such excess.

(c) DEMONSTRATION PROJECT SITES.—The demonstration project established under this section shall be conducted in not more than 5 sites in States selected by the Secretary that license or certify providers of services that furnish medical adult day-care services.

(d) DURATION.—The Secretary shall conduct the demonstration project for a period of 3 years.

(e) VOLUNTARY PARTICIPATION.—Participation of medicare beneficiaries in the demonstration project shall be voluntary. The total number of such beneficiaries that may participate in the project at any given time may not exceed 15,000.

(f) PREFERENCE IN SELECTING AGENCIES.—In selecting home health agencies to participate under the demonstration project, the Secretary shall give preference to those agencies that are currently licensed or certified through common ownership and control to furnish medical adult day-care services.

(g) WAIVER AUTHORITY.—The Secretary may waive such requirements of title XVIII of the Social Security Act as may be necessary for the purposes of carrying out the demonstration project, other than waiving the requirement that an individual be homebound in order to be eligible for benefits for home health services.

(h) EVALUATION AND REPORT.—The Secretary shall conduct an evaluation of the clinical and cost-effectiveness of the demonstration project. Not later than 6 months after the completion of the project, the Secretary shall submit to Congress a report on the evaluation, and shall include in the report the following:

(1) An analysis of the patient outcomes and costs of furnishing care to the medicare beneficiaries participating in the project as compared to such outcomes and costs to beneficiaries receiving only home health services for the same health conditions.

(2) Such recommendations regarding the extension, expansion, or termination of the project as the Secretary determines appropriate.

(i) DEFINITIONS.—In this section:

(1) HOME HEALTH AGENCY.—The term "home health agency" has the meaning given such term in section 1861(o) of the Social Security Act (42 U.S.C. 1395x(o)).

(2) MEDICAL ADULT DAY-CARE FACILITY.—The term "medical adult day-care facility" means a facility that—

> (A) has been licensed or certified by a State to furnish medical adult day-care services in the State for a continuous 2-year period;
>
> (B) is engaged in providing skilled nursing services and other therapeutic services directly or under arrangement with a home health agency;
>
> (C) is licensed and certified by the State in which it operates or meets such standards established by the Secretary to assure quality of care and such other requirements as the Secretary finds necessary in the interest of the health and safety of individuals who are furnished services in the facility; and
>
> (D) provides medical adult day-care services.

(3) MEDICAL ADULT DAY-CARE SERVICES.—The term "medical adult day-care services" means—

> (A) home health service items and services described in paragraphs (1) through (7) of section 1861(m) furnished in a medical adult day-care facility;
>
> (B) a program of supervised activities furnished in a group setting in the facility that—
>
>> (i) meet such criteria as the Secretary determines appropriate; and
>>
>> (ii) is designed to promote physical and mental health of the individuals; and
>
> (C) such other services as the Secretary may specify.

(4) MEDICARE BENEFICIARY.—The term "medicare beneficiary" means an individual entitled to benefits under part A of this title, enrolled under part B of this title, or both.

[CCH Explanation at ¶660.]

[¶10,810] ACT SEC. 704. TEMPORARY SUSPENSION OF OASIS REQUIREMENT FOR COLLECTION OF DATA ON NONMEDICARE AND NON-MEDICAID PATIENTS.

(a) IN GENERAL.—During the period described in subsection (b), the Secretary may not require, under section 4602(e) of the Balanced Budget Act of 1997 (Public Law 105-33; 111 Stat. 467) or otherwise under OASIS, a home health agency to gather or submit information that relates to an individual who is not eligible for benefits under either title XVIII or title XIX of the Social Security Act (such information in this section referred to as "non-medicare/medicaid OASIS information").

(b) PERIOD OF SUSPENSION.—The period described in this subsection—

(1) begins on the date of the enactment of this Act; and

(2) ends on the last day of the second month beginning after the date as of which the Secretary has published final regulations regarding the collection and use by the Centers for Medicare & Medicaid Services of non-medicare/medicaid OASIS information following the submission of the report required under subsection (c).

(c) REPORT.—

(1) STUDY.—The Secretary shall conduct a study on how non-medicare/medicaid OASIS information is and can be used by large home health agencies. Such study shall examine—

> (A) whether there are unique benefits from the analysis of such information that cannot be derived from other information available to, or collected by, such agencies; and
>
> (B) the value of collecting such information by small home health agencies compared to the administrative burden related to such collection.

In conducting the study the Secretary shall obtain recommendations from quality assessment experts in the use of such information and the necessity of small, as well as large, home health agencies collecting such information.

(2) REPORT.—The Secretary shall submit to Congress a report on the study conducted under paragraph (1) by not later than 18 months after the date of the enactment of this Act.

(d) CONSTRUCTION.—Nothing in this section shall be construed as preventing home health agencies from collecting nonmedicare/medicaid OASIS information for their own use.

[CCH Explanation at ¶670.]

[¶10,820] ACT SEC. 705. MEDPAC STUDY ON MEDICARE MARGINS OF HOME HEALTH AGENCIES.

(a) STUDY.—The Medicare Payment Advisory Commission shall conduct a study of payment margins of home health agencies under the home health prospective payment system under section 1895 of the Social Security Act (42 U.S.C. 1395fff). Such study shall examine whether systematic differences in payment margins are related to differences in case mix (as measured by home health resource groups (HHRGs)) among such agencies. The study shall use the partial or full-year cost reports filed by home health agencies.

(b) REPORT.—Not later than 2 years after the date of the enactment of this Act, the Commission shall submit to Congress a report on the study under subsection (a).

. . .

[CCH Explanation at ¶664.]

Subtitle B—Graduate Medical Education

. . .

[¶10,830] ACT SEC. 712. EXCEPTION TO INITIAL RESIDENCY PERIOD FOR GERIATRIC RESIDENCY OR FELLOWSHIP PROGRAMS.

(a) CLARIFICATION OF CONGRESSIONAL INTENT.—Congress intended section 1886(h)(5)(F)(ii) of the Social Security Act (42 U.S.C. 1395ww(h)(5)(F)(ii)), as added by section 9202 of the Consolidated Omnibus Budget Reconciliation Act of 1985 (Public Law 99-272), to provide an exception to the initial residency period for geriatric residency or fellowship programs such that, where a particular approved geriatric training program requires a resident to complete 2 years of training to initially become board eligible in the geriatric specialty, the 2 years spent in the geriatric training program are treated as part of the resident's initial residency period, but are not counted against any limitation on the initial residency period.

(b) INTERIM FINAL REGULATORY AUTHORITY AND EFFECTIVE DATE.—The Secretary shall promulgate interim final regulations consistent with the congressional intent expressed in this section after notice and pending opportunity for public comment to be effective for cost reporting periods beginning on or after October 1, 2003.

[CCH Explanation at ¶590.]

[¶10,840] ACT SEC. 713. TREATMENT OF VOLUNTEER SUPERVISION.

(a) MORATORIUM ON CHANGES IN TREATMENT.—During the 1-year period beginning on January 1, 2004, for purposes of applying subsections (d)(5)(B) and (h) of section 1886 of the Social Security Act (42 U.S.C. 1395ww), the Secretary shall allow all hospitals to count residents in osteopathic and allopathic family practice programs in existence as of January 1, 2002, who are training in non-hospital sites, without regard to the financial arrangement between the hospital and the teaching physician practicing in the non-hospital site to which the resident has been assigned.

(b) STUDY AND REPORT.—

(1) STUDY.—The Inspector General of the Department of Health and Human Services shall conduct a study of the appropriateness of alternative payment methodologies under such sections for the costs of training residents in non-hospital settings.

(2) REPORT.—Not later than 1 year after the date of the enactment of this Act, the Inspector General shall submit to Congress a report on the study conducted under paragraph (1), together with such recommendations as the Inspector General determines appropriate.

[CCH Explanation at ¶592.]

Subtitle C—Chronic Care Improvement

[¶10,850] ACT SEC. 721. VOLUNTARY CHRONIC CARE IMPROVEMENT UNDER TRADITIONAL FEE-FOR-SERVICE.

. . .

(b) REPORTS.—The Secretary shall submit to Congress reports on the operation of section 1807 of the Social Security Act, as added by subsection (a), as follows:

(1) Not later than 2 years after the date of the implementation of such section, the Secretary shall submit to Congress an interim report on the scope of implementation of the programs under subsection (b) of such section, the design of the programs, and preliminary cost and quality findings with respect to those programs based on the following measures of the programs:

(A) Quality improvement measures, such as adherence to evidence-based guidelines and rehospitalization rates.

(B) Beneficiary and provider satisfaction.

(C) Health outcomes.

(D) Financial outcomes.

(2) Not later than 3 years and 6 months after the date of the implementation of such section the Secretary shall submit to Congress an update to the report required under paragraph (1) on the results of such programs.

(3) The Secretary shall submit to Congress 2 additional biennial reports on the chronic care improvement programs conducted under such section. The first such report shall be submitted not later than 2 years after the report is submitted under paragraph (2). Each such report shall include information on—

(A) the scope of implementation (in terms of both regions and chronic conditions) of the chronic care improvement programs;

(B) the design of the programs; and

(C) the improvements in health outcomes and financial efficiencies that result from such implementation.

. . .

[CCH Explanation at ¶678.]

[¶10,870] ACT SEC. 723. CHRONICALLY ILL MEDICARE BENEFICIARY RESEARCH, DATA, DEMONSTRATION STRATEGY.

(a) DEVELOPMENT OF PLAN.—Not later than 6 months after the date of the enactment of this Act, the Secretary shall develop a plan to improve quality of care and reduce the cost of care for chronically ill medicare beneficiaries.

(b) PLAN REQUIREMENTS.—The plan will utilize existing data and identify data gaps, develop research initiatives, and propose intervention demonstration programs to provide better health care for chronically ill medicare beneficiaries. The plan shall—

(1) integrate existing data sets including, the Medicare Current Beneficiary Survey (MCBS), Minimum Data Set (MDS), Outcome and Assessment Information Set (OASIS), data from Quality Improvement Organizations (QIO), and claims data;

(2) identify any new data needs and a methodology to address new data needs;

(3) plan for the collection of such data in a data warehouse; and

(4) develop a research agenda using such data.

(c) CONSULTATION.—In developing the plan under this section, the Secretary shall consult with experts in the fields of care for the chronically ill (including clinicians).

(d) IMPLEMENTATION.—Not later than 2 years after the date of the enactment of this Act, the Secretary shall implement the plan developed under this section. The Secretary may contract with appropriate entities to implement such plan.

Subtitle D—Other Provisions

[¶ 10,880] ACT SEC. 731. IMPROVEMENTS IN NATIONAL AND LOCAL COVERAGE DETERMINATION PROCESS TO RESPOND TO CHANGES IN TECHNOLOGY.

(a) NATIONAL AND LOCAL COVERAGE DETERMINATION PROCESS.—

. . .

(2) EFFECTIVE DATE.—The amendments made by paragraph (1) shall apply to national coverage determinations as of January 1, 2004, and section 1862(l)(5) of the Social Security Act, as added by such paragraph, shall apply to local coverage determinations made on or after July 1, 2004.

(b) MEDICARE COVERAGE OF ROUTINE COSTS ASSOCIATED WITH CERTAIN CLINICAL TRIALS OF CATEGORY A DEVICES.—

. . .

(2) EFFECTIVE DATE.—The amendment made by paragraph (1) shall apply to routine costs incurred on and after January 1, 2005, and, as of such date, section 411.15(o) of title 42, Code of Federal Regulations, is superseded to the extent inconsistent with section 1862(m) of the Social Security Act, as added by such paragraph.

(3) RULE OF CONSTRUCTION.—Nothing in the amendment made by paragraph (1) shall be construed as applying to, or affecting, coverage or payment for a nonexperimental/investigational (category B) device.

(c) ISSUANCE OF TEMPORARY NATIONAL CODES.—Not later than July 1, 2004, the Secretary shall implement revised procedures for the issuance of temporary national HCPCS codes under part B of title XVIII of the Social Security Act.

[CCH Explanation at ¶ 796.]

[¶ 10,890] ACT SEC. 732. EXTENSION OF TREATMENT OF CERTAIN PHYSICIAN PATHOLOGY SERVICES UNDER MEDICARE.

Section 542(c) of BIPA (114 Stat. 2763A-551) is amended by inserting " , and for services furnished during 2005 and 2006" before the period at the end.

[¶ 10,900] ACT SEC. 733. PAYMENT FOR PANCREATIC ISLET CELL INVESTIGATIONAL TRANSPLANTS FOR MEDICARE BENEFICIARIES IN CLINICAL TRIALS.

(a) CLINICAL TRIAL.—

(1) IN GENERAL.—The Secretary, acting through the National Institute of Diabetes and Digestive and Kidney Disorders, shall conduct a clinical investigation of pancreatic islet cell transplantation which includes medicare beneficiaries.

(2) AUTHORIZATION OF APPROPRIATIONS.—There are authorized to be appropriated to the Secretary such sums as may be necessary to conduct the clinical investigation under paragraph (1).

(b) MEDICARE PAYMENT.—Not earlier than October 1, 2004, the Secretary shall pay for the routine costs as well as transplantation and appropriate related items and services (as described in subsection (c)) in the case of medicare beneficiaries who are participating in a clinical trial described in subsection (a) as if such transplantation were covered under title XVIII of such Act and as would be paid under part A or part B of such title for such beneficiary.

(c) SCOPE OF PAYMENT.—For purposes of subsection (b):

(1) The term "routine costs" means reasonable and necessary routine patient care costs (as defined in the Centers for Medicare & Medicaid Services Coverage Issues Manual, section 30-1), including immunosuppressive drugs and other followup care.

(2) The term "transplantation and appropriate related items and services" means items and services related to the acquisition and delivery of the pancreatic islet cell transplantation, notwithstanding any national noncoverage determination contained in the Centers for Medicare & Medicaid Services Coverage Issues Manual.

(3) The term "medicare beneficiary" means an individual who is entitled to benefits under part A of title XVIII of the Social Security Act, or enrolled under part B of such title, or both.

(d) CONSTRUCTION.—The provisions of this section shall not be construed—

(1) to permit payment for partial pancreatic tissue or islet cell transplantation under title XVIII of the Social Security Act other than payment as described in subsection (b); or

(2) as authorizing or requiring coverage or payment conveying—

(A) benefits under part A of such title to a beneficiary not entitled to such part A; or

(B) benefits under part B of such title to a beneficiary not enrolled in such part B.

[CCH Explanation at ¶783.]

[¶10,910] ACT SEC. 734. RESTORATION OF MEDICARE TRUST FUNDS.

(a) DEFINITIONS.—In this section:

(1) CLERICAL ERROR.—The term "clerical error" means a failure that occurs on or after April 15, 2001, to have transferred the correct amount from the general fund of the Treasury to a Trust Fund.

(2) TRUST FUND.—The term "Trust Fund" means the Federal Hospital Insurance Trust Fund established under section 1817 of the Social Security Act (42 U.S.C. 1395i) and the Federal Supplementary Medical Insurance Trust Fund established under section 1841 of such Act (42 U.S.C. 1395t).

(b) CORRECTION OF TRUST FUND HOLDINGS.—

(1) IN GENERAL.—The Secretary of the Treasury shall take the actions described in paragraph (2) with respect to the Trust Fund with the goal being that, after such actions are taken, the holdings of the Trust Fund will replicate, to the extent practicable in the judgment of the Secretary of the Treasury, in consultation with the Secretary, the holdings that would have been held by the Trust Fund if the clerical error involved had not occurred.

(2) OBLIGATIONS ISSUED AND REDEEMED.—The Secretary of the Treasury shall—

(A) issue to the Trust Fund obligations under chapter 31 of title 31, United States Code, that bear issue dates, interest rates, and maturity dates that are the same as those for the obligations that—

(i) would have been issued to the Trust Fund if the clerical error involved had not occurred; or

(ii) were issued to the Trust Fund and were redeemed by reason of the clerical error involved; and

(B) redeem from the Trust Fund obligations that would have been redeemed from the Trust Fund if the clerical error involved had not occurred.

(c) APPROPRIATION.—There is appropriated to the Trust Fund, out of any money in the Treasury not otherwise appropriated, an amount determined by the Secretary of the Treasury, in consultation with the Secretary, to be equal to the interest income lost by the Trust Fund through the date on which the appropriation is being made as a result of the clerical error involved.

(d) CONGRESSIONAL NOTICE.—In the case of a clerical error that occurs after April 15, 2001, the Secretary of the Treasury, before taking action to correct the error under this section, shall notify the appropriate committees of Congress concerning such error and the actions to be taken under this section in response to such error.

(e) DEADLINE.—With respect to the clerical error that occurred on April 15, 2001, not later than 120 days after the date of the enactment of this Act—

(1) the Secretary of the Treasury shall take the actions under subsection (b)(1); and

(2) the appropriation under subsection (c) shall be made.

[CCH Explanation at ¶793.]

[¶10,920] ACT SEC. 735. MODIFICATIONS TO MEDICARE PAYMENT ADVISORY COMMISSION (MEDPAC).

. . .

(d) ADDITIONAL REPORTS.—

(1) DATA NEEDS AND SOURCES.—The Medicare Payment Advisory Commission shall conduct a study, and submit a report to Congress by not later than June 1, 2004, on the need for current data, and sources of current data available, to determine the solvency and financial circumstances of hospitals and other medicare providers of services.

(2) USE OF TAX-RELATED RETURNS.—Using return information provided under Form 990 of the Internal Revenue Service, the Commission shall submit to Congress, by not later than June 1, 2004, a report on the following:

(A) Investments, endowments, and fundraising of hospitals participating under the medicare program and related foundations.

(B) Access to capital financing for private and for not-for-profit hospitals.

. . .

[CCH Explanation at ¶721.]

[¶10,930] ACT SEC. 736. TECHNICAL AMENDMENTS.

. . .

(b) PART B.—

. . .

(13) Section 128(b)(2) of BIPA (114 Stat. 2763A-480) is amended by striking "Not later that" and inserting "Not later than" each place it appears.

. . .

TITLE VIII—COST CONTAINMENT

Subtitle A—Cost Containment

[¶10,935] ACT SEC. 801. INCLUSION IN ANNUAL REPORT OF MEDICARE TRUSTEES OF INFORMATION ON STATUS OF MEDICARE TRUST FUNDS.

(a) DETERMINATIONS OF EXCESS GENERAL REVENUE MEDICARE FUNDING.—

(1) IN GENERAL.—The Board of Trustees of each medicare trust fund shall include in the annual reports submitted under subsection (b)(2) of sections 1817 and 1841 of the Social Security Act (42 U.S.C. 1395i and 1395t)—

(A) the information described in subsection (b); and

(B) a determination as to whether there is projected to be excess general revenue medicare funding (as defined in subsection (c)) for the fiscal year in which the report is submitted or for any of the succeeding 6 fiscal years.

(2) MEDICARE FUNDING WARNING.—For purposes of section 1105(h) of title 31, United States Code, and this subtitle, an affirmative determination under paragraph (1)(B) in 2 consecutive annual reports shall be treated as a medicare funding warning in the year in which the second such report is made.

(3) 7-FISCAL-YEAR REPORTING PERIOD.—For purposes of this subtitle, the term "7-fiscal-year reporting period" means, with respect to a year in which an annual report described in

paragraph (1) is made, the period of 7 consecutive fiscal years beginning with the fiscal year in which the report is submitted.

(b) INFORMATION.—The information described in this subsection for an annual report in a year is as follows:

(1) PROJECTIONS OF GROWTH OF GENERAL REVENUE SPENDING.—A statement of the general revenue medicare funding as a percentage of the total medicare outlays for each of the following:

(A) Each fiscal year within the 7-fiscal-year reporting period.

(B) Previous fiscal years and as of 10, 50, and 75 years after such year.

(2) COMPARISON WITH OTHER GROWTH TRENDS.—A comparison of the trend of such percentages with the annual growth rate in the following:

(A) The gross domestic product.

(B) Private health costs.

(C) National health expenditures.

(D) Other appropriate measures.

(3) PART D SPENDING.—Expenditures, including trends in expenditures, under part D of title XVIII of the Social Security Act, as added by section 101.

(4) COMBINED MEDICARE TRUST FUND ANALYSIS.—A financial analysis of the combined medicare trust funds if general revenue medicare funding were limited to the percentage specified in subsection (c)(1)(B) of total medicare outlays.

(c) DEFINITIONS.—For purposes of this section:

(1) EXCESS GENERAL REVENUE MEDICARE FUNDING.—The term " excess general revenue medicare funding" means, with respect to a fiscal year, that—

(A) general revenue medicare funding (as defined in paragraph (2)), expressed as a percentage of total medicare outlays (as defined in paragraph (4)) for the fiscal year; exceeds

(B) 45 percent.

(2) GENERAL REVENUE MEDICARE FUNDING.—The term "general revenue medicare funding" means for a year—

(A) the total medicare outlays (as defined in paragraph (4)) for the year; minus

(B) the dedicated medicare financing sources (as defined in paragraph (3))) for the year.

(3) DEDICATED MEDICARE FINANCING SOURCES.—The term "dedicated medicare financing sources" means the following:

(A) HOSPITAL INSURANCE TAX.—Amounts appropriated to the Hospital Insurance Trust Fund under the third sentence of section 1817(a) of the Social Security Act (42 U.S.C. 1395i(a)) and amounts transferred to such Trust Fund under section 7(c)(2) of the Railroad Retirement Act of 1974 (45 U.S.C. 231f(c)(2)).

(B) TAXATION OF CERTAIN OASDI BENEFITS.—Amounts appropriated to the Hospital Insurance Trust Fund under section 121(e)(1)(B) of the Social Security Amendments of 1983 (Public Law 98-21), as inserted by section 13215(c) of the Omnibus Budget Reconciliation Act of 1993 (Public Law 103-66).

(C) STATE TRANSFERS.—The State share of amounts paid to the Federal Government by a State under section 1843 of the Social Security Act (42 U.S.C. 1395v) or pursuant to section 1935(c) of such Act.

(D) PREMIUMS.—The following premiums:

(i) PART A.—Premiums paid by non-Federal sources under sections 1818 and section 1818A (42 U.S.C. 1395i-2 and 1395i-2a) of such Act.

(ii) PART B.—Premiums paid by non-Federal sources under section 1839 of such Act (42 U.S.C. 1395r), including any adjustments in premiums under such section.

Act Sec. 801(c)(3)(D)(ii) ¶10,935

(iii) PART D.—Monthly beneficiary premiums paid under part D of title XVIII of such Act, as added by section 101, and MA monthly prescription drug beneficiary premiums paid under part C of such title insofar as they are attributable to basic prescription drug coverage.

Premiums under clauses (ii) and (iii) shall be determined without regard to any reduction in such premiums attributable to a beneficiary rebate under section 1854(b)(1)(C) of such title, as amended by section 222(b)(1), and premiums under clause (iii) are deemed to include any amounts paid under section 1860D-13(b) of such title, as added by section 101.

(E) GIFTS.—Amounts received by the medicare trust funds under section 201(i) of the Social Security Act (42 U.S.C. 401(i)).

(4) TOTAL MEDICARE OUTLAYS.—The term "total medicare outlays" means total outlays from the medicare trust funds and shall—

(A) include payments made to plans under part C of title XVIII of the Social Security Act that are attributable to any rebates under section 1854(b)(1)(C) of such Act (42 U.S.C. 1395w-24(b)(1)(C)), as amended by section 222(b)(1);

(B) include administrative expenditures made in carrying out title XVIII of such Act and Federal outlays under section 1935(b) of such Act, as added by section 103(a)(2); and

(C) offset outlays by the amount of fraud and abuse collections insofar as they are applied or deposited into a medicare trust fund.

(5) MEDICARE TRUST FUND.—The term "medicare trust fund" means—

(A) the Federal Hospital Insurance Trust Fund established under section 1817 of the Social Security Act (42 U.S.C. 1395i); and

(B) the Federal Supplementary Medical Insurance Trust Fund established under section 1841 of such Act (42 U.S.C. 1395t), including the Medicare Prescription Drug Account under such Trust Fund.

(d) CONFORMING AMENDMENTS.—

(1) FEDERAL HOSPITAL INSURANCE TRUST FUND.—Section 1817(b)(2) (42 U.S.C. 1395i(b)(2)) is amended by adding at the end the following: " Each report provided under paragraph (2) beginning with the report in 2005 shall include the information specified in section 801(a) of Medicare Prescription Drug, Improvement, and Modernization Act of 2003.".

(2) FEDERAL SUPPLEMENTARY MEDICAL INSURANCE TRUST FUND.—Section 1841(b)(2) (42 U.S.C. 1395t(b)(2)) is amended by adding at the end the following: "Each report provided under paragraph (2) beginning with the report in 2005 shall include the information specified in section 801(a) of Medicare Prescription Drug, Improvement, and Modernization Act of 2003.".

(e) NOTICE OF MEDICARE FUNDING WARNING.—Whenever any report described in subsection (a) contains a determination that for any fiscal year within the 7-fiscal-year reporting period there will be excess general revenue medicare funding, Congress and the President should address the matter under existing rules and procedures.

[CCH Explanation at ¶765.]

[¶10,940] ACT SEC. 802. PRESIDENTIAL SUBMISSION OF LEGISLATION.

(a) IN GENERAL.—Section 1105 of title 31, United States Code, is amended by adding at the end the following new subsection:

(h)(1) If there is a medicare funding warning under section 801(a)(2) of the Medicare Prescription Drug, Improvement, and Modernization Act of 2003 made in a year, the President shall submit to Congress, within the 15-day period beginning on the date of the budget submission to Congress under subsection (a) for the succeeding year, proposed legislation to respond to such warning.

"(2) Paragraph (1) does not apply if, during the year in which the warning is made, legislation is enacted which eliminates excess general revenue medicare funding (as defined in section 801(c) of the Medicare Prescription Drug, Improvement, and Modernization Act of 2003) for the 7-fiscal-year reporting period, as certified by the Board of Trustees of each medicare trust fund (as defined in section 801(c)(5) of such Act) not later than 30 days after the date of the enactment of such legislation.".

(b) SENSE OF CONGRESS.—It is the sense of Congress that legislation submitted pursuant to section 1105(h) of title 31, United States Code, in a year should be designed to eliminate excess general revenue medicare funding (as defined in section 801(c)) for the 7-fiscal-year period that begins in such year.

[CCH Explanation at ¶768.]

[¶10,950] ACT SEC. 803. PROCEDURES IN THE HOUSE OF REPRESENTATIVES.

(a) INTRODUCTION AND REFERRAL OF PRESIDENT'S LEGISLATIVE PROPOSAL.—

(1) INTRODUCTION.—In the case of a legislative proposal submitted by the President pursuant to section 1105(h) of title 31, United States Code, within the 15-day period specified in paragraph (1) of such section, the Majority Leader of the House of Representatives (or his designee) and the Minority Leader of the House of Representatives (or his designee) shall introduce such proposal (by request), the title of which is as follows: "A bill to respond to a medicare funding warning." Such bill shall be introduced within 3 legislative days after Congress receives such proposal.

(2) REFERRAL.—Any legislation introduced pursuant to paragraph (1) shall be referred to the appropriate committees of the House of Representatives.

(b) DIRECTION TO THE APPROPRIATE HOUSE COMMITTEES.—

(1) IN GENERAL.—In the House, in any year during which the President is required to submit proposed legislation to Congress under section 1105(h) of title 31, United States Code, the appropriate committees shall report medicare funding legislation by not later than June 30 of such year.

(2) MEDICARE FUNDING LEGISLATION.—For purposes of this section, the term "medicare funding legislation" means—

(A) legislation introduced pursuant to subsection (a)(1), but only if the legislative proposal upon which the legislation is based was submitted within the 15-day period referred to in such subsection; or

(B) any bill the title of which is as follows: "A bill to respond to a medicare funding warning.".

(3) CERTIFICATION.—With respect to any medicare funding legislation or any amendment to such legislation to respond to a medicare funding warning, the chairman of the Committee on the Budget of the House shall certify—

(A) whether or not such legislation eliminates excess general revenue medicare funding (as defined in section 801(c)) for each fiscal year in the 7-fiscal-year reporting period; and

(B) with respect to such an amendment, whether the legislation, as amended, would eliminate excess general revenue medicare funding (as defined in section 801(c)) for each fiscal year in such 7-fiscal-year reporting period.

(c) FALLBACK PROCEDURE FOR FLOOR CONSIDERATION IF THE HOUSE FAILS TO VOTE ON FINAL PASSAGE BY JULY 30.—

(1) After July 30 of any year during which the President is required to submit proposed legislation to Congress under section 1105(h) of title 31, United States Code, unless the House of Representatives has voted on final passage of any medicare funding legislation for which there is an affirmative certification under subsection (b)(3)(A), then, after the expiration of not less than 30 calendar days (and concurrently 5 legislative days), it is in order to move to discharge any committee to which medicare funding legislation which has such a certification and which has been referred to such committee for 30 calendar days from further consideration of the legislation.

(2) A motion to discharge may be made only by an individual favoring the legislation, may be made only if supported by one-fifth of the total membership of the House (a quorum being present), and is highly privileged in the House. Debate thereon shall be limited to not more than one hour, the time to be divided in the House equally between those favoring and those opposing the motion. An amendment to the motion is not in order, and it is not in order to move to reconsider the vote by which the motion is agreed to or disagreed to.

(3) Only one motion to discharge a particular committee may be adopted under this subsection in any session of a Congress.

(4) Notwithstanding paragraph (1), it shall not be in order to move to discharge a committee from further consideration of medicare funding legislation pursuant to this subsection during a session of a Congress if, during the previous session of the Congress, the House passed medicare funding legislation for which there is an affirmative certification under subsection (b)(3)(A).

(d) FLOOR CONSIDERATION IN THE HOUSE OF DISCHARGED LEGISLATION.—

(1) In the House, not later than 3 legislative days after any committee has been discharged from further consideration of legislation under subsection (c), the Speaker shall resolve the House into the Committee of the Whole for consideration of the legislation.

(2) The first reading of the legislation shall be dispensed with. All points of order against consideration of the legislation are waived. General debate shall be confined to the legislation and shall not exceed five hours, which shall be divided equally between those favoring and those opposing the legislation. After general debate the legislation shall be considered for amendment under the five-minute rule. During consideration of the legislation, no amendments shall be in order in the House or in the Committee of the Whole except those for which there has been an affirmative certification under subsection (b)(3)(B). All points of order against consideration of any such amendment in the Committee of the Whole are waived. The legislation, together with any amendments which shall be in order, shall be considered as read. During the consideration of the bill for amendment, the Chairman of the Committee of the Whole may accord priority in recognition on the basis of whether the Member offering an amendment has caused it to be printed in the portion of the Congressional Record designated for that purpose in clause 8 of Rule XVIII of the Rules of the House of Representatives. Debate on any amendment shall not exceed one hour, which shall be divided equally between those favoring and those opposing the amendment, and no pro forma amendments shall be offered during the debate. The total time for debate on all amendments shall not exceed 10 hours. At the conclusion of consideration of the legislation for amendment, the Committee shall rise and report the legislation to the House with such amendments as may have been adopted. The previous question shall be considered as ordered on the legislation and amendments thereto to final passage without intervening motion except one motion to recommit with or without instructions. If the Committee of the Whole rises and reports that it has come to no resolution on the bill, then on the next legislative day the House shall, immediately after the third daily order of business under clause 1 of Rule XIV of the Rules of the House of Representatives, resolve into the Committee of the Whole for further consideration of the bill.

(3) All appeals from the decisions of the Chair relating to the application of the Rules of the House of Representatives to the procedure relating to any such legislation shall be decided without debate.

(4) Except to the extent specifically provided in the preceding provisions of this subsection, consideration of any such legislation and amendments thereto (or any conference report thereon) shall be governed by the Rules of the House of Representatives applicable to other bills and resolutions, amendments, and conference reports in similar circumstances.

(e) LEGISLATIVE DAY DEFINED.—As used in this section, the term "legislative day" means a day on which the House of Representatives is in session.

(f) RESTRICTION ON WAIVER.—In the House, the provisions of this section may be waived only by a rule or order proposing only to waive such provisions.

(g) RULEMAKING POWER.—The provisions of this section are enacted by the Congress—

(1) as an exercise of the rulemaking power of the House of Representatives and, as such, shall be considered as part of the rules of that House and shall supersede other rules only to the extent that they are inconsistent therewith; and

(2) with full recognition of the constitutional right of that House to change the rules (so far as they relate to the procedures of that House) at any time, in the same manner, and to the same extent as in the case of any other rule of that House.

[CCH Explanation at ¶771.]

[¶10,960] ACT SEC. 804. PROCEDURES IN THE SENATE.

(a) INTRODUCTION AND REFERRAL OF PRESIDENT'S LEGISLATIVE PROPOSAL.—

(1) INTRODUCTION.—In the case of a legislative proposal submitted by the President pursuant to section 1105(h) of title 31, United States Code, within the 15-day period specified in paragraph

Non-Code Provisions

(1) of such section, the Majority Leader and Minority Leader of the Senate (or their designees) shall introduce such proposal (by request), the title of which is as follows: "A bill to respond to a medicare funding warning." Such bill shall be introduced within 3 days of session after Congress receives such proposal.

(2) REFERRAL.—Any legislation introduced pursuant to paragraph (1) shall be referred to the Committee on Finance.

(b) MEDICARE FUNDING LEGISLATION.—For purposes of this section, the term "medicare funding legislation" means—

(1) legislation introduced pursuant to subsection (a)(1), but only if the legislative proposal upon which the legislation is based was submitted within the 15-day period referred to in such subsection; or

(2) any bill the title of which is as follows: "A bill to respond to a medicare funding warning.".

(c) QUALIFICATION FOR SPECIAL PROCEDURES.—

(1) IN GENERAL.—The special procedures set forth in subsections (d) and (e) shall apply to medicare funding legislation, as described in subsection (b), only if the legislation—

(A) is medicare funding legislation that is passed by the House of Representatives; or

(B) contains matter within the jurisdiction of the Committee on Finance in the Senate.

(2) FAILURE TO QUALIFY FOR SPECIAL PROCEDURES.—If the medicare funding legislation does not satisfy paragraph (1), then the legislation shall be considered under the ordinary procedures of the Standing Rules of the Senate.

(d) DISCHARGE.—

(1) IN GENERAL.—If the Committee on Finance has not reported medicare funding legislation described in subsection (c)(1) by June 30 of a year in which the President is required to submit medicare funding legislation to Congress under section 1105(h) of title 31, United States Code, then any Senator may move to discharge the Committee of any single medicare funding legislation measure. Only one such motion shall be in order in any session of Congress.

(2) DEBATE LIMITS.—Debate in the Senate on any such motion to discharge, and all appeals in connection therewith, shall be limited to not more than 2 hours. The time shall be equally divided between, and controlled by, the maker of the motion and the Majority Leader, or their designees, except that in the event the Majority Leader is in favor of such motion, the time in opposition thereto shall be controlled by the Minority Leader or the Minority Leader's designee. A point of order under this subsection may be made at any time. It is not in order to move to proceed to another measure or matter while such motion (or the motion to reconsider such motion) is pending.

(3) AMENDMENTS.—No amendment to the motion to discharge shall be in order.

(4) EXCEPTION IF CERTIFIED LEGISLATION ENACTED.—Notwithstanding paragraph (1), it shall not be in order to discharge the Committee from further consideration of medicare funding legislation pursuant to this subsection during a session of a Congress if the chairman of the Committee on the Budget of the Senate certifies that medicare funding legislation has been enacted that eliminates excess general revenue medicare funding (as defined in section 801(c)) for each fiscal year in the 7-fiscal-year reporting period.

(e) CONSIDERATION.—After the date on which the Committee on Finance has reported medicare funding legislation described in subsection (c)(1), or has been discharged (under subsection (d)) from further consideration of, such legislation, it is in order (even though a previous motion to the same effect has been disagreed to) for any Member of the Senate to move to proceed to the consideration of such legislation.

(f) RULES OF THE SENATE.—This section is enacted by the Senate—

(1) as an exercise of the rulemaking power of the Senate and as such it is deemed a part of the rules of the Senate, but applicable only with respect to the procedure to be followed in the Senate in the case of a bill described in this paragraph, and it supersedes other rules only to the extent that it is inconsistent with such rules; and

(2) with full recognition of the constitutional right of the Senate to change the rules (so far as relating to the procedure of the Senate) at any time, in the same manner, and to the same extent as in the case of any other rule of the Senate.

[CCH Explanation at ¶774.]

Subtitle B—Income-Related Reduction in Part B Premium Subsidy

[¶10,970] ACT SEC. 811. INCOME-RELATED REDUCTION IN PART B PREMIUM SUBSIDY.

. . .

(c) REPORTING REQUIREMENTS FOR SECRETARY OF THE TREASURY.—

(1) IN GENERAL.—Subsection (l) of section 6103 of the Internal Revenue Code of 1986 (relating to disclosure of returns and return information for purposes other than tax administration), as amended by section 105(e), is amended by adding at the end the following new paragraph:

(20) DISCLOSURE OF RETURN INFORMATION TO CARRY OUT MEDICARE PART B PREMIUM SUBSIDY ADJUSTMENT.—

(A) IN GENERAL.—The Secretary shall, upon written request from the Commissioner of Social Security, disclose to officers, employees, and contractors of the Social Security Administration return information of a taxpayer whose premium (according to the records of the Secretary) may be subject to adjustment under section 1839(i) of the Social Security Act. Such return information shall be limited to—

(i) taxpayer identity information with respect to such taxpayer,

(ii) the filing status of such taxpayer,

(iii) the adjusted gross income of such taxpayer,

(iv) the amounts excluded from such taxpayer's gross income under sections 135 and 911 to the extent such information is available,

(v) the interest received or accrued during the taxable year which is exempt from the tax imposed by chapter 1 to the extent such information is available,

(vi) the amounts excluded from such taxpayer's gross income by sections 931 and 933 to the extent such information is available,

(vii) such other information relating to the liability of the taxpayer as is prescribed by the Secretary by regulation as might indicate in the case of a taxpayer who is an individual described in subsection (i)(4)(B)(iii) of section 1839 of the Social Security Act that the amount of the premium of the taxpayer under such section may be subject to adjustment under subsection (i) of such section and the amount of such adjustment, and

(viii) the taxable year with respect to which the preceding information relates.

"(B) RESTRICTION ON USE OF DISCLOSED INFORMATION.—Return information disclosed under subparagraph (A) may be used by officers, employees, and contractors of the Social Security Administration only for the purposes of, and to the extent necessary in, establishing the appropriate amount of any premium adjustment under such section 1839(i)."

(2) CONFORMING AMENDMENTS.—

(A) Paragraph (3) of section 6103(a) of such Code, as amended by section 105(e)(2), is amended by striking "or (19)" and inserting "(19), or (20)".

(B) Paragraph (4) of section 6103(p) of such Code, as amended by section 105(e)(3), is amended by striking "(l)(16), (17), or (19)" each place it appears and inserting "(l)(16), (17), (19), or (20)".

(C) Paragraph (2) of section 7213(a) of such Code, as amended by section 105(f)(4), is amended by striking "or (19)" and inserting "(19), or (20)".

[CCH Explanation at ¶776.]

TITLE IX—ADMINISTRATIVE IMPROVEMENTS, REGULATORY REDUCTION, AND CONTRACTING REFORM

[¶ 10,980] ACT SEC. 900. ADMINISTRATIVE IMPROVEMENTS WITHIN THE CENTERS FOR MEDICARE & MEDICAID SERVICES (CMS).

. . .

(d) INCREASE IN GRADE TO EXECUTIVE LEVEL III FOR THE ADMINISTRATOR OF THE CENTERS FOR MEDICARE & MEDICAID SERVICES.—

(1) IN GENERAL.—Section 5314 of title 5, United States Code, is amended by adding at the end the following:

"Administrator of the Centers for Medicare & Medicaid Services.".

(2) CONFORMING AMENDMENT.—Section 5315 of such title is amended by striking "Administrator of the Health Care Financing Administration.".

(3) EFFECTIVE DATE.—The amendments made by this subsection take effect on January 1, 2004.

(e) CONFORMING AMENDMENTS RELATING TO HEALTH CARE FINANCING ADMINISTRATION.—

. . .

(3) AMENDMENTS TO THE INTERNAL REVENUE CODE OF 1986.—Section 6103(l)(12) of the Internal Revenue Code of 1986 is amended—

(A) in subparagraph (B), by striking "Health Care Financing Administration" in the matter preceding clause (i) and inserting "Centers for Medicare & Medicaid Services"; and

(B) in subparagraph (C)—

(i) by striking "HEALTH CARE FINANCING ADMINISTRATION" in the heading and inserting "CENTERS FOR MEDICARE & MEDICAID SERVICES"; and

(ii) by striking "Health Care Financing Administration" in the matter preceding clause (i) and inserting "Centers for Medicare & Medicaid Services".

(4) AMENDMENTS TO TITLE 10, UNITED STATES CODE.—Title 10, United States Code, is amended—

(A) in section 1086(d)(4), by striking "administrator of the Health Care Financing Administration" in the last sentence and inserting " Administrator of the Centers for Medicare & Medicaid Services"; and

(B) in section 1095(k)(2), by striking "Health Care Financing Administration" in the second sentence and inserting "Centers for Medicare & Medicaid Services".

(5) AMENDMENTS TO THE ALZHEIMER'S DISEASE AND RELATED DEMENTIAS SERVICES RESEARCH ACT OF 1992.—The Alzheimer's Disease and Related Dementias Research Act of 1992 (42 U.S.C. 11271 et seq.) is amended—

(A) in the heading of subpart 3 of part D to read as follows:

"Subpart 3—Responsibilities of the Centers for Medicare & Medicaid Services";

(B) in section 937 (42 U.S.C. 11271)—

(i) in subsection (a), by striking "National Health Care Financing Administration" and inserting "Centers for Medicare & Medicaid Services";

(ii) in subsection (b)(1), by striking "Health Care Financing Administration" and inserting "Centers for Medicare & Medicaid Services";

(iii) in subsection (b)(2), by striking "Health Care Financing Administration" and inserting "Centers for Medicare & Medicaid Services"; and

(iv) in subsection (c), by striking "Health Care Financing Administration" and inserting "Centers for Medicare & Medicaid Services"; and

(C) in section 938 (42 U.S.C. 11272), by striking "Health Care Financing Administration" and inserting "Centers for Medicare & Medicaid Services".

(6) MISCELLANEOUS AMENDMENTS.—

(A) REHABILITATION ACT OF 1973.—Section 202(b)(8) of the Rehabilitation Act of 1973 (29 U.S.C. 762(b)(8)) is amended by striking "Health Care Financing Administration" and inserting "Centers for Medicare & Medicaid Services".

(B) INDIAN HEALTH CARE IMPROVEMENT ACT.—Section 405(d)(1) of the Indian Health Care Improvement Act (25 U.S.C. 1645(d)(1)) is amended by striking "Health Care Financing Administration" in the matter preceding subparagraph (A) and inserting "Centers for Medicare & Medicaid Services".

(C) INDIVIDUALS WITH DISABILITIES EDUCATION ACT.—Section 644(b)(5) of the Individuals with Disabilities Education Act (20 U.S.C. 1444(b)(5)) is amended by striking "Health Care Financing Administration" and inserting "Centers for Medicare & Medicaid Services".

(D) THE HOME HEALTH CARE AND ALZHEIMER'S DISEASE AMENDMENTS OF 1990.—Section 302(a)(9) of the Home Health Care and Alzheimer's Disease Amendments of 1990 (42 U.S.C. 242q-1(a)(9)) is amended by striking "Health Care Financing Administration" and inserting "Centers for Medicare & Medicaid Services".

(E) THE CHILDREN'S HEALTH ACT OF 2000.—Section 2503(a) of the Children's Health Act of 2000 (42 U.S.C. 247b-3a(a)) is amended by striking " Health Care Financing Administration" and inserting "Centers for Medicare & Medicaid Services".

(F) THE NATIONAL INSTITUTES OF HEALTH REVITALIZATION ACT OF 1993.—Section 1909 of the National Institutes of Health Revitalization Act of 1993 (42 U.S.C. 299a note) is amended by striking "Health Care Financing Administration" and inserting "Centers for Medicare & Medicaid Services".

(G) THE OMNIBUS BUDGET RECONCILIATION ACT OF 1990.—Section 4359(d) of the Omnibus Budget Reconciliation Act of 1990 (42 U.S.C. 1395b-3(d)) is amended by striking "Health Care Financing Administration" and inserting "Centers for Medicare & Medicaid Services".

(H) THE MEDICARE, MEDICAID, AND SCHIP BENEFITS IMPROVEMENT AND PROTECTION ACT OF 2000.—Section 104(d)(4) of the Medicare, Medicaid, and SCHIP Benefits Improvement and Protection Act of 2000 (42 U.S.C. 1395m note) is amended by striking "Health Care Financing Administration" and inserting "Health Care".

(7) ADDITIONAL AMENDMENT.—Section 403 of the Act entitled, "An Act to authorize certain appropriations for the territories of the United States, to amend certain Acts relating thereto, and for other purposes", enacted October 15, 1977 (48 U.S.C. 1574-1; 48 U.S.C. 1421q-1), is amended by striking "Health Care Financing Administration" and inserting "Centers for Medicare & Medicaid Services".

[CCH Explanation at ¶801.]

Subtitle A—Regulatory Reform

[¶10,990] ACT SEC. 901. CONSTRUCTION; DEFINITION OF SUPPLIER.

(a) CONSTRUCTION.—Nothing in this title shall be construed—

(1) to compromise or affect existing legal remedies for addressing fraud or abuse, whether it be criminal prosecution, civil enforcement, or administrative remedies, including under sections 3729 through 3733 of title 31, United States Code (commonly known as the "False Claims Act"); or

(2) to prevent or impede the Department of Health and Human Services in any way from its ongoing efforts to eliminate waste, fraud, and abuse in the medicare program.

Furthermore, the consolidation of medicare administrative contracting set forth in this division does not constitute consolidation of the Federal Hospital Insurance Trust Fund and the Federal Supplementary Medical Insurance Trust Fund or reflect any position on that issue.

(b) DEFINITION OF SUPPLIER.—Section 1861 (42 U.S.C. 1395x) is amended by inserting after subsection (c) the following new subsection:

Supplier

Non-Code Provisions

"(d) The term 'supplier' means, unless the context otherwise requires, a physician or other practitioner, a facility, or other entity (other than a provider of services) that furnishes items or services under this title.".

[CCH Explanation at ¶825.]

[¶10,995] ACT SEC. 902. ISSUANCE OF REGULATIONS.

(a) REGULAR TIMELINE FOR PUBLICATION OF FINAL RULES.—

. . .

(2) EFFECTIVE DATE.—The amendment made by paragraph (1) shall take effect on the date of the enactment of this Act. The Secretary shall provide for an appropriate transition to take into account the backlog of previously published interim final regulations.

(b) LIMITATIONS ON NEW MATTER IN FINAL REGULATIONS.—

(1) IN GENERAL.—Section 1871(a) (42 U.S.C. 1395hh(a)), as amended by subsection (a), is amended by adding at the end the following new paragraph:

"(4) If the Secretary publishes a final regulation that includes a provision that is not a logical outgrowth of a previously published notice of proposed rulemaking or interim final rule, such provision shall be treated as a proposed regulation and shall not take effect until there is the further opportunity for public comment and a publication of the provision again as a final regulation.".

(2) EFFECTIVE DATE.—The amendment made by paragraph (1) shall apply to final regulations published on or after the date of the enactment of this Act.

. . .

[CCH explanation at ¶826.]

[¶11,000] ACT SEC. 904. REPORTS AND STUDIES RELATING TO REGULATORY REFORM.

(a) GAO STUDY ON ADVISORY OPINION AUTHORITY.—

(1) STUDY.—The Comptroller General of the United States shall conduct a study to determine the feasibility and appropriateness of establishing in the Secretary authority to provide legally binding advisory opinions on appropriate interpretation and application of regulations to carry out the medicare program under title XVIII of the Social Security Act. Such study shall examine the appropriate timeframe for issuing such advisory opinions, as well as the need for additional staff and funding to provide such opinions.

(2) REPORT.—The Comptroller General shall submit to Congress a report on the study conducted under paragraph (1) by not later than 1 year after the date of the enactment of this Act.

. . .

[CCH Explanation at ¶828.]

Subtitle B—Contracting Reform

[¶11,010] ACT SEC. 911. INCREASED FLEXIBILITY IN MEDICARE ADMINISTRATION.

. . .

(d) EFFECTIVE DATE; TRANSITION RULE.—

(1) EFFECTIVE DATE.—

(A) IN GENERAL.—Except as otherwise provided in this subsection, the amendments made by this section shall take effect on October 1, 2005, and the Secretary is authorized to take such steps before such date as may be necessary to implement such amendments on a timely basis.

(B) CONSTRUCTION FOR CURRENT CONTRACTS.—Such amendments shall not apply to contracts in effect before the date specified under subparagraph (A) that continue to retain the terms and conditions in effect on such date (except as otherwise provided under this Act, other than under this section) until such date as the contract is let out for competitive bidding under such amendments.

(C) DEADLINE FOR COMPETITIVE BIDDING.—The Secretary shall provide for the letting by competitive bidding of all contracts for functions of medicare administrative contractors for annual contract periods that begin on or after October 1, 2011.

(2) GENERAL TRANSITION RULES.—

(A) AUTHORITY TO CONTINUE TO ENTER INTO NEW AGREEMENTS AND CONTRACTS AND WAIVER OF PROVIDER NOMINATION PROVISIONS DURING TRANSITION.—Prior to October 1, 2005, the Secretary may, consistent with subparagraph (B), continue to enter into agreements under section 1816 and contracts under section 1842 of the Social Security Act (42 U.S.C. 1395h, 1395u). The Secretary may enter into new agreements under section 1816 prior to October 1, 2005, without regard to any of the provider nomination provisions of such section.

(B) APPROPRIATE TRANSITION.—The Secretary shall take such steps as are necessary to provide for an appropriate transition from agreements under section 1816 and contracts under section 1842 of the Social Security Act (42 U.S.C. 1395h, 1395u) to contracts under section 1874A, as added by subsection (a)(1).

(3) AUTHORIZING CONTINUATION OF MIP FUNCTIONS UNDER CURRENT CONTRACTS AND AGREEMENTS AND UNDER TRANSITION CONTRACTS.—Notwithstanding the amendments made by this section, the provisions contained in the exception in section 1893(d)(2) of the Social Security Act (42 U.S.C. 1395ddd(d)(2)) shall continue to apply during the period that begins on the date of the enactment of this Act and ends on October 1, 2011, and any reference in such provisions to an agreement or contract shall be deemed to include a contract under section 1874A of such Act, as inserted by subsection (a)(1), that continues the activities referred to in such provisions.

(e) REFERENCES.—On and after the effective date provided under subsection (d)(1), any reference to a fiscal intermediary or carrier under title XI or XVIII of the Social Security Act (or any regulation, manual instruction, interpretative rule, statement of policy, or guideline issued to carry out such titles) shall be deemed a reference to a medicare administrative contractor (as provided under section 1874A of the Social Security Act).

(f) SECRETARIAL SUBMISSION OF LEGISLATIVE PROPOSAL.—Not later than 6 months after the date of the enactment of this Act, the Secretary shall submit to the appropriate committees of Congress a legislative proposal providing for such technical and conforming amendments in the law as are required by the provisions of this section.

(g) REPORTS ON IMPLEMENTATION.—

(1) PLAN FOR IMPLEMENTATION.—By not later than October 1, 2004, the Secretary shall submit a report to Congress and the Comptroller General of the United States that describes the plan for implementation of the amendments made by this section. The Comptroller General shall conduct an evaluation of such plan and shall submit to Congress, not later than 6 months after the date the report is received, a report on such evaluation and shall include in such report such recommendations as the Comptroller General deems appropriate.

(2) STATUS OF IMPLEMENTATION.—The Secretary shall submit a report to Congress not later than October 1, 2008, that describes the status of implementation of such amendments and that includes a description of the following:

(A) The number of contracts that have been competitively bid as of such date.

(B) The distribution of functions among contracts and contractors.

(C) A timeline for complete transition to full competition.

(D) A detailed description of how the Secretary has modified oversight and management of medicare contractors to adapt to full competition.

[CCH Explanation at ¶ 829.]

[¶ 11,020] ACT SEC. 912. REQUIREMENTS FOR INFORMATION SECURITY FOR MEDICARE ADMINISTRATIVE CONTRACTORS.

. . .

(b) APPLICATION OF REQUIREMENTS TO FISCAL INTERMEDIARIES AND CARRIERS.—

(1) IN GENERAL.—The provisions of section 1874A(e)(2) of the Social Security Act (other than subparagraph (B)), as added by subsection (a), shall apply to each fiscal intermediary under section 1816 of the Social Security Act (42 U.S.C. 1395h) and each carrier under section 1842 of such Act (42 U.S.C. 1395u) in the same manner as they apply to medicare administrative contractors under such provisions.

(2) DEADLINE FOR INITIAL EVALUATION.—In the case of such a fiscal intermediary or carrier with an agreement or contract under such respective section in effect as of the date of the enactment of this Act, the first evaluation under section 1874A(e)(2)(A) of the Social Security Act (as added by subsection (a)), pursuant to paragraph (1), shall be completed (and a report on the evaluation submitted to the Secretary) by not later than 1 year after such date.

[CCH Explanation at ¶ 830.]

Subtitle C—Education and Outreach

[¶ 11,025] ACT SEC. 921. PROVIDER EDUCATION AND TECHNICAL ASSISTANCE.

(a) COORDINATION OF EDUCATION FUNDING.—

. . .

(3) REPORT.—Not later than October 1, 2004, the Secretary shall submit to Congress a report that includes a description and evaluation of the steps taken to coordinate the funding of provider education under section 1889(a) of the Social Security Act, as added by paragraph (1).

(b) INCENTIVES TO IMPROVE CONTRACTOR PERFORMANCE.—

. . .

(2) APPLICATION TO FISCAL INTERMEDIARIES AND CARRIERS.—The provisions of section 1874A(f) of the Social Security Act, as added by paragraph (1), shall apply to each fiscal intermediary under section 1816 of the Social Security Act (42 U.S.C. 1395h) and each carrier under section 1842 of such Act (42 U.S.C. 1395u) in the same manner as they apply to medicare administrative contractors under such provisions.

(3) GAO REPORT ON ADEQUACY OF METHODOLOGY.—Not later than October 1, 2004, the Comptroller General of the United States shall submit to Congress and to the Secretary a report on the adequacy of the methodology under section 1874A(f) of the Social Security Act, as added by paragraph (1), and shall include in the report such recommendations as the Comptroller General determines appropriate with respect to the methodology.

(4) REPORT ON USE OF METHODOLOGY IN ASSESSING CONTRACTOR PERFORMANCE.—Not later than October 1, 2004, the Secretary shall submit to Congress a report that describes how the Secretary intends to use such methodology in assessing medicare contractor performance in implementing effective education and outreach programs, including whether to use such methodology as a basis for performance bonuses. The report shall include an analysis of the sources of identified errors and potential changes in systems of contractors and rules of the Secretary that could reduce claims error rates.

(c) PROVISION OF ACCESS TO AND PROMPT RESPONSES FROM MEDICARE ADMINISTRATIVE CONTRACTORS.—

. . .

(3) APPLICATION TO FISCAL INTERMEDIARIES AND CARRIERS.—The provisions of section 1874A(g) of the Social Security Act, as added by paragraph (1), shall apply to each fiscal intermediary under section 1816 of the Social Security Act (42 U.S.C. 1395h) and each carrier under section 1842 of such Act (42 U.S.C. 1395u) in the same manner as they apply to medicare administrative contractors under such provisions.

[CCH Explanation at ¶ 831.]

[¶ 11,030] ACT SEC. 922. SMALL PROVIDER TECHNICAL ASSISTANCE DEMONSTRATION PROGRAM.

(a) ESTABLISHMENT.—

(1) IN GENERAL.—The Secretary shall establish a demonstration program (in this section referred to as the "demonstration program") under which technical assistance described in paragraph (2) is made available, upon request and on a voluntary basis, to small providers of services or suppliers in order to improve compliance with the applicable requirements of the programs under medicare program under title XVIII of the Social Security Act (including provisions of title XI of such Act insofar as they relate to such title and are not administered by the Office of the Inspector General of the Department of Health and Human Services).

(2) FORMS OF TECHNICAL ASSISTANCE.—The technical assistance described in this paragraph is—

(A) evaluation and recommendations regarding billing and related systems; and

(B) information and assistance regarding policies and procedures under the medicare program, including coding and reimbursement.

(3) SMALL PROVIDERS OF SERVICES OR SUPPLIERS.—In this section, the term "small providers of services or suppliers" means—

(A) a provider of services with fewer than 25 full-time-equivalent employees; or

(B) a supplier with fewer than 10 full-time-equivalent employees.

(b) QUALIFICATION OF CONTRACTORS.—In conducting the demonstration program, the Secretary shall enter into contracts with qualified organizations (such as peer review organizations or entities described in section 1889(g)(2) of the Social Security Act, as inserted by section 921(f)(1)) with appropriate expertise with billing systems of the full range of providers of services and suppliers to provide the technical assistance. In awarding such contracts, the Secretary shall consider any prior investigations of the entity's work by the Inspector General of Department of Health and Human Services or the Comptroller General of the United States.

(c) DESCRIPTION OF TECHNICAL ASSISTANCE.—The technical assistance provided under the demonstration program shall include a direct and in-person examination of billing systems and internal controls of small providers of services or suppliers to determine program compliance and to suggest more efficient or effective means of achieving such compliance.

(d) GAO EVALUATION.—Not later than 2 years after the date the demonstration program is first implemented, the Comptroller General, in consultation with the Inspector General of the Department of Health and Human Services, shall conduct an evaluation of the demonstration program. The evaluation shall include a determination of whether claims error rates are reduced for small providers of services or suppliers who participated in the program and the extent of improper payments made as a result of the demonstration program. The Comptroller General shall submit a report to the Secretary and the Congress on such evaluation and shall include in such report recommendations regarding the continuation or extension of the demonstration program.

(e) FINANCIAL PARTICIPATION BY PROVIDERS.—The provision of technical assistance to a small provider of services or supplier under the demonstration program is conditioned upon the small provider of services or supplier paying an amount estimated (and disclosed in advance of a provider's or supplier's participation in the program) to be equal to 25 percent of the cost of the technical assistance.

(f) AUTHORIZATION OF APPROPRIATIONS.—There are authorized to be appropriated, from amounts not otherwise appropriated in the Treasury, such sums as may be necessary to carry out this section.

[CCH Explanation at ¶ 833.]

[¶ 11,040] ACT SEC. 923. MEDICARE BENEFICIARY OMBUDSMAN.

. . .

(b) DEADLINE FOR APPOINTMENT.—By not later than 1 year after the date of the enactment of this Act, the Secretary shall appoint the Medicare Beneficiary Ombudsman under section 1808(c) of the Social Security Act, as added by subsection (a).

(c) FUNDING.—There are authorized to be appropriated to the Secretary (in appropriate part from the Federal Hospital Insurance Trust Fund, established under section 1817 of the Social Security Act (42 U.S.C. 1395i), and the Federal Supplementary Medical Insurance Trust Fund, established under section 1841 of such Act (42 U.S.C. 1395t)) to carry out section 1808(c) of such Act (relating to the Medicare Beneficiary Ombudsman), as added by subsection (a), such sums as are necessary for fiscal year 2004 and each succeeding fiscal year.

(d) USE OF CENTRAL, TOLL-FREE NUMBER (1-800-MEDICARE).—

(1) PHONE TRIAGE SYSTEM; LISTING IN MEDICARE HANDBOOK INSTEAD OF OTHER TOLL-FREE NUMBERS.—Section 1804(b) (42 U.S.C. 1395b-2(b)) is amended by adding at the end the following: "The Secretary shall provide, through the toll-free telephone number 1-800-MEDICARE, for a means by which individuals seeking information about, or assistance with, such programs who phone such toll-free number are transferred (without charge) to appropriate entities for the provision of such information or assistance. Such toll-free number shall be the toll-free number listed for general information and assistance in the annual notice under subsection (a) instead of the listing of numbers of individual contractors.".

(2) MONITORING ACCURACY.—

(A) STUDY.—The Comptroller General of the United States shall conduct a study to monitor the accuracy and consistency of information provided to individuals entitled to benefits under part A or enrolled under part B, or both, through the toll-free telephone number 1-800-MEDICARE, including an assessment of whether the information provided is sufficient to answer questions of such individuals. In conducting the study, the Comptroller General shall examine the education and training of the individuals providing information through such number.

(B) REPORT.—Not later than 1 year after the date of the enactment of this Act, the Comptroller General shall submit to Congress a report on the study conducted under subparagraph (A).

[CCH Explanation at ¶832.]

[¶11,050] ACT SEC. 924. BENEFICIARY OUTREACH DEMONSTRATION PROGRAM.

(a) IN GENERAL.—The Secretary shall establish a demonstration program (in this section referred to as the "demonstration program") under which medicare specialists employed by the Department of Health and Human Services provide advice and assistance to individuals entitled to benefits under part A of title XVIII of the Social Security Act, or enrolled under part B of such title, or both, regarding the medicare program at the location of existing local offices of the Social Security Administration.

(b) LOCATIONS.—

(1) IN GENERAL.—The demonstration program shall be conducted in at least 6 offices or areas. Subject to paragraph (2), in selecting such offices and areas, the Secretary shall provide preference for offices with a high volume of visits by individuals referred to in subsection (a).

(2) ASSISTANCE FOR RURAL BENEFICIARIES.—The Secretary shall provide for the selection of at least 2 rural areas to participate in the demonstration program. In conducting the demonstration program in such rural areas, the Secretary shall provide for medicare specialists to travel among local offices in a rural area on a scheduled basis.

(c) DURATION.—The demonstration program shall be conducted over a 3-year period.

(d) EVALUATION AND REPORT.—

(1) EVALUATION.—The Secretary shall provide for an evaluation of the demonstration program. Such evaluation shall include an analysis of—

(A) utilization of, and satisfaction of those individuals referred to in subsection (a) with, the assistance provided under the program; and

(B) the cost-effectiveness of providing beneficiary assistance through out-stationing medicare specialists at local offices of the Social Security Administration.

(2) REPORT.—The Secretary shall submit to Congress a report on such evaluation and shall include in such report recommendations regarding the feasibility of permanently out-stationing medicare specialists at local offices of the Social Security Administration.

[CCH Explanation at ¶835.]

[¶11,060] ACT SEC. 925. INCLUSION OF ADDITIONAL INFORMATION IN NOTICES TO BENEFICIARIES ABOUT SKILLED NURSING FACILITY BENEFITS.

(a) IN GENERAL.—The Secretary shall provide that in medicare beneficiary notices provided (under section 1806(a) of the Social Security Act, 42 U.S.C. 1395b-7(a)) with respect to the provision of post-hospital extended care services under part A of title XVIII of the Social Security Act, there shall be included information on the number of days of coverage of such services remaining under such part for the medicare beneficiary and spell of illness involved.

(b) EFFECTIVE DATE.—Subsection (a) shall apply to notices provided during calendar quarters beginning more than 6 months after the date of the enactment of this Act.

[CCH Explanation at ¶604.]

[¶11,070] ACT SEC. 926. INFORMATION ON MEDICARE-CERTIFIED SKILLED NURSING FACILITIES IN HOSPITAL DISCHARGE PLANS.

(a) AVAILABILITY OF DATA.—The Secretary shall publicly provide information that enables hospital discharge planners, medicare beneficiaries, and the public to identify skilled nursing facilities that are participating in the medicare program.

(b) INCLUSION OF INFORMATION IN CERTAIN HOSPITAL DISCHARGE PLANS.—

(1) IN GENERAL.—Section 1861(ee)(2)(D) (42 U.S.C. 1395x(ee)(2)(D)) is amended—

(A) by striking "hospice services" and inserting "hospice care and post-hospital extended care services"; and

(B) by inserting before the period at the end the following: " and, in the case of individuals who are likely to need post-hospital extended care services, the availability of such services through facilities that participate in the program under this title and that serve the area in which the patient resides".

(2) EFFECTIVE DATE.—The amendments made by paragraph (1) shall apply to discharge plans made on or after such date as the Secretary shall specify, but not later than 6 months after the date the Secretary provides for availability of information under subsection (a).

[CCH Explanation at ¶606.]

Subtitle D—Appeals and Recovery

[¶11,080] ACT SEC. 931. TRANSFER OF RESPONSIBILITY FOR MEDICARE APPEALS.

(a) TRANSITION PLAN.—

(1) IN GENERAL.—Not later than April 1, 2004, the Commissioner of Social Security and the Secretary shall develop and transmit to Congress and the Comptroller General of the United States a plan under which the functions of administrative law judges responsible for hearing cases under title XVIII of the Social Security Act (and related provisions in title XI of such Act) are transferred from the responsibility of the Commissioner and the Social Security Administration to the Secretary and the Department of Health and Human Services.

(2) CONTENTS.—The plan shall include information on the following:

(A) WORKLOAD.—The number of such administrative law judges and support staff required now and in the future to hear and decide such cases in a timely manner, taking into account the current and anticipated claims volume, appeals, number of beneficiaries, and statutory changes.

(B) COST PROJECTIONS AND FINANCING.—Funding levels required for fiscal year 2005 and subsequent fiscal years to carry out the functions transferred under the plan.

(C) TRANSITION TIMETABLE.—A timetable for the transition.

(D) REGULATIONS.—The establishment of specific regulations to govern the appeals process.

(E) CASE TRACKING.—The development of a unified case tracking system that will facilitate the maintenance and transfer of case specific data across both the fee-for-service and managed care components of the medicare program.

(F) FEASIBILITY OF PRECEDENTIAL AUTHORITY.—The feasibility of developing a process to give decisions of the Departmental Appeals Board in the Department of Health and Human Services addressing broad legal issues binding, precedential authority.

(G) ACCESS TO ADMINISTRATIVE LAW JUDGES.—The feasibility of—

(i) filing appeals with administrative law judges electronically; and

(ii) conducting hearings using tele- or videoconference technologies.

(H) INDEPENDENCE OF ADMINISTRATIVE LAW JUDGES.—The steps that should be taken to ensure the independence of administrative law judges consistent with the requirements of subsection (b)(2).

(I) GEOGRAPHIC DISTRIBUTION.—The steps that should be taken to provide for an appropriate geographic distribution of administrative law judges throughout the United States to carry out subsection (b)(3).

(J) HIRING.—The steps that should be taken to hire administrative law judges (and support staff) to carry out subsection (b)(4).

(K) PERFORMANCE STANDARDS.—The appropriateness of establishing performance standards for administrative law judges with respect to timelines for decisions in cases under title XVIII of the Social Security Act taking into account requirements under subsection (b)(2) for the independence of such judges and consistent with the applicable provisions of title 5, United States Code relating to impartiality.

(L) SHARED RESOURCES.—The steps that should be taken to carry out subsection (b)(6) (relating to the arrangements with the Commissioner of Social Security to share office space, support staff, and other resources, with appropriate reimbursement).

(M) TRAINING.—The training that should be provided to administrative law judges with respect to laws and regulations under title XVIII of the Social Security Act.

(3) ADDITIONAL INFORMATION.—The plan may also include recommendations for further congressional action, including modifications to the requirements and deadlines established under section 1869 of the Social Security Act (42 U.S.C. 1395ff) (as amended by this Act).

(4) GAO EVALUATION.—The Comptroller General of the United States shall evaluate the plan and, not later than the date that is 6 months after the date on which the plan is received by the Comptroller General, shall submit to Congress a report on such evaluation.

(b) TRANSFER OF ADJUDICATION AUTHORITY.—

(1) IN GENERAL.—Not earlier than July 1, 2005, and not later than October 1, 2005, the Commissioner of Social Security and the Secretary shall implement the transition plan under subsection (a) and transfer the administrative law judge functions described in such subsection from the Social Security Administration to the Secretary.

(2) ASSURING INDEPENDENCE OF JUDGES.—The Secretary shall assure the independence of administrative law judges performing the administrative law judge functions transferred under paragraph (1) from the Centers for Medicare & Medicaid Services and its contractors. In order to assure such independence, the Secretary shall place such judges in an administrative office that is organizationally and functionally separate from such Centers. Such judges shall report to, and be under the general supervision of, the Secretary, but shall not report to, or be subject to supervision by, another officer of the Department of Health and Human Services.

(3) GEOGRAPHIC DISTRIBUTION.—The Secretary shall provide for an appropriate geographic distribution of administrative law judges performing the administrative law judge functions transferred under paragraph (1) throughout the United States to ensure timely access to such judges.

(4) HIRING AUTHORITY.—Subject to the amounts provided in advance in appropriations Acts, the Secretary shall have authority to hire administrative law judges to hear such cases, taking into consideration those judges with expertise in handling medicare appeals and in a manner consistent with paragraph (3), and to hire support staff for such judges.

(5) FINANCING.—Amounts payable under law to the Commissioner for administrative law judges performing the administrative law judge functions transferred under paragraph (1) from the Federal Hospital Insurance Trust Fund and the Federal Supplementary Medical Insurance Trust Fund shall become payable to the Secretary for the functions so transferred.

(6) SHARED RESOURCES.—The Secretary shall enter into such arrangements with the Commissioner as may be appropriate with respect to transferred functions of administrative law judges to share office space, support staff, and other resources, with appropriate reimbursement from the Trust Funds described in paragraph (5).

(c) INCREASED FINANCIAL SUPPORT.—In addition to any amounts otherwise appropriated, to ensure timely action on appeals before administrative law judges and the Departmental Appeals Board consistent with section 1869 of the Social Security Act (42 U.S.C. 1395ff) (as amended by this Act), there are authorized to be appropriated (in appropriate part from the Federal Hospital Insurance Trust Fund, established under section 1817 of the Social Security Act (42 U.S.C. 1395i), and the Federal Supplementary Medical Insurance Trust Fund, established under section 1841 of such Act (42 U.S.C. 1395t)) to the Secretary such sums as are necessary for fiscal year 2005 and each subsequent fiscal year to—

(1) increase the number of administrative law judges (and their staffs) under subsection (b)(4);

(2) improve education and training opportunities for administrative law judges (and their staffs); and

(3) increase the staff of the Departmental Appeals Board.

(d) CONFORMING AMENDMENT.—Section 1869(f)(2)(A)(i) (42 U.S.C. 1395ff(f)(2)(A)(i)) is amended by striking "of the Social Security Administration".

[CCH Explanation at ¶901.]

[¶11,085] ACT SEC. 932. PROCESS FOR EXPEDITED ACCESS TO REVIEW.

. . .

(c) EXPEDITED REVIEW OF CERTAIN PROVIDER AGREEMENT DETERMINATIONS.—

. . .

(3) INCREASED FINANCIAL SUPPORT.—In addition to any amounts otherwise appropriated, to reduce by 50 percent the average time for administrative determinations on appeals under section 1866(h) of the Social Security Act (42 U.S.C. 1395cc(h)), there are authorized to be appropriated (in appropriate part from the Federal Hospital Insurance Trust Fund, established under section 1817 of the Social Security Act (42 U.S.C. 1395i), and the Federal Supplementary Medical Insurance Trust Fund, established under section 1841 of such Act (42 U.S.C. 1395t)) to the Secretary such additional sums for fiscal year 2004 and each subsequent fiscal year as may be necessary. The purposes for which such amounts are available include increasing the number of administrative law judges (and their staffs) and the appellate level staff at the Departmental Appeals Board of the Department of Health and Human Services and educating such judges and staffs on long-term care issues.

(d) EFFECTIVE DATE.—The amendments made by this section shall apply to appeals filed on or after October 1, 2004.

[¶11,086] ACT SEC. 933. REVISIONS TO MEDICARE APPEALS PROCESS.

. . .

(d) QUALIFIED INDEPENDENT CONTRACTORS.—

. . .

(4) EFFECTIVE DATE.—The amendments made by paragraphs (1) and (2) shall be effective as if included in the enactment of the respective provisions of subtitle C of title V of BIPA (114 Stat. 2763A-534).

(5) TRANSITION.—In applying section 1869(g) of the Social Security Act (as added by paragraph (2)), any reference to a medicare administrative contractor shall be deemed to include a reference to a fiscal intermediary under section 1816 of the Social Security Act (42 U.S.C. 1395h) and a carrier under section 1842 of such Act (42 U.S.C. 1395u).

[CCH Explanation at ¶906.]

[¶11,090] ACT SEC. 934. PREPAYMENT REVIEW.

. . .

(b) EFFECTIVE DATE.—

(1) IN GENERAL.—Except as provided in this subsection, the amendment made by subsection (a) shall take effect 1 year after the date of the enactment of this Act.

(2) DEADLINE FOR PROMULGATION OF CERTAIN REGULATIONS.—The Secretary shall first issue regulations under section 1874A(h) of the Social Security Act, as added by subsection (a), by not later than 1 year after the date of the enactment of this Act.

(3) APPLICATION OF STANDARD PROTOCOLS FOR RANDOM PREPAYMENT REVIEW.—Section 1874A(h)(1)(B) of the Social Security Act, as added by subsection (a), shall apply to random prepayment reviews conducted on or after such date (not later than 1 year after the date of the enactment of this Act) as the Secretary shall specify.

(c) APPLICATION TO FISCAL INTERMEDIARIES AND CARRIERS.—The provisions of section 1874A(h) of the Social Security Act, as added by subsection (a), shall apply to each fiscal intermediary under section 1816 of the Social Security Act (42 U.S.C. 1395h) and each carrier under section 1842 of such Act (42 U.S.C. 1395u) in the same manner as they apply to medicare administrative contractors under such provisions.

[CCH Explanation at ¶908.]

[¶11,095] ACT SEC. 935. RECOVERY OF OVERPAYMENTS.

(b) EFFECTIVE DATES AND DEADLINES.—

(1) USE OF REPAYMENT PLANS.—Section 1893(f)(1) of the Social Security Act, as added by subsection (a), shall apply to requests for repayment plans made after the date of the enactment of this Act.

(2) LIMITATION ON RECOUPMENT.—Section 1893(f)(2) of the Social Security Act, as added by subsection (a), shall apply to actions taken after the date of the enactment of this Act.

(3) USE OF EXTRAPOLATION.—Section 1893(f)(3) of the Social Security Act, as added by subsection (a), shall apply to statistically valid random samples initiated after the date that is 1 year after the date of the enactment of this Act.

(4) PROVISION OF SUPPORTING DOCUMENTATION.—Section 1893(f)(4) of the Social Security Act, as added by subsection (a), shall take effect on the date of the enactment of this Act.

(5) CONSENT SETTLEMENT.—Section 1893(f)(5) of the Social Security Act, as added by subsection (a), shall apply to consent settlements entered into after the date of the enactment of this Act.

(6) NOTICE OF OVERUTILIZATION.—Not later than 1 year after the date of the enactment of this Act, the Secretary shall first establish the process for notice of overutilization of billing codes under section 1893A(f)(6) of the Social Security Act, as added by subsection (a).

(7) PAYMENT AUDITS.—Section 1893A(f)(7) of the Social Security Act, as added by subsection (a), shall apply to audits initiated after the date of the enactment of this Act.

(8) STANDARD FOR ABNORMAL BILLING PATTERNS.—Not later than 1 year after the date of the enactment of this Act, the Secretary shall first establish a standard methodology for selection of sample claims for abnormal billing patterns under section 1893(f)(8) of the Social Security Act, as added by subsection (a).

[CCH Explanation at ¶909.]

[¶11,097] ACT SEC. 936. PROVIDER ENROLLMENT PROCESS; RIGHT OF APPEAL.

. . .

(b) EFFECTIVE DATES.—

(1) ENROLLMENT PROCESS.—The Secretary shall provide for the establishment of the enrollment process under section 1866(j)(1) of the Social Security Act, as added by subsection (a)(2), within 6 months after the date of the enactment of this Act.

(2) CONSULTATION.—Section 1866(j)(1)(C) of the Social Security Act, as added by subsection (a)(2), shall apply with respect to changes in provider enrollment forms made on or after January 1, 2004.

(3) HEARING RIGHTS.—Section 1866(j)(2) of the Social Security Act, as added by subsection (a)(2), shall apply to denials occurring on or after such date (not later than 1 year after the date of the enactment of this Act) as the Secretary specifies.

[CCH Explanation at ¶911.]

[¶11,100] ACT SEC. 937. PROCESS FOR CORRECTION OF MINOR ERRORS AND OMISSIONS WITHOUT PURSUING APPEALS PROCESS.

(a) CLAIMS.—The Secretary shall develop, in consultation with appropriate medicare contractors (as defined in section 1889(g) of the Social Security Act, as inserted by section 301(a)(1)) and representatives of providers of services and suppliers, a process whereby, in the case of minor errors or omissions (as defined by the Secretary) that are detected in the submission of claims under the programs under title XVIII of such Act, a provider of services or supplier is given an opportunity to correct such an error or omission without the need to initiate an appeal. Such process shall include the ability to resubmit corrected claims.

(b) DEADLINE.—Not later than 1 year after the date of the enactment of this Act, the Secretary shall first develop the process under subsection (a).

[CCH Explanation at ¶912.]

[¶11,110] ACT SEC. 938. PRIOR DETERMINATION PROCESS FOR CERTAIN ITEMS AND SERVICES; ADVANCE BENEFICIARY NOTICES.

. . .

(b) EFFECTIVE DATE; SUNSET; TRANSITION.—

(1) EFFECTIVE DATE.—The Secretary shall establish the prior determination process under the amendment made by subsection (a) in such a manner as to provide for the acceptance of requests for determinations under such process filed not later than 18 months after the date of the enactment of this Act.

(2) SUNSET.—Such prior determination process shall not apply to requests filed after the end of the 5-year period beginning on the first date on which requests for determinations under such process are accepted.

(3) TRANSITION.—During the period in which the amendment made by subsection (a) has become effective but contracts are not provided under section 1874A of the Social Security Act with medicare administrative contractors, any reference in section 1869(g) of such Act (as added by such amendment) to such a contractor is deemed a reference to a fiscal intermediary or carrier with an agreement under section 1816, or contract under section 1842, respectively, of such Act.

(4) LIMITATION ON APPLICATION TO SGR.—For purposes of applying section 1848(f)(2)(D) of the Social Security Act (42 U.S.C. 1395w-4(f)(2)(D)), the amendment made by subsection (a) shall not be considered to be a change in law or regulation.

Non-Code Provisions

(c) PROVISIONS RELATING TO ADVANCE BENEFICIARY NOTICES; REPORT ON PRIOR DETERMINATION PROCES.—

(1) DATA COLLECTION.—The Secretary shall establish a process for the collection of information on the instances in which an advance beneficiary notice (as defined in paragraph (5)) has been provided and on instances in which a beneficiary indicates on such a notice that the beneficiary does not intend to seek to have the item or service that is the subject of the notice furnished.

(2) OUTREACH AND EDUCATION.—The Secretary shall establish a program of outreach and education for beneficiaries and providers of services and other persons on the appropriate use of advance beneficiary notices and coverage policies under the medicare program.

(3) GAO REPORT ON USE OF ADVANCE BENEFICIARY NOTICES.—Not later than 18 months after the date on which section 1869(h) of the Social Security Act (as added by subsection (a)) takes effect, the Comptroller General of the United States shall submit to Congress a report on the use of advance beneficiary notices under title XVIII of such Act. Such report shall include information concerning the providers of services and other persons that have provided such notices and the response of beneficiaries to such notices.

(4) GAO REPORT ON USE OF PRIOR DETERMINATION PROCESS.—Not later than 36 months after the date on which section 1869(h) of the Social Security Act (as added by subsection (a)) takes effect, the Comptroller General of the United States shall submit to Congress a report on the use of the prior determination process under such section. Such report shall include—

(A) information concerning—

(i) the number and types of procedures for which a prior determination has been sought;

(ii) determinations made under the process;

(iii) the percentage of beneficiaries prevailing;

(iv) in those cases in which the beneficiaries do not prevail, the reasons why such beneficiaries did not prevail; and

(v) changes in receipt of services resulting from the application of such process;

(B) an evaluation of whether the process was useful for physicians (and other suppliers) and beneficiaries, whether it was timely, and whether the amount of information required was burdensome to physicians and beneficiaries; and

(C) recommendations for improvements or continuation of such process.

(5) ADVANCE BENEFICIARY NOTICE DEFINED.—In this subsection, the term "advance beneficiary notice" means a written notice provided under section 1879(a) of the Social Security Act (42 U.S.C. 1395pp(a)) to an individual entitled to benefits under part A or enrolled under part B of title XVIII of such Act before items or services are furnished under such part in cases where a provider of services or other person that would furnish the item or service believes that payment will not be made for some or all of such items or services under such title.

. . .

[CCH Explanation at ¶913.]

Subtitle E—Miscellaneous Provisions

[¶11,120] ACT SEC. 941. POLICY DEVELOPMENT REGARDING EVALUATION AND MANAGEMENT (E & M) DOCUMENTATION GUIDELINES.

(a) IN GENERAL.—The Secretary may not implement any new or modified documentation guidelines (which for purposes of this section includes clinical examples) for evaluation and management physician services under the title XVIII of the Social Security Act on or after the date of the enactment of this Act unless the Secretary—

(1) has developed the guidelines in collaboration with practicing physicians (including both generalists and specialists) and provided for an assessment of the proposed guidelines by the physician community;

(2) has established a plan that contains specific goals, including a schedule, for improving the use of such guidelines;

(3) has conducted appropriate and representative pilot projects under subsection (b) to test such guidelines;

(4) finds, based on reports submitted under subsection (b)(5) with respect to pilot projects conducted for such or related guidelines, that the objectives described in subsection (c) will be met in the implementation of such guidelines; and

(5) has established, and is implementing, a program to educate physicians on the use of such guidelines and that includes appropriate outreach. The Secretary shall make changes to the manner in which existing evaluation and management documentation guidelines are implemented to reduce paperwork burdens on physicians.

(b) PILOT PROJECTS TO TEST MODIFIED OR NEW EVALUATION AND MANAGEMENT DOCUMENTATION GUIDELINES.—

(1) IN GENERAL.—With respect to proposed new or modified documentation guidelines referred to in subsection (a), the Secretary shall conduct under this subsection appropriate and representative pilot projects to test the proposed guidelines.

(2) LENGTH AND CONSULTATION.—Each pilot project under this subsection shall—

(A) be voluntary;

(B) be of sufficient length as determined by the Secretary (but in no case to exceed 1 year) to allow for preparatory physician and medicare contractor education, analysis, and use and assessment of potential evaluation and management guidelines; and

(C) be conducted, in development and throughout the planning and operational stages of the project, in consultation with practicing physicians (including both generalists and specialists).

(3) RANGE OF PILOT PROJECTS.—Of the pilot projects conducted under this subsection with respect to proposed new or modified documentation guidelines—

(A) at least one shall focus on a peer review method by physicians (not employed by a medicare contractor) which evaluates medical record information for claims submitted by physicians identified as statistical outliers relative to codes used for billing purposes for such services;

(B) at least one shall focus on an alternative method to detailed guidelines based on physician documentation of face to face encounter time with a patient;

(C) at least one shall be conducted for services furnished in a rural area and at least one for services furnished outside such an area; and

(D) at least one shall be conducted in a setting where physicians bill under physicians' services in teaching settings and at least one shall be conducted in a setting other than a teaching setting.

(4) STUDY OF IMPACT.—Each pilot project shall examine the effect of the proposed guidelines on—

(A) different types of physician practices, including those with fewer than 10 full-time-equivalent employees (including physicians); and

(B) the costs of physician compliance, including education, implementation, auditing, and monitoring.

(5) REPORT ON PILOT PROJECTS.—Not later than 6 months after the date of completion of pilot projects carried out under this subsection with respect to a proposed guideline described in paragraph (1), the Secretary shall submit to Congress a report on the pilot projects. Each such report shall include a finding by the Secretary of whether the objectives described in subsection (c) will be met in the implementation of such proposed guideline.

(c) OBJECTIVES FOR EVALUATION AND MANAGEMENT GUIDELINES.—The objectives for modified evaluation and management documentation guidelines developed by the Secretary shall be to—

(1) identify clinically relevant documentation needed to code accurately and assess coding levels accurately;

Non-Code Provisions

(2) decrease the level of non-clinically pertinent and burdensome documentation time and content in the physician's medical record;

(3) increase accuracy by reviewers; and

(4) educate both physicians and reviewers.

(d) STUDY OF SIMPLER, ALTERNATIVE SYSTEMS OF DOCUMENTATION FOR PHYSICIAN CLAIMS.—

(1) STUDY.—The Secretary shall carry out a study of the matters described in paragraph (2).

(2) MATTERS DESCRIBED.—The matters referred to in paragraph (1) are—

(A) the development of a simpler, alternative system of requirements for documentation accompanying claims for evaluation and management physician services for which payment is made under title XVIII of the Social Security Act; and

(B) consideration of systems other than current coding and documentation requirements for payment for such physician services.

(3) CONSULTATION WITH PRACTICING PHYSICIANS.—In designing and carrying out the study under paragraph (1), the Secretary shall consult with practicing physicians, including physicians who are part of group practices and including both generalists and specialists.

(4) APPLICATION OF HIPAA UNIFORM CODING REQUIREMENTS.—In developing an alternative system under paragraph (2), the Secretary shall consider requirements of administrative simplification under part C of title XI of the Social Security Act.

(5) REPORT TO CONGRESS.—(A) Not later than October 1, 2005, the Secretary shall submit to Congress a report on the results of the study conducted under paragraph (1).

(B) The Medicare Payment Advisory Commission shall conduct an analysis of the results of the study included in the report under subparagraph (A) and shall submit a report on such analysis to Congress.

(e) STUDY ON APPROPRIATE CODING OF CERTAIN EXTENDED OFFICE VISITS.—The Secretary shall conduct a study of the appropriateness of coding in cases of extended office visits in which there is no diagnosis made. Not later than October 1, 2005, the Secretary shall submit a report to Congress on such study and shall include recommendations on how to code appropriately for such visits in a manner that takes into account the amount of time the physician spent with the patient.

(f) DEFINITIONS.—In this section—

(1) the term "rural area" has the meaning given that term in section 1886(d)(2)(D) of the Social Security Act (42 U.S.C. 1395ww(d)(2)(D)); and

(2) the term "teaching settings" are those settings described in section 415.150 of title 42, Code of Federal Regulations.

[CCH Explanation at ¶941.]

[¶11,140] ACT SEC. 943. TREATMENT OF HOSPITALS FOR CERTAIN SERVICES UNDER MEDICARE SECONDARY PAYOR (MSP) PROVISIONS.

(a) IN GENERAL.—The Secretary shall not require a hospital (including a critical access hospital) to ask questions (or obtain information) relating to the application of section 1862(b) of the Social Security Act (relating to medicare secondary payor provisions) in the case of reference laboratory services described in subsection (b), if the Secretary does not impose such requirement in the case of such services furnished by an independent laboratory.

(b) REFERENCE LABORATORY SERVICES DESCRIBED.—Reference laboratory services described in this subsection are clinical laboratory diagnostic tests (or the interpretation of such tests, or both) furnished without a face-to-face encounter between the individual entitled to benefits under part A or enrolled under part B, or both, and the hospital involved and in which the hospital submits a claim only for such test or interpretation.

. . .

[CCH Explanation at ¶794 and 943.]

[¶ 11,150] ACT SEC. 945. EMERGENCY MEDICAL TREATMENT AND LABOR ACT (EMTALA) TECHNICAL ADVISORY GROUP.

(a) ESTABLISHMENT.—The Secretary shall establish a Technical Advisory Group (in this section referred to as the "Advisory Group") to review issues related to the Emergency Medical Treatment and Labor Act (EMTALA) and its implementation. In this section, the term "EMTALA" refers to the provisions of section 1867 of the Social Security Act (42 U.S.C. 1395dd).

(b) MEMBERSHIP.—The Advisory Group shall be composed of 19 members, including the Administrator of the Centers for Medicare & Medicaid Services and the Inspector General of the Department of Health and Human Services and of which—

(1) 4 shall be representatives of hospitals, including at least one public hospital, that have experience with the application of EMTALA and at least 2 of which have not been cited for EMTALA violations;

(2) 7 shall be practicing physicians drawn from the fields of emergency medicine, cardiology or cardiothoracic surgery, orthopedic surgery, neurosurgery, pediatrics or a pediatric subspecialty, obstetrics-gynecology, and psychiatry, with not more than one physician from any particular field;

(3) 2 shall represent patients;

(4) 2 shall be staff involved in EMTALA investigations from different regional offices of the Centers for Medicare & Medicaid Services; and

(5) 1 shall be from a State survey office involved in EMTALA investigations and 1 shall be from a peer review organization, both of whom shall be from areas other than the regions represented under paragraph (4).

In selecting members described in paragraphs (1) through (3), the Secretary shall consider qualified individuals nominated by organizations representing providers and patients.

(c) GENERAL RESPONSIBILITIES.—The Advisory Group—

(1) shall review EMTALA regulations;

(2) may provide advice and recommendations to the Secretary with respect to those regulations and their application to hospitals and physicians;

(3) shall solicit comments and recommendations from hospitals, physicians, and the public regarding the implementation of such regulations; and

(4) may disseminate information on the application of such regulations to hospitals, physicians, and the public.

(d) ADMINISTRATIVE MATTERS.—

(1) CHAIRPERSON.—The members of the Advisory Group shall elect a member to serve as chairperson of the Advisory Group for the life of the Advisory Group.

(2) MEETINGS.—The Advisory Group shall first meet at the direction of the Secretary. The Advisory Group shall then meet twice per year and at such other times as the Advisory Group may provide.

(e) TERMINATION.—The Advisory Group shall terminate 30 months after the date of its first meeting.

(f) WAIVER OF ADMINISTRATIVE LIMITATION.—The Secretary shall establish the Advisory Group notwithstanding any limitation that may apply to the number of advisory committees that may be established (within the Department of Health and Human Services or otherwise).

. . .

[CCH Explanation at ¶ 945.]

[¶ 11,160] ACT SEC. 951. FURNISHING HOSPITALS WITH INFORMATION TO COMPUTE DSH FORMULA.

Beginning not later than 1 year after the date of the enactment of this Act, the Secretary shall arrange to furnish to subsection (d) hospitals (as defined in section 1886(d)(1)(B) of the Social Security Act, 42 U.S.C. 1395ww(d)(1)(B)) the data necessary for such hospitals to compute the number of patient days used in computing the disproportionate patient percentage under such section for that hospital for the current cost reporting year. Such data shall also be furnished to other hospitals which would qualify for additional payments under part A of title XVIII of the Social Security Act on the basis of such data.

. . .

[CCH Explanation at ¶510.]

[¶11,170] ACT SEC. 953. OTHER PROVISIONS.

(a) GAO REPORTS ON THE PHYSICIAN COMPENSATION.—

(1) SUSTAINABLE GROWTH RATE AND UPDATES.—Not later than 6 months after the date of the enactment of this Act, the Comptroller General of the United States shall submit to Congress a report on the appropriateness of the updates in the conversion factor under subsection (d)(3) of section 1848 of the Social Security Act (42 U.S.C. 1395w-4), including the appropriateness of the sustainable growth rate formula under subsection (f) of such section for 2002 and succeeding years. Such report shall examine the stability and predictability of such updates and rate and alternatives for the use of such rate in the updates.

(2) PHYSICIAN COMPENSATION GENERALLY.—Not later than 12 months after the date of the enactment of this Act, the Comptroller General shall submit to Congress a report on all aspects of physician compensation for services furnished under title XVIII of the Social Security Act, and how those aspects interact and the effect on appropriate compensation for physician services. Such report shall review alternatives for the physician fee schedule under section 1848 of such title (42 U.S.C. 1395w-4).

(b) ANNUAL PUBLICATION OF LIST OF NATIONAL COVERAGE DETERMINATIONS.—The Secretary shall provide, in an appropriate annual publication available to the public, a list of national coverage determinations made under title XVIII of the Social Security Act in the previous year and information on how to get more information with respect to such determinations.

(c) GAO REPORT ON FLEXIBILITY IN APPLYING HOME HEALTH CONDITIONS OF PARTICIPATION TO PATIENTS WHO ARE NOT MEDICARE BENEFICIARIES.—Not later than 6 months after the date of the enactment of this Act, the Comptroller General of the United States shall submit to Congress a report on the implications if there were flexibility in the application of the medicare conditions of participation for home health agencies with respect to groups or types of patients who are not medicare beneficiaries. The report shall include an analysis of the potential impact of such flexible application on clinical operations and the recipients of such services and an analysis of methods for monitoring the quality of care provided to such recipients.

(d) OIG REPORT ON NOTICES RELATING TO USE OF HOSPITAL LIFETIME RESERVE DAYS.—Not later than 1 year after the date of the enactment of this Act, the Inspector General of the Department of Health and Human Services shall submit a report to Congress on—

(1) the extent to which hospitals provide notice to medicare beneficiaries in accordance with applicable requirements before they use the 60 lifetime reserve days described in section 1812(a)(1) of the Social Security Act (42 U.S.C. 1395d(a)(1)); and

(2) the appropriateness and feasibility of hospitals providing a notice to such beneficiaries before they completely exhaust such lifetime reserve days.

[CCH Explanation at ¶953.]

TITLE X—MEDICAID AND MISCELLANEOUS PROVISIONS

Subtitle A—Medicaid Provisions

[¶11,180] ACT SEC. 1001. MEDICAID DISPROPORTIONATE SHARE HOSPITAL (DSH) PAYMENTS.

. . .

(e) CLARIFICATION REGARDING NON-REGULATION OF TRANSFERS.

(1) IN GENERAL. Nothing in section 1903(w) of the Social Security Act (42 U.S.C.1396b(w)) shall be construed by the Secretary as prohibiting a State's use of funds as the non-Federal share of expenditures under title XIX of such Act where such funds are transferred from or certified by a

publicly-owned regional medical center located in another State and described in paragraph (2), so long as the Secretary determines that such use of funds is proper and in the interest of the program under title XIX.

(2) CENTER DESCRIBED.

A center described in this paragraph is a publicly-owned regional medical center that—

(A) provides level 1 trauma and burn care services;

(B) provides level 3 neonatal care services;

(C) is obligated to serve all patients, regardless of 7 State of origin;

(D) is located within a Standard Metropolitan Statistical Area (SMSA) that includes at least 3 States, including the States described in paragraph (1);

(E) serves as a tertiary care provider for patients residing within a 125 mile radius; and

(F) meets the criteria for a disproportionate share hospital under section 1923 of such Act in at least one State other than the one in which the center is located.

. . .

[CCH Explanation at ¶1201.]

[¶11,190] ACT SEC. 1003. EXTENSION OF MORATORIUM.

(a) IN GENERAL.—Section 6408(a)(3) of the Omnibus Budget Reconciliation Act of 1989, as amended by section 13642 of the Omnibus Budget Reconciliation Act of 1993 and section 4758 of the Balanced Budget Act of 1997, is amended—

(1) by striking "until December 31, 2002", and

(2) by striking "Kent Community Hospital Complex in Michigan or."

(b) EFFECTIVE DATES.—

(1) PERMANENT EXTENSION.—The amendment made by subsection (a)(1) shall take effect as if included in the amendment made by section 4758 of the Balanced Budget Act of 1997.

(2) MODIFICATION.—The amendment made by subsection (a)(2) shall take effect on the date of enactment of this Act.

[CCH Explanation at ¶1207.]

Subtitle B—Miscellaneous Provisions

[¶11,200] ACT SEC. 1011. FEDERAL REIMBURSEMENT OF EMERGENCY HEALTH SERVICES FURNISHED TO UNDOCUMENTED ALIENS.

(a) TOTAL AMOUNT AVAILABLE FOR ALLOTMENT.—

(1) IN GENERAL.—Out of any funds in the Treasury not otherwise appropriated, there are appropriated to the Secretary $250,000,000 for each of fiscal years 2005 through 2008 for the purpose of making allotments under this section for payments to eligible providers in States described in paragraph (1) or (2) of subsection (b).

(2) AVAILABILITY.—Funds appropriated under paragraph (1) shall remain available until expended.

(b) STATE ALLOTMENTS.—

(1) BASED ON PERCENTAGE OF UNDOCUMENTED ALIENS.—

(A) IN GENERAL.—Out of the amount appropriated under subsection (a) for a fiscal year, the Secretary shall use $167,000,000 of such amount to make allotments for such fiscal year in accordance with subparagraph (B).

(B) FORMULA.—The amount of the allotment for payments to eligible providers in each State for a fiscal year shall be equal to the product of—

(i) the total amount available for allotments under this paragraph for the fiscal year; and

(ii) the percentage of undocumented aliens residing in the State as compared to the total number of such aliens residing in all States, as determined by the Statistics Division of the Immigration and Naturalization Service, as of January 2003, based on the 2000 decennial census.

(2) BASED ON NUMBER OF UNDOCUMENTED ALIEN APPREHENSION STATES.—

(A) IN GENERAL.—Out of the amount appropriated under subsection (a) for a fiscal year, the Secretary shall use $83,000,000 of such amount to make allotments, in addition to amounts allotted under paragraph (1), for such fiscal year for each of the 6 States with the highest number of undocumented alien apprehensions for such fiscal year.

(B) DETERMINATION OF ALLOTMENTS.—The amount of the allotment for each State described in subparagraph (A) for a fiscal year shall be equal to the product of—

(i) the total amount available for allotments under this paragraph for the fiscal year; and

(ii) the percentage of undocumented alien apprehensions in the State in that fiscal year as compared to the total of such apprehensions for all such States for the preceding fiscal year.

(C) DATA.—For purposes of this paragraph, the highest number of undocumented alien apprehensions for a fiscal year shall be based on the apprehension rates for the 4-consecutive-quarter period ending before the beginning of the fiscal year for which information is available for undocumented aliens in such States, as reported by the Department of Homeland Security.

(c) USE OF FUNDS.—

(1) AUTHORITY TO MAKE PAYMENTS.—From the allotments made for a State under subsection (b) for a fiscal year, the Secretary shall pay the amount (subject to the total amount available from such allotments) determined under paragraph (2) directly to eligible providers located in the State for the provision of eligible services to aliens described in paragraph (5) to the extent that the eligible provider was not otherwise reimbursed (through insurance or otherwise) for such services during that fiscal year.

(2) DETERMINATION OF PAYMENT AMOUNTS.—

(A) IN GENERAL.—Subject to subparagraph (B), the payment amount determined under this paragraph shall be an amount determined by the Secretary that is equal to the lesser of—

(i) the amount that the provider demonstrates was incurred for the provision of such services; or

(ii) amounts determined under a methodology established by the Secretary for purposes of this subsection.

(B) PRO-RATA REDUCTION.—If the amount of funds allotted to a State under subsection (b) for a fiscal year is insufficient to ensure that each eligible provider in that State receives the amount of payment calculated under subparagraph (A), the Secretary shall reduce that amount of payment with respect to each eligible provider to ensure that the entire amount allotted to the State for that fiscal year is paid to such eligible providers.

(3) METHODOLOGY.—In establishing a methodology under paragraph (2)(A)(ii), the Secretary—

(A) may establish different methodologies for types of eligible providers;

(B) may base payments for hospital services on estimated hospital charges, adjusted to estimated cost, through the application of hospital-specific cost-to-charge ratios;

(C) shall provide for the election by a hospital to receive either payments to the hospital for—

(i) hospital and physician services; or

(ii) hospital services and for a portion of the on-call payments made by the hospital to physicians; and

(D) shall make quarterly payments under this section to eligible providers.

If a hospital makes the election under subparagraph (C)(i), the hospital shall pass on payments for services of a physician to the physician and may not charge any administrative or other fee with respect to such payments.

(4) LIMITATION ON USE OF FUNDS.—Payments made to eligible providers in a State from allotments made under subsection (b) for a fiscal year may only be used for costs incurred in providing eligible services to aliens described in paragraph (5).

(5) ALIENS DESCRIBED.—For purposes of paragraphs (1) and (2), aliens described in this paragraph are any of the following:

(A) Undocumented aliens.

(B) Aliens who have been paroled into the United States at a United States port of entry for the purpose of receiving eligible services.

(C) Mexican citizens permitted to enter the United States for not more than 72 hours under the authority of a biometric machine readable border crossing identification card (also referred to as a "laser visa") issued in accordance with the requirements of regulations prescribed under section 101(a)(6) of the Immigration and Nationality Act (8 U.S.C. 1101(a)(6)).

(d) APPLICATIONS; ADVANCE PAYMENTS.—

(1) DEADLINE FOR ESTABLISHMENT OF APPLICATION PROCESS.—

(A) IN GENERAL.—Not later than September 1, 2004, the Secretary shall establish a process under which eligible providers located in a State may request payments under subsection (c).

(B) INCLUSION OF MEASURES TO COMBAT FRAUD AND ABUSE.—The Secretary shall include in the process established under subparagraph (A) measures to ensure that inappropriate, excessive, or fraudulent payments are not made from the allotments determined under subsection (b), including certification by the eligible provider of the veracity of the payment request.

(2) ADVANCE PAYMENT; RETROSPECTIVE ADJUSTMENT.—The process established under paragraph (1) may provide for making payments under this section for each quarter of a fiscal year on the basis of advance estimates of expenditures submitted by applicants for such payments and such other investigation as the Secretary may find necessary, and for making reductions or increases in the payments as necessary to adjust for any overpayment or underpayment for prior quarters of such fiscal year.

(e) DEFINITIONS.—In this section:

(1) ELIGIBLE PROVIDER.—The term "eligible provider" means a hospital, physician, or provider of ambulance services (including an Indian Health Service facility whether operated by the Indian Health Service or by an Indian tribe or tribal organization).

(2) ELIGIBLE SERVICES.—The term "eligible services" means health care services required by the application of section 1867 of the Social Security Act (42 U.S.C. 1395dd), and related hospital inpatient and outpatient services and ambulance services (as defined by the Secretary).

(3) HOSPITAL.—The term "hospital" has the meaning given such term in section 1861(e) of the Social Security Act (42 U.S.C. 1395x(e)), except that such term shall include a critical access hospital (as defined in section 1861(mm)(1) of such Act (42 U.S.C. 1395x(mm)(1)).

(4) PHYSICIAN.—The term "physician" has the meaning given that term in section 1861(r) of the Social Security Act (42 U.S.C. 1395x(r)).

(5) INDIAN TRIBE; TRIBAL ORGANIZATION.—The terms "Indian tribe" and "tribal organization" have the meanings given such terms in section 4 of the Indian Health Care Improvement Act (25 U.S.C. 1603).

(6) STATE.—The term "State" means the 50 States and the District of Columbia.

[CCH Explanation at ¶1208.]

[¶11,210] ACT SEC. 1012. COMMISSION ON SYSTEMIC INTEROPERABILITY.

(a) ESTABLISHMENT.—The Secretary shall establish a commission to be known as the "Commission on Systemic Interoperability" (in this section referred to as the "Commission").

(b) DUTIES.—

(1) IN GENERAL.—The Commission shall develop a comprehensive strategy for the adoption and implementation of health care information technology standards, that includes a timeline and prioritization for such adoption and implementation.

(2) CONSIDERATIONS.—In developing the comprehensive health care information technology strategy under paragraph (1), the Commission shall consider—

(A) the costs and benefits of the standards, both financial impact and quality improvement;

(B) the current demand on industry resources to implement this Act and other electronic standards, including HIPAA standards; and

(C) the most cost-effective and efficient means for industry to implement the standards.

(3) NONINTERFERENCE.—In carrying out this section, the Commission shall not interfere with any standards development of adoption processes underway in the private or public sector and shall not replicate activities related to such standards or the national health information infrastructure underway within the Department of Health and Human Services.

(4) REPORT.—Not later than October 31, 2005, the Commission shall submit to the Secretary and to Congress a report describing the strategy developed under paragraph (1), including an analysis of the matters considered under paragraph (2).

(c) MEMBERSHIP.—

(1) NUMBER AND APPOINTMENT.—The Commission shall be composed of 11 members appointed as follows:

(A) The President shall appoint 3 members, one of whom the President shall designate as Chairperson.

(B) The Majority Leader of the Senate shall appoint 2 members.

(C) The Minority Leader of the Senate shall appoint 2 members.

(D) The Speaker of the House of Representatives shall appoint 2 members.

(E) The Minority Leader of the House of Representatives shall appoint 2 members.

(2) QUALIFICATIONS.—The membership of the Commission shall include individuals with national recognition for their expertise in health finance and economics, health plans and integrated delivery systems, reimbursement of health facilities, practicing physicians, practicing pharmacists, and other providers of health services, health care technology and information systems, and other related fields, who provide a mix of different professionals, broad geographic representation, and a balance between urban and rural representatives.

(d) TERMS.—Each member shall be appointed for the life of the Commission.

(e) COMPENSATION.—

(1) RATES OF PAY.—Members shall each be paid at a rate not to exceed the daily equivalent of the rate of basic pay for level IV of the Executive Schedule for each day (including travel time) during which they are engaged in the actual performance of duties vested in the Commission.

(2) PROHIBITION OF COMPENSATION OF FEDERAL EMPLOYEES.—Members of the Commission who are full-time officers or employees of the United States or Members of Congress may not receive additional pay, allowances, or benefits by reason of their service on the Commission.

(3) TRAVEL EXPENSES.—Each member shall receive travel expenses, including per diem in lieu of subsistence, in accordance with applicable provisions under subchapter I of chapter 57 of title 5, United States Code.

(f) QUORUM.—A majority of the members of the Commission shall constitute a quorum but a lesser number may hold hearings.

(g) DIRECTOR AND STAFF OF COMMISSION; EXPERTS AND CONSULTANTS.—

(1) DIRECTOR.—The Commission shall have a Director who shall be appointed by the Chairperson. The Director shall be paid at a rate not to exceed the rate of basic pay for level IV of the Executive Schedule.

(2) STAFF.—With the approval of the Commission, the Director may appoint and fix the pay of such additional personnel as the Director considers appropriate.

(3) APPLICABILITY OF CERTAIN CIVIL SERVICE LAWS.—The Director and staff of the Commission may be appointed without regard to the provisions of title 5, United States Code, governing appointments in the competitive service, and may be paid without regard to the provisions of chapter 51 and subchapter III of chapter 53 of that title relating to classification and General Schedule pay rates, except that an individual so appointed may not receive pay in excess of level IV of the Executive Schedule.

(4) EXPERTS AND CONSULTANTS.—With the approval of the Commission, the Director may procure temporary and intermittent services under section 3109(b) of title 5, United States Code.

(5) STAFF OF FEDERAL AGENCIES.—Upon request of the Chairperson, the head of any Federal department or agency may detail, on a reimbursable basis, any of the personnel of that department or agency to the Commission to assist it in carrying out its duties under this Act.

(h) POWERS OF COMMISSION.—

(1) HEARINGS AND SESSIONS.—The Commission may, for the purpose of carrying out this Act, hold hearings, sit and act at times and places, take testimony, and receive evidence as the Commission considers appropriate.

(2) POWERS OF MEMBERS AND AGENTS.—Any member or agent of the Commission may, if authorized by the Commission, take any action which the Commission is authorized to take by this section.

(3) OBTAINING OFFICIAL DATA.—The Commission may secure directly from any department or agency of the United States information necessary to enable it to carry out this Act. Upon request of the Chairperson of the Commission, the head of that department or agency shall furnish that information to the Commission.

(4) GIFTS, BEQUESTS, AND DEVISES.—The Commission may accept, use, and dispose of gifts, bequests, or devises of services or property, both real and personal, for the purpose of aiding or facilitating the work of the Commission. Gifts, bequests, or devises of money and proceeds from sales of other property received as gifts, bequests, or devises shall be deposited in the Treasury and shall be available for disbursement upon order of the Commission. For purposes of Federal income, estate, and gift taxes, property accepted under this subsection shall be considered as a gift, bequest, or devise to the United States.

(5) MAILS.—The Commission may use the United States mails in the same manner and under the same conditions as other departments and agencies of the United States.

(6) ADMINISTRATIVE SUPPORT SERVICES.—Upon the request of the Commission, the Administrator of General Services shall provide to the Commission, on a reimbursable basis, the administrative support services necessary for the Commission to carry out its responsibilities under this Act.

(7) CONTRACT AUTHORITY.—The Commission may enter into contracts or make other arrangements, as may be necessary for the conduct of the work of the Commission (without regard to section 3709 of the Revised Statutes (41 U.S.C. 5)).

(i) TERMINATION.—The Commission shall terminate on 30 days after submitting its report pursuant to subsection (b)(3).

(j) AUTHORIZATION OF APPROPRIATIONS.—There is authorized to be appropriated such sums as may be necessary to carry out this section.

[CCH Explanation at ¶1209.]

[¶ 11,220] ACT SEC. 1013. RESEARCH ON OUTCOMES OF HEALTH CARE ITEMS AND SERVICES.

(a) RESEARCH, DEMONSTRATIONS, AND EVALUATIONS.—

(1) IMPROVEMENT OF EFFECTIVENESS AND EFFICIENCY.—

(A) IN GENERAL.—To improve the quality, effectiveness, and efficiency of health care delivered pursuant to the programs established under titles XVIII, XIX, and XXI of the Social Security Act, the Secretary acting through the Director of the Agency for Healthcare Research and Quality (in this section referred to as the "Director"), shall conduct and support research to meet the priorities and requests for scientific evidence and information identified by such programs with respect to—

(i) the outcomes, comparative clinical effectiveness, and appropriateness of health care items and services (including prescription drugs); and

(ii) strategies for improving the efficiency and effectiveness of such programs, including the ways in which such items and services are organized, managed, and delivered under such programs.

(B) SPECIFICATION.—To respond to priorities and information requests in subparagraph (A), the Secretary may conduct or support, by grant, contract, or interagency agreement, research, demonstrations, evaluations, technology assessments, or other activities, including the provision of technical assistance, scientific expertise, or methodological assistance.

(2) PRIORITIES.—

(A) IN GENERAL.—The Secretary shall establish a process to develop priorities that will guide the research, demonstrations, and evaluation activities undertaken pursuant to this section.

(B) INITIAL LIST.—Not later than 6 months after the date of the enactment of this Act, the Secretary shall establish an initial list of priorities for research related to health care items and services (including prescription drugs).

(C) PROCESS.—In carrying out subparagraph (A), the Secretary—

(i) shall ensure that there is broad and ongoing consultation with relevant stakeholders in identifying the highest priorities for research, demonstrations, and evaluations to support and improve the programs established under titles XVIII, XIX, and XXI of the Social Security Act;

(ii) may include health care items and services which impose a high cost on such programs, as well as those which may be underutilized or overutilized and which may significantly improve the prevention, treatment, or cure of diseases and conditions (including chronic conditions) which impose high direct or indirect costs on patients or society; and

(iii) shall ensure that the research and activities undertaken pursuant to this section are responsive to the specified priorities and are conducted in a timely manner.

(3) EVALUATION AND SYNTHESIS OF SCIENTIFIC EVIDENCE.—

(A) IN GENERAL.—The Secretary shall—

(i) evaluate and synthesize available scientific evidence related to health care items and services (including prescription drugs) identified as priorities in accordance with paragraph (2) with respect to the comparative clinical effectiveness, outcomes, appropriateness, and provision of such items and services (including prescription drugs);

(ii) identify issues for which existing scientific evidence is insufficient with respect to such health care items and services (including prescription drugs);

(iii) disseminate to prescription drug plans and MA-PD plans under part D of title XVIII of the Social Security Act, other health plans, and the public the findings made under clauses (i) and (ii); and

(iv) work in voluntary collaboration with public and private sector entities to facilitate the development of new scientific knowledge regarding health care items and services (including prescription drugs).

(B) INITIAL RESEARCH.—The Secretary shall complete the evaluation and synthesis of the initial research required by the priority list developed under paragraph (2)(B) not later than 18 months after the development of such list.

(C) DISSEMINATION.—

(i) IN GENERAL.—To enhance patient safety and the quality of health care, the Secretary shall make available and disseminate in appropriate formats to prescription drugs plans under part D, and MA-PD plans under part C, of title XVIII of the Social Security Act, other health plans, and the public the evaluations and syntheses prepared pursuant to subparagraph (A) and the findings of research conducted pursuant to paragraph (1). In carrying out this clause the Secretary, in order to facilitate the availability of such evaluations and syntheses or findings at every decision point in the health care system, shall—

(I) present such evaluations and syntheses or findings in a form that is easily understood by the individuals receiving health care items and services (including prescription drugs) under such plans and periodically assess that the requirements of this subclause have been met; and

(II) provide such evaluations and syntheses or findings and other relevant information through easily accessible and searchable electronic mechanisms, and in hard copy formats as appropriate.

(ii) RULE OF CONSTRUCTION.—Nothing in this section shall be construed as—

(I) affecting the authority of the Secretary or the Commissioner of Food and Drugs under the Federal Food, Drug, and Cosmetic Act or the Public Health Service Act; or

(II) conferring any authority referred to in subclause (I) to the Director.

(D) ACCOUNTABILITY.—In carrying out this paragraph, the Secretary shall implement activities in a manner that—

(i) makes publicly available all scientific evidence relied upon and the methodologies employed, provided such evidence and method are not protected from public disclosure by section 1905 of title 18, United States Code, or other applicable law so that the results of the research, analyses, or syntheses can be evaluated or replicated; and

(ii) ensures that any information needs and unresolved issues identified in subparagraph (A)(ii) are taken into account in priority-setting for future research conducted by the Secretary.

(4) CONFIDENTIALITY.—

(A) IN GENERAL.—In making use of administrative, clinical, and program data and information developed or collected with respect to the programs established under titles XVIII, XIX, and XXI of the Social Security Act, for purposes of carrying out the requirements of this section or the activities authorized under title IX of the Public Health Service Act (42 U.S.C. 299 et seq.), such data and information shall be protected in accordance with the confidentiality requirements of title IX of the Public Health Service Act.

(B) RULE OF CONSTRUCTION.—Nothing in this section shall be construed to require or permit the disclosure of data provided to the Secretary that is otherwise protected from disclosure under the Federal Food, Drug, and Cosmetic Act, section 1905 of title 18, United States Code, or other applicable law.

(5) EVALUATIONS.—The Secretary shall conduct and support evaluations of the activities carried out under this section to determine the extent to which such activities have had an effect on outcomes and utilization of health care items and services.

(6) IMPROVING INFORMATION AVAILABLE TO HEALTH CARE PROVIDERS, PATIENTS, AND POLICYMAKERS.—Not later than 18 months after the date of enactment of this Act, the Secretary shall identify options that could be undertaken in voluntary collaboration with private and public entities (as appropriate) for the—

(A) provision of more timely information through the programs established under titles XVIII, XIX, and XXI of the Social Security Act, regarding the outcomes and quality of patient care, including clinical and patient-reported outcomes, especially with respect to interventions and conditions for which clinical trials would not be feasible or raise ethical concerns that are difficult to address;

(B) acceleration of the adoption of innovation and quality improvement under such programs; and

(C) development of management tools for the programs established under titles XIX and XXI of the Social Security Act, and with respect to the programs established under such titles, assess the feasibility of using administrative or claims data, to—

(i) improve oversight by State officials;

(ii) support Federal and State initiatives to improve the quality, safety, and efficiency of services provided under such programs; and

(iii) provide a basis for estimating the fiscal and coverage impact of Federal or State program and policy changes.

(b) RECOMMENDATIONS.—

(1) DISCLAIMER.—In carrying out this section, the Director shall—

(A) not mandate national standards of clinical practice or quality health care standards; and

(B) include in any recommendations resulting from projects funded and published by the Director, a corresponding reference to the prohibition described in subparagraph (A).

(2) REQUIREMENT FOR IMPLEMENTATION.—Research, evaluation, and communication activities performed pursuant to this section shall reflect the principle that clinicians and patients should have the best available evidence upon which to make choices in health care items and services, in providers, and in health care delivery systems, recognizing that patient subpopulations and patient and physician preferences may vary.

(3) RULE OF CONSTRUCTION.—Nothing in this section shall be construed to provide the Director with authority to mandate a national standard or require a specific approach to quality measurement and reporting.

(c) RESEARCH WITH RESPECT TO DISSEMINATION.—The Secretary, acting through the Director, may conduct or support research with respect to improving methods of disseminating information in accordance with subsection (a)(3)(C).

(d) LIMITATION ON CMS.—The Administrator of the Centers for Medicare & Medicaid Services may not use data obtained in accordance with this section to withhold coverage of a prescription drug.

(e) AUTHORIZATION OF APPROPRIATIONS.—There is authorized to be appropriated to carry out this section, $50,000,000 for fiscal year 2004, and such sums as may be necessary for each fiscal year thereafter.

[CCH Explanation at ¶1210.]

[¶11,230] ACT SEC. 1014. HEALTH CARE THAT WORKS FOR ALL AMERICANS: CITIZENS HEALTH CARE WORKING GROUP.

(a) FINDINGS.—Congress finds the following:

(1) In order to improve the health care system, the American public must engage in an informed national public debate to make choices about the services they want covered, what health care coverage they want, and how they are willing to pay for coverage.

(2) More than a trillion dollars annually is spent on the health care system, yet—

(A) 41,000,000 Americans are uninsured;

(B) insured individuals do not always have access to essential, effective services to improve and maintain their health; and

(C) employers, who cover over 170,000,000 Americans, find providing coverage increasingly difficult because of rising costs and double digit premium increases.

(3) Despite increases in medical care spending that are greater than the rate of inflation, population growth, and Gross Domestic Product growth, there has not been a commensurate improvement in our health status as a nation.

(4) Health care costs for even just 1 member of a family can be catastrophic, resulting in medical bills potentially harming the economic stability of the entire family.

(5) Common life occurrences can jeopardize the ability of a family to retain private coverage or jeopardize access to public coverage.

(6) Innovations in health care access, coverage, and quality of care, including the use of technology, have often come from States, local communities, and private sector organizations, but more creative policies could tap this potential.

(7) Despite our Nation's wealth, the health care system does not provide coverage to all Americans who want it.

(b) PURPOSES.—The purposes of this section are—

(1) to provide for a nationwide public debate about improving the health care system to provide every American with the ability to obtain quality, affordable health care coverage; and

(2) to provide for a vote by Congress on the recommendations that result from the debate.

(c) ESTABLISHMENT.—The Secretary, acting through the Agency for Healthcare Research and Quality, shall establish an entity to be known as the Citizens' Health Care Working Group (referred to in this section as the "Working Group").

(d) MEMBERSHIP.—

(1) NUMBER AND APPOINTMENT.—The Working Group shall be composed of 15 members. One member shall be the Secretary. The Comptroller General of the United States shall appoint 14 members.

(2) QUALIFICATIONS.—

(A) IN GENERAL.—The membership of the Working Group shall include—

(i) consumers of health services that represent those individuals who have not had insurance within 2 years of appointment, that have had chronic illnesses, including mental illness, are disabled, and those who receive insurance coverage through medicare and medicaid; and

(ii) individuals with expertise in financing and paying for benefits and access to care, business and labor perspectives, and providers of health care.

The membership shall reflect a broad geographic representation and a balance between urban and rural representatives.

(B) PROHIBITED APPOINTMENTS.—Members of the Working Group shall not include Members of Congress or other elected government officials (Federal, State, or local). Individuals appointed to the Working Group shall not be paid employees or representatives of associations or advocacy organizations involved in the health care system.

(e) PERIOD OF APPOINTMENT.—Members of the Working Group shall be appointed for a life of the Working Group. Any vacancies shall not affect the power and duties of the Working Group but shall be filled in the same manner as the original appointment.

(f) DESIGNATION OF THE CHAIRPERSON.—Not later than 15 days after the date on which all members of the Working Group have been appointed under subsection (d)(1), the Comptroller General shall designate the chairperson of the Working Group.

(g) SUBCOMMITTEES.—The Working Group may establish subcommittees if doing so increases the efficiency of the Working Group in completing its tasks.

(h) DUTIES.—

(1) HEARINGS.—Not later than 90 days after the date of the designation of the chairperson under subsection (f), the Working Group shall hold hearings to examine—

(A) the capacity of the public and private health care systems to expand coverage options;

(B) the cost of health care and the effectiveness of care provided at all stages of disease;

(C) innovative State strategies used to expand health care coverage and lower health care costs;

(D) local community solutions to accessing health care coverage;

(E) efforts to enroll individuals currently eligible for public or private health care coverage;

(F) the role of evidence-based medical practices that can be documented as restoring, maintaining, or improving a patient's health, and the use of technology in supporting providers in improving quality of care and lowering costs; and

(G) strategies to assist purchasers of health care, including consumers, to become more aware of the impact of costs, and to lower the costs of health care.

(2) ADDITIONAL HEARINGS.—The Working Group may hold additional hearings on subjects other than those listed in paragraph (1) so long as such hearings are determined to be necessary by the Working Group in carrying out the purposes of this section. Such additional hearings do not have to be completed within the time period specified in paragraph (1) but shall not delay the other activities of the Working Group under this section.

(3) THE HEALTH REPORT TO THE AMERICAN PEOPLE.—Not later than 90 days after the hearings described in paragraphs (1) and (2) are completed, the Working Group shall prepare and make available to health care consumers through the Internet and other appropriate public channels, a report to be entitled, "The Health Report to the American People". Such report shall be understandable to the general public and include—

(A) a summary of—

(i) health care and related services that may be used by individuals throughout their life span;

(ii) the cost of health care services and their medical effectiveness in providing better quality of care for different age groups;

(iii) the source of coverage and payment, including reimbursement, for health care services;

(iv) the reasons people are uninsured or underinsured and the cost to taxpayers, purchasers of health services, and communities when Americans are uninsured or underinsured;

(v) the impact on health care outcomes and costs when individuals are treated in all stages of disease;

(vi) health care cost containment strategies; and

(vii) information on health care needs that need to be addressed;

(B) examples of community strategies to provide health care coverage or access;

(C) information on geographic-specific issues relating to health care;

(D) information concerning the cost of care in different settings, including institutional-based care and home and community-based care;

(E) a summary of ways to finance health care coverage; and

(F) the role of technology in providing future health care including ways to support the information needs of patients and providers.

(4) COMMUNITY MEETINGS.—

(A) IN GENERAL.—Not later than 1 year after the date of enactment of this Act, the Working Group shall initiate health care community meetings throughout the United States (in this paragraph referred to as "community meetings"). Such community meetings may be geographically or regionally based and shall be completed within 180 days after the initiation of the first meeting.

(B) NUMBER OF MEETINGS.—The Working Group shall hold a sufficient number of community meetings in order to receive information that reflects—

(i) the geographic differences throughout the United States;

(ii) diverse populations; and

(iii) a balance among urban and rural populations.

(C) MEETING REQUIREMENTS.—

(i) FACILITATOR.—A State health officer may be the facilitator at the community meetings.

(ii) ATTENDANCE.—At least 1 member of the Working Group shall attend and serve as chair of each community meeting. Other members may participate through interactive technology.

(iii) TOPICS.—The community meetings shall, at a minimum, address the following questions:

(I) What health care benefits and services should be provided?

(II) How does the American public want health care delivered?

(III) How should health care coverage be financed?

(IV) What trade-offs are the American public willing to make in either benefits or financing to ensure access to affordable, high quality health care coverage and services?

(iv) INTERACTIVE TECHNOLOGY.—The Working Group may encourage public participation in community meetings through interactive technology and other means as determined appropriate by the Working Group.

(D) INTERIM REQUIREMENTS.—Not later than 180 days after the date of completion of the community meetings, the Working Group shall prepare and make available to the public through the Internet and other appropriate public channels, an interim set of recommendations on health care coverage and ways to improve and strengthen the health care system based on the information and preferences expressed at the community meetings. There shall be a 90-day public comment period on such recommendations.

(i) RECOMMENDATIONS.—Not later than 120 days after the expiration of the public comment period described in subsection (h)(4)(D), the Working Group shall submit to Congress and the President a final set of recommendations.

(j) ADMINISTRATION.—

(1) EXECUTIVE DIRECTOR.—There shall be an Executive Director of the Working Group who shall be appointed by the chairperson of the Working Group in consultation with the members of the Working Group.

(2) COMPENSATION.—While serving on the business of the Working Group (including travel time), a member of the Working Group shall be entitled to compensation at the per diem equivalent of the rate provided for level IV of the Executive Schedule under section 5315 of title 5, United States Code, and while so serving away from home and the member's regular place of business, a member may be allowed travel expenses, as authorized by the chairperson of the Working Group. For purposes of pay and employment benefits, rights, and privileges, all personnel of the Working Group shall be treated as if they were employees of the Senate.

(3) INFORMATION FROM FEDERAL AGENCIES.—The Working Group may secure directly from any Federal department or agency such information as the Working Group considers necessary to carry out this section. Upon request of the Working Group, the head of such department or agency shall furnish such information.

(4) POSTAL SERVICES.—The Working Group may use the United States mails in the same manner and under the same conditions as other departments and agencies of the Federal Government.

(k) DETAIL.—Not more than 10 Federal Government employees employed by the Department of Labor and 10 Federal Government employees employed by the Department of Health and Human Services may be detailed to the Working Group under this section without further reimbursement. Any detail of an employee shall be without interruption or loss of civil service status or privilege.

(l) TEMPORARY AND INTERMITTENT SERVICES.—The chairperson of the Working Group may procure temporary and intermittent services under section 3109(b) of title 5, United States Code, at rates for individuals which do not exceed the daily equivalent of the annual rate of basic pay prescribed for level V of the Executive Schedule under section 5316 of such title.

(m) ANNUAL REPORT.—Not later than 1 year after the date of enactment of this Act, and annually thereafter during the existence of the Working Group, the Working Group shall report to Congress and make public a detailed description of the expenditures of the Working Group used to carry out its duties under this section.

(n) SUNSET OF WORKING GROUP.—The Working Group shall terminate on the date that is 2 years after the date on which all the members of the Working Group have been appointed under subsection (d)(1).

(o) ADMINISTRATION REVIEW AND COMMENTS.—Not later than 45 days after receiving the final recommendations of the Working Group under subsection (i), the President shall submit a report to Congress which shall contain—

(1) additional views and comments on such recommendations; and

(2) recommendations for such legislation and administrative actions as the President considers appropriate.

(p) REQUIRED CONGRESSIONAL ACTION.—Not later than 45 days after receiving the report submitted by the President under subsection (o), each committee of jurisdiction of Congress, the Committee on Finance of the Senate, the Committee on Health, Education, Labor, and Pensions of the Senate, the Committee on Ways and Means of the House of Representatives, the Committee on Energy and Commerce of the House of Representatives, Committee on Education and the Workforce of the House of Representatives, shall hold at least 1 hearing on such report and on the final recommendations of the Working Group submitted under subsection (i).

(q) AUTHORIZATION OF APPROPRIATIONS.—

(1) IN GENERAL.—There are authorized to be appropriated to carry out this section, other than subsection (h)(3), $3,000,000 for each of fiscal years 2005 and 2006.

(2) HEALTH REPORT TO THE AMERICAN PEOPLE.—There are authorized to be appropriated for the preparation and dissemination of the Health Report to the American People described in subsection (h)(3), such sums as may be necessary for the fiscal year in which the report is required to be submitted.

[CCH Explanation at ¶1211.]

[¶11,240] ACT SEC. 1015. FUNDING START-UP ADMINISTRATIVE COSTS FOR MEDICARE REFORM.

(a) IN GENERAL.—There are appropriated to carry out this Act (including the amendments made by this Act), to be transferred from the Federal Hospital Insurance Trust Fund and the Federal Supplementary Medical Insurance Trust Fund—

(1) not to exceed $1,000,000,000 for the Centers for Medicare & Medicaid Services; and

(2) not to exceed $500,000,000 for the Social Security Administration.

(b) AVAILABILITY.—Amounts provided under subsection (a) shall remain available until September 30, 2005.

(c) APPLICATION.—From amounts provided under subsection (a)(2), the Social Security Administration may reimburse the Internal Revenue Service for expenses in carrying out this Act (and the amendments made by this Act).

(d) TRANSFER.—The President may transfer amounts provided under subsection (a) between the Centers for Medicare & Medicaid Services and the Social Security Administration. Notice of such transfers shall be transmitted within 15 days to the authorizing committees of the House of Representatives and of the Senate.

. . .

[CCH Explanation at ¶1212.]

TITLE XI—ACCESS TO AFFORDABLE PHARMACEUTICALS

Subtitle A—Access to Affordable Pharmaceuticals

[¶ 11,250] ACT SEC. 1101. 30-MONTH STAY-OF-EFFECTIVENESS PERIOD.

(a) ABBREVIATED NEW DRUG APPLICATIONS.—Section 505(j) of the Federal Food, Drug, and Cosmetic Act (21 U.S.C. 355(j)) is amended—

(1) in paragraph (2)—

(A) by striking subparagraph (B) and inserting the following:

(B) NOTICE OF OPINION THAT PATENT IS INVALID OR WILL NOT BE INFRINGED.—

(I) AGREEMENT TO GIVE NOTICE.—An applicant that makes a certification described in subparagraph (A)(vii)(IV) shall include in the application a statement that the applicant will give notice as required by this subparagraph.

(II) TIMING OF NOTICE.—An applicant that makes a certification described in subparagraph (A)(vii)(IV) shall give notice as required under this subparagraph—

(I) if the certification is in the application, not later than 20 days after the date of the postmark on the notice with which the Secretary informs the applicant that the application has been filed; or

(II) if the certification is in an amendment or supplement to the application, at the time at which the applicant submits the amendment or supplement, regardless of whether the applicant has already given notice with respect to another such certification contained in the application or in an amendment or supplement to the application.

(III) RECIPIENTS OF NOTICE.—An applicant required under this subparagraph to give notice shall give notice to—

(I) each owner of the patent that is the subject of the certification (or a representative of the owner designated to receive such a notice); and

(II) the holder of the approved application under subsection (b) for the drug that is claimed by the patent or a use of which is claimed by the patent (or a representative of the holder designated to receive such a notice).

(IV) CONTENTS OF NOTICE.—A notice required under this subparagraph shall—

(I) state that an application that contains data from bioavailability or bioequivalence studies has been submitted under this subsection for the drug with respect to which the certification is made to obtain approval to engage in the commercial manufacture, use, or sale of the drug before the expiration of the patent referred to in the certification; and

"(II) include a detailed statement of the factual and legal basis of the opinion of the applicant that the patent is invalid or will not be infringed."; and

(B) by adding at the end the following subparagraph:

(D)(i) An applicant may not amend or supplement an application to seek approval of a drug referring to a different listed drug from the listed drug identified in the application as submitted to the Secretary.

(ii) With respect to the drug for which an application is submitted, nothing in this subsection prohibits an applicant from amending or supplementing the application to seek approval of a different strength.

"(iii) Within 60 days after the date of the enactment of the Medicare Prescription Drug, Improvement, and Modernization Act of 2003, the Secretary shall issue guidance defining the term 'listed drug' for purposes of this subparagraph."; and

(2) in paragraph (5)—

(A) in subparagraph (B)—

(i) by striking "under the following" and inserting "by applying the following to each certification made under paragraph (2)(A)(vii)"; and

(ii) in clause (iii)—

Non-Code Provisions 567

(I) in the first sentence, by striking "unless" and all that follows and inserting "unless, before the expiration of 45 days after the date on which the notice described in paragraph (2)(B) is received, an action is brought for infringement of the patent that is the subject of the certification and for which information was submitted to the Secretary under subsection (b)(1) or (c)(2) before the date on which the application (excluding an amendment or supplement to the application), which the Secretary later determines to be substantially complete, was submitted."; and

(II) in the second sentence—

(aa) by striking subclause (I) and inserting the following:

(I) if before the expiration of such period the district court decides that the patent is invalid or not infringed (including any substantive determination that there is no cause of action for patent infringement or invalidity), the approval shall be made effective on—

(aa) the date on which the court enters judgment reflecting the decision; or

"(bb) the date of a settlement order or consent decree signed and entered by the court stating that the patent that is the subject of the certification is invalid or not infringed;";

(bb) by striking subclause (II) and inserting the following:

(II) if before the expiration of such period the district court decides that the patent has been infringed—

(aa) if the judgment of the district court is appealed, the approval shall be made effective on—

(AA) the date on which the court of appeals decides that the patent is invalid or not infringed (including any substantive determination that there is no cause of action for patent infringement or invalidity); or

(BB) the date of a settlement order or consent decree signed and entered by the court of appeals stating that the patent that is the subject of the certification is invalid or not infringed; or

"(bb) if the judgment of the district court is not appealed or is affirmed, the approval shall be made effective on the date specified by the district court in a court order under section 271(e)(4)(A) of title 35, United States Code;";

(cc) in subclause (III), by striking "on the date of such court decision." and inserting "as provided in subclause (I); or";

(dd) by inserting after subclause (III) the following:

"(IV) if before the expiration of such period the court grants a preliminary injunction prohibiting the applicant from engaging in the commercial manufacture or sale of the drug until the court decides the issues of patent validity and infringement and if the court decides that such patent has been infringed, the approval shall be made effective as provided in subclause (II)."; and

(ee) in the matter after and below subclause (IV) (as added by item (dd)), by striking "Until the expiration" and all that follows;

(B) by redesignating subparagraphs (C) and (D) as subparagraphs (E) and (F), respectively; and

(C) by inserting after subparagraph (B) the following:

(C) CIVIL ACTION TO OBTAIN PATENT CERTAINTY.—

(i) **Declaratory judgment absent infringement action.**—

(I) IN GENERAL.—No action may be brought under section 2201 of title 28, United States Code, by an applicant under paragraph (2) for a declaratory judgment with respect to a patent which is the subject of the certification referred to in subparagraph (B)(iii) unless—

(aa) the forty-five day period referred to in such subparagraph has expired;

(bb) neither the owner of such patent nor the holder of the approved application under subsection (b) for the drug that is claimed by the patent or a use of which is claimed by the patent brought a civil action against the applicant for infringement of the patent before the expiration of such period; and

(cc) in any case in which the notice provided under paragraph (2)(B) relates to noninfringement, the notice was accompanied by a document described in subclause (III).

(II) **Filing of civil action.**—If the conditions described in items (aa), (bb), and as applicable, (cc) of subclause (I) have been met, the applicant referred to in such subclause may, in accordance with section 2201 of title 28, United States Code, bring a civil action under such section against the owner or holder referred to in such subclause (but not against any owner or holder that has brought such a civil action against the applicant, unless that civil action was dismissed without prejudice) for a declaratory judgment that the patent is invalid or will not be infringed by the drug for which the applicant seeks approval, except that such civil action may be brought for a declaratory judgment that the patent will not be infringed only in a case in which the condition described in subclause (I)(cc) is applicable. A civil action referred to in this subclause shall be brought in the judicial district where the defendant has its principal place of business or a regular and established place of business.

(III) **Offer of confidential access to application.**—For purposes of subclause (I)(cc), the document described in this subclause is a document providing an offer of confidential access to the application that is in the custody of the applicant under paragraph (2) for the purpose of determining whether an action referred to in subparagraph (B)(iii) should be brought. The document providing the offer of confidential access shall contain such restrictions as to persons entitled to access, and on the use and disposition of any information accessed, as would apply had a protective order been entered for the purpose of protecting trade secrets and other confidential business information. A request for access to an application under an offer of confidential access shall be considered acceptance of the offer of confidential access with the restrictions as to persons entitled to access, and on the use and disposition of any information accessed, contained in the offer of confidential access, and those restrictions and other terms of the offer of confidential access shall be considered terms of an enforceable contract. Any person provided an offer of confidential access shall review the application for the sole and limited purpose of evaluating possible infringement of the patent that is the subject of the certification under paragraph (2)(A)(vii)(IV) and for no other purpose, and may not disclose information of no relevance to any issue of patent infringement to any person other than a person provided an offer of confidential access. Further, the application may be redacted by the applicant to remove any information of no relevance to any issue of patent infringement.

(ii) COUNTERCLAIM TO INFRINGEMENT ACTION.—

(I) IN GENERAL.—If an owner of the patent or the holder of the approved application under subsection (b) for the drug that is claimed by the patent or a use of which is claimed by the patent brings a patent infringement action against the applicant, the applicant may assert a counterclaim seeking an order requiring the holder to correct or delete the patent information submitted by the holder under subsection (b) or (c) on the ground that the patent does not claim either—

(aa) the drug for which the application was approved; or

(bb) an approved method of using the drug.

(II) NO INDEPENDENT CAUSE OF ACTION.—Subclause (I) does not authorize the assertion of a claim described in subclause (I) in any civil action or proceeding other than a counterclaim described in subclause (I).

(iii) No DAMAGES.—An applicant shall not be entitled to damages in a civil action under subparagraph (i) or a counterclaim under subparagraph (ii).".

(b) APPLICATIONS GENERALLY.—Section 505 of the Federal Food, Drug, and Cosmetic Act (21 U.S.C. 355) is amended—

(1) in subsection (b)—

(A) by striking paragraph (3) and inserting the following:

(3) NOTICE OF OPINION THAT PATENT IS INVALID OR WILL NOT BE INFRINGED.—

(A) AGREEMENT TO GIVE NOTICE.—An applicant that makes a certification described in paragraph (2)(A)(iv) shall include in the application a statement that the applicant will give notice as required by this paragraph.

(B) TIMING OF NOTICE.—An applicant that makes a certification described in paragraph (2)(A)(iv) shall give notice as required under this paragraph—

(i) if the certification is in the application, not later than 20 days after the date of the postmark on the notice with which the Secretary informs the applicant that the application has been filed; or

(ii) if the certification is in an amendment or supplement to the application, at the time at which the applicant submits the amendment or supplement, regardless of whether the applicant has already given notice with respect to another such certification contained in the application or in an amendment or supplement to the application.

(C) RECIPIENTS OF NOTICE.—An applicant required under this paragraph to give notice shall give notice to—

(i) each owner of the patent that is the subject of the certification (or a representative of the owner designated to receive such a notice); and

(ii) the holder of the approved application under this subsection for the drug that is claimed by the patent or a use of which is claimed by the patent (or a representative of the holder designated to receive such a notice).

(D) CONTENTS OF NOTICE.—A notice required under this paragraph shall—

(i) state that an application that contains data from bioavailability or bioequivalence studies has been submitted under this subsection for the drug with respect to which the certification is made to obtain approval to engage in the commercial manufacture, use, or sale of the drug before the expiration of the patent referred to in the certification; and

(ii) include a detailed statement of the factual and legal basis of the opinion of the applicant that the patent is invalid or will not be infringed.; and

(B)(i) by redesignating paragraph (4) as paragraph (5); and

(ii) by inserting after paragraph (3) the following paragraph:

(4)(A) An applicant may not amend or supplement an application referred to in paragraph (2) to seek approval of a drug that is a different drug than the drug identified in the application as submitted to the Secretary.

(B) With respect to the drug for which such an application is submitted, nothing in this subsection or subsection (c)(3) prohibits an applicant from amending or supplementing the application to seek approval of a different strength.; and

(2) in subsection (c)(3)—

(A) in the first sentence, by striking "under the following" and inserting "by applying the following to each certification made under subsection (b)(2)(A)(iv)";

(B) in subparagraph (C)—

(i) in the first sentence, by striking "unless" and all that follows and inserting "unless, before the expiration of 45 days after the date on which the notice described in subsection (b)(3) is received, an action is brought for infringement of the patent that is the subject of the certification and for which information was submitted to the Secretary under paragraph (2) or subsection (b)(1) before the date on which the application (excluding an amendment or supplement to the application) was submitted.";

(ii) in the second sentence—

(I) by striking "paragraph (3)(B)" and inserting "subsection (b)(3)";

(II) by striking clause (i) and inserting the following:

(i) if before the expiration of such period the district court decides that the patent is invalid or not infringed (including any substantive determination that there is no cause of action for patent infringement or invalidity), the approval shall be made effective on—

(I) the date on which the court enters judgment reflecting the decision; or

"(II) the date of a settlement order or consent decree signed and entered by the court stating that the patent that is the subject of the certification is invalid or not infringed;";

(III) by striking clause (ii) and inserting the following:

(ii) if before the expiration of such period the district court decides that the patent has been infringed—

(I) if the judgment of the district court is appealed, the approval shall be made effective on—

(aa) the date on which the court of appeals decides that the patent is invalid or not infringed (including any substantive determination that there is no cause of action for patent infringement or invalidity); or

(bb) the date of a settlement order or consent decree signed and entered by the court of appeals stating that the patent that is the subject of the certification is invalid or not infringed; or

(II) if the judgment of the district court is not appealed or is affirmed, the approval shall be made effective on the date specified by the district court in a court order under section 271(e)(4)(A) of title 35, United States Code;;

(IV) in clause (iii), by striking "on the date of such court decision." and inserting "as provided in clause (i); or";

(V) by inserting after clause (iii), the following:

(iv) if before the expiration of such period the court grants a preliminary injunction prohibiting the applicant from engaging in the commercial manufacture or sale of the drug until the court decides the issues of patent validity and infringement and if the court decides that such patent has been infringed, the approval shall be made effective as provided in clause (ii).; and

(VI) in the matter after and below clause (iv) (as added by subclause (V)), by striking "Until the expiration" and all that follows; and

(iii) in the third sentence, by striking "paragraph (3)(B)" and inserting "subsection (b)(3)";

(C) by redesignating subparagraph (D) as subparagraph (E); and

(D) by inserting after subparagraph (C) the following:

(D) CIVIL ACTION TO OBTAIN PATENT CERTAINTY.—

(i) DECLARATORY JUDGMENT ABSENT INFRINGEMENT ACTION.—

(I) IN GENERAL

No action may be brought under section 2201 of title 28, United States Code, by an applicant referred to in subsection (b)(2) for a declaratory judgment with respect to a patent which is the subject of the certification referred to in subparagraph (C) unless—

(aa) the forty-five day period referred to in such subparagraph has expired;

(bb) neither the owner of such patent nor the holder of the approved application under subsection (b) for the drug that is claimed by the patent or a use of which is claimed by the patent brought a civil action against the applicant for infringement of the patent before the expiration of such period; and

(cc) in any case in which the notice provided under paragraph (2)(B) relates to noninfringement, the notice was accompanied by a document described in subclause (III).

(II) FILING OF CIVIL ACTION.—If the conditions described in items (aa), (bb), and as applicable, (cc) of subclause (I) have been met, the applicant referred to in such subclause may, in accordance with section 2201 of title 28, United States Code, bring a civil action under such section against the owner or holder referred to in such subclause (but not against any owner or holder that has brought such a civil action against the applicant, unless that civil action was dismissed without prejudice) for a declaratory judgment that the patent is invalid or will not be infringed by the drug for which the applicant seeks approval, except that such civil action may be brought for a declaratory judgment that the patent will not be infringed only in a case in which the condition described in subclause (I)(cc) is applicable. A civil action referred to in this subclause shall be brought in the judicial district where the defendant has its principal place of business or a regular and established place of business.

(III) OFFER OF CONFIDENTIAL ACCESS TO APPLICATION.—For purposes of subclause (I)(cc), the document described in this subclause is a document providing an offer of confidential access to the application that is in the custody of the applicant referred to in subsection (b)(2) for the purpose of determining whether an action referred to in subparagraph (C) should be brought. The document providing the offer of confidential access shall contain such restrictions as to persons entitled to access, and on the use and disposition of any information accessed, as would apply had a protective order been entered for the purpose of protecting trade secrets and other confidential business information. A request for access to an application under an offer of confidential access shall be considered acceptance of the offer of confidential access with the restrictions as to persons entitled to access, and on the use and disposition of any information accessed, contained in the offer of confidential access, and those restrictions and other terms of the offer of confidential access shall be considered terms of an enforceable contract. Any person provided an offer of confidential access shall review the application for the sole and limited purpose of evaluating possible infringement of the patent that is the subject of the certification under subsection (b)(2)(A)(iv) and for no other purpose, and may not disclose information of no relevance to any issue of patent infringement to any person other than a person provided an offer of confidential access. Further, the application may be redacted by the applicant to remove any information of no relevance to any issue of patent infringement.

(ii) COUNTERCLAIM TO INFRINGEMENT ACTION.—

(I) IN GENERAL.—If an owner of the patent or the holder of the approved application under subsection (b) for the drug that is claimed by the patent or a use of which is claimed by the patent brings a patent infringement action against the applicant, the applicant may assert a counterclaim seeking an order requiring the holder to correct or delete the patent information submitted by the holder under subsection (b) or this subsection on the ground that the patent does not claim either—

(aa) the drug for which the application was approved; or

(bb) an approved method of using the drug.

(II) NO INDEPENDENT CAUSE OF ACTION.—Subclause (I) does not authorize the assertion of a claim described in subclause (I) in any civil action or proceeding other than a counterclaim described in subclause (I).

(iii) NO DAMAGES.—An applicant shall not be entitled to damages in a civil action under clause (i) or a counterclaim under clause (ii).

(c) APPLICABILITY.—

(1) IN GENERAL.—Except as provided in paragraphs (2) and (3), the amendments made by subsections (a), (b), and (c) apply to any proceeding under section 505 of the Federal Food, Drug, and Cosmetic Act (21 U.S.C. 355) that is pending on or after the date of the enactment of this Act regardless of the date on which the proceeding was commenced or is commenced.

(2) NOTICE OF OPINION THAT PATENT IS INVALID OR WILL NOT BE INFRINGED.—The amendments made by subsections (a)(1) and (b)(1) apply with respect to any certification under subsection (b)(2)(A)(iv) or (j)(2)(A)(vii)(IV) of section 505 of the Federal Food, Drug, and Cosmetic Act (21 U.S.C. 355) submitted on or after August 18, 2003, in an application filed under subsection (b) or (j) of that section or in an amendment or supplement to an application filed under subsection (b) or (j) of that section.

(3) EFFECTIVE DATE OF APPROVAL.—The amendments made by subsections (a)(2)(A)(ii)(I) and (b)(2)(B)(i) apply with respect to any patent information submitted under subsection (b)(1) or (c)(2) of section 505 of the Federal Food, Drug, and Cosmetic Act (21 U.S.C. 355) on or after August 18, 2003.

(d) INFRINGEMENT ACTIONS.—Section 271(e) of title 35, United States Code, is amended by adding at the end the following:

(5) Where a person has filed an application described in paragraph (2) that includes a certification under subsection (b)(2)(A)(iv) or (j)(2)(A)(vii)(IV) of section 505 of the Federal Food, Drug, and Cosmetic Act (21 U.S.C. 355), and neither the owner of the patent that is the subject of the certification nor the holder of the approved application under subsection (b) of such section for the drug that is claimed by the patent or a use of which is claimed by the patent brought an action for infringement of such patent before the expiration of 45 days after the date on which the notice given under subsection (b)(3) or (j)(2)(B) of such section was received, the courts of the United States shall, to the extent consistent with the Constitution, have subject matter jurisdiction in any action brought by such person under section 2201 of title 28 for a declaratory judgment that such patent is invalid or not infringed.

[CCH Explanation at ¶ 1301.]

[¶ 11,260] ACT SEC. 1102. FORFEITURE OF 180-DAY EXCLUSIVITY PERIOD.

(a) IN GENERAL.—Section 505(j)(5) of the Federal Food, Drug, and Cosmetic Act (21 U.S.C. 355(j)(5)) (as amended by section 1101) is amended—

(1) in subparagraph (B), by striking clause (iv) and inserting the following:

(iv) 180-DAY EXCLUSIVITY PERIOD.—

(I) EFFECTIVENESS OF APPLICATION.—Subject to subparagraph (D), if the application contains a certification described in paragraph (2)(A)(vii)(IV) and is for a drug for which a first applicant has submitted an application containing such a certification, the application shall be made effective on the date that is 180 days after the date of the first commercial marketing of the drug (including the commercial marketing of the listed drug) by any first applicant.

(II) DEFINITIONS.—In this paragraph:

(aa) 180-DAY EXCLUSIVITY PERIOD.—The term '180-day exclusivity period' means the 180-day period ending on the day before the date on which an application submitted by an applicant other than a first applicant could become effective under this clause.

(bb) FIRST APPLICANT.—As used in this subsection, the term 'first applicant' means an applicant that, on the first day on which a substantially complete application containing a certification described in paragraph (2)(A)(vii)(IV) is submitted for approval of a drug, submits a substantially complete application that contains and lawfully maintains a certification described in paragraph (2)(A)(vii)(IV) for the drug.

(cc) SUBSTANTIALLY COMPLETE APPLICATION.—As used in this subsection, the term 'substantially complete application' means an application under this subsection that on its face is sufficiently complete to permit a substantive review and contains all the information required by paragraph (2)(A).

(dd) TENTATIVE APPROVAL.—

Non-Code Provisions

(AA) IN GENERAL.—The term 'tentative approval' means notification to an applicant by the Secretary that an application under this subsection meets the requirements of paragraph (2)(A), but cannot receive effective approval because the application does not meet the requirements of this subparagraph, there is a period of exclusivity for the listed drug under subparagraph (E) or section 505A, or there is a 7-year period of exclusivity for the listed drug under section 527.

"(BB) LIMITATION.—A drug that is granted tentative approval by the Secretary is not an approved drug and shall not have an effective approval until the Secretary issues an approval after any necessary additional review of the application."; and

(2) by inserting after subparagraph (C) the following:

(D) FORFEITURE OF 180-DAY EXCLUSIVITY PERIOD.—

(i) DEFINITION OF FORFEITURE EVENT.—In this subparagraph, the term 'forfeiture event', with respect to an application under this subsection, means the occurrence of any of the following:

(I) FAILURE TO MARKET.—The first applicant fails to market the drug by the later of—

(aa) the earlier of the date that is—

(AA) 75 days after the date on which the approval of the application of the first applicant is made effective under subparagraph (B)(iii); or

(BB) 30 months after the date of submission of the application of the first applicant; or

(bb) with respect to the first applicant or any other applicant (which other applicant has received tentative approval), the date that is 75 days after the date as of which, as to each of the patents with respect to which the first applicant submitted and lawfully maintained a certification qualifying the first applicant for the 180-day exclusivity period under subparagraph (B)(iv), at least 1 of the following has occurred:

(AA) In an infringement action brought against that applicant with respect to the patent or in a declaratory judgment action brought by that applicant with respect to the patent, a court enters a final decision from which no appeal (other than a petition to the Supreme Court for a writ of certiorari) has been or can be taken that the patent is invalid or not infringed.

(BB) In an infringement action or a declaratory judgment action described in subitem (AA), a court signs a settlement order or consent decree that enters a final judgment that includes a finding that the patent is invalid or not infringed.

(CC) The patent information submitted under subsection (b) or (c) is withdrawn by the holder of the application approved under subsection (b).

(II) WITHDRAWAL OF APPLICATION.—The first applicant withdraws the application or the Secretary considers the application to have been withdrawn as a result of a determination by the Secretary that the application does not meet the requirements for approval under paragraph (4).

(III) AMENDMENT OF CERTIFICATION.—The first applicant amends or withdraws the certification for all of the patents with respect to which that applicant submitted a certification qualifying the applicant for the 180-day exclusivity period.

(IV) FAILURE TO OBTAIN TENTATIVE APPROVAL.—The first applicant fails to obtain tentative approval of the application within 30 months after the date on which the application is filed, unless the failure is caused by a change in or a review of the requirements for approval of the application imposed after the date on which the application is filed.

(V) AGREEMENT WITH ANOTHER APPLICANT, THE LISTED DRUG APPLICATION HOLDER, OR A PATENT OWNER.—The first applicant enters into an agreement with another applicant under this subsection for the drug, the holder of the application for the listed drug, or an owner of the patent that is the subject of the certification under paragraph (2)(A)(vii)(IV), the Federal Trade Commission or the Attorney General files a complaint, and there is a final decision of the Federal Trade Commission or the court with regard to the complaint from which no appeal (other than a petition to the Supreme Court for a writ of certiorari) has been or can be taken that the agreement has violated the antitrust laws (as defined in section 1 of the Clayton Act (15 U.S.C. 12), except that the term includes section 5 of the Federal Trade Commission Act (15 U.S.C. 45) to the extent that that section applies to unfair methods of competition).

(VI) EXPIRATION OF ALL PATENTS.—All of the patents as to which the applicant submitted a certification qualifying it for the 180-day exclusivity period have expired.

(ii) FORFEITURE.—The 180-day exclusivity period described in subparagraph (B)(iv) shall be forfeited by a first applicant if a forfeiture event occurs with respect to that first applicant.

(iii) SUBSEQUENT APPLICANT.—If all first applicants forfeit the 180-day exclusivity period under clause (ii)—

(I) approval of any application containing a certification described in paragraph (2)(A)(vii)(IV) shall be made effective in accordance with subparagraph (B)(iii); and

(II) no applicant shall be eligible for a 180-day exclusivity period.

(b) EFFECTIVE DATE.—

(1) IN GENERAL.—Except as provided in paragraph (2), the amendment made by subsection (a) shall be effective only with respect to an application filed under section 505(j) of the Federal Food, Drug, and Cosmetic Act (21 U.S.C. 355(j)) after the date of the enactment of this Act for a listed drug for which no certification under section 505(j)(2)(A)(vii)(IV) of that Act was made before the date of the enactment of this Act.

(2) COLLUSIVE AGREEMENTS.—If a forfeiture event described in section 505(j)(5)(D)(i)(V) of that Act occurs in the case of an applicant, the applicant shall forfeit the 180-day period under section 505(j)(5)(B)(iv) of that Act without regard to when the first certification under section 505(j)(2)(A)(vii)(IV) of that Act for the listed drug was made.

(3) DECISION OF A COURT WHEN THE 180-DAY EXCLUSIVITY PERIOD HAS NOT BEEN TRIGGERED.—With respect to an application filed before, on, or after the date of the enactment of this Act for a listed drug for which a certification under section 505(j)(2)(A)(vii)(IV) of that Act was made before the date of the enactment of this Act and for which neither of the events described in subclause (I) or (II) of section 505(j)(5)(B)(iv) of that Act (as in effect on the day before the date of the enactment of this Act) has occurred on or before the date of the enactment of this Act, the term "decision of a court" as used in clause (iv) of section 505(j)(5)(B) of that Act means a final decision of a court from which no appeal (other than a petition to the Supreme Court for a writ of certiorari) has been or can be taken.

[CCH Explanation at ¶1301.]

[¶11,270] ACT SEC. 1103. BIOAVAILABILITY AND BIOEQUIVALENCE.

(a) IN GENERAL.—Section 505(j)(8) of the Federal Food, Drug, and Cosmetic Act (21 U.S.C. 355(j)(8)) is amended—

(1) by striking subparagraph (A) and inserting the following:

(A)(i) The term 'bioavailability' means the rate and extent to which the active ingredient or therapeutic ingredient is absorbed from a drug and becomes available at the site of drug action.

(ii) For a drug that is not intended to be absorbed into the bloodstream, the Secretary may assess bioavailability by scientifically valid measurements intended to reflect the rate and extent to which the active ingredient or therapeutic ingredient becomes available at the site of drug action.; and

(2) by adding at the end the following:

Non-Code Provisions

(C) For a drug that is not intended to be absorbed into the bloodstream, the Secretary may establish alternative, scientifically valid methods to show bioequivalence if the alternative methods are expected to detect a significant difference between the drug and the listed drug in safety and therapeutic effect..

(b) EFFECT OF AMENDMENT.—The amendment made by subsection (a) does not alter the standards for approval of drugs under section 505(j) of the Federal Food, Drug, and Cosmetic Act (21 U.S.C. 355(j)).

[CCH Explanation at ¶1301.]

[¶11,280] ACT SEC. 1104. CONFORMING AMENDMENTS.

Section 505A of the Federal Food, Drug, and Cosmetic Act (21 U.S.C. 355a) is amended—

(1) in subsections (b)(1)(A)(i) and (c)(1)(A)(i), by striking " (j)(5)(D)(ii)" each place it appears and inserting "(j)(5)(F)(ii)";

(2) in subsections (b)(1)(A)(ii) and (c)(1)(A)(ii), by striking " (j)(5)(D)" each place it appears and inserting "(j)(5)(F)"; and

(3) in subsections (e) and (l), by striking "505(j)(5)(D)" each place it appears and inserting "505(j)(5)(F)".

Subtitle B—Federal Trade Commission Review

[¶11,290] ACT SEC. 1111. DEFINITIONS.

In this subtitle:

(1) ANDA.—The term "ANDA" means an abbreviated drug application, as defined under section 201(aa) of the Federal Food, Drug, and Cosmetic Act.

(2) ASSISTANT ATTORNEY GENERAL.—The term "Assistant Attorney General" means the Assistant Attorney General in charge of the Antitrust Division of the Department of Justice.

(3) BRAND NAME DRUG.—The term "brand name drug" means a drug for which an application is approved under section 505(c) of the Federal Food, Drug, and Cosmetic Act, including an application referred to in section 505(b)(2) of such Act.

(4) BRAND NAME DRUG COMPANY.—The term "brand name drug company" means the party that holds the approved application referred to in paragraph (2) for a brand name drug that is a listed drug in an ANDA, or a party that is the owner of a patent for which information is submitted for such drug under subsection (b) or (c) of section 505 of the Federal Food, Drug, and Cosmetic Act.

(5) COMMISSION.—The term "Commission" means the Federal Trade Commission.

(6) GENERIC DRUG.—The term "generic drug" means a drug for which an application under section 505(j) of the Federal Food, Drug, and Cosmetic Act is approved.

(7) GENERIC DRUG APPLICANT.—The term "generic drug applicant" means a person who has filed or received approval for an ANDA under section 505(j) of the Federal Food, Drug, and Cosmetic Act.

(8) LISTED DRUG.—The term "listed drug" means a brand name drug that is listed under section 505(j)(7) of the Federal Food, Drug, and Cosmetic Act.

[CCH Explanation at ¶1320.]

[¶11,300] ACT SEC. 1112. NOTIFICATION OF AGREEMENTS.

(a) AGREEMENT WITH BRAND NAME DRUG COMPANY.—

(1) REQUIREMENT.—A generic drug applicant that has submitted an ANDA containing a certification under section 505(j)(2)(A)(vii)(IV) of the Federal Food, Drug, and Cosmetic Act and a brand name drug company that enter into an agreement described in paragraph (2) shall each file the agreement in accordance with subsection (c). The agreement shall be filed prior to the date of the first commercial marketing of the generic drug that is the subject of the ANDA.

(2) SUBJECT MATTER OF AGREEMENT.—An agreement described in this paragraph between a generic drug applicant and a brand name drug company is an agreement regarding—

(A) the manufacture, marketing or sale of the brand name drug that is the listed drug in the ANDA involved;

(B) the manufacture, marketing, or sale of the generic drug for which the ANDA was submitted; or

(C) the 180-day period referred to in section 505(j)(5)(B)(iv) of the Federal Food, Drug, and Cosmetic Act as it applies to such ANDA or to any other ANDA based on the same brand name drug.

(b) AGREEMENT WITH ANOTHER GENERIC DRUG APPLICANT.—

(1) REQUIREMENT.—A generic drug applicant that has submitted an ANDA containing a certification under section 505(j)(2)(A)(vii)(IV) of the Federal Food, Drug, and Cosmetic Act with respect to a listed drug and another generic drug applicant that has submitted an ANDA containing such a certification for the same listed drug shall each file the agreement in accordance with subsection (c). The agreement shall be filed prior to the date of the first commercial marketing of either of the generic drugs for which such ANDAs were submitted.

(2) SUBJECT MATTER OF AGREEMENT.—An agreement described in this paragraph between two generic drug applicants is an agreement regarding the 180-day period referred to in section 505(j)(5)(B)(iv) of the Federal Food, Drug, and Cosmetic Act as it applies to the ANDAs with which the agreement is concerned.

(c) FILING.—

(1) AGREEMENT.—The parties that are required in subsection (a) or (b) to file an agreement in accordance with this subsection shall file with the Assistant Attorney General and the Commission the text of any such agreement, except that such parties are not required to file an agreement that solely concerns—

(A) purchase orders for raw material supplies;

(B) equipment and facility contracts;

(C) employment or consulting contracts; or

(D) packaging and labeling contracts.

(2) OTHER AGREEMENTS.—The parties that are required in subsection (a) or (b) to file an agreement in accordance with this subsection shall file with the Assistant Attorney General and the Commission the text of any agreements between the parties that are not described in such subsections and are contingent upon, provide a contingent condition for, or are otherwise related to an agreement that is required in subsection (a) or (b) to be filed in accordance with this subsection.

(3) DESCRIPTION.—In the event that any agreement required in subsection (a) or (b) to be filed in accordance with this subsection has not been reduced to text, each of the parties involved shall file written descriptions of such agreement that are sufficient to disclose all the terms and conditions of the agreement.

[CCH Explanation at ¶ 1320.]

[¶ 11,310] ACT SEC. 1113. FILING DEADLINES.

Any filing required under section 1112 shall be filed with the Assistant Attorney General and the Commission not later than 10 business days after the date the agreements are executed.

[CCH Explanation at ¶ 1320.]

[¶ 11,320] ACT SEC. 1114. DISCLOSURE EXEMPTION.

Any information or documentary material filed with the Assistant Attorney General or the Commission pursuant to this subtitle shall be exempt from disclosure under section 552 of title 5, United States Code, and no such information or documentary material may be made public, except as may be relevant to any administrative or judicial action or proceeding. Nothing in this section is intended to prevent disclosure to either body of the Congress or to any duly authorized committee or subcommittee of the Congress.

[CCH Explanation at ¶ 1320.]

[¶ 11,330] ACT SEC. 1115. ENFORCEMENT.

(a) CIVIL PENALTY.—Any brand name drug company or generic drug applicant which fails to comply with any provision of this subtitle shall be liable for a civil penalty of not more than $11,000, for each day during which such entity is in violation of this subtitle. Such penalty may be recovered in a civil action brought by the United States, or brought by the Commission in accordance with the procedures established in section 16(a)(1) of the Federal Trade Commission Act (15 U.S.C. 56(a)).

(b) COMPLIANCE AND EQUITABLE RELIEF.—If any brand name drug company or generic drug applicant fails to comply with any provision of this subtitle, the United States district court may order compliance, and may grant such other equitable relief as the court in its discretion determines necessary or appropriate, upon application of the Assistant Attorney General or the Commission.

[CCH Explanation at ¶ 1320.]

[¶ 11,340] ACT SEC. 1116. RULEMAKING.

The Commission, with the concurrence of the Assistant Attorney General and by rule in accordance with section 553 of title 5, United States Code, consistent with the purposes of this subtitle—

(1) may define the terms used in this subtitle;

(2) may exempt classes of persons or agreements from the requirements of this subtitle; and

(3) may prescribe such other rules as may be necessary and appropriate to carry out the purposes of this subtitle.

[CCH Explanation at ¶ 1320.]

[¶ 11,350] ACT SEC. 1117. SAVINGS CLAUSE.

Any action taken by the Assistant Attorney General or the Commission, or any failure of the Assistant Attorney General or the Commission to take action, under this subtitle shall not at any time bar any proceeding or any action with respect to any agreement between a brand name drug company and a generic drug applicant, or any agreement between generic drug applicants, under any other provision of law, nor shall any filing under this subtitle constitute or create a presumption of any violation of any competition laws.

[CCH Explanation at ¶ 1320.]

[¶ 11,360] ACT SEC. 1118. EFFECTIVE DATE.

This subtitle shall—

(1) take effect 30 days after the date of the enactment of this Act; and

(2) shall apply to agreements described in section 1112 that are entered into 30 days after the date of the enactment of this Act.

[CCH Explanation at ¶ 1320.]

Subtitle C—Importation of Prescription Drugs

[¶ 11,370] ACT SEC. 1121. IMPORTATION OF PRESCRIPTION DRUGS.

(a) IN GENERAL.—Chapter VIII of the Federal Food, Drug, and Cosmetic Act (21 U.S.C. 381 et seq.) is amended by striking section 804 and inserting the following:

SEC. 804. IMPORTATION OF PRESCRIPTION DRUGS.

(a) DEFINITIONS.—In this section:

(1) IMPORTER.—The term 'importer' means a pharmacist or wholesaler.

(2) PHARMACIST.—The term 'pharmacist' means a person licensed by a State to practice pharmacy, including the dispensing and selling of prescription drugs.

(3) PRESCRIPTION DRUG.—The term 'prescription drug' means a drug subject to section 503(b), other than—

(A) a controlled substance (as defined in section 102 of the Controlled Substances Act (21 U.S.C. 802));

(B) a biological product (as defined in section 351 of the Public Health Service Act (42 U.S.C. 262));

(C) an infused drug (including a peritoneal dialysis solution);

(D) an intravenously injected drug;

(E) a drug that is inhaled during surgery; or

(F) a drug which is a parenteral drug, the importation of which pursuant to subsection (b) is determined by the Secretary to pose a threat to the public health, in which case section 801(d)(1) shall continue to apply.

(4) QUALIFYING LABORATORY.—The term 'qualifying laboratory' means a laboratory in the United States that has been approved by the Secretary for the purposes of this section.

(5) WHOLESALER.—

(A) IN GENERAL.—The term 'wholesaler' means a person licensed as a wholesaler or distributor of prescription drugs in the United States under section 503(e)(2)(A).

(B) EXCLUSION.—The term 'wholesaler' does not include a person authorized to import drugs under section 801(d)(1).

(b) REGULATIONS.—The Secretary, after consultation with the United States Trade Representative and the Commissioner of Customs, shall promulgate regulations permitting pharmacists and wholesalers to import prescription drugs from Canada into the United States.

(c) LIMITATION.—The regulations under subsection (b) shall—

(1) require that safeguards be in place to ensure that each prescription drug imported under the regulations complies with section 505 (including with respect to being safe and effective for the intended use of the prescription drug), with sections 501 and 502, and with other applicable requirements of this Act;

(2) require that an importer of a prescription drug under the regulations comply with subsections (d)(1) and (e); and

(3) contain any additional provisions determined by the Secretary to be appropriate as a safeguard to protect the public health or as a means to facilitate the importation of prescription drugs.

(d) INFORMATION AND RECORDS.—

(1) IN GENERAL.—The regulations under subsection (b) shall require an importer of a prescription drug under subsection (b) to submit to the Secretary the following information and documentation:

(A) The name and quantity of the active ingredient of the prescription drug.

(B) A description of the dosage form of the prescription drug.

(C) The date on which the prescription drug is shipped.

(D) The quantity of the prescription drug that is shipped.

(E) The point of origin and destination of the prescription drug.

(F) The price paid by the importer for the prescription drug.

(G) Documentation from the foreign seller specifying—

(i) the original source of the prescription drug; and

(ii) the quantity of each lot of the prescription drug originally received by the seller from that source.

(H) The lot or control number assigned to the prescription drug by the manufacturer of the prescription drug.

(I) The name, address, telephone number, and professional license number (if any) of the importer.

(J)(i) In the case of a prescription drug that is shipped directly from the first foreign recipient of the prescription drug from the manufacturer:

(I) Documentation demonstrating that the prescription drug was received by the recipient from the manufacturer and subsequently shipped by the first foreign recipient to the importer.

Non-Code Provisions

(II) Documentation of the quantity of each lot of the prescription drug received by the first foreign recipient demonstrating that the quantity being imported into the United States is not more than the quantity that was received by the first foreign recipient.

(III)(aa) In the case of an initial imported shipment, documentation demonstrating that each batch of the prescription drug in the shipment was statistically sampled and tested for authenticity and degradation.

(bb) In the case of any subsequent shipment, documentation demonstrating that a statistically valid sample of the shipment was tested for authenticity and degradation.

(ii) In the case of a prescription drug that is not shipped directly from the first foreign recipient of the prescription drug from the manufacturer, documentation demonstrating that each batch in each shipment offered for importation into the United States was statistically sampled and tested for authenticity and degradation.

(K) Certification from the importer or manufacturer of the prescription drug that the prescription drug—

(i) is approved for marketing in the United States and is not adulterated or misbranded; and

(ii) meets all labeling requirements under this Act.

(L) Laboratory records, including complete data derived from all tests necessary to ensure that the prescription drug is in compliance with established specifications and standards.

(M) Documentation demonstrating that the testing required by subparagraphs (J) and (L) was conducted at a qualifying laboratory.

(N) Any other information that the Secretary determines is necessary to ensure the protection of the public health.

(2) MAINTENANCE BY THE SECRETARY.—The Secretary shall maintain information and documentation submitted under paragraph (1) for such period of time as the Secretary determines to be necessary.

(e) TESTING.—The regulations under subsection (b) shall require—

(1) that testing described in subparagraphs (J) and (L) of subsection (d)(1) be conducted by the importer or by the manufacturer of the prescription drug at a qualified laboratory;

(2) if the tests are conducted by the importer—

(A) that information needed to—

(i) authenticate the prescription drug being tested; and

(ii) confirm that the labeling of the prescription drug complies with labeling requirements under this Act;

be supplied by the manufacturer of the prescription drug to the pharmacist or wholesaler; and

(B) that the information supplied under subparagraph (A) be kept in strict confidence and used only for purposes of testing or otherwise complying with this Act; and

(3) may include such additional provisions as the Secretary determines to be appropriate to provide for the protection of trade secrets and commercial or financial information that is privileged or confidential.

(f) REGISTRATION OF FOREIGN SELLERS.—Any establishment within Canada engaged in the distribution of a prescription drug that is imported or offered for importation into the United States shall register with the Secretary the name and place of business of the establishment and the name of the United States agent for the establishment.

(g) SUSPENSION OF IMPORTATION.—The Secretary shall require that importations of a specific prescription drug or importations by a specific importer under subsection (b) be immediately suspended on discovery of a pattern of importation of that specific prescription drug or by that specific importer of drugs that are counterfeit or in violation of any

Act Sec. 1121(a) ¶11,370

requirement under this section, until an investigation is completed and the Secretary determines that the public is adequately protected from counterfeit and violative prescription drugs being imported under subsection (b).

(h) APPROVED LABELING.—The manufacturer of a prescription drug shall provide an importer written authorization for the importer to use, at no cost, the approved labeling for the prescription drug.

(i) CHARITABLE CONTRIBUTIONS.—Notwithstanding any other provision of this section, section 801(d)(1) continues to apply to a prescription drug that is donated or otherwise supplied at no charge by the manufacturer of the drug to a charitable or humanitarian organization (including the United Nations and affiliates) or to a government of a foreign country.

(j) WAIVER AUTHORITY FOR IMPORTATION BY INDIVIDUALS.—

(1) DECLARATIONS.—Congress declares that in the enforcement against individuals of the prohibition of importation of prescription drugs and devices, the Secretary should—

(A) focus enforcement on cases in which the importation by an individual poses a significant threat to public health; and

(B) exercise discretion to permit individuals to make such importations in circumstances in which—

(i) the importation is clearly for personal use; and

(ii) the prescription drug or device imported does not appear to present an unreasonable risk to the individual.

(2) WAIVER AUTHORITY.—

(A) IN GENERAL.—The Secretary may grant to individuals, by regulation or on a case-by-case basis, a waiver of the prohibition of importation of a prescription drug or device or class of prescription drugs or devices, under such conditions as the Secretary determines to be appropriate.

(B) GUIDANCE ON CASE-BY-CASE WAIVERS.—The Secretary shall publish, and update as necessary, guidance that accurately describes circumstances in which the Secretary will consistently grant waivers on a case-by-case basis under subparagraph (A), so that individuals may know with the greatest practicable degree of certainty whether a particular importation for personal use will be permitted.

(3) DRUGS IMPORTED FROM CANADA.—In particular, the Secretary shall by regulation grant individuals a waiver to permit individuals to import into the United States a prescription drug that—

(A) is imported from a licensed pharmacy for personal use by an individual, not for resale, in quantities that do not exceed a 90-day supply;

(B) is accompanied by a copy of a valid prescription;

(C) is imported from Canada, from a seller registered with the Secretary;

(D) is a prescription drug approved by the Secretary under chapter V;

(E) is in the form of a final finished dosage that was manufactured in an establishment registered under section 510; and

(F) is imported under such other conditions as the Secretary determines to be necessary to ensure public safety.

(k) CONSTRUCTION.—Nothing in this section limits the authority of the Secretary relating to the importation of prescription drugs, other than with respect to section 801(d)(1) as provided in this section.

(l) EFFECTIVENESS OF SECTION.—

(1) COMMENCEMENT OF PROGRAM.—This section shall become effective only if the Secretary certifies to the Congress that the implementation of this section will—

(A) pose no additional risk to the public's health and safety; and

(B) result in a significant reduction in the cost of covered products to the American consumer.

(2) TERMINATION OF PROGRAM.—

(A) IN GENERAL.—If, after the date that is 1 year after the effective date of the regulations under subsection (b) and before the date that is 18 months after the effective date, the Secretary submits to Congress a certification that, in the opinion of the Secretary, based on substantial evidence obtained after the effective date, the benefits of implementation of this section do not outweigh any detriment of implementation of this section, this section shall cease to be effective as of the date that is 30 days after the date on which the Secretary submits the certification.

(B) PROCEDURE.—The Secretary shall not submit a certification under subparagraph (A) unless, after a hearing on the record under sections 556 and 557 of title 5, United States Code, the Secretary—

(i)(I) determines that it is more likely than not that implementation of this section would result in an increase in the risk to the public health and safety;

(II) identifies specifically, in qualitative and quantitative terms, the nature of the increased risk;

(III) identifies specifically the causes of the increased risk; and

(IV)(aa) considers whether any measures can be taken to avoid, reduce, or mitigate the increased risk; and

(bb) if the Secretary determines that any measures described in item (aa) would require additional statutory authority, submits to Congress a report describing the legislation that would be required;

(ii) identifies specifically, in qualitative and quantitative terms, the benefits that would result from implementation of this section (including the benefit of reductions in the cost of covered products to consumers in the United States, allowing consumers to procure needed medication that consumers might not otherwise be able to procure without foregoing other necessities of life); and

(iii)(I) compares in specific terms the detriment identified under clause (i) with the benefits identified under clause (ii); and

(II) determines that the benefits do not outweigh the detriment.

(m) AUTHORIZATION OF APPROPRIATIONS.—There are authorized to be appropriated such sums as are necessary to carry out this section.".

(b) CONFORMING AMENDMENTS.—The Federal Food, Drug, and Cosmetic Act is amended—

(1) in section 301(aa) (21 U.S.C. 331(aa)), by striking "covered product in violation of section 804" and inserting "prescription drug in violation of section 804"; and

(2) in section 303(a)(6) (21 U.S.C. 333(a)(6), by striking "covered product pursuant to section 804(a)" and inserting "prescription drug under section 804(b)".

[CCH Explanation at ¶1330.]

[¶11,380] ACT SEC. 1122. STUDY AND REPORT ON IMPORTATION OF DRUGS.

The Secretary, in consultation with appropriate government agencies, shall conduct a study on the importation of drugs into the United States pursuant to section 804 of the Federal Food, Drug, and Cosmetic Act (as added by section 1121 of this Act). Not later than 12 months after the date of the enactment of this Act, the Secretary shall submit to the appropriate committees of the Congress a report providing the findings of such study.

[CCH Explanation at ¶1330.]

[¶11,390] ACT SEC. 1123. STUDY AND REPORT ON TRADE IN PHARMACEUTICALS.

The President's designees shall conduct a study and report on issues related to trade and pharmaceuticals.

[CCH Explanation at ¶1330.]

TITLE XII—TAX INCENTIVES FOR HEALTH AND RETIREMENT SECURITY

[¶11,400] ACT SEC. 1201. HEALTH SAVINGS ACCOUNTS.

(a) IN GENERAL.—Part VII of subchapter B of chapter 1 of the Internal Revenue Code of 1986 (relating to additional itemized deductions for individuals) is amended by redesignating section 223 as section 224 and by inserting after section 222 the following new section:

SEC. 223. HEALTH SAVINGS ACCOUNTS.—

(a) DEDUCTION ALLOWED.—In the case of an individual who is an eligible individual for any month during the taxable year, there shall be allowed as a deduction for the taxable year an amount equal to the aggregate amount paid in cash during such taxable year by or on behalf of such individual to a health savings account of such individual.

(b) LIMITATIONS.—

(1) IN GENERAL.—The amount allowable as a deduction under subsection (a) to an individual for the taxable year shall not exceed the sum of the monthly limitations for months during such taxable year that the individual is an eligible individual.

(2) MONTHLY LIMITATION.—The monthly limitation for any month is $1/12$ of—

(A) in the case of an eligible individual who has self-only coverage under a high deductible health plan as of the first day of such month, the lesser of—

(i) the annual deductible under such coverage, or

(ii) $2,250, or

(B) in the case of an eligible individual who has family coverage under a high deductible health plan as of the first day of such month, the lesser of—

(i) the annual deductible under such coverage, or

(ii) $4,500.

(3) ADDITIONAL CONTRIBUTIONS FOR INDIVIDUALS 55 OR OLDER.—

(A) IN GENERAL.—In the case of an individual who has attained age 55 before the close of the taxable year, the applicable limitation under subparagraphs (A) and (B) of paragraph (2) shall be increased by the additional contribution amount.

(B) ADDITIONAL CONTRIBUTION AMOUNT.—For purposes of this section, the additional contribution amount is the amount determined in accordance with the following table:

For taxable years beginning in:	The additional contribution amount is:
2004	$500
2005	$600
2006	$700
2007	$800
2008	$900
2009 and thereafter	$1,000.

(4) COORDINATION WITH OTHER CONTRIBUTIONS.—The limitation which would (but for this paragraph) apply under this subsection to an individual for any taxable year shall be reduced (but not below zero) by the sum of—

(A) the aggregate amount paid for such taxable year to Archer MSAs of such individual, and

(B) the aggregate amount contributed to health savings accounts of such individual which is excludable from the taxpayer's gross income for such taxable year under section 106(d) (and such amount shall not be allowed as a deduction under subsection (a)).

Subparagraph (A) shall not apply with respect to any individual to whom paragraph (5) applies.

(5) SPECIAL RULE FOR MARRIED INDIVIDUALS.—In the case of individuals who are married to each other, if either spouse has family coverage—

(A) both spouses shall be treated as having only such family coverage (and if such spouses each have family coverage under different plans, as having the family coverage with the lowest annual deductible), and

(B) the limitation under paragraph (1) (after the application of subparagraph (A) and without regard to any additional contribution amount under paragraph (3))—

(i) shall be reduced by the aggregate amount paid to Archer MSAs of such spouses for the taxable year, and

(ii) after such reduction, shall be divided equally between them unless they agree on a different division.

(6) DENIAL OF DEDUCTION TO DEPENDENTS.— No deduction shall be allowed under this section to any individual with respect to whom a deduction under section 151 is allowable to another taxpayer for a taxable year beginning in the calendar year in which such individual's taxable year begins.

(7) MEDICARE ELIGIBLE INDIVIDUALS.— The limitation under this subsection for any month with respect to an individual shall be zero for the first month such individual is entitled to benefits under title XVIII of the Social Security Act and for each month thereafter.

(c) DEFINITIONS AND SPECIAL RULES.— For purposes of this section—

(1) ELIGIBLE INDIVIDUAL.—

(A) IN GENERAL.—The term 'eligible individual' means, with respect to any month, any individual if—

(i) such individual is covered under a high deductible health plan as of the 1st day of such month, and

(ii) such individual is not, while covered under a high deductible health plan, covered under any health plan—

(I) which is not a high deductible health plan, and

(II) which provides coverage for any benefit which is covered under the high deductible health plan.

(B) CERTAIN COVERAGE DISREGARDED.—Subparagraph (A)(ii) shall be applied without regard to—

(i) coverage for any benefit provided by permitted insurance, and

(ii) coverage (whether through insurance or otherwise) for accidents, disability, dental care, vision care, or long-term care.

(2) HIGH DEDUCTIBLE HEALTH PLAN.—

(A) IN GENERAL.—The term 'high deductible health plan' means a health plan—

(i) which has an annual deductible which is not less than—

(I) $1,000 for self-only coverage, and

(II) twice the dollar amount in subclause (I) for family coverage, and

(ii) the sum of the annual deductible and the other annual out-of-pocket expenses required to be paid under the plan (other than for premiums) for covered benefits does not exceed—

(I) $5,000 for self-only coverage, and

(II) twice the dollar amount in subclause (I) for family coverage.

(B) EXCLUSION OF CERTAIN PLANS.—Such term does not include a health plan if substantially all of its coverage is coverage described in paragraph (1)(B).

(C) SAFE HARBOR FOR ABSENCE OF PREVENTIVE CARE DEDUCTIBLE.—A plan shall not fail to be treated as a high deductible health plan by reason of failing to have a deductible for preventive care (within the meaning of section 1871 of the Social Security Act, except as otherwise provided by the Secretary).

(D) SPECIAL RULES FOR NETWORK PLANS.—In the case of a plan using a network of providers—

(i) ANNUAL OUT-OF-POCKET LIMITATION.—Such plan shall not fail to be treated as a high deductible health plan by reason of having an out-of-pocket limitation for services provided outside of such network which exceeds the applicable limitation under subparagraph (A)(ii).

(ii) ANNUAL DEDUCTIBLE.—Such plan's annual deductible for services provided outside of such network shall not be taken into account for purposes of subsection (b)(2).

(3) PERMITTED INSURANCE.—The term 'permitted insurance' means—

(A) insurance if substantially all of the coverage provided under such insurance relates to—

(i) liabilities incurred under workers' compensation laws,

(ii) tort liabilities,

(iii) liabilities relating to ownership or use of property, or

(iv) such other similar liabilities as the Secretary may specify by regulations,

(B) insurance for a specified disease or illness, and

(C) insurance paying a fixed amount per day (or other period) of hospitalization.

(4) FAMILY COVERAGE.—The term 'family coverage' means any coverage other than self-only coverage.

(5) ARCHER MSA.—The term 'Archer MSA' has the meaning given such term in section 220(d).

(d) HEALTH SAVINGS ACCOUNT.—For purposes of this section—

(1) IN GENERAL.—The term 'health savings account' means a trust created or organized in the United States as a health savings account exclusively for the purpose of paying the qualified medical expenses of the account beneficiary, but only if the written governing instrument creating the trust meets the following requirements:

(A) Except in the case of a rollover contribution described in subsection (f)(5) or section 220(f)(5), no contribution will be accepted—

(i) unless it is in cash, or

(ii) to the extent such contribution, when added to previous contributions to the trust for the calendar year, exceeds the sum of—

(I) the dollar amount in effect under subsection (b)(2)(B)(ii), and

(II) the dollar amount in effect under subsection (b)(3)(B).

(B) The trustee is a bank (as defined in section 408(n)), an insurance company (as defined in section 816), or another person who demonstrates to the satisfaction of the Secretary that the manner in which such person will administer the trust will be consistent with the requirements of this section.

(C) No part of the trust assets will be invested in life insurance contracts.

(D) The assets of the trust will not be commingled with other property except in a common trust fund or common investment fund.

(E) The interest of an individual in the balance in his account is nonforfeitable.

(2) QUALIFIED MEDICAL EXPENSES.—

(A) IN GENERAL.—The term 'qualified medical expenses' means, with respect to an account beneficiary, amounts paid by such beneficiary for medical care (as defined in section 213(d) for such individual, the spouse of such individual, and any dependent (as defined in section 152) of such individual, but only to the extent such amounts are not compensated for by insurance or otherwise.

(B) HEALTH INSURANCE MAY NOT BE PURCHASED FROM ACCOUNT.—Subparagraph (A) shall not apply to any payment for insurance.

(C) EXCEPTIONS.—Subparagraph (B) shall not apply to any expense for coverage under—

(i) a health plan during any period of continuation coverage required under any Federal law,

(ii) a qualified long-term care insurance contract (as defined in section 7702B(b)),

(iii) a health plan during a period in which the individual is receiving unemployment compensation under any Federal or State law, or

(iv) in the case of an account beneficiary who has attained the age specified in section 1811 of the Social Security Act, any health insurance other than a medicare supplemental policy (as defined in section 1882 of the Social Security Act).

(3) ACCOUNT BENEFICIARY.—The term 'account beneficiary' means the individual on whose behalf the health savings account was established.

(4) CERTAIN RULES TO APPLY.—Rules similar to the following rules shall apply for purposes of this section:

(A) Section 219(d)(2) (relating to no deduction for rollovers).

(B) Section 219(f)(3) (relating to time when contributions deemed made).

(C) Except as provided in section 106(d), section 219(f)(5) (relating to employer payments).

(D) Section 408(g) (relating to community property laws).

(E) Section 408(h) (relating to custodial accounts).

(e) TAX TREATMENT OF ACCOUNTS.—

(1) IN GENERAL.—A health savings account is exempt from taxation under this subtitle unless such account has ceased to be a health savings account. Notwithstanding the preceding sentence, any such account is subject to the taxes imposed by section 511 (relating to imposition of tax on unrelated business income of charitable, etc. organizations).

(2) ACCOUNT TERMINATIONS.—Rules similar to the rules of paragraphs (2) and (4) of section 408(e) shall apply to health savings accounts, and any amount treated as distributed under such rules shall be treated as not used to pay qualified medical expenses.

(f) TAX TREATMENT OF DISTRIBUTIONS.—

(1) AMOUNTS USED FOR QUALIFIED MEDICAL EXPENSES.—Any amount paid or distributed out of a health savings account which is used exclusively to pay qualified medical expenses of any account beneficiary shall not be includible in gross income.

(2) INCLUSION OF AMOUNTS NOT USED FOR QUALIFIED MEDICAL EXPENSES.—Any amount paid or distributed out of a health savings account which is not used exclusively to pay the qualified medical expenses of the account beneficiary shall be included in the gross income of such beneficiary.

(3) EXCESS CONTRIBUTIONS RETURNED BEFORE DUE DATE OF RETURN.—

(A) IN GENERAL.—If any excess contribution is contributed for a taxable year to any health savings account of an individual, paragraph (2) shall not apply to distributions from the health savings accounts of such individual (to the extent such distributions do not exceed the aggregate excess contributions to all such accounts of such individual for such year) if—

(i) such distribution is received by the individual on or before the last day prescribed by law (including extensions of time) for filing such individual's return for such taxable year, and

(ii) such distribution is accompanied by the amount of net income attributable to such excess contribution.

Any net income described in clause (ii) shall be included in the gross income of the individual for the taxable year in which it is received.

(B) EXCESS CONTRIBUTION.—For purposes of subparagraph (A), the term 'excess contribution' means any contribution (other than a rollover contribution described in paragraph (5) or section 220(f)(5)) which is neither excludable from gross income under section 106(d) nor deductible under this section.

(4) ADDITIONAL TAX ON DISTRIBUTIONS NOT USED FOR QUALIFIED MEDICAL EXPENSES.—

(A) IN GENERAL.—The tax imposed by this chapter on the account beneficiary for any taxable year in which there is a payment or distribution from a health savings account of such beneficiary which is includible in gross income under paragraph (2) shall be increased by 10 percent of the amount which is so includible.

(B) EXCEPTION FOR DISABILITY OR DEATH.—Subparagraph (A) shall not apply if the payment or distribution is made after the account beneficiary becomes disabled within the meaning of section 72(m)(7) or dies.

(C) EXCEPTION FOR DISTRIBUTIONS AFTER MEDICARE ELIGIBILITY.—Subparagraph (A) shall not apply to any payment or distribution after the date on which the account beneficiary attains the age specified in section 1811 of the Social Security Act.

(5) ROLLOVER CONTRIBUTION.—An amount is described in this paragraph as a rollover contribution if it meets the requirements of subparagraphs (A) and (B).

(A) IN GENERAL.—Paragraph (2) shall not apply to any amount paid or distributed from a health savings account to the account beneficiary to the extent the amount received is paid into a health savings account for the benefit of such beneficiary not later than the 60th day after the day on which the beneficiary receives the payment or distribution.

(B) LIMITATION.—This paragraph shall not apply to any amount described in subparagraph (A) received by an individual from a health savings account if, at any time during the 1-year period ending on the day of such receipt, such individual received any other amount described in subparagraph (A) from a health savings account which was not includible in the individual's gross income because of the application of this paragraph.

(6) COORDINATION WITH MEDICAL EXPENSE DEDUCTION.—For purposes of determining the amount of the deduction under section 213, any payment or distribution out of a health savings account for qualified medical expenses shall not be treated as an expense paid for medical care.

(7) TRANSFER OF ACCOUNT INCIDENT TO DIVORCE.—The transfer of an individual's interest in a health savings account to an individual's spouse or former spouse under a divorce or separation instrument described in subparagraph (A) of section 71(b)(2) shall not be considered a taxable transfer made by such individual notwithstanding any other provision of this subtitle, and such interest shall, after such transfer, be treated as a health savings account with respect to which such spouse is the account beneficiary.

(8) TREATMENT AFTER DEATH OF ACCOUNT BENEFICIARY.—

(A) TREATMENT IF DESIGNATED BENEFICIARY IS SPOUSE.—If the account beneficiary's surviving spouse acquires such beneficiary's interest in a health savings account by reason of being the designated beneficiary of such account at the death of the account beneficiary, such health savings account shall be treated as if the spouse were the account beneficiary.

(B) OTHER CASES.—

(i) IN GENERAL.—If, by reason of the death of the account beneficiary, any person acquires the account beneficiary's interest in a health savings account in a case to which subparagraph (A) does not apply—

(I) such account shall cease to be a health savings account as of the date of death, and

(II) an amount equal to the fair market value of the assets in such account on such date shall be includible if such person is not the estate of such beneficiary, in such person's gross income for the taxable year which includes such date, or if such person is the estate of such beneficiary, in such beneficiary's gross income for the last taxable year of such beneficiary.

(ii) SPECIAL RULES.—

(I) REDUCTION OF INCLUSION FOR PREDEATH EXPENSES.—The amount includible in gross income under clause (i) by any person (other than the estate) shall be reduced by the amount of qualified medical expenses which were incurred by the decedent before the date of the decedent's death and paid by such person within 1 year after such date.

(II) DEDUCTION FOR ESTATE TAXES.—An appropriate deduction shall be allowed under section 691(c) to any person (other than the decedent or the decedent's spouse) with respect to amounts included in gross income under clause (i) by such person.

(g) COST-OF-LIVING ADJUSTMENT.—

(1) IN GENERAL.—Each dollar amount in subsections (b)(2) and (c)(2)(A) shall be increased by an amount equal to—

(A) such dollar amount, multiplied by

(B) the cost-of-living adjustment determined under section 1(f)(3) for the calendar year in which such taxable year begins determined by substituting for 'calendar year 1992' in subparagraph (B) thereof—

(i) except as provided in clause (ii), 'calendar year 1997', and

(ii) in the case of each dollar amount in subsection (c)(2)(A), 'calendar year 2003'.

(2) ROUNDING.—If any increase under paragraph (1) is not a multiple of $50, such increase shall be rounded to the nearest multiple of $50.

(h) REPORTS.—The Secretary may require—

(1) the trustee of a health savings account to make such reports regarding such account to the Secretary and to the account beneficiary with respect to contributions, distributions, the return of excess contributions, and such other matters as the Secretary determines appropriate, and

(2) any person who provides an individual with a high deductible health plan to make such reports to the Secretary and to the account beneficiary with respect to such plan as the Secretary determines appropriate.

The reports required by this subsection shall be filed at such time and in such manner and furnished to such individuals at such time and in such manner as may be required by the Secretary.".

(b) DEDUCTION ALLOWED WHETHER OR NOT INDIVIDUAL ITEMIZES OTHER DEDUCTIONS.—Subsection (a) of section 62 of such Code is amended by inserting after paragraph (18) the following new paragraph:

(19) HEALTH SAVINGS ACCOUNTS.—The deduction allowed by section 223.".

(c) ROLLOVERS FROM ARCHER MSAS PERMITTED.—Subparagraph (A) of section 220(f)(5) of such Code (relating to rollover contribution) is amended by inserting "or a health savings account (as defined in section 223(d))" after "paid into an Archer MSA".

(d) EXCLUSIONS FOR EMPLOYER CONTRIBUTIONS TO HEALTH SAVINGS ACCOUNTS.—

(1) EXCLUSION FROM INCOME TAX.—Section 106 of such Code (relating to contributions by employer to accident and health plans) is amended by adding at the end the following new subsection:

(d) CONTRIBUTIONS TO HEALTH SAVINGS ACCOUNTS.—

(1) IN GENERAL.—In the case of an employee who is an eligible individual (as defined in section 223(c)(1)), amounts contributed by such employee's employer to any health savings account (as defined in section 223(d)) of such employee shall be treated as employer-provided coverage for medical expenses under an accident or health plan to the extent such amounts do not exceed the limitation under section 223(b) (determined without regard to this subsection) which is applicable to such employee for such taxable year.

(2) SPECIAL RULES.—Rules similar to the rules of paragraphs (2), (3), (4), and (5) of subsection (b) shall apply for purposes of this subsection.

(3) CROSS REFERENCE.—

"For penalty on failure by employer to make comparable contributions to the health savings accounts of comparable employees, see section 4980G.".

Act Sec. 1201(d)(1) ¶11,400

(2) EXCLUSION FROM EMPLOYMENT TAXES.—

(A) RAILROAD RETIREMENT TAX.—Subsection (e) of section 3231 of such Code is amended by adding at the end the following new paragraph:

(11) HEALTH SAVINGS ACCOUNT CONTRIBUTIONS.— The term 'compensation' shall not include any payment made to or for the benefit of an employee if at the time of such payment it is reasonable to believe that the employee will be able to exclude such payment from income under section 106(d)..

(B) UNEMPLOYMENT TAX.—Subsection (b) of section 3306 of such Code is amended by striking "or" at the end of paragraph (16), by striking the period at the end of paragraph (17) and inserting "; or", and by inserting after paragraph (17) the following new paragraph:

(18) any payment made to or for the benefit of an employee if at the time of such payment it is reasonable to believe that the employee will be able to exclude such payment from income under section 106(d)..

(C) WITHHOLDING TAX.—Subsection (a) of section 3401 of such Code is amended by striking "or" at the end of paragraph (20), by striking the period at the end of paragraph (21) and inserting "; or", and by inserting after paragraph (21) the following new paragraph:

(22) any payment made to or for the benefit of an employee if at the time of such payment it is reasonable to believe that the employee will be able to exclude such payment from income under section 106(d)..

(3) EMPLOYER CONTRIBUTIONS REQUIRED TO BE SHOWN ON W-2.—Subsection (a) of section 6051 of such Code is amended by striking "and" at the end of paragraph (10), by striking the period at the end of paragraph (11) and inserting ", and", and by inserting after paragraph (11) the following new paragraph:

(12) the amount contributed to any health savings account (as defined in section 223(d)) of such employee or such employee's spouse.

(4) PENALTY FOR FAILURE OF EMPLOYER TO MAKE COMPARABLE HEALTH SAVINGS ACCOUNT CONTRIBUTIONS.—

(A) IN GENERAL.—Chapter 43 of such Code is amended by adding after section 4980F the following new section:

SEC. 4980G. FAILURE OF EMPLOYER TO MAKE COMPARABLE HEALTH SAVINGS ACCOUNT CONTRIBUTIONS.

(a) GENERAL RULE.— In the case of an employer who makes a contribution to the health savings account of any employee during a calendar year, there is hereby imposed a tax on the failure of such employer to meet the requirements of subsection (b) for such calendar year.

(b) RULES AND REQUIREMENTS.— Rules and requirements similar to the rules and requirements of section 4980E shall apply for purposes of this section.

"(c) REGULATIONS.— The Secretary shall issue regulations to carry out the purposes of this section, including regulations providing special rules for employers who make contributions to Archer MSAs and health savings accounts during the calendar year.".

(B) CLERICAL AMENDMENT.—The table of sections for chapter 43 of such Code is amended by adding after the item relating to section 4980F the following new item:

Sec. 4980G. Failure of employer to make comparable health savings account contributions..

(e) TAX ON EXCESS CONTRIBUTIONS.—Section 4973 of such Code (relating to tax on excess contributions to certain tax-favored accounts and annuities) is amended—

(1) by striking "or" at the end of subsection (a)(3), by inserting "or" at the end of subsection (a)(4), and by inserting after subsection (a)(4) the following new paragraph:

(5) a health savings account (within the meaning of section 223(d)), and

(2) by adding at the end the following new subsection:

(g) EXCESS CONTRIBUTIONS TO HEALTH SAVINGS ACCOUNTS.— For purposes of this section, in the case of health savings accounts (within the meaning of section 223(d)), the term 'excess contributions' means the sum of—

(1) the aggregate amount contributed for the taxable year to the accounts (other than a rollover contribution described in section 220(f)(5) or 223(f)(5)) which is neither excludable from gross income under section 106(d) nor allowable as a deduction under section 223 for such year, and

(2) the amount determined under this subsection for the preceding taxable year, reduced by the sum of—

(A) the distributions out of the accounts which were included in gross income under section 223(f)(2), and

(B) the excess (if any) of—

(i) the maximum amount allowable as a deduction under section 223(b) (determined without regard to section 106(d)) for the taxable year, over

(ii) the amount contributed to the accounts for the taxable year.

For purposes of this subsection, any contribution which is distributed out of the health savings account in a distribution to which section 223(f)(3) applies shall be treated as an amount not contributed.".

(f) TAX ON PROHIBITED TRANSACTIONS.—

(1) Section 4975 of such Code (relating to tax on prohibited transactions) is amended by adding at the end of subsection (c) the following new paragraph:

(6) SPECIAL RULE FOR HEALTH SAVINGS ACCOUNTS.— An individual for whose benefit a health savings account (within the meaning of section 223(d)) is established shall be exempt from the tax imposed by this section with respect to any transaction concerning such account (which would otherwise be taxable under this section) if, with respect to such transaction, the account ceases to be a health savings account by reason of the application of section 223(e)(2) to such account.

(2) Paragraph (1) of section 4975(e) of such Code is amended by redesignating subparagraphs (E) and (F) as subparagraphs (F) and (G), respectively, and by inserting after subparagraph (D) the following new subparagraph:

(E) a health savings account described in section 223(d),

(g) FAILURE TO PROVIDE REPORTS ON HEALTH SAVINGS ACCOUNTS.—Paragraph (2) of section 6693(a) of such Code (relating to reports) is amended by redesignating subparagraphs (C) and (D) as subparagraphs (D) and (E), respectively, and by inserting after subparagraph (B) the following new subparagraph:

(C) section 223(h) (relating to health savings accounts),

(h) EXCEPTION FROM CAPITALIZATION OF POLICY ACQUISITION EXPENSES.—Subparagraph (B) of section 848(e)(1) of such Code (defining specified insurance contract) is amended by striking "and" at the end of clause (iii), by striking the period at the end of clause (iv) and inserting ", and", and by adding at the end the following new clause:

(v) any contract which is a health savings account (as defined in section 223(d)).

(i) HEALTH SAVINGS ACCOUNTS MAY BE OFFERED UNDER CAFETERIA PLANS.—Paragraph (2) of section 125(d) (relating to cafeteria plan defined) is amended by adding at the end the following new subparagraph:

(D) EXCEPTION FOR HEALTH SAVINGS ACCOUNTS.— Subparagraph (A) shall not apply to a plan to the extent of amounts which a covered employee may elect to have the employer pay as contributions to a health savings account established on behalf of the employee..

(j) CLERICAL AMENDMENT.—The table of sections for part VII of subchapter B of chapter 1 of such Code is amended by striking the last item and inserting the following:

Sec. 223. Health savings accounts.

Sec. 224. Cross reference.

(k) EFFECTIVE DATE.—The amendments made by this section shall apply to taxable years beginning after December 31, 2003.

[¶ 11,410] ACT SEC. 1202. EXCLUSION FROM GROSS INCOME OF CERTAIN FEDERAL SUBSIDIES FOR PRESCRIPTION DRUG PLANS.

(a) IN GENERAL.—Part III of subchapter B of chapter 1 of the Internal Revenue Code of 1986 is amended by inserting after section 139 the following new section:

SEC. 139A. FEDERAL SUBSIDIES FOR PRESCRIPTION DRUG PLANS.

"Gross income shall not include any special subsidy payment received under section 1860D-22 of the Social Security Act. This section shall not be taken into account for purposes of determining whether any deduction is allowable with respect to any cost taken into account in determining such payment.".

(b) ALTERNATIVE MINIMUM TAX RELIEF.—Section 56(g)(4)(B) of such Code is amended by inserting "or 139A" after "section 114".

(c) CONFORMING AMENDMENT.—The table of sections for part III of subchapter B of chapter 1 of such Code is amended by inserting after the item relating to section 139 the following new item:

"Sec. 139A. Federal subsidies for prescription drug plans.".

(d) EFFECTIVE DATE.—The amendments made by this section shall apply to taxable years ending after the date of the enactment of this Act.

[¶ 11,420] ACT SEC. 1203. EXCEPTION TO INFORMATION REPORTING REQUIREMENTS RELATED TO CERTAIN HEALTH ARRANGEMENTS.

(a) IN GENERAL.—Section 6041 of the Internal Revenue Code of 1986 (relating to information at source) is amended by adding at the end the following new subsection:

(f) SECTION DOES NOT APPLY TO CERTAIN HEALTH ARRANGEMENTS.— This section shall not apply to any payment for medical care (as defined in section 213(d)) made under—

(1) a flexible spending arrangement (as defined in section 106(c)(2)), or

(2) a health reimbursement arrangement which is treated as employer-provided coverage under an accident or health plan for purposes of section 106..

(b) EFFECTIVE DATE.—The amendment made by this section shall apply to payments made after December 31, 2002.

¶ 20,001
# Social Security Act Sections Added, Amended, or Repealed

Medicare Prescription Drug, Improvement, and Modernization Act of 2003

SSA section	Act section
1871(e)(2)(A)	903(c)
1108(f)	103(d)(2)
1114(i)	948(a)(1)
1117	900(e)
1117(a)	900(e)
1117(b)(1)	900(e)
1117(b)(3)	900(c)
1128(c)(3)(B)	949
1128B(b)(3)	101(e)(2)
1128B(b)(3)(C)	101(e)(8)
1128B(b)(3)(F)	237(d)(1)
1128B(b)(3)(F)	431(a)(1)
1128B(b)(3)(G)	237(d)(2)
1128B(b)(3)(G)	431(a)(2)
1128B(b)(3)(H)	237(d)(3)
1128B(b)(3)(H)	431(a)(3)
1140(a)(1)	900(e)(B)
1140(a)(1)(A)	900(e)(B)
1140(a)(1)(B)	900(e)(B)
1142(b)(3)	900(e)(C)
1144	103(g)
1144(a)(1)(A)	103(g)
1144(a)(1)(B)	103(g)
1144(a)(2)	103(g)
1144(a)(2)(A)	103(g)
1144(b)(1)(A)	103(g)
1144(b)(2)	103(g)
1154(a)(1)	109(a)
1154(a)(17)	109(b)
1154(e)(5)	948(d)
1802(b)(5)(B)	603
1805(b)(2)(B)(i)	735(b)
1805(b)(8)	735(a)
1805(c)(2)(B)	735(e)
1805(c)(2)(D)	735(c)(1)
1807	721(a)
1808	900
1808	923

SSA section	Act section
1812(a)(3)	512(a)(1)
1812(a)(3)	736(c)(1)
1812(a)(4)	512(a)(2)
1812(a)(5)	512(a)(3)
1814(a)	736(a)(1)(A)
1814(a)	736(c)(2)(A)
1814(a)(7)(A)(i)	736(a)(1)(B)(i)
1814(a)(7)(A)(i)(I)	408(b)
1814(a)(7)(A)(ii)	736(a)(1)(B)(ii)
1814(b)	736(a)(2)
1814(i)	946(b)
1814(i)(4)	512(b)
1814(l)	405(a)(1)
1814(l)(1)	405(g)(2)(A)
1814(l)(2)	405(g)(2)(B)
1815(e)(1)(B)	736(a)(3)
1815(e)(2)	405(c)(1)
1816	911(b)(1)
1816(a)	911(b)(2)
1816(b)	911(b)(3)
1816(c)	911(b)(4)
1816(c)(2)(B)(ii)(III)	736(a)(4)(A)
1816(c)(2)(B)(ii)(IV)	736(a)(4)(B)
1816(d)	911(b)(5)
1816(e)	911(b)(5)
1816(f)	911(b)(5)
1816(g)	911(b)(5)
1816(h)	911(b)(5)
1816(i)	911(b)(5)
1816(j)	911(b)(6)
1816(k)	911(b)(6)
1816(l)	911(b)(7)
1817(b)	900(e)(1)(D)
1817(k)(3)(A)(i)(I)	736(a)(5)(A)
1817(k)(3)(A)(ii)	736(a)(5)(A)
1817(k)(6)(B)	736(a)(6)
1818(a)	101(e)(5)
1818(d)(6)(A)	736(a)(7)(A)
1818(g)(2)(B)	736(a)(7)(B)
1819(b)(4)(C)(i)	736(a)(8)(A)
1819(d)(1)(A)	736(a)(8)(B)
1819(f)(2)	932(c)(2)(B)
1819(f)(2)(B)(iii)	736(a)(8)(C)
1819(f)(2)(B)(iii)	932(c)(2)
1820(c)(2)(B)(i)(II	405(h)(1)
1820(c)(2)(B)(iii)	405(e)(1)
1820(c)(2)(E)	405(g)(1)

Social Security Act Sections Added, Amended, or Repealed

SSA section	Act section
1820(f)	405(e)(2)
1820(g)(4)	405(f)(2)
1820(g)(5)	405(f)(2)
1820(h)	405(h)(2)(A)
1820(h)(3)	405(h)(2)(B)
1821(a)	706(a)(1)
1821(a)(2)	706(a)(2)
1833(a)(1)(D)	302(b)(2)(C)
1833(a)(1)(G)	626(c)
1833(a)(1)(S)	303(i)(3)(A)
1833(a)(1)(S)	642(b)
1833(a)(1)(T)	302(b)(2)(A)
1833(a)(1)(U)	302(b)(2)(B)
1833(a)(2)(E)(i)	614(b)
1833(a)(3)	237(a)
1833(b)	629
1833(g)(4)	624(a)(1)
1833(h)	942(b)
1833(h)(2)(A)(ii)(IV)	628
1833(h)(5)(D)	736(b)(1)
1833(i)(2)(A)	626(b)(1)(A)
1833(i)(2)(A)(i)	626(b)(1)(B)
1833(i)(2)(C)	626(a)
1833(i)(2)(D)	626(b)(2)
1833(m)(1)	413(b)(1)(A)
1833(m)(1)	413(b)(1)(B)
1833(m)(2)	413(b)(1)(C)
1833(m)(3)	413(b)(1)(C)
1833(m)(4)	413(b)(1)(C)
1833(o)(1)(B)	627(a)(1)
1833(o)(2)	627(a)(2)
1833(t)(1)(B)(iv)	614(a)
1833(t)(13)	411(b)(1)
1833(t)(13)	411(b)(2)
1833(t)(14)	621(a)(1)
1833(t)(16)(B)	621(a)(2)
1833(t)(16)(C)	621(b)(1)
1833(t)(2)(F)	621(b)(2)(A)
1833(t)(2)(G)	621(b)(2)(B)
1833(t)(2)(H)	621(b)(2)(C)
1833(t)(3)(C)(ii)	736(b)(2)
1833(t)(5)(E)	621(a)(3)
1833(t)(6)(D)(i)	621(a)(4)
1833(t)(6)(F)	622
1833(t)(7)(D)(i)	411(a)
1833(t)(9)(B)	621(a)(5)
1833(u)	413(a)

¶20,001

SSA section	Act section
1834(a)(1)(B)	302(d)(1)(A)
1834(a)(1)(C)	302(d)(1)(B)
1834(a)(1)(E)	302(a)(2)
1834(a)(1)(F)	302(d)(1)(C)
1834(a)(10)(B)	302(d)(1)(D)
1834(a)(14)(E)	302(c)(1)(A)(i)
1834(a)(14)(F)	302(c)(1)(A)(ii)
1834(a)(14)(G)	302(c)(1)(A)(iii)
1834(a)(14)(H)	302(c)(1)(A)(iii)
1834(a)(14)(I)	302(c)(1)(A)(iii)
1834(a)(14)(J)	302(c)(1)(A)(iii)
1834(a)(17)	302(a)(1)(A)
1834(a)(20)	302(a)(1)(B)
1834(a)(21)	302(c)(2)
1834(b)(4)(D)(iv)	736(b)(4)
1834(g)(1)	405(a)(1)
1834(g)(2)	405(d)(1)
1834(g)(5)	405(b)(1)
1834(h)(1)(B)	302(d)(2)(A)
1834(h)(1)(D)	302(d)(2)(B)
1834(h)(1)(H)	302(d)(2)(C)
1834(h)(4)(A)(ix)	302(c)(3)(C)
1834(h)(4)(A)(vii)	302(c)(3)(A)
1834(h)(4)(A)(viii)	302(c)(3)(B)
1834(h)(4)(A)(x)	302(c)(3)(C)
1834(h)(4)(C)	627(b)(1)
1834(l)(10)	414(a)(3)
1834(l)(11)	414(b)
1834(l)(12)	414(c)
1834(l)(13)	414(d)
1834(l)(14)	415(a)
1834(l)(2)(E)	414(a)(1)
1834(l)(8)	414(a)(2)
1834(m)(4)(C)(ii)(III)	736(b)(5)
1835(a)	736(c)(2)(B)
1838(a)(1)	736(b)(6)
1839(a)(2)	222(l)(2)(A)
1839(a)(2)	811(b)(1)
1839(a)(4)	736(b)(7)
1839(b)	625(a)(1)
1839(b)	811(b)(1)
1839(f)	811(b)(1)
1839(g)	105(a)
1839(g)(2)	105(a)
1839(h)	241(b)(2)(A)
1839(I)	811
1840(i)	222(l)(2)(B)

Social Security Act Sections Added, Amended, or Repealed

SSA section	Act section
1841	101(e)(3)
1841(a)	105(d)
1841(b)	900(e)(E)
1841(g)	105(d)
1842	911(c)(1)
1842(a)	911(c)(2)
1842(b)(1)	911(c)(3)
1842(b)(2)	911(c)(3)
1842(b)(3)	911(c)(3)
1842(b)(3)(A)	911(c)(3)(ii)
1842(b)(3)(B)	911(c)(3)(ii)
1842(b)(3)(B)	911(c)(3)(iii)
1842(b)(3)(C)	911(c)(3)(iv)
1842(b)(3)(D)	911(c)(3)(iv)
1842(b)(3)(E)	911(c)(3)(iv)
1842(b)(3)(F)	911(c)(3)(ii)
1842(b)(3)(G)	911(c)(3)(ii)
1842(b)(3)(H)	911(c)(3)(ii)
1842(b)(3)(H)	911(c)(3)(v)
1842(b)(3)(I)	911(c)(3)(vi)
1842(b)(3)(L)	911(c)(3)(ii)
1842(b)(3)(L)	911(c)(3)(vii)
1842(b)(3)(L)	911(c)(3)(viii)
1842(b)(5)	911(c)(3)(D)
1842(b)(6)	952
1842(b)(6)(A)	952
1842(b)(6)(D)(iv)	911(c)(3)E
1842(b)(7)	911(c)(3)(A)(ii)
1842(c)(1)	911(c)(4)(A)
1842(c)(2)(A)	911(c)(4)(B)
1842(c)(2)(B)(ii)(III)	736(b)(8)(A)
1842(c)(2)(B)(ii)(IV)	736(b)(8)(B)
1842(c)(3)(A)	911(c)(4)(C)
1842(c)(4)(A)	911(c)(4)(D)
1842(c)(5)	911(c)(4)(E)
1842(c)(6)	911(c)(4)(E)
1842(d)	911(c)(5)
1842(e)	911(c)(5)
1842(f)	911(c)(5)
1842(g)	911(c)(6)
1842(h)(2)	911(c)(7)(A)
1842(h)(3)(A)	911(c)(7)(B)
1842(h)(3)(B)	911(c)(7)(C)
1842(h)(5)(A)	911(c)(7)(D)
1842(h)(5)(B)(iii)	911(c)(7)(D)
1842(i)(2)	736(b)(9)
1842(l)(1)(A)(iii)	911(c)(8)(A)

¶ 20,001

SSA section	Act section
1842(l)(2)	911(c)(8)(B)
1842(o)(1)	303(b)(1)
1842(o)(1)(G)	305(a)
1842(o)(2)	303(i)(1)
1842(o)(4)	303(b)(2)
1842(o)(5)	303(e)(1)
1842(o)(6)	303(e)(2)
1842(o)(7)	303(g)(1)
1842(p)(3)(A)	911(c)(9)
1842(q)(1)(A)	911(c)(10)
1842(s)(1)	302(d)(3)(A)
1842(s)(2)(C)	627(b)(2)
1842(s)(3)	302(d)(3)(B)
1844(a)(1)(C)	811(b)(2)
1844(c)	222(l)(2)(C)
1844(c)	811(b)(2)
1847	302(b)(1)
1847A	303(c)(1)
1847B	303(d)(1)
1848(c)(2)(B)(ii)(II)	303(a)(1)(A)(i)
1848(c)(2)(B)(iv)	303(a)(1)(A)(ii)
1848(c)(2)(H)	303(a)(1)(B)
1848(c)(2)(I)	303(a)(1)(B)
1848(c)(2)(J)	303(a)(1)(B)
1848(d)(4)(B)	601(a)(2)
1848(d)(5)	601(a)(1)
1848(e)(1)(A)	412(1)
1848(e)(1)(A)	602(1)
1848(e)(1)(E)	412(2)
1848(e)(1)(G)	602(2)
1848(f)(2)(C)	601(b)(1)
1848(i)(1)(B)	303(g)(2)
1848(i)(3)(A)	736(b)(10)
1848(j)(3)	611(c)
1851(a)(1)	102(c)
1851(a)(2)(A)	221(a)
1851(a)(2)(A)(ii)	231(a)
1851(a)(3)(B)(ii)	222(l)(3)(D)
1851(b)(1)	222(l)(3)(A)
1851(d)(3)(F)	222(l)(3)(B)(i)
1851(d)(4)(A)(ii)	222(l)(3)(B)(ii)
1851(d)(4)(B)(i)	222(l)(3)(B)(iii)
1851(d)(4)(E)	222(l)(3)(B)(iv)
1851(e)(1)	102(a)
1851(e)(2)	102(a)
1851(e)(2)(B)(i)	102(a)
1851(e)(2)(C)(i)	102(a)

Social Security Act Sections Added, Amended, or Repealed

SSA section	Act section
1851(e)(3)(B)	102(a)
1851(e)(3)(C)	102(a)
1851(e)(3)(D)	102(a)
1851(e)(4)	102(a)
1851(e)(5)(A)(i)	233(d)(1)
1851(e)(5)(A)(ii)	233(d)(2)
1851(e)(5)(A)(iii)	233(d)(3)
1851(f)(1)	222(l)(3)(E)
1851(f)(3)	102(a)
1851(i)(1)	237(b)(2)(A)(i)
1851(i)(2)	221(d)(5)
1851(i)(2)	237(b)(2)(A)(ii)
1852(a)(1)	221(d)(3)(A)
1852(a)(1)	222(a)(2)
1852(a)(2)(C)	948(b)(2)
1852(a)(3)	222(a)(3)
1852(a)(5)	900 (e)(F)
1852(a)(6)	221(d)(3)(B)
1852(b)(1)(A)	222(l)(1)
1852(c)(1)(I)	233(a)(2)(A)
1852(c)(1)(I)	722(b)
1852(d)(4)(B)	211(j)
1852(e)	722(a)(1)
1852(e)(1)	233(a)(1)
1852(e)(1)	722(a)(2)
1852(e)(2)	722(a)(2)
1852(e)(2)(A)	233(a)(2)(B)
1852(e)(2)(B)	233(a)(2)(C)
1852(e)(3)	722(a)(2)
1852(e)(4)(B)(i)	722(a)(3)(A)
1852(e)(4)(B)(vii)	722(a)(3)(B)
1852(e)(5)	722(a)(4)
1852(g)(5)	940(b)(2)
1852(j)	102(b)
1852(j)(4)	222(h)(1)
1852(j)(4)(ii)	222(h)(2)
1852(j)(4)(iii)	222(h)(3)
1852(k)(1)	233(c)
1853(a)(1)(A)	222(e)(1)(B)
1853(a)(1)(B)	222(e)(1)(A)
1853(a)(1)(H)	222(i)
1853(a)(3)(C)(ii)	736(d)(1)(A)
1853(a)(3)(C)(iii)	736(d)(1)(B)
1853(a)(4)	237(b)(1)
1853(b)(1)	222(f)(1)
1853(b)(1)(B)(iii)	241(b)(1)(B)
1853(b)(3)	222(f)(2)

¶ 20,001

Social Security Act Sections Added, Amended, or Repealed

SSA section	Act section
1853(b)(4)	900(e)(1)(G)
1853(c)(1)	211(a)(2)
1853(c)(1)	221(d)(4)
1853(c)(1)(A)	211(b)(1)
1853(c)(1)(A)	211(c)(1)(A)
1853(c)(1)(B)(iv)	211(c)(1)(B)
1853(c)(1)(C)(iv)	211(c)(1)(C)
1853(c)(1)(C)(v)	211(c)(1)(D)
1853(c)(1)(D)	211(a)(1)
1853(c)(3)(A)	211(d)(1)
1853(c)(3)(E)	211(d)(2)
1853(c)(5)	211(b)(2)
1853(c)(5)	237(b)(2)(B)
1853(c)(5)	736(d)(1)(C)
1853(c)(6)(C)	211(c)(2)
1853(c)(7)	900(e)(1)(G)
1853(d)	221(d)(1)
1853(f)	101(e)(3)
1853(g)	211(e)(1)(A)
1853(g)(2)(B)	211(e)(1)(B)
1853(j)	222(d)
1853(j)(1)(A)	241(b)(1)(A)
1854	222(g)(1)(A)
1854(a)	222(g)(1)(B)
1854(a)(1)	222(a)(1)(A)
1854(a)(2)	222(g)(1)(C)
1854(a)(3)	222(g)(1)(D)
1854(a)(4)	222(g)(1)(E)
1854(a)(5)(A)	222(g)(1)(F)
1854(a)(5)(A)	900(e)(1)(H)
1854(a)(5)(B)	222(g)(1)(G)
1854(a)(6)	222(a)(1)(B)
1854(b)(1)(A)	222(b)(1)(A)
1854(b)(1)(A)	222(g)(1)(H)
1854(b)(1)(C)	222(b)(1)(B)
1854(b)(2)	222(b)(2)(A)
1854(b)(2)(A)	222(b)(2)(C)
1854(b)(2)(B)	222(b)(2)(C)
1854(b)(2)(C)	222(b)(2)(B)
1854(b)(2)(E)	222(b)(2)(D)
1854(b)(3)	222(b)(3)
1854(b)(4)	233(b)(1)
1854(b)(4)(A)	233(b)(2)
1854(b)(4)(C)	233(b)(3)
1854(c)	222(g)(2)
1854(d)(1)	222(g)(3)
1854(d)(1)	222(c)(1)

¶20,001 ©2004, CCH INCORPORATED

Social Security Act Sections Added, Amended, or Repealed

SSA section	Act section
1854(d)(2)	222(c)(2)
1854(d)(3)	222(c)(2)
1854(d)(4)	222(c)(2)
1854(e)(1)	222(g)(4)(A)
1854(e)(2)	222(g)(4)(B)
1854(e)(3)	222(g)(4)(C)
1854(e)(4)	222(g)(4)(D)
1854(f)	222(g)(5)(A)
1854(f)(1)(A)	222(g)(5)(B)
1854(g)	232(b)
1856(b)(3)	232(a)
1857(d)(1)	222(l)(3)(C)
1857(d)(4)(A)(ii)	900(e)(I)
1857(e)(2)(A)	222(k)(1)
1857(e)(2)(B)	222(k)(2)
1857(e)(2)(C)	222(k)(3)
1857(e)(2)(D)	222(k)(4)
1857(e)(2)(F)	222(k)(5)
1857(e)(3)	237(c)
1857(i)(1)	222(j)(1)
1857(i)(2)	222(j)(2)
1858	221(c)
1859(b)(4)	221(b)
1859(b)(5)	221(b)
1859(b)(6)	231(b)
1859(c)(5)	221(d)(2)
1859(f)	231(c)
1860C-1	241(a)
1860D-1	101(a)
1860D-2	101(a)
1860D-3	101(a)
1860D-4	101(a)
1860D-11	101(a)
1860D-12	101(a)
1860D-13	101(a)
1860D-14	101(a)
1860D-15	101(a)
1860D-16	101(a)
1860D-21	101(a)
1860D-22	101(a)
1860D-23	101(a)
1860D-24	101(a)
1860D-31	101(a)
1860D-41	101(a)
1860D-42	101(a)
1861(d)	901(b)
1861(s)(2)(A)	303(i)(2)

Social Security Act Sections Added, Amended, or Repealed

SSA section	Act section
1861(s)(2)(K)(i)	611(d)(2)
1861(s)(2)(K)(i)	736(b)(11)
1861(s)(2)(K)(ii)	611(d)(2)
1861(s)(2)(U)	611(a)(1)
1861(s)(2)(V)(iii)	611(a)(2)
1861(s)(2)(V)(iii)	612(a)(1)
1861(s)(2)(W)	611(a)(3)
1861(s)(2)(W)	612(a)(2)
1861(s)(2)(W)	613(a)(1)
1861(s)(2)(X)	612(a)(3)
1861(s)(2)(X)	613(a)(2)
1861(s)(2)(X)	642(a)(1)(A)
1861(s)(2)(Y)	613(a)(3)
1861(s)(2)(Y)	642(a)(1)(B)
1861(s)(2)(Z)	642(a)(1)(C)
1861(s)(7)	415(b)
1861(v)	736(c)(4)
1861(v)(1)(S)(ii)(III)	736(b)(3)
1861(v)(1)(U)	414(g)
1861(aa)(1)(B)	736(b)(12)
1861(dd)(2)(A)(i)	512(c)
1861(dd)(3)(B)	408(a)
1861(dd)(5)	946
1861(ee)(2)(D)	926(b)
1861(mm)	736(a)(10)
1861(tt)(1)	736(a)(11)
1861(tt)(2)	736(a)(11)
1861(ww)	611(b)
1861(xx)	612(b)
1861(yy)	613(b)
1861(zz)	642(a)(2)
1861(aaa)	706(b)
1862	948(a)(2)
1862(a)	731(a)(1)(A)
1862(a)(1)(H)	303(i)(3)(B)(i)
1862(a)(1)(I)	303(i)(3)(B)(ii)
1862(a)(1)(I)	611(d)(1)(A)(i)
1862(a)(1)(J)	303(i)(3)(B)(iii)
1862(a)(1)(J)	611(d)(1)(A)(ii)
1862(a)(1)(J)	612(c)(1)
1862(a)(1)(K)	611(d)(1)(A)(iii)
1862(a)(1)(K)	612(c)(2)
1862(a)(1)(K)	613(c)(1)
1862(a)(1)(L)	612(c)(3)
1862(a)(1)(L)	613(c)(2)
1862(a)(1)(M)	613(c)(3)
1862(a)(7)	611(d)(1)(B)

¶20,001 ©2004, CCH INCORPORATED

Social Security Act Sections Added, Amended, or Repealed

SSA section	Act section
1862(b)(1)(A)	301(c)(1)
1862(b)(2)(A)	301(b)(1)
1862(b)(2)(A)(ii)	301(a)(1)
1862(b)(2)(B)	301(a)(2)
1862(b)(2)(B)(ii)	301(b)(2)
1862(b)(2)(B)(iii)	301(b)(3)
1862(b)(3)(A)	301(c)(2)
1862(b)(5)(A)(ii)	900(e)(J)
1862(d)	944(a)
1862(k)(1)	950
1862(l)	731(a)(1)(B)
1862(m)	731(b)(1)
1865(b)(3)(B)	736(a)(12)
1866	936(a)(1)
1866(a)(1)	947(a)(1)
1866(a)(1)(O)	236(a)(1)
1866(a)(1)(R)	505(b)(1)
1866(a)(1)(S)	505(b)(2)
1866(a)(1)(S)	506(a)(1)
1866(a)(1)(T)	505(b)(3)
1866(a)(1)(T)	506(a)(2)
1866(a)(1)(U)	506(a)(3)
1866(b)	947(a)(2)
1866(b)(2)	736(a)(13)
1866(h)(1)	932(b)
1866(h)(1)	932(c)(1)
1866(j)	936(a)(2)
1866B(b)(7)(D)	736(c)(5)
1866C	646
1867(d)(1)(B)(ii)	736(a)(14)(A)
1867(d)(3)	944(c)
1867(d)(4)	944(b)
1867(e)(1)(B)	736(a)(14)(B)
1867(e)(2)	736(a)(14)(C)
1868	942(a)
1868	942(a)(1)
1869(a)	933(c)
1869(a)(3)(C)(i)	940(a)(2)
1869(a)(3)(C)(ii)	940(a)(1)
1869(b)	932
1869(b)	933(a)
1869(b)(1)(E)	940(b)(1)
1869(b)(1)(F)(ii)	932(a)(2)
1869(c)(3)	933(d)(1)(A)
1869(c)(3)(B)(i)	933(b)
1869(c)(3)(D)	933(d)(2)(A)
1869(c)(3)(E)	933(c)(2)

¶20,001

Social Security Act Sections Added, Amended, or Repealed

SSA section	Act section
1869(c)(3)(I)(ii)	948(b)(1)
1869(c)(3)(J)(i)	933(c)(4)
1869(c)(3)(K)	933(d)(1)(B)
1869(d)	933(c)(3)
1869(f)(2)(A)(I)	931(d)
1869(f)(4)	948(c)
1869(g)	933(d)(2)(B)
1869(h)	938
1869(i)	940A
1870(h)	939
1871(a)(3)	902(a)
1871(a)(4)	902(b)
1871(e)(1)(A)	903(a)
1871(e)(1)(A)	903(b)
1871(e)(1)(B)	903(b)
1871(e)(1)(C)	903(b)
1871(f)(1)	904
1874A	911(a)
1874A (f)	921
1874A(b)(3)(A)(i)	940A(b)
1874A(e)	912
1874A(g)	921(c)
1874A(h)	934(a)
1875(b)	101(e)(7)
1876(b)(5)(B)	940(b)(2)(B)
1876(c)(2)(B)	736(d)(2)(A)
1876(h)(5)	234
1876(j)(2)	736(d)(2)(B)
1877(b)	101(e)(8)
1877(d)(2)	507(a)(2)
1877(d)(3)(A)	507(a)(1)(A)(i)
1877(d)(3)(B)	507(a)(1)(A)(ii)
1877(h)(7)	507(a)(1)(B)
1880(e)(1)(A)	630
1881(b)(11)(B)	623(d)(3)
1881(b)(12)	623(d)(1)
1881(b)(13)	623(d)(1)
1881(b)(7)	623(a)
1881(b)(7)	623(b)(2)
1881(b)(7)	623(d)(2)
1882(d)(3)(A)(i)(II)	736(e)(1)
1882(d)(3)(B)(iii)(II)	736(e)(2)
1882(g)(1)	104(b)(2)(A)
1882(g)(2)(A)	736(e)(3)
1882(o)(1)	104(b)(2)(B)
1882(p)(2)(B)	736(e)(4)
1882(s)(3)(A)(iii)	736(e)(5)

Social Security Act Sections Added, Amended, or Repealed

SSA section	Act section
1882(s)(3)(C)(ii)	104(a)(2)(A)
1882(s)(3)(C)(iii)	104(a)(2)(B)
1882(v)	104(a)(1)
1882(w)	104(b)(1)
1883(a)(3)	405(a)(1)
1886(b)(3)(B)(i)(XIX)	501(a)(2)
1886(b)(3)(B)(i)(XIX)	501(a)(3)
1886(b)(3)(B)(i)(XVIII)	501(a)(1)
1886(b)(3)(B)(i)(XX)	501(a)(3)
1886(b)(3)(B)(vii)	501(b)
1886(b)(3)(I)(i)(I)	736(a)(9)
1886(b)(3)(I)(iii)	407(a)
1886(d)(12)	406(a)
1886(d)(13)	505(a)
1886(d)(2)(C)(i)	502(b)
1886(d)(2)(C)(iv)	402(b)(2)
1886(d)(3)	401(b)(2)(A)
1886(d)(3)(A)(iii)	401(b)(3)
1886(d)(3)(A)(iv)	401(a)(1)
1886(d)(3)(A)(iv)(II)	401(a)(2)
1886(d)(3)(D)	401(b)(1)(A)
1886(d)(3)(D)	401(b)(1)(B)
1886(d)(3)(D)	401(b)(2)(B)
1886(d)(3)(D)(i)	401(b)(1)(C)
1886(d)(3)(D)(ii)	401(b)(1)(D)
1886(d)(3)(D)(iii)	401(b)(1)(E)
1886(d)(3)(E)	403(a)(2)
1886(d)(3)(E)(i)	403(a)(1)(A)
1886(d)(3)(E)(ii)	403(a)(1)(B)
1886(d)(5)(B)(ii)	422(b)(1)(A)
1886(d)(5)(B)(ii)(IX)	502(a)(3)
1886(d)(5)(B)(ii)(VI)	502(a)(1)
1886(d)(5)(B)(ii)(VII)	502(a)(2)
1886(d)(5)(B)(ii)(VIII)	502(a)(3)
1886(d)(5)(B)(ii)(X)	502(a)(3)
1886(d)(5)(B)(ii)(XI)	502(a)(3)
1886(d)(5)(B)(ii)(XII)	502(a)(3)
1886(d)(5)(B)(ix)	422(b)(1)(C)
1886(d)(5)(B)(v)	422(b)(1)(B)
1886(d)(5)(F)	402(b)(1)
1886(d)(5)(F)(xiv)	402(a)
1886(d)(5)(K)(i)	503(b)(2)(A)
1886(d)(5)(K)(ii)(I)	503(b)(1)
1886(d)(5)(K)(ii)(III)	503(d)(1)
1886(d)(5)(K)(ix)	503(c)
1886(d)(5)(K)(vii)	503(a)
1886(d)(5)(K)(viii)	503(b)(2)(B)

¶20,001

Social Security Act Sections Added, Amended, or Repealed

SSA section	Act section
1886(d)(7)(A)	406(b)
1886(d)(9)(A)(i)	401(c)(1)(A)
1886(d)(9)(A)(i)	504(1)(A)
1886(d)(9)(A)(ii)	401(c)(1)(B)
1886(d)(9)(A)(ii)	504(1)(B)
1886(d)(9)(C)(i)	401(c)(2)(A)(i)
1886(d)(9)(C)(i)(II)	401(c)(2)(A)(ii)
1886(d)(9)(C)(ii)	401(c)(2)(B)
1886(d)(9)(C)(iii)	401(c)(2)(C)
1886(d)(9)(C)(iv)(I)	403(b)(1)
1886(d)(9)(C)(iv)(I)	403(b)(2)
1886(d)(9)(C)(iv)(II)	403(b)(3)
1886(d)(9)(E)	504(2)
1886(g)(3)(B)	736(a)(15)
1886(h)(2)(D)(iv)(I)	711(1)(A)(1)
1886(h)(2)(D)(iv)(II)	711(1)(A)(2)
1886(h)(3)(D)(ii)(III)	736(c)(6)
1886(h)(4)(F)(i)	422(a)(1)
1886(h)(4)(H)(i)	422(a)(2)
1886(h)(7)	422(a)(3)
1888(e)(12)	511(a)
1888(e)(2)(A)(i)(II)	410(a)(1)
1888(e)(2)(A)(iv)	410(a)(2)
1889	921
1889(b)	921(d)
1889(d)	921(e)
1889(g)	921(f)
1889(g)	921(f)
1889(c)	921(d)
1891(d)(1)	736(c)(3)
1893(a)	736(c)(7)
1893(f)	935(a)
1894(b)(3)	236(a)(2)
1894(b)(4)	236(a)(2)
1895(b)(3)(B)(i)	701(a)(1)
1895(b)(3)(B)(ii)(I)	701(a)(2)(A)
1895(b)(3)(B)(ii)(II)	701(a)(2)(B)
1895(b)(3)(B)(ii)(II)	701(a)(2)(D)
1895(b)(3)(B)(ii)(II)	701(b)(1)
1895(b)(3)(B)(ii)(III)	701(a)(2)(C)
1895(b)(3)(B)(ii)(III)	701(b)(2)
1895(b)(3)(B)(ii)(III)	701(b)(4)
1895(b)(3)(B)(ii)(IV)	701(b)(3)
1895(b)(3)(B)(iii)	701(a)(3)
1895(b)(3)(B)(iv)	701(a)(4)
1895(b)(5)	701(a)(5)
1896(b)(4)	736(c)(8)

Social Security Act Sections Added, Amended, or Repealed

SSA section	Act section
1897	1016
1902(a)(10)(E)(iv)	103(f)
1902(a)(64)	103(a)
1902(a)(65)	103(a)
1902(a)(65)	236(b)(1)(A)
1902(a)(66)	103(a)
1902(a)(66)	236(b)(1)(B)
1902(a)(67)	236(b)(1)(C)
1919(f)(2)	932(c)(2)(B)
1919(f)(2)(B)(iii)	932(c)(2)
1923(f)(3)	1001
1923(f)(3)(A)	1001(c)
1923(f)(5)	1001(b)
1923(f)(6)	1001(c)
1923(f)(7)	1001(c)
1923(j)	1001(d)
1927(a)(1)	303(i)(4)(A)
1927(b)(3)(A)(i)	303(i)(4)(B)(i)
1927(b)(3)(A)(ii)	303(i)(4)(B)(ii)
1927(b)(3)(A)(iii)	303(i)(4)(B)(iii)
1927(b)(3)(B)	303(i)(4)(C)(i)
1927(b)(3)(B)	303(i)(4)(C)(ii)
1927(b)(3)(D)	101(e)(4)
1927(b)(3)(D)	105(b)
1927(b)(3)(D)	303(i)(4)(D)(i)
1927(b)(3)(D)(i)	303(i)(4)(D)(ii)
1927(c)(1)(C)(i)	103(e)
1927(c)(1)(C)(i)(I)	1002
1927(c)(1)(C)(iii)	1002(b)
1927(e)(4)	900(e)(1)(K)
1927(f)(2)	900(e)(1)(L)
1927(g)(1)(B)(i)	101(e)(9)
1933(g)	103(f)
1934(b)(3)	236(b)(2)
1934(b)(4)	236(b)(2)
1935	103(a)
1935	103(b)
1935	103(c)
1935(a)	103(d)(1)
1935(c)(1)	103(d)(1)
1935(e)	103(d)(1)
201(g)	101(e)(3)
201(i)(1)	101(e)(3)
2104(g)(3)	900(e)(1)(M)
711(b)	432

¶20,001

¶ 20,010
Act Sections Amending Social Security Act Sections
Medicare Prescription Drug, Improvement, and Modernization Act of 2003

Act section	SSA section
101(a)	1860D-1
101(a)	1860D-2
101(a)	1860D-3
101(a)	1860D-4
101(a)	1860D-11
101(a)	1860D-12
101(a)	1860D-13
101(a)	1860D-14
101(a)	1860D-15
101(a)	1860D-16
101(a)	1860D-21
101(a)	1860D-22
101(a)	1860D-23
101(a)	1860D-24
101(a)	1860D-31
101(a)	1860D-41
101(a)	1860D-42
101(e)(2)	1128B(b)(3)
101(e)(3)	1841
101(e)(3)	1853(f)
101(e)(3)	201(g)
101(e)(3)	201(i)(1)
101(e)(4)	1927(b)(3)(D)
101(e)(5)	1818(a)
101(e)(7)	1875(b)
101(e)(8)	1128B(b)(3)(C)
101(e)(8)	1877(b)
101(e)(9)	1927(g)(1)(B)(i)
102(a)	1851(e)(1)
102(a)	1851(e)(2)
102(a)	1851(e)(2)(B)(i)
102(a)	1851(e)(2)(C)(i)
102(a)	1851(e)(3)(B)
102(a)	1851(e)(3)(C)
102(a)	1851(e)(3)(D)
102(a)	1851(e)(4)
102(a)	1851(f)(3)
102(b)	1852(j)

Act Sections Amending Social Security Act Sections

Act section	SSA section
102(c)	1851(a)(1)
103(a)	1935
103(a)	1902(a)(64)
103(a)	1902(a)(65)
103(a)	1902(a)(66)
103(b)	1935
103(d)(1)	1935(a)
103(d)(1)	1935(e)
103(d)(1)	1935(c)(1)
103(d)(2)	1108(f)
103(e)	1927(c)(1)(C)(i)
103(f)	1902(a)(10)(E)(iv)
103(f)	1933(g)
103(g)	1144
103(g)	1144(a)(1)(A)
103(g)	1144(a)(1)(B)
103(g)	1144(a)(2)
103(g)	1144(a)(2)(A)
103(g)	1144(b)(1)(A)
103(g)	1144(b)(2)
103(c)	1935
104(a)(1)	1882(v)
104(a)(2)(A)	1882(s)(3)(C)(ii)
104(a)(2)(B)	1882(s)(3)(C)(iii)
104(b)(1)	1882(w)
104(b)(2)(A)	1882(g)(1)
104(b)(2)(B)	1882(o)(1)
105(a)	1839(g)
105(a)	1839(g)(2)
105(b)	1927(b)(3)(D)
105(d)	1841(a)
105(d)	1841(g)
109(a)	1154(a)(1)
109(b)	1154(a)(17)
211(a)(1)	1853(c)(1)(D)
211(a)(2)	1853(c)(1)
211(b)(1)	1853(c)(1)(A)
211(b)(2)	1853(c)(5)
211(d)(1)	1853(c)(3)(A)
211(d)(2)	1853(c)(3)(E)
211(e)(1)(A)	1853(g)
211(e)(1)(B)	1853(g)(2)(B)
211(j)	1852(d)(4)(B)
211(c)(1)(A)	1853(c)(1)(A)
211(c)(1)(B)	1853(c)(1)(B)(iv)
211(c)(1)(C)	1853(c)(1)(C)(iv)
211(c)(1)(D)	1853(c)(1)(C)(v)

¶20,010 ©2004, CCH INCORPORATED

Act Sections Amending Social Security Act Sections

Act section	SSA section
211(c)(2)	1853(c)(6)(C)
221(a)	1851(a)(2)(A)
221(b)	1859(b)(4)
221(b)	1859(b)(5)
221(d)(1)	1853(d)
221(d)(2)	1859(c)(5)
221(d)(3)(A)	1852(a)(1)
221(d)(3)(B)	1852(a)(6)
221(d)(4)	1853(c)(1)
221(d)(5)	1851(i)(2)
221(c)	1858
222(a)(1)(A)	1854(a)(1)
222(a)(1)(B)	1854(a)(6)
222(a)(2)	1852(a)(1)
222(a)(3)	1852(a)(3)
222(b)(1)(A)	1854(b)(1)(A)
222(b)(1)(B)	1854(b)(1)(C)
222(b)(2)(A)	1854(b)(2)
222(b)(2)(B)	1854(b)(2)(C)
222(b)(2)(C)	1854(b)(2)(A)
222(b)(2)(C)	1854(b)(2)(B)
222(b)(2)(D)	1854(b)(2)(E)
222(b)(3)	1854(b)(3)
222(d)	1853(j)
222(e)(1)(A)	1853(a)(1)(B)
222(e)(1)(B)	1853(a)(1)(A)
222(f)(1)	1853(b)(1)
222(f)(2)	1853(b)(3)
222(g)(1)(A)	1854
222(g)(1)(B)	1854(a)
222(g)(1)(C)	1854(a)(2)
222(g)(1)(D)	1854(a)(3)
222(g)(1)(E)	1854(a)(4)
222(g)(1)(F)	1854(a)(5)(A)
222(g)(1)(G)	1854(a)(5)(B)
222(g)(1)(H)	1854(b)(1)(A)
222(g)(2)	1854(c)
222(g)(3)	1854(d)(1)
222(g)(4)(A)	1854(e)(1)
222(g)(4)(B)	1854(e)(2)
222(g)(4)(C)	1854(e)(3)
222(g)(4)(D)	1854(e)(4)
222(g)(5)(A)	1854(f)
222(g)(5)(B)	1854(f)(1)(A)
222(h)(1)	1852(j)(4)
222(h)(2)	1852(j)(4)(ii)
222(h)(3)	1852(j)(4)(iii)

¶20,010

Act Sections Amending Social Security Act Sections

Act section	SSA section
222(i)	1853(a)(1)(H)
222(j)(1)	1857(i)(1)
222(j)(2)	1857(i)(2)
222(k)(1)	1857(e)(2)(A)
222(k)(2)	1857(e)(2)(B)
222(k)(3)	1857(e)(2)(C)
222(k)(4)	1857(e)(2)(D)
222(k)(5)	1857(e)(2)(F)
222(l)(1)	1852(b)(1)(A)
222(l)(2)(A)	1839(a)(2)
222(l)(2)(B)	1840(i)
222(l)(2)(C)	1844(c)
222(l)(3)(A)	1851(b)(1)
222(l)(3)(B)(i)	1851(d)(3)(F)
222(l)(3)(B)(ii)	1851(d)(4)(A)(ii)
222(l)(3)(B)(iii)	1851(d)(4)(B)(i)
222(l)(3)(B)(iv)	1851(d)(4)(E)
222(l)(3)(C)	1857(d)(1)
222(l)(3)(D)	1851(a)(3)(B)(ii)
222(l)(3)(E)	1851(f)(1)
222(c)(1)	1854(d)(1)
222(c)(2)	1854(d)(2)
222(c)(2)	1854(d)(3)
222(c)(2)	1854(d)(4)
231(a)	1851(a)(2)(A)(ii)
231(b)	1859(b)(6)
231(c)	1859(f)
232(a)	1856(b)(3)
232(b)	1854(g)
233(a)(1)	1852(e)(1)
233(a)(2)(A)	1852(c)(1)(I)
233(a)(2)(B)	1852(e)(2)(A)
233(a)(2)(C)	1852(e)(2)(B)
233(b)(1)	1854(b)(4)
233(b)(2)	1854(b)(4)(A)
233(b)(3)	1854(b)(4)(C)
233(d)(1)	1851(e)(5)(A)(i)
233(d)(2)	1851(e)(5)(A)(ii)
233(d)(3)	1851(e)(5)(A)(iii)
233(c)	1852(k)(1)
234	1876(h)(5)
236(a)(1)	1866(a)(1)(O)
236(a)(2)	1894(b)(3)
236(a)(2)	1894(b)(4)
236(b)(1)(A)	1902(a)(65)
236(b)(1)(B)	1902(a)(66)
236(b)(1)(C)	1902(a)(67)

¶20,010

Act Sections Amending Social Security Act Sections

Act section	SSA section
236(b)(2)	1934(b)(3)
236(b)(2)	1934(b)(4)
237(a)	1833(a)(3)
237(b)(1)	1853(a)(4)
237(b)(2)(A)(i)	1851(i)(1)
237(b)(2)(A)(ii)	1851(i)(2)
237(b)(2)(B)	1853(c)(5)
237(d)(1)	1128B(b)(3)(F)
237(d)(2)	1128B(b)(3)(G)
237(d)(3)	1128B(b)(3)(H)
237(c)	1857(e)(3)
241(a)	1860C-1
241(b)(1)(A)	1853(j)(1)(A)
241(b)(1)(B)	1853(b)(1)(B)(iii)
241(b)(2)(A)	1839(h)
301(a)(1)	1862(b)(2)(A)(ii)
301(a)(2)	1862(b)(2)(B)
301(b)(1)	1862(b)(2)(A)
301(b)(2)	1862(b)(2)(B)(ii)
301(b)(3)	1862(b)(2)(B)(iii)
301(c)(1)	1862(b)(1)(A)
301(c)(2)	1862(b)(3)(A)
302(a)(1)(A)	1834(a)(17)
302(a)(1)(B)	1834(a)(20)
302(a)(2)	1834(a)(1)(E)
302(b)(1)	1847
302(b)(2)(A)	1833(a)(1)(T)
302(b)(2)(B)	1833(a)(1)(U)
302(b)(2)(C)	1833(a)(1)(D)
302(d)(1)(A)	1834(a)(1)(B)
302(d)(1)(B)	1834(a)(1)(C)
302(d)(1)(C)	1834(a)(1)(F)
302(d)(1)(D)	1834(a)(10)(B)
302(d)(2)(A)	1834(h)(1)(B)
302(d)(2)(B)	1834(h)(1)(D)
302(d)(2)(C)	1834(h)(1)(H)
302(d)(3)(A)	1842(s)(1)
302(d)(3)(B)	1842(s)(3)
302(c)(1)(A)(i)	1834(a)(14)(E)
302(c)(1)(A)(ii)	1834(a)(14)(F)
302(c)(1)(A)(iii)	1834(a)(14)(G)
302(c)(1)(A)(iii)	1834(a)(14)(H)
302(c)(1)(A)(iii)	1834(a)(14)(I)
302(c)(1)(A)(iii)	1834(a)(14)(J)
302(c)(2)	1834(a)(21)
302(c)(3)(A)	1834(h)(4)(A)(vii)
302(c)(3)(B)	1834(h)(4)(A)(viii)

¶20,010

Act section	SSA section
302(c)(3)(C)	1834(h)(4)(A)(ix)
302(c)(3)(C)	1834(h)(4)(A)(x)
303(a)(1)(A)(i)	1848(c)(2)(B)(ii)(II)
303(a)(1)(A)(ii)	1848(c)(2)(B)(iv)
303(a)(1)(B)	1848(c)(2)(H)
303(a)(1)(B)	1848(c)(2)(I)
303(a)(1)(B)	1848(c)(2)(J)
303(b)(1)	1842(o)(1)
303(b)(2)	1842(o)(4)
303(d)(1)	1847B
303(e)(1)	1842(o)(5)
303(e)(2)	1842(o)(6)
303(g)(1)	1842(o)(7)
303(g)(2)	1848(i)(1)(B)
303(i)(1)	1842(o)(2)
303(i)(2)	1861(s)(2)(A)
303(i)(3)(A)	1833(a)(1)(S)
303(i)(3)(B)(i)	1862(a)(1)(H)
303(i)(3)(B)(ii)	1862(a)(1)(I)
303(i)(3)(B)(iii)	1862(a)(1)(J)
303(i)(4)(A)	1927(a)(1)
303(i)(4)(B)(i)	1927(b)(3)(A)(i)
303(i)(4)(B)(ii)	1927(b)(3)(A)(ii)
303(i)(4)(B)(iii)	1927(b)(3)(A)(iii)
303(i)(4)(C)(i)	1927(b)(3)(B)
303(i)(4)(C)(ii)	1927(b)(3)(B)
303(i)(4)(D)(i)	1927(b)(3)(D)
303(i)(4)(D)(ii)	1927(b)(3)(D)(i)
303(c)(1)	1847A
305(a)	1842(o)(1)(G)
401(a)(1)	1886(d)(3)(A)(iv)
401(a)(2)	1886(d)(3)(A)(iv)(II)
401(b)(1)(A)	1886(d)(3)(D)
401(b)(1)(B)	1886(d)(3)(D)
401(b)(1)(C)	1886(d)(3)(D)(i)
401(b)(1)(D)	1886(d)(3)(D)(ii)
401(b)(1)(E)	1886(d)(3)(D)(iii)
401(b)(2)(A)	1886(d)(3)
401(b)(2)(B)	1886(d)(3)(D)
401(b)(3)	1886(d)(3)(A)(iii)
401(c)(1)(A)	1886(d)(9)(A)(i)
401(c)(1)(B)	1886(d)(9)(A)(ii)
401(c)(2)(A)(i)	1886(d)(9)(C)(i)
401(c)(2)(A)(ii)	1886(d)(9)(C)(i)(II)
401(c)(2)(B)	1886(d)(9)(C)(ii)
401(c)(2)(C)	1886(d)(9)(C)(iii)
402(a)	1886(d)(5)(F)(xiv)

Act Sections Amending Social Security Act Sections

Act section	SSA section
402(b)(1)	1886(d)(5)(F)
402(b)(2)	1886(d)(2)(C)(iv)
403(a)(1)(A)	1886(d)(3)(E)(i)
403(a)(1)(B)	1886(d)(3)(E)(ii)
403(a)(2)	1886(d)(3)(E)
403(b)(1)	1886(d)(9)(C)(iv)(I)
403(b)(2)	1886(d)(9)(C)(iv)(I)
403(b)(3)	1886(d)(9)(C)(iv)(II)
405(a)(1)	1814(l)
405(a)(1)	1834(g)(1)
405(a)(1)	1883(a)(3)
405(b)(1)	1834(g)(5)
405(c)(1)	1815(e)(2)
405(d)(1)	1834(g)(2)
405(e)(1)	1820(c)(2)(B)(iii)
405(e)(2)	1820(f)
405(f)(2)	1820(g)(4)
405(f)(2)	1820(g)(5)
405(g)(1)	1820(c)(2)(E)
405(g)(2)(A)	1814(l)(1)
405(g)(2)(B)	1814(l)(2)
405(h)(1)	1820(c)(2)(B)(i)(II
405(h)(2)(A)	1820(h)
405(h)(2)(B)	1820(h)(3)
406(a)	1886(d)(12)
406(b)	1886(d)(7)(A)
407(a)	1886(b)(3)(I)(iii)
408(a)	1861(dd)(3)(B)
408(b)	1814(a)(7)(A)(i)(I)
410(a)(1)	1888(e)(2)(A)(i)(II)
410(a)(2)	1888(e)(2)(A)(iv)
411(a)	1833(t)(7)(D)(i)
411(b)(1)	1833(t)(13)
411(b)(2)	1833(t)(13)
412(1)	1848(e)(1)(A)
412(2)	1848(e)(1)(E)
413(a)	1833(u)
413(b)(1)(A)	1833(m)(1)
413(b)(1)(B)	1833(m)(1)
413(b)(1)(C)	1833(m)(2)
413(b)(1)(C)	1833(m)(3)
413(b)(1)(C)	1833(m)(4)
414(a)(1)	1834(l)(2)(E)
414(a)(2)	1834(l)(8)
414(a)(3)	1834(l)(10)
414(b)	1834(l)(11)
414(c)	1834(l)(12)

¶20,010

Act section	SSA section
414(d)	1834(l)(13)
414(g)	1861(v)(1)(U)
415(a)	1834(l)(14)
415(b)	1861(s)(7)
422(a)(1)	1886(h)(4)(F)(i)
422(a)(2)	1886(h)(4)(H)(i)
422(a)(3)	1886(h)(7)
422(b)(1)(A)	1886(d)(5)(B)(ii)
422(b)(1)(B)	1886(d)(5)(B)(v)
422(b)(1)(C)	1886(d)(5)(B)(ix)
431(a)(1)	1128B(b)(3)(F)
431(a)(2)	1128B(b)(3)(G)
431(a)(3)	1128B(b)(3)(H)
432	711(b)
501(a)(1)	1886(b)(3)(B)(i)(XVIII)
501(a)(2)	1886(b)(3)(B)(i)(XIX)
501(a)(3)	1886(b)(3)(B)(i)(XIX)
501(a)(3)	1886(b)(3)(B)(i)(XX)
501(b)	1886(b)(3)(B)(vii)
502(a)(1)	1886(d)(5)(B)(ii)(VI)
502(a)(2)	1886(d)(5)(B)(ii)(VII)
502(a)(3)	1886(d)(5)(B)(ii)(IX)
502(a)(3)	1886(d)(5)(B)(ii)(VIII)
502(a)(3)	1886(d)(5)(B)(ii)(X)
502(a)(3)	1886(d)(5)(B)(ii)(XI)
502(a)(3)	1886(d)(5)(B)(ii)(XII)
502(b)	1886(d)(2)(C)(i)
503(a)	1886(d)(5)(K)(vii)
503(b)(1)	1886(d)(5)(K)(ii)(I)
503(b)(2)(A)	1886(d)(5)(K)(i)
503(b)(2)(B)	1886(d)(5)(K)(viii)
503(c)	1886(d)(5)(K)(ix)
503(d)(1)	1886(d)(5)(K)(ii)(III)
504(1)(A)	1886(d)(9)(A)(i)
504(1)(B)	1886(d)(9)(A)(ii)
504(2)	1886(d)(9)(E)
505(a)	1886(d)(13)
505(b)(1)	1866(a)(1)(R)
505(b)(2)	1866(a)(1)(S)
505(b)(3)	1866(a)(1)(T)
506(a)(1)	1866(a)(1)(S)
506(a)(2)	1866(a)(1)(T)
506(a)(3)	1866(a)(1)(U)
507(a)(1)(A)(i)	1877(d)(3)(A)
507(a)(1)(A)(ii)	1877(d)(3)(B)
507(a)(1)(B)	1877(h)(7)
507(a)(2)	1877(d)(2)

Act Sections Amending Social Security Act Sections

Act section	SSA section
511(a)	1888(e)(12)
512(a)(1)	1812(a)(3)
512(a)(2)	1812(a)(4)
512(a)(3)	1812(a)(5)
512(b)	1814(i)(4)
512(c)	1861(dd)(2)(A)(i)
601(a)(1)	1848(d)(5)
601(a)(2)	1848(d)(4)(B)
601(b)(1)	1848(t)(2)(C)
602(1)	1848(e)(1)(A)
602(2)	1848(e)(1)(G)
603	1802(b)(5)(B)
611(a)(1)	1861(s)(2)(U)
611(a)(2)	1861(s)(2)(V)(iii)
611(a)(3)	1861(s)(2)(W)
611(b)	1861(ww)
611(c)	1848(j)(3)
611(d)(1)(A)(i)	1862(a)(1)(I)
611(d)(1)(A)(ii)	1862(a)(1)(J)
611(d)(1)(A)(iii)	1862(a)(1)(K)
611(d)(1)(B)	1862(a)(7)
611(d)(2)	1861(s)(2)(K)(i)
611(d)(2)	1861(s)(2)(K)(ii)
612(a)(1)	1861(s)(2)(V)(iii)
612(a)(2)	1861(s)(2)(W)
612(a)(3)	1861(s)(2)(X)
612(b)	1861(xx)
612(c)(1)	1862(a)(1)(J)
612(c)(2)	1862(a)(1)(K)
612(c)(3)	1862(a)(1)(L)
613(a)(1)	1861(s)(2)(W)
613(a)(2)	1861(s)(2)(X)
613(a)(3)	1861(s)(2)(Y)
613(b)	1861(yy)
613(c)(1)	1862(a)(1)(K)
613(c)(2)	1862(a)(1)(L)
613(c)(3)	1862(a)(1)(M)
614(a)	1833(t)(1)(B)(iv)
614(b)	1833(a)(2)(E)(i)
621(a)(1)	1833(t)(14)
621(a)(2)	1833(t)(16)(B)
621(a)(3)	1833(t)(5)(E)
621(a)(4)	1833(t)(6)(D)(i)
621(a)(5)	1833(t)(9)(B)
621(b)(1)	1833(t)(16)(C)
621(b)(2)(A)	1833(t)(2)(F)
621(b)(2)(B)	1833(t)(2)(G)

¶20,010

Act Sections Amending Social Security Act Sections

Act section	SSA section
621(b)(2)(C)	1833(t)(2)(H)
622	1833(t)(6)(F)
623(a)	1881(b)(7)
623(b)(2)	1881(b)(7)
623(d)(1)	1881(b)(12)
623(d)(1)	1881(b)(13)
623(d)(2)	1881(b)(7)
623(d)(3)	1881(b)(11)(B)
624(a)(1)	1833(g)(4)
625(a)(1)	1839(b)
626(a)	1833(i)(2)(C)
626(b)(1)(A)	1833(i)(2)(A)
626(b)(1)(B)	1833(i)(2)(A)(i)
626(b)(2)	1833(i)(2)(D)
626(c)	1833(a)(1)(G)
627(a)(1)	1833(o)(1)(B)
627(a)(2)	1833(o)(2)
627(b)(1)	1834(h)(4)(C)
627(b)(2)	1842(s)(2)(C)
628	1833(h)(2)(A)(ii)(IV)
629	1833(b)
630	1880(e)(1)(A)
642(a)(1)(A)	1861(s)(2)(X)
642(a)(1)(B)	1861(s)(2)(Y)
642(a)(1)(C)	1861(s)(2)(Z)
642(a)(2)	1861(zz)
642(b)	1833(a)(1)(S)
646	1866C
701(a)(1)	1895(b)(3)(B)(i)
701(a)(2)(A)	1895(b)(3)(B)(ii)(I)
701(a)(2)(B)	1895(b)(3)(B)(ii)(II)
701(a)(2)(C)	1895(b)(3)(B)(ii)(III)
701(a)(2)(D)	1895(b)(3)(B)(ii)(II)
701(a)(3)	1895(b)(3)(B)(iii)
701(a)(4)	1895(b)(3)(B)(iv)
701(a)(5)	1895(b)(5)
701(b)(1)	1895(b)(3)(B)(ii)(II)
701(b)(2)	1895(b)(3)(B)(ii)(III)
701(b)(3)	1895(b)(3)(B)(ii)(IV)
701(b)(4)	1895(b)(3)(B)(ii)(III)
706(a)(1)	1821(a)
706(a)(2)	1821(a)(2)
706(b)	1861(aaa)
711(1)(A)(1)	1886(h)(2)(D)(iv)(I)
711(1)(A)(2)	1886(h)(2)(D)(iv)(II)
721(a)	1807
722(a)(1)	1852(e)

Act Sections Amending Social Security Act Sections

Act section	SSA section
722(a)(2)	1852(e)(1)
722(a)(2)	1852(e)(2)
722(a)(2)	1852(e)(3)
722(a)(3)(A)	1852(e)(4)(B)(i)
722(a)(3)(B)	1852(e)(4)(B)(vii)
722(a)(4)	1852(e)(5)
722(b)	1852(c)(1)(I)
731(a)(1)(A)	1862(a)
731(a)(1)(B)	1862(l)
731(b)(1)	1862(m)
735(a)	1805(b)(8)
735(b)	1805(b)(2)(B)(i)
735(c)(1)	1805(c)(2)(D)
735(e)	1805(c)(2)(B)
736(a)(1)(A)	1814(a)
736(a)(1)(B)(i)	1814(a)(7)(A)(i)
736(a)(1)(B)(ii)	1814(a)(7)(A)(ii)
736(a)(10)	1861(mm)
736(a)(11)	1861(tt)(1)
736(a)(11)	1861(tt)(2)
736(a)(12)	1865(b)(3)(B)
736(a)(13)	1866(b)(2)
736(a)(14)(A)	1867(d)(1)(B)(ii)
736(a)(14)(B)	1867(e)(1)(B)
736(a)(14)(C)	1867(e)(2)
736(a)(15)	1886(g)(3)(B)
736(a)(2)	1814(b)
736(a)(3)	1815(e)(1)(B)
736(a)(4)(A)	1816(c)(2)(B)(ii)(III)
736(a)(4)(B)	1816(c)(2)(B)(ii)(IV)
736(a)(5)(A)	1817(k)(3)(A)(i)(I)
736(a)(5)(A)	1817(k)(3)(A)(ii)
736(a)(6)	1817(k)(6)(B)
736(a)(7)(A)	1818(d)(6)(A)
736(a)(7)(B)	1818(g)(2)(B)
736(a)(8)(A)	1819(b)(4)(C)(i)
736(a)(8)(B)	1819(d)(1)(A)
736(a)(8)(C)	1819(f)(2)(B)(iii)
736(a)(9)	1886(b)(3)(I)(i)(I)
736(b)(1)	1833(h)(5)(D)
736(b)(10)	1848(i)(3)(A)
736(b)(11)	1861(s)(2)(K)(i)
736(b)(12)	1861(aa)(1)(B)
736(b)(2)	1833(t)(3)(C)(ii)
736(b)(3)	1861(v)(1)(S)(ii)(III)
736(b)(4)	1834(b)(4)(D)(iv)
736(b)(5)	1834(m)(4)(C)(ii)(III)

¶20,010

Act Sections Amending Social Security Act Sections

Act section	SSA section
736(b)(6)	1838(a)(1)
736(b)(7)	1839(a)(4)
736(b)(8)(A)	1842(c)(2)(B)(ii)(III)
736(b)(8)(B)	1842(c)(2)(B)(ii)(IV)
736(b)(9)	1842(i)(2)
736(c)(1)	1812(a)(3)
736(c)(2)(A)	1814(a)
736(c)(2)(B)	1835(a)
736(c)(3)	1891(d)(1)
736(c)(4)	1861(v)
736(c)(5)	1866B(b)(7)(D)
736(c)(6)	1886(h)(3)(D)(ii)(III)
736(c)(7)	1893(a)
736(c)(8)	1896(b)(4)
736(d)(1)(A)	1853(a)(3)(C)(ii)
736(d)(1)(B)	1853(a)(3)(C)(iii)
736(d)(1)(C)	1853(c)(5)
736(d)(2)(A)	1876(c)(2)(B)
736(d)(2)(B)	1876(j)(2)
736(e)(1)	1882(d)(3)(A)(i)(II)
736(e)(2)	1882(d)(3)(B)(iii)(II)
736(e)(3)	1882(g)(2)(A)
736(e)(4)	1882(p)(2)(B)
736(e)(5)	1882(s)(3)(A)(iii)
811	1839(i)
811(b)(1)	1839(a)(2)
811(b)(1)	1839(b)
811(b)(1)	1839(f)
811(b)(2)	1844(a)(1)(C)
811(b)(2)	1844(c)
900	1808
900(c)	1117(b)(3)
900(e)	1117
900(e)	1117(a)
900(e)	1117(b)(1)
900(e)(1)(B)	1140(a)(1)
900(e)(1)(B)	1140(a)(1)(A)
900(e)(1)(B)	1140(a)(1)(B)
900(e)(1)(C)	1142(b)(3)
900(e)(1)(D)	1817(b)
900(e)(1)(E)	1841(b)
900(e)(1)(G)	1853(b)(4)
900(e)(1)(G)	1853(c)(7)
900(e)(1)(H)	1854(a)(5)(A)
900(e)(1)(I)	1857(d)(4)(A)(ii)
900(e)(1)(J)	1862(b)(5)(A)(ii)
900(e)(1)(K)	1927(e)(4)

Act Sections Amending Social Security Act Sections

Act section	SSA section
900(e)(1)(L)	1927(f)(2)
900(e)(1)(M)	2104(g)(3)
900(e)(F)	1852(a)(5)
901(b)	1861(d)
902(a)	1871(a)(3)
902(b)	1871(a)(4)
903(a)	1871(e)(1)(A)
903(b)	1871(e)(1)(A)
903(b)	1871(e)(1)(B)
903(b)	1871(e)(1)(C)
903(c)	1871(e)(2)(A)
904	1871(f)(1)
911(10)	1842(q)(1)(A)
911(c)(4)(A)	1842(c)(1)
911(c)(4)(B)	1842(c)(2)(A)
911(c)(4)(C)	1842(c)(3)(A)
911(c)(4)(D)	1842(c)(4)(A)
911(c)(4)(E)	1842(c)(5)
911(c)(4)(E)	1842(c)(6)
911(c)(5)	1842(d)
911(c)(5)	1842(e)
911(c)(5)	1842(f)
911(c)(6)	1842(g)
911(c)(7)(A)	1842(h)(2)
911(c)(7)(B)	1842(h)(3)(A)
911(c)(7)(C)	1842(h)(3)(B)
911(c)(7)(D)	1842(h)(5)(A)
911(c)(7)(D)	1842(h)(5)(B)(iii)
911(c)(8)(A)	1842(l)(1)(A)(iii)
911(c)(8)(B)	1842(l)(2)
911(c)(9)	1842(p)(3)(A)
911(a)	1874A
911(b)(1)	1816
911(b)(2)	1816(a)
911(b)(3)	1816(b)
911(b)(4)	1816(c)
911(b)(5)	1816(d)
911(b)(5)	1816(e)
911(b)(5)	1816(f)
911(b)(5)	1816(g)
911(b)(5)	1816(h)
911(b)(5)	1816(i)
911(b)(6)	1816(j)
911(b)(6)	1816(k)
911(b)(7)	1816(l)
911(D)	1842(b)(5)
911(F)	1842(b)(7)

¶20,010

Act section	SSA section
911(c)(1)	1842
911(c)(2)	1842(a)
911(c)(3)	1842(b)(1)
911(c)(3)	1842(b)(2)
911(c)(3)	1842(b)(3)
911(c)(3)(ii)	1842(b)(3)(A)
911(c)(3)(ii)	1842(b)(3)(B)
911(c)(3)(ii)	1842(b)(3)(F)
911(c)(3)(ii)	1842(b)(3)(G)
911(c)(3)(ii)	1842(b)(3)(H)
911(c)(3)(ii)	1842(b)(3)(L)
911(c)(3)(iii)	1842(b)(3)(B)
911(c)(3)(iv)	1842(b)(3)(C)
911(c)(3)(iv)	1842(b)(3)(D
911(c)(3)(iv)	1842(b)(3)(E)
911(c)(3)(v)	1842(b)(3)(H)
911(c)(3)(vi)	1842(b)(3)(I)
911(c)(3)(vii)	1842(b)(3)(L)
911(c)(3)(viii)	1842(b)(3)(L)
911E	1842(b)(6)(D)(iv)
912	1874A(e)
921	1874A (f)
921	1889
921(d)	1889(b)
921(d)	1889(c)
921(e)	1889(d)
921(f)	1889(g)
921(f)	1889(g)
921(c)	1874A(g)
923	1808
926(b)	1861(ee)(2)(D)
931(d)	1869(f)(2)(A)(I)
932	1869(b)
932(a)(2)	1869(b)(1)(F)(ii)
932(b)	1866(h)(1)
932(c)(1)	1866(h)(1)
932(c)(2)	1819(f)(2)(B)(iii)
932(c)(2)	1919(f)(2)(B)(iii)
932(c)(2)(B)	1819(f)(2)
932(c)(2)(B)	1919(f)(2)
933(a)	1869(b)
933(b)	1869(c)(3)(B)(i)
933(c)(2)	1869(c)(3)(E)
933(c)(3)	1869(d)
933(c)(4)	1869(c)(3)(J)(i)
933(d)(1)(A)	1869(c)(3)
933(d)(1)(B)	1869(c)(3)(K)

Act Sections Amending Social Security Act Sections

Act section	SSA section
933(d)(2)(A)	1869(c)(3)(D)
933(d)(2)(B)	1869(g)
933(c)	1869(a)
934(a)	1874A(h)
935(a)	1893(f)
936(a)(1)	1866
936(a)(2)	1866(j)
938	1869(h)
939	1870(h)
940(a)(1)	1869(a)(3)(C)(ii)
940(a)(2)	1869(a)(3)(C)(i)
940(b)(1)	1869(b)(1)(E)
940(b)(2)	1852(g)(5)
940(b)(2)(B)	1876(b)(5)(B)
940A	1869(i)
940A(b)	1874A(b)(3)(A)(i)
942(a)	1868
942(a)(1)	1868
942(b)	1833(h)
944(a)	1862(d)
944(b)	1867(d)(4)
944(c)	1867(d)(3)
946	1861(dd)(5)
946(b)	1814(i)
947(a)(1)	1866(a)(1)
947(a)(2)	1866(b)
948(a)(1)	1114(i)
948(a)(2)	1862
948(b)(1)	1869(c)(3)(I)(ii)
948(b)(2)	1852(a)(2)(c)
948(d)	1154(e)(5)
948(c)	1869(f)(4)
949	1128(c)(3)(B)
950	1862(k)(1)
952	1842(b)(6)
952	1842(b)(6)(A)
1001	1923(f)(3)
1001(b)	1923(f)(5)
1001(c)	1923(f)(3)(A)
1001(c)	1923(f)(7)
1001(c)	1923(f)(6)
1001(d)	1923(j)
1002	1927(c)(1)(C)(i)(I)
1002(b)	1927(c)(1)(C)(iii)
1016	1897

¶20,010

¶ 20,020

Table of Amendments to Other Acts

Medicare Prescription Drug, Improvement, and Moderinization Act of 2003

Amended Act Sec.	H.R. 1 Sec.	Par. (¶)
Alzheimer's Disease and Related Dementias Services Research Act of 1992		
Subpart 3 of Part D, heading	900(e)(5)(A)	10,980
Sec. 937(a)	900(e)(5)(B)(i)	10,980
Sec. 937(b)(1)	900(e)(5)(B)(ii)	10,980
Sec. 937(b)(2)	900(e)(5)(B)(iii)	10,980
Sec. 937(c)	900(e)(5)(B)(iv)	10,980
Sec. 938	900(e)(5)(C)	10,980
An Act to Authorize Certain Appropriations for Territories of the U.S., to Amend Certain Acts Related Thereto, and for Other Purposes		
Section 403	900(e)(7)	10,980
Children's Health Act of 2000		
Sec. 2503(a)	900(e)(6)(E)	10,980
Federal Food, Drug and Cosmetic Act		
Sec. 505(b)(3)	1101(b)(1)(A)	11,250
Sec. 505(b)(4)	1101(b)(1)(B)(ii)	11,250
Sec. 505(c)(3)	1101(b)(2)(A)	11,250
Sec. 505(c)(3)(C)	1101(b)(2)(B)	11,250
Sec. 505(c)(3)(D)	1101(b)(2)(D)	11,250
Sec. 505(j)(2)(B)	1101(a)(1)(A)	11,250
Sec. 505(j)(2)(D)	1101(a)(1)(B)	11,250
Sec. 505(j)(5)(B)	1101(a)(2)(A)(i)	11,250
Sec. 505(j)(5)(B)(iii)	1101(a)(2)(A)(ii)	11,250
Sec. 505(j)(5)(B)(iv)	1102(a)(1)	11,260
Sec. 505(j)(5)(C)	1101(a)(2)(C)	11,250
Sec. 505(j)(5)(D)	1102(a)(2)	11,260
Sec. 505(j)(5)(E)	1101(a)(2)(B)	11,250
Sec. 505(j)(5)(F)	1101(a)(2)(B)	11,250
Sec. 505(j)(8)(A)	1103(a)(1)	11,270
Sec. 505(j)(8)(C)	1103(a)(2)	11,270
Sec. 505A(b)(1)(A)	1104(1),(2)	11,280
Sec. 505A(c)(1)(A)	1104 (1),(2)	11,280
Sec. 505A(e)(1)	1104(3)	11,280
Sec. 804	1121	11,370

Amended Act Sec.	H.R. 1 Sec.	Par. (¶)
Home Health Care and Alzheimer's Disease Amendments of 1990		
Sec. 302(a)(9)	900(e)(6)(D)	10,980
Indian Health Care Improvement Act		
Sec. 405(d)(1)	900(e)(6)(C)	10,980
Individuals with Disabilities Education Act		
Sec. 644(b)(5)	900(e)(6)(C)	10,980
Internal Revenue Code of 1986		
Sec. 56(g)(4)(B)	1202(b)	11,410
Sec. 62(a)(19)	1201(b)	11,400
Sec. 106(d)	1201(d)(1)	11,400
Sec. 125(d)(2)(D)	1201(i)	11,400
Sec. 139A	1202(a)	11,400
Sec. 220(f)(5)(A)	1201(c)	11,400
Sec. 223	1201(a)	11,400
Sec. 848(e)(1)(v)	1201(h)	11,400
Sec. 3231(e)(11)	1201(d)(2)(A)	11,400
Sec. 3306(b)(18)	1201(d)(2)(B)	11,400
Sec. 3401(a)(22)	1201(d)(2)(C)	11,400
Sec. 4973(a)(5)	1201(e)(1)	11,400
Sec. 4973(g)	1201(e)(2)	11,400
Sec. 4975(c)(6)	2101(f)(1)	11,400
Sec. 4975(e)(1)(E)	1201(f)(2)	11,400
Sec. 4980G	1201(d)(4)(A)	11,400
Sec. 6041(f)	1203(a)	11,420
Sec. 6051(a)(12)	1201(d)(3)	11,400
Sec. 6103(a)(3)	811(c)(2)(A)	10,970
Sec. 6103(a)(3)	105(e)(2)	10,020
Sec. 6103(l)(7)(D)(ii)	101(e)(6)	10,000
Sec. 6103(l)(12)(B)	900(e)(3)(A)	10,980
Sec. 6103(l)(12)(C)	900(e)(3)(B)	10,980
Sec. 6103(l)(19)	105(e)(1)	10,020
Sec. 6103(l)(20)	811(c)(1)	10,970
Sec. 6103(p)(4)	105(e)(3)	10,020
Sec. 6103(p)(4)	811(c)(2)	10,970
Sec. 6693(a)(2)	1201(g)	11,400

¶ 20,020

Amended Act Sec.	H.R. 1 Sec.	Par. (¶)	Amended Act Sec.	H.R. 1 Sec.	Par. (¶)
Sec. 7213(a)(2)	105(e)(4)	10,020	Sec. 916(c)(2)	900(e)(2)(C)(ii)	10,980
Sec. 7231(a)(2)	811(c)(2)(C)	10,970	Sec. 921(c)(3)(A)	900(e)(2)(D)	10,980
			Sec. 1318(a)(2)	900(e)(2)(E)	10,980

The Medicare, Medicaid, and SCHIP Benefits Improvement and Protection Act of 2000

Amended Act Sec.	H.R. 1 Sec.	Par. (¶)
Sec. 2102(a)(7)	900(e)(2)(F)	10,980
Sec. 2675(a)	900(e)(2)(G)	10,980
Sec. 104(d)(4)	900(e)(6)(H)	10,980

Rehabilitation Act of 1973

Sec. 202(b)(8)	900(e)(6)(A)	10,980

The National Institutes of Health Revitalization Act of 1993

Title 5, U.S.C.

Amended Act Sec.	H.R. 1 Sec.	Par. (¶)
Sec. 1909	900(e)(6)(F)	10,980
Sec. 5314	900(d)(1)	10,980
Sec. 5315	900(d)(2)	10,980

The Omnibus Budget Reconciliation Act of 1990

Title 10, U.S.C.

Amended Act Sec.	H.R. 1 Sec.	Par. (¶)
Sec. 4359(d)	900(e)(6)(G)	10,980
Sec. 1086(d)(4)	900(e)(4)(A)	10,980
Sec. 1095(k)(2)	900(e)(4)(B)	10,980

Public Health Service Act

Title 35, U.S.C.

Amended Act Sec.	H.R. 1 Sec.	Par. (¶)
Sec. 501(d)(18)	900(e)(2)(A)	10,980
Sec. 507(b)	900(e)(2)(B)	10,980
Sec. 271(e)	1101(d)	11,250
Sec. 916(b)(2)	900(e)(2)(C)(i)	10,980

¶ 20,030
Table of Act Sections Not Amending Social Security Act Sections
Medicare Prescription Drug, Improvement, and Modernization Act of 2003

	Paragraph
Definitions provided under the Federal Food, Drug, and Cosmetic Act (Act. Sec. 1111)	¶ 11,290
Notification of drug company agreements (Act. Sec. 1112)	¶ 11,300
Filing deadlines for drug company agreements (Act Sec. 1113)	¶ 11,310
Disclosure exemption (Act Sec. 1114)	¶ 11,320
Enforcement and civil penalty for drug company noncompliance (Act Sec. 1115)	¶ 11,330
Rulemaking power of the Federal Trade Commission (Act Sec. 1116)	¶ 11,340
Savings clause for legal proceedings (Act Sec. 1117)	¶ 11,350
Effective date (Act Sec. 1118)	¶ 11,360
Importation of drugs (Act Sec. 804)	¶ 10,960
Study and report on importation of drugs (Act Sec. 1122)	¶ 11,380
Study and report on trade in pharmaceuticals (Act Sec. 1123)	¶ 11,390
Health Savings Accounts (Act Sec. 223)	¶ 10,110
Short title (Act Sec. 1)	¶ 10,000
Technical aspects of prescription drug benefits (Act Sec. 101)	¶ 10,000
Medigap amendments (Act Sec. 104)	¶ 10,010
Prescription drug benefit and transition assistance (Act. Sec. 105)	¶ 10,020
Studies and reports (Act Sec. 107)	¶ 10,040
Grants to physicians for electronic drug prescription programs (Act Sec. 108)	¶ 10,050
Medicare quality improvement organizations (Act Sec. 109)	¶ 10,060
Conflict of interest study (Act Sec. 110)	¶ 10,070
Employment based retiree health coverage study (Act Sec. 111)	¶ 10,080
Medicare Advantage implementation (Act Sec. 201)	¶ 10,090
MEDPAC study (Act Sec. 211)	¶ 10,100

	Paragraph
Issuance of regulations and effective date (Act Sec. 223)	¶ 10,110
Specialized Medicare Advantage plans for special needs individuals (Act Sec. 231)	¶ 10,120
Health care performance measures; Report by IOM (Act Sec. 238)	¶ 10,180
Comparative Cost Adjustment program (Act Sec. 241)	¶ 10,190
Competitive acquisition; payment for durable medical equipment	¶ 10,210
Payment for covered outpatient drugs and biologicals (Act Sec. 303)	¶ 10,220
Extension of payment reform for covered outpatient drugs and biologicals (Act Sec. 304)	¶ 10,230
Payment for inhalation drugs (Act Sec 305)	¶ 10,240
Demonstration project for use recovery audit contractors (Act Sec. 306)	¶ 10,250
Pilot program for background checks on direct payment access (Act Sec. 307)	¶ 10,260
Equalizing urban and standardized payment amounts (Act. Sec. 401)	¶ 10,270
Hospital market basket updates (Act Sec. 404)	¶ 10,280
Critical access hospital program improvements (Act Sec. 405)	¶ 10,290
Rural hospice demonstration project (Act Sec. 409)	¶ 10,310
Rural community hospital demonstration program (Act Sec. 410A)	¶ 10,330
Physician scarcity; incentive payment program improvements (Act. Sec. 413)	¶ 10,340
Payment for rural and urban ambulance services (Act Sec. 414)	¶ 10,350

Table of Act Sections Not Amending Social Security Act Sections

	Paragraph
Clinical diagnostic laboratory tests for rural hospital outpatients (Act Sec. 416)	¶ 10,370
Demonstration project report on permitting skilled nursing facilities to be originating telehealth sites (Act Sec. 418)	¶ 10,390
One year increase for rural area home health care (Act Sec. 421)	¶ 10,400
Redistribution of unused resident positions; conforming amendments (Act Sec. 422)	¶ 10,410
Safe harbor for collaborative efforts that benefit medically underserved populations (Act Sec. 431)	¶ 10,420
MEDPAC study on rural hospital payment adjustments (Act Sec. 433)	¶ 10,430
Frontier extended stay clinic demonstration project (Act Sec. 434)	¶ 10,440
GAO report on payments under the prospective payment system for inpatient hospital services (Act Sec. 501)	¶ 10,450
Recognition of new medical technologies (Act Sec. 503)	¶ 10,470
Wage index adjustment reclassification reform (Act Sec. 505)	¶ 10,480
Inpatient hospital contract health services (Act Sec. 506)	¶ 10,490
Medicare limits on physician referrals; clarifications (Act Sec. 507)	¶ 10,500
One-time appeals process for hospital wage index classification (Act Sec. 508.1)	¶ 10,510
Portable diagnostic ultrasound services for beneficiaries in skilled nursing facilities (Act Sec. 513)	¶ 10,540
Access to physicians' services; GAO study (Act Sec. 604)	¶ 10,560
Demonstration-based review on physician practice expense geographic adjustment data (Act Sec. 605)	¶ 10,570
MEDPAC report on physicians' services payment (Act Sec. 606)	¶ 10,580
Hospital outpatient department payment reform (Act Sec. 621)	¶ 10,630

	Paragraph
Renal dialysis services payment (Act Sec. 623)	¶ 10,640
Two-year mortorium on therapy caps (Act Sec. 624)	¶ 10,650
Waiver of Part B late enrollment penalties for military retirees (Act Sec. 625)	¶ 10,660
Payment for ambulatory surgical center services (Act Sec. 626)	¶ 10,670
Demonstration project for prescription drug and biologicals (Act Sec. 641)	¶ 10,690
Surgical first assisting services of certified registered nurse first assistants (Act Sec. 643)	¶ 10,710
Vision impairments; studies (Act Sec. 645)	¶ 10,730
MEDPAC study; direct access to physical therapy services (Act Sec. 647)	¶ 10,740
Demonstration project; consumer directed chronic outpatient services (Act Sec. 648)	¶ 10,750
Demonstration program; Medicare care management performance (Act Sec. 649)	¶ 10,760
GAO study and report; Propaganda of concierge care (Act Sec. 650)	¶ 10,770
Demonstration program; Coverage of chiropractic services under Medicare (Act Sec. 651)	¶ 10,780
Demonstration project to clarify the definition of homebound (Act Sec. 702)	¶ 10,790
Demonstration project; Medical adult day care services (Act Sec. 703)	¶ 10,800
Temporary suspension of OASIS requirement for data collection on Non-Medicare and Non-Medicaid patients (Act Sec. 704)	¶ 10,810
Exception to initial residency period for geriatric residency or fellowship programs (Act Sec. 712)	¶ 10,830
Volunteer supervision (Act Sec. 713)	¶ 10,840
Voluntary chronic care improvement under traditional fee-for service (Act Sec. 721)	¶ 10,850
Chronically ill Medicare beneficiary research, data, and demonstration strategy (Act Sec. 723)	¶ 10,870

¶ 20,030

Table of Act Sections Not Amending Social Security Act Sections

	Paragraph
National and local coverage determination improvements to respond to new technology (Act Sec. 731)	¶10,880
Payment for pancreatic islet cell investigational transplants in clinical trials (Act Sec. 733)	¶10,900
Restoration of Medicare trust funds (Act Sec. 734)	¶10,910
MEDPAC modifications (Act Sec. 735)	¶10,920
Status of Medicare trust funds in annual report of Medicare Trustees (Act Sec. 801)	¶10,935
House of Representative procedures (Act Sec. 803)	¶10,950
Senate procedures (Act Sec. 804)	¶10,960
Regulatory reform reports and studies (Act Sec. 904)	¶11,000
Increased flexibility in Medicare administration (Act Sec. 911)	¶11,010
Requirements for information security for Medicare administrative contractors (Act Sec. 912)	¶11,020
Provider education and technical assistance (Act Sec. 921)	¶11,025
Demonstration program; small provider technical assistance (Act Sec. 922)	¶11,030
Medicare beneficiary ombudsman (Act Sec. 923)	¶11,040
Demonstration program; beneficiary outreach (Act Sec. 924)	¶11,050
Notices to beneficiaries concerning skilled nursing facility benefits (Act Sec. 925)	¶11,060
Transfer of responsibility for Medicare appeals (Act Sec. 931)	¶11,080
Expedited access to review process (Act Sec. 932)	¶11,085
Qualified independent contractors (Act Sec. 933)	¶11,086
Prepayment review (Act Sec. 934)	¶11,090
Recovery of overpayments (Act Sec. 935)	¶11,095
Provider enrollment process; effective dates (Act Sec. 936)	¶11,097

	Paragraph
Process for correcting minor errors and ommissions without pursuing appeals process (Act Sec. 937)	¶11,100
Advance beneficiary notices (Act Sec. 938)	¶11,110
Evaluation and management documentation guidelines (Act Sec. 941)	¶11,120
Treatment of hospitals for certain services under Medicare Secondary Payor (MSP) provisions (Act Sec. 943)	¶11,140
Establishment of the Emergency Medical Treatment and Labor Act (EMTALA) technical advisory group (Act Sec. 945)	¶11,150
Furnishing hospitals with information to compute DSH formula (Act Sec. 951)	¶11,160
Other provisions: GAO reports: physician compensation; annual publication list of national coverage determinations; and flexibility in applying home health conditions of participation to patients who are not Medicare beneficiaries. OIG report on notices relating to use of hospital lifetime reserve. (Act Sec. 953)	¶11,170
Medicare Disproportionate Share Hospital (DSH) Payments (Act Sec. 1001)	¶11,180
Federal reimbursement of emergency health services furnished to undocumented aliens (Act Sec. 1011)	¶11,200
Establishment of the Commission on Systemic Interoperability to develop health care information technology strategy and report (Act Sec. 1012)	¶11,210
Research on outcomes of health care items and services (Act Sec. 1013)	¶11,220
Establishment of the Citizens' Health Care Working Group (Act Sec. 1014)	¶11,230
Funding start-up administrative costs for Medicare Reform (Act Sec. 1015)	¶11,240

¶20,030

¶ 20,040
Social Security Act Sections to Explanation Table

SSA section	L & E Explanation Para	SSA section	L & E Explanation Para
1108(f)	205	1814(i)(4)	677
1114(i)	948	1814(l)(1)	578
1117	801	1814(l)(2)	578
1117(a)	801	1815(e)(2)	578
1117(b)(3)	801	1816	829
1117(b)(1)	801	1816(a)	829
1128(c)(3)(B)	949	1816(b)	829
1128B(b)(3)(F)	390	1816(c)	829
1128B(b)(3)(F)	798	1816(d)	829
1128B(b)(3)(G)	390	1816(e)	829
1128B(b)(3)(G)	798	1816(f)	829
1128B(b)(3)(H)	390	1816(g)	829
1128B(b)(3)(H)	798	1816(h)	829
1140(a)(1)	801	1816(i)	829
1140(a)(1)(A)	801	1816(j)	829
1140(a)(1)(B)	801	1816(k)	829
1142(b)(3)	801	1816(l)	829
1144	205	1817(b)	801
1144(a)(1)(A)	205	1819(f)(2)	905
1144(a)(1)(B)	205	1819(f)(2)(B)(iii)	905
1144(a)(2)	205	1820(c)(2)(B)(i)(II)	578
1144(a)(2)(A)	205	1820(c)(2)(B)(iii)	578
1144(b)(1)(A)	205	1820(c)(2)(E)	578
1144(b)(2)	205	1820(f)	578
1154(a)(1)	235	1820(g)(4)	578
1154(a)(17)	235	1820(g)(5)	578
1154(e)(5)	948	1820(h)	578
1802(b)(5)(B)	706	1820(h)(3)	578
1805(b)(2)(B)(i)	721	1821(a)	662
1805(b)(8)	721	1821(a)(2)	662
1805(c)(2)(B)	721	1833(a)(1)(D)	1002
1805(c)(2)(D)	721	1833(a)(1)(G)	594
1807	678		1004, 1006, 1009,
1808	801	1833(a)(1)(S)	1010
1808	832	1833(a)(1)(S)	760
1812(a)(3)	677	1833(a)(1)(T)	1002
1812(a)(4)	677	1833(a)(1)(U)	1002
1812(a)(5)	677	1833(a)(2)(E)(i)	754
1814(a)(7)(A)(i)(I)	671	1833(a)(3)	390
1814(i)	946	1833(b)	729

Social Security Act Sections to Explanation Table

SSA section	L & E Explanation Para	SSA section	L & E Explanation Para
1833(g)(4)	762	1834(h)(1)(D)	1002
1833(h)	795, 942	1834(h)(1)(H)	1002
1833(h)(2)(A)(ii)(IV)	756	1834(h)(4)(A)(ix)	1002
1833(i)(2)(A)	594	1834(h)(4)(A)(vii)	1002
1833(i)(2)(A)(i)	594	1834(h)(4)(A)(viii)	1002
1833(i)(2)(C)	594	1834(h)(4)(A)(x)	1002
1833(i)(2)(D)	594	1834(h)(4)(C)	761
1833(m)(1)	700	1834(l)(10)	596, 680
1833(m)(1)	700	1834(l)(11)	596, 680
1833(m)(2)	700	1834(l)(12)	596, 680
1833(m)(3)	700	1834(l)(13)	596, 680
1833(m)(4)	700	1834(l)(14)	598, 681
1833(o)(1)(B)	761	1834(l)(2)(E)	596, 680
1833(o)(2)	761	1834(l)(8)	596, 680
1833(t)(1)(B)(iv)	754	1839(a)(2)	376
1833(t)(13)	582	1839(a)(2)	776
1833(t)(13)	582	1839(b)	777
1833(t)(14)	547	1839(b)	776
1833(t)(16)(B)	547	1839(f)	776
1833(t)(16)(C)	545	1839(g)	215
1833(t)(2)(F)	545	1839(g)(2)	215
1833(t)(2)(G)	545	1839(h)	396
1833(t)(2)(H)	545	1840(i)	376
1833(t)(5)(E)	547	1841(a)	215
1833(t)(6)(D)(i)	547	1841(b)	801
1833(t)(6)(F)	547	1841(g)	215
1833(t)(7)(D)(i)	582	1842	829
1833(t)(9)(B)	547	1842(a)	829
1833(u)	700	1842(b)(1)	829
1834(a)(1)(B)	1002	1842(b)(2)	829
1834(a)(1)(C)	1002	1842(b)(3)	829
1834(a)(1)(E)	1002	1842(b)(3)(A)	829
1834(a)(1)(F)	1002	1842(b)(3)(B)	829
1834(a)(10)(B)	1002	1842(b)(3)(B)	829
1834(a)(14)(E)	1002	1842(b)(3)(C)	829
1834(a)(14)(F)	1002	1842(b)(3)(D)	829
1834(a)(14)(G)	1002	1842(b)(3)(E)	829
1834(a)(14)(H)	1002	1842(b)(3)(F)	829
1834(a)(14)(I)	1002	1842(b)(3)(G)	829
1834(a)(14)(J)	1002	1842(b)(3)(H)	829
1834(a)(17)	1002	1842(b)(3)(H)	829
1834(a)(20)	1002	1842(b)(3)(I)	829
1834(a)(21)	1002	1842(b)(3)(L)	829
1834(g)(2)	578	1842(b)(3)(L)	829
1834(g)(5)	578	1842(b)(3)(L)	829
1834(h)(1)(B)	1002	1842(b)(5)	829

Social Security Act Sections to Explanation Table

SSA section	L & E Explanation Para	SSA section	L & E Explanation Para
1842(b)(6)	952	1847B	1004, 1006, 1009, 1010
1842(b)(6)(A)	952		
1842(b)(6)(D)(iv)	829	1848(c)(2)(B)(ii)(II)	1004, 1006, 1009, 1010
1842(b)(7)	829		
1842(c)(1)	829	1848(c)(2)(B)(iv)	1004, 1006, 1009, 1010
1842(c)(2)(A)	829		
1842(c)(3)(A)	829	1848(c)(2)(H)	1004, 1006, 1009, 1010
1842(c)(4)	829		
1842(c)(5)	829	1848(c)(2)(I)	1004, 1006, 1009, 1010
1842(c)(6)	829		
1842(d)	829	1848(c)(2)(J)	1004, 1006, 1009, 1010
1842(e)	829	1848(d)(4)(B)	701
1842(f)	829	1848(d)(5)	701
1842(g)	829	1848(e)(1)(A)	708
1842(h)(2)	829	1848(e)(1)(A)	722
1842(h)(3)(A)	829	1848(e)(1)(E)	708
1842(h)(3)(B)	829	1848(e)(1)(G)	722
1842(h)(5)(A)	829	1848(f)(2)(C)	701
1842(h)(5)(B)(iii)	829		
1842(l)(1)(A)(iii)	829	1848(i)(1)(B)	1004, 1006, 1009, 1010
1842(l)(2)	829	1848(j)(3)	750, 1103
1842(o)(1)	1004, 1006, 1009, 1010	1851(a)(1)	200
1842(o)(1)(G)	1011	1851(a)(2)(A)	361
1842(o)(2)	1004, 1006, 1009, 1010	1851(a)(2)(A)(ii)	378
		1851(a)(3)(B)(ii)	376
1842(o)(4)	1004, 1006, 1009, 1010	1851(b)(1)	376
		1851(d)(3)(F)	376
1842(o)(5)	1004, 1006, 1009, 1010	1851(d)(4)(A)(ii)	376
		1851(d)(4)(B)(i)	376
1842(o)(6)	1004, 1006, 1009, 1010	1851(d)(4)(E)	376
		1851(e)(1)	200
1842(o)(7)	1004, 1006, 1009, 1010	1851(e)(2)	200
1842(p)(3)(A)	829	1851(e)(2)(B)(i)	200
1842(q)(1)(A)	829	1851(e)(2)(C)(i)	200
1842(s)(1)	1002	1851(e)(3)(B)	200
1842(s)(2)(C)	761	1851(e)(3)(C)	200
1842(s)(3)	1002	1851(e)(3)(D)	200
1844(a)(1)(B)	776	1851(e)(4)	200
1844(a)(1)(C)		1851(e)(5)(A)(i)	380
1844(c)	376	1851(e)(5)(A)(ii)	380
1844(c)	776	1851(e)(5)(A)(iii)	380
1847	1002	1851(f)(1)	376
1847A	1004, 1006, 1009, 1010	1851(f)(3)	200
		1851(i)(1)	390

¶20,040

Social Security Act Sections to Explanation Table

SSA section	L & E Explanation Para	SSA section	L & E Explanation Para
1851(i)(2)	390	1853(g)	355
1852(a)(1)	365	1853(g)(2)(B)	355
1852(a)(2)(c)	948	1853(j)	368
1852(a)(3)	365	1853(j)(1)(A)	396
1852(a)(5)	801	1854	371
1852(b)(1)(A)	376	1854(a)	371
1852(c)(1)(I)	380	1854(a)(1)	365
1852(c)(1)(I)	800	1854(a)(2)	371
1852(d)(4)(B)	360	1854(a)(3)	371
1852(e)	800	1854(a)(4)	371
1852(e)(1)	380	1854(a)(5)(A)	371
1852(e)(1)	800	1854(a)(5)(A)	801
1852(e)(2)	800	1854(a)(5)(B)	371
1852(e)(2)(A)	380	1854(a)(6)	365
1852(e)(2)(B)	380	1854(b)(1)(A)	366
1852(e)(3)	800	1854(b)(1)(A)	371
1852(e)(4)(B)(i)	800	1854(b)(1)(C)	366
1852(e)(4)(B)(vii)	800	1854(b)(2)	366
1852(e)(5)	800	1854(b)(2)(A)	366
1852(g)(5)	916	1854(b)(2)(B)	366
1852(j)	200	1854(b)(2)(C)	366
1852(j)(4)	372	1854(b)(2)(E)	366
1852(j)(4)(ii)	372	1854(b)(3)	366
1852(j)(4)(iii)	372	1854(b)(4)	380
1852(k)(1)	380	1854(b)(4)(A)	380
1853(a)(1)(A)	369	1854(b)(4)(C)	380
1853(a)(1)(B)	369	1854(c)	371
1853(a)(1)(H)	373	1854(d)(1)	371
1853(a)(4)	390	1854(d)(1)	376
1853(b)(1)	370	1854(d)(2)	376
1853(b)(1)(B)(iii)	396	1854(d)(3)	376
1853(b)(3)	370	1854(d)(4)	376
1853(b)(4)	801	1854(e)(1)	371
1853(c)(1)	351	1854(e)(2)	371
1853(c)(1)(A)	352	1854(e)(3)	371
1853(c)(1)(A)	353	1854(e)(4)	371
1853(c)(1)(B)(iv)	353	1854(f)	371
1853(c)(1)(C)(iv)	353	1854(f)(1)(A)	371
1853(c)(1)(C)(v)	353	1854(g)	379
1853(c)(1)(D)	351	1856(b)(3)	379
1853(c)(3)(A)	354	1857(d)(1)	376
1853(c)(3)(E)	354	1857(d)(4)(A)(ii)	801
1853(c)(5)	352	1857(e)(2)(A)	375
1853(c)(5)	390	1857(e)(2)(B)	375
1853(c)(6)(C)	353	1857(e)(2)(C)	375
1853(c)(7)	801		

¶20,040

Social Security Act Sections to Explanation Table

SSA section	L & E Explanation Para	SSA section	L & E Explanation Para
1857(e)(2)(D)	375	1861(s)(2)(Y)	755, 1016
1857(e)(2)(F)	375	1861(s)(2)(Y)	760
1857(e)(3)	390	1861(s)(2)(Z)	760
1857(i)(1)	374	1861(s)(7)	598, 681
1857(i)(2)	374	1861(v)(1)(U)	596, 680
1858	363	1861(aaa)	662
1859(b)(4)	362	1861(dd)(2)(A)(i)	677
1859(b)(5)	362	1861(dd)(3)(B)	671
1859(b)(6)	378	1861(dd)(5)	946
1859(f)	378	1861(ee)(2)(D)	606
1860C-1	396	1861(ww)	750, 1103
1860D-1	100	1861(xx)	753, 1014
1860D-2	130, 104, 105, 106, 107, 108	1861(yy)	755, 1016
1860D-3	109	1861(zz)	760
1860D-4	110, 111, 112, 113, 114	1862	948
1860D-11	115, 116	1862(d)	584
1860D-12	117	1862(a)	796
1860D-13	118	1862(a)(1)(H)	1004, 1006, 1009, 1010
1860D-14	119	1862(a)(1)(I)	1004, 1006, 1009, 1010
1860D-15	120	1862(a)(1)(I)	750, 1103
1860D-16	123	1862(a)(1)(J)	1004, 1006, 1009, 1010
1860D-21	125	1862(a)(1)(J)	750, 1103
1860D-22	127	1862(a)(1)(J)	753, 1014
1860D-23	129	1862(a)(1)(K)	750, 1103
1860D-24	131	1862(a)(1)(K)	753, 1014
1860D-31	150, 152, 154, 156, 158, 160, 162, 164, 166, 168, 170	1862(a)(1)(K)	755, 1016
1860D-41	175	1862(a)(1)(L)	753, 1014
1860D-42	178	1862(a)(1)(L)	755, 1016
1861(d)	825	1862(a)(1)(M)	755, 1016
1861(s)(2)(A)	1004, 1006, 1009, 1010	1862(a)(7)	750, 1103
1861(s)(2)(K)(i)	750, 1103	1862(b)(5)(A)(ii)	801
1861(s)(2)(K)(ii)	750, 1103	1862(k)(1)	950
1861(s)(2)(U)	750, 1103	1862(l)	796
1861(s)(2)(V)(iii)	750, 1103	1862(m)	796
1861(s)(2)(V)(iii)	753, 1014	1866(j)	911
1861(s)(2)(W)	750, 1103	1866	911
1861(s)(2)(W)	753, 1014	1866(a)(1)	947
1861(s)(2)(W)	755, 1016	1866(a)(1)(R)	570
1861(s)(2)(X)	753, 1014	1866(a)(1)(S)	570
1861(s)(2)(X)	755, 1016	1866(a)(1)(S)	572
1861(s)(2)(X)	760	1866(a)(1)(T)	570
		1866(a)(1)(T)	572

¶20,040

Social Security Act Sections to Explanation Table

SSA section	L & E Explanation Para	SSA section	L & E Explanation Para
1866(a)(1)(U)	572	1880(e)(1)(A)	730
1866(b)	947	1881(b)(11)(B)	759
1866(h)(1)	905	1881(b)(12)	759
1866C	785	1881(b)(13)	759
1867(d)(4)	584	1881(b)(7)	759
1867(d)(3)	584	1881(b)(7)	759
1868	795, 942	1881(b)(7)	759
1869(i)	916	1882(g)(1)	210, 215
1869(g)	907	1882(o)(1)	210, 215
1869(a)	906	1882(s)(3)(C)(ii)	210, 215
1869(a)(3)(C)(i)	916	1882(s)(3)(C)(iii)	210, 215
1869(a)(3)(C)(ii)	916	1882(v)	210, 215
1869(b)	903, 905	1882(w)	210, 215
1869(b)	906	1886(b)(3)(B)(i)(XIX)	560
1869(b)(1)(E)	916	1886(b)(3)(B)(i)(XIX)	560
1869(b)(1)(F)(ii)	903	1886(b)(3)(B)(i)(XVIII)	560
1869(c)(3)	907	1886(b)(3)(B)(i)(XX)	560
1869(c)(3)(K)	907	1886(b)(3)(B)(vii)	560
1869(c)(3)(B)(i)	906	1886(b)(3)(I)(iii)	505
1869(c)(3)(D)	907	1886(d)(12)	520
1869(c)(3)(E)	906	1886(d)(13)	570
1869(c)(3)(I)(ii)	948	1886(d)(2)(C)(i)	564
1869(c)(3)(J)(i)	906	1886(d)(2)(C)(iv)	510
1869(d)	906	1886(d)(3)	501
1869(f)(2)(A)(I)	901	1886(d)(3)(A)(iii)	501
1869(f)(4)	948	1886(d)(3)(A)(iv)	501
1869(h)	913	1886(d)(3)(A)(iv)(II)	501
1870(h)	915	1886(d)(3)(D)	501
1871(e)(1)(A)	827	1886(d)(3)(D)	501
1871(a)(3)	826	1886(d)(3)(D)	501
1871(a)(4)	826	1886(d)(3)(D)(i)	501
1871(e)(1)(B)	827	1886(d)(3)(D)(ii)	501
1871(e)(1)(C)		1886(d)(3)(D)(iii)	501
1871(e)(2)(A)	827	1886(d)(3)(E)	503
1871(f)(1)	828	1886(d)(3)(E)(i)	503
1874A(b)(3)(A)(i)	917	1886(d)(3)(E)(ii)	503
1874A(e)	830	1886(d)(5)(B)(ii)	588
1874A(f)	831	1886(d)(5)(B)(ii)(IX)	564
1874A(g)	831	1886(d)(5)(B)(ii)(VI)	564
1874A(h)	908	1886(d)(5)(B)(ii)(VII)	564
1876(b)(5)(B)	916	1886(d)(5)(B)(ii)(VIII)	564
1876(h)(5)	386	1886(d)(5)(B)(ii)(X)	564
1877(d)(2)	574	1886(d)(5)(B)(ii)(XI)	564
1877(d)(3)(A)	574	1886(d)(5)(B)(ii)(XII)	564
1877(d)(3)(B)	574	1886(d)(5)(B)(ix)	588
1877(h)(7)	574		

¶20,040

Social Security Act Sections to Explanation Table

SSA section	L & E Explanation Para	SSA section	L & E Explanation Para
1886(d)(5)(B)(v)	588	1895(b)(3)(B)(iii)	658
1886(d)(5)(F)	510	1895(b)(3)(B)(iv)	658
1886(d)(5)(F)(xiv)	510	1895(b)(5)	658
1886(d)(5)(K)(i)	566	1897	1215
1886(d)(5)(K)(ii)(I)	566	1902(a)(10)(E)(iv)	205
1886(d)(5)(K)(ii)(III)	566	1902(a)(64)	205
1886(d)(5)(K)(ix)	566	1902(a)(65)	205
1886(d)(5)(K)(vii)	566	1902(a)(66)	205
1886(d)(5)(K)(viii)	566	1919(f)(2)	905
1886(d)(7)(A)	504	1919(f)(2)(B)(iii)	905
1886(d)(9)(A)(i)	501	1923(f)(3)	1201
1886(d)(9)(A)(i)	568	1923(f)(3)(A)	1204
1886(d)(9)(A)(ii)	501	1923(f)(5)	1203
1886(d)(9)(A)(ii)	568	1923(f)(6)	1204
1886(d)(9)(C)(i)	501	1923(f)(7)	1204
1886(d)(9)(C)(i)(II)	501	1923(j)	1205
1886(d)(9)(C)(ii)	501	1927(a)(1)	1004, 1006, 1009, 1010
1886(d)(9)(C)(iii)	501	1927(b)(3)(A)(i)	1004, 1006, 1009, 1010
1886(d)(9)(C)(iv)(I)	503	1927(b)(3)(A)(ii)	1004, 1006, 1009, 1010
1886(d)(9)(C)(iv)(I)	503	1927(b)(3)(A)(iii)	1004, 1006, 1009, 1010
1886(d)(9)(C)(iv)(II)	503	1927(b)(3)(B)	1004, 1006, 1009, 1010
1886(d)(9)(E)	568	1927(b)(3)(B)	1004, 1006, 1009, 1010
1886(h)(2)(D)(iv)(I)	520, 521, 588	1927(b)(3)(D)	215
1886(h)(2)(D)(iv)(II)	520, 521, 588	1927(b)(3)(D)	1004, 1006, 1009, 1010
1886(h)(4)(F)(i)	588	1927(b)(3)(D)(i)	1004, 1006, 1009, 1010
1886(h)(4)(H)(i)	588	1927(c)(1)(C)(i)	205
1886(h)(7)	588	1927(c)(1)(C)(i)(I)	1206
1888(e)(12)	605	1927(c)(1)(C)(iii)	1206
1888(e)(2)(A)(i)(II)	610	1927(e)(4)	801
1888(e)(2)(A)(iv)	610	1933(g)	205
1889	831	1935	205
1889(d)	831	1935(a)	205
1889(e)	831	1935(c)(1)	205
1889(g)		1935(e)	205
1889(b)	831	2104(g)(3)	801
1889(c)	831	711(b)	799
1893(f)	909	1874A	829
1895(b)(3)(B)(i)	658		
1895(b)(3)(B)(ii)(I)	658		
1895(b)(3)(B)(ii)(II)	658		
1895(b)(3)(B)(ii)(II)	658		
1895(b)(3)(B)(ii)(II)	658		
1895(b)(3)(B)(ii)(III)	658		
1895(b)(3)(B)(ii)(III)	658		
1895(b)(3)(B)(ii)(III)	658		
1895(b)(3)(B)(ii)(IV)	658		

¶20,040

Topical Index

References are to CCH explanation paragraph numbers.

A

Access to affordable pharmaceuticals
. generic drugs in the marketplace . . . 1301
. Federal Trade Commission review of agreements . . . 1301
. re-importation of drugs . . . 1301

Adjustments to payment amounts for drugs and biologicals . . . 1009
. blood clotting factors . . . 1009
. pharmacy supplying fee . . . 1009
. prohibition of judicial review . . . 1009
. radiopharmaceutical payment . . . 1009
. revised drug and administration payments . . . 1009

Administration of Medicare program
. beneficiary outreach demonstration program . . . 835
. compliance with changes in regulations and policies . . . 827
. definition of supplier . . . 825
. improvement, regulatory reduction, and contracting reform . . . 801
. increased flexibility . . . 829
. issuance of regulations . . . 826
. Medicare beneficiary ombudsman . . . 832
. provider education and technical assistance . . . 831
. report and studies relating to regulatory reform . . . 828
. requirement for information security for contractors . . . 830

Adult day care services
demonstration as part of HHA episode of care . . . 660

Ambulance services
. air ambulance
. . coverage of rural air ambulance services . . . 598
. payment
. . rural and urban ambulance services . . . 596

Ambulatory surgical centers
. reimbursement
. . adjustment to payment for ASCs . . . 594

Appeals
. correction of minor errors and omissions . . . 912
. deceased beneficiary . . . 915
. expedited access to review . . . 903
. expedited review of SNF appeals . . . 905
. redeterminations
. . time limits . . . 915
. revision of process . . . 906
. transfer of responsibility . . . 901

Assignment and appeal rights
. outpatient drugs . . . 1006

Average Sales Price (ASP) methodology option
. drugs and biologicals . . . 1010

B

Beneficiaries
. savings calculation . . . 366
. special needs . . . 378

Bid amounts
. Medicare Advantage plans . . . 369

Brachytherapy devices
. payment for . . . 545

C

Cardiovascular screening blood tests
. coverage of . . . 753

Capitation rate
. change in budget neutrality . . . 352

Chronic care improvement
. fee-for-service . . . 678

Chronically ill beneficiaries
. demonstration strategy . . . 679

Clinical diagnostic laboratory tests
. payment . . . 756

Clinical laboratory services demonstration project . . . 1002

Comparative cost adjustment (CCA) program
. establishment . . . 396

Competition program
. bid submission . . . 365

Competitive acquisition programs
. guidelines . . . 1002

Competitive acquisition program for drugs and biologicals
. guidelines . . . 1006

Co-payments
. non-Medicare Advantage providers . . . 360

Cost containment
. House of Representatives procedures . . . 771
. Medicare financing sources . . . 765
. Medicare Trustee Annual Report . . . 765
. military retirees . . . 777
. Part B premium subsidy . . . 776
. presidential submission of legislation . . . 768
. Senate procedures . . . 774

Council for Technology and Innovation
. payment basis for new lab tests . . . 942

Coverage determinations
. improvements in process . . . 114

Criminal background checks
. skilled nursing facilities . . . 601

D

Dental claims
. supplemental coverage . . . 950

Dentists
. contracting authority . . . 706

Demonstration projects
. chiropractic services . . . 788
. consumer-directed outpatient services . . . 679
. frontier extended stay clinic . . . 593
. health care quality . . . 785
. Medicare care management performance . . . 786
. municipal health service . . . 387
. prescription drugs and biologicals . . . 710
. small provider technical assistance . . . 833
. telemedicine extension . . . 789
. vision care PPO networks . . . 792

Diabetes screening tests
. coverage of . . . 755

DIA

E

Education
. dissemination of enrollment information . . . 375

Emergency Medical Treatment and Active Labor Act (EMTALA)
. quality improvement organization review . . . 944
. screening and stabilization services . . . 944
. technical advisory group . . . 945

Extension of payment reform . . . 1008

F

Federally Qualified Health Centers (FQHC)
. wrap-around payment . . . 390

Federal Trade Commission (FTC)
. antitrust review . . . 1301

G

GAO study
. concierge care . . . 787
. report on physician compensation . . . 953

H

Hatch-Waxman Act
. changes . . . 1301

Health care infrastructure improvement
. financial assistance to cancer centers . . . 1215

Health care performance measures
. report . . . 394

Home health
. adult daycare coverage . . . 660
. change in annual PPS update date . . . 658
. definition of homebound . . . 650
. OASIS suspension for non-Medicare/Medicaid patients . . . 670
. payment increase for rural providers . . . 656
. religious nonmedical providers . . . 662

Hospice
. consultation services . . . 677
. nurse practitioners . . . 671
. providing core hospice services . . . 946
. rural area demonstration project . . . 675

Hospitals
. discharge notification requirements . . . 606

Hospital Insurance Trust Fund
. restoration of funds . . . 793

Hospital outpatient department
. functional equivalence test . . . 547
. payment reform . . . 547
. transition period . . . 547

I

Importation of drugs from Canada
. Food and Drug Administration (FDA) compliance . . . 1330

Income-related reduction in Part B premium subsidy
. inflation adjustment . . . 776
. subsidy percentages according to income . . . 776
. tax issues . . . 776

Indian hospitals and clinics
. services furnished . . . 730

Intravenous Immune Globulin (IVIG) treatment
. coverage . . . 760

Inpatient Prospective Payment System
. wage index adjustment . . . 570

J

Judicial review
. competitive acquisition program for drugs and biologicals . . . 1006

L

Local Medical Review Policies
. mediation process . . . 917

M

Mammography services
. payment . . . 754

Medicaid
. Medicare prescription drug benefit
. . amendments to Medicaid law . . . 205
. . coordination of benefits . . . 131
. . low-income individuals . . . 119
. . treatment of territories . . . 178
. Medicare prescription drug card assistance
. . determination of eligibility . . . 160
. . payment . . . 162
. . transitional assistance eligibility defined . . . 152
. . treatment of territories . . . 168

Medically underserved populations
. safe harbor . . . 798

Medicare administrative contractors
. definition and functions . . . 829

Medicare Advantage (MA) program
. implementation and transition . . . 350
. payments . . . 351
. quality improvement program . . . 800

Medicare Advantage (MA) plans
. assuring network adequacy . . . 363
. disclosure of information . . . 363
. effective date . . . 377
. employer sponsorship . . . 374
. e-prescribing . . . 200
. limitation on change in plan . . . 200
. MA regional and local plan rules . . . 362
. organizational and financial requirements . . . 363
. payment adjustments . . . 363
. plan entry funding . . . 363
. plan incentives . . . 363
. plan retention funding . . . 363
. regional benchmark amounts . . . 363
. required reports . . . 363
. risk corridors . . . 363
. single deductible and out-of-pocket limit . . . 363
. stabilization fund . . . 363
. uniform coverage determination . . . 363

Medicare medical savings accounts (MSAs)
. permanent option . . . 380

Medicare Payment Advisory Commission
. report on expenditures . . . 721

Medicare Secondary Payer (MSP)
. laboratory services . . . 943

Medigap
. benefit packages, new . . . 210
. prescription drug plan . . . 210
. . enrollment issues . . . 210
. . prohibitions . . . 210

MedPAC study
. adjusted average per capita cost (AAPCC) . . . 356
. cardio-thoracic surgeon . . . 705
. cost sharing structures . . . 358
. payment for physicians' services . . . 704
. physical therapy services . . . 791
. rural hospital payment adjustments . . . 586
. surgical First Assisting Services . . . 784

Military retirees
. waiver of late enrollment penalty . . . 777

N

National growth rate
. increase of minimum percentage . . . 353

New drugs or biologicals . . . 1006

Nurse practitioners
. hospice coverage . . . 671

O

Office of Rural Health Policy Improvement
. expansion of . . . 799

Optometrists
. contracting authority . . . 706

Occupational Safety and Health Administration (OSHA) Bloodborne Pathogens Standard . . . 947

Outcome Assessment and Information Set (OASIS)
. collection suspension for nonbeneficiaries . . . 670

Outpatient vision services
. payment furnished by vision rehabilitation professionals . . . 792

Overpayments
. recovery . . . 909

P

Part B deductible
. indexing deductible to inflation . . . 729

Payment for inhalation drugs . . . 1011

Payment rates
. revised Medicare Advantage payment rates . . . 359

Payment updates
. class III medical devices . . . 1002
. other payment issues . . . 1002

Pediatric facilities
. renal dialysis services . . . 759

Physician fee schedule adjustments, 2004 . . . 1004

Physician pathology services
. extension of treatment . . . 720

Physician scarcity
. incentive payment program . . . 700

Physicians' services
. evaluation and management
. . appropriate coding . . . 941
. . pilot project . . . 941
. GAO study on access to services . . . 703

Physicians' services payments
. conversion factor update . . . 701

Podiatrist
. contracting authority . . . 706

Premiums
. collection of . . . 367
. uniform premiums . . . 371

Prepayment review
. limitation on random reviews . . . 908
. non-random reviews . . . 908

Prescription drug benefit
. access to benefit
. . emergency . . . 111
. . negotiated prices . . . 111
. . pharmacy . . . 111
. . plans . . . 109
. alternative prescription drug coverage
. . actuarially equivalent . . . 106
. . deductible . . . 106
. . defined . . . 103, 106
. appeals
. . coverage determinations . . . 114
. . independent review . . . 114
. . reconsiderations . . . 114
. basic prescription drug coverage
. . defined . . . 103
. coinsurance . . . 104
. coordination of benefits . . . 131
. cost reimbursement contractors
. . application of Part D rules . . . 125
. covered Part D drug
. . defined . . . 108
. creditable coverage . . . 118
. deductible . . . 104
. disclosure of information . . . 120, 215
. electronic prescription drug program
. . establishment of standards . . . 113
. . grants to physicians for implementation . . . 230
. eligibility
. . creditable coverage . . . 118
. . eligible individuals . . . 100
. employer-sponsored programs
. . coverage requirements . . . 127
. . study and report . . . 240, 245
. . subsidy payment . . . 127
. enrollment
. . late enrollment penalty . . . 101, 118
. . process . . . 101
. fallback prescription drug plans
. . process . . . 116
. formularies
. . requirements . . . 111
. grievance procedures . . . 114
. incurred costs
. . defined . . . 105
. information to eligible individuals
. . dissemination by sponsor . . . 110
. . dissemination by Secretary . . . 102
. initial coverage limit . . . 104
. limited risk plans . . . 116
. Medicaid amendments . . . 205
. Medicare Advantage prescription drug (MA-PD) plan
. . application of Part D rules . . . 125
. . default enrollment rules . . . 125
. . private fee-for-service plans . . . 125
. Medicare Prescription Drug Account
. . establishment and rules . . . 123
. negotiated prices
. . beneficiary access . . . 107
. . disclosure to Secretary . . . 107
. out-of-pocket expenditures
. . annual threshold . . . 105
. . incurred costs . . . 105
. . third-party reimbursement . . . 105
. premium
. . adjustments to standardized bid . . . 120
. . base beneficiary premium defined . . . 118
. . collection of monthly premium . . . 118
. . late enrollment penalty . . . 118

Prescription drug benefit—continued
. premium—continued
.. low-income individuals . . . 119
.. payments to sponsors . . . 120
.. standardized bid amount . . . 118
. prescription drug plan
.. actuarial valuation . . . 115
.. appeals . . . 114
.. approval of plan . . . 115
.. bids and premiums . . . 115
.. contract requirements . . . 117
.. coordination of benefits . . . 115
.. cost and utilization management . . . 112
.. defined . . . 175
.. formularies . . . 111
.. grievance procedures . . . 114
.. medication therapy management . . . 112
.. payments to sponsors . . . 120
.. region defined . . . 115
.. risk corridors . . . 120
.. waiver of requirements . . . 117
. Program of All Inclusive Care to the Elderly (PACE)
.. application of Part D . . . 125
. qualified prescription drug coverage
.. alternative . . . 103
.. defined . . . 103
. qualifying plan
.. defined . . . 109
. reinsurance payment amount . . . 120
. reports to Congress . . . 178, 225
. risk corridors . . . 120
. standard prescription drug coverage
.. coinsurance . . . 104
.. deductible . . . 104
.. defined . . . 103
.. initial coverage limit . . . 104
. state pharmaceutical assistance programs
.. coordination of benefits . . . 129, 131
.. payments . . . 129
. subsidies
.. employer-sponsored programs . . . 127
.. premium for eligible individuals . . . 120
.. rules for low-income individuals . . . 119
. taxpayer data
.. disclosure of . . . 215
.. territorial residents . . . 119
. supplemental prescription drug coverage
.. defined . . . 103
. territories
.. coverage in . . . 178

Prescription drug discount card program
. American Indian, treatment of . . . 162
. beneficiary protections . . . 164
. contracting authority . . . 215
. disclosure and oversight . . . 166
. eligibility
.. eligible individuals defined . . . 152
.. procedures . . . 160
. enrollment
.. fees . . . 152
.. information . . . 154
.. late enrollment . . . 152
.. process . . . 152
. establishment of program . . . 150
.. funding . . . 170
. long-term care residents
.. transitional assistance . . . 162
. Medicaid needy
.. defined . . . 152
. negotiated prices . . . 158
. Part C plans
.. rules . . . 164

Prescription drug discount card program—continued
. prescription drug card sponsor responsibilities
.. application for endorsement . . . 164
.. information to enrollees . . . 154, 156
.. issuance of card . . . 154
.. negotiated prices, access to . . . 158
.. price differences, notification of . . . 156
.. qualifications . . . 164
.. requirements . . . 156, 158
.. prohibition on charges . . . 158
. sanctions . . . 166
. special transitional assistance eligible
.. defined . . . 152
.. determination of eligibility . . . 160
.. payment of enrollment fees and costs . . . 162
.. reconsideration . . . 160
. taxpayer data
.. disclosure of . . . 215
. territories
.. treatment of . . . 168
. transition
.. establishment of Commission . . . 220
.. rules for . . . 150
. transitional assistance account . . . 170
. transitional assistance eligible individual
.. American Indian, treatment of . . . 162
.. defined . . . 152
.. determination of eligibility . . . 160
.. long-term care residents . . . 162
.. payment of enrollment fees and costs . . . 162
.. reconsideration . . . 160

Prescription drug plans (PDPs)
. generally . . . 100

Prescription solicitation study . . . 1002

Preventive physical exams
. coverage of . . . 750

Professional education costs
. redistribution of unused resident positions . . . 588

Program Advisory and Oversight Committee establishment
. report . . . 1002

Program exclusion
. waiver . . . 949

Program of All-Inclusive Care for the Elderly (PACE)
. application of Part D . . . 125
. payment by providers . . . 388

Provider enrollment process
. appeals . . . 911

Q

Qualified independent contractors
. requirements . . . 907

Quality Improvement Organizations (QIOs)
. responsibilities, expanded
.. inclusion of Part C and Part D . . . 235
. study to evaluate program . . . 235

R

Reasonable cost contracts
. extension of . . . 386

Renal dialysis services
. case-mix adjusted prospective payment system . . . 759
. competitive bidding . . . 373

Rural hospitals
. hold harmless provision extension . . . 582

S

Skilled nursing facilities
. criminal background check . . . 601
. payment for AIDS patients . . . 605
. portable diagnostic ultrasound services . . . 608
. RHC FQHC exclusions from SNF-PPS . . . 610
. telehealth originating sites . . . 607

T

Therapy
. two-year extension of benefits caps . . . 762

Trust fund holdings
. correction . . . 793

U

Use recovery audit contractors demonstration project
. generally . . . 1012

W

Work geographic adjustment
. floor establishment . . . 708